Handbook of Applied Cognition

Handbook of Applied Cognition

Edited by
Francis T. Durso
University of Oklahoma, USA

Associate Editors
Raymond S. Nickerson
Tufts University, USA
Roger W. Schvaneveldt
New Mexico State University, Las Cruces, USA
Susan T. Dumais
Microsoft Corporation, USA
D. Stephen Lindsay
University of Victoria, Canada
Michelene T.H. Chi
University of Pittsburgh, USA

JOHN WILEY & SONS
Chichester • New York • Weinheim • Brisbane • Singapore • Toronto

Baffins Lane, Chichester,
West Sussex PO19 1UD, England

National 01243 779777
International (+44) 1243 779777
e-mail (for orders and customer service enquiries): cs-books@wiley.co.uk
Visit our Home Page on http://www.wiley.co.uk or http://www.wiley.com

Other Wiley Editorial Offices

John Wiley & Sons, Inc., 605 Third Avenue,
New York, NY 10158-0012, USA

WILEY-VCH Verlag GmbH, Pappelallee 3,
D-69469 Weinheim, Germany

Jacaranda Wiley Ltd, 33 Park Road, Milton,
Queensland 4064, Australia

John Wiley & Sons (Asia) Pte Ltd, 2 Clementi Loop #02-01,
Jin Xing Distripark, Singapore 129809

John Wiley & Sons (Canada) Ltd, 22 Worcester Road,
Rexdale, Ontario M9W 1L1, Canada

Library of Congress Cataloging-in-Publication Data

Handbook of applied cognition / editor, Francis T. Durso ; associate
editors, Raymond S. Nickerson . . . [et al.].
p. cm.
Includes bibliographical references and index.
ISBN 0-471-97765-9 (alk. paper)
1. Cognitive psychology. I. Durso, Francis Thomas.
II. Nickerson, Raymond S.
BF201.H36 1999
153—dc21 98-47298
CIP

British Library Cataloguing in Publication Data

A catalogue record for this book is available from the British Library

ISBN 0-471-97765-9

Typeset in 10/12pt Times by Mayhew Typesetting, Rhayader, Powys
Printed and bound in Great Britain by Bookcraft (Bath), Midsomer Norton, Somerset.
This book is printed on acid-free paper responsibly manufactured from sustainable forestry, in which at least two trees are planted for each one used for paper production.

Contents

About the Editors		ix
Contributors		xi
Reviewers		xvii
Preface		xix
SECTION 1	**OVERVIEWS**	1
Chapter 1	Applying Cognitive Psychology: Bridging the Gulf Between Basic Research and Cognitive Artifacts *Douglas J. Gillan & Roger W. Schvaneveldt*	3
Chapter 2	Applications of Attention Research *Wendy A. Rogers, Gabriel K. Rousseau & Arthur D. Fisk*	33
Chapter 3	Knowledge and Expertise *Neil Charness & Richard S. Schultetus*	57
Chapter 4	Memory Applied *David G. Payne, Celia M. Klin, James M. Lampinen, Jeffrey S. Neuschatz & D. Stephen Lindsay*	83
Chapter 5	Context, Process, and Experience: Research on Applied Judgment and Decision Making *Clarence C. Rohrbaugh & James Shanteau*	115
Chapter 6	Perspectives on Human Error: Hindsight Biases and Local Rationality *David D. Woods & Richard I. Cook*	141
Chapter 7	Applications of Social Cognition: Attitudes as Cognitive Structures *Leandre R. Fabrigar, Steven M. Smith & Laura A. Brannon*	173

SECTION 2 BUSINESS AND INDUSTRY 207

Chapter 8 The Cognitive Psychology and Cognitive Engineering of Industrial Systems 209
Neville Moray

Chapter 9 Cognitive Factors in Aviation 247
Christopher D. Wickens

Chapter 10 Situation Awareness 283
Francis T. Durso & Scott D. Gronlund

Chapter 11 Business Management 315
Stephen W. Gilliland & David V. Day

Chapter 12 Applied Cognition in Consumer Research 343
Joseph W. Alba & J. Wesley Hutchinson

SECTION 3 COMPUTERS AND TECHNOLOGY 375

Chapter 13 Devices that Remind 377
Douglas Herrmann, Brad Brubaker, Carol Yoder, Virgil Sheets & Adrian Tio

Chapter 14 Computer Supported Cooperative Work 409
Judith S. Olson & Gary M. Olson

Chapter 15 Cognitive Engineering Models and Cognitive Architectures in Human–Computer Interaction 443
Peter Pirolli

Chapter 16 Knowledge Elicitation 479
Nancy J. Cooke

SECTION 4 INFORMATION AND INSTRUCTION 511

Chapter 17 Statistical Graphs and Maps 513
Stephan Lewandowsky & John T. Behrens

Chapter 18 Instructional Technology 551
Richard E. Mayer

Chapter 19 Cognition and Instruction 571
Martin J. Dennis & Robert J. Sternberg

Chapter 20 Design Principles for Instruction in Content Domains: Lessons from Research on Expertise and Learning 595
Susan R. Goldman, Anthony J. Petrosino & Cognition and Technology Group at Vanderbilt

Chapter 21 Cognitive Psychology Applied to Testing 629
Susan E. Embretson

SECTION 5	**HEALTH AND LAW**	661
Chapter 22	Medical Cognition *Vimla L. Patel, Jose F. Arocha & David R. Kaufman*	663
Chapter 23	Designing Healthcare Advice for the Public *Patricia Wright*	695
Chapter 24	Cognitive Contributions to Mental Illness and Mental Health *Catherine Panzarella, Lauren B. Alloy, Lyn Y. Abramson & Karen Klein*	725
Chapter 25	The Natural Environment: Dealing with the Threat of Detrimental Change *Raymond S. Nickerson*	757
Chapter 26	Eyewitness Testimony *Daniel B. Wright & Graham M. Davies*	789
Chapter 27	Perspectives on Jury Decision-making: Cases with Pretrial Publicity and Cases Based on Eyewitness Identifications *Jennifer L. Devenport, Christina A. Studebaker & Steven D. Penrod*	819
Author Index		847
Subject Index		870

About the Editors

Frank Durso is professor of psychology and director of the University of Oklahoma's Human–Technology Interaction Center. He received his Ph.D. from SUNY, Stony Brook and his B.S. from Carnegie-Mellon University. He currently serves on editorial boards in applied cognition (*Applied Cognitive Psychology* [book review editor], *Cognitive Technology*, *Air Traffic Control Quarterly*) and is a member of the FAA Task Force on Flight Progress Strips. Dr Durso is a member of the Psychonomic Society, Human Factors & Ergonomics Society, ACM, SARMAC and the American Psychological Society (Fellow). He has served as president of the Southwestern Psychological Association and founded the Oklahoma Psychological Society. Dr Durso has received a Sigma Xi faculty research award and the Kenneth Crook Teaching Award. His applied work has focused on situation awareness and the cognitive processes of air-traffic control.

Raymond S. Nickerson received his Ph.D. in experimental psychology from Tufts University (1965). He was researcher and manager at Bolt Beranek and Newman Inc. for 25 years until he retired as senior vice president (1991). Dr Nickerson is a Fellow of the American Association for the Advancement of Science, American Psychological Association (Division 1, 3, 21). American Psychological Society, Human Factors and Ergonomics Society, and the Society of Experimental Psychologist, and a recipient of the Franklin V. Taylor award from APA's Engineering Psychology Division. Dr Nickerson was founding editor of the *Journal of Experimental Psychology: Applied* and past chair of the National Research Council's Committee on Human Factors. His scholarly books include: *Using Computers: Human Factors in Information Systems*; *Reflections of Reasoning*; *Looking Ahead: Human Factors Challenges in a Changing World.* Coauthor (with D. N. Perkins and E. E. Smith): *The Teaching of Thinking*. Editor: *Attention and Performance VIII*; *Emerging Needs and Opportunities for Human Factors Research.* Coeditor (with P. P. Zodhiates): *Technology in Education: Looking toward 2020.*

Roger Schvaneveldt is a professor of psychology and associate director of the Computing Research Laboratory at New Mexico State University. He received the Ph.D. in 1967 from the University of Wisconsin and was assistant and associate professor at the State University of New York at Stony Brook from 1967 to 1977. His research has addressed problems in concept learning, information processing, semantic memory, context and recognition, network scaling methodology and applications, and implicit learning. He has served on the editorial boards of *Memory and Cognition* and the *Journal of Experimental Psychology: Human Perception and Performance*. His current research interests are in knowledge engineering, aviation psychology, implicit learning, and dynamic systems.

Susan T. Dumais is a senior researcher in the Decision Theory and Adaptive Systems Group at Microsoft Research. Her research interests include algorithms and interfaces for improved information retrieval and classification, human–computer interaction, combining search and navigation, user modelling, individual differences, collaborative filtering, and organizational impacts of new technology. Before moving to Microsoft in 1997, she was a researcher and research manager at Bell Labs and Bellcore for 17 years. She received a B.A. in Mathematics and Psychology from Bates College, and a Ph.D. in Cognitive and Mathematical Psychology from Indiana University. She is a member of ACM, ASIS, the Human Factors and Ergonomic Society, and the Psychonomic Society, and serves on the editorial boards of *Information Retrieval*, *Human Computer Interaction (HCI)*, and the *New Review of Hypermedia and Multimedia (NRMH)*.

D. Stephen Lindsay is professor of psychology at the University of Victoria, British Columbia, Canada. He is a cognitive psychologist who earned his Ph.D. in 1987 from Princeton University. Much of his research has focused on memory source monitoring (e.g. studies of conditions under which witnesses mistake memories of postevent suggestions as memories of witnessed events). Lindsay co-edited, with J. Don Read, a 1997 book on the recovered-memories controversy, entitled *Recollections of Trauma: Scientific Evidence and Clinical Practice*.

Michelene T. H. Chi obtained her B.S. in mathematics and Ph.D. in psychology from Carnegie-Mellon University. She is a professor of the Department of Psychology and a senior scientist at the Learning, Research and Development Center, at the University of Pittsburgh. Among Dr Chi's honors are the Spencer Fellowship from the National Academy of Education, the Boyd McCandless Young Scientist Award from American Psychological Association, and a recognition of her 1981 paper on the representational differences between experts and novices as a Citation Classic. She was also a resident Fellow at the Center for Advanced Study in Behavioral Sciences in the 1996–97 academic year. Her current research centers on understanding how students learn complex concepts, such as those in science, and contrasting the effect of constructive learning on one's own versus learning under the guidance of a tutor. She also is involved in the cognitive assessment of learning in different contexts, such as assessing the effectiveness of learning from using computer simulations. In her research, she specializes in advancing a method that quantifies qualitative analyses of verbal (and video) data.

Contributors

Lyn Y. Abramson, Department of Psychology, University of Wisconsin, 1202 W Johnson Street, Madison, WI 53706, USA

Joseph W. Alba, Department of Marketing, University of Florida, 212 Bryan Hall, Gainesville, FL 32611-7155, USA

Lauren B. Alloy, Department of Psychology, Temple University, Philadelphia, PA 19122, USA

Jose F. Arocha, Centre for Medical Education, McGill University, 1110 Pine Avenue W, Montreal, Quebec, Canada, H3A 1A3

John T. Behrens, Division of Psychology in Education, College of Education, P O Box 870611, Tempe, AZ 85287-0611, USA

Laura A. Brannon, Department of Psychology, University of Oklahoma, Norman, OK 73019-2007, USA

Brad Brubaker, Department of Psychology, Indiana State University, Root Hall B-205, Terre Haute, IN 47809, USA

Neil Charness, Department of Psychology, Florida State University, Tallahassee, FL 32306-1270, USA

Cognition and Technology Group at Vanderbilt, Learning Technology Center, Vanderbilt University, Nashville, TN 37203, USA

Richard I. Cook, Department of Anesthesia and Critical Care, University of Chicago, Chicago, IL 60637, USA

Nancy J. Cooke, Department of Psychology, New Mexico State University, P O Box 30001, Las Cruces, NM 88003, USA

Graham M. Davies, Department of Psychology, University of Leicester, University Road, Leicester, LE1 7RH, UK

David V. Day, Department of Psychology, Pennsylvania State University, 643 Moore, University Park, PA 16802-3104, USA

Martin J. Dennis, Department of Psychology, Yale University, P O Box 208205, New Haven, CT 06520-8205, USA

Jennifer L. Devenport, Department of Psychology, California State University, Fullerton, P O Box 6846, Fullerton, CA 92834-6846, USA

Francis T. Durso, Department of Psychology, University of Oklahoma, Norman, OK 73019-0535, USA

Susan E. Embretson, Department of Psychology, University of Kansas, Lawrence, KS 66045, USA

Leandre R. Fabrigar, Department of Psychology, Queen's University, Kingston, Ontario, K7L 3N6, Canada

Arthur D. Fisk, School of Psychology, Georgia Institute of Technology, Atlanta, GA 30332-0170, USA

Douglas J. Gillan, Department of Psychology, New Mexico State University, Las Cruces, NM 88003, USA

Stephen W. Gilliland, Department of Management and Policy, University of Arizona, McClelland Hall 405U, Tucson, AZ 85721, USA

Susan R. Goldman, Learning Technology Center, Vanderbilt University, Nashville, TN 37203, USA

Scott D. Gronlund, Department of Psychology, University of Oklahoma, Norman, OK 73019-0535, USA

Douglas Herrmann, Psychology Department, Indiana State University, Terre Haute, NJ 47809, USA

J. Wesley Hutchinson, The Wharton School, University of Pennsylvania, 1400 Steinberg Hall, Philadelphia, PA 19104-63012, USA

David R. Kaufman, Department of Cognition and Development, Graduate School of Education, University of California, Berkeley, CA 94720, USA

Karen Klein, MCP Hahnemann University, Department of Clinical and Health Psychology, Broad & Vine Streets, Mail Stop 626, Philadelphia, PA 19102-1192, USA

Celia M. Klin, Department of Psychology, State University of New York, Binghamton, NY 13902-6000, USA

James M. Lampinen, Binghamton University, SUNY, P O Box 6000, Binghamton, NY 13902-6000, USA

Stephan Lewandowsky, Department of Psychology, University of Western Australia, Nedlands, WA 6907, Australia

D. Stephen Lindsay, Department of Psychology, University of Victoria, P O Box 3050, Victoria, BC, V8W 3H5, Canada

Richard E. Mayer, Department of Psychology, University of California, Santa Barbara, CA 93106-9660, USA

Neville Moray, Department of Psychology, University of Surrey, Guildford, Surrey, GU2 5XH, UK

Jeffrey S. Neuschatz, Department of Psychology, Binghamton University, Binghamton, NY 13902-6000, USA

Raymond S. Nickerson, Department of Psychology, Tufts University, Paige Hall, Medford, MA 02155, USA

Gary M. Olson, The School for Information, University of Michigan, Ann Arbor, MI, 48109, USA

Judith S. Olson, The School for Information, University of Michigan, Ann Arbor, MI, 48109, USA

Catherine Panzarella, MCP Hahnemann University, Department of Clinical and Health Psychology, Broad & Vine Streets, Mail Stop 626, Philadelphia, PA 19102-1192, USA

Vimla L. Patel, Centre for Medical Education, McGill University, 1110 Pine Avenue W, Montreal, Quebec, Canada, H3A 1A3

David G. Payne, Department of Psychology, State University of New York, Binghamton, NY 13902-6000, USA

Steven D. Penrod, Psychology and Law Program, University of Nebraska-Lincoln, Lincoln, NE 68588-0308, USA

Anthony J. Petrosino, Wisconsin Center for Educational Research, University of Wisconsin, Madison, USA

Peter Pirolli, Palo Alto Research Center, Xerox Corporation, 3333 Coyote Hill Road, Palo Alto, CA 94304, USA

Wendy A. Rogers, School of Psychology, Georgia Institute of Technology, Atlanta, GA 30332-0170, USA

Clarence C. Rohrbaugh, Department of Psychology, Bliemont Hall, 1101 Mid-Campus Drive, Kansas State University, Manhattan, KS 66506-5302, USA

Gabriel K. Rousseau, Department of Psychology, University of Georgia, Athens, GA 30602-3013, USA

Richard S. Schultetus, Department of Psychology, Florida State University, Tallahassee, FL 32306-1051, USA

Roger W. Schvaneveldt, Department of Psychology, New Mexico State University, Las Cruces, NM 88003, USA

James Shanteau, Department of Psychology, Kansas State University, 492 Bluemount Hall, Manhattan, KS 66506-5302, USA

Virgil Sheets, Department of Psychology, Indiana State University, Root Hall B-205, Terre Haute, IN 47809, USA

Steven M. Smith, Department of Psychology, Queen's University, Kingston, Ontario, Canada, K7L 3N6

Robert J. Sternberg, Department of Psychology, Yale University, P O Box 208205, New Haven, CT 06520-8205, USA

Christina A. Studebaker, Department of Psychology, Castleton State College, Castleton, VT 05735-9987, USA

Alan Tio, Department of Psychology, Indiana State University, Terre Haute, IN 47809, USA

Christopher D. Wickens, Institute of Aviation, University of Illinois, Willard Airport, Savoy, IL 61874, USA

David D. Woods, Cognitive Systems Engineering Laboratory, Institute for Ergonomics, The Ohio State University, Columbus, OH 43210-7852, USA

Daniel B. Wright, Department of Experimental Psychology, University of Bristol, Bristol, BS8 1TN, UK

Patricia Wright, School of Psychology, Cardiff University, Cardiff, CB2 2EF, UK

Carol Yoder, Psychology Department, Indiana State University, Terre Haute, IN 47809, USA

Reviewers

Erik M. Altmann
Michael Atwood
Ami L. Barile
Jonathan Baron
Marilyn Sue Bogner
Gretchen Chapman
Nancy Cooke
Jerry M. Crutchfield
Mary Czerwinski
Michael R. P. Dougherty
Baruch Fischhoff
David Foyle
Susan Fussell
Gerald Gardner
Douglas Gillan
Jane Goddman-Delahunty
Scott D. Gronlund
Jonathan Grudin
James Hartley
Reid Hastie
Kelly S. Bouas Henry
Douglas Hermann
Robert Hoffman
Margaret Intons-Peterson
Bonnie John
Shelia M. Kennison
Sara Kiesler
Adrienne Lee
Robert Lord
Carol Manning
Richard L. Marsh
Andrew Matthews
Gary McClelland
Peter M. Moertl
Neville Moray
Daniel Morrow
Geoffrey Norman
Ken Paap
Vimla Patel
Stephen Payne
Jenny L. Perry
Richard Reardon
Gary Reid
Clarence Rohrbaugh
David Roskos-Ewoldson
Tim Salthouse
Thomas Seamster
Zendal Segal
Priti Shah
James Shanteau
Paul Stern
Robert Sternberg
Tom Stewart
Robert Terry
Todd Truitt
Chris Wickens
Maria S. Zaragoza
Michael Zarate

Preface

During the past 40 years a large number of bright people have embraced the re-emergence of human mental functioning as a viable topic of scientific study. Indeed, the theories, models, and methodologies that have been developed to understand the human mind stand as tributes to the enthusiasm and intelligence of these scholars. Much of this progress has been in gaining an understanding of basic or fundamental cognitive functioning. Psychology has participated in, and often led, this initiative as one of the empirical arms of the cognitive science movement.

This *Handbook* explores another dimension of what it means to be interested in human mental functioning: the attempt to understand cognition in the uncontrolled world of interesting people. When I was first asked to edit this volume, I thought the timing was right for a number of reasons. First, a large amount of applied work was being conducted that was very strong, but not easily accessed – hidden in this specialty journal or tucked away in those proceedings. A *Handbook* devoted to applications of cognitive research could help bring this work to the notice of others. Second, exactly how to characterize basic research to applied researchers seemed a noble although difficult problem. Leaders in the applied community had routinely stated that basic cognitive research was not worth very much. Explicit condemnation of the value of cognitive psychology had been the topic of more than one thought-provoking address, including Don Norman's eloquent address at SARMAC, the organization that initiated this volume. Thus, for applied researchers, this volume offers a collection of chapters of successful and not-so-successful applications of basic principles. These chapters include reviews from the perspective of a basic cognitive process as well as reviews from the perspective of an applied domain. Third, basic research did not always appreciate the value of applied cognition, and even when cognitive research looked applied it was often what Doug Herrmann has called "applicable," not applied. More important than the under-appreciation of applied work, there did not seem to be the realization that good applied work was being conducted by people other than cognitive psychologists – a fact that should interest scientists who believe the empirical study of mind should be the province of cognitive psychology. Such a *Handbook* would supply a compendium of research that would move such debates from the general "useful/useless," "good/bad" debates to more sophisticated considerations of science, engineering, and mental functioning. Finally, and of most interest conceptually, a number of pressures on the current paradigm of cognitive psychology seemed to revolve around the ability to apply cognitive psychology. Debates occurred and are continuing on qualitative methods, hypothesis testing, situated cognition, the AI agenda, and Gibson. At their hearts, these debates confront various issues about the real-world applicability of what applied researchers would call academic cognitive psychology. As one looks over the pressures on cognitive psychology, the paradigm pressures seem to have a ring of familiarity.

Kuhnians amongst us would argue that cognitive psychology replaced neobehaviorism as the dominant paradigm in scientific psychology. In fact, a popular textbook of the early 1980s (Lachman, Lachman & Butterfield, 1979) stood out for its attempt to supply young cognitive psychologists a context from which to understand the demise of one paradigm and the rise of the other. Neobehaviorism had been under a number of paradigm pressures:

1. Models were attacked as becoming overly complex sequences of Ss and Rs.
2. Concepts like reinforcement and stimulus control looked circular outside the laboratory.
3. Applied researchers challenged fundamental assumptions of neobehaviorism by making it clear that humans were not passive recipients of impinging events.
4. Advances in technology (i.e. computer science) provided new opportunities, but neobehaviorists tended to ignore or under-utilize the new technology.
5. Finally, and perhaps most critical, neobehaviorism was not making advances in areas it should have (like language and perception) but, importantly, other disciplines were.

Today, modern cognitive psychology is buffeted by paradigm pressures just as its predecessor was. Several of these points are eloquently discussed elsewhere in the literature. In my view, the pressures seem surprisingly reminiscent:

1. Cognitive psychology's typical method of explanation is the construction of underlying mechanisms (e.g. short-term memory) and not by inducing abstract categories for the experimental variables (e.g. this is a force, this is a mass). The proliferation of cognitive models is apparent. From the perspective of the applied community, large amounts of effort and talent have been spent on relatively small, model-specific problems.
2. Like reinforcement and stimulus control, cognitive constructs are often not well specified in the applied arena. Consider elaborative rehearsal versus maintenance rehearsal. Although they are important additions to our theories of short-term memory and are supported by ingenious laboratory experiments, it is difficult for the applied researcher to employ the concepts. An air-traffic controller remembers one plane, but not another. The first must have undergone elaborative rehearsal because it is remembered better, and so on.

3. It is becoming clear that, not only are humans active processors of events, but that humans impinge on events as well as being impinged by them. The fact that humans control and modify their environment, have choices about what to look at and what to do, is not only abundantly clear in a field setting, but becomes critical in any attempt to apply basic research to an applied problem. Typically, when an expert is doing his or her job, the experimental intervention is the least interesting part of the environment; in the laboratory it is often the most interesting, if not only, part of the environment. This assertion is perhaps made most clearly by the distributed cognition initiatives. An important part of a human's environment is often other humans. We could say that such issues are the responsibility of social cognition, but that is just second millenium thinking. Besides, many social psychologists have affirmed their intent to become more like cognitive psychologists, making it difficult for cognitive psychologists to become more like them.
4. New technologies today include virtual reality and high fidelity simulations. Ignoring these technologies makes sense within the current cognitive paradigm where the environment plays a role secondary to internal cognition. However, to cash out the promise of cognitive psychology in the applied marketplace will require complex, dynamic, interactive, yet controllable environments. Use of these technologies can take advantage of new methodologies and statistical procedures for the understanding of sequential data.
5. Despite these paradigm pressures, if neobehaviorism could have made reasonable contributions to language and perception, not only might Chomsky have read *Verbal Behavior* before he reviewed it, but neobehaviorism may have participated in a Hegelian synthesis rather than being the paradigm lost. How well is cognitive psychology doing in the applied arena? The answer is not a simple one. The many chapters of this *Handbook* are attempts to characterize cognitive research in applied settings, but not necessarily applied cognitive psychology. Several of the chapters do not rely much on cognitive psychology and make that point explicitly. Several other chapters have easily imported the findings and views of cognitive psychology into their applied domains. In addition, several authors draw heavily from social psychology. The domains covered in this *Handbook* clearly vary from relatively new areas about which little is understood, to large, well-researched, well-understood domains.

The *Handbook* begins with a chapter on applying cognitive psychology and then continues with six chapters that overview applied research from perspectives familiar to most cognitive psychologists. These overviews are followed by chapters that focus on particular applied domains. These domains fall roughly into four broad arenas: business and industry, computers and technology, information and instruction, and health and law, but it will be clear that issues raised in one section of the *Handbook* will echo in others.

There are a number of people who were critical to the production of this volume. The panel of associate editors served as vital advisers and coordinated helpful reviews for a number of the chapters. Several of the early drafts were reviewed by my graduate-level Applied Cognition class; these discussions often helped me clarify my view of the chapters. Many colleagues agreed to review chapters often within impossibly short timeframes, and the chairs of the Psychology Department, Ken Hoving and Kirby Gilliland, were gracious in allowing me access to departmental resources. I was director of the University of Oklahoma's Human–Technology Interaction Center while this volume was being produced, and appreciate the support of my HTIC colleagues during the past year. My graduate students were tolerant of the demands placed on me by this task. Patience and tolerance were particularly plentiful from the people at Wiley, Comfort Jegede and Melanie Phillips, who held my hand throughout the process. My assistants, Paul Linville and Helen Fung, were absolutely invaluable, with special thanks to Paul who was my right hand through all but the final phase of the project. Finally, thanks to the great loves of my life, Kate Bleckley who found the time to continue her degree at GaTech while giving me editorial assistance, cognitive aid, and emotional support, and to my son, Andy, who took time from being a teenager to let me know he thinks it's cool I'm editing a book.

The contributions of the authors speak for themselves in the pages that follow.

F. T. D.
June 23, 1998
University of Oklahoma

REFERENCES

Chomsky, N. (1959). A review of Skinner's *Verbal Behavior*. *Language*, 35, 26–58.

Lachman, R., Lachman, J.L. & Butterfield, E.C. (1979). *Cognitive Psychology and Information Processing: An Introduction*. Hillsdale, NJ: Lawrence Erlbaum.

Section 1

Overviews

Chapter 1

Applying Cognitive Psychology: Bridging the Gulf Between Basic Research and Cognitive Artifacts

Douglas J. Gillan and Roger W. Schvaneveldt
New Mexico State University

Applied cognitive psychology occupies the large gulf between basic cognitive psychology and the development of useful and usable cognitive artifacts. Cognitive artifacts are human-made objects, devices, and systems that extend people's abilities in high-level perception; encoding and storing information in memory, as well as retrieving it from memory; thinking, reasoning, and problem solving; and the acquisition, comprehension, and production of language. Cognitive artifacts range from simple and ubiquitous objects, such as maps and graphs, to complex and rare objects, such as nuclear power plant control rooms and aircraft flight decks. They also include prosthetic systems used to augment the capabilities of persons with cognitive disabilities. Complex relations link basic cognitive psychology to these cognition-aiding tools; furthermore, developing a discipline of applied cognitive psychology that helps to bridge the gulf between them remains a work in progress. Because of its importance, this set of complex interrelations between basic cognitive research, applied cognitive research, and the design and development of cognitive artifacts serves as the first theme of this chapter.

We conceive of applied cognitive psychology as a multidimensional matrix. The dimensions of this matrix include:

Handbook of Applied Cognition, Edited by F. T. Durso, R. S. Nickerson, R. W. Schvaneveldt, S. T. Dumais, D. S. Lindsay and M. T. H. Chi.

1. the cognitive processes and abilities that underlie performance in real-world tasks and laboratory-based simulations of those tasks (e.g. signal detection, object perception, depth perception, memory encoding and storage, retrieval, reasoning, language production, discourse comprehension)
2. those tasks in which cognition plays a central role (e.g. human–computer interaction, aviation, medical diagnosis, process control)
3. methodologies, including research methods (e.g. observational, experimental, and statistical methods), modeling and simulation methods (including mental modeling), and design methods (e.g. task analysis, knowledge acquisition, prototyping, usability engineering)
4. theories and models of cognition.

A second theme of this chapter concerns selected aspects of those dimensions; we address this theme pervasively throughout the chapter rather than in a single section. Finally, we hope that this chapter, as well as this entire book can serve as a springboard for additional thinking about applied cognitive psychology that will lead to advances in the area such that this multidimensional matrix may look somewhat different in the future; accordingly, the third theme of the chapter (also distributed throughout the chapter) addresses our ideas about the future of applied cognitive psychology.

FROM BASIC SCIENCE TO COGNITIVE ARTIFACT: USING APPLIED COGNITIVE PSYCHOLOGY TO BRIDGE THE GULF

Technology Transfer, Need-based Design, and Designer-initiated Design

What is the relation between basic research and its application? The classic approach to this relation comes out of the logical positivist tradition which proposed that scientists could predict and explain the occurrence of an event by applying deductive logic to a set of scientific laws and a set of empirical observations (for a review, see Bechtel, 1988). The predicted or explained event might be either the outcome of a laboratory experiment or a practical application. This approach to applications, which we call technology transfer, suggests that applying basic science involves a two-step process: in step 1, basic research discovers laws of nature which, in step 2, get translated by engineering design and testing, as well as specific applied research studies, into the design of artifacts to meet some real-world need. The story of the development of the atomic bomb follows this pattern – from physical theory beginning with Einstein, to basic research that tested the theory, to the applied research and engineering of the Manhattan Project that transferred the knowledge into the technological artifact of a bomb that met a military purpose during the Second World War.

In cognitive psychology, the development of a LISP (a high-level programming language) tutor based on Anderson's ACT* theory and associated basic research (Anderson, 1995; Anderson & Reiser, 1985) followed the technology transfer approach. Anderson and his colleagues developed an account of skill acquisition based on ACT* and conducted experiments to test the theory. The theory proposed that a skill consists of numerous elements represented as condition–action rules (also known as procedures or production rules). Many of the sequential elements of a skill are connected because the action of one rule serves as a condition of another. According to ACT*, as a learner successfully completes a task (e.g. writing a line of LISP code) the procedures that produced the performance are retained in long-term memory; in addition, skill acquisition involves improvements in the application of general strategies and the organization of information. Finally, Anderson's theory of skill acquisition suggests that transfer of a skill to a novel situation will be based on the commonality of the elements (i.e. procedures) between the training and novel situations. One part of testing the ACT* account of skill acquisition involved developing a computer-based LISP tutor. The development of the tutor involved: (a) identifying the procedures necessary for writing LISP code – approximately 500 condition–action rules, (b) representing the rules in the computer-based tutor, and (c) designing the tutor to monitor the learner's ability to write LISP functions that correspond to the production rules such that the tutor could indicate success or correct errors by giving advice and asking questions. The design of the tutor derived directly from the theory. Research showed that students learned LISP faster when trained by the tutor than when trained in a traditional classroom situation (Anderson, 1995).

The counterexamples to the technology transfer approach seem to outnumber the examples (e.g. Carroll & Campbell, 1989). For example, the Romans did not wait for the development of physical theories to build bridges all over the known world; *and* the bridges were so well designed and built that some still stand today. Thus, the artifact preceded the scientific explanation and experimental tests. We might call this the need-based approach: a need (e.g. crossing a river) stimulates technological development (e.g. building bridges). The development methodology may include trial-and-error testing of designs, which may eventually lead to abstraction of general laws of nature that underlie the technology (e.g. mechanical principles).

The graphical user interface (GUI) and associated methods of direct manipulation in computer systems provide an example of need-based design related to cognitive psychology. The movement of computer use from a few highly trained users to masses of people due to the marketing of personal computers created a need for new methods of human–computer interaction. To meet this need, designers at Xerox developed the Alto and Star interfaces (Bewley, Roberts, Schroit & Verplanck, 1983). The design of the Star began with a set of objectives:

1. base the overall design on a conceptual model that is familiar to the users
2. the interaction should involve seeing and pointing at displayed objects, not remembering and typing commands
3. what you see should be what you get

4. a set of commands should be available to the user in every application
5. the user should be able to interact with an interface which is simple and uses consistent operations which always lead to the same outcome
6. the interface should permit a degree of user tailoring (Bewley et al., 1983).

System designers developed and employed interface objects and approaches such as the "desktop" metaphor, the mouse, and windows to meet these objectives. They also conducted specific research to address human factors issues that arose related to graphical interfaces and direct manipulation devices (for example Card, English & Burr, 1978); however, the designers did not systematically apply a relevant knowledge base of basic theory and empirically based knowledge of perception, cognition, and motor performance to create the interface.

Despite the overwhelming success of GUIs and direct manipulation both in increasing usability of computers and in market share, they have stimulated only a small amount of either basic or applied cognitive research designed to examine how such interfaces work. One study by Smilowitz (1995) investigated the role of metaphors in the use of computers. She showed that for a task in which people had to search for information on the World Wide Web, an interface based on a library metaphor improved performance over a nonmetaphorical interface, whereas an interface based on a travel metaphor did not improve performance. She found that the advantage of the library metaphor over the travel metaphor was a function of the mapping of the elements of the source domain (i.e. the library) to the target domain (i.e. the World Wide Web); increasing the mapping between travel as the source domain and the World Wide Web improved users' performance.

In contrast to technology transfer and need-based design, designers sometimes create technological artifacts primarily because of the emergence of a new technology. Thus the design is preceded by neither basic research nor users' needs. This approach, which we call designer-initiated, represents the third way in which basic science relates to application. A recent example of this approach concerns the development of virtual reality (VR). Developments in display, input and tracking technologies, as well as the improvements in computer processing speed, memory and storage capacity, converged to make it possible to provide an immersive experience for users that could simulate many different environments. Other than perhaps certain science fiction writers (e.g. Gibson, 1984), potential users did not identify a strong *a priori* need for VR. Only after VR systems became available did people begin to identify many potential uses, such as for simulation and visualization (Bayarri, Fernandez & Perez, 1996; Bryson, 1996). Nor did basic research in vision or cognition point the way for VR. Instead, the cognitive principles that underlie users' interactions with VR remain to be determined by basic researchers (see Wickens & Baker, 1995). In this case, technology became available and designers decided to see what they could do with it. Other recent information age artifacts – multimedia authoring systems like HyperCard® and heads-up displays – also follow this pattern.

What role might basic cognitive psychology play in the need-initiated and designer-initiated approaches? One piece of evidence that cognitive psychology has a critical role to play in the various design approaches is that user interface designers with training in cognition create more usable designs (Bailey, 1993).

(We discuss additional implications of this finding below.) Another role for basic cognitive psychology involves the reverse of the traditional flow from science to its application. Once users establish that a designed system is usable, cognitive researchers could identify the underlying cognitive processes or principles that make this artifact usable. In other words, the success or failure of cognitive artifacts could be used as a rich source of hypotheses about cognition – using the cognitive artifacts as implicit theories about human cognition (see Carroll & Campbell, 1989). Recent research on graph comprehension (for an extensive review, see Lewandowsky & Behrens, 1999, this volume) could be viewed in this light. Graphs are very successful cognitive artifacts which were developed beginning with Lambert and Playfair in the late 1700s without the benefit of basic research in cognition (Tilling, 1975). Since the mid 1980s, several psychological researchers, as well as statisticians and economists, have begun to specify the perceptual and cognitive operations involved in reading a graph. In many cases, this research has resulted in improvements in graphical displays and the methods by which people read them, as discussed by Lewandowsky & Behrens (1999, this volume).

Like basic science in the need-initiated and designer-initiated approaches, applied cognitive research also follows from design in these approaches. As in the development of the Xerox Star, applied cognitive research is essential for answering specific questions that arise during the design process.

Cognitive psychologists – perhaps because of the influence of the logical positivist tradition – have been slow to recognize that ideas for research might come from observing how users interact with artifacts or from analyzing what makes some artifacts usable and others unusable. In contrast, Hutchins's *Cognition in the Wild* (1995a) provides an excellent counterexample to the usual neglect of observation and analysis of people interacting with artifacts (we review this work in greater detail below). In addition, many cognitive psychologists have also ignored ways in which the concepts and principles of cognition might be applied even in the traditional technology transfer approach. This observation should not be taken as an indictment of basic researchers, many of whose time and resources are consumed by the problems of their basic research. Nor should readers assume that the picture is hopelessly bleak: refer to counterexamples in subsequent chapters in this book. Reports of research by Anderson (1990), the Cognition and Technology Group at Vanderbilt University (1992), Glaser (1984), Kintsch & Vipond (1979), Norman (1983), and Kieras & Polson (1985) also serve as selected counterexamples among several possibilities.

There is also a major movement to relate basic research in memory to real-world applications. Three books have recently provided comprehensive reviews of the work in applied memory research (Hermann, McEvoy, Hertzog, Hertel & Johnson, 1996a, b; Payne & Conrad, 1997). We will not attempt to duplicate those reviews here. The application of the research in applied memory often involves information and influence, not the design of cognitive artifacts. For example, one important application of research on false memories has been to influence the interpretation of recovered memories in both psychotherapeutic and legal settings (as reviewed in special issues of *Applied Cognitive Psychology*, Grossman & Pressley, 1994, and *Current Directions in Psychological Science*,

Lynn & Payne, 1997). In contrast, because much of our work has been in engineering psychology and human–computer interaction, the focus that we have selected for this chapter is on bridging the gulf between basic research and the design of artifacts.

Finally, we believe that the failure to apply basic cognitive research should be seen as a system failure – there are few people prepared to bridge the gulf between basic cognitive research and applications and fewer still who have the incentive to do so. That system failure serves as the focus of the following section of this chapter.

Applied Cognition as an Intermediary between Basic Cognition and Design

Imagine if other basic sciences resembled cognitive psychology in its relatively low rate of translating research into applications during the past 50 years: we would live in a world without gene and drug therapies based on biological research; documents would be laboriously typed in triplicate because the micro-miniaturization of technology necessary for personal computers and the development of the laser necessary for laser writers would not have been derived from physics research; the idea of sending astronauts to the moon would still be the province of science fiction. Why, then, has basic cognitive psychology had less applied impact than many of its scientific counterparts? One important factor is that cognitive psychology, unlike those other sciences, has not had a large contingent of people knowledgeable about cognition involved in transferring principles and empirical findings from basic research to design, and communicating design needs and the results of design tests concerning usability to basic researchers. In recent years, as cognitive psychologists have taken positions in industry (for example, as usability engineers involved in the design of user interfaces for computers), a cadre of these intermediaries has emerged. However, the size of this cadre is still small relative to the other sciences, and much usability design work needs to be done.

These intermediaries can help bridge gaps between basic research and design in six areas: (1) philosophy, (2) mission, (3) timeline, (4) reward structure, (5) activity, and (6) means of communication with the world. The importance of bridging the gaps goes beyond communicating research findings. Such gaps have also led to mutual distrust between basic cognitive psychologists and designers of cognitive artifacts, with the result of a paucity of meaningful communication of any type. (For additional discussion of the reasons for the science–technology gulf related to cognition, see Gillan & Bias, 1992; Landauer, 1992; Long, 1996; Norman, 1995; Plyshyn, 1991.)

Philosophy

During the past twenty years or so, basic cognitive psychology has been dominated by issues such as the architecture of cognition (e.g. Anderson, 1983, 1993; McClelland & Rumelhart, 1986; Rumelhart & McClelland, 1986), the number of different memory systems (Tulving, 1985), modularity of the mind (Fodor, 1983), genetic determinism in language processing (Pinker, 1994), and neuropsychological correlates of cognition (e.g. Squire, Knowlton & Musen, 1993). These issues, with their emphasis on the structure of cognition, resemble the issues that concerned the structuralists at the end of the last century (see also Wilcox, 1992). Issues concerning cognitive structure may have motivated cognitive psychologists to stress model building and theory to the exclusion of applications. In the early part of this century, functionalism served as perhaps the most important alternative to the theoretical focus of structuralism. Carr (1925) outlined the seven principles of functionalism, one of which was the importance of practical applications as an integral part of theory development and testing. Likewise, the related philosophical approach of pragmatism (James, 1907), with its focus on the utility of knowledge as a validity criterion for theories also provides a strong alternative to structuralism. Applied cognitive psychologists, especially in design organizations, may serve as a functionalist/pragmatist tonic to structuralism in basic cognitive psychology.

Mission and Timeline

Among the missions of basic scientists are: to operationally define and describe selected phenomena; to determine the empirical and predictive relations of a selected set of variables within a phenomenon; and to investigate the causal factors underlying the empirical relations of variables within a phenomenon. In contrast, the mission of artifact designers is to create a useful artifact or system (cf. Petroski, 1992, 1996). As a consequence of this difference in mission, the timelines of science and design differ. Science, except in periods of great theoretical upheaval, is relatively static (e.g. Kuhn, 1970). A program of scientific research may take years to explore the relations among the many theoretical constructs underlying a phenomenon. In contrast, design enterprises tend to need immediate answers to problems (Allen, 1977; Norman, 1995) and, consequently, show dramatic changes in short periods of time. Often, Simon's (1957) principle of satisficing – of reaching a solution to a problem that is not perfect but good enough – is grudgingly accepted by science, whereas, with time at a premium, satisficing is critical for design.

Reward Contingencies

Scientists and designers operate under different motivational conditions. Allen (1977) has proposed that scientists and designers have different loci of rewards – scientists are intrinsically motivated, whereas designers are extrinsically motivated. However, the stereotypes at the base of Allen's proposal contrast the self-sacrificing scientist with the acquisitive practitioner. These stereotypes fail to capture the complex motives of real people in real jobs. In our experience, designers are often motivated by the opportunity to create elegant and useful artifacts, and basic research does not immunize people from the motivations of extrinsic rewards. Rather, different occupations have different reward contingencies, so people adjust their behavior according to those contingencies. Both groups receive similar extrinsic rewards – status and money. Scientists receive status in their research organization or in the larger world of cognitive psychology and receive money in terms of grants and contracts (as well as increased salary) primarily by publishing reports of their research. Designers receive status and money for producing designs. Publishing papers may be permitted or even encouraged in a designer's organization, but more often are not encouraged. Successful designs and money-making products are reinforced in those organizations.

Activities

The differences in mission, timeline, and reward contingencies in turn result in a variety of different activities in science and design. One important difference is the available time for searching and reading the literature and reflecting on its meaning. The rapid schedule of design projects often means that designers need to begin design activities, such as task analysis and prototyping, very early in a project. Designers have little time for either a general or a directed reading of the literature (Mulligan, Altom & Simkin, 1991). On the other hand, scientists must read extensively prior to, during, and after a research project in order to complete the research and get it published. Scientists also often engage in general reading in their field to help generate new ideas.

Communication

All of the aforementioned differences manifest themselves as differences in the means by which designers and scientists communicate with the world (see also Allen, 1977). Basic researchers in cognitive psychology communicate the results of their work either by writing research reports which are published in journals, or by giving talks at conferences. These various forums are public outlets for a specific type of information – novel findings of theoretical, methodological, or empirical interest. Although public, these media tend to require effort to find because they tend to be housed in libraries at universities and other research centers. In contrast, designers communicate by means of various design instruments – prototypes; documents describing guidelines, standards, or specifications; and final designs. The information in these media rarely find wide distribution because (a) the design organization has concerns about security and competitive advantage, (b) designers lack the time to produce a document for a general readership, and (c) the methods and data from any given successful design usually provide information that is of little interest to journals traditionally read by scientists (although see Bewley et al., 1983, for an example of a paper describing design processes and lessons learned). So, typically, even if researchers wanted to find out about the development of designs, they would have difficulty.

Distrust

A particularly unfortunate consequence of the division between research and application is the distrust and even disdain that each group may show for the other (Gillan & Bias, 1992). Designers may believe that scientists are out of touch with the real world and unable to produce a straight answer in anything approaching a timely fashion. One belief among scientists is that designers are doing a poor imitation of science and are too ignorant of the basic facts and procedures of science to do better. This distrust and disdain may be a natural consequence of the differences in mission, rewards, timelines, activities and communication between the two groups. However, these negative feelings further inhibit the dialogue between basic cognitive psychology and the designers of cognitive artifacts.

Tools to Help Applied Cognitive Psychology Bridge the Gulf between Basic Research and Design

When science and technology fail to communicate, both disciplines suffer. The damage to cognitive psychology due to its failure to communicate with designers of cognitive artifacts can be twofold: (a) it risks being self-referential and minimally related to issues of real-world interest (for discussions, see Carroll, 1990; Gillan, 1990), and (b) researchers may miss theoretically critical variables (Broadbent, 1980; Chapanis, 1988). The damage for the design of cognitive artifacts and of interfaces can also be twofold: (a) by remaining ignorant of the psychological processes that underlie the design of cognitive artifacts, designers may miss opportunities for novel designs; and (b) designers may produce interfaces that either don't work well or that require a greater number of costly iterations in the design process before they work.

Although they often don't realize it, basic cognitive psychologists and the designers of cognitive artifacts are involved in a unique kind of cooperative work (Gillan & Bias, 1992). However, because the cooperation between the groups involves primarily the flow of information, as opposed to interpersonal contact, they need never work face-to-face. In addition, the flow of information between designers and cognitive researchers will often involve a relatively long time lag. Another feature of this cooperative work is that integration of information from disparate sources is desired. Such an integration of information can foster exciting interchanges between research findings and design needs and might lead to a consensus. The temporal delay in communication between scientists and designers may be desirable to the extent that it permits the different sources of information to interact and coalesce.

The information flow between cognitive psychology and its related design disciplines needs to be improved in both directions. Below we propose tools that can improve that flow of information. The first two tools, guidelines and design analysis models, help with the technology transfer from basic research to applications, whereas the other tools could be used to improve both the flow of ideas from research to applications and from applications to research.

Guidelines

One important method for getting relevant research information to designers is by means of design guidelines (for examples, see Gillan, Wickens, Hollands &

Carswell, 1998; Kosslyn, 1994; Mayhew, 1992). Most guidelines are compiled as a hard copy document that provides specific procedural advice for design. That advice derives from science in two ways: first, from the application of generally relevant basic research or theory, and second, from applying directly related research findings. In addition, guidelines come from analyses of the end user's needs and from practice-based knowledge. For example, Gillan et al. (1998) provide advice for graph design to authors of papers in publications of the Human Factors and Ergonomics Society. They provide a guideline based on the general application of the Gestalt law of similarity:

> People tend to perceive similar-looking objects as part of a coordinated unit. Design implications include:
>
> - Use similar patterns or shapes to indicate data from similar conditions in a study.
> - Do not use similar patterns or shapes for indicators for conditions intended to be distinguished.

In contrast, a guideline generated from specific research findings (Gillan & Lewis, 1994; Gillan & Neary, 1992; Milroy & Poulton, 1978) is:

> Readers need to be able to determine the relations among elements of the graph quickly. Design implications include:
>
> - Place indicators that will be compared close together.
> - If the reader will perform arithmetic operations on indicators, place the indicators near the numerical labels either by placing labeled axes on both sides of the graph or by placing the numerical values next to the indicators.
> - Place verbal labels close to the axis they label.
> - Place labels close to the indicators to which they refer.

Although most sets of guidelines are paper-based, they might also be incorporated into design tools that could provide the designer with just-in-time design guidance. For example, user interface prototyping tools provide a designer with technological capabilities like libraries of design components (e.g. display objects for text and graphics and user input objects such as menus or data forms), as well as the ability to link user actions to system responses and feedback. However, prototyping tools have not typically constrained or guided design on the basis of scientific principles. Prototyping tools could serve as valuable technology transfer tools if they incorporated design guidelines based on basic research in cognitive psychology and relevant applied research in cognitive engineering. Those guidelines might be organized in a hypermedia data base which a designer could access during design. For example, user interface designers arranging objects on a screen might want to know how to organize the objects based on psychological principles. The tool used to prototype the designs could provide the designers with direct access to guidelines based on psychological research, such as the Gestalt laws of perceptual organization (e.g. Koffka, 1935). Because the guidelines would be used by designers, they should be accessible by such terms as screen organization and display arrangement as well as by their scientific nomenclature, e.g. Gestalt laws or perceptual organization.

Design Analysis Models

A few applied researchers (Elkind, Card, Hochberg & Huey, 1990; Lohse, 1993; Tullis, 1984, 1997) have pointed the way for another type of tool that could communicate research findings to designers in a timely and useful manner – design analysis models. An excellent example is Tullis's program for analyzing tabular displays. Tullis's program analyzes displays based on a model of how people read alphanumeric tables. The model focuses on the global and local density of the display, the size of groups of characters, and the horizontal and vertical alignment of starting points of groups. Tullis derived the model from the research literature (Tullis, 1983) and conducted further research to support the model (Tullis, 1984). Finally, Tullis (1986) implemented the model in software that (a) examines display parameters relevant to the model, and (b) provides designers with both the model's predictions of users' performance with that design and suggestions for modifications to improve the design. By using this software, a designer can make use of research information without having to become directly familiar with that information. In addition, by using the software and receiving feedback describing which features of the design were consistent and which were inconsistent with the model, designers may implicitly learn to design consistent with the model.

Other display designs appear to be good candidates for analytical tools like Tullis's. For example, a promising application of this approach is Lohse's (1993) analysis software for statistical graphs, called UCIE. Other types of displays – for example, spreadsheets, maps, text, menu layouts and icons – are ripe for this approach. The further development of the analytical tools for design will first require development of models of the underlying psychological processes.

For design analysis tools to play an important role in communications between basic cognitive psychology and design, applied cognitive psychologists have to do what Tullis and Lohse have done – develop a model by applying findings from the basic psychological literature to a given interface, test the model, and write the software that incorporates the model and performs on-line analyses. For this to happen, corporations or government agencies with an interest in improving the quality and efficiency of designs will need to fund the research and development.

Gatekeepers

Allen (1977) proposes that one way in which science communicates with design is through technological gatekeepers – people in the design organization who read the relevant scientific literature, interpret the results for their design implications, and communicate those results and/or interpretations to their design colleagues. In the case of cognitive psychology and the design of both cognitive artifacts and user interfaces, the gate needs to be hinged so that the flow of information is bidirectional. Thus, gatekeepers are also needed to pass design information to the research community. However, as we noted above, designers tend not to communicate through publications, but through design. Thus, these gatekeepers would need to keep current with interface design innovations, not the literature.

In addition, for designers to affect the direction of research, an outlet for discussion of design needs, successes and failures will be required.

One of the major difficulties for the technological gatekeeper is trying to keep current with research while operating under the informational and incentive constraints of a design organization. Applied cognitive researchers in academia, government or other research institutions can help this process of gatekeeping. First, applied cognitive psychologists could publish general papers in journals that designers read. Examples of contact with practitioners through this route include discussions of the cognitive processes underlying: (a) human error (e.g. Bias & Gillan, 1997; Norman, 1983, 1990); (b) active learning (e.g. Carroll, 1984); (c) problem solving (e.g. Singley, 1990); and (d) analysis of bad designs (for example, Norman, 1988). Second, applied cognitive psychologists could make information widely available on the World Wide Web. The Bad Design Web Site at http://www.baddesigns.com/ (Darnell, 1996) provides an excellent example of this approach. Third, forums in which researchers and designers interact directly (e.g. Bias, 1994) may be valuable ways for gatekeepers to keep up with basic and applied research, and with its translation into design.

In addition to human gatekeepers, the gatekeepers between cognitive psychology and design could be electronic – for example, based on current computer bulletin board technology. Bias, Gillan & Tullis (1993) describe a case study in which an electronic gatekeeper was used as part of a user interface design project. The electronic gatekeeper in this case consisted largely of entries from designers describing current designs, guidelines and specifications, usability and other relevant test results, and issues that were raised during design and needs for information. Greater involvement by applied cognitive psychologists who could translate basic and applied research into design ideas or guidance would also have been useful.

Human Resources in Bridging the Gulf between Basic Science and Cognitive Artifact

Applying research and theory from the experimental laboratory directly to practical problems meets with mixed success. Above, we have considered several reasons for the difficulty in going from research and theory to practice. With the limited success of directly applying the fruits of cognitive research, it may seem surprising that people trained in academic settings to do theoretically driven basic research on cognition often are very successful at working in applied settings. Over the last two decades, an increasing number of psychologists trained in cognitive psychology have taken positions in industry involved in the design and evaluation of products. It is interesting that the results of research in cognitive psychology are difficult to apply, while the students trained to do cognitive research are in demand in industry.

Some evidence supporting the soundness of hiring candidates with training in psychology was provided in a study reported by Bailey (1993). He had several different individuals develop software systems for filing and retrieving recipes. Half of the developers had been trained in computer science, and the other half in some aspect of psychology or human factors. Each developer was given feedback about the usability of his or her system in the form of a videotape of users attempting to use the system. With this feedback, the developers revised their designs over three cycles in an attempt to improve usability. Bailey's study showed that those designers with some background in psychology produced the more usable designs at the outset. He also showed that iterative design leads to improved usability even though new problems are often introduced with new iterations.

Why does training in cognitive psychology and human factors produce effective designers of cognitive artifacts? The difficulty of directly applying cognitive research and theory suggests that psychologists do not simply acquire and apply a set of algorithmic principles as a mechanical engineer might. Rather, we hypothesize first, that cognitive psychologists have learned general skills, including how to think about the thinking of others, anticipating specific difficulties in performing tasks, and designing tasks that people can perform; second, that these skills transfer to the design and evaluation of cognitive artifacts; and third, that applying these skills in design situations increases the likelihood that usable artifacts will result.

Students' experience conducting research in cognitive psychology teaches them to design experimental tasks that are appropriate for the individuals under study. Preparing instructions for participants in research requires considering what knowledge the participants bring to the task, as well as how to direct them to perform the task in terms understandable to them. This training in communicating with relatively naive individuals about various complex tasks may transfer to the task of designing cognitive artifacts. A usable product must communicate the ways in which a user can interact with it. To create an artifact that communicates which actions are appropriate at what times, a good designer will need to consider the potential mental states of the users at various stages in learning about and using the artifact. We propose that training in cognitive psychology increases a student's ability to identify users' potential mental states and to predict what behaviors would result from those mental states.

THE VALUE OF APPLIED COGNITIVE PSYCHOLOGY

Above, we have discussed the complex and difficult interrelations between basic cognitive psychology, applied cognitive psychology, and the development of cognitive artifacts. Implicit in that discussion is that the enterprise of applying cognitive psychology, including both research and design, has value. However, such an important point should not be left to inference. Accordingly, in this section, we discuss the specific benefits of applied cognitive psychology, both for basic cognitive psychology and for the industries that develop and market cognitive artifacts.

Applied Cognition can Benefit Basic Cognitive Psychology

Perhaps the most common metaphor in cognitive psychology has been "the mind is a computer." Like other metaphors in science, it has played a valuable role in helping reveal connections and similarities between a known entity, computers, and an unknown one, the mind. However, to realize the full value of a metaphor, one must recognize its limitations, as well as its applicability (Halasz & Moran, 1982). Thus, although minds and computers both process information, computer designs have been shaped by market forces, whereas the mind has been shaped by natural selection to help individuals meet goals such as attracting a fit mate, raising offspring, finding food and water, and avoiding predation. The goals of human cognition have expanded beyond those directly related to survival and reproduction to include goals related to the tasks of the workplace and of modern communities. Accordingly, analyses of cognition would be improved by considering the context from which the goals of cognition emerge.

Context and Cognition

The book, *Cognition in the Wild* (Hutchins, 1995a), deals with "ecological cognition" rather than applied cognition, *per se*. However, Hutchins's conception of ecological cognition relates to the analysis of context in cognition. In the book and his paper, "How a cockpit remembers its speeds" (Hutchins, 1995b), he emphasizes the importance of the structure of the environment in terms of both the physical properties of tools and information sources, and the interactions among different individuals in his analysis of cognition in the airplane cockpit and the bridge of a ship. He argues that cognition is a property not just of individuals, but also of the entire system of individuals in a team and the environment in which they operate. To focus solely on cognition in the heads of single individuals is to miss much of importance about why the environment comes to be structured the way it is, how the structure of the environment contributes to cognitive processes, and how and why cooperating individuals communicate with each other. In Hutchins's view, maps, instruments, and tools are part of the cognitive system, and they not only shape the cognition of the people involved, but they also accomplish such cognitive processes as remembering, computing, attending and making decisions. Although one might argue with the details of Hutchins's analysis, we agree with his message that observing cognition in context reveals much of importance that may be overlooked in the confines of a laboratory.

The approach of situated cognition (e.g. Suchman, 1987; see also Neisser, 1982) also analyzes the context of cognition to include: goals; task-related knowledge; the structure of the task, including collaborative cognition; the availability of cognitive tools and resources, including cognitive artifacts; the physical environment in which cognition occurs (or at least the mental representation of that environment); and the specific content of the cognition (e.g. Choi & Hannafin, 1995; Lave, 1988). The idea of situated cognition has had a substantial impact on educational psychology and instructional design (e.g. Young, 1993), as well as on artificial intelligence (see Winograd & Flores, 1986), but less on cognitive psychology (although see Greeno, Moore & Smith, 1993).

The concept of situation links basic and applied research in cognition. Basic and applied cognitive research, like everyday cognition in the home, classroom and workplace, occur in particular contexts. The experimental control that underlies both basic and applied research involves trade-offs between eliminating irrelevant context that primarily increases noise in the data or introduces confounds, and including relevant context that increases the generalizability of the results and conclusions of the research to those everyday situations (for recent discussion, see Payne & Blackwell, 1997; Vicente, 1997). Any kind of research, basic or applied, should benefit from identifying irrelevant and relevant contexts.

Cognition occurs in a context generated by the thinker's needs, knowledge and skills, as well as the physical and social/cultural worlds. The relative importance of those factors may vary across different cognitive processes but, as researchers, we believe that such variations will turn out to be systematic and understandable. Thus, research that treats a participant's goals and knowledge as irrelevant might be generalizable to other situations, but frequently would be limited to the narrow and impoverished situation of the research. Likewise, one complaint about applied studies is that they also take place in a specific context, thereby making generalization difficult (e.g. Banaji & Crowder, 1989). In addition, at this point in our understanding of the effects of context on cognitive processes, any cognitive study that attempts to manipulate context may have expended wasted effort and generated noisy data with little increase in generality. Accordingly, an important goal of research in cognition (especially applied cognition) should be to determine the conditions under which context is theoretically and experimentally meaningful. In other words, we need to develop theories and research programs that address context as a critical theoretical construct in cognitive psychology. As a consequence, the study of applied cognition could blaze trails necessary for progress in basic cognitive psychology.

Guiding Basic Research

Applied cognition serving as a trailblazer for basic cognitive research would entail a return to the historical roots of cognitive psychology. A major push toward the modern emphasis on cognitive processes resulted from the attempts of psychologists to apply their psychological knowledge to the war effort in the Second World War (cf. Lachman, Lachman & Butterfield, 1979). Much to the distress of many of these psychologists, the knowledge from years of laboratory research and the theories developed to account for the findings of this research proved to be of little use in confronting the real problems of training, human performance, and the usability of complex machinery. Some of these researchers (Donald Broadbent and Paul Fitts are notable examples among many possible) took this challenge to develop some new ways of approaching the applied problems they faced. For example, Broadbent's interest in divided attention was instigated by his experiences as a pilot with the RAF. At that time, all radio communication was conducted on a single radio frequency such that simultaneous messages were frequently present and one had to understand a particular message out of the stream present. This was difficult, but apparently just possible. Broadbent believed that this phenomenon merited systematic investigation which he subsequently undertook (Broadbent, 1958).

Broadbent consistently advocated keeping psychological research in touch with problems found in practical affairs, as in the following passage:

> Briefly, I do not believe that one should start with a model of man and then investigate those areas in which the model predicts particular results. I believe one should start from practical problems, which at any one time will point us toward some part of human life. (Broadbent, 1980, pp. 117–18)

He also proposed that models can be useful if they are tested in conjunction with applied problems because reducing the number of potential models for application can be helpful. A major reason for starting from practical problems is that they "throw up the bits of human life which involve the major variables." For example, Broadbent noted that years of laboratory research had failed to identify the time of day as a major factor in human performance. This observation had little theoretical value for most models of performance, but once noticed, of course, the result demands some explanation from performance theories.

Broadbent's message is that focusing on real problems can help solve real problems, and for the benefit of basic science, real problems provide a way of identifying the important factors that must be included in any serious scientific analysis of human performance. Confining research investigations to puzzles that arise in the laboratory can easily come to be focused on the details of research paradigms rather than on the phenomena in the world that call for understanding. To the degree that the study of cognition covers more of the interesting cognitive phenomena in the world, the science of cognition will benefit from maintaining contact with practical problems.

In a related vein, Greenwald, Pratkanis, Leippe & Baumgardner (1986) discuss the influence of confirmation bias in research motivated by theory. Among other consequences, a bias toward finding confirmation for a theory leads researchers to focus on discovering situations in which the predictions of theories hold. Although in the course of confirming the theory, several conditions are discovered in which the predictions do not hold, the focus on the theory leads to discounting these nonconfirming conditions. Of course, when the theory is later applied to predict outcomes in some practical situation, it is quite likely that one of the nonconfirming conditions will be encountered again. Greenwald et al. argue that much could be gained from more emphasis on explicitly identifying limiting conditions for theories in addition to simply finding confirmation for the theory. Feedback from applied research to basic research could help supply an understanding of such limiting conditions.

Applied Cognition can Produce Economic Benefits

One important reason that people buy many products and services is that these systems perform functions that their users either cannot do at all or cannot do as well on their own. In other words, people purchase functionality (e.g. Davis, Bagozzi & Warshaw, 1989) designed to extend either their physical or cognitive abilities. Much economic activity centers around purchasing devices to extend our physical capabilities – for example, cars, trains, and planes transport us and goods faster and with less effort than we can by walking; construction equipment multiplies the forces that we can exert to dig, lift, etc.; furnaces and air conditioners warm and cool us better than muscular exertion and sweating. The functionality of these systems focuses on the body rather than the mind; however, cognition is involved in the usability of these systems both as we learn how to use them and, later, as we process information and make decisions during their use.

People also buy many systems to extend their cognitive abilities. For example, reference books extend people's ability to store information – thus, the popular student lament, "Why should I learn this fact [or definition, or formula] when I can look it up in a book?" Similarly, parents videotape their child's performance in a Christmas pageant as a way to extend their memory (e.g. Norman, 1992). Businesses which spend billions of dollars a year for graphics and presentation software (Verity, 1988) are paying to have information presented in a format that makes it easy to learn or to use in solving problems. Some of those same businesses also pay for researchers and consultants to make masses of data understandable. And, of course, individuals, companies and governments spend billions of dollars on computers to extend their arithmetic, mathematical problem solving, and symbol manipulation abilities, as well as to store and present information. Thus, many of the artifacts that people have created throughout history have had a cognitive purpose. Certainly, one goal of research in applied cognitive psychology should be to understand how people use these cognitive artifacts. A second goal should be to use the knowledge from basic cognitive research and from the study of the processes involved in using cognitive artifacts to both improve the current cognitive artifacts and design novel artifacts to meet other cognitive needs.

Functionality probably provides the initial impetus for consumers to purchase an artifact. However, if users have difficulty accessing the functions, the artifacts typically will not survive in a competitive marketplace. Access to functionality is commonly known as usability (e.g. Nielsen, 1993).

A common life course of an artifact is initial high functionality and low usability followed by relatively slow growth in functionality and rapid growth in usability (Gentner, 1990). Factors that underlie the shift in focus to usability may include feedback from users and competitors recognizing that usability is an area in which they have leverage. Mini- and micro-computers provide a prominent example of the importance of usability. Operating system software such as Microsoft Windows® and the Macintosh® operating system, both of which are sold largely on the basis of ease of use, are now the largest selling software, despite arguably greater functionality by less usable operating systems (for example, UNIX-based systems).

The application of cognitive psychology has the potential to increase the functionality of cognitive artifacts and the usability of any artifact that involves human interaction. From the viewpoint of the manufacturer of the artifact, increasing usability should improve product quality which in turn may translate into higher sales and improved profitability. Another path to improved profits involves reducing the costs associated with an artifact; applied cognition has a role to play in cost reduction as well as in quality improvement. For example, taking into account a user's cognitive processes (e.g. limitations in working memory or the factors that direct attention in visual displays) early in the design of a product may decrease the need for expensive redesigns later in the design process (see Bias & Mayhew, 1994, for a general discussion of the cost-benefit analysis of usability).

Usability and Productivity

Landauer's (1995) book, *The Trouble with Computers*, builds a convincing argument that, contrary to the popular wisdom, computers have not led to improved growth of productivity. He marshals considerable evidence in support of this claim:

> Beginning around 1985, a few economists began to sing the blues about a disappointing love affair between American business and computers. Since then, the refrain of these soloists has turned into a chorus. I have replayed here all the major themes: the downturn of productivity growth over time coincident with widespread computerization, the concentration of growth failures in industries most heavily involved, the failure of labor productivity in services to respond positively to lavish information technology, the long-term lack of correlation of business success with investment in this new technology. And we have looked closely, wherever a view was to be had, at the direct effects of computers as they try to lend a hand to people at work. Almost everything points to the conclusion that computers have failed to work wonders for productivity. (Landauer, 1995, pp. 76–7)

Landauer goes on to argue that the limited usability of computers is probably a major contributor to their failure to improve productivity; an implication of this argument is that the potential economic benefits from applied cognitive psychology influence not just individual companies, but the economic well-being of the entire country.

The failures of usability in millions of individual interactions add up to a huge net loss of time, effort and money and a consequent decrease in the Gross National Product. At the heart of that decreased productivity is an experience that all computer users have had – the frustration of failing to accomplish some simple task using a computer because we couldn't figure out how to get the computer to do just what we wanted. A recent experience exemplifies this frustration: in creating a graph using a high level graph drawing application, we were unable to change the display of numerical values on an axis; after hours of failing to change the default values, we gave up and accepted those values. Hours of productive time were lost to produce a product of lower quality than was desired (and than was potentially realizable). Even more serious problems arise for individuals, as well as for entire companies, when a hard drive crashes without an adequate backup. How many hours have been spent trying unsuccessfully to recover data from a crashed disk? How many hours of work have been lost from the crashed disks?

Should designers make computers easier to use? Should the design of computers protect users from disasters from which they often fail to protect themselves? At one level, one might be hard pressed to find anyone who would answer "No" to these questions. On the other hand, in most development projects, the reality of schedule and development costs often work against usability. Yet, real progress seems to have been made in improving usability. For those who can remember, compare the usability of the system on your desk to the mainframes we used in the past. If your memory is very good, you might even remember Hollerith cards, the major input method of most mainframes in the distant past. Running a program required carrying punched cards to the computer center, often through the rain or freezing cold, giving the cards to the computer operator, and waiting around or coming back later to pick up the output. Especially memorable are those human–computer interactions that ended with the printout telling the user about omitting a required period – "Why didn't it just put in the period if it knew I had left it out?" Working with today's desktop computers is certainly superior to that experience. So usability has improved enough so that computer use is available to more people for more tasks – who would attempt word processing using the punch card interface? However, if Landauer's analysis is correct, the increase in usability of computers has not kept pace with the expanded bases of users and tasks.

To continue to improve usability will require more work on understanding how to accomplish usability as a general proposition. In practice, accomplishing usability as a general proposition translates into identifying and following methods of design and system development that result in usable systems. Experimental cognitive psychology can contribute to this endeavor in a number of ways. First, although the problems of understanding human cognition are hard, to the extent we make progress in understanding those cognitive processes involved in human–computer interaction, including memory, language and communication, problem solving, we should gain some insights into what might constitute successful designs. Second, as we proposed above, training people to think systematically about human cognition and human behavior can have a positive impact on designing more usable systems. Third, the methods we develop for studying cognition in the laboratory may facilitate the process of interface design and testing. In the next section, we discuss ways in which methods from basic cognitive psychology can benefit applied cognitive research and design.

METHODOLOGY FOR BASIC AND APPLIED RESEARCH

As we suggested above, experience in basic cognitive research may increase researchers' skill in thinking about and adjusting to people's cognitive abilities and inclinations, which results in greater skill in taking user needs into account during the design process. When researchers design experiments, they must think about how tasks and situations will be interpreted by the participants, and must accommodate the tasks and situations to those interpretations. Individuals with such training may also be able to influence others in the course of their work. To the extent that more of the people working on designing cognitive artifacts become sensitive to user considerations, it should have a positive impact on the usability of those products. Of course, good intentions alone are unlikely to ensure usability. This is where methods of observation, measurement, and assessment become important. We often hear from former students working in industry that they indeed do use the methods they learned in pursuing their graduate studies. They often recommend increasing the time devoted to the study of methods and measurement.

Methods are often used in somewhat different ways in basic and applied research, especially in applied research that occurs as part of the design process. Despite those differences, having the ability to discriminate good from bad research is likely to help designers and usability evaluators conduct useful studies, even when the details of the procedure must accommodate such demands of the applied setting as schedule-driven limitations on time and the number of participants.

Applying Scaling Methods

Both authors of this chapter have substantial experience working with scaling methods in basic research and applied settings (see Gillan, Breedin & Cooke, 1992; Schvaneveldt, 1990). Accordingly, we have chosen to use the application of these methods to exemplify the various ways in which methods that have been developed to address basic research issues can provide useful tools for applications.

Psychometric methods, such as multidimensional scaling, cluster analysis, and network-development algorithms, were developed to investigate perception and knowledge organization. In multidimensional scaling methods (Kruskal, 1964; Shepard, 1962a, b) stimuli of various kinds are located as points in a low-dimensional space according to the perceived similarities or dissimilarities among the stimuli. Methods which produce clusters of stimuli include hierarchical methods (Johnson, 1967), overlapping clusters (Shepard & Arabie, 1979), tree structures (Butler & Corter, 1986; Cunningham, 1978; Sattath & Tversky, 1977), and networks (Feger & Bien, 1982; Hutchinson, 1981; Schvaneveldt & Durso, 1981; Schvaneveldt, Dearholt & Durso, 1988; Schvaneveldt, Durso & Dearholt, 1989). Applied researchers and usability engineers and instructional designers have identified ways in which they could use these methods to address their specific needs.

Many of the psychometric methods begin with proximity data: similarity, relatedness, distance, and correlation data, all of which indicate the degree to which things "belong together." Proximity is a general term which represents these concepts as well as other measurements, both subjective and objective, of the relationship between pairs of entities. Proximity data can be obtained in many ways. Judgments of similarity, relatedness, or association between entities are frequently used in the study of human cognition. Investigations of social processes often make use of proximity measures such as liking between pairs of individuals and frequency of communication between individuals or groups of individuals. Proximities can also be obtained from measures of co-occurrence, sequential dependency, correlation and distance. Of course, there are potentially as many proximity data points as there are pairs of entities, so even with small sets of entities, there can be many proximities. Scaling methods reduce this complexity by providing representations which capture some aspects of the structure in the set of proximities.

Because we are most familiar with network models, we discuss the use of such models as an example. As psychological models, networks entail the assumption that concepts and their relations can be represented by a structure consisting of nodes (concepts) and links (relations). Networks can be used to model heterogeneous sets of relations on concepts such as those found in semantic networks (e.g. Collins & Loftus, 1975; Meyer & Schvaneveldt, 1976; Quillian, 1969). More generally, networks highlight salient relations among concepts. One particular approach to producing networks from proximity data is known as the Pathfinder method (Schvaneveldt, 1990; Schvaneveldt & Durso, 1981; Schvaneveldt et al., 1988, 1989).

Applications of Pathfinder Networks

Applications of Pathfinder networks include studies of the differences in knowledge between experts and novices, predicting course performance from the similarity of networks between teachers and students, and to help with designing user interfaces. In a Pathfinder network, the nodes represent the original objects used in the distance measures, links represent relations between objects, and a weight associated with the link and derived from the original proximity data reflects the strength of the relation. A completely connected network can be used to represent (without any data reduction) the original distance data. One of the benefits of the Pathfinder algorithm, however, is in its data reduction properties. The algorithm eliminates various links in order to reduce the data and facilitate comprehension of the resulting network. Basically, if a link exceeds the minimum strength criterion set by the analyst (be it experimenter or designer), that link is included by the algorithm if the minimum distance path (chain of one or more links) is greater than or equal to the distance indicated by the proximity estimate for that pair.

Experts and novices differ in knowledge organization (e.g. Chase & Simon, 1973; Chi, Feltovich & Glaser, 1981; McKeithen, Reitman, Rueter & Hirtle, 1981; Reitman, 1976; Schvaneveldt, Durso, Goldsmith, Breen, Cooke, Tucker & DeMaio, 1985); Pathfinder networks can be used to capture these expert–novice differences in conceptual structure. For example, Schvaneveldt et al. (1985) asked expert (USAF instructor pilots and Air National Guard pilots) and novice (USAF undergraduate pilot trainees) fighter pilots to judge the relatedness of concepts taken from two flight domains. The networks derived from the proximity data showed meaningful differences between the novices and the experts. Similar results have been obtained in several other studies including investigations of computer programming (Cooke & Schvaneveldt, 1988), physics (Schvaneveldt, Euston, Sward & Van Heuvelen, 1992), British Railways (Gammack, 1990), and electronics trouble-shooting (Rowe, Cooke, Hall & Halgren, 1996).

A related application of Pathfinder networks concerns the assessment of student knowledge through the organization of course-related concepts in networks derived from students' ratings of the relatedness of course concepts (Acton, Johnson & Goldsmith, 1994; Goldsmith, Johnson & Acton 1991; Gomez, Hadfield & Housner, 1996; Gonzalvo, Canas & Bajo, 1994; Housner, Gomez & Griffey, 1993a, b; Johnson, Goldsmith & Teague, 1994). Goldsmith et al. (1991) found that the similarity of student and instructor networks was a better predictor of exam performance than were correlations between the student and instructor relatedness ratings or measures based on the use of multidimensional scaling. Goldsmith et al. (1991) concluded that the networks captured the configural character of the relationships among concepts, and this configural pattern is particularly sensitive to student knowledge. Housner et al. (1993a) found similar results using prospective teachers enrolled in pedagogy courses. Knowledge of key pedagogical concepts was organized more consistently and was more similar to the instructor's organization after completion of the course than it was in the beginning of the course.

Gonzalvo et al. (1994) used the configural properties of Pathfinder networks to predict the acquisition of conceptual knowledge in the domain of history of psychology. They conducted a fine-grained analysis of the relationship of the concepts in Pathfinder networks to students' abilities to define these concepts. Each concept in the instructor and student networks was assessed structurally in terms of the concepts to which it was directly linked. Well-structured concepts in the student networks were defined as those sharing greater degrees of similarity (in terms of direct links to the same set of concepts) with those links found in instructor networks. Ill-structured concepts were defined as those sharing less student-to-instructor link similarity. Gonzalvo et al. found positive correlations between the goodness of students' definitions of concepts and the structural similarity of their concepts to the concepts in the instructor networks, as well as an increase in the number of well-structured concepts at the end as compared to the beginning of the course.

Thus, many studies attest to the relation of network structure to student performance in the classroom. It is also of value to know how course exams and network structure relate to the ability to generalize knowledge to an applied setting. Gomez et al. (1996) investigated this issue. Like other studies, they found a positive relationship between course performance and network similarity to the course instructor for prospective math teachers enrolled in an elementary mathematics teaching methods course. They also found that the similarity of student and instructor networks predicted students' ability to apply the knowledge obtained in the course in a simulated teaching task. Thus, in addition to predicting the recall of knowledge (as reflected in traditional course assessment measures), network structure also predicts the quality of the application of knowledge (as reflected in a simulated teaching task).

Interface designers have demonstrated the value of Pathfinder networks in designing user interfaces. For example, Roske-Hofstrand and Paap (1986) used Pathfinder networks derived from relatedness ratings by pilots to design a system of menu panels in an information retrieval system used by pilots. The Pathfinder-based system led to superior performance in using the retrieval system by the target users of the system. A similar application of Pathfinder to a menu-based version of the MS-DOS operating system was reported by Snyder, Paap, Lewis, Rotella,

Happ, Malcus & Dyck (1985). Snyder et al. reported significantly faster learning of operating system commands with a menu organized according to a Pathfinder network. Several other studies (Branaghan, McDonald & Schvaneveldt, 1991; Gillan, Breedin & Cooke, 1992; Kellogg & Breen, 1990; McDonald, Dearholt, Paap & Schvaneveldt, 1986; McDonald & Schvaneveldt, 1988) used Pathfinder network scaling in conjunction with other scaling methods to design and/or analyze various aspects of computer–user interfaces. A major theme in those studies was the use of empirical techniques to define users' models of systems. These models were then incorporated into the user interface or compared with existing interfaces. The results generally showed that users were more effective using interfaces derived from Pathfinder networks than interfaces created by professional designers but without the benefit of Pathfinder.

As a case study, the use of Pathfinder in applied settings illustrates two key points. First, a method developed to address issues in basic research can be useful in a wide range of different applied settings. In contrast, methods developed to meet specific applied needs may work well in those settings that closely resemble the original one, but might not work across very different tasks. Second, despite the many differences that divide basic researchers from practitioners, the two sides of the gulf also share important features: at issue with Pathfinder is that both are often concerned with ways to measure constructs that can't be observed directly – people's cognitive states and processes.

CONCLUSION

Designing and building bridges is hard work. Despite the difficulties inherent in trying to apply cognitive psychology, many reasons compel us to attempt application of the research and theory in the field. Sometimes the applications flow from professionals trained in the research, theory and methodology of cognition who are demonstrably adept at conceiving of and recognizing good design. We need to improve the communication channels between researchers and practitioners to improve the application of research. The research community also benefits from both successful and unsuccessful applications of basic principles. Research should also stay informed about the real problems in the world and attempt to encompass these problems in their research and theory. Much good work in cognitive psychology has managed to proceed in this way. More good work in the future will flow from considering the relation between science and practice.

ACKNOWLEDGMENTS

We wish to thank our many colleagues and collaborators for their positive influence on our ideas about applied cognitive psychology. Special acknowledgment is due to Randolph Bias, who has helped identify many of the issues in applying cognitive psychology in the real world and who provided helpful comments on an earlier version of this chapter.

REFERENCES

Acton, W. H., Johnson, P. J. & Goldsmith, T. E. (1994). Structural knowledge assessment: comparison of referent structures. *Journal of Educational Psychology*, 86, 303–11.

Allen, T. J. (1977). *Managing the Flow of Technology: Technology Transfer and Dissemination of Technological Information within the R & D Organization*. Cambridge, MA: MIT Press.

Anderson, J. R. (1983). *The Architecture of Cognition*. Cambridge, MA: Harvard University Press.

Anderson, J. R. (1990). Analysis of student performance with the LISP tutor. In N. Frederiksen, R. Glaser, A. Lesgold & M. Shafto (Eds), *Diagnostic Monitoring of Skill and Knowledge Acquisition* (pp. 27–50). Hillsdale, NJ: Lawrence Erlbaum.

Anderson, J. R. (1993). *Rules of the Mind*. Hillsdale, NJ: Lawrence Erlbaum.

Anderson, J. R. (1995). *Cognitive Psychology and its Implications* (4th edn). New York: Freeman.

Anderson, J. R. & Reiser, B. J. (1985). The LISP Tutor. *Byte*, 10, 159–75.

Bailey, G. (1993). Iterative methodology and designer training in human–computer interface design. *Proceedings of INTERCHI '93 Conference on Human Factors in Computing Systems* (pp. 24–9). Amsterdam: Association of Computing Machinery.

Banaji, M. R. & Crowder, R. G. (1989). The bankruptcy of everyday memory. *American Psychologist*, 44, 1185–93.

Bayarri, S., Fernandez, M. & Perez, M. (1996). Virtual reality for driving simulation. *Communications of the ACM*, 39 (5), 72–6.

Bechtel, W. (1988). *Philosophy of Science: An Overview for Cognitive Science*. Hillsdale, NJ: Lawrence Erlbaum.

Bewley, T. L., Roberts, T. L., Schroit, D. & Verplanck, W. L. (1983). Human factors testing in the design of Xerox 8010 "Star" office workstation. In *Human Factors in Computing Systems: Proceedings of CHI 1983* (pp. 72–7). New York: Association for Computing Machinery.

Bias, R. G. (1994). User interface navigation: and a model for explicit research–practice interaction. In *Proceedings of the Human Factors and Ergonomics Society 38th annual meeting* (p. 255). Santa Monica, CA: Human Factors and Ergonomics Society.

Bias, R. G. & Gillan, D. J. (1997). Human error: but which human? *Disaster Recovery Journal*, 10 (3), 43–4.

Bias, R. G., Gillan, D. J. & Tullis, T. S. (1993). Three usability enhancements to the human factors–design interface. In G. Salvendy & M. J. Smith (Eds), *Proceedings of the Fifth International Conference on Human–Computer Interaction: HCI International '93* (pp. 169–74). Amsterdam: Elsevier.

Bias, R. G. & Mayhew, D. J. (Eds) (1994). *Cost-justifying Usability*. Boston, MA: Academic Press.

Branaghan, R., McDonald, J. & Schvaneveldt, R. (1991). Identifying tasks from protocol data. Paper presented at CHI '91, New Orleans, May.

Broadbent, D. E. (1958). *Perception and Communication*. London: Pergamon Press.

Broadbent, D. E. (1980). The minimization of models. In A. Chapman & D. Jones (Eds), *Models of Man*. Leicester: The British Psychological Society.

Bryson, S. (1996). Virtual reality in scientific visualization. *Communications of the ACM*, 39 (5), 62–71.

Butler, K. A. & Corter, J. E. (1986). The use of psychometric tools for knowledge acquisition: a case study. In W. Gale (Ed.), *Artificial Intelligence and Statistics*. Reading, MA: Addison-Wesley.

Card, S. K., English, W. K. & Burr, B. J. (1978). Evaluation of mouse, rate-controlled isometric joystick, step keys, and text keys for text selection on a CRT. *Ergonomics*, 21, 601–13.

Carr, H. A. (1925). *Psychology: A Study of Mental Activity*. New York: Longmans Green.

Carroll, J. M. (1984). Minimalist training. *Datamation*, 30/18, 125–36.

Carroll, J. M. (1990). *The Nurnberg Funnel: Designing Minimalist Instruction for Practical Computer Skill*. Cambridge, MA: MIT Press.

Carroll, J. M. & Campbell, R. L. (1989). Artifacts as psychological theories: the case of human–computer interaction. *Behaviour and Information Technology*, 8, 247–56.

Chapanis, A. (1988). Some generalizations about generalization. *Human Factors*, 30, 253–67.

Chase, W. G. & Simon, H. A. (1973). Perception in chess. *Cognitive Psychology*, 4, 55–81.

Chi, M. T. H., Feltovich, P. J. & Glaser, R. (1981). Categorization and representation of physics problems by experts and novices. *Cognitive Science*, 5, 121–52.

Choi, J.-I. & Hannafin, M. (1995). Situated cognition and learning environments: roles, structures, and implications for design. *Educational Technology Research & Design*, 43, 53–69.

Cognition and Technology Group at Vanderbilt University (1992). Anchored instruction in science and mathematics: theoretical basis, developmental projects, and initial research findings. In R. A. Duschl & R. J. Hamilton (Eds), *Philosophy of Science, Cognitive Psychology, and Educational Theory and Practice* (pp. 244–73). Albany NY: SUNY Press.

Collins, A. M. & Loftus, E. F. (1975). A spreading activation theory of semantic processing. *Psychological Review*, 82, 407–28.

Cooke, N. M. & Schvaneveldt, R. W. (1988). Effects of computer programming experience on network representations of abstract programming concepts. *International Journal of Man–Machine Studies*, 29, 407–27.

Cunningham, J. P. (1978). Free trees and bidirectional trees as representations of psychological distance. *Journal of Mathematical Psychology*, 17, 165–88.

Darnell, M. (1996). The Bad Design Web site (on-line). Available World Wide Web: http://www.baddesigns.com/.

Davis, F. D., Bagozzi, R. P. & Warshaw, P. R. (1989). User acceptance of computer technology: a comparison of two theoretical models. *Management Science*, 35, 982–1003.

Elkind, J. I., Card, S. K., Hochberg, J. & Huey, B. M. (1990). *Human Performance Models for Computer-aided Engineering*. Boston: Academic Press.

Feger, H. & Bien, W. (1982). Network unfolding. *Social Networks*, 4, 257–83.

Fodor, J. (1983). *The Modularity of Mind*. Cambridge, MA: MIT Press/Bradford Books.

Gammack, J. G. (1990). Expert conceptual structure: the stability of Pathfinder representations. In R. Schvaneveldt (Ed.), *Pathfinder Associative Networks: Studies in Knowledge Organization*. Norwood, NJ: Ablex.

Gentner, D. R. (1990). Why good engineers (sometimes) create bad interfaces. In *Human Factors in Computing Systems: Proceedings of CHI 1990* (pp. 277–82). New York: Association for Computing Machinery.

Gibson, W. (1984). *Neuromancer*. New York: Berkley Publications.

Gillan, D. J. (1990). Computational human factors. *Contemporary Psychology*, 35, 1126–8.

Gillan, D. J. & Bias, R. G. (1992). The interface between Human Factors and design. *Proceedings of the Human Factors Society 36th Annual Meeting* (pp. 443–7). [Reprinted (1996) in G. Perlman, G. K. Green & M. S. Wogalter (Eds), *Human Factors Perspectives on Human–Computer Interaction* (pp. 296–300). Santa Monica, CA: Human Factors and Ergonomics Society.]

Gillan, D. J., Breedin, S. D. & Cooke, N. M. (1992). Network and multidimensional representations of the declarative knowledge of human–computer interface design experts. *International Journal of Man–Machine Studies*, 36, 587–615.

Gillan, D. J. & Lewis, R. (1994). A componential model of human interaction with graphs. I. Linear regression modeling. *Human Factors*, 36, 419–40.

Gillan, D. J. & Neary, M. (1992). A componential model of human interaction with graphs. II. The effect of distance between graphical elements. In *Proceedings of the Human Factors Society 36th Annual Meeting* (pp. 365–8). Santa Monica, CA: Human Factors Society.

Gillan, D. J., Wickens, C., Hollands, J. G. & Carswell, C. M. (1998). Guidelines for presenting quantitative data in HFES publications. *Human Factors*, 40, 28–41.

Glaser, R. (1984). Education and thinking: the role of knowledge. *American Psychologist*, 39, 93–104.

Goldsmith, T. E., Johnson, P. J. & Acton, W. H. (1991). Assessing structural knowledge. *Journal of Educational Psychology*, 83, 88–96.

Gomez, R. L., Hadfield, O. D. & Housner, L. D. (1996). Conceptual maps and simulated teaching episodes as indicators of competence in teaching elementary mathematics. *Journal of Educational Psychology*, 88, 572–85.

Gonzalvo, P., Canas, J. & Bajo, M. (1994). Structural representations in knowledge acquisition. *Journal of Educational Psychology*, 86, 601–16.

Greeno, J., Moore, J. & Smith, D. (1993). Transfer of situated learning. In D. Detterman & R. Sternberg (Eds), *Transfer on Trial: Intelligence, Transfer, and Instruction* (pp. 99–167). Norwood, NJ: Ablex.

Greenwald, A. G., Pratkanis, A. R., Leippe, M. R. & Baumgardner, M. H. (1986). Under what conditions does theory obstruct research progress? *Psychological Review*, 93, 216–29.

Grossman, L. R. & Pressley, M. (1994). Recovery of memories of childhood sexual abuse (Special Issue). *Applied Cognitive Psychology*, 8 (4).

Halasz, F. & Moran T. P. (1982). Analogy considered harmful. In *Proceedings of Human Factors in Computer Systems Conference* (pp. 383–6). National Bureau of Standards, Gaithersburg, Maryland.

Herrmann, D., McEvoy, C., Hertzog, C., Hertel, P. & Johnson, M. (Eds) (1996a). *Basic and Applied Memory: Vol. 1. Theory in Context*. Mahwah, NJ: Erlbaum.

Herrmann, D., McEvoy, C., Hertzog, C., Hertel, P. & Johnson, M. (Eds) (1996b). *Basic and Applied Memory: Vol. 2. New Findings*. Mahwah, NJ: Erlbaum.

Housner, L. D., Gomez, R. L. & Griffey, D. (1993a). Pedagogical knowledge in prospective teachers: relationships to performance in a teaching methodology course. *Research Quarterly for Exercise & Sport*, 64, 167–77.

Housner, L. D., Gomez, R. L. & Griffey, D. (1993b). A Pathfinder analysis of pedagogical knowledge structures: a follow-up investigation. *Research Quarterly for Exercise & Sport*, 64, 291–9.

Hutchins, E. (1995a). *Cognition in the Wild*. Cambridge, MA: MIT Press.

Hutchins, E. (1995b). How a cockpit remembers its speeds. *Cognitive Science*, 19, 265–88.

Hutchinson, J. W. (1981). Network representations of psychological relations. Unpublished doctoral dissertation, Stanford University, Palo Alto, CA.

James, W. (1907). *Pragmatism: A New Name for Some Old Ways of Thinking*. New York: Longmans, Green.

Johnson, P. J., Goldsmith, T. E. & Teague, K. W. (1994). Locus of the predictive advantage in Pathfinder-based representations of classroom knowledge. *Journal of Educational Psychology*, 86, 617–26.

Johnson, S. C. (1967). Hierarchical clustering schemes. *Psychometrika*, 32, 241–54.

Kellogg, W. A. & Breen, T. J. (1990). Using Pathfinder to evaluate user and system models. In R. Schvaneveldt (Ed.), *Pathfinder Associative Networks: Studies in Knowledge Organization*. Norwood, NJ: Ablex.

Kieras, D. E. & Polson, P. G. (1985). An approach to the formal analysis of user complexity. *International Journal of Man–Machine Studies*, 22, 365–94.

Kintsch, W. & Vipond, D. (1979). Reading comprehension and readability in educational practice and psychological theory. In L. G. Nilsson (Ed.), *Perspectives on Memory Research*. Hillsdale, NJ: Erlbaum.

Koffka, K. (1935). *Principles of Gestalt Psychology*. New York: Harcourt Brace.

Kosslyn, S. M. (1994). *Elements of Graph Design*. New York: W. Freeman.

Kruskal, J. B. (1964). Nonmetric multidimensional scaling: a numerical method. *Psychometrika*, 29, 115–29.

Kuhn, T. (1970). *The Structure of Scientific Revolutions* (2nd edn). Chicago: University of Chicago Press.

Lachman, R., Lachman, J. L. & Butterfield, E. C. (1979). *Cognitive Psychology and Information Processing: An Introduction*. Hillsdale, NJ: Erlbaum.
Landauer, T. K. (1992). Let's get real, a position paper on the role of cognitive psychology in the design of humanly useful and usable systems. In J. C. Carroll (Ed.), *Designing Interaction* (pp. 60–73). Cambridge: Cambridge University Press.
Landauer, T. (1995). *The Trouble with Computers: Usefulness, Usability, and Productivity*. Cambridge, MA: MIT Press.
Lave, J. (1988). *Cognition in Practice: Mind, Mathematics, and Culture in Everyday Life*. Cambridge: Cambridge University Press.
Lewandowsky, S. & Behrens, J. T. (1999). Statistical graphs and maps. In F. T. Durso, R. S. Nickerson, R. W. Schvaneveldt, S. T. Dumais, D. S. Lindsay & M. T. H. Chi (Eds), *Handbook of Applied Cognition*, chapter 17. Chichester: John Wiley.
Lohse, G. L. (1993). A cognitive model for understanding graphical perception. *Human–Computer Interaction*, 8, 313–34.
Long, J. (1996). Specifying relations between research and the design of human–computer interactions. *International Journal of Human–Computer Studies*, 44, 875–920.
Lynn, S. J. & Payne, D. G. (1997). Memory as a theater of the past (Special Issue). *Current Directions in Psychological Science*, 6 (3).
Mayhew, D. J. (1992). *Principles and Guidelines in Software User Interface Design*. Englewood Cliffs, NJ: Prentice-Hall.
McClelland, J. L. & Rumelhart, D. E. (Eds) (1986). *Parallel Distributed Processing: Explorations in the Microstructure of Cognition* (Vol. 2). Cambridge, MA: MIT Press/Bradford Books.
McDonald, J. E., Dearholt, D. W., Paap, K. R. & Schvaneveldt, R. W. (1986). A formal interface design methodology based on user knowledge. *Proceedings of CHI '86*, 285–90.
McDonald, J. E. & Schvaneveldt, R. W. (1988). The application of user knowledge to interface design. In R. Guindon (Ed.), *Cognitive Science and its Applications for Human–Computer Interaction*. Hillsdale, NJ: Erlbaum.
McKeithen, K. B., Reitman, J. S., Rueter, H. H. & Hirtle, S. C. (1981). Knowledge organization and skill differences in computer programmers. *Cognitive Psychology*, 13, 307–25.
Meyer, D. E. & Schvaneveldt, R. W. (1976). Meaning, memory structure and mental processes. *Science*, 192, 27–33.
Milroy, R. & Poulton, E. C. (1978). Labeling graphs for increased reading speed. *Ergonomics*, 21, 55–61.
Mulligan, R. M., Altom, M. W. & Simkin, D. K. (1991). User interface design in the trenches: some tips on shooting from the hip. In *Human Factors in Computing Systems: CHI '91 Conference Proceedings* (pp. 232–6). Reading, MA: Addison-Wesley.
Neisser, U. (Ed.) (1982). *Memory Observed: Remembering in Natural Contexts*. San Francisco: Freeman.
Nielsen, J. (1993). *Usability Engineering*. Cambridge, MA: AP Professional.
Norman, D. A. (1983). Design rules based on analyses of human error. *Communications of the ACM*, 26, 254–8.
Norman, D. A. (1988). *The Psychology of Everyday Things*. New York: Basic Books. [Published 1989 in paperback as *The Design of Everyday Things*. New York: Doubleday.]
Norman, D. A. (1990). Commentary: human error and the design of computer systems. *Communications of the ACM*, 33, 4–7.
Norman, D. A. (1992). *Turn Signals are the Facial Expressions of Automobiles*. Reading, MA: Addison-Wesley.
Norman, D. A. (1995). On differences between research and design. *Ergonomics in Design*, April, 35–6.
Payne, D. G. & Blackwell, J. M. (1997). Toward a valid view of human factors research: response to Vicente (1997). *Human Factors*, 39, 329–31.

Payne, D. G. & Conrad, F. G. (Eds) (1997). *Intersections in Basic and Applied Memory Research*. Mawah, NJ: Erlbaum.
Petroski, H. (1992). *The Evolution of Useful Things*. New York: Knopf.
Petroski, H. (1996). *Invention by Design*. Cambridge, MA: Harvard University Press.
Pinker, S. (1994). *The Language Instinct*. New York: William Morrow.
Plyshyn, Z. W. (1991). Some remarks on the theory–practice gap. In J. M. Carroll (Ed.), *Designing Interaction*. Cambridge: Cambridge University Press.
Quillian, M. R. (1969). The teachable language comprehender: a simulation program and theory of language. *Communications of the ACM*, 12, 459–76.
Reitman, J. S. (1976). Skilled perception in Go: deducing memory structures from interresponse times. *Cognitive Psychology*, 8, 336–56.
Roske-Hofstrand, R. J. & Paap, K. R. (1986). Cognitive networks as a guide to menu organization: an application in the automated cockpit. *Ergonomics*, 29, 1301–11.
Rowe, A. L., Cooke, N. J., Hall, E. P. & Halgren, T. L. (1996). Toward an online assessment methodology: building on the relationship between knowing and doing. *Journal of Experimental Psychology: Applied*, 2, 31–47.
Rumelhart, D. E. & McClelland, J. L. (Eds) (1986). *Parallel Distributed Processing: Explorations in the Microstructure of Cognition* (Vol. 1). Cambridge, MA: MIT Press/Bradford Books.
Sattath, S. & Tversky, A. (1977). Additive similarity trees. *Psychometrika*, 42, 319–45.
Schvaneveldt, R. W. (Ed.) (1990). *Pathfinder Associative Networks: Studies in Knowledge Organization*. Norwood, NJ: Ablex.
Schvaneveldt, R. W. & Durso, F. T. (1981). General semantic networks. Paper presented at the annual meetings of the Psychonomic Society, Philadelphia.
Schvaneveldt, R. W., Dearholt, D. W. & Durso, F. T. (1988). Graph theoretic foundations of Pathfinder networks. *Computers and Mathematics with Applications*, 15, 337–45.
Schvaneveldt, R. W., Durso, F. T. & Dearholt, D. W. (1989). Network structures in proximity data. In G. Bower (Ed.), *The Psychology of Learning and Motivation: Advances in Research and Theory*, Vol. 24 (pp. 249–84). New York: Academic Press.
Schvaneveldt, R., Euston, D., Sward, D. & Van Heuvelen, A. (1992). Physics expertise and the perception of physics problems. Paper presented at the 33rd Annual Psychonomic Society Meetings, St Louis, November.
Schvaneveldt, R., Durso, F., Goldsmith, T., Breen, T., Cooke, N., Tucker, R. & DeMaio, J. (1985). Measuring the structure of expertise. *International Journal of Man–Machine Studies*, 23, 699–728.
Shepard, R. N. (1962a). Analysis of proximities: multidimensional scaling with an unknown distance function. I. *Psychometrika*, 27, 125–40.
Shepard, R. N. (1962b). Analysis of proximities: multidimensional scaling with an unknown distance function. II. *Psychometrika*, 27, 219–46.
Shepard, R. N. & Arabie, P. (1979). Additive clustering: representation of similarities as combinations of discrete overlapping properties. *Psychological Review*, 86, 87–123.
Simon, H. A. (1957). *Models of Man: Social and Rational*. New York: Wiley.
Singley, M. K. (1990). The reification of goal structures in a calculus tutor: effects on problem-solving performance. *Interactive Learning Environments*, 1, 102–23.
Smilowitz, E. D. (1995). Metaphors in User Interface Design: An Empirical Investigation. Unpublished doctoral dissertation, New Mexico State University, Las Cruces.
Snyder, K., Paap, K., Lewis, J., Rotella, J., Happ, A., Malcus, L. & Dyck, J. (1985). Using cognitive networks to create menus. IBM Technical Report No. TR 54.405, Boca Raton, FL.
Squire, L. R., Knowlton, B. & Musen, G. (1993). The structure and organization of memory. *Annual Review of Psychology*, 44, 453–95.
Suchman, L. A. (1987). *Plans and Situated Actions: The Problem of Human–Machine Communication*. Cambridge: Cambridge University Press.
Tilling, L. (1975). Early experimental graphs. *British Journal for the History of Science*, 8, 193–213.

Tullis, T. S. (1983). The formatting of alphanumeric displays: a review and analysis. *Human Factors*, 25, 657–82.

Tullis, T. S. (1984). Predicting the usability of alphanumeric displays. Ph.D. dissertation, Rice University. Lawrence, KS: The Report Store.

Tullis, T. S. (1986). *Display Analysis Program* (Version 4.0). Lawrence, KS: The Report Store.

Tullis, T. S. (1997). Screen design. In M. G. Helander, T. K. Landauer, & P. V. Prasad (Eds), *Handbook of Human–Computer Interaction* (pp. 503–31).

Tulving, E. (1985). How many memory systems are there? *American Psychologist*, 40, 385–98.

Verity, J. W. (1988). The graphics revolution. *Business Week*, November 28, 142–53.

Vicente, K. J. (1997). Heeding the legacy of Meister, Brunswick, and Gibson: toward a broader view of human factors research. *Human Factors*, 39, 323–8.

Wickens, C. D. & Baker, P. (1995). Cognitive issues in virtual reality. In W. Barfield & T. Furness (Eds), *Virtual Environments and Advanced Interface Design*. New York: Oxford Press.

Wilcox, S. B. (1992). Functionalism then and now. In D. A. Owens & M. Wagner (Eds), *Progress in Modern Psychology: The Legacy of American Functionalism* (pp. 31–51). Westport, CT: Praeger.

Winograd, T. & Flores, F. (1986). *Understanding Computers and Cognition*. Norwood, NJ: Ablex.

Young, M. F. (1993). Instructional design for situated learning. *Educational Technology Research & Design*, 41, 43–58.

Chapter 2

Applications of Attention Research

Wendy A. Rogers, Gabriel K. Rousseau and Arthur D. Fisk
Georgia Institute of Technology

Pierre is a chef in an up-market downtown restaurant. It is early evening and the diners are beginning to arrive. He is extremely busy. He is preparing a new dish tonight – duck and orange flambé – that requires perfect timing. In addition, he must remember to stir the bouillabaisse every few minutes, check the soufflé in the oven, and finish combining the ingredients for the Caesar's salad. Amidst all of this, Pierre must also monitor the activities of the sous-chef, the dessert chef, and the other aides in the kitchen.

Peter is a professional football quarterback. On this Sunday afternoon, his team is competing for the championship of their division. On any given play he must transmit information in the huddle to his teammates, receive the ball, scan the field in search of an open player, avoid the opposing players who are trying to tackle him, find his receiver, and throw the ball. And, all of this must be done in the midst of thousands of screaming fans.

Pierre and Peter are both engaging in attention-demanding tasks. Pierre is dividing his attention among his many tasks, alternately focusing his attention on the various dishes he is cooking, shifting attention among his staff members, and so on. Peter must focus his attention on his teammates in the huddle and block out the noises of the crowd. When he is ready to throw a pass, he must selectively attend to the open receiver, while at the same time dividing his attention between his task and the oncoming rushers.

These examples illustrate the complexity of the term attention. Given the many activities and processes that involve attention, how then should one define attention? Psychologists have come to the conclusion that there are "varieties of attention" (e.g. Parasuraman & Davies, 1984) – that is, attention is a construct that is representative of different processes.

Handbook of Applied Cognition, Edited by F. T. Durso, R. S. Nickerson, R. W. Schvaneveldt, S. T. Dumais, D. S. Lindsay and M. T. H. Chi.

One major function of attention is to enable us to select certain information for processing. Selective attention involves filtering stimulus information. The classic example of selective attention was termed the "cocktail party problem" by Cherry (1953). Imagine yourself at a cocktail party (or in any other crowded room where a number of conversations are occurring simultaneously). How is it that you are able to selectively attend to the conversation in which you are involved?

Selective attention is affected by the ease with which the target information can be distinguished from the other stimulus information in the environment. Imagine trying to find your sister in a crowd of people. The task would be easier if your sister were 5'6" tall and she were standing amidst a group of 4-year-olds; or if your sister were brunette and she was in a room of blondes. Selective attention is also aided by expectation or instruction. If I tell you that your sister is in the left side of the room, you will be able to locate her more quickly.

In a focused attention task, the individual knows where the target will appear, but distracting information is also present. Focused attention involves concentration – that is, intense processing of information from a particular source. Focusing of attention involves blocking out external sources of stimulus information. Sometimes we get so involved in a task that we forget where we are and are oblivious to what is going on around us. Other times it is more difficult to focus attention on the task at hand. Variables such as interest, motivation, and fatigue can all influence our ability to successfully focus attention.

Sustained attention refers to one's ability to actively process incoming information over a period of time – that is, focusing attention for an extended interval. Sustained attention has been most often measured in vigilance tasks in which an observer must respond to infrequent signals over an extended period of time. Real-world examples of vigilance tasks include a submarine officer monitoring the radar screen for unfamiliar blips, an assembly line inspector searching for defective products, and a mother listening for her baby's cry.

Dividing attention and switching attention are other aspects of the construct of attention. They are considered together because it is difficult to differentiate between the true division of attention and the rapid switching between tasks. For example, consider reading the newspaper and watching television. Is limited attention really simultaneously "divided" between the two tasks or does attention actually switch back and forth between the two, attending more to the television when something interesting is happening and switching to the newspaper during the commercials?

Thus far we have been discussing tasks that require attention. However, an important component of skill acquisition is the ability to "automatize" task components such that they no longer require attention. Consider a novice driver trying to carry on a conversation. His or her attempts are intermittent because inexperienced drivers must focus most of their attention on the task of driving, especially at critical junctures of switching gears or turning a corner. More experienced drivers, however, are able to perform these activities while talking, changing the radio, or planning their day. One fundamental difference between a novice and a skilled driver is the amount of attention required for the task components. Consistent components such as changing gears become automatized with extensive practice. However, even for skilled drivers, the overall task of driving is not automatic as evidenced by the fact that other activities cease when the driver is in heavy traffic or an unfamiliar neighborhood.

OVERVIEW OF CHAPTER

The focus of this chapter will be to review how these various aspects of the construct of attention have been empirically investigated in the laboratory. We will provide specific examples of how the information acquired from controlled laboratory studies has had direct relevance to real-world tasks. Because the study of attention is historically rooted in the tradition of understanding practically relevant issues, we will begin with a brief historical overview of research in the field. We will then provide a sampling of areas of attention research that have been demonstrated to have practical relevance. Within each section we will provide background on the topic, a description of the fundamental attentional limit being addressed by research in that area, an overview of the methodological approaches that have been used, and lastly, solutions and success stories for that aspect of attentional research.

HISTORICAL REVIEW

The realization that attention was an important concept in psychology dates back at least to the beginning of this century. William James ([1890] 1950) is noted for his musings about various aspects of attention. A review of the attention literature was published in *Psychological Bulletin* as early as 1928 by Dallenbach. Books with attention in the title appeared as early as 1903 (Ribot's *Psychology of Attention*) and 1908 (Titchener's *Lectures on the Elementary Psychology of Feeling and Attention*). In addition, experimental research was being carried out on topics in attention as early as 1896 by Solomons and Stein, and 1899 by Bryan and Harter. Clearly, then, the study of attention has a long and distinguished history.

Although the study of attention issues had an early start in the field of experimental psychology, as with many "cognitively oriented" topics, it received scant focus during the early part of the century when behaviorism was the dominant theme in psychology (especially in the United States). However, psychologists and engineers in the military during the Second World War began to investigate such topics. Much of this early research was continued after the war and served as the basis for theories of attention. One set of studies conducted by Cherry (1953) assessed how individuals are able to selectively attend to speech when two simultaneous messages are presented (one to each ear) – the cocktail party problem we referred to earlier. Cherry used a shadowing task to study the cocktail party problem in the laboratory. In a shadowing experiment the subject wears headphones and separate messages are presented to each ear. One story might be read and presented to the left ear and a completely different story read and presented to the right ear. The task is to attend to only one message and ignore the other. To ensure that the subject really is listening to the message that he or she is supposed to be listening to, they are required to shadow the message – repeat it back when they hear it. Cherry found that with some practice subjects could successfully concentrate on just one message.

Cherry (1953) also assessed the extent of awareness of the unattended message. He manipulated the characteristics of the ignored message. He would later ask subjects if they noticed anything peculiar about the unattended message. There were four manipulations of the unattended message: from speech to pure tone; from male voice to female voice (changes frequency); from normal speech to reversed speech; from English to German. Subjects only noticed the change from speech to pure tone and from male to female voice. Changing the meaningfulness of the unattended message by reversing the speech or presenting it in a foreign language was not noticed by the subjects. This experiment suggested that subjects filter the messages on the basis of the physical properties alone and not on an analysis of the meaning of the messages.

Broadbent (1957, 1958) proposed a model of attention that was based in part on the data reported by Cherry (1953), as well as on many studies Broadbent himself had carried out. According to Broadbent's early model, the human has a limited capacity and there is a need for a selective operation. Such selection is based primarily on sensory information (i.e. physical properties of the stimuli). Thus, the filter is very early in the system; hence, this model is called the *early selection* model of attention. However, subsequent studies revealed that subjects were sometimes able to process more than just the physical properties of an unattended message, such as semantic content (e.g. Gray & Wedderburn, 1960; Treisman, 1960), or one's own name (Moray, 1959). Treisman thus modified the early selection theory to account for these data and proposed an *attenuated filter model* whereby not all of the incoming information was filtered on the basis of physical features alone, but some information was analyzed further (e.g. Treisman & Geffen, 1967). The information that was processed further would be that which was particularly relevant to the current task or to the individual. However, on the basis of neurophysiological data such as cortical evoked responses, Deutsch & Deutsch (1963) proposed what is referred to as the *late selection model* wherein all information was processed for meaning and the bottleneck or the filter occurred at the level of the response. That is, although all information may be analyzed, it is only possible to respond to one source of information at a time and thus the bottleneck is at the response stage (see also Corteen & Wood, 1972; Norman, 1968).

All of the models discussed thus far had the common feature of proposing a bottleneck at some stage of information processing. Kahneman (1973) put forth the suggestion that cognitive operations were far more flexible than bottleneck theories would allow. He proposed a capacity model of attention wherein humans have a limited capacity of attention that can be flexibly allocated to the demands of the task (or tasks) at hand. Such allocations would be controlled by enduring dispositions (reflexes), momentary intentions, demands and arousal. Moreover, the capacity available would vary with the arousal level of the individuals. Kahneman's theory represented a dramatically different way of thinking about attention. His model allowed for flexibility and the allocation of attentional "resources," although he did not initially use this term.

Throughout the 1970s and early 1980s, many studies were carried out to investigate the ability to engage in two tasks simultaneously (for a review, see Wickens, 1984). The results of these studies revealed that a single, undifferentiated pool of resources could not account for the patterns of data. Thus, theories of multiple resources have been proposed (e.g. Navon & Gopher, 1979; Wickens, 1980, 1984). For example, Wickens (1980) proposed the following three-dimensional classification of resources: stages of processing (perceptual/central versus response stage), codes of processing (verbal versus spatial), and modalities of input and response (visual versus auditory, manual versus vocal). One cogent criticism of multiple resources theory is the difficulty of determining the limits of potential pools of resources. Navon (1984) cautioned that the idea of resources might be like the proverbial soup stone, with little meat.

Concurrent with assessments of the limits of attention have been studies of how such limits can be overcome via practice and the development of automatic processes. Early studies of the effects of practice were conducted by Solomons & Stein (1896) and Bryan & Harter (1899). The seminal research on the defining characteristics of automatic processes and the boundary conditions under which such processes develop was carried out by Shiffrin & Schneider (1977; Schneider & Shiffrin, 1977). This research program and the subsequent developments are reviewed in great detail by Shiffrin (1988) and we describe it in more depth later in the chapter.

In the 1990s, theoretical issues in attention are being studied in the traditional manner as well in two emerging areas: computational modeling and neurophysiological assessments. Both of these avenues of research are being used to investigate some of the basic perspectives on attention. For example, Meyer & Kieras (1997) have developed a computational theory of executive cognitive processes that allows them to assess the existence of central bottlenecks. Their data suggest that there is not a central response-selection bottleneck, but peripheral bottlenecks may exist for the production of movements.

In the neurophysiological arena, Posner and his colleagues (reviewed in Posner, 1992) are finding that the attention system appears to involve separable networks (perhaps analogous to multiple resources) that subserve different aspects of attention such as orienting or detecting. For example, Posner & Petersen (1990) propose that a posterior brain system mediates attention to spatial locations whereas an anterior system mediates attention to cognitive operations. Thus, different components of attentional processing may be controlled by different brain regions (see also Cowan, 1995).

We have provided only a cursory review of the history of attention research. Recent historical reviews of research on attention in experimental psychology are provided by LaBerge (1990), Underwood (1993) and Meyer & Kieras (1997). LaBerge provides a historical review in the context of William James's perspectives on attention. The Underwood reference is an introduction to an excellent two-volume collection of many of the classic research articles in attentional research. The Meyer & Kieras review is part of their introduction to a comprehensive computational model of cognitive processing. These reviews provide chronological perspectives on the major foci of research on attention (see also Shiffrin, 1988).

The topic of attention has continued to be highly researched in the field of experimental psychology. One indicator of its prevalence in the field is the fact that "Attention" is the third most common session title for papers presented at the annual meetings of the Psychonomic Society, following "Information Processing" and "Vision," respectively (Dewsbury, 1997). Thus, through the years that these meetings have been held (1960 to the present), attention research has remained an active research area. We turn next to a description of research in several areas of attention that are most relevant to the focus of this book; namely, the application of cognitive findings to areas of technology, business, industry and education.

SAMPLES OF APPLIED ATTENTION RESEARCH

As discussed above, research in attention has its roots in real-world problems as evidenced by James's ruminations on attentional capabilities, Cherry's focus on the cocktail party problem, and Broadbent's efforts to understand the capabilities of individuals such that they could perform tasks more safely. We turn now to contemporary examples of how attention research is being applied to address human capabilities and limitations outside the laboratory. As will be clear from our discussion, not only are there varieties of attention, there are also varieties of approaches to the empirical assessment of attention.

Automaticity and Training

A major applied goal of the field of attention is to aid in the principled approach to training, especially to the training of high-performance skills. High performance skills are defined here as having three important characteristics (see Schneider, 1985, for more detail):

1. the learner expends considerable time and effort learning the skill
2. a large number of individuals never attain the requisite performance level, even with a high degree of motivation
3. there are easily identifiable qualitative differences in performance between a novice and an expert within the domain.

The example we point to later is that of training American football quarterbacks (Walker & Fisk, 1995).

From an applied cognition perspective, this approach to training high performance skill assumes that as an individual transitions from novice performance to that of an expert, cognitive (and attentional) requirements change across identifiable phases or stages. Such an approach is well grounded in basic human performance and attentional theory (e.g. Anderson, 1982, 1983; Fitts, 1964, [1965] 1990; Shiffrin & Schneider, 1977). As the learner transitions through these phases, from so-called controlled processing to automatic processing (Schneider & Shiffrin, 1977), the major components of the task require less intervention of attention for successful task performance.

For more than a century, psychologists have realized the importance of making aspects of a task habitual or automatized, thereby reducing the amount of attention required for performance of the overall task (Bryan & Harter, 1899; James, [1890] 1950; Solomons & Stein, 1896). Since these early studies, much experimental work has been conducted to understand the characteristics of such automatism (for reviews see Fisk & Rogers, 1992; Shiffrin, 1988). The importance of an approach to training that capitalizes on automatization or overlearning has been reported in reviews of the training literature (Goldstein, 1986; Howell & Cooke, 1989).

Skilled performance of most complex tasks requires the coordination and integration of many components. Consider either the task of driving a manual shift automobile or piloting a jet fighter aircraft. One must coordinate the components of the task. The complexity of the full task can be overwhelming for the novice. For the expert, many of the task components no longer require attention (they have become automatized); those task components can be performed with ease and concurrently with other task components.

Logan (1985) referred to automatization as the hands and feet of skill. There are certain characteristics that define whether something is a controlled (attention demanding) or automatic process (Schneider, Dumais & Shiffrin, 1984; Shiffrin & Dumais, 1981). Controlled processes are required for the performance of novel tasks, as well as for tasks that are varied in nature and require the devotion of attention. For example, in the task of driving, monitoring the behavior of other vehicles on the road is dominated by task components that demand attention. Some controlled processes consume attentional resources such that it becomes difficult to perform other task components concurrently. Consider the concentration involved in merging onto a busy highway: generally, conversation stops, the driver tunes out the sounds of the radio, and attention is focused on the component task of merging successfully. Controlled processes are serial in nature, meaning that they are carried out in a step-by-step fashion. Anderson (1982) likened novice performance on some tasks to following a recipe. The requirement to perform controlled processes serially results in their being performed slowly and under the explicit control of attention.

The characteristics of automatic processes are nearly opposite those of controlled processes. After extensive and consistent practice some task components may become automatized. As a result, because they no longer require step-by-step application, they are performed faster, are more efficient, and are generally more accurate. Automatized task components generally do not require devotion of attentional resources and, hence, may be performed in parallel with other tasks. Another characteristic of automatic processes is that, once initiated they tend to run to completion unless a conscious effort is made to inhibit them. A simplistic example is that when handwriting the word "bitter", you will dot the "i" and cross the "t"s, and it is rather difficult to inhibit this process while maintaining your normal writing speed. Automatic processes can occur without intention in the presence of eliciting stimuli.

There are many benefits of automatic processing: (a) attentional requirements are minimized, enabling one to perform more than one task at a time; (b) performance becomes fast, efficient, and accurate; and (c) performance becomes resistant to potentially deleterious effects of stress (Hancock, 1984, 1986), fatigue, and vigilance situations (Fisk & Schneider, 1981). Recent research also suggests that automatized components of tasks are better retained up to 16 months, with no intervening practice, than controlled process (and strategic) task components (Fisk, Hertzog, Lee, Rogers & Anderson-Garlach, 1994; Fisk & Hodge, 1992).

For the purposes of illustration, our examples have been described in the context of relatively simple tasks. Many training situations involve tasks that are much more complex. For example, consider training supervisors in nuclear power plants, anti-air warfare controllers on board a Navy ship, or quarterbacks of an NFL American football team. Although such tasks are complex, the basic principles gleaned from fundamental attention (and automaticity) research are applicable. The majority of tasks performed outside the laboratory are actually combinations of controlled and automatic processing components. Consequently, focusing on the components that can become automatic with proper training can have significant benefits for overall performance (Rogers, Maurer, Salas & Fisk, 1997). Performance will be enhanced and more cognitive resources will be available for the strategic aspects of the overall task. As an example, consider a recent training system for quarterbacks derived directly from the psychological principles developed from basic laboratory research.

Training American Football Quarterbacks

Certainly, the quarterback of a football team receives practice. How can applied psychological science contribute to training a football quarterback to make better decisions? A first step is to analyze the quarterback's job via task analysis. There appear to be four primary cognitive and perceptual processes that a quarterback must perform. First, given a play, the quarterback must remember the pass pattern that each of the receivers is expected to run. Next, as the quarterback leaves the huddle and goes to the line of scrimmage, he must visually scan the defense to determine what defensive set is being faced. This is a dynamic process because the opposing team will attempt to hide the defense for the play. Based on the quarterback's decision about the defensive set, he must remember the "read sequence" for the receivers. This sequence is specified in advance and directs the quarterback's visual search. Finally, once the ball is snapped, the quarterback must then look at each of the receivers and determine which one is open and which one is the optimal receiver given the situational context of the game.

Given this analysis, it is possible to categorize this list of tasks into two major types: retrieval tasks (remember the pass pattern and the receiver read sequence) and perceptual judgment tasks (recognizing the defensive set and making a judgment about which receiver is open). In addition, "situational awareness" comes into play in the decision making process. For example, on a third down and short-yardage play, the quarterback should choose a safe pass that gains the necessary yardage. On the other hand, if it is second down and one yard, the optimal receiver may more likely be a "deep" receiver.

Further analysis revealed that quarterbacks (even in the NFL) have few opportunities to train on the visual task that faces them each week during the game. In fact, over the course of a season, there is limited practice, only a small percentage of which is spent practicing with full offensive and defensive teams. Given that this practice is distributed over hundreds of different offensive plays and defensive set combinations, and that a team is trying to train three or four quarterbacks, a college or professional quarterback actually has few repetitions with a specific scenario before a play occurs in an actual game. In many ways, training a quarterback presents a classic training problem facing those in applied psychology.

Based on the literature, Walker & Fisk (1995) reasoned that performance on the field could be significantly improved through training that focused on developing automatic processing of the information retrieval and perceptual judgment components of the overall task. Considering analysis of the quarterback task and on previous research (Fisk & Eggemeier, 1988; Kirlik, Walker, Fisk & Nagel, 1996; Schneider, 1985), it became clear that specialized training was required to develop automatic processes of critical task components. The following were the keys to effective training:

- identification of consistent task components
- development of part-task training for those consistent components
- training that afforded a high number of repetitions and immediate, task specific feedback
- training for task recomposition (putting the individual skills together)
- targeting of skill deficiencies for focused remedial training.

A training simulator was developed that allowed guided part-task training opportunities. The simulator facilitated players receiving the equivalent of a year's practice on critical, consistent components over the course of just a couple of weeks of one-hour training sessions. The simulator also afforded visual search practice that enhanced decision making based on visually presented cues likely to occur in the real game situation. The part-task training included:

- retrieval of correct read sequences – the player would receive the play and the defensive set and respond by pressing the receiver buttons in the correct order
- recognizing defensive sets – the player would see defensive sets from the line of scrimmage and report the correct name of the defensive set
- determining correctness of the called play – the play is given and the defensive set is shown; the player accepts the play or calls a new play
- situation awareness training – the player is given a situation (goal line, third down and long, etc.) and must retrieve and enter the correct play and/or select the optimum receiver
- determine when a receiver is open – this is a dynamic process; the player learns to recognize visual cues that allow anticipation of when or if a receiver will be open to receive a pass.

In addition, full task, simulator training was provided that allowed "putting the components together." Real-time feedback was given concerning play selection, optimum receiver choice, and optimum decision time. Also, the performance data were logged to allow analysis of player performance and need for remedial training.

Laboratory evaluations of the use of visual enhancements in training through football simulations and other tasks that are dependent on visual judgments have proven successful (e.g. Kirlik et al., 1996; Walker, Fisk & Phipps, 1994). These techniques of isolating consistent components of the task during training to develop component automatic processes have increased the rate of acquisition and promoted the transfer of skills to real-world situations. In addition, the response to the system is quite positive from both quarterbacks and coaches (see *Sports Illustrated*, 1994).

Vigilance

Vigilance refers to the ability to sustain attention on a task for an extended period of time. The impetus for research on vigilance or sustained attention began during the Second World War. The need to perform repetitive tasks, such as viewing radar screens, for extended periods of time led to concerns regarding declines in performance. Because of the dire nature of the consequences of a failure (e.g. missing the detection of an enemy plane), vigilance became a prominent focus of study. Since the war, many researchers have devoted their efforts to the study of vigilance to determine the limits under which individuals may sustain their attention before decrements ensue. In fact, well over one thousand research articles have been published on this topic.

There have been two primary findings in the vigilance literature regarding the likelihood of decrements. First, the existence of a decrement will depend on whether the task relies on one's ability to maintain information active in memory, that is, working memory (Parasuraman, 1979, 1985). Simultaneous tasks that require no short-term storage of information do not evidence a vigilance decrement. These types of tasks present all the necessary information to make a decision at the same time. For example, a symbol appears on a radar screen and the operator signals that a target has been detected. In contrast, successive tasks require holding information active in memory and using it in conjunction with additional information before making a decision, and decrements do occur on these types of tasks. For example, a radar operator may need to track the motion of an object before confirming that it is a target. In this instance, the operator must maintain in memory the prior locations of the object and integrate them with the current position before making a decision. In addition to successive tasks, the frequency of targets also affects vigilance. Decrements are likely to be found for higher event rates, where targets occur at least 24 times an hour (Parasuraman & Davies, 1977), although the basis of the decrement has not been clearly established (Warm & Jerison, 1984).

There is some dispute over the generalizability of vigilance decrements. In 1987, Adams contended that researchers have been overzealous in their study of vigilance, and have found very little of any significance. He suggested that simulation is the key to successfully generalizing findings about vigilance beyond the laboratory. Methodology may be a factor in conclusions drawn regarding decrements in sustained attention. Laboratory tasks have been criticized because they are often shorter in length than actual work shifts would be. Further, as a consequence of experimental control, the introduction of signals to be detected is often much more regular or frequent than in the real-world tasks (Weiner, 1987). Another possible factor is that experimental participants may not be as motivated to perform well during vigilance tasks compared to workers because the costs of a vigilance decrement are unlikely to be as severe as those in actual work environments. Thus, the concern is that laboratory tasks may not be representative of real-world vigilance tasks.

Some researchers have successfully integrated laboratory control with more ecological tasks. For example, Pigeau, Angus, O'Neill & Mack (1995) used the NORAD aircraft detection system to examine sustained attention effects on the detection of targets by radar operators. Pigeau et al. were able to inject simulated aircraft into a live radar stream, thus being able to control the occurrence of targets while maintaining the validity of the task. They found a decrement in vigilance, but this effect was largely due to the type of shift workers were in, with the midnight shift workers suffering most from a decline in vigilance. In general, Pigeau et al. concluded that laboratory tasks appear to inflate the vigilance decrement, although it does exist.

Vigilance research that allows for realistic task performance as well as experimental control, appears to offer hope for better understanding this construct. The role of other factors, such as environmental and task characteristics that lead to decrements in performance remain to be determined. Such topics include boredom, motivation, skill level, stress, task complexity and cognitive factors (for a review, see Warm, 1984). Further, the prevalence of vigilance-type tasks is actually on the increase as computer automation becomes more frequent in workplaces. Fundamental aspects of work are changing, emphasizing monitoring rather than active performance (e.g. air traffic control, nuclear power plant systems, operating aircraft, some human–computer interaction and industry tasks). Therefore, the generalization of vigilance research to many new tasks merits investigation.

Optimal Feature Search

Over the last decade the number of computers in the workplace has burgeoned as has the menu-driven navigation of these systems. To perform many tasks, computer users must navigate through a hierarchy of menu options before completing their search. For example, to print a document, most word processors require the user to open a file menu, locate the print option, and then proceed to further options nested under the print menu before the document can be routed as output. In this example, only several levels must be traversed. Other menu procedures or systems may require even more extended navigation. As the number of steps increases, so too does the amount of time required for successful navigation. Researchers have turned to the role of attention in an attempt to minimize the amount of time required to perform these functions. Specifically, the manner in which attention may be attracted to the appropriate menu options has been studied.

Many aspects of computer menu search are similar to problems addressed in research on visual search. In the standard visual search paradigm, a word is given to a participant and he or she must search for this target amidst a display containing several words (i.e. distractors). During initial practice, the number of items presented in the display will greatly influence the speed with which the target word will be found. With continued practice, if the relationships among the targets and distractors are consistent, attention will quickly be drawn to the target items (Shiffrin, 1988).

Fisher, Coury, Tengs & Duffy (1989) have enumerated some aspects of attention and visual search that are akin to task characteristics of menu navigation. Considering these similarities to visual search, recommendations for menu design can be made. For example, users typically must engage in serial search. That is, users, particularly novices, will have to examine each menu item individually, rather than examining all options at the same time (i.e. in parallel). In addition, menu search will be self-terminating, meaning that the search comes to an end when the user finds the target menu option. These characteristics of visual search underlie several mathematical models that may be used to optimize menu navigation.

Although empirical research on menu navigation has been conducted, in many instances, the number of potential combinations of menu options is far too great to study exhaustively. Fisher and his colleagues (e.g. Fisher, Yungkurth & Moss, 1990; Fisher et al., 1989) have described some mathematical techniques to determine the optimal number of menu options and levels when designing menu-driven systems, some of which have been empirically supported (see also Paap & Roske-Hofstrand, 1986). Among the suggestions are that menu items should be organized semantically instead of ensuring that the same number of items appear under each menu heading. Also, frequently used options should require fewer steps to locate in the hierarchy than less frequently used options. Highlighting particular options with different colors may be a useful method for drawing attention to them. Bear in mind that these recommendations are most relevant for novice users, as more experienced users will eventually quickly recall the appropriate manner in which to traverse the menu options. However, these recommendations may facilitate the transition from novice to skilled menu user.

As Fisher et al. (1989) argued, by reducing menu search times by 70% and assuming that the menu is accessed one million times in a year, 2000 work hours may be saved. Thus, great savings in productivity may be achieved through consideration of the optimal manner in which to design menu systems. Menu-based systems are becoming more prevalent in a variety of environments in addition to offices. For instance, menu systems are used in automatic teller machines and on-line library systems. To the extent that designers heed knowledge of visual search and how to draw attention to important information when it is needed, these technologies will be easier for workers and consumers to use.

Dual and Multiple Tasks

Multiple task performance refers to the ability to receive and process information from several sources at the same time. In other words, time-sharing is required to coordinate the performance of several tasks. The ability to perform multiple tasks has been a topic of study for over one hundred years, dating back to work by Binet in the 1890s (Brookings & Damos, 1991), though research waned during the period between the World Wars. Around the time of the Second World War, the complexity of new technologies led to a rekindling of interest on the study of multiple task performance. The fundamental interest of researchers throughout the last century has been the factors that constrain the performance of multiple tasks, such as individual differences and task complexity.

The nature of the tasks will greatly affect the ability to perform them concurrently. For example, searching for a specific street sign while driving in a new environment will be more difficult than doing both activities in a familiar area. In the first instance, the driver must navigate an unfamiliar road while also searching for a street. In contrast, familiarity with the environment will allow for more attention to be devoted to searching for the street. Thus, the manner in which different tasks are combined will determine the ease with which they may be performed at the same time.

A range of task characteristics, apart from experience, will affect multiple task performance. Ultimately, the combination of tasks usually results in one of three different possibilities (Wickens & Carswell, 1997):

1. the tasks will be performed as well when performed in tandem as when they are performed singly
2. the level of performance for one task will decline when performed in conjunction with other tasks
3. the tasks will require serial processing, in which attention must be shifted between each task rather than performing them at the same time.

Researchers who have emphasized the theoretical implications of multiple task performance on human information processing have developed a number of models to understand performance limitations such as the single channel hypothesis, bottleneck theories, and resource models. (For extensive reviews of the debate regarding the strengths and weaknesses of these models, see Meyer and Kieras, 1997; Pashler, 1994.) From the applied standpoint, researchers have been concerned with determining what aspects of tasks result in performance decrements. In other words, when does the workload go beyond the information processing capacity of the task performer? There have been a variety of attempts to examine the construct of workload. Unlike some constructs where a single methodology has become the standard, workload has not been so constrained. In fact, three primary methods of assessing performance limitations are used, namely:

- performance-based assessments – for example examining whether declines in performance occur when the task becomes more demanding or when a secondary task must also be performed

- physiological measures – for example examining measures of heart rate or electrical activity in the brain as an index of workload
- subjective indexes – for example asking someone to rate the amount of effort they are expending to perform a task.

(See Eggemeier, Wilson, Kramer & Damos, 1991; Tsang & Wilson, 1997.)

The researcher who wishes to assess workload has a number of methods at his or her disposal. Tsang and Wilson (1997) have provided a series of guidelines for selecting appropriate measures. Besides methodological and theoretical considerations, pragmatics and cost play prominent roles. Subjective reports are among the least expensive and simplest measures to adopt, although these methods may be susceptible to biases or inaccurate assessments. On the other hand, physiological measures, although expensive, are useful for providing a continuous index of workload; for example, electrodes may continually monitor brain activity. Additionally, performance measures may provide the most objective measure of changes in workload, because they can be used to determine if people are maintaining performance at an optimal or acceptable level. Tradeoffs associated with the different techniques highlight the importance of using multiple measures to assess workload. That is, different measures should be used to provide specificity in determining what particular aspects of a task are most demanding. For example, when examining the performance of multiple tasks that require motor control, as well as both auditory and visual attention, researchers may be able to isolate the specific component (e.g. visual attention) that contributes most to workload.

Regardless of the type of workload assessments used, there are certain methodological factors that should be considered to optimize the accuracy of the measures. O'Donnell & Eggemeier (1986) enumerated five such factors regarding the use of workload measures:

1. *sensitivity* – whether the measure can detect subtle changes in workload
2. *diagnosticity* – the ability to determine the source of workload limitations, such as in perceptual processing or in motor responses
3. *intrusiveness* – the degree to which the workload measure interferes with the task(s) being performed
4. *implementation* – the ease or difficulty related to employing the workload measures
5. *operator acceptance* – whether participants are willing to properly use the workload measure.

Although researchers may not be able to optimize all of these aspects of workload measures using a single measure, they will increase the likelihood of attaining meaningful information from their experiments through consideration of these factors.

The study of multiple task performance offers insight into the limits of attention with regard to time-sharing. Workload measures provide a number of ways for assessing the ability of workers to achieve acceptable levels of performance. Through the use and careful selection of workload measures, researchers will gain a better understanding of how multiple task performance may be optimized.

Useful Field of View

Useful field of view (UFOV) refers to the size of the visual area that may be perceived from a glance (Sanders, 1970). One of the most fundamental aspects of the UFOV is the detection of objects in the periphery, to which attention may then be focused. Larger visual fields will allow for earlier detection of peripheral objects than smaller visual fields, thus allowing for more time to respond. Task characteristics, such as the duration of presentation, competing demands on attention, target salience and distance of target from central vision will also affect the ease with which information is perceived in the visual field (Ball & Owsley, 1991).

Many activities rely on early detection of peripheral objects or motion. One such task is driving. Because of the high speed of vehicles and the danger of accidents, it is important for drivers to be able to detect objects, such as oncoming traffic or pedestrians as quickly as possible. Driving has been one of the main areas of applied research on UFOV.

Researchers who investigate age-related changes in the visual system have found that as people grow older the size of the UFOV declines (Owsley, Ball, Sloane, Roenker & Bruni, 1991). In other words, older individuals have a smaller visual field, which means they may be slower to detect peripheral visual signals than young adults. Because of this age-related decline, there have been efforts to examine the consequences of having a smaller visual field on driving. The typical methods of studying this issue include: (a) classifying individuals according to visual field and comparing their accident rates over a fixed period of time (e.g. the last five years) using retrospective and/or police reports; or (b) having individuals perform a variety of driving tasks using a simulator. The strength of the relationship between driving ability and UFOV is largely determined by the experimental methods. Driving simulators usually evidence little or no declines in driving ability that are related specifically to visual field (Szlyk, Seiple & Viana, 1995). On the other hand, Szlyk et al., Owsley et al. (1991) and Ball & Owsley (1991) have been able to use UFOV as a good predictor of accident histories, particularly for accidents at intersections, which would presumably carry the greatest risk due to reduced visual field size. Not only has UFOV been used successfully as a predictor of accidents, but restricted UFOVs can be improved through training by as much as 133% after only five days of instruction (Ball, Beard, Roenker, Miller & Griggs, 1988). Visual field has been shown to be a better predictor of accident risk than visual acuity. Thus, an understanding of UFOV may be useful for determining the success with which people will be able to perform tasks that rely heavily on the integration of vision and attention.

Individual Differences

The importance of understanding individual differences in psychological variables was well-stated by Adams (1989) as follows:

> Performance on tasks without concern for individual differences would reflect the processes that define general laws of behavior. Measures from individuals in these

> same tasks would give human variation in the processes, and this would lead to general laws that include the prediction of individual behavior, which should be the goal of psychology. (Adams, 1989, p. 16)

Basically, Adams argued that our knowledge is incomplete if we ignore the irrefutable fact of individual differences.

Individual Differences and Selection

There are practical applications of understanding individual differences in abilities. First is selection. An important problem in business, industry and the military is selecting the right people for the right jobs. Different jobs require different abilities: the abilities required to be a pilot are very different from the abilities required to be a lathe operator, which in turn are very different from the abilities required to be a graphic artist. The task of selection has benefited from theoretical understanding of the relationships between abilities and performance for various tasks and classes of skills. Seminal work in the area was conducted by Fleishman and his colleagues in the 1950s through the 1970s (e.g. Fleishman & Hempel, 1954, 1955; Fleishman, 1966, 1972), and continued into the 1980s and 1990s by various scholars such as Ackerman (1988, 1990), Ackerman, Kanfer & Goff (1995), Fleishman & Mumford (1989), Kyllonen & Stephens (1990), Kyllonen, Tirre & Christal (1991), Kyllonen & Woltz (1989), Woltz (1988), and Woltz & Shute (1993). These researchers utilized an individual differences approach to examine the extent to which abilities predict performance. The basic tenet of much of this research is that the abilities that are most predictive of successful performance are dependent on whether the goal is to predict the performance of a novice, a person with an intermediate amount of practice, or an expert. From a practical perspective there are thus two problems: is the goal to predict who will do well during the early stages of training, or is the goal to predict who will ultimately perform the job/ task/ skill at the most superior level? The answer to this question will influence the choice of ability variables used to make the selection.

With respect to attentional abilities, much success has been gained in the domain of selecting individuals best suited for the job of being a pilot. An initial question was whether it was possible to measure individual differences in attentional abilities and whether such differences were correlated with real-world tasks. Gopher (1982) demonstrated quite convincingly an affirmative answer to both questions. He used a dichotic listening test as a measure of selective attention and found reliable individual differences. More importantly, for purposes of selection, he found that individual differences in attention were correlated with individual differences in performance in a flight training program. Moreover, the predictability of the attention measure was significant even after controlling for the traditional pilot-selection test battery measures. Auditory and visual selective attention tests have since been used to illustrate the relationship between individual differences in attention and individual differences in a variety of real-world tasks such as piloting an airplane, driving and monitoring tasks (for a review, see Arthur, Strong, Jordan, Williamson, Shebilske & Regian, 1995). In addition, these attention measures are predictive of performance throughout practice for complex tasks that require considerable controlled processing even after practice (e.g. Arthur et al. 1995).

Individual Differences and Training

Training is another domain in which knowledge of individual differences in abilities can be informative. For example, Eberts & Brock (1987) suggest that the degree to which computer-aided instruction will be successful is dependent on the trainer's ability to accurately assess the individual student's level of ability. Then the difficulty level of the task can be tailored to the individual student to ensure that he or she is capable of doing the task yet sufficiently challenged to maintain motivated performance. More generally, Cronbach & Snow (1977) have shown that the degree to which an individual will benefit from a particular training program may be dependent on his/her ability level. Such "aptitude–treatment interactions" must be considered to maximize the benefits of training regimes.

The *Space Fortress* game has been used extensively to study individual differences in the acquisition of complex skills (see the special issue of *Acta Psychologica*, 1989, Volume 71, for a selection of research in this area). The game simulates dynamic aviation environments, is complex and representative of many real-world tasks in the military and other job settings. The game is controlled by a computer program that has 50 parameters that can be varied to influence the complexity and nature of the task (Mane & Donchin, 1989). The complexity of the task incorporates many aspects of attention such as the ability to divide and/or switch attention between aspects of the task, the ability to selectively attend to the most critical aspects of the task at a given point in the game, and the ability to sustain attention across the trials of the game. Arthur et al. (1995) demonstrated that individual differences in visual attention are predictive of individual differences in performance on *Space Fortress*.

Understanding the importance of attention to the *Space Fortress* task has led to the development of training protocols that minimize the attentional demands initially (e.g. Gopher, Weil & Siegel, 1989). Thus, trainees can become successful at performing the *Space Fortress* game. Importantly, the attention allocation strategies thus acquired during training on *Space Fortress* transfer to actual flight performance. Gopher, Weil & Bareket (1994) provided Israeli Air Force flight school cadets with ten hours of training on *Space Fortress*. Compared to cadets who did not receive such training, cadets with game experience yielded significantly better flight performance (performance measures were flights scored by flight instructors blind to condition). Moreover, their advantage actually increased for more advanced flights. Similar benefits of *Space Fortress* training have been reported by Hart & Battiste (1992) for helicopter trainees. Gopher et al. argued that the efficient attention control strategies developed during practice with the *Space Fortress* game transferred to the flight situation. The benefits of *Space Fortress* training have been so successful that the game has been incorporated as part of the Air Force's regular training program.

Individual Differences and Goal-setting

Improvements in training programs are due in part to the motivation of the individual trainee. One method to increase motivation is to provide goals for the participant to aim for during the training programs. However, there is a complex relationship between the benefits of such goals and the basic abilities of the individual trainee. To explain this relationship, Kanfer & Ackerman (1989) have developed a framework based on Kahneman's (1973) model of attentional capacity. They suggest that attentional capacity is an inter-individual difference attribute and that attentional resources can be allocated across different activities. Resources can be allocated to off-task activities (e.g. daydreaming), on-task activities (e.g. aspects of performing the task itself), and self-regulatory activities (e.g. monitoring if goals are being met). According to Kanfer & Ackerman, low ability participants have fewer available attentional resources. Thus, providing these individuals with task goals may interfere with task performance because they must allocate resources to monitoring their performance.

The importance of the Kanfer & Ackerman (1989) work has been to demonstrate that individual differences in attentional resources have a direct influence on the success of instructional manipulations. They used a computer simulation of an air traffic control task to investigate the relationships between individual differences in abilities (i.e. attentional resources), the presence of task goals, and performance on the complex air traffic control task. Their result clearly supported the predictions of their model. That is, low ability participants did not benefit from interventions designed to engage motivational processes because their resources were devoted to performing the task. Kanfer & Ackerman thus recommend that such motivational strategies not be provided to low ability individuals until they have had the opportunity to learn the basics of the task at hand.

Later research by Kanfer & Ackerman demonstrated that another method to allow low ability individuals to benefit from goal-setting motivational manipulations was to provide them with spaced (i.e. distributed) practice (Kanfer, Ackerman, Murtha, Dugdale & Nelson, 1994). The basis for this finding was that during the spaces between trials, individuals could devote their attentional resources to the self-regulatory activities that would enable them to benefit from the goal-setting manipulation. This type of research demonstrates the importance of understanding individual differences in attention as they may affect instructional design for complex tasks.

SUMMARY AND CONCLUSIONS

The goals of the chapter were as follows: (a) to provide a historical context for attention research in experimental psychology; (b) to illustrate the complexity of the construct of attention; and (c) to provide concrete examples of how attention research has been successfully applied to the solution of real-world problems.

Much of the initial empirical work in the field of attention began in the context of the Second World War, whereby psychologists and engineers were attempting to solve critical problems. For example, designing aircraft cockpits that did not overload the psychological capabilities of the pilot could mean the difference between life and death. Since that time, attention researchers have continued the tradition of applying laboratory-derived solutions to real-world problems. As we have illustrated in our review, such applications have been very successful.

The contributions of attention research have been as varied as the construct of attention itself. For example, the training of high performance skills has benefited in a number of ways, including: (a) determining how to automatize consistent components of the task; (b) developing training programs suitable to the capabilities of the trainees; (c) discovering how to assess workload to monitor the performance of trainees; and (d) designing motivational interventions that are appropriate to the attentional capabilities of the learner. Other applications of attention research include understanding the concept of sustained attention (via vigilance research) to minimize performance decrements, relying on understanding of visual search strategies to optimize computer menu design, and assessing the useful field of view to predict whether older adults are likely to be involved in motor vehicle accidents (and providing training to minimize such accident predispositions).

Psychological researchers must focus on the theoretical interpretations of their data, consider the practical relevance of their science, and understand the symbiotic relationship between experiments conducted in the laboratory and real-world problems. Attention research provides an excellent example of how this approach has been successful in increasing our understanding of cognitive functions and solving problems in the everyday lives of individuals.

ACKNOWLEDGMENTS

The authors were supported in part by grants from the National Institute of Health (National Institute on Aging) Grants P50 AG-11715 and R01 AG-07654. We would like to acknowledge the helpful comments of Frank Durso, Roger Schvaneveldt and Ken Paap on the initial draft of the chapter.

REFERENCES

Ackerman, P. L. (1988). Determinants of individual differences during skill acquisition: cognitive abilities and information processing. *Journal of Experimental Psychology: General*, 117, 288–318.

Ackerman, P. L. (1990). A correlational analysis of skill specificity: learning, abilities, and individual differences. *Journal of Experimental Psychology: Learning, Memory, and Cognition*, 16, 883–901.

Ackerman, P. L., Kanfer, R. & Goff, M. (1995). Cognitive and noncognitive determinants and consequences of complex skill acquisition. *Journal of Experimental Psychology: Applied*, 1, 270–304.

Adams, J. A. (1987). Criticisms of vigilance research: a discussion. *Human Factors*, 29, 737–40.

Adams, J. A. (1989). Historical background and appraisal of research on individual differences in learning. In R. Kanfer, P. L. Ackerman & R. Cudeck (Eds), *Abilities, Motivation, and Methodology: The Minnesota Symposium on Learning and Individual Differences* (pp. 3–22). Hillsdale, NJ: Erlbaum.

Anderson, J. R. (1982). Acquisition of cognitive skill. *Psychological Review*, 89, 369–406.

Anderson, J. R. (1983). *The Architecture of Cognition*. Cambridge, MA: Harvard University Press.

Arthur, W., Strong, M. H., Jordan, J. A., Williamson, J. E., Shebilske, W. L. & Regian, J. W. (1995). Visual attention: individual differences in training and predicting complex task performance. *Acta Psychologica*, 88, 3–23.

Ball, K. & Owsley, C. (1991). Identifying correlates of accident involvement for the older driver. Special Issue: Safety and mobility of elderly drivers: Part I. *Human Factors*, 33, 583–95.

Ball, K., Beard, B., Roenker, D., Miller, R. & Griggs, D. (1988). Age and visual search: expanding the useful field of view. *Journal of the Optical Society of America*, 5, 2210–19.

Broadbent, D. E. (1957). A mechanical model for human attention and immediate memory. *Psychological Review*, 64, 205–15.

Broadbent, D. E. (1958). *Perception and Communication*. London: Pergamon Press.

Brookings, J. B. & Damos, D. L. (1991). Individual differences in multiple-task performance. In D. L. Damos (Ed.), *Multiple Task Performance* (pp. 363–86). Washington, DC: Taylor & Francis.

Bryan, W. L. & Harter, N. (1899). Studies on the telegraphic language: the acquisition of a hierarchy of habits. *Psychological Review*, 6, 345–75.

Cherry, E. C. (1953). Some experiments on the recognition of speech, with one and with two ears. *Journal of the Acoustical Society of America*, 25, 975–9.

Corteen, R. S. & Wood, B. (1972). Autonomic responses to shock-associated words in an unattended channel. *Journal of Experimental Psychology*, 94, 308–13.

Cowan, N. (1995). *Attention and Memory: An Integrated Framework*. New York: Oxford University Press.

Cronbach, L. J. & Snow, R. E. (1977). *Aptitudes and Instructional Methods: A Handbook for Research on Interactions*. New York: Irvington.

Dallenbach, K. M. (1928). Attention. *Psychological Bulletin*, 25, 493–511.

Deutsch, J. A. & Deutsch, D. (1963). Attention: some theoretical considerations. *Psychological Review*, 70, 80–90.

Dewsbury, D. A. (1997). History of the Psychonomic Society III: the meetings of the Psychonomic Society. *Psychonomic Bulletin & Review*, 4, 350–8.

Eberts, R. E. & Brock, J. F. (1987). Computer-assisted and computer-managed instruction. In G. Salvendy (Ed.), *Handbook of Human Factors* (pp. 976–1011). New York: John Wiley & Sons.

Eggemeier, F. T., Wilson, G. F., Kramer, A. F. & Damos, D. L. (1991). Workload assessment in multi-task environments. In D. L. Damos (Ed.), *Multiple Task Performance* (pp. 207–16). Washington, DC: Taylor & Francis.

Fisher, D. L., Coury, B. G., Tengs, T. O. & Duffy, S. A. (1989). Minimizing the time to search visual displays: the role of highlighting. *Human Factors*, 31, 167–82.

Fisher, D. L., Yungkurth, E. J. & Moss, S. M. (1990). Optimal menu hierarchy design: syntax and semantics. *Human Factors*, 32, 665–83.

Fisk, A. D. & Eggemeier, F. T. (1988). Application of automatic/controlled processing theory to training tactical command and control skills: 1. Background and task analytic methodology. *Proceedings of the Human Factors Society 32nd Annual Meeting*. Santa Monica, CA: Human Factors Society.

Fisk, A. D., Hertzog, C., Lee, M. D., Rogers, W. A. & Anderson-Garlach, M. M. (1994). Long-term retention of skilled visual search: do young adults retain more than old adults? *Psychology and Aging*, 9, 206–15.

Fisk, A. D. & Hodge, K. A. (1992). Retention of trained performance in consistent mapping search after extended delay. *Human Factors*, 34, 147–64.

Fisk, A. D. & Rogers, W. A. (1992). The application of consistency principles for the assessment of skill development. In W. Regian & V. Shute (Eds), *Cognitive Approaches to Automated Instruction* (pp. 171–94). Hillsdale, NJ: Erlbaum.

Fisk, A. D. & Schneider, W. (1981). Controlled and automatic processing during tasks requiring sustained attention: a new approach to vigilance. *Human Factors*, 23, 737–50.

Fitts, P. M. (1964). Perceptual-motor skill learning. In A. W. Melton (Ed.), *Categories of Human Learning* (pp. 243–85). New York: Academic Press.
Fitts, P. M. ([1965] 1990). Factors in complex skill training. In M. Venturino (Ed.), *Selected Readings in Human Factors* (pp. 275–95). Santa Monica, CA: Human Factors Society.
Fleishman, E. A. (1966). Human abilities and the acquisition of skill. In E. A. Bilodeau (Ed.), *Acquisition of Skill* (pp. 147–67). NY: Academic Press.
Fleishman, E. A. (1972). On the relation between abilities, learning, and human performance. *American Psychologist*, 27, 1017–32.
Fleishman, E. A. & Hempel, W. E. (1954). Changes in factor structure of a complex motor test as a function of practice. *Psychometrika*, 18, 239–52.
Fleishman, E. A. & Hempel, W. E. (1955). The relation between abilities and improvement with practice in a visual discrimination reaction task. *Journal of Experimental Psychology*, 49, 301–12.
Fleishman, E. A. & Mumford, M. D. (1989). Abilities as causes of individual differences in skill acquisition. *Human Performance*, 2, 201–23.
Goldstein, I. L. (1986). *Training in Organizations: Needs Assessment, Development and Evaluation* (2nd edn). Monterey, CA: Brooks/Cole.
Gopher, D. (1982). A selective attention test as a predictor of success in flight training. *Human Factors*, 24, 173–83.
Gopher, D., Weil, M. & Bareket, T. (1994). Transfer of skill from a computer game trainer to flight. *Human Factors*, 36, 387–405.
Gopher, D., Weil, M. & Siegel, D. (1989). Practice under changing priorities. *Acta Psychologica*, 71, 147–79.
Gray, J. A. & Wedderburn, A. A. I. (1960). Grouping strategies with simultaneous stimuli. *Quarterly Journal of Experimental Psychology*, 12, 180–4.
Hancock, P. M. A. (1984). Environmental stressors. In J. S. Warm (Ed.), *Sustained Attention in Human Performance* (pp. 134–77). New York: John Wiley & Sons.
Hancock, P. M. A. (1986). Sustained attention under thermal stress. *Psychological Bulletin*, 99, 263–81.
Hart, S. G. & Battiste, V. (1992). Flight test of a video game trainer. In *Proceedings of the Human Factors Society 36th Annual Meeting* (pp. 1291–5). Santa Monica, CA: Human Factors Society.
Howell, W. C. & Cooke, N. J. (1989). Training the human information processor: a review of cognitive models. In I. L. Goldstein (Ed.), *Training and Development in Organizations* (pp. 121–82). San Francisco: Jossey-Bass.
James, W. ([1890] 1950). *The Principles of Psychology* (Vol. 1). New York: Holt, Rhinehart & Winston.
Kahneman, D. (1973). *Attention and Effort*. Englewood Cliffs, NJ: Prentice-Hall.
Kanfer, R. & Ackerman, P. L. (1989). Motivation and cognitive abilities: an integrative/aptitude–treatment interaction approach to skill acquisition. *Journal of Applied Psychology Monograph*, 74, 657–90.
Kanfer, R., Ackerman, P. L., Murtha, T. C., Dugdale, B. & Nelson, L. (1994). Goal setting, conditions of practice, and task performance: a resource allocation perspective. *Journal of Applied Psychology*, 79, 826–35.
Kirlik, A., Walker, N., Fisk, A. D. & Nagel, K. (1996). Supporting perception in the service of dynamic decision making. *Human Factors*, 38, 288–99.
Kyllonen, P. C. & Stephens, D. L. (1990). Cognitive abilities as determinants of success in acquiring logic skill. *Learning and Individual Differences*, 2, 129–60.
Kyllonen, P. C. & Woltz, D. J. (1989). Role of cognitive factors in the acquisition of cognitive skill. In R. Kanfer, P. L. Ackerman & R. Cudeck (Eds), *Abilities, Motivation, and Methodology* (pp. 239–80). Hillsdale, NJ: Erlbaum.
Kyllonen, P. C., Tirre, W. C. & Christal, R. E. (1991). Knowledge and processing speed as determinants of associative learning. *Journal of Experimental Psychology: General*, 120, 57–79.
LaBerge, D. L. (1990). Attention. *Psychological Science*, 1, 156–62.

Logan, G. D. (1985). Skill and automaticity: relations, implications, and future directions. *Canadian Journal of Psychology*, 39, 367–86.

Mane, A. & Donchin, E. (1989). The *Space Fortress* game. *Acta Psychologica*, 71, 17–22.

Meyer, D. E. & Kieras, D. E. (1997). A computational theory of executive cognitive processes and multiple task performance: Part 1. Basic mechanisms. *Psychological Review*, 104, 3–65.

Moray, N. (1959). Attention in dichotic listening: affective cues and the influence of instructions. *Quarterly Journal of Experimental Psychology*, 11, 56–60.

Navon, D. (1984). Resources – a theoretical soup stone? *Psychological Review*, 91, 216–34.

Navon, D. & Gopher, D. (1979). On the economy of the human processing system. *Psychological Review*, 86, 214–55.

Norman, D. A. (1968). Towards a theory of memory and attention. *Psychological Review*, 75, 522–36.

O'Donnell, R. D. & Eggemeier, F. T. (1986). Workload assessment methodology. In K. R. Boff & L. Kaufman (Eds), *Handbook of Perception and Human Performance* (Vol. 2) (pp. 1–49). New York: John Wiley & Sons.

Owsley, C., Ball, K., Sloane, M. E., Roenker, D. L & Bruni, J. R. (1991). Visual/cognitive correlates of vehicle accidents in older adults. *Psychology and Aging*, 6, 403–15.

Paap, K. R. & Roske-Hofstrand, R. J. (1986). The optimal number of menu options per panel. *Human Factors*, 28, 377–85.

Parasuraman, R. (1979). Memory load and event rate control sensitivity decrements in sustained attention. *Science*, 205, 924–7.

Parasuraman, R. (1985). Sustained attention: a multifactorial approach. In M. I. Posner & O. S. M. Marin (Eds), *Attention and Performance XI* (pp. 493–511). Hillsdale, NJ: Erlbaum.

Parasuraman, R. & Davies, D. R. (1977). A taxonomic analysis of vigilance performance. In R. R. Mackie (Ed.), *Vigilance: Theory, Operational Performance, and Physiological Correlates* (pp. 559–74). New York: Plenum.

Parasuraman, R. & Davies, D. R. (1984). *Varieties of Attention*. Orlando: Academic Press.

Pashler, H. (1994). Dual-task interference in simple tasks: data and theory. *Psychological Bulletin*, 116, 220–44.

Pigeau, R. A., Angus, R. G., O'Neill, P. & Mack, I. (1995). Vigilance latencies to aircraft detection among NORAD surveillance operators. *Human Factors*, 37, 622–34.

Posner, M. I. (1992). Attention as a cognitive and neural system. *Current Directions in Psychological Science*, 1, 11–14.

Posner, M. I. & Petersen, P. T. (1990). The attention system of the human brain. *Annual Review of Neuroscience*, 13, 25–42.

Ribot, Th. (1903). *The Psychology of Attention*. Chicago: Open Court Publishing.

Rogers, W. A., Maurer, T. J., Salas, E. & Fisk, A. D. (1997). Task analysis and cognitive theory: controlled and automatic processing task analytic methodology. In J. K. Ford, S. W. J. Kozlowski, K. Kraiger, E. Salas & M. S. Teachout (Eds), *Improving Training Effectiveness in Work Organizations* (pp. 19–45). Mahwah, NJ: Erlbaum.

Sanders, A. F. (1970). Some aspects of the selective process in the functional field of view. *Ergonomics*, 13, 101–17.

Schneider, W. (1985). Training high performance skills: fallacies and guidelines. *Human Factors*, 27, 285–300.

Schneider W. & Shiffrin, R. M. (1977). Controlled and automatic human information processing: I. Detection, search and attention. *Psychological Review*, 84, 1–66.

Schneider, W., Dumais, S. T. & Shiffrin, R. M. (1984). Automatic processes and attention. In R. Parasuraman & D. R. Davies (Eds), *Varieties of Attention* (pp. 1–27). Orlando, FL: Academic Press.

Shiffrin, R. M. (1988). Attention. In R. C. Atkinson, R. J. Herrnstein & R. D. Luce (Eds), *Stevens' Handbook of Experimental Psychology* (pp. 739–811). New York: John Wiley & Sons.

Shiffrin, R. M. & Dumais, S. T. (1981). The development of automatism. In J. A.

Anderson (Ed.), *Cognitive Skills and their Acquisition* (pp. 111–40). Hillsdale, NJ: Erlbaum.

Shiffrin, R. M. & Schneider, W. (1977). Controlled and automatic human information processing: II. Perceptual learning, automatic attending, and a general theory. *Psychological Review*, 84, 127–90.

Solomons, L. & Stein, G. (1896). Normal motor automatism. *Psychological Review*, 3, 492–512.

Sports Illustrated (1994). Inside the South. September 12.

Szlyk, J. P., Seiple, W. & Viana, M. (1995). Relative effects of age and compromised vision on driving performance. Special Issue: Telecommunications. *Human Factors*, 37, 430–6.

Titchener, E. B. (1908). *Lectures on the Elementary Psychology of Feeling and Attention*. New York: Arno Press.

Treisman, A. M. (1960). Contextual cues in selective listening. *Quarterly Journal of Experimental Psychology*, 12, 242–8.

Treisman, A. & Geffen, G. (1967). Selective attention: perception of response? *Quarterly Journal of Experimental Psychology*, 19, 1–17.

Tsang, P. & Wilson, G. F. (1997). Mental workload. In G. Salvendy (Ed.), *Handbook of Human Factors and Ergonomics* (pp. 417–49). New York: John Wiley & Sons.

Underwood, G. (1993). Introduction. *The Psychology of Attention: Volume 1* (pp. xiii–xxi). New York: New York University Press.

Walker, N. & Fisk, A. D. (1995). Human factors goes to the gridiron: developing a quarterback training system. *Ergonomics in Design*, 3, July, 8–13.

Walker, N., Fisk, A. D. & Phipps, D. (1994). Perceptual rule based skills: when rule-training hinders learning. *Proceedings of the Human Factors and Ergonomics Society 38th Annual Meeting*. Santa Monica, CA: Human Factors and Ergonomics Society.

Warm, J. S. (1984). *Sustained Attention in Human Performance*. New York: John Wiley & Sons.

Warm, J. S. & Jerison, H. J. (1984). The psychophysics of vigilance. In J. S. Warm (Ed.), *Sustained Attention in Human Performance* (pp. 15–59). New York: John Wiley & Sons.

Weiner, E. L. (1987). Application of vigilance research: rare, medium, or well done? *Human Factors*, 29, 725–36.

Wickens, C. D. (1980). The structure of attentional resources. In R. S. Nickerson (Ed.), *Attention and Performance VIII* (pp. 239–57). Hillsdale, NJ: Erlbaum.

Wickens, C. D. (1984). Processing resources in attention. In R. Parasuraman & D. R. Davies (Eds), *Varieties of Attention* (pp. 63–102). Orlando, FL: Academic Press.

Wickens, C. D. & Carswell, C. M. (1997). Information processing. In G. Salvendy (Ed.), *Handbook of Human Factors and Ergonomics* (pp. 89–129). New York: John Wiley & Sons.

Woltz, D. J. (1988). An investigation of the role of working memory in procedural skill acquisition. *Journal of Experimental Psychology: General*, 117, 319–31.

Woltz, D. J. & Shute V. J. (1993). Individual differences in repetition priming and its relationship to declarative knowledge acquisition. *Intelligence*, 17, 333–59.

Chapter 3

Knowledge and Expertise

Neil Charness and Richard S. Schultetus
Florida State University

The study of expert performance has considerable relevance to applied cognition. First, it provides an important context for education and training. If we can develop a deep understanding of expertise, we will be in a better position to promote and even accelerate its development through more effective instruction and training. Second, such an understanding may facilitate the building of expert systems, artificial intelligence (AI) programs that can perform at the same levels as the best humans (and perhaps surpass them). Third, both lines of research lead to the promise of synergy for systems that combine human experts with AI experts.

As early work in AI on expert systems made clear, "knowledge is power" (e.g. Feigenbaum, 1989). The right type of knowledge could almost eliminate the need to search for solutions through immense problem spaces. However, when it comes to human expertise, it is now apparent that it takes thousands of hours of deliberate practice to acquire sufficient knowledge to perform at world class levels (e.g. Charness, Krampe & Mayr, 1996; Ericsson, Krampe & Tesch-Römer, 1993; Simon & Chase, 1973). Much of that time is undoubtedly devoted to acquiring broad yet flexible knowledge in the form of both declarative information about the domain and procedures for applying that information to task performance.

We begin our chapter with attempts to define "expertise" and "knowledge". We review techniques for assessing both concepts, in the process highlighting the dimensions of recognition versus search for the application of knowledge. We also discuss the costs and benefits of knowledge. We briefly examine some of the techniques for assessing amount and organization of knowledge. Finally, we explore the techniques used to encode the knowledge of human experts into expert systems.

Handbook of Applied Cognition, Edited by F. T. Durso, R. S. Nickerson, R. W. Schvaneveldt, S. T. Dumais, D. S. Lindsay and M. T. H. Chi.
Published 1999 by John Wiley & Sons Ltd.

Domain-related chapters in this volume can be expected to provide more detailed information about specific areas of expertise. We emphasize knowledge and expertise, and do not deal directly with the interrelated topics of skill acquisition and knowledge acquisition. The origin of human knowledge has been a persistent concern for many disciplines (e.g. philosophy) as well as for sub-fields within cognitive science (developmental theory, psycholinguistics). Applied psychologists are more concerned with the pragmatics of how to facilitate knowledge acquisition processes in order to educate people or to build expert system programs. Excellent recent reviews of skill acquisition can be found in Ericsson & Lehmann (1996), Van Lehn (1996) and Ericsson (1996).

We deal here with knowledge and expertise solely from the perspective of the individual. There is also a pressing need for better models at the social level of description when trying to understand the expertise of teams, cases of two or more individuals collaborating on a project (e.g. Baltes & Staudinger, 1996; Hinsz, Tindale & Vollrath, 1997).

DEFINITIONS OF EXPERTISE AND KNOWLEDGE

Expertise

Curiously, there was little attempt to define expert performance in early compendiums on expertise (e.g. Chi, Glaser & Farr, 1988). Ericsson & Charness (1994) and Ericsson and Smith (1991) defined expert performance as "consistently superior performance on a specified set of representative tasks for the domain that can be administered to any subject." ("Any subject" is meant to refer to someone with at least minimal skill in the domain of interest. We would not want to put a college undergraduate into the cockpit of a fighter jet for a study of pilot expertise. Typically, studies contrast novices with experts, not beginners with experts.)

One useful way to reference superior performance is with respect to the normal distribution. We can consider those who are positive outliers, two or more standard deviations above the mean, as experts. Experts should be consistent, or reliable, ruling out one-time performances, such as fund managers picking stocks that out-perform market averages in one year, but not in subsequent years. Tasks should be representative ones for the domain. An expert chess player would be asked to solve chess problems, such as finding the best move from an unfamiliar chess position. An expert typist would be expected to transcribe a document with a high net-words-per-minute rate. The degree of superiority of the expert is what ought to differentiate her or him from a merely skilled performer.

Using "outlier" as part of the operational definition of superior performance is not without weaknesses. For one, superiority then depends largely on who constitutes the reference group. If, for instance, one included everyone who knew how to play chess, then even a relatively weak tournament player might be considered an expert. Similarly, most adult readers would be considered experts compared to children who are beginning to learn to read. Another weakness is that many examples of skilled performance may not end up having experts because the pool of individuals is too small to have outliers (e.g. in some naturalistic decision making situations with only one key decision maker; see Zsambok & Klein, 1997). However, the focus of this chapter is on expertise, not skilled performance.

Although the above definition of expertise is restrictive, it has advantages. We can contrast the use of consistently superior performance as a marker of expertise with other approaches such as peer nomination and level of domain experience. One might speak to peers or to a professional association representing the individual to try to determine the expertise level of a prospective professional, such as a lawyer, physician, or dentist. Given the difficulty of validating such peer assessments, some might prefer to rely on certification procedures (for example: Is my physician certified for surgery?) to establish expertise in such domains. Ideally, certification procedures will make use of representative tasks from the domain (e.g. medical diagnosis of diseases, knowledge of operating procedures, within the specialty area). In other cases, all the professional association may be able to report is that the association has never censured the individual in question, or that the individual has won an award.

Another common, but risky technique for identifying expertise is relying on experience as an index. For instance, expertise in psychology might be operationalized by years of training. Thus, a study purporting to examine expertise in psychology might designate undergraduates as novices, and graduate students or psychology professors as experts. Experience, however, may be only loosely associated with expertise. The number of hours spent playing chess is more weakly associated with expertise than is the number of hours spent seriously studying the game (Charness, Krampe & Mayr, 1996). A similar finding has been shown for instrumental music performance (e.g. Ericsson et al., 1993).

The type of practice that seems most effective for producing experts, *deliberate practice* (Ericsson & Charness, 1994), typically involves solitary study with the aim of improving performance. The range of activities considered deliberate practice can be quite broad as there tends to be substantial variability in task demands across domains. However, these activities tend to be things like reading, which can be used to expand the knowledge base; problem solving, for the application of knowledge and heuristics; and drills to refine the more elementary skills. Deliberate practice is considered to require a great deal of effort, so it is usually not conducted for longer than four hours a day (Ericsson et al., 1993).

The sobering finding from virtually all the studies that have attempted to estimate the time spent in deliberate practice is that thousands of hours are required to become an expert, and to reach top-level (world championship) performance the requirement is typically closer to 10 000 hours. So, if your goal is to train to expert levels quickly, for most semantically rich tasks, ones that require a large knowledge base, this will simply not be possible. Also, given the huge investment in time required for the achievement of the very highest levels of skill it is critical that candidates have adequate external support. Aside from financial support that facilitates access to relevant materials and elite coaching, it also seems necessary for family and coaches to support trainees to maintain the motivation necessary to adhere to rigorous practice regimens.

Fortunately, people can expect to make large improvements in their performance early on in practice. Performance usually follows a power function (Newell

& Rosenbloom, 1981) with rapid early improvement followed by steadily diminishing returns. Part of the reason for the declining rate of improvement is that experts must learn to recognize and be prepared to respond flexibly to rarely occurring patterns. People may need to devote considerable time or practice trials to add such rare patterns to the knowledge base underlying expert performance.

Finally, it should be kept in mind that each domain has a different set of demands and, consequently, each requires different skills. This is a critical feature in determining how best to quantify performance and in deciding what types of tasks would be most representative of the domain. It may also be important in terms of exploring the structure of the underlying knowledge base. In many instances, the speed of performance is of less importance (e.g. painting and writing) so the knowledge base does not necessarily need to be organized for fast retrieval. In sports or medicine, however, access to information may be required almost instantly and so these knowledge systems need to be organized accordingly. In a domain such as management, communication skills and social skills may be critically important.

Knowledge

The *Concise Oxford Dictionary* definition of knowledge is: "Knowing, familiarity gained by experience; person's range of information." Although this definition incorporates some of the features of knowledge, we feel that it omits at least one critical feature.

Information processing systems act effectively when they make correct, and timely, decisions. They have two basic ways to accomplish this. First, they can activate prior stored knowledge by matching a description of the current situation to a past situation – a fast process. Second, they may discover that the current situation is not identical to a past situation and then use available knowledge and computational ability (engaging in what Newell, 1990, termed "knowledge search") to discover an appropriate course of action. Much of the computation supports the classic process of problem solving (Newell & Simon, 1972). Thus, the two ends of the continuum are bounded by: (a) relatively effortless recognition-driven retrieval linked to appropriate actions, and (b) effortful knowledge retrieval and conscious computation.

The necessary information to respond appropriately can either be innate or acquired. Simple organisms with limited adaptive capacity rely more strongly on hard-wired circuits for adaptive behavior (thermostats, one-celled organisms). More complex organisms (humans, well-programmed computers) rely on both hardware and acquired software for adaptive behavior.

Although there is a tendency to see knowledge as a product or outcome, it is worth keeping in mind the philosophical distinction between "knowing that" and "knowing how," which corresponds roughly to the psychological distinction between declarative and procedural knowledge. In reality, it is very difficult to make a clean partition between data and program for information processing systems (e.g. Anderson, 1978).

Perhaps a better way to bound the concept of knowledge is to identify characteristic features. We define knowledge as: acquired information that can be activated in a timely fashion in order to generate an appropriate response. We use the term "acquired" to distinguish acquired knowledge from innate structures and processes, such as reflexes, that can and do result in appropriate behavior.

The feature of timely activation is sometimes overlooked. Of course, in sports domains such as running or swimming, speed is the most important criterion for success. Even in cognitive domains such as television quiz shows, speed (together with appropriate accuracy) can be the determining factor in success. In the academic world, we do not credit a student with knowledge if they approach us after an exam ends with the correct answer to a question (the "I knew it, but couldn't remember it" or "tip of the tongue" problem).

With problem-solving performance by physics novices and experts, speed of solution is sometimes a major differentiating factor (e.g. Simon & Simon, 1978), given that both groups solve the problem (eventually). Speed is most certainly a factor in medicine, especially in those cases where the physician must make a correct decision quickly, as in medical emergencies.

It may seem trivial to note in the definition that knowledge enables an organism to make an appropriate response. Nonetheless, it is worth underlining the view that an increase in knowledge ought to enable an organism to tune its behavior so that it is better adapted to its environment.

KNOWLEDGE AND SEARCH

As wonderful as it is, the human brain has notable limitations. Finding these parameters or information processing constants has driven the field of cognitive psychology for decades. One such limitation is learning rate. Compared with the very recent invention, the digital computer, when learning in rote fashion, humans acquire and store information very slowly: 5 to 10 seconds to store a new chunk (Simon, 1974). We store and manipulate only a few chunks at a time: Miller's (1956) famous 7 (plus or minus two) parameter. Compared with digital computers we compute very slowly, with the fastest operation being around 40 ms to compare two internal symbols in a memory search task (Sternberg, 1975), or approximately 200 ms to recognize a familiar pattern such as a printed word. Card, Moran & Newell (1983) delineated these and other information processing constants.

In recent years, however, the limits for information processing seem to have stretched considerably when considering expert performance. Work on the role of memory in chess expertise (Charness, 1976) was among the first to show that information extracted by skilled individuals from briefly presented domain displays is not held in short-term memory. Rather it seems to be stored directly in long-term memory, or what has come to be called long-term working memory (Ericsson & Kintsch, 1995). Long-term working memory allows experts to bypass the normal limits on information processing, such as Miller's 7 (plus or minus two) chunks for short-term memory capacity. Long-term working memory contains domain-specific specialized retrieval structures that enable skilled individuals to directly encode new information into an interference-resistant, rapidly access-

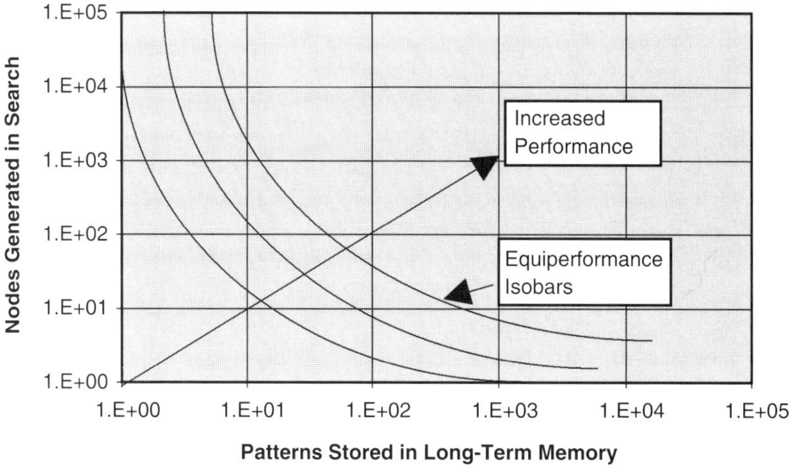

Figure 3.1 Knowledge-search equivalence patterns for performance.

ible state. Another formalism used to model the extraordinary memory performance of experts is "templates" (e.g. Richman, Staszewski & Simon, 1995).

Nonetheless, traditional information processing limitations mean that outside our domains of expertise we usually can respond quickly only when recognizing what to do, rather than when searching through a problem space to solve a problem. In short, for humans, acquiring accessible knowledge is the royal road to refined adaptation.

We now discuss a conceptualization introduced by Berliner (1981) and elaborated on by Newell (1989, 1990): the role of knowledge versus search in intelligent behavior.

Figure 3.1 portrays the space representing the trade-off between knowledge and search. Adding in the (implicit) time dimension fleshes things out further. Systems can reach the same goal or level of performance by very different routes. They can have prepared knowledge that is simply triggered under the right circumstances (patterns, in Figure 3.1), or they can engage in search through a problem space. For instance, in the schematic space of Figure 3.1, you can reach the same point on the performance curve by doing one computation with 1000 available facts or by knowing one fact and doing 1000 computations. If you memorized all the two-digit multiplicands (e.g. 1 × 1 through 99 × 99) rather than the usual times tables (1 × 1 through 12 × 12) you could quickly retrieve the answer to 98 × 98 (9604). Otherwise, you would need to use your addition knowledge and usual times-table knowledge to answer the question by doing many computations. There are also intermediate strategies that rely on learning a different algorithm than the one typically taught for paper and pencil calculations (e.g. Charness & Campbell, 1988). Usually, recognition is faster than search (computation) for humans so adults tend to capitalize on their vast acquired knowledge reserves to act appropriately in real time.

Sometimes, raw computational power surpasses knowledge-weighted strategies for solving problems. The trade-off between direct retrieval and computation

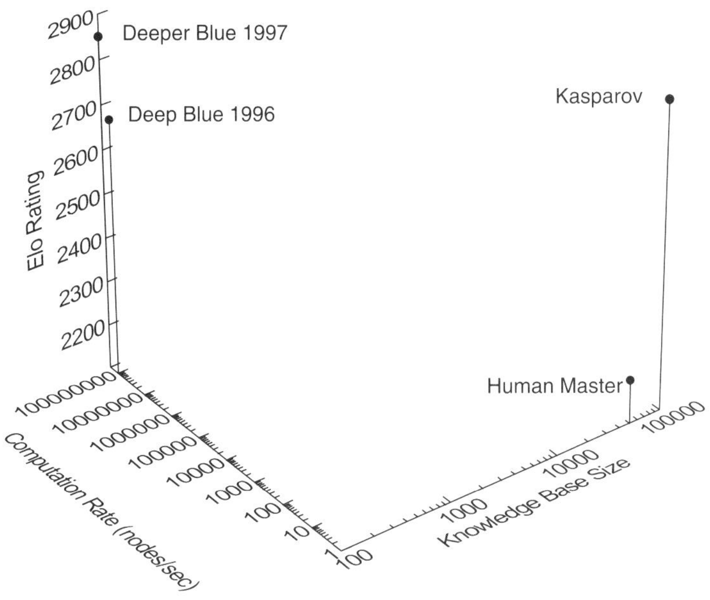

Figure 3.2 Humans and computers in knowledge vs. search space for chess.

is shown nicely with the isobars for performance in Figure 3.1. It is the reason why very slow computing humans in their role as chess players can compete on nearly equal terms with computer systems that search 200 million nodes per second compared to the human estimate of one node per second, or less (Charness, 1981).

Figure 3.2 depicts that relationship for the domain of chess playing, showing human champion Garry Kasparov plotted against IBM's chess machine, Deep Blue 96 and Deeper Blue 97, in the knowledge versus search space. For comparison, we've also plotted a master player, a chess expert at 2–3 standard deviations above the mean for rated chess players. We've estimated the machine's performance ratings from Kasparov's annual rating in both years (approximately 2800: see Elo, 1986, for a discussion of the chess rating system) and the match outcomes.

Man and machine stand literally at opposite corners in this space. (We do not imply that Deeper Blue does not have a great deal of knowledge (procedures) relevant to chess; however, much of the program's code deals with ways to manage search processes, or is in the form of static databases of opening moves and endgame play.) Nonetheless, Deeper Blue 97 surpassed the performance of World Chess Champion Garry Kasparov in part because it could project far enough into the game tree to permit it to make "wise" choices for moves. Brute force computations can sometimes triumph over hard-won acquired knowledge. Humans are remarkable at acquiring knowledge, albeit slowly, but are very slow and potentially inaccurate at serial computation tasks (e.g. try serial subtraction by 7s starting from 256). Further, they have less than perfect retrieval from memory, a possible explanation for Kasparov's choice of a questionable move during the opening phase of Game 6 that ultimately cost him the match.

Nonetheless, it is amazing to contemplate how effectively slow, but very knowledgeable humans can compete against well-programmed computing devices with minimal knowledge but prodigious search capability. As numerous studies of expertise have shown (e.g. Chase & Simon, 1973a, b), superior pattern-matching capabilities account for much of the human's prowess.

KNOWLEDGE: PROS AND CONS

More knowledge is not always a good feature (e.g. Charness & Bieman-Copland, 1992). Problems associated with increases in knowledge can be seen for access, acquisition and persistence.

Access

For knowledge to be useful, it must be readily accessible. Unfortunately, as computer scientists who design databases have noted, the larger the database, the greater the access time for a query. Generally, although it depends on organizational features, retrieval time increases as a linear function of the logarithm of number of data records. There are ways around this dilemma, particularly by using pre-compiled indexes to speed search. Unfortunately, learning organisms such as humans do not have the luxury of assembling all their knowledge at once and then compiling it. Rather, they must add knowledge in real time (interpret it) from an environment that usually does not package it neatly.

Slow access with increased database size leads us to the "paradox of the expert" (e.g. Anderson, 1990). How are experts able to mobilize their knowledge as quickly as they do, given that retrieval time should increase with the size of the knowledge base? To address this question properly, we need to consider some potential architectures for human information processing. Most common architectures assume that semantic information is represented in some type of network structure, and that there is an indexing mechanism to access the information.

Three primary architectures for indexing knowledge have been proposed to account for human thinking: symbolic processing models such as EPAM (e.g. Feigenbaum & Simon, 1984); neural networks, also termed parallel distributed processing models (e.g. McClelland and Rumelhart, 1988); and hybrid systems, such as Anderson's (1983) ACT architecture, Newell's SOAR architecture (Newell, 1990), or Hummel & Holyoak's (1997) LISA analogical reasoning system. An EPAM-like indexing system can either use serial binary tests (e.g. Feigenbaum & Simon, 1984) or sequential n-ary (e.g. Richman et al., 1995) parallel tests to branch from node to node in the space of tests that define the entries to long-term memory information. In the former case, there is an expected slowing in time to access information from bigger nets than smaller nets, but it can be very small (Gobet, personal communication). Speed depends in part on the time to carry out the test, which is often assumed to be around 10 ms, a small time charge relative to time charges for other processes. In the latter case there is, potentially, very little difference in semantic memory access time between large and small nets.

Parallel distributed processing (PDP) models offer another approach. They are composed of units and connections, much as the brain is composed of neurons, axons and dendrites; however, they operate by assigning connection weights rather than neurotransmitters. PDP-style models would be expected to show very small differences between large and small pattern sets given that all that changes are the connection weights assigned to the units in the network. It seems likely, though, that the size of the network necessary to make accurate classifications might be expected to increase for larger domains of knowledge. Thus, there might be concomitant increases in the time to settle into a state representing the recognized pattern.

Based on such architectures, experts might be expected to be slightly slower to access any piece of their extensive knowledge base than those who are less expert, but the differences could be difficult to detect under ordinary circumstances. Other factors that are more critical to rapid access, such as frequency of occurrence, and recency of access (e.g. Anderson, 1990) will likely prove to be more important. In systems such as ACT, frequency of occurrence affects the strength of information traces. Strength affects access time. Thus, a system with many items in a highly accessible state will promote faster access than a system with fewer but less strong traces. Given that experts are usually in contact with their knowledge base more intensively, and usually more recently than their less-expert counterparts (due to greater current deliberate practice), they should have faster access to such primed knowledge.

In summary, although more knowledge should mean slower access, human information processing systems seem more affected by factors such as frequency and recency of access than by the size of the knowledge base when it comes to retrieving information.

Acquisition

According to one line of research, the more you know, the more difficult it is to acquire new information: a process called proactive interference (Underwood, 1957). This phenomenon was first shown for the learning of word and paired-associate lists. Although this effect is powerful, it depends on the way that information is organized and seems to be most relevant to the acquisition of episodic information. For instance, release from proactive inhibition takes place in list learning experiments when word categories are shifted (e.g. Wickens, Born & Allen, 1963). Learning mechanisms such as EPAM (Feigenbaum & Simon, 1984) provide a straightforward interpretation of such effects. Namely, it should be more difficult to index new information that is highly related to old information, given that the system needs to create more sophisticated tests for differences.

Conversely, at least theoretically, there is also a "snowball effect" for how having some knowledge makes it possible to acquire further knowledge more easily. Assuming an appropriate organizational structure, a system having a lot of knowledge, even unrelated knowledge, can acquire new information more effectively. The Landauer & Dumais (1997) latent semantic analysis (LSA) model demonstrates how learning may be tightly coupled with the context of all available information. Vocabulary learning in LSA depends on extracting and refining appropriate dimensions for lexical items. New words are not just related to words appearing in the same context, but differentiated from all known words that do not occur in the target word's context.

Landauer & Dumais give the following example. Assume that an expert is learning in a given domain, studying three hours a day for ten years and reading/encoding 240 words per minute. The expert encounters a new word on the 2 000 001st 70-word paragraph. The expert might be expected to gain 0.56 in probability correct for a new word, whereas a novice might gain only 0.14 probability correct for the same unfamiliar word, a 4:1 advantage for the expert.

At this point, we can only speculate about the balance of positive and negative effects of prior knowledge on the acquisition of new knowledge. We certainly need a more detailed theory about transfer (e.g. Singley & Anderson, 1989) to make specific predictions for a given task. We do know that the rate of skill improvement decreases as a power function from low to high levels of practice (Newell & Rosenbloom, 1981). This seems more likely to be a function of diminishing opportunities to acquire new chunks, rather than being due to the build up of proactive interference. We merely wish to point out that there may be both the expected benefits of knowledge and some costs when it comes to encoding new information. This leads us to a related problem: persistence of knowledge.

Persistence

One problem with knowing something, perhaps best represented in a cognitive architecture such as a production system (Newell & Simon, 1972), is that it tends to be activated whenever its conditions match the current situation. Duncker (1945) and other early researchers of problem solving demonstrated examples of premature closure effects, such as "functional fixedness" that trap people into blindly applying old techniques when a more efficient one is possible. "Tried and true" solutions to problems become automated and unless there is a conscious effort to break set, even experts may fail to realize that more efficient solutions are possible. A good example of this in chess is Saariluoma's (1992) finding that even strong master players used a stereotypic checkmating theme, the smothered mate, to solve a chess problem when a shorter mate was possible. If the ability to "break set" declines with increased accumulation of knowledge, this might explain declines in creativity as measured by psychometric test materials (Ruth & Birren, 1985) or creative output in a profession (Simonton, 1997).

Other examples of potentially negative effects of persistent knowledge are priming and inhibition failure. Priming refers to the facilitation observed when you process a new item following the processing of a related item (e.g. making a word/non-word judgment for a string such as "nurse", following a lexical judgment for the string "doctor" compared to the string "book"). One negative consequence is that records of past thinking activity can capture your train of thought all too easily. Perhaps this problem is partially responsible for the problem that some older adults have with telling and retelling the same story to a weary listener (Jennings & Jacoby, 1997).

Inhibition failure refers to the inability to end processing of an item quickly in order to process another item (e.g. suppress a context-irrelevant meaning for a word). Such persistence of knowledge (e.g. Hasher, Stolzfus, Zacks & Rypma, 1991) may also be a factor in the increasing rigidity of older adults evident in longitudinal studies (e.g. Schaie, Dutta & Willis, 1991).

Still, on balance, it is almost always better to have more knowledge than less knowledge, as Miller (1956) pointed out in his famous paper describing the chunking process. Those with more and larger patterns can encode information more quickly and accurately than those with fewer and smaller patterns. The same advantage holds true for more complex programs consisting of mental (and physical) procedures. Humans are generally faster when implementing an existing program than when trying to build one from scratch. Retrieval is almost always faster than computation.

APPROACHES TO ESTIMATING THE SIZE OF THE KNOWLEDGE BASE

It is sometimes useful to try to estimate the size of a knowledge base. For instance, for building expert systems, it is helpful to know the size of the domain in order to choose an appropriate tool set (hardware and software). Methods for estimating the size of an expert's knowledge base appear to fall into two categories: direct and indirect.

Direct Methods

Direct methods make the same basic assumption that standard test theory does. They assume that there is a universe of knowledge and that by sampling items from that universe, it is possible to estimate how much knowledge the individual possesses. Much as we do with testing in school situations, we can assume that if we sampled (randomly) from the universe of course material and a student achieves 80% correct on the test, then that student must know about 80% of the universe of knowledge in that course. We go one step further with direct methods. Given that we know the number of entries in the knowledge source (for instance, lexical entries in a dictionary), we can multiply the number of entries by 0.80 to estimate the number of lexical items in someone's vocabulary.

Oldfield (1963, 1966) was one of the first investigators to use this technique. By asking students to provide definitions for words taken from a large dictionary, he determined that typical college undergraduates must have a working knowledge base of some 100 000 English words.

There are a number of potential problems with this technique for estimating knowledge base size. For one, dictionary size tends to have undue influence on the final number. As well, we cannot be sure that inferential processes are not supplementing the expected recognition processes. For instance, knowledge of prefixes, suffixes, morphemes, foreign language words and some inference processing can enable people to generate a definition for an unknown English-like word. (Define "autoilluminator".)

Another approach to direct measurement is to pick domains where the person's strategies and knowledge can be encoded as moderate-sized production systems. A good example is provided by the Pirolli & Wilson (1998) models of the acquisition of LISP programming skills by adults, and balance-beam reasoning by children and adults. A combined approach of using production system models to define the knowledge in the domain together with Rasch scaling techniques can do a fine job of identifying the model of a particular individual or group and the difficulty of the domain items.

Things become much more complicated when attempting to define domains of knowledge broader than lexical entries. If we wanted to estimate your knowledge of psychology, for instance, how would we proceed? Psychology is a very big field. Much of the knowledge may not be in a passive declarative format, but in an active, generative format, similar to a grammar. A psychologist may know how to treat patients, how to design good experiments, ways to critique manuscripts, how to write grant proposals, in addition to being able to answer questions that might be found on undergraduate exams about subject matter in psychology. We could go to a set of encyclopedic sources (e.g. all the books classified as psychology texts in a library), but then deciding on how much information is present in those sources and how to sample it would be a daunting task.

Indirect Methods

Indirect methods for estimating knowledge base size have evolved through simulating recall patterns of skilled individuals. The classic task used is a paradigm of brief exposure followed by recall. As Chase & Simon (1973a, b) pointed out in the domain of chess playing, structured chess positions are recalled more successfully than random ones. Also, more skilled players outperform less skilled ones primarily on the structured positions. The original theory assumed that strong and weak players had equivalent short-term memory capacity. Players were assumed to recognize chess positions as chunks of familiar clusters of pieces. Hence, skilled players, possessing more and larger chunks, ought to recall more pieces. If each chunk encoded five chess pieces for a skilled player, but a single piece for an unskilled one, five chunks of short-term memory would yield 25 pieces for the expert, but only five pieces for the novice. The advantage would be seen primarily for structured chess positions that are composed mostly of familiar chunks, as opposed to random ones, which, by definition, lack such familiar structures.

Simulation studies of chess recall (Gobet, 1993; Gobet & Simon, 1996; Simon & Gilmartin, 1973) have led to the conclusion that an EPAM-style network consisting of nodes and links, indexing in the region of 50 000–100 000 patterns can adequately simulate master-level recall. Chess players probably have access to a vocabulary of chess patterns that is of the same order of magnitude as that for word patterns by adult native speakers of English.

Similarly, Richman et al. (1995) used EPAM-like structures supplemented by retrieval structures in long-term memory to simulate the performance of an expert in digit span. This simulation was able to achieve excellent recall (100+ digits) with a network of 3000–3500 chunks of information in the form of clusters of 3–5 digits.

These techniques for estimating the size of a knowledge base have different strengths and weaknesses. Direct methods, such as sampling from knowledge sources, usually result in estimates that are a function of the size of the dictionary, given that proportion correct scores from the subset of items actually tested are multiplied by the number of items in the source. Simulations may represent knowledge quite differently than does the human, leading to underestimates or overestimates. Multiple and, hopefully, converging techniques are required in this enterprise.

APPROACHES TO ASSESSING KNOWLEDGE ORGANIZATION

Knowledge structures can be represented as semantic networks in the form of connected graphs (e.g. Collins & Loftus, 1975; Collins & Quillian, 1969) or linked-list structures (e.g. Newell & Simon, 1972), with entities as units (nodes) and relations as the links between units. A number of different structures have been proposed to represent semantic information. Chang (1986) provides a good overview. *Frames* or *schemas* represent structures with a combination of predetermined or default values and free nodes that can bind new information to the structure. *Images* maintain first or second-order isomorphism (e.g. Kosslyn & Pomerantz, 1977; Shepard & Chipman, 1970) with spatial arrays in the real world in terms of the types of operations permissible (such as mental rotation). *Propositions* represent list-like structures that have truth values, for instance "the ball is red" might be represented as red (ball). Finally, neural nets represent information in terms of connection weights between nodes (McClelland & Rumelhart, 1988).

Simulations have also been used to assess knowledge base organization. An early example was the Collins & Quillian (1969) TLC model for assessing how quickly concepts and their properties are referenced when answering questions such as "Is a canary yellow?", or "Does a canary fly?" Latency to respond is used as an index of the distance between concepts and properties. Here, as in other simulations, there is a broad set of assumptions underlying the translation of latencies to levels in a hierarchy of concepts.

Work that Chi and colleagues completed on people of different experience levels solving physics problems indicated that experts classify problems quite differently than novices. Experts sorted problems based on deep structure similarity (physics principles related to problem-solving activities, such as conservation of energy), whereas novices sorted the problems based on surface structure similarity, such as whether an inclined plane was present (Chi, Feltovich & Glaser,

1981). Such work supports the idea that experts have a different organizational structure for domain knowledge. They not only know more facts and procedures, but also organize this information in more complex relational structures.

Patel and colleagues (e.g. Patel, Arocha & Kaufman, 1994; Patel & Groen, 1986) have used a variety of techniques to model the reasoning behavior of medical experts. They make use of problem-solving tasks and think aloud techniques as well as probe techniques such as asking for explanations of cases. Verbal statements are converted to propositional representations and then to semantic networks representing the knowledge structures and reasoning processes used in medical diagnosis.

Reitman Olson & Biolski (1991) provide an excellent guide to a range of techniques for uncovering the structure of knowledge in experts. These involve approaches such as protocol analysis of verbal reports (Ericsson & Simon, 1993), clustering techniques for recall order, and multidimensional scaling procedures. Such direct techniques as scaling category terms from a knowledge domain remain underutilized, probably because of the large number of terms in a given domain and the number of dyads or triads of terms that would be needed to make the required number of ratings.

We turn now to the applied question of methodology for building expert systems, AI programs that encapsulate the knowledge and reasoning abilities of human experts.

METHODOLOGICAL APPROACHES TO EXTRACTING KNOWLEDGE

When a character is injured in an old movie, someone inevitably shouts, "Is there a doctor in the house?" With advances in computer hardware, programming techniques, and storage media the day may not be far off when someone replies, "Yes, I have a doctor" and pulls out a laptop computer. Of course, the laptop wouldn't actually be a board-certified physician, it would be an *expert system*, or a system that attempts to simulate expert performance. It would prompt the user for input – symptoms, perhaps – and direct the user through a process of elimination until the root of the problem could be identified. It might then suggest a line of action to remedy the situation, which would then be implemented by the user. Though far less dramatic than the Hollywood version, such a system would be useful nonetheless, and a logical extension of the very earliest expert systems such as MYCIN (Shortliffe, 1976).

Constructing an expert system is essentially expertise research in that it requires one to collate a sufficiently large knowledge base and a set of heuristics to guide search and solve problems. Returning to the example of the Deep Blue chess machine for a moment; its knowledge base was constructed by humans so we could simply ask the engineers how much "knowledge" the system has, how it is organized, and how Deep Blue retrieves and manipulates the information. Unfortunately, this does not work well for human chess masters as they do not have ready access to that kind of information.

To understand how knowledge is used, we must utilize a number of knowledge elicitation techniques (e.g. Hoffman, Shadbolt, Burton & Klein, 1995) that include interviews, verbal reports (protocol analysis), reaction time (RT) measures, eye-movement (EM) tasks, and conceptual sorting techniques. Note that none of these methods is fool-proof, so researchers typically adopt a converging methodology, in which a hypothesis is supported when multiple techniques converge on the same explanation.

Interviews

The structure of an interview determines the type of data that will be elicited during a session. If it has a general agenda, or none at all, the discussion will tend to be unfocused and the resulting data will be of little use in terms of establishing relationships among domain concepts or inferring problem-solving strategies. However, these can be useful for the initial stages of investigation, where the primary goal may be to learn more about the domain, identify areas for further study, or to get a feel for what methods might be most appropriate for exploring the domain.

Structured interviews, discussion of case studies, and the like vary in their degree of focus and can range from discussions of general concepts to very specific applications of them. Whereas unstructured interviews require little preparation on the part of the elicitor, structured interviews require increasingly more preparation as the focus of the discussion narrows. Discussing a particular scenario, for instance, requires that the elicitor understand enough about the domain to present a realistic example. Note, however, that more focused discussions tend to yield more manageable and complete data and so sessions of this type are useful for defining the knowledge base and may give some insights into knowledge organization.

Structuring interviews

Wood & Ford (1993; see also Ford & Wood, 1992) outlined a general strategy for conducting interviews that begins with general declarative knowledge and moves toward making inferences about procedural knowledge. While their strategy was directed specifically toward the design of expert systems, it is also quite relevant to the early stages in researching knowledge organization.

Descriptive elicitation is aimed at gathering a large body of declarative knowledge about the domain. It should include the appropriate terminology used within the domain with complete definitions of special terms, as well as examples and anything else that helps define the problem space. They emphasize that the elicitor should record information provided by the expert precisely to avoid the potential influence of reductive biases.

Once the major domain concepts have been laid out and the relevant terminology defined, the next step should be to integrate the concepts, expanding on them as necessary. This process of elaboration and organization is called *structured expansion*. Wood & Ford (1993) recommend that questions in this stage should be:

- phrased using domain terminology
- long, to encourage longer responses
- asked in a setting or context in which the expert typically engages in problem solving.

By presenting questions in this manner, the length and detail of the responses are said to be much improved and are also less likely to be influenced by translation errors or reductive biases.

At this point the researcher should have enough information to begin exploring procedural knowledge, in what Wood & Ford refer to as *scripting*. While this can be done in a variety of ways, Wood and Ford suggest verbal reports (see below) since the elicitor has already acquired the terminology and declarative knowledge to present reasonable problems and then to analyze the resulting protocols.

Verbal reports

While interviews are often useful for eliciting domain knowledge from experts, they tend to be poor tools for understanding how information is used to solve problems. Verbal reports, by contrast, are well suited for this purpose. Verbal report techniques require that the expert solve domain-relevant problems and provide an account, either during problem solving or immediately following it, of the procedures and information employed. Reports given during problem solving are called concurrent or "think aloud" techniques, while those given afterwards are called retrospective reports.

Concurrent verbal reports may be good measures of on-line processing, since the expert must describe problem solving as it occurs. While this can force the expert to make explicit processes that would have otherwise been overlooked, there is considerable debate as to what impact concurrent reports have on processing. That is, the act of giving a concurrent report may interrupt the expert's problem solving and thereby change the process. Also, if tasks within the expert's domain involve communication or frequent verbalizations, concurrent reports will either seriously interfere with task performance or they will not even be possible (Bainbridge, 1979).

To avoid the possibility of task interference, retrospective reports may be taken following problem solving, usually immediately after each trial or problem so it will be fresh in the expert's mind. One criticism of such reports is that the only information available to the expert is that which occurred late in the problem and remains in short-term memory. Anything beyond this represents a reconstructive effort on the part of the expert so a complete report can be given. (If long-term working memory has been used to encode problem details, however, such information may be well maintained over an extended interval between encoding and report.) Another concern is that the expert may believe that he or she follows a certain strategy and may provide a verbal report that is consistent with this, hence giving the elicitor a potentially incorrect account of processing.

Perhaps the most serious criticism of verbal reports is that the expert may not be aware of many processes and so they will be left out of the reports (Bainbridge, 1990; Smith, Normore & Denning, 1991). Ericsson & Simon (1984, 1993) made several suggestions to improve the quality of verbal reports, which include instructing the expert on how to give reports and walking the expert through a few practice problems. In spite of their limitations and criticisms, verbal reports are still among the more common techniques for problem solving and have much to offer in terms of describing the strategies used by experts during problem solving.

Reaction time measures

For the reasons given above, it may be desirable to use an indirect method to get at knowledge organization and search strategies. Here, reaction times may be a useful alternative. This is probably the most common approach in experimental psychology because of the ease and flexibility of the technique. Tasks can quickly be created to explore a multitude of phenomena and the reaction time (RT) data is often very accurate and easy to manage.

With regard to your comprehension of this chapter, we could take what we know about your vocabulary and create several alternative organization schemes for that knowledge. We could then test these using simple RT tasks. The Collins & Quillian (1969) study mentioned earlier is a good example of a model that has been supported by RT data. Unfortunately, other models have been proposed that are also consistent with their data (Smith, Shoben & Rips, 1974), which illustrates the primary weakness of RT data – it often lends itself to multiple interpretations.

Eye-movement tasks

The recording of eye movements is one of the more recently acquired techniques for process tracing given that it requires relatively sophisticated equipment. There are a few variations in implementation. Electrooculography uses a set of strategically placed electrodes to record the movements of eye muscles and hence the movements of the eye itself. Some systems project an infrared beam of light onto the purkinje cells in the retina, which reflect the beam back out of the eye to the point of fixation. Other variations are also available which vary in accuracy, flexibility, and range of display types. Perhaps the most important breakthrough has been the development of head-free systems that compensate for head movements, so the subject can move freely and even give concurrent verbal reports without severely affecting eye-tracking accuracy. There are, however, no simple guidelines for how to align the verbal data stream with the visual (fixation) stream.

Self-reports are limited by the subjective nature of the data and are poorly suited for uncovering tacit knowledge or strategies. On the other hand, RT measures are useful for exploring tacit knowledge, but patterns of reaction times are frequently open to several interpretations. Eye-movement (EM) data falls somewhere between the two, providing a detailed record of EM patterns, which can be interpreted much like a verbal report, and most of the newer systems also provide RT data as well.

For example, EM data are an excellent way of understanding how you are able to comprehend this chapter. By recording the eye movements of subjects as they read sentences and short paragraphs, it is possible to develop models of text integration and better understand how concepts are linked during reading. By looking at fixation times and locations we can begin to see how attention is being allocated – looking at regressive eye movements, re-fixating previously read material, we can begin to make inferences regarding your strategy for integrating concepts.

A good example involves garden-path sentences, which lead the reader to misinterpret the meaning of the sentence, for example: "The cotton clothing is usually made of grows in Mississippi" (Pinker, 1994). Frazier & Rayner (1982) found that readers spent a significant amount of time fixating the point of ambiguity of garden-path sentences; in this case, that would be at "cotton clothing". This is important since we can infer that readers integrate the words as they read the sentence, otherwise they would not have made a mistake. When they realize the sentence makes no sense, they return to the point of ambiguity and attempt to resolve the problem. One could use EM records to observe similar patterns when integrating concepts across text or when using context to learn an unfamiliar word.

Obviously, eye tracking can be used only for visual tasks. It is also important to keep in mind that EM data, while more descriptive than RT data, is still open to interpretation. The data may indicate that a subject was fixating on a particular feature of the display, but the reason for that fixation is only speculative – it could reflect encoding, comparison, forgetting (if it's re-fixated), etc. Verbal reports, either concurrent or retrospective, can aid interpretation.

Conceptual techniques

These methods are aimed at identifying the relationships among domain concepts and often these concepts are then arranged or grouped into a network or hierarchical arrangement. A simple task of this sort would be having an expert arrange a set of cards, each one representing a domain concept, as they relate to one another. Of course, they are often more complex than this and are frequently computer guided, so the process can be more interactive. AQUINAS is an example of an interactive automated system that guides the expert through the construction of a repertory grid, one type of conceptual technique. Because the process is interactive, the expert is kept informed as to the state of the knowledge base and is permitted to make revisions as needed.

Conceptual techniques require little introspection from the expert and so may be viewed as somewhat more objective than either interviews or protocols. They also produce more structured data so analysis is simplified and the combination of data from multiple experts is facilitated. Their primary weakness is that the tasks involved do not resemble domain-related tasks, so they may not provide as much insight into concept organization as one would hope (Geiwitz, Kornell & McCloskey, 1990). Also, since their purpose is to explore functional relationships among concepts, the set of concepts must be relatively complete. The result is that the scope of conceptual methods tends to be restricted to reduce the number of concepts examined at any given time, making them difficult to use with large or complex domains.

Does the system work?

This is perhaps the least developed area in the creation of expert or knowledge-based systems – can someone actually use the system? While a great deal of time and effort has gone into gathering the information and programming knowledge bases and retrieval structures, relatively little effort has been directed toward usability. Unfortunately, the quality of the user interface can make even the best-performing system virtually useless if it is designed for the wrong user.

Systems can be designed for a number of uses, such as data mining, training, and augmenting human performance. For systems that perform lengthy searches or process large quantities of information, the user interface may not be critical as interactions with the system may be relatively brief and infrequent. However, systems for medical diagnosis would need a very efficient, user-friendly interface so the user could quickly get the type of information needed.

Werner (1996) suggested a number of criteria that an expert or knowledge-based system should meet, which includes not only the completeness and correctness of the knowledge base, but also human interaction issues as well. Assuming the system is capable of performing its intended function, attention should next be focused on the nature of the commands required of the user. Are they easy to learn? Are there too many? Are some redundant or unnecessary? The system should include only as many commands as necessary and they should be logically organized or labeled to minimize the user's learning time. Next, Werner emphasizes the importance of the user being in control of the system – that is, knowing what the computer has provided or is requesting and knowing how to interact with it at that point. Finally, the system should be capable of dealing with unexpected or rare situations, perhaps by providing a reasonable solution but definitely by indicating that the requested information is beyond its knowledge. This is extremely important in that it avoids the possibility of a system actually making a problem worse by providing incorrect or unreliable information in unusual and potentially unpredictable cases.

People (but not many computer programs) can exhibit knowledge about their own knowledge processes, termed metacognition (Nelson, 1996). That is, they have a monitoring function that enables them to make judgments about their progress in problem solving. Experts are more likely to be well calibrated (e.g. Keren, 1987) than less-skilled individuals in terms of judging the probable outcome of their planned actions. Experts are more likely to know that they do not know something and may be better at using colleagues or external information sources to help them solve domain-related problems.

SUMMARY

While the bulk of expertise research has been directed toward understanding knowledge and retrieval operations, one of the largest (and perhaps most successful) applications has been the creation of expert systems. The process of exploring a domain and creating an expert system is called *knowledge engineering*, which is described in detail by Cooke (1999, this volume). The ultimate goal of this endeavor is to produce computerized "experts" for a variety of domains.

Although expert systems have generally been tailored to relatively specialized domains, there are also projects with more ambitious goals. To try to approximate human reasoning in its broadest sense, one artificial intelligence project has attempted to encode very large amounts of knowledge, equivalent to the content of encyclopedias. Lenat (1990) and colleagues have been exploring how to encode such massive amounts of information, pairing large numbers of propositions with a flexible inference engine that can reason validly about the world. The goal is to have the system behave intelligently across a broad set of domains.

One of the virtues of building expert systems is that when a successful program is produced it automatically passes the *sufficiency* test as a model of expert performance. Still, a successful artificial intelligence program need not perform a task the same way a human does (e.g. the Deeper Blue chess program) and will thus fail the *necessity* requirement of a successful simulation. Nonetheless, the techniques employed to study expert performance in humans (protocol analysis, categorization techniques) do seem to transfer well to the task of building expert systems. Further, the building of expert systems holds the promise of advancing both the theoretical side of cognition as well as its application.

Finally, the recognition of how long it takes to develop an expert should make us even more appreciative of the amazing feats that human experts perform. The tremendous time cost involved in acquiring expertise should also spur us to consider how best to develop artificial experts that can augment our own abilities. The distributed knowledge system represented by a human expert's recognition capabilities and an artificial intelligence expert system's speed of computation potentially gives us the best of both routes to knowledge.

APPLIED ISSUES

From our review, we have highlighted several areas where basic research on expertise and knowledge can be applied immediately. There are also some areas where further development is needed.

1. *Developing criteria for assessing expertise.* Although the definition of expertise as "consistently superior performance on a specified set of representative tasks for the domain that can be administered to any subject" is an improvement over earlier attempts to use peer nomination or experience as criteria, much work remains to be done. We need better scaling of expertise in most human work environments. For many fields of practical importance

there seems to be little agreement on how to measure expertise, for instance in teaching (e.g. Greenwald, 1997) and in financial advice (e.g. Bédard & Chi, 1993; Camerer & Johnson, 1991). More needs to be done to find good sets of representative tasks that can be brought into the laboratory and quickly administered. Otherwise, we have to rely on reputation and experience to identify experts – a hazardous way to proceed.

2. *Improvement in the data analytic tools for assessing knowledge.* We have outlined some of the main techniques for probing knowledge structures. In almost every case, there is a need to refine the available tools to make them easier to administer and easier to manage the data that is collected. One example is finding ways to automate the alignment of eye-fixation records and verbal report records.
3. *Eliciting knowledge to build expert systems, or perhaps to store accumulated knowledge.* Expert systems have immediate commercial value, though the tools for creating them are still fairly rudimentary and not very easy to work with. Nonetheless, even small organizations might benefit from systematic recording of the accumulated knowledge of long-term employees using the elicitation techniques described above.
4. *Training human experts.* The work outlining the importance of deliberate practice indicates that simply having employees perform their tasks will not be likely to lead to improvements in their overall competence. Take the example of word processing expertise, what Card, Moran & Newell (1980) termed a "routine cognitive skill." Maintenance practice will probably make people perform more efficiently (power law of practice). But, if you want trainees to excel, they need to have time away from routine work assignments to build up their knowledge base about commands, and to learn to create procedures for chaining together commands to solve word processing problems. Similarly, work on expertise indicates that it is necessary to provide supportive learning conditions that enhance motivation and include access to skilled coaching. Further, there is considerable room in the area of training to produce more expert tutors to help move students along the path to expertise more efficiently. Development of better intelligent tutoring systems (e.g. Barns, Parlett & Luckhardt Redfield, 1991) may be an effective technique to accomplish this goal.
5. *Building hybrid human–computer experts.* By taking advantage of superior human pattern matching capability and superior machine speed for search, it is possible to build hybrid, distributed expert systems that may reach higher levels of competence than either human or artificial intelligence experts. Similar collaborative efforts in noncompetitive environments, such as medical diagnosis, may also help human diagnosticians avoid the slips (Norman, 1981), and reasoning errors (Kahneman & Tversky, 1984) that humans seem prey to, perhaps resulting in better diagnosis.

Of course, one of the problems that still must be surmounted in any collaborative relationship is trust in the reliability (knowledge and expertise?) of the partner. For instance, human drivers are not yet certain that in-vehicle navigation computer systems provide reliable information (Kantowitz, Hanowski & Kantowitz,

1997). Experienced pilots sometimes have difficulty monitoring the state of complex automated aircraft (Sarter & Woods, 1997). Such work points to the necessity to explore both the social and cognitive dynamics in collaborative expert systems.

ACKNOWLEDGMENTS

This work was supported by a grant from the National Institute on Aging (NIA 5R01 AG13969-02) to Neil Charness. We appreciate helpful comments from Francis Durso, Timothy Salthouse, and three anonymous reviewers.

REFERENCES

Anderson, J. R. (1978). Arguments concerning representations for mental imagery. *Psychological Review*, 85, 249–77.

Anderson, J. R. (1983). *The Architecture of Cognition*. Cambridge, MA: Harvard University Press.

Anderson, J. R. (1990). *The Adaptive Character of Thought*. Hillsdale, NJ: Lawrence Erlbaum.

Bainbridge, L. (1979). Verbal reports as evidence of the process operator's knowledge. *International Journal of Man–Machine Studies*, 11, 411–36.

Bainbridge, L. (1990). Verbal protocol analysis. In J. R. Wilson & E. N. Corlett (Eds), *Evaluation of Human Work: A Practical Ergonomics Methodology* (pp. 161–79). London: Taylor & Francis.

Baltes, P. B. & Staudinger, U. M. (Eds) (1996). *Interactive Minds: Life-span Perspectives on the Social Foundation of Cognition*. New York: Cambridge University Press.

Barns, H., Parlett, J. W. & Luckhardt Redfield, C. (1991). *Intelligent Tutoring Systems. Evolutions in Design*. Hillsdale, NJ: Erlbaum.

Bédard, J. & Chi, M. T. H. (1993). Expertise in auditing. *Auditing*, 12, Supplemental, 21–45.

Berliner, H. J. (1981). Search vs. knowledge: an analysis from the domain of games. Paper presented at the NATO symposium on Human and Artificial Intelligence, Lyon, France, October. Available as CMU-CS-82-103 from Computer Science Department, Carnegie-Mellon University.

Camerer, C. F. & Johnson, E. J. (1991). The process–performance paradox in expert judgment: how can experts know so much and predict so badly? In K. A. Ericsson & J. Smith (Eds), *Toward a General Theory of Expertise: Prospects and Limits* (pp. 195–217). New York: Cambridge University Press.

Card, S. K., Moran, T. P. & Newell, A. (1980). Computer text-editing: an information-processing analysis of a routine cognitive skill. *Cognitive Psychology*, 12, 32–74.

Card, S. K., Moran, T. P. & Newell, A. (1983). *The Psychology of Human–Computer Interaction*. Hillsdale, NJ: Lawrence Erlbaum.

Chang, T. M. (1986). Semantic memory: facts and models. *Psychological Bulletin*, 99, 199–220.

Charness, N. (1976). Memory for chess positions: resistance to interference. *Journal of Experimental Psychology: Human Learning and Memory*, 2, 641–53.

Charness, N. (1981). Search in chess: age and skill differences. *Journal of Experimental Psychology: Human Perception and Performance*, 7, 467–76.

Charness, N. & Bieman-Copland, S. (1992). The learning perspective: adulthood. In R. J. Sternberg & C. A. Berg (Eds), *Intellectual Development* (pp. 301–27). New York: Cambridge University Press.

Charness, N. & Campbell, J. I. D. (1988). Acquiring skill at mental calculation in adulthood: a task decomposition. *Journal of Experimental Psychology: General*, 117, 115–29.
Charness, N., Krampe, R. & Mayr, U. (1996). The role of practice and coaching in entrepreneurial skill domains: an international comparison of life-span chess skill acquisition. In K. A. Ericsson (Ed.), *The Road to Excellence: The Acquisition of Expert Performance in the Arts and Sciences, Sports and Games* (pp. 51–80). Mahwah, NJ: Erlbaum.
Chase, W. G. & Simon, H. A. (1973a). The mind's eye in chess. In W. G. Chase (Ed.), *Visual Information Processing* (pp. 215–81). New York: Academic Press.
Chase, W. G. & Simon, H. A. (1973b). Perception in chess. *Cognitive Psychology*, 4, 55–81.
Chi, M. T. H., Feltovich, P. J. & Glaser, R. (1981). Categorization and representation of physics problems by experts and novices. *Cognitive Science*, 5, 121–52.
Chi, M. T. H., Glaser, R. & Farr, M. J. (Eds) (1988). *The Nature of Expertise*. Hillsdale, NJ: Lawrence Erlbaum.
Collins, A. M. & Loftus, E. F. (1975). A spreading–activation theory of semantic processing. *Psychological Review*, 82, 407–28.
Collins, A. M. & Quillian, M. R. (1969). Retrieval time from semantic memory. *Journal of Verbal Learning and Verbal Behavior*, 8, 240–7.
Cooke, N. J. (1999). Knowledge elicitation. In Durso, F. T., Nickerson, R. S., Schvaneveldt, R. W., Dumais, S. T., Lindsay, D. S. & Chi, M. T. H. (Eds), *Handbook of Applied Cognition* (chapter 16). Chichester: John Wiley.
Duncker, K. (1945). On problem solving. *Psychological Monographs*, 58 (5), No. 270.
Elo, A. E. (1986). *The Rating of Chessplayers, Past and Present* (2nd edn). New York: Arco.
Ericsson, K. A. (Ed.) (1996). *The Road to Excellence: The Acquisition of Expert Performance in the Arts and Sciences, Sports, and Game*. Mahwah, NJ: Erlbaum.
Ericsson, K. A. & Charness, N. (1994). Expert performance: its structure and acquisition. *American Psychologist*, 49, 725–47.
Ericsson, K. A. & Kintsch, W. (1995). Long-term working memory. *Psychological Review*, 102, 211–45.
Ericsson, K. A., Krampe, R. Th & Tesch-Römer, C. (1993). The role of deliberate practice in the acquisition of expert performance. *Psychological Review*, 100, 363–406.
Ericsson, K. A. & Lehmann, A. C. (1996). Expert and exceptional performance: evidence of adaptation to task constraints. *Annual Review of Psychology*, 47, 273–305.
Ericsson, K. A. & Simon, H. A. (1984). *Protocol Analysis: Verbal Reports as Data*. Cambridge, MA: MIT Press.
Ericsson, K. A. & Simon, H. A. (1993). *Protocol Analysis: Verbal Reports as Data* (rev. edn). Cambridge, MA: MIT Press.
Ericsson, K. A. & Smith, J. (Eds) (1991). Prospects and limits of the empirical study of expertise: an introduction. In K. A. Ericsson & J. Smith (Eds), *Studies and Expertise: Prospects and Limits* (pp. 1–38). New York: Cambridge University Press.
Feigenbaum, E. A. (1989). What hath Simon wrought? In D. Klahr & K. Kotovsky (Eds), *Complex Information Processing: The Impact of Herbert A. Simon* (pp. 165–82). Hillsdale, NJ: Lawrence Erlbaum.
Feigenbaum, E. A. & Simon, H. A. (1984). EPAM-like models of recognition and learning. *Cognitive Science*, 8, 305–36.
Ford, J. M. & Wood, L. E. (1992). Structuring and documenting interactions with subject-matter experts. *Performance Improvement Quarterly*, 5 (1), 2–24.
Frazier, L. & Rayner, K. (1982). Making and correcting errors during sentence comprehension: eye movements in the analysis of structurally ambiguous sentences. *Cognitive Psychology*, 14 (2), 178–210.
Geiwitz, J., Kornell, J. & McCloskey, B. (1990). *An Expert System for the Selection of Knowledge Acquisition Techniques*. Technical Report 785-2. Santa Barbara, CA: Anacapa Sciences.

Gobet, F. (1993). *Les Mémoires d'un Joueur d'Échecs*. Saint-Paul Fribourg Suisse: Editions Universitaires Fribourg Suisse.

Gobet, F. & Simon, H. A. (1996). Templates in chess memory: a mechanism for recalling several boards. *Cognitive Psychology*, 31, 1–40.

Greenwald, A. G. (1997). Validity concerns and usefulness of student ratings of instruction. *American Psychologist*, 52, 1182–6.

Hasher, L., Stolzfus, E. R., Zacks, R. T. & Rypma, B. (1991). Age and inhibition. *Journal of Experimental Psychology: Learning, Memory & Cognition*, 17, 163–9.

Hinsz, V. B., Tindale, R. S. & Vollrath, D. A. (1997). The emerging conceptualization of groups as information processors. *Psychological Bulletin*, 121, 43–64.

Hoffman, R. R., Shadbolt, N. R., Burton, A. M. & Klein, G. (1995). Eliciting knowledge from experts: a methodological analysis. *Organizational Behavior and Human Decision Processes*, 62, 129–58.

Hummel, J. E. & Holyoak, K. J. (1997). Distributed representations of structure: a theory of analogical access and mapping. *Psychological Review*, 104, 427–66.

Jennings, J. M. & Jacoby, L. L. (1997). An opposition procedure for detecting age-related deficits in recollection: telling effects of repetition. *Psychology and Aging*, 12, 352–61.

Kahneman, D. & Tversky, A. (1984). Choices, values, and frames. *American Psychologist*, 38, 341–50.

Kantowitz, B. H., Hanowski, R. J. & Kantowitz, S. C. (1997). Driver acceptance of unreliable traffic information in familiar and unfamiliar settings. *Human Factors*, 39, 164–76.

Keren, G. (1987). Facing uncertainty in the game of bridge: a calibration study. *Organizational Behavior and Human Decision Processes*, 39, 98–114.

Kosslyn, S. M. & Pomerantz, J. R. (1977). Imagery, propositions, and the form of internal representations. *Cognitive Psychology*, 9, 52–76.

Landauer, T. K. & Dumais, S. T. (1997). A solution to Plato's problem: the latent semantic analysis theory of acquisition, induction, and representation of knowledge. *Psychological Review*, 104, 211–40.

Lenat, D. B. (1990). *Building Large Knowledge-based Systems: Representation and Inference in the Cyc Project*. Reading, MA: Addison-Wesley.

McClelland, J. L. & Rumelhart, D. E. (1988). *Explorations in Parallel Distributed Processing. A Handbook of Models, Programs, and Exercises*. Cambridge, MA: MIT Press.

Miller, G. A. (1956). The magical number seven, plus or minus two: some limits on our capacity for processing information. *Psychological Review*, 63, 81–97.

Nelson, T. O. (1996). Consciousness and metacognition. *American Psychologist*, 51, 102–16.

Newell, A. (1989). Putting it all together. In D. Klahr & K. Kotovsky (Eds), *Complex Information Processing: The Impact of Herbert A. Simon* (pp. 399–440). Hillsdale, NJ: Lawrence Erlbaum.

Newell, A. (1990). *Unified Theories of Cognition*. Cambridge, MA: Harvard University Press.

Newell, A. & Rosenbloom, P. S. (1981). Mechanisms of skill acquisition and the power law of practice. In J. R. Anderson (Ed.), *Cognitive Skills and their Acquisition* (pp. 1–55). Hillsdale, NJ: Lawrence Erlbaum.

Newell, A. & Simon, H. A. (1972). *Human Problem Solving*. Englewood Cliffs, NJ: Prentice-Hall.

Norman, D. A. (1981). Categorization of action slips. *Psychological Review*, 88, 1–15.

Oldfield, R. C. (1963). Individual vocabulary and semantic currency: a preliminary study. *British Journal of Social and Clinical Psychology*, 2, 122–30.

Oldfield, R. C. (1966). Things, word and the brain. *Quarterly Journal of Experimental Psychology*, 18, 340–53.

Patel, V. L. & Groen, G. J. (1986). Knowledge based solution strategies in medical reasoning. *Cognitive Science*, 10, 91–116.

Patel, V. L., Arocha, J. F. & Kaufman, D. R. (1994). Diagnostic reasoning and medical expertise. *The Psychology of Learning and Motivation*, 31, 187–252.

Pinker, S. (1994). *The Language Instinct* (p. 212). New York: William Merrow and Co.

Pirolli, P. & Wilson, M. (1998). A theory of the measurement of knowledge content, access, and learning. *Psychological Review*, 105, 58–82.

Reitman Olson, J. & Biolski, K. J. (1991). Techniques for representing expert knowledge. In K. A. Ericsson & J. Smith (Eds), *Toward a General Theory of Expertise: Prospects and Limits* (pp. 240–85). New York: Cambridge University Press.

Richman, H. B., Staszewski, J. J. & Simon, H. A. (1995). Simulation of expert memory using EPAM IV. *Psychological Review*, 102, 305–30.

Ruth, J. & Birren, J. E. (1985). Creativity in adulthood and old age: relations to intelligence, sex and mode of testing. *International Journal of Behavioral Development*, 8, 99–109.

Saariluoma, P. (1992). Error in chess: the apperception–restructuring view. *Psychological Research*, 54, 17–26.

Sarter, N. B. & Woods, D. D. (1997). Team play with a powerful and independent agent operational experiences and automation surprises on the Airbus A-320. *Human Factors*, 39, 553–69.

Schaie, K. W., Dutta, R. & Willis, S. L. (1991). The relationship between rigidity–flexibility and cognitive abilities in adulthood. *Psychology and Aging*, 6, 371–83.

Shepard, R. N. & Chipman, S. (1970). Second-order isomorphism of internal representations: shapes of states. *Cognitive Psychology*, 1, 1–17.

Shortliffe, E. H. (1976). *Computer-based Medical Consultations: MYCIN*. New York: Elsevier.

Simon, D. P. & Simon, H. A. (1978). Individual differences in solving physics problems. In R. Siegler (Ed.), *Children's Thinking: What Develops?* (pp. 325–48). Hillsdale, NJ: Lawrence Erlbaum.

Simon, H. A. (1974). How big is a chunk? *Science*, 183, 482–8.

Simon, H. A. & Chase, W. G. (1973). Skill in chess. *American Scientist*, 61 (4), 394–403.

Simon, H. A. & Gilmartin, K. (1973). A simulation of memory for chess positions. *Cognitive Psychology*, 5, 29–46.

Simonton, D. K. (1997). Creative productivity: a predictive and explanatory model of career trajectories and landmarks. *Psychological Review*, 104, 66–89.

Singley, M. K. & Anderson, J. R. (1989). *The Transfer of Cognitive Skill*. Cambridge, MA: Harvard University Press.

Smith, P. J., Normore, L. F. & Denning, R. (1991). Knowledge acquisition techniques: a case study in the design of a reference materials access tool. *Proceedings of the Human Factors Society 35th Annual Meeting*, pp. 273–7, San Francisco, CA.

Smith, E. E., Shoben, E. J. & Rips, L. J. (1974). Structure and process in semantic memory: a featural model for semantic decisions. *Psychological Review*, 81, 214–41.

Sternberg, S. (1975). Memory scanning: new findings and current controversies. *Quarterly Journal of Experimental Psychology*, 27, 1–32.

Underwood, B. J. (1957). Interference and forgetting. *Psychological Review*, 64, 49–60.

Van Lehn, K. (1996). Cognitive skill acquisition. *Annual Review of Psychology*, 47, 513–39.

Werner, A. (1996). Importance of the quality of human–software interaction in expert systems. *Behavior and Information Technology*, 15 (5), 331–5.

Wickens, D. D., Born, D. G. & Allen, C. K. (1963). Proactive inhibition and item similarity in short-term memory. *Journal of Verbal Learning and Verbal Behavior*, 2, 440–5.

Wood, L. E. & Ford, J. M. (1993). Structuring interviews with experts during knowledge elicitation. *International Journal of Intelligent Systems*, 8, 71–90.

Zsambok, C. E. & Klein, G. (Eds) (1997). *Naturalistic Decision Making*. Mahwah, NJ: Erlbaum.

Chapter 4

Memory Applied

David G. Payne, Celia M. Klin, James M. Lampinen, Jeffrey S. Neuschatz
Binghamton University
and
D. Stephen Lindsay
University of Victoria

Memory can broadly be defined as the retention of information over time. For humans and other biological organisms, memory can be operationally defined as changes in behavior caused by events in the rememberers' past. These definitions point to the fact that memory plays a key role in many aspects of everyday life, but they do not make it clear how integral memory is to virtually all cognitive processes. To appreciate the effect of memory on everyday life, consider what would happen if one's memory suddenly stopped working entirely. Imagine, for example, a person who has an accident that causes damage to the brain, resulting in dense amnesia. After the accident, what would life be like for this person? Perhaps your first impulse is to imagine that such a catastrophe might leave the victim wandering around mumbling "Who am I?", perhaps asking people "Where am I?" or looking for clues such as a name on an ID card.

While these might be reasonable questions for the victim to ask, the fact the person is able to ask them shows that they have not suffered a *complete* loss of memory. A person with no memory whatsoever would be unable to produce or understand language, because those skills rely on memory for the semantics, vocabulary, etc. of one's language. Even trying to read the information on their driver's license would be impossible, since reading requires matching visual patterns on the license with knowledge of the language stored in memory. Our hapless victim would even have trouble wandering around, because walking is

Handbook of Applied Cognition, Edited by F. T. Durso, R. S. Nickerson, R. W. Schvaneveldt, S. T. Dumais, D. S. Lindsay and M. T. H. Chi.

also a complex, learned skill. Without any support from memory the person would be unable to speak, read, walk, or even crawl.

This hypothetical scenario makes clear the absurdity of the notion that a single chapter could provide a comprehensive review of research and applied work dealing with human memory. Every chapter in this book includes (explicitly or not) discussions of the role of memory in applied psychology. This chapter provides a brief survey of general theoretical approaches in contemporary memory research, a discussion of lay persons' naïve theories of memory, and a description of some of the real-world domains in which memory research has successfully been applied. We will also discuss some of the issues relevant to the basic/applied research distinction as it applies to memory.

The remainder of this chapter is organized as follows. The first section deals with theoretical and metatheoretical issues regarding memory, including the major contemporary memory theories and several of the important "kinds" of memory that have been identified. The second section deals with common metaphors used for memory, the implicit theories lay persons have about memory, and the effects of such everyday beliefs about memory. The third section reviews several substantive research areas in which inroads have been made towards understanding how memory functions in important everyday situations. The fourth section discusses issues concerning applying theories derived from basic research to everyday memory situations. In the final section we describe a new memory metaphor that we think offers considerable advantages over previous metaphors.

THEORETICAL VIEWS ON MEMORY

Contemporary Models of Memory

Cognitive psychologists have developed a number of very sophisticated theories of human memory. In this section we summarize the main features of three of the primary theoretical approaches to human memory.

Information Processing Models

Traditional cognitive approaches to memory draw heavily on an analogy to digital computers as symbol-manipulating devices. According to this metaphor, the mind/brain codes events into internal, symbolic representations, or traces, which can then be stored, retrieved, combined with other symbols, and transformed in various ways. For example, if the word "fish" is foveally presented, the retina will code the pattern of contrasts in the light into an electrochemical pattern, which is further processed (i.e. recoded into different electrochemical "languages") by other brain processes. By such accounts, the internal, symbolic representation of a particular instance of reading the word "fish" exists in a specific location in the brain (e.g. it may be copied into long-term memory), just as a word processing file symbolically represents text (i.e. the file does not consist of letters and words *per se*, but rather of more abstract computer code that symbolically represents letters and words) and is stored in some particular location on a computer hard drive.

Brains and computers differ in a great many ways, of course, and cognitive models that describe memory in terms of symbolic representations do not deny this; they do imply, however, that memories consist of "traces" that symbolically code or represent past cognitions. Most representational models also imply that the structures and processes of memory *per se* are distinct from other sorts of cognitive structures and processes (e.g. perceptual processes, decision making). As we will argue later in the chapter, this assumption may be convenient for the memory researcher, but it appears to be at odds with the way memory functions in the real world.

Connectionism

In their pure form, connectionist models (also known as parallel distributed processing models or neural network models: Rumelhart & McClelland, 1986) reject the idea that cognitive processes give rise to internal symbolic representations that are stored in particular locations in the brain. In connectionist models, information in memory is distributed across a network composed of a large number of densely interconnected simple processing units. Lindsay & Read (1995b) offered the following apt analogy to describe the architecture and processes involved in a connectionist model: imagine a spider web composed of millions of fibers, with some fibers anchored on input units (e.g. sensory receptors) and others anchored on output units (e.g. motor-control enactors). Sensory stimulation causes fibers connected to the receptors to vibrate, with the amount of vibration of each input fiber corresponding to an aspect or feature of the stimulus (e.g. for visual stimuli, some input fibers vibrate a lot if the stimulus is red, others if it is blue, others if it has a curved edge, etc.). A pattern of vibration propagates throughout the entire web, with the amount of vibration in different parts of the web determined by the pattern of input vibration and by the strengths of the connections between fibers. Any particular pattern of input vibrations is ultimately transformed into a corresponding (but different) pattern of output vibrations.

Using simple feedback mechanisms, connectionist networks can modify the connections between fibers (tightening or loosening connections so that transmission of vibration is amplified or muted) to learn new input/output relations while maintaining previously learned ones (e.g. Gluck & Bower, 1988). Thus the network learns to produce particular patterns of output vibration in response to particular patterns of input; the memory of the event is represented in the pattern of weighted connections between fibers in the entire network, and "thinking" about that event is represented by a particular pattern of vibration throughout the network. If given an input about some aspects of a past stimulus, such networks naturally "retrieve" a close approximation of the response to the complete stimulus (analogous to responding on a cued recall test).

As a metaphor for memory, connectionist networks have many advantages over traditional representational models. They capture, in an elegant and rather natural manner, the way memories of similar events can interfere with one another, cue one another, or become blended together (depending on specifics of the memories and the cues; e.g. Eich, 1985; Metcalfe, 1990, 1991). The connectionist metaphor assumes that remembering is not a process of retrieving records from a special library where they have been stored, separate from the rest of mental life. Rather, in connectionist models memory is viewed as a byproduct of the processes that give rise to and constitute ongoing cognition, and memories are represented as subtle and complex changes in those processes. Thus memory is not neatly and cleanly separated from perceiving, thinking, imagining, and other aspects of mental life, and the experience of remembering does not reduce to simply locating and reading off an encapsulated record of a past experience but rather involves partially recreating a prior pattern of activation across an entire network.

Despite these advantages, a rather severe limitation of the connectionist memory metaphor is that they generally fail to make *a priori* predictions about the effects of various factors on memory performance. Traditional representational models (e.g. Atkinson & Shiffrin, 1968) are quite explicit about the manner in which various factors should affect encoding, storage, and retrieval, and thus researchers can derive and test predictions of the models. (This is somewhat less true of more recent, and more complicated models such as Raaijmakers & Shiffrin's, 1981, SAM (search of associated memory) model.) For applied researchers, this difficulty in deriving predictions from the connectionist models is more than a simple inconvenience, for it makes it difficult to use the connectionist metaphor as a basis for real-world applications (e.g. design of memory remediation programs).

Functional Models

The final class of memory models we consider are the functional models. What differentiates functional models from traditional information processing models is that functional models do not postulate a specific architecture and set of processes presumed to underlie memory. Rather, functional models describe important functional relations between large classes of variables that have been shown to exert a major influence on memory performance. Perhaps the best known functional model is the levels of processing framework proposed by Craik & Lockhart (1972). This model proposes that the deeper an event is processed (with depth defined as extent of meaningful analysis) at encoding, the better the retention of the event. The levels of processing framework identified a fundamental fact concerning human memory, namely that the nature and extent of the processing an event receives during encoding exerts a tremendous effect on memory for that event. This has been shown to hold with different materials (e.g. words, pictures, faces), subject populations (e.g. children, young adults, older adults), and types of retention measures (e.g. recall vs. recognition). (For a review, see Cermak & Craik, 1979.) The levels of processing framework has also had an impact in the applied domain (e.g. Heiman, 1987; Herrmann, 1992).

Despite its success, there are problems with the levels framework. From an applied perspective, one of the main shortcomings of the levels of processing view is that it says nothing about the manner in which memory will be expressed. That is, the levels framework focuses exclusively on encoding processes and is mute on the role of retrieval processes in affecting memory performance. An alternative functionalist view, the transfer appropriate processing view proposed by Morris, Bransford & Franks (1977; see also Bransford, Franks, Morris & Stein, 1979) remedies this situation by proposing that encoding processes will aid memory to the extent that the processes engaged at encoding match, or are appropriate for, the processes required by the retrieval task (cf. Tulving's encoding specificity principle, e.g. Tulving, 1983). The concept of transfer appropriate processing illustrates the way in which functionalist models attempt to account for memory phenomena by identifying lawful relationships between observable variables (as opposed to detailed postulations regarding internal mechanisms.) (See Watkins, 1990, for further arguments supporting functionalist approaches to memory theory.)

Types of Memory

Another important aspect of contemporary memory research and theorizing is the notion of different "kinds" of memory. Just as the early information processing models made distinctions between short-term and long-term memory, modern theorists find it useful to contrast different types of memory that differ on one or more dimensions. Over the last several decades a number of distinctions have been proposed between different types of memory, and several of these distinctions have proven to be both influential and useful in understanding and affecting memory in the real world. In this section we briefly review two of these distinctions.

Episodic versus Semantic Memory

Tulving (1972, 1983) proposed an extremely influential distinction between what he argued were two different types of memory: episodic and semantic memory. Episodic memory, according to Tulving, encodes and stores information about autobiographical experiences (i.e. memory for personally experienced episodes situated in particular spatial/temporal contexts in one's past). Semantic memory, in contrast, stores all of our knowledge but does not maintain information regarding how, when, or where that knowledge was acquired. In operational terms, episodic memory is assessed by asking the rememberer to recall or recognize events that occurred in a specific context, such as words in a to-be-remembered list. Semantic memory can be measured in a number of ways, such as asking general knowledge questions (e.g. "What Vice President of the United States once misspelled potato during a school spelling bee?").

Since its introduction in 1972 the episodic/semantic distinction has attracted a great deal of attention, and there have been intense debates over the correct theoretical interpretation of differences between episodic and semantic tasks. For example, some have argued that episodic and semantic memory reflect the operation of distinct, albeit highly interrelated, memory systems (Tulving, 1983) whereas others have held that the differences between episodic and semantic memory tasks can be accounted for without postulating distinct memory systems (e.g. Johnson & Chalfonte, 1994; Squire, 1994). Still others have proposed additional distinct memory systems, such as a memory system for sensory information (e.g. Cowan, 1995; Tulving & Schacter, 1990).

Despite these theoretical disputes, there is agreement among memory researchers that the semantic/episodic distinction is useful. Regardless of whether autobiographical recollections and semantic knowledge are served by qualitatively distinct memory systems or reflect different kinds of uses of a single memory system, these two categories of memories are functionally and phenomenologically distinct. While the furore over the episodic/semantic distinction has settled down in recent years, many of the same issues have been played out in discussions of the related distinction between implicit and explicit memory.

Implicit versus Explicit Memory

Graf & Schacter (1985) introduced the terms implicit and explicit memory to distinguish between two forms of memory that are revealed in different types of memory tasks. To illustrate these two forms of memory, consider an experiment reported by Tulving, Schacter & Stark (1982). In this study subjects first saw a long list of words followed by two memory tests, a recognition test and a word fragment completion test. The recognition test involved presenting subjects with words from the study list mixed in with extralist distracter words, and the subject's task was to indicate which words had appeared in the study list. For the word fragment completion test subjects were given word fragments (e.g. A _ _ A _ _ IN) and their task was simply to fill in the missing letters to create any English word (e.g. ASSASSIN). Some of the word fragments corresponded to words from the study list and the remainder were extralist items. Performance in the word fragment completion test was assessed by comparing the probability of completing the fragments corresponding to list words versus extralist words; higher completion rates for the studied items represent a *priming effect*.

Subjects completed the recognition and word fragment completion tests soon after the list was presented and also seven days later. Tulving et al. (1982) found that, not surprisingly, performance on the recognition test decreased significantly across the seven-day retention interval. In contrast, there was virtually no decrease in the magnitude of the priming effect observed in the word fragment completion test. This pattern of data represents a functional dissociation: increasing the retention interval affected recognition performance but not performance in the word fragment completion test. (Similarly, in a much earlier study by Warrington & Weiskrantz, 1970, amenstic patients, who performed very poorly on recall and recognition tests, benefited as much as normal subjects from prior exposure to words that could be used on a subsequent word-stem completion test.)

Graf & Schacter (1985) used the terms implicit and explicit memory to describe the two forms of memory evidenced in the recognition and word fragment completion tests: "For descriptive purposes, we use the terms 'implicit' and 'explicit' memory to distinguish between these forms of memory. Implicit memory is revealed when performance on a task is facilitated in the absence of conscious recollection; explicit memory is revealed when performance on a task requires conscious recollection of previous experiences" (p. 501).

Since Graf and Schacter introduced these terms there has been a tremendous amount of research reported comparing implicit and explicit memory, and much of this work has shown that there are important functional dissociations between these two forms of memory. As was the case with the episodic/semantic memory distinction, there have also been a number of different theoretical accounts offered for this distinction. The two primary types of accounts that have attracted the greatest attention are the processing theories (e.g. Blaxton, 1989; Roediger, 1990) and the systems theories (e.g. Schacter, 1987; Squire, 1994). (For comprehensive reviews of the implicit/explicit distinction and the alternative theoretical accounts of the dissociations between implicit and explicit memory, see Schacter, 1987; Roediger & McDermott, 1993; Kelley & Lindsay, 1996.) According to the processing view, differences between implicit and explicit forms of memory reflect differences in the types of information required to perform the retention tests. Systems theories hold that there are distinct underlying memory systems that are tapped when completing implicit versus explicit tests. From an applied prospective, both views hold promise for helping to understand memory in the real world.

MEMORY METAPHORS, IMPLICIT THEORIES AND BELIEFS ABOUT MEMORY

As the scenario involving the amnesic at the beginning of the chapter makes clear, memory manifests itself in many different ways. Given the complexity of human memory it is not surprising that scholars and laypersons have employed many different types of explanatory mechanisms to account for memory. The theories described in the last section represent explanations developed by scientists based on laboratory and clinical research. But nonscientists also develop explanations for how memory operates. In this section we review some popular memory metaphors and evidence suggesting that these metaphors, along with the implicit theories people have about memory, affect memory performance in important ways.

Memory Metaphors

Lakoff & Johnson (1980) argued convincingly that people frequently employ metaphors in their attempts to understand the world, and that the metaphors we employ serve to structure the ways we think, perceive, and act. Roediger (1980) noted that the primary type of memory metaphor used in cognitive psychology was a spatial metaphor (although, as noted earlier, spatial metaphors are giving way to the connectionist metaphor and to functionalist approaches among memory theorists). Lay people often describe memory as akin to a library, with memories of specific events being similar to books stored on the library shelf. Remembering an event then involves searching the library for the appropriate book; forgetting involves a failure to locate the sought-after book (perhaps because it is no longer in the library, or perhaps because it simply cannot be found).

From an applied perspective, there are four important consequences of embracing a spatial metaphor for memory. First, because a storehouse metaphor implies that for any given event a memory is or is not stored and is or is not accessible, these metaphors focus attention on the *quantity* of information remembered, and downplay other aspects of the normal functioning of memory, such as the qualitative characteristics and accuracy of memories. Recent empirical and theoretical work (e.g. Koriat & Goldsmith, 1994; Payne, Elie, Blackwell & Neuschatz, 1996; Roediger & McDermott, 1995) shows that there are often large discrepancies between what people remember and what actually occurred. Second, a spatial metaphor implies that for each experience there is a corresponding "memory trace" that encodes all aspects of that experience into a unitized bundle. It is not clear how ongoing experience would be divided into such discrete bundles, and evidence (e.g. Chalfonte & Johnson, 1996) indicates that memories of different aspects of an event are less tightly bound together than such a metaphor suggests. Third, spatial metaphors imply that memory is separate and distinct from other cognitive and metacognitive factors, and here again there is evidence, some of which we review later, that argues against this notion. Fourth, the spatial metaphors do not in themselves capture the role that extra-memorial factors (e.g. motivation, attention, health) play in affecting memory (Herrmann & Searleman, 1990).

Implicit Theories

As Sternberg (1985) noted, "Implicit theories are constructions by people (whether psychologists or laypersons) that reside in the minds of those individuals. Such theories need to be discovered rather than invented [as explicit theories are] because they already exist, in some form, in people's heads" (p. 608). In the applied domain, implicit memory theories can play a major role in affecting how people approach the task of memorizing a set of materials, what they do when attempting to recollect past events, and how confident they are that they will remember events experienced under certain circumstances.

Memory metaphors and implicit memory theories exert a very strong influence on memory in the real world, even when they are at odds with what is known about memory from scientific research. To illustrate these points, consider one of the oldest and best established principles from the memory literature, the spacing effect (Dempster, 1988). Over a century ago, Jost (1897, cited in Hintzman, 1974) inferred from Ebbinghaus' ([1885] 1964) data that learning is improved if practice is spread out in time rather than massed together. Following this initial observation, there have been hundreds of studies examining the spacing effect and the distribution of practice (Hintzman, 1974; Payne & Wenger, 1992).

Given the robustness of the spacing effect, one might expect individuals' implicit theories of memory to reflect this effect. However, the available evidence indicates that lay people have erroneous ideas regarding spacing effects. For example, Modigliani & Hedges (1987) presented subjects with lists of 20 words and required some subjects to rehearse the items aloud during list presentation. Modigliani & Hedges examined rehearsal patterns and found that when people are given free rein over how they rehearse, they do so in a manner analogous to massed presentation.

It is possible, of course, that the subjects in the Modigliani & Hedges (1987) study were aware of the benefits of spacing but they were unable to alter their rehearsal patterns. Data reported by Zechmeister & Shaughnessy (1980), however, argue against this view. Zechmeister & Shaughnessy presented subjects with common nouns to study. Some of the items appeared only once whereas others were repeated, either massed together or spaced throughout the list. When subjects were asked to estimate the likelihood that they would be able to recall particular list items when tested later, they rated the massed items as more likely to be recalled than the spaced items. These self-report data suggest that subjects believe that rehearsing/studying items in a massed fashion is an effective way to commit information to memory, whereas the literature on the spacing effect shows clear evidence of the benefits of distributed practice for long-term retention. Thus erroneous implicit theories can lead to sub-optimal memory-task performance.

In addition to the data regarding the spacing effect there are many other findings in the memory literature that suggest that people have invalid implicit theories about how memory operates. For example, people often use rote repetition when attempting to memorize materials, although systematic research indicates that rote repetition is an extraordinarily poor technique for memorization (e.g. Craik & Lockhart, 1972). As another example, Garry, Loftus, Brown & DeBreuil (1997) recently examined lay persons' beliefs about memory and how these beliefs correlated with their behaviors. Garry et al. found that a portion of their subjects held beliefs that are at odds with the results of scientific studies (e.g. 16% of the subjects surveyed reported they believed that people can recollect prebirth experiences). Garry et al. also showed that constellations of these beliefs are correlated with real-world behaviors such as engaging in memory-recovery techniques during psychotherapy.

As a final example, evidence indicates that under some circumstances individuals are vulnerable to illusions of remembering. False memories may arise from external suggestive influences (as in the eyewitness misinformation effect: e.g. Loftus & Palmer, 1974) or when the products of spontaneous internal cognitions (e.g. associations, fantasies, dreams) are mistaken as memories of actual events (e.g. Johnson, Hashtroudi & Lindsay, 1993; Kelley & Jacoby, 1998; Lindsay & Kelley, 1996; Roediger & McDermott, 1995). People are often very confident in false memories, and sometimes claim to remember details of the episode in which the event supposedly occurred (e.g. Payne et al., 1996; for a review, see Lampinen, Neuschatz & Payne, 1997). It is likely that mistaken beliefs about memory contribute to vulnerability to illusory memories.

The general conclusion that emerges from these and other studies is that people are often quite inaccurate in their beliefs regarding memory. The invalid beliefs presumably reflect people's implicit theories about memory, and these memory beliefs are correlated with at least some aspects of performance in everyday situations. One of the challenges for applied workers is to translate laboratory research into programs to better educate people, with the aim of improving memory in applied settings.

APPLICABLE AND APPLIED MEMORY RESEARCH

In this section, we review several literatures within the memory field that have forged links between basic research and theorizing and how memory operates in the real world.

Metamemory

People often make decisions based on what they feel they know. For example, students preparing for final exams must assess how well they have mastered the materials in their different courses in order to prepare effectively. Although such memory assessments are made frequently in everyday life, for much of this century psychologists largely ignored these processes. Fortunately, the past 30 years has seen a healthy interest in metamemory, or what we believe about what we know.

Metamemory judgments, judgments about what information exists in memory, can often be made quickly, based on the familiarity of a memory cue, such as a question (e.g. Glenberg, Sanocki, Epstein & Morris, 1987; Schwartz & Metcalfe, 1992). Despite disagreements regarding the exact nature of the processes underlying metamemory judgments, there is general agreement that there are many circumstances in which people can monitor and evaluate the contents of their memory with relative success. For example, "feeling of knowing" judgments for items that cannot be recalled are often good predictors of future recognition accuracy (e.g. Hart, 1965; Metcalfe, Schwartz & Joaquim, 1993).

Although metamemory judgments are relatively accurate, they are far from perfect. While retrieval fluency, or familiarity, provides a generally adequate index of how well something is known, it can also be misleading. For example, Reder (1987) found that subjects were more likely to predict that they could answer general knowledge questions (e.g. "What is the term in golf for scoring one under par?") if some of the words in the question (e.g. golf, par) had appeared earlier in the experiment, making the question seem more familiar. However, this increased confidence was not accompanied by improved performance; the familiarity manipulation had no effect on subjects' actual ability to answer the questions.

Examples of "illusions of knowing" have also been well documented outside the laboratory. For example, Bjork (1996) analyzed study-skills training programs, and found that a number of features are commonly present in these programs that work to increase learners' perceptions of competence, while lowering their actual competence. These include the use of massed practice, excessive feedback, fixed conditions of training, and limited opportunities for retrieval practice. To remedy the mismatch between trainees' competence and confidence, Bjork recommended that the conditions of training should be varied to better reflect the challenges the learner will face in the post-training environment, practice should be spaced, and feedback should be reduced.

Understanding the factors that influence the accuracy, and inaccuracy, of metamemory assessments has important implications for eyewitness testimony, particularly in light of the fact that jurors give a great deal of weight to witness confidence. Cutler, Penrod & Stuve (1988) found that of ten witness and identification variables, only witness confidence had a reliable effect on jurors' judgments regarding the probability that an identification was correct. Unfortunately, this faith in witnesses' metamemory abilities is somewhat misguided, as there is often a weak correlation between witnesses' confidence and their accuracy (Wells & Murray, 1984). In a meta-analysis of 35 studies, Bothwell at al. (1987) found the correlation between eyewitness confidence and accuracy to be only 0.25.

A number of studies have attempted to identify specific moderator variables that qualify this accuracy–confidence relationship in eyewitnesses' metacognitive judgments. For example, Deffenbacher (1980) proposed that the correlation between accuracy and confidence varies with the optimality of the conditions during the encoding and retrieval stages, with more optimal conditions leading to stronger accuracy–confidence correlations. Bothwell et al. (1987) found some support for this prediction in their meta-analysis: increasing exposure to the target face during the original event increased the correlation between accuracy and confidence. A meta-analysis by Sporer, Penrod, Read & Cutler (1995) showed that the accuracy–confidence correlation is stronger when analyses are restricted to choosers (those who make an identification) than when both choosers and non-choosers are included. Dunning & Stern (1994) showed that there were significant differences in the decision processes of subjects who made accurate versus inaccurate identifications: accurate witnesses were more likely to state that their judgments were based on automatic processes (e.g. the face seemed to "just pop out" of the display), whereas inaccurate eyewitnesses were more likely to employ a process of elimination as they viewed the photos. These findings suggest ways in which suspect identification procedures could be amended to enhance the correlation between witnesses' confidence and accuracy.

Eyewitness Memory

Misinformation Effects

In addition to studying eyewitnesses' metacognitive assessments, basic and applied researchers have examined a host of other factors that affect the accuracy of eyewitness memory. The effect that has attracted the greatest attention over the last 25 years is the misinformation effect, originally demonstrated by Loftus and her colleagues. In their classic studies, Loftus & Palmer (1974) showed subjects a film of a traffic accident involving two cars. After watching the film, subjects were asked to estimate how fast the cars were going when the accident occurred. For different groups of subjects the verb used in the speed question ("How fast were the cars going when they . . .?") was "contacted," "hit," "bumped," "collided," or "smashed." Loftus & Palmer found that the magnitude of the speed estimate was directly related to the form of the verb. If the verb implied a minor collision (e.g. "contacted") the speed estimates were fairly low but if the verb implied a more violent accident (e.g. "smashed"), then subjects' speed estimates were much higher. A second important finding was that subjects' reports of what they remembered from the filmed event was also affected by the form of the question. Subjects who were asked the question that implied a more violent accident were more likely to report that they remembered seeing broken glass in the filmed event than were subjects who were asked the question implying a less serious accident. (In fact, there was no broken glass.)

The implication of these studies is that witnesses' recollections can be affected by the way they are questioned or by other sources of postevent misinformation. But *how* is memory affected? According to the changed trace hypothesis, the postevent information in some way alters or overwrites the original information in memory (e.g. Loftus, 1979; Loftus & Loftus, 1980). Conversely, the multiple trace hypothesis holds that the original information is not lost from memory, but rather the postevent information is added to memory and in some way interferes with the retrieval of old information at test (e.g. Bonto & Payne, 1991; Chandler, 1989, 1991). As argued by McCloskey & Zaragoza (1985), standard tests of the eyewitness misinformation effect are ambiguous with regard to whether post-event information has any effect at all on ability to remember the corresponding event details. While the debate over the mechanisms responsible for producing the misinformation effect is far from settled, much of the extant evidence favors the multiple trace hypothesis (Chandler, 1989, 1991).

The postevent misinformation effect has also been studied in more naturalistic settings. For example, Bruck, Ceci, Francouer & Barr (1995) repeatedly gave subjects misleading information indicating that a vaccination had been given by a nurse rather than by a doctor. On the fourth and final interview, 31 out of 32 misled children indicated that the vaccination was indeed administered by the nurse. Peters (1987) reported similar results regarding children's memory of dental visits.

Effects of Stress on Memory

Another eyewitness memory topic that has received considerable attention is the effect of stress during encoding. This is a topic with obvious real-world implications (e.g. many crimes occur in high-stress situations). One hypothesis regarding the relationship between stress and memory is the Yerkes–Dodson (1908) law, which predicts that stress will enhance performance up to a threshold, after which further increases in stress will impair memory performance. Although laboratory studies indicate that stress and emotionality do affect memory, the pattern of results is much more complex than would be predicted by the Yerkes–Dodson law. In any case, it is difficult to generalize laboratory findings to real-world situations because the stress levels studied in the laboratory are far lower than those that occur in many real-world events. To avoid this problem, researchers have examined memory for naturally occurring, extremely stressful events such as natural disasters (Parker, Bahrick, Lundy, Fivush & Levitt, 1998), hospital procedures (Goodman & Schaaf, 1997; Howe, Courage & Peterson, 1994), and crimes (Yuille & Cutshall, 1986). In these extremely stressful situations, researchers have generally found that people's memories are quite accurate and resistant to forgetting. For example, Parker et al. (1998) interviewed children who had low, moderate, or high exposure to stress during Hurricane Andrew.

Exposure to stress was defined by how much damage occurred to the children's homes. Although hurricane exposure definitely affected stress levels, it did not affect the children's memory for the hurricane itself. (There were effects of stress on the recall of events after the hurricane, but these are difficult to interpret due to differences in the amount of information subjects at the different stress levels had to recall.)

Researchers have also examined how memory for stressful events changes over time. Despite what one might expect based on laboratory research, Yuille & Cutshall (1986) demonstrated that adult witnesses' memory for a violent crime involving a fatal shooting was very accurate even after a six-month retention interval, and Parker et al. (1998) reported that children's long-term memory of Hurricane Andrew was also quite accurate. Such findings indicate that, relative to memory for laboratory events (e.g. word lists, films, etc.), memory for dramatic life events is robust. This does not mean that the fundamental mechanisms of memory for real-life events differ from those of laboratory events, nor does it mean that dramatic life events are never forgotten or misremembered. On the contrary, there is ample evidence both for forgetting (e.g. Williams, 1994) and misremembering (e.g. Loftus & Ketcham, 1994) of dramatic life events, and we see little reason to assume that the mechanisms of such memory errors differ qualitatively from the mechanisms that underlie memory errors for laboratory events. Differences between laboratory and observational studies of highly stressful natural events do, however, underscore the fact that absolute levels of performance vary dramatically across situations.

In summary, research does not support the Yerkes–Dodson "law" that high levels of stress impair memory. In a review of this literature, Christianson (1992) argued that the evidence indicates complex interactions between degree of stress or emotionality, type of information, retention interval, and form of test. In general, central details of highly stressful events tend to be remembered unusually well whereas peripheral details of highly stressful events tend to be remembered poorly.

Methods to Enhance Eyewitness Memory

Efforts to improve eyewitness memory have benefited from the interaction of basic and applied memory research. There are many reasons why it is important to develop procedures that maximize the accuracy and completeness of eyewitness memory. Eyewitnesses' performance on identification tasks is particularly important, because thousands of people become criminal suspects as a result of eyewitness identifications each year (Goldstein, Chance & Schneller, 1989). Some of these identifications are inaccurate and lead to wrongful convictions (Wells & Bradfield, in press). The National Institute of Justice recently examined 28 cases of people who had been released from prison due to the introduction of new incontrovertible DNA evidence. In 24 of these cases the primary evidence against the defendant was multiple eyewitness identification from lineups or photo spreads (Wells & Bradfield, in press). Of course, in other cases witnesses fail to identify the perpetrator. The Good Lineup Practices Subcommittee of the American

Psychology/Law Society is currently drafting a White Paper with recommendations for improving the accuracy and usefulness of identification evidence (further information is available on the Internet at http://www.unl.edu/ap-ls/).

There is also a need to enhance the accuracy and completeness of eyewitnesses' verbal accounts. Although law enforcement personnel spend a great deal of time interviewing witnesses, several surveys in the 1970s and 1980s showed that no more than 2% of law enforcement personnel received any formal training in how to interview (Rand Corporation, 1975, and Sanders, 1986, both cited in Geiselman & Fisher, 1997), and observational studies of actual police interviews indicate that they often use sub-optimal techniques (Geiselman & Fisher, 1997).

As a result of these and other factors, Geiselman, Fisher and their colleagues (e.g. Geiselman, Fisher, MacKinnon & Holland, 1986) developed the Cognitive Interview as a forensic tool for enhancing eyewitness memory. In its original version, the cognitive interview was designed to take advantage of two well-established memory principles. The first principle is that memories are assumed to consist of multiple features (e.g. Underwood, 1969) and therefore the effectiveness of a memory enhancement procedure will depend on the extent to which the retrieval cues provided overlap with those features stored in memory (e.g. Tulving & Thomson, 1973). The second principle holds that there may be several retrieval paths to a memory trace and hence different retrieval cues may lead to the retrieval of different information (Tulving, 1974).

The original Cognitive Interview consisted of four general retrieval techniques, along with more specific techniques designed to elicit specific types of information (e.g. license plate numbers, names). Two of the four general methods are designed to increase the overlap of features stored at encoding with those provided at retrieval: (a) mentally reinstating the physical and personal context in which the event took place (Bower, Gilligan & Monteiro, 1981), and (b) encouraging witnesses to report all information regardless of its perceived importance (Smith, 1983). The remaining two techniques encourage the use of multiple retrieval routes: (a) recounting events in different temporal orders (e.g. backwards and forwards: Loftus & Fathi, 1985), and (b) reporting the events from a variety of perspectives (e.g. burglar and homeowner; Anderson & Pichert, 1978).

The Cognitive Interview has met with success, both in terms of application and in generating research. In terms of research, at least 45 experiments on the Cognitive Interview or variants of the procedure have been reported (Memon, 1998). In commenting on their ten years of work with the Cognitive Interview, Geiselman & Fisher (1997) noted that they have offered over a hundred workshops to local and federal law enforcement agencies in the United States. The Cognitive Interview is either required or included as part of standard training for numerous organizations in the United States as well as in the United Kingdom. The Cognitive Interview has also passed an important test in the legal system. Geiselman & Fisher (1997) reported that in a "hearing on the admissibility of interview evidence gained with the cognitive interview (CI), the presiding judge in California ruled CI to pass the test" (p. 292). We score this as a major victory for those seeking to export principles from the laboratory to the real world.

A related topic that has received extensive research attention is forensic interviewing of child witnesses. In most cases of child sexual assault, the child victim and the perpetrator are the only witnesses, and there is no clear medical evidence. Thus great weight rests on the accuracy and completeness of children's reports when abuse is suspected. Here too, interactions between basic and applied research are providing bases for improved interview techniques and means of assessing the accuracy of particular reports (for recent reviews, see a special issue of *Applied Cognitive Psychology* edited by Ornstein & Davies, 1997, and Poole & Lindsay, 1998).

Mnemonics

Mnemonics, or memory aids, are strategies used to enhance memory. Mnemonics are of particular use for difficult memory tasks such as learning face-name associations (e.g. McCarty, 1980) and foreign language acquisition (e.g. Gruneberg, 1992), and for populations prone to memory impairments such as the aged (e.g. Verhaeghen, Marcoen & Goossens, 1992) and Korsakoff patients (e.g. Cermak, 1980). Mnemonics include external aids, such as making lists or writing on a calendar (Intons-Peterson & Fournier, 1986), as well as internal aids, such as alphabetic searching, the method of loci (associating to-be-remembered items with familiar locations), the pegword method (memorizing a series of number-word associations, such as "one is a bun, two is a shoe . . ." and then associating each to-be-remembered item with a "pegword"), and rhymes ("Thirty days has September . . .").

Although there are questions regarding the practicality of using internal mnemonics outside of a few tasks (e.g. memorizing a shopping list, foreign vocabulary, or names of new acquaintances), there is considerable evidence that when used, mnemonics are effective in enhancing recall compared with normal "rote" learning methods. For example, McCarty (1980) investigated the usefulness of mnemonics in learning face-name associations, a notoriously difficult task. The mnemonic involved selecting words that phonologically resembled the person's name, and associating these words with some prominent feature of the person's face. For example, in a task in which subjects learned to associate photographs with proper names, they were told to associate the photograph of "Wagner" (who had prominent cheeks) with the word "wagon," and were told to "visualize covered *wagons* bumping over his cheeks." In an immediate recall task, subjects who received this mnemonic instruction were significantly more likely to recall the name associated with the photograph (55% correct) than subjects in a variety of control conditions (12–23% correct). McCarty pointed out that it is unclear if the usefulness of the face-name mnemonic would work in everyday situations in which people have to create their own related words and visual images, and memory of the names is needed for a longer time period after acquisition.

Gruneberg (e.g. 1985) developed foreign language courses which utilize "the linkword language system." In this system, to learn the Italian word for fly, "mosca," for example, the learner might imagine flies invading "Moscow." Foreign language learners have reported that the keyword method was faster, easier and more enjoyable than conventional methods (Gruneberg & Sykes, 1991).

The keyword method has also been shown to aid in learning new vocabulary terms in one's native language. McDaniel & Pressley (1989) found that subjects who learned new English words with the keyword method outperformed subjects in a context group, who learned the new vocabulary words in the context of a three sentence story. Impressively, not only were the definitions of the words more likely to be recalled (76% vs. 53%), but comprehension of passages using the new vocabulary words was better for the keyword group, with no decrease in reading speed. The fact that the improvement in memory also enhanced comprehension shows yet again the extent to which memory influences performance on other cognitive tasks.

While these and other studies attest to the effectiveness of mnemonics across a variety of tasks and populations, there is also evidence that suggests that such techniques are rarely used. Several studies (e.g. Harris, 1980; Intons-Peterson & Fournier, 1986; Park, Smith & Cavanaugh, 1990) have found that people generally prefer external memory aids (e.g. writing out a grocery list) to using mnemonics. For example, Cermak (1980) demonstrated that alcoholic Korsakoff patients could improve their memory performance with mnemonics, but the patients quickly forgot the mnemonic techniques. Harris (1980) interviewed subjects regarding what memory strategies they used, and found that external aids (e.g. writing memos, putting something in a special place) were used far more frequently than internal aids (e.g. first letter mnemonics, rhymes, method of loci). Finally, Park et al. (1990) collected self-reports regarding the use of memory strategies from memory researchers, all of whom should be well aware of the potential benefits of using mnemonics, and compared these with self-reports from other psychologists, who were not experts in memory, and non-psychologist university faculty. Results indicated little use of formal mnemonic techniques across all three groups, with memory researchers' pattern of mnemonic use very similar to that of the other groups.

Overall, then, mnemonics have been shown to be quite effective, but people – even savvy memory researchers – rarely employ them. The general lack of effective use of mnemonics may be due to two factors: they require substantial effort to learn and some effort to use properly (Gruneberg, 1985) and existing mnemonics are useful only in a limited variety of tasks.

Above and beyond specific mnemonic tasks, basic research suggests that people can enhance their real-world memory performance in at least three ways. Firstly, when encountering to-be-remembered information, pay attention. It may sound painfully obvious, but many failures to remember reflect a failure to pay attention when the event occurred (e.g. when a new acquaintance was introduced). Memory performance can be enhanced by focusing attention on the to-be-remembered material, processing it "deeply" (i.e. thinking about its meaning), forming visual images of it, and integrating the new material with prior knowledge. Secondly, capitalize on the phenomenon of transferring appropriate processing by matching memorization technique to testing technique. That is, study by doing what it is you want to be able to do later (e.g. study differently for a multiple-choice test than for an essay test) and make the ambient conditions in which you study similar to those in which you will be tested. Thirdly, when an initial retrieval effort fails, try a different tack. (For a discussion of related techniques to enhance retention of texts, see Thomas & Robinson, 1972.)

Prospective Memory

Memory enables recollection of past events, but it can also enable remembering to do things in the future. Thus we might try to remember to take the laundry to the dry cleaners on the way home from work, take medication every three 3 hours, or send Uncle Bob a get-well card. Remembering in the future is known as prospective memory, and in recent years there has been a steady increase in our understanding of the factors that affect prospective memory. For example, one assumption that is often made about prospective memory is that constant reminders will improve performance. However, Guynn, McDaniel & Einstein (1998) found that reminders are effective only under certain circumstances. Specifically, reminders improved performance only if the person is reminded of the target event as well as the action that needs to be performed. For example, if one has to relay a message to another person, then thinking about both the person and the action will increase the likelihood that one will carry out the task (Harris, 1980).

It is a commonplace fact that some individuals perform more poorly on prospective tasks than others. Do individual differences in internal mnemonic processes contribute to such differences, or are they due primarily to individual differences in the use of external memory aids? To address this question, Marsh, Hicks & Landau (1998) asked a group of students to identify all the goals that they had to achieve for an upcoming week as well as whether they typically wrote down these goals on a calendar or daily planner. Marsh et al. referred to those subjects who reported using daily planners as "recorders." Marsh et al. randomly assigned half of the recorders and non-recorders to use daily planners in which they were to write down their plans for the week. Subjects completed more of their future plans when they used the external memory aid regardless of whether they were recorders or non-recorders.

In addition, Marsh et al. (1998) explored the relationship between performance in free recall, perception of accuracy of memory (a metamemory assessment), and prospective memory. Marsh et al. found that recorders recalled fewer items on a free recall task and rated their memory as being less accurate than non-recorders. These data suggest that recorders realize that they have rather poor memories and attempt to compensate for this by using an external memory aid such as a daily planner. This represents another case of metamemorial awareness affecting how people solve real-world prospective memory tasks.

Prospective memory tasks are extremely common in everyday life. Understanding how people achieve these tasks can help applied workers create interventions, training regimes, etc. that help people improve performance in these important tasks. There have already been several notable successes in this regard (e.g. Camp, Foss, Stevens & O'Hanlon, 1996; Park & Kidder, 1996) and we look forward to further applications.

Psychotherapy and Memory

No recent issue has been more contentious than the question of whether traumatic memories that are recovered in therapy are likely to be accurate (Berliner & Williams, 1994; Lindsay & Read, 1995a; Loftus, 1993). On the one hand, psychologists have only relatively recently come to grips with the prevalence and damage caused by childhood physical and sexual abuse (Finkelhor & Browne, 1988; Finkelhor & Dzubia-Leatherman, 1994). Because of that, many are understandably wary about appearing to discount claims of abuse based on recovered-memory experiences. On the other hand, the emerging theoretical picture of how memory operates that was sketched earlier in this chapter provides ample reason to be cautious in assuming that any memory, even a memory for a traumatic event, is necessarily accurate (Payne & Blackwell, 1998).

The issue of recovered memories arises out of clinical approaches dating back to Freud ([1896] 1962) that assume that childhood trauma produces psychopathology and that recovering long forgotten memories of abuse can ameliorate these problems. Recently, some clinical psychologists proposed that psychotherapy with child abuse victims requires an uncovering of memories of abuse and that this includes some clients who initially claim to have no memory of abuse (e.g. Briere, 1992). It is important to note too, however, that Briere suggested caution in doing so, so as not to pressure clients into reporting abuse when none exists. Briere argued that therapies aimed at recovering memories have a number of specific advantages, including allowing the therapist to obtain data on what happened and the clients' response to the abuse, "emotional catharsis," allowing the client to view abuse from an adult perspective and lessening the painfulness of the abuse through repeated recall.

Are painful childhood events such as physical and sexual abuse actually ever forgotten and then later recovered? There appears to be ample evidence that the answer to this question is yes. Indeed, what is contentious about this sub-issue is not so much whether it is possible to forget abuse, but rather technical issues concerning the mechanisms through which this forgetting occurs. In particular, debate between some memory psychologists and some therapists appears to focus on whether the forgetting is due to a mechanism of "repression" or whether other mechanisms can account for the loss of memory for traumatic events (Loftus & Ketcham, 1994).

The evidence for a repression mechanism *per se* is rather limited (Holmes, 1994). Indeed, if we consider in detail the components of the definition of repression we can see why it may be difficult in principle to provide evidence for this construct. The term repression appears to refer, in part, to a type of amnesia that occurs in reaction to psychological trauma or stress and whose purpose is to protect the individual from anxiety (Loftus & Ketcham, 1994). This part of the definition is clearly difficult to test empirically; it may be possible to show that forgetting painful events decreases anxiety but it is unclear how one would show that forgetting occurred "in order" to decrease anxiety.

Because of these conceptual and definitional issues, we believe that it makes more sense to reframe the central issue. For the social and legal issues being discussed in the recovered memory debate, it is not really crucial whether "repression" ever occurs. What matters is whether accurate memories of long-forgotten traumatic events can later be recovered.

Even the staunchest critics of recovered memories agree that people sometimes forget dramatic and even traumatic childhood experience (e.g. Loftus & Ketcham, 1994). This claim is supported by two recent prospective studies of victims of child abuse. Williams (1994) found that 32% of 129 women who had experienced a documented instance of abuse as children failed to report the documented instance of abuse as adults (even though they were willing and able to report other embarrassing events – indeed, 88% of the sample reported one or more instance of childhood sexual abuse). Although it is possible that a portion of the cases in which the documented instance of abuse was not reported involved (a) failure to report rather than failure to remember the abuse, (b) women who were very young when the abuse occurred, and (c) women whose abuse was relatively non-memorable, Williams argues that most of these cases reflect genuine forgetting of childhood traumas. These arguments are further supported by similar findings in another prospective study by Widom (1997).

Retrospective studies suggest that forgotten abuse can sometimes later be remembered. In some studies, women in therapy have been asked if there was ever a period in their life when they could not remember the abuse that they now remember. In most studies a substantial proportion of women report periods of having no memory for the abuse (e.g. Briere & Conte, 1993). In some of these studies some women have provided some degree of corroborating evidence that the abuse actually occurred (e.g. Herman & Schatzow, 1987). Some of these studies have been criticized on the grounds that the questions may have been worded in an ambiguous way (Loftus, 1993) but even studies conducted by some of these critics have found substantial rates of reports of prior periods of not remembering abuse in women who now claim to remember being abused (Loftus, Polonsky & Fullilove, 1994).

Furthermore, there is now substantial case evidence that previously forgotten memories that are later recovered are sometimes true. Ross Cheit (1998) has archived many of these cases at

http://www.brown.edu/Departments/Taubman_Center/Recovmem/Archive.html.

Overall, then, both the existing survey research and case evidence suggest that it is possible that people may forget childhood abuse incidents and recall them years later, although the precise mechanisms through which this occurs are unclear.

Things would be easier if we could simply accept all recovered memory claims at face value. However, the situation is not so simple, as there is also ample evidence that practices engaged in by some therapists can lead to the creation of false memories of abuse. There is debate about the frequency with which such practices occur but it is clear that some therapists have engaged in memory recovery practices that raise the risk of creating false memories (Lindsay & Read, 1995a). For example, in her book *Repressed Memories*, Fredrickson (1992) urged readers who lack a memory for abuse to repeatedly imagine incidents of abuse and for one year to treat these imagined events as if they really happened. Substantial laboratory evidence suggests that this sort of repeated imagining of events can lead to false memories that seem subjectively compelling (Ceci, Crotteau-Huffman, Smith & Loftus, 1994; Hyman, Husband & Billings, 1995).

Laboratory studies suggest that the practice of repeatedly asking subjects to recall events that never happened can lead to the creation of false memories for entire events. But is it possible for people to falsely recall events of a traumatic nature that never happened? It would obviously be unethical to attempt to produce false memories for childhood abuse. However, there appears to be substantial case evidence of memory distortion even for traumatic events. For example, Garry & Loftus (1994) report a case in which a woman claimed to have been repeatedly abused in a ritualistic fashion over a number of years and of having been raped by her father. According to her claim the rape resulted in a pregnancy and eventual birth of a child who was later murdered. However, review of medical records and photographs from the time demonstrated that the girl had never been pregnant.

Other clear evidence of the creation of false memories of traumatic events comes from cases in which people claim to remember being abducted and probed by aliens (Newman & Baumeister, 1996). Many of these cases occur after months of therapy with practitioners inclined to believe in alien abduction and with the use of suggestive interview techniques such as hypnosis. It seems clear to us that if a memory recovery technique leads to the recovery of memories for alien abductions, then that memory recovery technique should be used very cautiously indeed (if at all). (For recent reports representing a variety of perspectives on the recovered-memory controversy, see an edited volume by Read & Lindsay, 1997.)

Consumer Memory

Researchers interested in attitude change and advertising have long recognized the importance of memory for producing attitude change and influencing consumer brand choice and product use (Keller, 1987). An advertisement, no matter how entertaining or convincing, will have little effect on consumer behavior unless consumers remember the content of the ad, the brand being advertised, etc. Towards this goal, companies place multiple ads for the same products in the same magazines or on the same television networks. Assuming that the purpose of these ads is to increase consumers' memory for the product, brandname, etc., this raises the obvious question of how the ads should be placed to best maximize their effectiveness. As we indicated earlier, basic research on memory suggests that when events are repeated the information is most memorable when presented in a spaced rather than massed fashion (Hintzman, 1974). Additionally, Glenberg (1976) found that the number of intervening items that is optimal for memory performance is contingent on how long information has to be remembered. In particular, at short retention intervals people remember more when fewer intervening items are used between each successive presentation but at longer retention intervals memory is better when more items intervene between each successive presentation.

Inspired by this finding in the basic memory literature, Singh, Mishra, Bendapudi & Linville (1994) investigated the effects of spaced presentation on memory for television ads. They compared recall and recognition of brand name information for advertisements that were shown twice with either a short lag (one intervening item) or a long lag (four intervening items). Subjects were tested either shortly after viewing the advertisements or on the next day. Consistent with the findings of basic memory research, at short delays subjects recalled and recognized more brand names when the short lag was used but at long delays subjects recalled and recognized more brand names when long lags were used.

Another principle of basic memory research that has been applied to consumer memory is the encoding specificity principle (Tulving & Thomson, 1973). According to the encoding specificity principle, memory will be best when the cues available when people attempt to remember information match the cues available when they initially learned information. In terms of consumer memory, consideration of encoding specificity is important because advertisers are not merely interested in improving memory for a product in general but rather are interested in having consumers remember product information at the moment they are making a buying decision. It would thus be useful if companies could manipulate the cues available when consumers are shopping such that they are similar to the cues available in the advertisement.

To evaluate this possibility, Keller (1987) presented subjects with a series of print ads about products. The ads were created such that subjects who remembered the ads' content should prefer the target products over the filler products. Subjects were later shown a mock-up of a product's box that either included a cue from the ad or failed to include such a cue. Subjects who saw the mock-up containing the cue rated the product more favorably than did those who saw the mock-up without the cue. Note that in this study an implicit measure of memory (preference) was used rather than the more typically used explicit measures of recall or recognition. This is important in that many consumer choices are made based on preferences rather than on explicit recall of advertisements.

A final example of a finding from basic memory research that has been used by researchers interested in consumer memory is the picture superiority effect (Nelson, Reed & Walling, 1976). Because both recall and recognition are better for pictures than words, advertisers almost always include more pictorial and verbal information in ads (Houston, Childers & Heckler, 1987). An important question is how visual and verbal information should best be integrated to maximize the memorability of ad content and product names. Lutz & Lutz (1977) compared the effects of interactive and non-interactive pictures on memory for brand names. Interactive pictures were defined as images in which the product name and the product were combined into a single interactive image. For instance, the ad for Rocket Messenger Service showed a messenger carrying a package and being propelled by a rocket. Non-interactive images were pictures that illustrated either the product name or the product itself but did not combine both in an interactive fashion. For example, OBear Abrasive Saws was illustrated by showing a picture of a bear standing to the right of a giant "O." Subjects were later presented with lists of products and were asked to provide the brand name associated with it. Subjects were better able to recall the brand names when they had seen the interactive images than when they had seen the non-interactive images.

APPLYING LABORATORY-BASED THEORIES TO REAL-WORLD PROBLEMS

Some memory researchers (e.g. Herrmann & Raybeck, 1997; Neisser, 1978) have suggested that there is little hope that laboratory-based theories can be translated into usable prescriptions for improving memory in the real world. In this section, we review some of the factors that are likely to affect how well we are able to achieve this goal.

It is not unreasonable to hope that the theories developed based on laboratory findings can be used in addressing real-world problems, and happily there are many examples of the ways in which factors identified in basic memory theories can be creatively applied when addressing real-world memory problems (e.g. Camp & Foss, 1997; Geiselman & Fisher, 1997; Glisky & Schacter, 1987). Unfortunately, there are also numerous counterexamples of basic theories failing when they are moved from the laboratory to the real world (e.g. Yuille & Cutshall, 1986).

In this section we consider factors that influence the success or failure of basic theories of memory in real-world applications. It is important to note that in both cases – successes and failures – there are a chain of assumptions, inferences, etc. between the basic research theory and the application of that theory to solve a real-world problem.

First, the theory must have identified factors that exert a powerful influence over memory performance, and these factors must have been tested under a wide range of conditions. Basic researchers strive to keep conditions as constant and controlled as possible, and this high degree of experimental control can result in demonstrations of effects that are statistically significant but that are either (a) restricted to a very constrained set of conditions or (b) small in magnitude. When small or non-robust effects are used as the basis for formulating theories, generalization of those theories to real-world situations is likely to fail. There are simply too many factors that simultaneously affect behavior in the real world for small or non-robust factors isolated in the laboratory to exert a detectable influence. Although the theory may have identified factors that influence behavior under laboratory conditions, the effect may be so small that it can be observed only in the laboratory. This would seem to be the case for many quantitative theories that are based on small reaction time differences between conditions of interest. That is, a 20 millisecond difference may be important in terms of testing the theory's predictions, but it may not have a practical effect in many real-world settings. This is one of the reasons why many memory researchers have argued that memory must be studied in naturalistic settings (e.g. Conway, 1993; Neisser, 1978).

A quick glance through any of the basic cognitive psychology journals provides ample evidence that laboratory research typically involves conditions, materials, tasks, etc. that are far removed from conditions one would encounter in the real world. This does not mean that the research reported in these articles is without value. Many of the more advanced sciences (especially the physical sciences) have made important discoveries by studying phenomena under conditions that seldom if ever occur in the "real world" (see Banaji & Crowder, 1989). However, for basic memory research to generalize beyond the laboratory, important contextual features must be identified and incorporated into basic research. Several recent applied models (e.g. Herrmann & Searleman, 1990) have made this point quite clear.

A second reason why a basic memory theory may fail in a real-world setting is that the factors identified by the theory do not have a close correspondence with variables in the real world. For example, Norman, Brooks, Coblentz & Babcock (1992) showed that basic theories of categorization failed to predict performance in a simulated real-world task, in this case diagnosing X-ray features when the X-rays are supplemented with patient case histories. The fact that subjects' performance in these tasks is different from what would be predicted from laboratory-based theories indicates that there is some aspect of the tasks or environments that differed between the simple laboratory tasks and the more complex simulated real-world task. If factors such as the emotional state of the individual, cultural biases, and health factors are not accounted for in basic theories then the theory is unlikely to provide an adequate explanatory framework for applied work.

Finally, there must be straightforward means for mapping the constructs of the theory onto real-world factors that can be manipulated. In addition, the theory must be comprehensible to people outside the specialized area in which it was devised and tested. It is unfortunate that many of the theories and models proposed by cognitive psychologists include constructs and variables for which there appears to be no direct correspondence to factors in the real world. This is especially true of constructs in connectionist models such as "hidden units," "connection weights," and "patterns of connectivity." While these theories and models may be useful basic research tools, it is unlikely that the concepts invoked in the theory can be translated into strategies and techniques that can be used to solve real-world human memory problems.

AN ALTERNATIVE MEMORY METAPHOR

In the previous sections we outlined the factors that allow a memory theory, model, or metaphor to serve a useful function for applied researchers. As we argued in the introduction, the implicit metaphors and explicit models we use to conceptualize memory can serve to elucidate our understanding of memory but they can also limit us by causing us to focus on certain sets of questions and ignoring others. The traditional storehouse metaphor of memory served a useful function for addressing some applied problems, especially problems whose main focus concerns the quantity of information that people are able to retrieve. However, these gains have come at a cost because the storehouse metaphor focuses attention on the accurate storage and retrieval of information but does not naturally lead one to ask questions concerning topics such as the malleability of memory or the generation of false memories.

In this final section we review an alternative to the traditional storehouse metaphor, the perception/re-perception model of memory proposed by Payne & Blackwell (1998). This model shares many similarities with the source monitoring model proposed by Johnson and her co-workers (e.g. Johnson et al., 1993) and extended by Lindsay (1994), and is also related to Jacoby's "attributional" approach to the phenomenology of remembering (e.g. Jacoby, Kelley & Dywan, 1989). The model suggests that memory processes can usefully be thought of as analogous to perceptual processes. What is normally called "encoding" in the memory literature can be replaced by perception – that is, interpreting sensory signals (Craik & Lockhart, 1972, made a similar suggestion) – and what is normally called "retrieval" can be thought of as re-perceiving the stimulus event.

Perceiving and recollecting share many common features. In perception, people encounter information in the world, they transform that information, and they interpret the information based on pre-existing categories, general knowledge, and decision making processes. So too, in remembering people encounter the products of cognitive processes (e.g. retrieval) and interpret that information in various ways. At the most basic level both memory and perceptual tasks involve the creation of an internal representation of the external world and the use of this representation to guide behavior. These representations often need to be retained across periods of delay. Subjects in perception experiments sometimes are required to compare two temporally distinct stimuli. Subjects in memory experiments may be asked to perform similar comparisons but typically across longer intervals.

According to the perception/re-perception model, memory is not most usefully conceptualized as the storage and retrieval of inert traces but rather involves the active interpretation of internal representations that arose from past sensory, perceptual, and conceptual processes. These internal representations are not clearly separate and distinct from the sensory and perceptual processes that gave rise to them. Rather the same basic representations and processes used in performing what are traditionally viewed as perceptual tasks are also used when performing memory tasks. The act of remembering thus involves the re-perception of internal representations that are created from our experiences with the world around us.

The perception/re-perception model is a more natural metaphor for addressing many of the applied questions reviewed in this chapter. The model naturally focuses attention on memory accuracy in that just as the perceptual system can give rise to convincing perceptual illusions the re-perception process can give rise to convincing memory illusions. This point of emphasis is a marked improvement over the storehouse metaphor's emphasis on the retrieval of inert memory traces. The perception/re-perception model also allows us to understand memory illusions as reflecting the normal processes by which we interpret the world around us. This emphasis makes examining the errors made by eyewitnesses, or clients in psychotherapy, a natural and legitimate object of both basic and applied research.

In addition to these advantages of this alternative metaphor the perception/re-perception model also emphasizes the close relation between encoding (perception) and retrieval (re-perception) processes. This provides a new way of conceptualizing transfer appropriate processing and understanding issues such as why reinstating the original context can aid eyewitness retrieval in the cognitive interview, or why reinstating the context of an advertisement can change product evaluations.

As argued in the introduction, both implicit memory metaphors and explicit memory models guide the way both applied researchers and the lay public think about memory. Models and metaphors influence the range of questions asked, the predictions people make, and the way data are interpreted. The perception/re-perception model provides an alternative to the traditional storehouse metaphor of memory in which memory processes involve the transfer of inert traces between storage registers. This metaphor provides novel interpretations to old-standing findings and also forces us to ask new questions about memory content, memory processes and memory illusions. The ability of the model to pose new questions, to serve as a heuristic for both applied and theoretical work, is perhaps the greatest strength of the model.

The perception/re-perception model is in a sense both a step forward and a retreat in the establishment of memory models. It represents a step forward in that it serves a useful heuristic function, causing us to ask questions that might not otherwise be asked. It is a retreat in that in its current guise it is a functional model rather than a formally stated explicit model postulating storage systems, retrieval processes and so forth. In some sense what we are suggesting is that memory researchers study memory in a manner similar to how we have studied the sensory and perceptual systems, namely by seeking to specify the transfer functions that relate behavior to real-world events. Such an approach would likely lead to theoretical and conceptual advances that serve the needs and interests of both basic and applied memory researchers.

ACKNOWLEDGMENT

We thank Francis Durso, Robyn Reichert, Scott Gronlund, and Michael J. Wenger for helpful comments on early versions of this manuscript.

REFERENCES

Anderson, R. C. & Pichert, J. W. (1978). Recall of previously unrecallable information following a shift in perspective. *Journal of Verbal Learning and Verbal Behavior*, 17, 1–12.

Atkinson, R. C. & Shiffrin, R. M. (1968). Human memory: a proposed system and its control processes. In K. W. Spence & J. T. Spence (Eds), *The Psychology of Learning and Motivation* (pp. 89–105). New York: Academic Press.

Banaji, M. R. & Crowder, R. G. (1989). The bankruptcy of everyday memory. *American Psychologist*, 44, 1185–93.

Berliner, L. & Williams, L. M. (1994). Memories of child sexual abuse: a response to Lindsay and Read. *Applied Cognitive Psychology*, 8, 379–88.

Bjork, R. A. (1996). Memory and metamemory considerations in the training of human beings. In J. Metcalfe & A. P. Shimamura (Eds), *Metacognition: Knowing about Knowing* (pp. 185–205). Cambridge: MIT Press.

Blaxton, T. A. (1989). Investigating dissociations among memory measures: support for a transfer-appropriate processing framework. *Journal of Experimental Psychology: Learning, Memory, and Cognition*, 15, 657–68.

Bonto, M. A. & Payne, D. G. (1991). Role of environmental context in eyewitness memory. *American Journal of Psychology*, 104, 117–34.

Bothwell, R. K., Deffenbacher, K. A. & Brigham, J. C. (1987). Correlation of eyewitness accuracy and confidence: optimality hypothesis revisited. *Journal of Applied Psychology*, 72, 691–5.

Bower, G. H., Gilligan, S. G. & Monteiro, K. P. (1981). Selectivity of learning caused by affective states. *Journal of Experimental Psychology: General*, 110, 451–73.

Bransford, J. D., Franks, J. J., Morris, C. D. & Stein, B. S. (1979). Some general con-

straints on learning and memory research. In L. S. Cermak & F. I. M. Craik (Eds), *Levels of Processing in Human Memory* (pp. 331–54). Hillsdale, NJ: Lawrence Erlbaum.
Briere, J. (1992). *Child Abuse Trauma: Theory and Treatment of the Lasting Effects*. Newbury Park, CA: Sage.
Briere, J. & Conte, J. (1993). Self-reported amnesia for abuse in adults molested as children. *Journal of Traumatic Stress*, 6, 21–31.
Bruck, M., Ceci, S. J., Francouer, E. & Barr, R. (1995). "I hardly cried when I got my shot!" Influencing children's reports about a visit to the pediatrician. *Child Development*, 66, 193–208.
Camp, C. J. & Foss, J. W. (1997). Designing ecologically valid memory interventions for persons with dementia. In D. G. Payne & F. G. Conrad (Eds), *Intersections in Basic and Applied Memory Research* (pp. 311–25). Mahwah, NJ: Lawrence Erlbaum.
Camp, C. J., Foss, J. W., Stevens, A. B. & O'Hanlon, A. M. (1996). Improving prospective memory performance in persons with Alzheimer's disease. In M. Brandimonte, G. O. Einstein & M. A. McDaniel (Eds), *Prospective Memory: Theory and Applications*. Mahwah, NJ: Lawrence Erlbaum.
Ceci, S. J., Crotteau-Huffman, M., Smith, E. & Loftus, E. F. (1994). Repeatedly thinking about non-events. *Consciousness & Cognition*, 3, 388–407.
Cermak, L. S. (1980). Improving retention in alcoholic Korsakoff patients. *Journal of Studies on Alcohol*, 41, 159–69.
Cermak, L. S. & Craik, F. I. M. (Eds) (1979). *Levels of Processing in Human Memory*. Hillsdale, NJ: Lawrence Erlbaum.
Chalfonte, B. L. & Johnson, M. K. (1996). Feature memory and binding in young and older adults. *Memory and Cognition*, 24, 403–16.
Chandler, C. C. (1989). Specific retroactive interference in modified recognition test: evidence for an unknown cause of interference. *Journal of Experimental Psychology: Learning, Memory, and Cognition*, 15, 256–65.
Chandler, C. C. (1991). How memory for an event is influenced by related events: interference in modified recognition tests. *Journal of Experimental Psychology: Learning, Memory, and Cognition*, 17, 115–25.
Cheit, R. (1998). The Recovered Memory Project. http://www.brown.edu/Departments/Taubman_Center/Recovmem/Archive.html (online document).
Christianson, S. A. (1992). Remembering emotional events: potential mechanisms. In S. A. Christianson (Ed.), *The Handbook of Emotion and Memory: Research and Theory*. Hillsdale, NJ: Lawrence Erlbaum Associates.
Conway, M. A. (1993). Method and meaning in memory research. In G. M. Davies & R. H. Logie (Eds), *Memory in Everyday Life* (pp. 499–524). New York: North-Holland.
Cowan, N. (1995). *Attention and Memory: An Integrated Framework*. New York: Oxford.
Craik, F. I. M. & Lockhart, R. S. (1972). Levels of processing: a framework for memory research. *Journal of Verbal Learning and Verbal Behavior*, 11, 671–84.
Cutler, B. L., Penrod, S. D. & Stuve, T. E. (1988). Juror decision making in eyewitness identification cases. *Law and Human Behavior*, 12, 41–55.
Deffenbacher, K. A. (1980). Eyewitness accuracy and confidence: can we infer anything about their relationship? *Law and Human Behavior*, 4, 243–60.
Dempster, F. N. (1988). The spacing effect: a case study in the failure to apply the results of psychological research. *American Psychologist*, 43, 627–34.
Dunning, D. & Stern, L. B. (1994). Distinguishing accurate from inaccurate eyewitness identifications via inquiries about decision processes. *Journal of Personality and Social Psychology*, 5, 818–35.
Ebbinghaus, H. ([1885] 1964). *Memory: A Contribution to Experimental Psychology* (H. A. Ruger & C. E. Bussenius, Trans.). New York: Dover.
Eich, J. M. (1985). Levels of processing, encoding specificity, elaboration, and CHARM. *Psychological Review*, 92, 1–38.
Finkelhor, D. & Browne, A. (1988). Assessing the long-term impact of child sexual abuse: a review and conceptualization. In E. T. Hotaling, D. Finkelhor, J. T. Kirkpatrick &

M. A. Strauss (Eds), *Family Abuse and its Consequences: New Directions in Research* (pp. 270–89). Newbury Park, CA: Sage.
Finkelhor, D. & Dzubia-Leatherman, J. (1994). Victimization of children. *American Psychologist*, 49, 173–83.
Fredrickson, R. (1992). *Repressed Memories: A Journey to Recovery from Sexual Abuse*. New York: Simon & Schuster.
Freud, S. ([1896] 1962). The aetiology of hysteria. In J. Strachey (Ed. and Trans.), *The Standard Edition of the Complete Psychological Works of Sigmund Freud* (Vol. 3, pp. 191–221). Toronto: Clark, Irwin.
Frye v. United States, 293 F1013 34 ALR 145 (DC Cir., 1923)
Garry, M. & Loftus, E. F. (1994). Repressed memories of childhood trauma: could some of them be suggested? *USA Today*, 122 (January), 82–4.
Garry, M., Loftus, E. F., Brown, S. W. & DeBreuil, S. C. (1997). Womb with a view: memory beliefs and memory-work experiences. In D. G. Payne & F. G. Conrad (Eds), *Intersections in Basic and Applied Memory Research* (pp. 233–55). Mahwah, NJ: Lawrence Erlbaum.
Geiselman, R. E. & Fisher, R. P. (1997). Ten years of cognitive interviewing. In D. G. Payne & F. G. Conrad (Eds), *Intersections in Basic and Applied Memory Research* (pp. 291–310). Mahwah, NJ: Lawrence Erlbaum.
Geiselman, R. E., Fisher, R. P., MacKinnon, D. P. & Holland, H. L. (1986). Enhancement of eyewitness memory with the cognitive interview. *American Journal of Psychology*, 99, 385–401.
Glenberg, A. M. (1976). Monotonic and nonmonotonic lag effects in paired-associate and recognition memory paradigms. *Journal of Verbal Learning and Verbal Behavior*, 15, 1–16.
Glenberg, A. M., Sanocki, T., Epstein, W. & Morris, C. (1987). Enhancing calibration of comprehension. *Journal of Experimental Psychology: General*, 116, 119–36.
Glisky, E. L. & Schacter, D. L. (1987). Acquisition of domain-specific knowledge in organic amnesia: training for computer-related work. *Neuropsychologia*, 25, 893–906.
Gluck, M. A. & Bower, G. H. (1988). From conditioning to category learning: an adaptive network model. *Journal of Experimental Psychology: General*, 117, 227–47.
Goodman, G. S. & Schaaf, J. M. (1997). Over a decade of research on children's eyewitness testimony: What have we learned? Where do we go from here? *Applied Cognitive Psychology*, 11, S5–S20.
Goldstein, A. G., Chance, J. E. & Schneller, G. R. (1989). Frequency of eyewitness identification in criminal cases: a survey of prosecutors. *Bulletin of the Psychonomic Society*, 27, 71–4.
Graf, P. & Schacter, D. L. (1985). Implicit and explicit memory for new associations in normal and amnesic subjects. *Journal of Experimental Psychology: Learning, Memory and Cognition*, 11, 501–18.
Gruneberg, M. M. (1985). *Computer Linkword: French, German, Spanish, Italian, Greek, Russian, Dutch, Portuguese, Hebrew*. Penfield, New York: USA Artworx Inc.
Gruneberg, M. M. (1992). The practical application of memory aids: knowing how, knowing when, and knowing when not. In M. M. Gruneberg and P. E. Morris (Eds), *Aspects of Memory*, Vol. 1: *The Practical Aspects* (2nd edn) (pp. 168–95). London: Routledge.
Gruneberg, M. M. & Sykes, R. N. (1991). Individual differences and attitudes to the keyword method of foreign language learning. *Language Learning Journal*, 4, 60–2.
Guynn, M. E., McDaniel, M. & Einstein, G. O. (1998). Prospective memory: when memory fails. *Memory and Cognition*, 26, 287–98.
Harris, J. E. (1980). Memory aids people use: two interview studies. *Memory and Cognition*, 8, 31–8.
Hart, J. T. (1965). Memory and the feeling-of-knowing experience. *Journal of Educational Psychology*, 56, 208–16.
Heiman, M. (1987). Learning to learn: a behavioral approach to improving thinking. In

D. N. Perkins, J. Lochhead & J. Bishop (Eds), *Thinking: The Second International Conference* (pp. 431–52). Hillsdale, NJ: Lawrence Erlbaum.
Herman, J. L. & Schatzow, E. (1987). Recovery and verification of memories of childhood sexual trauma. *Psychoanalytic Psychology*, 4, 1–14.
Herrmann, D. J. (1992). *Super Memory: A Quick Action Program for Memory Improvement*. Avenel, NJ: Outlet Book Company.
Herrmann, D. & Raybeck, D. (1997). A clash of cultures: basic and applied cognitive research. In D. G. Payne & F. G. Conrad (Eds), *Intersections in Basic and Applied Memory Research* (pp. 25–44). Mahwah, NJ: Lawrence Erlbaum.
Herrmann, D. J. & Searleman, A. (1990). The new multimodal approach to memory improvement. In G. H. Bower (Eds), *Advances in Learning and Motivation* (pp. 175–205). New York: Academic Press.
Hintzman, D. L. (1974). Theoretical implications of the spacing effect. In R. L. Solso (Ed.), *Theories in Cognitive Psychology: The Loyola Symposium* (pp. 77–99). Potomac, MD: Erlbaum.
Holmes, D. S. (1994). Is there evidence for repression? Doubtful. *Harvard Mental Health Letter*, 10, 4–6.
Houston, M. J., Childers, T. L. & Heckler, S. E. (1987). Picture–word consistency and the elaborative processing of advertisements. *Journal of Marketing Research*, 24, 359–69.
Howe, M. L., Courage, M. L. & Peterson, C. (1994). How can I remember when "I" wasn't there: long-term retention of traumatic experiences and emergence of the cognitive self. *Consciousness and Cognition*, 3, 327–55.
Hyman, I. E. Jr, Husband, T. H. & Billings, F. J. (1995). False memories of childhood experiences. *Applied Cognitive Psychology*, 9, 181–97.
Intons-Peterson, M. J. & Fournier, J. (1986). External and internal memory aids: when and how often do we use them? *Journal of Experimental Psychology: General*, 115, 267–80.
Jacoby, L. L., Kelley, C. M. & Dywan, J. (1989). Memory attributions. In H. L. Roediger, III & F. I. M. Craik (Eds), *Varieties of Memory and Consciousness: Essays in Honour of Endel Tulving* (pp. 391–422). Hillsdale, NJ: Lawrence Erlbaum Associates.
Johnson, M. K. & Chalfonte, B. L. (1994). Binding complex memories: the role of activation and the hippocampus. In D. L. Schacter & E. Tulving (Eds), *Memory Systems 1994*. Cambridge, MA: MIT Press.
Johnson, M. K., Hashtroudi, S. & Lindsay, D. S. (1993). Source monitoring. *Psychological Bulletin*, 114, 3–28.
Keller, K. L. (1987). Memory factors in advertising: the effect of advertising retrieval cues on brand evaluations. *Journal of Consumer Research*, 14, 316–33.
Kelley, C. M. & Jacoby, L. L. (1998). Subjective reports and process dissociation: fluency, knowing, and feeling. *Acta Psychologica*, 98, 127–40.
Kelley, C. M. & Lindsay, D. S. (1996). Conscious and unconscious memory. In E. L. Bjork and R. A. Bjork (Eds), *Handbook of Perception and Cognition: Memory* (2nd edn) (pp. 31–63). Academic Press: New York.
Koriat, A. & Goldsmith, M. (1994). Memory in naturalistic and laboratory contexts: distinguishing the accuracy-oriented and quantity-oriented approaches to memory assessment. *Journal of Experimental Psychology: General*, 123, 297–315.
Lakoff, G. & Johnson, M. (1980). *Metaphors We Live By*. Chicago, IL: The University of Chicago Press.
Lampinen, J. M., Neuschatz, J. S. & Payne, D. G. (1997). Memory illusions and consciousness: exploring the phenomenology of true and false memories. *Current Psychology*, 16, 181–224.
Lindsay, D. S. (1994). Memory source monitoring and eyewitness testimony. In D. F. Ross, J. D. Read & M. P. Toglia (Eds), *Adult Eyewitness Testimony: Current Trends and Developments* (pp. 27–55). New York: Cambridge University Press.
Lindsay, D. S. & Kelley, C. M. (1996). Creating illusions of familiarity in a cued-recall remember/know paradigm. *Journal of Memory and Language*, 35, 197–211.
Lindsay, D. S. & Read, J. D. (1995a). "Memory work" and recovered memories of

childhood sexual abuse: scientific evidence and public, professional and personal issues. *Psychology, Public Policy and the Law*, 1, 846–908.

Lindsay, D. S. & Read, J. D. (1995b). Memory, remembering, and misremembering. *PTSD Research Quarterly*, 6, 1–7.

Loftus, E. F. (1979). Reactions to blatantly contradictory information. *Memory & Cognition*, 7, 409–20.

Loftus, E. F. (1993). The reality of repressed memories. *American Psychologist*, 48, 518–37.

Loftus, E. F. & Fathi, D. C. (1985). Retrieving multiple autobiographical memories. *Social Cognition*, 3, 280–95.

Loftus, E. F. & Ketcham, K. (1994). *The Myth of Repressed Memory: False Memories and Allegations of Sexual Abuse*. New York: St. Martin's Press.

Loftus, E. F. & Loftus, G. R. (1980). On the permanence of stored information in the human brain. *American Psychologist*, 35, 409–20.

Loftus, E. F. & Palmer, J. C. (1974). Reconstruction of an automobile deconstruction: an example of the interaction between language and memory. *Journal of Verbal Learning and Verbal Behavior*, 13, 585–9.

Loftus, E. F., Polonsky, S. & Fullilove, M. T. (1994). Memories of childhood sexual abuse: remembering and repressing. *Psychology of Women Quarterly*, 18, 67–84.

Lutz, D. A. & Lutz, R. J. (1977). Effects of interactive imagery on learning: applications to advertising. *Journal of Applied Psychology*, 62, 493–8.

Marsh, R. L., Hicks, J. L. & Landau J. D. (1998). An investigation of everyday prospective memory. *Memory and Cognition*, 26, 633–43.

McCarty, D. L. (1980). Investigation of a visual imagery mnemonic device for acquiring face–name associations. *Journal of Experimental Psychology: Human Learning and Memory*, 2, 145–55.

McCloskey, M. & Zaragoza, M. S. (1985). Misleading postevent information and memory for events: arguments and evidence against memory impairment hypotheses. *Journal of Experimental Psychology: General*, 114, 1–16.

McDaniel, M. A. & Pressley, M. (1989). Keyword and context instruction of new vocabulary meanings: effects on text comprehension and memory. *Journal of Educational Psychology*, 2, 204–13.

Memon, A. (1998). Telling it all: the cognitive interview. In A. Memon, A. Vrij & R. Bull (Eds), *Psychology and Law: Truthfulness, Accuracy and Credibility* (pp. 170–87).

Metcalfe, J. (1990). Composite Holographic Associative Recall Model (CHARM) and blended memories in eyewitness testimony. *Journal of Experimental Psychology General*, 119, 145–60.

Metcalfe, J. (1991). Recognition failure and the composite memory trace in CHARM. *Psychological Review*, 98, 529–53.

Metcalfe, J., Schwartz, B. L. & Joaquim, S. G. (1993). The cue-familiarity heuristic in metacognition. *Journal of Experimental Psychology: Learning, Memory and Cognition*, 19, 851–61.

Modigliani, V. & Hedges, D. G. (1987). Distributed rehearsals and the primacy effect in single-trial free recall. *Journal of Experimental Psychology Learning, Memory, and Cognition*, 13, 426–36.

Morris, C. D., Bransford, J. D. & Franks, J. J. (1977). Levels of processing versus transfer appropriate processing. *Journal of Verbal Learning and Verbal Behavior*, 16, 519–33.

Neisser, U. (1978). Memory: what are the important questions? In M. M. Gruneberg, P. E. Morris & R. N. Sykes (Eds), *Practical Aspects of Memory* (pp. 3–24). London: Academic Press.

Nelson, D. L., Reed, V. S. & Walling, J. R. (1976). Pictorial superiority effect. *Journal of Experimental Psychology: Human Learning & Memory*, 2, 523–8.

Newman, L. S. & Baumeister, R. F. (1996). Toward an explanation of the UFO abduction phenomenon: hypnotic elaboration, extraterrestrial sadomasochism, and spurious memories. *Psychological Inquiry*, 7, 99–126.

Norman, G. R., Brooks, L. R., Coblentz, C. L. & Babcock, C. J. (1992). The correlation of feature identification and category judgments in diagnostic radiology. Special Issue: Memory and cognition applied. *Memory and Cognition*, 20, 344–55.

Ornstein, P. A. & Davies, G. (1997). Memory and suggestibility in child witnesses: the NATO conference. *Applied Cognitive Psychology*, 11, Special Issue.

Park, D. C. & Kidder, D. P. (1996). Prospective memory and medication adherence. In M. Brandimonte, G. O. Einstein & M. A. McDaniel (Eds), *Prospective Memory: Theory and Applications*. Mahwah, NJ: Lawrence Erlbaum.

Park, D. C., Smith, A. D. & Cavanaugh, J. C. (1990). Metamemories of memory researchers. *Memory and Cognition*, 18, 321–7.

Parker, J. F., Bahrick, L., Lundy, B., Fivush, R. & Levitt, M. (1998). Effects of stress on children's memory for a natural disaster. In C. P. Thompson, D. J. Herrmann, J. D. Read, D. Bruce, D. G. Payne & M. P. Toglia (Eds), *Eyewitness Memory Theoretical and Applied Perspectives* (pp. 31–54). Mahwah, NJ: Lawrence Erlbaum.

Payne, D. G. & Blackwell, J. M. (1998). Truth in memory: caveat emptor. In S. Lynn & K. McConkey (Eds), *Truth in Memory* (pp. 32–61). New York: Guilford Press.

Payne, D. G. & Wenger, M. J. (1992). Improving memory through practice. In D. J. Herrmann, H. Weingartner, A. Searleman & C. McEvoy (Eds), *Memory Improvement: Implications for Memory Theory* (pp. 187–209). New York: Springer-Verlag.

Payne, D. G., Elie, C. J., Blackwell, J. M. & Neuschatz, J. S. (1996). Memory illusions: recalling, recognizing, and recollecting events that never occurred. *Journal of Memory and Language*, 35, 261–85.

Peters, D. P. (1987). The impact of naturally occurring stress on children's memory. In S. J. Ceci, M. P. Toglia & D. F. Ross (Eds), *Children's Eyewitness Memory* (pp. 121–41). New York: Springer-Verlag.

Poole, D. A. & Lindsay, D. S. (1998). Assessing the accuracy of young children's reports: lessons from the investigation of childhood sexual abuse. *Journal of Applied and Preventative Psychology*, 7, 1–26.

Raaijmakers, J. G. W. & Shiffrin, R. M. (1981). Search of associative memory. *Psychological Review*, 88, 93–134.

RAND Corporation. (1975). The criminal investigation process (RAND Corporation Tech. Report No. R-1777-DOJ, Vols. 1–3). Santa Monica, CA: RAND Corporation.

Read, J. D. & Lindsay, D. S. (Eds) (1997). *Recollections of Trauma: Scientific Research and Clinical Practice*. New York: Plenum.

Reder, L. M. (1987). Strategy selection in question answering. *Cognitive Psychology*, 19, 90–138.

Roediger, H. L. III (1980). Memory metaphors in cognitive psychology. *Memory and Cognition*, 8, 231–46.

Roediger, H. L. III (1990). Implicit memory: retention without remembering. *American Psychologist*, 45, 1043–56.

Roediger, H. L. III & McDermott, K. B. (1993). Implicit memory in normal human subjects. In F. Boller & J. Grafman (Eds), *Handbook of Neuropsychology*. Amsterdam: Elsevier.

Roediger, H. L. III & McDermott, K. B. (1995). Creating false memories: remembering words not presented in lists. *Journal of Experimental Psychology: Learning, Memory and Cognition*, 21, 803–14.

Rumelhart, D. E. & McClelland, J. L. (1986). *Parallel Distributed Processing: Explorations of the Microstructure of Cognition*. Cambridge, MA: MIT Press.

Sanders, G. S. (1986). On increasing the usefulness of eyewitness research. *Law and Human Behavior*, 10, 333–5.

Schacter, D. L. (1987). Implicit memory: history and current status. *Journal of Experimental Psychology: Learning, Memory and Cognition*, 13, 501–18.

Schwartz, B. L. & Metcalfe, J. (1992). Cue familiarity but not target retrievability enhances feeling-of-knowing judgments. *Journal of Experimental Psychology: Learning, Memory and Cognition*, 18, 1074–83.

Singh, S. N., Mishra, S., Bendapudi, N. & Linville, D. (1994). Enhancing memory of

television commercials through message spacing. *Journal of Marketing Research*, 31, 384–92.
Smith, M. (1983). Hypnotic memory enhancement of eyewitnesses: does it work? *Psychological Bulletin*, 94, 384–407.
Sporer, S. L., Penrod, S., Read, J. D. & Cutler, B. (1995). Choosing, confidence, and accuracy: a meta-analysis of the confidence–accuracy relation in eyewitness identification studies. *Psychological Bulletin*, 118, 315–27.
Squire, L. R. (1994). Declarative and nondeclarative memory: multiple brain systems supporting learning and memory. In D. L. Schacter & E. Tulving (Eds), *Memory Systems 1994*. Cambridge, MA: MIT Press.
Sternberg, R. J. (1985). Implicit theories of intelligence, creativity, and wisdom. *Journal of Personality and Social Psychology*, 49, 607–27.
Thomas, E. L. & Robinson, H. A. (1972). *Improving Reading in Every Class: A Sourcebook for Teachers*. Boston, MA: Allyn & Bacon.
Tulving, E. (1972). Episodic and semantic memory. In E. Tulving & W. Donaldson (Eds), *Organization of Memory* (pp. 381–403). New York: Academic Press.
Tulving, E. (1974). Cue-dependent forgetting. *American Scientist*, 62, 74–82.
Tulving, E. (1983). *Elements of Episodic Memory*. Oxford: Oxford University Press.
Tulving, E. & Schacter, D. L. (1990). Priming and human memory. *Science*, 247, 301–6.
Tulving, E. & Thomson, D. M. (1973). Encoding specificity and retrieval processes in episodic memory. *Psychological Review*, 80, 352–73.
Tulving, E., Schacter, D. L. & Stark, H. A. (1982). Priming effects in word-fragment completion are independent of recognition memory. *Journal of Experimental Psychology Learning, Memory, and Cognition*, 8, 336–42.
Underwood, B. J. (1969). Attributes of memory. *Psychological Review*, 76, 559–73.
Verhaeghen, P., Marcoen, A. & Goossens, L. (1992). Improving memory performance in the aged through mnemonic training: a meta-analytic study. *Psychology and Aging*, 7, 242–51.
Warrington, E. K. & Weiskrantz, L. (1970). Amnesic syndrome: consolidation or retrieval? *Nature*, 228, 628–30.
Watkins, M. (1990). Mediationism and the obfuscation of memory. *American Psychologist*, 45, 320–35.
Wells, G. L. & Bradfield, A. L. (1998). "Good, you identified the suspect." Feedback to eyewitnesses distorts their reports of the witnessing experience. *Journal of Applied Psychology*, 83, 360–76.
Wells, G. L. & Murray, D. M. (1984). Eyewitness confidence. In G. L. Wells & E. F. Loftus (Eds), *Eyewitness Testimony: Psychological Perspectives*. Cambridge: Cambridge University Press.
Widom, C. S. (1997). Accuracy of adult recollections of early childhood abuse. In J. D. Read & D. S. Lindsay (Eds), *Recollections of Trauma: Scientific Research and Clinical Practice* (pp. 49–70). New York: Plenum.
Williams, L. M. (1994). Recall of childhood trauma: a prospective study of women's memories of child sexual abuse. *Journal of Consulting and Clinical Psychology*, 62, 1167–76.
Yerkes, R. M. & Dodson, J. D. (1908). The relation of strength of stimulus to rapidity of habit-information. *Journal of Comparative Neurology of Psychology*, 18, 459–82.
Yuille, J. C. & Cutshall, J. L. (1986). A case study of eyewitness memory of a crime. *Journal of Applied Psychology*, 71, 291–301.
Zechmeister, E. B. & Shaughnessy, J. J. (1980). When you know that you know and when you think that you know but you don't. *Bulletin of the Psychonomic Society*, 15, 41–4.

Chapter 5

Context, Process, and Experience: Research on Applied Judgment and Decision Making

Clarence C. Rohrbaugh and James Shanteau
Kansas State University

Human judgment and decision making research has made inroads through applications to business, government, social policy, and medical decision making. Recent trends in applied decision research, as Cooksey (1996) suggests, have begun to "incorporate the constraining impact that the human condition has upon decision processes unfolding in their natural context." This constraining impact reflects such variables as situational context, cognitive processing modes, and personal experiences.

Research on decision making had its roots in the 1950s and 1960s in economic theory. Often called the "rational man" approach, normative decision theory is concerned with the discrepancies between how choices under risk should be made and how they are actually made. With the introduction in the 1970s of multi-attribute utility (MAU) analysis, decision theoretic researchers also began investigating subjective values and weighting functions. At the same time, other psychologists were exploring how people make judgments and draw inferences. Descriptive research focused on the variables that influence various types of judgments. These analyses provided numerous insights into how judgments are formed and how they can be modeled.

More recently, research on heuristics and biases (H & B) combined elements of these two traditions. Studies in the H & B tradition examine heuristics (rules

Handbook of Applied Cognition, Edited by F. T. Durso, R. S. Nickerson, R. W. Schvaneveldt, S. T. Dumais, D. S. Lindsay and M. T. H. Chi.

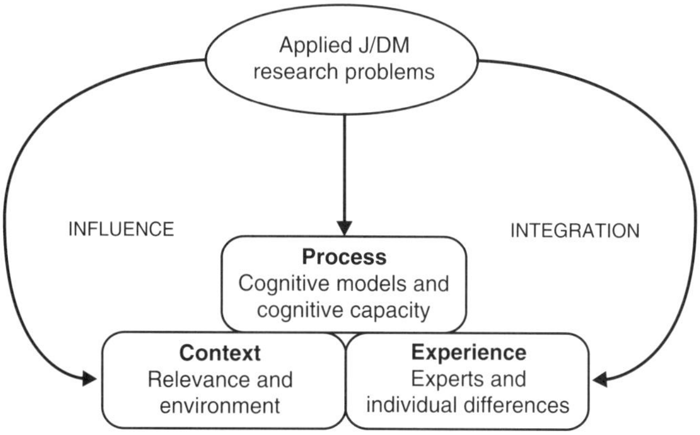

Figure 5.1 Chart showing how applied research on judgment and decision making (J/DM) leads to consideration of the separate influence and joint integration of context, process, and experience.

of thumb) used by decision makers and the biases that can arise from the use of heuristics. (Much of the H & B work is concerned with the affect of task stimulus manipulation. However, the work of Fischhoff (1975) and Fischhoff & Beyth (1975) on hindsight bias is an example of H & B work that focuses on evidence of the use of heuristics to solve decision problems that appear to be unaffected by task stimulus.) Specifically, H & B looks at how individuals' responses in specific decision situations deviate from normatively expected outcomes. As noted by Dawes (1996), H & B research is the study of anomalies of decision making that can occur when subjects systematically solve a problem other than the one they want to solve.

In a recent review, Mellers, Schwartz & Cooke (1998) ask "why" deviations from normative expectations are observed. The contextual, cognitive, and personal elements of the judgment or decision process become likely candidates for the answer to this question. "Contextual" elements refer to environmental variables that are external to the individual and have an impact on cognitive processes. "Cognitive" elements refer to the information processing strategies used to evaluate and combine various sources of inputs. "Personal" elements refer to the influence of internally developed mechanisms for handling a given situation. The integration of contextual, cognitive, and personal elements is an essential component in the study of judgment and decision making, particularly as seen from the perspective of applied research.

Our focus is on research that examines how contextual, cognitive, and personal variables (and their interaction) influence the decision process. As illustrated in Figure 5.1, this chapter is categorized by context, process, and experience. The first section covers research looking at the influence of context on the perceived relevance or irrelevance of information in various decision situations; some issues included are strategy selection, framing, and the environment. The second section describes work on mental models, risk, and affect; this includes studies that provide evidence of policy use, the effects of feedback, and cognitive capacity. The third section covers research focused on the knowledge, skills, and preferences an individual brings to a decision situation; these variables contribute to the development of decision processes and are precipitated by factors such as expertise and individual differences. Each section includes examples of research and application.

CONTEXT

In this section we discuss three major concepts: the impact of critical elements in a decision situation, including image and utility theory; applications and limitations of framing effects; and assessment of environmental factors and training to cope with environmentally induced difficulties. However, except for image theory, little effort has been made to integrate these concepts into a more comprehensive structure.

Contextual Impact

Traditional decision research has disregarded the impact of context on problem perception, outcomes, and methods used in the study of decision making. This oversight can result in meaningless data or responses to questions other than those asked in the study. When context is ignored in the choice of decision research methods, the results can be quite misleading.

As an example, Fischhoff (1996) examined risk taking among adolescents. The first step in his study was to replicate experiments previously conducted using adults. Results showed a similar pattern of observed responses between teens and adults. Considering the real-world behavior of teens, the results "were so similar as to raise the suspicion that the method had shaped the message" (p. 233). Fischhoff went on to say that "we set minimalist problems before subjects and expect them to resist the temptation to impute a context." Payne, Bettman & Johnson (1992) as well as many other researchers agree that the environment, stimulus context, and other factors have a major influence on decisions. Many researchers have begun to include context in their models of decision making but few studies attempt to explain which contextual components are important in a decision situation and why some contextual components are more relevant than others.

Image Theory

Einhorn & Hogarth (1981) argued that individuals make use of mental simulation to evaluate options by making adjustment strategies from known situations to new situations. Klein & Crandall (1995) incorporate this concept into the Recognition-Primed Decision Model (RPDM). They argue that events are perceived as either typical or not typical and a course of action is evoked based on that perception. Image theory (Beach, 1990) makes use of a similar idea. This descriptive theory assumes that the decision maker possesses an image of the goal and an image of the strategy to reach that goal. The screening of options is based on the compatibility of an option with standards established by the goal and strategy images. The work of Dunegan (1993) provides evidence that environmental condition or context affects the perceptions of compatibility between options and strategies. More precisely, cognitive modes shift from controlled processes under negative or stressful conditions to more automatic processes under positive conditions. (In contrast to the work of Dunegan (1993), the manipulation of positive and negative environmental conditions did not have a significant effect when Beach et al. (1996) used a similar manipulation. Beach suggested that the between-subject manipulation used in their study and the within-manipulation used in the Dunegan (1993) study may be the source of difference in results.)

Utility theory can be invoked to describe the changes an individual makes in the utilities and/or weights of decision options (Mellers & Cooke, 1994; Tversky & Simonson, 1993). Utility theory states that individuals consider the values of potential outcomes and the chance of those outcomes being delivered. A study by Beach, Puto, Heckler, Naylor & Marble (1996) provided evidence that differential weighting of options in image theory accounted for observed screening decisions more accurately than other weighting techniques. Tversky & Simonson (1993) suggested that changes in global context would affect attribute weight. The global context in image theory would come from the set of options being screened. Therefore, if the set of options differs in size or composition between similar decision situations, the attribute weights of a given option will differ. Image theory assumes context within imagined courses of action and thus can identify the impact of context on the decision maker's response.

Utility Theory

The Simple Multi-Attribute Rating Technique (SMART) may also identify the impact of context if the assumption is made that context influences the ranking or weighting of attributes. As described by Edwards & Barron (1994), SMART is prescriptive in nature and designed to provide the "best" choice. Edwards has clearly stated that SMART is not descriptive. The specification of alternatives, attributes, and ranks in its various forms is an effort to determine what is relevant to the decision maker and situation. The reduction or elimination of judgmental errors and the simple forms of elicitation used allow for the application of SMART in areas such as market research or policy analysis (Edwards & Barron, 1994). Revised versions of SMART include the Simple Multi-Attribute Rating Technique with Swing weights (SMARTS), and the Simple Multi-Attribute Rating Technique Exploiting Ranks (SMARTER) (Edwards & Barron, 1994).

A need to design studies and use methods that account for the impact of context has recently been recognized in the study of decision making. The approaches mentioned can be useful for inclusion of context in the measurement of behavior in applied situations. The contextual relevance is reflected in the decision maker's responses or choices. However, misinterpretation of information or behavior may occur when the influence of context on problem perception is ignored or assumed. Specifically, making assumptions based on normative standards can be problematic.

Framing Effects

Research on framing effects has provided evidence of how normatively irrelevant variables can affect decision making. A frame includes the context provided by the stimulus. Typically, the researcher defines the context included in the decision situation. Framing or the editing phase of a choice process, according to Kahneman & Tversky (1979), consists of the preliminary analysis of options, their outcomes and contingencies, and the coding of those outcomes as gains or losses. Tversky & Kahneman (1981) also refer to framing in a more general context as the description of options. This "description" does not change the value of the cues but does change the reference point from which cues are judged. Framing effects were first studied using verbal scenarios such as the "Asian disease" problem (Tversky & Kahneman, 1981). Later studies provided evidence of these same effects under other conditions.

When They Occur

Johnson, Hershey, Meszaros & Kunreuther (1993) described the preferences for automobile insurance coverage of drivers from New Jersey and Pennsylvania. Drivers in both states were offered approximately the same coverage at the same rates. In New Jersey the drivers had to purchase the right to sue for an additional cost and in Pennsylvania declining the right to sue was presented as a cost reduction. In Pennsylvania 75% of drivers paid for the right to sue whereas fewer than 50% of New Jersey drivers paid for the right to sue. This demonstrates framing since, based on normative standards, there should be no influence from the format in which insurance information was presented. Framing effects have also been reported in studies of product price displays in supermarkets (Kleinmuntz & Schkade, 1993), economic business threats (Highhouse, Paese & Leatherberry, 1996), health care financing (Schweitzer, 1995), group decision making (Paese, Bieser & Tubbs, 1993), auditing (Johnson, Jamal & Berryman, 1991), and other situations (for a review, see Schneider, Levin, Gaeth & Conlon, 1995).

Why They Occur

Previous research has identified various types of framing effects (Schneider, Levin & Gaeth, 1997). Recent efforts are directed at methods by which these framing effects might be reduced or eliminated. One such method is the introduction of a causal schema (Jou, Shanteau & Harris, 1996). Schemata or general knowledge structures provide individuals with a referent about events and relationships between events. Relationships between events may not be understood when an event occurs that does not fit the individual's knowledge structures. When this occurs, according to Berkeley & Humphreys (1982), mental representations are constructed by the individual that differ from that of the experimenter, which results in framing effects. Jou, Shanteau & Harris (1996) found that framing effects were reduced or eliminated when subjects were provided with a causal schema in conjunction with the decision problem.

Dawes (1996) refers to frames in terms of the category in which problems are placed. These categories are a form of mental accounting and are dependent on how an individual views a decision situation. For example, the purchase of an item may create budget categories in which the purchase could be considered a gift for a loved one or a luxury item for the subject. The cost is the same, but an individual is more likely to make the purchase when it is a gift. In gambling, an individual is often more willing to spend "house money" than personal funds – without considering that the "house money" is his or hers. Another important category mentioned by Dawes is the status quo. The desire to leave the current state unchanged is more frequently endorsed when it is the default option. In this case, individuals are less willing to make a change. A person may express concern for getting a flu shot when that person has been receiving a shot for years because it has become the status quo. This decision to obtain the shot is therefore based more on the status quo than on consideration of the risks and benefits from the shot. The cumulative evidence from these studies shows that the effects of framing can be modeled by judgment analysis based on cognitive modes and levels of thought.

Recent meta-analysis by Kuhberger (1997) and Schneider, Levin & Gaeth (in press) show that the strength of framing effects is less in applied settings than under laboratory conditions. The typical framing study involves presentation of risky and riskless choices in a hypothetical decision scenario. The choices are mutually exclusive and subjects choose a single option. The positive and negative framing of the independent options generally result in different choices. Applied settings seldom offer this dichotomy of choices. However, studies conducted in applied settings commonly frame risk in terms of action versus inaction where the choices are not independent, e.g. Meyerowitz & Chaiken's (1987) presentation of the consequences of doing a breast self-exam or not doing a self-exam where the consequences are not dichotomous. As deviations from typical independent choice tasks increase, therefore, it appears the impact of framing effects decreases.

Environment

The context in which information is presented or made available has a strong influence on the response to that information. Factors such as pre-existing response patterns, time pressure, saliency, affect, and perceived risk can all impact the decisions made. The work of Slovic (1975) and Tversky, Sattath & Slovic (1988) provided evidence that reasoning played a prominent role in the formation of responses. "Reasoning" was defined as the consideration of arguments and justification in a choice. Participants were asked to match different pairs of options so that they became equal in value, and then to choose between these options. Their choice often did not agree with matching – a preference reversal. Instead, the chosen option was justified as superior on the most important dimension or attribute. Thus, seeing how participants justify their choices provides an indication of what is relevant and what is not.

Based on this line of research, Tversky, Sattath & Slovic (1988) formulated the prominence hypothesis, which says that more prominent attributes are given greater weight in choice than in matching. Slovic (1995) cites the influence of prominence on decision construction, risky choice, and preference reversal. This shows that some attributes in a choice situation are more relevant to the decision maker, where relevance is determined by the context in which attributes are presented (Tversky, Sattath & Slovic, 1988).

Assessment

Kleinmuntz & Schkade (1993) examined the impact of context and suggested that improvements in decision making could be made by evaluating and changing the environment. This view is reflected in the Naturalistic Decision Making (NDM) approach (Klein, 1997). NDM emphasizes the interface between decision makers and their environment (Klein, Kaempf, Wolf, Thordsen & Miller, 1997). A key step is the identification of decision requirements through a cognitive task analysis. Such an analysis identifies the key decisions (go–no go, buy–sell, launch–hold, etc.) and determines from experts how the decision is made or how relevant information is identified and integrated into the decision process.

Recently, NDM was applied to study the decision making of Navy AEGIS cruiser commanders. Decisions regarding the intent of an unidentified approaching aircraft require rapid and accurate assessment and integration of relevant information (i.e. situation awareness). After identification of tasks involved, a cognitive task analysis was performed using the critical incident method (Klein, Calderwood & MacGregor, 1989). This method makes use of participant interviews, including clarification of cues and actions in previously experienced non-routine events. All events were charted according to time and sequence of decisions. The identification of critical decision requirements helped designers better understand how AEGIS operators used workstation displays. Researchers have successfully applied this method to nursing (Crandall & Getchell-Reiter, 1993) and software programming (Riedl, Weitzenfeld, Freeman, Klein & Musa, 1991).

Training

Applied research such as NDM attempts to identify environmental factors that are most relevant in a given decision situation. However, the approach is only applicable to problems with clearly defined goals. The use of ad-hoc interviews and verbal protocols can lead to reliance on untestable assumptions about cognitive processes (Shanteau & Pounds, 1996; for a discussion of the strengths and weaknesses of verbal protocols, see Payne, 1994). Training to improve assessment can focus on either the identification of key decision elements, or the elimination of irrelevant information. As an example of the former, Crandall & Getchell-Reiter (1993) determined the critical assessment indicators in the recognition of stressed neonatal infants. These key decision elements were then incorporated into a training program for new NICU nurses. To illustrate the latter approach, Gaeth & Shanteau (1984) attempted to improve decision making by eliminating irrelevant decision elements. They looked at evaluations by soil judges based on the recognition of extraneous factors, such as excessive moisture, which often interferes with accurate identification. Soil judges were given training sessions in which the interfering element was identified, formal definitions of irrelevant information were provided, and suggestions were given to help the judges minimize the impact of irrelevant information. Significant increases in soil identification accuracy were found both immediately after the training and in follow-up studies over a 12 to 21 month period. Shanteau, Grier, Johnson & Berner (1991) reported similar results from a parallel effect to train student nurses.

Regardless of the training methods used, information is a key element in the decision process. Fischhoff & Downs (1996) stated that people can only act in their own best interest when they have the right information and they know how good that information is. The difficulty is in determining how an individual identifies the "right" information. Image theory (see above) provides one answer: compare goal and strategy images to select relevant information and appropriate strategies. When context is taken into account, decision theory can provide another means for determining the "goodness" of information.

PROCESS

Mellers, Ordonez & Birnbaum (1992) argue, "the process by which subjects combine information depends on the task, the stimulus context, and individual difference factors" (p. 367). The impact of these factors is covered in the following section that discusses:

1. models of decision making based on memory, personal policies, justification, and feedback
2. effects of risk on the decision making process
3. influence of affect on the decision process.

Some of the research cited in this section has yet to be applied to real-world settings. However, the influence of task and context consideration is evident. This influence should lead to an understanding of decision processes and has the potential for use of these process models in applied settings. Many of the models and approaches discussed in this section describe the impact of personal relevance: that is, individuals bring to any decision problem an internal mental process influenced by memory and emotions that interact with the external environment and problem context.

Decision Models

The work of Gigerenzer (1996, 1997; Gigerenzer & Goldstein, 1996) focuses on a domain specific theory about how inferences are made in social contexts. This work refers to Simon's (1990) notion of satisficing, which suggests that an individual uses heuristic decision procedures to overcome limitations of memory and time. One of these procedures involves making decisions based on selecting the first option that is satisfactory to the decision maker rather than selecting the optimal or best choice. Gigerenzer & Goldstein (1996) contend that a set of fast and frugal algorithms (although non-optimal) can produce as many correct inferences in less time as traditional models of rational inference. To provide evidence for this contention, a "take the best" (TTB) algorithm was compared with rational algorithms in making inferences in a two alternative choice task. This algorithm makes use of a framework that Gigerenzer & Goldstein (1996) call a theory of probabilistic mental models (PMM). "A PMM is an inductive device that uses limited knowledge to make fast inferences" (p. 652).

The results of their studies provide empirical evidence that TTB outperforms traditional methods (such as weighted linear models). While this approach takes into consideration the effects of memory and cognitive load, it is parsimonious compared to attempts that include a broader range of complexities to describe behavior (e.g. Busemeyer & Townsend, 1993; Cooksey, 1996).

Memory

The work of Dougherty et al. (in press) outlines a cognitive processing model for judgments of likelihood that also accounts for major heuristics. The theory addresses prior probability or "category likelihood," conditional probabilities or "category membership" based on multiple data, and compound or chained likelihoods. They propose that memory involves two subprocesses: first, a decomposition mechanism that functions as a conditional memory search, and, second, recall in the form of schema-based memory activation. The conditional memory component of the model and memory activation values or "echo intensity" can simulate many of the heuristics. While this model is still in its development stage, it is a commendable effort to create an integrated theory of the underlying cognitive processes of likelihood judgments. They have moved beyond the isolated explanations found in work on heuristics and have begun the process of integrating decades of memory research into the field of judgment and decision making.

Policy Use

The environment in which a decision is made can dictate the type of internal decision processes that take place. Decision behavior has been separated into three distinct classes: automatic, intuitive, and deliberative (Beach, Jungermann & DeBruyn, 1996). *Automatic* is the rapid activation of a preexisting decision process in response to recognition of a familiar situation; this method is called rule or policy following. *Intuitive* is a process that identifies the compatibility of a decision option's most salient features with the decision maker's standards and involves the ability to imagine what would happen if each of the options is adopted. *Deliberative* requires the most elaborative use of structured imagination – decision options are screened and incompatible or unacceptable options are eliminated; the decision process does not always involve clearly defined problems or alternatives and the decision maker may find it easier to rely on policy driven action by doing what was done previously in similar situations. Each class of decision behavior is dependent on the interaction of the environment and problem context with the availability and activation of specific cognitive processes.

When no policy is available, mental representations or cognitive scenarios must be constructed (Jungermann, 1985) to represent possible actions or events that can connect the present situation with an expected or desired future situation. Thuring & Jungermann (1986) present a four-stage model that includes activation of situation relevant knowledge, followed by construction of a mental model, simulation of possible scenarios, and ending with selection of a single plan of action or decision. Activation of situation relevant knowledge is dependent on past experience and other internal variables. The concept of personal relevance can account for why an individual might identify specific knowledge as salient to the situation.

Policy driven decisions are produced by familiar tasks such as driving to work every day or assembly line work. This familiarity can also lead to reduced awareness of the environment and potential hazards. Research on the development of internal decision processes and the determinants of relevant factors that trigger those processes is needed to identify methods of overcoming automatic policy activation or encouraging a more deliberative process appropriate to the situation.

Justification

A concern for justification can lead to inappropriate support of continued expenditures based on previous investment rather than expected benefit. This has been labeled the sunk cost effect. According to economic analysis, previously incurred costs should be ignored when they do not affect the outcomes of future decisions (Yates, 1990). However, people often allude to previous costs when giving reasons for future investment. Hogarth & Kunreuther (1995) refer to this reasoning as the process of decision justification. This is an example of how the decision process can influence reliance on irrelevant factors. Prior investment can change the process from normative to one that places greater importance on justification of prior behavior.

The sunk cost effect was explained by Arkes & Blumer (1985) in terms of wastefulness – individuals are unwilling to change a course of action because of previous investments of time or money. For their study, participants were presented with one of two scenarios. In one scenario, the owner of a printing company spends $200,000 on trucks instead of modern printing equipment; one week later a bankrupt competitor offers to sell the owner modern printing equipment for $10,000 that is better than the equipment the owner could have bought for the $200,000. In the second scenario, the $200,000 is spent on the modern printing press equipment. Participants were asked to take the place of the owner and decide whether $10,000 should be taken from savings to purchase the printing equipment. In the truck purchase version 77% of participants said they would buy the printing equipment, but only 53% of participants said that they would in the second version. The decision process used by many subjects was influenced by the desire to avoid appearing wasteful.

Harrison & Shanteau (1993) found that advanced accounting students, who were familiar with differential-cost concepts, were also susceptible to the sunk cost effects reported by Arkes & Blumer (1985). However, these students were able to avoid the effect when familiar accounting formats were used. This familiarity may provide a match between the problem context and the activation of appropriate and relevant decision policies.

Effects of Feedback

Feedback during the decision process can be either detrimental or beneficial. Doherty, Schiavo, Tweney & Mynatt (1981) examined data selection in complex tasks in which irrelevant information interfered with data selection (also see Shanteau, 1975). Results of their study provided evidence that feedback reduced but did not eliminate selection of non-diagnostic data. However, Diehl & Sterman (1995) found that cognitive capacity could be taxed by feedback. They asked participants to handle product sales by managing an inventory. As time delays and the complexity of feedback increased, participants' performance deteriorated. These effects have also been observed in studies of perceived medical risk. One interpretation of such results might be that feedback can increase cognitive load beyond an individual's capacity to make use of the information (Hammond, 1996).

The results of these studies provide information regarding the maximum amount of information useful to a decision maker in specific tasks. A key question is what determines the relevant factors participants use when they reach maximum cognitive load? McClelland, Stewart, Judd & Bourne (1987) reported better memory for chosen alternatives and suggested that the process used to select alternatives was critical to making the choice. If this is the case, then identification of processes for the selection of information in decision situations would integrate research on justification, feedback effects, risk, and many other areas covered in this chapter.

While much of the work covered in this chapter refers to the decision process as choices between alternatives, the imposition of a framework or broader theory requires a more inclusive definition of process. Svenson (1996) suggests that the search and creation of decision alternatives are a significant process in real-life decision making. This process approach is described in his differentiation and consolidation theory that outlines a generic framework and includes both pre- and post-decision processes.

Risk

Studies of risk are most commonly performed under laboratory conditions in which subjects make choices between uncertain options. In an effort to identify the generalizability of laboratory studies on risk, Wiseman & Levin (1996) examined whether risky choices differed between real and hypothetical situations. They found no significant differences in choices. In the "real situations," participants were exposed to the consequences of their choices. The consequences involved proofreading for shorter or longer periods of time based on the flip of a coin. In the hypothetical condition, participants were not required to proofread for a specified period of time based on a coin flip.

In contrast to Wiseman and Levin, marketing research shows that people say they are interested in risk information in hypothetical settings, but actually make little use of this information in real situations (Anderson, 1983). The difference between what an individual states or chooses hypothetically and what is stated or chosen in reality depends on the context. The relevant factors differ between the situations (real and hypothetical) and across different types of situations. In the studies mentioned, consequences change from short term in the Wiseman & Levin study to long term in the Anderson study. The length of time between an action and its consequence is obviously relevant.

Jungermann, Schutz & Thuring (1988) found that many people do not understand the information on drug package inserts. Fischer & Jungermann (1996) conducted an experiment to investigate whether the format of information about drug risks affected the perceived risk. Leaflets about the risks of drug use were prepared in either a numerical format or an equivalent verbal format. Interactions were found between mode of presentation and seriousness of risk. With mild side-effects, numerically described formats were rated riskier than verbal formats. With severe side-effects, the opposite was observed. Wallsten, Fillenbaum & Cox (1986) suggested that representation of numerical information with verbal labels is more vague with high and medium probabilities and that people prefer to avoid vagueness. This provides evidence that although relevant information may be desired by the decision maker, it may be obscured by the context.

Source

Jungermann, Pfister & Fischer (1996) investigated the credibility of sources of information about chemical risks in five European countries. The sources' trustworthiness depended on perceived honesty and competence. Political and administrative sources were among the least trusted. However, type of information influenced preference. For example, respondents preferred information about the safety risks of a product from the company making the product. In contrast, respondents preferred information regarding the health risks from scientists. Clearly, knowledge of the role that information sources play in risk judgments is necessary for understanding of the decision process.

Divide and Conquer

The primary method used to improve decision processes involves ranking and weighting of the separate risks, attributes, and alternatives. Fischhoff (1996) suggests a six-stage process for risk evaluation that includes: defining and categorizing, identifying relevant attributes, describing the risks, selecting rankers, performing the rankings, and providing detailed descriptions. These procedures were initially designed as a method for federal agencies to prioritize risks by separating technical risks identified by experts and perceived risks identified by citizens (Hammond & Adelman, 1976).

Perceived risks are characterized by three primary dimensions (Fischhoff, 1996). Response to risk is mediated by the number of people affected; an individual may not be willing to use a drug if one person in 100 is harmed, but if that number is one in 10,000 the individual might feel safe taking the drug. Knowledge or lack of information also affects response to risk; people have a strong desire for knowledge and often feel more confident when they can obtain more information. Dread can be defined by the potential for catastrophe an individual or group feels about an event or act; while the definition is dependent on the context of the situation, its inclusion as a measure of negative response to the risks involved is essential to any comprehensive model.

Connolly & Srivastava (1995) found that tasks affect the causal structure connecting attributes and overall evaluations or ranks. Mediating dimensions or elements in the decision process can be identified as perceived levels of risk, knowledge, control, and sense of dread (or other emotional components). Each element may have a level of acceptability. The point at which any of these elements becomes acceptable or unacceptable is established by relevance to the individual.

Affect

The work of Kahn & Isen (1993) and Nygren, Isen, Taylor & Dulin (1996) provide evidence that positive affect promotes such things as variety seeking, including seeking additional options. Moreover, positive affect can lead to overestimating the likelihood of positively perceived events while underestimating the likelihood of negatively perceived events. People in positive moods deliberate longer and use more information, while those in negative moods generally employ simpler decision strategies (Mano, 1994). Also, negative affect increases use of attribute-based comparisons over alternative-based comparisons (Luce, Bettman & Payne, 1997).

Research has clearly shown the impact of affect on decision processes. However, work is needed on individual susceptibility to the manipulations of affect as well as how affect interacts with other factors. Affect should be integrated into a more complete model of decision behavior based on the various influences of what an individual brings to the decision situation.

In this section we have discussed decision making in terms of behavioral models, including attempts to account for the influence of memory on the decision process. The determination of what is relevant to the decision and to the individual becomes more difficult when policy use, risk, and the source of information are taken into account. These and other factors, such as experience, are necessary components for a complete model of applied decision making that describes the interaction of contextual, cognitive, and personal elements.

EXPERIENCE

Hamm (1993) suggested investigating the processes by which task characteristics influence the use of particular decision strategies. This in turn requires attention to individual differences in weights, values, risk perceptions, and preferences. However, particular attention should be paid to differences that result from personal experience, including expertise. This section looks at research that describes experts and seeks to identify measurable qualities of expertise; identifies some effects of experience on decision making in applied settings; and describes research strategies for investigating the impact of individual differences on decision behavior.

Experts

The study of experts provides an excellent example of individual–difference research in judgment and decision making. Experts necessarily are experienced individuals, although not all experienced individuals are experts. Experts are identified as the most capable and successful individuals within a specific domain. Shanteau (1992) found that superior performance of experts was reflected, in part, by their ability to distinguish relevant from irrelevant information.

The growth of information technology and the cognitive sciences has generated an intense interest in the identification and elicitation of expert knowledge. Studies of experts have ranged from preschool children (Means & Voss, 1985) to chess masters (Chase & Simon, 1973), but as Hoffman, Shadbolt, Burton & Klein (1995) have suggested, "expertise is not a simple category." Shanteau (1988) outlined a partial list of characteristics of experts, including:

1. highly developed perceptual/attentional abilities
2. ability to decompose and simplify complex problems
3. greater creativity when faced with novel problems
4. ability to communicate their expertise to others
5. strong sense of self-confidence in their abilities
6. extensive, up-to-date content knowledge.

Research on experts has been conducted simultaneously in two nonoverlapping research streams. The first, primarily conducted by cognitive psychologists, involved analyses of memory and problem-solving skills of experts. Since the early work with chess masters (deGroot, 1965), experts were believed to hold sway within their domain because of their superior ability to recall patterns of relevant information from that domain (Chase & Simon, 1973). To identify the limitations of this ability, later researchers used the presentation of random domain information. Results suggest that experts' memory recall advantage over novices is eliminated under these conditions (Cooke, Atlas, Lane & Berger, 1993; Ericsson & Charness, 1994). A more extensive discussion of this line of research appears in the chapter by Charness & Schultetus (1999, this volume).

The other research stream flowed from analyses conducted by decision researchers. The early work on clinical judgment focused on a search for rules or formulas (Elstein, 1976). In an early study of experts, Hughes (1917; see also Wallace, 1923) analyzed the judgment strategies of corn judges. Later work shifted to psychometric analyses, often reporting that clinical judgment had low levels of validity and reliability (e.g. Oskamp, 1962).

More recent research has focused on calibration and information use. Calibration is a measure of the goodness of fit between the quantity of correct responses and the individual's probability estimates of that quantity (Spence, 1996). Early research revealed mixed results for experts. Weather forecasters appear to be very well calibrated (Murphy & Winkler, 1977) with values approaching 1.0 (Stewart, Roebber & Bosart, 1997). However, doctors' diagnoses tend to be poorly calibrated and are, instead, overconfident (Christensen-Szalanski & Bushyhead, 1981).

Many suggestions have been offered to explain these disparate findings. O'Connor (1989) argued that experts dealt with different loss functions, e.g. doctors might perceive a greater risk in a false negative. Another possibility stems from possible methodological differences or familiarity with elicitation measures (Spence, 1996). Mahajan (1992) suggested that experts were "cognitive misers." That is, they truncate their information searches and overlook diagnostic information. Spence (1996) provided evidence that experts' best estimates were better than novices', but when asked to provide confidence ranges around those estimates, their ranges were often too narrow.

Shanteau (1992) offered an account that may explain some seeming inconsistencies in studies of experts. He argued that performance of experts is closely connected to task domain. In some domains, such as weather forecasting, experts perform quite well (Stewart et al., 1997). In other domains, such as clinical psychology, experts perform less well (Dawes, 1988). He attributed this difference, among other things, to stability of stimuli and availability of relevant information.

Another issue concerns how the public perceives information from experts. Fischhoff (1994) relates a story of severe weather conditions that, based on strong indicators, had been clearly forecast and broadcast to the public. In spite of the warnings, there were numerous deaths, injuries, and accidents. Subsequently, efforts were made to discover how best to communicate information such that users understand what experts mean. Errors of communication can occur from ambiguity regarding the predicted event, relevance to the user, and issues of trust and context. A key message in Fischhoff's (1994) work is that when expert information is provided to the public, the recipient's understanding of this information should be elicited and identified to establish its concurrence with the presented information.

Experience Effects

As well as studies of experts, there have been numerous studies of how experience influences decision making. The work of Weber (1997) provides one example. Structured interviews were used to identify farmers' beliefs regarding climate changes and expectations of future changes in precipitation and temperature over the next 20 to 30 years. The data covered a broad range of information including a section on each farmer's attitudes and opinions, years of experience as a farmer, and recollections of weather in past years. Farmers with more experience, and who had seen many more fluctuations in the weather, were less likely to believe in contributors to current weather patterns or future climate change. A significant association was found between belief in global warming and predictions of temperature changes. Weber (1997) concluded that prior expectations are a determining factor for identification of relevant personal and contextual variables.

There have been many studies of the diagnostic ability of doctors. For example, Weber, Bockenholt, Hilton & Wallace (1993) found that experience affected the diagnostic hypothesis generation of physicians by increasing the availability of similar cases. The strength of a hypothesis increased when similar cases with the same hypothesis had been seen before. The generation of hypotheses by physicians proceeded from general to more specific in nature consistent with the frequency of experience. This experience effect has also been revealed in expert–novice studies by Camerer & Johnson (1991) and Joseph & Patel (1990).

Kirschenbaum (1992) observed an effect of experience on the information-gathering strategies of naval officers. Increased decision accuracy was found in sonar detection tasks for experienced officers compared to officer candidates. Experience can both broaden and focus the recognition of available options, as found in Beyth-Marom & Fischhoff's (1996) work on adolescent risk decisions. As adolescents increase their knowledge or experience, they become better at option generation and consequence production.

However, the acquisition of new knowledge is heavily influenced by the individual's current domain knowledge (Arkes & Freedman, 1984). Anderson, Marchant, Robinson & Schadewald (1990) provided evidence that knowledge also affects the integration of new information. Using three different instructional methods (presentation of cases, concepts, or examples), Anderson et al. provided new tax-related information to accounting participants with different levels of accounting knowledge. Results of the application of this new knowledge indicated that prior knowledge affected the impact of various instructional methods.

Studies of experts provide a notable example of individual differences in decision performance. The impact can be seen in the ability to identify relevant information, the structured generation of hypothesis, the application of content knowledge, and superior information-gathering strategies.

Individual Differences

The importance of individual differences varies by area of study. In the field of career choice and counseling, for instance, individual differences are the cornerstone of research. Topological methods are used to categorize individuals according to preference, skill, and ability. This information is integrated with skill and ability requirements of various occupations to provide an individual with viable career options. Unlike most research in judgment and decision making, career decision research seldom goes beyond topological methods to describe or prescribe the choice process.

Rohrbaugh (1996) investigated the impact of two instruments used as career decision aids on college students who were uncomfortable with their current career status. One instrument was an adaptation of multi-attribute rating techniques, and the other asked students for comparisons between career desires and preferred television characters. The latter is a more socially integrative approach, while the former uses formal decision analysis. Results indicated an interaction between gender and instructional method. Gender differences have also been shown to affect the relative importance of career-related attributes (Gati, Osipow & Givon, 1995). Results of such studies indicate the need for a better understanding of gender-specific differences in the identification of relevant information during the decision process.

Individual differences can be categorized as an individual's problem construction ability (Reiter-Palmon, Mumford, Boes & Runco, 1996). Participants were presented with a series of ambiguous and poorly defined problem-solving tasks. Problem construction ability was measured by the quality and originality of problem restatement. Results show that individuals with greater problem construction ability produce solutions of higher quality. The researchers suggest that this is at least partly due to metacognitive skills.

Lopes (1996) advanced a theory of Security-Potential and Aspiration (SP/A) to describe the preferences and reasoning of individuals making risky decisions. The aspiration component of SP/A involves maximizing probability for achieving some aspiration level. This suggests that individuals establish self-imposed targets of success (or goals) and that differences between individuals might be measured by this aspiration level. Although Lopes' focus is on risk, her research confirms the need to include the effects of individual differences in any descriptive theory of decision making.

Smith & Levin (1996) examined the effect of levels of cognition on decision making. Assuming that increases in thinking reduce susceptibility to irrelevant variables, Smith & Levin (1996) identified individuals with a high/low need for cognition (NFC). Both groups were given a situation based on Tversky & Kahneman's (1981) "ticket problem." Participants in the low NFC group displayed significantly greater susceptibility to the effects of problem framing. In a related study by Cacioppo, Petty & Kao (1984), participants were randomly assigned to one of two frames in a medical problem taken from McNeil, Pauker, Sox & Tversky (1982). Results showed that individuals with high NFC are less susceptible to effects of framing.

The importance of individual difference research is evident in the work of Saks & Hastie (1978). Research in the judicial system has shown inconsistency among judges for sentencing in criminal cases with identical circumstances. Sentencing policies are related to such individual differences among judges as political, religious, and educational background. Hastie (1993) also examined work on individual decision criteria in jury decision making and found an individual's story structure to be the most predictive of the verdicts. Group decision research in applied settings has influenced jury selection, committee decision making styles, and government policy. See Hastie (1993) for a review on theories of jury decision making and Steckel, Corfman, Curry, Gupta & Shanteau (1991) for an outline on problems in modeling group decisions.

The studies discussed in this section all relate individual differences to cognitive processing strategies. These differences relate to experience, need for cognition, and problem construction ability. The effort to measure and categorize individual differences produces questions such as: What constitutes a meaningful category of individual difference in decision making? Should cognitive process, independent of outcome, be used as a measure of individual difference? The connecting theme of individual differences is what the decision makers consider relevant to their problem.

FROM CONTEXT TO COGNITION: HOW DOES IT COME TOGETHER?

The growth of decision research is dependent on an empirically supportable structure that will not isolate applied research from basic research (or descriptive methods from prescriptive methods). We have provided examples of several research issues and suggested the unifying concept of relevance as central to the integration of research approaches. The importance of this integration rests on a clearer understanding of what constitutes relevant factors and what influences those factors have before, during, and after the decision process.

We have also argued that the application of what is learned from research will benefit from a recognition of the interrelationship of context, process, and experience. The ability, for example, to map common decision elements using "fast and frugal" methods could lead to identification of key environmental variables. These three variables cross all domains and could find application to any situation that requires a decision. Our view of how the relevance of information is influenced by context, process, and experience is illustrated in Figure 5.2. As can be seen, we believe that relevance (or diagnosticity) of information is key to understanding applied research on decision making. And relevance is, in turn, influenced by the interaction of context, process, and experience.

Svenson (1996) makes the distinction between a process approach that examines changes in the rules, representations, and values and a structural approach that relates input variables to choices. The more common structural approach has provided a useful framework for decision research. However, greater effort is needed to investigate the processing aspects of decision making.

Currently, the field of decision research would benefit from a research approach that, first, identifies relevant problem context and considers the influence of context on the decision process; second, considers a wider variety of variables, such as memory and feedback in addition to risk and utility; third, attempts to identify variables such as experience and individual differences that influence decision processes.

The applied research of Hammond and his colleagues (summarized in Hammond, 1996) nicely illustrates the importance of an interactive view of applied research. Based on Brunswick's (1956) analysis of perceptual processes, Hammond (1966) developed cognitive continuum theory (CCT). According to CCT, judgments fall along a continuum ranging from analytic at one end to intuitive at the other, with quasi-rational in between. Hammond, Hamm, Grassia & Pearson (1987) argued that accuracy of expert judgment will be greatest when there is a correspondence between task properties and cognitive properties: "At some point on the cognitive continuum, performance will be best and accuracy will fall off as the expert becomes either more analytic or more intuitive."

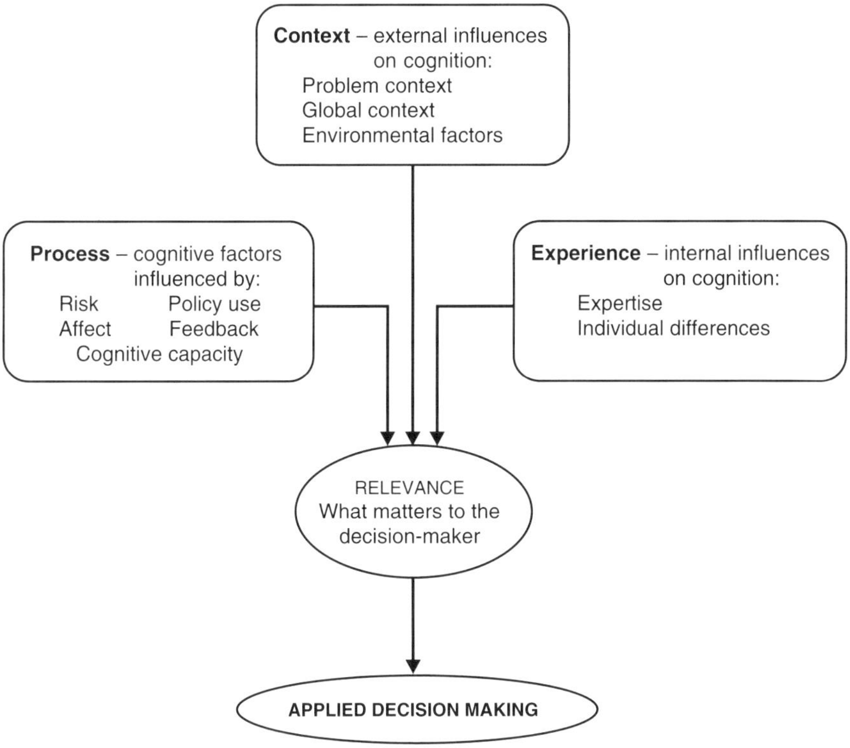

Figure 5.2 Diagram of how variables that influence context, process, and experience combine to determine relevance in applied decision making.

The element that ties all of the issues in this chapter is the transition from basic to applied research. From a decade of subjective expected utility (1960s) to two decades of H & B (1970s and 1980s), basic research has dictated what would find its way into application. Unfortunately, findings that were strong and consistent in basic research often proved to be weak and inconclusive in applied research. The connection between applied and basic research has been tenuous.

However, the tables may be turning – applied research may now be leading the way. For instance, applied researchers have long faced the problem of individual differences; basic researchers are just now beginning to notice. We believe an integrated basic/applied research approach will take the lead in the next decade of decision research.

ACKNOWLEDGMENTS

Preparation of this manuscript was supported, in part, by a National Science Foundation Grant (DMI 96-12126) to both authors and by support from the Institute for Social and Behavioral Research at Kansas State University to the second author.

The authors wish to thank Michael Dougherty, Frank Durso, and Ward Edwards for their helpful comments and suggestions on earlier versions of the manuscript.

REFERENCES

Anderson, J. R. (1983). *The Architecture of Cognition*. Cambridge, MA: Harvard University Press.

Anderson, U., Marchant, G., Robinson, J. & Schadewald, M. (1990). Selection of instructional strategies in the presence of related prior knowledge. *Issues in Accounting Education*, 5, 41–57.

Arkes, H. R. (1996). The psychology of waste. *Journal of Behavioral Decision Making*, 9, 213–24.

Arkes, H. R. & Freedman, M. R. (1984). A demonstration of the costs and benefits of expertise in recognition memory. *Memory and Cognition*, 84–9.

Beach, L. R. (1990). *Image Theory: Decision Making in Personal and Organizational Contexts*. Chichester: John Wiley.

Beach, L. R., Jungermann, H. & DeBruyn, E. E. J. (1996). Imagination and planning. In L. R. Beach (Ed.), *Decision Making in the Workplace: A Unified Perspective* (pp. 143–54). Mahwah, NJ: Lawrence Erlbaum.

Beach, L. R., Puto, C. P., Heckler, S. E., Naylor, G. & Marble, T. A. (1996). Differential versus unit weighting of violations, framing, and the role of probability in image theory's compatibility test. *Organizational Behavior and Human Decision Processes*, 65, 77–82.

Berkeley, D. & Humphreys, P. (1982). Structuring decision problems and the "bias heuristic." *Acta Psychologica*, 50, 201–52.

Beyth-Marom, R. & Fischhoff, B. (1996). Adolescents' decisions about risks: a cognitive perspective. In J. Schulenberg, J. Maggs & K. Hurnelmans (Eds), *Health Risks and Developmental Transaction During Adolescence* (pp. 110–35). New York: Cambridge University Press.

Brunswick, E. (1956). *Perception and the Representative Design of Psychological Experiments* (2nd edn). Berkeley, CA: University of California Press.

Busemeyer, J. R. & Townsend, J. T. (1993). Decision field theory: a dynamic–cognitive approach to decision making in an uncertain environment. *Psychological Review*, 100, 432–59.

Cacioppo, J. T., Petty, R. E. & Kao, C. F. (1984). The efficient assessment of need for cognition. *Journal of Personality Assessment*, 48, 306–7.

Camerer, C. & Johnson, E. J. (1991). The process–performance paradox in expert judgment: how can experts know so much and predict so badly? In A. Ericsson & J. Smith (Eds), *Toward a General Theory of Expertise: Prospects and Limitations* (pp. 101–29). Cambridge: Cambridge University Press.

Charness, N. & Schultetus, R. S. (1999). Knowledge and expertise. In F. T. Durso, R. S. Nickerson, R. W. Schvaneveldt, S. T. Dumais, D. S. Lindsay & M. T. H. Chi (Eds), *Handbook of Applied Cognition* (chapter 3). Chichester: John Wiley & Sons.

Chase, W. G. & Simon, H. A. (1973). Perception in chess. *Cognitive Psychology*, 4, 55–81.

Christensen-Szalanski, J. J. J. & Bushyhead, J. B. (1981). Physicians' use of probabilistic information in a real clinical setting. *Journal of Experimental Psychology: Human Perception and Performance*, 7, 928–35.

Connolly, T. & Srivastava, J. (1995). Cues and components in multiattribute evaluation. *Organizational Behavior and Human Decision Processes*, 64, 219–28.

Cooke, N. J., Atlas, R. S., Lane, D. M. & Berger, R. C. (1993). Role of high-level knowledge in memory for chess positions. *American Journal of Psychology*, 106, 321–51.

Cooksey, R. W. (1996). *Judgment Analysis: Theory, Methods, and Applications*. San Diego, CA: Academic Press.

Crandall, B. & Getchell-Reiter, K. (1993). Critical decision method: a technique for eliciting concrete assessment indicators from the "intuition" of NICU nurses. *Advances in Nursing Sciences*, 16, 42–51.

Dawes, R. M. (1988). *Rational Choice in an Uncertain World*. San Diego, CA: Harcourt, Brace, Jovanovich.

Dawes, R. M. (1996). Behavioral decision making and judgment. In D. Gilbert, S. Fiske & G. Lindzey (Eds), *The Handbook of Social Psychology*. Boston, MA: McGraw-Hill.
deGroot, A. D. (1965). *Thought and Choice in Chess*. The Hague: Mouton.
Diehl, E. & Sterman, J. D. (1995). Effects of feedback complexity on dynamic decision making. *Organizational Behavior and Human Decision Processes*, 62, 198–215.
Doherty, M. E., Schiavo, M. B., Tweney, R. D. & Mynatt, C. R. (1981). The influence of feedback and diagnostic data on pseudodiagnosticity. *Bulletin of the Psychonomic Society*, 18, 191–4.
Dougherty, M. R., Gettys, C. F. & Ogden, E. E. (in press). MINERVA-DM: a memory processes model for judgments of likelihood.
Dunegan, K. J. (1993). Framing, cognitive modes, and image theory: toward an understanding of a glass half full. *Journal of Applied Psychology*, 78, 491–503.
Edwards W. & Barron, F. H. (1994). SMARTS and SMARTER: improved simple methods for multiattribute utility measurement. *Organizational Behavior and Human Decision Processes*, 60, 306–25.
Einhorn, H. J. & Hogarth, R. M. (1981). Behavioral decision theory: processes of judgment and choice. *Annual Review of Psychology*, 32, 53–88.
Elstein, A. S. (1976). Clinical judgment: psychological research and medical practice. *Science*, 194, 696–700.
Ericsson, K. A. & Charness, N. (1994). Expert performance: its structure and acquisition. *American Psychologist*, 49, 725–47.
Fischer, K. & Jungermann, H. (1996). Rarely occurring headaches and rarely occurring blindness: is rarely = rarely? *Journal of Behavioral Decision Making*, 9, 153–72.
Fischhoff, B. (1975). Hindsight (does not equal) foresight: the effect of outcome knowledge on judgment under uncertainty. *Journal of Experimental Psychology: Human Perception and Performance*, 1, 288–99.
Fischhoff, B. (1994). Acceptable risk: a conceptual proposal. *Risk: Health, Safety and Environment*, 1, 1–28.
Fischhoff, B. (1996). The real world: what good is it? *Organizational Behavior and Human Decision Processes*, 65, 232–48.
Fischhoff, B. & Beyth, R. (1975). "I knew it would happen": remembered probabilities of once-future things. *Organizational Behavior and Human Performance*, 13, 1–16.
Fischhoff, B. & Downs, J. (1996). Accentuate the relevant. Paper presented at the NIDA Workshop on Basic Research Approaches to Behavioral Treatment, Bethesda, MD.
Gaeth, G. J. & Shanteau, J. (1984). Reducing the influence of irrelevant information on experienced decision makers. *Organizational Behavior and Human Decision Processes*, 33, 263–82.
Gati, I., Osipow, S. H. & Givon, M. (1995). Gender differences in career decision making: the content and structure of preferences. *Journal of Counseling Psychology*, 42, 204–16.
Gigerenzer, G. (1996). Rationality: why social context matters. In P. B. Baltes and U. M. Staudinger (Eds), *Interactive Minds: Life-span Perspectives on the Social Foundation of Cognition*. Cambridge: Cambridge University Press.
Gigerenzer, G. (1997). Bounded rationality: models of fast and frugal inference. *Swiss Journal of Economics and Statistics*, 133.
Gigerenzer, G. & Goldstein, D. (1996). Reasoning the fast and frugal way: models of bounded rationality. *Psychological Review*, 103, 650–9.
Hamm, R. M. (1993). Explanations for common responses to the blue/green cab probabilistic inference word problem. *Psychological Reports*, 72, 219–42.
Hammond, K. R. (1966). Probabilistic functionalism: Egon Brunswik's integration of the history, theory and method of psychology. In K. R. Hammond (Ed.), *The Psychology of Egon Brunswik*. New York: Holt.
Hammond, K. R. (1996). *Human Judgment and Social Policy: Irreducible Uncertainty, Inevitable Error, Unavoidable Justice*. New York: Oxford University Press.
Hammond, K. R. & Adelman, L. (1976). Science, values, and human judgment: integration of facts and values requires the scientific study of human judgment. *Science*, 194, 389–96.

Hammond, K. R., Hamm, R. M., Grassia, J. & Pearson, T. (1987). Direct comparison of the efficacy of intuitive and analytic cognition in expert judgment. *IEEE Transactions on Systems, Man and Cybernetics*, 17 (5), 753–70.
Harrison, P. & Shanteau, J. (1993). Do sunk cost effects generalize to cost accounting students? *Advances in Management Accounting*, 2, 171–86.
Hastie, R. (1993). *Inside the Juror: The Psychology of Juror Decision Making*. New York: Cambridge University Press.
Highhouse, S., Paese, P. W. & Leatherberry, T. (1996). Contrast effects on strategic-issue framing. *Organizational Behavior and Human Decision Processes*, 65, 95–105.
Hoffman, R. R., Shadbolt, N. R., Burton, A. M. & Klein, G. (1995). Eliciting knowledge from experts: a methodological analysis. *Organizational Behavior and Human Decision Processes*, 62, 129–58.
Hogarth, R. M. & Kunreuther, H. (1995). Decision making under ignorance: arguing with yourself. *Journal of Risk and Uncertainty*, 10, 15–36.
Hughes, H. D. (1917). An interesting corn seed experiment. *The Iowa Agriculturalist*, 17, 424–5.
Johnson, E. J., Hershey, J., Meszaros, J. & Kunreuther, H. (1993). Framing, probability distortions, and insurance decisions. *Journal of Risk and Uncertainty*, 7, 35–51.
Johnson, P. E., Jamal, K. & Berryman, R. G. (1991). Effects of framing on auditor decisions. *Organizational Behavior and Human Decision Processes*, 50, 75–105.
Joseph, G. M. & Patel, V. L. (1990). Domain knowledge and hypothesis generation in diagnostic reasoning. *Medical Decision Making*, 10, 31–46.
Jou, J., Shanteau, J. & Harris, R. J. (1996). An information processing view of framing effects: the role of causal schemas in decision making. *Memory and Cognition*, 24, 1–15.
Jungermann, H. (1985). Inferential processes in the construction of scenarios. *Journal of Forecasting*, 4, 321–7.
Jungermann, H., Pfister, H. & Fischer, K. (1996). Credibility, information preferences, and information. *Risk Analysis*, 16, 251–61.
Jungermann, H., Schutz, H. & Thuring, M. (1988). Mental models in risk assessment: informing people about drugs. *Risk Analysis*, 8, 147–55.
Kahn, B. E. & Isen, A. M. (1993). The influence of positive affect on variety seeking among safe, enjoyable products. *Journal of Consumer Research*, 20, 257–70.
Kahneman, D. & Tversky, A. (1979). Prospect theory: an analysis of decision under risk. *Econometrica*, 47, 263–91.
Kirschenbaum, S. S. (1992). Influence of experience on information-gathering strategies. *Journal of Applied Psychology*, 77, 343–52.
Klein, G. A. (1997). An overview of naturalistic decision making. In C. E. Zsambok and G. Klein (Eds), *Naturalistic Decision Making. Expertise: Research and Application* (pp. 49–59). Mahwah, NJ: Lawrence Erlbaum.
Klein, G. A., Calderwood, R. & MacGregor, D. (1989). Critical decision method for eliciting knowledge. *IEEE Transactions on Systems, Man, and Cybernetics*, 19, 462–72.
Klein, G. A. & Crandall, B. W. (1995). The role of mental simulation in problem solving and decision making. In P. Hancock, J. Flach, J. Caird & K. Vincente (Eds), *Local Applications of the Ecological Approach to Human–Machine Systems* (pp. 325–58). Hillsdale, NJ: Lawrence Erlbaum.
Klein, G., Kaempf, G. L., Wolf, S., Thordsen, M. & Miller, T. (1997). Applying decision requirements to user-centered design. *International Journal of Human–Computer Studies*, 46, 1–15.
Kleinmuntz, D. N. & Schkade, D. A. (1993). Information displays and decision processes. *Psychological Science*, 4, 221–7.
Kuhberger, A. (1998). The influence of framing on risky decisions: a meta-analysis. *Organizational Behavior and Human Decision Processes*, 75, 23–54.
Lopes, L. L. (1996). When time is of the essence: averaging, aspiration, and the short run. *Organizational Behavior and Human Decision Processes*, 65, 179–89.
Luce, M., Bettman, J. & Payne, J. W. (1997). Choice processing in emotionally difficult decisions. *Journal of Experimental Psychology: LMC*, 23, 384–405.

Mahajan, J. (1992). The overconfidence effect in marketing management predictions. *Journal of Marketing Research*, 29, 329–42.
Mano, H. (1994). Risk taking, framing effects, and affect. *Organizational Behavior and Human Decision Processes*, 57, 38–58.
McClelland, G. H., Stewart, B. E., Judd, C. M. & Bourne, L. E., Jr (1987). Effects of choice task on attribute memory. *Organizational Behavior and Human Decision Processes*, 40, 235–54.
McNeil, B. J., Pauker, S. G., Sox, H. C. & Tversky, A. (1982). On the elicitation of preferences for alternative therapies. *New England Journal of Medicine*, 306, 1259–62.
Means, M. L. & Voss, J. F. (1985). Star wars: a developmental study of expert and novice knowledge structures. *Journal of Memory and Language*, 24, 746–57.
Mellers, B. A. & Cooke A. D. J. (1994). Trade-offs depend on attribute range. *Journal of Experimental Psychology: HPP*, 20, 1055–67.
Mellers, B. A., Ordonez, L. D. & Birnbaum, M. H. (1992). A change-of-process theory for contextual effects and preference reversals in risky decision making. *Organizational Behavior and Human Decision Processes*, 52, 331–69.
Mellers, B. A., Schwartz, A. & Cooke, D. J. (1998). Judgment and decision making. *Annual Review of Psychology*, 49, 447–77.
Meyerowitz, B. E. & Chaiken, S. (1987). The effect of message framing on breast self-examination attitudes, intentions, and behavior. *Journal of Personality and Social Psychology*, 52, 500–10.
Murphy, A. H. & Winkler, P. (1977). Can weather forecasters formulate reliable probability forecasts of precipitation and temperature? *National Weather Digest*, 2, 2–9.
Nygren, T. E., Isen, A. M., Taylor, P. J. & Dulin, J. (1996). The influence of positive affect on the decision rule in risk situations: focus on outcome (and especially avoidance of loss) rather than probability. *Organizational Behavior and Human Decision Processes*, 66, 59–72.
O'Connor, M. J. (1989). Models of human behavior and confidence in judgment: a review. *International Journal of Forecasting*, 5, 159–69.
Oskamp, S. (1962). The relationship of clinical experience and training methods to several criteria of clinical prediction. *Psychological Monograph*, 76.
Paese, P. W., Bieser, M. & Tubbs, M. E. (1993). Framing effects and choice shifts in group decision making. *Organizational Behavior and Human Decision Processes*, 56, 149–65.
Payne, J. W. (1994). Thinking aloud: insights into information processing. *Psychological Science*, 5 (41), 245–8.
Payne, J. W., Bettman, J. R. & Johnson, E. J. (1992). Behavioral decision research: a constructive processing perspective. *Annual Review of Psychology*, 43, 87–131.
Reiter-Palmon, R., Mumford, M. D., Boes, J. O. & Runco, M. A. (1996). Problem construction and creativity: the role of ability, cue consistency, and active processing. Unpublished manuscript.
Riedl, T. R., Weitzenfeld, J. S., Freeman, J. T., Klein, G. A. & Musa, J. (1991). What we have learned about software engineering expertise. *Proceedings of the Fifth Software Engineering Institute (SEI) Conference on Software Engineering Education*. New York: Springer-Verlag.
Rohrbaugh, C. C. (1996). Career decision structure: Improving vocational decision making with decision skills training. Unpublished master's thesis, Kansas State University, Manhattan.
Saks, M. J. & Hastie, R. (1978). Social psychology in court: the judge. In H. R. Arkes and K. R. Hammond (Eds), *Judgment and Decision Making* (pp. 255–74). New York: Cambridge University Press.
Schneider, S. L., Levin, I. P. & Gaeth, G. J. (1997). Understanding the different types of positive/negative information framing effects. Paper presented at the 9th Annual Convention of the American Psychological Society, Washington, DC.
Schneider, S. L., Levin, I. P. & Gaeth, G. J. (in press). Framing effects in valence-based information processing: a broader perspective and typology. *Psychological Bulletin*.

Schneider, S. L., Levin, I. P., Gaeth, G. J. & Conlon, A. B. (1995). All frames are not created equal: a topology of valence framing effects. Paper presented at Meetings of the Psychonomic Society, Los Angeles, CA.
Schweitzer, M. (1995). Multiple reference points, framing, and the status quo bias in health care financing decisions. *Organizational Behavior and Human Decision Processes*, 63, 69–72.
Shanteau, J. (1975). Averaging versus multiplying combination rules of inference judgment. *Acta Psychologica*, 39, 83–9.
Shanteau, J. (1988). Psychological characteristics and strategies of expert decision makers. *Acta Psychologica*, 68, 203–15.
Shanteau, J. (1992). How much information does an expert use? Is it relevant? *Acta Psychologica*, 81, 71–86.
Shanteau, J., Grier, M., Johnson, J. & Berner, E. (1991). Teaching decision-making skills to student nurses. In J. Baron & R. V. Brown (Eds), *Teaching Decision Making to Adolescents* (pp. 185–206). Hillsdale, NJ: Lawrence Erlbaum Associates.
Shanteau, J. & Pounds, J. (1996). The pendulum swings. *American Journal of Psychology*, 109, 635–44.
Simon, H. A. (1990). Invariants of human behavior. *Annual Review of Psychology*, 41, 1–19.
Simonson, I. (1992). The influence of anticipating regret and responsibility on purchase decisions. *Journal of Consumer Research*, 19, 105–18.
Slovic, P. (1975). Choice between equally valued alternatives. *Journal of Experimental Psychology: Human Perception and Performance*, 1, 280–7.
Slovic, P. (1995). The construction of preference. *American Psychologist*, 50, 364–71.
Smith, S. M. & Levin, I. P. (1996). Need for cognition and choice framing effects. *Journal of Behavioral Decision Making*, 9, 283–90.
Spence, M. T. (1996). Problem-solver characteristics affecting the calibration of judgments. *Organizational Behavior and Human Decision Processes*, 67, 271–9.
Stewart, T. R., Roebber, P. J. & Bosart, L. F. (1997). The importance of the task in analyzing expert judgment. *Organizational Behavior and Human Decision Processes*, 69, 205–19.
Steckel, J. H., Corfman, K. P., Curry, D. J., Gupta, S. & Shanteau, J. (1991). Prospects and problems in modeling group decisions. *Marketing Letters*, 2, 231–40.
Svenson, O. (1996). Decision making and the search for fundamental psychological regularities: what can be learned from a process perspective? *Organizational Behavior and Human Decision Processes*, 65, 252–67.
Thuring, J. & Jungermann, H. (1986). Constructing and running mental models for inferences about the future. In B. Brehmer, H. Jungermann, P. Lourens & G. Sevon (Eds), *New Directions in Decision Research* (pp. 163–74). Amsterdam: Elsevier.
Tversky, A. & Kahneman, D. (1981). The framing of decisions and the rationality of choice. *Science*, 221, 453–8.
Tversky, A., Sattath, S. & Slovic, P. (1988). Contingent weighting in judgment and choice. *Psychological Review*, 95, 371–84.
Tversky, A. & Simonson, I. (1993). Context-dependent preferences. *Management Science*, 39, 1179–89.
Wallace, H. A. (1923). What is in the corn judge's mind? *Journal of the American Society of Agronomy*, 15, 300–24.
Wallsten, T. S., Fillenbaum, S. & Cox, J. (1986). Base rate effects on the interpretation of probability and frequency expressions. *Journal of Memory and Language*, 25, 571–87.
Weber, E. U. (1997). Perception and expectation of climate change: precondition for economic and technological adaptation. In M. Bazerman, D. Messick, A. Tenbrunsel & K. Wade-Benzoni (Eds), *Psychological Perspectives to Environmental and Ethical Issues in Management* (pp. 314–41). San Francisco, CA: Jossey-Bass.

Weber, E. U., Bockenholt, U., Hilton, D. J. & Wallace, B. (1993). Determinants of diagnostic hypothesis generation: effects of information, base rates, and experience. *Journal of Experimental Psychology: Learning, Memory, and Cognition*, 19, 1151–64.

Wiseman, D. B. & Levin, I. P. (1996). Comparing risky decision making under conditions of real and hypothetical consequences. *Organizational Behavior and Human Decision Processes*, 66, 241–50.

Yates, J. F. (1990). *Judgment and Decision Making*. Englewood Cliffs, NJ: Prentice Hall.

Chapter 6

Perspectives on Human Error: Hindsight Biases and Local Rationality

David D. Woods
The Ohio State University
and
Richard I. Cook
University of Chicago

INTRODUCTION

Early Episodes of "Human Error"

Consider the following two case studies where some stakeholders reacted to failure by attributing the cause to "human error," but where more careful examination showed how a combination of factors created the conditions for failure. Here, the term stakeholders refers to all of the different groups that are affected by an accident in that domain and by changes to operations, regulations, equipment, policies, etc. as a result of reactions to that accident. For example, an accident in aviation affects the public as consumers of the service, the FAA as regulators of the industry, pilots as practitioners, air traffic controllers as practitioners, air carrier organizations as providers of the service, manufacturers of the aircraft type as equipment designers, other development organizations that develop other equipment such as avionics, navigation aids, and software, and other groups as well.

Handbook of Applied Cognition, Edited by F. T. Durso, R. S. Nickerson, R. W. Schvaneveldt, S. T. Dumais, D. S. Lindsay and M. T. H. Chi.

Case 1:

- In 1796 the astronomer Maskelyne fired his assistant Kinnebrook because the latter's observations did not match his own (see Boring, 1950).
- Bessel, another astronomer, studied the case empirically and identified systematic factors which produced imprecise observations. By systematic factors, we mean the behavior is not random but lawful, i.e. there are empirical regularities, factors that influence behavior are external to individuals (system properties), these factors have an effect because they influence the physical, cognitive and collaborative activities of practitioners, and, finally, because there are regularities, there are predictable effects.

The implicit assumption was that one person (the assistant) was the source of failure whether due to some inherent trait or to lack of effort on his part. Bessel broke free of this assumption and empirically examined individual differences in astronomical observations. He found that there were wide differences across observers given the methods of the day. The techniques for making observations at this time required a combination of auditory and visual judgments. Those judgments were shaped by the tools of the day, pendulum clocks and telescope hairlines, in relation to the demands of the task. Dismissing Kinnebrook did not change what made the task difficult, did not eliminate individual differences, and did not make the task less vulnerable to sources of imprecision. Progress was based on searching for better methods for making astronomical observations, re-designing the tools that supported astronomers, and re-designing the tasks to change the demands placed on human judgment.

Case 2:

- In 1947 investigations of military aviation accidents concluded that pilot errors were the cause of the crashes.
- Fitts & Jones empirically studied pilot performance in the cockpit and showed how systematic factors in interpreting instruments and operating controls produced misassessments and actions not as intended (see Fitts & Jones, 1947).

The implicit assumption was that the person closest to the failure was the cause. Investigators saw that the aircraft was in principle flyable and that other pilots were able to fly such aircraft successfully. They could show how the necessary data were available for the pilot to correctly identify the actual situation and act in an appropriate way. Since the pilot was the human closest to the accident who could have acted differently, it seemed obvious to conclude that the pilot was the cause of the failure.

Fitts and his colleague empirically looked for factors that could have influenced the performance of the pilots. They found that, given the design of the displays and layout of the controls, people relatively often misread instruments or operated the wrong control, especially when task demands were high. The misreadings and misoperations were design-induced in the sense that researchers could link properties of interface design to these erroneous actions and assessments. In other words, the "errors" were not random events, rather they resulted from understandable, regular, and predictable aspects of the design of the tools practitioners used.

The researchers found that misreadings and misoperations occurred, but did not always lead to accidents due to two factors. First, pilots often detected these errors before negative consequences occurred. Second, the misreadings and misoperations alone did not lead directly to an accident. Disaster or near misses usually occurred only when these errors occurred in combination with other factors or other circumstances.

In the end, the constructive solution was not to conclude that pilots err, but rather to understand principles and techniques for the design of visual displays and control layout. Changing the artifacts used by pilots changed the demands on human perception and cognition and changed the performance of pilots.

Erratic People or System Factors?

While historical, the above episodes encapsulate current, widespread beliefs in many technical and professional communities and the public in general about the nature of human error and how systems fail. In most domains today, from aviation to industrial processes to transportation systems to medicine, when systems fail we find the same pattern as was observed in these earlier cases.

1. Stakeholders claim failure is "caused" by unreliable or erratic performance of individuals working at the sharp end* who undermine systems which otherwise worked as designed (for example, see the recent history of pilot-automation accidents in aviation; Billings, 1996; Woods & Sarter, in press). The search for causes tends to stop when we can find the human or group closest to the accident who *could have acted differently* in a way that would have led to a different outcome. These people are seen as the source or "cause" of the failure, that is, the outcome was due to "human error." When stakeholders see erratic people as the cause of bad outcomes, they respond by calls to remove these people from practice, to provide remedial training to other practitioners, to urge other practitioners to try harder, and to regiment practice through policies, procedures, and automation.

2. However, researchers look more closely at the system in which these practitioners – "a person engaged in the practice of a profession or occupation" (Webster's, 1990) – are embedded and their studies reveal a different picture. Their results show how popular beliefs that such accidents are due simply to isolated blunders of individuals mask the deeper story – a story of multiple contributors that create the conditions that lead to operator errors. Reason (1990, p. 173) summarizes the results: "Rather than being the main instigators of an

* It has proven useful to depict complex systems such as health care, aviation and electrical power generation and others as having a sharp and a blunt end (Reason, 1990). At the sharp end, practitioners interact with the underlying process in their roles as pilots, spacecraft controllers, and, in medicine, as nurses, physicians, technicians, and pharmacists. At the blunt end of a system are regulators, administrators, economic policy makers, and technology suppliers. The blunt end of the system controls the resources and constraints that confront the practitioner at the sharp end, shaping and presenting sometimes conflicting incentives and demands (Reason, 1997).

accident, operators tend to be the inheritors of system defects . . . Their part is that of adding the final garnish to a lethal brew whose ingredients have already been long in the cooking." The empirical results reveal regularities in organizational dynamics and in the design of artifacts that produce the potential for certain kinds of erroneous actions and assessments by people working at the sharp end of the system (Reason, 1997; Woods, Johannesen, Cook & Sarter, 1994).

For example, one basic finding from research on disasters in complex systems (e.g. Reason, 1990) is that accidents are not due to a single failure or cause. Accidents in complex systems only occur through the concatenation of multiple small factors or failures, each necessary but only jointly sufficient to produce the accident. Often, these small failures or vulnerabilities are present in the organization or operational system long before a specific incident is triggered. All complex systems contain such "latent" factors or failures, but only rarely do they combine to create an accident (Reason, 1997).

This pattern of multiple, latent factors occurs because the people in an industry recognize the existence of various hazards that threaten to cause accidents or other significant consequences, and they design defenses that include technical, human, and organizational elements. For example, people in health care recognize the hazards associated with the need to deliver multiple drugs to multiple people at unpredictable times in a hospital setting and use computers, labeling methods, patient identification cross-checking, staff training, and other methods to defend against misadministrations. Accidents in these kinds of systems occur when multiple factors join together to create the trajectory for an accident by eroding, bypassing or breaking through the multiple defenses. Because there are a set of contributors, multiple opportunities arise to redirect the trajectory away from disaster. The research has revealed that an important part of safety is enhancing opportunities for people to recognize that a trajectory is heading closer to a poor outcome and to recover before negative consequences occur (Rasmussen, 1986). Factors that reduce error tolerance or block error detection and recovery degrade system performance.

Behind the Label Human Error

Based on this pattern in the data, researchers see that the label "human error" should serve as the starting point for investigating how systems fail, not as a conclusion. In other words, human performance is shaped by systematic factors, and the scientific study of failure is concerned with understanding how these factors shape the cognition, collaboration and ultimately the behavior of people in various work domains.

This research base has identified some of these regularities. In particular, we know about how a variety of factors make certain *kinds* of erroneous actions and assessments predictable (e.g. Hollnagel, 1993; Norman, 1983; Norman, 1988). Our ability to predict the timing and number of erroneous actions is very weak, but our ability to predict the kind of errors that will occur, when people do err, is often good. For example, when research pursues this deeper story behind the label "human error," we find imbalances between the demands practitioners face and the resources available to meet the demands of that field of activity (Rasmussen, 1986). These demand–resource imbalances can affect the development of necessary expertise (Feltovich, Ford & Hoffman, 1997), how the system brings additional expertise to bear especially when more difficult problems emerge, how people cope with multiple pressures and demands (Klein, 1998), how the system supports cooperative work activities especially when the tempo of operations increases, and how organizational constraints hinder or aid practitioners when they face difficult tradeoffs and dilemmas (Weick & Roberts, 1993).

This chapter will explore only a small portion of the issues that come to the fore when one goes behind the label human error. The space of social, psychological, technological, and organizational issues is large in part because people play such diverse roles in work environments and because work environments themselves vary so much.

Two Perspectives: Studying the Factors that Affect Human Performance and Studying Reactions to Failure

The chapter revolves around an ambiguity in the label human error. The two historical episodes introduced at the beginning of the chapter illustrate this ambiguity.

When we use the label human error we are sometimes referring to the processes and factors that influence the behavior of the people in the situation. From this perspective investigators are trying to understand the factors that lead up to erroneous actions and assessments. In this sense, the label human error points at all of the factors that influence human performance – in particular, the performance of the practitioners working in some field of activity. In the examples at the beginning of the chapter, Bessel and Fitts followed up the incidents with this kind of investigation. Understanding human performance is a very large subject (in part the subject of much of this volume) and here we will examine only a few of the relevant issues – predominately cognitive factors, but also how those cognitive processes are shaped by artifacts, coordination across multiple people, and organizational pressures.

While the above constitutes the bulk of this chapter, the label human error can refer to a different class of psychological issues and phenomena. After-the-fact, stakeholders look back and make judgments about what led to the accident or incident. In the examples at the beginning of the chapter, Maskelyne and the authors of the aviation accident reports reacted after-the-fact with the judgment that individuals were the cause of the accidents. Labeling a past action as erroneous is a judgment based on a different perspective and on different information than what was available to the practitioners in context. In other words, this judgment is a process of causal attribution, and there is an extensive body of research about the social and psychological factors which influence these kinds of attributions of causality (e.g. Baron & Hershey, 1988; Fischhoff, 1975; Hilton, 1990; Kelley, 1973). From this perspective, error research studies the social and psychological processes which govern our *reactions to failure* as stakeholders in the system in question (Tasca, 1990; Woods et al., 1994, ch. 6).

Our reactions to failure as stakeholders are influenced by many factors. One of the most critical is that, after an accident, we know the outcome and, working backwards, what were critical assessments or actions that, if they had been different, would have avoided that outcome. It is easy for us with the benefit of hindsight to say, "How could they have missed *x*?", or "How could they have not realized that *x* obviously would lead to *y*?"

Studies have consistently shown that people have a tendency to judge the quality of a process by its outcome (Baron & Hershey, 1988; Caplan, Posner & Cheney, 1991; Lipshitz, 1989). In a typical study, two groups are asked to evaluate human performance in cases with the same descriptive facts but with the outcomes randomly assigned to be either bad or neutral. Those with knowledge of a poor outcome judge the same decision or action more severely. This is referred to as the *outcome bias* (Baron & Hershey, 1988) and has been demonstrated with practitioners in different domains. For example, Caplan, Posner & Cheney (1991) found an inverse relationship between the severity of outcome and anesthesiologists' judgments of the appropriateness of care. The judges consistently rated the care in cases with bad outcomes as substandard while viewing the same behaviors with neutral outcomes as being up to standard even though the care (i.e. the preceding human performance) was identical. The information about outcome biased the evaluation of the process that was followed.

Other research has shown that once people have knowledge of an outcome, they tend to view the outcome as having been more probable than other possible outcomes. Moreover, people tend to be largely unaware of the modifying effect of outcome information on what they believe they could have known in foresight. These two tendencies collectively have been termed the *hindsight bias*. Fischhoff (1975) originally demonstrated the hindsight bias in a set of experiments that compared foresight and hindsight judgments concerning the likelihood of particular socio-historical events. Basically, the bias has been demonstrated in the following way: participants are told about some event, and some are provided with outcome information. At least two different outcomes are used in order to control for one particular outcome being *a priori* more likely. Participants are then asked to estimate the probabilities associated with the several possible outcomes. Participants given the outcome information are told to ignore it in coming up with their estimates, i.e. "to respond as if they had not known the actual outcome," or in some cases are told to respond as they think others without outcome knowledge would respond. Those participants with the outcome knowledge judge the outcomes they had knowledge about as more likely than the participants without the outcome knowledge, even when those making the judgments have been warned about the phenomenon and been advised to guard against it (Fischhoff, 1982). Experiments on the hindsight bias have shown that: (a) people overestimate what they would have known in foresight, (b) they also overestimate what others knew in foresight, and (c) they actually misremember what they themselves knew in foresight.

Taken together, the outcome and hindsight biases have strong implications for error analyses.

- Decisions and actions having a negative outcome will be judged more harshly than if the *same* process had resulted in a neutral or positive outcome. We can expect this result even when judges are warned about the phenomenon and have been advised to guard against it.
- Judges will tend to believe that people involved in some incident knew more about their situation than they actually did. Judges will tend to think that people should have seen how their actions would lead up to the outcome failure.

One sense of studying "human error", then, involves understanding how social and psychological processes such as hindsight and outcome biases shape our reactions to failure as stakeholders in the failed system. In a narrow sense, the outcome and hindsight biases refer to specific experimental findings from different test paradigms. In a broader sense, both of these experimental results, and other results, refer to a collection of factors that influence our reactions to failures based on information that is available only after the outcome is known. In the context of error analysis, we have used the label "hindsight bias" to refer to the broader perspective of a judge looking back in hindsight to evaluate the performance of others (Woods et al., 1994). Both specific experimental results illustrate ways in which people with the benefit of hindsight can misperceive and misanalyze the factors that influenced the behavior of the people working in the situation before outcome was known. In general, we react, after the fact, as if the knowledge we now possess was available to the operators then. This oversimplifies or trivializes the situation confronting the practitioners, and masks the processes affecting practitioner behavior before-the-fact. As a result, hindsight and outcome bias blocks our ability to see the deeper story of systematic factors that predictably shape human performance.

There is limited data available about the reactions of stakeholders to failure (but see, Tasca, 1990, and the review in Woods et al., 1994, ch. 6). This perspective shifts the focus of investigation from studying sharp end practitioners to studying stakeholders. It emphasizes the need to collect data on reactions to failure and to contrast those reactions after-the-fact to results on the factors that influence human performance before-the-fact derived from methods that reduce hindsight biases. Such studies can draw from the conceptual base created by experimental studies on the social and psychological factors in judgments of causal attribution such as hindsight biases.

The main portion of this chapter will focus on the deeper story behind the label human error of factors that influence human performance, especially some of the cognitive factors. Then, we will return to hindsight and outcome bias to illustrate several misconceptions about cognition that arise often when incidents are reviewed with knowledge of outcome.

COGNITIVE FACTORS AND HUMAN PERFORMANCE

What cognitive factors affect the performance of practitioners in complex settings like medicine, aviation, telecommunications, process plants, and space mission control? There are many ways one could organize classes of cognitive factors relevant to human performance (e.g. Rasmussen, 1986; Norman, 1988; Reason, 1990). Different aspects of cognition will be relevant to various settings and situations. For example, one area of human performance is concerned with slips of action such as capture errors or omissions of isolated acts (e.g. Byrne & Bovair, 1997; Norman, 1981; Reason & Mycielska, 1982). We have found it useful to teach people about cognitive factors and error by using the concept of bounded or local rationality (Simon, 1957).

Local Rationality

At work, groups of practitioners pursue goals and match procedures to situations, but they also

- resolve conflicts
- anticipate hazards
- accommodate variation and change
- cope with surprise
- work around obstacles
- close gaps between plans and real situations
- detect and recover from miscommunications and misassessments.

In these activities practitioners at the sharp end block potential accident trajectories. In other words, people actively contribute to safety when they can carry out these roles successfully. "Error" research on human performance tries to identify factors that undermine practitioners' ability to do these activities successfully. The question then becomes how can the same processes result in success some of the time but result in failure in other circumstances (Rasmussen, 1986).

The concept of bounded rationality is very useful for helping us think about how people can form intentions and act in ways that later events will reveal are erroneous. Peoples' behavior in the work situations can be considered as consistent with Newell's principle of rationality – that is, practitioners use their knowledge to pursue their goals (Newell, 1982). But there are bounds to the data that they pick up or search out, bounds to the knowledge that they possess, bounds to the knowledge that they activate in a particular context, and there may be multiple goals which conflict (Simon, 1957). In other words, people's behavior can be seen as "rational," though possibly erroneous, when seen from the point of view of their knowledge, their mindset, and the multiple goals they are trying to balance (Rasmussen, Duncan & Leplat, 1987). Rationality here does not mean consistent with external, global standards such as models, policies or procedures; rationality in Newell's principle is defined locally from the point of view of the people in a situation as they use their knowledge to pursue their goals based on their view of the situation. As a result, for the context of error, we will refer to the concept that human rationality is limited or bounded as "local" rationality (Woods et al., 1994).

Fundamentally, human (and real machine) problem solvers possess finite capabilities. They cannot anticipate and consider all the possible alternatives and information that may be relevant in complex problems. This means that the rationality of finite resource problem solvers is local in the sense that it is exercised relative to the complexity of the environment in which they function (Klein, Orasanu & Calderwood, 1993; Klein, 1998). It takes effort (which consumes limited computational resources) to seek out evidence, to interpret it (as relevant), and to assimilate it with other evidence. Evidence may come in over time, over many noisy channels. The process may yield information only in response to diagnostic interventions. Time pressure, which compels action (or the *de facto* decision not to act), makes it impossible to wait for all evidence to accrue. Multiple goals may be relevant, not all of which are consistent. It may not be clear, in foresight, which goals are the most important ones to focus on at any one particular moment in time. Human problem solvers cannot handle all the potentially relevant information, cannot activate and hold in mind all of the relevant knowledge, and cannot entertain all potentially relevant trains of thought. Hence, rationality must be local – attending to only a subset of the possible evidence or knowledge that could be, in principle, relevant to the problem.

The role for "error" research, in the sense of understanding the factors that influence human performance, is to understand how limited knowledge (missing knowledge or misconceptions), how a limited and changing mindset, and how multiple interacting goals shaped the behavior of the people in the evolving situation. In other words, this type of error research reconstructs what the view was like or would have been like had we stood in the same situation as the participants. If we can understand how their knowledge, their mindset, and their goals guided the behavior of the participants, then we can see how they were vulnerable to err given the demands of the situation they faced. We can see new ways to help practitioners activate relevant knowledge, shift attention to the critical focus among multiple tasks in a rich, changing data field, and recognize and balance competing goals.

Given that people use their knowledge to pursue their goals, but also that there are bounds to their knowledge, limits to their mindset and multiple not always consistent goals to achieve, one can learn about the performance of practitioners at the sharp end by looking at factors that affect:

- how knowledge relevant to the situation at hand is called to mind – knowledge in context
- how we come to focus on one perspective or one part of a rich and changing environment, and how we shift that focus across multiple events over time – mindset
- how we balance or make tradeoffs among multiple interacting goals – interacting goals.

We have found it useful to group various findings and concepts into these three classes of cognitive factors that govern how people form intentions to act (Cook & Woods, 1994). Problems in the coordination of these cognitive functions, relative to the demands imposed by the field of activity, create the potential for mismanaging systems towards failure. For example, in terms of knowledge factors, some of the possible problems are buggy knowledge (e.g. incorrect model of device function), inert knowledge, and oversimplifications (Spiro, Coulson, Feltovich & Anderson, 1988). In terms of mindset, one form of breakdown occurs when an inappropriate mindset takes hold or persists in the face of evidence which does not fit this assessment. Failures very often can be traced back to dilemmas and tradeoffs that arise from multiple interacting and sometimes conflicting goals. Practitioners by the very nature of their role at the sharp end of systems must implicitly or explicitly resolve these conflicts and dilemmas as they are expressed in particular situations (Cook & Woods, 1994).

Knowledge in Context

Knowledge factors refer to the process of bringing knowledge to bear to solve problems in context:

- what knowledge practitioners possess about the system or process in question (is it correct, incomplete, or erroneous, i.e. "buggy"?)
- how this knowledge is organized so that it can be used flexibly in different contexts, and
- the processes involved in calling to mind the knowledge relevant to the situation at hand.

Knowledge of the world and its operation may be complete or incomplete and accurate or inaccurate. Practitioners may act based on inaccurate knowledge or on incomplete knowledge about some aspect of the complex system or its operation. When the mental model that practitioners hold of such systems is inaccurate or incomplete, their actions may well be inappropriate. These mental models are sometimes described as "buggy." The study of practitioners' mental models has examined the models that people use for understanding technological, physical, and physiological processes. Several volumes are available which provide a comprehensive view of research on this question (see Chi, Glaser & Farr, 1988; Feltovich, Ford & Hoffman, 1997; Gentner & Stevens, 1983).

Note that research in this area has emphasized that mere possession of knowledge is not enough for expertise. It is also critical for knowledge to be organized so that it can be activated and used in different contexts (Bransford, Sherwood, Vye & Rieser, 1986). Thus, Feltovich, Spiro & Coulson (1989) and others emphasize that one component of human expertise is the *flexible* application of knowledge in *new* situations.

There are multiple overlapping lines of research related to the activation of knowledge in context by humans performing in complex systems. These include the problem of inert knowledge, and the use of heuristics, simplifications, and approximations.

Going behind the label "human error" involves investigating how knowledge was or could have been brought to bear in the evolving incident. Any of the above factors could influence the activation of knowledge in context – for example, did the participants have incomplete or erroneous knowledge? Were otherwise useful simplifications applied in circumstances that demanded consideration of a deeper model of the factors at work in the case? Did relevant knowledge remain inert? We will briefly sample a few of the issues in this area.

Activating Relevant Knowledge in Context: The Problem of Inert Knowledge

Lack of knowledge or buggy knowledge may be one part of the puzzle, but the more critical question may be factors that affect whether relevant knowledge is activated and utilized in the actual problem solving context (e.g. Bransford, Sherwood & Riesser, 1986). The question is not just does the problem solver know some particular piece of domain knowledge, but does he or she call it to mind when it is relevant to the problem at hand and does he or she know how to utilize this knowledge in problem solving? We tend to assume that if a person can be shown to possess a piece of knowledge in one situation and context, then this knowledge should be accessible under all conditions where it might be useful. In contrast, a variety of research results have revealed dissociation effects where knowledge accessed in one context remains inert in another (Gentner & Stevens, 1983; Perkins & Martin, 1986).

Thus, the fact that people possess relevant knowledge does not guarantee that this knowledge will be activated when needed. The critical question is not to show that the problem solver possesses domain knowledge, but rather the more stringent criterion that situation-relevant knowledge is accessible under the conditions in which the task is performed. Knowledge that is accessed only in a restricted set of contexts is called *inert knowledge*. Inert knowledge may be related to cases that are difficult to handle, not because problem solvers do not know the individual pieces of knowledge needed to build a solution, but because they have not confronted previously the need to join the pieces together.

Results from accident investigations often show that the people involved did not call to mind all the relevant knowledge during the incident although they "knew" and recognized the significance of the knowledge afterwards. The triggering of a knowledge item *X* may depend on subtle pattern recognition factors that are not present in every case where *X* is relevant. Alternatively, that triggering may depend critically on having sufficient time to process all the available stimuli in order to extract the pattern. This may explain the difficulty practitioners have in "seeing" the relevant details when the pace of activity is high.

One implication of these results is that training experiences should exercise knowledge in the contexts where it is likely to be needed.

Oversimplifications

People tend to cope with complexity through simplifying heuristics. Heuristics are useful because they are usually relatively easy to apply and they minimize the cognitive effort required to produce decisions. These simplifications may be useful approximations that allow limited resource practitioners to function robustly over a variety of problem demand factors or they may be distortions or misconceptions that appear to work satisfactorily under some conditions but lead to error in others. Feltovich et al. (1989) call the latter "oversimplifications."

In studying the acquisition and representation of complex concepts in biomedicine, Feltovich et al. (1989) found that various oversimplifications were held by some medical students and even by some practicing physicians. They found that ". . . bits and pieces of knowledge, in themselves sometimes correct, sometimes partly wrong in aspects, or sometimes absent in critical places, interact with each other to create large-scale and robust misconceptions" (Feltovich et al., 1989, p. 162). Examples of kinds of oversimplification include (see Feltovich, Spiro & Coulson, 1993):

- seeing different entities as more similar than they actually are
- treating dynamic phenomena as static
- assuming that some general principle accounts for all of a phenomenon
- treating multidimensional phenomena as unidimensional or according to a subset of the dimensions
- treating continuous variables as discrete
- treating highly interconnected concepts as separable
- treating the whole as merely the sum of its parts.

Feltovich and his colleagues' work has important implications for the teaching and training of complex material. Their studies and analyses challenge the view of instruction that presents initially simplified material in modules that decompose complex concepts into their simpler components with the belief that these will eventually "add up" for the advanced learner (Feltovich et al., 1993). Instructional analogies, while serving to convey certain aspects of a complex phenomenon, may miss some crucial ones and mislead on others. The analytic decomposition misrepresents concepts that have interactions among variables. The conventional approach may produce a false sense of understanding and inhibit pursuit of deeper understanding because learners may resist learning a more complex model once they already have an apparently useful simpler one (Spiro et al., 1988). Feltovich and his colleagues have developed the theoretical basis for a new approach to advanced knowledge acquisition in ill-structured domains (Feltovich, Spiro & Coulson, 1997).

Why do practitioners utilize simplified or oversimplified knowledge? These simplifying tendencies may occur because of the cognitive effort required in demanding circumstances (Feltovich et al., 1989). Also, simplifications may be adaptive, first, because the effort required to follow more "ideal" reasoning paths may be so large that it would keep practitioners from acting with the speed demanded in actual environments. This has been shown elegantly by Payne, Bettman & Johnson (1988) and by Payne, Johnson, Bettman & Coupey (1990) who demonstrated that simplified methods will produce a higher proportion of correct choices between multiple alternatives under conditions of time pressure.

In summary, heuristics represent effective and necessary adaptations to the demands of real workplaces (Rasmussen, 1986). The issue may not always be the shortcut or simplification itself, but instead whether practitioners know the limits of the shortcuts, can recognize situations where the simplification is no longer relevant, and have the ability to use more complex concepts, methods, or models (or the ability to integrate help from specialist knowledge sources) when the situation they face demands it.

Mindset

"Everyone knows what attention is. It is the taking possession by the mind, in a clear and vivid form, of one out of what seem several simultaneously possible objects or trains of thought" (James, [1890] 1950, 403–4). We are able to focus, temporarily, on some objects, events, actions in the world or on some of our goals, expectations or trains of thought *while remaining sensitive to new objects or events that may occur*. We can refer to this broadly as a state of attentional focus or mindset (LaBerge, 1995).

Mindset is not fixed, but shifts to explore the world and to track potentially relevant changes in the world (LaBerge, 1995). In other words, one re-orients attentional focus to a newly relevant object or event from a previous state where attention was focused on other objects or on other cognitive activities (such as diagnostic search, response planning, communication to others). New stimuli are occurring constantly; any of these could serve as a signal that we should interrupt ongoing lines of thought and re-orient attention. This re-orientation involves disengagement from a previous focus and movement of attention to a new focus. Interestingly, this control of attentional focus can be seen as a skillful activity that can be developed through training (Gopher, 1991) or supported (or undermined) by the design of artifacts and intelligent machine agents (Woods 1995; Patterson, Watts, & Woods, in press).

A basic challenge for practitioners at work is where to focus attention next in a changing world (Woods & Watts, 1997). Which object, event, goal, or line of thought we focus on depends on the interaction of two sets of activity. One of these is goal or knowledge directed, endogenous processes (often called attentional set) that depend on the observer's current knowledge, goals and expectations about the task at hand. The other set of processes are stimulus- or data-driven where attributes of the stimulus world (unique features, transients, new objects) elicit attentional capture independent of the observer's current mindset (Yantis, 1993). These salient changes in the world help guide focus of attention or mindset to relevant new events, objects, or tasks.

These two kinds of processes combine in a cycle – what Neisser (1976) called the perceptual cycle – where unique events in the environment shift the focus of attention or mindset, call to mind knowledge, trigger new lines of thought. The activated knowledge, expectations, or goals in turn guides further exploration and action. This cycle is a crucial concept for those trying to understand human performance in the workplace (e.g. Jager Adams, Tenney & Pew, 1995).

There are a variety of interesting psychological phenomena that can be organized under the label "mindset." Examples include:

- attentional control and loss of situation awareness (Durso & Gronlund, 1999, this volume; Gopher, 1991; Jager Adams et al., 1995)

- revising assessments as new evidence occurs, for example in garden path problems and in failures to revise, such as fixation effects (Johnson, Moen & Thompson, 1988; De Keyser & Woods, 1990)
- framing effects and the representation effect (Johnson, Jamal & Berryman, 1991; Zhang & Norman, 1994; Zhang, 1997)
- juggling multiple lines of thought and activity in time including breakdowns in workload management and thematic vagabonding (Dorner, 1983).

There are a variety of problems that can occur in synchronizing mindset to goals and priorities in a changing world depending on problem demands, skill levels, coordinative structures, and the artifacts available to support performance, for example:

- Irrelevant stimuli may intrude on a primary task, e.g. distraction – a breakdown in selective attention.
- One's mindset may be too easily interrupted, as in thematic vagabonding – a breakdown in attention switching. Thematic vagabonding refers to one form of loss of coherence where multiple interacting themes are treated superficially and independently so that the person or team jumps incoherently from one theme to the next (Dorner, 1983).
- One's mindset may be too hard to interrupt and re-focus, i.e. fixating on one view of the problem – a breakdown in attention switching.
- Attention may be captured by irrelevant stimuli, or relevant stimuli fail to capture attention in a cognitively noisy workplace, e.g. habituation to nuisance alarms or high rates of false alarms (Getty, Swets, Pickett & Gonthier, 1995; Woods, 1995).
- Breakdowns can occur in setting priorities or making tradeoffs, e.g. shedding the wrong task under high workload – a breakdown in attention switching.

When the goal of the investigator is to understand the factors that shape human performance, a critical step is to trace out how an individual's mindset or a group's mindset develops and changes as the incident evolves. Often this involves understanding how the mindset of different individuals or groups interact and remain encapsulated. This analysis reveals the cues which attracted attention, how did they match the expectations of the observers, what was called to mind, what lines of thought were triggered, and how those goals and issues guided further exploration and action, which in turn generates new cues. This analysis reveals the kinds of attentional challenges produced by the evolving problem and the kinds of attentional breakdowns that occurred.

Loss of Situation Awareness

Situation awareness is a label that is often used to refer to many of the cognitive processes involved in forming and changing mindset (e.g. Durso & Gronlund, 1999, this volume; Jager Adams et al., 1995). Maintaining situation awareness necessarily requires shifts of attention to inform and modify a coherent picture or model of the situation the practitioners face. Anticipating how the situation may develop or change in the future state is a particularly important aspect.

Breakdowns in these cognitive processes can lead to operational difficulties in handling the demands of dynamic, event-driven incidents. In aviation circles this is known as "falling behind the plane" and in aircraft carrier flight operations it has been described as "losing the bubble" (Roberts & Rousseau, 1989). In each case what is being lost is the operator's internal representation of the state of the world at that moment and the direction in which the forces active in the world are taking the system that the operator is trying to control.

Fischer, Orasanu & Montvalo (1993) examined the juggling of multiple threads of a problem in a simulated aviation scenario. More effective crews were better able to coordinate their activities with multiple issues over time; less effective crews traded one problem for another. More effective crews were sensitive to the interactions between multiple threads involved in the incident; less effective crews tended to simplify the situations they faced and were less sensitive to the constraints of the particular context they faced. Less effective crews "were controlled by the task demands" and did not look ahead or prepare for what would come next. As a result, they were more likely to run out of time or encounter other cascading problems. Interestingly, there were written procedures for each of the problems the crews faced. The cognitive work associated with managing multiple threads of activity goes beyond the activities needed to merely follow the rules.

This study illustrates how breakdowns in attentional control result from how task demands human abilities to shift and focus attention in a changing task world (Gilson, 1995).

Failures to Revise Situation Assessments: Fixation or Cognitive Lockup

Diagnostic problems fraught with inherent uncertainties are common, especially when evidence arrives over time and situations can change. Incidents rarely spring full blown and complete; rather incidents evolve. Practitioners make provisional assessments and form expectancies based on partial and uncertain data. These assessments are incrementally updated and revised as more evidence comes in. Furthermore, situation assessment and plan formulation are not distinct sequential stages, but rather they are closely interwoven processes with partial and provisional plan development and feedback leading to revised situation assessments (Woods, 1994).

As a result, it may be necessary for practitioners to entertain and evaluate what turn out later to be erroneous assessments. Problems arise when the revision process breaks down and the practitioner becomes fixated on an erroneous assessment, missing, discounting, or re-interpreting discrepant evidence (e.g. De Keyser & Woods, 1990; Gaba & DeAnda, 1989; Johnson et al., 1981, 1988). These *failures to revise* situation assessment as new evidence comes in have been referred to as functional fixations, cognitive lockup and cognitive hysteresis. The operational teams involved in several major accidents (e.g. the one on Three Mile Island) seem to have exhibited this pattern of behavior (Woods et al., 1987).

In cases of fixation, the initial situation assessment tends to be appropriate, in the sense of being consistent with the partial information available at that early stage of the incident. As the incident evolves, however, people fail to revise their assessments in response to new evidence, evidence that indicates an evolution away from the expected path. The practitioners become fixated on the old assessment and fail to revise their situation assessment and plans in a manner appropriate to the data now present in their world. Thus, a *fixation* occurs when practitioners fail to revise their situation assessment or course of action and maintain an inappropriate judgment or action *in the face of opportunities to revise*. Thus, fixations represent breakdowns in the process of error detection and recovery where people discount discrepant evidence and fail to keep up with new evidence or a changing situation.

Several criteria need to be met in order to describe an event as a fixation. One critical feature is that there is some form of *persistence* over time in the behavior of the fixated person or team. Second, opportunities to revise are cues, available or potentially available to the practitioners, that could have started the revision process if observed and interpreted properly. In part, this feature distinguishes fixations from simple cases of inexperience, lack of knowledge, or other problems that impair error detection and recovery. The basic defining characteristic of fixations is that the immediate problem-solving context has biased the practitioners' mindset in some direction inappropriately. In naturally occurring problems, the context in which the incident occurs and the way the incident evolves activates certain kinds of knowledge as relevant to the evolving incident. This knowledge, in turn, affects how new incoming information is interpreted – a framing effect. After the fact or after the correct diagnosis has been pointed out, the solution seems obvious, even to the fixated person or team.

There are certain types of problems that may encourage fixations by mimicking other situations, in effect, leading practitioners down a *garden path* (Johnson et al., 1988; Johnson, Jamal & Berryman, 1991; Johnson, Grazioli, Jamal & Zualkernan, 1992; Roth, Woods & Pople, 1992). In garden path problems "early cues strongly suggest [plausible but] incorrect answers, and later, usually weaker cues suggest answers that are correct" (Johnson, Moen & Thompson, 1988). It is important to point out that the erroneous assessments resulting from being led down the garden path are not due to knowledge factors. Rather, they seem to occur because "a problem-solving process that works most of the time is applied to a class of problems for which it is not well suited" (Johnson et al., 1988). This notion of garden path situations is important because it identifies a task genotype (Hollnagel, 1993) in which people become susceptible to fixations. The problems that occur are best attributed to the interaction of particular environmental (task) features and the heuristics people apply (local rationality given difficult problems and limited resources), rather than to a generic weakness in the strategies used. The way that a problem presents itself to practitioners may make it very easy to entertain plausible but in fact erroneous possibilities.

Fixation may represent the downside of normally efficient and reliable cognitive processes given the cognitive demands of dynamic situations and cases where diagnosis and response happen in parallel (Woods, 1994). It is clear that in demanding situations where the state of the monitored process is changing rapidly, there is a potential conflict or tradeoff between the need to revise the situation assessment and the need to maintain coherence. Not every change is important; not every signal is meaningful. The practitioner whose attention is constantly shifting from one item to another may not be able to formulate a complete and coherent picture of the state of the system (thematic vagabonding in Dorner, 1983). Conversely, the practitioner whose attention does not shift may miss cues and data that are critical to updating the situation assessment. This latter condition may lead to fixation.

Given the kinds of cognitive processes that seem to be involved in fixation, there are a variety of techniques that, in principle, may reduce this form of breakdown. Data on successful and unsuccessful revision of erroneous situation assessments show that it usually takes a person with a fresh point of view on the situation to break a team or individual out of a fixation (Woods et al., 1987). Note that this result reveals a distributed, multi-agent component to cognition at work. Thus, one can change the architecture of the distributed system to try to ensure a fresh point of view, i.e. one that is unbiased by the immediate context. Another approach is to try to develop distributed system architectures where one person or group criticizes the assessments developed by the remainder of the group (e.g. a devil's advocate team member as in Schwenk & Cosier, 1980). A third direction is predicated on the fact that poor feedback about the state and behavior of the monitored process, especially related to goal achievement, is often implicated in fixations and failures to revise. Thus, one can provide practitioners with new *kinds* of representations about what is going on in the monitored process (see Woods et al., 1987, for examples from nuclear power which tried this in response to the Three Mile Island accident).

Interacting Goals

Another set of factors that effect cognition at work is strategic in nature. People have to make tradeoffs between different but interacting or conflicting goals, between values or costs placed on different possible outcomes or courses of action, or between the risks of different errors. They must make these tradeoffs while facing irreducible uncertainty, risk, and the pressure of limited resources (e.g. time pressure; opportunity costs). One may think of these tradeoffs in terms of simplistic global examples, such as safety versus economy. Tradeoffs also occur on other kinds of dimensions. In responding to an anomaly in domains such as aircraft or space vehicles, for example, there is a tradeoff with respect to when to commit to a course of action. Practitioners have to decide whether to take corrective action early in the course of an incident with limited information, to delay the response and wait for more data to come in, to search for additional findings, or to ponder additional alternative hypotheses.

Practitioners also trade off between following operational rules or taking action based on reasoning about the case itself (cf. Woods et al., 1987). Do the standard rules apply to this particular situation when some additional factor is present that complicates the textbook scenario? Should we adapt the standard plans or should we stick with them regardless of the special circumstances?

Strategic tradeoffs can also involve coordination among people and machine agents in the distributed human–machine cognitive system (Woods et al., 1994, chapter 4). A machine expert recommends a particular diagnosis or action, but what if your own evaluation is different? What is enough evidence that the machine is wrong to justify disregarding the machine expert's evaluation and proceeding on your own evaluation of the situation?

Criterion setting on these different tradeoffs may not always be a conscious process or an explicit decision made by individuals. The criterion adopted may be an emergent property of systems of people, either small groups or larger organizations. The criterion may be fairly labile and susceptible to influence or relatively stable and difficult to change. The tradeoffs may create explicit choice points for practitioners embedded in an evolving situation, or may influence performance indirectly, for example by shifting a team's mindset in a particular direction (e.g. Layton, Smith & McCoy, 1994).

Goal Conflicts

Multiple goals are simultaneously relevant in actual fields of practice. Depending on the particular circumstances in effect in a particular situation, the means to influence these multiple goals will interact, potentially producing conflicts between different goals. Expertise consists, in part, of being able to negotiate among interacting goals by selecting or constructing the means to satisfy all sufficiently or by deciding which goals to focus on and which goals to relax or sacrifice in a particular context.

However, practitioners may fail to meet this cognitive demand adequately. An adequate analysis of human performance and the potential for error requires explicit description of the interacting goals, the tradeoffs being made, and the pressures present that shift the operating points for these tradeoffs (Cook & Woods, 1994).

Finding potential conflicts, assessing their impact, and developing robust strategies may be quite difficult. Consider the anesthesiologist. Practitioners' highest level goal (and the one most often explicitly acknowledged) is to protect patient safety. But that is not the only goal. There are other goals, some of which are less explicitly articulated. These goals include reducing costs, avoiding actions that would increase the likelihood of being sued, maintaining good relations with the surgical service, maintaining resource elasticity to allow for handling unexpected emergencies, and others.

In a given circumstance, the relationships between these goals can produce conflicts. In the daily routine, for example, maximizing patient safety and avoiding lawsuits create the need to maximize information about the patient through preoperative workup. The anesthetist may find some hint of a potentially problematic condition and consider further tests that may incur costs, risks to the patient, and a delay of surgery. The cost-reduction goal provides an incentive for a minimal preoperative workup and the use of same-day surgery. This conflicts with the other goals. The anesthetist may be squeezed in this conflict – gathering the additional information, which in the end may not reveal anything important, will cause a delay of surgery and decrease throughput.

Given these external pressures, some medical practitioners will not follow up hints about some aspect of the patient's history because to do so would impact the usual practices relative to throughput and economic goals. However, failing to acquire the information may reduce the ill-defined margin of safety and, in a specific case, the omission may turn out to be a contributor to an incident or accident. Other practitioners will adopt a conservative stance and order tests for minor indications even though the yield is low. This may affect the day's surgical schedule, the hospital's and the surgeons' economic goals, and the anesthesiologist's relationship with the surgeons. In either case, the nature of the goals and pressures on the practitioner are seldom made explicit and rarely examined critically.

Analyses of past disasters frequently find that goal conflicts played a role in the accident evolution, especially when they place practitioners in double binds. In one tragic aviation disaster, the Dryden Ontario crash (Moshansky, 1992), several different organizational pressures to meet economic goals, along with organizational decisions to reduce resources, created a situation which placed a pilot in a double bind. Demand for the flight created a situation where the flight either could carry all of the passengers awaiting transport or carry enough fuel to reach their destination, but not both (no other aircraft was available to meet demand). The captain decided to offload passengers and make a direct trip; the company (a regional carrier) overruled him, deciding to offload fuel and make a refueling stop at Dryden on the way to their destination.

After landing at Dryden weather was within nominal standards but a freezing rain had begun. Any delays increased the probability of wing ice. After landing, the crew had to keep engines running (a "hot" fuel) or they would have been unable to restart them, (a) because the aircraft had departed with an inoperative auxiliary power unit; and (b) due to the lack of equipment to restart jet engines at this airport. However, deicing is not permitted with an engine running because of other safety concerns. Several factors led to delays (e.g. they delayed on the ramp waiting for another aircraft to land). The captain attempted to take off, and the aircraft crashed because its wings were contaminated with ice.

The immediate reaction was that a pilot error was responsible. In hindsight, there were obvious threats which it appeared the pilot recklessly disregarded. However, this view drastically oversimplified the situation the pilot faced. The actual accident investigation went deeper and found that organizational factors and specific circumstances placed the pilot in a goal conflict and double bind (note the report needed four volumes to lay out all of the different organizational factors and how they created the latent conditions for this accident).

One critical part of the investigation was understanding the situation from the point of view of the practitioners in the situation. When the investigators reconstructed the view of the evolving situation from the vantage point of a pilot, the captain's dilemmas became clear. Deciding not to take off would strand a full plane of passengers, disrupt schedules, and lose money for the carrier. Such a decision would be regarded as an economic failure with potential sanctions for the pilot. On the other hand, the means to accommodate the interacting constraints of the weather threat and refueling process were not available due to organizational choices not to invest in or cut back on equipment at peripheral airports such as

Dryden. The air carrier was new to jet service and provided minimal support for the flight crew in terms of guidance or from company dispatch.

The accident investigation identified multiple, latent organizational factors which created the dilemmas. These included factors at the levels of:

- the regional carrier – e.g. new to jet operations but with inadequate investment in expertise and infrastructure to support these operations
- the relationship between the regional carrier and the parent carrier – e.g. the parent organization distanced itself from operations and safety issues in its newly acquired subsidiary; the regional carrier minimized communication to preserve its autonomy
- regulatory oversight – e.g. breakdowns due to increased workload in a deregulated environment coupled with major staff and budget cuts.

As in this case, constraints imposed by organizational or social context can create or exacerbate competition between goals. Organizational pressures that generated competition between goals were an important factor in the breakdown of safety barriers in the system for transporting oil through Prince William Sound that preceded the *Exxon Valdez* disaster (National Transportation Safety Board, 1990).

It should not be thought that the organizational goals are necessarily simply the written policies and procedures of the institution. Indeed, the messages received by practitioners about the nature of the institution's goals may be quite different from those that management acknowledges. How the organization reacts to incidents, near misses and failures can send sharp end practitioners potent if implicit messages about how to tradeoff conflicting goals (Rochlin et al., 1987). These covert factors are especially insidious because they affect behavior and yet are unacknowledged. For example, the Navy sent an implicit but very clear message to its commanders by the differential treatment it accorded to the commander of the *Stark* following that incident (US House of Representatives Committee on Armed Services, 1987) as opposed to the *Vincennes* following that incident (US Department of Defense, 1988).

Goal conflicts also can arise from intrinsic characteristics of the field of activity. An example from cardiac anesthesiology is the conflict between the desirability of a high blood pressure to improve cardiac perfusion (oxygen supply to the heart muscle) and a low one to reduce cardiac work. The blood pressure target adopted by the anesthetist to balance this tradeoff depends in part on the practitioner's strategy, the nature of the patient, the kind of surgical procedure, anticipating potential risks (e.g. the risk of major bleeding), and the negotiations between different people in the operating room team (e.g. the surgeon who would like the blood pressure kept low to limit the blood loss at the surgical site).

Because local rationality revolves around how people pursue their goals, understanding performance at the sharp end depends on tracing interacting multiple goals and how they produce tradeoffs, dilemmas, and double binds. In this process the investigator needs to understand how the tradeoffs produced by interacting goals are usually resolved. Practitioners in a field of activity may usually apply standard routines without deliberating on the nature of a dilemma, or they may work explicitly to find ways to balance the competing demands. The typical strategies for resolving tradeoffs, dilemmas and interacting goals, whether implicit in organizational practices or explicitly developed by practitioners, may be:

- robust – work well across a wide range of circumstance but still not guarantee a successful outcome
- brittle – work well under a limited set of conditions but break down when circumstances create situations outside the boundary conditions
- poor – very vulnerable to breakdown.

Understanding where and how goal conflicts can arise is a first step. Organizations can then examine how to improve strategies for handling these conflicts, even though ultimately there may be no algorithmic methods that can guarantee successful outcomes in all cases.

Problem Demands

In the above discussion, one should notice that it is difficult to examine cognition at work without also speaking of the demands that situations place on individuals, teams, and more distributed, coordinated activity (Rasmussen, 1986). The concept of local rationality captures this idea that cognitive activity needs to be considered in light of the *demands* placed on practitioners by characteristics of the incidents and problems that occur. These problem demands vary in type and degree. One incident may present itself as a textbook version of a well-practiced plan while another may occur accompanied by several complicating factors which together create a more substantive challenge to practitioners. One case may be straightforward to diagnose, while another may represent a garden path problem (e.g. Johnson et al., 1988; Roth et al., 1992). One case may be straightforward because a single response will simultaneously satisfy the multiple relevant goals, while another may present a dilemma because multiple important goals conflict.

Understanding the kinds of problem demands that can arise in a field of activity can reveal a great deal about the knowledge activation, attentional control or handling of multiple goals that is needed for successful performance. In other words, problem demands shape the cognitive activities of any agent or set of agents who might confront that incident. This perspective implies that one must consider what features of domain incidents and situations increase problem demands (coupling; escalation; time pressure; sources of variability, and in particular unanticipated variability; variations in tempo, including rhythms of self-paced and event-driven activity; conflicting goals; uncertainty). The expression of expertise and error, then, is governed by the interplay of problem demands inherent in the field of activity and the resources available to bring knowledge to bear in pursuit of the critical goals. Analyses of the potential for failure look for mismatches in this demand–resource relationship (Rasmussen, 1986). Two examples of demand factors are coupling and escalation.

Coupling

One demand factor that affects the kinds of problems that arise is the degree of coupling in the underlying system (Perrow, 1984). Increasing the coupling in a system increases the physical and functional interconnections between parts (Rasmussen, 1986). This has a variety of consequences but among them are effects at a distance, cascades of disturbances, side effects of actions (Woods, 1994). Several results follow from the fact that apparently distant parts are coupled.

- Practitioners must master new knowledge demands, e.g. knowing how different parts of the system interact physically or functionally. Greater investments will be required to avoid buggy, incomplete or oversimplified models. However, many of these interconnections will be relevant only under special circumstances. The potential for inert knowledge may go up.
- An action or a fault may influence a part of the system that seems distant from the area of focus. This complicates the diagnostic search process, for example, the ability to discriminate red herrings from important "distant" indications will be more difficult (e.g. the problem in Roth et al., 1992). In hindsight the relevance of such distant indications will be crystal clear, while from a practitioners' perspective the demand is to discriminate irrelevant data from the critical findings to focus on.
- A single action will have multiple effects. Some of these will be the intended or main effects while others will be "side" effects. Missing side-effects in diagnosis, planning, and adapting plans in progress to cope with new events is a very common form of failure in highly coupled systems.
- A fault will produce multiple disturbances and these disturbances will cascade along the lines of physical and functional interconnection in the underlying monitored process. This also complicates diagnostic search (evidence will come in over time), but, importantly, it will increase the tempo of operations.

Escalation

A related demand factor is phenomenon of escalation which captures a fundamental correlation between the situation, the cognitive demands, and the penalties for poor human–machine interaction (Woods et al., 1994; Woods & Patterson, in press): the greater the trouble in the underlying process or the higher the tempo of operations, the greater the information processing activities required to cope with the trouble or pace of activities.

As situations diverge from routine or textbook, the tempo of operations escalates and the cognitive and cooperative work needed to cope with the anomalous situation escalates as well. As a result, demands for monitoring, attentional control, information gathering, and communication among team members (including human–machine communication) all tend to go up with the unusualness, tempo, and criticality of situations. More knowledge and more specialist knowledge will need to be brought to bear as an incident evolves and escalates. This occurs through the technological and organizational structures used to access knowledge stored in different systems, places, or people. More lines of activity and thought will arise and need to be coordinated (Woods, 1994). The potential for goals to interact and conflict will go up. Focusing on the most critical goals may be needed to make tradeoff decisions. Plans will need to be put into effect to cope with the anomalous situation, but some practitioners will need to evaluate how well contingency plans match the actual circumstances or how to adapt them to the specific context.

If there are workload or other burdens associated with using a computer interface or with interacting with an autonomous or intelligent machine agent, these burdens tend to be concentrated at the very times when the practitioner can least afford new tasks, new memory demands, or diversions of his or her attention away from the job at hand to the interface *per se* (e.g. the case of cockpit automation; Billings, 1996). This means the penalties for poor design will be visible only in beyond-textbook situations. Since the system will seem to function well much of the time, breakdowns in higher tempo situations will seem mysterious after-the-fact and attributed to "pilot error" (see Woods & Sarter, in press, for this process in the case of cockpit automation).

COGNITION IN CONTEXT

While many of the factors discussed in the previous sections appear to be aspects of an individual's cognitive processes – i.e. knowledge organization, mental model, attention, judgment under uncertainty – we quickly find in work environments that these cognitive activities occur in the context of other practitioners, supported by artifacts of various types, and framed by the demands of the organization (Moray, 1999, this volume). While research on errors often began by considering the cognition of individuals, investigations quickly revealed one had to adopt a broader focus. For example, the more researchers have looked at success and failure in complex work settings, the more they have realized that a critical part of the story is how resources and constraints provided by the blunt end shape and influence the behavior of the people at the sharp end (Rochlin et al., 1987; Hirschhorn, 1993; Reason, 1998).

When investigators studied cognition at work, whether on flightdecks of commercial jet airliners, in control centers that manage space missions, in surgical operating rooms, in control rooms that manage chemical or energy processes, in control centers that monitor telecommunication networks, or in many other fields of human activity, first, they did not find cognitive activity isolated in a single individual, but rather they saw cognitive activity distributed across multiple agents (Hutchins, 1995; Resnick, Levine & Teasley, 1991). Second, they did not see cognitive activity separated in a thoughtful individual, but rather as a part of a stream of activity (Klein, Orasanu & Calderwood, 1993). Third, they saw these sets of active practitioners embedded in larger group, professional, organizational, or institutional contexts which constrain their activities, set up rewards and punishments, define goals which are not always consistent, and provide resources (e.g. Hutchins, 1990). Moments of individual cognition punctuated this larger flow, and they were set up and conditioned by the larger system and communities of practice in which that individual was embedded.

Fourth, they observed phases of activity with transitions and evolution. Cognitive and physical activity varied in tempo, with periods of lower activity and more self-paced tasks interspersed with busy, externally paced operations where task performance was more critical. These higher tempo situations created greater need for cognitive work and at the same time often created greater constraints on cognitive activity (e.g. time pressure, uncertainty, exceptional circumstances, failures, and their associated hazards). They observed that there are multiple consequences at stake for the individuals, groups, and organizations involved in the field of activity or affected by that field of activity – such as economic, personal, and safety goals.

Fifth, they noticed that tools of all types are everywhere. Almost all activity was aided by external artifacts, some fashioned from traditional technologies and many built in the computer medium (Norman, 1993). More in-depth observation revealed that the computer technology was often poorly adapted to the needs of the practitioner. The computer technology used was clumsy in that the computer-based systems made new demands on the practitioner, demands that tended to congregate at the higher tempo or higher criticality periods. Close observation revealed that people and systems of people (operators, designers, regulators, etc.) adapted their tools and their activities continuously to respond to indications of trouble or to meet new demands. Furthermore, new machines were not used as the designers intended, but were shaped by practitioners to the contingencies of the field of activity in a locally pragmatic way (Woods et al., 1994, ch. 5).

These kinds of observations about cognition at work have led some to propose that cognition can be seen as fundamentally public and shared, distributed across agents, distributed between external artifacts and internal strategies, embedded in a larger context that partially governs the meanings that are made out of events (Hutchins, 1995; Norman, 1993; Winograd & Flores, 1987). Understanding cognition, then, depends as much on studying the context in which cognition is embedded and the larger distributed system of artifacts and multiple agents, as on studying what goes on between the ears – a distributed cognitive system perspective (Hutchins, 1995).

Hughes, Randall & Shapiro (1992) illustrate this distributed cognitive system viewpoint in their studies of the UK air traffic control system and the reliability of this system:

> If one looks to see what constitutes this reliability, it cannot be found in any single element of the system. It is certainly not to be found in the equipment . . . for a period of several months during our field work it was failing regularly. . . . Nor is it to be found in the rules and procedures, which are a resource for safe operation but which can never cover every circumstance and condition. Nor is it to be found in the personnel who, though very highly skilled, motivated, and dedicated, are as prone as people everywhere to human error. Rather we believe it is to be found in the cooperative activities of controllers across the "totality" of the system, and in particular in the way that it enforces the active engagement of controllers, chiefs, and assistants with the material they are using and with each other. (Hughes, Randall & Shapiro, 1992, p. 5)

Success and failure belong to the larger operational system and not simply to an individual. Failure involves breakdowns in cognitive activities which are distributed across multiple practitioners and influenced by the artifacts used by those practitioners. This is perhaps best illustrated in processes of error detection and recovery which play a key role in determining system reliability in practice. In most domains, recovery involves the interaction of multiple people cross-stimulating and cross-checking each other (e.g. see Billings, 1996, for aviation; Rochlin et al., 1987, for air carrier operations; also see Seifert & Hutchins, 1992).

HINDSIGHT AND COGNITIVE FACTORS

Now that we have explored some of the factors that affect human performance, the way in which our knowledge of outcome biases attributions about causes of accidents becomes clearer. With knowledge of outcome, reviewers oversimplify the situation faced by practitioners in context (Woods et al., 1994). First, reviewers, after-the-fact, assume that if people demonstrate knowledge in some context, then that knowledge should be available in all contexts. However, research on human performance shows that calling to mind knowledge is a significant cognitive process. Education research has focused extensively on the problem of inert knowledge – knowledge that can be demonstrated in one context (e.g. test exercises) is not activated in other contexts where it is relevant (e.g. ill-structured problems). Inert knowledge consists of isolated facts that are disconnected from how the knowledge can be used to accomplish some purpose. This research emphasizes the need to "conditionalize" knowledge to its use in different contexts as a fundamental training strategy.

Second, reviewers, after-the-fact, assume that if data are physically available, then their significance should be appreciated in all contexts. Many accident reports have a statement to the effect that all of the data relevant in hindsight were physically available to the people at the sharp end, but the people did not find and interpret the right data at the right time. Hindsight biases reviewers, blocking from view all of the processes associated with forming and shifting mindset as new events occur, the attentional demands of the situation, and the factors that led to a breakdown in synchronizing mindset in a changing world. Instead of seeing the mindset related factors and how they shape human performance, reviewers in hindsight are baffled by the practitioners' inability to see what is obvious to all after-the-fact. In this explanatory vacuum reviewers in hindsight fall back on other explanations, for example, a motivational or effort factor (the people involved in an incident didn't "try hard enough") and try to improve things by a carrot and stick approach of exhortations to try harder combined with punishments for failure.

Third, since reviewers after-the-fact know which goal was the most critical, they assume that this should have been obvious to the practitioners working before-the-fact. However, this ignores the multiple interacting goals that are always present in systems under resource pressure, goals that sometimes co-exist peacefully but which sometimes work against each other. If practitioner actions that are shaped by a goal conflict contribute to a bad outcome in a specific case, then it is easy for post-incident evaluations to say that a "human error" occurred – e.g. the practitioners should have delayed the surgical procedure to investigate the hint. The role of the goal conflict may never be noted; therefore, post-accident changes cannot address critical contributors, factors that can contribute to other incidents.

To evaluate the behavior of the practitioners involved in an incident, it is important to elucidate the relevant goals, the interactions among these goals, and the factors that influence how practitioners make tradeoffs in particular situations. The role of these factors is often missed in evaluations of the behavior of practitioners. As a result, it is easy for organizations to produce what appear to be solutions that in fact exacerbate conflict between goals rather than help practitioners handle goal conflicts in context. In part, this occurs because it is difficult for many organizations (particularly in regulated industries) to admit that goal conflicts and tradeoff decisions exist. However distasteful to admit or whatever public relations problems it creates, denying the existence of goal interactions does not make such conflicts disappear and is likely to make them even tougher to handle when they are relevant to a particular incident.

Debiasing and Studying Human Error

Hindsight biases fundamentally undermine our ability to understand the factors that influenced practitioner behavior. Given knowledge of outcome, reviewers will tend to *oversimplify* the problem-solving situation that was actually faced by the practitioner. The dilemmas, the uncertainties, the tradeoffs, the attentional demands, and double binds faced by practitioners may be missed or under-emphasized when an incident is viewed in hindsight. Typically, hindsight biases make it seem that participants failed to account for information or conditions that "should have been obvious" or behaved in ways that were inconsistent with the (now known to be) significant information. Possessing knowledge of the outcome, because of hindsight biases, trivializes the situation confronting the practitioner, who cannot know the outcome before-the-fact, and makes the "correct" choice seem crystal clear.

Because hindsight biases mask the real dilemmas, uncertainties, and demands practitioners confront, the result is a distorted view of the factors contributing to the incident or accident. In this vacuum, we can only see human performance after an accident or near miss as irrational, willing disregard (for what is now obvious to us and to them), or even diabolical. This seems to support the belief that human error often is the cause of an accident and that this judgment provides a satisfactory closure to the accident. When the label human error ends the investigation, the only response left is to search for the culprits and once they have been identified, remove them from practice, provide remedial training, replace them with technology, while new policies and procedures can be issued to keep other practitioners in line.

The difference between these everyday or "folk" reactions to failure and investigations of the factors that influence human performance is that researchers see the label human error as the starting point for investigations and use methods designed to remove hindsight biases to see better the factors that influenced the behavior of the people in the situation. When this is done, from Bessel's observations to Fitts' studies to today's investigations of computerized cockpits and other domains, the results identify the multiple deeper factors that lead to erroneous actions and assessments. These deeper factors will still be present even if the people associated with the failure are removed from practice. The vulnerabilities remain despite injunctions for practitioners to be more careful in the future. The injunctions or punishments that follow the accident may even exacerbate some of the vulnerabilities resident in the larger system.

We always can look back at people, episodes or cases in any system and using one or another standard identify any number of "errors," that is, violations of that standard. The key to safety is not minimizing or eradicating an infection of error (Rasmussen, 1990). Effective, robust, "high reliability" systems are able to recognize trouble before negative consequences occur. This means that processes involved in detecting that a situation is heading towards trouble and re-directing the situation away from a poor outcome is an important part of human performance related to safety versus failure. Evidence of difficulties, problems, incidents is an important form of information about the organization and operational system that is necessary for adaptive and constructive change (Reason, 1997). Studying cognitive factors, coordinative activities, and organizational constraints relative to problems demands in a particular domain is a crucial part of generating this base of information. Successful, "high reliability" organizations value, encourage, and generate such flows of information without waiting for accidents to occur (Rochlin, LaPorte & Roberts, 1987).

SUMMARY

Considering the topic "human error" quickly led us to two different perspectives.

"Human error" in one sense is a label invoked by stakeholders after-the-fact in a psychological and social process of causal attribution. Psychologists and others have studied these processes and in particular found a pernicious influence of knowledge of outcome, such as outcome and hindsight biases, that obscures the factors that shape human performance. Studying "human error" from this perspective is the study of how stakeholders react to failure.

"Human error" in another sense refers to the processes that lead up to success and failure (or potential failures) of a *system*. Researchers, using techniques to escape the hindsight bias, have studied such work domains and the factors that influence the performance of the people who work in those systems. In this chapter, we have reviewed a portion of the results using one heuristic structure: knowledge in context, mindset, and goal conflicts.

However, there is an irony in these research results. In focusing on cognitive factors behind the label human error, processes that would seem to reside only within individuals, researchers instead found:

- a critical role for understanding the demands posed by problems, e.g. coupling and escalation (Perrow, 1984; Rasmussen, 1986)

- that artifacts shape cognition (Woods et al., 1994, ch. 5; Zhang & Norman, 1994)
- that coordination across practitioners is an essential component of success (Hutchins, 1995; Resnick, Levine & Teasley, 1991)
- that organizations create or exacerbate constraints on sharp end practitioners (Reason, 1998; Rochlin et al., 1987).

When one investigates the factors that produce "human error" in actual work environments, our view of cognition expands. "Cognition in the wild," as Hutchins (1995) puts it, is distributed across people, across people and machines, and constrained by context.

REFERENCES

Baron, J. & Hershey, J. (1988). Outcome bias in decision evaluation. *Journal of Personality and Social Psychology*, 54, 569–79.

Billings, C. E. (1996). *Aviation Automation: the Search for a Human-Centered Approach*. Hillsdale, NJ: Lawrence Erlbaum.

Boring, E. G. (1950). *A History of Experimental Psychology* (2nd edn). New York: Appleton-Century-Crofts.

Bransford, J., Sherwood, R., Vye, N. & Rieser, J. (1986). Teaching and problem solving: research foundations. *American Psychologist*, 41, 1078–89.

Byrne, M. D. & Bovair, S. (1997). A working memory model of a common procedural error. *Cognitive Science*, 21, 31–61.

Caplan, R., Posner, K. & Cheney, F. (1991). Effect of outcome on physician judgments of appropriateness of care. *Journal of the American Medical Association*, 265, 1957–60.

Chi, M. T. H., Glaser, R. & Farr, M. (1988). *The Nature Of Expertise*. Hillsdale, NJ: Lawrence Erlbaum.

Cook, R. I. & Woods, D. D. (1994). Operating at the "sharp end": the complexity of human error. In M. S. Bogner (Ed.), *Human Error in Medicine*. Hillsdale, NJ: Lawrence Erlbaum.

De Keyser, V. & Woods, D. D. (1990). Fixation errors: failures to revise situation assessment in dynamic and risky systems. In A. G. Colombo & A. Saiz de Bustamante (Eds), *System Reliability Assessment*. The Netherlands: Kluwer Academic, 231–51.

Dorner, D. (1983). Heuristics and cognition in complex systems. In R. Groner, M. Groner & W. F. Bischof (Eds), *Methods of Heuristics*. Hillsdale NJ: Lawrence Erlbaum.

Durso, F. T. & Gronlund, S. D. (1999). Situation awareness. In F. T. Durso, R. S. Nickerson, R. W. Schvaneveldt, S. T. Dumais, D. S. Lindsay & M. T. H. Chi (Eds), *Handbook of Applied Cognition* (chapter 10). Chichester: John Wiley.

Feltovich, P. J., Ford, K. M. & Hoffman, R. R. (1997). *Expertise in Context*. Cambridge, MA: MIT Press.

Feltovich, P. J., Spiro, R. J. & Coulson, R. (1989). The nature of conceptual understanding in biomedicine: the deep structure of complex ideas and the development of misconceptions. In D. Evans & V. Patel (Eds), *Cognitive Science In Medicine: Biomedical Modeling*. Cambridge, MA: MIT Press.

Feltovich, P. J., Spiro, R. J. & Coulson, R. (1993). Learning, teaching and testing for complex conceptual understanding. In N. Fredericksen, R. Mislevy and I. Bejar (Eds), *Test Theory For A New Generation Of Tests*. Hillsdale, NJ: Lawrence Erlbaum.

Feltovich, P. J., Spiro, R. J. & Coulson, R. (1997). Issues of expert flexibility in contexts characterized by complexity and change. In P. J. Feltovich, K. M. Ford & R. R. Hoffman (Eds), *Expertise in Context*. Cambridge, MA: MIT Press.

Fischer, U., Orasanu, J. M. & Montvalo, M. (1993). Efficient decision strategies on the flight deck. In *Proceedings of the Seventh International Symposium on Aviation Psychology*. Columbus, OH. April.

Fischhoff, B. (1975). Hindsight ≠ foresight: the effect of outcome knowledge on judgment under uncertainty. *Journal of Experimental Psychology: Human Perception and Performance*, 1, 288–99.

Fischhoff, B. (1982). For those condemned to study the past: heuristics and biases in hindsight. In D. Kahneman, P. Slovic & A. Tversky (Eds), *Judgment under Uncertainty: Heuristics and Biases*. Cambridge, MA: Cambridge University Press.

Fitts, P. M. & Jones, R. E. (1947). Analysis of factors contributing to 460 "pilot-error" experiences in operating aircraft controls (Memorandum Report TSEAA-694-12). Wright Field, OH: US Air Force Air Materiel Command, Aero Medical Laboratory.

Gaba, D. M. & DeAnda, A. (1989). The response of anesthesia trainees to simulated critical incidents. *Anesthesia and Analgesia*, 68, 444–51.

Gentner, D. & Stevens, A. L. (Eds) (1983). *Mental Models*. Hillsdale, NJ: Lawrence Erlbaum.

Getty, D. J., Swets, J. A., Pickett, R. M. & Gonthier, D. (1995). System operator response to warnings of danger: a laboratory investigation of the effects of predictive value of a warning on human response time. *Journal of Experimental Psychology: Applied*, 1, 19–33.

Gilson, R. D. (Ed.) (1995). Special Section on Situation Awareness. *Human Factors*, 37, 3–157.

Gopher, D. (1991). The skill of attention control: acquisition and execution of attention strategies. In *Attention and Performance XIV*. Hillsdale, NJ: Lawrence Erlbaum.

Hilton, D. (1990). Conversational processes and causal explanation. *Psychological Bulletin*, 197, 65–81.

Hirschhorn, L. (1993). Hierarchy vs. bureaucracy: the case of a nuclear reactor. In K. H. Roberts (Ed.), *New Challenges To Understanding Organizations*. New York: Macmillan.

Hollnagel, E. (1993). *Human Reliability Analysis: Context and Control*. London: Academic Press.

Hughes, J., Randall, D. & Shapiro, D. (1992). Faltering from ethnography to design. *Computer Supported Cooperative Work (CSCW) Proceedings*, November, 1–8.

Hutchins, E. (1990). The technology of team navigation. In J. Galegher, R. Kraut & C. Egido (Eds), *Intellectual Teamwork: Social and Technical Bases of Cooperative Work*. Hillsdale, NJ: Lawrence Erlbaum.

Hutchins, E. (1995). *Cognition in the Wild*. Cambridge, MA: MIT Press.

Jager Adams, M., Tenney, Y. J. & Pew, R. W. (1995). Situation awareness and the cognitive management of complex systems. *Human Factors*, 37, 85–104.

James, W. (1850). *The Principles of Psychology*. New York: H. Holt and Company.

Johnson, P. E., Duran, A. S., Hassebrock, F., Moller, J., Prietula, M., Feltovich, P. J. & Swanson, D. B. (1981). Expertise and error in diagnostic reasoning. *Cognitive Science*, 5, 235–83.

Johnson, P. E., Grazioli, S., Jamal, K. & Zualkernan, I. (1992). Success and failure in expert reasoning. *Organizational Behavior and Human Decision Processes*, 53, 173–203.

Johnson, P. E., Jamal, K. & Berryman, R. G. (1991). Effects of framing on auditor decisions. *Organizational Behavior and Human Decision Processes*, 50, 75–105.

Johnson, P. E., Moen, J. B. & Thompson, W. B. (1988). Garden path errors in diagnostic reasoning. In L. Bolec & M. J. Coombs (Eds), *Expert System Applications*. New York: Springer-Verlag.

Kelley, H. H. (1973). The process of causal attribution. *American Psychologist*, 28, 107–28.

Klein, G. A. (1998). *Sources of Power: How People Make Decisions*. Cambridge, MA: MIT Press.

Klein, G. A., Orasanu, J. & Calderwood, R. (Eds) (1993). *Decision Making in Action: Models and Methods*. Norwood, NJ: Ablex.

LaBerge, D. (1995). *Attentional Processing: the Brain's Art of Mindfulness*. Cambridge, MA: Harvard University Press.

Layton, C., Smith, P. & McCoy, E. (1994). Design of a cooperative problem-solving system for enroute flight planning: an empirical evaluation. *Human Factors*, 36, 94–119.
Lipshitz, R. (1989). "Either a medal or a corporal": the effects of success and failure on the evaluation of decision making and decision makers. *Organizational Behavior and Human Decision Processes*, 44, 380–95.
Moray, N. (1999). The cognitive psychology and cognitive engineering of industrial systems. In F. T. Durso, R. S. Nickerson, R. W. Schvaneveldt, S. T. Dumais, D. S. Lindsay & M. T. H. Chi (Eds), *Handbook of Applied Cognition* (chapter 8). Chichester: John Wiley.
Moshansky, V. P. (1992). *Final Report of the Commission of Inquiry into the Air Ontario Crash at Dryden, Ontario*. Ottawa: Minister of Supply & Services, Canada.
National Transportation Safety Board (1990). *Marine Accident Report: Grounding of the U.S. Tankship Exxon Valdez on Bligh Reef, Prince William Sound, near Valdez, Alaska, March 24, 1989*. Report no. NTSB/MAT-90/04. Springfield, VA: National Technical Information Service.
Neisser, U. (1976). *Cognition and Reality: Principles and Implications of Cognitive Psychology*. San Francisco, CA: W. H. Freeman.
Newell, A. (1982). The knowledge level. *Artificial Intelligence*, 18, 87–127.
Norman, D. A. (1981). Categorization of action slips. *Psychological Review*, 88, 1–15.
Norman, D. A. (1983). Design rules based on analysis of human error. *Communications of the ACM*, 26, 254–8.
Norman, D. A. (1988). *The Psychology of Everyday Things*. New York, NY: Basic Books.
Norman, D. A. (1993). *Things That Make Us Smart*. Reading, MA: Addison-Wesley.
Patterson, E. S., Watts-Perotti, J. C. & Woods, D. D. (in press). Voice loops as coordination aids in space shuttle mission control. *Computer Supported Cooperative Work*.
Payne, J. W., Bettman, J. R. & Johnson, E. J. (1988). Adaptive strategy selection in decision making. *Journal of Experimental Psychology: Learning, Memory and Cognition*, 14, 534–52.
Payne, J. W., Johnson, E. J., Bettman, J. R. & Coupey, E. (1990). Understanding contingent choice: a computer simulation approach. *IEEE Transactions on Systems, Man, and Cybernetics*, 20, 296–309.
Perkins, D. & Martin, F. (1986). Fragile knowledge and neglected strategies in novice programmers. In E. Soloway & S. Iyengar (Eds), *Empirical Studies of Programmers*. Norwood, NJ: Ablex.
Perrow, C. (1984). *Normal Accidents: Living with High Risk Technologies*. New York: Basic Books.
Rasmussen, J. (1986). *Information Processing and Human–Machine Interaction: an Approach to Cognitive Engineering*. New York: North-Holland.
Rasmussen, J. (1990). The role of error in organizing behavior. *Ergonomics*, 33, 1185–99.
Rasmussen, J., Duncan, K. & Leplat, J. (1987). *New Technology and Human Error*. Chichester: John Wiley.
Reason, J. (1990). *Human Error*. Cambridge: Cambridge University Press.
Reason, J. (1997). *Managing the Risks of Organizational Accidents*. Brookfield, VT: Ashgate Publishing.
Reason, J. & Mycielska, K. (1982). *Absent Minded? The Psychology of Mental Lapses and Everyday Errors*. Englewood Cliffs, NJ: Prentice Hall.
Resnick, L., Levine, J. & Teasley, S. D. (1991). *Perspectives on Socially Shared Cognition*. New York: American Psychological Association.
Roberts, K. H. & Rousseau, D. M. (1989). Research in nearly failure-free, high-reliability organizations: having the bubble. *IEEE Transactions in Engineering Management*, 36, 132–9.
Rochlin, G., LaPorte, T. R. & Roberts, K. H. (1987). The self-designing high reliability organization: aircraft carrier flight operations at sea. *Naval War College Review*, Autumn, 76–90.
Roth, E. M., Woods, D. D. & Pople, H. E. Jr (1992). Cognitive simulation as a tool for cognitive task analysis. *Ergonomics*, 35, 1163–98.

Schwenk, C. & Cosier, R. (1980). Effects of the expert, devil's advocate and dialectical inquiry methods on prediction performance. *Organizational Behavior and Human Decision Processes*, 26.

Seifert, C. M. & Hutchins, E. (1992). Error as opportunity: learning in a cooperative task. *Human–Computer Interaction*, 7, 409–35.

Simon, H. (1957). *Models of Man (Social and Rational)*. New York: John Wiley.

Spiro, R. J., Coulson, R. L., Feltovich, P. J. & Anderson, D. K. (1988). Cognitive flexibility theory: advanced knowledge acquisition in ill-structured domains. *Proceedings of the Tenth Annual Conference of the Cognitive Science Society*. Hillsdale, NJ: Lawrence Erlbaum.

Tasca, L. (1990). The social construction of human error. Unpublished Doctoral Dissertation, State University of New York at Stony Brook, August.

US Department of Defense (1988). *Report of the Formal Investigation into the Circumstances Surrounding the Downing of Iran Air Flight 655 on 3 July 1988*. Washington, DC: Department of Defense.

US House of Representatives Committee on Armed Services (1987). *Report on the Staff Investigation into the Iraqi Attack on the USS Stark*. Springfield, VA: National Technical Information Service.

Webster's New International Dictionary. New York: Merriam.

Weick, K. E. & Roberts, K. H. (1993). Collective mind and organizational reliability: the case of flight operations on an aircraft carrier deck. *Administration Science Quarterly*, 38, 357–81.

Winograd, T. & Flores, F. (1987). *Understanding Computers and Cognition*. Reading, MA: Addison-Wesley.

Woods, D. D. (1994). Cognitive demands and activities in dynamic fault management: abduction and disturbance management. In N. Stanton (Ed.), *Human Factors of Alarm Design*. London: Taylor & Francis.

Woods, D. D. (1995). The alarm problem and directed attention in dynamic fault management. *Ergonomics*, 38 (11), 2371–93.

Woods, D. D., Johannesen, L., Cook, R. I. & Sarter, N. B. (1994). *Behind Human Error: Cognitive Systems, Computers and Hindsight*. Crew Systems Ergonomic Information and Analysis Center, WPAFB, Dayton, OH.

Woods, D. D., O'Brien, J. & Hanes, L. F. (1987). Human factors challenges in process control: the case of nuclear power plants. In G. Salvendy (Ed.), *Handbook of Human Factors/Ergonomics* (1st edn). New York: John Wiley.

Woods, D. D. & Patterson, E. S. (in press). How unexpected events produce an escalation of cognitive and coordinative demands. In P. A. Hancock & P. Desmond (Eds), *Stress, Workload and Fatigue*. Hillsdale, NJ: Erlbaum.

Woods, D. D. & Sarter, N. B. (in press). Learning from automation surprises and going sour accidents. In N. Sarter & R. Amalberti (Eds), *Cognitive Engineering in the Aviation Domain*. Hillsdale, NJ: Erlbaum.

Woods, D. D. & Watts, J. C. (1997). How not to have to navigate through too many displays. In M. G. Helander, T. K. Landauer & P. Prabhu (Eds), *Handbook of Human–Computer Interaction* (2nd edn). Amsterdam: Elsevier Science.

Yantis, S. (1993). Stimulus-drive attention capture. *Current Directions in Psychological Science*, 2, 156–61.

Zhang, J. (1997). The nature of external representations in problem solving. *Cognitive Science*, 21, 179–217.

Zhang, J. & Norman, D. A. (1994). Representations in distributed cognitive tasks. *Cognitive Science*, 18, 87–122.

Chapter 7

Applications of Social Cognition: Attitudes as Cognitive Structures

Leandre R. Fabrigar and Steven M. Smith
Queen's University
and
Laura A. Brannon
University of Oklahoma

One of the most important developments in social psychology has been the rise of the social cognitive approach (see Fiske & Taylor, 1991; Devine, Hamilton & Ostrom, 1994). Although precisely defining this broad approach is difficult (see Ostrom, 1984), Sherman, Judd & Park (1989) cast social cognition as a conceptual and empirical approach to understanding social psychological phenomena by investigating their operative cognitive structures and processes. Hamilton, Devine & Ostrom (1994) elaborated upon this definition by noting four characteristic features.

First, social cognition research directly examines the cognitive structures and processes underlying social psychological phenomena. In contrast, social phenomena had been addressed previously with less attention toward direct testing of specific hypotheses regarding underlying structure and process. Furthermore, recent research has exploited theory and methods from cognitive psychology. Thus, a second feature has been to frame social phenomena in terms of information-processing models. That is, social processes (e.g. person perception, group decision making) are viewed from the standpoint of a person who must attend to information, encode it, interpret it, integrate it, and store it, and access it for subsequent use. A third feature is to assume that basic information processing

Handbook of Applied Cognition, Edited by F. T. Durso, R. S. Nickerson, R. W. Schvaneveldt, S. T. Dumais, D. S. Lindsay and M. T. H. Chi.

principles can to some degree be generalized across social and non-social contexts. Finally, social cognition is indeed an approach rather than a content area; it is a way of thinking about and investigating different social phenomena rather than an empirical domain in its own right.

Researchers have long examined a variety of different types of cognitive structures (e.g. stereotypes, self-concept) and processes (e.g. inter-group relations, impression formation) thought to be relevant to social phenomena. However, probably no construct has been more central and enduring in social psychological research than attitude (see McGuire, 1985). And as has been the case with other constructs and the processes, the study of attitudes has been influenced by the social cognitive perspective.

Our review of theory and applications related to attitudes illustrates the social cognitive approach. We focus on attitudes because this construct has played a central role in the theoretical and applied social psychological literatures (see Dawes & Smith, 1985; Rajecki, 1990) and because attitudes are a particular type of cognitive structure that has been found to exert a powerful impact on social information processing and social behavior. We also concentrate on attitude because this construct has been ubiquitous both explicitly and implicitly within a variety of applied literatures. For example, business administration researchers have long been interested in how managers' social attitudes and beliefs might bias decisions regarding the hiring and evaluation of employees. Lawyers and legal scholars have been interested in anticipating how jurors' social attitudes influence their propensity to render a particular verdict and in predicting which jurors are likely to be especially influential during deliberations. Marketing researchers have examined to what extent product attitudes influence purchasing behavior and how consumer attitudes can be effectively changed via advertising. Political campaign strategists have been interested in how different types of attitudes influence voting behavior and in developing campaigns for influencing attitudes toward candidates. Finally, health professionals have long been concerned with the impact of attitudes and beliefs on health related behaviors (e.g. smoking, drug use, condom use, dietary behaviors) and how such behaviors can be changed.

Thus, our chapter differs from some of the other chapters in this book in that we concentrate on a specific construct and several processes related to this construct rather than on a particular applied context. Our goal is to highlight basic psychological principles of attitudes and note how these principles can have practical implications for a variety of applied settings. In pursuing this goal, we address three major themes that have guided attitude research. We begin our review with a discussion of how attitudes are structured and the consequences of different structural properties. Next, we examine how attitudes direct information processing and behavior. Finally, we review literature on attitude formation and change processes.

It is important to note that our review is more illustrative than comprehensive. The attitudes literature is vast and it is impossible to do full justice to it within the constraints of a single chapter. Thus, we have chosen to highlight selected models and findings that have played a central role in theory and application or that provided good illustrations of how social cognition has influenced attitude research.

ATTITUDE STRUCTURE

One major reason that professionals in applied settings are interested in attitudes is that they often wish to use attitudes to predict people's future decisions and behaviors. Additionally, professionals in applied settings sometimes wish to change attitudes so as to influence subsequent decisions and behaviors. As we will see, research on attitude structure can provide important insights into how to accomplish both of these objectives. Specifically, knowing the structure of an attitude can assist in gauging:

- how likely it is that the attitude will influence behaviors/judgments
- what types of behaviors/judgments the attitude is most likely to influence
- how susceptible the attitude is likely to be to persuasive attempts
- what types of persuasive appeals are likely to be most successful in changing the attitude.

What is an Attitude?

Most contemporary social psychologists use the term attitude to refer to a relatively general and enduring evaluation of some object, person, issue, or concept along a dimension ranging from negative to positive (e.g. Petty & Cacioppo, 1986a; Zanna & Rempel, 1988).[1] This definition implies that attitudes can be thought of as having two inherent properties (Krosnick & Petty, 1995): valence and extremity. Valence refers to whether the evaluation is negative or positive, and extremity refers to the degree to which the evaluation deviates from neutrality.

A second implication is that attitudes are global evaluations (e.g. ice cream is extremely good, country music is slightly bad) and therefore can be differentiated from specific beliefs and emotions. For example, specific emotions (e.g. happiness, anger) and specific traits (e.g. useful, dangerous) which might be associated with an object have both valence and extremity but are not general evaluations of an object. Attitudes are presumed to provide an overall summary evaluation of an object that might be derived from the specific beliefs a person has about the object and the specific emotions a person associates with the object.

Finally, attitudes are relatively enduring and, unlike moods and other constructs referring to psychological states, constitute reasonably stable evaluations that are presumed to be stored in long-term memory.

---

[1] Note that the terms "attitude object" and "object" are used to refer to any target of evaluation. People can hold attitudes towards virtually any type of target including but not limited to physical objects (e.g. microwave ovens, thunderbird automobiles), other people (e.g. one's mother, the President of the United States), classes of people (e.g. police officers, the French), policy positions (e.g. legalized abortion, capital punishment), or abstract concepts (e.g. freedom, compassion). Thus, the use of these terms is not restricted to attitudes toward physical objects.

Types of Attitude Structure

In the sections that follow, we review a variety of structural properties of attitudes which can be organized under two broad categories (Eagly & Chaiken, 1995, 1998): intra–attitudinal structure (i.e. structural properties of a single attitude), and inter-attitudinal structure (i.e. structural properties among multiple attitudes).

Accessibility

Attitude accessibility is the likelihood that an attitude will be automatically activated from memory upon merely encountering the attitude object (Fazio, 1989, 1995). Accessibility reflects the strength of association in memory between a representation of an object and the evaluation of that object along a dimension ranging from negative to positive. Thus, an attitude can be regarded as a simple semantic network in which the object and the evaluation are linked nodes.

Like more complex semantic networks (see Anderson, 1983), attitudes have the property of spreading activation. That is, activation of one node (i.e. the object) can spread to other linked nodes (i.e. the evaluation) as a function of the strength of the associative link. When the object–evaluation link is strong, the attitude will be highly accessible such that merely encountering the object will activate the evaluation. When the object–evaluation link is weak, encountering the object will be unlikely to activate the evaluation. Accessibility is typically assessed by measuring response latencies to attitude statements presented on computers with the inference being that greater speed in responses implies greater accessibility (see Fazio, 1995).

Accessibility is an important structural property of attitudes because it is a determinant of the strength of attitudes (Fazio, 1989, 1995). Attitudes are said to be strong when they are persistent over time, resistant to persuasion, influence information processing and judgments, and direct behavior (Krosnick & Petty, 1995).[2] According to Fazio (1989, 1990), accessibility is a determinant of strength because an evaluation is unlikely to have effects if it is not activated upon encountering the object. Thus, accessibility has been found to be positively related to the stability of attitudes toward political candidates and social issues (Grant, Button & Noseworthy, 1994; Hodges & Wilson, 1993). Increased accessibility has also been associated with increased resistance to persuasion about social issues (Bassili, 1996; Bassili & Fletcher, 1991; however, see Fabrigar, Priester, Petty & Wegener, 1998). We will also see that the impact of attitudes on information processing, judgments, and behaviors increases with enhanced attitude accessibility.

[2] Krosnick and Petty (1995) have suggested that the various properties of attitudes which have been found to be associated with the strength of an attitude can be classified as falling into four categories, i.e.: (1) aspects of the attitude, (2) aspects of attitude structure, (3) subjective beliefs about attitudes and attitude objects, and (4) the processes by which attitudes are formed and changed. In this chapter, we focus on structure and process properties related to strength.

Affective/Cognitive Bases

Theoretical discussions of attitude structure have long postulated that affect and cognition are important bases of attitudes (Smith, 1947; Katz & Stotland, 1959; Rosenberg & Hovland, 1960; Petty & Cacioppo, 1986a; Zanna & Rempel, 1988).[3]

Affect refers to evaluatively laden *emotions* that an individual associates with an attitude object, and cognition refers to evaluatively laden *characteristics* that an individual believes the attitude object possesses (e.g. Ostrom, 1969; Breckler, 1984; Crites, Fabrigar & Petty, 1994; Eagly, Mladinic & Otto, 1994). Of course, some attitudes can be based predominantly on affect and others predominantly on cognition (e.g. Breckler & Wiggins, 1989; Crites et al., 1994; Fabrigar & Petty, 1999). An affective attitude can be thought of as an attitude in which the attitude object has strong associative links in memory to various emotions but for which there are relatively few characteristics associated with the object and/or the associative links between the characteristics and the object are relatively weak. Thus, the global evaluation is likely to be primarily determined by affect. In contrast, cognitive attitudes are those in which the object has strong associative links with various characteristics but for which there are relatively few emotions associated with the object and/or the associative links between the emotions and the object are relatively weak. Thus, the global evaluation associated with such objects is likely to be predominantly derived from cognition.

Knowing the primary basis of the attitude is useful because the effectiveness of different types of persuasive appeals can be influenced by the degree to which the attitude is based on affect or cognition. Persuasive appeals may be more effective when they match the basis of the attitude rather than mismatch it (Edwards, 1990; Edwards & von Hippel, 1995; Fabrigar & Petty, in press). For example, persuasion that is affective in nature is more successful against affective attitudes than cognitive attitudes. Such affective/cognitive persuasion matching effects have been demonstrated for attitude objects such as consumer products, job applicants, animals, and ideographs. In contrast, other experiments with consumer products and puzzles have suggested that affective or cognitive persuasive appeals work better when they mismatch the basis of the attitude (Millar & Millar, 1990).

Although there have been attempts to resolve the apparent inconsistency between experiments demonstrating affective/cognitive matching versus mismatching effects (Millar, 1992; Millar & Millar, 1993; Messé, Bodenhausen & Nelson, 1995), none of these have been entirely satisfactory (Fabrigar & Petty, in press). Perhaps future research will show that attitude strength and argument strength determine when matching versus mismatching effects occur (see Edwards, 1990; Millar & Millar, 1990; Petty, Gleicher & Baker, 1991; Fabrigar & Petty, 1999).

Affective and cognitive bases of attitudes can also determine the extent to which attitudes will influence behavior. Millar & Tesser (1986, 1989) have suggested that behaviors can be classified as consummatory (intrinsically rewarding, such as

[3] Although some theories have postulated a third basis of attitudes (the behavioral component), we focus on the affective and cognitive bases of attitudes because they have received more empirical attention.

playing tennis because the game is enjoyable) versus instrumental (obtaining some goal extrinsic to the behavior itself, such as studying just to obtain a good grade). Research suggests that attitudes based on affect tend to predict consummatory behaviors better than instrumental behaviors, whereas cognitive attitudes tend to predict instrumental behaviors better than consummatory behaviors (Millar & Tesser, 1986, 1989).

Functional Bases of Attitudes

Theorists have long postulated that attitudes vary in the functions they serve (e.g. Katz, 1960; Kelman, 1958; Smith, Bruner & White, 1956). Among some of these attitude functions are the knowledge function (i.e. helping organize one's social world), the utilitarian function (i.e. assisting a person obtain rewards and avoid punishments), the value-expressive function (i.e. aiding in the expression of core values), the social-adjustive function (i.e. facilitating social interactions), and the ego-defensive function (i.e. enhancing or maintaining self-esteem).

It is possible to conceptualize attitude functions in structural terms (i.e. in terms of the type of characteristics or traits an individual most strongly associates with the attitude object in memory). For instance, attitude objects most strongly linked in memory to basic values might result in attitudes that serve a value-expressive function. Attitude objects most strongly associated in memory with traits that have practical benefits or costs might serve a utilitarian function and so on. Factors such as personality, situational context, and the nature of the object can all serve to influence the extent to which certain types of characteristics are strongly associated with an attitude object (Shavitt, 1989; see also Brannon & Brock, 1994; Brock, Brannon & Bridgwater, 1990).

One important benefit of knowing the function an attitude serves is that persuasive messages have been found to be more effective if they directly target the functional basis of the attitude than if they target a function that is not the basis of the attitude. For example, Shavitt (1990) asked people to list their thoughts regarding different attitude objects (e.g. coffee, the Republican Party, homosexuals) and then content coded these thoughts to determine if certain objects tended to serve particular functions. Persuasive messages that addressed the function typically associated with an attitude object were more successful in changing attitudes toward the object than persuasive messages that addressed a function not typically associated with the attitude object.

Snyder & DeBono (1985) measured a personality trait known as self-monitoring. This trait reflects the extent to which a person relies on external cues in their social context (i.e. high self-monitoring) versus internal psychological cues (i.e. low self-monitoring) as a guide to reaching decisions and performing behaviors. Snyder & DeBono reasoned that high self-monitors would be more likely than low self-monitors to form attitudes for social-adjustive reasons, whereas low self-monitors would be more likely than high self-monitors to form utilitarian or value-expressive attitudes. Participants were exposed to a persuasive message regarding a brand of alcoholic beverage that was designed to focus on either the image (social-adjustive features) or the quality (utilitarian properties) of the product. Consistent with their predictions, image advertisements tended to work better on high than low self-monitors and quality advertisements tended to work better on low than high self-monitors (see also Snyder & DeBono, 1989).

Interestingly, functional matching does not always lead to enhanced persuasion. Petty & Wegener (1998) demonstrated that messages which match the functional basis of the attitude engender more motivation to extensively elaborate the message (i.e. to carefully scrutinize the merits of the arguments) than messages which mismatch the functional basis of the attitude. Thus, functional matching enhanced persuasion for consumer products when the arguments were strong but decreased persuasion when the arguments were weak.

Knowledge

Another structural property of attitudes that has received considerable attention among attitude researchers is knowledge. Knowledge is typically defined as the amount of attitude-relevant information that a person can retrieve from memory (Davidson, 1995; Wood, Rhodes & Biek, 1995). It is usually assessed by asking people to list all the information they know about the attitude object and all the experiences they have had with respect to the attitude object.

Knowledge is conceptualized as a structural property (e.g. Krosnick & Petty, 1995) because the amount of attitude-relevant information that a person is capable of retrieving is likely to be a function of the number of attributes or characteristics associated with the object in memory as well as the strength of these associations. When numerous attributes are associated with the object and the strength of these associations is high, people are likely to be able to retrieve large amounts of attitude-relevant information from memory.

As will be reviewed later, research has supported the notion that attitudes based on extensive knowledge influence information processing and behavior more than attitudes based on relatively little knowledge (for reviews, see Davidson, 1995; Wood et al., 1995).

Intra-attitudinal Consistency (Ambivalence)

A global evaluation can be thought of as a summary of the extent to which an object is evaluated both negatively and positively. In some cases, one of these components is likely to be much stronger than the other (e.g. the object has a strong positive evaluation and no negative evaluation) thereby resulting in an attitude that is evaluatively consistent. In other cases, both components might be relatively strong leading to a summary evaluation based on evaluatively inconsistent components. Attitudes of this sort are said to be high in ambivalence (Kaplan, 1972; Scott, 1968). Evaluative consistency can also be conceptualized as a within-attitude basis property (e.g. affective consistency) or a between-attitude basis property (Chaiken, Pomerantz & Giner-Sorolla, 1995; Thomson et al., 1995).

Intra-attitudinal consistency (i.e. consistency within a single attitude) in its many forms has been a structural feature that has generated much interest in domains such as racial attitudes, health behaviors, consumer products, and social issues.

Intra-attitudinal consistency is an important determinant of attitude strength (Chaiken et al., 1995; Eagly & Chaiken, 1995; Thomson et al., 1995). Some work has examined the manner in which positive and negative evaluations are related to one another and how these evaluations should best be combined to form an index of ambivalence (e.g. Breckler, 1994; Cacioppo, Gardner & Berntson, 1997; Katz & Hass, 1988; Priester & Petty, 1996; Scott, 1969; Thomson et al., 1995). Research has also examined the degree to which intra-attitudinal consistency influences attitude stability and susceptibility to persuasion. Consistent with an attitude strength perspective, as inconsistency in attitudes increases, attitudes become less stable (Chaiken et al., 1995; Norman, 1975; Rosenberg, 1968) and more susceptible to social influence (Chaiken & Baldwin, 1981; Chaiken et al., 1995; Norman, 1975; Rosenberg, 1968). Finally, increases in inconsistency are also associated with less impact of attitudes on judgments and behavior (Fazio & Zanna, 1978; Moore, 1980; Norman, 1975; Sparks, Hedderly & Shepherd, 1992; however, see Jonas, Diehl & Bromer, 1997).

Inter-attitudinal Consistency

Another structural property of an attitude is the extent to which it is associated with other attitudes in memory and the degree to which the target attitude is evaluatively consistent with linked attitudes. Although inter-attitudinal structure has been discussed by social psychologists (e.g. Eagly & Chaiken, 1995, 1998; Festinger, 1957; Judd & Krosnick, 1989; McGuire, 1989; McGuire & McGuire, 1991), relatively little empirical work has been conducted. This work has suggested that increases in variables such as domain expertise and attitude importance are related to stronger associations and consistency among political attitudes in memory (Judd & Downing, 1990; Judd & Krosnick, 1989). Other research has found that frequent activation of an attitude toward a social issue can enhance the extremity and accessibility of attitudes towards other social issues linked to it in memory (Judd, Drake, Downing & Krosnick, 1991). Judd et al. (1991) explained these effects in terms of semantic network representations of inter-attitudinal structure and noted that these effects have implications for understanding when question context effects will occur in surveys.

Summary and Applied Implications

In applied contexts, attitudes are often assessed in order to predict future behaviors or decisions. It is not enough to simply know a person's attitude. It is also useful to know the structure of the attitude because attitudes with certain structural properties (e.g. high accessibility, extensive knowledge, high intra-attitudinal consistency) are much more likely than attitudes which lack these properties to influence judgments and behavior. Also, some structural features of attitudes (affective/cognitive bases) might also provide insight into what types of behaviors (e.g. consummatory versus instrumental) the attitude is likely to influence. Thus, information concerning attitude structure might assist in improving prediction of behavior. For example, political pollsters often assess attitudes in order to predict citizens' voting and reactions to legislation. Pollsters could potentially improve their predictions by using attitude structure measures to better differentiate between those citizens whose political attitudes are likely to translate into political action and those who are unlikely to act on their attitudes.

Researchers in many applied contexts also often attempt to develop campaigns to change attitudes (e.g. advertising campaigns for products, public health campaigns). Some structural properties of attitudes (e.g. accessibility, intra-attitudinal consistency) can provide information regarding the extent to which an attitude is likely to be resistant to persuasion. Thus, attitude structure measures might be used to aid in targeting persuasive campaigns. For example, marketing professionals conducting advertising campaigns for products could use structural measures to identify if specific segments of the public have product attitudes that are likely to be especially susceptible to change. This in turn could allow them to more efficiently target their advertising.

Another benefit of attitude structure measures might be in assessing the likely effectiveness of persuasive campaigns. Communication researchers have often noted that informational campaigns can change attitudes without necessarily resulting in changes in behavior (see Backer, Rogers & Sopory, 1992). The structure literature suggests that when developing and testing campaign messages, it might be useful to assess the impact of message on structural properties of the attitude as well as the attitude itself. For example, a health professional testing different messages to be used in an anti-smoking campaign might want to assess not only if the messages change attitudes, but also if they produce attitudes that possess structural properties associated with strong attitude–behavior consistency.

Finally, some structural properties of attitudes (e.g. affective/cognitive bases, functional bases) can provide assistance in determining what type of persuasive information will be most successful in changing a particular attitude. For example, if a market researcher determines that attitudes toward a certain product tend to have a particular functional basis, this can provide a guide as to what types of information should be included in the message.

THE IMPACT OF ATTITUDES ON INFORMATION PROCESSING AND BEHAVIOR

A second major theme that has dominated attitude research is understanding the processes by which attitudes influence information processing and behavior. This research provides guidance for understanding when an attitude will be likely to influence information processing/behavior, what types of attitudes are most likely to influence a given behavior, and what other psychological constructs must be taken into account when using attitudes to predict behaviors/judgments.

Attitudes and Information Processing

Festinger (1957) provided one of the earliest detailed discussions and empirical investigations of the impact of attitudes on information processing. Festinger hypothesized that individuals are motivated to maintain consistency among elements in their cognitive structures. Thus, he reasoned that people should be motivated to incorporate information which is congruent with their attitudes and to avoid information which is incongruent. These effects were labeled "congeniality effects" and were expected to occur at the exposure, attention, perception, judgment and memory stages of information processing (Eagly & Chaiken, 1998). However, determining precisely which step in information processing an attitude has influenced can be difficult. Thus, Eagly & Chaiken (1993) have argued that most empirical research which addresses the impact of attitudes on information processing can be categorized into one of the following three broad groups:

1. those which address selective exposure and attention processes
2. those which address selective perception and judgment processes
3. those concerning selective memory processes.

Selective Exposure and Attention

Exposure to and attention toward new information are separate steps in information processing (McGuire, 1985). The exposure step involves seeking out information in an active manner, whereas the attention step involves the process whereby individuals attend to information to which they have been exposed (Eagly & Chaiken, 1993). Festinger (1957) hypothesized that if a person holds two cognitions which are incongruent, negative arousal (i.e. dissonance) is produced. Festinger also proposed that one situation which often produces dissonance is when a person is forced to choose between two equally attractive alternatives. He suggested that one way a person might reduce dissonance in such a situation is by selectively exposing him or herself to information that supports the decision made.

For example, Ehrlich, Guttman, Schonbach & Mills (1957) found that car owners who had recently made a car purchase read more ads about the cars they had purchased than they did ads for cars they had considered but decided not to buy. Although some reviews of later literature concluded that selective exposure effects did not occur (Sears, 1965), more recent reviews (Cotton, 1985; Frey, 1986) have concluded that these effects do occur and that some inconsistencies might have been due to failing to account for moderators of selective exposure effects.

For instance, Lowin (1967) demonstrated that ease of message refutation moderated selective exposure effects. Lowin mailed offers of political brochures to supporters of Goldwater and Johnson in the 1964 presidential campaign. The brochures (supporting or opposing the candidates) were represented by a series of arguments that were either easy or difficult to refute. Hard-to-refute, supportive information and easy-to-refute, nonsupportive information were preferred to easy-to-refute, supportive information and hard-to-refute, nonsupportive information. Thus, this study suggested that individuals did not simply prefer attitude consistent information. Instead, they wanted strong attitude consistent information, thereby giving their views added validity, as well as weak attitude inconsistent information, thus suggesting that alternative views were fallacious.

Other types of exposure and attention effects have also been found. Roskos-Ewoldsen & Fazio (1992) argued that people would be more likely to attend to objects for which they had highly accessible (that is, strong) attitudes than objects for which they had relatively inaccessible (weak) attitudes because the activation of an attitude conveys to a person that the object has hedonic relevance. Consistent with this, they demonstrated that people noticed and attended to objects more when their attitudes towards those objects were high in accessibility versus low in accessibility. Another attitude strength variable that has been found to influence exposure effects is attitude importance. In a study by Berent & Krosnick (1993) described by Boninger, Krosnick, Berent & Fabrigar (1995), participants were asked to evaluate political candidates based on statements the candidates had made on six policy issues. The participants were told they could hear the candidates' statements about only three issues. Berent & Krosnick (1993) found that people chose to hear statements relevant to attitudes which were particularly important to them at the expense of information relevant to less important attitudes.

Selective Perception and Judgment

As with selective exposure and attention, selective perception and judgment can be conceptualized as two distinct processes. Perception can be defined as the encoding of information, whereas judgment can be defined as drawing conclusions about the meaning or relevance of information (Eagly & Chaiken, 1993). As with earlier steps in information processing, Festinger (1957) postulated that motivation to maintain consistency would encourage people to perceive and evaluate that information in a manner consistent with their preexisting attitudes. Sherif & Hovland (1961), on the other hand, discussed these effects in terms of assimilation and contrast. They argued that attitudes serve as judgmental anchors such that new information is interpreted in relation to those attitudes. When encountering information which is close to their own attitudes, people assimilate or minimize the dissimilarity of that information whereas, when encountering information which is distant from their own attitudes, they contrast or exaggerate the dissimilarity or negativity of the information.

Empirical research has provided clear support for the general claim that people usually evaluate messages negatively which are counter to their preexisting attitudes. In a classic study, Lord, Ross & Lepper (1979) demonstrated biased perception and judgment of information regarding capital punishment. Participants who either favored capital punishment or opposed it were presented with the results of two fabricated studies. One study supported the efficacy of capital punishment as a deterrent to crime whereas the other undermined it. As predicted by selectivity principles, participants rated the study that agreed with their own point of view as more convincing and more rigorous than the study which disagreed with their views. In another classic study, Hastorf & Cantril (1954) had Princeton and Dartmouth students watch a film of a football game. Students were asked to note any rule infractions (whether the referee called them or not). While both groups of students noted the same number of infractions for the Princeton team, Princeton students cited more infractions to the Dartmouth team than the Dartmouth students did, demonstrating selective perception and judgment of the Dartmouth team's actions.

Other studies have demonstrated different types of bias effects. For instance, Vallone, Ross & Lepper (1985) showed pro-Israeli and pro-Arab individuals previously televised news reports concerning a massacre in two refugee camps in Lebanon. Both pro-Israeli and pro-Arab participants rated the programs and the people responsible for them as biased against their side. Furthermore, partisans reported different perceptions and recollections of the actual programs, remembering more negative references to their side than positive ones. They also evaluated the media's sample facts and arguments differently. The authors labeled this reaction the "hostile media bias." The authors suggested that this reaction occurred because, even though the program was essentially neutral in its reporting, this neutrality was sufficiently different from the participants' own views to be contrasted and thus seen as biased against them.

Not surprisingly, selectivity effects have been found to be particularly likely to occur when attitudes are held strongly. For instance, Houston & Fazio (1989) demonstrated that people whose attitudes toward capital punishment were more accessible engaged in biased processing to a greater degree than people whose attitudes were not as accessible. Likewise, Fazio & Williams (1986) found that people whose attitudes toward presidential candidates were highly accessible engaged in more biased processing regarding the candidates' performance in presidential debates than did people with attitudes low in accessibility.

Selective Memory

Congeniality effects in memory might occur simply because people are more likely to attend to attitudinally congenial information, and recall is facilitated by active attention (Eagly & Chaiken, 1993). Alternatively, people may forget or even distort attitudinally incongruent information in an attempt to reduce the dissonance it produces (Festinger, 1957). For example, Echabe & Rovira (1989) found that participants who had been presented with information about AIDS later showed better recall of information which was congruent with their preexisting attitudes. Further, participants distorted incongruent information to make it more compatible with their own attitudes.

However, people also employ active strategies such as counterarguing incongruent information which could result in enhanced memory for incongruent information (Eagly & Chaiken, 1998). Several studies (e.g. Cacioppo & Petty, 1979; Johnson & Judd, 1983) have demonstrated better memory for attitudinally incongruent information. More recent investigations of selective memory have focused on how structural features of the attitude may influence memory. For example, Pratkanis (1989) found that bipolar attitudes (i.e. when knowledge concerns both sides of an issue, rather than only one) resulted in better recollection of extreme information regardless of its congruency with the attitude.

The Impact of Attitudes on Behavior

Specificity of Attitudes

The failure of many early studies to produce strong correlations between attitudes and behaviors (Wicker, 1969) was due largely to a lack of correspondence in specificity between the attitude and behavior being measured. Fishbein & Ajzen (1975; Ajzen & Fishbein, 1980) argued that behaviors could be broken down into four components:

1. the action performed – e.g. driving, wearing a cross
2. the target of the action – e.g. a car, a person
3. the context in which the behavior is performed – e.g. on a city street, in church
4. the time at which the behavior is performed – e.g. in the morning, on Sundays.

In addition, each of these components can be singular or multiple (e.g. single or multiple contexts or times). Once these components and their elements are combined the behavior has been properly specified. In order to best predict a specified behavior, Fishbein & Ajzen argued that the attitude measured must correspond to the behavior of interest on each of these components. Consistent with this reasoning, they demonstrated that very general attitudes toward religion did poorly at predicting specific religious behaviors but did relatively well at predicting general patterns of religious behavior (Fishbein & Ajzen, 1974).

Weigel & Newman (1976) measured general attitudes toward the environment in telephone interviews of a random sample of small-town New Englanders and the extent to which the sample engaged in pro-environmental behaviors. The specific behaviors included actions such as signing petitions, participating in local clean-up efforts, and recycling. Attitude–behavior correlations were usually weak for general attitudes predicting single behaviors (average r of .32). In contrast when the behaviors were combined into a general behavioral index, the correlation was quite high, $r = .62$. Thus, if general patterns of behavior across multiple types of behavior are of interest, general attitudes are a useful predictor.

Likewise, Davidson & Jaccard (1979) demonstrated that increasing the specificity of the measured attitude had a powerful impact on the ability to predict specific behaviors. These authors were interested in predicting women's use of birth control pills in a two-year period. As the specificity of the question increased from "attitude toward birth control" to "attitude toward using birth control pills in the next two years" the attitude–behavior relationship increased from an r of .08 to an r of .57.

Attitude Strength

Strong attitudes should exert a greater impact on behaviors than weak attitudes. For example, Fazio & Williams (1986) found that attitudes toward presidential candidates were more predictive of subsequent behavior (i.e. voting for the candidate) when attitude accessibility was high rather than low. Similarly, Bassili (1995) found that voting intentions were more predictive of self-reported voting behavior when the accessibility of voting intention was high rather than low. Fazio, Powell & Williams (1989) measured people's attitudes toward ten consumer items and measured their response latency to the attitude items. Participants were then allowed to choose five of the items to keep. Participants with highly accessible attitudes showed greater attitude–behavior correspondence than those with less accessible attitudes.

Attitude-relevant knowledge has also been found to moderate the attitude–behavior relation. Kallgren & Wood (1986) found that people who had substantial knowledge about environmental issues showed a greater degree of attitude–behavior consistency (as measured by petition signing and participation in a recycling project) than those who had less knowledge. In three studies, Davidson, Yantis, Norwood & Montano (1985) also showed that amount of knowledge moderated attitude behavior consistency. They found that participants' attitudes toward the candidates predicted voting behavior to a greater degree for people who had more knowledge of the candidates than for those who had less. In a third study examining attitudes toward influenza vaccinations and actually getting a vaccination, the authors found that increased knowledge resulted in a stronger attitude–behavior relationship.

A final strength-related property of attitudes to be discussed in the context of the attitude–behavior relation is the amount of elaboration of attitude relevant information (Petty & Cacioppo, 1986a, 1986b; Petty, Haugtvedt & Smith, 1995). Elaboration refers to the extent to which an individual engages in careful scrutiny of information directly relevant to the attitude. Brown (1974) measured high school students' attitudes about breaking various laws (e.g. drug and traffic laws) and found that students who reported a greater degree of thinking about the laws had stronger attitude–behavior consistency than students who reported less thinking. Similarly, Shestowsky, Wegener & Fabrigar (1998) found that individuals high in need for cognition (a personality trait reflecting an individual's intrinsic enjoyment of engaging in effortful cognitive activity and thus associated with extensive elaboration) were more active and successful in influencing other group members to adopt their views in a jury decision-making task than were people who were low in need for cognition. High need for cognition people have also been found to have attitudes that are more predictive of the votes for presidential candidates than do people low in need for cognition (Cacioppo, Petty, Kao & Rodriguez, 1986). Finally, Petty, Cacioppo & Schumann (1983) found that consumer product attitudes changed via high elaboration were more predictive of behavioral intentions than were attitudes changed via low elaboration.

Models of Attitude Behavior Prediction

A third important development in understanding the processes by which attitudes influence behavior has been the emergence of attitude–behavior theories. The theory of reasoned action (TORA: Fishbein & Ajzen, 1975; Ajzen & Fishbein, 1980) and its successor, the theory of planned behavior (TPB: Ajzen, 1985, 1987, 1991) are two of the best known of these theories. As can be seen in Panel A of

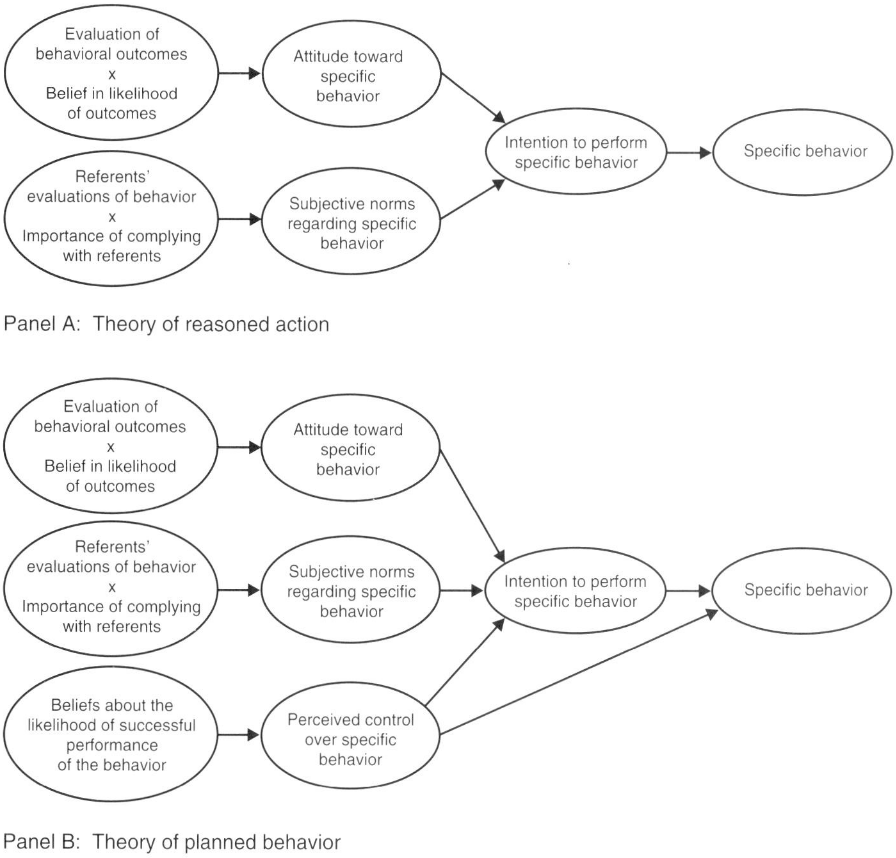

Figure 7.1 Diagram representations of the theory of reasoned action (Panel A), adapted from *Understanding Attitudes and Predicting Social Behavior,* Ajzen & Fishbein, 1980, p. 84, by permission of Prentice-Hall, Inc. Upper Saddle River, NJ.; and the theory of planned behavior (Panel B), adapted from Ajzen, 1987, p. 46).

Figure 7.1, an important determinant of behavior in TORA is behavioral intention – a decision to perform the specific behavior in question. The model further specifies that these intentions are determined by attitudes and subjective norms. The attitude referred to in the model is the attitude toward the specific behavior in question (e.g. purchasing a Porsche automobile) rather than the target of the behavior (e.g. a Porsche automobile). This attitude is assumed to be a function of beliefs that the behavior leads to certain outcomes and evaluations of those outcomes (e.g. purchasing a Porsche will bankrupt me and this would be bad). Subjective norms refer to the degree to which the individual's perception that other people important to the individual either approve or disapprove of the individual performing the behavior and the individual's motivation to comply with the wishes of these specific significant others (e.g. my father would approve of me purchasing a Porsche and his opinion is important to me). Thus, in this model, attitudes do play an important role in behavior but their effect is indirect (via intention), and they are not the sole determinant of behavior.

The model has been used in hundreds of studies to predict behaviors such as consumer behavior (Fishbein & Ajzen, 1980), voting in elections (Fishbein, Ajzen & Hinkle, 1980), smoking (Norman & Tedeschi, 1989), seat belt use (Stasson & Fishbein, 1990) and performing testicular self-exams (Steffen, 1990) to name just a few. Typically, studies of this sort have measured attitudes, subjective norms, intentions, and behavior, and then used regression analyses to assess the relations among these constructs.

Although reviews (e.g. Sheppard, Hartwick & Warshaw, 1988) have provided evidence for the predictive utility of TORA, one main criticism is that the model is designed to measure and predict only volitional behavior, and has no mechanism to account for behaviors which require skills, resources, or opportunities that are not necessarily under a person's control (Liska, 1984). Other criticisms revolved around neglect of the role of external variables such as past behaviors, moral obligations, and self-identity, which could affect behavioral intentions and behaviors (e.g. Bentler & Speckart, 1979; Schwartz & Tessler, 1972; Biddle, Bank & Slavings, 1987).

In an attempt to address some of the concerns regarding the theory of reasoned action, Ajzen (1985, 1987, 1991: theory of planned behavior) introduced "perceived behavioral control," which is defined as one's perception of the difficulty of performing a particular behavior. As can be seen in Panel B of Figure 7.1, increased perceived behavioral control is postulated to lead to intentions to perform the behavior as well as a direct increase in likelihood of performing the behavior. Madden, Ellen & Ajzen (1992) examined ten different behaviors ranging from health behaviors (e.g. exercise, taking vitamin supplements) to household chores (e.g. doing laundry, washing one's car) to consumer behaviors (e.g. renting video cassettes, shopping). Including perceived behavior control tended to improve prediction of intentions and behaviors, and especially for behaviors that people regarded as largely beyond their control (see also, Ajzen, 1991; Hausenblas, Carron & Mack, 1997).

One of the most recent models of attitude–behavior relations is the MODE model (Fazio, 1990). This model suggests that when a person is motivated and able to deliberate regarding the behavior, the process by which attitudes influence behavior will be similar to that proposed by the TORA (see panel A of Figure 7.2). That is, when motivation and ability are high, attitudes *toward the specific behavior* will influence behavior via intentions.

However, when motivation and/or ability are low, the process unfolds as outlined in Panel B of Figure 7.2. First, if the attitude is sufficiently accessible, the attitude *toward the object* is activated upon encountering the attitude object. Once activated, the attitude biases processing of incoming information so that perceptions of the object become attitudinally consistent. These perceptions of the object lead, in part, to the definition of the event relevant to the behavior. The definition of the event is also dependent on the perceived norms which define the behavioral context and the definition determines the nature of the behavior. Approach behaviors result from primarily positive perceptions, and avoidance behaviors result from primarily negative perceptions. Note that this entire sequence does not require deliberative thought: behavior simply follows from the definition of the event that has been biased by the attitude.

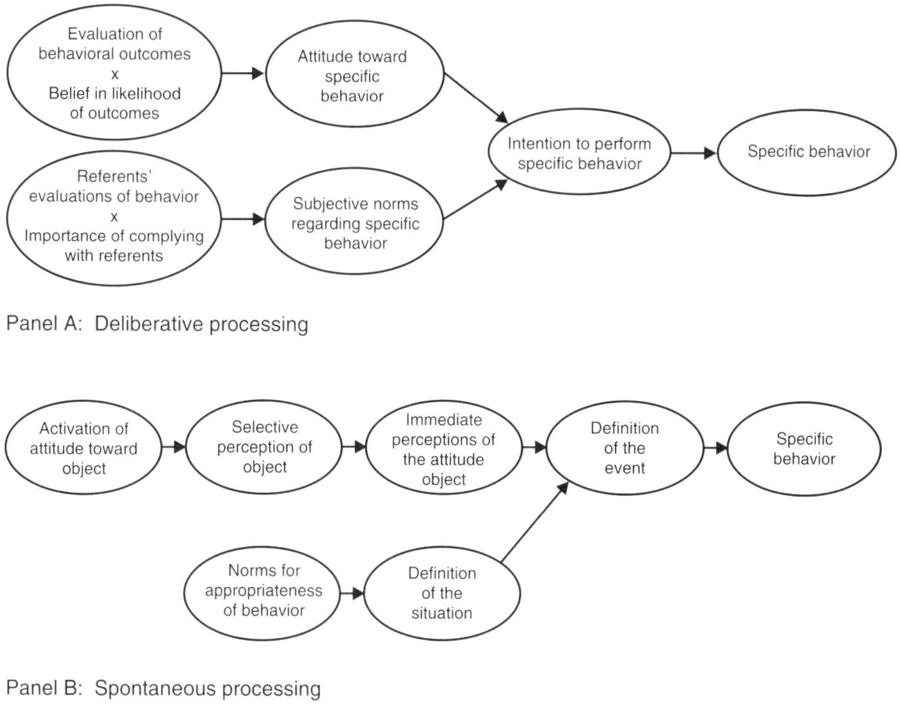

Figure 7.2 Diagram representations of the MODE model (Panel A), adapted from *Understanding Attitudes and Predicting Social Behavior,* Ajzen & Fishbein, 1980, p. 84, by permission of Prentice-Hall, Inc. Upper Saddle River, NJ.; (Panel B), adapted from Fazio, 1990, p. 84).

Sanbonmatsu & Fazio (1990) demonstrated that as motivation or the opportunity to use available information decreased, preexisting general attitudes guided decisions. However, when motivation and opportunity were high, individuals used information directly relevant to the specific behavior. In another study, Schuette & Fazio (1995) found that participants who did not have the motivation or opportunity to consider object relevant information made judgments congruent with their existing highly accessible general attitudes, whereas participants who did have the motivation and opportunity made judgments based on the attributes of the attitude object.

Summary and Applied Implications

The literature on the impact of attitudes on information processing and behavior has several practical implications for the applied tasks of predicting future judgments/behaviors and changing attitudes. With respect to prediction, as with the attitude structure literature, this research highlights the importance of assessing the strength of an attitude in addition to the attitude itself.

A second important lesson of this literature is that when using attitudes to predict future outcomes, a researcher should carefully consider the specificity of that which he or she wants to predict and the conditions under which the decisions or behaviors are likely to occur. For example, if a health professional wishes to predict future health-related behaviors for a target group, he or she should consider the specificity of the behavior of interest and whether that behavior is likely to occur under conditions of deliberative thought. If the behavior is very specific and likely to occur under careful deliberation (e.g. choosing to obtain a flu vaccination this year), assessing attitudes toward the specific behavior (e.g. attitudes toward flu vaccinations this year) is likely to work best. However, if the goal is to predict a general pattern of behaviors (e.g. exercising) and/or there is likely to be little deliberative thought prior to the behavior, more general attitudes toward the target of the behaviors should be assessed (e.g. attitudes toward exercising in general rather than a specific type of exercise activity). Additionally, this literature suggests that applied professionals should not only consider attitudes but also subjective norms and perceived behavioral control when predicting behavior.

This research also has implications for designing communication campaigns to change behaviors. For example, if a manager wishes to implement a program to discourage employees from taking extended lunch breaks, the manager should concentrate his or her campaign on attitudes specific to that behavior as well as on subjective norms and perceived behavioral control relevant to this behavior. A campaign that focuses on more general work behavior-related attitudes or which does not address how the behavior is perceived by others and the extent to which employees have direct control over the behavior is likely to be less successful in changing the behavior.

Finally, the research on the impact of attitudes on information processing also has important implications for designing communication campaigns. Anyone involved in transmitting information to the public (e.g. marketers, health professionals, politicians, lawyers) will have their messages attended to, interpreted, and remembered as function of the recipients' attitudes. Thus, communicators should attempt to identify what preexisting attitudes in their target audience are likely to bias processing of the message and in what manner these biases are likely to occur. A communicator could then construct a message such that these biases are directly addressed and counterarguments for them are included.

ATTITUDE CHANGE PROCESSES

One of the major areas of attitude research which has been of interest to those in applied settings is the topic of attitude change. The literature on this topic is vast and numerous theories of attitude change have been proposed (e.g. see Eagly & Chaiken, 1993). Thus, a comprehensive review of this work is not possible within the confines of our chapter.

Instead, we have chosen to focus on one of the most recent information processing theories of attitude change, the elaboration likelihood model (ELM: Petty & Cacioppo, 1986a, b). We have chosen this theory because it has been an influential perspective and because it provides an integrative framework for organizing much of the attitude change literature. We have also chosen to highlight this theory because it provides a good example of how recent persuasion theories have come to focus more directly on the cognitive processes underlying attitude change (Fiske & Taylor, 1991). However, the ELM is by no means the only theory of this sort. Another influential information processing theory of attitude change is the heuristic-systematic model (HSM: Chaiken, Liberman & Eagly, 1989). Although the ELM and HSM differ in certain respects, they also share a number of features and can generally account for the same empirical findings (see Petty, Wegener & Fabrigar, 1997). Thus, for the sake of brevity and simplicity, we confine our discussion to the framework of the ELM.

The Elaboration Continuum

Basic Concepts

Elaboration, conceived as a continuum (Petty & Cacioppo, 1986a, b), refers to the process by which people carefully scrutinize and think about the central merits of attitude relevant information. Elaboration is not simply learning information about the attitude object but rather entails cognitive responding: deriving inferences from, making evaluations of, and forming reactions to attitude-relevant information.

The ELM holds that when elaboration is extensive, attitudes are formed or changed as a function of the cognitive responses (elaborations) people generate in reaction to attitude-relevant information: the "central route" to persuasion. Under conditions in which elaboration is unlikely to occur, the ELM predicts that attitudes will be formed or changed via peripheral cues: features of the persuasion context that are not directly related to the central merits of attitude-relevant information but provide a low-effort basis for arriving at an attitude. For instance, if the source of a message was highly credible, this could be used as a simple cue to infer that the advocacy should be accepted: the "peripheral route" to persuasion.

The central and peripheral routes to persuasion can be thought of as the extreme endpoints on a continuum reflecting amount of elaboration. The greater the amount of elaboration, the greater the impact of cognitive responses on attitude change and the less the impact of peripheral cues (Petty, Cacioppo & Goldman, 1981). Under moderate elaboration conditions, both cognitive responses and peripheral cues will exert some impact on attitude change.

Determinants of Elaboration

The ELM holds that in order for extensive elaboration to occur, people must be both *motivated* and *able* to expend cognitive resources to scrutinize attitude-relevant information. Perhaps the most widely studied motivation variable is personal involvement.[4] In one well-known experiment, Petty et al. (1983)

[4] Although some researchers have suggested that it is productive to distinguish among different types of involvement (Johnson & Eagly, 1989, 1990), we do not emphasize such a distinction in our review (see Petty & Cacioppo, 1990).

manipulated involvement for advertisements about disposable razors by leading some participants to believe they would later be allowed to select from one of several brands of razors and others to believe that they would be selecting a different type of product. Participants were also randomly assigned to receive either strong (compelling) or weak (specious) arguments in favor of the target product (people who are attending to and elaborating on the message should be influenced by its quality to a greater extent than people who are not elaborating on the message). Finally, half of the participants were told that the product was endorsed by famous people (i.e. professional athletes) and the other half by nonfamous people. Under high involvement, the quality of the arguments was a powerful determinant of how much attitude change occurred, thereby suggesting that people were carefully elaborating the messages. Additionally, under high involvement, who endorsed the product had no impact on the amount of attitude change. In contrast, under low involvement, argument quality had much less influence on attitude change, and the product endorser exerted a substantial impact on attitude change thereby suggesting that little elaboration took place. Other determinants of motivation to elaborate such as personal responsibility, number of message sources, and personality traits (e.g. need for cognition) have produced similar patterns of results (for reviews, see Petty & Cacioppo, 1986a, b; Petty, Priester & Wegener, 1994).

Variables affecting ability to elaborate have also been examined. For example, Petty, Wells & Brock (1976) had participants listen to a message while performing a task that varied in how distracting it was. Low distraction allowed people to elaborate the messages; therefore, the quality of the arguments in the message was an important determinant of attitude change. In contrast, argument quality had virtually no impact on attitude change under high distraction where little elaboration of the message occurred. Other factors influencing ability to elaborate have also been examined such as message repetition, message recipient posture, and topic-relevant knowledge (for reviews, see Petty & Cacioppo, 1986a, b; Petty et al., 1994; Wood et al., 1995). These experiments have sometimes examined the impact of these variables in applied contexts such as product advertisements and political persuasion.

The Multiple Roles of Variables in Persuasion Contexts

The Four Roles in Persuasion

Another central tenet of the ELM is that variables can influence persuasion by serving in one or more of four possible roles (see Petty & Cacioppo, 1986a, b). Specifically, under conditions where background factors render motivation and/or ability to elaborate as low, a variable can influence persuasion by serving as a *cue*. Under conditions where motivation and/or ability to elaborate are moderate, a variable can influence persuasion by *determining the amount of elaboration* that takes place. Finally, under conditions where motivation and ability to elaborate are high, a variable can serve to *bias the direction of elaboration*. That is, variables exerting positive bias will encourage a person to generate positive cognitive responses to the message and variables exerting negative bias will encourage a person to generate negative cognitive responses to the message. Such bias will be particularly likely to occur when the quality of the arguments in a persuasive message is somewhat ambiguous rather than clearly strong or weak (Chaiken & Maheswaran, 1994). Alternatively, under high elaboration conditions, a variable might also serve as a central *argument* for or against the advocacy if the variable is directly relevant to the attitude object (e.g. an attractive source promoting a beauty product).

Importantly, the role any given variable is likely to serve can be predicted based on whether background factors are likely to create conditions of low, moderate, or high elaboration. To illustrate these principles, we discuss how several well-known persuasion variables can be conceptualized as serving multiple roles.

Multiple Roles of Affect (Mood)

In recent years, the role of mood states in information processing has been of central interest to researchers in the domain of attitude research, as well as social cognition research more generally (e.g. see Fiske & Taylor, 1991; Schwarz, 1990). The ELM postulates that mood could serve any of four possible roles (for detailed discussions, see Petty et al., 1991, 1994). Under low elaboration, mood influences persuasion as a peripheral cue such that people infer that positive mood implies agreement with the message and negative mood implies disagreement with the message. In contrast, under high elaboration, if mood is directly relevant to the attitude object under consideration (e.g. "this music makes me happy"), it could serve as a central argument. Alternatively, mood could influence persuasion under high elaboration by biasing the valence of cognitive responses. For example, in many contexts mood might facilitate the generation of cognitive responses congruent with the current mood state.

Petty, Schumannn, Richman & Strathman (1993) reported results that supported the notion that mood influenced attitude change via different processes under high and low elaboration. Under low involvement, participants' mood had no influence on the cognitive responses generated in reaction to a television advertisement concerning a brand of pen, but mood did have a direct influence on post-message attitudes. These findings suggested that mood influenced persuasion by serving as a peripheral cue. In contrast, under high involvement, mood did not have a direct impact on post-message attitudes but instead exerted a substantial impact on the valence of cognitive responses to the advertisement, which in turn strongly influenced post-message attitudes.

Under moderate elaboration conditions, mood serves as a determinant of amount of elaboration. One view of how mood influences elaboration is the hedonic contingency perspective (e.g. Wegener, Petty & Smith, 1995; for different perspectives, see Forgas, 1995; Mackie & Worth, 1989; Schwarz, 1990). People who are in a positive mood are particularly sensitive to hedonic contingencies of processing persuasive messages. If there is clear reason to expect that the message will maintain their positive mood, individuals in a positive mood will be likely to engage in extensive elaboration. However, if it appears that the message will be unpleasant or the hedonic consequences are unclear, positive mood people will engage in relatively little elaboration so as to avoid harming their mood. In contrast, because it is relatively unlikely that a message will make a person in a negative mood feel worse, and it is possible that the message will make them feel better, people in a negative mood are likely to engage in relatively high levels of elaboration regardless of hedonic contingencies.

Multiple Roles of Source Attractiveness and Expertise

Two of the most widely studied persuasion variables are source (communicator) attractiveness and expertise. The ELM postulates that under low elaboration people might use the attractiveness or expertise of the message source as a peripheral cue such that people will tend to agree with highly attractive and/or expert sources more than sources who lack these characteristics. Importantly, these source effects will occur relatively independent of the content of the message. Under moderate elaboration conditions, people might be more likely to elaborate a message for a highly expert source than a low credible source because there is little reason to scrutinize information from a person who lacks expertise on the topic. Likewise, people might be more prone to elaborate messages for people who are attractive than unattractive because such people are better liked. Finally, under high elaboration, increases in expertise and attractiveness of sources might bias the elaboration of the message in a positive direction if the arguments are of ambiguous quality (see Chaiken & Maheswaran, 1994). Alternatively, if the attractiveness of the source or some aspect of the source's expertise were directly relevant to the message topic, attractiveness and expertise might also serve as a central argument for the advocacy (for recent reviews, see Petty et al., 1994, 1997).

Moore, Hausknecht & Thamodaran (1986) manipulated elaboration by varying the pace at which participants were exposed to product advertisements (faster pace allows less opportunity for elaboration). Under a rapid pace (i.e. low elaboration condition), argument quality had very little impact on persuasion but source expertise had substantial impact, thereby suggesting that source expertise was used as a peripheral cue. Under a moderate pace (i.e. moderate elaboration condition), argument quality had a greater impact on persuasion for high expertise sources than low expertise sources. This finding suggested that increased source expertise resulted in increased elaboration of messages. Finally, under a slow pace (i.e. high elaboration condition), argument quality had more impact and source expertise less impact than the fast pace condition.

In an experiment on source attractiveness (Shavitt, Swan, Lowrey & Wanke, 1994), Shavitt and her colleagues manipulated the attractiveness of the message source, motivation to elaborate an advertisement, and the relevancy of the salient central features of the advertised product to attractiveness. When elaboration was low, the attractiveness of the source influenced attitude change regardless of whether attractiveness was relevant to the central features of the product: attractiveness served as a peripheral cue. In contrast, under high elaboration, source attractiveness only influenced attitude change if attractiveness was relevant to the central features of the product (e.g. the public image of the product was made salient). Therefore, attractiveness appeared to function as a central argument when it was relevant to the attitude object and elaboration was high.

Group Process Variables

Several variables of direct relevance to group life have been examined within the context of the ELM (see Petty et al., 1994). One such variable is the status of the source as a member of a numerical majority or minority. Traditional research on this variable has concentrated on issues such as whether majorities or minorities have greater impact (e.g. Levine, 1989; Tanford & Penrod, 1984) and whether majorities and minorities influence attitudes via different processes (e.g. Moscovici, 1980). The ELM predicts that the manner in which majority/minority sources influence attitude change will vary as a function of the level of elaboration.

When elaboration is low, numerical majority/minority source status is likely to serve as a simple cue. For example, all other things being equal, people engaging in little elaboration might be more likely to accept the advocacy of a majority source than a minority source because high social consensus could serve as a simple cue to support the advocacy. Under moderate elaboration, majority/minority status might serve to influence the amount of elaboration. Recent research (Baker & Petty, 1994) has suggested that elaboration of messages is enhanced when a majority source advocates a position that is counter-attitudinal to the target (recipient) of the message or when a minority source advocates a position that is pro-attitudinal to the target of the message. This enhanced elaboration effect occurs under these conditions because finding that one's position is in the minority is generally surprising to most people and thus motivates them to elaborate the message. In contrast, when a majority source advocates a pro-attitudinal position or a minority source advocates a counter-attitudinal position, this is seen as less surprising and thus is less likely to motivate elaboration. When elaboration is high, majority/minority source status might serve to bias elaboration. For example, Trost, Maas & Kenrick (1992) found that a message advocated by a minority source was relatively effective when the topic was of low relevance but a message advocated by a minority source was less effective than that advocated by the majority when the topic was of high relevance. Thus, majority/minority status appeared to act as a biasing factor in elaboration. Alternatively, Petty et al. (1994) suggested that when social consensus is of central relevance to the topic, majority/minority status might also serve as a central argument under high elaboration.

Another set of factors relevant to group contexts is whether a message comes from multiple sources and whether there are multiple targets of the message (i.e. whether a person believes that he or she is the only one receiving the message or whether he or she believes others are also receiving the message). Under low elaboration, one might expect the fact that arguments come from multiple sources, versus a single source, to enhance persuasion by providing a basis to infer social consensus, which in turn could be used as a cue to accept the advocacy. However, there seems no clear basis to expect that the number of targets of the message should serve as a cue. Under moderate conditions, elaboration has been found to be enhanced when the message is seen as coming from several sources versus a single source. However, this effect only occurs if the sources are seen as independent of one another (e.g. Harkins & Petty, 1987). One explanation that has been advanced for this effect is that information coming from multiple independent sources is seen as more valid because it is based on a variety of perspectives. In contrast, increasing the number of targets of persuasion has been found to lead to less elaboration of messages (e.g. Petty, Harkins & Williams, 1980). This effect has been postulated to occur because people feel less personally responsible for evaluating the adequacy of the message when they know others are also evaluating the message. Finally, under high elaboration conditions, one might expect that knowing a message comes from multiple independent sources versus a single source could bias elaboration in a positive manner because the message is seen as representing multiple perspectives.

A final group variable that will be discussed in the context of the ELM is group polarization. When individuals who have attitudes of similar valence toward a topic discuss the topic in a group, postdiscussion attitudes become more extreme (e.g. see Myers & Lamm, 1976). The ELM suggests several mechanisms for this effect depending upon level of elaboration. Under low elaboration, merely discovering that others share your opinion might serve as a cue that your attitude is appropriate and thus enhance a person's confidence in the attitude. This in turn might make a person willing to endorse a more extreme position. On the other hand, under moderate elaboration conditions, the act of discussing the topic in a group might enhance elaboration of the issue. Research has suggested that mere thought about a topic will tend to produce attitude consistent thoughts, which will in turn enhance the extremity of the attitude (Tesser, 1978). Finally, under high elaboration, learning that others share your opinion might further bias a person to generate attitude consistent thoughts, which would enhance attitude extremity. Alternatively, because people will tend to generate arguments consistent with their attitudes, group discussion might result in a person learning additional arguments in support of the position from other members thereby making the attitude more extreme. This explanation is similar to the persuasive arguments explanation for group polarization (see Myers & Lamm, 1976).

Consequences of Elaboration

Another important postulate of the ELM is that the greater the amount of elaboration during attitude formation and change, the stronger the resulting attitude will be (see Petty et al., 1995). For example, research has suggested that attitudes associated with high elaboration are more predictive of behavior in contexts such as obeying community laws (Brown, 1974), reaching decisions in jury deliberation tasks (Shestowsky et al., 1998), voting for presidential candidates (Cacioppo et al., 1986), and choosing consumer products (Petty et al., 1983) than are attitudes associated with low elaboration.

Increased elaboration has also been associated with greater attitude change persistence. For example, Haugtvedt & Petty (1992) exposed high and low need for cognition people to an advertisement about a telephone answering machine and then measured their post-message attitudes. Two days later they re-measured their attitudes towards the product. Although attitudes for high and low need for cognition participants were equivalent immediately following the message, attitudes for the high need for cognition participants (those who enjoy thinking and spontaneously engage in elaboration across situations) were substantially more persistent over time than those of low need for cognition participants (those who don't enjoy thinking, and tend to elaborate only when provided with sufficient external motivation). Increased personal involvement has been found to be associated with greater attitude persistence within the context of advertisements for bicycles (Haugtvedt & Strathman, 1990).

Finally, enhanced elaboration has also been found to produce attitudes that are more resistant to counter-persuasion. For instance, Haugtvedt & Petty (1992) found that high need for cognition participants who received an initial message about a food additive were more resistant to a subsequent opposing message than were low need for cognition participants. Similarly, Haugtvedt & Wegener (1994) found that people who received an initial message about nuclear power under high involvement conditions were more resistant to a second opposing message than were people who received the initial message under low involvement conditions.

Summary and Applied Implications

Applied professionals have often been primarily interested in establishing what variables enhance or inhibit persuasion without necessarily being interested in the processes by which these variables have their influence. The ELM illustrates the value of carefully attending not only to whether a variable influences the amount of persuasion, but also to the cognitive processes by which the variable influences attitude change.

First, the ELM highlights that some attitude change is likely to be more consequential than other attitude change. If change occurs as a result of extensive elaboration, then attitudes are likely to be strong; on the other hand, if change occurs as a result of peripheral cues, then attitudes are likely to be weak. Therefore, in most cases, developers of communication campaigns should strive to create conditions that provide both motivation and ability to extensively elaborate messages. The ELM provides guidance with respect to a number of variables that have been found to influence elaboration. Interestingly, applied researchers (e.g. Rogers & Storey, 1987) have noted that campaigns are often unsuccessful when they fail to establish the conditions likely to foster elaboration of the message (e.g. personal relevance). Thus, when testing persuasive messages to be used for campaigns, applied researchers should assess not only the amount of attitude change produced by the messages but also the extent to which this change was a result of elaboration versus peripheral cues.

The ELM further suggests that when designing each feature of a message and persuasion context, applied professionals should carefully consider how each feature is likely to influence persuasion across a wide range of possible levels of elaboration. Ideally, practitioners should build in features that will be likely to enhance persuasion via all four possible roles. For example, when a company selects a spokesperson for its product, they should select someone who is not only credible and likeable but also directly relevant to the product. Thus, regardless of background elaboration, this spokesperson can enhance persuasion by serving as a peripheral cue, a motivation to elaborate, a positive bias on elaboration, or a central argument. The large research literature under the auspices of ELM and other theories has identified a number of variables that could be of use to practitioners in this regard.

EPILOGUE

This chapter has examined attitudes within the framework of the social cognition revolution. Attitudes were conceived of as cognitive structures and a number of important properties of such structures were discussed. Next, the psychological processes by which attitudes influence information processing and behavior were examined. Finally, the processes by which attitudes are formed and changed was addressed from the perspective of one recent information processing theory of attitude formation and change, the ELM. In examining each of these topics, we highlighted how basic principles from attitude research could be used to assist in the prediction and change of behavior in a variety of applied contexts including health, marketing, politics, and business management.

ACKNOWLEDGMENTS

Preparation of this chapter was supported by a grant from the Social Sciences and Humanities Research Council of Canada to Leandre R. Fabrigar. The authors would like to thank Frank Durso, David Roskos-Ewoldsen, and an anonymous reviewer for their helpful comments on an earlier version of this chapter.

REFERENCES

Ajzen, I. (1985). From intentions to actions: a theory of planned behavior. In J. Kuhl & J. Beckman (Eds), *Action Control: From Cognition to Behavior* (pp. 11–39). Heidelberg: Springer.

Ajzen, I. (1987). Attitudes, traits, and actions: dispositional prediction of behavior in personality and social psychology. *Advances in Experimental Social Psychology*, 20, 1–63.

Ajzen, I. (1991). The theory of planned behavior. *Organizational Behavior and Human Decision Processes*, 50, 179–211.

Ajzen, I. & Fishbein, M. (1980). *Understanding Attitudes and Predicting Social Behavior*. Englewood Cliffs, NJ: Prentice Hall.

Anderson, J. R. (1983). *The Architecture of Cognition*. Cambridge, MA: Harvard University Press.

Backer, T. E., Rogers, E. M. & Sopory, P. (1992). *Designing Health Communication Campaigns: What Works?* Newbury Park, CA: Sage.

Baker, S. M. & Petty, R. E. (1994). Majority and minority influence: source–position imbalance as a determinant of message scrutiny. *Journal of Personality and Social Psychology*, 67, 5–19.

Bassili, J. N. (1995). Response latency and the accessibility of voting intentions: what contributes to accessibility and how it affects vote choice. *Personality and Social Psychology Bulletin*, 21, 686–95.

Bassili, J. N. (1996). Meta-judgmental versus operative indexes of psychological attributes: the case of measures of attitude strength. *Journal of Personality and Social Psychology*, 71, 637–53.

Bassili, J. N. & Fletcher, J. F. (1991). Response-time measurement in survey research. *Public Opinion Quarterly*, 55, 331–46.

Bentler, P. M. & Speckart, G. (1979). Models of attitude–behavior relations. *Psychological Review*, 86, 452–64.

Berent, M. K. & Krosnick, J. A. (1993). Attitude importance and the organisation of attitude-relevant knowledge in memory. Unpublished manuscript, Ohio State University, Columbus.

Biddle, B. J., Bank, B. J. & Slavings, R. L. (1987). Norms, preferences, identities and retention decisions. *Social Psychology Quarterly*, 50, 322–37.

Boninger, D. S., Krosnick, J. A., Berent, M. K. & Fabrigar, L. R. (1995). The causes and consequences of attitude importance. In R. E. Petty & J. A. Krosnick (Eds), *Attitude Strength: Antecedents and Consequences* (pp. 159–90). Mahwah, NJ: Erlbaum.

Brannon, L. A. & Brock, T. C. (1994). Test of Schema Correspondence Theory of persuasion: effects of matching an appeal to actual, ideal, and product "selves." In E. M. Clark, T. C. Brock & D. W. Stewart (Eds), *Attention, Attitude, and Affect in Response to Advertising* (pp. 169–88). Hillsdale, NJ: Lawrence Erlbaum.

Breckler, S. J. (1984). Empirical validation of affect, behavior, and cognition as distinct components of attitude. *Journal of Personality and Social Psychology*, 47, 1191–205.

Breckler, S. J. (1994). A comparison of numerical indexes for measuring attitude ambivalence. *Educational and Psychological Measurement*, 54, 350–65.

Breckler, S. J. & Wiggins, E. C. (1989). Affect versus evaluation in the structure of attitudes. *Journal of Experimental Social Psychology*, 25, 253–71.

Brock, T. C., Brannon, L. A. & Bridgwater, C. (1990). Message effectiveness can be increased by matching appeals to recipients' self-schemas: laboratory demonstrations and a national field experiment. In S. Agres, J. Edell & T. Dubitsky (Eds), *Emotion in Advertising: Theoretical and Practical Explorations* (pp. 285–315). Westport, CT: Quorum Books.

Brown, D. W. (1974). Adolescent attitudes and lawful behavior. *Public Opinion Quarterly*, 38, 98–106.

Cacioppo, J. T., Gardner, W. L. & Berntson, G. (1997). Beyond bipolar conceptualizations and measures: the case of attitudes and evaluative space. *Personality and Social Psychology Review*, 1, 3–25.

Cacioppo, J. T. & Petty, R. E. (1979). Effects of message repetition and position on cognitive response, recall, and persuasion. *Journal of Personality and Social Psychology*, 37, 97–107.

Cacioppo, J. T., Petty, R. E., Kao, C. F. & Rodriguez, R. (1986). Central and peripheral routes to persuasion: an individual difference perspective. *Journal of Personality and Social Psychology*, 51, 1032–43.

Chaiken, S. & Baldwin, M. W. (1981). Affective–cognitive consistency and the effect of salient behavioral information on the self-perception of attitudes. *Journal of Personality and Social Psychology*, 41, 1–12.

Chaiken, S., Liberman, A. & Eagly, A. H. (1989). Heuristic and systematic processing within and beyond the persuasion context. In J. S. Uleman & J. A. Bargh (Eds), *Unintended Thought* (pp. 212–52). New York: Guilford.

Chaiken, S. & Maheswaran, D. (1994). Heuristic processing can bias systematic processing: effects of source credibility, argument ambiguity, and task importance on attitude judgment. *Journal of Personality and Social Psychology*, 66, 460–73.

Chaiken, S., Pomerantz, E. M. & Giner-Sorolla, R. (1995). Structural consistency and attitude strength. In R. E. Petty & J. A. Krosnick (Eds), *Attitude Strength: Antecedents and Consequences* (pp. 387–412). Mahwah, NJ: Erlbaum.

Cotton, J. L. (1985). Cognitive dissonance in selective exposure. In D. Zillmann & J. Bryant (Eds), *Selective Exposure to Communication* (pp. 11–33). Hillsdale, NJ: Erlbaum.
Crites, S. L. Jr, Fabrigar, L. R. & Petty, R. E. (1994). Measuring the affective and cognitive properties of attitudes: conceptual and methodological issues. *Personality and Social Psychology Bulletin*, 20, 619–34.
Davidson, A. R. (1995). From attitudes to actions to attitude change: the effects of amount and accuracy of information. In R. E. Petty & J. A. Krosnick (Eds), *Attitude Strength: Antecedents and Consequences* (pp. 315–36). Mahwah, NJ: Erlbaum.
Davidson, A. R. & Jaccard, J. J. (1979). Variables that moderate the attitude–behavior relation: results of a longitudinal survey. *Journal of Personality and Social Psychology*, 37, 1364–76.
Davidson, A. R., Yantis, S., Norwood, M. & Montano, D. E. (1985). Amount of information about the attitude object and attitude–behavior consistency. *Journal of Personality and Social Psychology*, 49, 1184–98.
Dawes, R. M. & Smith, T. L. (1985). Attitude and opinion measurement. In G. Lindzey & E. Aronson (Eds), *The Handbook of Social Psychology* (3rd edn, vol. 1, pp. 509–66). New York: Random House.
Devine, P. G., Hamilton, D. L. & Ostrom, T. M. (Eds) (1994). *Social Cognition: Impact on Social Psychology*. San Diego: Academic Press.
Eagly, A. H. & Chaiken, S. (1993). *The Psychology of Attitudes*. Fort Worth, TX: Harcourt, Brace, Jovanovich.
Eagly, A. H. & Chaiken, S. (1995). Attitude strength, attitude structure, and resistance to change. In R. E. Petty & J. A. Krosnick (Eds), *Attitude Strength: Antecedents and Consequences* (pp. 413–32). Mahwah, NJ: Erlbaum.
Eagly, A. H. & Chaiken, S. (1998). Attitude structure and function. In D. Gilbert, S. Fiske & G. Lindzey (Eds), *The Handbook of Social Psychology* (4th edn). New York: McGraw-Hill.
Eagly, A. H., Mladinic, A. & Otto, S. (1994). Cognitive and affective bases of attitudes toward social groups and social policies. *Journal of Experimental Social Psychology*, 30, 113–37.
Echabe, A. E. & Rovira, D. P. (1989). Social representations and memory: the case of AIDS. *European Journal of Social Psychology*, 19, 543–51.
Edwards, K. (1990). The interplay of affect and cognition in attitude formation and change. *Journal of Personality and Social Psychology*, 59, 202–16.
Edwards, K. & von Hippel, W. (1995). Hearts and minds: the priority of affective versus cognitive factors in person perception. *Personality and Social Psychology Bulletin*, 21, 996–1011.
Ehrlich, D., Guttman, I., Schonbach, P. & Mills, J. (1957). Postdecision exposure to relevant information. *Journal of Abnormal and Social Psychology*, 54, 98–102.
Fabrigar, L. R. & Petty, R. E. (1999). The role of the affective and cognitive bases of attitudes in susceptibility to affectively and cognitively based persuasion. *Personality and Social Psychology Bulletin*, 25, 91–107.
Fabrigar, L. R., Priester, J. R., Petty, R. E. & Wegener, D. T. (1998). The impact of attitude accessibility on elaboration of persuasive messages. *Personality and Social Psychology Bulletin*, 24, 339–52.
Fazio, R. H. (1989). On the power and functionality of attitudes: the role of attitude accessibility. In A. R. Pratkanis, S. J. Breckler & A. G. Greenwald (Eds), *Attitude Structure and Function* (pp. 153–79). Hillsdale, NJ: Erlbaum.
Fazio, R. H. (1990). Multiple processes by which attitudes guide behavior: the MODE model as an integrative framework. *Advances in Experimental Social Psychology*, 23, 75–109.
Fazio, R. H. (1995). Attitudes as object-evaluation associations: determinants, consequences, and correlates of attitude accessibility. In R. E. Petty & J. A. Krosnick (Eds), *Attitude Strength: Antecedents and Consequences* (pp. 247–82). Mahwah, NJ: Erlbaum.
Fazio, R. H., Powell, M. C. & Williams, C. J. (1989). The role of attitude accessibility in the attitude-to-behavior process. *Journal of Consumer Research*, 16, 280–8.

Fazio, R. H. & Williams, C. J. (1986). Attitude accessibility as a moderator of the attitude–perception and attitude–behavior relations: an investigation of the 1984 presidential election. *Journal of Personality and Social Psychology*, 51, 505–14.

Fazio, R. H. & Zanna, M. P. (1978). Attitudinal qualities relating to the strength of the attitude–behavior relationship. *Journal of Experimental Social Psychology*, 14, 398–408.

Festinger, L. (1957). *A Theory of Cognitive Dissonance*. Stanford: Stanford University Press.

Fishbein, M. & Ajzen, I. (1974). Attitudes towards objects as predictors of single and multiple behavioral criteria. *Psychological Review*, 81, 59–74.

Fishbein, M. & Ajzen, I. (1975). *Belief, Attitude, Intention, and Behavior: an Introduction to Theory and Research*. Reading, MA: Addison-Wesley.

Fishbein, M. & Ajzen, I. (1980). Predicting and understanding consumer behavior: attitude–behavior correspondence. In I. Ajzen & M. Fishbein (Eds), *Understanding Attitudes and Predicting Social Behavior* (pp. 148–72). Englewood Cliffs, NJ: Prentice Hall.

Fishbein, M., Ajzen, I. & Hinkle, R. (1980). Predicting and understanding voting in American elections: effects of external variables. In I. Ajzen & M. Fishbein (Eds), *Understanding Attitudes and Predicting Social Behavior* (pp. 173–95). Englewood Cliffs, NJ: Prentice Hall.

Fiske, S. T. & Taylor, S. E. (1991). *Social Cognition* (2nd edn). New York: McGraw-Hill.

Forgas, J. (1995). Mood and judgment: the affect–infusion model (AIM). *Psychological Bulletin*, 117, 39–66.

Frey, D. (1986). Recent research on selective exposure to information. In L. Berkowitz (Ed.), *Advances in Experimental Social Psychology* (vol. 19, pp. 41–80). San Diego, CA: Academic Press.

Grant, M. J., Button, C. M. & Noseworthy, J. (1994). Predicting attitude stability. *Canadian Journal of Behavioural Science*, 26, 68–84.

Hamilton, D. L., Devine, P. G. & Ostrom, T. M. (1994). Social cognition and classic issues in social psychology. In P. G. Devine, D. L. Hamilton & T. M. Ostrom (Eds), *Social Cognition: Impact on Social Psychology* (pp. 1–13). San Diego: Academic Press.

Harkins, S. G. & Petty, R. E. (1987). Information utility and the multiple source effect. *Journal of Personality and Social Psychology*, 52, 260–8.

Hastorf, A. & Cantril, H. (1954). They saw a game: a case study. *Journal of Abnormal and Social Psychology*, 49, 129–34.

Haugtvedt, C. P. & Petty, R. E. (1992). Personality and persuasion: need for cognition moderates persistence and resistance of attitude changes. *Journal of Personality and Social Psychology*, 63, 308–19.

Haugtvedt, C. P. & Strathman, A. (1990). Situational personal relevance and attitude persistence. *Advances in Consumer Research*, 17, 766–9.

Haugtvedt, C. P. & Wegener, D. T. (1994). Message order effects in persuasion: an attitude strength perspective. *Journal of Consumer Research*, 21, 205–18.

Hausenblas, H. A., Carron, A. V. & Mack, D. E. (1997). Application of the theories of reasoned action and planned behavior to exercise behavior: a meta-analysis. *Journal of Sport and Exercise Psychology*, 19, 36–51.

Hodges, S. D. & Wilson, T. D. (1993). Effects of analyzing reasons on attitude change: the moderating role of attitude accessibility. *Social Cognition*, 11, 353–66.

Houston, D. A. & Fazio, R. H. (1989). Biased processing as a function of attitude accessibility: making objective judgments subjectively. *Social Cognition*, 7, 51–66.

Johnson, B. T. & Eagly, A. H. (1989). Effects of involvement on persuasion: a meta-analysis. *Psychological Bulletin*, 106, 290–314.

Johnson, B. T. & Eagly, A. H. (1990). Involvement and persuasion: types, traditions, and the evidence. *Psychological Bulletin*, 107, 375–84.

Johnson, J. T. & Judd, C. M. (1983). Overlooking the incongruent: categorisation biases in the identification of political statements. *Journal of Personality and Social Psychology*, 45, 978–96.

Jonas, K., Diehl, M. & Bromer, P. (1997). Effects of attitudinal ambivalence on

information processing and attitude intention consistency. *Journal of Experimental Social Psychology*, 33, 190–210.
Judd, C. M. & Downing, J. W. (1990). Political expertise and the development of attitude consistency. *Social Cognition*, 8, 104–24.
Judd, C. M., Drake, R. A., Downing, J. W. & Krosnick, J. A. (1991). Some dynamic properties of attitude structures: context-induced response facilitation and polarization. *Journal of Personality and Social Psychology*, 60, 193–202.
Judd, C. M. & Krosnick, J. A. (1989). The structural bases of attitude consistency. In A. R. Pratkanis, S. J. Breckler & A. G. Greenwald (Eds), *Attitude Structure and Function* (pp. 99–128). Hillsdale, NJ: Erlbaum.
Kallgren, C. A. & Wood, W. (1986). Access to attitude-relevant information in memory as a determinant of attitude–behavior consistency. *Journal of Experimental Social Psychology*, 22, 328–38.
Kaplan, K. J. (1972). On the ambivalence–indifference problem in attitude theory and measurement: a suggested modification of the semantic differential technique. *Psychological Bulletin*, 77, 361–72.
Katz, D. (1960). The functional approach to the study of attitudes. *Public Opinion Quarterly*, 24, 163–204.
Katz, I. & Hass, R. G. (1988). Racial ambivalence and American value conflict: correlational and priming studies of dual cognitive structures. *Journal of Personality and Social Psychology*, 55, 893–905.
Katz, D. & Stotland, E. (1959). A preliminary statement of a theory of attitude structure and change. In S. Koch (Ed.), *Psychology: A Study of a Science* (vol. 3, pp. 423–75). New York: McGraw-Hill.
Kelman, H. C. (1958). Compliance, identification, and internalization: three processes of attitude change. *Journal of Conflict Resolution*, 2, 51–60.
Krosnick, J. A. & Petty, R. E. (1995). Attitude strength: an overview. In R. E. Petty & J. A. Krosnick (Eds), *Attitude Strength: Antecedents and Consequences* (pp. 1–24). Mahwah, NJ: Erlbaum.
Levine, J. M. (1989). Reaction to opinion deviance in small groups. In P. B. Paulus (Ed.), *Psychology of Group Influence* (2nd edn, pp. 187–231). Hillsdale, NJ: Erlbaum.
Liska, A. E. (1984). A critical examination of the causal structure of the Fishbein/Ajzen attitude–behavior model. *Social Psychology Quarterly*, 47, 61–74.
Lord, C. G., Ross, L. & Lepper, M. R. (1979). Biased assimilation and attitude polarization: the effects of prior theories on subsequently considered evidence. *Journal of Personality and Social Psychology*, 37, 2098–109.
Lowin, A. (1967). Approach and avoidance as alternative modes of selective exposure to information. *Journal of Personality and Social Psychology*, 6, 1–9.
Mackie, D. M. & Worth, L. T. (1989). Processing deficits and the mediation of positive affect in persuasion. *Journal of Personality and Social Psychology*, 57, 27–40.
Madden, T. J., Ellen, P. S. & Ajzen, I. (1992). A comparison of the theory of planned behavior and the theory of reasoned action. *Personality and Social Psychology Bulletin*, 18, 3–9.
McGuire, W. J. (1985). Attitudes and attitude change. In G. Lindzey & E. Aronson (Eds), *Handbook of Social Psychology* (3rd edn, vol. 2, pp. 233–346). New York: Random House.
McGuire, W. J. (1989). The structure of individual attitudes and attitude systems. In A. R. Pratkanis, S. J. Breckler & A. G. Greenwald (Eds), *Attitude Structure and Function* (pp. 37–69). Hillsdale, NJ: Erlbaum.
McGuire, W. J. & McGuire, C. V. (1991). The content, structure, and operation of thought systems. In R. Wyer & T. Srull (Eds), *Advances in Social Cognition* (vol. 4, pp. 1–78). Hillsdale, NJ: Erlbaum.
Messé, L. A., Bodenhausen, G. V. & Nelson, T. D. (1995). Affect–cognition congruence and attitude change: a re-examination. Paper presented at the annual convention of the American Psychological Society, New York.

Millar, M. G. (1992). Effects of experience on matched and mismatched arguments and attitudes. *Social Behavior and Personality*, 20, 47–56.
Millar, M. G. & Millar, K. U. (1990). Attitude change as a function of attitude type and argument type. *Journal of Personality and Social Psychology*, 59, 217–28.
Millar, M. G. & Millar, K. U. (1993). Changing breast self-examination attitudes: influences of repression–sensitization and attitude–message match. *Journal of Research in Personality*, 27, 301–14.
Millar, M. G. & Tesser, A. (1986). Effects of affective and cognitive focus on the attitude–behavior relation. *Journal of Personality and Social Psychology*, 51, 270–6.
Millar, M. G. & Tesser, A. (1989). Effects of affective–cognitive consistency and thought on the attitude–behavior relation. *Journal of Experimental Social Psychology*, 25, 189–202.
Moore, M. (1980). Validation of attitude toward any practice scale through the use of ambivalence as a moderator variable. *Education and Psychological Measurement*, 40, 205–8.
Moore, D. L., Hausknecht, D. & Thamodaran, K. (1986). Time compression, response opportunity, and persuasion. *Journal of Consumer Research*, 13, 85–99.
Moscovici, S. (1980). Toward a theory of conversion behavior. In L. Berkowitz (Ed.), *Advances in Experimental Social Psychology* (vol. 13, pp. 209–39). New York: Academic Press.
Myers, D. G. & Lamm, H. (1976). The group polarization phenomenon. *Psychological Bulletin*, 83, 602–27.
Norman, R. (1975). Affective–cognitive consistency, attitudes, conformity, and behavior. *Journal of Personality and Social Psychology*, 32, 83–91.
Norman, N. M. & Tedeschi, J. T. (1989). Self-presentation, reasoned action, and adolescents' decisions to smoke cigarettes. *Journal of Applied Social Psychology*, 19, 543–58.
Ostrom, T. M. (1984). The sovereignty of social cognition. In R. S. Wyer Jr & T. K. Srull (Eds), *Handbook of Social Cognition* (vol. 1, pp. 1–38). Hillsdale, NJ: Erlbaum.
Ostrom, T. M. (1969). The relationship between affective, behavioral, and cognitive components of attitude. *Journal of Experimental Social Psychology*, 5, 12–30.
Petty, R. E. & Cacioppo, J. T. (1986a). *Communication and Persuasion: Central and Peripheral Routes to Attitude Change*. New York: Springer-Verlag.
Petty, R. E. & Cacioppo, J. T. (1986b). The elaboration likelihood model of persuasion. In L. Berkowitz (Ed.), *Advances in Experimental Social Psychology* (vol. 19, pp. 123–205). New York: Academic Press.
Petty, R. E. & Cacioppo, J. T. (1990). Involvement and persuasion: tradition versus integration. *Psychological Bulletin*, 107, 367–74.
Petty, R. E. & Wegener, D. T. (1998). Matching versus mismatching attitude functions: implications for scrutiny of persuasive messages. *Personality and Social Psychology Bulletin*, 24, 227–40.
Petty, R. E., Cacioppo, J. T. & Goldman, R. (1981). Personal involvement as a determinant of argument-based persuasion. *Journal of Personality and Social Psychology*, 41, 847–55.
Petty, R. E., Cacioppo, J. T. & Schumann, D. (1983). Central and peripheral routes to advertising effectiveness: the moderating role of involvement. *Journal of Consumer Research*, 10, 134–48.
Petty, R. E., Gleicher, F. & Baker, S. M. (1991). Multiple roles for affect in persuasion. In J. Forgas (Ed.), *Emotion and Social Judgments* (pp. 181–200). New York: Pergamon Press.
Petty, R. E., Harkins, S. G. & Williams, K. D. (1980). The effects of group diffusion of cognitive effort on attitudes: an information processing view. *Journal of Personality and Social Psychology*, 38, 81–92.
Petty, R. E., Haugtvedt, C. P. & Smith, S. M. (1995). Elaboration as a determinant of attitude strength: creating attitudes that are persistent, resistant, and predictive of

behavior. In R. E. Petty & J. A. Krosnick (Eds), *Attitude Strength: Antecedents and Consequences* (pp. 93–130). Mahwah, NJ: Erlbaum.

Petty, R. E., Priester, J. R. & Wegener, D. T. (1994). Cognitive processes in attitude change. In R. S. Wyer & T. K. Srull (Eds), *Handbook of Social Cognition* (2nd edn, vol. 2, pp. 69–142).

Petty, R. E., Wegener, D. T. & Fabrigar, L. R. (1997). Attitudes and attitude change. *Annual Review of Psychology*, 48, 609–47.

Petty, R. E., Wells, G. L. & Brock, T. C. (1976). Distraction can enhance or reduce yielding to propaganda: thought disruption versus effort justification. *Journal of Personality and Social Psychology*, 34, 874–84.

Petty, R. E., Schumann, D. W., Richman, S. A. & Strathman, A. J. (1993). Positive mood and persuasion: different roles for affect under high- and low-elaboration conditions. *Journal of Personality and Social Psychology*, 64, 5–20.

Pratkanis, A. R. (1989). The cognitive representation of attitudes. In A. R. Pratkanis, S. J. Breckler & A. G. Greenwald (Eds), *Attitude Structure and Function* (pp. 71–98). Hillsdale, NJ: Erlbaum.

Priester, J. R. & Petty, R. E. (1996). The gradual threshold model of ambivalence: relating the positive and negative bases of attitudes to subjective ambivalence. *Journal of Personality and Social Psychology*, 71, 431–49.

Rajecki, D. W. (1990). *Attitudes*. Sunderland, MA: Sinauer Associates.

Rogers, E. M. & Storey, J. D. (1987). Communication campaigns. In C. R. Berger & S. H. Chaffee (Eds), *Handbook of Communication Science* (pp. 817–46). Newbury Park, CA: Sage.

Rosenberg, M. J. (1968). Hedonism, inauthenticity, and other goals toward expansion of a consistency theory. In R. P. Abelson, E. Aronson, W. J. McGuire, T. M. Newcomb, M. J. Rosenberg & P. H. Tannenbaum (Eds), *Theories of Cognitive Consistency: A Sourcebook* (pp. 73–111). Chicago: Rand McNally.

Rosenberg, M. J. & Hovland, C. I. (1960). Cognitive, affective, and behavioral components of attitude. In M. J. Rosenberg, C. I. Hovland, W. J. McGuire, R. P. Abelson & J. W. Brahm (Eds), *Attitude Organization and Change* (pp. 1–14). New Haven, CT: Yale University Press.

Roskos-Ewoldsen, D. R. & Fazio, R. H. (1992). On the orienting value of attitudes: attitude accessibility as a determinant of an object's attraction of visual attention. *Journal of Personality and Social Psychology*, 18, 19–25.

Sanbonmatsu, D. M. & Fazio, R. H. (1990). The role of attitudes in memory-based decision making. *Journal of Personality and Social Psychology*, 59, 614–22.

Schuette, R. A. & Fazio, R. H. (1995). Attitude accessibility and motivation as determinants of biased processing: a test of the MODE model. *Personality and Social Psychology Bulletin*, 21, 704–10.

Schwarz, N. (1990). Feelings as information: informational and motivational functions of affective states. In R. M. Sorrentino & E. T. Higgins (Eds), *Handbook of Motivation and Cognition: Foundations of Social Behavior* (vol. 2, pp. 527–61). New York: Guilford Press.

Schwartz, S. H. & Tessler, R. C. (1972). A test of a model for reducing attitude–behavior discrepancies. *Journal of Personality and Social Psychology*, 24, 225–36.

Scott, W. A. (1968). Attitude measurement. In G. Lindsey & E. Aronson (Eds), *The Handbook of Social Psychology* (vol. 2, pp. 204–73). Reading, MA: Addison-Wesley.

Scott, W. A. (1969). Structure of natural cognitions. *Journal of Personality and Social Psychology*, 12, 261–78.

Sears, D. O. (1965). Biased indoctrination selectivity of exposure to new information. *Sociometry*, 28, 363–76.

Shavitt, S. (1989). Operationalizing functional theories of attitude. In A. R. Pratkanis, S. J. Breckler & A. G. Greenwald (Eds), *Attitude Structure and Function* (pp. 311–37). Hillsdale, NJ: Erlbaum.

Shavitt, S. (1990). The role of attitude objects in attitude functions. *Journal of Experimental Social Psychology*, 26, 124–48.

Shavitt, S., Swan, S., Lowrey, T. M. & Wanke, M. (1994). The interaction of endorser attractiveness and involvement in persuasion depends on the goal that guides message processing. *Journal of Consumer Psychology*, 3, 137–62.

Sheppard, B. H., Hartwick, J. & Warshaw, P. R. (1988). The theory of reasoned action: a meta-analysis of past research with recommendation for modifications and future research. *Journal of Consumer Research*, 15, 325–43.

Sherif, M. & Hovland, C. I. (1961). *Social Judgment: Assimilation and Contrast Effects in Communication and Attitude Change*. New Haven, CT: Yale University Press.

Sherman, S. J., Judd, C. M. & Park, B. (1989). Social cognition. In M. R. Rosenzweig & L. W. Porter (Eds), *Annual Review of Psychology* (vol. 40, pp. 281–326). Palo Alto, CA: Annual Reviews.

Shestowsky, D., Wegener, D. T. & Fabrigar, L. R. (1998). Need for cognition and interpersonal influence: individual differences in impact on dyadic decisions. *Journal of Personality and Social Psychology*, 74, 1317–28.

Smith, M. B. (1947). The personal setting of public opinions: a study of attitudes toward Russia. *Public Opinion Quarterly*, 11, 507–23.

Smith, M. B., Bruner, J. S. & White, R. W. (1956). *Opinions and Personality*. New York: Wiley.

Snyder, M. & DeBono, K. G. (1985). Appeals to images and claims about quality: understanding the psychology of advertising. *Journal of Personality and Social Psychology*, 49, 586–97.

Snyder, M. & DeBono, K. G. (1989). Understanding the functions of attitudes: lessons from personality and social behavior. In A. R. Pratkanis, S. J. Breckler & A. G. Greenwald (Eds), *Attitude Structure and Function* (pp. 339–59). Hillsdale, NJ: Erlbaum.

Sparks, P., Hedderly, D. & Shepherd, R. (1992). An investigation into the relationship between perceived control, attitude variability and the consumption of two common foods. *European Journal of Social Psychology*, 22, 55–71.

Stasson, M. & Fishbein, M. (1990). The relation between perceived risk and preventative action: a within-subject analysis of perceived driving risk and intentions to wear seatbelts. *Journal of Applied Social Psychology*, 20, 1541–57.

Steffen, V. J. (1990). Men's motivation to perform the testicle self-exam: effects of prior knowledge and an educational brochure. *Journal of Applied Social Psychology*, 20, 681–702.

Tanford, S. & Penrod, S. (1984). Social influence model: a formal integration of research on majority and minority influence processes. *Psychological Bulletin*, 95, 189–225.

Tesser, A. (1978). Self-generated attitude change. In L. Berkowitz (Ed.), *Advances in Experimental Social Psychology* (vol. 11, pp. 290–338). New York: Academic Press.

Thomson, M. M., Zanna, M. P. & Griffin, D. W. (1995). Let's not be indifferent about (attitudinal) ambivalence. In R. E. Petty & J. A. Krosnick (Eds), *Attitude Strength: Antecedents and Consequences* (pp. 361–86). Mahwah, NJ: Erlbaum.

Trost, M. R., Maass, A. & Kenrick, D. T. (1992). Minority influence: personal relevance biases cognitive processes and reverses private acceptance. *Journal of Experimental Social Psychology*, 28, 234–54.

Vallone, R. P., Ross, L. & Lepper, M. R. (1985). The hostile media phenomenon: biased perception and perceptions of media bias in coverage of the Beirut massacre. *Journal of Personality and Social Psychology*, 49, 577–85.

Wegener, D. T., Petty, R. E. & Smith, S. M. (1995). Positive mood can increase or decrease message scrutiny: the hedonic contingency view of mood and message processing. *Journal of Personality and Social Psychology*, 69, 5–15.

Weigel, R. H. & Newman, L. S. (1976). Increasing attitude–behavior correspondence by broadening the scope of the behavioral measure. *Journal of Personality and Social Psychology*, 33, 793–802.

Wicker, A. W. (1969). Attitudes versus actions: the relationship of verbal and overt behavioral responses to attitude objects. *Journal of Social Issues*, 25, 41–78.

Wood, W., Rhodes, N. & Biek, M. (1995). Working knowledge and attitude strength: an information processing analysis. In R. E. Petty & J. A. Krosnick (Eds), *Attitude Strength: Antecedents and Consequences* (pp. 283–314). Mahwah, NJ: Erlbaum.

Zanna, M. P. & Rempel, J. K. (1988). Attitudes: a new look at an old concept. In D. Bar-Tal & A. W. Kruglanski (Eds), *The Social Psychology of Knowledge* (pp. 315–34). Cambridge: Cambridge University Press.

Section 2

Business and Industry

Chapter 8

The Cognitive Psychology And Cognitive Engineering of Industrial Systems

Neville Moray
University of Surrey

Cognitive activity in industrial human–machine systems had already been extensively studied by the 1960s. Lees (1974) provided a bibliography of several hundred articles relevant to human–machine interaction in process control, while Edwards and Lees (1974b) cited over one hundred *pages* of references on the same topic. For one entering the field, the following references are *sine qua non*: Edwards & Lees, 1974a; Rasmussen, 1986; Rasmussen, Pejtersen & Goodstein, L., 1995; Salvendy, 1997; Singleton, 1978. Collectively they provide an introduction to cognition in continuous process control systems (CPCS) and discrete manufacturing systems (DMS).

Cognition at work takes place in the world as much as in the head and is an example of "cultural cognition" (Hutchins, 1995). Consider Figure 8.1. Academic cognitive research is typically found in the shaded region, but the dynamics of organizations, and the constraints imposed by the outer levels in Figure 8.1, are always as important as cognitive abilities in determining performance in real tasks, while at the center the ergonomics of control rooms and the factory floor constrain the information available and the possibilities for action.

Handbook of Applied Cognition, Edited by F. T. Durso, R. S. Nickerson, R. W. Schvaneveldt, S. T. Dumais, D. S. Lindsay and M. T. H. Chi.

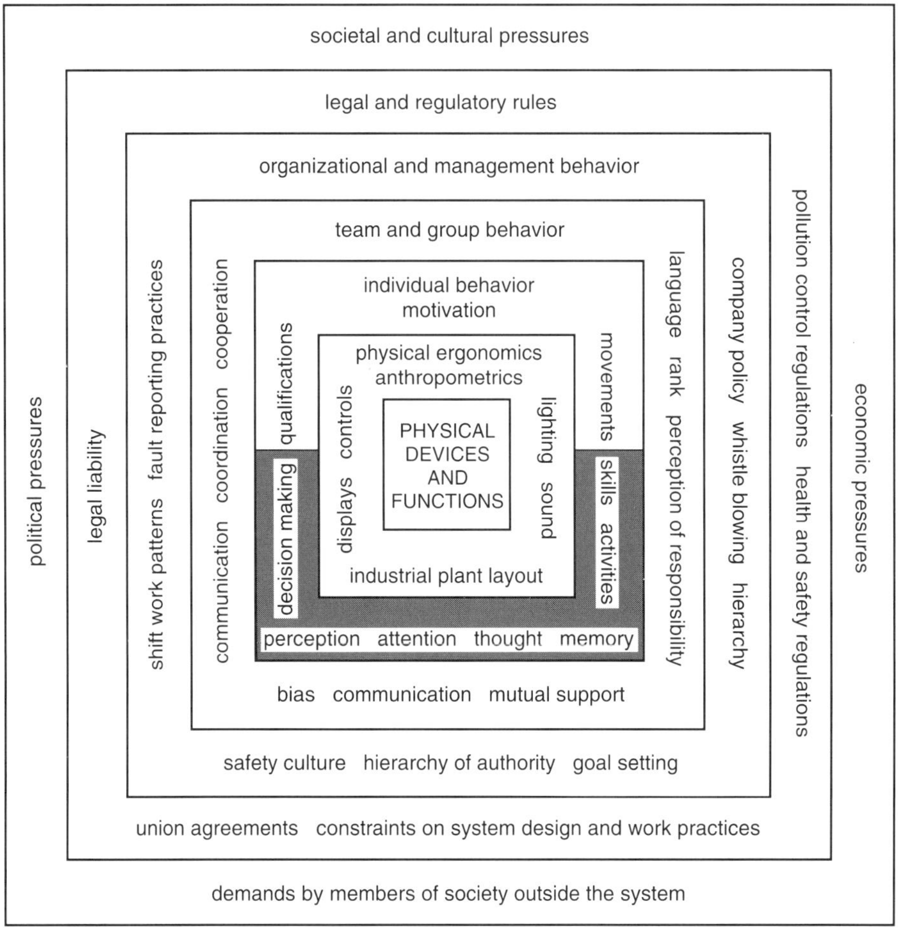

Figure 8.1 Constraints on Cognitive Behavior

CHARACTERISTICS OF INDUSTRIAL SYSTEMS

Progress towards increased industrial automation is continuous, but it is also widely accepted that humans should be retained in heavy industry, either as symbiotic partners with automation, for sociopolitical reasons, or both (Kuo & Hsu, 1990; Vierling, 1990). Humans are retained particularly as agents in fault management when plants may enter states which were not foreseen in design. Because we are concerned with cognition in human–machine *systems*, rather than human cognition *tout court*, cognition in industrial settings can only be understood in terms of the constraints on behavior imposed by the task environment (Hutchins, 1995; Rasmussen et al., 1995; Simon, 1981; Vicente, 1999). We need, therefore, first to examine the characteristics of industrial systems themselves. Four particularly important characteristics of industrial systems are their size, their complexity, their temporal characteristics, and the mode of control.

Size

Size is significant in two respects. The first is physical size: a worker cannot know what is happening in all parts of a plant, since the latter may extend over many hectares, and only a subset of information is displayed in the control room. Even in industries with a single control room operator there is cooperation between operator, maintenance and field personnel, management, etc., above all during abnormal or fault conditions. It may take many minutes to retrieve information and may involve cooperation through telephonic or other means of communication, as well as access to the information displayed in the control room.

Secondly, the functional size of a system is measured by its degrees of freedom, which is also one measure of the cognitive load on workers. Systems can be analyzed to find a minimal set of variables sufficient to describe and control the plant, and the number of entries in such a list is defined as its degrees of freedom. Any controller, human or otherwise, must be able to measure and act upon a correctly chosen set of variables at least equal to the degrees of freedom of the system. In a nuclear power plant (NPP) control room there may be 1000–2000 displays and controls, or several *hundred* pages of computerized displays. An NPP may be several square kilometers in extent and many meters high, and contain hundreds of thousands of parts. Such a plant has 40–50 degrees of freedom.

Complexity

There is no agreed definition of complexity, but it certainly includes the notion of many subsystems, parts and components which are interconnected. A major cognitive consequence of the complexity of industrial systems is that it is often difficult to know what will happen when one aspect of a system is changed. Any changes to a variable often propagate throughout many parts of the system, often with long delays, so that the correlations and causal relations are difficult to perceive, understand and predict.

Coupling is the physical causal origin of correlation among variables. If two parts of a system are coupled, change in one part affects the other. Perrow (1984) maintains that it is tight coupling which causes modern complex industrial systems to be so hazardous in the face of human error. One reason expert personnel with long experience of a system seldom intervene in its operation is that any intervention, even if locally successful in reducing the impact of a disturbance, may have widespread effects throughout the system due to coupling, and therefore produce undesirable effects distant in time and space. Human and machine intelligence, rather than physical force, are coupled through the human–machine interface.

Temporal Characteristics

Industrial systems operate in "real time." In modern DMS large inventories of stock are seldom held, so any order must be completed rapidly in response to the client's demand, a matter of months, days, hours, or minutes, depending on the product. In CPCS there are both explicit and implicit deadlines. Although CPCS may run continuously for many months, rates of heating and cooling can be altered; casting and annealing metal have particular tempos; and in highly dynamic processes such as nuclear fission it may be necessary to shut down a reactor within a few seconds.

The time constant of a system can be thought of informally as the shortest time over which a variable varies significantly, or as the inverse of the highest frequency present in the bandwidth of the system. The time constants of annealing metal are long – of the order of hours, while events in the fuel rods of a nuclear power reactor are of the order of microseconds. Scheduling dynamics have time constants of many hours, although individual machines used in DMS may have short time constants. The time constants of complex systems may not be immediately obvious. Fast transient impulses may perturb what is generally a slow process (Crossman, 1974; Crossman & Cooke, 1974). If there are components with very short time constants, the system may none the less be buffered by others acting as integrators, providing the equivalent of inertia, and a longer effective time constant.

The emphasis on "real time" reflects an important difference between laboratory environments and the industrial world. A failure to decrease the rate of energy generation in a system with a short time constant when the dynamics change because of a fault can cause anything from minor economic loss to catastrophic failure and death. Action must be taken by deadlines even without complete information, in the face of risk and hazard, and whether or not operators are confident that what they are doing is correct. By contrast, the start-up of an NPP or a petrochemical refinery takes several *days*, during which dozens or even hundreds of people are involved in more or less continuous decision making, day and night, with people changing shift, sharing information, and supporting one another's cognitive activity over many hours at a time.

To describe individual and group cognition and the dynamics of the cognitive tasks requires a knowledge of the rate at which the plant processes evolve, the timing of the arrival of information, the distribution in time and space of personnel, and the properties of communication channels involved. The rate at which people can make decisions is constrained by the rate at which physical events unfold and the way in which information is displayed, often more than by the psychological characteristics of the operators. Domain knowledge is essential for understanding cognition in real-world systems.

Modes of Control

In most modern plants some tasks are performed by fully automatic closed loop controllers, but distributed control is common, with tactical and strategic decisions being left to humans. Both open loop and closed loop control may be present.

A characteristic of expertise is a change from closed to open loop predictive control (Crossman & Cooke, 1974; Kelly, 1964; Moray, Lootsteen & Pajak,

1986). But a major problem of automation is that operators are no longer a component of the closed loop, and often become for long periods observers of the system rather than actors in it. This can produce an "out of the loop syndrome," such that if operators must suddenly take control they are out of touch with the state of the plant and with its dynamics (Endsley & Kiris, 1995). It is difficult for operators to retain the necessary expertise for skill-based behavior (see below, pp. 21) if they are not in the loop (Edwards & Lees, 1974a; Singleton, 1978; Wickens, 1991).

Automation and Robotics

Robotics often refers to zoomorphic mechanical devices with moving parts which perform the physical tasks of humans, while automation in its more general sense does not require the presence of a physical simulacrum (Sheridan, 1992). Important systems characteristics include the type and degree of automation and the quality of "function allocation," the partition of control between human and machine intelligence. Poor allocation of function ("clumsy automation") means that automation makes the work of operators harder, not easier (Wiener & Curry, 1980). Bainbridge (1983) noted that what is automated is what is well understood by engineers, leaving the less understandable, more difficult tasks for human operators.

Differences among Industrial Systems

There are differences between CPCS and DMS which have important consequences for cognition. In CPCS coupling is tight. If a valve is opened, pressure is transmitted through the system at the speed of sound, and since liquids are incompressible, flows are changed instantaneously (except for viscous fluids). Temperature differences cause continuous energy fluxes across boundaries according to the laws of thermodynamics. Some parts of such systems, however, may have lags or delays, so that a change in one component may take many minutes or even hours to appear in another part of the system (Moray, 1997b).

In DMS, coupling is looser. A change in the activity of one numerically controlled machine has no direct effect on others. If an automated guided vehicle (AGV) drops off a pallet on one conveyor it has no effect on others. If an AGV halts it may not indicate a fault: the scheduling algorithm may indicate that such a pause will support optimal performance some hours hence. Often the state of the plant is not readily observable. Temporal delays do not provide an error signal in the same way as do pressure or temperature differences in a chemical process. Above all, causality in scheduling is final causality, goal directed causality, rather than material causality (to use Aristotelian terms). A pallet moves from one machine to another not because a pressure pushes it, but because it is required at the next station in order that something may be done to it. Scheduling pulls events through a DMS, whereas Newtonian physics pushes events through a CPCS.

Table 8.1 Differences between continuous process control and discrete manufacturing

Process control	Discrete manufacturing
Newtonian physical causality	Goal-directed causality
Tight and continuous coupling	Distributed and loose coupling
Continuous display of error signal as feedback synchronous in real time	Error signal ambiguous, intermittent and asynchronous
Intervention tends to produce global propagation of effects	Intervention can be very local and with little or no propagation
Strong control theory models available	No accepted strong models available
Time, physical processes, and couplings continuous and synchronous	Time, physical processes, causal and causal couplings discrete and asynchronous
Fundamental problem is the control of physical processes, mass/energy balances and chemical reactions, in real time and closed loop	Fundamental problem is the control of planning and scheduling, mainly off line and feed-forward
Usually sequentially continuous	Partly parallel due to multiple machines, but sequential due to scheduling constraints
Often require control long after the process has been stopped due to thermal inertia, residual heat and reactivity, secondary reactions	Often can be stopped quickly, and individual subsystems closed down without affecting others

The profound differences between continuous and discrete production technology, summarized in Table 8.1, require different operator mental models supported by different kinds of displays and aids, and co-operation between human and machine demands different kinds of reasoning in the two cases.

To summarize, the characteristics of industrial systems most relevant to cognitive engineering include:

- system size
- system complexity
- system dynamics (time constraints, bandwidth)
- system decomposition into subsystems and components
- intrasystem coupling
- closed loop and open loop control characteristics
- degree of automation
- style of automation
- observability
- modelability
- bases for function allocation
- modes of human–machine coupling
- quality of human–machine interface
- less than complete display of information

CONCEPTUAL FRAMEWORKS

Abstraction Hierarchy, Decision Ladder, Part–Whole Decomposition

The work of Rasmussen has become increasingly influential in cognitive engineering, accepted by engineers, psychologists and ergonomists (Rasmussen, 1986; Rasmussen et al., 1995). He proposes five conceptual frameworks:

- the abstraction hierarchy
- the means–ends hierarchy
- part–whole decomposition
- the decision ladder
- the work domain framework.

The first three describe the engineering properties of human–machine systems, the fourth is a heuristic (or perhaps a model) of cognitive activities in human–machine systems, and the last provides a sociotechnical view of work. Only the first four will be described here.

Abstraction Hierarchy (AH)

Any complex system can be considered at different levels of abstraction (Rasmussen, 1986). See Table 8.2 for the hierarchy and applications to CPCS and DMS. The most concrete description, *physical form*, lists physical components. In a control room it will be a description of switches, sliders, knobs, meters, pen recorders, computer screens, etc. Such a description concentrates on a system's anatomy or topography, the simplest components of the system, but does not define what the system is for or what it does. The next level is *physical function*, where one identifies physical subsystems – a certain set of switches and displays comprise a pump. Some function is evident – conveyors are to move things; valves control flows. But we still do not know the purpose of the system. At the level of *general function*, we no longer think of the physical characteristics of components, but of local purpose. This subsystem is a cooling system; that one controls the flow of fuel to the heating system; that switch activates a conveyor to move parts to a milling machine. Above that is the level of *abstract function*. This part of the plant is to provide energy; that part to transform or transport the energy; this part to assemble components; that part to deliver them to storage. Finally, we have the most abstract level of all: the level which defines the purpose of the entire system – to generate electricity, to manufacture light bulbs.

Maintenance personnel typically think about the lower levels of physical form and physical function. Management are directly concerned only with the highest levels of abstraction. Operators use predominantly intermediate levels. The AH

Table 8.2 Rasmussen's abstraction hierarchy

Typical operations	Means–ends relations	Characteristic modes of thought	Process control operations	Discrete manufacturing
Produce and sell electricity to make a profit for the business	GOALS AND CONSTRAINTS	Necessary and sufficient properties to link the performance of the system and its design goals Language in terms of demands of environment	Produce 2000 liters of pasteurized juice per day	Make 168 items in 12 hours to fill order
Run the plant at high power to follow the real time demands	ABSTRACT FUNCTION	Necessary and sufficient characteristics to prioritize according to design specifications and set points for mass–energy balances Language in terms of abstract general properties, not specific to a particular plant	Heat, pasteurize and cool juice; collect spoiled juice, avoid emptying system or running pumps dry; maintain mass–energy balance	Fulfill scheduling plans
Control local properties such as temperature, energy generation, coolant flows, etc.	GENERAL FUNCTION	Necessary and sufficient properties to identify functions which must be controlled without regard to the particular instantiations of those functions in this particular plant	Heat steam; pump feedstock; pump steam; raise temperature of feedstock in heat exchanger; maintain inventory of juice in vat; sense temperature of juice	Schedule action sequences on current jobs

		Language in terms of well-known input–output relations and transfer functions		
Use particular subsystems to control flows, pressures, core reactivity, etc. Start a pump, change rod positions	PHYSICAL PROCESSES AND ACTIVITIES	Necessary and sufficient properties to control particular work activities, choice and use of equipment, predict the results of intervention, diagnose and maintain subsystems Language related to physical systems and processes	Control rate of pumps; control temperature of steam; control energy supply to boiler; switch flow according to temperature; exchange energy in heat exchangers	Movement by AGV, machining, inspection, assembly, pallet loading and unloading
Open a valve, change the position of a switch	PHYSICAL FORM AND RELATIONS IN THE CONTROL ROOM	Necessary and sufficient properties to categorize, identify, and operate a particular component, and to physically explore the topology of the system Language related to the designer's and architect's specification of the system	Vats, pumps, pipes, heater, switches, thermometers, heat exchangers, displays, controls, etc.	AGV, pallets, numerically controlled machines, inspection cell, robots, parts for assembly, etc.

can be applied to all systems, including commercial or economic systems (Rasmussen et al., 1995). To solve different kinds of problems, or to communicate with colleagues with different responsibilities, one must shift between conceptual levels, for what can be thought in the language of one level cannot be thought in another. Consider the difference between the meaning of "urgent" applied to product delivery dates of a manager or when an operator controls a chemical reaction, or the fact that during fault diagnosis operators shift between topographic search (in which they search for the part of the plant which is faulty at the level of physical form), and symptomatic search (in which they try to interpret functional changes in the behavior of variables) (Rasmussen, 1986).

Means–Ends Hierarchy

Each level of the AH represents the goal or end which the level below subserves as a means, so that the AH is also a means–ends hierarchy. Problem solving often requires switching conceptual frameworks – look for a means, at a lower level, to serve the end perceived to exist at a higher. When moving down the hierarchy we move from social, economic and psychological goals to physical goals. High up the hierarchy goals are concerned with purpose. Low down they are concerned with physical causality (Rasmussen, 1986).

Part–Whole Decomposition (PWD)

Orthogonal to the abstraction hierarchy is part–whole decomposition. At each AH level one can think about the system at different levels of detail. At the highest level of the AH, for example, there are plans for production by the whole plant, by different subdivisions, by different assembly lines or individual machines or individual worker; at the level of physical form one might look for a leak in the overall appearance of a room containing a reaction vessel, or at the finest level examine a particular welded seam to see if its integrity is intact. For further details see Rasmussen (1986, p. 119).

AH and PWD represent the context of operators' cognitive and physical behavior when interacting with human–machine systems, but they are not descriptions of behavior. They provide conceptual frameworks to support cognitive and physical task analyses, and to define the informational and control needs of automatic controllers and human operators. The means–ends hierarchy on the other hand includes both psychological and physical teleologies.

The Decision Ladder (DL)

Cognitive behavior in human–machine interaction is summarized in the decision ladder (DL), (Rasmussen, 1986) a version of which is shown in Figure 8.2. The word "operator" here and throughout this chapter is used generically to refer to

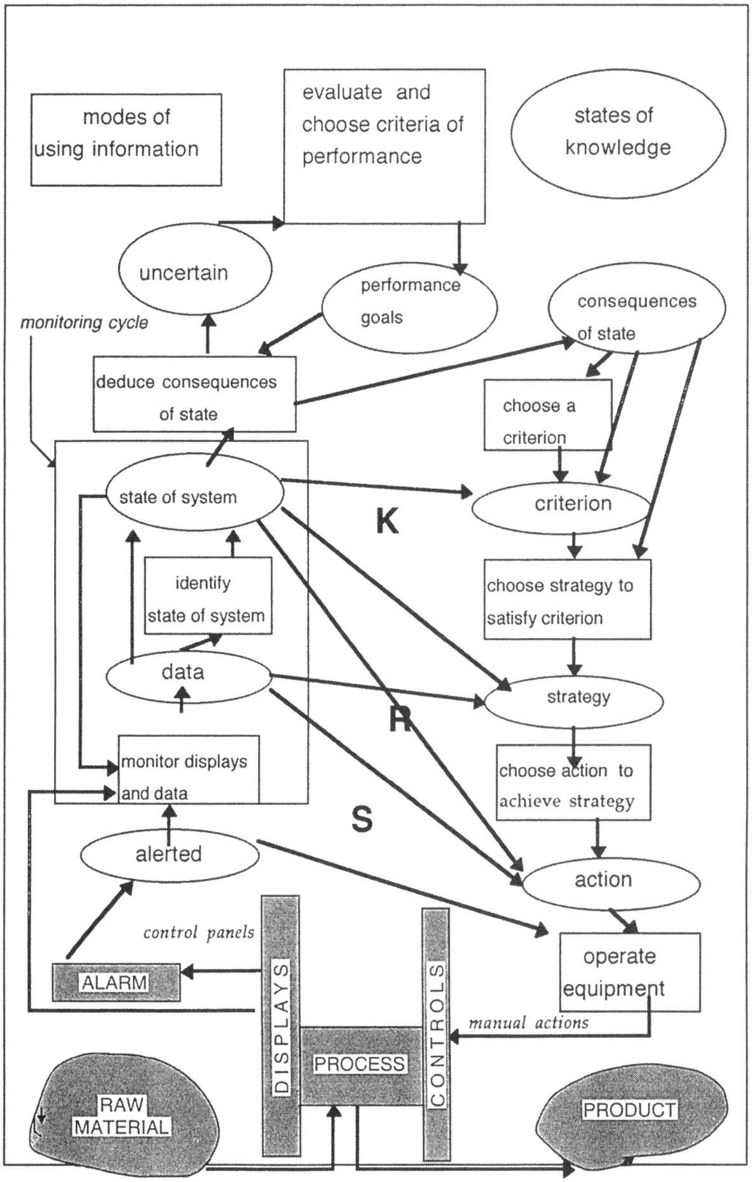

Figure 8.2 Rasmussen's Decision Ladder

a traditional control room operator, to someone monitoring a discrete manufacturing process while walking about the floor of a factory, to a maintenance technician, a supervisor, a manager – in fact to anyone who performs cognitive tasks in industrial or commercial contexts. The DL shows the cycle of cognitive activity from the receipt of information from displays through various kinds of decision making, to the selection of plans and actions on the plant. It will be discussed in more detail below.

SBB, RBB, and KBB

Rasmussen assigns behavior to one of three categories: skill-based, rule-based, or knowledge-based behavior (SBB, RBB and KBB). This taxonomy has found very widespread acceptance as a heuristic among engineers and engineering psychologists. It summarizes many psychological ideas at a level which is useful for systems design and analysis.

SBB appears after prolonged practice or where there is a high degree of stimulus–response compatibility, and is typical of perceptual–motor skills. It can probably be identified with the automatic processing described by Shiffrin & Schneider (1977). SBB is typically effortless, highly efficient, fast, and prone only to errors of the kind called "slips" by Reason (1990). It involves little or no deliberate thought. It is typical of expert operators in high bandwidth manual control, such as driving or piloting skills, or in overlearned rapid discrete responses to alarms. Since industrial operators may have thousands of hours' practice, SBB can probably appear even when there is not consistent mapping between information and response (see also Durso, Cooke, Breen & Schvaneveldt, 1987).

RBB appears when using procedures, whether written or known by heart. It is typically modeled in so-called expert systems: "If Condition A, then do *X*. If Condition B, then do *Y*." (Such rule-based systems are sometimes called "production systems" in cognitive science. It is important to note that this is a different meaning from industrial production in the sense of manufacturing.) Conditions can be recognized perceptually, or may require inference. They may be as simple as a temperature, or may be complex, such as there being a certain percentage of jobs completed and one numerically controlled lathe out of three faulty with only four hours left to complete an order. Field studies suggest that people typically choose to work with RBB and avoid deep reasoning if possible. RBB errors may arise either from errors of state recognition, or from errors of selection of action, and are prone both to "lapses" of working memory and to both of Reason's proposed "mistake" mechanisms – pattern matching and frequency gambling (Reason, 1990).

KBB occurs when neither SBB nor RBB is possible. The operators find themselves in a situation which seems completely novel. The state of the system cannot be identified, or there is no well-specified rule to follow. They must reason deeply to understand the state of the system and to decide what to do. Academic cognitive psychology has typically been concerned with KBB (Johnson-Laird, 1983), because it requires logical reasoning. It is extremely rare in real work in real time industrial systems, and is most often seen in fault management, although even here, as emphasized by studies of naturalistic decision making (Klein, Orasanu, Calderwood & Zsambok, 1993), deep reasoning is avoided by experts. KBB errors are typically "mistakes" (Reason, 1990), rare but with significant consequences (Woods & Roth, 1988).

Signals, Signs, and Symbols

Rasmussen suggests that SBB, RBB, and KBB imply different semiotics, respectively signals, signs, and symbols.

A single displayed variable value may have several meanings. Rasmussen (1986) gives the example of a meter and its associated control. During normal operation the position of the pointer is read with respect to the set-point, the commanded value. If the observed value is too high, the operator responds with SBB using the deviation from the set-point as an error *signal* in closed-loop control, and turns the control knob to null out the disturbance and return the pointer to the set-point. If the plant is in an unusual state, such as start-up, the pointer may have a different expected value. The temperature of a subsystem may rise only late in the start-up process. If operators know that the plant is in the expected-low-temperature state, they should not use the control to try to drive the instrument reading to the normal set-point. A reading far from normal requires one action during start-up, and a different response in normal operating mode. Hence RBB is required: "If the plant is cold, do not use the control to force the pointer to the normal set-point. If the plant is in full power operating mode, null any error to drive the pointer to the normal set-point." In this case Rasmussen describes the displayed information as a *sign*. Signs indicate contexts within which different RBBs are appropriate.

Finally, operators may find that the indicator reading is quite abnormal, a value which they have never seen, which was not included in training, and which makes no sense – there are no well-defined rules to follow. The first response might be to press the "calibrate" button to make sure that the meter is properly set up. If the abnormal reading persists, the displayed information is *symbolic* of something that requires KBB, reasoning, experiments, perhaps further information.

SBB, RBB, and KBB describe behavior: signals, signs, and symbols describe the logical status of displayed information which supports choices of adaptive behavior. Novices typically begin by using KBB or RBB, depending on their training and the design of the human–machine interface, and progress at least to a stable pattern of performance at RBB. If the bandwidth of the system is high, if stimulus response compatibility is high, and if behavior can be practiced sufficiently, operators will often achieve SBB. (See, for example, Crossman & Cooke, 1974; Moray et al., 1986. For a related model of skill acquisition, see McRuer & Krendel, 1957.)

Sociotechnical factors also affect modes of behaviour. If training and operating procedures emphasize the absolute primacy of rules, with no freedom on the part of operators to diverge from the formal regulations imposed by management, action will be extremely constrained. A managerial regime which punishes infringement of tightly written operating procedures may prevent operators taking any action at all. Operators can justify inaction because it is no longer their responsibility to cope with unforeseen events (use KBB), only to follow instructions (RBB). On the other hand, a liberal regime where creativity is encouraged will permit the maximum use of human intelligence in the face of unforeseen events. But flexibility has a price: it can lead operators to put the system into unforeseen states. This balance between creativity and prescription is central to the design problem of sociotechnical systems (Hollnagel, 1993, 1998; Reason, 1990; Zuboff, 1988).

Sociotechnical Aspects of Cognition in Work

Almost never do workers work alone, and this implies a social dimension to information processing. Moray, Sanderson & Vicente (1992) describe a case where telephone communication was as important as an elaborate computer-based information system in the analysis of nuclear power incidents, and where cognition was distributed over a team of more than ten people during emergency management. De Keyser (1981) noted that steel mill workers relied extensively on telephone messages to confirm control room displays even when given a modern computer-based control room. Several papers from the 1960s in Edwards & Lees (1974) make the same point (Crossman, 1974; Englestadt, 1974; Lees, 1974). Hutchins' (1995) study of cognition in ship navigation is a classic account of these phenomena. The work of Rochlin, LaPorte & Roberts (1987) shows how even in a sociotechnical system which might be expected to be prone to failure, good sociotechnical organization can produce a remarkably high level of safe performance. To properly set the DL in a work context, one would have to use several DLs, each representing a different person, and each coupled to the other as a source of information and control.

THE COGNITIVE ECOLOGY OF THE INDUSTRIAL DOMAIN

To apply a theory of cognition to a real work situation requires a task analysis, both of action and cognition, to define the environmental constraints and the cognitive behavior required for industrial tasks (Kirwan & Ainsworth, 1992; Vicente, 1999).

In a short introduction such as this we cannot consider ergonomic and organizational factors. We can, however, identify several cognitive activities which are typical of many industrial tasks.

Planning and Scheduling

Planning and scheduling support behavior under time constraints. In DMS scheduling is the central operation, requiring a rich mental model of the process and interaction with sophisticated computer programs, since scheduling algorithms are often computationally extremely demanding. (For the relation of psychology to scheduling see Dessouky, Moray & Kijowski, 1995.) In CPCS and hybrid systems planning is critical. Bainbridge (1974) provides both a transcript of a verbal protocol in a CPCS in which an operator handles problems of time estimation, and a flow chart of the decision cycles which use time estimation to control the process. French and Belgian engineering psychologists in particular emphasize the crucial role of time as a cognitive variable in industrial processes (Cellier, De Keyser & Valot, 1996; De Cortis, 1988; De Keyser, 1981; De Keyser et al., 1987; Hoc, 1995, 1996), and earlier relevant studies can be found in Edwards & Lees (1974).

Monitoring

In supervisory control (Sheridan, 1992, 1997), operators' primary task is to monitor the system to ensure that the system state is close to the desired state.

Monitoring involves attention, pattern recognition, dynamic attention allocation, decision making, and perceptual–motor control. Attention and pattern recognition are used to provide information needed to decide to intervene manually if the system diverges from its desired state or if windows of opportunity to increase efficiency can be found. In systems such as steel mills some state variables can be monitored directly, the noise, color and appearance of the hot metal, vibrations, etc., providing what De Keyser (1981) calls "informal information." In traditional NPP control rooms there are 1000–2000 displays and controls spread across a wall 20 meters or more long, or several *hundred* pages of information presented on computer screens. In DMS, some information may be displayed on a central computer console, with local displays on various pieces of equipment scattered around the plant requiring operators to visit them to acquire information.

Constraint Recognition

The system state space is the industrial equivalent of the problem space discussed in artificial intelligence. The degrees of freedom define a multidimensional space of temperature, pressure, flow rates, mass inventory, queue length, machining time, etc. Within this space lie constraint boundaries. These define regions of acceptable operation or conditions requiring intervention. Recent developments in display design put great emphasis on displaying constraint boundaries in order to support creative responses by operators (Rasmussen et al., 1995; Reising & Sanderson, 1996; Vicente, 1992, 1998; Vicente et al., 1996; Woods, 1988; Woods & Roth, 1988). Diagnosis and fault management in particular require an operator to understand the causal structure of the system and knowledge of where the plant state locus lies in relation to constraint boundaries.

Allocation of Function

Deciding when to intervene in a highly automated system requires three kinds of knowledge:

1. the characteristics of the mechanical and automated system
2. the intentions of the designer (Why does the equipment behave in this way? What is the purpose of this pump in this location, and if it is malfunctioning, in what other way can the same result be achieved?)

3. the relative abilities of the human operator and the mechanized or automated systems. This is the problem of allocation of function between human and machine.

With increasing machine intelligence adaptive allocation includes a social relation involving mutual trust and an understanding of mutual authority between human and machine. Methods of function allocation such as "Fitts' List," based on the comparative abilities of humans and machines, are no longer satisfactory. This is a topic of increasing importance (Inagaki, 1993, 1995; Moray et al., 1994; Parasuraman & Riley, 1997; Rouse, 1988; Scerbo, 1996; Sheridan, 1997; Woods, 1988; Woods & Roth, 1988).

Communication and Coordination

Cognitive processes supporting coordination and communication are of the utmost importance. There is a constant flow of information among those running a plant, those supervising them and those performing maintenance. During major emergencies radical departures from normal practice may be needed. The strategic goals of management and executives may have time constants of weeks or even years: the tactical goals of operators have time constants of the order of minutes or hours; the action goals of operators or maintenance technicians during an emergency may lie in the range of seconds. (Managing the supply of electricity for the Ukraine involves decision making on a time scale of decades, but the transient that destroyed Chernobyl involved processes with time constants of fractions of a second.)

Social and Motivational Factors

Effective cognition involves social dynamics and motivation. A workforce which understands the long-term goals of management, and which trusts the management, is likely to work well, make good decisions, pay close attention to its task, and develop good patterns of communication which support coordination and mutual understanding. A management which is sensitive to the needs of the workforce, and trusts the operators, is more likely to be prepared to invest in equipment and training, and to allow creative experiment, than one which is not (Rasmussen et al., 1995; Zuboff, 1988). Reason (1990, 1997) has pointed out that many violations of work rules are not malicious, but represent the accumulated "work wisdom" arising from practice and expertise. If management is willing to accept violations as experiments in good faith, and if also "whistle blowing" to identify problems is acceptable, then the dynamics of social interaction in the workplace will support efficient performance of cognitive tasks. In this regard, research by Rochlin, LaPorte & Roberts (1987) on effective systems is particularly interesting and lists characteristics of systems which promote error detection and safe operation, arising from self-organizing properties of human–machine systems rather than the application of rigid rule structures.

Mental Models

Operators use mental models whose existence has long been taken for granted by engineers and psychologists in human–machine systems research (Edwards & Lees, 1974). For reviews of mental models in industrial contexts, see: Bainbridge, 1991; Moray, 1997a, 1998; Rutherford, Rogers & Bibby, 1992; Wilson & Rutherford, 1989. For comparable classical laboratory work, see: Gentner & Stevens, 1983; Johnson-Laird, 1983.

One can use Rasmussen's classification of behavior to clarify the meaning of operator mental models. In SBB mental models can be identified with human operator transfer functions (McRuer & Krendel, 1976; Sheridan & Ferrell, 1974; Young, 1969, 1973). At the level of RBB mental models are probably look-up tables entered by pattern recognition fed by direct perception of displays, or by calculations on an array of multivariate state space variables (Beishon, 1974; Dutton & Starbuck, 1971). In other cases they are the remembered contents of rule sets constructed in the mind. KBB models are probably a mental representation of the system in the form of verbal (declarative) knowledge, and also sets of mental images.

In this last sense, models for KBB, operators' mental models most resemble those discussed in basic research (Gentner & Stevens, 1983; Johnson-Laird, 1983). There are however, important differences. In academic research experiments subjects can form exact and complete mental models, isomorphic to the problem. The entire universe which they model is the set of data provided by the experimenter. By contrast, the mental models of workers in complex systems are not isomorphs, but homomorphs, many-to-one mappings in which information is lost in the interests of simplification and mental economy. While most accounts of mental models in laboratory research seem to imply that mental models exist in working memory, most engineering psychologists think of them as long-term representations of operating experience. Mental models reside in long-term memory, whence they may be recalled in whole or in part, for use in working memory.

Mental models of real systems are always incomplete and imperfect. Workers never experience all the possible states of even a simple system. Operators may form multiple models of a given system, representing final cause, material cause, etc. Indeed, the abstraction hierarchy can be thought of as progressively more compact mental models, since one can form mental models of mental models (Moray, 1989, 1997a, 1998). Workers frequently modify their mental models on the basis of experience so that the relation between their different ways of thinking about a system change. There is empirical evidence that models which can support normal operation may not generalize to abnormal operation, even in quite simple systems.

It is frequently stated that interface design, procedures, and training, should support operators' mental models (e.g. Wickens, 1991). However, this should only be done *if the models are correct*, and it is one of the tasks of cognitive engineering to ensure that mental models are as accurate as possible. Clearly this involves training, although training deliberately centered on model creation has not been much explored. A major part of expertise aquisition is the construction of good mental models.

Fault Detection and Management

One of the most important roles of human operators is the detection, diagnosis and management of faults (Rasmussen & Rouse, 1981). This is a subset of problem solving in a dynamic environment where the problem may change rapidly, and where the outcomes involve high hazards and payoffs. Generally, faults propagate so that a single localized failure rapidly produces a cascade of further problems, requiring the operators to change frames of reference and problem spaces dynamically. This is particularly difficult because people seem to think about only one problem at a time, and are unable or unwilling to switch between concurrent problems (Moray & Rotenberg, 1989; Wei, 1998; Weiringa, 1997; Woods, 1994).

All industrial systems possess extensive alarm systems, but these are often insufficient, especially in large systems, to support fault management. Sensors can fail, or minor faults become accepted as chronic plant states and so hide important changes. As Reason (1990) and many others have noted, the "defense in depth" design philosophy of many hazardous industrial systems may make it harder to manage faults. Such systems are designed with much redundancy, so that no one failure, or even several are sufficient to challenge plant safety. The problem is that the steady degradation of safety systems may be hidden until the moment of catastrophic failure. There is one well-documented case where no less than seven safety systems failed simultaneously, although a probabilistic risk assessment of such an event would suggest, due to redundancy, that its probability is less than 10^{-14}, which one would normally regard as zero. Such events constitute "fundamental surprises" (Lanir, 1986; Sarter, Woods & Billings, 1997) arising from "resident pathogens" (Reason, 1990, 1997). In large systems alarms and sensors are often faulty and "cry wolf" constantly, so that when the real fault occurs it may go unnoticed (Kemeny, 1979).

In a classical paper Bainbridge (1983) spoke of the "ironies of automation" whereby engineers automate all that they can understand, leaving to the humans those tasks which are too difficult to be automated. Hence automation often makes human tasks harder. This has been discussed under the title "clumsy automation," particularly in aviation (Rasmussen et al., 1995; Wiener & Curry, 1980; Woods, 1988; see also Norman, 1990).

COGNITIVE ACTIVITIES IN THE DL CYCLE

We can relate cognition in industrial tasks to laboratory research by examing the activities of an individual using Rasmussen's DL (see Figure 8.2), starting at the bottom left element of the figure and considering each of the information processing activities in turn.

Alarm

A typical event initiating the DL cycle is an alarm which alerts the operator to monitor information and may cause a rapid SBB response, such as to hit an emergency shut-down switch. The automatic, "thoughtless" skill-based path from signal detection to action is indicated by the arrow marked S. Such SBB is error prone if the relation between perception and action violates either stimulus–response compatability, or stimulus–response population stereotypes. (NPP regulations commonly require operators to monitor the automatic safety systems for 20 minutes before intervening because of the high probability of error under stress.)

Another response to an alarm is to scan displays and acquire data from indicators, computer screens, the physical appearance of material such as molten steel, the position or movement of an object on a conveyor belt or the number of items in a queue. Such observations in response to an alarm support decision making when there is no SBB available.

Coupling causes difficulty. It is extremely rare for a single alarm to appear. At least in CPCS an abnormal state is almost certain to propagate disturbances throughout the plant. Several hundred alarms occurred during the first minute in the accident at Three Mile Island, and by the end of two or three minutes almost every alarm was illuminated (Kemeny, 1979). Such a state carries no diagnostic information save that "something is wrong." The problem of cascading alarms is discussed by Woods (1994) and reviews of alarms and warnings have recently appeared (Laughery, Wogalter & Young, 1995; Stanton, 1994). De Keyser (1981) and De Keyser et al. (1987) report that workers in a steel mill sometimes took action to correct a situation before the alarm sounded and used the alarm as a form of feedback to monitor the state of the process.

Monitor Displays and Data

To monitor a system is to distribute attention over sources of information to keep track of plant state. To sample is to observe a single source of data. A monitoring cycle typically takes several seconds, since operators must scan a computer screen or a large control panel using head and eye movements, page through computer displays, walk around the control room, speak to colleagues directly or by telephone, or glance down through a window to see what is happening on the plant floor. These behaviors, not details of central nervous system physiology, are the mechanisms of attention relevant to industrial work.

Attention in real work situations differs greatly from attention in laboratory studies. There may be hundreds or thousands of displays and controls distributed over many square meters of wall space in traditional control rooms, and several hundred pages of computer images in computer-generated displays. The values of variables are more or less strongly correlated one with another due to physical coupling. There are no well-defined trials. The duration of "stimuli" is indefinite and often at the choice of the observer, or may change too rapidly to track during faults (at Three Mile Island the hard copy print-out was running nearly an hour behind the events (Kemeny, 1979)!). The actions of operators change what will happen next. The duration of a display may depend entirely on how long the observer chooses to keep it on a screen. Values change continuously when they are not being observed.

There is no fixed value of attention switching time and no limit to how long it may take to switch attention. If someone has to walk across a room, turn their eyes, head or body, or use a mouse or keyboard to call up a page of data, the time taken to switch attention may be several seconds or longer. Both from theory (Moray, 1986; Senders, 1983; Sheridan & Ferrell, 1974) and empirical data, it is known that the greater the precision required in reading a display, the lower the signal to noise ratio of the display, and the more complex the display, the longer it takes to process the visual input. The fixation duration of eye movements, once a source is selected, has a lower limit of perhaps 200 milliseconds, but the upper limit is again indeterminate, and may be several seconds or more (for example, if the observer fixates a changing display and tries to estimate its mean value).

The main factors determining the rate of sampling are the rate of growth of uncertainty (due either to forgetting or the bandwidth of system events) and the expected value of significant events. If an observation shows a variable to be close to a constraint boundary, the next attentional sample will be taken earlier (Leermakers, 1995; Senders, 1983). The interval before the next sample will be reduced if a positive payoff is associated with the observation, and lengthened if observations are costly (Kvalseth, 1977). Sampling is also used to update mental models.

The control of attention may be under conscious control (RBB or KBB) or may become skill-based and unconscious after prolonged experience of a system with stable statistical properties. Mental models may drive attention, and a particularly interesting case arises in what has been called "cognitive lockup" or "cognitive tunnel vision" (Moray, 1981, 1986), seen both in laboratory and field studies (Edwards & Lees, 1974a; Kemeny, 1979; Rasmussen & Rouse, 1981). When a fault is detected the first plausible hypothesis as to its cause tends to be adopted, attention becomes locked onto the suspect subsystem, and observers try to confirm the hypothesis, rather than test it (Klein et al., 1993; Reason, 1990; Zsambok & Klein, 1997). Other parts of the system are neglected so that later faults tend to remain untreated. Usually thought of as an error, cognitive tunnel vision may better be regarded as a rational strategy based on an operator's realization that a fault first propagates within a tightly coupled subsystem. Iosif (1968, 1969a, b) provides evidence from his work on a fossil fuel power plant that mental models partition the plant into such subsystems. He found that operator attention was distributed very unequally over subsystems, and that within each subsystem only one or two variables were sampled frequently, suggesting that those components were conveying enough information to reduce the sampling of others due to correlation among variables.

Identify State of System

Rasmussen's frames of reference emphasize pattern recognition, above all in RBB. Because of the weaknesses of human reasoning (Johnson-Laird, 1983; Kahneman, Slovic & Tversky, 1982), which are worse under stress and time pressure, it is now believed that displays should support direct pattern recognition rather than reasoning, because "solving a problem simply means representing it so as to make the solution transparent" (Simon, 1981, p. 153), and because of people's known preference for RBB. In addition to recognizing the current state, workers must also be able to recognize the past dynamic history of the plant, predict its future trajectory through state space, and to recognize where the plant is in relation to the physical and sociotechnical constraint boundaries.

State identification is equivalent to complex pattern recognition. Models of sequential decision making and the theory of signal detection (TSD) can be used to model event detection and state identification in industrial applications (Moray, 1986). A different approach from that usually used in TSD laboratory studies is needed, since the detection of drifts or the onset of instability in a CPCS involve the detection of continuous signals (Taylor, Lindsay & Forbes, 1967). (For industrial applications of TSD see Drury & Sinclair, 1983; Swets, 1987; Swets & Pickett, 1982.) Jerison (1967) has argued that values of β as high as 10 or 20 are unrealistic in laboratory experiments and invalidate TSD as a model for perception, but calculating β with costs and payoffs in the real world can lead to values of an order of magnitude greater. To trip (shut down) a power plant can cost a utility hundreds of thousands of dollars a day, while not tripping the plant can result, in the limit, in catastrophic failure with costs running into many millions of dollars and severe social consequences including death to employees and others. Very high values of β are realistic. Moray (1982) found high values of β when using TSD to predict the probability of failing to notice abnormal states of a component during the development of a fault in an NPP.

Displays and Cognition

What kind of displays best support the role of the human in complex industrial human–machine systems? It has been suggested that different display formats may suit different users and that each user could reconfigure the interface to their preferred layout, symbology, and mode of presentation. Such proposals bear a potential for severe accident. If teams, not individuals, control complex processes, flexible adaptability could result in confusion. Many graphs and displays look superficially similar, and an operator might glance at displayed data without realizing that a colleague had reconfigured the displays. Moray and Gaines (Moray, 1992) evaluated a flexible adaptable control panel for ships' engine rooms, and noted that an experienced operator lost track of display–control relationships after reconfiguring them. We do not at present know how to choose an appropriate level of adaptability and flexibility in computerized control rooms. See Kragt (1992) for examples of control room design.

Designing Displays

Bennett & Flach (1992) provide an interesting introduction to the choice of displays using the simple hydraulic system shown in Figure 8.3. Two inputs are controlled by valves, V1 and V2, with flow rates shown on the meters I1 and I2. At the output is a valve V3 and its flow meter O. The meter T shows the temperature of the fluid in the reservoir, whose fluid inventory is shown by the meter R. The system goal G1 is to hold the value of *R* at a particular set point

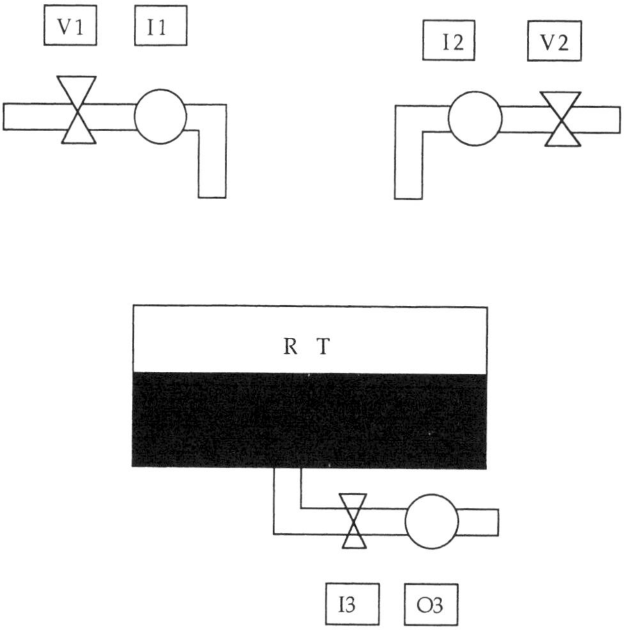

Figure 8.3 Bennett and Flach's hydraulic system to demonstrate interface design options

and goal G2 is to achieve a specified flow rate through the system. (Multiple simultaneous goals are a common feature of industrial processes.) The relation between the valve settings and the flow rates are given by:

$$I1 = k1.V1 \quad (1)$$
$$I2 = k2.V2 \quad (2) \text{ and}$$
$$O = k3.V3 \quad (3)$$

which can be rearranged to give

$$k1 = I1/V1 \quad (1a)$$
$$k2 = I2/V2 \quad (2a) \text{ and}$$
$$k3 = O/V3 \quad (3a)$$

to show the invariants.

Changes in the content of the reservoir are governed by the equation,

$$dR/dt = (V1 + V2) - V3 \qquad (4)$$

which can be also expressed in terms of ks and I's.

Together the values of the variables and the state equations (1)–(4) completely describe the system. How should they be displayed?

In Figure 8.4, Bennett & Flach offer six solutions to the display problem. In A, B, and E the circles represent meters. C represents a mimic diagram, in which the

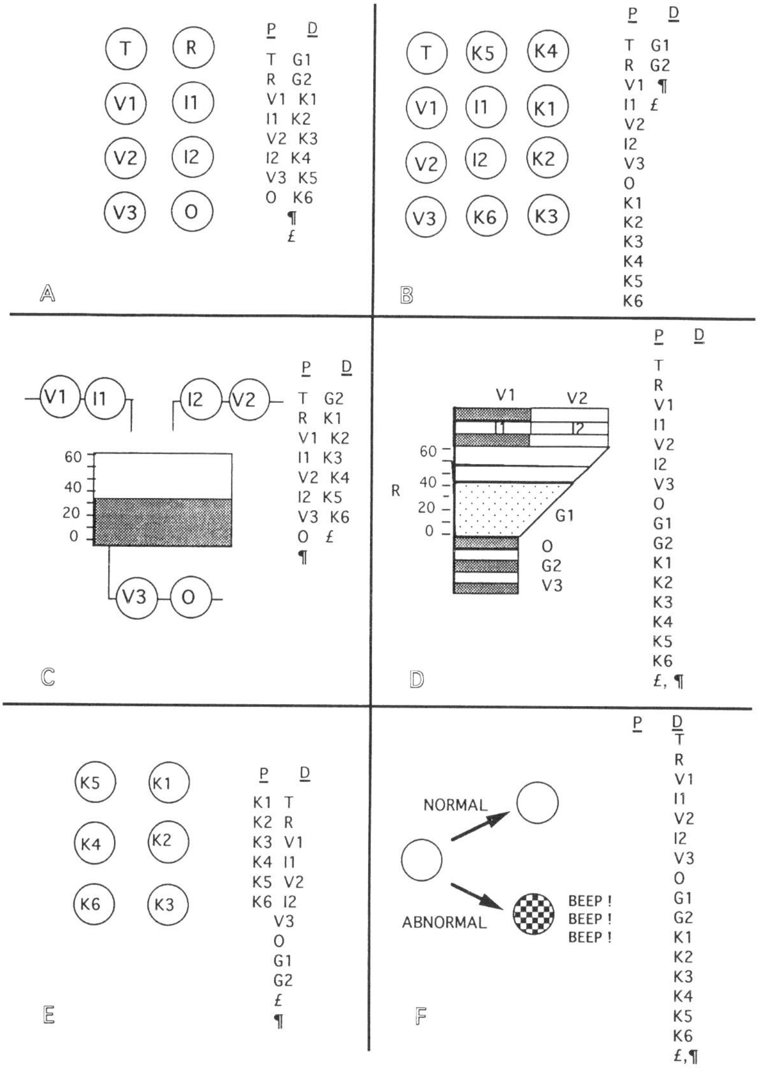

Figure 8.4 Bennett and Flach proposals for displays

circles are again meters or digital indicators. In F the circles represent lamps which may be illuminated or dark. D represents an "ecological interface display" (EID), to be discussed in more detail later. The columns in each display labelled P and D show respectively: values which are directly perceptible from the display without any thought (P), and the values which must be derived from the displayed values by calculation (D).

It is unusual to display values such as *k*1–*k*3, but such information is useful diagnostically. These *k*s should be constant, since they are system invariants, part of the hardware definition. If *k*3 is abnormally high, it implies that the flow is lower than expected for the given valve setting, which in turn indicates either that something is blocking the outflow pipe or that there is a fault in the sensor measuring the reservoir level, and that therefore the pressure head is lower than indicated. If *k* values are not displayed the operator must calculate the ratio of I to V in order to check for constant *k*, that is, use KBB. Entries in the D column rely on human reasoning and increase mental workload.

Bennett & Flach do not discuss temporal information. Process operators like trend displays, which represent the (recent) past history of the process, and which allow them to extrapolate trends into the future (Edwards & Lees, 1974a, b). In the past trend graphs were produced by pen recordings, and more recently as computer graphs (Hansen, 1995; Woods, 1986). Extrapolation into the future can be supported by predictor displays. These were originally proposed by Zeiboltz (Kelley, 1964), and are becoming increasingly common (Hansen, 1995; Sheridan, 1992, 1997; Wickens, 1991).

Currently it is believed that, if possible, workers should work at the SBB or RBB level, and avoid KBB, hence it is desirable to maximize the entries in the (P) column. Cognitive engineering should not always support thought and reasoning – it may be sometimes better to avoid it in favor of rules and recognition based skills (see the quotation from Simon given above).

There is no space to treat the design of displays in detail, but two classes need special emphasis, displays based on emergent features, and so-called "ecological" displays.

"Emergent Feature" Displays

For discussions of emergent features see: Buttigieg & Sanderson, 1991; Carswell & Wickens, 1987; Sanderson et al., 1989. Perhaps the best-known industrial example of an integrated display with emergent features is the so-called "star" diagram, in which several variables are simultaneously displayed along the radii of a star, each having its zero value at the center of the circle, and normalized so that when each variable is at its expected value one can draw a polygon of constant radius joining up the values (Coekin, 1969; see Sheridan, 1997, for an advanced form of this display). Any abnormality distorts the polygon.

Although attractive in principle as a multivariable display, the use of star displays is problematic. There is no simple way to decide which variables to include in a star. Some configurations may be easier than others to read. Scaling to make radii equal when the plant state is normal may mean that changes in some variables are less perceptible than others. Some events may be easier to recognize when certain variables are on adjacent radii, but for others it may be better to have a different sequence. Nothing is known about how to optimize such displays. Little evaluation has been done. Woods et al. (1981) showed that detection of abnormalities was good with star displays (although they did not seem to aid diagnosis), but one group of users actively disliked a star display because it was *difficult* to recognize abnormal conditions: in a real system there is always enough drift or disturbance present to ensure that the variables do not fall on the "normal" circle even when the plant is operating normally.

"Ecological" Displays

The most important recent development in display design is referred to as ecological interface displays (EID). Consider Example D in Figure 8.4. The *form* of the display directly presents the values of all the system state variables, inputs and outputs, *and the relations among them*. The geometry shows the system state in the shapes of the components of the display. Again, we may quote Simon (1981): "solving a problem simply means representing it so as to make the solution transparent."

Consider how the display supports the perception that the output goal is satisfied. By suitable scaling, the length of the bars O, V3 and G2 can be made equal when the goal G2 is satisfied. Then the vertical straight line bounding the end of O, V3, and G2 is a directly perceptible indicator that the output flow goal is satisfied regardless of their quantitative values.

Similarly we can scale all the variables and relations to produce a display in which all information is P, and none D. A system running normally is then represented by a vertical rectangle, and any departure from normality by a geometrical deformation of the rectangle. Furthermore, by choosing the geometry appropriately, the distortions indicate their cause. In example D of Figure 8.4 the reservoir is filling (the inflow to the reservoir is greater than the outflow), and the shape of the trapezoid resembles something which is increasing (filling) because of the slope of the line on the right-hand end of the trapezoid. (Were it emptying, it would slope the other way.) This form of display allows an assessment of system state without quantitative calculations, using perception rather than cognition.

Vicente (1999) summarizes thus the philosophy of EID as applied to large-scale systems:

> The approach . . . is based on an ecological perspective which demands that system design begin with, and be driven by, an explicit analysis of the constraints that the work environment imposes on behavior. Only by adopting such a perspective can designers ensure that the content and structure of the interface is compatible with the constraints that actually govern the work domain . . . The desired objective of this approach is to ensure that workers will acquire a veridical mental model of the work domain, so that their understanding corresponds, as closely as possible, to the actual behavior of the system with which they are interacting (e.g. the nuclear power plant). This is not to say that cognitive considerations are not important, . . . Psychological factors come into play, but only after ecological constraints have been satisfied. After all, if ecological compatibility has not been established, then the design is doomed from the start, as the preceding examples have shown. . . . The argument for the ecological perspective . . . generalizes meaningfully to any application domain where there is an external reality – outside of the person and the computer – that imposes dynamic, goal-relevant constraints on meaningful behavior. . . . For these correspondence-driven work domains, workers' mental models should correspond with this external reality. The only way to accomplish this objective efficiently is to adopt an ecological perspective by starting and driving the system design process by conducting an analysis of work constraints. (Vicente, 1999)

The aim in EID is not to provide quantitative information about the values of variables (that is, "data"), but to show the users where they are in constraint space. The display should support all kinds of behavior (SBB, RBB, and KBB), and modes of thought at all levels of the abstraction hierarchy (physical form, physical function, general form, general function, high level goals). This will allow the maximum freedom for workers to navigate in state space.

The importance of EIDs from a cognitive perspective is its insistence on perception rather than reasoning as the basis of adaptive behavior. Several important reviews have been published (Flach et al., 1995; Hancock et al., 1995; Vicente, 1999), but there is considerable confusion in the literature about the relation between EID and Gibson's original description of the ecological psychology and adaptive behavior in the natural world (e.g. Gibson, 1986).

It is clear that originally Gibson was concerned with perceptual-motor skills in natural environments, and proposed a "strong" ecological psychology which is best regarded as dealing with only such situations. As the human operator becomes increasingly remote from manual control of high bandwidth systems, strong ecological psychology becomes less and less relevant, and a careful reading of Gibson suggests that he explicitly excluded environments typical of industrial systems. Efforts such as those of Shaw, Flascher & Kadar (1995) to justify ecological psychology on the basis of dimensional analysis and the discovery of force related invariance are irrelevant, since through a human–machine interface any force, however small, can cause any acceleration, however great, by realizing appropriate interface transfer functions. The sense in which Rasmussen, Vicente, Sanderson and others use the term "ecological" should be clearly distinguished from Gibson's original use. An interface is ecological when it displays perceptually the relevant system invariances.

There may be a "natural" or "canonical" representation which provides the natural geometry for the display (Beltracchi, 1987; Vicente et al., 1996). Rasmussen et al. (1995) place great emphasis on looking for such displays. But research on cross-cultural display stereotypes suggests that there are very large cultural differences, and that gestalten which seem completely "natural" are often learned, and may have different meanings in different cultures. EIDs are *not* instantly understandable, nor do they instantly provide affordances to all viewers, as Gibson claims for the ecology of the natural world. EIDs provide affordance for experts with domain knowledge, and even domain experts must have the symbology of the displays explained to them. Although intended for recognition-based behavior, paradoxically the design of EIDs is a fascinating challenge for *cognitive* psychology.

Deduce Consequences of State: Evaluate and Choose Criteria of Performance

Tracking the state of the system in an industrial process is equivalent to "situation awareness" in other domains (Endsley, 1995; Endsley & Kiris, 1995). However, due to the complexity and size of industrial systems, abnormal situations and faults may not allow operators to identify system state. They then proceed up the DL to the highest levels, and use KBB to develop strategies. Here they use the displayed data and information as inputs for reasoning using mental models, trying to find a way to act on the plant to drive it to a state which *is* understood, or at least is relatively safe and stable, and will provide time to develop strategies and tactics which lead to appropriate action.

Special Aspects of DMS: Scheduling

The phrase "mental model" has many meanings (Moray, 1997a, 1998) but studies in industrial settings, particularly when scheduling is involved and because RBB is preferred to KBB, suggest that in such systems mental models have a characteristic form. In their classic paper "Charlie's Run-Time Estimator", Dutton & Starbuck (1971) provide a particularly clear account of practical cognition and an operator's mental model in a plant functioning normally. "Charlie" was responsible for scheduling in a factory making cloth, controlling a machine on which cloth was formed, and then cut longitudinally ("ripped") and transversely ("cut"). His task was to estimate the time it would take to fill orders. Dutton & Starbuck worked with him for a year, measuring his behavior objectively and conducting interviews, taking verbal protocols, etc.

The total number of possibilities is extremely large, of the order of several thousand combinations – the product of the number of variables and their range of values – but Charlie was able to perform very accurate mental estimates of how long orders would take, apparently taking into account the following variables:

1. The kind of cloth being produced.
2. The raw material of which the cloth was to be made.
3. The set up of the ripper (which makes the longitudinal cuts).
4. The number of changes of width required.
5. The speed of the machine in yards per hour.
6. The average length of rips.
7. The sum of rip length.
8. The value of this sum divided by the speed.
9. "Several other factors."

Charlie considered the variables in an almost invariable sequence, indicating a methodical approach to his mental calculations. Dutton & Starbuck constructed two models of Charlie's behavior. One was a quantitative engineering model, based on their observations, and the second was based on Charlie's own account of what he was doing.

The quantitative equation was:

$$T = aR + (b + gW)L$$

where

T = The sum of the times for the segments scheduled
R = The number of "ripper set-ups" used
W = The weight per square yard of the cloth
L = The length in yards of the material to be produced

a = Time required for "set-up"
$b + gW$ = time per yard produced.

The model based on what Charlie told them of how he worked was equivalent to:

$$T = L/S \tag{1}$$

where

$$S = f(A, \text{type of cloth, texture, properties of material}) \tag{2}$$

and

S = speed measured in yards/hour
A = mean length of a "rip"

(Note that $S = 1/(a/A + b + gW)$ even if Charlie was unaware of the fact.)

Dutton & Starbuck comment, "Charlie thus uses two non-linear relations, of which one is quite complex, in order to construct a simple linear relation." This latter is then used to schedule the task. The authors remark that relation (1) seems to be a description of a mental model rather than a true equation, and (2) is effectively a very large multidimensional look-up table, with between 2000 and 5000 entries. Very large mental look-up tables probably cause less mental workload than calculations. Charlie seems to be using a combination of RBB (the look-up table) and KBB (reasoning), based on a mental model or models built up by long experience, which enables him to finesse the need for direct calculation. (See also Beishon, 1974.)

Charlie's task appears to have been one in which scheduling was completed prior to the beginning of the run. Sanderson and her group (Buss, 1988; Sanderson, 1989; Seiler, 1994; Singalewitch, 1992) have revealed some of the subtleties of dynamic intervention in their studies on the acquisition of scheduling skills. They developed optimal algorithms for a simulated DMS, and investigated how operators acquire supervisory control skills in scheduling. After some hours of practice, the combination of human and optimal automation showed an increase in output of around 15% over automation alone, despite the fact that the algorithm was optimal in the strong mathematical sense over the time horizon of the production run. This tendency for hybrid human–machine systems to be better than either alone is well attested (Sanderson, 1989).

The operators seemed to operate rationally but opportunistically on a short time horizon. For example, they might halt an empty AGV on its way to a distant destination because they could see that a task was about to be completed at an intermediate location. By pausing until this latter was finished, the AGV could transport it to another intermediate destination on the way to the AGV's final destination as algorithmically programmed with a time horizon of the complete task, due to last nearly an hour. The time lost in the short delay was more than compensated by avoiding an extra circuit of the track to deal subsequently with the second job. Short time horizon opportunistic intervention improved the overall performance of the human–machine combination over either automation or manual control alone. Sanderson and her group found that if they added the opportunistic rule-based strategies to the long time horizon algorithm, automated control approached, but never completely matched the symbiotic behaviour. (It should be emphasized that industrial scheduling is increasingly automated, and the opportunities for short-term intervention by operators is decreasing.)

An excellent analysis of the human role in DMS based on field studies will be found in Wiers (1997). His analysis broadly supports the results quoted above from laboratory and earlier field studies. For a general review of the human factors of manufacturing see Karwowski et al. (1997).

THE ROLE OF THE HUMAN IN AUTOMATION: "FUNCTION ALLOCATION"

The final topic of this chapter is a central topic in human–machine interaction and the design of human–machine systems. Function allocation is the decision as to which aspects of a process shall be performed by humans and which by automation, and when allocation should alter (Grote et al., 1995; Inagaki, 1993, 1995; Parasuraman & Riley, 1997; Sheridan, 1992, 1997; Wei, 1998; Weiringa, 1997). There is even a social dimension to this problem, since a psychodynamics of trust exists between human and machine which closely resembles that between humans and influences how people interact with automation (Lee & Moray, 1992, 1994; Muir, 1994; Muir & Moray, 1996; Riley, 1994, 1996; Tan & Lewandowsky, 1996).

Traditionally allocation of function was done by listing the abilities of humans and those of machines, and deciding which agent performed which tasks best. Such an approach is inadequate. Rather, as any agent, human or otherwise, becomes overloaded, it should call on other agents for assistance, function allocation being performed dynamically in real time. Several taxonomies of function allocation for modern automation have been proposed (Sheridan, 1997; Wei, 1998). Sheridan & Verplanck's (1978) taxonomy is shown in Table 8.3. Surprisingly little research has been done on which levels are preferable (but see Moray, Inagaki & Ioth, 1999). Intuitively it is clear that the center of the figure maximizes symbiosis of human and machine intelligence at the cost of added workload due to communication and coordination.

The most common approach to dynamic allocation of function is based on task queuing as a measure of overload (Rouse, 1988). As the queue of tasks lengthens, the machine can either intervene or can ask the humans if they wish to offload some tasks. Whatever system is chosen, ultimate authority must normally reside with the human (but for an exception, see Inagaki, 1993, 1995). For limitations of excessive automation see Bainbridge (1983), Weiner & Curry (1980), and Woods (1988).

Several strategic models for deciding on allocation have been proposed in addition to simple queueing (Moray, 1986; Sheridan, 1992).

Table 8.3 Sheridan & Verplanck's Levels of Automation

Level of human–machine interaction	Human functions	Machine functions
Whole task done by human except for actual operation by machine	DETERMINE possible actions	
	SELECT action	
	INITIATE action →	PERFORM action
Computer suggests options	REQUEST possible actions →	
		DISPLAY possible actions
	SELECT action ←	
	INITIATE action →	PERFORM action
Computer suggests options and proposes one of them	(REQUEST possible actions) →	
		DISPLAY possible actions
	←	
	ASK for suggestion →	
		PROPOSE an action
	←	
	SELECT action (perhaps a different one)	
	INITIATE action →	PERFORM action
Computer chooses an action and performs it if human approves	(REQUEST possible actions) →	
		RETRIEVE possible actions
	←	PROPOSE action
	APPROVE action	
	→	PERFORM action
Computer chooses an action and performs it unless human disapproves	(REQUEST possible actions) →	
		RETRIEVE possible actions
	←	PROPOSE action
	(DISAPPROVE action)	
	→	PERFORM action
Computer chooses an action, performs it, and informs human	(REQUEST possible actions) →	
		RETRIEVE possible actions
		SELECT action
		INITIATE action
	←	INFORM human
Computer chooses an action, performs it, and informs human if it thinks he/she needs to know	(REQUEST possible actions) →	
		RETRIEVE possible actions
		SELECT action
		INITIATE action
	←	(INFORM human)
• • • • • •		• • • • • •
• • • • • •		• • • • • •
Computer does everything autonomously	(REQUEST possible actions) →	
		RETRIEVE possible actions
		SELECT action
		INITIATE action

Operators should take over a function if they can perform the task better than the automatic systems and vice versa. This has led to the first models of how people decide whether they are competent to take control (Lee & Moray, 1992, 1994; Muir 1994; Muir & Moray, 1996; Parasuraman & Riley, 1997; Riley, 1994, 1996; Tan & Lewandowsky, 1996). Muir used the social psychology and sociology of trust to construct a general model, and Lee & Moray (1992, 1994) predicted intervention with a quantitative time series model of trust and self-confidence as a function of the system dynamics and disturbances. Tan & Lewandowsky (1996) compared trust between human and machine to that between human and human, and Raeth (personal communication) has shown that these models can be extended predictively to tasks in other domains. Wei, Macwan & Weiringa (1998) have developed a new scale for the degree of automation, and related it both to system performance and to the mental effort required of operators. Although their study was of a laboratory task, it had enough engineering face validity to suggest that their measure may be valid in more general contexts, and provide a tool for relating system characteristics to cognitive load. This will provide another tool for deciding on allocation of function, since there seems to be a level of automation above which increasing automation yields little return. Wei (1998) has validated the measure using a version of PASTEURISER, a laboratory CPCS (Lee & Moray, 1992).

SUMMARY

The aim of this chapter has been to introduce, in a very elementary way, four ideas.

First, it is possible to carry out both field studies and experiments on cognitive behavior in real or realistic settings. Experimental work can be performed in the field, in simulators, or in the laboratory using "microworlds," realistic tasks which are sufficiently complex to call up realistic behavior from operators (Buss, 1988; Lee & Moray, 1992, 1994; Muir 1994; Sanderson, 1989; Seiler, 1994; Singalewitch, 1992). Rasmussen et al. (1995, pp. 219–24) provide a particularly insightful discussion of the conditions under which laboratory studies are likely to produce ecologically valid results.

Second, it is possible to find parallels between many concepts investigated in the cognitive psychology laboratory and behavior in field settings.

Third, on the other hand, little laboratory research can be currently applied to systems design because of the oversimplified research settings used in the laboratory, which frequently prevent realistic behavior from appearing.

Fourth, applied cognitive research is a rich and fascinating field, with enormous importance to productivity, safety, and the job satisfaction of workers in an increasingly technological world. It provides deeply challenging intellectual problems for researchers, and a vivid setting for testing the predictive power of cognitive models, computational or otherwise. It further provides an outstanding opportunity to synthesize different fields of psychology, experimental, social and organizational, and in so doing give a richer meaning to "cognition". The real world is the ultimate challenge for any psychological theory.

REFERENCES

Bainbridge, L. (1974). Analysis of protocols from a process control task. In E. Edwards and F. Lees (Eds), *The Human Operator in Process Control* (pp. 146–58). London: Taylor & Francis.
Bainbridge, L. (1983). The ironies of automation. *Automatica*, 19, 755–79.
Bainbridge, L. (1991). Mental models in cognitive skills: the example of industrial process control. In A. Rutherford and Y. Rogers (Eds), *Models in the Mind*. New York: Academic Press.
Beishon, R. J. (1974). An analysis and simulation of an operator's behaviour in controlling continuous baking ovens. In E. Edwards and F. Lees (Eds), *The Human Operator in Process Control* (pp. 79–90). London: Taylor and Francis.
Beltracchi, L. (1987). A direct manipulation interface for water-based Rankine cycle heat engines. *IEEE Transactions of Systems, Man and Cybernetics*. SMC-17, 478–87.
Bennett, K. B. & Flach, J. M. (1992). Graphical displays: implications for divided attention, focussed attention and problem solving. *Human Factors*, 34 (5), 513–33.
Buss, T. (1988). Operator fault management in a small computer integrated manufacturing system. M.Sc. Thesis, Engineering Psychology Research Laboratory, Department of Mechanical and Industrial Engineering, University of Illinois at Urbana-Champaign.
Buttigieg, M. & Sanderson, P. M. (1991). Emergent features in visual display design for two types of failure detection tasks. *Human Factors*, 33 (6), 631–51.
Carswell, C. M. & Wickens, C. D. (1987). Information integration and the object display: an interaction of task demands and display superiority. *Ergonomics*, 30, 511–27.
Cellier, J-M., De Keyser, V. & Valot, C. (1996). *La gestion du temps dans les environnements dynamiques*. Paris: Presses Universitaires de France.
Coekin, J. A. (1969). A versatile presentation of parameters for rapid recognition of total state. *International Symposium on Man–Machine Systems*. (58-MMS 4). New York: IEEE Conference Record 69.
Crossman, E. R. & Cooke, F. W. (1974). Manual control of slow response systems. In E. Edwards & F. Lees, (Eds), *The Human Operator in Process Control* (pp. 51–66). London: Taylor & Francis.
Crossman, E. R. (1974). Automation and skill. In E. Edwards & F. Lees (Eds), *The Human Operator in Process Control* (pp. 1–24). London: Taylor & Francis.
De Cortis, F. (1988). Dimension temporelle de l'activité cognitive lors des démarrages de systèmes complexes. *Le Travail Human*, 51, 1215–38.
De Keyser, V. (1981). La fiabilité humaine dans les processus continus, les centrales thermo-éléctriques et nucléaires. Technical Report 720-ECI-2651-C-(0) GCE-DGXII, CERI, Bruxelles.
De Keyser, V., De Cortis, F., Housiaux, A. & Van Daele, A. (1987) Les communications hommes–machines dans les systèmes complexes. Appendice, Technical Report Contrat No. 8, Actions Nationales de Recherche En Soutien A Fast. Université de Liège, Belgium.
Dessouky, M. I., Moray, N. & Kijowski, B. (1995). Taxonomy of scheduling systems as a basis for the study of strategic behavior. *Human Factors*, 37 (3), 443–72.
Drury, C. G. & Sinclair, M. A. (1983). Human and machine performance in an inspection task. *Human Factors*, 25, 391–9.
Durso, F. T., Cooke, N. M., Breen, T. J. & Schvaneveldt, R. W. (1987). Is consistent mapping necessary for high-speed search? *Journal of Experimental Psychology: Learning, Memory and Cognition*, 13 (2), 223–9.
Dutton, J. M. & Starbuck, W. (1971). Finding Charlie's run-time estimator. In J. M. Dutton and W. Starbuck (Eds), *Computer Simulation of Human Behavior*. New York: Wiley.
Edwards, E. & Lees, F. (1974a). *The Human Operator in Process Control*. London: Taylor & Francis.

Edwards, E. & Lees, F. (1974b). *Process Control*. London: Institute of Chemical Engineers.

Endsley, M. R. (1995). Towards a theory of situation awareness in dynamic systems. *Human Factors*, 37 (1), 32–64.

Endsley, M. R. & Kiris, E. O. (1995). The out-of-the-loop performance problem and level of control in automation. *Human Factors*, 37 (2), 381–94.

Englestadt, P. H. (1974). Socio-technical approach to problems of process control. In E. Edwards & F. Lees (Eds), *The Human Operator in Process Control*. London: Taylor & Francis.

Flach, J., Hancock, P., Caird, J. & Vicente, K. (1995). *Local Applications of the Ecological Approach to Human–Machine Systems* (vol. 2). Hillsdale, NJ: Lawrence Erlbaum.

Gentner, D. & Stevens, A. L. (1983). *Mental Models*. Hillsdale, NJ: Lawrence Erlbaum.

Gibson, J. J. (1986). *The Ecological Approach to Visual Perception*. Hillsdale, NJ: Lawrence Erlbaum.

Grote, G. S., Weik, T., Wafler, T. & Zolch, M. (1995). Criteria for the complementary allocation of functions in automated work systems and their use in simultaneous engineering projects. *International Journal of Industrial Ergonomics*, 16, 367–82.

Hancock, P., Flach, J., Caird, J. & Vicente, K. (1995). *Global Applications of the Ecological Approach to Human–Machine Systems* (vol. 1). Hillsdale, NJ: Lawrence Erlbaum.

Hansen, J.-P. (1995). Representation of system invariants by optical invariants in configural displays for process control. In P. Hancock, J. Flach, J. Caird & K. Vicente (Eds), *Local Applications of the Ecological Approach to Human–Machine Systems* (pp. 208–33). Hillsdale, NJ: Lawrence Erlbaum.

Hoc, J.-M. (1995). Planning in diagnosing a slow process. *Zeitschrift für psychologie*, 203, 111–5.

Hoc, J.-M. (1996). *Supervision et controle de processus: la cognition en situation dynamique*. Grenoble: Presses Universitaires de Grenoble.

Hollnagel, E. (1993). *Human Reliability Analysis: Context and Control*. London: Academic Press.

Hollnagel, E. (1998). *Cognitive Reliability and Error Analysis Method*. Amsterdam: Elsevier.

Hutchins, E. (1995). *Cognition in the Wild*. Cambridge, MA: MIT Press.

Inagaki, T. (1993). Situation-adaptive degree of automation for system safety. *Proceedings of IEEE International Workshop on Robot and Human Communication* (pp. 231–6).

Inagaki, T. (1995). Situation-adaptive responsibility allocation for human-centered automation. *Transactions of the Society of Instrument and Control Engineers*, 31 (3), 292–8.

Iosif, G. (1968). La stratégie dans la surveillance des tableaux de commande. I. Quelques facteurs déterminants de caractère objectif. *Revue Roumanien de Science Social-Psychologique*, 12, 147–61.

Iosif, G. (1969a). La stratégie dans la surveillance des tableaux de commande. I. Quelques facteurs déterminants de caractère subjectif. *Revue Roumanien de Science Social-Psychologique*, 13, 29–41.

Iosif, G. (1969b). Influence de la correlation fonctionelle sur parametres technologiques. *Revue Roumanien de Science Social-Psychologique*, 13, 105–10.

Jerison, H. (1967). Signal detection theory in the analysis of human vigilance. *Human Factors*, 9, 285–8.

Johnson-Laird, P. N. (1983). *Mental Models*. Cambridge, MA: Harvard University Press.

Kahneman, D., Slovic, P. & Tversky, A. (Eds) (1982). *Judgement Under Uncertainty: Heuristics and Biases*. Cambridge: Cambridge University Press.

Karwowski, W., Warnecke, H. J., Hueser, M. & Salvendy, G. (1997). Human factors in manufacturing. In G. Salvendy (Ed.), *Handbook of Human Factors* (2nd edn, pp. 1876–925). New York: Wiley.

Kelly, C. (1964). *Manual and Automatic Control*. New York: Wiley.

Kemeny, J. G. (Ed.) (1979). *The President's Commission on the Accident at Three Mile Island*. Washington, DC: US Government Printing Office.

Kirwan, B. & Ainsworth, L. K. (1992). *A Guide to Task Analysis*. London: Taylor & Francis.
Klein, G. A., Orasanu, J., Calderwood, R. & Zsambok, C. E. (1993). *Decision Making in Action: Models and Methods*. Norwood, NJ: Ablex.
Kragt, H. (1992). *Enhancing Industrial Performance: Experiences of Integrating the Human Factor*. London: Taylor & Francis.
Kuo, W. & Hsu, J. P. (1990). Update: simultaneous engineering design in Japan. *Industrial Engineering*, 22, 23–8.
Kvalseth, T. (1977). Human information processing in visual sampling. *Ergonomics*, 21, 439–54.
Lanir, Z. (1986). *Fundamental Surprise*. Eugene, OR: Decision Research.
Laughery, K. R., Wogalter, M. S. & Young, S. L. (1995). Human factors perspectives on warnings. Santa Monica, CA: Human Factors and Ergonomics Society.
Lee, J. D. & Moray, N. (1992) Trust, control strategies and allocation of function in human–machine systems. *Ergonomics*, 35, 1243–70.
Lee, J. D. & Moray, N. (1994) Trust, self confidence and operators' adaptation to automation. *International Journal of Human–Computer Studies*, 40, 153–84.
Leermakers, T. (1995). *Monitoring Behaviour*. Eindhoven: Eindhoven University of Technology.
Lees, F. (1974). Research on the process operator. In E. Edwards & F. Lees (Eds), *The Human Operator in Process Control* (pp. 386–425). London: Taylor & Francis.
McRuer, D. T. & Krendel, E. (1957). *Dynamic Response of the Human Operator*. (WADC TR-56-254). Dayton, OH: Wright-Patterson AFB.
McRuer, D. T. & Krendel, E. (1976). *Mathematical Models of Human Pilot Behavior*. NATO AGARDograph No. 188. Brussels.
Moray, N. (1981). The role of attention in the detection of errors and the diagnosis of failures in man–machine systems. In J. Rasmussen and W. B. Rouse (Eds), *Human Detection and Diagnosis of System Failures*. New York: Plenum Press.
Moray, N. (1982). *Subjective Criteria Used by Nuclear Power Plant Operators in Making Decisions About the Normality of their Equipment*. 15th Proceedings of Human Factors Association of Canada, Toronto.
Moray, N. (1986). Monitoring behavior and supervisory control. In K. R. Boff, L. Kaufman & J. P. Thomas (Eds), *Handbook of Perception and Human Performance* (ch. 45). New York: Wiley.
Moray, N. (1989). A lattice theory approach to the structure of mental models. *Philosophical Transactions of the Royal Society of London*, series B, 327, 447–593.
Moray, N. (1992). Flexible interfaces can promote operator error. In H. Kragt (Ed.), *Enhancing Industrial Performance* (pp. 49–64). London: Taylor & Francis.
Moray, N. (1997a). Models of Models of . . . Mental Models. In T. B. Sheridan and T. Van Lunteren (Eds), *Perspectives on the Human Controller* (pp. 271–85). Mahwah, NJ: Lawrence Erlbaum.
Moray, N. (1997b). Human factors in process control. In G. Salvendy (Ed.), *Handbook of Human Factors* (2nd edn, pp. 1944–71). New York: Wiley.
Moray, N. (1998). Mental models in theory and practice. *Attention and Performance XVII*, Beit Oren, Israel.
Moray, N. & Rotenberg, I. (1989). Fault management in process control: eye movements and action. *Ergonomics*, 32, 1319–42.
Moray, N., Inagaki, T. & Ioth (in preparation).
Moray, N., Lee, J. D. & Hiskes. D. (1994). Why do people intervene in the control of automated systems? *Proceedings of the 1st Conference on the Human Factors of Automated Systems*. Washington, DC, February.
Moray, N., Lee, J. D. & Muir, B. M. (1995). Trust and human intervention in automated systems. In J.-M. Hoc, C. Cacciabue & E. Hollnagel (Eds), *Expertise and Technology: Cognition and Human–Computer Interaction*. Lawrence Erlbaum.
Moray, N., Lootsteen, P. & Pajak, J. (1986). Acquisition of process control skills. *IEEE Transactions on Systems, Man and Cybernetics*, SMC-16, 497–504.

Moray, N., Sanderson, P. M. & Vicente, K. J. (1992). Cognitive task analysis of a complex work domain: a case study. *Reliability Engineering and Systems Safety*, 36, 207–16.

Muir, B. M. (1994). Trust in automation: Part 1 – Theoretical issues in the study of trust and human intervention in automated systems. *Ergonomics*, 37 (11), 1905–23.

Muir, B. M. & Moray, N. (1996). Trust in automation. Part II. Experimental studies of trust and human intervention in a process control simulation. *Ergonomics*, 39 (3), 429–61.

Neisser, U. (1976). *Cognition and Reality*. New York: Freeman.

Norman, D. (1990). *The Design of Everyday Things*. New York: Doubleday.

Parasuraman, R. & Riley, V. (1997). Humans and automation: use, misuse, disuse, abuse. *Human Factors*, 39 (2), 230–53.

Perrow, C. (1984). *Normal Accidents*. New York: Basic Books

Rasmussen, J. (1986). *Information Processing and Human–Machine Interaction: An Approach to Cognitive Engineering*. Amsterdam: North-Holland.

Rasmussen, J. & Rouse, W. B. (Eds) (1981). *Human Detection and Diagnosis of System Failures*. New York: Plenum Press.

Rasmussen, J., Pejtersen, A.-M. & Goodstein, L. (1995). *Cognitive Engineering: Concepts and Applications*. New York: John Wiley.

Reason, J. (1990). *Human Error*. Cambridge: Cambridge University Press.

Reason, J. (1997). *Managing Risks of Organizational Accidents*. Aldershot: Ashgate.

Reising, D. V. C. & Sanderson, P. M. (1996). Work domain analysis of a pasteurisation plant: building an abstraction hierarchy representation. *Proceedings of the Human Factors and Ergonomics Society 40th Annual Meeting*.

Riley, V. (1994). A theory of operator reliance on automation. In M. Mouloua & R. Parasuraman (Eds), *Human Performance in Automated Systems: Recent Research and Trends* (pp. 8–14). Hillsdale, NJ: Lawrence Erlbaum.

Riley, V. (1996). Operator reliance on automation. In M. Mouloua & R. Parasuraman (Eds), *Human Performance in Automated Systems: Theory and Applications* (pp. 19–35). Hillsdale, NJ: Lawrence Erlbaum.

Rochlin, E., LaPorte, T. & Roberts, K. (1987). The self-designing high reliability organisation: aircraft flight operation at sea. *Naval War College Review*, Autumn, 76–91.

Rouse, W. B. (1988). Adaptive aiding for human–computer control. *Human Factors*, 30, 431–8.

Rutherford, A., Rogers, Y. & Bibby, P. A. (Eds) (1992). *Models in the Mind*. London: Academic Press.

Salvendy, G. (Ed.) (1997). *Handbook of Human Factors*. New York: John Wiley.

Sanderson, P. M. (1989). The human planning and scheduling role in advanced manufacturing systems: an emerging human factors role. *Human Factors*, 31 (6), 635–66.

Sanderson, P. M. & Moray, N. (1990). The human factors of scheduling behavior. In W. Karwowski & M. Rahini (Eds), *Ergonomics of Hybrid Automated Systems, II*. Amsterdam: Elsevier.

Sanderson, P. M., Flach, J. M., Buttigieg, M. A. & Casey, E. J. (1989). Object displays do not always support better integrated task performance. *Human Factors*, 31 (2), 183–98.

Sarter, N. B., Woods, D. D. & Billings, C. E. (1997) Automation surprises. In G. Salvendy (Ed.), *Handbook of Human Factors* (pp. 1026–43). New York: John Wiley.

Scerbo, M. S. (1996). Theoretical perspectives on adaptive automation. In R. Parasuraman & M. Moulova (Eds), *Automation and Human Performance: Theory and Application*. Hillsdale, NJ: Lawrence Erlbaum.

Seiler, M. (1994). The effects of heterarchical vs. hierarchical scheduling algorithms on human operator behavior in discrete manufacturing systems. M.Sc. thesis, Engineering Psychology Research Laboratory, Department of Mechanical and Industrial Engineering, University of Illinois at Urbana-Champaign.

Senders, J. W. (1983). *Visual Sampling Processes*. Katholieke Hogeschool Tilburg, Netherlands and Hillsdale, NJ: Lawrence Erlbaum.

Senders, J. W. & Monty, R. A. (Eds) (1978). *Eye Movements in the Higher Psychological Functions*. Hillsdale, NJ: Lawrence Erlbaum.
Shaw, R. E., Flascher, O. M. & Kadar, E. E. (1995). Dimensionless invariants for intentional systems: measuring the fit of vehicular activities to environmental layout. In J. Flach, P. Hancock, J. Caird & K. Vicente (Eds), *Global Perspectives on the Ecology of Human–Machine Systems* (vol. 1, pp. 293–358). Hillsdale, NJ: Lawrence Erlbaum.
Sheridan, T. B. (1992). *Telerobotics, Automation, and Human Supervisory Control*. Cambridge, MA: MIT Press.
Sheridan, T. B. (1997). Supervisory control. In G. Salvendy (Ed.), *Handbook of Human Factors* (2nd edn, pp. 1295–327). New York: John Wiley.
Sheridan, T. B. & Ferrell, W. R. (1974). *Man–Machine Systems*. Cambridge, MA: MIT Press.
Sheridan, T. B. & Verplanck, W. L. (1978). *Human and Computer Control of Undersea Teleoperators*. Technical Report, Man–Machine Systems Laboratory, Department of Mechanical Engineering, Massachusetts Institute of Technology, Cambridge, MA.
Shiffrin, R. M. & Schneider, W. (1977). Controlled and automatic human information processing II: perceptual learning, automatic attending, and a general theory. *Psychological Review*, 84, 127–90.
Simon, H. (1981). *The Sciences of the Artificial*. Cambridge, MA: MIT Press.
Singalewitch, H. (1992). Learning strategies in a computer integrated manufacturing simulation. M.Sc. thesis, Engineering Psychology Research Laboratory, Department of Mechanical and Industrial Engineering, University of Illinois at Urbana-Champaign.
Singleton, W. T. (Ed.) (1978). *The Study of Real Skills*. London: Academic Press.
Stanton, N. (Ed.) (1994). *Human Factors in Alarm Design*. London: Taylor & Francis.
Swets, J. (1996). *Signal Detection Theory and ROC Analysis in Psychology and Diagnostics*. Marwah, NJ: Lawrence Erlbaum.
Swets, J. & Pickett, R. (1982). *Evaluation of Diagnostic Systems*. New York: Academic Press.
Tan, G. & Lewandowsky, S. (1996). A comparison of operator trust in humans versus machines. *INTERNET: CybErg International Electronic Conference. http://www.curtin.edu.au/conference/*
Taylor, M., Lindsay, P. H. & Forbes, S. M. (1967). Quantification of shared capacity processing in auditory and visual discrimination. *Acta Psychologica*, 27, 223–31.
Vicente, K. J. (1992). Ecological interface design: theoretical foundations. *IEEE Transactions on Systems, Man, and Cybernetics*, SMC-22 (4), 589–606.
Vicente, K. J. (1998). Improving dynamic decision making in complex systems through ecological interface design: a research overview. *Systems Dynamics Review*, 12, 251–279.
Vicente, K. J. (1999). *Cognitive Work Analysis: Towards Safe, Productive and Healthy Computer-based Work*. Marwah, NJ: Lawrence Erlbaum.
Vicente, K. J., Moray, N., Lee, J. D., Rasmussen, J. D., Jones, B. G., Brock, R. & Djemil, T. (1996). Evaluation of a Rankine cycle display for nuclear power plant monitoring and diagnosis. *Human Factors*, 38 (3), 506–22.
Vierling, A. E. (1990). Machines can only produce as efficiently as the people who operate them. *Industrial Engineering*, 22, 24–6.
Wei, Z.-G. (1998). *Mental Load and Performance at Different Automation Levels*. Delft: University of Delft.
Wei, Z.-G., Macwan, A. P. & Weiringa, P. A. (1998). A quantitative measure for the degree of automation and its relation to system performance and mental load. *Human Factors*, 40, 277–95.
Weiringa, P. A. (1997). Operator support and supervisory control. In T. B. Sheridan & T. Van Lunteren (Eds), *Perspectives on the Human Controller* (pp. 251–60). Mahwah, NJ: Lawrence Erlbaum.
Wickens, C. D. (1991). *Engineering Psychology and Human Performance*. New York: HarperCollins.
Wiener, E. L. & Curry, R. E. (1980). Flight-deck automation: promises and problems. *Ergonomics*, 23 (10), 995–1011.

Wiers, V. C. S. (1997). *Human–Computer Interaction in Production Scheduling*. Eindhoven: Institute for Business Engineering and Technology Application.

Wilson, J. R. & Rutherford, A. (1989). Mental models: theory and application in human factors. *Human Factors*, 31, 617–34.

Woods, D. D. (1986). Human factors challenges in process control: the case of nuclear power plants. In G. Salvendy (Ed.), *Handbook of Human Factors*. New York: John Wiley.

Woods, D. D. (1988). Coping with complexity: the psychology of human behavior in complex systems. In L. P. Goodstein, H. B. Andersen & S. E. Olsen (Eds), *Tasks, Errors and Mental Models*. New York: Taylor & Francis.

Woods, D. D. (1994). Cognitive demands and activities in dynamic fault management: abductive reasoning and disturbance management. In N. Stanton (Ed.), *Human Factors in Alarm Design* (pp. 63–92). London: Taylor & Francis.

Woods, D. D. & Roth, E. M. (1988). Cognitive systems engineering. In M. Helander (Ed.), *Handbook of Human–Computer Interaction*. Amsterdam: North-Holland Elsevier.

Woods, D. D., Wise, J. A. & Hanes, L. F. (1981). An evaluation of nuclear power plant safety parameter display systems. *Proceedings of the Human Factors Society, 25th Annual Meeting*.

Young, L. R. (1969). On adaptive manual control. *IEEE Transactions on Man–Machine Systems*, MMS-10, 292–331.

Young, L. R. (1973). Human control capabilities. In J. F. Parker Jr & V. R. West (Eds), *Bioastronautics Data Book*. Washington, DC: National Aeronautics and Space Administration.

Zsambok, C. E. & Klein, G. (1997). *Naturalistic Decision Making*. Marwah, NJ: Lawrence Erlbaum.

Zuboff, S. (1988). *In the Age of the Smart Machine*. New York: Basic Books.

Chapter 9

Cognitive Factors in Aviation

Christopher D. Wickens
University of Illinois at Urbana-Champaign

This chapter describes the task of flying an aircraft from a cognitive perspective as involving a time-shared collection of four meta tasks: aviating, navigating, communicating, and systems management. The pilot is described within an information processing framework and then each of the four meta tasks are described in detail, considering their implications for displays, pilot error and automation. We then consider the cognitive constructs of decision making, situation awareness, procedures following and mental workload, which apply across all four meta tasks. The last section addresses the cognitive issues as pilots deal with aircraft automation.

COGNITIVE FACTORS IN AVIATION

Flying an aircraft is one of the greatest challenges to the cognitive capabilities of humans, involving as it does the knowledge of how to control a vehicle that defies the natural forces of gravity. From the standpoint of cognitive psychology, the task of flying will be considered from three different but intersecting perspectives:

- the cognitive analysis of the different tasks a pilot must carry out (Seamster, Redding & Kaempf, 1997)
- a description of the physical characteristics of the aircraft system that is the focus of those tasks
- a representation of the pilot's information processing structures that are most critical, in different combinations, to achieving those tasks.

In the following pages, we first describe the physical characteristics of airplane flight that impose so heavily upon the pilot's cognitive capabilities. Then, after rep-

Handbook of Applied Cognition, Edited by F. T. Durso, R. S. Nickerson, R. W. Schvaneveldt, S. T. Dumais, D. S. Lindsay and M. T. H. Chi.

resenting the pilot as an information processing system, we describe the cognitive demands imposed by the following aviation task categories: aviating, navigating, communicating, and systems management. Within each category, we discuss ways in which the design of aircraft and of the airspace is evolving to remediate (but sometimes exacerbate) those demands. Then we address four general issues, falling within the purview of cognitive psychology, that transcend the different task categories: aeronautical decision making, situation awareness, following procedures, and the interplay between mental workload and task management.

THE AIRCRAFT AS A DYNAMIC SYSTEM

Effective control of any complex dynamic system depends on the operator possessing an accurate mental model of the system from which to establish expectancies of system response (Bellenkes, Wickens & Kramer, 1997). The foundations of the mental model of the aircraft are based in its dynamics, represented schematically in Figure 9.1(a) which presents a graphics presentation of the aircraft. Figure 9.1(b) presents a more schematic and abstract version of its dynamic elements. As shown in both figures, the aircraft can be characterized first by control of its attitude (orientation or rotation) in three dimensional space, a vector defined by pitch, bank (or roll), and yaw. As shown in the middle row of Figure 9.1(b), as the aircraft moves forward, its attitude parameters then produce rates of change: vertical velocity generally being influenced by pitch, and heading change being influenced primarily by roll. Changes in forward movement (acceleration) are primarily influenced by the thrust from the aircraft. As shown in the next row of Figure 9.1(b), the changes along the vertical, heading, and forward motion (longitudinal) dimensions, produce new positions in altitude, heading and airspeed. Finally, as shown in the bottom row, heading and airspeed produce lateral deviations (from a desired flight path), and longitudinal position along the flight path, respectively. This causal sequence of aircraft dynamic behavior is represented by the three embedded control loops in Figure 9.1(b). These may be referred to as inner loop, middle loop and outer loop control.

As shown in Figure 9.1(a), in most aircraft the pilot has direct control over pitch, bank and thrust. Using these parameters the pilot must perform two fundamental tasks which we shall discuss in more detail later: maintaining stable flight control or aviating (to avoid stalling the aircraft such that it falls out of the air), and navigating to reach certain points in three dimensional space and avoid other regions (bad weather, terrain, other aircraft). Because the aviation task is accomplished by maintaining an adequate velocity of airflow relative to the wings' orientation, it depends critically on control of attitude and airspeed. On the other hand, the navigation task is based on control of the variables altitude, lateral deviation, and longitudinal position, at the bottom level of Figure 9.1(b), since these are the variables that define positions in the 3D airspace.

Three characteristics of these tasks impose very complex cognitive demands on the pilot. First, as noted, control of the attitude parameters of pitch and roll must serve two (not always compatible) tasks: preventing stall, and using these parameters to influence rate of change which will in turn influence position, in

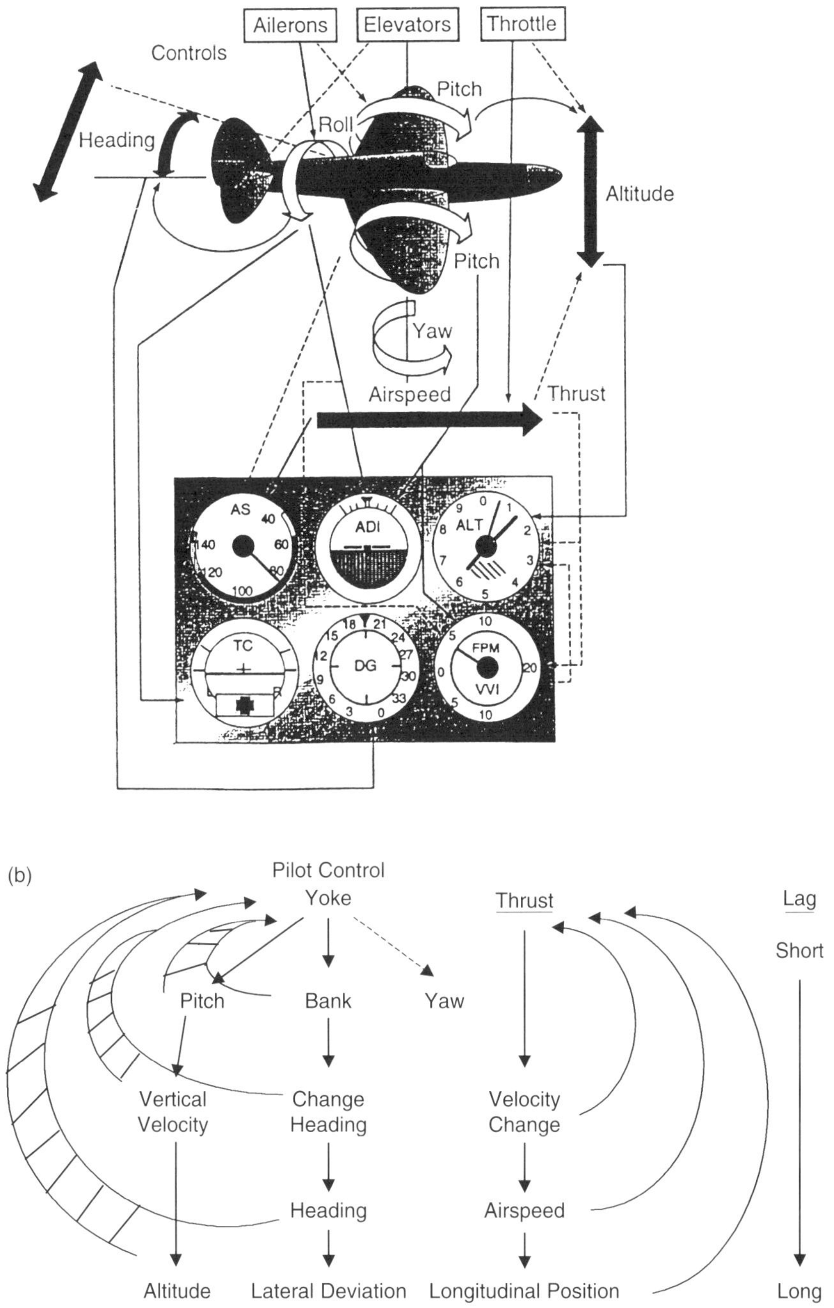

Figure 9.1 A representation of flight dynamics: (a) shows the relation between flight control inputs (top), the movement and rotation of the aircraft (middle), and how these movements are displayed to the pilot (bottom). The thin lines represent sources of "cross-coupling" between axes of flight. (b) Represents the flight axes in more schematic form. The pilot directly controls inner loop variables at the top, to affect control of middle and outer loop variables toward the bottom.

order to satisfy navigational goals. Second, control of the outer loop navigational variables is sluggish. This is shown by the causal sequence of arrows in Figure 9.1(b). The pilot must control inner loop parameters to influence mid loop parameters, and use these in turn to influence outer loop parameters. As a result, the latter change slowly; they have a greater lag. The control of sluggish systems is a cognitive challenge, because it requires a great degree of mental prediction and extrapolation (Wickens, 1986, 1992). Third, as reflected in the dashed arrows in Figure 9.1(a), the causal effects of control variables is not as simple as the representation in Figure 9.1(b) suggests. The three axes of flight show considerable crosstalk, such that, for example, changes in bank affect pitch (the aircraft will pitch down if its wings are not level), and changes in pitch affect airspeed (pitch down increases airspeed), which itself affects vertical velocity.

It should be noted, too, that many aspects of these dynamics will be modified by particular aircraft characteristics. The control loop delays of large transport aircraft are much longer (more sluggish) than of light aircraft, and some aircraft, such as helicopters or hovercraft, have the ability to halt forward flight altogether – but this capability produces even greater complexity in their dynamics.

The pilot who must accomplish these two fundamental tasks can be represented by the information processing model shown in Figure 9.2. Information bearing on aircraft state is processed by the senses, where its quality may or may not be degraded by environmental factors. The pilot's experience, represented in long-term memory, is then brought to bear to perceive or interpret the information, via top-down processing and the template matching, in order to understand the current state of the aircraft and its systems. Such information may need to be temporarily maintained in working memory prior to the selection and execution of an action. In some cases the new information may require permanent storage in long-term memory, the residence of pilot expertise. The cognitive skills possessed by the expert pilot are, in turn, employed to guide selective attention (Gopher, 1992) to form expectancies that aid top-down perceptual processing and categorization, and to assist in the selection of appropriate actions.

The model shown in Figure 9.2 also contains three additional features, not generally represented in more traditional information processing models. First, the concept of situation awareness (Endsley, 1995; Garland & Endsley, 1997; see below and Durso & Gronlund, 1999, this volume) – which has achieved considerable attention in aviation circles – characterizes information which can rapidly be brought to mind regarding the dynamically evolving situation in the airspace. It embodies that information, regarding a particular situation, that can be perceived, is held in working memory, and can be rapidly retrieved from a larger capacity memory store, referred to as long-term working memory (LTWM) (Kintsch & Ericsson, 1995). This LTWM component is the second feature. Third, we have explicitly represented aeronautical decision making (Orasanu, 1993; see below), shown within the oval as a process that involves both diagnosis and situation assessment in working memory, as well as the choice of action (Wickens, 1992).

As we noted above and will look at further below, the pilot must, at a minimum, bring these processes to bear on the tasks of aviation and navigation. But these core tasks often spawn others. Because the airspace must usually be shared with other users, it is necessary to communicate with other aircraft, or with air traffic

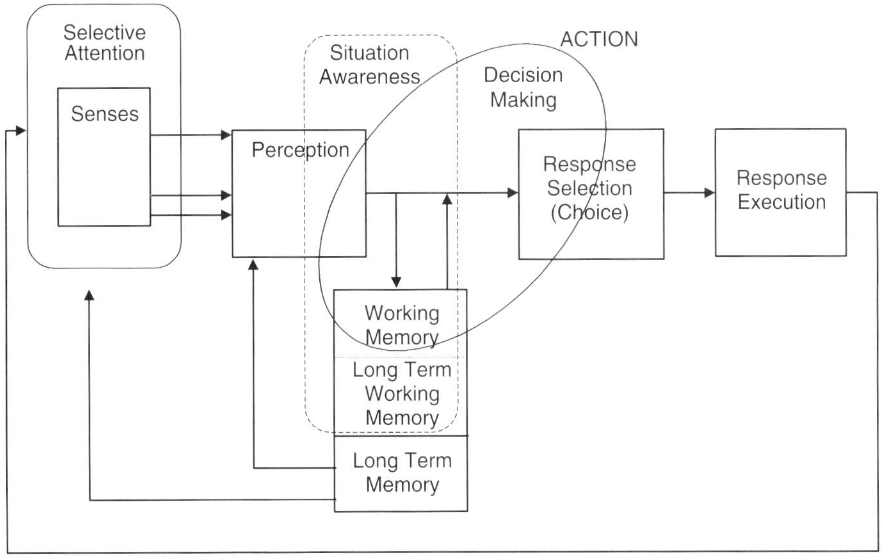

Figure 9.2 Representation of the pilot as an information processing system.

control, to avoid collision. Because the aircraft itself depends on the functioning of many other mechanical, and electrical *systems*, it is often necessary for the pilot to understand what those systems are doing (systems management). Finally, carrying out the aviation, navigation, communications, and systems subtasks generally requires knowledge of very specific procedures. The pilot must both accomplish tasks within these various categories, as well as prioritize among them (Schutte & Trujillo, 1996), a prioritization scheme that generally dictates a hierarchy of aviate, navigate, communicate, systems management, but often may need to temporarily deviate from it. We discuss each of these major task categories in the following sections, before discussing cognitive issues brought about by their automation.

AVIATE: MAINTAINING STABILITY

As shown in Figure 9.1(a), the requirement to maintain adequate airflow over the wings, to avoid stalling and to direct the aircraft in a way that satisfies the outer loop navigational goals, is a complex process. A pilot may rely on one of two generic sources of visual information to accomplish this: visual contact information, and flight instrument information. Visual contact information is provided by the view outside the aircraft, using a number of fundamental perceptual invariants (Gibson, 1979; Warren & Wertheim, 1990) to update the pilot's attitude awareness. For example, the angle, and vertical location on the windscreen of the horizon line provide an accurate representation of bank and pitch, respectively. When flying toward or along a textured surface, the pilot may use the texture gradient to judge altitude changes, and may use texture flow to judge ground speed, and the orientation of the flight path relative to the ground plane (Larish & Flach, 1990).

While such holistic or ecological visual cues are intuitive and can rapidly be perceived (Owen, 1991), many of them are imprecise, subject to visual illusion (Leibowitz, 1988) and of course may be unavailable at night or in poor weather. Furthermore, since they are all based on ground features, none of them offer reliable information regarding velocity through the air (airspeed vector) which is a critical variable for preventing stall. As a consequence of these shortcomings, all conventional aircraft have been equipped with a minimum standard set of (generally six) instruments, shown at the bottom of Figure 9.1(a).

Examination of cockpit visual scanning (Bellenkes et al., 1997; Fitts, Jones & Milton, 1950; Harris & Christhilf, 1980) has revealed important differences between the six flight instruments, in terms of the frequency and dwell duration with which they are scanned, and how these differences in turn are affected by pilot skill levels. These skill-related differences implicate changes in the pilot's mental model of the flight dynamics. For example, a repeated finding from cockpit scanning research is that the attitude directional indicator or "artificial horizon," shown in the upper center of the instrument panel, is the most important instrument. It is visited most frequently, and the eyeballs dwell there longest when it is visited. Two reasons can be offered for its importance:

1. It is the only instrument which offers two channels of information integrated into one – the horizon line both pitches and banks, hence conveying the two most critical aspects of attitude.
2. As noted in Figure 9.1(b), pitch and bank represent the most rapidly changing inner loop information (highest bandwidth) which simultaneously serves two goals: maintaining stability, and influencing the middle and outer loop parameters to affect navigational goals.

Collectively, these features establish the ADI as both the most important and the most informative instrument, hence, explaining its scanning parameters.

In a study of novice–expert differences in visual instrument scanning, Bellenkes et al. (1997) have noted the much greater frequency and longer dwells with which novice pilots fixate the ADI in comparison to experts, a characterization that avails the novices less "free time" to inspect the other instruments. Two further differences between the two pilot groups were revealed in how they chose to deploy this "free time" away from the ADI. First, experts appeared to be more sensitive to the crosscoupling between axes, depicted in Figure 9.1(a), by "checking" instruments that might reflect deviations in one axis of flight, during the time in which another axis was changed (i.e. pitch down when banking the aircraft). Second, experts appeared more sensitive to the predictive aspects of certain instruments, checking for example the vertical velocity indicator to cue them for an anticipated change in altitude. As we have noted, the skills of prediction and anticipation are some of the most critical that any operator of sluggish dynamic systems must possess.

In conclusion, studies of visual scanning have provided valuable insight into a skilled pilot's mental model, and hence into the procedural knowledge of the inner

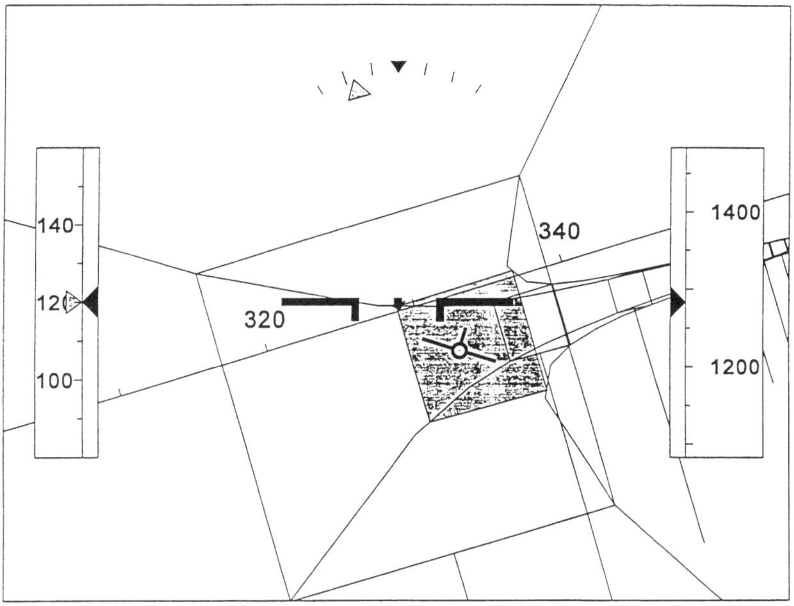

Figure 9.3 Example of a 3-dimensional "highway in the sky" flight instrument (from Theunissen, 1997).

loop flight dynamics necessary for the aviate subtask. Such studies also reveal a major source of visual attention demand in the cockpit. The scanning costs here are substantial enough that aircraft designers have pursued three avenues to alleviate these attention demands. First, capitalizing on electronic display technology, efforts are being made to improve the symbology by providing more integrated and cognitively compatible information. Figure 9.3 provides an example in which predictive information is explicitly presented (rather than needing to be cognitively derived), via the 3-dimensional "tunnel in the sky" extending into the future (Theunissen, 1997). Furthermore, vertically-oriented instruments representing airspeed and altitude have replaced "round dial" ones, hence, presenting a more cognitively compatible representation of these linear quantities (Roscoe, 1968).

Second, many aircraft can present this critical flight information in a "head up" location, superimposed on the outside world, hence in theory reducing the attention demands away from the visual view outside the cockpit (Figure 9.4; Weintraub & Ensing, 1992; Wickens, 1997). However, research has suggested that the mere superimposition of two channels of visual information (the instruments, and the visual world beyond) does not necessarily support effective divided attention between those channels (Neisser & Becklen, 1975; Wickens & Long, 1995). In particular, the perception of unexpected and non-salient events that are viewed in or through an HUD (head-up display) image appears to suffer (Wickens, 1997). However, when HUDs can be designed such that their instruments overlay or "conform" to features of the world beyond, like the horizon line shown in Figure 9.4, then pilots may effectively "fuse" HUD information with the

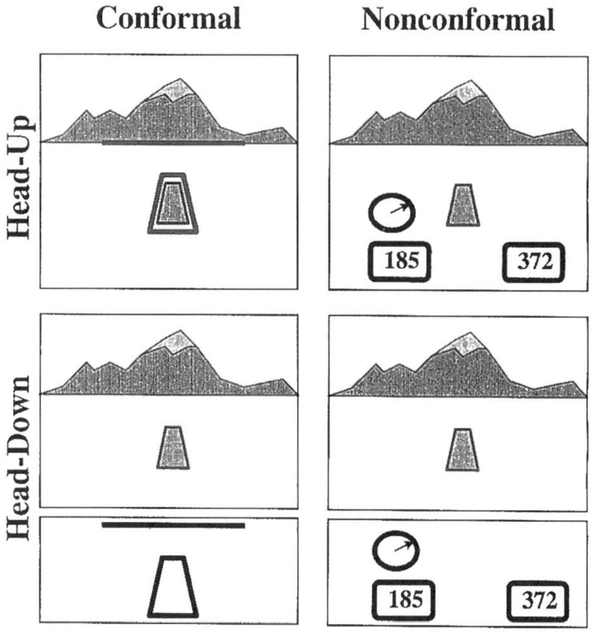

Figure 9.4 Example of a head-up display. The instrument panel containing both conformal (the horizon line and runway outline) and nonconformal information (the round dial gauges) is superimposed on the view of the "far" domain.

environmental information, creating a single visual "object." Research in visual attention has shown the extent to which attention can be more readily divided across the features of one object (Duncan, 1984; Kramer & Jacobson, 1991) than of several. Hence, not surprisingly, HUDs with conformal imagery appear to do a better job of supporting the division of attention between instruments and the far domain (Martin-Emerson & Wickens, 1997; Wickens & Long, 1995).

Third, designers have pursued the option of using autopilots to control the short lag, high bandwidth inner loop variables of pitch and bank, as well as the mid loop variables of heading change (turn) and altitude change. Most commercial cockpits are equipped with such autopilot equipment, accessed through a mode control panel at the top of the instrument panel and just below the windscreen, or through a flight management system. Such automation does not relieve the pilot from needing to be aware of these inner loop variables, but does unburden the need for the continuous monitoring necessary for active manual control.

NAVIGATION

The pilot's navigational task is critical. Several examples of controlled flight into terrain or CFIT (Strauch, 1997; Wiener, 1977) have exemplified the dangers when a pilot flying a perfectly stable airplane loses awareness of his or her three-dimensional position with respect to the terrain. Less severe in their consequences but still of major concern are instances in which pilots, often flying in good weather with adequate visibility of the terrain (visual meteorological conditions, or VMC), have landed at the wrong airport (Antunano, Mohler & Gosbee, 1989). In the previous section we explained how pilots could control their position in 3D space via the control of inner loop variables. In this section we consider the cognitive factors involved in understanding or maintaining spatial awareness of their actual position and of the locational goals: of paths and destinations to pursue, and of hazards – such as weather, air traffic and terrain – to avoid (Wickens, 1998). Such aviation navigational issues can be addressed in two different contexts:

- in visual contact flight the pilot has the terrain in sight, and navigates by virtue of a map, while searching the airspace for possible traffic
- in instrument flight (which must be assumed in poor visibility and at night but may also be characteristic of much flight in VMC), the pilot navigates by reference to navigational instruments.

Visual Flight: The Role of Navigational Checking

In visual flight, the pilot's navigational task is supported by a map, generally a two-dimensional paper display. As a flight proceeds, the pilot continuously updates his or her awareness of location, by confirming a correspondence between the image of the terrain perceived in the forward field of view, and an inferred position represented on the map (Aretz, 1991). This process of confirmation may be described as pilotage (Hickox & Wickens, 1997; Schreiber, Wickens, Renner, Alton & Hickox, 1998; Williams et al., 1996; Figure 9.5). If correspondence is confirmed, positional awareness is maintained. If it is not confirmed, the pilot may be considered lost.

The task of navigational checking has many similarities with image comparison or perceptual matching tasks examined in cognitive psychology (e.g. Cooper, 1980; Posner, 1978; Shepard & Cooper, 1982; Shepard & Hurwitz, 1984), in which the objective is to establish the congruence or identity of two images after some cognitive transformation such as mental rotation. The cost of the transformation can be established from the increase in response time for judgments of congruence when the transformation is required (e.g. when two images are rotated with respect to each other). In navigational checking, three mental transformations are typically required to bring the frame of reference of the map into congruence with the frame of reference of the forward view:

1. *zooming*, to bring the large global scale of the map into congruence with the more local view forward
2. *lateral mental rotation*, if the map is held in a north up orientation while the pilot is heading in a direction other than north
3. *envisioning*, in order to imagine the three-dimensional appearance of the terrain, represented on the two-dimensional map.

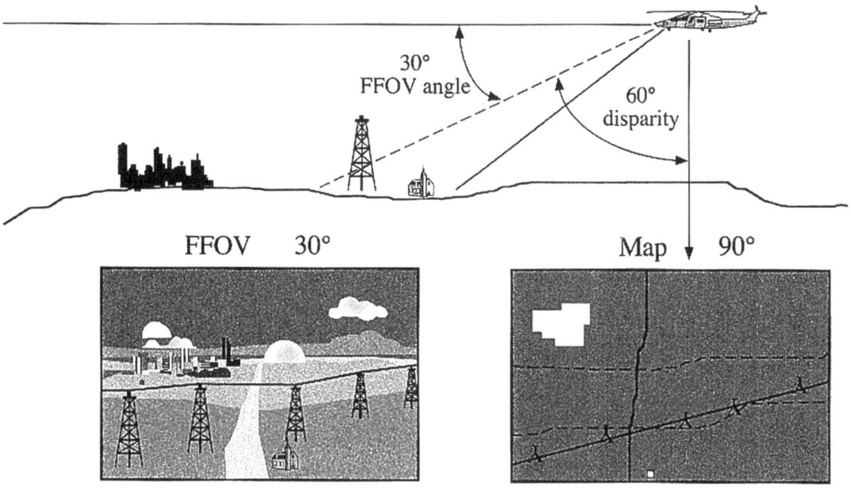

Figure 9.5 Representation of the navigational checking task. A forward field of view (left) must be compared with a map view (right) to assure their congruence or correspondence.

Several investigators have established that the costs of lateral mental rotation of pilot viewpoint in navigational checking follow generally the same function as those costs observed with simpler two-dimensional images (Aretz, 1991; Aretz & Wickens, 1992; Schreiber et al., 1998), although the slope of those functions is typically steeper, and it is the case that many pilots choose to maintain their paper maps in a rotated "track up" orientation, hence obviating the need for mental rotation (Williams, Hutchinson & Wickens, 1996). Envisioning a 2D (planar) map, to create a 3D image for comparison may also be conceived as a form of mental rotation; a vertical rotation around the axis through the wings of the aircraft. However, the time function of such rotation appears to be different than that explained by physical rotation, and is better described by a comparison of differences projected onto the 2D image plane (Hickox & Wickens, 1996, 1997; Schreiber et al., 1998). It also appears to be the case that the need for scene rotation depends on the nature of the scene content. If the scene contains primarily viewpoint independent features (Biederman et al., 1982), such as linear and parallel roads, whose orthogonal or parallel grid-like structure can be understood across any viewpoint, then vertical transformation costs are reduced, compared to scenes that contain viewpoint dependent features, such as terrain or irregularly flowing rivers (Hickox & Wickens, 1996, 1997).

The findings of transformation costs in navigational checking have a direct bearing on the development of electronic maps to support visual navigation (Hickox & Wickens, 1997); to minimize these costs, such maps should rotate laterally, should present the world in a 3D perspective (Olmos, Liang & Wickens, 1997), and should be somewhat similar in scale to the forward view observed by the pilot (although they may be somewhat larger in scope, to facilitate prediction and planning). We discuss more features of electronic map design below.

Instrument Flight

Traditional navigational displays to assist the pilot when the terrain cannot be viewed have not served the pilot's cognitive processes very well. A digital display of distance along a track, to or from a fixed navigational beacon presents inconsistent information, sometimes indicating the distance to a beacon being approached, and sometimes indicating the distance from a beacon that has been passed. The pilot's awareness of lateral deviation from the ground track must be perceived from an analog indicator that violates principles of motion compatibility (Roscoe, 1968), depicting a moving flight path symbol and a stationary aircraft symbol. Finally, the indication of altitude, obtained from the traditionally analog round dial altimeter is obtained from a third location in the cockpit, and registers altitude above sea level, rather than above ground level. Thus, to obtain a true 3D sense of position the pilot must integrate three sources of differently represented, separately located, and inconsistently represented information, a task that imposes heavily on working memory, and cognitive information integration capabilities (Wickens & Carswell, 1995).

Fortunately, good human factors assistance has been applied to improve navigational awareness in the design of dynamic electronic maps. For example, most modern transport cockpits are equipped with integrated representations of position in the lateral and longitudinal axes, the so-called horizontal situation display (Fadden, Braune & Wiedemann, 1991; Gabriel, 1993). Furthermore, such maps are designed to rotate to a track-up orientation in order to always maintain congruence between the visual representation of position and the manual control of that position (e.g. a leftward position on the map is pursued by a leftward movement of the control). This map rotation is as beneficial in instrument flight as it is in visual flight (Wickens, Liang, Prevett & Olmos, 1996). Current technology allows the aircraft position to be established on the basis of satellite-based communications (the global positioning system, or GPS) rather than ground-based navigational beacons.

Less certain in instrument flight than in visual flight, however, is the potential value of a 3D or perspective view of the navigational space (Merwin et al., 1997; Wickens & Prevett, 1995; Wickens et al., 1996). While such a view does not hinder the appreciation of position along the flight path, it does appear to disrupt the precise estimate of location of ownship, relative to other air hazards such as traffic, weather or terrain. This disruption appears to reflect directly the ambiguity with which perspective displays represent differences in position along the viewing axis of the display (McGreevy & Ellis, 1986).

A final cognitive issue concerning the design of maps, whether electronic or paper, concerns *clutter*. In fact, the design of such a map represents a constant tension between the pilot's desire for a variety of classes of information, generally all represented within the same spatial framework, and the disruption that multiple layers of closely packed information imposes on the ability to focus attention (Kramer & Jacobson, 1991). Some designers have chosen to address issues of clutter by developing computer-based decluttering tools, in which a switch can turn off classes of information deemed temporarily irrelevant (Mykityshyn, Kuchar & Hansman, 1994). However, such devices invite the danger of "out of sight, out of mind." That is, the pilot may erase information that at the time may appear irrelevant (in order to aid focused attention on the relevant), only to forget the existence of that erased information at a time when it suddenly becomes directly relevant to a navigational decision. For example, a pilot might declutter weather information, and hence fail to realize the approach of hazardous weather.

Navigational Automation

Automation has been applied to address the cognitive demands of navigation in several forms. First, as we have already noted, computer image processors have contributed valuably to the integrated electronic display of position and hazard information, as well as offering the mixed benefits of decluttering. Second, as we discuss later in the chapter, the flight management system (FMS) provides automated control and guidance for the aircraft to seek higher (outerloop) navigational goals. For example, the pilot can "set in" particular 3D fixes, which the autopilots will then automatically seek. Such devices do not necessarily obviate concerns about navigational awareness, as the recent crash of a commercial airliner using an FMS tragically illustrates (Strauch, 1997). Finally, automated monitoring systems have been installed in many aircraft, to warn the pilot of close encounters with the terrain (the ground proximity warning system, or GPWS), and with other air traffic (the traffic alert and collision avoidance system, or TCAS). The strengths and weaknesses of such automated devices, in terms of their impact on cognitive processes, will be discussed later in the chapter.

COMMUNICATIONS

Cockpit communications can be categorized into three sorts. First, the pilot and air traffic controller are both involved in an intricate network of ground–air voice communications which is particularly, although not exclusively, focused on the navigational subtask. Second, personnel within the flight deck (i.e. pilot and co-pilot) must often communicate between themselves. Third, pilots may communicate with an on-board "mission" crew, such as flight attendants on a commercial flight (Chute & Wiener, 1995). Flight deck communications, whether within the aircraft or with the ground, are highly vulnerable to human error. Nagel (1988) estimated that over half of the incidents reported in NASA's Aviation Safety Reporting System (a human factors incident database) could be characterized by breakdowns in information transfer. Such breakdowns may occasionally result in tragedy, as when a communications error led the pilot of a 747 aircraft to mistakenly believe that he had been granted clearance for takeoff

(Hawkins, 1993) when in fact another 747 was still on the runway. The resulting collision of the two jumbo jets cost over 500 lives.

While the absolute frequency of incorrect air–ground communications is relatively small – estimated to be approximately 10% (Cardosi, 1993; Morrow, Lee & Rodvold, 1993) – this number is still large enough to warrant serious concern for its causes, many of which are based on cognitive factors. We focus our discussion here most directly on air–ground communications, rather than intracockpit communications, because the former have generally been better analyzed and studied and proceduralized, while the latter are more heavily influenced by characteristics of social and personality psychology (Foushee, 1984; Wiener, Kanki & Helmreich, 1993).

Task analysis of the communications process reveals that a "unit" of communications generally includes:

1. a *transmission* typically from controller to pilot relaying an instruction (e.g. "United 486, climb to flight level 210 and turn to heading 180; anticipate climb to 240")
2. a subsequent *readback* or acknowledgment which contains the source, and repeats back all the key features of the transmission ("Roger; United 486 flight level 210, heading 180 anticipate 240")
3. a *covert monitoring* of the readback by the message transmitter (in this example the air traffic controller) to insure that the message sent was accurately read back by the recipient. Such an accurate readback is implicitly assumed by the controller to indicate that the pilot will comply with the instruction.

One class of errors in the process are procedural in which, for example, a readback is incomplete or missing altogether, or in which a controller fails to deliver instructions in standard terminology. A second class of errors are transmission errors, in which a communication is heard incorrectly. In some cases this error may be detected (by the transmitter) in the readback; in other cases it may not be. The vulnerabilities in the communications process can readily be linked to four well-known characteristics of human information processing: procedural knowledge, workload, expectancies and working memory limitations, and we describe the interlocking influences of these factors as follows.

As we noted above, standard communications procedures are prescribed for both pilot and controller. Yet circumstances, often resulting from lack of experience, sometimes lead these to be violated, perhaps via an incomplete readback (Morrow et al., 1993) or an improper sequence as described above. Also controllers may sometimes deliver a single message that is considerably longer than that which is procedurally recommended (Morrow et al., 1993).

The likelihood of both controller and pilot procedural errors may be amplified by the effects of high cognitive workload and time pressure. For example, higher cockpit workload may lead the pilot to truncate, and possibly eliminate the appropriate readback, whereas high controller workload (coupled with the time cost required to initiate and complete each communications exchange), may lead the controller to deliver a long string of instructions in a single message, rather than dividing this string across two or more shorter communications. This choice is made for the sake of efficiency because the single message will shorten the total amount of time the controller must deal with each individual aircraft. For the pilot, and particularly, the controller, high workload can eliminate careful read-back monitoring (Redding, 1992).

The cognitive bias of top-down processing, which causes us to hear what we expect to hear can itself amplify the influence of the factors described above. Whenever the bottom-up signal quality of communications is made more difficult (e.g. by low acoustic quality, or by a rapidly spoken long string) the pilot's bias will be to hear the expected string. Thus, if an unexpected or unusual item is delivered in the communications, an error in understanding is invited. Furthermore, the controller expects the pilot to read back the transmission as it was delivered. Hence, in the monitoring component of the transmission sequence, the controller may fail to detect a pilot's incorrect readback; what Monan (1986) has described as the "hearback" problem.

Finally, the limited capacity of working memory is clearly evident in the communications transmission errors that are observed (Loftus, Dark & Williams, 1979; Morrow et al., 1993). The contents of any sequence of instructions must be maintained in working memory until it is fully read back, and beyond that, until it is either written down, entered into a computer, or actually executed. The more chunks that a transmission contains, or the more rapidly it is delivered (hence, leading to less opportunity for deeper encoding of each chunk), the greater is the chance of forgetting. Such forgetting may often result from confusion, such as a pilot transposing digits (115 vs. 151), or even confusing the three critical message components – heading, airspeed and flight level – all of which are generally expressed as three-digit numbers. The relationship between message length and communications vulnerability in air traffic control has been clearly established, both in the laboratory (Loftus et al., 1979) and in the analysis of real-time communications tapes from ATC centers (Morrow et al., 1993).

Solutions to such communications problems can readily be found in two approaches. Clearly, the training and enforcement of standardized procedures can have a major beneficial impact. This may involve both the standardization of full readbacks, as well as reminders to controllers to maintain both message length and the rate of speech at a reasonable level. Computer-based automation has also been sought to remediate communications problems in the form of data link (Kerns, 1991, 1994; Wickens, Mavor, Parasuraman & McGee, 1998), a digitized communications system whereby instructions flow between ground and air over digital channels, rather than voice-base radio telephone. Such a system has at least two cognitive advantages over the conventional radio channels. First, because communications data would be available (and therefore preservable) electronically in the cockpit, it can be printed and maintained, hence off-loading the limited capacity working memory system. Second, because of its availability in digital form, it may be displayed in a multimedia fashion, hence capitalizing both on human's facility with redundant information (Garner & Morton, 1969; e.g. a message simultaneously spoken by digitized voice and printed text), and on certain principles of cognitive display compatibility (e.g. a spatial trajectory instruction can be represented spatially on an electronic navigation display, rather than, or in addition to, being presented in verbal form; Hahn & Hansman, 1992).

Of course, the data link system may impose some problems of its own, related for example to the workload of composing messages via keyboard, or to the absence of non-linguistic components of the voice (Wickens, Mavor, Parasuraman & McGee, 1998).

As we noted at the outset of this section, intra-cockpit communications are also important. Traditionally, these have been examined more from within the framework of social psychology (Foushee, 1984; Wiener, Kanki & Helmreich, 1993), than that of cognitive psychology, because of the heavy influence of personality factors in driving communications effectiveness. Furthermore, some recent attention has been given to the role of non-linguistic visual factors in communications, such as pointing and gesturing (Segal, 1995).

SYSTEMS MONITORING AND MANAGEMENT

The fourth major task domain within the cockpit is that associated with monitoring (and occasional control over) aircraft systems. In some presentations of the pilot's task hierarchy, which typically emphasize "aviate; communicate; navigate", this fourth component is neglected entirely. Such neglect results in part because system monitoring and management generally is a relatively low bandwidth task, which requires little overt action (e.g. monitoring fuel consumption and occasionally switching fuel tanks; or monitoring the health of navigational systems). However, as with many other process monitoring tasks (Moray, 1986, 1997; Parasuraman, 1987), the task of systems monitoring takes on tremendous importance on the rare occasions when systems do malfunction. In such cases the speed of detection becomes a critical factor, as does the speed and accuracy with which diagnosis and selection of remedial action are accomplished (Rasmussen & Rouse, 1981).

In this domain, designers of automation have provided a valuable service by providing pictorially based, easy to interpret graphics of many aspects of systems monitoring tasks. Furthermore, to attenuate the clutter associated with the massive number of systems to monitor on the modern transport aircraft, as well as to allow integrated depiction of textual and status information, designers have gone to menu-based multifunction displays, in which multiple pages of information can be examined (albeit sequentially) through a single viewport. While this centralized computer-based graphics image capability has many advantages, it also raises some important cognitive issues regarding the structure of the computer database (Seidler & Wickens, 1992; Wickens & Seidler, 1997), and the extent to which this organizational structure matches the pilot's cognitive model of systems relatedness (Roske-Hofstrand & Paap, 1986; Seamster, Redding & Kaempf, 1997). Where the design mismatches the pilot's mental model, added time costs in navigating through the database are invited.

A final cognitive issue raised by the consideration of aircraft systems concerns the pilot's ability to rapidly execute the appropriate procedures, should systems be diagnosed to have failed. Such a concern makes relevant the more general cognitive issue of aviation procedural knowledge, for both routine as well as emergency circumstances, an issue we deal with later.

COGNITIVE FRAMEWORK FOR TASK MANAGEMENT

In the previous pages, we have described four "meta tasks," each of which may challenge the pilot's cognitive capabilities in retrieving, or processing information. Across all of these, and integrating them is a network of four additional cognitive concepts: decision making, situation awareness, procedures, and mental workload, each of which will be described in more detail in the following sections.

AERONAUTICAL DECISION MAKING

The pilot must make decisions regarding a variety of actions, across all four levels of the task hierarchy. These might include, for example, a split-second decision at low altitude of whether to increase airspeed to avoid a stall, or to pull up to increase distance from the ground (aviate); a decision to climb, descend, or turn, to avoid bad weather (navigate); a decision of whether or not to request further clarification of a slightly ambiguous instruction, delivered by an overworked and impatient controller (communicate); or a decision to shut down a possibly overheating engine (systems) management. In general, all such decisions can be mapped onto three general stages of information processing:

1. acquiring information
2. using that information to update a mental picture or diagnosis of the state of the world (situation awareness)
3. choosing a course of action. In many aviation circumstances such a choice will have high risks.

The study of aeronautical decision making (Jensen, 1981; Orasanu, 1993) has proceeded along three approaches. In one approach, investigators have noted many of the parallels between the pilot as a decision maker (Mosier, Palmer & Degani, 1992), and the classic heuristics and biases demonstrated both within the laboratory and beyond in ground-based decision making (Slovic, Fischhoff & Lichtenstein, 1977; Tversky & Kahneman, 1974; Wallsten, 1980; Wickens, 1992; Yates, 1990). Such an approach can readily be applied in hindsight, to analyze the causes of major accidents, such as the crash of an Air Florida flight in Washington DC, in which pilots inappropriately decided to proceed with a takeoff in bad weather (O'Hare & Roscoe, 1990). It can also be applied to characterize the causes of reliably and repeatedly observed classes of errors in judgments such as the tendency of many general aviation pilots who are licensed or intending to fly only in good weather (Visual Flight Rules) to fly into bad weather (instrument meteorological conditions; Griffin & Rockwell, 1987). Under these circumstances, decision heuristics related to availability (Tversky & Kahneman, 1974), and biases related to both cognitive tunneling, and hypothesis confirmation (anchoring; Wickens, 1992), can be used to account for the poor judgment (Mosier et al., 1998). That is, the pilot becomes fixated or anchored on the initial hypothesis that the weather is acceptable along the filed flight plan and fails to seek or process information suggesting that it is not.

A second approach following a more recent trend in the study of aeronautical decision making has examined the process within the framework of expertise in decision making (Klein, 1997; Zsambok & Klein, 1997), particularly as carried out within the time-critical environment of the cockpit or air traffic control workstation. Such an approach focuses less on the biases than on the adaptive and appropriate strategies which enable the majority of such decisions to be acceptable ones. In particular, Klein's (1997) model of recognition primed decision making has considered the effective and relatively automatic manner by which situations are diagnosed in a process by which the current perceptual cues are matched with a vast array of similar situations that are immediately retrievable from long-term memory.

Third, a hybrid approach to aeronautical decision making that bridges the gap between the classical heuristics/biases view, and the conception of naturalistic decision making, is one that tries to analyze the differences between effective and less effective decision makers in complex aviation simulations (O'Hare, 1992; Orasanu & Fischer, 1997; Stokes, Kemper & Kite, 1997; Wickens, Stokes, Barnett & Hyman, 1993). For example, more effective decision makers tend to be better at time management, task management and be more proactive, anticipating and preparing for future uncertainties (Orasanu & Fischer, 1997). They also tend to be more selective in applying different decision strategies, given the nature of the decision problem (Berlin et al., 1982; O'Hare & Roscoe, 1990; Trollip & Jensen, 1991).

Whichever approach is taken to modeling or describing aeronautical decision making, the remediations designed to improve decision quality have generally taken one of three forms:

1. Decision aids in the cockpit or air traffic control facility may be provided, using artificial intelligence or expert systems technology to assist diagnosis and recommend solutions, or using other technology to provide interactive planning tools (Layton, Smith & McCoy, 1994; Wickens, 1998).
2. Alternatively, the increased flexibility of computer-driven display systems, can provide more effective and integrated displays of necessary information, in a way that supports situation awareness. Great strides, for example, are being made in developing better graphic weather displays, diagnostic displays for system management or, for the air traffic controller, displays to facilitate the more optimal scheduling and ordering of traffic (Erzberger et al., 1993).
3. Various programs have been developed to improve pilot decision making through training, making pilots aware of hazardous or ineffective strategies (Jensen, 1997; Trollip & Jensen, 1991).

SITUATION AWARENESS

Situation awareness – understanding the state of affairs upon which a decision should be based – is not a concept that originated in cognitive psychology to be applied to aviation. Rather, situation awareness is a concept that is expressed in a language comfortable to aviators and air traffic controllers; it has direct relevance to aviation, because of the class of accidents that can be characterized by a loss of situation awareness (Sarter & Woods, 1995; Strauch, 1997); and the concept is one that can generate specific remediating solutions through displays and training. Hence, researchers in aviation psychology have sought to identify the set of cognitive structures that underlie the situation awareness concept (Adams, Tenney & Pew, 1995; Dominguez, 1994; Durso & Gronlund, 1999, this volume; Endsley, 1995).

Endsley (1995) has characterized three levels of awareness about a situation:

1. *perceiving* or attending to events and changes in the evolving, dynamic environment of, for example, the airspace (navigational awareness), or the cockpit automation system (mode awareness)
2. *understanding* or interpreting the meaning of those events
3. *projecting* or predicting the future implications of those changes.

In essence, the higher levels of situation awareness depend on achievement of the lower levels. Thus, projection of the future flight path depends on understanding the present location, and that understanding depends on perceiving and attending to relevant sources of navigational information. Thus, situation awareness may be lost by breakdowns in any of the three processes (Jones & Endsley, 1996). For example:

- an air traffic controller may fail to perceive that an aircraft has exceeded its assigned altitude – level 1 failure
- the controller may perceive the overshoot, but not understand how large the departure is – level 2 failure
- the controller may understand the size of the departure, but not project that the excessive climb will put it in the path of a distant aircraft currently depicted on the far side of the radar display – level 3 failure.

Researchers have emphasized the important distinction between the situation awareness concept, which supports the *potential* to carry out effective actions on the one hand, and the choice and execution of those actions themselves (Endsley, 1995; Wickens, 1996). Thus, for example, a pilot flying with an accurate automation-based flight director will be able to fly a very accurate approach (good flight control actions), yet may have very poor awareness of the absolute location of the flight path in space and its proximity to other hazards, even as he or she is properly exercising the control actions dictated by the flight director. Yet should those other hazards, not in the forward flight path, suddenly become relevant because of a need to rapidly change the flight path, the pilot with poor navigational hazard awareness may suffer, while the one whose hazard awareness is good, will not. Thus, an important characteristic of situation awareness is its support for the response to unexpected, rather than routine, events (Wickens, 1995).

Researchers have also tried to distinguish between the *product* of situation awareness, and the *process* of maintaining that awareness (Adams et al., 1995). The product or contents of situation awareness can be defined as that material characterizing the dynamic changing situation of interest (e.g. hazards, systems or tasks) that is either in working memory or may be rapidly retrieved from "long-term working memory" (Kintsch & Ericsson, 1995; see Durso and Gronlund, 1999, this volume). Wickens (1996) has distinguished between three important categories of aviation relevant material about which a pilot should be aware:

- external (geographical) *hazards*
- internal aircraft *systems* (including automation modes)
- that status of *tasks* that must be performed.

In contrast to the product, the process of maintaining hazard, system, or task awareness depends critically on two other cognitive structures: long-term memory and attention. Long-term memory structures are necessary to provide a framework or mental model within which the newly arriving information can readily be interpreted (the understanding component of situation awareness). The mental model may also provide rules that are the basis for predicting future state from present information (i.e. supporting the predictive functions at level 3 of situation awareness). For example, the skilled pilot's mental model of flight dynamics provides a framework for anticipating a change in altitude following a sudden change in the ADI and vertical speed indicator. Long-term memory may also contain the information storage and retrieval strategies necessary for the operation of long-term working memory (Kintsch & Ericsson, 1995); and it may provide knowledge of scanning or information access strategies necessary to direct selective attention to different channels in the environment (Bellenkes et al., 1997). However, all of these properties of long-term memory can readily be distinguished from the contents of situation awareness by their bandwidth. Long-term memory structures are by their nature of low bandwidth: slowly acquired and equally slowly forgotten (i.e. time constants in the order of hours, days or years). In contrast, the contents or product of situation awareness is of higher bandwidth, with time constants in the order of seconds or minutes.

Secondly, situation awareness is critically dependent on the process of selective attention, to direct the eyes (or other processing channels) to the appropriate locations where new and changing information may be acquired (Adams et al., 1995; Bellenkes et al., 1997; Carbonnell, Ward & Senders, 1968; Sarter & Woods, 1995; Senders, 1964; Sheridan, 1972). But here again, the distinction between selective attention as a supporting process, and situation awareness as the product of that process is crucial. Selective attention can be misguided, and can focus on information sources that have little or nothing to do with the evolving situation. While product and process may be distinguished, it is important to recognize that properties of the two process mechanisms, long-term memory and attentional skills, are critical for discriminating the ability to maintain situation awareness between novices and experts. However, expertise must not be treated as synonymous with high situation awareness. Thus, the expert may be as capable as the novice of losing situation awareness, because: (a) high workload directs selective attention to the wrong channels, or (b) displays provide non-salient information regarding the changing situation, or even (c) the experts' well-ingrained knowledge structures foster expectancy-driven (and incorrect) processing of unexpected information.

The construct of situation awareness has practical implications in two directions. First, distinctions between novices' and experts' situation awareness on the basis of attention and long-term memory differences embody guidance as to the sorts of training programs that can improve the ability to maintain situation awareness. For example, attentional skills necessary to update the pilot's mental model regarding newly arriving information may be trained (Gopher, 1992; Gopher, Weil & Bareket, 1994).

Second, display technology can often be harnessed in the interest of providing a more interpretable picture of the dynamics of rapidly evolving events, exemplified by the displays for navigational hazard awareness discussed earlier, and the display guidance for attention control which we will discuss in the context of automation mode awareness in a later section (Sarter & Woods, 1995, 1997).

PROCEDURES AND CHECKLISTS

Cockpit procedures, relevant to all levels of the task hierarchy, depend on a vast array of declarative knowledge, nearly all of which is backed up by published federal air regulations (known as FARs), operating manuals, and checklists. The various procedures, such as setting up navigational instruments, dealing with a malfunctioning instrument, filing a flight plan, or checking the status of the aircraft prior to engine start, have two general attributes: *how* they should be carried out, and *when* they should be done. Because of human frailties in both declarative knowledge (how), and prospective memory (when) (Harris & Wilkins, 1982), an absolutely critical memory support for the pilot is the checklist (Degani & Wiener, 1993). The pilot will have several checklists for both routine and emergency procedures (Figure 9.6), each listing the nature of the procedure (characterizing the "how"), in the sequential order in which it should be accomplished (characterizing the "when"), thus providing what Norman (1988) has designated as "knowledge in the world."

Yet even such a valuable support as the checklist is vulnerable to certain cognitive frailties. Two in particular are related to expectancy-driven processing and selective attention. As an example of expectancy-driven processing, it is possible that a checklist might ask the pilot to "check that switch *X* is on." If the normal state of switch *X is* in the "on" position, the pilot may "see" the switch in that state based on expectancy alone, rather than making a careful evaluation based on bottom-up visual inspection of the switch itself. In this example the tendency for the top-down processing is reinforced by the greater facility with which people judge "true positive" responses in a word–picture comparison task which characterizes the information processing demands of the checklist item (Carpenter & Just, 1975; Clark & Chase, 1972).

Selective attention also plays a role in checklist following, as the pilot's eyes must move down the list from item to item. Here the orderly sequence may be disrupted and such disruption is more likely under time pressure. For a single pilot following the list, the eyes must move away to assure that the item is in the appropriate "checked" state. And even in a two pilot crew, the pilot reading the

■ INTERMEDIATE STOP ITEMS
▲ S/O'S FUNCTION
NO CHALLENGE

B-727 PILOT'S CHECKLIST ▲
(-232 & -247 Modified) Delta

FAA APPROVED
DATE: 3-15-88

FIRST FLIGHT OF DAY CHECK THE FOLLOWING:

STANDBY RUDDER	FLIGHT DIRECTORS
ANTI-SKID	STAB TRIM
ANTI-ICE	AUTOPILOT
PITOT HEAT	

BEFORE START

■ A/C STATUS & LOGBOOK .... CK
■ FUEL REQD .... —— ON BOARD ——
OXY MASK/REG/INTERPHONE .... CK
STANDBY RUDDER .... OFF
FLIGHT CONTROL SWITCHES .... ON
ANTI-SKID .... OFF
STALL WARNING .... CK
INSTRUMENT COMPARATOR .... CK
EMERGENCY EXIT LIGHTS .... ARMEO
#2 ENG ACCESS DOOR LIGHT .... OFF
ENGINE START SWITCHES .... OFF
■ SEAT BELT & NO SMOKING .... ON
■ WINDOW HEAT .... ON
ANTI-ICE .... CLOSED
PITOT HEAT .... OFF
INTERIOR & EXTERIOR LIGHTS .... SET
■ NAVIGATION LIGHTS [247] .... ON
■ ENGINE FIRE WARNING SYSTEMS .... CK
ALT & FLT INSTS .... SET/CROSSCX
COMPASS SELECTORS .... SLAVED
GPWS .... CK
STATIC SOURCE SELECTORS .... NORMAL
MACH AIRSPEED WARNING .... CK
INDICATOR LIGHTS & APD .... CK
ENGINE INSTRUMENTS .... CK
LANDING GEAR .... DOWN, IN, 3 GREEN
■ RADAR & TRANS .... CK & SET
FLIGHT DIRECTORS .... STBY
SPEED BRAKE .... DETENT
REV, THROTTLES & START LEVERS .... DOWN,CLOSED & CUTOFF
FLAPS .... UP
STAB TRIM .... NORMAL
AUTOPILOT .... OFF
■ RADIOS & NAV INSTS .... CK & SET
■ RUDDER & AILERON TRIM .... ZERO
STANDBY POWER .... CK
■ CABIN & S/O PREFLIGHT .... COMPLETE
■▲ AUTOPILOT TEST SW .... NORMAL
■▲ CIRCUIT BREAKERS .... CK
■ DEPARTURE BRIEFING .... COMP

BEFORE DISPATCH

▲ #2 SYS B HYD PUMP .... ON
▲ APU & BATT CHARGER .... START & CK
▲ PACK(S) .... AS REQD

ENGINE START

▲ DOOR WARNING LIGHTS .... CK
▲ PACKS .... BOTH OFF
▲ GALLEY POWER .... OFF
▲ FUEL SYSTEM .... SET
BEACON .... ON
PARKING BRAKE .... AS REQD
PNEUMATIC PRESSURE .... —— PSI

AFTER START

▲ ELEC SYSTEM .... CH & SET
▲ EXTERNAL POWER & AIR .... REMOVE
▲ GALLEY POWER .... ON
▲ FUEL SYSTEM .... SET
▲ SYS A & B HYD PUMPS .... CH & ON
▲ ENG 2/APU BLEEDS .... AS REQD
▲ PACKS .... AS REQD
▲ COCKPIT DOOR .... LOCKED (PRIOR TO T/O)
ENGINE INSTRUMENTS .... CK
ENGINE ANTI-ICE .... AS REQD

TAXI

T/O DATA COMPUTED RWY... ... —USING RWY—
AUTO PACK TRIP LT .... REQD OR NOT REQD
PITOT HEAT .... ON
AIRSPD & EPR BUGS .... SET/CROSSCK
AIRSPD WARN SWS .... SET, 3 —— (A OR B)
ALT & FLT INSTS .... SET/CROSSCK
STAB TRIM .... —— UNITS

When Delayed Start is Desired

DELAYED ENGINE START

▲ PACKS .... BOTH OFF
▲ GALLEY POWER .... OFF
▲ FUEL SYSTEM .... SET
PNEUMATIC PRESS .... —— PSI

DELAYED AFTER START

▲ ELEC SYSTEM .... CK & SET
▲ GALLEY POWER .... ON
▲ FUEL SYSTEM .... SET FOR TAKEOFF
▲ SYS A HYD PUMPS .... CK & ON
▲ ENG 2/APU BLEEDS .... CLOSE
▲ PACKS .... ON
ENGINE INSTRUMENTS .... CK
ENGINE ANTI-ICE .... AS REQD

TAXI (CONTINUED)

▲ FUEL HEAT .... AS REQD
▲ FLT GRD SWITCH .... FLT
▲ F/O ALT VIBRATOR C/B (232) .... IN
SHOULDER HARNESS .... ON
FLAPS .... —— GREEN LIGHT
FLIGHT CONTROLS .... CK
NAV INSTRUMENTS .... SET

BEFORE TAKEOFF

TAKEOFF BRIEFING .... COMP
FLIGHT ATTENDANTS .... NOTIFIED/ACKD
ANTI-SKID .... ON
CONTINUOUS IGNITION [232] .... ON
START SWITCHES [247] .... FLT START
NAV LIGHTS [232]/STROBE [247] .... ON
TRANSPONDER .... ON
▲ APU MASTER SWITCH .... OFF
▲ FUEL HEAT .... OFF
▲ APU LIGHT .... OFF
▲ AUTO PACK TRIP SWITCH .... NORMAL
▲ CSD OIL COOLER [247] .... GROUND OFF

Figure 9.6 A typical pilot checklist.

list may often wish to glance at the other pilot in order to provide a redundant check (and guard against expectancy-driven processing: Degani & Wiener, 1993). Yet such a diversion can disrupt the orderly sequential flow of attention down the list, as it did tragically in 1987 when pilots of a commercial airliner taxiing prior to takeoff at Detroit Airport had their attention disrupted from the checklist by a required procedural change directed from air traffic control

(Wiener, 1988). When attention returned to the list, it did so one item beyond the last item prior to the interruption. The missing item turned out to be the critical one of setting the flaps and slats for takeoff. This omission compromised the amount of lift generated by the plane, and left it with insufficient altitude to clear obstructions after it left the runway. Over one hundred lives were lost in the resulting crash.

As with so many of the vulnerabilities we have described above, automation, along with good human factors, is suggested as a remediation for some of the problems with checklists (Bresley, 1995; Degani & Wiener, 1993; Palmer & Degani, 1991). For example, electronic checklists can require that each item be actively "checked" by the pilot providing a machine-readable input (e.g. a touch screen overlaying the list), and hence offering a monitoring device that could prevent the error of omission described above (Mosier, Palmer & Degani, 1992; Palmer & Degani, 1991). While such an approach would not address the problems associated with expectancy-driven processing, these could be addressed, in some circumstances, by sensors in the aircraft that could sense and self-report their state (e.g. the switch in the previous example could report that it is in the "off" position, and alert or suggest that the pilot should turn it "on"). However, it appears that the most effective solution to preventing checklist violations is through straightforward training and motivational incentives to treat the list with utmost importance (Hawkins, 1993).

TASK MANAGEMENT AND WORKLOAD

As we have noted, checklists are reminders that prescribe ways and sequences of performing particular tasks. However, they do not often provide guidance of how to prioritize among different tasks (although items toward the end of a checklist may implicitly be considered to be of lower priority, because of the possibility that they will be omitted if the list is terminated prematurely because of time pressure: Degani & Wiener, 1993). While the inherent priority ordering of "aviate, navigate, communicate, systems manage" hierarchy provides general guidance, there are obviously times when such an ordering needs to be temporarily restructured, as when, for example, a possible engine malfunction requires that "systems management" be brought to the top of the hierarchy. This then is the fundamental cognitive issue of executive control or task management (Gopher, 1992; Gopher & Koriat, 1998) and one that is inexorably linked to the issue of mental workload. We will, therefore, discuss these two concepts in consort.

The concern for pilot (and to a lesser extent controller) mental workload has been long standing (Eggemeier, 1988; Roscoe, 1987; Tsang & Wilson, 1997; Williges & Wierwille, 1979). Mental workload, like situation awareness, is a construct that has great intuitive meaning to the operator (pilot or controller), but presents considerable challenges for precise definition and objective measurement. Like situation awareness, mental workload defines the *potential* to perform, rather than the performance itself. If a pilot is said to have high mental workload, this does not necessarily imply that performance itself is deficient. Rather, the pilot is assumed to have very little "spare capacity" with which to deal with the potential for further increases in task demands. When, however, mental work overload *does* occur, performance will break down. Following Norman & Bobrow (1975), researchers have carefully distinguished between performance breakdowns attributable to mental workload overload (when the demand for cognitive resources exceeds the available supply), and those attributable to the absence of adequate sensory data or knowledge (e.g. a communications transmission is garbled by static, or the pilot forgets procedures). These two sorts of limits have been referred to as "resource limits" and "data limits" respectively (Norman & Bobrow, 1975).

Space does not permit a discussion of all the many issues associated with the measurement and prediction of mental workload (see Tsang & Wilson, 1997, for a recent review). We only note here that *time* availability is perhaps one of the greatest drivers of mental workload (Hendy, Liao & Milgram, 1997), particularly in the high tempo time-critical cockpit environment; but other factors, such as, for example, the complexity of an ATC display that cannot easily be represented by time, are also important contributors to mental workload.

More recently, attention is beginning to be focused on the critical link between mental workload and task management strategies. Researchers have conceptualized the link between these two entities in a closed loop model of workload, in which the pilot or air traffic controller seeks to maintain workload at some optimal, homeostatic value, by seeking tasks to perform when workload drops to a low level, and adopting workload reduction strategies when workload becomes excessive (Hart & Wickens, 1990; Sperandio, 1976). At issue is what the high workload strategies may be, the extent to which they can be classified as "adaptive" or maladaptive, and how one can predict the conditions in which one strategy or the other is chosen. For example, under high workload, the pilot or controller may choose to continue to perform multiple tasks, but at a degraded level, to change the strategy of task performance to one demanding fewer resources (e.g. by chunking or using less precise information) (Sperandio, 1976), to build up a lag or queue of unperformed tasks until workload recedes, or to shed tasks altogether. In the latter case, task shedding can be defined as more or less optimal, depending on whether it is low or high priority tasks (respectively) that are abandoned (Raby & Wickens, 1994).

As with poor situation awareness, *post hoc* analysis of many accidents can attribute these to poor task management strategies under high workload (Chou, Madhavan & Funk, 1996; Funk, 1991). A particularly prevalent finding is the failure to monitor altitude (navigation) or sometimes even attitude (aviation) when the pilot deals with an unexpected system failure; and hence crashes into the terrain in either a controlled or uncontrolled manner respectively (Wiener, 1977). It is assumed that appropriate cockpit task management is a skill that can be learned (Gopher, 1992), and, therefore, trained (Gopher, Weil & Bareket, 1994). And it has been established that differences in task management seem to discriminate between good and poor performing crews in complex emergency or high workload situations (Orasanu & Fischer, 1997; Orasanu & Strauch, 1994; Raby & Wickens, 1994). However, the specific manner in which environmental and informational properties interact with cognitive task importance hierarchies, in order to influence the decision of what task to perform when, remains poorly understood.

A few basic assertions regarding this relationship can be stated with some confidence however:

(a) There is a cost for switching between tasks (Moray, 1986; Sheridan, 1972), and so there is a tendency to remain with a lower priority task longer than optimal (i.e. to avoid switching), if the need to perform one of higher priority suddenly arises.
(b) Different physical or salient sensory reminders or annunciators to perform a task will be more likely to trigger a switch to that task, than less salient properties, or purely memorial representations (Wickens & Seidler, 1997).
(c) In contrast to computer optimization models, pilots (or people in general) do not tend to maintain elaborate and highly optimal planning strategies for task management (Laudeman & Palmer, 1995; Raby & Wickens, 1994). This simplification results perhaps because applying such strategies themselves is a source of high cognitive workload (Tulga & Sheridan, 1980), and hence, would be self-defeating at the very time it might be most necessary.
(d) As a correlate of (c), pilots tend to be more *proactive* when workload is modest (i.e. establishing various contingency plans), and more *reactive* when workload becomes high (Hart & Wickens, 1990).
(e) There is a good possibility that well-designed automation can provide support for the pilot's task management skills, by monitoring the pilot's performance, and providing reminders if high priority tasks are "dropped" (Funk, 1991; Funk & Braune, 1997; Wiener & Curry, 1980). However, this possibility, as with previous examples of automation described above, raises further concerns about the cognitive issues in automation, a topic which we will now address.

COGNITIVE ISSUES IN AUTOMATION

The previous sections have all alluded in one way or another to ways in which computer-based automation might be introduced to address some of the cognitive vulnerabilities of the pilot or controller. However, the past two decades of experimental aviation research, coupled with both accident and incident analyses, have revealed that automation does not provide a universal benefit (Billings, 1996; Sarter & Woods, 1995, 1997; Wiener & Curry, 1980). And while the benefits of automation to both flight safety and efficiency provided by devices such as collision warnings and autopilots have far outweighed the costs, it is true nevertheless that some of the costs that *have* been observed can be directly attributed to cognitive problems of understanding and memory. We address these below.

It is important first to note that automation can accomplish a large number of functions that bridge the task hierarchy described above. For example, autopilots can stabilize the aircraft (aviate); they can also provide guidance to fixed waypoints in space, as well as warn pilots of hazards to avoid (navigate). Automation such as data link may provide digital channels of information between ground and air (communicate), and may integrate and diagnose systems information

Table 9.1 Levels of automation of:

Information collection and representation		Decision and choice	Response execution
HIGH:	All Features	All auto	
↑	4 Features	Auto chooses, informs human	Auto executes
	3 Features	Auto chooses unless human vetos	
	2 Features	Auto suggests best option	
		Auto suggests few options	
	1 Feature	Auto suggests many options	Human executes
LOW:	No features	All manual	

Features = filtering, integration, transformation, reliability check inferencing

(systems). As we have also noted, automation may monitor and actually carry out checklist actions (procedures), and has the capability even to monitor pilot task performance (task management).

The duties of automation can also be represented within an information processing framework, shown in Table 9.1 (Wickens, Mavor, Parasuraman & McGee, 1998). According to such a framework, automation may be trichotomized in terms of whether its functions are designed primarily to (a) collect and represent information for the human user, (b) choose or recommend actions for the human user, or (c) execute those actions. Furthermore, the first two features can be defined by ordinal scales, characterizing the levels of automation. For example, the level of automation of information collection and representation can be defined by the number of computer-based operations carried out on the raw data: examples of these operations include data filtering, data inferencing (i.e. prediction and interpolation), data integration (e.g. derived quantities from separate variables like time-to-contact based on speed and distance); data reliability checking (and reporting); and data graphics rendering. Generally speaking, the more such operations or features that a device contains, the higher is the level of information collection automation.

The middle column of the table indicates that the level of automation of decision and choice can be represented essentially in terms of the increasing constraints that are imposed on the human as to what options can be selected (Sheridan, 1987). Finally, automation of response execution can often be represented by a dichotomous scale. For example, in an automation data link communication system, the computer executes the response (conveying a message between the ground and the air), whereas in a conventional system, the operator speaks. There is not really any middle ground. It should be noted that the automation levels of choice can be performed on tasks for which there are varying degrees of risk; this risk is defined jointly by the probability or uncertainty that the recommended or chosen action may be incorrect, and by the cost to safety if the action *is* incorrect (Wickens et al., 1998). An example of a high-risk decision would be to put an aircraft on a different flight trajectory in a crowded airspace. An example of a lower risk decision would be to shift the flow of fuel to an alternate tank, in order to restore balance.

Within the framework described above, we may identify three important potential problems with automation, each with direct implications for human cognition (see Billings, 1996; Parasuraman & Riley, 1997; Wickens et al., 1997, 1998, for more exhaustive discussions which incorporate the three concerns described below). The three concerns are somewhat interrelated: the first addresses the causes of too little trust in automation; the second concerns issues at high levels of automation of choice; while the third concerns the consequences of too much trust.

Mistrust: The Mental Model and Situation Awareness

When automation fails to act as it is intended or expected, users may come to distrust it, and abandon it or perhaps intervene inappropriately (Parasuraman & Riley, 1997; Sarter & Woods, 1997). Two automation devices discussed in the previous pages have lent themselves to foster distrust, but by different mechanisms. First, collision warning devices, either for protection against terrain collision (ground proximity warning system – GPWS) or mid-air collision (traffic alert and collision warning system – TCAS) have, following their introduction, induced an annoying number of "alarm false alarms" – that is, alerts that were unnecessary because the algorithms upon which they were based could not discriminate a real collision trajectory from one that was not (e.g. the pilot was about to alter course, whereas the alarm system issued its alarm assuming that a straight course would be continued). As any user may have experienced with other alarm systems of this sort, the annoyance can lead to a distrust or "cry wolf" syndrome, whereby true and legitimate alarms are disregarded, or are not treated with as much urgency as they deserve.

A more complex aviation automation system that has fostered distrust for somewhat different reasons is the flight management system, or FMS, which has been the subject of a series of recent investigations by Sarter & Woods (1992, 1994, 1995, 1997). Briefly, as introduced earlier, the FMS is a complex series of autopilots, that can engage in both inner loop and outer loop control, along all three axes of flight, and hence can provide automated action choice and execution for both aviation and navigation. The cognitive issue of mistrust here is driven by the extent to which the pilots fail to understand and appreciate the momentary actions of the FMS, leading to the perception that it is doing things that were not intended or requested (i.e. is unreliable). In this case the cause is somewhat different than that of the alarm false alarm, and is based on the fact that the complex linkages and couplings between the various autopilots in the FMS are poorly understood by the pilot, and often configured differently from the way a pilot might fly the aircraft by hand. Hence the pilot's mental model of automation is wanting. Contributing further to this deficiency is the fact that the displays of the state of automation, and its current and pending actions are poorly integrated; state changes (e.g. the autopilot brings the aircraft to level flight at a previously commanded altitude) are not indicated by salient indicators, and the displays that do exist do not provide any integrated spatial representation of the aircraft's trajectory along the three flight axes. As a result the FMS does not support good automation mode awareness. If the pilot has inadequate mode awareness, it is more likely that the aircraft will perform unpredicted actions, as if on its own (autonomy), and if the pilot has a poor spatial representation of FMS behavior, it becomes difficult for him or her to develop an adequate mental model, which, as discussed above, provides one of the supporting structures for maintaining system mode awareness (Sarten & Woods, 1997).

Levels of Automation and Overtrust: The Generation Effect versus Workload

The action choice scale depicted in Table 9.1 presents a wide range of automation levels. Ostensibly, increasing levels of automation, by decreasing the degree and extent of options available to the pilot or controller, should simplify the choice and so reduce the cognitive workload. Similar claims can be made for higher levels of automation of information integration, if these are implemented reliably and with sensitivity to pilot or controller information needs, and preferred format. However, the downside of increasing levels of automation of action choice is related to what Slamecka & Graf (1978) have labeled as "the generation effect" (see also Hopkin, 1995). That is, operators are better able to remember the nature of options if they themselves have actively selected the options, than if another agent (human or machine) made the same choices, which the operators passively observed. Consider the following three examples, each of which contrasts active (low automation) choice with passive (high automation) choice:

1. contrast a situation in which the pilot actively checks an item on a checklist (low automation) with one in which the computer checks and informs the operator (high automation)
2. contrast a system in which the computer offers a series of options to the air traffic controller on how to manage a traffic problem (lower automation) with one in which the computer recommends only a single solution which the controller can accept or reject (higher automation)
3. contrast a system in which data link delivers a printed message to the pilot, which the pilot must approve and manually enter into the FMS (lower automation) with one in which the uplinked flight plan will automatically be loaded into the FMS, if the pilot presses a single button (higher automation), or even one in which the flight plan will be automatically flown unless the pilot intervenes to veto it (highest automation).

In all three of the above cases, the higher automation option reduces cognitive load (Van Gent, 1997); the responsible operator *should* be carefully attending to and reviewing the actions that the automation is choosing (or reviewing the other alternatives that the automation does not recommend); and yet the fact that a greater component of the action is not performed by the operator will render the memory for that operation at a lower strength, and thus render the information less available should it suddenly be needed. This memory deficit related to the generation effect (Slamecka & Graf, 1978) may offset any benefits that might be offered by the lower level of workload at the higher automation levels.

Complacency and Overtrust

The consequences of the generation effect are not severe unless a rapid manual intervention is required, should either the automation itself fail, or should a system failure occur with which the automation is unable to cope (e.g. the autopilot may be unable to fly a severely crippled airliner). Under these conditions rapid manual intervention is required, but may be hampered by deficiencies in any of three processes: detection, diagnosis and intervention. These processes are all related in one respect or another to the excessively high level of trust in an automation system which is quite reliable (Lee & Moray, 1992; Parasuraman & Riley, 1997). Such overtrust fosters what has been called complacency (Parasuraman, Molloy & Singh, 1993). The effects of complacency on each of the three processes of detection, diagnosis, and intervention can directly be related to different cognitive phenomena.

In the first place, if automation is highly reliable, the occurrence of its "failure" will be a very unlikely event. People are simply slow (and/or unlikely) to detect events that are unexpected, whether these are routine stimuli in the laboratory (Fitts & Posner, 1967; Posner, 1978) or failures of automated systems (Parasuraman, 1987; Parasuraman et al., 1993; Wickens & Kessel, 1981). Second, because of the generation effect at high levels of action choice automation, people will have reduced situation awareness of the state of either the automated system, the process that it is managing, or the raw data that it is processing, once an abnormality is noticed (Endsley & Kiris, 1995; Mosier et al., 1998). This degraded awareness will be amplified by poor displays. It was poor automation mode awareness of this sort that caused a pilot to produce a tragically inappropriate maneuver on a landing near Nagoya Japan (Sekigawa & Mecham, 1996), and it was poor hazard awareness of this sort that led a transport aircraft to crash into the terrain near Cali Columbia (Strauch, 1997). Third, it is likely that a pilot or controller who consistently uses automation that is highly reliable, might – through forgetting – lose some of the precise skills necessary to appropriately intervene should manual action be required (Lee & Moray, 1992). Given the differential nature of forgetting curves for different kinds of material, such "deskilling" could be most likely to occur if procedural skills are automated, rather than those involving perceptual motor coordination.

Together, then, all three human processes – detection, awareness or diagnosis, and manual intervention – might be expected to degrade if complacency develops with highly reliable, "overtrusted" automation. An irony is that the more reliable the automation actually is, the greater could be the likelihood of slow, inappropriate, and poorly coordinated intervention, should the system eventually fail (Bainbridge, 1983; Lee & Moray, 1992).

The above discussion of problems with automation should not lead to a conclusion that automation should be abandoned. As noted, many aspects of automation have undoubtedly contributed in a positive way to safety and efficiency. TCAS, for example, has undoubtedly saved many lives, and its failures (alarm false alarms) are responsible for no deaths. What this discussion does highlight, however, is that the introduction of automation should proceed with a clear understanding of how its representation, training, and reliability can influence the effectiveness of its use; and how particular human factors approaches related to good displays, appropriate choice of levels, and appropriate training, can mitigate the consequences of the occasional failures that may be observed.

CONCLUSIONS

In this chapter, we have described how cognitive psychology can be applied to understanding the behavior of the individual pilot's perception, attention, understanding, and decision making. Yet a broader view of the national airspace reveals that this is only one component of the many factors that affect the safety and efficiency of flight, and the broader picture makes relevant two additional domains related to cognitive psychology: cognitive engineering and social cognition. On the one hand, the pilot is a participant in an organization with multiple interacting agents: air traffic controllers, nearby aircraft in the airspace, airline dispatchers and schedulers, and various automated systems. Space does not allow us to address here the fascinating applications of cognitive engineering (Rasmussen, Pejtersen & Goodstein, 1995; Moray, 1999, this volume) to understanding these relations, nor to examining in depth the many fascinating cognitive issues in air traffic control. These are well discussed in Durso, Hackworth, Truitt, Crutchfield, Nikolic & Manning (1998), Hopkin (1995), Seamster, Redding & Kaempf (1997), and Wickens, Mavor & McGee (1997).

On the other hand, pilot communications, which we briefly discussed earlier in the chapter, are influenced by a large number of social factors, that go well beyond the influences of bottom-up and top-down processing, and represent the content of the discipline of personality and social psychology and, in particular, social cognition. Within the domain of aviation, these are embodied in the general study of crew resource management (Wiener, Kanki & Helmreich, 1993).

The relevance of both cognitive engineering and social cognition suggest that cognition in aviation extends well beyond the cognition of the individual pilot's perception, awareness and decision making. Yet while the latter factors are not sufficient, they remain absolutely necessary for understanding the issues of air safety.

REFERENCES

Adams, M. J., Tenney, Y. J. & Pew, R. W. (1995). Situation awareness and the cognitive management of complex systems. *Human Factors*, 37 (1), 85–104.

Antunano, M. J., Mohler, S. R. & Gosbee, J. W. (1989). Geographic disorientation: approaching and landing at the wrong airport. *Aviation, Space and Environmental Medicine*, 55, 996–1004.

Aretz, A. J. (1991). The design of electronic map displays. *Human Factors*, 33 (1), 85–101.

Aretz, A. J. & Wickens, C. D. (1992). The mental rotation of map displays. *Human Performance*, 5 (4), 303–28.

Bainbridge, L. (1983). Ironies of automation. *Automatica*, 19 (6), 775–9.

Bellenkes, A. H., Wickens, C. D. & Kramer, A. F. (1997). Visual scanning and pilot

expertise: the role of attentional flexibility and mental model development. *Aviation, Space, and Environmental Medicine*, 68 (7), 569–79.
Biederman, I., Mezzanotte, R. J. & Rabinowitz, J. C. (1982). Scene perceptions; detecting and judging objects undergoing relational violations. *Cognitive Psychology*, 14, 143–77.
Billings, C. (1996). *Toward a Human Centered Approach to Automation*. Englewood Cliffs, NJ: Lawrence Erlbaum.
Bresley, B. (1995). 777 flight deck design. *Airliner*, April–June, 1–9.
Carbonnell, J. R., Ward, J. L. & Senders, J. W. (1968). A queuing model of visual sampling: experimental validation. *IEEE Trans. on Man–Machine Systems*, MMS-9, 82–7.
Cardosi, K. M. (1993). Time required for transmission of time-critical air traffic control messages in an en route environment. *The International Journal of Aviation Psychology*, 3 (4), 303–14.
Carpenter, P. A. & Just, M. A. (1975). Sentence comprehension: a psycholinguistic processing model of verification. *Psychological Review*, 82 (1), 45–73.
Chou, C., Madhavan, D. & Funk, K. (1996). Studies of cockpit task management errors. *International Journal of Aviation Psychology*, 6, 307–20.
Chute, R. D. & Wiener, E. L. (1995). Cockpit–cabin communication: I. A tale of two cultures. *The International Journal of Aviation Psychology*, 5 (3), 257–76.
Clark, H. H. & Chase, W. G. (1972). On the process of comparing sentences against pictures. *Cognitive Psychology*, 3, 472–517.
Cooper, L. A. (1980). Recent themes in visual information processing: a selected overview. In R. A. Nickerson (Ed.), *Attention and Performance* (pp. 319–45). Hillsdale, NJ: Lawrence Erlbaum.
Degani, A. & Wiener, E. L. (1993). Cockpit checklists: concepts, design and use. *Human Factors*, 35 (4), 345–60.
Dominguez, C. (1994). Can SA be defined? In M. Vidulich, C. Dominguez, E. Vogel & G. McMillan (Eds), *Situation Awareness: Papers and Annotated Bibliography (U)*, Interim Report AL/CF-TR-1994-0085. Wright-Patterson AFB, OH: Armstrong Laboratory, Air Force Materiel Command.
Durso, F. T. & Gronlund, S. D. (1999). Situation awareness. In F. T. Durso, R. S. Nickerson, R. W. Schvaneveldt, S. T. Dumais, D. S. Lindsay & M. T. H. Chi (Eds) *Handbook of Applied Cognition* (chapter 10). Chichester: John Wiley.
Durso, F. T., Hackworth, C. A., Truitt, T. R., Crutchfield, J., Nikolic, D. & Manning, C. A. (1998). Situation awareness as a predictor of performance for en route air traffic controllers. *Air Traffic Control Quarterly*, 6 (1), 1–20.
Duncan, J. (1984). Selective attention and the organization of visual information. *Journal of Experimental Psychology: General*, 113, 501–17.
Eggemeier, F. T. (1988). Properties of workload assessment techniques. In P. A. Hancock and N. Meshkati (Eds), *Human Mental Workload*. Amsterdam: North Holland.
Endsley, M. R. (1995). Toward a theory of situation awareness in dynamic systems. *Human Factors*, 37 (1), 85–104.
Endsley, M. R. & Kiris, E. O. (1995). The out-of-the-loop performance problem and level of control in automation. *Human Factors*, 37 (2), 381–94.
Erzberger, H., Davis, T. J. & Green, S. (1993). Design of center-TRACON automation system. *AGARD Conference Proceedings 538: Machine Intelligence in Air Traffic Management* (pp. 11–1/11–12). Seine, France: Advisory Group for Aerospace Research and Development.
Fadden, D. M., Braune, R. & Wiedemann, J. (1991). Spatial displays as a means to increase pilot situational awareness. In S. R. Ellis, M. K. Kaiser & A. J. Grunwald (Eds), *Pictorial Communication in Virtual and Real Environments* (pp. 173–81). London: Taylor & Francis.
Fitts, P., Jones, R. E. & Milton, E. (1950). Eye movements of aircraft pilots during instrument landing approaches. *Aeronautical Engineering Review*, 9, 24–9.
Fitts, P. M. & Posner, M. I. (1967). *Human Performance*. Pacific Palisades, CA: Brooks/Cole.

Foushee, H. C. (1984). Dyads and triads at 35,000 feet: factors affecting group process and aircrew performance. *American Psychology*, 39, 885–93.

Funk, K. (1991). Cockpit task management: preliminary definitions, normative theory, error taxonomy, and design recommendations. *The International Journal of Aviation Psychology*, 1 (4), 271–86.

Funk, K. H. & Braune, R. (1997). Expanding the functionality of existing airframe systems monitors: the agenda manager. In R. Jensen & L. Rakovan (Eds), *Proceedings of the 9th International Symposium on Aviation Psychology*. Columbus, OH: Ohio State University.

Gabriel, R. F. (1993). Cockpit automation. *Human Factors for Flight Deck Certification Personnel Final Report* (DOT/FAA/RD-93/5 – DOT/VNTSC-FAA-93-4; pp. 209–41). Washington, DC: Federal Aviation Administration, Research and Development Service.

Garland, D. J. & Endsley, M. R. (1997). *Situation Awareness Analysis and Measurement*. Mahwah, NJ: Lawrence Erlbaum.

Garner, W. R. & Morton, J. (1969). Perceptual independence: definitions, models, and experimental paradigms. *Psychological Bulletin*, 72, 233–59.

Gibson, J. J. (1979). *The Ecological Approach to Visual Perception*. Boston, MA: Houghton Mifflin.

Gopher, D. (1992). The skill of attention control: acquisition and execution of attention strategies. In D. E. Meyer & S. Kornblum (Eds), *Attention and Performance XIV: Synergies in Experimental Psychology, Artificial Intelligence, and Cognition Neuroscience – A Silver Jubilee*. Cambridge, MA: MIT Press.

Gopher, D. & Koriat, A. (Eds) (1998). *Attention and Performance* (vol. 16). Orlando, FL: Academic Press.

Gopher, D., Weil, M. & Bareket, T. (1994). Transfer of skill from a computer game trainer to flight. *Human Factors*, 36 (4), 387–405.

Griffin, W. C. & Rockwell, T. H. (1987). A methodology for research on VFR flight into IMC. In R. Jensen (Ed.), *Proceedings of the Fourth International Symposium on Aviation Psychology*. Columbus, OH: Ohio State University.

Hahn, E. C. & Hansman, R. J. (1992). Experimental studies on the effect of automation and pilot situational awareness in the datalink ATC environment. *SAE AEROTECH Conference and Exposition*. Warrendale, PA: Society of Automotive Engineers, Inc.

Harris, R. L. Sr & Christhilf, D. M. (1980). What do pilots see in displays? *Proceedings of the 24th Annual Meeting of the Human Factors Society* (pp. 22–6). Santa Monica, CA: Human Factors Society.

Harris, J. R. & Wilkins, A. J. (1982). Remembering to do things: a theoretical framework and an illustrative experiment. *Human Learning*, 1, 123–36.

Hart, S. G. & Wickens, C. D. (1990). Workload assessment and prediction. In H. R. Booher (Ed.), *MANPRINT: An Approach to Systems Integration* (pp. 257–96). New York: Van Nostrand Reinhold.

Hawkins, F. H. (1993). *Human Factors in Flight*. Brookfield, VT: Ashgate.

Hendy, K. C., Liao, J. & Milgram, P. (1997). Combining time and intensity effects in assessing operator information-processing load. *Human Factors*, 39, 30–47.

Hickox, J. & Wickens, C. D. (1996). *Navigational Checking: A Model of Elevation Angle Effects, Image Complexity, and Feature Type*. University of Illinois Institute of Aviation Technical Report (ARL-96-4/NAWC-ONR-96-1). Savoy, IL: Aviation Res. Lab.

Hickox, J. C. & Wickens, C. D. (1997). 3D electronic maps, design implications for the effects of elevation angle disparity, complexity, and feature type. *Proceedings of the 41st Annual Meeting of the Human Factors and Human Factors Society*. Santa Monica, CA: Human Factors and Ergonomics Society.

Hopkin, D. (1995). *Human Factors in Air Traffic Control*. London: Taylor & Francis.

Jensen, R. S. (1981). Prediction and quickening in perspective displays for curved landing approaches. *Human Factors*, 23, 333–64.

Jensen, R. S. (1997). Risk management in general aviation: making your own rules. In

R. S. Jensen & L. Rakovan (Eds), *Proceedings of the 9th International Symposium on Aviation Psychology*. Columbus, OH: Ohio State University.
Jones, D. G. & Endsley, M. R. (1996). Sources of situation awareness errors in aviation. *Aviation, Space, and Environmental Medicine*, 67 (6), 507–12.
Kerns, K. (1991). Data-link communication between controllers and pilots: a review and synthesis of the simulation literature. *The International Journal of Aviation Psychology*, 1 (3), 181–204.
Kerns, K. (1994). *Human Factors in ATC/Flight Deck Integration: Implications of Data Link Simulation Research* (MP 94W0000098). McLean, VA: The Mitre Corporation.
Kintsch, W. & Ericsson, K. A. (1995). Long term working memory. *Psychological Review*, 102, 211–45.
Klein, G. (1997). The recognition-primed decision (RPD) model: looking back, looking forward. In C. E. Zsambok & G. Klein (Eds), *Naturalistic Decision Making*. Hillsdale, NJ: Lawrence Erlbaum.
Kramer, A. F. & Jacobson, A. (1991). Perceptual organization and focused attention: the role of objects and proximity in visual processing. *Perception and Psychophysics*, 50, 267–84.
Larish, J. F. & Flach, J. M. (1990). Sources of optical information useful for perception of speed of rectilinear self-motion. *Journal of Experimental Psychology: Human Perception & Performance*, 16, 295–302.
Laudeman, I. V. & Palmer, E. A. (1995). Quantitative measurement of observed workload in the analysis of aircrew performance. *The International Journal of Aviation Psychology*, 5 (2), 187–98.
Layton, C., Smith, P. J. & McCoy, C. E. (1994). Design of a cooperative problem-solving system for en-route flight planning: an empirical evaluation. *Human Factors*, 36 (4), 94–119.
Lee, J. & Moray, N. (1992). Trust, control strategies and allocation of function in human–machine systems. *Ergonomics*, 35, 1243–70.
Leibowitz, H. (1988). The human senses in flight. In E. Wiener & D. Nagel (Eds), *Human Factors in Aviation* (pp. 83–110). San Diego, CA: Academic Press.
Loftus, G., Dark, V. & Williams, D. (1979). Short-term memory factors in ground controller/pilot communication. *Human Factors*, 21, 169–81.
Martin-Emerson, R. & Wickens, C. D. (1997). Superimposition, symbology, visual attention, and the head-up display. *Human Factors*, 39 (4), 581–601.
McGreevy, M. W. & Ellis, S. R. (1986). The effect of perspective geometry on judged direction in spatial information instruments. *Human Factors*, 28, 439–56.
Merwin, D., O'Brien, J. V. & Wickens, C. D. (1997). Perspective and coplanar representation of air traffic: implications for conflict and weather avoidance. *Proceedings of the 9th International Symposium on Aviation Psychology*. Columbus, OH: Dept. of Aerospace Engineering, Applied Mechanics, and Aviation, Ohio State University.
Monan, W. P. (1986). *Human Factors in Aviation Operations: The Hearback Problem* (NASA Contractor Report 177398). Moffett Field, CA: NASA Ames Res. Ctr.
Moray, N. (1986). Monitoring behavior and supervisory control. In K. R. Boff, L. Kaufman & J. P. Thomas (Eds), *Handbook of Perception and Performance*, Vol. II (pp. 40–1/40–51). New York: John Wiley.
Moray, N. (1997). Human factors in process control. In G. Salvendy (Ed.), *The Handbook of Human Factors and Ergonomics* (2nd edn). New York: John Wiley.
Moray, N. (1999). The cognitive psychology and cognitive engineering of industrial systems. In F. T. Durso, R. S. Nickerson, R. W. Schvaneveldt, S. T. Dumais, D. S. Lindsay & M. T. H. Chi (Eds), *Handbook of Applied Cognition* (chapter 8). Chichester: John Wiley.
Morrow, D., Lee, A. & Rodvold, M. (1993). Analysis of problems in routine controller–pilot communication. *The International Journal of Aviation Psychology*, 3 (4), 285–302.
Mosier, K. L., Palmer, E. A. & Degani, A. (1992). Electronic checklists: implications for

decision making. *Proceedings of the 36th Annual Meeting of the Human Factors Society* (pp. 7–11). Santa Monica, CA: Human Factors Society.
Mosier, K. L., Skitka, L. J., Heers, S. & Burdick, M. (1998). Automation bias: decision making and performance in high-tech cockpits. *The International Journal of Aviation Psychology*, 8, 47–63.
Mykityshyn, M. G., Kuchar, J. K. & Hansman, R. J. (1994). Experimental study of electronically based instrument approach plates. *The International Journal of Aviation Psychology*, 4 (2), 141–66.
Nagel, D. C. (1988). Pilot error. In E. L. Wiener & D. C. Nagel (Eds), *Human Factors in Aviation*. San Diego, CA: Academic Press.
Neisser, U. & Becklen, R. (1975). Selective looking: attention to visually specified events. *Cognitive Psychology*, 7, 480–94.
Norman, D. (1988). *The Psychology of Everyday Things*. New York: Basic Books.
Norman, D. A. & Bobrow, D. G. (1975). On data-limited and resource-limited processes. *Cognitive Psychology*, 7, 44–64.
O'Hare, D. (1992). The "artful" decision maker: a framework model for aeronautical decision making. *The International Journal of Aviation Psychology*, 2 (3), 175–91.
O'Hare, D. & Roscoe, S. N. (1990). *Flightdeck Performance: The Human Factor*. Ames, IA: Iowa State University Press.
Olmos, O., Liang, C.-C. & Wickens, C. D. (1997). Electronic map evaluation in simulated visual meteorological conditions. *International Journal of Aviation Psychology*, 7 (1), 37–66.
Orasanu, J. M. (1993). Decision-making in the cockpit. In E. L. Wiener, B. G. Kanki & R. L. Helmreich (Eds), *Cockpit Resource Management* (pp. 137–73). San Diego, CA: Academic Press.
Orasanu, J. & Fischer, U. (1997). Finding decisions in natural environments: the view from the cockpit. In C. E. Zsambok & G. Klein (Eds), *Naturalistic Decision Making* (pp. 343–57). Mahwah, NJ: Lawrence Erlbaum.
Orasanu, J. & Strauch, B. (1994). Temporal factors in aviation decision making. *Proceedings of the 38th Annual Meeting of the Human Factors and Ergonomics Society*. Santa Monica, CA: Human Factors and Ergonomics Society.
Owen, D. H. (1991). Perception and control of changes in self-motion: a functional approach to the study of information and skill. In R. Warren & A. H. Wertheim (Eds), *Perception and Control of Self-motion* (pp. 289–322). Hillsdale, NJ: Lawrence Erlbaum.
Palmer, E. & Degani, A. (1991). Electronic checklists: evaluation of two levels of automation. *Proceedings of the 6th International Symposium on Aviation Psychology*. Columbus, OH: The Ohio State University, Department of Aviation.
Parasuraman, R. (1987). Human–computer monitoring. *Human Factors*, 29, 695–706.
Parasuraman, R., Molloy, R. & Singh, I. L. (1993). Performance consequences of automation-induced complacency. *International Journal of Aviation Psychology*, 3 (1), 1–23.
Parasuraman, R. & Riley, V. (1997). Humans and automation: use, misuse, disuse, abuse. *Human Factors*, 39, 230–53.
Posner, M. I. (1978). *Chronometric Explorations of the Mind*. Hillsdale, NJ: Lawrence Erlbaum.
Raby, M. & Wickens, C. D. (1994). Strategic workload management and decision biases in aviation. *International Journal of Aviation Psychology*, 4 (3), 211–40.
Rasmussen, J. & Rouse, W. (Eds) (1981). *Human Detection and Diagnosis of System Failures*. New York: Plenum Press.
Rasmussen, J., Pejtersen, A. & Goodstein, L. (1995). *Cognitive Engineering: Concepts and Applications*. New York: John Wiley.
Redding, R. E. (1992). Analysis of operational errors and workload in air traffic control. *Proceedings of the 36th Annual Meeting of the Human Factors Society* (pp. 1321–5). Santa Monica, CA: Human Factors Society.
Roscoe, S. N. (1968). Airborne displays for flight and navigation. *Human Factors*, 10, 321–32.

Roscoe, S. N. (Ed.) (1987). *The Practical Assessment of Pilot Workload* (AGARDograph #282). Essex, England: Specialised Printing Services.

Roske-Hofstrand, R. J. & Paap, K. R. (1986). Cognitive networks as a guide to menu organization: an application in the automated cockpit. *Ergonomics*, 29, 1301–11.

Sarter, N. B. & Woods, D. D. (1992). Pilot interaction with cockpit automation: operational experiences with the flight management system. *The International Journal of Aviation Psychology*, 2 (4), 303–21.

Sarter, N. B. & Woods, D. D. (1994). Pilot interaction with cockpit automation II: an experimental study of pilots' model and awareness of the flight management system. *The International Journal of Aviation Psychology*, 4 (1), 1–28.

Sarter, N. B. & Woods, D. D. (1995). How in the world did we ever get into that mode? Mode error and awareness in supervisory control. *Human Factors*, 37 (1), 5–19.

Sarter, N. B. & Woods, D. D. (1997). Team play with a powerful and independent agent: operational experiences and automation surprises on the Airbus A-320. *Human Factors*, 39 (4), 553–69.

Schreiber, B. T., Wickens, C. D., Renner, G. J., Alton, J. & Hickox, J. C. (1998). Navigational checking using 3D maps: the influence of elevation angle, azimuth, and foreshortening. *Human Factors*, 40 (2), 209–23.

Schutte, P. C. & Trujillo, A. C. (1996). Flight crew task management in non-normal situations. *Proceedings of the 40th Annual Meeting of the Human Factors and Ergonomics Society* (pp. 244–8). Santa Monica, CA: Human Factors and Ergonomics Society.

Seamster, T. L., Redding, R. E. & Kaempf, G. L. (1997). *Applied Cognitive Task Analysis in Aviation*. Brookfield, VT: Ashgate.

Segal, L. D. (1995). Designing team workstations: the choreography of teamwork. In P. Hancock, J. Flach, J. Caird & K. Vicente (Eds), *Location Applications of the Ecological Approach to Human–Machine Systems* (vol. 2) (pp. 392–415). Hillsdale, NJ: Lawrence Erlbaum.

Seidler, K. & Wickens, C. D. (1992). Distance and organization in multifunction displays. *Human Factors*, 34, 555–69.

Sekigawa, E. & Mecham, M. (1996). Pilots, A300 systems cited in Nagoya crash. *Aviation Week and Space Technology*, 145 (5), 29 July, 36–7.

Senders, J. W. (1964). The human operator as a monitor and controller of multidegree of freedom systems. *IEEE Trans. on Human Factors in Electronics*, HFE-5, 2–6.

Shepard, R. N. & Cooper, L. A. (1982). *Mental Images and their Transformations*. Cambridge, MA: MIT Press/Bradford Books.

Shepard, R. N. & Hurwitz, S. (1984). Upward direction, mental rotation, and discrimination of left and right turns in maps. In S. Pinker (Ed.), *Visual Cognition* (pp. 163–93). Cambridge, MA: MIT Press.

Sheridan, T. (1972). On how often the supervisor should sample. *IEEE Trans. on Systems, Science, and Cybernetics*, SSC-6, 140–5.

Sheridan, T. B. (1987). Supervisory control. In G. Salvendy (Ed.), Handbook of Human Factors. New York: John Wiley.

Slamecka, N. J. & Graf, P. (1978). The generation effect: dilineation of a phenomena. *Journal of Experimental Psychology: Human Learning and Memory*, 4, 592–604.

Slovic, P., Fischhoff, B. & Lichtenstein, S. (1977). Behavioral decision theory. *Annual Review of Psychology*, 28, 1–39.

Sperandio, J. C. (1976). From the plane space to the air mobile space: experimental comparison between two displays of spatio temporal information. *Le Travail Humain*, 30, 130–54.

Stokes, A. F., Kemper, K. & Kite, K. (1997). Aeronautical decision making. In C. Zsambok & G. Klein (Eds), *Naturalistic Decision Making*. Mahwah, NJ: Lawrence Erlbaum.

Strauch, B. (1997). Automation and decision making: lessons learned from the Cali accident. *Proceedings of the 41st Annual Meeting of the Human Factors & Ergonomics Society* (pp. 195–9). Santa Monica, CA: Human Factors & Ergonomics Society.

Theunissen, E. (1997). Integrated design of a man–machine interface for 4-D navigation. Doctoral dissertation, Faculty of Electrical Engineering, Delft University of Technology. Delft, The Netherlands.
Trollip, S. R. & Jensen, R. S. (1991). *Human Factors for General Aviation*. Englewood, CO: Jeppesen Sanderson.
Tsang, P. & Wilson, G. (1997). Mental workload. In G. Salvendy (Ed.), *The Handbook of Human Factors and Ergonomics* (2nd edn). New York: John Wiley.
Tulga, M. K. & Sheridan, T. B. (1980). Dynamic decisions and workload in multitask supervisory control. *IEEE Trans. on Systems, Man, and Cybernetics*, SMC-10, 217–32.
Tversky, A. & Kahneman, D. (1974). Judgment under uncertainty: heuristics and biases. *Science*, 185, 1124–31.
Van Gent, R. N. H. W. (1997). *Human Factors Issues with Airborne Data Link: Towards Increased Crew Acceptance for Both En-route and Terminal Flight Operations* (NLR Technical Publication TP 95666 L). Amsterdam: National Aerospace Laboratory NLR.
Wallsten, T. S. (1980). *Cognitive Processes in Choice and Decision Behavior*. Hillsdale, NJ: Lawrence Erlbaum.
Warren, R. & Wertheim, A. H. (Eds) (1990). *Perception and Control of Self-motion*. Hillsdale, NJ: Lawrence Erlbaum.
Weintraub, D. J. & Ensing, M. J. (1992). *Human Factors Issues in Head-up Display Design: The Book of HUD* (SOAR CSERIAC State of the Art Report 92-2). Dayton, OH: Crew System Ergonomics Information Analysis Center, Wright-Patterson Air Force Base.
Wickens, C. D. (1986). The effects of control dynamics on performance. In K. R. Boff, L. Kaufman & J. P. Thomas (Eds), *Handbook of Perception and Performance* (vol. II) (pp. 39–1/39–60). New York: John Wiley.
Wickens, C. D. (1992). *Engineering Psychology and Human Performance* (2nd edn). New York: HarperCollins.
Wickens, C. D. (1995). The tradeoff of design for routine and unexpected performance: implications of situation awareness. In D. J. Garland & M. R. Endsley (Eds), *Proceedings of the International Conference on Experimental Analysis and Measurement of Situation Awareness* (pp. 57–64). Daytona Beach, FL: Embry-Riddle Aeronautical University Press.
Wickens, C. D. (1996). Situation awareness: impact of automation and display technology. *AGARD Conference Proceedings 575: Situation Awareness: Limitations and Enhancement in the Aviation Environment* (pp. K2–1/K2–13). Neuilly-Sur-Seine, France: Advisory Group for Aerospace Research & Development.
Wickens, C. D. (1997). Attentional issues in head-up displays. In D. Harris (Ed.), *Engineering Psychology and Cognitive Ergonomics: Integration of Theory and Application*. London: Avebury Technical.
Wickens, C. D. (1998). Frame of reference for navigation. In D. Gopher and A. Koriat (Eds), *Attention and Performance* (vol. 16). Orlando, FL: Academic Press.
Wickens, C. D. & Carswell, C. M. (1995). The proximity compatibility principle: its psychological foundation and relevance to display design. *Human Factors*, 37 (3), 473–94.
Wickens, C. D. & Kessel, C. (1981). Failure detection in dynamic systems. In J. Rasmussen and W. Rouse (Eds), *Human Detection and Diagnosis of System Failures*. New York: Plenum Press.
Wickens, C. D., Liang, C.-C., Prevett, T. & Olmos, O. (1996). Electronic maps for terminal area navigation: effects of frame of reference and dimensionality. *International Journal of Aviation Psychology*, 6 (3), 241–71.
Wickens, C. D. & Long, J. (1995). Object- vs. space-based models of visual attention: implications for the design of head-up displays. *Journal of Experimental Psychology: Applied*, 1 (3), 179–94.
Wickens, C. D., Mavor, A. S. & McGee, J. P. (Eds) (1997). *Flight to the Future: Human Factors in Air Traffic Control*. Washington, DC: National Academy Press.
Wickens, C. D., Mavor, A., Parasuraman, R. & McGee, J. M. (1998). *The Future of Air*

Traffic Control: Human Operators and Automation. Washington, DC: National Academy Press.
Wickens, C. D. & Prevett, T. (1995). Exploring the dimensions of egocentricity in aircraft navigation displays. *Journal of Experimental Psychology: Applied*, 1 (2), 110–35.
Wickens, C. D. & Seidler, K. S. (1997). Information access in a dual-task context: testing a model of optimal strategy selection. *Journal of Experimental Psychology: Applied*, 3 (3), 196–215.
Wickens, C. D., Stokes, A., Barnett, B. & Hyman, F. (1993). The effects of stress on pilot judgment in a MIDIS simulator. In O. Svenson & A. J. Maule (Eds), *Time Pressure and Stress in Human Judgment and Decision Making* (pp. 271–92). New York: Plenum Press.
Wiener, E. L. (1977). Controlled flight into terrain accidents: system-induced errors. *Human Factors*, 19, 171–81.
Wiener, E. L. (1988). Cockpit automation. In E. L. Wiener & D. C. Nagel (Eds), *Human Factors in Aviation* (pp. 433–61). San Diego, CA: Academic Press.
Wiener, E. L. & Curry, R. E. (1980). Flight deck automation: promises and problems. *Ergonomics*, 23 (10), 995–1011.
Wiener, E. L., Kanki, B. C. & Helmreich, R. L. (Eds) (1993). *Cockpit Resource Management*. San Diego, CA: Academic Press.
Williams, H., Hutchinson, S. & Wickens, C. D. (1996). A comparison of methods for promoting geographic knowledge in simulated aircraft navigation. *Human Factors*, 38 (1), 50–64.
Williges, R. C. & Wierwille, W. W. (1979). Behavioral measures of aircrew mental workload. *Human Factors*, 21, 549–74.
Yates, J. F. (1990). *Judgment and Decision Making*. Englewood Cliffs, NJ: Prentice Hall.
Zsambok, C. E. & Klein, G. (Eds) (1997). *Naturalistic Decision Making*. Mahwah, NJ: Lawrence Erlbaum.

Chapter 10

Situation Awareness

Francis T. Durso and Scott D. Gronlund
University of Oklahoma

Situation awareness (SA) is a term that emerged from aviation psychology to describe the component of tactical flight operations that involves the pilot's understanding. Expanding SA to an operator's comprehension of a complex system has extended SA research to other domains in which the environment is dynamically changing and in which the operator is responsible for maintaining or achieving particular states or goals. A dynamic environment, one that will change whether or not the operator takes action, helps restrict the number of domains to which one could interestingly speak of SA. Likewise, requiring that the operator has a goal, helps insure that SA will be a vital part of that hypothetical scenario. SA research can be found on fighter pilots (e.g. Endsley, 1993), air traffic controllers (e.g. Durso, Hackworth, Truitt, Crutchfield, Nikolic & Manning, 1998a; Durso, Truitt, Hackworth, Crutchfield & Manning, 1998b; Gronlund, Ohrt, Dougherty, Perry & Manning, in press), nuclear power plant operators (e.g. Hogg, Folleso, Strand-Volden & Torralba, 1995), anesthesiologists (e.g. Gaba, Howard & Small, 1995), military commanders (e.g. Federico, 1995), automobile drivers (e.g. Gugerty, 1997), electronic warfare tacticians (e.g. Randel & Pugh, 1996), chess experts (e.g. Durso et al., 1995), video game players (e.g. Vidulich, McCoy & Crabtree, 1995), and so on (see Vidulich, Dominguez, Vogel & McMillan, 1994, for other examples).

The prominent role of SA is at least in part due to the increasingly cognitive nature of the tasks we ask operators to perform. Failure in such complex cognitive tasks due to loss of SA can have devastating results (see Casey, 1993). Several case studies (e.g. Cheung, Money & Sarkar, 1995) and analyses of existing databases (e.g. Jones & Endsley 1996; Durso et al., 1998b) point to a loss of SA as an important precursor to performance failure. For example, controlled-flight

Handbook of Applied Cognition, Edited by F. T. Durso, R. S. Nickerson, R. W. Schvaneveldt, S. T. Dumais, D. S. Lindsay and M. T. H. Chi.

into terrain (CFIT) accidents killed nearly 5000 people from 1978 to 1992 (Woodhouse & Woodhouse, 1995). According to Woodhouse & Woodhouse, 74% of these accidents were due to a lack of awareness on the part of the flight crew, as opposed to non-adherence or proficiency/skill failure. Similarly, Durso et al. (1998b; see also Rodgers & Nye, 1993) reported that 62% of the en route operational errors in 1993 were made by air traffic controllers who were unaware that an error was developing.

Because the term SA emerged from the pilot/practitioner and only later attracted the interest of researchers, it exists in the literature in a form where it is sometimes treated as familiar to everyone and other times treated as beyond definition. It is sometimes a construct, sometimes a phenomenon; sometimes a process, sometimes a product. A formal definition of SA has received considerable attention in the literature. At the broadest level, researchers and practitioners have used the term "situation awareness" in a way that makes it synonymous with the cognitive activities necessary to operate in or control a dynamic environment. In this most general use, anything relevant to cognitive psychology is relevant to an understanding of SA. At the opposite extreme, the definition is one that is specific to a domain or environment. System-specific definitions have the advantage of being easily applied to improve the operator or the system, but the disadvantage, from a scientific perspective, of a lack of generalizability.

Most researchers have approached SA from a position between these two extremes. These middle positions typically remain very general, but some kinds of cognitive activity are assumed to be outside of SA. A representative definition at this level is one proposed by Dominguez (1994), who explicitly borrowed from Endsley (1990) and Carroll (1992):

> Continuous extraction of environmental information, integration of this information with previous knowledge to form a coherent mental picture, and the use of that picture in directing further perception and anticipating future events.

The definition is noteworthy both for what it contains and what it omits. Clearly SA remains within the domain of cognitive psychology. It involves all of the processes one would expect to see in a description of any complex cognitive activity, although the idea of directing future perception and anticipating future events is perhaps more prominent in this definition than it might be in definitions of cognitive activities that involve static inputs. As with most definitions of SA, this one does not equate SA with performance nor with workload. Also consistent with several definitions in the literature, decision making and subsequent actions are not components of SA. Finally, Dominguez's (1994) definition is noncommittal on how seriously the term *awareness* should be treated in *situation awareness*. Although we would allow automatic and veiled processes as well as tacit knowledge to be part of SA (preferring the term situation assessment), others in the literature take the constraints imposed by the term "awareness" more seriously (e.g. Endsley, 1995b).

Problems with defining SA have slowed theoretical development. Although there are no theories of SA in the archival literature, there are frameworks from which theories are likely to emerge. Two of these frameworks capture the spirit of several others: Endsley's (1995b) information processing framework and Adams, Tenney & Pew's (1995) neo-Gibsonian view. As one would expect, the information processing framework considers SA as emerging from a complex of component cognitive processes; the neo-Gibsonian view considers SA as the product (and process) of the cycle of perceptual exploration of environmental structure, which modifies the existing schemata that directs the perceptual exploration. It is interesting that two of the frameworks paramount in basic cognitive research, often existing in tension or as mutually exclusive alternatives, are reflected in this applied area. We suspect that future SA work will continue to struggle with the information processing/neo-Gibsonian distinction. SA invites the principled synthesis of an approach that focuses on the environment with one that focuses on the operator.

If SA involves a changing environment monitored by an operator with goals to be achieved, what are its limits? We believe that both the environment and the operator help define the limits. The environment places an upper limit on the degree of SA that can be achieved: SA cannot be greater than the predictability of the system the operator controls. When free flying moths detect the ultrasonic pulse of a predatory bat, they fly a random flight path (Roeder, 1962); such evasive actions make the predictability of the system low, thus limiting the bat's SA.

Although the highest level of SA that can be achieved is determined by the environment, the lowest level is determined by the operator. SA cannot be lower than the divided attention capacity of the operator. In a situation where the operator is not attending to the task at all, divided attention could serve to maintain a minimal level of SA. The fortunate driver broken from reverie by the police siren chasing someone else can understand this lower limit. The controller separating traffic in one part of the sector when the conflict alert flashes on another part of the display understands it as well. Recognizing that simple attentional processes can be operating is important in keeping SA from becoming synonymous with being awake. For example, when we orient to the waiter who dropped the dishes, it is because of our attentional mechanisms, not because we had good SA. Such boundary conditions help address Charness' (1995) queries about what is *not* SA.

In summary, SA is sometimes thought to involve all the cognitive processes underlying control of a dynamic environment, and at other times to involve most of those processes, eliminating some, such as decision making or automatic processing, from the mix of SA components. Our attempts to constrain when the term SA should be applicable led to two hypothetical boundary conditions: an upper level determined by the predictability of the environment to a lower level determined by attentional capacity.

In this chapter, we review the literature on SA from the perspective of cognitive psychology. We begin by detailing the various methodologies that have been used. We then focus on the empirical findings that bear on our understanding of SA. We do this by partitioning the literature into sections that correspond roughly to major sub-areas of cognitive psychology: attention, pattern recognition, working memory, knowledge structures, and decision making. In the course of reviewing the literature, we found that this young field was able to supply fewer empirical findings than is needed to develop a coherent theory. Due to the lack of research involving dynamic environments, we sometimes rely on studies using static environments that we think are likely to generalize to dynamic situations. Time will tell if we are correct in generalizing the particular studies we discuss. Finally, we discuss SA research conducted in three arenas of practical concern: automation, training, and teamwork.

METHODOLOGIES OF SA

Although formal definitions and analytical thinking provide an important backdrop against which to understand SA, empirical measurement is critical to a scientific understanding of it. Amongst the debate and confusion over a formal definition of SA, a number of operational (in the scientific sense) definitions have been developed, tested, and compared. From a workshop sponsored by the US Nuclear Regulatory Commission, Gravell & Schopper (1994) report the consideration of some 20 measures. Subsequent proposals and domain-specific procedures make the list longer.

Several proposed classifications have helped to bring order to the available methods. Gravell & Schopper (1994) suggested six measures: retrospective (memory), concurrent, subjective, process, performance, and signal detection theoretic. Adams et al. (1995) suggest three categories: on-line indices, indirect probes, and model-based approaches. Hoffman (1997) suggested two orthogonal dimensions: on-line vs. off-line measurement crossed with direct vs. indirect measurement. Modifying Sarter & Woods (1995; Wickens, 1996), we consider three general approaches to the assessment of SA: subjective measures, query methods, and implicit performance measures.

Subjective Measures

Perhaps the most straightforward measure of SA would be to ask the system operator. Cognitive psychologists have been appropriately warned about self-reports (e.g. Nisbett & Wilson, 1977), and applied researchers have also recognized this and other concerns with subjective measures. For example, Vidulich (1995) discusses "the 6-o'clock problem", where aviators believe they have clear flying but, in fact, are about to be locked by fighters at their 6-o'clock position. In fact, Vidulich's point fits within a broader scheme depicted in Figure 10.1.

This broader perspective also helps explain why, despite valid reasons to eschew self-report in basic research, applied research must consider subjective judgments of SA. Regardless of how good an operator's SA is, if the operator does not recognize the high level of SA he or she enjoys, mistrust and concerns about the system or situation will be an important part of the operator's job satisfaction and performance.

The most often used self-report measure of SA is Taylor's (1990) SA rating technique (SART). The procedure is a relatively straightforward set of either eleven (originally ten) or four (originally three) Likert scales. For example, the

	Actual SA high	Actual SA low
Subjective SA high	Accurate evaluation of a system or situation	Dangerous system or situation awareness, the "6-o'clock" problem
Subjective SA low	Untrustworthy system or disquieting situation	Accurate evaluation of a poor system or situation

Figure 10.1 Subjective measures of situation awareness

short form of SART (Taylor, Finnie & Hoy, 1997) asked participants to judge demand on attentional resources, supply of attentional resources, understanding of the situation, and SA on a 7-point scale. Some of the scales capture subjective impressions of workload (e.g. Selcon, Taylor & Koritas, 1991), but others were intended to capture more cognitive dimensions. There is some empirical work showing that input variables have their impact on different SART subscales (Selcon et al., 1991). In a study by Vidulich et al. (1995), as mission difficulty increased, the attentional-demand rating increased. On the other hand, the availability of tools to aid SA affected the understanding scale. In Crabtree, Marcelo, McCoy & Vidulich (1993), attentional-demand ratings were affected by factors that affected how easily a tank could be located, but not by factors that affected how easily the tank could be eliminated (i.e. size of the tank's vulnerable area). Interestingly, no factor affected the overall SA rating.

Query Methods

The first, and most popular, of these methods was developed by Endsley (1990): the SA global assessment technique (SAGAT). In SAGAT, the experimenter – presumably after gaining considerable understanding of the domain from experts about what is important (see Endsley, 1993; Endsley & Rodgers, 1994; Pritchett & Hansman, 1993) – compiles a database of questions. At random points during the control of a simulation, the simulation is stopped, and all information is removed from the operator while he or she answers a set of randomly selected queries. Accuracy is the dependent variable. SAGAT has often been useful in comparing complete systems (e.g. Hogg et al., 1995; Endsley & Kiris, 1995; Uytterhoeven, de Vlaminck & Javaux, 1995).

Much of the initial work was designed to determine if the methodology interfered with normal processing. Concerns had been raised (e.g. Sarter & Woods, 1991) that SAGAT was intrusive and relied too heavily on memory. Endsley (1994) provided evidence that SAGAT scores were comparable whether the queries were asked immediately (20 seconds) after the interruption or 6 minutes afterward. If one is willing to assume that no memorial decay occurs in the first 20 seconds, then this is evidence that the memory component was not a factor in SAGAT (Endsley, 1994; but see Gugerty, 1998).

Another point that emerged from consideration of the memory component of SAGAT was that to have SA does not necessarily require memorial access to all relevant information. Durso et al. (1998a) proposed that knowing where to find a particular piece of information in the environment could be indicative of good SA, even if the information was not available in memory. In fact, if a piece of information was immediately available in the environment, it might be a poor idea to use limited resources to remember it. In concert with this thinking, Durso et al. measured the time required to answer questions about chess positions that remained visible to the player. Response time could be distinguished between novice, intermediate, and expert players. When Durso et al. (1998a) later applied this situation-present assessment method (SPAM) to air traffic controllers, both SPAM and SAGAT were able to predict various measures of performance of air traffic controllers.

Implicit Performance

Although we agree that merely measuring performance is not a useful way to understand SA, the third general method for assessing SA uses particular performance indices as an implicit measure of SA (e.g. Pritchett, Hansman & Johnson, 1996; Sarter & Woods, 1991; Wickens, 1996). For example, an experimenter would embed operationally relevant information into a high-fidelity simulation (or that information may naturally be embedded). Discovery of that information would indicate good SA by virtue of the changes in behavior that such a discovery would naturally involve. In addition, some specific subtasks naturally occurring in the mission might prove to be useful implicit performance measures. Paraphrasing Wickens (1996), a subtask that could be performed well by an operator with SA, but poorly by one without SA, is a viable candidate for an implicit SA measure.

Implicit performance measures can be found in a number of studies. Andre, Wickens, Moorman & Boschelli (1991) had participants try to fly to the eight different waypoints in three-dimensional space. On random occasions, the display would blank and the participants would be thrown into an unpredictable bank and pitch angle; SA was measured by the accuracy with which they initiated an appropriate turn. Busquets, Parrish, Williams & Nold (1994) asked participants to land on one runway and a second aircraft was to land on the other runway. However, that second aircraft would sometimes deviate and try to land on the operator's runway. The measure of SA was the time to take action to avoid the second aircraft.

COGNITIVE FACTORS

In a study of F-15 pilots, Caretta, Perry & Ree (1996) used a number of cognitive, psychomotor, and personality factors to predict the 31 supervisory/peer ratings on the Air Force's SA battery. Caretta et al. found that four cognitive, two psychomotor, and one personality variable were reliable predictors. The cognitive factors were verbal working memory, spatial reasoning, divided attention, and spatial working memory. The psychomotor factors were aiming, attention RT, and rate control. The personality factor was conscientiousness. Of particular interest was the finding that once flight experience was controlled, only the four cognitive factors remained as predictors. Similarly, Bolstad (1991) had 21 Northrop employees fly a person-in-the-loop simulation while SA was assessed using on-line queries (Endsley, 1993). Best predictors included measures of attention sharing, memory, encoding speed, dot estimation, and scores on the Group Embedded Figures Test (Witkin, Goodenough & Oltman, 1979). Again, cognitive factors tended to be important predictors of SA.

These results certainly argue for the centrality of cognition in SA. Although experience plays a role, it seems only to distinguish the conscientious pilot with "good hands" from his or her peers. Distinguishing among pilots with the same amount of experience seems to depend only on cognitive factors.

Although we find the psychomotor and personality effects interesting, the purpose of this chapter leads us to turn now to a more detailed consideration of relevant cognitive processes. Empirical study of the constituent cognitive processes of SA is critical to making it a viable explanatory construct. Without such study, SA can be, and has been, criticized as a circular construct with little explanatory power (Flach, 1995).

Attention

Few studies in cognitive psychology proper take seriously the importance of the environment in understanding the cognitive processing that occurs. Typically, in the laboratory, the environment is quite impoverished. This impoverished state includes the fact that most laboratory participants have little choice in where to apply their attentional resources. With skilled operators controlling complex environments, attention becomes a critical cognitive component.

Directing attention to the appropriate aspects of the environment depends on both an understanding of the system and the physical characteristics of the environment. Ideally, an experienced operator will find him or herself in a clear environment working with a well-designed system where they should have little problem employing time-tested strategies to sample the environment. Experienced operators can attend to the relevant cues, ignoring irrelevant ones (Ericsson & Lehman, 1996). Search through complex displays for targets can be quite efficient. Even when unexpected events occur, they sometimes "pop-out" (Johnston & Dark, 1986). Thus, experts seem adroit at directing attention across often complex displays.

Eye movement research allows direct assessment of scanning patterns which in turn allows assessment of where attention is being allocated (peripheral vision and uncorrelated attention effects notwithstanding). In a wide variety of situations, eye movements occur at a rate of about 2.5 per second, with a gaze duration of a little less than 500 milliseconds (Moray, 1990). In addition, operators tend to make rapidly repeated visits to a faulty subsystem, rather than increasing the gaze duration for each visit (Moray & Rotenberg, 1989). This finding stands in sharp contrast to the impression one receives from research on eye movements during reading. In the latter case, good readers tend *not* to revisit a word, and gaze duration seems to vary with the cognitive processing required at that point in the sentence (Just & Carpenter, 1980). The scanning strategy used by operators of dynamic environments obviously works, although it is remarkable that the limited gaze durations can supply sufficient information. Part of the resolution of this puzzle lies with top-down knowledge and the structured environment, allowing knowledge to fill in what observation did not register; or, more eloquently, allowing "correlation to substitute for observation" (Moray, 1990, p. 1204). Both Gibsonian invariants and physics limit the information needed for encoding, keeping the system within the abilities of the skilled operator.

However, the strategies governing the sampling of the environment may falter (Wickens, 1992). As one example, stressors can narrow the attentional field (Baddeley, 1972), leading to the ignoring of potentially important peripheral information that fails to otherwise attract attention due to the oversampling of dominant information (Broadbent, 1971) or the breakdown of data sampling strategies. In a study by Wellens (1993), SA was also harmed as communication broke down due to time stress. If several successive emergencies occurred, the dispatcher often allocated some nominal resources to all the emergencies rather than fully understanding what resources (if any) were necessary.

However, SA can be influenced for the better by the design changes made to the environment. Good design aids can benefit SA by attracting attention to important stimuli that might otherwise go unnoticed. Human factors specialists have made considerable efforts designing alarms, warnings, and alerts (e.g. Wickens, 1992). Good design aids can also include making visible otherwise unforeseen hazards, such as weather, or other aircraft in poor visibility. System designers have taken advantage of our understanding of human attentional processes with varying degrees of success. However, it is not always apparent that a design aid will facilitate SA. For example, the head-up display (HUD) used in aviation (e.g. Weintraub & Ensing, 1987) is not trivially transferred to other environments, such as automobiles (Ward & Parkes, 1994).

Although a great deal of effort is appropriately expended to ensure that SA alarms, warnings, and alerts meet human factors constraints, attention is not always directed by bottom-up influences. Operators control their distribution of attention, and most training programs recognize the importance of developing an efficient strategy for distributing attention across the cockpit or radar screen. Typically these top-down influences aid by priming lower-level processes. Expecting a stimulus can prime, or initiate partial processing of, the stimulus before it physically appears in the environment. However, top-down influences can also have negative consequences. For example, operators tend to become locked on the initial fault of a multiple-fault failure (Moray & Rotenberg, 1989), not attending to the second fault until some time later.

Finally, in addition to top-down or priming influences that allow the efficient use of attention, with sufficient practice, some processing will place fewer demands on limited attentional resources. Automatic processing can occur provided there has been sufficient practice and provided the mapping between the input and the cognitive response is consistent (Schneider & Shiffrin, 1977). In fact, mapping need only be partially consistent for benefits of automaticity to accrue (Durso, Cooke, Breen & Schvaneveldt, 1987) and these benefits have been shown to last through nine years of disuse (Cooke, Durso & Schvaneveldt, 1994). Whether these automatic processes are viewed as part of SA or as supportive of SA depends in large part on whether one takes a general or more restricted view of SA. Minimally, as Endsley (1995b) has argued, automatic processing can free up resources that can in turn be used in SA.

In summary, the operator in a complex environment must determine the items in the environment on which to focus. This is aided both by well-designed bottom-up alerting devices and displays, and well-practiced top-down scanning patterns coupled with priming or automatic detection. Attention is often allocated efficiently, but not always (e.g. time pressure, information overload, cognitive tunnel-vision).

Pattern Recognition

Perception is generally recognized as a critical component of SA. In addition to its prominence in most definitions, perception has been implicated as a frequent cause of loss of SA. A cognitive look at perception would tend to focus on pattern recognition processes, those processes by which the operator categorizes cues extracted from the environment.

Perceptual errors have been implicated in a number of aviation errors. Jones & Endsley (1996) classified reports from the ASRS, a database of pilots' voluntary reports. They identified 262 pilot SA errors from the 143 selected incidents and classified them along three levels (see Endsley, 1995b). Although Level 1 SA is often equated in the literature with perception, it is more accurately the processing of individual units within the situation. For example, in Jones & Endsley, failures at Level 1 did include perception, but also implicated attentional and even higher-level processes (e.g. memory loss). Thus Level 1 is, to use an analogy from the reading comprehension literature, word-level information prior to combining the words into phrases. Level 2 SA refers to comprehension of the current situation, and Level 3 SA refers to projection into the future.

Although Jones & Endsley (1996) used a scoring system biased to score incidents as Level 1, it seems safe to conclude that a larger percentage of SA errors (72%) were due to failures to process information about individual units than were due to difficulties in putting this unit information together or using it to predict the future (28%). A closer look at the Level 1 errors suggests that they were due to both perceptual and attentional failures. Similarly, Durso et al. (1998b) reported that, for controllers who were unaware that an error was developing, operational errors were due to attentional or perceptual failures about equally often and together accounted for about half of the errors, with memory failures and thinking errors (e.g. faulty assumptions, reasoning) accounting for the other half.

Understanding the role of pattern recognition in SA will ultimately depend on an understanding of the dynamic environments. Several viable approaches could be followed to reach this goal. Analytic modeling (e.g. Veldhuyzen & Stassen, 1977) has yielded detailed descriptions of systems; however, the relationship between such analytic descriptions and the cognitive mechanisms is lacking. Gibsonian-inspired studies could try to identify the invariances in stimuli within a particular environment (e.g. a MiG's wake) that could afford perception and ultimately SA. For example, Smith & Hancock (1995) speculate that a "risk-space" may be such an invariance. Work by a few researchers does confirm the suspicion that such invariances are present in particular environments. Kass, Herschler & Companion (1991) trained civilians to recognize different elliptically shaped tank-muzzle flashes. Training, especially training with only essential stimulus cues, was successful in improving SA as measured by the accuracy with which the operator could locate the tank.

Secrist & Hartman (1993) also investigated the trainability of pattern recognition for briefly presented stimuli. Unlike Kass et al.'s, the Secrist & Hartman stimuli were symbols (e.g. ♣♦♥♠) only arbitrarily related to the task. Secrist & Hartman's subjects learned to classify the symbols in different ways. On detect-trials, the subject indicated whether something or nothing was presented. On recognize-trials, the subject made essentially a friend vs. foe decision – that is, was the symbol one of four previously designated targets, or was it one of five distractors? The third type of classification asked subjects to identify which of the four targets was presented. When masked stimuli were presented for 33 milliseconds, the ability to detect a target was comparable to the ability to recognize the target. In other words, participants were able to classify a stimulus as a foe as easily as they could decide that something was there. Clearly, if an expert can classify a stimulus as easily as he or she can detect it, then SA should be better than that of a novice who could merely detect it. Similarly, Druckman & Bjork (1991; Means, Salas, Crandall & Jacobs, 1993) showed that experts recognized cues more quickly and completely, and could detect important features of a stimulus more readily. Lipshitz & Ben Shaul (1997) showed that expert gunboat commanders were better at distinguishing between legitimate and bogus targets. Stokes, Kemper & Kite (1997) found that expert pilots identified more relevant cues.

Other than speeding up classification, improving classification, or freeing attentional resources for other tasks, gleaning information quickly from perceptual inputs can improve SA by providing a look at the future. Research in how experts process events (see Ericsson & Lehmann, 1996) suggests that experts can glean advance cues that allow them to anticipate the immediate future. Wright, Pleasants & Gomez-Meza (1990) asked NCAA volleyball players and students taking a physical activity class to view short clips of a setter and to determine which spiker was the intended recipient of the set. Experts outperformed novices for film clips that ended 167 milliseconds before the setter touched the ball. Such anticipatory advantages are not new to coaches: Day (1980) indicated that skilled tennis players can utilize advance cues such as racquet angle, weight transfer, and ball toss to determine the likely terminal location of a ball. In a controlled demonstration of this proposition, Abernethy & Russell (1987) showed that prediction was degraded in expert badminton players when the arm of the server was occluded.

If the pattern recognition process of experts supplies information about the future, it may be that perception and Endsley's other levels of SA are more inextricable than SA theories would suggest. In cognitive psychology, perception of a pattern is tantamount to categorizing that pattern. Furthermore, because we know that categorization leads to the automatic activation of constituent components not presented, including activation of related concepts (e.g. Meyer & Schvaneveldt, 1971), it is difficult to indicate where perception ends and understanding begins. And, if research on advance cues is correct, perception may lead quickly and directly to decisions about the future, a critical assumption underlying the recognition-primed decisions of naturalistic decision making (see Zsambok & Klein, 1997). Finally, it may be the case that highly skilled operators can perceive an entire situation in the sense that the entire situation is recognized as a typical pattern that has been previously experienced. In addition to other differences, experts may spend more of their time assessing the situation, whereas novices are more likely to be engaged in option evaluation (Calderwood, Crandall & Baynes, 1988; Randel & Pugh, 1996). In the Lipshitz & Ben Shaul (1997) study, the expert gunboat commanders collected more information from more sources on more varied aspects of the situation, considered the other boats' role in battle, and communicated more frequently with friendly boats. Finally, Federico (1995) asked expert and novice tactical naval officers to judge the similarity of various situations. Experts ascribed more importance to similar contexts than did the novices, who attributed more weight to background knowledge. If Federico's findings hold, it would suggest that experts are more context dependent than are novices. In such a case, SA would depend not only on the categorization of the stimulus but on the context in which that categorization takes place.

Such a possibility harkens back to James ([1890] 1950). To James, if we activated the concept of a MiG, the activation would overlap with activations from the immediate past. Thus, we think of a MiG in a particular context and it is this context + concept amalgam that drives the activation of other information, which in turn overlaps with the existing activation. A window of awareness (controlled by attention according to James) on these overlapping distributions gives us the discrete thought of, in our example, a MiG, but it is a thought of a MiG that depends heavily on whether we have recently been thinking about airshows or combat. To James, what seems like a discrete thought to us is a peek at a composite of many concepts that contribute to an amorphous activation. If James's introspection holds, SA will depend not only on the patterns we recognize, but on the temporal context in which we recognize those patterns.

The current literature supplied some insight into the role of pattern recognition in SA. When perceptual processes fail, SA fails. When perceptual processes are particularly attuned, SA seems superior. Specific cues obviously exist in particular domains, but few studies have identified and taken advantage of specific knowledge in designing studies to assess perceptual and attentional processes in SA. It is critical that specific knowledge is available, because experts seem able to tune into the relevant information in their domain. Obviously, processing the relevant cues (and ignoring irrelevant or less diagnostic ones) can have a positive impact on SA in a number of ways. Knowing the critical cues in an environment can speed encoding, facilitate the categorization of the stimuli, and can even help project into the immediate future. There is some evidence that experience allows a stimulus to be categorized specifically as accurately as it could be categorized generically (simply detected). There is also evidence that, once the relevant information from the dynamic environment is identified, it can be used in training by focusing novices on the relevant information. Finally, experts seem to take a more global perspective from which, according to naturalistic decision making, a response is primed; experts may even consider an amalgam broader than the situation itself, one that includes the context as well.

Working Memory

Most dynamic environments are represented spatially and humans are quite able to take advantage of spatial presentations. Some researchers (Hasher & Zacks, 1979) have even suggested that the ability to represent spatial information is an innate automatic process. For tasks that are clearly spatial, such as flying a fighter plane, multiple regression analyses have implicated spatial working memory and spatial reasoning (Caretta et al., 1996) as relevant to SA. The value of spatial representations is also apparent in a number of studies designed to compare different frames of reference for pilots (e.g. Barfield, Rosenberg & Furness, 1995) and air traffic controllers (e.g. Wickens, Mavor & McGee, 1997).

In addition, some work has demonstrated more directly the value of spatial representations. For example, Hess, Detweiler & Ellis (1994), expanding Yntema's (1963) classic experiment, had undergraduates monitor several attributes of one spaceship or one attribute of several spaceships. In the ship-by-attribute-grid condition, every object-attribute pair had a particular location on the screen. In the window condition, the same windows were used to present information about all object-attribute pairs. As might be expected, responses to periodic queries about the ships were more accurate in the grid condition, and the advantage of the grid was more apparent the longer the delay between the ship's update and the query.

Working memory (WM), especially spatial working memory, seems at first blush to be a critical component of SA. Although psychometric dissections of SA sometimes implicate the role of WM (e.g. Caretta et al., 1996), consideration of the literature suggests that the relationship between SA and trait-based measures of WM or between SA and state-based WM is not a ubiquitous one. For example, given the strong degree of correspondence between decision making and SA (e.g. Zsambok & Klein, 1997), it is surprising that Barnett (1989) found little relationship between aeronautical decision performance and WM. Furthermore, Mogford & Tansley (1991) measured the performance of ATC trainees and found that none of the memory tests they used (list learning, running memory, or complex figures) predicted performance. Beringer & Hancock (1989) found no effect of memory load on performance – participants concurrently performed a dual-task: monitoring a map and canceling presented stimulus items. In the map monitoring task, participants had to monitor the progress of an "automated" flight and verbally report when the aircraft crossed various waypoints. The system periodically failed and participants had to reconstruct the entire flight path by manually tracing the route segments. The cancellation task was either conducted immediately or delayed, the latter inducing a memory load. The delayed cancellation task caused only a temporary disruption to performance of the map task which quickly dissipated with practice. In a test of the validity of SAGAT, Endsley (1995a) showed that what was remembered about a scenario was unaffected by a delay of up to several minutes. It is unlikely that information residing in WM could survive that delay. Thus, the need to store information temporarily in WM is not sufficient to produce an effect on SA.

The correlation between measures of WM and SA that is sometimes found may not be driven by the storage of information, but rather by the processing of that information. Early conceptualizations of short-term memory focused largely on its ability to store information (e.g. Atkinson & Shiffrin, 1968). However, much evidence has now accumulated (e.g. Baddeley, 1986) demonstrating that a short-term memory system includes a processor or executive in addition to storage structures. Baddeley & Hitch (1974) proposed a model of WM that includes a central executive responsible for processing, along with two subsystems responsible for the temporary storage of auditory/verbal and visual/spatial information; Meyer & Kieras (1997) have also proposed a model of (in part) the central executive. The importance of the executive role of WM is evident from a study by Yee, Hunt & Pellegrino (1991). With a public-safety dispatching task, Yee et al. identified some college students with a superior ability to coordinate tasks independent of an ability to deal with either task separately. Lee, Anderson & Matessa (1995) examined the effects of extensive practice in an air traffic control simulation and found that the improved performance was the result of improved strategies. Improved processing and better strategies resulted in improved SA.

There are at least four general strategies that experienced operators could use to ensure that demands on WM do not exceed its resources and which could reduce the correlation between WM and SA. All of these strategies depend on the operator processing the inputs as domain-relevant meaningful stimuli. Remembering only a subset of the possible information is one means to ensure that the limited capacity of WM is not exceeded. Shanteau (1992) showed that the most important factor in expert judgment was not the amount of information used but the type of information. Experts knew what was important and what was not. In another example, Gugerty (1998) showed that as the memory load in a driving simulation increased (the number of cars surrounding the operator's car), the locations of only cars closest to the operator's car were remembered, presumably because these cars would be considered most hazardous to the operator's own car. Similarly, Gronlund et al. (in press) showed that air traffic controllers remembered more flight data about important flights (i.e. those that were in conflict or potential conflict). Sperandio (1971, 1978) showed that controllers dealt with only the most relevant variables associated with a flight.

In addition to holding only the important information in WM, the load on WM can be reduced by reorganizing the incoming information into richer "chunks" of related information (Miller, 1956). Support for the importance of chunking information is apparent, because experts show better memory for stimuli from their domain if this information is meaningful (e.g. Vicente, 1992), but not if that information is randomly rearranged (cannot readily be chunked). Borgeaud & Abernethy (1987) had expert and novice volleyball players view dynamic game sequences on videotape. Experts recalled the position of players better than did novices in a structured game situation, but there was no difference for unstructured game situations (for similar findings from basketball see Allard & Starkes, 1991). Stokes et al. (1997) found that expert pilots were better than novice pilots at reconstructing radio call sequences, but there was no difference if the call sequences were scrambled.

A third means by which the amount of information impinging on WM can be reduced is through the "gistification" of relevant data. For example, rather than remembering the exact speed of two aircraft, a controller might remember that one is faster than the other. Brainerd & Reyna (1990) have shown that there is no relationship between memory for verbatim features of a static task and subsequent reasoning regarding that domain.

Finally, the load on WM can be reduced by restructuring of the environment. Gruen (1996) examined the strategies of office workers for handling interruptions and found that various external cues were used as reminders. Examples are placing a checkmark to indicate where you stopped in a manual, and stacking a pile of papers perpendicular to the other papers in the pile. Xiao, Milgram & Doyle (1997) found that anesthesiologists configured the workplace spatially through the placement of various triggering (retrieval) cues. Hutchins (1995) showed that navigators reduced cognitive load by virtue of the environmental restructuring produced by the person preceding them in the sequence of processing.

It is clear that focusing on important information, chunking together meaningful information, gistifying detailed information, and restructuring the environment, serve to lessen the load on WM while it improves the assessment of the current situation and supports more accurate anticipation of the future situation. With these strategies, it may seem surprising that tests of WM capacity ever correlate with SA.

Given that these strategies are likely to be most efficiently used by experts, it may prove to be the case that WM and SA correlate less as expertise increases. Stokes (1991) argued that WM was important only when an operator failed to match the current situation to a course of action. It was only in the event of this inability to match that the operator utilized an alternative strategy using real-time computational and inferential processes that were heavily dependent on WM. Similarly, Endsley (1997) has argued that novices are more dependent on WM than experts and that experts do not need WM unless they find themselves in novel situations.

At a mechanism level, we suggest experts do not rely on WM but on long-term working memory (LT-WM) for the maintenance of information supporting SA. LT-WM is a construct introduced by Ericsson & Kintsch (1995) in which pointers in WM point to information stored in long-term memory. This allows experts to store information rapidly in, and to retrieve information efficiently from, long-term memory. The majority of the experts reviewed by Ericsson & Kintsch also maintain a strong spatial character to these retrieval structures. For example, an expert waiter could remember the dinner orders of up to 20 patrons around a table by utilizing their location at the table.

In summary, recent theorizing suggests that operators in dynamic environments capitalize on the spatial nature of their tasks through development of

LT-WM retrieval structures. Furthermore, we argued that the correlation that is sometimes found between WM and SA is the result not of the storage capacity of WM (which can be circumvented by LT-WM) but by the executive processing capabilities (task management) of WM. We identified four general processing strategies whereby experienced operators can reduce the information load on WM:

- remember only the "important" information
- reorganize information into richer "chunks"
- "gistification"
- restructuring the environment.

The ability to use any of these strategies requires that the operator be a task expert, which is consistent with the argument that WM (or at least its storage capability) is more important to the novice than to the expert.

Mental Models

Much of the recent research in cognitive science has been directed at gaining a better understanding of long-term knowledge structures (see Charness & Schuletus, 1999, this volume). Applied researchers have recognized and discussed such knowledge structures and how they can be applied (e.g. Rasmussen, 1986). An important characteristic of knowledge structures is that many of these structures "expect" certain attributes to co-occur with other attributes. For example, in a frame system (Minsky, 1975), a kitchen frame "knows," in a sense, that a refrigerator is present and that an octopus is an unlikely possibility. Or, the verb "shot" (Schank, 1972) carries with it the idea that some instrument of the shooting must exist, if only implicitly, and that unless the context suggests otherwise, the instrument is more likely to be a gun than a Welsh longbow. This ability to expect or predict allows knowledge structures some top-down processing capabilities. These expectations can, in turn, affect not only higher cognitive processes, but fundamental processes such as attention (e.g. Friedman, 1979) and perception (e.g. Warren, 1970) as well.

The knowledge structure most central to SA is the mental model. The construct has yielded some confusion in the literature, although efforts have helped to reduce this confusion (e.g. Wilson & Rutherford, 1989). Several researchers have pointed out the need to treat the mental model as distinct from other knowledge structures, and Moray (1996) has pointed out that the mental model relevant to operators of dynamic, complex systems differs from the mental model of a static object and from the mental model of an abstract syllogism (Johnson-Laird, 1983). Although all of these mental models share some characteristics, such as a loss of information in moving from the reality to the model, they differ as a function of the task and the environment in which the operator and task are embedded. The mental model of a dynamic, complex system is one that represents the functional or causal connections relevant to the system. In our view, the mental model can be thought of as a representation of the typical causal interconnections involving actions and environmental events that influence the functioning of the system. In this sense, the mental model is a long-term memory, knowledge structure.

Of more interest to SA, the confluence of the mental model and the environment gives rise to what Van Dijk & Kintsch (1983) refer to as a situation model. In a situation model, some slots in the mental model are filled with values gleaned from the environment and other slots are filled from the operator's expectations. The situation model can then be "run" to determine the projected outcome of the operator's planned action. This distinction between a mental model and a situation model is important for several reasons.

First, the mental model, but not the situation model, is difficult to modify once established.

Second, the mental model can give rise to thousands of situation models, depending on the environmental inputs. Thus, attempts in the literature to equate SA and mental models is part of the past confusion. Endsley (1995b) more appropriately equates SA with a situation model, which she considers "a schema depicting the current state of the system model." We agree that the situation model gives rise to SA, but we stop short of equating the two, primarily because the equation is not well specified; for example, what are the implications for awareness of the cognitive representation if one holds that SA contains only information about which the operator is aware. [Others (e.g. Brewer, 1987) have argued that mental models are the creation of the moment and that schemata are stored and activated. We believe that, for experts, the mental model is stored, and that instantiation processes create, for the moment, a token of the mental model that we have referred to as the situation model.]

Third, issues related to the specificity of mental models (e.g. Rouse & Morris, 1986; Wickens, 1984) become mute: the apparent richness of problem-solving behavior (e.g. metaphors, analogies) would be due to the mental model, and the apparent specificity due to the situation model. The mental model can be "run" (De Kleer & Brown, 1983) to produce an outcome for an idealized system; the situation model can be "run" to produce the expected outcome for the current system.

Fourth, we suspect that the situation model is run in LT-WM to allow, for example, predictions into the near future. Although LT-WM is a relatively new construct, it is our suspicion that the construct will ultimately prove necessary for an understanding of a number of cognitive results, including expertise effects and SA.

Because the existence of mental models is often considered self-evident, there has been little empirical work on knowledge (mental models) and SA. Thus, although basic research suggests that mental models will affect many cognitive processes, there are few direct tests of this in SA research. Nevertheless, some work does infer the properties of mental models that develop after different types of training (e.g. Kessel & Wickens, 1982). Some work gives naïve operators particular mental models and then determines, for example, the type of errors they would tend to make (e.g. Dayton, Gettys & Unrein, 1989). Some work determines the system model analytically and fits it to human performance data (e.g. Veldhuyzen & Stassen, 1977). Finally, some work attempts to discern the structure of the mental model using cognitive task analysis or other knowledge elicitation techniques (see Cooke, 1999, this volume). For example, using regression analyses, Mogford (1994) showed that memory of altitude and heading were predictors of success in ATC radar training, whereas memory of speed was counterproductive, suggesting that altitude and direction were important parts of the controller's "picture," or mental model. Stout (1995) analyzed mental models by comparing graph structures using the Pathfinder scaling algorithm (Schvaneveldt, Durso & Dearholt, 1989) from undergraduates operating as members of teams flying a low-fidelity helicopter simulation. Teams whose members had similar Pathfinder graphs planned better and engaged in more efficient communication.

Some research has made the effort to understand the general structure of mental models needed for control of dynamic systems. For example, Moray (1987) has argued that when systems become complex, operators, in an effort to reduce processing load, create mental models that fall at different levels within a lattice defined by different levels of information specification. The idea is similar to the gistification ideas put forth by Brainerd & Reyna (1990). Operators form homomorphs between their models and the actual environment that preserve different degrees of information specification. For example, an air traffic controller's situation model might maintain the relative altitudes between two aircraft while a situation model at a different level in the lattice representation might maintain absolute altitudes.

Problems resulting from the improper use of situation models can arise in at least three ways:

1. Of foremost importance, the wrong situation model could be instantiated, leading to misinterpretation. Such misinterpretation can be resistant to change as its top-down influences will lead the operator to search for and interpret incoming cues according to the misinterpretation.
2. This is related to Moray's (1987) lattice theory – an operator may be at the wrong level within the lattice. A situation may arise that requires the operator to know more detailed knowledge than is available at this level of the lattice (e.g. the air traffic controller might know the relative altitudes of two aircraft but needs to know their absolute altitudes).
3. The operator could inappropriately adhere to the situation model in the face of evidence to the contrary, leading to dramatic reductions of SA (e.g. Taylor et al., 1997).

In summary, knowledge is a critical component of SA. The details of the knowledge architecture include the distinction between a mental model and a situation model. The former can exist at a general, abstract level, transcending any particular instantiation; the latter exists in a specific circumstance that arises from the environment and predictions/expectations made by the operator.

Naturalistic Decision Making

Researchers studying decision making in complex environments, most recently Klein (1989; for a recent review, see Zsambok & Klein, 1997), have focused on the diagnosis (as opposed to choice) phase of decision making, advancing the argument that in many real-world tasks the choice phase is relatively trivial. For instance, across a wide range of domains (e.g. firefighters, chess players, air traffic controllers, pilots, etc.) it has been demonstrated that operators do not enumerate all possible alternatives (Gettys, Pliske, Manning & Casey, 1987). Rather, decision making in these environments focuses instead on assessing the situation (see Patel, Arocha & Kaufman, 1999, this volume, for a discussion of forward reasoning). According to Klein, once a situation is assessed, the appropriate course of action will usually be apparent without deliberation. In other words, assessing the situation and retrieving what to do about it are typically part and parcel of the same process. For example, Kaempf, Klein, Thordsen & Wolf (1996) found that 87% of the decisions of command-and-control officers were made in this manner; only 12% involved situations in which the environment did not provide sufficient information, forcing inferences or what Klein (1993) calls storybuilding.

The decisions that follow immediately from situation assessment are called recognition primed decisions. They occur only when the current situation is similar to a typical situation from the past, thus this form of decision making is especially apparent in experts who have probably experienced all typical situations. Consequently, experts spend most of their time assessing the situation whereas novices are more likely to be engaged in option evaluation (Calderwood et al., 1988; Randel & Pugh, 1996). Stokes et al. (1997) found that experts identified more relevant cues of the situation; Xiao et al. (1997) found that the points of consideration identified by anesthesiologists as they plan for an operation helped them select a focus of attention that would keep them away from irrelevant cues. This is important because Nisbett, Zukier & Lemley (1981) showed that consideration of irrelevant information dilutes reliance on relevant information. As we discussed earlier, several studies have shown that experts use cues more efficiently and diagnostically than do novices (e.g. Druckman & Bjork, 1991; Lipshitz & Ben Shaul, 1997; Means et al., 1993).

Storybuilding is also an important component task for the operator in a complex environment. Some have even equated storybuilding with situation assessment or SA (e.g. Oransanu, Dimges & Fischer, 1993). Roth (1997) found that nuclear power plant workers constructed a mental representation of the situation using storybuilding and used the resulting mental representation to anticipate future problems. Xiao et al. (1997) completed a field study of anesthesiologists and showed that they begin their planning activities by compiling and reviewing points for consideration (future problems to be avoided, alleviated, or solved). The use of storybuilding to interpret the situation supports a focus on the future, suggesting that anticipation of future problems should be indicative of good SA.

An appreciation of the future does appear to be indicative of good SA. For example, Hogg et al. (1995) found that answers to questions comparing the current process state of a nuclear power plant with past, present and future states all contributed to SA, but understanding the future had the strongest relationship. Durso et al. (1998a) used measures tapping the present and future to predict objective performance (a count of the number of actions remaining at the end of a scenario) in an air traffic simulation. The better able to answer queries about the future, the more efficient was the controller; he or she had fewer control actions remaining. However, the better the appreciation of the present situation, the less efficient was the controller and the more actions remained at the end of the scenario. Apparently, controllers who focused on the present did so at the cost of the future.

Having a plan for upcoming events seems generally sound, but a plan can sometimes interfere with SA. People are prone to a confirmation bias (Mynatt, Doherty & Tweney, 1978), a tendency to try to confirm their beliefs/hypotheses or execute a plan, failing to heed contradictory evidence. Operators in complex, dynamic environments are no exception. Taylor et al. (1997) showed a bias to execute a plan despite evidence that the plan should be abandoned. Participants performed a simulation task requiring coordination of a multi-aircraft attack on a target. The degree of pre-flight preparation varied from minimal to complete (i.e. rehearsal and automation of the plan). The latter group was more likely to lose track of its primary mission directive (survival) indicating plan over-adherence. Subjective SA (measured by SART) showed that the complete group rated their workload as lower and their SA higher than the minimal group. Although this was consistent with the participants' performance on the secondary mission directive (attacking the target), it contradicted their performance on the primary mission directive (staying alive).

In summary, experts in complex domains spend much of their time assessing the situation, using cues more efficiently and diagnostically than novices. The decision to be made follows directly from the assessment of the situation, assuming the situation is a typical one. If the situation is not typical, the operator will engage in storybuilding to aid interpretation. A focus on the future seems particularly important, usually improving SA, but sometimes reducing it.

PRACTICAL ISSUES

We have described a variety of cognitive factors and their impact on SA. We turn next to a discussion of three issues relevant to controlling complex systems that has received attention in the literature: the impact of automation on SA, the training of SA, and the distribution of SA across members of a team.

Automation

Wickens (1996) distinguished between two types of SA relevant to interface design: hazard SA and automation-relevant SA. Much research has been directed at interface design in support of hazard SA (for a review, see Wickens, 1996; for an example, see McCann & Foyle, 1996). Considerable work has investigated how

SA of hazards (for the pilot, hazards include weather, terrain, other aircraft, etc.) is affected by various display characteristics, including display scale, eye-point elevation, map rotation, and display dimensionality. Less research has been conducted on automation-relevant SA, although there are obvious directions to pursue. We can begin with a first principle like Billings (1991): automation that reduces workload will likely benefit SA. Support for this idea was found by Vortac, Edwards, Fuller & Manning (1993). They compared performance of air traffic controllers required to manage flight progress strips versus an automation–analog group for whom some of the tasks involved with managing flight strips were eliminated. No differences were found on various performance, attentional, and retrospective memory measures. However, the automation–analog group performed better on future-looking activities (e.g. granting prospective requests, planning), perhaps because automation reduced the workload and the controller redirected those cognitive resources at future-looking activities.

However, much research directed at the effect of automation on SA has shown that automation decreases an operator's SA (e.g. Carmody & Gluckman, 1993; Endsley, 1994). A study by Endsley & Kiris (1995) is representative. They implemented different levels of automation in a driving decision task. Decisions were slower on the first trial after the failure of the automation than it was for the manual condition, although performance recovered on the next trial. More interesting, despite decreased Level 2 SA for the automation condition (reflecting poorer understanding of the situation), operator confidence was higher than in the manual condition.

In what ways does automation decrease SA? Research by Sarter & Woods (1992) on the flight management system (FMS) used by pilots provides some insight. Sarter & Woods (1994) conducted simulation studies that showed that pilots often revealed inadequate SA of the FMS when it was configured in unusual states. Pilots often failed to understand what the system was doing and why, or pilots failed to realize the current mode. Automation can also make the operator a passive monitor of the system rather than an active participant in its control (i.e. taking them out of the control loop). Consequently, over reliance on the automation could lead to complacency (Parasuraman, Molloy & Singh, 1993).

An automation deficit was also observed by Ballas, Heitmeyer & Perez (1992). They designed a dual tracking/choice task that resembled tasks performed in complex aircraft. The tracking task required the cursor to be kept on a target. The choice situation was partially automated by an on-board computer that took over the choice task whenever the tracking task became difficult. When the tracking task became easy again, the choice task was returned to the operator and an automation deficit (slowed choice performance) was observed. Kieras & Meyer (1995) suggested that the automation deficit could be reduced if the priority of the objects requiring classification in the choice task was available (i.e. represented) at the time that responsibility for the automated task was returned to the operator. Under manual control, the operator would have naturally maintained this priority, but under automation it was not necessary. In this view, the automation deficit was the result of poor SA regarding the prioritization of these objects which a better interface could have improved.

Good automation, then, must serve many roles. It should:

- reduce operator workload, while keeping the operator in the loop for certain aspects of the task – this should help maintain important aspects of the task in the operator's memory.
- make the operator aware of the mode of the system so that the operator is able to ascertain what the system will do next.
- keep track of relevant information to ease any automation deficit.

The challenge is clear. Good automation requires an understanding of the operator, the task requirements, and the environment.

Training SA

Training in complex dynamic environments should occur in a training environment that contains all the relevant features of the performance environment; this is referred to as embedded training by Cannon-Bowers & Bell (1997). This makes simulation necessary because only it can provide the necessary realism in a setting in which the characteristics of the problems and the situational cues are controlled and feedback provided (e.g. see Means et al., 1993). Context-driven training of this sort can enhance the SA skills necessary for effective recognition-primed decision making (Robertson & Endsley, 1995) by explicitly building the experiential repertoires and situational schemata of students (Stokes et al., 1997). Another way of achieving this is through cognitive apprenticeships in which experts lead students through a series of constructive activities that allow the trainee to work closely with an expert in the actual environment (Druckman & Bjork, 1991). Similarly, "exploratory" training of an automated system (Sarter & Woods, 1995) would expose the operators to the entire range of possible activities of the system and thereby improve their mental model of the system, assuming the interface affords a veridical model of the work environment (Vicente, 1997). The result of receiving appropriate simulator training or practice as a cognitive apprentice is to begin to equip the operator with the necessary schemata and mental models to perform the job adequately. Once that foundation is in place, situation assessment can take place, which, according to the recognition-primed decision model of Klein (1997), leads directly to the selection of the appropriate course of action.

Once an underlying model exists and the operator is able to make recognition-primed decisions, the need for effective training remains. Cohen, Freeman & Thompson (1997) highlighted two related problems that might arise, even in experts, that would serve to harm SA. One problem is that operators may fail to consider conflicting information (Taylor et al., 1997). Alternatively, Cohen (1993) discussed that it is also inappropriate to abandon a hypothesis prematurely. Cohen et al. believed that SA could be improved with appropriate training directed at alleviating these two related problems by training metarecognitional skills to supplement pattern recognition. These skills include identifying key assessments and their recognitional support, checking stories and plans for completeness, elaborating stories to explain a conflicting cue rather than discarding it, etc. The group that received the training considered more factors in their evaluations, considered better factors (i.e. considered fewer irrelevant factors), and noticed more factors that conflicted with the assessment. Training operators to perform in complex, dynamic environments requires extensive experience in that environment to acquire the necessary knowledge structures. But once that is accomplished, training should focus on the evaluation of alternative explanations for situation assessment and the handling of conflicting data.

Training can also focus on particular cognitive or behavioral components suspected of playing a role in SA. For example, Shapiro & Raymond (1989), using the video game *Space Fortress* (Donchin, 1994), compared an efficient eye movement group to an inefficient eye movement group and a control group that simply played the video game. The efficient group was trained to minimize repetitive saccades to previously processed stimuli or irrelevant stimuli. The efficient group showed superior performance. Driskell, Salas & Hall (1994) trained experienced Navy officers either to (a) systematically scan all relevant items of evidence and review the information prior to making a decision, or (b) scan only the items necessary to make a decision, and only review the items if necessary. Performance was worse in the former condition. The ability to not resample already understood information (Shapiro & Raymond, 1989) and to focus on relevant information (Driskell et al., 1994) should be beneficial to SA.

Vidulich et al. (1995) used direct measures of SA in a study of attentional control training based on *Space Fortress*. Training transferred to a commercial air combat simulation package, leading to more kills than did placebo training. Of interest, however, is that neither SART nor SAGAT measures of SA were affected by attentional control training. Because these SA measures were affected by other manipulations (e.g. the presence of SA tools), it is unlikely that the measures were simply insensitive. Instead, the results suggest that attentional control may have its effect on performance without the mediation of SA. Although particular training procedures might implicate SA as an intermediate mechanism that influences performance, it is important to confirm SA's presumed role.

Training in complex environments must take place in context. This allows the novice operator to begin to acquire the experiential repertoires and mental models to support recognition-primed decision making. The accumulation of this aggregation of repertoires and mental models can be facilitated by focused training of particular cognitive and behavioral task components. Once the operator has sufficient experience and has achieved a level of expertise, the goal of training shifts to helping the operator remain a critical evaluator of the evolving situation, appropriately considering conflicting observations – in other words, strategies for maintaining their SA.

Distributed SA

When interest in SA extends to situations in which several operators are working in unison to accomplish a common goal, another dimension, a social dimension, becomes important. Social psychologists have studied small group behavior for years (for an overview, see Levine & Moreland, 1990), and more recently investigators have become interested in assessing the extent to which people in social interactions share the same understanding of the situation. For example, Ickes (1997) and colleagues have been studying "empathic accuracy," the accuracy with which one member of a social interaction knows the feelings of the other. Typically, surreptitious video recordings are made of spontaneous interactions that occur between members of a dyad "waiting to participate in an experiment." One member of the dyad later indicates when and what he or she was thinking at particular points during the interaction; the other member of the dyad attempts to identify what their partner was thinking at those same points in time. Stinson & Ickes (1992) showed, for example, that individuals with an interaction history (i.e. friends) were better able to divine their partner's thoughts than were people without a history (i.e. strangers). This finding and others about gender interactions are not surprising to anyone who has been married for 20 years; nevertheless, such procedures from social psychology help place such folk wisdom under empirical scrutiny.

Some empirical scrutiny has been given to task-directed social interactions with the goal of determining what makes for a team with good SA. Wickens (1996) argued that task SA (the ability to maintain awareness of a to-be-performed task or set of tasks) is crucial in a multi-operator environment with shared responsibility for certain tasks. Yet, team SA is more than the aggregate of the individual team member's SA. It must include knowledge shared by team members (e.g. Blickensderfer, Cannon-Bowers & Salas, 1997). Stout (1995) investigated the relationship among the mental models of team members (as measured by Pathfinder associative networks: Schvaneveldt, 1990) and found that crew members whose mental models were similar demonstrated better SA by more often anticipating when a fellow crew member needed particular information. Crews with more similar mental models also were rated higher in their planning behavior. Prince, Salas & Stout (1995) identified the three highest and lowest scoring teams according to the total of their individual SAGAT scores; the higher scoring teams identified more potential problems and did so sooner. Good performing flight crews also make more statements relating to situation assessment (Orasanu, 1995).

CONCLUSIONS

Difficult to define, but easy to recognize, situation awareness is a testbed that can be used to determine if cognitive theory can "scale-up." It can be used by cognitive psychologists to determine if the mechanisms induced from our controlled laboratory experiments, and held out as fundamental, are in fact important constituents of a complex process – a cognitive process so evident, despite its complexity, that it was identified by the pilots and operators who rely on it.

Despite problems in establishing a consensus definition, researchers have offered research methodologies that have led to some empirical understanding of SA. Appropriate allocation of attention by experience or design together with various resource-reducing strategies in WM allows recognition of mission-critical cues and the instantiation of the appropriate situation model which can then facilitate recognition-primed decisions. The interrelations among such constituent cognitive processes are obviously intricate. The operator must have the experiential repertoires and mental models in place to generate situation models to perform their task. Appropriate training can facilitate acquisition of these repertoires and models. The repertoires, in turn, help skilled operators process critical cues and ignore others, which aids in reducing information load. Appropriate automation can aid in the identification of cues and the reduction of load, as can cognitive strategies such as encoding relational information and anticipating the future – all strategies that may rely on the establishment of LT-WM, a memory structure that is the interface between what the operator knows and what the world presents. Here, knowledge categorizes stimuli and situations, allowing operators to make rapid and accurate decisions. If team members agree on the categorization of the situation, team SA and performance seem to be enhanced.

In this way, the literature has depicted SA with broad brush strokes. As empirical work continues to accumulate, we suspect several theories of SA will emerge from the existing cognitive frameworks which, in turn, will guide additional SA research.

ACKNOWLEDGMENTS

The authors are grateful to Carol Manning, Chris Wickens, Robert Hoffman, Todd Truitt, Mike Dougherty, Jerry Crutchfield, Jenny Perry, Peter Moertl, Paul Linville, and two anonymous reviewers under the editorship of Roger Schvaneveldt.

REFERENCES

Abernethy, B. & Russell, D. G. (1987). The relationship between expertise and visual search strategies in a racquet sport. *Human Movement Science*, 6, 283–319.

Adams, M. J., Tenney, Y. J. & Pew, R. W. (1995). Situation awareness and the cognitive management of complex systems. *Human Factors*, Special issue: Situation Awareness, 37, 85–104.

Allard, F. & Starkes, J. L. (1991). Motor-skill experts in sports, dance, and other domains. In K. A. Ericsson & J. Smith (Eds), *Toward a General Theory of Expertise: Prospects and Limits* (pp. 126–52). New York: Cambridge University Press.

Andre, A. D., Wickens, C. D., Boorman, L. & Boschelli, M. M. (1991). Display formatting techniques for improving situation awareness in the aircraft cockpit. *International Journal of Aviation Psychology*, 1, 205–18.

Atkinson, R. C. & Shiffrin, R. M. (1968). Human memory: a proposed system and its control processes. In K. W. Spence & J. T. Spence (Eds), *The Psychology of Learning and Motivation: Advances in Research and Theory* (Vol. 2) (pp. 89–195). New York: Academic Press.

Baddeley, A. D. (1972). Selective attention and performance in dangerous environments. *British Journal of Psychology*, 63, 537–46.

Baddeley, A. (1986). *Working Memory*. Oxford: Clarendon Press/Oxford University Press.

Baddeley, A. D. & Hitch, G. (1974). *Working Memory*. In G. Bower (Ed.), *Recent Advances in Learning and Motivation*, 8, New York: Academic Press, 47–89.

Ballas, J. A., Heitmeyer, C. L. & Perez, M. A. (1992). Direct manipulation and intermittent automation in advanced cockpits (Technical Report NRL/FR/5534–92-9375). Washington DC: Naval Research Laboratory.

Barfield, W., Rosenberg, C. & Furness, T. A. (1995). Situation awareness as a function of frame of reference, computer-graphics eyepoint elevation, and geometric field of view. *International Journal of Aviation Psychology*, 5, 233–56.

Barnett, B. (1989). Modeling information processing components and structural knowledge representations in pilot judgment. Unpublished doctoral dissertation, University of Illinois, Urbana-Champaign.

Beringer, D. & Hancock, P. A. (1989). Exploring situational awareness: a review and the effects of stress on rectilinear normalization. In *Proceedings of the Fifth International Symposium on Aviation Psychology*, 2, 646–51.

Billings, C. E. (1991). *Human-centered Aircraft Automation: A Concept and Guidelines* (NASA Technical Memorandum 103885). Moffett Field, CA: NASA-Ames Research Center.

Blickensderfer, E., Cannon-Bowers, J. A. & Salas, E. (1997). Training teams to self-correct: an empirical evaluation. Paper presented at the Meeting of the Society for Industrial and Organizational Psychology, St Louis, MO (April 10–13).

Bolstad, C. A. (1991). Individual pilot differences related to situation awareness. *Proceedings of the Human Factors Society*, 35, 52–6.

Borgeaud, P. & Abernethy, B. (1987). Skilled perception in volleyball defense. *Journal of Sport Psychology*, 9, 400–6.

Brainerd, C. J. & Reyna, V. F. (1990). Gist is the grist: fuzzy-trace theory and the new intuitionism. *Developmental Review*, 10, 3–47.

Brewer, W. F. (1987). Schemas versus mental models in human memory. In M. Peter (Ed.), *Modelling Cognition* (pp. 187–97). Chichester: John Wiley.

Broadbent, D. E. (1971). *Decision and Stress*. London: Academic Press.

Busquets, A. M., Parrish, R. V., Williams, S. P. & Nold, D. E. (1994). Comparison of pilots' acceptance and spatial awareness when using EFIS vs. pictorial display formats for complex, curved landing approaches. In R. D. Gilson, D. J. Garland & J. M. Koonce (Eds), *Situational Awareness in Complex Systems: Proceedings of a CAHFA Conference* (pp. 139–67). Daytona Beach, FL: Embry-Riddle Aeronautical University Press.

Calderwood, R., Crandall, B. W. & Baynes, T. H. (1988). *Protocol Analysis of Expert/Novice Command Decision-making During Simulated Fire Ground Incidents*. Yellow Springs, OH: Klein Associates, Inc.

Cannon-Bowers, J. A. & Bell, H. H. (1997). Training decision makers for complex environments: implications of the naturalistic decision making perspective. In C. E. Zsambok & G. Klein (Eds), *Naturalistic Decision Making. Expertise: Research and Applications* (pp. 99–110). Mahwah, NJ: Lawrence Erlbaum.

Carmody, M. A. & Gluckman, J. P. (1993). Task specific effects of automation and automation failure on performance, workload, and situational awareness. In *Proceedings of the 7th International Symposium on Aviation Psychology* (Vol. 1) (pp. 167–71). Columbus, OH: Ohio State University.

Carretta, T. R., Perry, D. C. & Ree, M. J. (1996). Prediction of situational awareness in F-15 pilots. *International Journal of Aviation Psychology*, 6, 21–41.

Carroll, L. A. (1992). Desperately seeking SA. *TAC Attack (TAC SP 127-1)*, 32, March, 5–6.

Casey, S. (1993). *Set Phasers on Stun and other True Tales of Design, Technology, and Human Error*. Santa Barbara, CA: Aegean Publishing.

Charness, N. (1995). Expert performance and situation awareness. In D. J. Garland & M. R. Endsley (Eds), *Experimental Analysis and Measurement of Situation Awareness* (pp. 35–41). Daytona Beach: Embry-Riddle Aeronautical University Press.

Charness, N. & Schuletus, R. S. (1999). Knowledge and expertise. In F. T. Durso, R. S. Nickerson, R. W. Schvaneveldt, S. Dumais, D. S. Lindsay & M. T. H. Chi (Eds), *Handbook of Applied Cognition* (chapter 3). Chichester: John Wiley.

Cheung, B., Money, K. & Sarkar, P. (1995). Loss of aviation situation awareness in the Canadian forces. *AGARD Conference Proceedings*, 575, 1.1–1.8.
Cohen, M. S. (1993). The naturalistic basis of decision biases. In G. A. Klein, J. Orasanu, R. Calderwood & C. E. Zsambok (Eds), *Decision Making in Action: Model and Methods* (pp. 51–99). Norwood, NJ: Ablex.
Cohen, M. S., Freeman, J. T. & Thompson, B. B. (1997). Training the naturalistic decision maker. In C. E. Zsambok & G. Klein (Eds), *Naturalistic Decision Making. Expertise: Research and Applications* (pp. 257–68). Mahwah, NJ: Lawrence Erlbaum.
Cooke, N. J. (1999). Knowledge elicitation. In F. T. Durso, R. S. Nickerson, R. W. Schvaneveldt, S. T. Dumais, D. S. Lindsay & M. T. H. Chi (Eds), *Handbook of Applied Cognition* (chapter 16). Chichester: John Wiley.
Cooke, N. J., Durso, F. T. & Schvaneveldt, R. W. (1994). Retention of skilled search after nine years. *Human Factors*, 36, 597–605.
Crabtree, M. S., Marcelo, R. A. Q., McCoy, A. L. & Vidulich, M. A. (1993). An examination of a subjective situational awareness measure during training on a tactical operations simulator. *Proceedings of the 7th International Symposium on Aviation Psychology*, 2, 891–5.
Day, L. (1980) Anticipation in junior tennis players. In J. Groppel & R. Sears (Eds), *Proceedings of International Symposium on the Effective Teaching of Racquet Sports* (pp. 107–16). Urbana-Champaign: University of Illinois.
Dayton, T., Gettys, C. F. & Unrein, J. T. (1989). Theoretical training and problem detection in a computerized database retrieval task. *International Journal of Man–Machine Studies*, 30, 619–37.
De Kleer, J. & Brown, J. S. (1983). Assumptions and ambiguities in mechanistic mental models. In D. Gentner & A. L. Stevens (Eds), *Mental Models*. New Jersey: Erlbaum.
Dominguez, C. (1994). Can SA be defined? In M. Vidulich, C. Dominguez, E. Vogl & G. McMillan (Eds), *Situation Awareness: Papers and Annotated Bibliography* (pp. 5–15). AL/CF-TR-1994-0085, Armstrong Laboratory.
Donchin, E. (1994). Video games as research tools: the *Space Fortress* game. *Behavior Research Methods, Instruments & Computers*, 27, 217–23.
Driskell, J. E., Salas, E. & Hall, J. K. (1994). The effect of vigilant and hyper-vigilant decision training on performance. Paper presented at the 1994 Annual Meeting of the Society of Industrial and Organizational Psychology.
Druckman, D. & Bjork, R. A. (1991). *In the Mind's Eye: Enhancing Human Performance*. Washington, DC: National Academy Press.
Durso, F. T., Cooke, N. M., Breen, T. J. & Schvaneveldt, R. W. (1987). Is consistent mapping necessary for high speed search? *Journal of Experimental Psychology: Learning, Memory & Cognition*, 13, 223–9.
Durso, F. T., Hackworth, C., Truitt, T. R., Crutchfield, J., Nikolic, D. & Manning, C. A. (1998a). Situation awareness as a predictor of performance in en route air traffic controllers. *Air Traffic Control Quarterly*.
Durso, F. T., Truitt, T. R., Hackworth, C., Crutchfield, J. & Manning, C. A. (1998b). En route operational errors and situation awareness. *International Journal of Aviation Psychology*.
Durso, F. T., Truitt, T. R., Hackworth, C. A., Crutchfield, J. M., Nikolic, D., Moertl, P. M., Ohrt, D. & Manning, C. A. (1995). Expertise and chess: a pilot study comparing situation awareness methodologies. In D. J. Garland & M. R. Endsley (Eds), *Experimental Analysis and Measurement of Situation Awareness* (pp. 295–304). Daytona Beach: Embry-Riddle Aeronautical University Press.
Endsley, M. R. (1990). Predictive utility of an objective measure of situation awareness. *Proceedings of the Human Factors Society*, 34, 41–5.
Endsley, M. R. (1993). A survey of situation awareness requirements in air-to-air combat fighters. *International Journal of Aviation Psychology*, 3, 157–68.
Endsley, M. R. (1994). Situation awareness in dynamic human decision making: measurement. In R. D. Gilson, D. J. Garland & J. M. Koonce (Eds), *Situational*

Awareness in Complex Systems: Proceedings of a CAHFA Conference (pp. 139–67). Daytona Beach, FL: Embry-Riddle Aeronautical University Press.
Endsley, M. R. (1995a). Measurement of situation awareness in dynamic systems. *Human Factors*, 37, 65–84.
Endsley, M. R. (1995b). Toward a theory of situation awareness in dynamic systems. *Human Factors*, 37, 32–64.
Endsley, M. R. (1997). The role of situation awareness in naturalistic decision making. In G. K. Caroline & E. Zsambok (Eds), *Naturalistic Decision Making. Expertise: Research and Applications* (pp. 269–83). Mahwah, NJ: Lawrence Erlbaum.
Endsley, M. R. & Kiris, E. O. (1995). The out-of-the-loop performance problem and level of control in automation. *Human Factors*, 37, 381–94.
Endsley, M. R. & Rodgers, M. D. (1994). Situation awareness information requirements for en route air traffic control. *FAA Office of Aviation Medicine Reports*, 94, 27–34.
Ericsson, K. A. & Kintsch, W. (1995). Long term working memory. *Psychological Review*, 102, 211–45.
Ericsson, K. A. & Lehmann, A. C. (1996). Expert and exceptional performance: evidence of maximal adaptation to task constraints. *Annual Review of Psychology*, 47, 273–305.
Federico, P. (1995). Expert and novice recognition of similar situations. *Human Factors*, 37, 105–22.
Flach, J. M. (1995). Situation awareness: proceed with caution. *Human Factors*, 37, 149–57.
Friedman, A. (1979). Framing pictures: the role of knowledge in automized encoding and memory for gist. *Journal of Experimental Psychology: General*, 108, 316–55.
Gaba, D. M., Howard, S. K. & Small, S. D. (1995). Situation awareness in anesthesiology. *Human Factors*, 37, 20–31.
Gettys, C. F, Pliske, R. M., Manning, C. & Casey, J. T. (1987). An evaluation of human act generation performance. *Organizational Behavior & Human Decision Processes*, 39, 23–51.
Gravelle, M. & Schopper, A. W. (1994). Measures and methods for characterizing operator performance in nuclear power plant control rooms: workshop findings and recommendations. US Nuclear Regulatory Commission Report #NRC FIN W6104.
Gronlund, S. D., Ohrt, D. D., Dougherty, M. R. P., Perry, J. L. & Manning, C. A. (in press). Role of memory in air traffic control. *Journal of Experimental Psychology: Applied*.
Gruen, D. M. (1996). The role of external resources in the management of multiple activities. Unpublished doctoral dissertation, San Diego, CA.
Gugerty, L. J. (1997). Situation awareness during driving: explicit and implicit knowledge in dynamic spatial memory. *Journal of Experimental Psychology: Applied*, 3, 42–66.
Gugerty, L. J. (1998). Evidence from a partial report task for forgetting in dynamic spatial memory. *Human Factors*.
Hasher, L. & Zacks, R. T. (1979). Automatic and effortful processes in memory. *Journal of Experimental Psychology: General*, 108, 356–88.
Hess, S. M., Detweiler, M. C. & Ellis, R. D. (1994). The effects of display layout on monitoring and updating system states. *Proceedings of the Human Factors and Ergonomics Society*, 38, 1336–9.
Hoffman, R. R. (1997). The elicitation of expert knowledge in domains involving perceptual skill, mental workload, and situation awareness. Unpublished manuscript.
Hogg, D. N., Folleso, K., Strand-Volden, F. & Torralba, B. (1995). Development of a situation awareness measure to evaluate advanced alarm systems in nuclear power plant control rooms. *Ergonomics*, 11, 2394–413.
Hutchins, E. (1995). *Cognition in the Wild*. Cambridge, MA: MIT Press.
Ickes, W. J. (Ed.) (1997). *Empathic Accuracy*. New York: Guilford Press.
James, W. ([1890] 1950). *Principles of Psychology*. New York: Dover.
Johnson-Laird, P. N. (1983). *Mental Models*. Cambridge, MA: Harvard University Press.
Johnston, W. A. & Dark, V. J. (1986). Selective attention. *Annual Review of Psychology*, 37, 43–75.

Jones, D. G. & Endsley, M. R. (1996). Sources of situation awareness errors in aviation. *Aviation, Space, and Environmental Medicine*, 67, 507–12.

Just, M. A. & Carpenter, P. A. (1980). A theory of reading: from eye fixations to comprehension. *Psychological Review*, 87, 329–54.

Kaempf, G. L., Klein, G., Thordsen, M. L. & Wolf, S. (1996). Decision making in complex naval command-and-control environments. *Human Factors*, 38, 220–31.

Kass, S. J., Herschler, D. A. & Companion, M. A. (1991). Training situational awareness through pattern recognition in a battlefield environment. *Military Psychology*, 3, 105–12.

Kessel, C. J. & Wickens, C. D. (1982). The transfer of failure-detection between monitoring and controlling dynamic systems. *Human Factors*, 24, 49–60.

Kieras, D. E. & Meyer, D. E. (1995). An overview of the EPIC architecture for cognition and performance with application to human–computer interaction. Technical Report 95/ONR-EPIC-5.

Klein, G. A. (1989). Recognition-primed decisions. In W. B. Rouse (Ed.), *Advances in Man–Machine Systems Research* (Vol. 5) (pp. 47–92). Greenwich, CT: JAI.

Klein, G. (1993). *Naturalistic Decision Making – Implications for Design*. SOAR 93-01 (Contract No. DLA900-88-0393). Dayton, OH: CSERIAC.

Klein, G. (1997). An overview of naturalistic decision making applications. In C. E. Zsambok & G. Klein (Eds), *Naturalistic Decision Making Expertise: Research and Applications*. Mahwah, NJ: Lawrence Erlbaum.

Lee, F. J., Anderson, J. R. & Matessa, M. P. (1995). Components of dynamic skill acquisition. *Proceedings of the Cognitive Science Society*, 17, 506–11.

Levine, J. M. & Moreland, R. L. (1990). Progress in small group research. *Annual Review of Psychology*, 41, 585–634.

Lipshitz, R. & Ben Shaul, O. (1997). Schemata and mental models in recognition-primed decision making. In E. Zsambok & C. G. Klein (Eds), *Naturalistic Decision Making. Expertise: Research and Applications* (pp. 293–303). Mahwah, NJ: Lawrence Erlbaum.

McCann, R. S. & Foyle, D. C. (1996). Scene-linked symbology to improve situation awareness. *AGARD Conference Proceedings*, 16.1–16.11.

Means, B., Salas, E., Crandall, B. & Jacobs, T. O. (1993). Training decision makers for the real world. In G. A. Klein, J. Orasanu, R. Calderwood & C. E. Zsambok (Eds), *Decision Making in Action: Models and Methods*. Norwood, NJ: Ablex.

Meyer, D. E. & Kieras, D. E. (1997). A computational theory of executive cognitive processes and multiple-task performance: I. Basic mechanisms. *Psychological Review*, 104, 3–65.

Meyer, D. E. & Schvaneveldt, R. W. (1971). Facilitation in recognizing pairs of words: evidence of a dependence between retrieval operations. *Journal of Experimental Psychology*, 90, 227–34.

Miller, G. A. (1956). The magical number seven, plus or minus two: some limits on our capacity for processing information. *Psychological Review*, 63, 81–97.

Minsky, M. L. (1975). A framework for representing knowledge. In P. Winston (Ed.), *The Psychology of Computer Vision*. New York: McGraw-Hill.

Mogford, R. H. (1994). Mental models and situation awareness in air traffic control. In R. D. Gilson, D. J. Garland & J. M. Koonce (Eds), *Situational Awareness in Complex Systems* (pp. 199–207). Embry-Riddle Aeronautical University Press.

Mogford, R. H. & Tansley, B. W. (1991) The importance of the air traffic controller's picture. *Proceedings of the Human Factors Association of Canada*, 24, 135–40.

Moray, N. (1987). Intelligent aids, mental models, and the theory of machines. *International Journal of Man–Machine Studies*, 27, Special Issue: Cognitive engineering in dynamic worlds, 619–29.

Moray, N. (1990). Designing for transportation safety in the light of perception, attention, and mental models. *Ergonomics*, 33, 1201–13.

Moray, N. (1996). Mental models in theory and practice. In D. Gopher (Ed.), *Attention and Performance XX*. Tel Aviv.

Moray, N. & Rotenberg, I. (1989). Fault management in process control: eye movements and action. *Ergonomics*, 11, 1319–42.
Mynatt, C. R., Doherty, M. E. & Tweney, R. D. (1978). Consequences of confirmation and disconfirmation in a simulated research environment. *Quarterly Journal of Experimental Psychology*, 30, 395–406.
Nisbett, R. E. & Wilson, T. D. (1977). Telling more than we can know: verbal reports on mental processes. *Psychological Review*, 84, 231–59.
Nisbett, R. E., Zukier, H. & Lemley, R. E. (1981). The dilution effect: nondiagostic information weakens the implications of diagnostic information. *Cognitive Psychology*, 13, 248–77.
Orasanu, J. (1995). Evaluating team situation awareness through communication. In D. J. Garland & M. R. Endsley (Eds), *Experimental Analysis and Measurement of Situation Awareness* (pp. 295–304). Daytona Beach: Embry-Riddle Aeronautical University Press.
Oransanu, J., Dimges & Fischer, U. (1993). Decision errors in the cockpit. *Proceedings of the Human Factors and Ergonomics Society 37th Annual Meeting* (pp. 363–7). Santa Monica, CA: Human Factors and Ergonomics Society.
Parasuraman, R., Molloy, R. & Singh, I. L. (1993) Performance consequences of automation-induced "complacency". *International Journal of Aviation Psychology*, 3, 1– 23.
Patel, V. L., Arocha, J. F. & Kaufman, D. R. (1999). Medical cognition. In F. T. Durso, R. S. Nickerson, R. W. Schvaneveldt, S. T. Dumais, D. S. Lindsay & M. T. H. Chi (Eds), *Handbook of Applied Cognition* (chapter 22). Chichester: John Wiley.
Prince, C., Salas, R. & Stout, R. J. (1995). Situation awareness: team measures, training, and methods. In D. J. Garland & M. R. Endsley (Eds), *Experimental Analysis and Measurement of Situation Awareness* (pp. 295–304). Daytona Beach: Embry-Riddle Aeronautical University Press.
Pritchett, A. & Hansman, R. J. (1993). Preliminary analysis of pilot ratings of "party line" information importance. *Proceedings of the 7th International Symposium on Aviation Psychology*, 1, 360–6.
Pritchett, A. R., Hansman, R. J. & Johnson, E. N. (1996). Use of testable responses for performance-based measurement of situation awareness. In D. J. Garland & M. R. Endsley (Eds), *Experimental Analysis and Measurement of Situation Awareness*. Daytona Beach: Embry-Riddle Aeronautical University Press.
Randel, J. M. & Pugh, H. L. (1996). Differences in expert and novice situation awareness in naturalistic decision making. *International Journal of Human–Computer Studies*, 45, 579–97.
Rasmussen, J. (1986). *Information Processing and Human–Machine Interaction*. Amsterdam: North-Holland.
Robertson, M. M. & Endsley, M. R. (1995). A methodology for analyzing team situation awareness in aviation maintenance. In D. J. Garland & M. R. Endsley (Eds), *Experimental Analysis and Measurement of Situation Awareness* (pp. 313–20). Daytona Beach: Embry-Riddle Aeronautical University Press.
Rodgers, M. D. & Nye, L. G. (1993). Factors associated with the severity of operational errors at air route traffic control centers. In M. D. Rodgers (Ed.), *An Examination of the Operational Error Database for Air Route Traffic Control Centers* (DOT/FAA/AM-93/22, pp. 11–25). Washington, DC: Federal Aviation Administration.
Roeder, K. D. (1962). The behavior of free flying moths in the presence of artificial ultrasonic pulses. *Animal Behavior*, 10, 300–4.
Roth, E. M. (1997). Analysis of decision making in nuclear power plant emergencies: an investigation of aided decision making. In C. E. Zsambok & G. Klein (Eds), *Naturalistic Decision Making. Expertise: Research and Applications* (pp. 175–82). Mahwah, NJ: Lawrence Erlbaum.
Rouse, W. B. & Morris, N. M. (1986). On looking into the black box: prospects and limits in the search for mental models. *Psychological Bulletin*, 100, 349–63.

Sarter, N. B. & Woods, D. D. (1991) Situation awareness: a critical but ill-defined phenomenon. *International Journal of Aviation Psychology*, 1, 45–57.
Sarter, N. B. & Woods, D. D. (1992). Pilot interaction with cockpit automation: operational experiences with the flight management system. *International Journal of Aviation Psychology*, 2, 303–21.
Sarter, N. B. & Woods, D. D. (1994). Pilot interaction with cockpit automation: II. An experimental study of pilots' model and awareness of the flight management system. *International Journal of Aviation Psychology*, 4, 1–28.
Sarter, N. B. & Woods, D. D. (1995). How in the world did we ever get into that mode? Mode error and awareness in supervisory control. *Human Factors*, 37, 5–19.
Schank, R. C. (1972). Conceptual dependency: a theory of natural language understanding. *Cognitive Science*, 3, 552–631.
Schneider, W. & Shiffrin, R. M. (1977). Controlled and automatic human information processing: I. Detection, search, and attention. *Psychological Review*, 84, 1–66.
Schvaneveldt, R. W. (Ed.) (1990). *Pathfinder Associative Networks: Studies in Knowledge Organization*. Norwood, NJ: Ablex.
Schvaneveldt, R. W., Durso, F. T. & Dearholt, D. W. (1989). Network structures in proximity data. In G. Bower (Ed.), *The Psychology of Learning and Motivation* (pp. 249–84). New York: Academic Press.
Secrist, G. E. & Hartman, B. O. (1993). Situational awareness: the trainability of the near-threshold information acquisition dimension. *Aviation, Space & Environmental Medicine*, 64, 885–92.
Selcon, S. J., Taylor, R. M. & Koritas, E. (1991). Workload or situational awareness?: TLX vs. SART for aerospace systems design evaluation. *Proceedings of the Human Factors Society*, 35, 62–6.
Shanteau, J. (1992). Competence in experts: the role of task characteristics. *Organizational Behavior and Human Decision Processes*, 53, 252–66.
Shapiro, K. L. & Raymond, J. E. (1989). Training of efficient oculomotor strategies enhances skill acquisition. *Acta Psychologica*, 71, 217–42.
Smith, K. & Hancock, P. A. (1995). Situation awareness is adaptive, externally directed consciousness. *Human Factors*, 37, 137–48.
Sperandio, J. C. (1971). Variation of operator's strategies and regulating effects on workload. *Ergonomics*, 14, 511–17.
Sperandio, J. C. (1978). The regulation of working methods as a function of workload among air traffic controllers. *Ergonomics*, 21, 195–200.
Stinson, L. & Ickes, W. (1992). Empathic accuracy in the interactions of male friends versus male strangers. *Journal of Personality & Social Psychology*, 62, 787–97.
Stokes, A. F. (1991). Flight management training and research using a micro-computer flight decision simulator. In R. Sadlowe (Ed.), *PC-based Instrument Flight Simulation – A First Collection of Papers* (pp. 47–52). New York: American Society of Mechanical Engineers.
Stokes, A. F., Kemper, K. & Kite, K. (1997). Aeronautical decision making, cue recognition, and expertise under time pressure. In C. E. Zsambok & G. Klein (Eds), *Naturalistic Decision Making. Expertise: Research and Applications*. Mahwah, NJ: Lawrence Erlbaum.
Stout, R. J. (1995). Planning effects on communication strategies: a shared mental models perspective. *Proceedings of the Human Factors and Ergonomics Society 39th Annual Meeting* (pp. 1278–82). Santa Monica, CA.
Taylor, R. M. (1990). Situational awareness rating technique (SART): the development of a tool for aircrew systems design. In AGARD-CP-478, *Situational Awareness in Aerospace Operations* (pp. 3-1–3-17). Neuilly Sur Seine, France, April.
Taylor, R. M., Finnie, S. & Hoy, C. (1997). Cognitive rigidity: the effects of mission planning and automation on cognitive control in dynamic situations. Presented at the 9th International Symposium on Aviation Psychology, April, Columbus, OH.
Uytterhoeven, G., de Vlaminck, M. & Javaux, D. (1995). Situation awareness evaluation for an operator support system in a nuclear power plant. In D. J. Garland & M. R.

Endsley (Eds), *Experimental Analysis and Measurement of Situation Awareness* (pp. 275–82). Daytona Beach: Embry-Riddle Aeronautical University Press.
Van Dijk, T. A. & Kintsch, W. (1983). *Strategies of Discourse Comprehension*. New York: Academic Press.
Veldhuyzen, W. & Stassen, H. G. (1977). The internal model concept: an application to modeling human control of large ships, 19, 367–80.
Vicente, K. J. (1992). Memory recall in a process control system: a measure of expertise and display effectiveness. *Memory & Cognition*, 20, Special Issue: Memory and Cognition Applied, 356–73.
Vicente, K. J. (1997). Memory recall in a process control system: a measure of expertise and display effectiveness. *Memory & Cognition*, 20, 356–73.
Vidulich, M. (1995). Subjective measures of situation awareness: the "6 o'clock problem". Paper presented at the International Conference on Experimental Analysis and Measurement of Situation Awareness, Daytona Beach, FL, November.
Vidulich, M., Dominguez, C., Vogel, E. & McMillan, G. (1994). Situation Awareness: Papers and Annotated Bibliography. Armstrong Laboratory Technical Report, AL/CF-TR-1994-0085.
Vidulich, M. A., McCoy, A. L. & Crabtree, M. S. (1995). Attentional control and situational awareness in a complex air combat simulation. In *Situation Awareness: Limitations and Enhancement in the Aviation Environment* (pp. 18.1–18.5). Brussels: AGARD Conference Proceedings.
Vortac, O. U., Edwards, M. B., Fuller, D. K. & Manning, C. A. (1993). Automation and cognition in air traffic control: an empirical investigation. *Applied Cognitive Psychology*, 7, 631–51.
Ward, N. J. & Parkes, A. M. (1994). Head-up displays and their automotive application: an overview of the human factors issues. *Accident Analysis and Prevention*, 26I, 703–18.
Warren, R. M. (1970). Perceptual restoration of missing speech sounds. *Science*, 167, 392–3.
Weintraub, D. J. & Ensing, M. (1987). *Human Factors in Head-up Display Design: The Book of HUD*. Ann Arbor, MI: CSERIAC, University of Michigan.
Wellens, A. R. (1993). Group situation awareness and distributed decision making: from military to civilian applications. In N. J. Castellan Jr (Ed.), *Individual and Group Decision Making: Current Issues* (pp. 267–91). Hillsdale, NJ: Lawrence Erlbaum.
Wickens, C. D. (1984). *Engineering Psychology and Human Performance*. Columbus, OH: Merrill.
Wickens, C. D. (1992). *Engineering Psychology and Human Performance* (2nd edn). New York: HarperCollins.
Wickens, C. D. (1996). Situation awareness: impact of automation and display technology. In *Situation Awareness: Limitations and Enhancement in the Aviation Environment* (pp. k2.1–k2.13). Brussels: AGARD Conference Proceedings.
Wickens, C. D., Mavor, A. S. & McGee, J. P. (Eds) (1997). *Flight to the Future: Human Factors in Air Traffic Control*. National Academy Press: Washington, DC.
Wilson, J. R. & Rutherford, A. (1989). Mental models: theory and application in human factors. *Human Factors*, 31, 617–34.
Witken, H. A., Goodenough, D. R. & Oltman, P. K. (1979). Psychological differentiation: current status. *Journal of Personality and Social Psychology*, 37, 1127–45.
Woodhouse, R. & Woodhouse, R. A. (1995). Navigation errors in relation to controlled flight into terrain (CFIT) accidents. *8th International Symposium on Aviation Psychology*. Columbus, OH, April.
Wright, D. L., Pleasants, F. & Gomez-Meza, M. (1990). Use of advanced visual cue sources in volleyball. *Journal of Sport & Exercise Psychology*, 12, 406–14.
Xiao, Y., Milgram, P. & Doyle, D. J. (1997). Planning behavior and its functional role in interactions with complex systems. *Transactions on Systems, Man, and Cybernetics – Part A: Systems and Humans*, 27, 313–24.
Yee, P. L., Hunt, E. & Pellegrino, J. W. (1991). Coordination cognitive information: task

effects and individual differences in integrating information from several sources. *Cognitive Psychology*, 23, 615–80.

Yntema, D. B. (1963). Keeping track of several things at once. *Human Factors*, 5, 7–17.

Zsambok, C. E. & Klein, G. (Eds) (1997). *Naturalistic Decision Making Expertise: Research and Applications*. Mahwah, NJ: Lawrence Erlbaum.

Chapter 11

Business Management

Stephen W. Gilliland
University of Arizona
and
David V. Day
Pennsylvania State University

Cognitive psychology has a long history of application in the field of business management. In 1958, March & Simon suggested that people are influenced by the organizations within which they work, and in turn organizations are shaped and defined by the people who work there. Further, they suggested that humans are complex information processors whose operations include decision making and problem solving, but whose capacity for processing and attention is limited. This notion of "bounded rationality" has been incorporated into many subsequent theories of management and organizational theory (cf. Walsh, 1988).

Since the work of March & Simon, cognitive psychology has influenced many areas of research in management, organizational behavior, and industrial/organizational psychology. In the 1960s and 1970s, research on employment interviews examined the impact of stereotypes and positive and negative information on interviewer decisions (Schmitt, 1976). Research on performance appraisal in the 1980s was dominated by studies of cognitive processes involved in acquiring performance information and generating ratings (Ilgen, Barnes-Farrell & McKellin, 1993). More recently, cognitive psychology has shaped the study of leadership (Lord & Maher, 1991), motivation (Kanfer & Ackerman, 1989), and training (Kraiger, Ford & Salas, 1993). So widespread has been this influence of cognitive psychology that in 1991 the Academy of Management established an interest group for managerial and organizational cognition. Members of this group study how individuals in organizations make sense of their experiences and how such processes interact with behaviors. Major topics of study come straight

Handbook of Applied Cognition, Edited by F. T. Durso, R. S. Nickerson, R. W. Schvaneveldt, S. T. Dumais, D. S. Lindsay and M. T. H. Chi.

Table 11.1 Cognitive Applications to Business Management Research

Domains of business management	Business management research area	Cognitive processes examined
Micro business management	• Interviewing • Performance appraisal • Decision making • Motivation • Training	• Information acquisition • Knowledge representation • Evaluation • Decision making
Macro business management	• Leadership perceptions • Strategic leadership • Organizational sensemaking	• Knowledge representation • Decision making

from cognitive psychology and include: attention, attribution, decision making, information processing, learning, memory, mental representations and images, perceptual and interpretative processes, social construction, and symbols.

The field of business management is often divided into two major domains that represent micro and macro levels of management. The micro side of management focuses on individual processes and decisions. Specific areas of study include individual motivation and decision making, training and development, and human resource practices such as selection and performance appraisal. The macro side of management focuses on organizational functioning and those individuals and decision makers (e.g. business leaders) who directly impact aspects of organizational functioning and related outcomes. Specific areas of study include leadership, strategic decision making, and organizational structure and culture. Although cognitive psychology has had the greatest influence on the micro side of management, recent research on macro issues has adopted a cognitive perspective.

The types of cognitive processes that have been examined in the field of business management are fairly representative of the field of cognitive psychology and include: information acquisition, representation, evaluation, and decision making. Table 11.1 provides an overview of the main management issues that have been examined from a cognitive perspective and also identifies the cognitive processes that have been considered. As can be seen, the micro issues of management have considered the range of cognitive processes from acquisition and representation to evaluation and decision making. Macro issues of management have tended to focus predominantly on knowledge representation and decision making. It is important to realize that although the cognitive processes considered are taken from cognitive psychology, the level of detail in examining these issues is often quite different. The "chunks" of information examined in micro-management research are considerably larger than those examined in traditional cognitive psychology and the chunks are even larger in macro-management research.

It is also important to consider the different goals of cognitive psychology and management research. Although the cognitive issues studied in business management are similar to those of cognitive psychology, the orientation and goals of this research are fundamentally different. Generally, the goal of much cognitive psychology is to understand human mental processes and the extent to which different contextual stimuli influence and shape these processes. In the field of business management, the goal is often to study organizations and the people, processes, and procedures that exist in organizations. Cognitive processes are studied as a means of gaining greater understanding of the way people respond to organizational demands. Most basically, then, whereas cognitive psychologists use contextual stimuli to understand cognitive processes, management researchers use cognitive processes to understand reactions to contextual stimuli.

One of the goals of this chapter is to share with applied cognitive researchers the theories and research methods that are used in cognitive management research. Although management researchers have tended to borrow theories from cognitive psychology, it is possible that applied cognitive researchers will be able to borrow some of the methods from cognitive management research.

This chapter is organized around the micro and macro domains of management research. For each domain, we examine the areas within which cognitive research has been applied. We also present examples of the different research methods used. Our review is not meant to be comprehensive, but rather to provide an overview with relevant examples of current research. For most of the topics we consider, detailed reviews of cognitive research are available and are cited in our presentation.

COGNITIVE APPROACHES TO MICRO ISSUES IN BUSINESS MANAGEMENT

Cognitive psychology can be found in most areas of micro research in business management and some researchers have even discussed the "cognitive revolution" of organizational behavior (Ilgen, Major & Tower, 1994). Rather than examine all of these areas, we focus our discussion on five research areas that have applied both cognitive theories and also cognitive psychology's research methods. These areas are: interviewing, performance appraisal, decision making, motivation, and training.

Interviewing

Employment interviews continue to be the most commonly used procedure for selecting among job applicants. The basic interview process involves:

1. collecting information from a job applicant
2. integrating and evaluating that information to form an impression of the applicant
3. making a hiring decision.

Researchers have long acknowledged the influence of a variety of cognitive biases on this judgment and decision process, including stereotyping, overweighing of negative information, primacy effects, and contrast effects (e.g. Wright, 1969). Considerable research in the 1960s and 1970s was aimed at demonstrating these influences. For example, Farr (1973) manipulated the order of positive and negative information that was present for hypothetical job applicants and found strong effects on participants' evaluations of the applicants. Much of this research has been criticized for being overly "microanalytical" and not generalizable to actual interview settings (e.g. Arvey & Campion, 1982; Schmitt, 1976).

More recent research has continued to investigate the cognitive processes of interviewers but has adopted an integrated perspective in which cognitive processes are considered in conjunction with social processes and interview outcomes (Dipboye, 1992). This work includes recent developments in cognitive psychology and considers information search processes, knowledge structures of the interviewer, interviewer attention, information categorization, attribution processes, information recall, judgments of applicant fit, and final decision making. Macan & Dipboye (1990) provide a good example of this more integrated approach to studying the interview process. They collected data from actual interviewers and job applicants at multiple points in the interview process and demonstrated the impact of interviewers' pre-interview impressions on post-interview evaluations. While this study demonstrates the overall influence of pre-interview impressions, it does not address specific cognitive processes that are involved. In a separate study, Macan and Dipboye (1988) focused on the information acquisition stage and demonstrated that interviewers ask different questions of applicants based on their credentials. These findings suggest that one way in which pre-interview impressions may influence post-interview evaluations is in the interview questioning (information gathering) phase.

Although Dipboye (1992) has done an effective job of outlining cognitive processes of interviewers, this cognitive perspective has not revolutionized interview research. Rather, research has identified a number of biases and limitations with interview judgments and then the focus has shifted toward ways of minimizing these limitations and improving the validity of interview judgments. By standardizing and structuring interview questions and scoring procedures the validity of interviews can be greatly improved (Campion, Palmer & Campion, 1997). Thus, current research designed to understand the interview process has taken a back seat to research designed to improve the interview process.

Performance Appraisal

By far, the greatest "cognitive revolution" in the micro side of business management has occurred in the area of performance appraisal. Like interviews, performance appraisals are a standard feature in most jobs in most organizations. Also like interviews, performance appraisals have been criticized for being overly subjective and prone to biases and errors (Cardy & Dobbins, 1994; Landy & Farr, 1980). In 1980, Landy & Farr published a major review of performance appraisal research that shifted the focus of research away from rating scales and rater training to the study of cognitive processes in appraisals. Other reviews in the early 1980s further developed this cognitive perspective (e.g. DeNisi, Cafferty

& Meglino, 1984; Ilgen & Feldman, 1983) and dozens of research studies were conducted on raters' cognitive processes. This research can be roughly sorted into three phases: attention and observation, storage and memory, and recall and evaluation (for a thorough review, see Ilgen et al., 1993).

Attention and Observation

Attention and observation is the process through which raters acquire information on the ratee and is of demonstrated importance to appraisal accuracy. Research demonstrates that attention and observation can be influenced by:

- characteristics of the ratee (e.g. prototypicality)
- the rater (e.g. knowledge of the ratee's job)
- the rating scale (e.g. types of rating dimensions)
- the setting (e.g. purpose of the appraisal) (Ilgen et al., 1993).

Although much of this research infers attention and observation from recall, some research has more directly examined information acquisition (e.g. Werner, 1994).

For example, Kozlowski & Ford (1991) used a process tracing procedure to monitor information search. Information on hypothetical ratees was presented in a computer controlled information matrix (e.g. *n* ratees by *n* dimensions of information) and raters were able to acquire as much information as they needed to complete their evaluations. The computer recorded the amount of information raters accessed for each ratee. This study demonstrated that the amount of information that participants accessed was a function of both the amount of prior knowledge raters had of each ratee and whether the ratee's prior performance was good or poor.

These process tracing methods are useful in that they enable the researcher to isolate the pre-decision information search processes, but it is reasonable to question the external validity of this research. Does searching for information on a computer have any correspondence to the observation of performance of a subordinate on the job?

Storage and Memory

Performance appraisals typically occur some time after job performance is actually observed, so information encoding and memory can also influence appraisal accuracy. As with attention and observation, research indicates that encoding and memory are influenced by characteristics of the ratee, rater, scale, and setting. Also similar to attention and observation research is that much research has indirectly examined encoding and memory through measures of recall.

One interesting study that was able to examine both cognitive processes and practical applications considered the role of diary keeping in performance appraisal (DeNisi, Robbins & Cafferty, 1989). In a laboratory study, raters kept diaries of job performance information that were organized by ratee, by task, or by whatever system the rater chose. Cognitive storage was inferred from the structure of recalled information (by computing adjusted ratio of clustering indices – ARC). Information that was presented in an unstructured format tended to be organized in memory in the same pattern as it was organized in the performance diary. Further, raters preferred organizing information in diaries (and therefore in memory) by ratees, rather than by tasks, and this tended to result in more accurate recall and performance ratings. DeNisi & Peters (1996) recently replicated this finding in a field experiment with managers who kept diaries for three months and then rated actual subordinates.

Recall and Evaluation

The final cognitive process examined in performance appraisal research is recall and evaluation. By far, this is the stage that has received the most research attention, probably because it is the most important stage from a practical perspective of rater accuracy. Researchers have examined a variety of issues, including:

- ratee characteristics (e.g. race and gender)
- rater characteristics (e.g. intelligence and confidence)
- types of scale
- purpose of the appraisals (see Ilgen et al., 1993).

With an applied sample of subordinates rating their middle level managers, Mount & Thompson (1987) examined the influence of congruence with a cognitive schema on the quality of performance ratings. Congruence was defined in terms of the extent to which managers' behavior matched subordinates' schema of how a manager should behave (on dimensions such as scheduling and assigning work efficiently). Quality of performance ratings was assessed in terms of the difference between the subordinates' ratings and the averaged ratings of all subordinates, the manager's supervisor, and a self-rating by the manager. Congruence was related to rating accuracy, with greater accuracy occurring when performance was congruent with the subordinate's schema. While many interesting results have emerged from this research, rather than developing a coherent picture of the process of recall and evaluation, we have ended up with a laundry list of factors that can influence recall and evaluation.

After approximately a decade of cognitive research on performance appraisals, many researchers criticized this direction in appraisal research for making little contribution to the improvement of performance appraisals in organizations (e.g. Murphy & Cleveland, 1991). Ilgen and colleagues (1994) suggest that this criticism is valid, but is also misdirected in that cognitive research was not intended to offer direct solutions to appraisal problems, but rather to gain an understanding of rating processes. Intervention or solution-oriented research can then build on the understanding provided by cognitive research, and in the process this may develop further understanding of the cognitive processes.

Sulsky & Day (1992, 1994) provide a good example of this next step in performance appraisal research with their studies of frame-of-reference training.

Prior research has demonstrated that giving raters a common schema or frame-of-reference for conducting the ratings can improve rating accuracy. Sulsky & Day's research demonstrate that these gains do not come through improved memory of individual behaviors (recognition accuracy was actually lower as a result of the training) or organization and storage of information (assessed by the clustering of free-recall data). After examining accuracy and memory effects over time, Sulsky & Day suggested that frame-of-reference training may promote on-line impression formation (Hastie & Park, 1986), and these impressions are retained in memory and accessed when making ratings. Without frame-of-reference training, raters may use more memory-based judgment and rely on degraded memories of specific individual behaviors. These results provide practical suggestions for improving rating accuracy and also have theoretical implications in terms of the link between memory and judgment.

Decision Making

Decision making research spans the entire range of applied cognitive psychology and is addressed in detail in a separate chapter in this volume (see Rohrbaugh & Shanteau, 1999, this volume). In the area of business management this research has addressed individual decisions such as job search and job choice (Stevens & Beach, 1996), or employee turnover (Lee & Mitchell, 1994), as well as organizational decisions regarding company culture (Weatherly & Beach, 1996), facility location/relocation (Gilliland, Wood & Schmitt, 1994), and business strategy (addressed later in this chapter). There is also a sizable body of research that addresses basic decision-making processes using business management decisions. For example, Gilliland & Schmitt (1993) examined the influence of information redundancy on pre-decision information search behavior in a simulated job choice decision. Cognitive processes including information acquisition, storage and recall, combination and evaluation, and decision making have all been considered in both the basic and, to a lesser extent, the applied decision research.

Research methods in management decision making are also widely varied. A number of researchers have used process tracing techniques to investigate pre-decision information search (for a review, see Ford, Schmitt, Schechtman, Hults & Doherty, 1989). With this technique, information on decision alternatives must be accessed by decision makers, such that the amount and order of information accessed, as well as the time spent examining each piece of information are recorded. Amount, order, and access time all provide evidence of pre-decision information search strategies, and the effects of various contextual constraints on these strategies can be examined.

Policy capturing techniques have also been a common means of examining decision behavior, but instead of focusing on information search processes, policy capturing addresses information combination and evaluation processes. With policy capturing, judgments or decisions are regressed on the information cues presented to decision makers. The regressions weights associated with information cues are interpreted as indicators of the importance of each cue. For example, Hitt & Barr (1989) investigated information combination in managerial selection decisions by presenting line and staff managers videotaped presentations of hypothetical job applicants. Job-relevant and job-irrelevant variables were manipulated across the applicants. Policy capturing with main effects for job-relevant and job-irrelevant variables, as well as higher order interactions, was used to examine information combination in the prediction of favorability ratings and starting salary recommendations. One interesting methodological advance in the policy capturing literature is the use of meta-analytic techniques to test hypotheses about clusters of decision makers (Viswesvaran, Schmidt & Deshpande, 1994). In addition to process tracing and policy capturing, many other methods have been used to study decision processes. Unfortunately, much of the decision-making literature exists in isolated pockets without common theory or even common research methods to unite it.

One theory of decision making that attempts to unify formal models of decision making with cognitive notions of schemas and mental representations is Beach and Mitchell's image theory (Beach, 1990, 1996; Mitchell & Beach, 1990). This theory suggests that decisions result from matching alternatives with decision makers' images of what they value, what they want to achieve, and how they plan to get there. If the alternative violates these images it is screened out of the decision process and does not receive further evaluation. If the alternative matches these images, and is the only alternative available, it is adopted. Finally, if more than one alternative matches these images then they are evaluated more thoroughly and formally to see which alternative is most "profitable." This intuitive model of decision making helps explain and unite many different observations and results in the decision literature. It has also been applied to a variety of managerial and organizational decisions (for a summary, see Beach, 1996).

Motivation

Vroom introduced expectancy theory to organizational researchers in 1964, and since that time cognitive and social cognitive theories have dominated motivation research. Much of the research and theories of the 1970s and 1980s have been integrated into "metatheories" or integrative models that rely heavily on cognitive psychology (for a recent review, see Kanfer, 1994). Examples include control theory, goal-setting theory, and the resource allocation model. Based on the work of Carver & Scheier (1981), control theory is a theory of self-regulation based on negative feedback loops and a drive to reduce the discrepancies between one's standards (goals) and perceived performance. These control loops are nested in hierarchies, such that discrepancy reduction in short-term goals can lead to the attainment of long-term goals. Klein (1989) provided a thorough review of control theory in the area of work motivation and a number of researchers have demonstrated support for the basic control theory mechanisms (e.g. Campion & Lord, 1982; Hollenbeck, 1989).

Goal-setting theory has been developed by Locke & Latham (1990) and suggests that task performance is directed by conscious goals that individuals set and try to attain. Over 400 studies of the basic goal-setting process demonstrate that specific, difficult goals lead to greater performance than vague "do your best" goals or easy goals. Self-efficacy, goal commitment, feedback, and a variety of situational constraints are all central to the goal-setting process. Goals have been demonstrated to influence behavior through individual effort, persistence, direction of attention, and strategy development. For example, Gilliland & Landis (1992) assigned easy or difficult quality and quantity goals to participants completing a complex, multi-trial decision task. In addition to observed effects of goals on performance quality, goals also influenced decision strategy development.

With both control theory and goal-setting theory, recent interest appears to have waned or at least shifted to different problems and issues. For example, control theory has been applied to the study of stress in organizations (Edwards, 1992). Current research on goal setting has focused on the effectiveness of goals with complex tasks. Research has demonstrated that with some complex tasks, goal setting can actually inhibit performance (perhaps because the goals limit effective strategy search and development). In an interesting study, DeShon & Alexander (1996) distinguished between complex tasks that require explicit versus implicit learning and demonstrated that when the process is explicit, goal setting can be effective with complex tasks. This research demonstrates the power of cognitive theories (in this case explicit versus implicit learning) for explaining complex and unusual results.

The resource allocation model proposed by Kanfer & Ackerman (1989) relies heavily on cognitive psychology and suggests that motivation is the process of allocating a limited pool of time and effort to various tasks. This integrative model includes the basic notions of goal-setting and control theories, as well as cognitive processes such as resource limitations and skill acquisition and attention. In a series of studies, Kanfer & Ackerman (1989) demonstrated support for the basic processes in their model and demonstrated that the effectiveness of goal setting is dependent on both ability and the individual's stage in the learning process. Although these researchers have conducted additional research on this model (Kanfer, Ackerman, Murtha, Dugdale & Nelson, 1994), it has not been widely adopted.

Training

The area of training is the most recent area of micro business management to apply theories and methods of cognitive psychology. In 1989, Howell & Cooke demonstrated how current research in cognitive psychology on information processing, memory, and problem solving have relevance for research on training. The appropriateness of this application is evidenced by the widespread application of cognitive psychology to the field of instructional design. However, training researchers have been slow to adopt this cognitive perspective.

More recently, Kraiger et al. (1993) developed a model for training evaluation that was based heavily on cognitive psychology. Three types of learning outcomes were proposed:

- *cognitive* outcomes, which include verbal knowledge, knowledge organization, and cognitive strategies.

- *skill-based* outcomes are defined in terms of compilation and automaticity outcomes since they may be based on theories of skill development that suggest a progression from initial acquisition, through compilation, to automaticity.
- *affective* outcomes, which include attitudinal reactions and motivation.

In addition to defining these types of training outcomes, Kraiger and colleagues (1993) propose methods for measuring these outcomes. For example, knowledge organization can be assessed in terms of mental models (Johnson-Laird, 1983), or patterns of association among related concepts. The Pathfinder analytical technique, which creates a link-weighted network based on ratings of relatedness, is one approach that can be used to assess these models. Trainees' models can be compared to a prototype or the instructor's model to examine the impact of training on knowledge organization.

Given that this extension of cognitive psychology to training evaluation is relatively recent, work adopting this framework has not yet been published, although some research has been presented at national conferences on this topic. For example, Braverman & Goldstein (1997) examined changes in trainees' mental models as a result of training. Expected changes were observed in trainees' mental models, but these changes were unrelated to transfer of training to the performance setting. This is clearly an area to watch for developments in applied cognitive research.

Summary

It is clear that cognitive psychology has been applied to many areas of micro business management research. Areas such as motivation and decision making have long been dominated by interest in cognitive processes. However, in other areas of micro business management research, there appears to be a life cycle for interest in the cognitive perspective. Interview researchers borrowed some basic concepts of cognitive biases, and after investigating these biases, attention was turned toward looking at how to improve the interview process. Similarly, in performance appraisal research, cognitive psychology was adopted to understand the appraisal process, but after approximately a decade of research attention turned to more practical investigations of performance appraisal. In the area of training, researchers have only recently adopted the cognitive perspective and it will be interesting to see if a similar cycle occurs in that area. As with training, researchers in macro issues of business management have only recently applied a cognitive perspective.

COGNITIVE APPROACHES TO MACRO ISSUES IN BUSINESS MANAGEMENT

In contrast to the micro side of business management that applies cognitive psychology to study individual performance and decision making, research on macro issues in business management focuses on organization-wide decisions and performance. Specific areas in which cognitive approaches have been adopted include: leadership perceptions, strategic leadership, and organizational sense-making.

Leadership Perceptions

It is not an overstatement to conclude that the body of leadership literature is both vast and diverse, with more than 3000 published studies on the topic (Bass, 1990). Despite the multi-disciplinary appeal of leadership, relatively few approaches have considered the cognitive processes of leaders or followers as primary mechanisms in the leadership process. One notable exception is the model of leadership perceptions advanced by Lord and associates (e.g. Lord, Binning, Rush & Thomas, 1978; Lord, Foti & De Vader, 1984; Lord & Maher, 1991). The central tenet of Lord's theory is that leadership is the process of being perceived by others as a leader (Lord & Maher, 1991, p. 11). Although there are many ways by which leaders are able to influence followers and ultimately enhance individual, group, and organizational performance, these leadership processes are predicated on followers' granting of another latitude for influence to occur. To be effective as a leader, an individual first must be perceived by others as leader-like; otherwise, followers resist or reject an aspiring leader's influence attempts.

The cognitive foundation of Lord's model of leadership perceptions is categorization theory (Cantor & Mischel, 1979; Rosch, 1978). People develop leadership prototypes as part of their implicit leadership theories (ILTs), which are used in categorizing others as leaders (Lord et al., 1984). The more a target's traits, behaviors, or performance matches a perceiver's leadership prototype, or is consistent with other aspects of the perceiver's ILT, the greater the likelihood that the target will be perceived as a leader. Leadership perceptions are formed through either relatively automatic recognition-based processes using prototype matching, or by means of more controlled, inferential processing using comprehensive causal (i.e. attributional) analysis (Lord & Maher, 1991). Whereas traits and behaviors are used as the primary data source in recognition-based leadership perceptions, events and outcomes are the primary determinants of whether or not someone is seen as a leader based on inferential processes (see Figure 11.1).

An ingenious example of the importance of ILTs and inferential processes in the formation of leadership perceptions is found in investigations of the *performance cue* effect (e.g. Binning & Lord, 1980; Lord et al., 1978; Phillips & Lord, 1982). In these studies, participants observe a videotaped group interaction and are subsequently asked to evaluate the designated leader using a standard leadership questionnaire (e.g. Leader Behavior Description Questionnaire: Stogdill, 1963). Participants are told that the videotaped group either performed second best or second worst of twenty or more participating groups. Given that all participants watched the identical videotaped group it was thought that any differences associated with the performance cue would indicate a leadership rating bias in the direction of participants' ILTs. Results consistently showed that

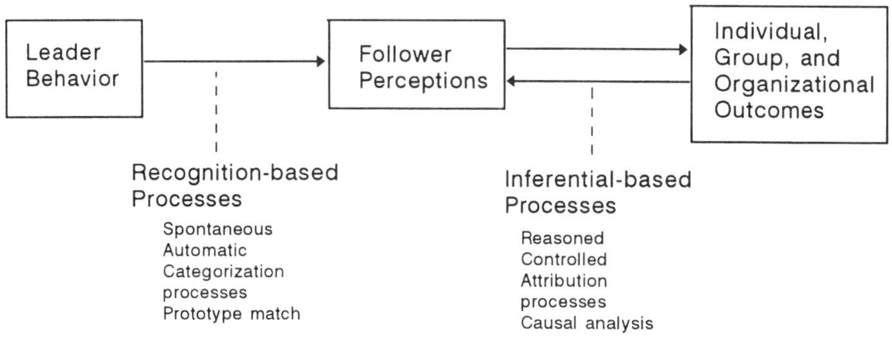

Figure 11.1 The influences of recognition- and inference-based processes on leadership perceptions of followers.

those participants who were told that they were observing a high-performing group rated the leader's behavior more positively than those who supposedly observed a poor-performing group.

Effective group performance is a central aspect of many individual's ILTs. When group – or organization (Meindl & Ehrlich, 1987) – performance is thought to be good, observers subsequently infer that a likely reason for this effectiveness is strong leadership. The performance cue literature is important in demonstrating that followers are not objective processors of leader behavior, and that salient outcomes and events often bias leadership perceptions. An implication of such findings is that data gathered using questionnaire-based measures of leadership are suspect.

Additional research has demonstrated that leadership perceptions can also be formed at encoding, consistent with a recognition-based route to leadership perceptions. While watching a videotape in which a target person interacted with two other group members, Cronshaw & Lord (1987) had participants depress a hand-held button when they saw "meaningful" behavior. The definition of what constituted meaningful behavior was deliberately left ambiguous to assess participants' natural encoding of stimuli. The prototypicality of leader behavior was manipulated on the tape by scripting various numbers of prototypical and antiprototypical leader behaviors. In addition to the on-line measure of encoding, written ratings were collected of participants' general leadership impression (i.e. the primary measure of leadership perceptions) as well as open- and close-ended causal ascriptions. Results were interpreted as supporting a recognition-based categorization process in explaining leadership perceptions over a more controlled attributional model. This supports the proposition that categorization is the primary process in determining leadership perceptions, given that it is relatively automatic and occurs prior to attributional reasoning (see also Smith & Miller, 1983). These results also demonstrate the value of measuring leadership perceptions in an on-line fashion.

The topic of changes in leadership perceptions has been the focus of recent research. Hanges, Lord, Day, Sipe, Smith & Brown (1997) adopted dynamical systems theory, which is concerned with the nature and study of change in social systems (Vallacher & Nowak, 1994a), as a theoretical framework in studying gender effects on changes in leadership perceptions. Similar to the methods of Cronshaw & Lord (1987), an on-line measure of leadership perceptions was used. The measurement instrument was adopted from previous work evaluating attitudes as a stream of social judgments (Vallacher & Nowak, 1994b). While watching a series of nine videotaped vignettes of a four-person decision-making group, study participants were asked to move a computer's cursor to indicate their perceptions of who was the group leader. Measures were taken ten times per second, and the distance between the cursor and the target of interest (either a male or female leader) was used as an inverse measure of how strongly the target was perceived as leader (cf. Hovland, Janis & Kelley, 1953). In addition, four process measures (i.e. velocity, acceleration, stability, and shifts-in-leadership) were developed to help quantify each participant's pattern of cursor movements within each vignette. The Hanges et al. (1997) study explored whether raters would identify and categorize a female emerging as group leader as quickly as they identify a male emerging as group leader. In addition, the specific type of change process was of interest. It was hypothesized that raters would hold to the perception of a male leader, as a female leader began emerging, until evidence was overwhelming, which would lead to a sudden, discontinuous change in perceptions. The change from a female to a male emergent leader was hypothesized to be a smoother and more continuous process. Data were modeled using mathematical catastrophe theory techniques (Cobb, 1981; Thom, 1975).

The results of the Hanges et al. (1997) study supported the value of the Lord model of leadership perceptions in understanding gender bias in leadership evaluation. Even though participants watched and evaluated the same vignettes, they were more sensitive to leadership behaviors exhibited by a male than a female emergent leader. The female leader had to exhibit more leadership behaviors before participants began to change their leadership ratings. The use of an on-line measure in this study was especially helpful in providing information that was unobtainable using traditional leadership questionnaires. In particular, the on-line measure provided data that avoided problems associated with inferential processes (i.e. attributional biases associated with participants' ILTs) and were sufficiently sensitive to demonstrate support for discontinuous as well as continuous change patterns.

In summary, research investigating the cognitive influences on leadership perceptions has helped to integrate and apply a wide range of cognitive principles including categorization, encoding and perception, attribution, dynamical systems theory, gender bias, and discontinuous change and catastrophe modeling. None of the many other leadership approaches have adopted such a cognitively grounded orientation to the topic. This is due in large part to the guiding theoretical assumption that leadership is primarily a perceptually based phenomenon, as compared with other approaches that view it as a quality of the leader (e.g. behavioral style or trait), the match between leader style and follower or situational characteristics, or the relationship that develops between a leader and a follower. Another area of leadership that has become increasingly infused with cognitive theory is strategic leadership theory.

Strategic Leadership

Strategic leadership theory is primarily concerned with the influence of top-level managers on organizations, including individual decision making, organizational policy, and strategy. A fundamental assumption of this approach is that organizations are a reflection of top managers (Hambrick & Mason, 1984), and that aspects of executives' cognitions, personality, and personal agendas shape the strategic direction and performance of organizations (Cannella & Monroe, 1997). The origination of strategic leadership theory has often been credited to Child (1972), who first proposed a formal strategic choice model, although interest in top-level executives and their effects on contemporary business organizations can be traced as far back as Barnard (1938). More recently, organizational scholars have argued for the importance of managerial cognition in strategic decision making (Schwenk, 1988; Stubbart, 1989). Despite such urgings, many basic aspects of managerial thinking remain under-researched.

There are comprehensive reviews of the managerial cognition literature (e.g. Ungson, Braunstein & Hall, 1981; Walsh, 1995), as well as of the more specific topic of strategic decision making (Cowan, Fiol & Walsh, 1992). Day & Lord (1988) also outline how the cognitive structures and processes of top-level managers can affect organizational performance. (Refer to these sources for comprehensive reviews of the relevant literature.) The focus of this chapter is on the recent empirical literature, with a particular emphasis on the various methodologies used to study managerial cognition at upper organizational levels. Because of the challenges associated with access to and assessment of top-level managers, many of the more traditional laboratory methods used to understand cognitive processing are infeasible. Out of necessity, researchers have been innovative in their approaches, using both quantitative and qualitative techniques (for a review of methods for mapping strategic thought, see Huff, 1990).

Quantitative Methods

Several studies have examined the perceptual processes of top-level managers using card sorting procedures (Rosenberg, 1982) to uncover the problem categories used by executives. Walsh (1988) had 121 senior level managers sort through a set of 50 cards, each with a different factor thought to be broadly related to the success of organizations (e.g. profitability, product line, strategic planning) to help articulate their "belief structures." Managers were asked to:

1. sort cards into two piles (important versus relatively unimportant factors to success)
2. sort the important pile into smaller categories of related factors
3. rank the categories in terms of their perceived importance.

The content of managers' belief structures was identified using individual differences multidimensional scaling (i.e. IDSORT). The effects of these belief structures on managerial information processing was assessed by examining the problem identifications, information use, and information requests from a case analysis completed by participants. Contrary to the widely held notion of bounded rationality (i.e. selective perception based on functional speciality; Dearborn & Simon, 1958; March & Simon, 1958), managers tended to have complex belief structures that did not constrain their conceptualizations of organizational issues. That is, analyses across several content groups (human relations, accounting/finance, marketing, and generalists) revealed no significant differences in the type of information used to solve a business case, and only limited support for the proposition that managers would search for additional information that was from the same content domain as their belief structures' content.

Cowan (1990) attempted to develop a taxonomy of organizational problems using a similar card sorting procedure. His approach involved a problem generation phase, followed by a "free" sorting phase (i.e. no guidelines or a priori categories were imposed) that was completed by a second sample of executives. Multidimensional scaling was used to examine the underlying structure of the 78 problem statements. Results suggested six bipolar dimensions as the best fitting solution:

- marketing–human resources
- operations–marketing
- production–MIS
- strategic–customer
- accounting–communications
- management–external/environmental.

The dimensions were then combined into an overall organizational problem classification structure, demonstrating the strength of links between problem dimensions. A practical implication of this type of classification structure is in training management students (e.g. MBAs) to develop a meaningful taxonomy for classifying business problems.

Day & Lord (1992) used sorting times as well as the mean number and variability of problem categories in comparing the knowledge structures of experts (i.e. chief executive officers in the machine tool industry) and novices (i.e. MBA students). Experts were shown to engage in substantially faster categorizations than novices – over five minutes faster across the 28 problems – and to have greater variability in the number of categories used to sort the problems. For experts, the number of categories was positively related to the number of different product and service offerings of their organizations. These findings suggest a link between the cognitive knowledge structures of top-level managers and organizational strategy, although the causal direction cannot be determined from these correlational data.

The repertory grid technique (Fransella & Bannister, 1977; Kelly, 1955) has also been suggested as a technique for eliciting the content and structure of cognitive systems (Reger, 1990). It was originally proposed as a collection of semistructured interview techniques that allow a researcher to extract the cognitive structure used by a strategic decision maker to interpret a given situation, and allows the respondent to provide definitions about the content elements and underlying cognitive structure. It is a technique best suited for idiographic interpretation. Despite the advantages associated with the repertory grid technique (e.g. it does not impose the researcher's cognitive frame) it has not been widely used.

Borman (1987) used a variant of the repertory grid technique in eliciting the content of categories used by a sample of US Army officers in making performance judgments. The officers independently generated a list of "personal work constructs" that were thought to differentiate between effective and ineffective noncommissioned officers. Participants then rated the similarity of their constructs with a reference set of performance, ability, and personal characteristics concepts. Correlations were computed between similarity ratings and the resulting matrix was eventually factor analyzed, yielding six interpretable content factors. Borman's study is unusual in that it adopted an exploratory, inductive, and primarily descriptive approach in an attempt to understand the content of performance categories used by experts in a domain to judge the work performance of subordinates.

Another recommended technique for mapping strategic thought quantitatively is content analysis. As with the repertory grid procedure, there are numerous possible versions of the general technique using either written communication, interview transcripts, or other verbal protocols. Analysis is typically conducted on two levels: the manifest content, which examines surface characteristics of words (e.g. frequency counts); and latent content, which is concerned with the underlying semantics of the text (Erdener & Dunn, 1990). A relevant application of content analysis was reported by Isenberg (1986), who compared the "think aloud" protocols of general managers and undergraduate business students as they solved a short business case. The protocols (ranging from 767 to 4490 words in length; mean = 1910) were scored using a 17-category coding scheme that included dimensions such as information focus (requests or repeats specific information), clarifies, and evaluates. Managers were found to be more action-oriented than students in that their protocols reflected more immediate action planning. In addition, the managers used fewer words to reflect on the task process than students, and engaged in more conditional reasoning. An advantage of using this type of content analysis approach is that it allows for greater insight into the cognitive processes of managers, and not just the content of their strategic thinking.

Finally, a number of studies have provided insight into strategic thinking through the use of survey questionnaires. Thomas & McDaniel (1990) tested the hypothesis that organizational strategy and the information processing structure of top management teams in the hospital industry were related to the strategic issue labels used by CEOs. Strategic labeling is extremely important in strategic leadership because it is used to categorize and evaluate strategic issues. For example, labeling an issue in relatively positive terms might denote a perceived strategic opportunity, whereas labeling the same issue in negative terms would denote a perceived threat (Dutton & Jackson, 1987). In this study, information processing structure was measured with nine survey items (e.g. Can decision making be characterized as participative? Is there a free and open exchange of ideas among group members about strategic issues?) that were scaled using a seven-point Likert format. Responses across the nine items were scored such that higher scores indicated a "high capacity for information processing" (p. 295). Results demonstrated empirical linkages between information processing capacity and different strategy types. However, questions can be raised regarding how well cognitive information processing can be measured using survey questionnaires. Additional *process*-oriented research is needed before any strong claims can be made of a link between top-management team information processing and organizational strategy. Furthermore, future researchers should consider testing hypothesized linkages between information processing, strategy, and firm performance.

Questionnaire-based approaches have also been used to study the cognitive categorization and perceptual accuracy (e.g. Sutcliffe, 1994) of top managers. For example, Porac and associates (Porac & Thomas, 1994; Porac, Thomas, Wilson, Paton & Kanfer, 1995) used a variety of objective rating procedures to capture the underlying structure used by managers in defining and categorizing rival firms. This type of questionnaire-based research is more appropriate for enlightening researchers on issues of content, structure, and accuracy, but less so when the central focus is on cognitive processes.

Qualitative Methods

A trend has steadily developed toward the more accepted use of qualitative methods in the study of managerial cognition and strategic thought. Most qualitative research uses some form of grounded theory (Glaser & Strauss, 1967) and inductive methods to impose meaning on a given topic (e.g. Butterfield, Trevino & Ball, 1996; Eisenhardt, 1989). Qualitative studies typically are not concerned with hypothesis testing; instead, such studies have theory development through thick description, explanation, and critique as the primary objective. The main source of data for qualitative studies tends to be the interview, but can also take the form of written materials and observations. There are four predominant techniques of analysis – ethnomethodology, semiotic analysis, dramaturgical analysis, and deconstruction (Feldman, 1995) – which have been used (albeit sparingly) in the recent literature on managerial and organizational cognition.

Ethnography assumes that organizational and occupational norms shape individual and collective cognition. Ethnomethodologists are concerned with how fundamental norms and beliefs (i.e. culture) are developed, maintained, and changed (Feldman, 1995). The actual content of such norms is of less perceived value than the processes that shape their development and use. The specific methods of ethnography have their origins in anthropology and sociology, but have also been used successfully to understand (retrospectively) the thought processes and decision making of individuals.

A recent and highly acclaimed example of this type of work is Diane Vaughan's (1996) book, *The Challenger Launch Decision*. For her analysis, Vaughan read interview transcripts and conducted her own interviews of administrators, managers, and engineers who played key roles in the space shuttle's launch decision; she also reviewed previous published and unpublished accounts of the incident and analyzed documents from NASA, Morton Thiokol (manufacturer of the O-ring), and the Marshall Space Flight Center. Her primary data sources consisted of more than 122 000 pages of transcripts, reports, and documentation. The result is a "brilliant and disturbing book" (Sagan, 1997) that uncovers an incremental descent into poor judgment supported by a culture of high-risk technology and the gradual normalization of deviance. It is a stunning and provocative assessment of how culture shapes cognition (also see Hutchins, 1995, for an analysis of how Navy culture shapes the cognitions of ship navigators).

Semiotics is "concerned with everything that can be taken as a sign" where a sign substitutes for something else (Eco, 1976, p. 3). A fundamental assumption of the semiotic approach is that surface signs are manifestations of underlying culture (Feldman, 1995). An introduction to method and a detailed presentation of steps in carrying out narrative semiotic analysis is provided by Fiol (1990), who has used the technique to reach a deeper understanding of the corporate language used in joint venturing (Fiol, 1989). An overarching goal of semiotics is not to lead the researcher to discover new facts, but to consider relationships that had not been previously acknowledged (Feldman, 1995).

There are three primary methods that have been used by semioticians for interpreting qualitative data:

1. Semiotic *clustering* (Manning, 1987) is based on constructing a table with three columns:

- competing meanings – i.e. denotative meanings or signs
- connotative meanings – i.e. metaphor and metonymy
- institutional concerns – i.e. organizational issues related to denotative and connotative meanings.

The table should help a researcher make connections between the issues represented in the three columns. Feldman (1995) provides an example of how semiotic cluster analysis can be used to link the common ways that people talk about buildings (denotative meaning), what people really mean by these terms (connotative meanings), and the relationships to important issues in residence education.

2. *Chain* analysis is often used to map how underlying meaning and structure are represented in commonplace signs. Barley (1983) employed a chain analysis in examining the semiotics of funeral work, with a particular interest in the kinds of signs used by funeral directors to make funeral scenes appear natural and normal. The overall goal of directors – what might be termed an institutional concern – was to alleviate the stress of survivors by attempting to "recreate metaphorically the system of metonymical signs that we take as indices of peaceful sleep" (p. 403). Building his chain analysis on the assumption that signs are relatively meaningless unless they can be contrasted with other signs in a system, Barley compared the domains of a living sleeping person with that of a dead person using the basic semiotic tools of denotation, connotation, metonymy, metaphor, and opposition.

3. The semiotic *square* was developed by Greimas (1987). The square is used to describe a system of rules, or a so-called grammar based on *contradictories* (i.e. oppositions), through which meaning is produced. The four basic components of a semiotic square are:

- things that are prescribed
- things that are prohibited
- things that are not prescribed
- things that are not prohibited.

Although too complex to describe in sufficient detail here (see Feldman, 1995, pp. 33–9; for applications, see Greimas, 1987, pp. 48–62), the square is especially useful in illuminating oppositions. Feldman claims that perhaps the best use of a semiotic square "is in exploring the differences between sets of rules at different levels or in different parts of an organization" (p. 40).

It is important to recognize that the different semiotic methods can be used in conjunction with each other in constructing interpretations. Whereas all three methods assume that signs are manifestations of an underlying structure and that opposition is an important concern in understanding this structure, it is likely that the various methods will lead to differing interpretations of the underlying structure. A predominant theme in organizational semiotics, however, is that macro-level phenomena profoundly shape individuals' perceptions and interpretations of their work environment.

Dramaturgical analysis is based on the metaphor of performance (e.g. organizational rituals) as producers of meaning (Feldman, 1995). On the other hand, the deconstruction analytical technique (as compared with literary theory) is accomplished through a close reading of a text – whether it be a verbal exchange, action, or a written document – to open it so that the reader "can see the pattern of conflicting relationships" (Kilduff, 1993, p. 16). Neither technique has been widely used in the organizational literature, although there are precedents (e.g. Martin, 1990). Boje (1995) used aspects of dramaturgy and deconstruction in his analysis of the stories told by one of the most visible storytelling organizations in the world: Walt Disney enterprises. The dramaturgical aspects concern the public performances of key stakeholders such as Walt and Roy Disney, Michael Eisner, and Jack Kinney (former Disney artist who wrote a critical account of the early years at Disney) with deconstruction aimed primarily at surfacing previously marginalized voices and stories within the Disney organization. A key message in the article is that there are many struggling stories within this – or any – organization, which mask meaning not only for internal actors but also for external customers.

Recent work has taken a dramaturgical perspective on charismatic leadership (Gardner & Avolio, 1998). In particular, the roles of the environment (set), the leader (actor), and followers (audience) contribute jointly to constructing a charismatic relationship. This is an especially interesting approach because it is based on the assumption that leadership is an emergent, relational phenomenon that is played out around leader impression management and follower identification within a particular environmental backdrop or setting. As such, charismatic leadership is not the sole property of an actor (i.e. leader), or completely explainable as an attributional bias on the part of perceivers (i.e. followers). Instead, charisma emerges through expressive behavior as a natural part of social interaction.

Organizational Sensemaking

There has been a recent move from basic cognitive research on managerial and organizational issues to a more eclectic, context-specific – and perhaps post-modern – means of understanding organizational sensemaking. As defined by Weick (1995), the concept of sensemaking literally means "the making of sense" (p. 4). A prominent interpretation of sensemaking involves the study of how stimuli are placed within some social framework or frame-of-reference as a means of actively structuring objects and events. Sensemaking research is not bound by the traditional methods and practices of cognitive psychology. Instead, it seeks to understand the functioning of people in their natural environments; as such, sensemaking is inherently a context-specific process.

Sensemaking is grounded in both individual and social activity. It is enactive and ongoing, but at the same time retrospective. Of the seven properties of sensemaking proposed by Weick (1995), two in particular differentiate it from basic cognitive psychology. Sensemaking is thought to be grounded in identity construction, which means that it is concerned with relational issues of voice, justice, and power (Sampson, 1993), and not only with processes that occur "in the head." In addition, the fundamental criterion of sensemaking is that it is driven by plausibility rather than accuracy. As a result, it is oriented toward an interpretivist, as compared with a functionalist, scientific paradigm (Gioia & Pitre, 1990). Within an interpretivist paradigm, meaning is socially constructed and "truth" is relative. Different individuals are likely to make sense of the same event in very different ways.

The sensemaking literature is in the early stages of development, and relatively few studies taking this orientation have been published to date; however, there are several notable examples with relevance to the central issues of leadership and strategic thought. Gioia & Thomas (1996) used qualitative and quantitative methods to understand identity, image, and strategic issue interpretation among top management teams in higher education. Their study progressed from an inductive, grounded theory approach (case study) to a theory-driven and generalizable study of over 600 executives from more than 350 colleges and universities (questionnaire surveys). The results of the Gioia & Thomas study help clarify the effects of perceptions of organizational identity and image (especially desired future organization image) on the sensemaking processes of top management teams during strategic change. Those authors also suggest that important issues are interpreted as either political or strategic, contrary to previous theory suggesting common use of the issue categories of threat and opportunity (Dutton & Jackson, 1987).

In an interesting, longitudinal study of organizational sensemaking, Dutton & Dukerich (1991) examined the Port Authority of New York and New Jersey and its dealings with the issue of homelessness. Of particular interest was how individuals in that organization made sense of a nontraditional and emotional strategic issue. The theoretical framework for examining this case was grounded in organization *identity* (i.e. what organizational members believe to be its central, enduring, and distinctive characteristics) and organization *image* (i.e. the way that organization members believe others see the organization). Their research method included open-ended interviews with key informant-employees, and a review of all internal documents and published articles pertinent to the Port Authority's stance on the homeless issue, as well as other qualitative data sources. The authors provided a credible analysis of how the homeless were gradually re-interpreted from a threat (i.e. police-security issue) to a moral responsibility (i.e. homeless in transportation facilities are unique and need advocates). A notable aspect of this study is in how it bridged a longstanding gap between individual motivations (microprocesses) and patterns of organizational change (macro responses).

Arguably the most compelling study of sensemaking in the organizational literature analyzed the Mann Gulch fire disaster that resulted in the death of 13 smokejumpers in 1949. Weick (1993) used Norman Maclean's (1992) carefully researched book on the subject (*Young Men and Fire*) to attempt a better understanding of sensemaking and leadership as part of a disintegrating organization. Weick provides a close reading (although not a formal deconstruction) of Maclean's book, and proposes four sources of organizational resilience (improvisation, virtual role systems, the attitude of wisdom, and norms of respectful interaction) grounded in the Mann Gulch incident. These resilience sources are thought to make organizations less vulnerable to sensemaking interruptions and deter disintegration. Weick's analysis is a clear example of how a qualitative, grounded method can lead to profound insight into individual sensemaking and "cognition in the wild" (Hutchins, 1995).

CONCLUSIONS

The research reviewed in this chapter demonstrates that theories and methods from cognitive psychology have been applied to many areas of business management. An important question to ask at this point is how valuable has this application been for business management, and also has it been of value for cognitive psychology. We believe that cognitive psychology has been useful for helping us understand underlying human processes involved in many aspects of business management. Examples include understanding biases in interviewer decisions and understanding processes involved in enhancing rating accuracy in performance appraisals. However, for many areas of business management, practical application is as important and in some cases more important than understanding. This is particularly the case with the micro side of business management. Understanding interview and appraisal processes is important to the extent that it leads to applications that reduce biases and enhance accuracy. From this perspective of developing practical applications, cognitive psychology has not been particularly useful. Furthermore, researchers and practitioners alike have questioned the importance of process outcomes such as accuracy, arguing that the primary goal in interviews is to assess person–organization fit and that appraisals are used mainly for motivational purposes in organizations. Understanding cognitive processes is not seen as relevant for these purposes.

It appears that within different areas of business management, interest in applied cognition builds when attention is turned toward understanding and wanes when attention turns toward practical application. In those areas of business management that are primarily driven by practical concerns, such as interviewing and performance appraisal, we see that the "life cycle" for the cognitive approach was about ten years, after which researchers shifted their focus to practical applications. A possible reason for this short life cycle is that translation of much cognitive research to practical application is very difficult. Additionally, many applied researchers question the external validity of laboratory research, which has dominated cognitive research. After initial cognitive research fails to translate into field experiments and practical consulting applications, researchers tend to turn their attention to problems and issues that can be more directly translated to application. In areas that are not as focused on practical applications – such as motivation and decision making – the life cycle for cognitive research appears to be much longer.

If these trends are generalizable, we would expect to see a short (ten-year?) interest in cognitive psychology among researchers studying training and development, since this area is oriented toward practical applications. However, some of the areas in the macro side of business management – such as organizational sensemaking – are oriented primarily toward understanding and, therefore, interest in cognitive approaches may be much more lasting.

The relatively short life cycle for cognitive research in some of the areas of business management is problematic for a number of reasons. First, most management researchers are not well trained in cognitive methodology, such that the retooling required to do good cognitive work can be a lengthy process. Second, conducting good cognitive research can be more difficult and time consuming than questionnaire-based applied research. Related to this is the fact that fundamental advances in any field, and especially cognitive psychology, usually take more than ten years to see full potential. Researchers may be giving up in an area before fundamental advances are realized. A final problem with relatively short life cycles is that it discourages integration across different areas of cognitive management research. This is a problem that has been highlighted in a number of places throughout this chapter.

It is also useful to consider what, if anything, the area of business management has contributed to cognitive psychology. One could argue that any application of cognitive theories and methods to a new domain is a contribution, but we are more interested in the extent to which business management has influenced or changed theories and methods of cognitive psychology. It is our impression that there has been relatively little influence of business management research on cognitive psychology. This is not to say that such a contribution could not be made. Some of the theories and research methods being developed in the macro side of business management are new, innovative, and potentially useful for other cognitive or applied cognitive researchers. However, an important difference between cognitive research in business management and most basic cognitive research in psychology is that in business management we are primarily concerned with the role of context on cognitive processes. Organizational context drives business management research. In basic cognitive psychology, a dominant approach is to identify and understand cognitive processes that generalize across people and situations. Given the fundamental difference in orientation, we may never see the applied areas of business management making contributions that are returned to cognitive psychology.

REFERENCES

Arvey, R. D. & Campion, J. E. (1982). The employment interview: a summary and review of recent research. *Personnel Psychology*, 35, 281–322.

Barley, S. R. (1983). Semiotics and the study of occupational and organizational culture. *Administrative Science Quarterly*, 28, 393–413.

Barnard, C. I. (1938). *The Functions of the Executive*. Cambridge, MA: Harvard University Press.

Bass, B. M. (1990). *Bass and Stogdill's Handbook of Leadership: A Survey of Theory and Research*. New York: Free Press.

Beach, L. R. (1990). *Image Theory: Decision Making in Personal and Organizational Contexts*. Chichester: John Wiley.

Beach, L. R. (1996). *Decision Making in the Workplace: A Unified Perspective*. Mahwah, NJ: Erlbaum.

Binning, J. F. & Lord, R. G. (1980). Boundary conditions for performance cue effects on group process ratings: familiarity versus type of feedback. *Organizational Behavior and Human Performance*, 26, 115–30.

Boje, D. M. (1995). Stories of the storytelling organization: a postmodern analysis of Disney as "*Tamara*-land." *Academy of Management Journal*, 38, 997–1035.

Borman, W. C. (1987). Personal constructs, performance schemata, and "folk theories" of subordinate effectiveness: explorations in an army officer sample. *Organizational Behavior and Human Decision Processes*, 40, 307–22.

Braverman, E. P. & Goldstein, I. L. (1997). Investigating relationships between trainees' mental models and transfer of training. Presented at the 12th annual conference of the Society for Industrial and Organizational Psychology, St Louis.

Butterfield, K. D., Trevino, L. K. & Ball, G. A. (1996). Punishment from the manager's perspective: a grounded investigation and inductive model. *Academy of Management Journal*, 39, 1479–512.

Campion, M. A. & Lord, R. G. (1982). A control system conceptualization of the goal setting and changing process. *Organizational Behavior and Human Performance*, 30, 265–87.

Campion, M. A., Palmer, D. K. & Campion, J. E. (1997). A review of structure in the selection interview. *Personnel Psychology*, 50, 655–702.

Cannella, A. A. Jr & Monroe, M. J. (1997). Contrasting perspectives on strategic leaders: toward a more realistic view of top managers. *Journal of Management*, 23, 213–37.

Cantor, N. & Mischel, W. (1979). Prototypes in person perception. *Advances in Experimental Social Psychology*, 12, 3–51.

Cardy, R. L. & Dobbins, G. H. (1994). *Performance Appraisal: Alternative Perspectives*. Cincinnati, OH: South-Western.

Carver, C. S. & Scheier, M. F. (1981). *Attention and Self-regulation: A Control Theory Approach to Human Behavior*. New York: Springer-Verlag.

Child, J. (1972). Organizational structure, environment, and performance: the role of strategic choice. *Sociology*, 6, 1–22.

Cobb, L. (1981). Parameter estimation for the cusp catastrophe model. *Behavioral Science*, 26, 75–8.

Cowan, D. A. (1990). Developing a classification structure for organizational problems: an empirical investigation. *Academy of Management Journal*, 33, 366–90.

Cowan, D. A., Fiol, M. C. & Walsh, J. P. (1992). A midrange theory of strategic choice processes. In R. L. Phillips & J. G. Hunt (Eds), *Strategic Leadership: A Multi-organizational-level Perspective* (pp. 63–79). Westport, CT: Quorum Books/Greenwood.

Cronshaw, S. F. & Lord, R. G. (1987). Effects of categorization, attribution, and

encoding processes on leadership perceptions. *Journal of Applied Psychology*, 72, 97–106.
Day, D. V. & Lord, R. G. (1988). Executive leadership and organizational performance: suggestions for a new theory and methodology. *Journal of Management*, 14, 111–22.
Day, D. V. & Lord, R. G. (1992). Expertise and problem categorization: the role of expert processing in organizational sense-making. *Journal of Management Studies*, 29, 35–47.
Dearborn, D. C. & Simon, H. A. (1958). Selective perception: a note on the department identifications of executives. *Sociometry*, 21, 140–4.
DeNisi, A. S. & Peters, L. H. (1996). Organization of information in memory and the performance appraisal process: evidence from the field. *Journal of Applied Psychology*, 81, 717–37.
DeNisi, A. S., Cafferty, T. P. & Meglino, B. M. (1984). A cognitive view of the performance appraisal process: a model and research propositions. *Organizational Behavior and Human Performance*, 33, 360–96.
DeNisi, A. S., Robbins, T. & Cafferty, T. P. (1989). The organization of information used for performance appraisals: the role of diary-keeping. *Journal of Applied Psychology*, 74, 124–9.
DeShon, R. P. & Alexander, R. A. (1996). Goal setting effects on implicit and explicit learning of complex tasks. *Organizational Behavior and Human Decision Processes*, 65, 18–36.
Dipboye, R. L. (1992). *Selection Interviews: Process Perspectives*. Cincinnati, OH: South-Western.
Dutton, J. E. & Dukerich, J. M. (1991). Keeping an eye on the mirror: image and identity in organizational adaptation. *Academy of Management Journal*, 34, 517–54.
Dutton, J. E. & Jackson, S. E. (1987). Categorizing strategic issues: links to organizational actions. *Academy of Management Review*, 12, 76–90.
Eco, U. (1976). *A Theory of Semiotics*. Bloomington, IN: University of Indiana.
Edwards, J. R. (1992). A cybernetic theory of stress, coping, and well-being in organizations. *Academy of Management Review*, 17, 238–74.
Eisenhardt, K. M. (1989). Making fast strategic decisions in high-velocity environments. *Academy of Management Journal*, 32, 543–76.
Erdener, C. B. & Dunn, C. P. (1990). Content analysis. In A. S. Huff (Ed.), *Mapping Strategic Thought* (pp. 291–300). Chichester: John Wiley.
Farr, J. L. (1973). Response requirements and primacy-recency effects in a simulated selection interview. *Journal of Applied Psychology*, 58, 228–33.
Feldman, M. S. (1995). Strategies for interpreting qualitative data. In Sage University Paper Series on Qualitative Research Methods, Vol. 33. Thousand Oaks, CA: Sage.
Fiol, C. M. (1989). A semiotic analysis of corporate language: organizational boundaries and joint venturing. *Administrative Science Quarterly*, 34, 277–303.
Fiol, C. M. (1990). Narrative semiotics: theory, procedure and illustration. In A. S. Huff (Ed.), *Mapping Strategic Thought* (pp. 377–402). Chichester: John Wiley.
Ford, J. K., Schmitt, N., Schechtman, S., Hults, B. M. & Doherty, M. L. (1989). Process tracing methods: contributions, problems, and neglected research questions. *Organizational Behavior and Human Decision Processes*, 43, 75–117.
Fransella, F. & Bannister, D. (1977). *A Manual for Repertory Grid Technique*. New York: Academic Press.
Gardner, W. L. & Avolio, B. J. (1998). The charismatic relationship: a dramaturgical perspective. *Academy of Management Review*, 23, 32–58.
Gilliland, S. W. & Landis, R. S. (1992). Quality and quantity goals in a complex decision task: strategies and outcomes. *Journal of Applied Psychology*, 77, 672–81.
Gilliland, S. W. & Schmitt, N. (1993). Information redundancy and decision behavior: a process tracing investigation. *Organizational Behavior and Human Decision Processes*, 54, 157–80.
Gilliland, S. W., Wood, L. & Schmitt, N. (1994). The effects of alternative labels on decision behavior: the case of corporate site selection decisions. *Organizational Behavior and Human Decision Processes*, 58, 406–27.

Gioia, D. A. & Pitre, E. (1990). Multiparadigm perspectives on theory building. *Academy of Management Review*, 15, 584–602.
Gioia, D. A. & Thomas, J. B. (1996). Identity, image, and issue interpretation: sensemaking during strategic change in academia. *Administrative Science Quarterly*, 41, 370–403.
Glaser, B. G. & Strauss, A. L. (1967). *The Discovery of Grounded Theory*. Chicago: Aldine.
Greimas, A. J. (1987). *OM meaning: Selected Writings on Semiotic Theory*. Minneapolis, MN: University of Minnesota.
Hambrick, D. C. & Mason, P. (1984). Upper echelons: the organization as a reflection of its top managers. *Academy of Management Review*, 9, 193–206.
Hanges, P. J., Lord, R. G., Day, D. V., Sipe, W. P., Smith, W. C. & Brown, D. J. (1997). Leadership and gender bias: Dynamic measures and nonlinear modeling. Manuscript submitted for publication.
Hastie, R. & Park, B. (1986). The relationship between memory and judgment depends on whether the judgment task is memory-based or on-line. *Psychological Review*, 93, 256–68.
Hitt, M. A. & Barr, S. H. (1989). Managerial selection decision models: examination of configural cue processing. *Journal of Applied Psychology*, 74, 53–61.
Hollenbeck, J. R. (1989). Control theory and the perception of work environments: the effects of focus of attention on affective and behavioral reactions to work. *Organizational Behavior and Human Decision Processes*, 43, 406–30.
Hovland, C., Janis, I. & Kelley, H. H. (1953). *Communication and Persuasion*. New Haven, CT: Yale University.
Howell, W. C. & Cooke, N. J. (1989). Training the human information processor: a review of cognitive models. In I. L. Goldstein (Ed.), *Training and Development in Organizations*. San Francisco: Jossey-Bass.
Huff, A. S. (Ed.) (1990). *Mapping Strategic Thought*. Chichester: John Wiley.
Hutchins, E. (1995). *Cognition in the Wild*. Cambridge, MA: MIT.
Ilgen, D. R. & Feldman, J. M. (1983). Performance appraisal: a process focus. In L. L. Cummings & B. M. Staw (Eds), *Research in Organizational Behavior*, vol. 5. Greenwich, CT: JAI Press.
Ilgen, D. R., Barnes-Farrell, J. L. & McKellin, D. B. (1993). Performance appraisal process research in the 1980s: what has it contributed to appraisals in use? *Organizational Behavior and Human Decision Processes*, 54, 321–68.
Ilgen, D. R., Major, D. A. & Tower, S. L. (1994). The cogntive revolution in organizational behavior. In J. Greenberg (Ed.), *Organizational Behavior: The State of the Science*. Hillsdale, NJ: Erlbaum.
Isenberg, D. J. (1986). Thinking and managing: a verbal protocol analysis of managerial problem solving. *Academy of Management Journal*, 29, 775–88.
Johnson-Laird, P. (1983). *Mental Models*. Cambridge, MA: Harvard University Press.
Kanfer, R. (1994). Work motivation: new directions in theory and research. In C. L. Cooper & I. T. Robertson (Eds), *Key Reviews in Managerial Psychology: Concepts and Research for Practice*. Chichester: John Wiley.
Kanfer, R. & Ackerman, P. L. (1989). Motivation and cognitive abilities: an integrative/aptitude-treatment interaction approach to skill acquisition. *Journal of Applied Psychology*, 74, 657–90.
Kanfer, R., Ackerman, P. L., Murtha, T. C., Dugdale, B. & Nelson, L. (1994). Goal setting, conditions of practice, and task performance: a resource allocation perspective. *Journal of Applied Psychology*, 79, 826–35.
Kelly, G. A. (1955). *The Psychology of Personal Constructs*. New York: Norton.
Kilduff, M. (1993). Deconstructing *Organizations*. *Academy of Management Review*, 18, 13–31.
Klein, H. (1989). An integrated control theory model of work motivation. *Academy of Management Review*, 14, 150–72.
Kozlowski, S. W. J. & Ford, J. K. (1991). Rater information acquisition processes: tracing

the effects of prior knowledge, performance level, search constraints, and memory demands. *Organizational Behavior and Human Decision Processes*, 49, 282–301.

Kraiger, K., Ford, J. K. & Salas, E. (1993). Application of cognitive, skill-based, and affective theories of learning outcomes to new methods of training evaluation. *Journal of Applied Psychology*, 78, 311–28.

Landy, F. J. & Farr, J. L. (1980). Performance ratings. *Psychological Bulletin*, 87, 72–107.

Lee, T. W. & Mitchell, T. R. (1994). An alternative approach: the unfolding model of voluntary employment turnover. *Academy of Management Review*, 19, 51–89.

Locke, E. A. & Latham, G. P. (1990). *A Theory of Goal Setting and Task Performance*. New York: Prentice-Hall.

Lord, R. G., Foti, R. J. & De Vader, C. (1984). A test of leadership categorization theory: internal structure, information processing, and leadership perceptions. *Organizational Behavior and Human Performance*, 34, 343–78.

Lord, R. G., Binning, J. F., Rush, M. C. & Thomas, J. C. (1978). The effect of performance cues and leader behavior on questionnaire ratings of leadership behavior. *Organizational Behavior and Human Performance*, 21, 27–39.

Lord, R. G. & Maher, K. J. (1991). *Leadership and Information Processing: Linking Perceptions and Performance*. Boston, MA: Unwin Hyman.

Macan, T. M. & Dipboye, R. L. (1988). The effects of interviewers' initial impressions on information gathering. *Organizational Behavior and Human Decision Processes*, 42, 364–87.

Macan, T. M. & Dipboye, R. L. (1990). The relationship of the interviewers' preinterview impressions to selection and recruitment outcomes. *Personnel Psychology*, 43, 745–69.

Maclean, N. (1992). *Young Men and Fire*. Chicago: University of Chicago.

Manning, P. K. (1987). *Semiotics and Fieldwork*. Newbury Park, CA: Sage.

March, J. G. & Simon, H. A. (1958). *Organizations*. New York: John Wiley.

Martin, J. (1990). Deconstructing organizational taboos: the suppression of gender conflict in organizational stories. *Organizational Science*, 1, 339–59.

Meindl, J. R. & Ehrlich, S. B. (1987). The romance of leadership and the evaluation of organizational performance. *Academy of Management Journal*, 30, 78–102.

Mitchell, T. R. & Beach, L. R. (1990). ". . . Do I love thee? Let me count . . ." Toward an understanding of intuitive and automatic decision making. *Organizational Behavior and Human Decision Processes*, 47, 1–20.

Mount, M. K. & Thompson, D. (1987). Cognitive categorization and quality of performance ratings. *Journal of Applied Psychology*, 72, 240–6.

Murphy, K. R. & Cleveland, J. N. (1991). *Performance Appraisal: An Organizational Perspective*. Boston, MA: Allyn & Bacon.

Phillips, J. S. & Lord, R. G. (1982). Schematic information processing and perceptions of leadership in problem-solving groups. *Journal of Applied Psychology*, 67, 486–92.

Porac, J. F. & Thomas, H. (1994). Cognitive categorization and subjective rivalry among retailers in a small city. *Journal of Applied Psychology*, 79, 54–66.

Porac, J. F., Thomas, H., Wilson, F., Paton, D. & Kanfer, A. (1995). Rivalry and the industry model of Scottish knitwear producers. *Administrative Science Quarterly*, 40, 203–27.

Reger, R. K. (1990). The repertory grid technique for eliciting the content and structure of cognitive constructive systems. In A. S. Huff (Ed.), *Mapping Strategic Thought* (pp. 301–9). Chichester: John Wiley.

Rohrbaugh, C. C. & Shanteau, J. (1999). Context, process, and experience: research on applied judgment and decision making. In F. T. Durso, R. S. Nickerson, R. W. Schvaneveldt, S. T. Dumais, D. S. Lindsay & M. T. H. Chi (Eds), *Handbook of Applied Cognition* (chapter 5). Chichester: John Wiley.

Rosch, E. (1978). Principles of categorization. In E. Rosch & B. Lloyd (Eds), *Cognition and Categorization* (pp. 27–47). Hillsdale, NJ: Erlbaum.

Rosenberg, S. (1982). The method of sorting in multivariate research with applications selected from cognitive psychology and person perception. In H. Hirschenberg & L. G.

Humphreys (Eds), *Multivariate Applications in the Social Sciences* (pp. 117–42). Hillsdale, NJ: Erlbaum.

Sagan, S. D. (1997). Review of the book *The Challenger Launch Decision. Administrative Science Quarterly*, 42, 401–5.

Sampson, E. E. (1993). Identity politics: challenges to psychology's understanding. *American Psychologist*, 48, 1219–30.

Schmitt, N. (1976). Social and situational determinants of interview decisions. Implications for the employment interview. *Personnel Psychology*, 29, 79–101.

Schwenk, C. R. (1988). The cognitive perspective on strategic decision making. *Journal of Management Studies*, 25, 41–55.

Smith, E. R. & Miller, F. D. (1983). Mediation among attributional inferences and comprehension processes: initial findings and a general method. *Journal of Personality and Social Psychology*, 44, 492–505.

Stevens, C. K. & Beach, L. R. (1996). Job search and job selection. In L. R. Beach (Ed.), *Decision Making in the Workplace: A Unified Perspective*. Mahwah, NJ: Erlbaum.

Stogdill, R. M. (1963). *Manual for the Leader Behavior Description Questionnaire – Form XII*. Columbus, OH: Bureau of Business Research, Ohio State University.

Stubbart, C. I. (1989). Managerial cognition: a missing link in strategic management research. *Journal of Management Studies*, 26, 325–47.

Sulsky, L. M. & Day, D. V. (1992). Frame-of-reference training and cognitive categorization: an empirical investigation of rater memory issues. *Journal of Applied Psychology*, 77, 501–10.

Sulsky, L. M. & Day, D. V. (1994). Effects of frame-of-reference training on rater accuracy under alternative time delays. *Journal of Applied Psychology*, 79, 535–43.

Sutcliffe, K. M. (1994). What executives notice: accurate perceptions in top management teams. *Academy of Management Journal*, 37, 1360–78.

Thom, R. (1975). *Structural Stability and Morphogenesis: An Outline of a General Theory of Models*. Reading, MA: W. A. Benjamin.

Thomas, J. B. & McDaniel, R. R. Jr (1990). Interpreting strategic issues: effects of strategy and the information-processing structure of top management teams. *Academy of Management Journal*, 33, 286–306.

Ungson, G. R., Braunstein, D. N. & Hall, P. D. (1981). Managerial information processing: a research review. *Administrative Science Quarterly*, 26, 116–34.

Vallacher, R. R. & Nowak, A. (Eds) (1994a). *Dynamical Systems in Social Psychology*. San Diego, CA: Academic Press.

Vallacher, R. R. & Nowak, A. (1994b). The stream of social judgment. In R. R. Vallacher & A. Nowak (Eds), *Dynamical Systems in Social Psychology* (pp. 251–77). San Diego, CA: Academic Press.

Vaughan, D. (1996). *The Challenger Launch Decision: Risky Technology, Culture, and Deviance at NASA*. Chicago: University of Chicago.

Viswesvaran, C., Schmidt, F. L. & Deshpande, S. P. (1994). A meta-analytic method for testing hypotheses about clusters of decision makers. *Organizational Behavior and Human Decision Processes*, 58, 304–21.

Vroom, V. H. (1964). *Work and Motivation*. New York: John Wiley.

Walsh, J. P. (1988). Selectivity and selective perception: an investigation of managers' belief structures and information processing. *Academy of Management Journal*, 31, 873–96.

Walsh, J. P. (1995). Managerial and organizational cognition: notes from a trip down memory lane. *Organization Science*, 6, 280–312.

Weatherly, K. A. & Beach, L. R. (1996). Organizational culture and decision making. In L. R. Beach (Ed.), *Decision Making in the Workplace: A Unified Perspective*. Mahwah, NJ: Erlbaum.

Weick, K. E. (1993). The collapse of sensemaking in organizations: the Mann Gulch disaster. *Administrative Science Quarterly*, 38, 628–52.

Weick, K. E. (1995). *Sensemaking in Organizations*. Thousand Oaks, CA: Sage.

Werner, J. M. (1994). Dimensions that make a difference: examining the impact of in-role and extrarole behaviors on supervisory ratings. *Journal of Applied Psychology*, 79, 98–107.

Wright, O. R. (1969). Summary of research on the selection interview since 1964. *Personnel Psychology*, 22, 391–413.

Chapter 12

Applied Cognition in Consumer Research

Joseph W. Alba
University of Florida
and
J. Wesley Hutchinson
University of Pennsylvania

Cognitive psychology has been a pervasive influence on consumer research. In this chapter we review the models, methods, and empirical results obtained from research pertaining to consumer cognition. We organize these topics into two main problem areas: the cognitive antecedents of decision making, and decision-making processes. The antecedents of consumer decision making constitute an eclectic set of topics that are seldom integrated into a common framework. These topics include consumer response to marketing actions (such as advertising and pricing), information search (in memory as well as the external environment), and consumer expertise. Research on these cognitive antecedents tends to be descriptive in nature and draws from the mnemonic, interpretive, perceptual, and learning effects traditionally examined by cognitive psychologists. In contrast, research on decision processes tends to be concerned with methods for discerning the nature of the decision process and deviations from normative behavior. Such research draws on psychometrics and economics in addition to cognitive psychology.

COGNITIVE ANTECEDENTS OF DECISION MAKING

From the perspective of economics and management science, the inputs to decision making are well-specified by the definition of the decision problem.

Handbook of Applied Cognition, Edited by F. T. Durso, R. S. Nickerson, R. W. Schvaneveldt, S. T. Dumais, D. S. Lindsay and M. T. H. Chi.

From a cognitive perspective, however, the inputs to real-world decision making are ill-specified and could include information available in the immediate environment, knowledge retrieved from memory, and inferences based on a combination of internal and external inputs. Even the awareness that a problem exists or that a decision needs to be made cannot be taken for granted. Our review focuses on two broad categories of cognitive antecedents to consumer decision making: buyer responses to the marketing actions of sellers, and the results of goal-oriented buyer behaviors.

Consumer Responses to Marketing Actions

It is traditionally held that firms have four general tools for influencing consumer choices: advertising (and related promotional devices), pricing, distribution and physical display of the product, and the product itself. Most research that has investigated the cognitive antecedents of decision making has focused on the first two tools. Distribution has received far less formal investigation, although managerial heuristics often make assumptions about consumer information processing. Product has been studied in a variety of contexts and is an inherent component of the normative approaches to decision making described later. In this section we discuss consumer response to products primarily under the rubric of brand equity.

Advertising

In its best form, advertising conveys information that consumers can use in making purchase decisions. Managers' concerns tend to revolve around the effectiveness of their advertising and the return on their dollar investments. Behavioral scientists, on the other hand, have mainly investigated the role advertising plays in persuasion. One area in which these interests converge is in the study of ad recall. The prevailing wisdom, supported by anecdotal and proprietary research, is that memory for advertising can be extremely low. In part, the problem is one of limited attention and encoding failure. Ads are typically viewed in a distracting, uninvolved setting. Academic research has generally examined more favorable climates in which attention, per se, is not a limiting factor but where competitive effects loom large. Consistent with basic memory research, memory for information contained in advertisements appears to be governed by proactive, retroactive, and output interference. Moreover, these effects are moderated by such real-world considerations as the modality of the message, message variability, cognitive structure (expertise) of the receiver, processing involvement, cues present at the time of recall, and the evaluative and semantic similarity of competing ad messages (Alba & Chattopadhyay, 1985a, 1986; Burke & Srull, 1988; Keller, 1991; Pieters & Bijmolt, 1997; Unnava, Burnkrant & Erevelles, 1994; Unnava & Sirdeshmukh, 1994).

More provocative than the pure mnemonics of advertising is the question of how advertising influences consumers. A broad construal of consumer learning argues that the market needs to convey information about three types of decision inputs: search attributes, experience attributes, and credence attributes (Darby & Karni, 1973). Search attributes can be evaluated based on inspection and represent the types of cues traditionally studied by cognitive and decision researchers. Thus, search attributes include ingredients, technical specifications, and price – attributes that should be most compatible with traditional advertising formats. Experience attributes cannot be assessed fully from description and therefore must be directly experienced. Flavor is a classic example. Rare by comparison, credence attributes represent information that cannot be obtained personally within a reasonable period of time and therefore must be described by another party. For example, the efficacy of competing brands of toothpaste is difficult to evaluate, and one may take an expert's advice in lieu of conducting an error-prone time-series experiment.

Those who subscribe to a *caveat emptor* philosophy of regulation point to the relative rarity of credence attributes and argue that consumers have access to nearly complete information, which in turn affords consumers the opportunity to make optimal decisions – irrespective of their level of exposure to advertising and the content of that advertising. *Caveat emptor* is less consistent with the findings and intuitions of decision researchers. The issue is not whether rational agents can make optimal decisions or should bear the responsibility for those decisions; rather, it is a question of consumers' ability to learn from the environment (Alba & Hutchinson, 1991; Hoch & Deighton, 1989). Those who view consumers as imperfect learners argue that advertising may exert a variety of influences that enhance or distort the accurate accrual of product beliefs even in the case of search and experience attributes. For search attributes, advertising may "frame" the buying decision by altering the importance weights applied to the different attributes that constitute the decision rule. In some cases, advertisements may successfully change decisions by persuading consumers to place greater or lesser weight on different product attributes, by defining the ideal point for a product category, or by inhibiting recall and consideration of particular decision criteria (Alba & Chattopadhyay, 1985b; Krugman, 1965).

A worrisome effect of advertising is its potential to influence experience. A growing body of evidence suggests that conceptually driven processes guide the evaluation and choice of options when product quality is ambiguous, regardless of how ambiguity is instantiated. For example, expectations guide choice when objective information is voluminous (Deighton, 1984), the choice set is efficient (Ha & Hoch, 1989), and when tactile information (Hoch & Ha, 1986) fails to indicate a clearly superior alternative. More worrisome is the finding that expectations may guide evaluation of taste goods when the alternatives are not entirely ambiguous (Hoyer & Brown, 1990; Levin & Gaeth, 1988). Insofar as advertising creates the expectations that guide information search and perceptions of product experience, it is inappropriate to argue that advertising uniformly enhances market efficiency and consumer welfare.

Brand Equity

Consumers process advertising and other information but ultimately make purchases, typically, from competing brands. Consumer reactions to brands and the efforts firms make on behalf of their brands are pivotal in determining the competitive dynamics of the market.

Brand names can constitute one of the greatest assets of a firm, as revealed by the monetary value placed on a name vis-à-vis a firm's tangible assets (see Aaker, 1991). On the surface, the extraordinary sums paid by firms to purchase established brand names may seem paradoxical in a world in which true product uniqueness is becoming increasingly difficult to maintain. However, consider the following cognition-based assets of a strong brand name.

Awareness

A simple definition of brand equity consists of three components: awareness, meaning, and loyalty. The first component is important for two reasons. First, the familiarity aspect of awareness can have affective implications (Moore & Hutchinson, 1985; Zajonc, 1980). Second, and perhaps more important given that consumers have basic awareness of many competing options, is the memory aspect of awareness. Consumers must make choices from large choice sets. Later in this chapter we will discuss the importance to a brand of being perceived and recognized in a stimulus-based choice set and recalled in a memory-based choice set. For present purposes it is sufficient to note that mere inclusion in the consumer's choice set is an enormously powerful predictor of consumer choice (Hauser, 1978). Insofar as a salient brand name can ensure recognition or recall at the time of choice, the economic value of the awareness component of brand equity is considerable.

Meaning

Environmental noise and cognitive limitations similarly raise the value of the meaning component of brand equity. The origin of branding was as a signal of quality. Brands continue to serve this function – and much more. When consumers lack the resources or ability to assess relative quality across offerings, brands provide heuristic value and enhance consumer welfare (whenever the signals are accurate). Competition, commoditization, and elementary strategic considerations have sharpened the signaling value of brands. Many brands do not signal mere unidimensional quality; they also convey specific meanings by acting as a label for a market position (e.g. *Ivory* dishwashing liquid is gentle to your hands). In a multidimensional product space, brands represent different positions in the space. When the dimensions are product benefits, brands facilitate choice by distinguishing one offering from another on a meaningful decision criterion. Moreover, if a brand becomes synonymous with a benefit and consumers use brand names heuristically, the brand may dominate its competitors – even when it lacks true competitive superiority as defined by objective product specifications (i.e. the signal is inaccurate). Thus, a brand can represent a competitive advantage that is very slow to erode due to the cognitive limitations of consumers. In a dense and dynamic information environment, it is difficult for consumers to research products thoroughly on a routine basis.

Finally, brands possess not only present value but also potential value. When brands take on specific meanings, they enable firms to extend into other product classes using the brand name as a source of leverage. The brand image or meaning provides a source of differentiation in the new category (e.g. *Ivory* shampoo is gentle to your hair). The true signaling power of a brand is revealed by a brand's ability to facilitate entry into a category in which the firm possesses no structural competence. For example, *Brinks* is persuasive as a provider of home security systems even though such systems lack manufacturing synergy with *Brinks*'s original service. Brand meanings can be sufficiently strong that they dominate other persuasive inputs into decision making. Broniarczyk & Alba (1994a) demonstrated that when a brand's meaning (or specific association) fits the category into which it intended to extend, the meaning is a stronger determinant of the attractiveness of the extension than the affect associated with the brand name or the similarity of the original and new categories.

Loyalty

Brand loyalty is a cherished goal of most firms. Loyal consumers provide a consistent and predictable revenue stream and are likely to exhibit less price sensitivity than other consumers. Interestingly, little is known about the causal determinants of consumer loyalty in general, and firms often cannot assess the reasons for loyalty and defection within their own customer populations. In part, the difficulty in addressing these issues stems from the fact that many plausible and independent factors may enhance loyalty, most of which are cognitively based.

The endpoints of the range of possible causes correspond to both professional and lay beliefs about loyalty. At one end is pure brand utility, consistent with economic models of human preference. Consumers remain loyal to a brand because it provides greater utility than competing brands. At the other end of the spectrum is loyalty as emotional attachment (Fournier, 1998; Jacoby, 1971). Between these poles are a variety of rational, semi-rational, and irrational reasons why consumers exhibit brand loyalty – or more generally a "status quo bias" (see Samuelson & Zeckhauser, 1988).

Somewhat closer to the utility perspective is loyalty driven by the costs of switching. In such instances consumers remain loyal not because the chosen brand is superior but because net utility for the chosen brand is higher when search costs and learning costs associated with switching to a competing brand are factored into the decision.

Loyalty may obtain also from (over)confidence that one's chosen brand is objectively superior to other options. Confidence-based loyalty, as in other manifestations of overconfidence, may be driven by asymmetric knowledge about the chosen and nonchosen brands. Greater knowledge about a satisfactory incumbent brand has been shown to result in erroneous beliefs about its superiority over competing brands (Kardes & Kalyanaram, 1992; Muthukrishnan, 1995).

Properly viewed as irrational is loyalty due to sunk costs (cf. Staw, 1976). Consumers may make an investment and then forego superior alternatives to avoid loss of the initial investment or the appearance of wastefulness that accompanies replacement of a still-functional product (cf. Arkes & Blumer, 1985).

Independent of the sunk cost mentality, people appear to place greater value on a good when it is in their possession than when it is not. In a typical experimental demonstration, such mere-possession or endowment effects are reflected in higher prices demanded by individuals when selling a good compared to the purchase prices individuals would pay to obtain the same good (Kahneman, Knetsch & Thaler, 1990; Thaler, 1980). The difference between the selling and purchase prices can be staggering and does not necessarily require actual possession. Mere-possession effects have recently been reported with coupons, which provide only an option to purchase (Sen & Johnson, 1997). Insofar as consumers overvalue possessed goods, their likelihood of purchasing replacements to obtain greater utility is reduced as well.

Lastly, it would be surprising if purchase deviated from other human behavior with regard to risk aversion. Consumers may remain loyal to a brand due to the risks associated with switching to another vendor. Similarly, consumers may be motivated to choose a particular option to avoid regret associated with choosing a different option. As Simonson (1992) argues, conventional options represent the norm and may prompt greater regret if foregone in favor of an option that ultimately proves to be less attractive. In the consumer world, the conventional option may be the market leader or the brand generally purchased by an individual.

In sum, there are a variety of reasons for loyalty but no easy way to distinguish the cause of loyalty in any given situation. In fact, it is likely that multiple causes come to bear on most decisions. Advertising can prompt loyalty in ways independent of taste manipulation by communicating higher utility, creating warm images and feelings, instilling asymmetric knowledge, and suggesting a default option.

Pricing

Pricing represents one of the most fundamental decisions faced by firms (e.g. Smith & Nagle, 1994). Consider a simple case in which a consumer assesses the attractiveness of a price for a particular good. A rational agent would compare the (positive) utility of consuming the product to the (negative) utility of paying its price and choose the product if the net utility is positive. In principle, these utilities could be measured in dollars, and the equilibrium behavior of markets – individuals and firms – could be inferred. Although it is certainly true that consumers implicitly (if not explicitly) consider the utility provided by a good when making a purchase decision, their reactions to prices are likely to be influenced by psychological factors in addition to the purely economic trade-offs involved. Two frequently studied areas of psychological influence are reference prices and mental accounting.

Reference Prices

The attractiveness of a price is often assessed as a function of its comparison to some other price, typically called a reference price (Winer, 1986). The difference between the real and reference price reflects the "transaction utility" derived from a purchase that is incremental to the utility derived from consumption. If an observed price is well above a reference price, transaction utility is low and consumers may forego purchase. The problem for firms lies not exclusively in consumers' failure to behave on the basis of their acquisition utility but also in understanding and adjusting to the reference points adopted by consumers.

A problem faced by any firm that interacts with consumer markets is that consumers are inherently heterogeneous. In the present context, this implies that consumers may have different reference points (see below) or, moreover, may rely on different types of information when deciding whether a particular price is a "good deal." *A priori*, it would seem reasonable to believe that most consumers examine the stated price of a desired good and then compare it to the price paid for the item in a previous period – particularly in the case of frequently purchased goods. Indeed, one segment of consumers (sometimes referred to as "price vigilantes") may engage in precisely such behavior. Other consumers appear far less interested in putting forth such effort, which results in two different outcomes. First, a significant proportion of consumers simply ignore price information (Dickson & Sawyer, 1990). Second, for those consumers who do examine prices, impressions appear stimulus-based rather than memory-based. Due to consumers' low attention to and/or poor recall of past prices, price perceptions are often driven by cues present at the point of purchase (cf. Lattin & Bucklin, 1989; Mayhew & Winer, 1992). Thus, explicit information about a price reduction exerts a large influence on behavior. It is perhaps not surprising that memory takes a back seat to stimulus information given the task faced by the consumer. The number of "stimulus list items" and the dynamic nature of prices makes for a daunting memory task. Thus, it seems reasonable to rely on vendor-supplied assistance. The risk, of course, is that vendors do not always operate in the consumers' interest and may exploit the malleability of consumer impressions by supplying artificially high reference points (cf. Urbany, Bearden & Weilbaker, 1988), signaling a price reduction without actually reducing the price (Inman, McAlister & Hoyer, 1990; cf. Kalwani, Yim, Rinne & Sugita, 1990), or by citing the frequency rather than the depth of price reduction (Alba, Broniarczyk, Shimp & Urbany, 1994).

Despite the research focus on how consumers evaluate a price relative to "normal" or past price, it has been properly noted by Jacobson & Obermiller (1990) that the utility-maximizing consumer will view a price relative to anticipated future prices because the purely economic decision is to buy now or wait for a lower price (foregoing the benefits of a current purchase). An interesting aspect of this observation from a cognitive perspective is that it introduces the notion of extrapolation. In the context of price reductions (e.g. coupons, sales), the consumer's task is to estimate deal frequency and inter-deal interval. Research indicates that traditional overestimation of low frequencies and underestimation of high frequencies is replicated in a purchasing context (Krishna, 1991). In a broader context, Jacobson & Obermiller (1990) report that extrapolation is not described by a rational expectations model and that consumers are more likely to base predictions of future prices on the most recent price than on the trend in the price history. This result is consistent with findings from other forecasting contexts (Bolger & Harvey, 1995). When combined with the human tendency to underestimate exponential growth (e.g. Wagenaar & Timmers, 1979), the phenomenon of "sticker shock" is easy to understand in purchase situations characterized by long interpurchase intervals.

Mental Accounting

Consumers confronted with sticker shock may feel that a price is unfair because it is well above expectations. Although discussion of reference prices typically focuses on the previous price of a good or the current price of competing goods, a much more frustrating reference point for firms wishing to engage in rational, utility-driven pricing is the consumer's perception of the vendor's costs (Kahneman, Knetsch & Thaler, 1986). Consumers who perceive that a vendor's prices are well above costs may forego purchase even if the purchase would provide sufficient utility in terms of benefits to justify the vendor's price.

A final peculiarity of human behavior driven by monetary reference points is that consumers treat money as less fungible than it is (Prelec & Lowenstein, 1998; Thaler, 1985). People possess a total personal wealth but often divide that wealth into budgetary categories that are psychologically determined. Each "mental" category has its own reference point. Thus, although $100 is a constant, it will be deemed an acceptable or unacceptable expenditure depending on the category from which it is mentally subtracted. In the context of the family food budget, a $100 meal might be considered expensive; however, if the meal is purchased while the family is on vacation, the perception might be much different if the price is mentally subtracted from the vacation budget. Clearly, there are instances in which the reference points provided by different mental accounts can lead to inconsistent behavior.

Goal-oriented Consumer Behaviors

We consider two broad classes of activities undertaken by consumers in an effort to acquire informational inputs for decision making. The first consists of searching the external environment for relevant factual information. The second consists of searching the internal environment, including the retrieval from memory of explicit factual information and the use of knowledge that may have been learned implicitly and applied unconsciously. Before reviewing consumer research in these areas we briefly review the literature on optimal search and learning, which serves as a normative reference point for many descriptive studies.

Optimal Information Search and Learning

Consumer research has been influenced by work in economics and statistics that attempts to describe how utility-maximizing consumers should behave in acquiring information. Two types of problems have been the main foci of information search and learning. The optimal search problem is typically defined as one in which previously unknown information is revealed with certainty. The search process is modeled as drawing a sample of a given size from some population that varies in the values being optimized. The consumer then decides either to choose the best option in that sample or draw a new sample. The act of drawing a sample is assumed to have a cost (based on factors such as search effort and the opportunity cost of time).

Price search is a classic example. Consider a consumer who is shopping for apples. The consumer might draw a sample of prices by visiting a grocery store and examining the prices of the different types of apples available at the store. Having acquired this information, the consumer would either buy apples at that store or visit another store. For most search problems of this type, the optimal policy is to first determine the optimal sample size for each draw and then continue drawing samples until the best current option is better than or equal to a specific value (e.g. McKenna 1987; Stigler, 1961). This value, often called a *reservation value*, is the statistically expected value of continued search. The actual computation of the sample size and the reservation value can be quite complex, but the rule itself is simple. A number of researchers have examined variations of this problem tailored to realistic consumer situations (Feinberg & Huber, 1996; Hauser & Wernerfelt, 1990; Moorthy, Ratchford & Talukdar, 1997; Roberts & Lattin, 1991). Optimal search has also been examined experimentally. Similar to other empirical tests of optimal decision making, humans are found to respond to manipulated variables in ways that are directionally correct but often not precisely optimal (e.g. Meyer & Assuncao, 1990).

Learning problems are typically defined as uncertainty reduction, and Bayesian updating defines optimal behavior. Both classic and recent research in psychology have documented the ways in which humans deviate from Bayesian learning (e.g. Gigerenzer & Hoffrage, 1995; Grether, 1980; Kruschke, 1996; March, 1996; Tversky & Koehler, 1994). Although Bayesian learning has frequently been assumed in the normative models developed in economics and marketing, direct empirical tests in consumer contexts have been rare (Chatterjee & Eliashberg, 1990; Lippman & McCardle, 1991; Roberts & Urban, 1988). Instead, most consumer research on both information search and learning has been primarily descriptive and has examined cognitive models without explicit reference to optimal behavior other than to identify the key trade-off between the cost and benefits of information acquisition. This is, however, an area of increasing activity.

Information Search Behavior

Consumer researchers have long been interested in search behavior for obvious reasons. Optimal decisions require knowledge, and all of the requisite knowledge is not obtainable from advertising. However, a common finding is that consumers engage in less than exhaustive search (Newman, 1977; Urbany, Dickson & Wilkie, 1989). As in the case of brand loyalty, the reasons are sometimes rational and sometimes the result of human frailty.

External Search

Failure to search is likely due to a combination of cognitive and motivational forces. From a strictly cognitive perspective, search may be inhibited by knowledge deficits. Although knowledge deficits should motivate information acquisition, novices may search least of all because they lack the ability to conduct an appropriate search. As shown in shopping and nonshopping contexts alike, the ability to ask a useful question depends on one's pre-existing knowledge (Brucks, 1985; Miyake & Norman, 1979). Expertise leads to deeper investigation of alternatives, particularly when the optimal choice is not obvious, *a priori*. However, very high levels of knowledge may inhibit search if it allows consumers to rely on prior evaluations or restrict search to the most diagnostic information available (Johnson & Russo, 1984).

The reservation value search rule described earlier should lead to satisfactory outcomes if the consumer can make reasonably accurate assessments of the benefits and costs of additional search. In most cases, this assessment is very difficult because the future is uncertain, and the sources of uncertainty are many. Somewhat paradoxically, uncertainty often increases the optimal amount of search because in future decisions one selects the best option (not the average); thus, uncertainty tends to increase the expected value of a future choice. However, actual behavior can differ. For example, Urbany et al. (1989) identify a significant segment of consumers who admit to knowing little about how to make optimal decisions within a product class but simultaneously express great confidence in being able to identify the best brand. They refer to this segment as the "blissfully uninformed." Not surprisingly, this segment engages in the least amount of product search.

Errors in reasoning also may play a role in suboptimal search behavior. For example, consistent with the assumption of a nonlinear value function (e.g. Kahneman & Tversky, 1979; Thaler, 1985), consumers may perform less price search when the potential price saving is computed on a high base price than a low base price (cf. Grewal & Marmorstein, 1994). Consumers also may forego choice and investigate other options when a choice option is *added* to the choice set (cf. Dhar, 1997; Tversky & Shafir, 1992). Finally, consumers may overgeneralize from very limited product experience (Hoch & Deighton, 1989), consistent with biases observed in other contexts (Shaklee & Fischhoff, 1982; Tversky & Kahneman, 1974). If the experience is negative, further sampling of the option may be quickly but prematurely terminated.

Internal Search

It is natural to think about search in terms of the external environment. Indeed, when the decision task is completely "stimulus-based," as in some supermarket contexts, consumers can view a relatively complete set of brands and inspect product specifications for all or most of the desired attribute information. In other instances, however, there may be no or only incomplete stimulus information, and the decision must be based partially or exclusively on retrieved options and attributes (Alba, Hutchinson & Lynch, 1991).

Several studies have examined the role of memory processes in the formation of consideration sets. (Early consumer research discovered that people frequently do not consider all possible alternatives when making actual choices. More or less independently, econometric analysis developed sophisticated statistical models of heterogeneity in both preferences and the choice set across individuals.

For a review, see Shocker, Ben-Akiva, Boccara & Nadungadi, 1991.) Nedungadi (1990) asked subjects to make a memory-based choice from a familiar product category. His results showed that unobtrusive priming of a brand in a nonsalient subcategory dramatically increased choice probabilities for that brand and for non-primed brands in the same subcategory. The results also showed that recall, but not rated preference, was similarly enhanced.

Alba & Chattopadhyay (1985a, 1986) showed that a consumer's consideration set can be manipulated via provision of a subset of available brands, not unlike recall inhibition achieved through part-list cuing.

Mitra & Lynch (1995) showed how the effects of advertising on memory for product information can affect price sensitivity. Advertising enhanced the retrieval of more alternatives at the time of choice and allowed the consumer to exhibit greater price sensitivity (i.e. recall and choose acceptable low-priced items; cf. Shapiro, MacInnis & Heckler, 1997). However, the content of advertising also differentiated items, essentially giving consumers retrievable information to justify choosing higher priced options.

Kardes & Kalyanaram (1992) used multiple experimental sessions over several weeks to simulate the development of consideration sets in new markets. Their results provided empirical support for the hypothesis that there are enduring primacy effects on both memory and preference that provide a partial explanation of the "first-mover advantage" often observed in real markets.

Hutchinson, Raman & Mantrala (1994) developed and empirically estimated a stochastic model of brand name recall. Retrieval time was found to be inversely related to prior usage (which presumably reflects consideration and preference), the overall presence of the products in the marketplace (similar to frequency of instantiation; Barsalou, 1985), and the marketing efforts of manufacturers (e.g. amount of money spent advertising the brand). Together, the above studies demonstrate how basic memory processes affect brand recall and ultimate consumer choice.

Once a consumer has constructed a set of brands for consideration, there remains the task of making a final choice. Not all attribute information is recalled equally well, and traditional memory factors, such as perceptual salience, repetition, elaboration, and interference influence inputs into the decision (for more extensive discussions, see Alba & Hutchinson, 1987; Petty & Cacioppo, 1981). Similarly, the decision itself may influence the type of information that is subsequently recalled. For example, research suggests that attributes of chosen alternatives are preferentially recalled over attributes of nonchosen alternatives (Biehal & Chakravarti, 1982) and reasons that support a decision are preferentially recalled over contradictory reasons (Dellarosa & Bourne, 1984). Traditional rehearsal and cuing explanations have been offered for these effects as well. In recent years, however, effort has shifted away from understanding the nature of attribute recall and toward determining whether consumers engage in internal attribute search during decision making.

Although it might appear intuitive that consumers would search memory for attribute information when making memory-based decisions, the issue is noteworthy precisely because numerous studies have reported evidence to the contrary. Specifically, a majority of studies report a weak correlation between attribute recall and persuasion. A widely accepted explanation of this outcome is that most judgments are made upon receipt of information. Once formed, they may be retrieved directly without reliance on memory for the attributes on which they are based. On the presumably rare occasions in which an initial judgment is not generated, significant correlations between judgment and attribute recall should obtain (see Hastie & Park, 1986).

Although "judgment-referral" has been implicated in many decision contexts, consumer research has shown it to be an incomplete account of decision making. One simple reason is that memory for product judgments is subject to the same constraints as memory for other types of information. For example, in the context of judgments for multiple options, interference may reduce the retrievability of one's judgment of any particular option (Baumgardner, Leippe, Ronis & Greenwald, 1983; Keller, 1991).

More important than interference, however, is the nature of the task confronting the consumer. Unlike social judgment, purchase situations frequently require consumers to make a choice among competing options rather than an assessment of a single target. A key moderator of the use of prior judgments vis-à-vis product attributes is the "diagnosticity" of the recalled information (Feldman & Lynch, 1988). In some consumer choice contexts, global judgments will not be sufficient to discriminate among alternatives. Most competing brands are evaluatively good in some sense. Unless consumers are satisficing, the relative assessments required to establish preferences may require more precise inputs. Hence, consumers may attempt to recall more specific information. Empirical support for this more complex relationship comes from two studies (Chattopadhyay & Alba, 1988; Lynch, Marmorstein & Weigold, 1988). Those studies show that consumers will rely on overall evaluations rather than specific attributes when only a single alternative is being judged or when the overall evaluations are sufficiently different and can discriminate among options. However, when comparative judgments or choices are made and the global evaluations are not diagnostic, attribute recall predicts preference.

Of course, much depends on the precision of memory. When specific attributes cannot be recalled but a decision must be made nonetheless, consumers will retrieve and use whatever information is deemed next most diagnostic. Such information may include memorable peripheral cues and abstract summaries of specific attributes, which can result in choice of inferior options (Alba, Marmorstein & Chattopadhyay, 1992).

Learning and the Development of Consumer Expertise

Information search and exposure to products do not ensure the development of expertise or improvements in decision quality. We briefly consider consumer knowledge across the broad spectrum from familiarity to true expertise.

Familiarity

Researchers in both marketing and psychology have found evidence that "mere" familiarity has a positive effect on attitudes and choices. For example, the classic mere exposure effect has been demonstrated in consumer situations involving brand names and product packages (Janiszewski, 1993; see also Gordon & Holyoak, 1983; Kunst-Wilson & Zajonc, 1980; Obermiller, 1985; Zajonc & Markus, 1982). Additionally, Moore & Hutchinson (1985) found evidence that familiarity mediates the delayed positive effect of affective reactions to advertising (regardless of whether the initially affective response was positive or negative). Finally, many researchers have found that typicality generally has a positive effect on brand preferences, although preferences for novelty and moderate levels of schema incongruity have also been reported (Barsalou, 1985; Gordon & Holyoak, 1983; Loken & Ward, 1990; Martindale & Moore, 1988; Nedungadi & Hutchinson, 1985; Veryzer & Hutchinson, 1998).

Learning and Prediction

We noted how advertising, when used as an information source, can shape consumer opinion and lead to suboptimal decisions. Fortunately, consumers have other options available to them. However, there is scant evidence that consumers are highly informed or are rapid learners, regardless of information source. Surveys of consumers' factual knowledge can produce disappointing results (Alba & Hutchinson, 1991), and rule learning does not appear to be a particular strength of consumers (Hutton, Mauser, Filiatrault & Ahtola, 1986). Although there is no well-developed literature on consumer learning, the available evidence suggests that, as with other topics discussed thus far, failure to learn appropriate rules stems from a combination of poor logic, low motivation, and information processing constraints.

One of the few studies to examine consumer learning of multiattribute rules revealed two interesting effects (Meyer, 1987). First, despite multiple learning trials, consumers are more likely to learn how exemplars are associated with positive and negative product outcomes than the underlying attribute rule that governs quality outcomes. Second, consumers are quicker to learn exemplars that lead to a positive outcome than to a negative outcome. Although the use of exemplars as an optimizing strategy can be criticized (see Hutchinson & Alba, 1997), exemplar heuristics are not rare and a "positive-exemplar heuristic" can be viewed as reasonable if consumers adopt a "good-enough" criterion for product choice. If known similar cases have resulted in good outcomes, approximations of those cases also are likely to produce good outcomes.

A similar explanation may be provided for consumers' tendency to draw erroneous conclusions from advocacy messages such as advertisements (see Hoch & Deighton, 1989). A brand may stake a claim to superiority by promoting an attribute it shares with its competitors. Hoch & Deighton's example of *Folgers*' "mountain grown" coffee serves as a good illustration. High quality coffees are grown in mountainous regions. This is true for *Folgers* as well as its high quality competitors. By promoting "mountain grown" as a reason to purchase, *Folgers* commits no sin even though consumers are unlikely to understand that the attribute does not apply uniquely to *Folgers* (cf. Kruschke, 1996). Nonetheless, if the attribute is causal, use of it may result in unwarranted loyalty to *Folgers* but may not necessarily result in a loss of welfare.

Processing constraints also may contribute to the formation of erroneous rules. Cognitive psychologists have long distinguished between analytic and holistic categorization processes (Brooks, 1978; Kemler Nelson, 1984). The former refers to correct categorization based (typically) on a single diagnostic attribute; the latter refers to classification based on an object's overall similarity to other category instances. Hutchinson & Alba (1991) demonstrated, however, that when meaningful product information is used to construct stimuli, and salience varies significantly across attributes, classification is neither analytic nor holistic. Rather, decisions are based on a small subset of salient attributes that typically includes both diagnostic and nondiagnostic information. Limiting cases were "pseudoanalytic" insofar as a single salient, but nondiagnostic, attribute was used (see also Russo & Dosher, 1983).

Consumer learning can also be inhibited by conceptually driven processes. As in other areas of human endeavor, consumers possess strong prior beliefs (or prejudices) about the state of the world, including beliefs about brand superiority, country-of-origin effects, and the price–quality relationship. Consumers are prone to cling to these beliefs even in the face of contradictory data, especially, as in the case of pseudoanalytic processing, when the environment imposes processing constraints. For example, consider the case of the price–quality relationship. Independent tests report low empirical correlations in some product categories (Lichtenstein & Burton, 1989), yet consumers appear to rely heavily on price as a signal of quality. Laboratory research indicates that consumers are most biased by their prior beliefs when perception and recall of price and quality information is made difficult (Pechmann & Ratneshwar, 1992) or when the density and presentation format of the information provide consumers with latitude to engage in confirmatory processing (Broniarczyk & Alba, 1994b, c).

The research described above suggests that, when left to their own devices, consumer learning can be inefficient and errorful. However, as with investigation of decision making in general, there is a tendency to accentuate the negative (Christensen-Szalanski & Beach, 1984). Consumers can learn, even without formal attempts to educate them. A recent study demonstrates that the mere provision of a "consumption vocabulary," operationalized as a set of attribute labels and descriptions, can result in improvements on several learning dimensions (West, Brown & Hoch, 1996). In comparison to consumers who inspect a novel category without such linguistic assistance, consumers provided merely with a vocabulary are more likely to learn about additional dimensions not included in the vocabulary, engage in more complex decision making, show consistency in their preferences over time, and exhibit a greater ability to describe the bases for their preferences.

Between-Groups Differences in Expertise

Consumer researchers and marketing managers have had a long-standing interest in the cognitive effects of extensive experience with specific products. In particular, whenever innovative products are introduced, the entire population must learn about the costs and benefits of that product. Moreover, consumers differ widely in knowledge about even well-established products and brands, depending on their personal experiences. For example, one might be very knowledgeable about motorcycles but not sewing machines, or about one's favorite soft drink but not the favorite of one's spouse. These differences have important implications for issues ranging from information search to product safety (cf. Chi, Glaser & Farr, 1988). Thus, there is a growing interest in the areas of consumer expertise and knowledge. Alba & Hutchinson (1987) reviewed a broad spectrum of consumer and cognitive research in an attempt to characterize consumer expertise and distinguish it from product familiarity. Although the constructs are clearly related, they define familiarity to be "the number of product-related experiences that have been accumulated by the consumer" and expertise as "the ability to perform product-related tasks successfully." From this perspective, most early research in this area used measures of familiarity or ownership, whereas more recent research has included measures of expertise (Brucks, 1986).

As discussed earlier, research on external information search suggests an inverted-U relationship with consumer expertise (i.e. the highest levels of search occur at moderate levels of expertise). Expert–novice comparisons among consumers have also found expert-superiority effects in the size and structure of memory for brand names and factual information (Hutchinson, 1983; Mitchell & Dacin, 1996), the ability to match products to usage situations correctly (Mitchell & Dacin, 1996), and the ability to predict market prices (Spence & Brucks, 1997). Similarly, a number of studies have examined how various consumer-related abilities develop during childhood (Brucks, Armstrong & Goldberg, 1988; John, 1997; Macklin, 1996). One finding that is common to many of these studies is that experts are able to identify the most diagnostic inputs for decision making, thereby reducing their effort and increasing their accuracy. In some instances, however, these benefits are offset by diminished search activity and overconfidence.

CONSUMER DECISION MAKING

Consumer research has focused much of its attention on how individuals make purchase decisions. There are many other types of decisions that consumers make, including what information is needed, where and when to shop prior to purchase, how to use or consume previously purchased products, and when such products are no longer needed. However, the purchase decision is central to most business applications because that transaction marks the point at which money changes hands and an effect is exerted on the buyer, the seller, and the economy as a whole.

Models of Preference and Choice

Although there are many variations, the standard model of the purchase decision is a stage model in which the consumer first recognizes a need, collects information (either from memory or from external sources), combines that information in some way to form product preferences, chooses a specific product, and finally consumes the product (thus achieving the initial goal and obtaining feedback that can be used in future decisions). Typically the chosen product is most preferred among those available; however, in some models, memory failures, cognitive biases, or information processing errors can result in the choice of less preferred alternatives. Need recognition, information acquisition, and consumption are often assumed to encompass a wide variety of activities that may occur over an extended period of time (see earlier discussions). The act of purchase, however, is typically a singular event. Thus, a very common research paradigm is to control both motivation and information experimentally and then measure preferences or observe choice behavior (usually without consumption feedback). In many ways, this conforms to the traditional stimulus–response paradigms used in cognitive psychology. There is a fundamental difference, however. In typical cognitive tasks, the experimenter knows or defines a "correct" response *a priori* and subsequently assesses performance in terms of measures such as accuracy or decision times (for correct responses) that are computed in the same way for all subjects. For most purchase tasks, "correctness" is fundamentally problematic because different individuals have different needs and goals and, therefore, value choice alternatives differently. Although some paradigms contrive methods to control such heterogeneity (e.g. by asking subjects to make a purchase for a hypothetical individual with explicitly defined values), most consumer research must include measures of individual preferences. Often, and especially in academic research, these measures provide methodological controls for testing other hypotheses of interest (e.g. factors that change preferences, affect comprehension and recall, etc.). Equally often, and especially in commercial applications, measures of preference and choice are of direct interest because they guide managerial decisions about what products and services to develop and what prices to charge.

Measuring Consumer Preference

The measurement models used for assessing consumer preferences derive from two research domains in psychology: attitude formation and psychometric analysis. In particular, fundamental measurement (Krantz, Luce, Suppes & Tversky, 1971), information integration (Anderson, 1981), expectancy-value (Fishbein & Ajzen, 1975), and multiattribute utility theory (Carroll, 1980; Keeney & Raiffa, 1976) have been highly influential, and the methods of those paradigms are often directly applied in consumer research.

Three general approaches to measuring preferences are most common. First, the survey methods of attitude and public opinion research are commonly employed to assess consumer preferences for actual or hypothetical products and consumer perceptions (or beliefs) about the attributes products possess. Preference measures are then modeled as a function of attribute perceptions and other variables using some appropriate statistical methods (e.g. Lilien, Kotler & Moorthy, 1992). For example, Bagozzi (1982) reports a field application of Fishbein & Ajzen's (1975) model that employs causal modeling. Additionally, it is not uncommon to assess purchase intention and to validate these intentions with measures of actual behavior. This validation step has been a focus of research activity in both academic and commercial applications (Jamieson & Bass, 1989; Urban & Katz, 1983).

The second general approach to measuring preferences is conjoint analysis. Although influenced by the classic work of Krantz & Tversky (e.g. 1971) on axiomatic foundations and Anderson (1981; Lynch, 1985) on model-testing, marketing research has developed an extensive academic literature on the design, analysis, and validation of data from conjoint experiments. These methods have been widely applied in commercial settings to guide product development and understand how identifiable groups of consumers (often called segments) differ in product preferences (e.g. Carroll & Green, 1995; Green & Srinivasan, 1990; Louviere, 1988). The typical conjoint analysis experiment requires subjects to rate or rank 10–30 hypothetical products described (verbally and/or visually) in terms of nominal scale attributes. The complete set of describable products (i.e. all possible combinations of attribute values) is prohibitively large, so an orthogonal fraction is used and the main effects of each attribute on preference (called part-worths) are estimated.

The third approach uses psychometric methods such as factor analysis, multidimensional scaling, and joint space analysis to represent preferences among existing products as distances from an ideal product in an underlying space (Carroll, 1980). The main goal of these analyses is to uncover the features or dimensions that consumers naturally use to organize products. As with conjoint analysis, marketing researchers began applying these methods and developing specialized versions in parallel with their development in psychology in the 1970s (e.g. Cooper, 1983; Shepard, Romney & Nerlove, 1972). As in psychology, the psychometric methods used to uncover cognitive structure have been complemented by more experimental research on natural categories and graded structure (Bettman & Sujan, 1987; Hutchinson et al., 1994; Nedungadi & Hutchinson, 1985; Ratneshwar & Shocker, 1991; Urban, Hulland & Weinberg, 1993).

Context Effects

As a result of the widespread use of these preference scaling methods, consumer researchers have also investigated many of the context effects that have been identified in the cognitive literature. Two of these have been particularly important not only because of their implications for models of the judgment process but also because they highlight systematic sources of measurement error that have pragmatic implications as well. First, there are the effects of stimulus range and frequency that were first noted by Parducci (1965; see also Gescheider, 1988). The focus in this research is on the separation of the effects of "response language" from those of psychological impressions. Presumably, the latter are a more valid indicator of true preferences. To the extent that the stimulus range affects psychological impressions (even transiently), consumers are at risk to be biased in their decisions by the specific set of alternatives available. In general, consumer research supports the existence of range effects at both levels (i.e. response language and psychological impressions); however, these effects appear to be reduced substantially by experience (Lynch, Chakravarti & Mitra, 1991). Thus, novice consumers are at greater risk than experts (see also Alba & Hutchinson, 1987).

The second important context effect that has influenced consumer researchers is preference reversal (e.g. Schkade & Johnson, 1989; Tversky, Slovic & Kahneman, 1990). The basic finding is that willingness-to-pay measures of preference (in which subjects report specific prices in dollars that create indifference between two alternatives) are systematically reversed when subjects (possibly the same subjects) are presented with a discrete choice. This result is problematic for both the economic theory of rational consumer behavior and commercial applications of preference measurement (e.g. conjoint analysis). In marketing, there has been considerable research on the development of measurement methods in which subjective ratings and discrete choices produce consistent and reliable estimates of preference (Louviere, 1988). In general, such convergence is possible, but researchers must be vigilant about the differences between preference and choice tasks.

Predicting Consumer Choice in Real and Simulated Markets

In recent years, there has been a widespread trend toward collecting and modeling discrete choice data in the laboratory and the field. The impetus for this trend is simply that consumers participate in markets by making choices. Few real-world behaviors resemble the types of judgments measured by ratings scales, and research on attitude–behavior consistency cautions against taking rating scale responses at face value (Petty, Unnava & Strathman, 1991).

As in the case of preference modeling, consumer choice modeling has been strongly influenced by work in psychology (especially Luce, 1959; Tversky, 1972) and in econometrics (especially McFadden, 1986). Often called the Bradley–Terry–Luce model (after independent development by Bradley & Terry, 1957 and Luce, 1959) in the psychological literature, the *attraction model* of aggregate and individual level choice is ubiquitous. In its simplest form, the probability of choosing item x from the set of choice alternatives A is $\mathrm{v}(x)/\sum_{y \in \mathrm{A}} \mathrm{v}(y)$ where v is a positive-valued function that represents the attractiveness of each item. There is abundant evidence in both psychology (e.g. Tversky & Sattath, 1979) and consumer research (e.g. Kahn, Moore & Glazer, 1987) that this model fails to account for key aspects of both aggregate and individual level choice. In particular, the model exhibits the formal property of independence from irrelevant alternatives. (Often abbreviated as IIA, this property requires that the addition of one or more choice alternatives decreases the choice probabilities for existing alternatives by a constant percentage.) However, it is frequently observed that a new choice alternative draws its share disproportionately from alternatives that are similar to it, as when a conservative Independent Party candidate hurts the Republican candidate more than the Democratic candidate in an election. This is called the *similarity effect* and was first described by Debreu (1960). A wide array of more sophisticated models have been developed in a number of disciplines to account for these and other known choice phenomena. It is beyond the scope of this chapter to review these models; however, excellent reviews of the consumer choice literature can be found in Corstjens & Gautschi (1983), McFadden (1986), and Meyer & Kahn (1991).

Despite its failure as a complete model of choice, the attraction model is often a good and easily estimated approximation. As such, it has proved to be a widely used "work horse" as part of more complex models in need of a decision-making component. The exponential, or multinomial logit, version of the attraction model has proved especially useful in this regard as it has in cognitive models of memory and classification (e.g. see Nosofsky, 1984) mainly because of its mathematical and statistical properties. The most influential application of this model in consumer research is the analysis of scanner panel data by Guadagni & Little (1983).* These researchers examined purchases of regular ground coffee over a two-year time period and showed that a multinomial logit model that incorporated price, promotion, and brand loyalty (as measured by past purchases) provided an excellent predictive model of future purchases, including conditions of changed price and promotion. The model is very rudimentary from a cognitive perspective and can be thought of as a simple response model for stimuli defined by price and promotion plus a simple learning component (similar to associative reinforcement models such as Kruschke, 1996, and Rescorla & Wagner, 1972). In fact, more recent and sophisticated statistical models that distinguish between structural state dependence, habit persistence, and unobserved heterogeneity are relatively simple from a cognitive perspective (e.g. Roy, Chintagunta & Haldar, 1996). However, they establish important benchmarks for testing cognitively based models with observations of real choice behavior in a complex environment.

Dynamic aspects of choice, especially choice-switching behavior, have been extensively studied by consumer researchers (see Hutchinson & Meyer, 1994; Meyer & Kahn, 1991). A central problem has been to identify systematic deviations from patterns of switching that would result from simple zero-order stochastic processes (i.e. random variations without true statistical dependence on prior choices, learning, etc.). The main sources of such deviations that have been postulated are cognitive in nature and include behavioral reinforcement from consumption, brand loyalty, attribute satiation effects, and need for variety (Hutchinson, 1986; Kahn, Kalwani & Morrison, 1986; Lattin & McAlister, 1985; Menon & Kahn, 1995). Hutchinson (1986) reviews the formal properties of brand switching models from a perspective similar to that used in mathematical psychology for single-occasion choice models.

The explicit incorporation of population heterogeneity into models of choice behavior has proven to be particularly important and is often ignored in cognitive research (although there are certainly exceptions). The basic insight from a wide variety of research is that observed market-level behavior, and estimated choice model parameters, can strongly suggest dynamic properties, such as those discussed earlier, that are spurious or distorted when heterogeneity in the population is ignored. In particular, heterogeneity in preference induces an aggregate pattern of choice that exhibits significant apparent inertia or purchase

* Scanner panel data is derived from samples of consumers who, for a fee, allow all of their food store purchases to be tracked electronically – providing an unobtrusive method for observing actual choice behavior as it occurs in the marketplace. Such data are collected by a marketing research firm, analyzed, and sold to manufacturers. However, a number of academic release data sets have stimulated intensive research activity over the past 10 to 15 years.

habit (Roy et al., 1996). If not explicitly modeled, this inertia can mask consumer sensitivities to available information and tendencies to seek variety.

Finally, an increasing amount of research on choice behavior uses simulated markets and the methods of experimental economics (Camerer & Ho, 1999; Lopes 1994; Meyer & Assuncao, 1990). Unlike the paradigms used in cognitive and social psychology, these experiments place a premium on creating real markets in which significant amounts of money are provided as incentives. Also, few concurrent measures are observed other than the inputs to the market and the choice behavior of participants. The manipulations across conditions of the experiment are typically those suggested by economic theory regarding how populations of optimizing consumers should behave when the market comes to an equilibrium. A fair, though necessarily simplistic, summary of many results is that simulated markets respond in directions that are consistent with economic theory, but the precise points of the observed equilibria may exhibit systematic biases (Camerer, 1987; Hutchinson & Meyer, 1994). The initial market activity prior to the equilibria are typically of limited interest to experimental economists; however, to cognitive researchers and a growing number of economists studying market evolution, this period of learning and problem solving seems particularly fertile ground (Camerer & Ho, 1999; Lopes, 1994).

Heuristics and Biases in Risky Decision Making

The previous section describes how the models and methods of cognitive psychology have been applied and extended to understand consumer preferences and choices among options that are known with certainty. In this section, we briefly review aspects of the large, multidisciplinary literature on risky decision making that have most influenced consumer research and then discuss two unique contributions of consumer research to the decision-making literature.

The Influence of Behavioral Decision Theory

There are many excellent reviews of behavioral decision theory (e.g. Mellers, Schwartz & Cooke, 1998; Payne, Bettman & Johnson, 1993), so we will not attempt to provide a comprehensive summary here. Rather, we will describe the ways in which this research has affected consumer research. That consumers are limited in their ability to conform to the strategic, rational behavior of economic theory has been widely accepted in marketing for a long time as a result of both academic research (e.g. Simon, 1955; Tversky & Kahneman, 1974) and practitioner observations about market phenomena (e.g. Howard & Sheth, 1969; Krugman 1965). At a very general level, most consumer research adopts a perspective that reflects these limitations. One recent articulation of this perspective is the adaptive decision-making framework of Payne et al. (1993). Drawing on work in cognitive psychology, organizational behavior, and consumer research, these authors propose that choices in the marketplace result from a process of strategy selection. Consumers are able to use a wide variety of strategies to make any given decision. These strategies range from conscious, explicit rules to unconscious, automatic processes that serve as decision heuristics. The strategies vary in the effort they require and the accuracy with which they achieve decision objectives. Consumers choose among strategies based on their assessment of the effort–accuracy trade-off. This choice may not be strictly optimal, but it is assumed to generally be adaptive and intelligent (Payne et al., 1993). A key implication of this approach is that as decision tasks become more complex, simplifying strategies are more likely to be adopted. Simpler strategies are generally less accurate and more susceptible to the biasing effects of task and context variables.

Within the adaptive decision-making framework, the most influential work has been that of Simon (1955; Newell & Simon, 1972) and Tversky & Kahneman (1974). Many early (and still widely used) models of consumer behavior used Simon's problem-solving framework (e.g. Bettman, 1979; Howard & Sheth, 1969). Similarly, many consumer-oriented tasks have been used to replicate and extend results on framing (Thaler, 1985), agenda effects (Kahn et al., 1987), and loss aversion (Hardie, Johnson & Fader, 1993). In fact, these effects can be viewed as a more theoretical account of well-known marketing practices in advertising to "position" a product by influencing the relative salience of attribute information.

Finally, in addition to behavioral decision theory, models of consumer decision making have been strongly influenced by recent work on social judgment and attitude change. In particular, the elaboration-likelihood model of Petty, Cacioppo & Schumann (1983; Petty et al., 1991) and the accessibility-diagnosticity model of Feldman & Lynch (1988; Lynch et al., 1988) have received considerable attention. Both models are close in spirit to the adaptive decision-making model discussed earlier. For example, numerous consumer studies have examined how peripheral and central routes to persuasion are manifest in mass media advertising and how their effects are moderated by the consumer's level of involvement either with the product or the decision, per se (Petty et al., 1991).

Some Unique Contributions of Consumer Research

Most decision-making research is properly regarded as part of a broader, multidisciplinary effort in which core problems are addressed from a variety of perspectives. In addition to making progress on these core problems, the unique perspectives of each discipline often lead to unique contributions. In this section, we briefly describe two such contributions of the consumer perspective: choice context effects and methods for tracing cognitive processes during decision making.

Choice Context Effects

As discussed earlier, research on choice behavior quickly rejected simple attraction models because the principle of independence from irrelevant alternatives is frequently violated. Moreover, the systematic nature of the violations due to similarity effects motivated the development of a broad array of models in psychology and econometrics. Virtually all of these models satisfy the property of *regularity* (i.e. choice probabilities can only decrease or remain unchanged whenever a new alternative is added to the choice set). However, consumer researchers have found several manipulations of the stimulus context that result in systematic violations of regularity. All of these effects involve choices between two or three items that vary on two dimensions. The first of these, called *attraction* or *decoy effects*, arises when a two-item choice set is expanded by the addition of a third item that is dominated by one, but not the other, of the original two items (Huber, Payne & Puto, 1982). For example, the original set might contain items that differ in price and quality such that the higher quality item is also higher in price (i.e. neither item dominates the other). If a third item is added that is similar to the high-price item but slightly higher in price and slightly lower in quality, then a decoy effect arises. Few subjects choose the new item because it is dominated by the original high-price item. However, the original high-price item is chosen more frequently when the third item is present than when it is absent – a violation of regularity. The explanation of this effect is still a matter of intense debate, but there can be no doubt that it is a serious problem for traditional models of choice that are not context-sensitive (see Heath & Chatterjee, 1995).

More recently, Simonson (1989; Simonson & Tversky, 1992) has demonstrated violations of IIA and regularity without using dominated alternatives. As an example, assume that most people choose the lower priced item in the two-item set described earlier. If a third item is added that is higher in price and quality than the original high-price item by an amount that is approximately equal to that which separated the original two, the original high-price item benefits significantly and often in violation of regularity. This has been dubbed the *compromise effect* because the original high price item looks like a mid-price item in the new choice set. Again, the explanation for this effect is controversial; however, Tversky & Simonson (1993) have developed a model in which loss-aversion is the main explanatory principle.

Process Tracing

The ability of decision makers to provide accurate verbal descriptions of the processes that led to their choices has been a matter of significant debate (Ford, Schmitt, Schechtman, Hults & Doherty, 1989; Nisbett & Wilson, 1977). While acknowledging the problems of process tracing, consumer researchers have expended considerable effort developing techniques and methods of analysis for verbal protocols (Bettman & Park, 1980; Biehal & Chakravarti, 1986). More significantly, consumer researchers have been active in developing nonverbal methods that trace the information used by decision makers. For example, matrix-format stimulus displays are often used in an experimental paradigm that requires subjects to choose a spatial location and thereby acquire a specific piece of information (Jacoby, Chestnut, Weigl & Fisher, 1976; Payne et al., 1993). These displays are similar to the product-by-attribute tables frequently found in magazine advertising, but the entries of the table are revealed sequentially as the subject chooses them and the information history recorded and analyzed for consistency with various decision strategies. Alternatively, researchers have used eye-tracking methods to recover similar data in a more naturalistic manner (Russo, 1978). Most recently, consumer researchers have become very active in gathering and analyzing information acquisition data from computer on-line services (Alba et al., 1997; Hauser, Urban & Weinberg, 1993). Surprisingly, many of the laboratory methods that produced unnatural decision environments for consumers in the 1970s are very natural for "electronic consumers" of the 1990s.

CONCLUSIONS AND FUTURE DIRECTIONS

Our overly simple model of consumer behavior argues that consumers are exposed to information, react to information, and make decisions based on that information. Our objective has not been to develop a model but to illustrate the cognitive influences on a category of human endeavor that is an integral part of everyday life. In addition, we have tried to describe the points of overlap between cognitive psychology and consumer research. In some cases, such as in the study of memory, consumer research has contextualized some basic effects first reported in the cognitive literature; in other cases, such as in the study of information search, the influence could easily flow in the opposite direction; in yet other cases, such as in the study of loyalty and preference, the influence is, or should be, mutual. These bi-directional influences pertain not only to substantive findings about behavior, but also to the procedural domains of experimental method and psychophysical measurement.

We hope that our description of consumer research has been even-handed in terms of consumer welfare. Most researchers and practitioners believe that, in the long term, a firm's success is more likely to be driven by accurate and timely understanding of consumer preferences than by manipulation of those preferences. However, it is nonetheless the case that firms occasionally attempt to exploit deficits in consumer information processing described in the preceding pages.

To conclude with an emerging issue, recent developments in information technology may provide a shock to the competitive environment that will have fundamental implications for consumer welfare – as well as the study of consumer cognition. Specifically, developments in electronic shopping do much more than enhance shopping convenience. Predictions about "frictionless" commerce are based on the assumption that electronic formats can provide consumers with accesses to an extremely large number of choice options and an abundance of information about each of those options (see Alba et al., 1997). In principle, the availability of full information should reduce the potential for deception. In reality, the issue will be unresolved until externally valid empirical investigation is possible. Although prior research provides guidance regarding how consumers may react to such quantities of information, it provides only a starting point for understanding consumer use of information screening devices envisioned for electronic environments (Negroponte, 1995) or the implications of those devices for decision making (Widing & Talarzyk, 1993).

REFERENCES

Aaker, D. A. (1991). *Managing Brand Equity*. New York: Free Press.

Alba, J. W., Broniarczyk, S. M., Shimp, T. A. & Urbany, J. E. (1994). The influence of prior beliefs, frequency cues, and magnitude cues on consumers' perceptions of comparative price data. *Journal of Consumer Research*, 21, 219–35.

Alba, J. W. & Chattopadhyay, A. (1985a). Effects of context and part-category cues on recall of competing brands. *Journal of Marketing Research*, 22, 340–9.

Alba, J. W. & Chattopadhyay, A. (1985b). The effects of part-list cuing on attribute recall: problem framing at the point of retrieval. In E. C. Hirschman & M. B. Holbrook (Eds), *Advances in Consumer Research* (Vol. 12) (pp. 410–13). Provo, UT: Association for Consumer Research.

Alba, J. W. & Chattopadhyay, A. (1986). Salience effects in brand recall. *Journal of Marketing Research*, 23, 363–9.

Alba, J. W. & Hutchinson, J. W. (1987). Dimensions of consumer expertise. *Journal of Consumer Research*, 13, 411–54.

Alba, J. W. & Hutchinson, J. W. (1991). Public policy implications of consumer knowledge. In P. N. Bloom (Ed.), *Advances in Marketing and Public Policy* (Vol. 2) (pp. 1–39). Greenwich, CT: JAI Press.

Alba, J. W., Hutchinson, J. W. & Lynch, J. G. Jr (1991). Memory and decision making. In T. S. Robertson & H. H. Kassarjian (Eds), *Handbook of Consumer Behavior* (pp. 1–49). Englewood Cliffs, NJ: Prentice-Hall.

Alba, J., Lynch, J., Weitz, B., Janiszewski, C., Lutz, R., Sawyer, A. & Wood, S. (1997). Interactive home shopping: consumer, retailer, and manufacturer incentives to participate in electronic marketplaces. *Journal of Marketing*, 61, 38–53.

Alba, J. W., Marmorstein, H. & Chattopadhyay, A. (1992). Transitions in preference over time: the effects of memory on message persuasiveness. *Journal of Marketing Research*, 29, 406–16.

Anderson, N. H. (1981). *Foundations of Information Integration Theory*. New York: Academic Press.

Arkes, H. R. & Blumer, C. (1985). The psychology of sunk cost. *Organizational Behavior and Human Decision Processes*, 35, 124–40.

Bagozzi, R. P. (1982). A field investigation of causal relations among cognitions, affect, intentions, and behavior. *Journal of Marketing Research*, 19, 562–84.

Barsalou, L. W. (1985). Ideals, central tendency, and frequency of instantiation as determinants of graded structure. *Journal of Experimental Psychology: Learning, Memory, and Cognition*, 11, 629–54.

Baumgardner, M. H., Leippe, M. R., Ronis, D. L. & Greenwald, A. G. (1983). In search of reliable persuasion effects: II. Associative inference and persistence of persuasion in a message-dense environment. *Journal of Personality and Social Psychology*, 45, 524–37.

Bettman, J. R. (1979). *An Information Processing Theory of Consumer Choice*. Reading, MA: Addison-Wesley.

Bettman, J. R. & Park, C. W. (1980). Effects of prior knowledge and experience and phase of the choice process on consumer decision processes: a protocol analysis. *Journal of Consumer Research*, 7, 234–48.

Bettman, J. R. & Sujan, M. (1987). Effects of framing on evaluation of comparable and noncomparable alternatives by expert and novice consumers. *Journal of Consumer Research*, 14, 141–54.

Biehal, G. & Chakravarti, D. (1982). Information-presentation format and learning goals as determinants of consumers' memory retrieval and choice processes. *Journal of Consumer Research*, 8, 431–41.

Biehal, G. & Chakravarti, D. (1986). Consumer's use of memory and external information in choice: macro and micro perspectives. *Journal of Consumer Research*, 13, 382–405.

Bolger, F. & Harvey, N. (1995). Rationality of expectations in judgmental extrapolation of time series. In J.-P. Caverni, M. Bar-Hillel, F. H. Barron & H. Jungermann (Eds),

Contributions to Decision Making – I (pp. 121–134). Amsterdam: North-Holland/ Elsevier.

Bradley, R. A. & Terry, M. E. (1957). Rand analysis of incomplete blocks designs, I: the method of paired comparisons. *Biometrika*, 39, 324–45.

Broniarczyk, S. M. & Alba, J. W. (1994a). The importance of the brand in brand extension. *Journal of Marketing Research*, 31, 214–28.

Broniarczyk, S. M. & Alba, J. W. (1994b). The role of consumers' intuitions in inference making. *Journal of Consumer Research*, 21, 393–407.

Broniarczyk, S. M. & Alba, J. W. (1994c). Theory versus data in prediction and correlation tasks. *Organizational Behavior and Human Decision Processes*, 57, 117–39.

Brooks, L. (1978). Nonanalytic concept formation and memory for instances. In E. Rosch and B. B. Lloyd (Eds), *Cognition and Categorization* (pp. 169–211). Hillsdale, NJ: Erlbaum.

Brucks, M. (1985). The effects of product class knowledge on information search behavior. *Journal of Consumer Research*, 12, 1–16.

Brucks, M. (1986). A typology of consumer knowledge content. In R. J. Lutz (Ed.), *Advances in Consumer Research* (Vol. 13) (pp. 58–63). Provo, UT: Association for Consumer Research.

Brucks, M., Armstrong, G. M. & Goldberg, M. E. (1988). Children's use of cognitive defenses against television advertising: a cognitive response approach. *Journal of Consumer Research*, 14, 471–82.

Burke, R. R. & Srull, T. K. (1988). Competitive interference and consumer memory for advertising. *Journal of Consumer Research*, 15, 55–68.

Camerer, C. F. (1987). Do biases in probability judgments matter in markets? Experimental evidence. *American Economic Review*, 77, 981–97.

Camerer, C. & Ho, T.-H. (1999). Experience-weighted attraction learning in games: a unifying approach. Unpublished manuscript.

Carroll, J. D. (1980). Models and methods for multidimensional analysis of preferential choice (or other dominance) data. In E. D. Lantermann & H. Feger (Eds), *Similarity and Choice* (pp. 234–89). Bern, Germany: Hans Huber.

Carroll, J. D. & Green, P. E. (1995). Psychometric methods in marketing research: part I, conjoint analysis. *Journal of Marketing Research*, 32, 385–91.

Chatterjee, R. & Eliashberg, J. (1990). The innovation diffusion process in a heterogeneous population: a micromodeling approach. *Management Science*, 36, 1057–79.

Chattopadhyay, A. & Alba, J. W. (1988). The situational importance of recall and inference in consumer decision making. *Journal of Consumer Research*, 15, 1–12.

Chi, M. T. H, Glaser, R. & Farr, M. J. (1988). *The Nature of Expertise*. Hillsdale, NJ: Erlbaum.

Christensen-Szalanski, J. J. J. & Beach, L. R. (1984). The citation bias: fad and fashion in the judgment and decision literature. *American Psychologist*, 39, 75–8.

Cooper, L. (1983). A review of multidimensional scaling in marketing research. *Applied Psychological Measurement*, 7, 427–50.

Corstjens, M. L. & Gautschi, D. A. (1983). Formal choice models in marketing. *Marketing Science*, 2, 19–56.

Darby, M. R. & Karni, E. (1973). Free competition and the optimal amount of fraud. *Journal of Law and Economics*, 16, 66–86.

Debreu, G. (1960). Review of the book R. D. Luce, *Individual Choice Behavior: A Theoretical Analysis*. *American Economic Review*, 50, 186–8.

Deighton, J. (1984). The interaction of advertising and evidence. *Journal of Consumer Research*, 11, 763–70.

Dellarosa, D. & Bourne, L. E. Jr (1984). Decisions and memory: differential retrievability of consistent and contradictory evidence. *Journal of Verbal Learning and Verbal Behavior*, 23, 669–82.

Dhar, R. (1997). Consumer preferences for a no-choice option. *Journal of Consumer Research*, 24, 215–31.

Dickson, P. R. & Sawyer, A. G. (1990). The price knowledge and search of supermarket shoppers. *Journal of Marketing*, 54, 42–53.
Feinberg, F. M. & Huber, J. (1996). A theory of cutoff formation under imperfect information. *Management Science*, 42, 65–84.
Feldman, J. M. & Lynch, J. G. Jr (1988). Self-generated validity and other effects of measurement on belief, attitude, intention, and behavior. *Journal of Applied Psychology*, 73, 421–35.
Fishbein, M. & Ajzen, I. (1975). *Belief, Attitude, Intention, and Behavior: An Introduction to Theory and Research*. Reading, MA: Addison-Wesley.
Ford, J. K., Schmitt, N., Schechtman, S. L., Hults, B. M. & Doherty, M. L. (1989). Process tracing methods: contributions, problems, and neglected research questions. *Organizational Behavior and Human Decision Processes*, 43, 75–117.
Fournier, S. (1998). Consumers and their brands: developing relationship theory in consumer research. *Journal of Consumer Research*, 24, 343–73.
Gescheider, G. A. (1988). Psychophysical scaling. *Annual Review of Psychology*, 39, 169–200.
Gigerenzer, G. & Hoffrage, U. (1995). How to improve bayesian reasoning without instruction: frequency formats. *Psychological Review*, 102, 684–704.
Gordon, P. C. & Holyoak, K. J. (1983). Implicit learning and generalization of the 'mere exposure' effect. *Journal of Personality and Social Psychology*, 45, 492–500.
Green, P. E. & Srinivasan, V. (1990). Conjoint analysis in marketing: new developments with implications for research and practice. *Journal of Marketing*, 54, 3–19.
Grether, D. M. (1980). Bayes rule as a descriptive model: the representativeness heuristic. *Quarterly Journal of Economics*, 537–57.
Grewal, D. & Marmorstein, H. (1994). Market price variation, perceived price variation, and consumers' price search decisions for durable goods. *Journal of Consumer Research*, 21, 453–60.
Guadagni, P. M. & Little, J. D. C. (1983). A logit model of brand choice calibrated on scanner data. *Marketing Science*, 2, 203–38.
Ha, Y.-W. & Hoch, S. J. (1989). Ambiguity, processing strategy, and advertising-evidence interactions. *Journal of Consumer Research*, 16, 354–60.
Hastie, R. & Park, B. (1986). The relationship between memory and judgment depends on whether the judgment task is memory-based or on-line. *Psychological Review*, 93, 258–68.
Hardie, B. G. S., Johnson, E. J. & Fader, P. S. (1993). Modeling loss aversion and reference dependence effects on brand choice. *Marketing Science*, 12, 378–94.
Hauser, J. R. (1978). Testing the accuracy, usefulness, and significance of probabilistic models: an information-theoretic approach. *Operations Research*, 26, 406–21.
Hauser, J. R. & Wernerfelt, B. (1990). An evaluation cost model of consideration sets. *Journal of Consumer Research*, 16, 393–408.
Hauser, J. R., Urban, G. L. & Weinberg, B. W. (1993). How consumers allocate their time when searching for information. *Journal of Marketing Research*, 30, 452–66.
Heath, T. B. & Chatterjee, S. (1995). Asymmetric decoy effects on lower quality versus higher quality brands: meta-analytic and experimental evidence. *Journal of Consumer Research*, 22, 268–84.
Hoch, S. J. & Deighton, J. (1989). Managing what consumers learn from experience. *Journal of Marketing*, 53, 1–20.
Hoch, S. J. & Ha, H.-Y. (1986). Consumer learning: advertising and the ambiguity of product experience. *Journal of Consumer Research*, 13, 221–33.
Howard, J. A. & Sheth, J. N. (1969). *The Theory of Buyer Behavior*. New York: John Wiley.
Hoyer, W. D. & Brown, S. P. (1990). Effects of brand awareness on choice for a common, repeat-purchase product. *Journal of Consumer Research*, 17, 141–8.
Huber, J., Payne, J. W. & Puto, C. (1982). Adding asymmetrically dominated alternatives: violations of regularity and the similarity hypothesis. *Journal of Consumer Research*, 9, 90–8.

Hutchinson, J. W. (1983). Expertise and the structure of free recall. In R. P. Bagozzi & A. M. Tybout (Eds), *Advances in Consumer Research* (Vol. 10) (pp. 585–9). Provo, UT: Association for Consumer Research.

Hutchinson, J. W. (1986). Discrete attribute models of brand switching. *Marketing Science*, 5, 350–71.

Hutchinson, J. W. & Alba, J. W. (1991). Ignoring irrelevant information: situational determinants of consumer learning. *Journal of Consumer Research*, 18, 325–45.

Hutchinson, J. W. & Alba, J. W. (1997). Heuristics and biases in the 'eye-balling' of data: the effects of context on intuitive correlation assessment. *Journal of Experimental Psychology: Learning, Memory, and Cognition*, 23, 591–621.

Hutchinson, J. W. & Meyer, R. J. (1994). Dynamic decision making: optimal policies and actual behavior in sequential choice problems. *Marketing Letters*, 5, 369–82.

Hutchinson, J. W., Raman, K. & Mantrala, M. (1994). Finding choice alternatives in memory: probability models of brand name recall. *Journal of Marketing Research*, 31, 441–61.

Hutton, R. B., Mauser, G. A., Filiatrault, P. & Ahtola, O. T. (1986). Effects of cost-related feedback on consumer knowledge and consumption behavior: a field experimental approach. *Journal of Consumer Research*, 13, 327–36.

Inman, J. J., McAlister, L. & Hoyer, W. D. (1990). Promotion signal: proxy for a price cut? *Journal of Consumer Research*, 17, 74–81.

Jacobson, R. & Obermiller, C. (1990). The formation of expected future price: a reference price for forward-looking consumers. *Journal of Consumer Research*, 16, 420–32.

Jacoby, J. (1971). A model for multi-brand loyalty. *Journal of Advertising Research*, 11, 25–30.

Jacoby, J., Chestnut, R. W., Weigl, K. C. & Fisher, W. (1976). Pre-purchase information acquisition: description of a process methodology, research paradigm, and pilot investigation. In B. B. Anderson (Ed.), *Advances in Consumer Research* (Vol. 3) (pp. 306–14). Provo, UT: Association for Consumer Research.

Jamieson, L. F. & Bass, F. M. (1989). Adjusting stated intention measures to predict trial purchase of new products: a comparison of models and methods. *Journal of Marketing Research*, 26, 336–45.

Janiszewski, C. (1993). Preattentive mere exposure effects. *Journal of Consumer Research*, 20, 376–92.

John, D. R. (1997). Out of the mouth of babes: what children can tell us. In M. Brucks and D. MacInnis (Eds), *Advances in Consumer Research* (Vol. 24) (pp. 1–5). Provo, UT: Association for Consumer Research.

Johnson, E. J. & Russo, J. E. (1984). Product familiarity and learning new information. *Journal of Consumer Research*, 11, 542–50.

Kahn, B. E., Kalwani, M. U. & Morrison, D. M. (1986). Measuring variety seeking and reinforcement behaviors using panel data. *Journal of Marketing Research*, 23, 89–100.

Kahn, B., Moore, W. M. & Glazer, R. (1987). Experiments in constrained choice. *Journal of Consumer Research*, 14, 96–113.

Kahneman, D. & Tversky, A. (1979). Prospect theory: an analysis of decision under risk. *Econometrica*, 47, 263–91.

Kahneman, D., Knetsch, J. L. & Thaler, R. (1986). Fairness as a constraint on profit seeking: entitlements in the market. *American Economic Review*, 76, 728–41.

Kahneman, D., Knetsch, J. L. & Thaler, R. H. (1990). Experimental tests of the endowment effect and the coarse theorem. *Journal of Political Economy*, 98, 1325–48.

Kalwani, M. U., Yim, C. K., Rinne, H. J. & Sugita, Y. (1990). A price expectations model of customer brand choice. *Journal of Marketing Research*, 27, 251–62.

Kardes, F. R. & Kalyanaram, G. (1992). Order-of-entry effects on consumer memory and judgment: an information integration perspective. *Journal of Marketing Research*, 29, 343–57.

Keeney, R. L. & Raiffa, H. (1976). *Decisions with Multiple Objectives: Preferences and Value Tradeoffs*. New York: Wiley.

Keller, K. L. (1991). Memory and evaluation effects in competitive advertising environments. *Journal of Consumer Research*, 17, 463–76.
Kemler Nelson, D. G. (1984). The effect of information on what concepts are acquired. *Journal of Verbal Learning and Verbal Behavior*, 23, 734–59.
Krantz, D. H. & Tversky, A. (1971). Conjoint measurement analysis of composition rules in psychology. *Psychological Review*, 78, 151–69.
Krantz, D. H., Luce, R. D., Suppes, P. & Tversky, A. (1971). *Foundations of Measurement* (Vol. 1). New York: Academic Press.
Krishna, A. (1991). Effect of dealing patterns on consumer perceptions of deal frequency and willingness to pay. *Journal of Marketing Research*, 28, 441–51.
Krugman, H. E. (1965). The impact of television advertising: learning without involvement. *Public Opinion Quarterly*, 39, 349–56.
Kruschke, J. K. (1996). Base rates in category learning. *Journal of Experimental Psychology: Learning, Memory, and Cognition*, 22, 2–26.
Kunst-Wilson, W. R. & Zajonc, R. B. (1980). Affective discrimination of stimuli that cannot be recognized. *Science*, 207, 557–8.
Lattin, J. M. & Bucklin, R. E. (1989). Reference effects of price and promotion on brand choice behavior. *Journal of Marketing Research*, 26, 299–310.
Lattin, J. M. & McAlister, L. (1985). Using a variety-seeking model to identify substitute and complementary relationships among competing products. *Journal of Marketing Research*, 22, 330–9.
Levin, I. P. & Gaeth, G. J. (1988). How consumers are affected by the framing of attribute information before and after consuming the product. *Journal of Consumer Research*, 15, 374–8.
Lichtenstein, D. R. & Burton, S. (1989). The relationship between perceived and objective price-quality. *Journal of Marketing Research*, 26, 429–43.
Lilien, G. L., Kotler, P. & Moorthy, K. S. (1992). *Marketing Models*. Englewood Cliffs, NJ: Prentice Hall.
Lippman, S. A. & McCardle, K. (1991). Uncertain search: a model of search among technologies of uncertain values. *Management Science*, 37, 1474–90.
Loken, B. & Ward, J. (1990). Alternative approaches to understanding the determinants of typicality. *Journal of Consumer Research*, 17, 111–26.
Lopes, L. L. (1994). Psychology and economics: perspectives on risk, cooperation, and the marketplace. *Annual Review of Psychology*, 45, 197–227.
Louviere, J. L. (1988). *Analyzing Decision Making: Metric Conjoint Analysis*. New York: Sage.
Luce, R. D. (1959). *Individual Choice Behavior*. New York: Wiley.
Lynch, J. G. Jr (1985). Uniqueness issues in the decompositional modeling of multiattribute overall evaluations: an information integration perspective. *Journal of Marketing Research*, 22, 1–19.
Lynch, J. L. Jr, Chakravarti, D. & Mitra, A. (1991). Contrast effects in consumer judgments: changes in mental representations or in the anchoring of rating scales? *Journal of Consumer Research*, 18, 284–97.
Lynch, J. L. Jr, Marmorstein, H. & Weigold, M. F. (1988). Choices from sets including remembered brands: use of recalled attributes and prior overall evaluations. *Journal of Consumer Research*, 15, 169–84.
Macklin, M. C. (1996). Preschoolers' learning of brand names from visual cues. *Journal of Consumer Research*, 23, 251–61.
March, J. G. (1996). Learning to be risk averse. *Psychological Review*, 103, 309–19.
Martindale, C. & Moore, K. (1988). Priming, prototypicality, and preference. *Journal of Experimental Psychology: Human Perception and Performance*, 14, 661–70.
Mayhew, G. E. & Winer, R. S. (1992). An empirical analysis of internal and external reference prices using scanner data. *Journal of Consumer Research*, 19, 62–70.
McFadden, D. (1986). The choice theory approach to marketing research. *Marketing Science*, 5, 275–97.
McKenna, C. J. (1987). Theories of individual search behaviour. In J. D. Hey & P. J.

Lambert (Eds), *Surveys in the Economics of Uncertainty* (pp. 91–109). Oxford: Blackwell.

Mellers, B. A., Schwartz, A. & Cooke, A. D. J. (1998). Judgment and decision making. *Annual Review of Psychology*, 49, 447–77.

Menon, S. & Kahn, B. E. (1995). The impact of context on variety seeking in product choices. *Journal of Consumer Research*, 22, 285–95.

Meyer, R. J. (1987). The learning of multiattribute judgment policies. *Journal of Consumer Research*, 14, 155–73.

Meyer, R. J. & Assuncao, J. (1990). The optimality of consumer stockpiling strategies. *Marketing Science*, 9, 18–41.

Meyer, R. J. & Kahn, B. E. (1991). Probabilistic models of consumer choice. In T. S. Robertson & H. H. Kassarjian (Eds), *Handbook of Consumer Behavior* (pp. 85–123). Englewood Cliffs, NJ: Prentice-Hall.

Mitchell, A. A. & Dacin, P. A. (1996). The assessment of alternative measures of consumer expertise. *Journal of Consumer Research*, 23, 219–39.

Mitra, A. & Lynch, J. G. Jr (1995). Toward a reconciliation of market power and information: theories of advertising effects on price elasticity. *Journal of Consumer Research*, 21, 644–60.

Miyake, N. & Norman, D. (1979). To ask a question, one must know enough to know what is not known. *Journal of Verbal Learning and Verbal Behavior*, 18, 357–64.

Moore, D. L. & Hutchinson, J. W. (1985). The influence of affective reactions to advertising: direct and indirect mechanisms of attitude change. In L. Alwitt & A. A. Mitchell (Eds), *Psychological Processes and Advertising Effects: Theory, Research, and Application* (pp. 65–87). Hillsdale, NJ: Erlbaum.

Moorthy, S., Ratchford, B. T. & Talukdar, D. (1997). Consumer information search revisited: theory and empirical analysis. *Journal of Consumer Research*, 23, 263–78.

Muthukrishnan, A. V. (1995). Decision ambiguity and incumbent brand advantage. *Journal of Consumer Research*, 22, 98–109.

Nedungadi, P. (1990). Recall and consumer consideration sets: influencing choice without altering brand evaluations. *Journal of Consumer Research*, 17, 263–76.

Nedungadi, P. & Hutchinson, J. W. (1985). The prototypicality of brands: relationships with brand awareness, preference and usage. In E. C. Hirschman & M. B. Holbrook (Eds), *Advances in Consumer Research* (Vol. 12) (pp. 498–503). Provo, UT: Association for Consumer Research.

Negroponte, N. (1995). *Being Digital*. New York: Alfred A. Knopf.

Newell, A. & Simon, H. A. (1972). *Human Problem Solving*. Englewood Cliffs, NJ: Prentice-Hall.

Newman, J. W. (1977). Consumer external search: amounts and determinants. In A. A. Woodside, J. Sheth & P. Bennett (Eds), *Consumer and Industrial Buying Behavior* (pp. 79–94). New York: Elsevier.

Nisbett, R. & Wilson, T. D. (1977). The halo effect: evidence for unconscious alteration of judgments. *Journal of Personality and Social Psychology*, 35, 250–6.

Nosofsky, R. M. (1984). Choice, similarity, and the context theory of classification. *Journal of Experimental Psychology: Learning, Memory, and Cognition*, 10, 104–14.

Obermiller, C. (1985). Varieties of mere exposure: the effects of processing style and repetition on affective responses. *Journal of Consumer Research*, 12, 17–30.

Parducci, A. (1965). Category judgment: a range-frequency model. *Psychological Review*, 72, 407–18.

Payne, J. W., Bettman, J. R. & Johnson, E. J. (1993). *The Adaptive Decision Maker*. Cambridge: Cambridge University Press.

Pechmann, C. & Ratneshwar, S. (1992). Consumer covariation judgments: theory or data driven? *Journal of Consumer Research*, 19, 373–86.

Petty, R. E. & Cacioppo, J. T. (1981). *Attitudes and Persuasion: Classic and Contemporary Approaches*. Dubuque, IA: William C. Brown.

Petty, R. E., Cacioppo, J. T. & Schumann, D. (1983). Central and peripheral routes to

advertising effectiveness: the moderating role of involvement. *Journal of Consumer Research*, 10, 135–46.
Petty, R. E., Unnava, R. H. & Strathman, A. J. (1991). Theories of attitude change. In T. S. Robertson & H. H. Kassarjian (Eds), *Handbook of Consumer Behavior* (pp. 241–80). Englewood Cliffs, NJ: Prentice-Hall.
Pieters, R. G. M. & Bijmolt, T. H. A. (1997). Consumer memory for television advertising: a field study of duration, serial position, and competition effects. *Journal of Consumer Research*, 23, 362–72.
Prelec, D. & Lowenstein, G. (in press). The red and the black: mental accounting of savings and debt. *Marketing Science*.
Ratneshwar, S. & Shocker, A. D. (1991). Substitution in use and the role of usage context in product category structures. *Journal of Marketing Research*, 28, 281–95.
Rescorla, R. A. & Wagner, A. R. (1972). A theory of Pavlovian conditioning: variations in the effectiveness of reinforcement and nonreinforcement. In A. H. Black & W. F. Prokasy (Eds), *Classical Conditioning II: Current Research and Theory* (pp. 64–99). New York: Appleton-Century-Crofts.
Roberts, J. H. & Lattin, J. M. (1991). Developing and testing of a model of consideration set composition. *Journal of Marketing Research*, 28, 281–95.
Roberts, J. H. & Urban, G. (1988). Modeling multiattribute utility, risk, and belief dynamics for new consumer durable brand choice. *Management Science*, 34, 167–85.
Roy, R., Chintagunta, P. K. & Haldar, S. (1996). A framework for investigating habits, "the hand of the past," and heterogeneity in dynamic brand choice. *Marketing Science*, 15, 280–99.
Russo, J. E. (1978). Eye fixations can save the world: critical evaluation and comparison between eye fixations and other information processing methodologies. In H. K. Hunt (Ed.), *Advances in Consumer Research* (Vol. 5) (pp. 561–70). Ann Arbor, MI: Association for Consumer Research.
Russo, J. E. & Dosher, B. A. (1983). Strategies for multiattribute binary choice. *Journal of Experimental Psychology: Learning, Memory, and Cognition*, 9, 676–96.
Samuelson, W. & Zeckhauser, R. (1988). Status quo bias in decision making. *Journal of Risk and Uncertainty*, 1, 7–59.
Schkade, D. A. & Johnson, E. J. (1989). Cognitive processes in preference reversals. *Organizational Behavior and Human Decision Processes*, 44, 203–31.
Sen, S. & Johnson, E. J. (1997). Mere-possession effects without possession in consumer choice. *Journal of Consumer Research*, 24, 105–17.
Shaklee, H. & Fischhoff, B. (1982). Strategies of information search in causal analysis. *Memory & Cognition*, 10, 520–30.
Shapiro, S., MacInnis, D. J. & Heckler, S. E. (1997). The effects of incidental ad exposure on the formation of consideration sets. *Journal of Consumer Research*, 24, 94–104.
Shepard, R. N., Romney, A. K. & Nerlove, S. B. (1972). *Multidimensional Scaling: Theory and Applications in the Behavioral Sciences* (Vols 1 & 2). New York: Seminar Press.
Shocker, A., Ben-Akiva, M., Boccara, B. & Nedungadi, P. (1991). Consideration set influences on consumer decision making and choice: issues, models, and suggestions. *Marketing Letters*, 2, 181–98.
Simon, H. (1955). A behavioral model of rational choice. *Quarterly Journal of Economics*, 69, 99–118.
Simonson, I. (1989). Choice based on reasons: the case of attraction and compromise effects. *Journal of Consumer Research*, 16, 105–18.
Simonson, I. (1992). The influence of anticipating regret and responsibility on purchase decisions. *Journal of Consumer Research*, 19, 158–74.
Simonson, I. & Tversky, A. (1992). Choice in context: tradeoff contrast and extremeness aversion. *Journal of Marketing Research*, 29, 281–95.
Smith, G. E. & Nagle, T. T. (1994). Financial analysis for profit-driven pricing. *Sloan Management Review*, 35, 71–84.
Spence, M. T. & Brucks, M. (1997). The moderating effects of problem characteristics on experts' and novices' judgments. *Journal of Marketing Research*, 34, 233–47.

Staw, B. M. (1976). Knee-deep in the big muddy: a study of escalating commitment to a chosen course of action. *Organizational Behavior and Human Performance*, 16, 27–44.
Stigler, G. J. (1961). The economics of information. *Journal of Political Economy*, 69, 213–25.
Thaler, R. (1980). Toward a positive theory of consumer choice. *Journal of Economic Behavior and Organization*, 1, 39–60.
Thaler, R. (1985). Mental accounting and consumer choice. *Marketing Science*, 4, 199–214.
Tversky, A. (1972). Elimination by aspects: a theory of choice. *Psychological Review*, 79, 281–99.
Tversky, A. & Kahneman, D. (1974). Judgment under uncertainty: heuristics and biases. *Science*, 185, 1124–31.
Tversky, A. & Koehler, D. (1994). Support theory: a nonextensional representation of subjective probability. *Psychological Review*, 101, 547–67.
Tversky, A. & Sattath, S. (1979). Preference trees. *Psychological Review*, 86, 542–73.
Tversky, A. & Shafir, E. (1992). Choice under conflict: the dynamics of deferred decision. *Psychological Science*, 3, 358–61.
Tversky, A. & Simonson, I. (1993). Context dependent preferences. *Management Science*, 39, 1179–89.
Tversky, A., Slovic, P. & Kahneman, D. (1990). The determinants of preference reversal. *American Economic Review*, 80, 204–17.
Unnava, H. R. & Sirdeshmukh, D. (1994). Reducing competitive ad interference. *Journal of Marketing Research*, 31, 403–11.
Unnava, H. R., Burnkrant, R. E. & Erevelles, S. (1994). Effects of presentation order and communication modality on recall and attitude. *Journal of Consumer Research*, 21, 481–90.
Urban, G. L. & Katz, G. M. (1983). Pre-test-market models: validation and managerial implications. *Journal of Marketing Research*, 20, 221–34.
Urban, G., Hulland, J. S. & Weinberg, B. D. (1993). Premarket forecasting of new consumer durable goods: modeling categorization, elimination, and consideration phenomena. *Journal of Marketing*, 57, 47–64.
Urbany, J. E., Bearden, W. O. & Weilbaker, D. C. (1988). The effect of plausible and exaggerated reference prices on consumer perceptions and price search. *Journal of Consumer Research*, 15, 95–110.
Urbany, J. E., Dickson, P. R. & Wilkie, W. L. (1989). Buyer uncertainty and information search. *Journal of Consumer Research*, 16, 208–15.
Veryzer, R. W. & Hutchinson, J. W. (1998). The influence of unity and prototypicality on aesthetic responses to new product designs. *Journal of Consumer Research*, 24, 374–94.
Wagenaar, W. A. & Timmers, H. (1979). The pond-and-duckweed problem: three experiments on the misperception of exponential growth. *Acta Psychologica*, 43, 239–51.
West, P. W., Brown, C. L. & Hoch, S. J. (1996). Consumption vocabulary and preference formation. *Journal of Consumer Research*, 23, 120–35.
Widing, R. E. II & Talarzyk, W. W. (1993). Electronic information systems for consumers: an evaluation of computer-assisted formats in multiple decision environments. *Journal of Marketing Research*, 30, 125–41.
Winer, R. S. (1986). A reference price model of brand choice for frequently purchased products. *Journal of Consumer Research*, 13, 250–6.
Zajonc, R. B. (1980). Feeling and thinking: preferences need no inference. *American Psychologist*, 35, 151–75.
Zajonc, R. B. & Markus, H. (1982). Affective and cognitive factors in preferences. *Journal of Consumer Research*, 9, 123–31.

Section 3

Computers and Technology

Chapter 13

Devices that Remind

Douglas Herrmann, Brad Brubaker, Carol Yoder, Virgil Sheets and Alan Tio
Indiana State University

Everyone has various things that have to be done every day. Everything that we have to do has to be done within a certain time frame. Sometimes the time frame is precise. Other times the time frame is indefinite but even in these cases there is the hope that what needs to be done will be done sooner than later. On some days, the number of responsibilities that we have to do is more than one's schedule permits. On other days the number of responsibilities is not so great. Whether our scheduling is heavy or light, some things to be done are critical to work or home life and hence must be accomplished on time.

Sometimes the forgetting of an intention has serious consequences, personal and professional. Forgetting can disrupt, and sometimes even destroy, personal relationships. Failing to send flowers or buy a gift on anniversaries, birthdays, and other occasions may render the forgetter as not truly in love with the potential recipient. Arriving late or not arriving at all for an important date has been known to lead to the end of love affairs. At work, forgetting can result in being fired, demoted, or at least not promoted. In the military, forgetting to lock a safe with confidential information can lead to a court martial. In civilian life, forgetting to lock a safe which leads to a theft may result in financial liability for the loss (if one wants to retain the job), or possibly an arrest if the person who left the safe unlocked is seen as potentially criminally involved. Clearly, remembering intentions can be difficult.

To ensure that we do all the things that we have to do, we rely on our memory to remind us or we can arrange for the environment to do the reminding. The kind of memory that we rely on to remind us was called "memory for the future" by Aristotle (Cole, 1993; Herrmann & Chaffin, 1988). Today, psychologists call

Handbook of Applied Cognition, Edited by F. T. Durso, R. S. Nickerson, R. W. Schvaneveldt, S. T. Dumais, D. S. Lindsay and M. T. H. Chi.

this kind of memory "prospective," contrasting it with a person's retrospective memory, which is memory for the past (Harris, 1980a, b; Hitch & Ferguson, 1991; Hunter, 1957; Meacham, 1988; Searleman & Herrmann, 1994). Statements about prospective memory are common in daily communication. For example, the statement "Let's meet for lunch at 12 at the Angus" or "Would you please not forget to get the car washed this week" refer to upcoming events.

Just as we often forget events from our past, we also forget future events. Prospective memory is unsuccessful when a person forgets to execute an intended act, at a certain time, or within an expected interval (Einstein & McDaniel, 1996; Kvavilashvili & Ellis, 1996). Because prospective memory performance often depends on carrying out an intended act on or about a certain time, successful performance of a prospective memory task often requires access to an external clock or a watch. Consequently, much of the research on prospective memory has made a timing device available to subjects in the interval during which the intention is retained (Ceci & Bronfenbrenner, 1985; Harris, 1984; Harris & Wilkins, 1982).

If we do not want the added responsibilities of time monitoring, there are devices that will remind us when necessary. Reminding devices, such as the string tied around one's fingers, have been used for centuries, but they do not indicate what you are supposed to do. A variety of other devices exist now that indicate not only what to do but also alert us to when to do it. The first goal of this chapter is to review research on devices (Norman, 1991) that remind people of prospective memory tasks. Another goal of this chapter is to identify the properties of the most effective reminder now available (according to the ease of use and outcomes), a palmtop computerized reminder, called a personal data assistant (PDA).

Many devices have been developed to facilitate prospective memory. Almost all of these devices assist memory some time. In some cases, people swear that the devices have saved them from terribly embarrassing consequences. Some companies are recommending these devices for their employees and these devices have become part and parcel of cognitive rehabilitation (Parente & Herrmann, 1996). In this chapter we explain the effectiveness of reminding devices, ranging from artifacts created out of materials in a person's home to the electronic reminders currently sold in electronic stores and in catalogs. We begin by examining the kinds of intentions that people experience in everyday life. Next, we review prospective memory theories and consider what the theories have to say about the effectiveness of reminding devices.

Finally, we review the range of prospective memory aids, with special consideration of the palmtop computerized reminder called a personal data assistant (Shelly, Cashman, Waggoner & Waggoner, 1997). We have focused on PDAs because they have emerged as one of the most useful kinds of external memory aids for adults in general (Herrmann & Petro, 1990) and for individuals with neurological impairment (Parente & Herrmann, 1996). If the PDA's effectiveness could be better understood, this understanding might channel better use of PDAs and external memory aids overall. It will be seen that the effectiveness of reminding devices has indeed contributed to our understanding of the cognitive processes that underlie prospective memory performance.

PROSPECTIVE MEMORY THEORY

Prospective Memory Types

Prospective memory research was not formally launched until 1980 (Brandimonte, Einstein & McDaniel, 1996). At that time, Harris published the first of a series of papers that pointed out that memory could be aided externally (by the sight of objects or by hearing sounds) as well as internally (by searching the contents of one's memory). Subsequently, it was confirmed that people preferred to rely more on external aids than on internal aids (Harris, 1980a, b, 1984; Intons-Peterson, 1993; Intons-Peterson & Fournier, 1986; Intons-Peterson & Newsome, 1992; Meacham & Leiman, 1982; Meacham & Singer, 1977; Morris, 1992; Winograd, 1988).

Initially, research treated all prospective memory tasks as alike. However, it was soon recognized that there are different kinds of intentions that need to be distinguished from each other (Kvavilashvili & Ellis, 1996).

First, intentions differ according to how the intended act is to be executed. In some cases, an intention is to be executed precisely, whereas other intentions could be executed within an interval. For example, most people feel that they should arrive on time for an appointment with their boss, whereas they feel they can arrive a few minutes early or late for a recreational event, such as an evening of playing cards. In the words of Ellis (1988) who first pointed out this distinction, some intentions must be executed precisely, like a *pulse* in time, whereas other intentions may be executed anywhere in a broad interval or on a *step* in time.

A second distinction recognized as important concerns whether or not the date and time of day is critical to an intention. Appointments typically occur at a certain time (of the day and on a certain date), whether or not the interval that brackets that time is narrow or broad. These intentions are time based. However, there are many other intentions where the time of day and the date is irrelevant to the execution of the intention. For example, when a person notices that the gas gauge in their car is near empty, the intention to buy gas triggered by the gauge must be executed soon – irrespective of the time that the gauge is low. Similarly, the sight of the newspaper sitting on the front step elicits the intention to pick the paper up and bring it in. No one decides to fill their gas tank or pick up their newspaper according to the date on a calendar or the time on a clock. Instead, such intentions are event based (the needle on a gas gauge; the appearance of the newspaper on the front step).

A third distinction pertains to cultural expectations for prospective memory performance. Four kinds of prospective memory tasks have played a role in western culture (Aveni, 1989; Cole, 1993; Mpofu, D'Amico & Cleghorn, 1996). These kinds, defined in Table 13.1, differ in terms of their goals and according to the temporal requirements of intentions.

Temporal Aspects of Intentions

Comparison of the kinds of intentions in Table 13.1 reveals that prospective memory tasks are defined temporally according to three parameters (Barnard &

Table 13.1 Kinds of prospective memory tasks

Momentary intentions	An intention to perform an act in the next few minutes
Chores	An intention to perform a certain act within a window of time (most phone calls; things to be taken from one place to another; errands)
Appointments	An intention to meet one or more persons at a certain time
Deadlines	An intention to perform a certain act at a certain time (accomplishing certain tasks at work; taking prescribed medicine)

Harrison, 1989). Three temporal parameters describe an intention. An intention involves a *retention interval* (T_{rtn}) that spans the time from when the intention was *formed* (T_f) to the time the intended act is to be carried out, i.e. the *time of response* (T_r). A response is judged as successful if it occurs in an expected interval of time. This *response window* is bounded by a lower limit (T_{rl}) and an upper limit (T_{ru}). Responses prior to this window are early; responses after this window are late. As mentioned earlier, the width of the window varies from being precise, i.e. a simple point in time (wherein T_{rl} and T_{ru} are identical), to being broad (Ellis, 1988).

When a person arranges for a warning signal to remind him or herself to perform an intended act, the temporal characteristics are added to the mental representation of an intention (Brandimonte, Einstein & McDaniel, 1996). The user typically sets a warning signal to go off shortly before an appointment is to be met. Once the signal is sounded, the user has to perform the intended act shortly thereafter (Doerner, 1986). The length of time that occurs between the sounding of a signal and the time when the intended response is supposed to be made can be assumed to affect the likelihood that the person will actually carry out the intended act (Fraisse, 1963). This interval is called here the *anticipatory interval* (T_a) because the warning signal anticipates the time that an action is to be executed. Typically the anticipatory interval is substantially shorter than the retention interval. The retention interval is too long to maintain continual attention. If the anticipatory interval is made relatively brief, a person can remain aware of the intended act and carry it out.

Figure 13.1 illustrates these temporal properties of an intention task whose remembering is aided by an active reminder. Specifically, the table shows an intention with a retention interval (T_{rtn}), bounded by the time the intention was formed (T_{rtn}) to the time the intended response is to be carried out (T_r), within a response window bounded by time limits below (T_{rl}) and above (T_{ru}) the expected time of response. A warning signal is set to go off (at T_a) so a person may anticipate that a response is to be made at T_r.

Any intention which is aided by a reminder requires a person to understand and remember three temporal properties: the retention interval, the anticipatory interval, and the response window. Some intentions have a long retention interval and a long anticipatory interval, such as remembering to mail a birthday card to arrive before, or on, the intended date. For this task a person may need to be reminded five or six days in advance of the birthday to allow for sufficient time to buy a card and get it in the mail. Other intentions have short retention intervals

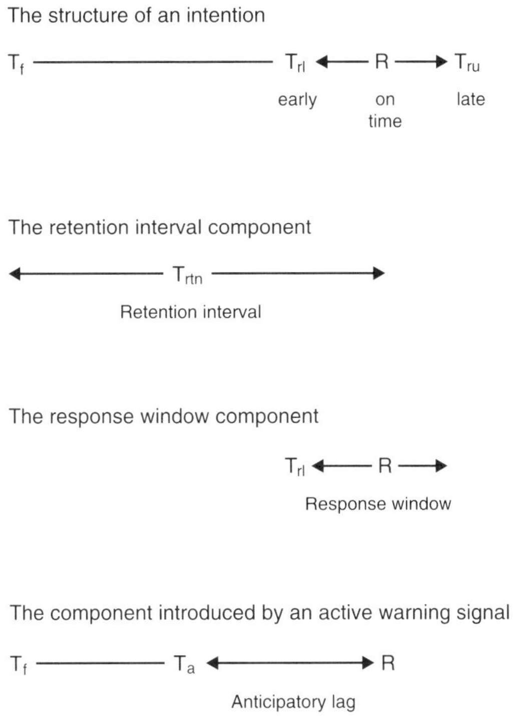

Figure 13.1 The temporal structure of an intention and its components, defined according to time markers, T_f (time of intention formation), T_a (time of active reminding), the ideal timely response (R) which is to be performed at a specified time (T_r), the response interval (the time of lower bound, T_{rl}, and the time of upper bound, T_{ru}), and the retention interval (T_{rtn}).

and anticipatory intervals such as remembering to take your coffee out of the microwave oven where you put it 30 seconds ago to reheat. If the anticipatory interval is short and the person is actively monitoring, the person is alerted to respond almost immediately. If the interval is short and the person is monitoring passively, the alarm may take the person off guard. If the anticipatory interval is long and the person is actively monitoring, then he or she finds the alarm of little usefulness because the time to perform is so far off. If the interval is long and the person is monitoring passively, the alarm may rouse a person to be prepared by the time to perform arrives (Brandimonte, 1991). Table 13.2 summarizes the different effects of anticipatory intervals of different durations.

As if time demands were not enough, remembering to perform future tasks may be jeopardized by other intervening tasks. Often a person does not have just one task to remember. For example, we may not only have to pick up some milk at the grocery store but also pick up the dry cleaning and put gas in the car. The number of tasks we have to do is sometimes called the prospective task load. The more tasks that make up a person's prospective load, the more prospective memory tasks that person must retain simultaneously. As the prospective task load increases, the temporal constraints on a person's remembering multiply.

Table 13.2 Temporal properties of an intention cued by an active reminder

Retention window	The duration of time (T_{rtn}) after an intention has been formed (T_f) up to the time that an action is to be performed (time-to-perform: T_r)
Anticipatory lag	The duration in time (T_a) that begins just after a reminder alarm has been set off and ends at the response time (T_r) that an action is to be performed
Response window	Interval of time ($T_{ru} - T_{rl}$) in which a response is held to have been performed on time (T_r). The response may occur before the approach zero, requiring a precise response (pulse) or be greater than zero (steps). The response window typically forms a symmetric bracket about T_r but asymmetric intervals may be used
Prospective task load	The number of other mental tasks that a person has to carry out around the same time as the T_p. An increase in load above one task may impose an increase in retention intervals, anticipatory lags, and times of execution

When we encode an intention or are given a task to perform, we determine the time by which the task needs to be done. We refer to the statement that describes the action a person intends to do as a directive, because the statement directs a person to respond at a certain time. A directive for momentary intentions and chores are typically stated vaguely, e.g. "sometime soon." In contrast, appointments and deadlines usually involve a directive that explicitly states the time of responding and often a statement of the boundaries of the response window which is typically short.

The temporal properties of intentions differ. Momentary intentions involve a brief retention interval and a very brief response; the retention interval of momentary intentions is typically so brief that there usually is not time to arrange for a warning signal. Appointments, chores, and deadlines usually involve substantial retention intervals. Appointments and chores usually use symmetric response windows, whereas deadlines necessarily require an asymmetric response window. For example, intervals typically precede or include the intended act (delivering a report to one's boss in time for the report to be presented at a board meeting; or cooking something but not burning it). Sometimes the response window includes or follows the intended act (as in redirecting a plane to change its course in time to avert a collision).

Prospective Memory Processing

Processing Stages

A prospective memory task is readily describable in several stages. According to Ellis (1996), these stages include:

1. the formation and encoding of an intended act
2. an interval in which the intention is held in memory

3. a retrieval interval in which the individual retrieves the intention and prepares to execute the intended act
4. a response window in which a response, if it occurs, is considered appropriate
5. and an evaluation of the effects of the intended act.

Because the intention is retained in memory and retrieved presumably by cues in the same manner as retrospective memories, the prospective memory includes a retrospective component.

The prototypical memory experience involves an implicit retrieval with an "ah ha" reaction (e.g. "Oh, no, I am supposed to be at Mary's house for dinner in five minutes"). In contrast, retrospective remembering experiences are often characterized as intentional. However, intentionality does not define the difference between retrospective memory; both prospective memory and retrospective memory may be elicited implicitly or explicitly (Goschke & Kuhl, 1996). For example, instead of an ah-ha experience, people may ask themselves "What should I be doing now?", and explicitly search memory for the intention they suspect they have. Nevertheless, the prospective memory experience that everyone fears is when one has lost awareness of what is to be done. Thus, the most important challenge to research on prospective memory is to determine why unconscious intentions do not surface on time and how to make them do so.

Remembering Intentions

Time itself has been thought to be mentally represented in at least four ways (Friedman, 1990). For example, a person may decide (in the absence of a warning signal) that it is time to carry out a certain act because a *time tag* associated with the act alerts us to action ("pick up the kids at 4:30"). A person may decide it is time to act because of the sense that enough time has passed since the intention was formed (the *conveyor belt* model). Another possibility is that a person notices that an intention has declined in *memory strength* to a degree that suggests the time has arrived when an intention is to be carried out. An *inference* may allow a person to conclude it is time to act ("If the sun is above the trees it must be about time for the kids to get out of school; I better go").

In addition to these conceptualizations, Tulving (1983) proposed an associative "reminding" model in which cues in the environment lead to the remembering of a prior memory. This model is easily extended to prospective memory whereby cues that are associated directly or indirectly with an intention lead to remembering the intention. A recent variation of the reminding model assumes that two processes underlie prospective remembering (Herrmann et al., 1997b). First, intentions are held in memory in either one of two states: an aware state or an unaware state. Intentions in the unaware state may emerge into awareness by the stimulation of one or more cues. Once the intention is in the aware state, the individual monitors the environment for when the intended act is to be carried out.

One way to conceive of the two states of remembering is in terms of monitoring processes. For example, a dual process model of intention retrieval assumes that there are two types of monitoring processes that may alert us to perform an intended act (Herrmann et al., 1997b). In passive monitoring, a person has encoded an appointment previously and is implicitly aware that he or she has a task coming up in the near future. However, the person is not preoccupied with thinking about the task. As relevant cues increase and as the time of the intended act approaches, the individual shifts to active monitoring when the memory of the intention emerges into explicit and conscious awareness (Goschke & Kuhl, 1996; Michon & Jackson, 1984).

In terms of the models of time passage (Friedman, 1990), passive monitoring appears to conform to a strength model, inference, and/or reminding model. Either the strength reaches a critical level in the unconscious that triggers a shift to active monitoring or a cue in the environment triggers such a shift. In either case, the individual goes from being unaware to being aware that action is imminent. Once engaged in active monitoring, the person attempts to continually monitor the clock in order to execute the intended act at the planned time. Active monitoring appears to conform to a conveyor belt model.

Reminders

Execution of a response requires a person's memory to alert him or her when the response window has arrived. Because the response window occurs at a certain point in time, many people fear they will forget to perform the intended act. People are renowned for having a poor memory of time, for both past and future events (Brewer, 1994; Herrmann, 1994; Wagenaar, 1986). Consequently, many people deliberately arrange for cues to alert them during the retention interval to respond when intended.

The key to successful prospective remembering lies in effective cuing of an intention at the appropriate time. Such cuing may occur internally (as may result from a biological clock or recognition of physiological cues associated with an intention). However, internal cues are well known to fail. For example, appointments have been missed by nearly everyone because people assume they will spontaneously remember to respond but then they do not.

Active and Passive Reminders

Harris (1978) pointed out that reminding devices differ in how they attract attention. A passive reminder, such as a notepad with an intention written on it, will remind a person of what is to be done, i.e. if that person looks at the notepad and reads it. If a person spies the notepad, he or she may choose to look at it. But if the person is looking somewhere else, he or she will not be reminded.

An active reminder will attract attention readily. For example, a signal sounded by an alarm clock attracts attention and will continue to sound until it is turned off. Similarly, a warning light that shines brightly and in a pulsating fashion will also attract attention until it is turned off. Once the alarm or warning light is turned off, the individual must remain conscious of the intention until it has to be executed.

The active reminder, i.e. a signal, is the most effective means for eliciting a prospective memory (Harris, 1980a, b; Leirer, Morrow, Tanke & Pariante, 1991; Park & Kidder, 1996). Two different monitoring processes may underlie reminding, as raised from the very first research on prospective memory. Harris & Wilkins (1982) required subjects to perform an intentional task of recording specified time intervals while they viewed a movie. These subjects had the task of shifting attention from watching a movie to performing an intentional task of record keeping. Inspired by Harris & Wilkins' (1982) research, Ceci & Bronfenbrenner (1985; also reported in Ceci, Baker & Bronfenbrenner, 1988) had adolescents perform two intentions with a precise time requirement: bake some cupcakes and recharge a battery, both of which had a precise time of task performance. The subjects were allowed to do other things in the waiting period. Apparently, they shifted from passive monitoring to active monitoring just before the time of task execution, in order to avoid making an error. Subjects seem to engage in a passive form of monitoring as compared to the heightened consciousness typical of vigilance and other attention tasks.

A Model of Prospective Memory Involving Reminding

Only a couple of models of prospective memory have been advanced. One model proposes that responding to a prospective memory task is based on a series of processes: the encoding of the intention, a delay, performance interval (called here the response window), execution of the response, and evaluation of how one performed (Ellis, 1996).

A second model assumes that responding to a prospective memory task depends critically on active and passive monitoring that occurs during the retention interval or, in the terms of the stage model above, during the delay and part of the performance interval (Herrmann et al., 1997b). The model holds that prospective memories of intentions are monitored passively and that the passive process will with some probability elicit active monitoring prior to the time of performing the intended act. A signal ensures better performance in two ways. The signal can produce a shift from passive to active processing. In addition, if the signal occurs while a person is actively monitoring, the signal indicates to this person the amount of time remaining until the time to perform the response. Active reminders serve to trigger the emergence of an intention, alerting a person to an upcoming intention, thereby eliciting active monitoring of the intention, and leading to the execution of the intended task. Figure 13.2 illustrates a two-stage monitoring process that consists of active monitoring and passive monitoring, as well as the relationship between these two kinds of monitoring.

This model is consistent with many of the findings that have been accumulated regarding PDAs. For example, people are more likely to forget an intention if an alarm goes off too far in advance. When this occurs, people slip back into passive monitoring which is not as reliable as active monitoring in alerting a person to respond on time. People are more likely to fail to execute a response on time if the alarm goes off at the time of responding. When this occurs, active monitoring processes require time to be elicited, making the person respond after the desired time.

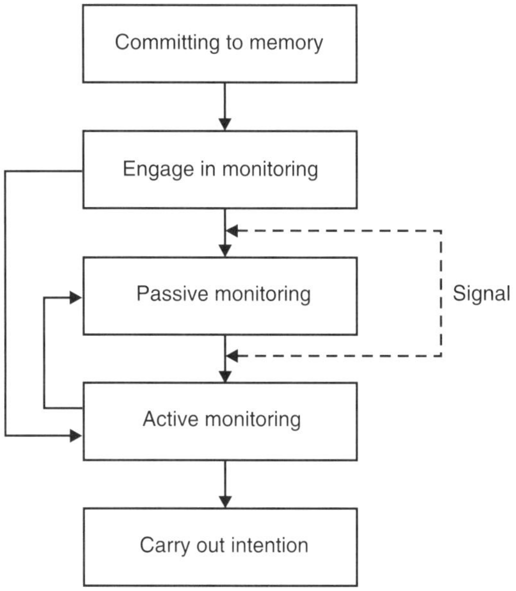

Figure 13.2 A model of prospective remembering based on active and passive monitoring (see Herrmann et al., 1997b).

The model explains why passive reminders (Lipman, Caplan, Schooler & Lee, 1995) are not as effective as active reminders. A passive reminder does not alert a user to temporal information, leaving the person in the passive monitoring state. The user must periodically check a clock (Ceci & Bronfenbrenner, 1985) in order to perform scheduled intentions when planned.

An active cue, such as a sound or light, alerts a person at or near the time of execution and places him or her in active monitoring. Auditory or visual warning signals free people from clock-checking and allow them to devote their minds to other activities (Ceci & Bronfenbrenner, 1985; Harris & Wilkins, 1982). The model explains why auditory cues have an advantage over visual cues. With auditory cues, people do not have to direct their senses toward the origin of the stimulus. The auditory cue puts the person into active monitoring. For a visual cue to work, it must be actually seen. If it is not seen, the person stays in passive monitoring.

The anticipatory interval can be expected to affect the two kinds of monitoring processes differently. If the anticipatory interval is very short, the person engaged in active monitoring can proceed directly to responding. If the anticipatory interval is very short and the person is engaged in passive monitoring, the person will have to use time to shift to active processing and may end up responding past the time expected for a response. If the anticipatory interval is long, the person engaged in active monitoring will recognize that the warning signal is coming too early to be useful. If the anticipatory interval is long and the person is engaged in passive monitoring, this person will shift to active processing; the time to make this shift may allow this person enough time to get ready to respond. If a person

Table 13.3 The effect of duration of anticipatory interval and whether a person is actively or passively monitoring prospective intentions

Duration of anticipatory interval	Kind of monitoring process	
	Active	Passive
Short	Right on!	Huh!!
Long	Why so early?	Enough time to get ready

has more than one intention to deal with, the load for passive and active monitoring is increased. Additionally, a load of two or more intentions raises the problem that a person must determine which intention is being signaled by a warning signal.

KINDS OF REMINDING DEVICES

While it has long been known that experimenters can influence memory performance by manipulating physical characteristics of stimuli, the control that subjects have on their memory performance by similar manipulations has been recognized only recently (Harris, 1984). At the simplest level there are two kinds of reminding devices: passive aids and active aids.

Passive Reminding Devices

There are many memory aids that people themselves devise naturally. These aids typically involve making a novel use of mundane objects in the environment. Harris (1980a, b) asked people about how often they used each of several external memory aids, such as tying a string on one's finger, putting a rubberband on one's wrist, and writing on a memory pad. Passive aids usually help memory but in a manner unrelated to the object's normal use. For example, although a rubberband may serve as a reminder when worn on one's wrist, its purpose (as manufactured) is to bind things together, not to serve as a memory aid. Table 13.4 lists several passive aids that people devise to remind them.

Some passive memory aids may be purchased. Notepads, calendars, diaries, and day planners have been the primary way for people to keep track of their intentions for centuries. For example, Kelly & Chapinis (1982) interviewed professionals about their use of calendars. The majority of those interviewed reported that calendars were essential to their lives. Some people maintained two or more calendars. Some people used their calendar to plan the current day and the next day whereas other people planned for more than a year in advance. Some people rarely changed their calendar whereas others changed them often.

Analogous to a notepad, there are now note recorders that record brief messages on a computer chip. These devices do not come with a warning signal to alert the user of things to do.

Table 13.4 Examples of passive reminders

- Ask someone to remind you of what you should do when the time arrives
- Rubberband on wrist
- Bulletin board
- Calendar
- String on finger
- Switch ring to other hand
- Switch watch to other wrist, wallet to another pocket
- Turn ring over
- Turn watch over
- Wear unusual arrangement of clothes, jewellery, or accessories to remind you of something to do
- Writing on one's hand

Source: From Herrmann & Petro (1990), based on Harris (1978) and Intons-Peterson & Fournier (1986).

Active Reminding Devices

Active reminders provide warning signals at a designated time. These aids have been useful in the investigation and treatment of memory problems in neurologically impaired patients, elderly who have suffered memory deficits, and in normal adults who want to improve their everyday memory performance.

Reminding devices eliminate the need for people to remember intentions over long time periods; people need only remember the intention after the alarm reminds them to execute the intention. The warning signal "externalizes" the intention (Gorayska & Mey, 1996), capturing the user's attention and ensuring that the intention is activated in conscious memory at the appropriate time.

Nonportable Devices

Electrical Timers

Electrical timers that run off commercial electricity are helpful to monitor all manner of chores. They can be set for whatever interval is desired. When the alarm signals, the user either remembers what is next or knows at least that something needs to be done. An alarm clock is the simplest example of such timers. Complex electrical timers will turn on the furnace, lights in various places throughout the house, and turn on the sprinkling system to water the lawn.

Computer Calendars

Computerized calendars consist of spread sheets, organized in the manner of a paper calendar, that are operated on a personal computer. The software permits entering appointments and chores, which then can be printed out. They can be set for whatever interval is desired. When the alarm signals, the user either remembers what is next or knows at least that something needs to be done. The potential for computer devices to assist in reminding people of their intentions was recognized almost two decades ago (Kelly & Chapinis, 1982). Programs were quickly developed for personal computers that facilitate keeping a calendar of one's intentions (Beard, Palanianppan, Humm, Banks, Nair & Shan, 1990; Grief, 1982). The cues provided by such programs were usually passive in that the user has to call up the program and look at the screen in order to be cued to remember.

In the past few years, the computer calendars have become very sophisticated. They provide visual and auditory alarms of what needs to be done. With a printer, it is possible to print out one's schedule for the day or week, and with e-mail, to send the schedule to a colleague, secretary, or other interested party. In a study that compared users of computer calendars with users of day planners, it was found that the computer calendar users almost never forgot appointments whereas the day planner users forgot much more often (Phegley, 1997).

Portable Reminders

Battery Powered or Mechanical Timers

These devices are commonly used in cooking but they also can be set to remind the user of any impending task.

Interval Reminders

Some reminding devices allow users to select a time such as 8:00 or 8:30 a.m. and the device will produce an auditory signal at the selected interval. These devices have the advantage that they do not require the user to key in the numbers of the time of an appointment. However, they do not provide a directive that characterizes what needs to be done.

Watches

In recent years, several reminding watches (or memo watches) have been sold by companies such as Seiko, Casio, and others. These wristwatches store the date and time of appointments and activate an alarm to remind a client when the date and time arrive. The alarm is accompanied by a directive that is exhibited on the screen of the watch. Once a watch is on someone's wrist, it is there until removed. Consequently, it is not as easy to misplace as other devices. Some reminder watches can download and upload files on either an Apple or IBM computer. One can plan a schedule on a computer with directives and dates and then transmit to the watch.

Wearable computers, in the form of watches or laptops, also can be used to remind one of what to do. As size decreases, portability increases. However, as size decreases, use of the device's controls becomes more difficult (Naugle, Prevy, Naugle & Delaney, 1988). A critical issue is whether or not a person has to return to a main computer to enter appointments. Some people do not mind having to do so, but many people will not use a device unless they can record an appointment at the time the intention is formed.

Personal Data Assistants (PDAs)

These palmtop or credit-card size computerized devices have special functions that enable individuals to better remember their intentions. These devices are called personal data assistants because they typically aid not only prospective memory tasks but also can be programmed to retain other information such as phone numbers and memos. Most of these products require that the user key in the time of tasks and a few letters or words to identify the purpose of the task. Later the device reminds the user of their intention by a warning signal, such as an audible beep, that is presented along with the message that was entered about what is to be done. Some reminding devices have the user speak into the device the time and purpose of the task and others have the user write onto a pad that converts a person's script to a printed directive (Herrmann, Yoder, Wells & Raybeck, 1996).

The primary advantage of PDAs over other reminding devices is that the PDA is portable, provides an active signal to remind people of what to do, and presents a message in case the signal is not sufficient to prompt the person to remember the intention. On the basis of self reports, people report that they remember intentions twice as well with active reminders than passive reminders (Harris, 1984; Intons-Peterson, 1993). The only comparison that has been made between people that use active aids and people who use passive aids indicated that the active aids lead to about 10% better performance than people who use passive aids only (Phegley, 1997). However, this difference may reflect individual differences only. Experimental research is needed on the difference between active and passive reminders.

People

Many people ask a good friend, colleague, or spouse to remind them of intentions at the scheduled time. Some people believe that another person makes the best active reminder. However, this assumption is predicated on a good relationship between the person who needs to remember and the other person (Gentry & Herrmann, 1990; Kobayashi & Maruno, 1994). It also presumes that the other person has a good memory.

PERSONAL DATA ASSISTANTS

This section provides a comprehensive analysis of the use and effectiveness of the personal data assistant. We focus on this particular kind of reminding device because the PDA represents the state of the art in reminding devices. As such, it merits investigation to determine if it delivers what it promises. Specifically, is the PDA better than other active reminders and, moreover, is it better than passive reminders? Presently, more research has been done on PDAs than on any other active reminder.

This section begins by examining the physical characteristics of PDAs and the operation of a PDA. Then we review the effectiveness of PDAs as reminders, the facts of PDA usage, and findings on factors that affect the effectiveness of PDAs.

Physical Characteristics of a PDA

PDAs differ in size and weight. Most are smaller than a video tape cassette (Herrmann et al., 1996). Palmtops necessarily use keyboards that are too small for human fingers to use with standard typing format. The auditory signals of PDAs are almost universally loud enough for normal hearing users to hear in a typical environment. All PDAs provide a written directive on the screen when the signal is presented. The signal and the written cue work better than memory alone because physical stimuli are usually more compelling than the ideas that might lead to performing an intended act (Searleman & Herrmann, 1994).

Operation of a PDA

The user of a PDA follows this sequence:

- The user forms an intention.
- The user keys in the time of the event and a directive describing the event.
- An alarm is set for the intention.
- The user picks up the PDA and puts it in his or her pocket or purse.
- At some point, the warning signal sounds. The user will then do one of two things: If the user knows what the alarm is for, he or she may respond accordingly. If the user does not know what the alarm is for, he or she will check the directive and then respond.

Use of PDAs

Prevalence of Users of PDAs

In a study of graduate students, approximately 5% reported using a PDA (Herrmann, Sheets, Wells & Yoder, 1997a). In another study, 15% of business people, 14% of the professors, and 7% of the students reported owning a PDA (Tio, 1997). However, of the individuals owning PDAs, only half reported using them.

In yet another study where subjects made use of a PDA for about two months, only 10% of them indicated that they would continue to use them (Herrmann et al., 1997a). However, very few people (less than 5%) ever try to use a personal data assistant in the first place. Thus, only a small percentage of the population actually used these devices on a regular basis. Taking all of the results together, it appears that PDAs, either in their current form or in some future form, are not likely to be the major answer to prospective memory failures. Many people feel that their day planner is enough to meet their obligations. Some people do not even use a day planner. However, while PDAs may not be the answer to prospective memory problems of the population, it will be seen below that PDAs are definitely the answer for people with impaired prospective memory and people who live very active lives.

Ease of Learning to Use a PDA

College students reported that it was easy to learn how to use the device (Herrmann et al., 1997b). Generally, subjects learn to press the appropriate buttons in about 15 minutes. If used daily, subjects became skilled in keying in appointments in about a week (Herrmann et al., 1997a).

Entering in Appointment Information

The majority of new PDA users complained that entering scheduling information on the reminder's keyboard was more time-consuming than handwriting the information in a planner (Grief, 1982; Herrmann et al., 1997b). Using a keyboard requires concentration that interferes with concurrent tasks such as making conversation.

Personal data assistants which involve vocal records of intentions (Lynch, 1995) overcome the keyboard problems but these devices can be embarrassing, such as when the PDA announces personal information in the presence of others who should not know this information. Personal data assistants that permit handwritten messages on a screen fail to operate accurately some of the time, although clearly practice at writing messages can decrease this problem substantially on recent PDAs.

Representation of Time

The representation of time has been a problem from the very first computer calendars, which were first designed for PCs. People complained that the early computer calendars did not look like a paper calendar or planner. As a result, browsing a computer calendar was judged odd and not as easy to use as a paper calendar or day planner (Grief, 1982; Payne, 1993). Today people seem to feel similarly about PDAs. The visual representation of time and the difficulties of accessing the different levels of time (day, week, month) is the primary reason that people decide not to use a PDA (Herrmann et al., 1997b).

Different PDAs represent information about intentions in different ways. All PDAs represent different aspects of intention information at different levels (Grief, 1982; Herrmann et al., 1997b; Payne, 1993). The day level is primary in the representation of intentions in all PDAs. Most PDAs present just a list of appointments for a day. The amount of time that spans between appointments is not shown spatially as it is in a day timer. Most of our subjects have found a list of appointments not as useful as a day planner because a list obscures relative temporal information. Alternatively, some planners present a screen with equal space allocated for each hour.

Expertise

The more that people use a PDA, the more skilled they become in its use. Part of this skill may be due to having acquired more experience at trying to remember certain appointments and ascertaining how to optimize the PDA's function for one's particular uses (Andrzejewski, Moore, Corvette & Herrmann, 1991). Another part of this skill is increased skill at using the keys and screen.

Prospective Memory Performance

Facilitation of Remembering After being Reminded by a PDA

Although a warning signal would seem to guarantee that the user remembers the intention, people still may fail to carry out the intended act after hearing it (Ellis, 1996). Since the signal precedes the time of action by a brief anticipatory interval, typically minutes or seconds, it may seem surprising that people would ever forget to carry out the intention. Nevertheless, such forgetting occurs (Herrmann et al., 1996). The rest of this section is devoted to explaining the conditions and factors that give rise to this forgetting. For example, in our research, successful remembering and execution of assigned intentions is typically about 50%. In everyday life, people typically remember around 90% or better of their intentions (Andrzejewski et al., 1991).

Whatever a person's characteristic rate of remembering, the critical question is whether or not remembering with a PDA is better than remembering with a day planner or some other passive reminder. One study, cited earlier, indicates that experienced users of PDAs remember their appointments better than those who use a day planner (Phegley, 1997). Another study in which subjects used a PDA for over two months found that most subjects felt that the PDA helped them to remember to perform intentions better than other methods (Herrmann et al., 1997a).

However, just because people can use a PDA effectively does not mean that they will continue to use them. In one study, only three out of 18 subjects who used a PDA for two months indicated that they would use these devices in the future. A similar result was obtained in an earlier study of 20 employees of IBM who also preferred paper calendars to the use of PDAs (Payne, 1993).

Finally, PDAs permit the recording of appointments years in advance. Paper calendars are typically annual. Annual appointments are, therefore, more likely to be registered accurately year after year with a PDA.

Interference with Prospective Memory Performance

In some cases, the use of a PDA may actually lead to poorer prospective memory performance. PDAs may fail the user in a variety of ways. Because the user has given the responsibility for remembering an appointment over to the PDA, they tend to think less about the appointment than they would if they had to remember it on their own. Thus, if the alarm does not sound or if the user does not hear the alarm, it is less likely that the user will spontaneously remember the appointment than if the user had expected to have to remember the appointment all along (Payne, 1993).

An alarm may not sound properly because the appointment was not encoded properly. Some alarms are too brief or not loud enough to be noticed amidst a background. When the warning signal is not present, people forget prospective intentions. Sometimes cues present at input diabolically disappear at output. Many of our subjects have reported that they failed to make an appointment because the alarm went off when they were in the shower, asleep, or in a different room than the PDA. Payne (1993) similarly reported that some of his subjects did not meet appointments because the PDA was out of hearing range. Sometimes a PDA will fail to sound an alarm because the batteries have expired. Other times, a user will misread the directive in the PDA screen.

When one has many close appointments, the alarms attached to these appointments create problems. When too many alarms sound, there is a tendency to ignore some of them. Also, there is another tendency to conclude that an alarm is for one of the other appointments and not check the directive. Alarms alert users but do not inform them.

Students in our research preferred to use a written planner instead of a PDA (Herrmann et al., 1997a, b). Similarly, computer-experts in another study also preferred paper calendars to the use of PDAs (Payne, 1993).

Ironically, some people find that they miss the satisfaction of personally remembering appointments that the PDA signals. Conversely, some people find they become anxious when they anticipate that an alarm should go off.

Conditions of Use

Optimal use of the PDA, as mentioned above, may exceed that achieved with a day planner. Even if it does not, the PDA reduces mental stress due to not having to think about the intention during the retention interval. Nevertheless, PDA use is vulnerable to disruption by various factors. In order to avoid forgetting an intention after a warning signal has sounded, a person must remain focused on the intention to resist being disrupted by these factors. The factors that have been found to interfere with maintaining such focus may result in forgetting.

Temporal Variables

No research has investigated the effect of the retention interval and the response window on prospective memory performance. However, four studies have investigated the prospective memory performance of groups of psychology students, undergraduate and graduate, who were provided with a PDA to carry. The number of late appointments and missed appointments was greatest at the shortest (2 minutes) and longest (20 minutes) intervals and least at the intermediate interval

(10 minutes). Consistent with these data, the subjects also reported that the best anticipatory interval was the intermediate one. It is plausible that warning signals can come too close to the time of responding, not providing enough time to respond in a timely fashion. It is plausible that warning signals can come too early, allowing one to forget that a response needs to be made.

The conditions that dispose people to be late are not necessarily the same as the conditions that lead to a missed appointment. In two studies, the likelihood of being late did not covary with the likelihood of missing appointments (Herrmann et al., 1997a, b). Lateness appears to be the consequence of poor monitoring and poor organizational skills. Missed appointments are usually due to forgetting. There are probably several reasons that intentions may be forgotten: poor encoding of the intention, poor motivation to perform the response, presence of distractions at the time the response is to be made, and other factors.

Research is needed to determine the best way to remind someone for a short interval versus a long interval. Some people report that a kitchen timer is more useful than a PDA for an intention with a brief retention interval. For example, if someone drops by and asks you to come visit in five minutes, a kitchen timer is easier to set than recording this appointment in a PDA.

Time of Day

Prior research has found that people recall information less well in the evening than earlier in the day (Eysenck & Folkard, 1980; Folkard, 1979; Folkard & Monk, 1980; Harma, Illmarinen, Knauth & Rutenfranz, 1988; Humphreys & Revelle, 1984; Revelle, Humphreys, Simon & Gilliland, 1980). Similarly, subjects in our research responded less frequently to warning signals later in the day than earlier in the day (Herrmann et al., 1997a, b). Subjects reported that their performance was lower in the evening than in the morning because they were fatigued in the evening (Mullin, Herrmann & Searleman, 1993) and because they were involved in activities that led them to ignore the PDA's signal. Similar results were obtained by Leirer, Tanke & Morrow (1994) for the effects of time of day on simulated medication and appointment adherence.

Social Context

Because interest in gadgets is more common in men, it is not surprising that PDAs are used primarily by males. The auditory signal of most PDAs are loud enough for normal hearing users to find the warning signal (a beep) annoying to people other than the user. Also, in some situations, any audible reminder may be inappropriate (such as at a board meeting, or a funeral). Continued beeping leads the user of a PDA to disattend to the beep. In addition, some users report that they came to feel anxious when they heard the signal because it suggested something must be done. Because the signal came to be anxiety evoking, these users began to ignore the signal.

User Readiness

To perform an intended act when a warning signal appears, people need to be physically and emotionally ready to perform. People are more absentminded when fatigued, stressed, short on sleep, undernourished, have taken certain medications (especially those that make people drowsy), ill, emotionally upset, inebriated, or under the influence of controlled substances (Herrmann, 1996; Herrmann & Parente, 1994; Parente & Herrmann, 1996).

Individual Differences

People differ in their desire to use PDAs and some people are more prone to cognitive failures than others (Broadbent, Cooper, Fitzgerald & Parkes, 1982). Research has also shown that people vary in the mechanical/conceptual skill to use devices (Weil & Rosen, 1994; cf. Plude & Schwartz, 1996). Research has shown that individuals differ in their ability to perform prospective memory tasks as a function of practice at the task (Andrzejewski et al., 1991) and personality characteristics (Searleman, 1996). Cultural background also is known to affect the way a person conceives of time and prospective memory (Aveni, 1989). A person's prospective memory ability is partially dependent on developmental history (Beal, 1985).

There are ample findings of *age differences* in prospective memory (Einstein & McDaniel, 1996; Mantyla, 1994; Maylor, 1990). Time-based memory performance decreases with age, apparently because advanced age impairs spontaneous retrieval. Hence, as we age, there may be greater need for active reminders (although see Schumann-Hengsteler, Scheffler & Trotscher, 1993). Previous research indicates that older subjects prefer devices that have an active reminding characteristic if these devices are not too difficult to use (Chute & Bliss, 1994; Petro, Herrmann, Burrows & Moore, 1991; Schumann-Hengsteler et al., 1993).

Individuals with neurological impairments often experience difficulty with remembering intentions (Grafman, 1989). As a result, rehabilitation procedures have been developed to address difficulties in planning and reminding (Bendiksen & Bendiksen, 1996; Camp, Foss, Stevens & O'Hanlon, 1996; Cockburn, 1996; Herrmann, 1996) by training clients in the use of PDAs (Bourgeois, 1993; Fowler, Hart & Sheehan, 1972; Jones & Adam, 1979; Kapur, 1995; Kurlychek, 1983; Lynch, 1995; Naugle et al., 1988; Sandler & Harris, 1991; West, 1989).

Our research and other research in the literature (e.g. the use of paper calendars, Kelly & Chapinis, 1982, and PDAs, Payne, 1993) suggest the profile of individuals who will or will not use a PDA. These profiles are shown in Table 13.5. In brief, the individual who will use a PDA regularly is one whose work and home impose many demands on him or her, who likes gadgets, who is easily fatigued, who tends to forget appointments, is ambitious, and can afford a PDA. People who are technophobic will not be expected, for obvious reasons, to want a PDA (Weil & Rosen, 1994). Highly organized individuals remember intended acts in time more than less organized individuals (Searleman, 1996). Individuals with a relaxed pace of life will forget intended acts less often than individuals with a hectic schedule of appointments (Reason, 1988).

Table 13.5 Characteristics of people who will or will not buy and use a personal data assistant for reminding

	People who will buy and use a PDA for reminding	People who will not buy and use a PDA for reminding
Cognitive load	Many appointments Some appointments are very important	Few appointments No appointments are really important
Tastes	Likes gadgets	Dislike gadgets
Well being	Easily fatigued	Not easily fatigued
Habits	Forgetful of appointments Dislikes asking others to remind them of appointments Likes being reminded, and being around others being reminded, by beepts Ambitious (type A)	A good memory for appointments Doesn't mind asking others to remind them of appointments Does not like being reminded by beeps or having to hear others reminding by beeps Not ambitious (type B)
Finances	Has surplus funds	Short on funds

Life-style and occupation can be expected also to influence the decision to use an active reminder. In a recent study (Tio, 1997), faculty members reported almost always having more appointments and job responsibilities than business people and students. Professors reported that they engaged in planning, wrote their schedule down, and made lists more often than business people and students, who reported engaging in these behaviors about equally. More professors and business people reported owning a PDA than did students.

DISCUSSION

Prospective memory is very important to everyday life. An accurate prospective memory facilitates the management of one's activities. Successful prospective memory performance assures those people who are close to us that we respect and care for them. An inaccurate prospective memory leads to tardy performance and can offend colleagues and a boss, as well as family and friends.

The existence of active reminding devices highlights the major difficulty of prospective memory: arranging the environment to provide the cues that will lead the intention to emerge into awareness at the appropriate time. Passive reminders will cause a timely emergence of an intention in some people all of the time and in many people most of the time. Nevertheless, everyone has some or many appointments that they dare not forget. An active reminder seems to give an individual the best chance at remembering such appointments.

The research question is not whether a PDA is better than a passive system such as a day planner, but which system is most appropriate for different people. The likelihood that a person will use a PDA in their possession depends on several factors: the physical characteristics of PDAs; the ease of operation of a

PDA; the manner in which the PDA represents time; the temporal properties of the intention to be remembered; the degree to which the warning signal will attract attention; and individual differences that favor the use of a PDA.

Active reminders can remind people effectively of intentions they would forget otherwise. These devices eliminate the need for people to remember intentions over long time periods. People need only remember the intention after the warning signal reminds them to execute the intention. Additionally, the warning signal of the PDA "externalizes" the intention (Gorayska & Mey, 1996), thereby ensuring that the intention is activated in conscious memory at or near the appropriate time.

Although a warning signal helps a person remember an intention, people still may forget to carry out the intended act after hearing the cue (Ellis, 1996). Even if the signal briefly precedes the time of expected responding by just a few minutes or seconds, people may forget to carry out the intention (Herrmann, 1996). To avoid forgetting, a person must remain focused on an intention after a warning signal. Variables that have been identified which detract from maintaining such focus may result in forgetting. These variables include a long retention interval, a long anticipatory interval, an unimportant intention, a time of response late in the day, a schedule crowded with other intentions and warning signals, placing the PDA in another room, social acceptance of the warning signal, user fatigue, and excessive user emotions. Additionally, PDAs are most likely to be used as a reminding device by a certain kind of person, someone with a positive mental attitude towards these devices and a life-style in need of external reminding.

Prospective Memory Theory

Research with PDAs expands our understanding of how people plan and remember intentions. Active reminders are useful in part because they alert people to intentions that would otherwise be forgotten. When cues in the environment lead an intention to emerge in consciousness (Tulving, 1983), the rememberer must monitor the intention until the time for action arises. Regardless of the model of time representation and perception (time tags, memory strength, inference, or conveyor belt), the two-process model of memory monitoring appears to provide a reasonable account of prospective memory, especially when active reminders are involved. At any time, a person remains unaware of many impending obligations. A warning signal eliminates the need either to assess how much time has passed already or to detect a time tag, assess the strength of the intention, or to draw an inference. Instead, the warning signal alerts the user to the nature of the impending appointment.

A warning signal changes a time-based task to an event-based task (Einstein & McDaniel, 1996). Without a warning signal, a time-based task requires a person to keep track of the passage of time and to remember that an intention should be carried out at a certain time. As the time to respond approaches, the person shifts between passive and active monitoring. When the time to respond is imminent, the person remains in active monitoring and executes the response on time. In an event-based task, some cue in the environment alerts a person that action is needed (in a manner similar to how a low gas gauge alerts a driver to fill up with gas). If a warning signal is used to carry out a time-based task, the signal can alert a person to respond in the same way that a cue alerts a person in an event-based task. For a signal to change a time-based task to an event-based task, the signal must alert the user just before the time to respond in order to eliminate the monitoring that is crucial to time-based tasks. If a warning signal sounds and a person must still keep track of time prior to responding, the task remains time-based. Alternatively, if the warning signal prompts a person to respond as soon as is feasible, the task has become event-based where the signal is the event that leads a person to respond.

Broader Implications

The research reviewed here holds implications beyond PDAs as reminding devices. Warning signals occur in a variety of situations in society. The effectiveness of other warning signals can be assumed to depend on the temporal, social, and individual variables discussed here. Without a warning signal, a person must rely on memory to encode an intention, retain it until the approximate time to carry out the intended act, and to alert him or herself to respond at the appropriate time. The precise values of the temporal properties of the anticipatory interval, the retention interval, and the response window obviously vary from one situation to another. Here are some examples of such situations:

- Operators of complex machinery (such as construction equipment) require precise performance at certain points in time. The operators form intentions and carry out acts within retention and response windows. Where active alarms are provided, operators also track the anticipatory intervals. Both the retention interval and the response window are short and may be followed by additional signaling if the response is not executed.
- Pilots of planes, trains, and ships must execute certain actions precisely at certain points in time. The equipment they operate provides visual and auditory alarms. Also guidance systems – such as air controllers for airplanes, trainyard switch operators, and ship guidance systems – have to respond to warning signals (Vortac, Barile, Albright, Truitt, Manning & Bain, 1996). Directives are often provided to guide the appropriate action.
- Physicians, nurses, and other health care professionals have to administer treatments at specified times within limited intervals. Computer prompting of physicians has been shown in certain situations to result in more effective treatment interventions (Harris, O'Malley, Fletcher & Knight, 1990). Patients must take medications on schedule (Baddeley, Lewis & Nimmo-Smith, 1978; Park & Kidder, 1996) and visit their doctor (Leirer, Morrow, Pariante & Sheikh, 1991; Leirer, Morrow, Tanke & Pariante, 1991). A variety of directives (e.g. written reminders, phone contact) may be used along with a choice of artifacts.
- Chefs and cooks must heat foods and mix ingredients at precise times. As a result, they usually use alarms to remind them of what to do when. In turn,

the cooks typically provide a visual and auditory warning to alert waiters and waitresses that meal items are ready to be served.

- Construction workers must heed alarms that signal dangerous conditions. For example, a crane may signal that too much weight is being lifted. Concrete must be allowed a certain amount of time to set before it may support additional weight. Timing these and other procedures is critical to building safe structures.
- Domestic life now involves a variety of memory friendly devices that present signals (Herrmann & Petro, 1990; Petro et al., 1991). As mentioned earlier, microwaves are equipped to signal when a cooking cycle is over. Cars provide signals that alert drivers and passengers to turn off lights, fasten seat belts, and to add fuel and oil; clothes dryers signal when they are ready to turn off.
- Victims of head injury and other neurological impairments often benefit greatly by the use of PDAs (Parente & Herrmann, 1996; Kapur, 1995). In most cases, PDAs have to be programmed by caregivers or healthcare professionals. Nevertheless, the sound of a warning signal brings order to a life that otherwise is often unmanageable.

These examples show that prospective memory is an integral part of everyday life, extending beyond everyday chores and appointments. The reminding function of PDAs may be seen to be applicable also to the psychological processes of scheduling, alerting, warning, and executing intentions in general. Thus, as we come to better understand devices such as PDAs, we expand our understanding of not only prospective memory (Brandimonte et al., 1996), but also cognitive processes in general and how these processes depend on active and passive monitoring.

Training People to Use Reminding Devices

When considering whether to train someone in the use of a PDA, it is important to remember that only about 15% of people persist in using these devices after having a chance to use them. In order to decide whether to train a person in the use of a reminding device, it is necessary to consider their life-style, personality, and attitudes towards reminding devices (Herrmann, 1996). Individuals with a simple life will have little need for a PDA even if they believe these devices will be useful. Disorganized individuals might profit from the use of a PDA (Searleman, 1996), but not if they are happy with their approach to life. Similarly, people who are technophobic will normally not want a PDA. Convincing a disorganized individual who is happy with his or her disorganization or a strongly technophobic individual to use a PDA is probably an impossible task.

Nevertheless, sometimes disorganized people and technophobic people decide that they need a reminding device. Disorganized people who want some help with meeting their obligations will need supervised training in the use of the device. PDAs are highly organized. Disorganized people will only come to use them if they can become comfortable with the structure provided by PDAs. Such comfort requires a systematic acquisition process that is as easy as possible. For example, the use of the PDA by a disorganized person will require daily review of the use of the device for at least one or two weeks. A few discouraging experiences trying to figure out the controls on a PDA are usually enough to make the disorganized person quit.

Technophobic people who want to use a PDA will also need training and considerable supervision. It is important to ascertain the origin of the person's technophobia. Many older people claim they are technophobic but their belief may originate simply from a lack of exposure to technology (Plude & Schwartz, 1996). Often when such people are acquainted with technology, they take to it readily. Some people have a vendetta with devices of all types. If orientation to a PDA and a brief period of usage does not seem to change this attitude, it is unlikely that further training and supervision will result in continued use of these devices. The technophobic person's use of a PDA should be reviewed at least twice a day for a week, followed by daily review of the use of the device for at least another week or two. Some technophobic people will quit use of a PDA after one or two discouraging experiences trying to figure out the controls on a PDA.

In some situations, a person may supervise the entry of intentions into a PDA. For example, an employer may want employees to cary PDAs in order that they carry out certain work assignments. In such situations, it may be easier if the employer leads the employees through the steps of entering the appropriate information. Additionally, supervised registration of intentions in a PDA may ensure accuracy. Most people do not mind being reminded by a PDA if the warning signal alerts them to do work that they really want to do.

The controls of a PDA that many people find annoying are even more troublesome for some neurologically impaired individuals (Parente & Herrmann, 1996; Kapur, 1995). If a neurologically impaired person suffers motor problems in the use of their hands, this person should not be asked to try to learn to enter intentions (Naugle et al., 1988). Instead, their intentions should be entered by a caregiver or a healthcare professional. Before trying to train a neurologically impaired person in the use of a PDA, it is useful to understand the impairment (Cockburn, 1996) and to ask family members about this person's habits prior to the impairment. If a person would not have used a reminding device prior to some injury, disease, or disorder, it is unlikely that training after the impairment will lead them to use such a device. However, neurological impairments sometimes change a person from being closed to such devices to being open to them. Indeed, some of the people who demonstrate the greatest skill in the use of a PDA are those who have become neurologically impaired. If a neurologically impaired person has good insight into lost functions, they usually are good candidates for training to use a PDA. Over a period of time, they may improve in their use of the device and in prospective memory generally (Lynch, 1995; McKitrick, Camp & Black, 1992; Sohlberg, White, Evans & Mateer, 1992). Nevertheless, some neurologically impaired people will respond to a warning signal provided by a PDA. Such people should have their intentions entered by a caregiver or a healthcare professional.

An Ideal Reminding Device

The research reviewed here indicates the design properties of the reminding device of the future. First, an ideal reminding device will fit easily into a shirt pocket. Devotees of PDAs will accept larger devices, but most other people are not as committed to gadgets. If a reminding device is larger than the datebook that a person is in the habit of using, this person will stick with the datebook (even after using a PDA to good effect).

Second, an ideal reminding device will be relatively inexpensive. Devices that can be "bundled" with extra options (such as fax, outputting to a printer) may put off consumers. Many people want a device that is not only easy to use and affordable, but also easy to understand when deciding to buy.

Third, an ideal reminding device will record directives to respond in handwriting, typed print, and orally, as well as being able to switch from each of these modes to the other modes. Currently, the conversion of speech to text is less than ideal. Similarly, the conversion of cursive writing to text is far from perfect too. Conversion from text to a voice message is pretty accurate, although no reminders have this capability at this time. Different modes of recording are needed because different social situations make certain modes more convenient to use. If a person is alone, an oral record is very convenient. When with others, writing or print is often more discrete than making an oral record. If it is necessary that a message be precise, a printed record may be more desirable than a handwritten record.

Fourth, an ideal reminding device will use signals that remind someone overtly (as is now done with beepers) and signals that remind someone covertly (such as with vibration, now done by pagers). People often do not care if others know that they have impending intentions but sometimes everyone wants to keep their plans private.

Fifth, an ideal reminding device will have the capability to announce an intention audibly or to present it in print in the device's viewing window. Again, people often do not care if others overhear certain mundane intentions. However, everyone has some plans that are their own business; the ideal reminding device will allow the user to designate that some messages should be presented in print only.

CONCLUSIONS

This chapter has reviewed research on the use of passive and active reminders on prospective memory, with a particular focus on PDAs as reminding devices. Because most PDAs do not permit recording of intentions as naturally and quickly as a passive reminder, such as a paper calender, most people prefer passive reminders over PDAs. Thus, although a PDA can render a person smarter at remembering intentions (Norman, 1993), PDAs require a user to acquire considerable knowledge so that he or she may use the PDA in an effective fashion (Norman, 1988).

REFERENCES

Andrzejewski, S. J., Moore, C. M., Corvette, M. & Herrmann, D. (1991). Prospective memory skills. *Bulletin of the Psychonomic Society*, 29, 304–6.

Aveni, A. F. (1989). *Empires of Time: Calendars, Clocks, and Cultures.* New York: Basic Books.

Baddeley, A., Lewis, V. & Nimmo-Smith, I. (1978). When did you last . . .? In M. M. Gruneberg, P. E. Morris & R. N. Sykes (Eds), *Practical Aspects of Memory: Current Research and Issues* (pp. 371–6). London: Academic Press.

Barnard, P. & Harrison, M. (1989). Integrating cognitive and system models in human–computer interaction. In A. Sutcliffe & L. Macaulay (Ed.), *People and Computers V.* New York: Cambridge University Press.

Beal, C. R. (1985). Development of knowledge about the use of cues to aid prospective retrieval. *Child Development*, 56, 631–42.

Beard, D., Palanianppan, M., Humm, A., Banks, D., Nair, A. & Shan, Y. P. (1990). A visual calendar for scheduling group meetings. *Proceedings of CSCW '90*, 279–90. New York: ACM.

Bendiksen, M. & Bendiksen, I. (1996). Multi-modal memory rehabilitation for the toxic solvent injured population. In D. Herrmann, M. Johnson, C. McEvoy, C. Hertzog & P. Hertel (Eds), *Basic and Applied Memory Research: Practical Applications* (pp. 469–80). Mahwah, NJ: Erlbaum.

Bourgeois, M. (1993). Effects of memory aids on the dyadic conversations of individuals with dementia. *Journal of Applied Behavior Analysis*, 26, 77–87.

Brandimonte, M. A. (1991). Remembering the future. *Giornale Italiano di Psicologia*, 18, 351–74.

Brandimonte, M. A., Einstein, G. & McDaniel, M. (Eds) (1996). *Prospective Memory: Theory and Applications.* Hillsdale, NJ: Erlbaum.

Broadbent, D. E., Cooper, P. F., Fitzgerald, P. & Parkes, K. R. (1982). The Cognitive Failures Questionnaire (CFQ) and its correlates. *British Journal of Psychology*, 21, 1–16.

Brewer, W. (1994). The validity of autobiographical recall. In N. Schwarz & S. Sudman (Eds), *Autobiographical Memory and the Validity of Retrospective Reports.* New York: Springer Verlag.

Camp, C. J., Foss, J. W., Stevens, A. B. & O'Hanlon, A. M. (1996). Improving prospective memory task performance in persons with Alzheimer's disease. In M. Brandimonte, G. Einstein & McDaniel (Eds), *Prospective Memory: Theory and Applications.* Hillsdale, NJ: Erlbaum.

Ceci, S. J. & Bronfenbrenner, U. (1985). "Don't forget to take the cupcakes out of the oven": prospective memory, strategic time-monitoring, and context. *Child Development*, 56, 152–64.

Ceci, S. J., Baker, J. G. & Bronfenbrenner, U. (1988) Prospective remembering, temporal calibration, and context. In M. Gruneberg, P. Morris & R. Sykes (Eds), *Practical Aspects of Memory: Current Research and Issues*, vol. 2. Chichester: John Wiley.

Chute, D. L. & Bliss, M. E. (1994). Prosthesis ware: concepts and caveats for microcomputer-based aids to everyday living. Special Issue: technology and environmental issues for the elderly. *Experimental Aging Research*, 20, 229–38.

Cockburn, J. (1996). Assessment and treatment of prospective memory deficits. In M. A. Brandimonte, G. Einstein & M. McDaniel (Eds), *Prospective Memory: Theory and Applications.* Hillsdale, NJ: Erlbaum.

Cole, M. (1993). Remembering the future. In G. Harman (Ed.), *Conceptions of the Human Mind: Essays in Honor of George A. Miller.* Hillsdale, NJ: Erlbaum.

Doerner, D. (1986). Memory systems and the regulation of behavior. In E. van der Meer & J. Hoffmann (Eds), *Knowledge Aided Information Processing.* Amsterdam: North Holland.

Einstein, G. O. & McDaniel, M. A. (1996). Remembering to do things: remembering a forgotten topic. In D. Herrmann, C. McEvoy, C. Hertzog, P. Hertel & M. Johnson (Eds), *Basic and Applied Memory: New Findings on the Practical Aspects of Memory* (pp. 333–42). Englewood Cliffs, NJ: Erlbaum.

Ellis, J. A. (1988). Memory for future intentions: investigating pulses and steps. In M. M. Gruneberg, P. E. Morris & R. N. Sykes (Eds), *Practical Aspects of Memory: Current Research and Issues* (pp. 371–6). Chichester: John Wiley.

Ellis, J. (1996). Prospective memory or the realization of delayed intentions. In M. Brandimonte, G. Einstein & M. McDaniel (Eds), *Prospective Memory: Theory and Applications*. Hillsdale, NJ: Erlbaum.

Eysenck, M. W. & Folkard, S. (1980). Personality, time of day, and caffeine: some theoretical and conceptual problems in Revelle et al. *Journal of Experimental Psychology: General*, 109, 32–41.

Folkard, S. (1979). Time of day and level of processing. *Memory & Cognition*, 7, 247–52.

Folkard, S. & Monk, T. H. (1980). Circadian rhythms in human memory. *British Journal of Psychology*, 71, 295–307.

Fowler, R., Hart, J. & Sheehan, M. (1972) A prosthetic memory: an application of the prosthetic environment concept. *Rehabilitation Counselling Bulletin*, 15, 80–5.

Fraisse, P. (1963). *The Psychology of Time*. Translated by J. Leith. Westport, Connecticut: Greenwood Press.

Friedman, W. (1990). *About Time: Inventing the Fourth Dimension*. Cambridge, MA: MIT Press.

Gentry, M. & Herrmann, D. J. (1990). Memory contrivances in everyday life. *Personality and Social Psychology Bulletin*, 18, 241–53.

Gorayska, B. & Mey, J. L. (1996). Of minds and men. In B. Gorayska & J. L. Mey (Eds), *Cognitive Technology: In Search of a Human Interface*. Amsterdam: Elsevier.

Goschke, T. & Kuhl, J. (1996). Remembering what to do: explicit and implicit memory for intentions. In M. Brandimonte, G. Einstein & M. McDaniel (Eds), *Prospective Memory: Theory and Applications*. Hillsdale, NJ: Erlbaum.

Grafman, J. (1989). Plans, actions, and mental sets: managerial knowledge units in the frontal lobes. In E. Perelman (Ed.), *Integrating Theory and Practice in Clinical Neuropsychology* (pp. 93–138). Hillsdale, NJ: Erlbaum.

Grief, I. (1982). The user interface of a personal calendar program. In Y. Vassiliou (Ed.), *Human Factors and Interactive Computer Systems*. Norwood, NJ: Ablex.

Harma, M. I., Illmarinen, J., Knauth, P. & Rutenfranz, J. (1988). Physical training intervention in female shift workers: II. The effects of intervention on the circadian rhythms of alertness, short-term memory, and body temperature. *Ergonomics*, 31, 51–63.

Harris, J. E. (1978). External memory aids. In P. E. Gruneberg, P. E. Morris & R. N. Sykes (Eds), *Practical Aspects of Memory*. London, New York: Academic Press.

Harris, J. E. (1980a). Memory aids people use: two interview studies. *Memory and Cognition*, 8, 31–8.

Harris, J. E. (1980b). We have ways of helping you to remember. *Journal of the British Association for Service to the Elderly*, 17 (May), 21–7.

Harris, J. E. (1984). Remembering to do things: a forgotten topic. In J. E. Harris & P. E. Morris (Eds), *Everyday Memory, Actions, and Absentmindedness*. London: Academic Press.

Harris, J. E. & Wilkins, A. J. (1982). Remembering to do things: a theoretical framework and an illustrative experiment. *Human Learning*, 1, 123–36.

Harris, R. P., O'Malley, M. S., Fletcher, S. W. & Knight, B. P. (1990). Prompting physicians for preventive procedures: a five-year study of manual and computer reminders. *American Journal of Preventive Medicine*, 6, 145–52.

Herrmann, D. (1994). The validity of retrospective reports as a function of the directness of retrieval processes. In N. Schwarz & S. Sudman (Eds), *Autobiographical Memory and the Validity of Retrospective Reports*. New York: Springer Verlag.

Herrmann, D. (1996). Improving prospective memory. In M. Brandimonte, G. Einstein & M. McDaniel (Eds), *Prospective Memory: Theory and Applications*. Hillsdale, NJ: Erlbaum.

Herrmann, D. & Chaffin, R. (1988). *Memory in a Historical Perspective*. New York: Springer Verlag.

Herrmann, D. & Parente, R. (1994). A multi-modal approach to cognitive rehabilitation. *NeuroRehabilitation*, 4, 133–42.

Herrmann, D. J. & Petro, S. (1990) Commercial memory aids. *Applied Cognitive Psychology*, 4, 439–50.

Herrmann, D., Sheets, V., Wells, J. & Yoder, C. (1997a). Palmtop computerized reminding devices: the effectiveness of the temporal properties of warning signals. *AI & Society*, 11, 71–84.

Herrmann, D., Sheets, V., Yoder, C., Wells, J. & Brubaker, B. (1997b). Reminding as a function of the temporal properties of intentions. In B. Gorayska & J. Mey (Eds), *Cognitive Technology: In Search of a Humane Interface*. Advances in Psychology 113. Amsterdam: Elsevier/North Holland.

Herrmann, D., Yoder, C., Wells, J. & Raybeck, D. (1996). Portable electronic scheduling and reminding devices. *Cognitive Technology*, 1, 36–44.

Hitch, G. & Ferguson, J. (1991). Prospective memory for future intentions: some comparisons with memory for past events. *European Journal of Cognitive Psychology*, 3, 285–95.

Humphreys, M. S. & Revelle, W. (1984). Personality, motivation, and performance: a theory of the relationship between individual differences and information processing. *Psychological Review*, 91, 153–84.

Hunter, I. M. L. (1957). *Memory*. Harmondsworth: Penguin.

Intons-Peterson, M. J. (1993). External memory aids and their relation to memory. In C. Izawa (Ed.), *Cognitive Psychology Applied* (pp. 142–66). Mahwah, NJ: Erlbaum.

Intons-Peterson, M. J. & Fournier, J. (1986). External and internal memory aids: when and how often do we use them? *Journal of Experimental Psychology: General*, 115, 267–80.

Intons-Peterson, M. J. & Newsome, G. L. (1992). External memory aids: effects and effectiveness. In D. J. Herrmann, H. Weingartner, A. Searleman & C. L. McEvoy (Eds), *Memory Improvement: Implications for Memory Theory* (pp. 101–21). New York: Springer Verlag.

Jones, G. & Adam, J. (1979). Towards a prosthetic memory. *Bulletin of the British Psychological Society*, 32, 165–7.

Kapur, N. (1995). Memory aids in the rehabilitation of memory disordered patients. In A. D. Baddeley, B. A. Wilson & F. N. Watts (Eds), *Handbook of Memory Disorders* (pp. 533–56). New York: John Wiley.

Kelly, J. F. & Chapinis, A. (1982). How professional persons keep their calendars: implications for computerization. *Journal of Occupational Psychology*, 55, 241–56.

Kobayashi, K. & Maruno, S. (1994). The role of other persons in prospective memory: dependence on other persons inhibits remembering and execution of a task. *Japanese Journal of Psychology*, 64, 482–7.

Kurlychek, R. T. (1983). Use of a digital alarm chronograph as a memory aid in early dementia. *Clinical Gerontologist*, 1, 93–4.

Kvavilashvili, L. & Ellis, J. (1996). Varieties of intention: some distinctions and classifications. In M. Brandimonte, G. Einstein & M. McDaniel (Eds), *Prospective Memory: Theory and Applications*. Hillsdale, NJ: Erlbaum.

Leirer, V. O., Morrow, D. G., Pariante, G. M. & Sheikh, J. I. (1991). Elder's non-adherence, its assessment and computer assisted instruction for medication recall training. *Journal of the American Gerontological Society*, 36, 877–84.

Leirer, V. O., Morrow, D. G., Tanke, E. D. & Pariante, G. M. (1991). Elder's non-adherence: its assessment and medication reminding by voice mail. *The Gerontologist*, 31, 514–20.

Leirer, V. O., Tanke, E. D. & Morrow, D. G. (1994). Time of day and naturalistic prospective memory. *Experimental Aging Research*, 20, 127–34.

Lipman, P. D., Caplan, L. J., Schooler, C. & Lee, J. (1995). Inside and outside the mind: the effects of age, organization, and access to external sources on retrieval of life events. *Applied Cognitive Psychology*, 9, 289–306.

Lynch, W. J. (1995). You must remember this: assistive devices for memory impairment. *Journal of Head Trauma Rehabilitation*, 10, 94–7.

Mantyla, T. (1994). Remembering to remember: adult age differences in prospective memory. *Journal of Gerontology*, 49, 276–82.

Maylor, E. (1990). Age and prospective memory. *Quarterly Journal of Experimental Psychology*, 42, 471–93.

McKitrick, L. A., Camp, C. J. & Black, F. W. (1992). Prospective memory intervention in Alzheimer's disease. *Journals of Gerontology*, 47, P337–P343.

Meacham, J. A. (1988). Interpersonal relations and prospective remembering. In M. M. Gruneberg, P. E. Morris & R. N. Sykes (Eds), *Practical Aspects of Memory: Current Research and Issues* (pp. 371–6). Chichester: John Wiley.

Meacham, J. A. & Leiman, B. (1982). Remembering to perform future actions. In U. Neisser (Ed.), *Memory Observed: Remembering in Natural Contexts* (pp. 327–36). San Francisco: Freeman.

Meacham, J. A. & Singer, J. (1977). Incentive effects in prospective remembering. *Journal of Psychology*, 97, 191–7.

Michon, J. A. & Jackson, J. L. (1984). Attentional effort and cognitive strategies in the processing of temporal information. In J. Gibbon & L. Allan (Eds), *Timing and Time Perception*. Annals of the New York Academy of Sciences, volume 423. New York: New York Academy of Sciences.

Morris, P. E. (1992). Prospective memory: remembering to do things. In M. M. Gruneberg & P. E. Morris (Eds), *Aspects of Memory: The Practical Aspects*. London: Routledge.

Mpofu, E., D'Amico, M. & Cleghorn, A. (1996). Time management practices in African culture: correlates with college academic grades. *Canadian Journal of Behavioural Science*, 28, 102–12.

Mullin, P., Herrmann, D. J. & Searleman, A. (1993). Forgotten variables in memory research. *Memory*, 15, 43–64.

Naugle, R., Prevy, M., Naugle, C. & Delaney, R. (1988). New digital watch as a compensatory device for memory dysfunction. *Cognitive Rehabilitation*, 6, 22–3.

Norman, D. (1988). *Psychology of Everyday Things*. New York: Basic Books.

Norman, D. (1991). Cognitive artifacts. In J. M. Carroll (Ed.), *Designing Interaction: Psychology and the Human Computer Interface*. Cambridge: Cambridge University Press.

Norman, D. (1993). *Things that Make Us Smart: Defending Human Attributes in the Age of the Machine*. New York: Addison-Wesley.

Parente, R. & Herrmann, D. (1996). *Retraining Cognition*. Gaithersburg: Aspen.

Park, D. C. & Kidder, D. P. (1996). Prospective memory and medication adherence. In M. Brandimonte, G. Einstein & McDaniel (Eds), *Prospective Memory: Theory and Applications*. Hillsdale, NJ: Erlbaum.

Payne, S. J. (1993). Understanding calendar use. *Human Computer Interaction*, 8, 83–100.

Petro, S., Herrmann, D., Burrows, D. & Moore, C. (1991). Usefulness of commercial memory aids as a function of age. *International Journal of Aging and Human Development*, 33, 295–309.

Phegley, L. (1997). Computerized reminding devices versus the paper planner: how effective are they? Unpublished manuscript. Indiana State University, Terre Haute, IA.

Plude, D. J. & Schwartz, L. K. (1996). The promise of Compact Disc-interactive technology for memory training with the elderly. In D. Herrmann, C. McEvoy, C. Hertzog, P. Hertel & M. Johnson (Eds), *Basic and Applied Memory: New Findings on the Practical Aspects of Memory* (pp. 333–42). Englewood Cliffs, NJ: Erlbaum.

Reason, J. (1988). *Human Error*. Oxford: Oxford University Press.

Revelle, W., Humphreys, M. S., Simon, L. & Gilliland, K. (1980). The interactive effect of personality, time of day, and caffeine: a test of the arousal model. *Journal of Experimental Psychology: General*, 109, 1–31.

Sandler, A. B. & Harris, J. L. (1991). Use of external aids with a head injured patient. *The American Journal of Occupational Therapy*, 46, 163–6.

Schumann-Hengsteler, R., Scheffler, S. & Trotscher, B. (1993). Memory aids in the everyday lives of young and old adults. *Zeitschrift fur Gerontologie*, 26, 89–96.

Searleman, A. (1996). Personality variables and prospective memory performance. In D. Herrmann, C. McEvoy, C. Hertzog, P. Hertel & M. Johnson (Eds), *Basic and Applied*

Memory: New Findings on the Practical Aspects of Memory (pp. 333–42). Englewood Cliffs, NJ: Erlbaum.

Searleman, A. & Herrmann, D. (1994). *Memory from a Broader Perspective*. New York: McGraw Hill.

Shelly, G. B., Cashman, T. J., Waggoner, G. A. & Waggoner, W. C. (1997). *Discovering Computers: A Link to the Future*. Cambridge, MA: Course Technology.

Sohlberg, M. M., White, O., Evans, E. & Mateer, C. (1992). An investigation of the effects of prospective memory training. *Brain Injury*, 6, 139–54.

Tio, A. (1997). Use of personal data assistants in business and academe. Unpublished research. Indiana State University.

Tulving, E. (1983). *Elements of Episodic Memory*. Oxford: Oxford University Press.

Vortac, O. U., Barile, A. L., Albright, C. A., Truitt, T. R., Manning, C. A. & Bain, D. (1996). Automation of flight data in air traffic control. In D. Herrmann, C. McEvoy, C. Hertzog, P. Hertel & M. Johnson (Eds), *Basic and Applied Memory: Theory in Context* vol. 1. Mahwah, NJ: Erlbaum.

Wagenaar, W. A. (1986). My memory: a study of autobiographical memory over six years. *Cognitive Psychology*, 18, 225–52.

Weil, M. M. & Rosen, L. D. (1994). The psychological impact of technology from a global perspective: a study of technological sophistication and technophobia in university students from twenty-three countries. In *Human Behavior*, vol. 11, pp. 95–133.

West, R. L. (1989). Planning and practical memory training for the aged. In L. W. Poon, D. C. Rubin & B. A. Wilson (Eds), *Everyday Cognition in Adulthood and Late Life* (pp. 573–97). New York: Cambridge University Press.

Winograd, E. (1988). Some observations on prospective memory. In M. M. Gruneberg, P. E. Morris & R. N. Sykes (Eds), *Practical Aspects of Memory: Current Research and Issues* (pp. 371–6). Chichester: John Wiley.

Chapter 14

Computer Supported Cooperative Work

Judith S. Olson and Gary M. Olson
University of Michigan

We are social animals. We began by living in clusters and cooperating in our hunting and gathering. We still reside in communities and cooperate in work; we just do it differently. Over the millennia, we have invented tools and processes to help us cooperate, such as standardized time zones, telegraph and train signaling, paper filing and accounting systems. We cooperate and coordinate by meeting. We converse face-to-face, by telephone, and paper mail. We use blackboards, flip charts, slides, acetate overheads, and duplicated paper handouts.

But the speed of change in these tools has accelerated since the advent of accessible personal and now interpersonal computing. Technology is changing how we cooperate and coordinate. We still meet face-to-face, but people project computer generated slides (e.g. from PowerPoint), take notes on laptops, show Web sites and stored files, and share applications in real time (e.g. spreadsheets to help us come to agreement on a budget). People converse over long distance via chat boxes (which allow people to connect to others in real time, conversing by typing and reading), audio teleconferences, videoconferences, sometimes showing slides or projected work objects at all locations. And, people use fax, email, attachments (which are whole formatted files, e.g. a Word document or an Excel spreadsheet, that are bundled in a coded form with an email message; the recipient of the message can then "open" the file from the email message and turn it into the full, editable format on their computers), voicemail, Lotus Notes (which allows people to easily store documents in an organized, searchable way, and to converse asynchronously while maintaining the conversational "threads"), or intranets (which are web sites totally internal to an organization, serving as

Handbook of Applied Cognition, Edited by F. T. Durso, R. S. Nickerson, R. W. Schvaneveldt, S. T. Dumais, D. S. Lindsay and M. T. H. Chi.

central sources of documents, workflow support, etc.) to manage our asynchronous coordinated work. With the advent of these technologies, we have fundamentally changed how our collaborations can take place. Today, people can successfully plan a global conference without ever meeting face-to-face; large corporations form world-wide teams of experts (attempting to achieve what they call "Virtual Collocation"); people telecommute; and some organizations function entirely with mobile technology (that is laptops with modem connections, cellular phones, portable printers, and other devices that do not require any "hard wiring" to facilities) without the necessity of any physical offices.

Computer Supported Cooperative Work (CSCW) is the study of how people work together using computer and communication technologies. This name emerged in the mid-1980s, first referring to a series of biannual meetings that constitute the principal forum for researchers in this area and now referring to the whole area of research. CSCW is a broadly interdisciplinary field, drawing from computer science, management information systems, information science, psychology, sociology, and anthropology. Within psychology there is participation from the cognitive, social, and organizational perspectives as well as findings to inform these fields. These many perspectives offer a mixture of theories and methods, often sparking healthy debate, some of which is reviewed later in this chapter.

The field of CSCW is huge and growing. We cannot cover it all in this chapter. We have chosen a range of examples to illustrate the issues; our goal is not to be exhaustive in this survey. In this chapter we will examine CSCW research from a psychological perspective. We will do this through the following topics:

- an initial framework that helps define the overall issues in the area, including a brief survey of the kinds of technologies that have been developed for CSCW applications
- a review of how CSCW relates to cognitive psychology along with the various critiques of psychological theories and methods and their implications
- a survey of representative empirical findings to date on what happens when people use CSCW technologies.

AN INITIAL FRAMEWORK

Just as it is impossible to answer the single overarching question, "How do computers affect people?" it is equally impossible to answer the question, "How do computers affect groups, organizations, and society?" The only possible answer is that "it depends." Before we present the empirical findings, it is imperative to adopt a vocabulary for the particular. If "it depends," what does it depend on?

Figure 14.1 shows a simple conceptual framework of the things that need to be described before we can sort out the various results. In this diagram, there are four major determinants of the process the group members engage in and the eventual outcome. We have intentionally simplified the complexity of the real

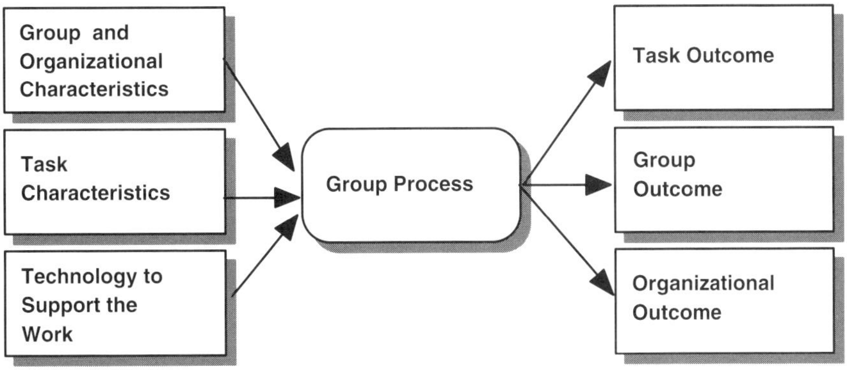

Figure 14.1 A simplified representation of the relationship between technology and behavioral consequences in group work. (After Kraemer & Pinsonneault, 1990, and Olson & Olson, 1997.)

world for tutorial purposes. The world is not this neat and certainly not this linear; there are interesting interactions and feedback loops to explore. We present the framework briefly here; it is detailed elsewhere (Olson & Olson, 1997).

The Group

The same technology can have a remarkably different effect on groups that have different compositions, relationships, organizations, and contexts of time and location. A group that has members with similar and appropriate task skills will function differently than one that is heterogeneous. How these skills are used will differ in the presence of various technologies. We know, for example, that strangers whose language skills are not fluent benefit from videoconferencing whereas established groups who are fluent and share cultural backgrounds do just as well over audioconferencing (Gabarro, 1990; Veinott, Olson, Olson & Fu, 1997; Williams, 1997). Similarly, those groups that have established trust in each other can function cooperatively via email, where those that have not established this trust quickly dissipate into non-cooperative behavior (Rocco, 1998). Technologies also fit or misfit with the group's communication structure (whether it takes place through hierarchical paths only or by free dissemination), and may be adopted or not depending on the organization's reward structure, work norms, or routines (Orlikowski & Gash, 1994).

The Task

Tasks are described in everyday vernacular with such words as brainstorming, design, teaching, or decision making, etc. But, if we are to understand how technologies support various kinds of tasks, this level of description is too coarse-grained. For example, some technologies support the generation of ideas and critiques well, but not the clarification of ideas nor the organization of the ideas into a scheme or frame, all of which are part of design tasks. Most macro tasks are made up of a mixture of smaller task units, and it is at that level that we believe tasks need to be described.

Tasks differ in the nature of the material, whether it consists of abstract ideas or concrete objects. The core activities themselves and their flow are differentially supported by technology. The work involves various amounts of exchange of information, planning, gathering or generating information, discussing to come to agreement, and planning and producing a product. Each of these subtasks may be supported by a different technology. There are also different dependencies among group members in performing the joint activity. Technologies that support group members' awareness of the moment by moment work of each other may help in highly dependent work, called tightly-coupled work, but may indeed impede loosely-coupled work because it is distracting. And tasks differ on something akin to difficulty, having to do both with the number of constraints that have to be satisfied and with their familiarity to the group members themselves. Technologies that make esoteric problems simple via representations, or those that compute constraint satisfaction can differentially support tasks that differ on this key feature.

Group interactions also have more social goals such as learning about the others, learning to trust them, finding empathy, etc. As we will relate later, many of the newsgroups and on-line chat sessions are not intended to get work done, but rather to have social exchange.

The Technologies

Technologies for group work fall into clusters on two major dimensions:

- the setting in which the interaction takes place: the location and timing of the interaction, and
- what the technology supports: the object or the conversation.

First, technologies are intended for support of work that is either in the same or different time and the same or different location (Bullen & Bennett, 1996). In Figure 14.2, real-time work is depicted on the right-hand side, with people meeting either face-to-face or remotely by videoconferencing. Some groups may display the agenda electronically and take minutes by typing changes to the agenda in real time. Some groups may use a group decision support system (GDSS) that helps them brainstorm ideas anonymously, create criteria on which to evaluate alternative ideas, and then rank order or vote on the ideas. Remote participants converse by audioconferencing or videoconferencing. In more informal settings, remote participants may engage in a discussion in a chat session, MUD (multi-users dungeons, i.e. the original application of a shared game) or MOO (MUD-object oriented, the underlying programming language that supports the activity; this technology is described in more detail later in the chapter), by typing their

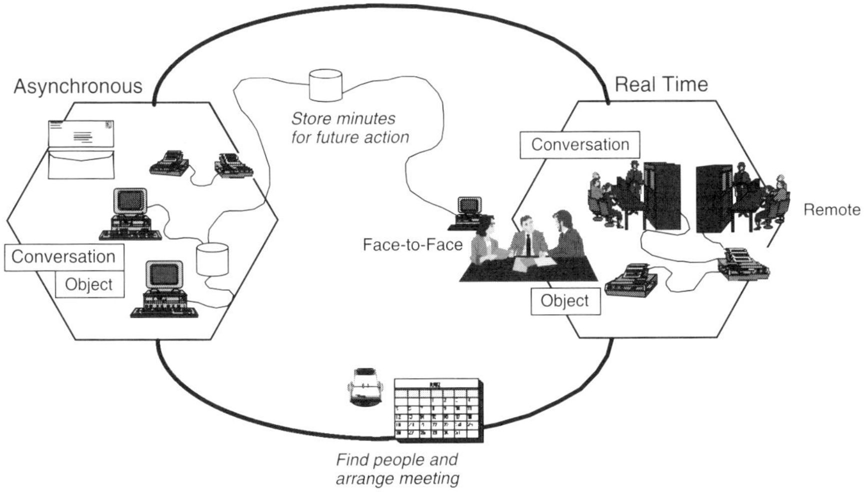

Figure 14.2 Representation of real-time and asynchronous work, transitions between them, and support of conversation and objects

contribution to a conversation and having it appear on all group members' screens at the same time as soon as the utterance is completed.

The arc at the top of the figure depicts the transition to asynchronous work. At the end of their meeting they may store their meeting minutes on a server for each to access, perhaps from which to make their own to-do lists.

On the left side of Figure 14.2 is represented asynchronous work, where people work independently on the project, conversing over email and shipping files to each other electronically for approval or editing. The arc at the bottom represents the transition back to real-time work. Electronic calendars search for time when people can meet. Electronic Rolodexes keep track of people's contact information and background information to help determine whom to invite to a meeting.

The second dimension refers to what the technology is supporting. Technologies variously support the object of work (like a proposal that is being developed by the group or the patient undergoing surgery) and/or the conversation on these objects. When people are face-to-face, it is usually easy for people to refer to the objects of the conversation and to maintain context. In supporting asynchronous work with today's technology, one can send files to one another (the objects) and converse by email, but it is difficult to specify in the conversation exactly what is being referred to. And, sometimes email itself often serves a dual function, both sending an object (e.g. a list of courses offered in the next semester's curriculum) and engaging in conversation about it (e.g. asking for comments on proposed ideas).

Table 14.1 lists various technologies in this scheme, including both commercial products and a few of the better-known prototype systems. The table is organized to cluster the technologies that support real time vs. asynchronous work, and within real-time a distinction is made between those that are face-to-face and those that are remote.

Table 14.1 Various technologies to support different group work settings, and to support conversation and/or sharing of objects

Work situation	Example products	Example prototype systems
Real-time		
Support of face-to-face conversation		
Decision support systems	• Vantana, • Group Systems V	• SAMM (Dickson et al., 1992); • NICK (Ellis et al., 1991)
Support of remote conversation		
Chat boxes, MUDs and MOOs	• Unix Talk • LambdaMOO	• UARC ChatBoxes (Finholt & Olson, 1997) • LambdaMOO (Curtis, 1996)
Video conference	• PictureTel, VTel	• VideoWindow (Kraut et al., 1990)
Desktop audio	• Placeware	• Mbone
Desktop video	• ProShare, • CU-See Me • NetMeeting	• Hydra (Buxton et al., 1997) • Forum (Isaacs et al., 1995) • Cruiser (Fish et al., 1993) • Montage (Tang et al., 1994) • Rave (Gaver et al., 1992) • MERMAID (Sakata et al., 1996)
Support of shared work objects		
Object camera	• PictureTel Object Camera	
Computer whiteboards	• SoftBoard, • LiveBoard, • Netmeeting, • ProShare	• Commune (Minneman & Bly, 1991) • Clearboard (Ishii & Kobayashi, 1994) • Forum (Isaacs et al., 1994) • Tivoli (Pedersen et al., 1993)
Shared editors	• Aspects	• GROVE (Ellis, Gibbs & Rein, 1991) • Cognoter (Stefik et al., 1987) • ShrEdit (Olson & Olson, 1996) • DOLPHIN (Streitz et al., 1994) • SEPIA (Haake & Wilson, 1994) • DistEdit (Knister & Prakash, 1990) • MMConf (Crowley et al., 1990)
Application sharing	• ProShare, • NetMeeting, • Timbuktu, • Point to Point, • Shared-X	
Asynchronous work		
Support of conversation		
Email	• many kinds, including The Coordinator (Winograd, 1988)	
Filters for email		• LENS (Malone et al., 1989)
Video email	• NeXTStep, • Vistium	
Structured conversational database	• Lotus Notes conversation database, • Confer, • Netnews	
Revision control system, notes attached to stored file	• RCS	
Design rationale capture		• gIBIS (Conklin & Begeman, 1988) • QOC (MacLean et al., 1996)

continues

Table 14.1 *(continued)*

Work situation	Example products	Example prototype systems
Support of objects		
Shared file server	• Transport by FTP • Fetch • Lotus Notes	
Group authoring including hypertext systems	• MSWord Revisions, • For Comment	• PREP (Neuwirth et al., 1990) • DOLPHIN (Streitz et al., 1994) • SEPIA (Haake et al., 1994) • Quilt (Leland et al., 1988), • see review by Michailidis & Rada (1995, 1996)
Project management	• MacProject	
Workflow systems	• Lotus Notes	• Freeflow (Dourish et al., 1996)
Transitions between modes of work		
Electronic calendars	• Meeting Maker, • PROFs	
Awareness servers	• CU-See Me	• Cruiser (Fish et al., 1993) • Montage (Tang et al., 1994) • Rave (Gaver et al., 1992) • VideoWindow (Fish et al., 1996) • Media Space (Harrison et al., 1997; Olson & Bly, 1991) • Thunderwire (Hindus et al., 1996) • Olivetti badges

As one might guess, these technologies differ on a number of specifics, each of which has the potential of making significant differences in behavior. Unfortunately, many systems have been built but never formally evaluated, some have been evaluated only by the builders, and some have been evaluated in case studies, without any comparative evaluation. But it would be hard to enumerate all the possibilities of various designs and their consequences. It will be a long time before we understand the full set of interactions. Some researchers are beginning to do evaluation, and from them we can see trends, which we review below. Some trends confirm what we know about social psychology and communication, some are surprises warranting further investigation. Others, especially the emergent processes and far-reaching social impact, are new and bear examination by researchers in the more basic behavioral sciences.

The Process

The nature of the group, the kind of task they are engaged in and the features of the technology affect how people behave, the focus of the center box in Figure 14.1. This process in turn affects the quality of the product, what group members have learned, and how they feel about each other. Some researchers look for effects of groupware on the details of the process. To date, researchers have focused most on the content of the conversations in interactions, the gestures that accompany them, and various timing and participation measures. For example, some look in the content at the depth and breadth of the discussion and the time spent in various activities, distinguishing those related to the task itself from those related to the organization of the activity and those in socializing or digression. Some catalog the turntaking activity, including the number and kinds of interruptions people generate. And some code the affect of each utterance, and how wide the participation is in the activity and the organizational roles of those that participate (e.g. whether he or she is someone with authority and power or not).

Measures of Effects

The literature on the effectiveness of groupware assesses impact in a number of different ways. These are illustrated in the right side of Figure 14.1. Many studies measure the task outcome, counting the number of ideas or the quality of the product. These are measures that are often taken in comparative laboratory studies. It is difficult to measure task outcome in field settings because "success" depends on many things outside the group's control. Success is not often attributable solely to the adoption of a particular technology. Some people measure the participants' attitudes about the quality of the work, but it is well known that attitudes and performance are not always correlated (Eagly & Chaiken, 1998; Petty & Wegener, 1998). This well-established phenomenon has been shown in CSCW settings as well (e.g. Kottemann, Davis & Remus, 1994).

Other studies focus on group outcomes, assessing how technology affects people's understanding of what they decide, commitment to these decisions, satisfaction with the process or product, or the follow-on attitudes. Some technologies (e.g. video) may affect the willingness of people to work together in the future. Others, like email or chats, may make people feel more connected to others or more isolated. Few studies focus on organizational outcomes, longer-term effects of the adoption and use of various technologies. Technologies may change a person's status in the organization, loyalty to the organization, learning (knowledge and skills), and work norms.

A few emerging studies are now focusing on how technologies change an entire section of society, addressing issues about people's sense of community. Studies on electronic communities and collaboratories are few, often take a long time to conduct, and are far-reaching in their evidence for change. But they are important not only for their implications for basic theory, but also more practically for policy formation and informing decisions about whether to fund large projects (Are they worth it? What are the unintended consequences? Rochlin, 1997; Sproull & Kiesler, 1991; Tenner, 1996).

PSYCHOLOGY AND CSCW

As mentioned at the beginning of the chapter, CSCW is a multidisciplinary field, and psychology is only one of a number of behavioral fields that have influenced research and theory. In fact, psychology has not necessarily provided the dominant conceptual and methodological ideas in CSCW, a state of affairs that some have suggested has impeded progress in CSCW (Finholt & Teasley, 1998).

The various social sciences that contribute to CSCW have not always been happy partners. Cognitive psychology has been singled out for criticism both theoretically and methodologically by CSCW researchers from other social science traditions. Interestingly, many who were trained as cognitive psychologists who are among the most active CSCW researchers have become much more methodologically and theoretically eclectic.

Psychology has come in for two classes of criticisms. The first is theoretical. Psychology has been criticized for seeking principles at too abstract a level of generality, at only the individual level, and thus failing to pay sufficient attention to the details of social and physical context (e.g. Suchman, 1987; Lave, 1988). An extensive debate over this has appeared in the published literature (e.g. Vera & Simon, 1993, and an entire issue of *Cognitive Science* devoted to comments on their article). One result has been to widen the scope of cognitive theories and of the phenomena that are studied. Emerging theoretical perspectives such as distributed cognition represent attempts to incorporate a more explicit treatment of social and physical contexts into a psychological account of the kind of behavior seen with CSCW systems. A related move is to examine the cognitive behavior of aggregates of individuals, such as groups or organizations. We will look at these in more detail below.

A related criticism is methodological. Many areas of psychology depend on laboratory experiments for empirical evaluation of ideas. Critics charge that the situations and subjects used in many psychological experiments are not representative of typical group work. In contrast, much of the empirical work in CSCW is based on field observations, including ethnographic methods. Indeed, the methods of sociology and anthropology have played a major role in defining the empirical strategies of many CSCW researchers. Finholt & Teasley (1998) note how little of the research published in the meetings on CSCW have used experimental methods. They stress the value for CSCW research of using "reliable and proven measures of human behavior" drawn from psychological research in order to more quickly accumulate knowledge across studies. We have argued in more detail elsewhere (Olson, Olson, Storrøsten & Carter, 1993; Olson & Olson, 1997) that the external validity of experimental methods can be improved considerably. Improvement comes from the careful selection of tasks and subjects, and by coordinated field and laboratory investigations that explicitly analyze the similarities and differences between the two kinds of situations. Another research strategy is to conduct quasi-experiments in the field, using the kinds of design and analysis strategies discussed in Cook & Campbell (1979).

In the remainder of this section we present several approaches to the description of cognition that are representative of the new ways of conceptualizing cognitive activity.

Distributed Cognition

A theoretical perspective known as distributed cognition (e.g. Hutchins, 1990, 1991, 1995a, b; Wertsch, 1985, 1991) provides a framework for examining cognitive activity in its social and physical contexts. Cognitive processes and representations are characterized not only in terms of activity inside the heads of individuals but in the patterns of activity across individuals and in the material artifacts that mediate this activity. Hutchins has provided detailed accounts of cognitive activity in team settings to illustrate how this might work (e.g. shipboard navigation in Hutchins 1990, 1995a; flying a modern commercial jet in Hutchins, 1995b).

All of the traditional phenomena of cognitive psychology are manifested in the interactions of individuals with their social and material world. In this view, the social setting and the artifacts serve to help us with:

- short-term memory (e.g. moving a ruler down a recipe to remind us of the steps already accomplished and to help us find what to do next; checking off where we are in a long list of numbers that have to be entered in a database; after an interruption, asking the person we had been talking with to remind us what the topic was)
- calculation (e.g. using paper and pencil to do multiplication; constructing special tables to pre-calculate commonly encountered problems; using armies of individuals to calculate bomb trajectories in the Second World War)
- long-term memory (e.g. remembering where to find a book or who else knows something rather than committing to memory the contents of the book; jointly giving each other hints until a word or past event or name can be recalled)
- attention (e.g. designing a large newspaper graphic to alert everyone to the fact that daylight savings time is at hand and our clocks have to change, and a checklist to help us remember all the steps to go through to change the clocks; cheerleaders using gestures to orchestrate a cheer)
- cognitive representation (e.g. plotting data in a graph so we can visually inspect it and gain insight through perceptual processing).

The most important implication of the theory of distributed cognition is that we can *design* the artifacts and the social processes to embody cognition. The field of CSCW is exactly about this act of design. How do we design the artifacts that support our needs in distributed cognition? How do we understand what is missing when we use certain kinds of technology that affect distributed cognition? The goal is to design new technology-based artifacts, or to design the processes that help distributed cognition thrive in new ways. But the idea of distributed cognition is also a new way of thinking that has significant implications for mainstream psychological theory.

Groups as Information Processors

The idea that cognition happens outside the head of an individual is expanded by Hinsz, Tindale & Vollrath (1997), who consider groups as collective information processors. According to this view, groups perform a variety of cognitive tasks, such as problem solving, judgment, inference and decision making. These tasks involve activities that occur both inside individuals and shared among the minds. Their view of the components of group activity are depicted in Figure 14.3. Their

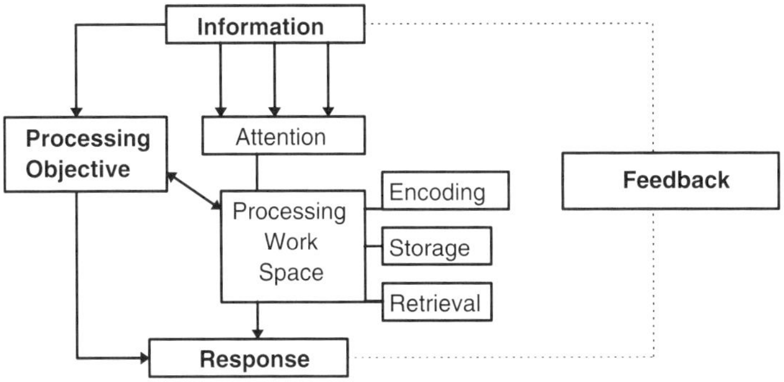

Figure 14.3 Outline of a generic information processing model for groups (from Hinsz et al., 1997). Copyright © 1997 by the American Psychological Association. Reprinted with permission

view compares well with our framework in Figure 14.1, collapsing some of the distinctions we make and expanding others. The inputs to their group process include only *Information* and *Processing Objectives*, where ours delineates aspects of the group membership, the task in its environment or context, and the technology in use. Our outcomes are broader than their *Response and Feedback*, delineating task outcomes, group outcomes and organizational outcomes. The value in their framework, however, is that they expand what is going on in our Process component to include things familiar to cognitive psychologists. The group attends, uses processing workspace, encodes, stores, and retrieves information in order to solve problems and make decisions. Their review of the small group behavior literature follows these constructs, as illustrated in the following.

- *Processing objectives*: It matters whether the individuals share the same goal and the context in which the work is viewed (e.g. juries act differently depending on who they are accountable to). Whether the group thinks that the group's goal is relationship-building or task-processing determines the ways in which people try to persuade each other.
- *Attention*: How do groups direct each others' attention to the material or issues at hand? How does the distribution of information among the group members influence who directs attention to what? For example, it appears that information must be held by at least two people in the group before it will be brought to the attention of the group as a whole. And, various kinds of information will be attended to depending on the time allowed to do a task. Under short time pressure, only task-related information is brought to bear and group members keep their coming-in positions more strongly. Under more relaxed time pressure, the group focuses more on the quality of the outcome, bringing together more of the group's individual ideas, spending time on comparing and contrasting them.
- *Encoding*: How are individual representations of the information combined by the group? There are shared or unshared mental models of the problem and of the process the group will undergo to solve the problem. Often

heterogeneous people will not share the criteria that are to be brought to bear in making a decision, making the process difficult and consensus less likely.

- *Storage*: Presumably groups have the potential of storing greater amounts of information than individuals because there are more heads involved. There is overhead in remembering the information shared by others as well as the individual items.
- *Retrieval*: Because more than one person stores a piece of information, members can correct the errors of others. But group members also both stimulate recall and inhibit it by group actions (e.g. distracting from recall by changing the topic or helping recall by generating cues). The brainstorming literature, showing that more ideas are generated when group members think individually and later sum their responses, illustrates how these two factors interact (Gallupe, Bastianutti & Cooper, 1991; Hymes & Olson, 1992).
- *Processing*: How do groups use a workspace? What techniques, rules, procedures, etc. do they adopt to get the work done? For example, individuals in a risky decision making situation will take the risk of either no loss or a huge loss in favor of a sure moderate loss. Groups exaggerate this tendency. Also groups exaggerate the tendency to ignore base rates in probabilistic judgments. Groups use rules more consistently (probably having a watchdog in the group) and are less variable in judgments.
- *Response*: If the group thinks there is one correct response, they share more of the individually-held information during discussion than if they believe there is no correct response. Groups assigned a unanimous rule remain more committed to a previously chosen alternative than groups assigned a majority rule.
- *Feedback*: How does a group learn or change from feedback? The literature shows us that failure is typically attributed to someone else in the group or to the situation, but positive feedback is attributed to the group as a whole.
- *Overall*: Although some basic level of shared knowledge is necessary for groups to function, there is no perfect correlation between amount of shared knowledge and group effectiveness.

The authors synthesize from the findings two overarching questions about small group behavior:

1. How do groups identify and apply the resources that group members bring to the task?
2. What are the processes by which these resources are combined to produce the outcome?

Hinsz et al. (1997) highlight the importance of doing research with variously designed technologies to reveal how these processes work. Hirokawa (1990), for example, argues that the more a decision-making task requires the members to collectively process information, the more important communication is for the group to succeed at the task. It is likely that if a technology reduced the information processing demands (e.g. by showing the output of a simulation or the results of complicated calculations), the groups need to communicate less. That is, appropriately built technology may not only elucidate the hypothesized processes active in a theory of group cognition, but also in the end be useful for practical purposes.

Also, because technology in group contexts often allows us to capture fine grained behavior (e.g. the content of a chat or threaded discussion), we are able to test various models of the microprocesses in interactions. For example, Hutchins (1991) developed a distributed connectionist model to examine how the confirmatory bias could arise in groups. And Thagard (1989) has conducted an analysis of research on juries, using a constraint satisfaction model. These models have ways of representing the pattern of communication in groups (e.g. who talks to whom) so a finer analysis of how information is processed through discussion is an appropriate test venue. There are testable hypotheses about how people process pieces of information that can be examined in CSCW contexts.

Establishing and Using Common Ground

Researchers on the psychology of language have already begun a dialog with those in CSCW. Together they have learned the importance of conversational conventions, and have gained a clear notion of what it means to make an utterance in the context of an ongoing conversation of a particular type (e.g. Clark, 1996; Clark & Brennan, 1991; O'Conaill, Whittaker & Wilbur, 1997). For example, if we are conversing to come to an agreement on an issue, there are a number of steps we must go through, including offering, counter-offering, accepting, and agreeing that we are done. These conversational conventions are easy to keep track of when we are face-to-face, where immediate prior actions and the goal of the interaction are still in memory. But when we engage in an elongated conversation and when we conduct many of them interleaved, as we do in email, memory is put to the test. Our conventions must change if we are to manage it all. These ideas have been explored in research on communication among remote members of groups working together via video connections (see the edited collection of Finn, Sellen & Wilbur, 1997, for a number of examples). The social aspects of conversation, how we read the signals from our conversational partner about when it is our turn, etc. are similarly important (Fussell & Benimoff, 1995). When video conferences delay our speech and our partner is off-screen, conversational disruption is predictable.

CSCW also speaks to social and organizational psychologists, especially about how people categorize other individuals and the context they interact in. This categorization drives people's ability to predict others' actions and behave appropriately (McCauley, Stitt & Segal, 1980). People judge each other's intelligence by age and dress (e.g. we speak more slowly and simply to young children, and dress to be accepted in the culture we visit); they gauge their expectations by the context in which they encounter other people (e.g. in the US, we expect to be served in order of appearance when we queue for service); they infer power and intent by a person's loudness and physical stature. All of these are characteristics that are disrupted in today's long-distance technologies. For example, people encounter those from other cultures over videoconferencing and misinterpret their behaviors. They mis-assess their intelligence because they dress differently and appear far away and are hard to hear.

Organizational Cognition

In a long tradition going back at least as far as March & Simon (1958) organizations have been described as information processing systems. Thus, it is not surprising that the vocabulary of cognition has been applied to the organization: knowledge (Nonaka & Takeuchi, 1995), collective intelligence (Weick, 1993; Weick & Roberts, 1993), routines (Cohen & Bacdayan, 1994; Cyert & March, 1963), learning (Argyris, 1992; Senge, 1990), and memory (Walsh, 1995; Walsh & Ungson, 1991). These descriptions are particularly relevant to CSCW, since information technology's role in organizations is typically to alter the way in which information processing is done.

One important characteristic of cognitive activity that is as true of organizations as of individual minds is that some of the knowledge is explicit and easily accessible while other knowledge is more tacit and procedural (Anderson, 1982). Organizational routines are "multi-actor, interlocking, reciprocally-triggered sequences of actions" that are "a major source of the reliability and speed of organizational performance [Cohen & Bacdayan, 1994, p. 554]." Routines at the organizational level are naturally built from cognitive procedures at the individual level, and share the characteristics of tacitness and automaticity. Based on these cognitive foundations we would expect routines to exhibit gradual acquisition, resistance to change, automatic invocation in response to social and physical cues, and limited access to verbal descriptions by the participants. Not surprisingly, they are a key element in the organizational response to new technologies.

FINDINGS ABOUT BEHAVIOR CHANGES WITH THESE TECHNOLOGIES

In the following section, we review some of the key findings that have implications for both the applied world and basic psychological research. We point to various reviews of the literature, where they exist, for a more complete discussion of the topic. We present the results using the technology/situation categorizations in Table 14.1, highlighting the features in Figure 14.1 within each category. That is, when appropriate, we describe specifically what *group* characteristics were present in the study, the *task* they undertook, and the details of the *technology*. We then describe the aspects of the *process* measured and the *outcomes*.

Support for Face-to-face Conversations

Technology has supported face-to-face meetings in a variety of ways. Some embed some support for cognitive processes involved in problem solving and decision making. These structure the process of discussion (e.g. embodying nominal group technique or brainstorming), guide the way criteria are developed for decision making (e.g. embodying stakeholder analysis), and determine how voting is accomplished (e.g. anonymously, with various voting and ranking algorithms). Others are more free form. They allow people to create, view, and edit the object under discussion. These support the conversational grounding, the context and referents of the work.

Group Decision Support Systems (GDSS) are one common kind of face-to-face system that structure the group's problem-solving and decision processes. GDSSs are built on decision support systems designed to aid individual decision-makers by adding a series of group tools to coordinate the decision making. These systems are designed to support large heterogeneous *groups* engaged in decision-making tasks, where their *task* consists of brainstorming alternatives and deciding among them. Most GDSSs require the services of a facilitator and someone to retrieve, run, and store results from one subtask to the other (e.g. Nunamaker et al., 1991). The attention of the group members is focused as it should be on the decisions they are making, not on the complex task of orchestrating the technology and the group.

There have been a number of experimental evaluations of such systems, and there are several literature reviews that attempt to draw general conclusions from this work (Hollingshead, McGrath & O'Connor, 1993; Kraemer & Pinsonneault, 1990; McLeod, 1992). These reviews conclude that the structured meeting support systems typically affect various *processes* that in turn affect outcomes. Because many of these systems allow anonymous input, they typically produce meetings with more equal participation. Decision quality increases with the GDSS, but meetings require more time, and produce decisions that are less satisfying to the participants than traditionally supported meetings.

Support for Remote Real-time Conversation

Remote real-time conversation is most typically supported by the telephone. When there are more than two people conversing, speaker phones or more sophisticated audioconferencing services are used. Two other modes are used and studied in CSCW: real-time chat or MUDs and MOOs, and videoconferencing. These, of course, differ enormously on the amount of information that can be conveyed by both the sender and the receiver. They have very different effects on the progress and content of the conversations that ensue. We will review first the work on text-based conversation modes, then the audio and videoconferencing studies.

Text-based Conversation

Real-time text-based conversation is typically supported by one window on the computer into which the person types the utterance, which is then broadcast to all participants with the person's name tagged on the front. In MUDs and MOOs, people type not only their contribution to the conversation, but typically other descriptions of their actions, e.g. "Judy smiles," "George glances at Gary and waves", as well. In more complicated, sophisticated MUDs and MOOs, users can query about a person's background, and various descriptions of places, like rooms, doors, and corridors, are available for display as well. Participants program the system to display these descriptions, creating clever descriptions of places and actions in the imagined world. This playfulness accounts for a large part of the appeal. Although MUDs and MOOs began in the fantasy and game world, there are occasions when they are used for serious purposes, for meeting remotely and inexpensively in real time about various issues of mutual concern.

There are a number of ethnographic accounts of the interactions that occur in MUDs and MOOs. These studies center mainly on the issues of identity, since players can describe themselves as another gender or creature. Curtis (1996) describes experiences of identity and interaction in his famous LambdaMOO, noting how surprised people are at the responses they get from others when they describe themselves in various ways. People respond helpfully to those that describe themselves in non-powerful ways, aggressively when described powerfully. Communities in different MOOs develop their own rules of etiquette, finding the need for shared understanding of the cultural norms essential for smooth interactions. There are a number of potentially interesting research topics to pursue in this arena about trust, identity, and social organizations (Turkle, 1995).

One chat system with a serious purpose has been studied in detail. In the Upper Atmospheric Research Collaboratory (UARC), scientists share in real-time displays of scientific instruments that are collecting and representing data on the atmosphere worldwide (Olson et al., 1998). The scientists converse using chat boxes, with sometimes as many as 15 people actively participating, and as many as 30 "lurking." An analysis of the conversational threads in the UARC chat box showed that there were no more confusions in content and progress than naturally occurring in a large free-form discussion face-to-face, even though there were sometimes eight topics being discussed at once. Furthermore, more people were able to participate than in face-to-face conversation (McDaniel, Olson & Magee, 1996). The fact that the chat box allows the user to scroll back through the typed conversation to review context, supporting the memory of the user, likely accounts for this advantage.

Audio and Video Conferencing

A classic early study of conversations over various media showed that the quality of the product was significantly better in audio over text-based chat, but that video did not increase it further (Chapanis & Ochsman, 1972). Yet, ever since Picturephone (a commercial product that allowed regular telephone users to see the called party as well as be seen by them (Wish, 1975)), designers have continued to explore the use of video connections to support people working at a distance. In spite of the commercial failure of Picturephone and the lack of evidence that video connectivity does anything to enhance simultaneous group work at a distance (Egido, 1988), people persist in using video.

Room-based videoconferencing systems are commercially available (e.g. Picturetel), and continue to be extensively deployed in organizations. Desktop videoconferencing systems running over networks or ISDN lines have become available (e.g. Intel's ProShare system). Some experimental video systems are intended to support two or more co-workers while they engage in close work (Tang & Minneman, 1990). CAVECAT (Mantei et al., 1991) put the faces of the co-workers in small windows on a single screen. And both Hydra (Buxton, Sellen & Sheasby, 1997) and the set-up used in the Olson study (Olson, Olson & Meader, 1995) presented each remote speaker on a different screen and arranged them in a semi-circle as if each person was seated around a table. Commune (Minneman & Bly, 1991) show both user and drawing surface separately, whereas ClearBoard (Ishii & Kobayashi, 1994) blends the two by arranging people on either side of the object under discussion, as if looking through glass.

Unfortunately, many more video systems have been built than have been studied. However, a recent collection of reports of video-mediated communications (Finn, Sellen & Wilbur, 1997) show some interesting results. A study with a well-designed videoconferencing set-up showed that small established *groups* doing a design *task* can produce *output* that is indistinguishable in quality from face-to-face groups. However, the video-supported groups are less satisfied, and a detailed analysis of the process of conversation showed that they spend much more time organizing themselves than they do when meeting face-to-face (Olson, Olson & Meader, 1995). In this study, video was not a big advantage over audio only, probably because these were established groups whose behavior and opinions are well conveyed by voice.

Other detailed comparisons of groups using video connections to support their conversations (pairs of people completing a map-following task or negotiating alternative travel plans) showed that behavior in video and audio-only conditions did not differ, but both differed from face-to-face (Anderson et al., 1997). Those subjects who had only audio reported not knowing what was transpiring when there was silence at the other end.

Some of these effects are explained by a deeper understanding of the ways in which meaning is conveyed visually in a conversation (Whittaker & O'Conaill, 1997). Visible cues help people determine whose turn it is next to talk, what people are talking about (by gesture or presence of an object), whether their message is being received accurately, and whether someone is paying attention or not. In audioconferencing, these cues are missing, causing disruptions in turn-taking and feedback.

These cues are present in videoconferencing, but there are more subtle effects on conversation. Unfortunately, most commercial video systems produce a delay in the transmission of video, and most additionally delay the audio so that it is synchronized with the video stream. This delay, often on the order of one second, has a well-known disruptive effect on conversation. Just as loss of visual cues affects turn-taking in audioconferencing, delays produce similar effects. Sometimes the backchannels are misinterpreted because they appear at points different from when they were uttered (Ruhleder & Jordan, 1997). (Backchannel responses are those that a listener utters during the speaker's speech to signal to the speaker that he or she understands or not, agrees or not, etc. They consist of short grunts and "uh huhs" or head nods and furled brows.) Other work suggests that delay will affect the time to complete tasks as well as the participants' understanding of what they did (Kraut et al., 1982; Oviatt & Cohen, 1991). Indeed, when given the choice, people report that the delay in audio matters more than the asynchrony of video and audio (Isaacs & Tang, 1997).

Many of the studies reported above involve two people working on a joint task. There are other uses for remote video. Several people have experimented with remote presentations. The speaker broadcasts the presentation by video and audio and can gesture with a telepointer or mark the presentation with digital ink (Isaacs et al., 1994). In one such system, called Forum, the audience also has the opportunity to interact, asking questions or voting on various presenter-posed questions. Use of this system over a variety of presentations showed that there was a larger audience viewing but poorer interaction, mainly because the audience could split their attention with other tasks (e.g. doing email). Audiences liked this, but speakers preferred face-to-face. Because the speakers did not have visual contact with the audience, they reported missing the normal feedback signals of whether the audience was engaged or not. Presenters heard neither laughter nor applause. Interestingly, speakers tended to overestimate the quality of their talk when it was face-to-face and underestimate it in Forum.

Support for Face-to-face and Remote Real-time Sharing of Objects

A number of systems support sharing of an editable object, such as a document or drawing. Unlike GDSSs, they do not structure the process, but rather allow the conversation to move as it will. Systems in this class include Cognoter in the Colab at Xerox PARC (Stefik et al., 1987), ShrEdit (Olson et al., 1993), and a commercial product, Aspects (Group Technologies, 1990). Application-sharing through the use of ProShare and NetMeeting, and screen-sharing offered by Shared-X, Timbuktu, or Point-to-Point are simple but powerful collaborative tools. Like flip charts and whiteboards, these tools do not dictate the group process but rather provide editable, visible support for whatever the group dictates is useful at the time.

Studies of the use of these technologies by small established *groups* doing design *tasks* show that the *quality* of the work is higher with these technologies than that with traditional support – with whiteboard paper and pencil – but groups were slightly less *satisfied* (Olson et al., 1993). A detailed *process* analysis showed that the computer-supported groups, surprisingly, explored fewer options than the whiteboard groups while achieving higher quality. The tool was thought to help keep the groups more focused on the core issues, to have them waste less time on less important topics, and to capture what was said as they worked. This work was extended to evaluate the same technology in groups that were not collocated. In a second study, similar groups doing the same design task sat in different offices connected with both a shared editor and either video and audio or audio-only connections. The quality of the work was nearly the same as that of groups meeting face-to-face using the shared editor (Olson, Olson & Meader, 1995).

Exploring a very different setting, Posner & Baecker and colleagues (Mitchell et al., 1995; Posner & Baecker, 1992) used Aspects, a shared editor, with *groups* of four sixth-grade students engaged in the *task* of writing articles for their class magazine over the course of 12 weeks. The students were shown various methods of conducting shared writing: using a scribe, writing in parallel and then joining the document, and joint writing (simultaneously seeing what others write as you write). Unlike traditional cognitive psychology experiments, there was no control group. However, important observations were made about how the shared editor affected the group. Students were often concerned with issues of ownership and control, puzzling over whether someone can change what another has written, for example. And, since people often work out of view of one another, there were numerous episodes of being confused as to who could see what. Clearly the invisibility of others' work and the ability of others to freely edit one's work violated norms that appear as early as sixth grade. However, the result was a rich experience for the students to learn to work out ways to involve everyone in the production of a joint process, an early lesson in cooperative behavior.

The LiveBoard, a large pen-based computer display much like an electronic whiteboard or flip chart (Elrod et al., 1992) has been evaluated in an extended case study of a *group* whose *task* it was to manage intellectual property issues. The team used the LiveBoard in conjunction with laptop notetaking and audio records for a period of two years. Their persistent use of the technology suggested that it was useful support for their work (voting with their feet). Comments and suggestions they had along the way were incorporated into valued feature changes (Moran et al., 1996). They suggested that the system recognize various constructions that the team member recognized, such as lists, regions of the board, and outlines. By having the tool support the marks in the way the team members understood them, e.g. by having items in a list dragged around to re-arrange them and having the rest of the list adjust position automatically around the moved item, the support for distributed cognition was smoother.

Nardi (Nardi et al., 1995) observed a highly functional surgical team coordinate their work by having access to the surgeon's view of the surgery itself displayed on a monitor viewable by all. By seeing the progress of the surgery and both expected and unexpected actions, Nardi observed that the staff could smoothly prepare for the next step without the need for conversation. Using video in this way was seen as vastly superior to their previous coordination from only vague signals from their co-workers' words and gestures, many of which were confusing or absent under stress.

Unfortunately, many of the reports on these new group technologies for real-time support do not evaluate them with real groups doing real work, whether in a case study or in a comparative evaluation. The research has been more focused on the rationale behind the design and the various implementation challenges to be overcome. Although many of the rationales imply models of cognition and coordination, they are not well developed enough to be of use to psychologists.

Asynchronous Support of Conversation

It is generally agreed that electronic mail is one groupware application that has seen wide success (Anderson, Bikson, Law & Mitchell, 1995; O'Hara-Devereaux & Johansen, 1994; Satzinger & Olfman, 1992; Sproull & Kiesler, 1991). The widespread dissemination of networks and personal computers has led to extensive use of email in organizations and from home. Now that email is widespread, it has many of the characteristics of other widespread communication technologies such as the telephone. Because it works across heterogeneous hardware and software, it offers the possibility of universal service (Anderson et al., 1995). With the use of standard attachments (e.g. MIME) and common representation formats (e.g. Postscript, binhex, uucode, rtf) it is increasingly easy to send complex, multimedia documents through email, a feature made even easier through the use of HTML and the World Wide Web (Schatz & Hardin, 1994). Email spans the barriers of space and time, and the use of distribution lists offers broadcast access to widespread communities. Demographic data on network connections, email use, and general connectivity all show the wide adoption of electronic communication as a common form of human contact (Garton & Wellman, 1995).

Electronic mail has a number of well-known effects on human behavior. Because of email's power to reach many subscribers quickly, it has changed the culture of the organizations in which it resides: it changes who talks to whom (Sproull & Kiesler, 1991), what kind of person is heard from (Finholt, Sproull & Kiesler, 1990), and the tone of what is said (Sproull & Kiesler, 1991). With email, people who were previously thought to be under-performers find a voice. They are no longer impeded by shyness or difficulty with social interaction; they can speak without seeing other people. On the other side of the coin, forgetting that there is a human reading the message at the other end, and in the absence of feedback from the recipient, people tend to "flame," to write asocial emotive messages that are either shocking, upsetting or offensive to the reader. Arrow et al. (1996) and Hollingshead et al. (1993) suggest, however, that these effects dissipate in time.

As for its effect on the work itself, people vary widely in how they use it (Mackay, 1989). Several studies have found that email is not only useful for direct communication, but people also find it especially useful for managing time, tasks, and information flow (Carley & Wendt, 1991; Mackay, 1989). But, because email systems were not designed to support these secondary tasks, they support them poorly. Users spend enormous amounts of time managing their inboxes (Whittaker & Sidner, 1996). Clearly something more is required.

With people subscribing to listserves and bulletin boards, conversational threads are lost in the volume. Readers are confused because it is hard to reinstate a context. Some attempt to reinstate the context by replying with the previous message attached, but after two or three such replies, the message is long and unwieldy. In response to these problems, some email systems organize messages by topic, making the conversational threading visible. For example, Lotus Notes conversation databases do this. The "sender" appends his/her reply visually near the item to which he/she is responding, creating a visually organized thread. The Coordinator (Winograd, 1987–88) asks the sender of a message to declare the action that the recipient is expected to make, by designating the message as a request, a commitment or promise, background information, etc. Studies of the use of the Coordinator suggest that this kind of formalization of conversational patterns at best fits only some kinds of organizational situations, and is problematic in many others (Bikson et al., 1988). In the Information LENS, the user can generate rules by which the incoming mail could be sorted into folders that can later be examined by the reader in some priority order (Malone et al., 1989). LENS provides organization over collected email, but the burden of organizing falls on the receiver, not the sender.

A very important new line of research addresses the consequence of the use of remote technologies to the development and loss of trust. Recently, Rocco (1998) watched groups of six play a game that is a variant of prisoner's dilemma. In this game individuals repeatedly decide what to invest in a common pool, and receive benefits either by cooperating (where everyone gets some positive benefit) or by "defecting," making a move that is personally beneficial but at the cost of making others lose. She found that groups who were able to occasionally talk to each other face-to-face about the optimal strategy ended in achieving benefit through cooperation; those who discussed things by email defected more often. Importantly, however, those groups that met prior to the game and conducted a team-building activity eventually cooperated even when they were restricted to email for their discussion. This opens up a line of questions about what other technologies (e.g, videoconferencing) afford the same cooperative, trustful behavior that face-to-face does, to what extent and under what conditions.

Asynchronous Support of Sharing of Objects

A variety of objects are shared in the conduct of work. Documents such as workplans, proposals, requirements, etc. are often authored by many over time. People store finished documents like the quarter-end financial statement for others to access. Some people are experimenting with storing what are called design rationales to help people who come later on a project to understand earlier thinking. And project management systems and workflow systems support the coordination of various stages of work.

Collaborative Authoring of Documents

Much of group work currently consists of individuals writing documents (e.g. system requirements, policy proposals, project proposals) and then soliciting comments from many different people and making changes, iterating several times. Today this activity involves a lot of paper drafts and a great deal of time simply entering edits. The standard word processors (e.g. MSWord) now have revision features that make edits visible (cross outs of previous words, new additions marked differently) and allow easy acceptance of the edits and production of a clean copy. There are many more sophisticated systems developed to support collaborative writing that are prototypes, not commercial products. These include For Comment (Edwards, Levine & Kurland, 1986), Quilt (Leland, Fish & Kraut, 1988), the PREP Editor (Neuwirth et al., 1990), and SEPIA (Haake & Wilson, 1994). See Posner & Baecker (1992) and Michailidis & Rada (1995) for extensive reviews of such tools.

Plowman (1995) describes how talk and writing interact when collaborating authors develop the ideas for their text, implying a need for informal support at this stage of writing. A study of the use of the PREP editor also supported the need for flexibility in the technology to support the difference phases and preferences of collaborating authors (Kaufer et al., 1995; Neuwirth et al., 1994; Wojahn et al., 1998). At some points in the text, authors chose to attach voice commentary, and at others they wanted to explain their ideas by rewriting the text.

Design Rationale

A number of systems are intended to support groups of designers in the complex task of designing an object like an automobile or airplane. Most of these systems aim to capture the argumentation that occurs during the design process, linking the questions of consideration with the alternative solutions that were proposed as well as the evaluative discussion that accompanied it. There is a strong belief that this kind of system would help designers in two ways. It would help designers remember more alternatives and therefore consider them more fully. And later, it would also be a memory source to help those other team members that have to maintain and/or alter the system. By retrieving the rationale behind an earlier decision, the maintainers could spend less time rediscovering why some unused alternatives would not work (Moran & Carroll, 1996). The most well known of these systems is gIBIS (Conklin & Begeman, 1988) which uses a hypertext linking structure to organize the various issues, alternatives, and criteria in the design rationale. QOC is a similar method and system (MacLean et al., 1996).

The capture of design rationale has not been totally successful, likely because it is a classic case of misaligned benefits. The person benefiting from the information is not the person who has to invest time and effort by entering it (Conklin & Burgess-Yakemovic, 1996; Grudin, 1988; Shum, 1996). Also, the representation does not always fit the discussion. We have found that discussions do not always follow one issue at a time, and alternatives and criteria sometimes relate in braided ways. But, when the diagramming/procedure of design rationale is followed, indeed the designers that come on the project later use it with some success. An analysis of their discussions showed that half their questions are design rationale questions, and half of these are answered by the design rationale documentation. Difficulties arise in that the originator does not always anticipate what later designers might need (and therefore ignores rationales actually discussed) and some design decisions are made without rationale and are accepted without discussion (Karsenty, 1996).

Repositories of Shared Knowledge

Other types of coordination are possible with applications like Lotus Notes. A group can keep open issues lists in a form accessible to all interested parties, and construct workflow systems that automatically route information to the right people for additions and approvals. Some organizations are viewing Notes as repositories of corporate knowledge, capturing people's experience on previous projects, their heuristics for decision making (e.g. pricing policies and exception handling), boilerplate for various kinds of proposals, etc.

Two extensive case studies have shown the organizational consequences of introducing these kinds of technologies. In the first (Orlikowski & Gash, 1994), consultants were asked to share their knowledge about various clients and engagements in a large Notes database so that others could benefit from their experience and insights. Two key issues prevented successful adoption. First, although consultants had to bill all their working hours to various clients, there was no account for them to use to bill the time devoted to data entry and learning of Notes. Second, consultants were promoted on the basis of their skill advantage over their co-workers, discouraging them from sharing their knowledge. So in this case the accounting/billing of time and the assessment of credit was misaligned with the capability the technology afforded, the objective of its introduction and the goals of its use. In a successful case in our experience, sales people shared their client contacts with each other. This sharing prevented the embarrassing occasions when a single client was being told different stories by two different sales people. This use fit the incentive scheme in which sales people received commissions on total sales as well as their individual sales.

In the second case study, software designers used Notes to keep their open issue list and to share information about future features or potential solutions to bugs (Olson & Teasley, 1996). Their use of the system initially rose and then declined over 12 months. Interviews of the group members revealed that the team members were less and less inclined to use the application because they thought the manager was not participating. They saw no activity on his part and assumed he did not value their use of the system. In truth, the manager was participating regularly; he read the material but did not write. Unfortunately, Notes does not make reading activity visible in the interface.

Workflow Applications

Workflow applications allow people to design, execute and manage coordinated activities over a network. A process involving several people, like the reporting, approval, and payment of travel expenses, would be supported electronically. Initial reporting would be done in an electronic document, transferred to another, signatures obtained for approval, and records kept of not only where a particular document is in the process, but who is responsible for it and when it was received or completed.

Workflow applications have often resulted from business process re-engineering efforts, where teams examine a business activity and find ways to make it more efficient. Often, efficiency comes with some technology to either store documents for many people to access (eliminating paper), or some stages of processing being eliminated, automated, or supported. Not only does workflow have a bad reputation among workers because it displaces workers, but it also is often conceived as the ideal work process, both rigid and dictatorial. Many of the systems do not support the flexibility and judgment that often accompanies real coordinated work and therefore fall into disuse (e.g. Abbott & Sarin, 1994).

One other aspect of workflow applications has also generated user resistance. Because applications can track the status of various documents and procedures, management can monitor the work of employees. In many countries, such monitoring is disallowed by powerful worker organizations (Prinz & Kolvenbach, 1996). In the US, it is not disallowed, but certainly unwelcome. In a team where workflow was a new concept, the team members misunderstood how important it was to be accurate in assigning responsibility to various subtasks (like who will handle a particular bug fix). They did not know the full range of views available to the manager to monitor work. One team member, the one most often assigned the first task in a series, came to realize that there was a potential for managerial monitoring. The management report would look as if he alone were responsible for delays, when in fact the real work was being done by others down the line. This feature made him less and less eager to use the application (Olson & Teasley, 1996). In general, managerial monitoring is a feature that is known to disincline people from using groupware (Markus, 1983).

Support for the Transition between Asynchronous and Real-time Work: Awareness Support and Calendars

Group work is a mixture of synchronous and asynchronous activities. People meet to plan the work, assign individuals to do various subtasks. These people coordinate and clarify as they go, and periodically meet to align goals and plan next steps. They move often between individual subtasks and coordination or clarification in real time. The following technologies would support these transitions.

First, project management software captures decisions made in meetings about who is doing what, and what the linkages or dependencies are between subtasks. These technologies help calculate the consequences of changes to the plan (by calculating the critical path) and indicate to team members who is waiting for work. Open issues lists and project management software are the tools to support the transition from real-time meetings to parallel, more independent work. These technologies suffer only from the time and effort involved in keeping them up to date; like writing and distributing meeting minutes, it requires someone to do it.

More difficult is the transition from asynchronous to synchronous work, both accessing an individual so that one can converse or negotiate in real time, and calling meetings. Recognizing how difficult this is, some organizations expect workers to be at their desks at all time (and thus reachable at all times). Others schedule standing meetings, expecting full attendance whether one's expertise is needed or not. In lieu of these rash solutions, some have adopted some technologies to help people locate others or to assess when they can reach them so they can make contact.

One of the most comprehensive of these systems is Montage (Tang, Isaacs & Rua, 1994). Montage, like Cruiser (Fish et al., 1993), allows video "glances" into team members' offices so one can assess whether they are available for a phone or video conversation. If the glance instead reveals that the intended person is not there or not available, the seeker has several options. The seeker can leave an email message, can view the person's calendar to see when he/she might return or where they might be reached. Or the seeker can leave a "sticky note" on the screen of the person being sought, attracting the team member's attention immediately upon their return. In an evaluation of Montage which was deployed in a distributed workgroup, the results showed that people glanced at each other nearly 3 times a day, and 3/4 of those were unacknowledged (people were there but they did not respond to connect in a real time video link). The connections when made were short (a little over a minute). And, although the additional access to calendars, email and sticky notes were used infrequently, people reported afterwards valuing them highly.

Other uses of video to allow awareness of team members' activity have been tried. The VideoWindow at Bellcore was intended to encourage both ordinary meeting and casual interactions from remote sites over coffee (Fish, Kraut & Chalfonte, 1990). RAVE, a suite of systems at Rank Xerox EuroPARC (Gaver et al., 1992), was intended to support awareness of global activity, glances into individuals' offices, and point-to-point contact for close intense work. Long-term use of video connectivity was analyzed in the Portland Experiment (Olson & Bly, 1991). All of these systems have been studied within research lab settings, where modest amounts of sustained use were found. It would be extremely useful to have studies of these systems carried out in other kinds of organizational settings.

All of the implementations of awareness through video raise issues of privacy. Various solutions have been proposed, including introducing reciprocity (you are only on camera when you can see the person viewing you), warning (the sound of a "squeaky door opening" or footsteps coming serves as a signal of an impending glance), viewee control over camera position, and showing recent snapshots as opposed to live immediate action (see Hudson & Smith, 1996 for a discussion). One awareness system, called Thunderwire (Hindus et al., 1996), used open audio instead of video. In use, most difficulties pointed to the interpretation of silence. People realized the need for designing new norms in announcing oneself (because the hearers are blind), and negotiating inattention and withdrawal.

On-line calendars afford awareness as well as ease in scheduling meetings. PROFs calendar and Meeting Maker are two popular implementations; both allow designation of who can write and who can read the calendar, as well as control over private portions of the calendar, where viewers can see that the person is busy, but not what they are doing. Although Grudin (1988) has designated this application as the quintessential misalignment of costs and benefits (the individual has to keep the calendar up to date if it is going to be of benefit to others), many organizations have since adopted it successfully (Grudin & Palen, 1995; Mosier & Tammaro, 1997). A culture of sharing and accessibility supports the successful adoption of on-line calendars (Ehrlich, 1987; Lange, 1992).

Efforts to Support Communities

A number of recent projects investigated the needs of large-scale communities, both through user-centered design and by merely deploying a flexible technology and watching its use. Two main thrusts are relevant here: the development of collaboratories, and the study of home/community use of the World Wide Web.

A collaboratory is the "combination of technology, tools and infrastructure that allow scientists to work with remote facilities and each other as if they were co-located" (Lederberg & Uncapher, 1989, p. 6). A National Research Council (1993) report defines a collaboratory as a "center without walls, in which the nation's researchers can perform their research without regard to geographical location – interacting with colleagues, accessing instrumentation, sharing data and computational resources [and] accessing information in digital libraries" (National Research Council, 1993, p. 7). A simplified form of these definitions describes a collaboratory as the use of computing and communication technology to achieve the enhanced access to colleagues and instruments provided by a shared physical location, but in a domain where potential collaborations are not constrained by temporal or geographic barriers.

One such collaboratory effort is the Upper Atmospheric Research Collaboratory, a set of technologies that allow space scientists studying the upper atmosphere to view real-time data from various instruments (like incoherent scatter radar) around the world. They can align these views with models of what should be going on, and converse through a chat facility with the other scientists or graduate students, and share their configuration views with others to support their ongoing conversation. Finholt & Olson (1997) present a review of the concept of a collaboratory and describe some preliminary findings. For example, they found that UARC theorists and data analysts are working together where they did not before. Also graduate students have access to remote mentors and can experience real-time data collection, where previously they might get to go to a site once in their graduate training (Olson et al., 1998). Their network of colleagues has shifted with use of the collaboratory, and it is expected that publication authorship will shift as well. The issue, really, is whether science is progressing faster or not, and since there is no real control group for this effort, we do not know.

An earlier collaboratory supporting molecular biologists studying the *C. elegans* nematode, affectionately called the Worm Community, illustrated both the difficulty of getting a community started and the important emergent attitudes about various participants' willingness to share (Schatz, 1991–92; Star & Ruhleder, 1994). Various disciplines develop their own cultures about joint work, credit, and need for immediate communication, and will be variously successful in adopting this and other new capability, like digital libraries (Covi, 1996). There are now efforts underway to support medical radiology and AIDS clinicians and bench scientists in collaboratories. It is likely that collaboratory interactions in science will become a routine aspect of scientific practice, with important implications not just for the practices of scientists but also for the training of graduate students.

In contrast to this well planned, user-centered development of technologies evident in collaboratories, there are efforts to install various technologies in designated communities. The intent is to learn by various evaluation strategies what people value and what they might need in the future. Two such efforts are the HomeNet in the Pittsburgh area (Kraut et al., 1996) and another is the

Blacksburg Electronic Village in Virginia (Carroll & Rosson, 1996). These systems have been installed for a few years and data collection has progressed to a point of revealing trends in behavior. They are finding that teenage males are by far the heaviest users, although there is evidence that access to electronic mail for keeping up personal conversations and contacts is valued by all.

Pointers to the Past and Future Research in this Area

A number of sources exist that review subsets of the technologies and associated group behavior in greater depth. They are well worth pursuing if one wants more detail and deeper analysis of cognition in CSCW. Six large volumes are anthologies of studies in this area:

- *Readings in Groupware and Computer Supported Cooperative Work*, edited by Baecker (Baecker, 1993)
- *Groupware: Software for Computer Supported Cooperative Work*, edited by Marca & Bock (1992)
- *Groupware and Authoring*, edited by Rada (1996)
- *Video Mediated Communication*, edited by Finn, Sellen & Wilbur (1997)
- *Intellectual Teamwork: Social and Technological Foundations of Cooperative Work*, edited by Galegher, Kraut & Egido (1990)
- *Computer Supported Cooperative Work: a Book of Readings*, edited by Greif (1988)

These excellent volumes plus the *Proceedings on Computer Supported Cooperative Work (CSCW)* and the *European Computer Supported Cooperative Work (ECSCW)*, the conferences that alternate meeting bi-annually, provide both the basics and the continuing progress in this exciting field. Several journals also publish CSCW work: *Computer Supported Cooperative Work*, *Human–Computer Interaction*, *ACM Transaction on Information Systems*, *Communication of the ACM*, and *ACM Transactions on Computer–Human Interaction*.

ACKNOWLEDGMENTS

Work behind this chapter was supported in part by a grant from the Natural Data Types Research Council at Intel, National Science Foundation (Grant No. IRI-8902930), and Corporate Partnership between CREW and Steelcase, Inc. We are grateful for the comments on an earlier version from Stephanie Teasley, Lisa Covi, Ruben Mendoza, and six anonymous reviewers under Susan Dumais' editorship.

REFERENCES

Abbott, K. R. and Sarin, S. K. (1994). Experiences with workflow management: issues for the next generation. *Proceedings of the Conference on Computer Supported Cooperative Work*, 113–20.

Anderson, A. H., O'Malley, C., Doherty-Sneddon, G., Langton, S., Newlands, A., Mullin, J., Fleming, A. M. & Van der Velden, J. (1997). The impact of VMC on collaborative problem solving: an analysis of task performance, communicative process, and user satisfaction. In K. Finn, A. Sellen & S. B. Wilbur (Eds), *Video Mediated Communication* (pp. 133–55). Mahwah, NJ: Lawrence Erlbaum.

Anderson, J. R. (1982). Acquisition of cognitive skill. *Psychological Review*, 89, 369–406.

Anderson, R. H., Bikson, T. K., Law, S. A. & Mitchell, B. M. (1995). *Universal Access to E-mail: Feasibility and Societal Implications*. Santa Monica, CA: RAND.

Argyris, C. (1992). *On Organizational Learning*. Cambridge, MA: Blackwell.

Arrow, H., Berdahl, J. L., Bouas, K. S., Craig, K. M., Cummings, A., Lebei, L., McGrath, J. E., O'Connor, K. M., Rhoades, J. A. & Schlosser, A. (1996). Time, technology, and groups: an integration. *Computer Supported Cooperative Work*, 4, 253–61.

Baecker, R. M. (1993). *Readings in Groupware and Computer-Supported Cooperative Work*. San Mateo, CA: Morgan Kaufman.

Bikson, T. K., Bair, J. H., Barry, R. & Grantham, C. E. (1988). Communication, coordination, and group performance. *Proceeding of the ACM Conference on Computer Supported Cooperative Work (CSCW '88)*, panel discussion.

Bullen, C. V. & Bennett, J. L. (1996). Groupware in practice: an interpretation of work experiences. In R. Kling (Ed.), *Computerization and Controversy* (2nd edn) (pp. 348–82). New York: Academic Press.

Buxton, W. A. S., Sellen, A. J. & Sheasby, M. C. (1997). Interfaces for multi-party videoconferences. In K. Finn, A. Sellen & S. B. Wilbur (Eds), *Video Mediated Communication* (pp. 385–400). Mahwah, NJ: Lawrence Erlbaum.

Carley, K. & Wendt, K. (1991). Electronic mail and scientific communication: a study of the Soar extended research group. *Knowledge: Creation, Diffusion, Utilization*, 12, 406–40.

Carroll, J. M. & Rosson, M. B. (1996). Developing the Blacksburg Electronic Village. *Communications of the ACM*, 39 (12), 69–74.

Chapanis, A. & Ochsman, R. N. (1972). Studies in interactive communication: 1. the effects of four communication modes on the behavior of teams during cooperative problem solving. *Human Factors*, 14, 487–509.

Clark, H. H. (1996). *Using Language*. Cambridge: Cambridge University Press.

Clark, H. H. & Brennan, S. E. (1991). Grounding in communication. In L. Resnick, J. M. Levine & S. D. Teasley (Eds), *Perspectives on Socially Shared Cognition* (pp. 127–49). Washington, DC: APA.

Cohen, M. D. & Bacdayan, P. (1994). Organizational routines are stored as procedural memory: evidence from a laboratory study. *Organizational Science*, 5, 554–68.

Conklin, J. & Begeman, M. (1988). gIBIS: a hypertext tool for exploratory policy discussion. *ACM Transactions on Office Information Systems*, 6 (4), 303–31.

Conklin, E. J. & Burgess-Yakemovic, K. C (1996). A process-oriented approach to design rationale. In T. P. Moran & J. M. Carroll (Eds), *Design Rationale: Concepts, Techniques & Use* (pp. 393–428). Mahwah, NJ: Lawrence Erlbaum.

Cook, T. D. & Campbell, D. T. (1979). *Quasi-experimentation: Design and Analysis Issues for Field Settings*. Boston, MA: Houghton Mifflin.

Covi, L. (1996). Material mastery: how university researchers use digital libraries for scholarly communication. Unpublished Ph.D. thesis, University of California, Irvine, CA.

Crowley, T., Milazzo, P., Baker, E., Forsdick, H. & Tomlinson, R. (1990). MMConf: an infrastructure for building shared multimedia applications. *Proceedings of Computer Supported Cooperative Work (CSCW '90)*, pp. 329–42.

Curtis, P. (1996). MUDding: social phenomena in text-based virtual realities. In P. Ludlow (Ed.), *High Noon on the Electronic Frontier: Conceptual Issues in Cyberspace*. Cambridge, MA: MIT Press.

Cyert, R. M. & March, J. G. (1963). *A Behavioral Theory of the Firm*. Englewood Cliffs, NJ: Prentice-Hall.

Dickson, G. W., Poole, M. S. & DeSanctis. G. (1992). An overview of the GDSS research project and the SAMM system. In R. P. Bostrom, R. T. Watson & S. T. Kinney (Eds), *Computer Augmented Teamwork: A Guided Tour* (pp. 163–70). New York: Van Nostrand Reinhold.

Dourish, P., Holmes, J., MacLean, A., Marqvardsen, P. & Zbyslaw, A. (1996). Freeflow: mediating between representation and action in workflow systems. *Proceedings of the Conference on Computer Supported Cooperative Work (CSCW '96)*, pp. 190–8.

Eagly, A. H. & Chaiken, S. (1998). Attitude structure and function. In D. T. Gilbert, S. T. Fiske & G. Lindzey (Eds), *The Handbook of Social Psychology* (pp. 269–322). Boston, MA: McGraw-Hill.

Edwards, M. U., Levine, J. A. & Kurland, D. M. (1986). ForComment. Broderbund.

Egido, C. (1988). Videoconferencing as a technology to support group work: a review of its failures. *Proceedings of the Conference on Computer Supported Cooperative Work*, 13–24.

Ehrlich, S. F. (1987). Strategies for encouraging successful adoption of office communication systems. *ACM Transactions on Office Information Systems*, 5, 340–57.

Ellis, C. A., Gibbs, S. J. & Rein, G. L. (1991). Groupware: some issues and experiences. *Communications of the ACM* (34), 38–58.

Elrod, S., Bruce, R., Gold, R., Goldberg, D., Halasz, F., Janssen, W., Lee, D., McCall, K., Pedersen, E., Pier, K., Tang, J. & Welch, B. (1992). LiveBoard: a large interactive display supporting group meetings, presentations, and remote collaboration. *Proceedings of Human Factors in Computing Systems (CHI '92)*, pp. 599–607.

Finholt, T. A. & Olson, G. M. (1997). From laboratories to collaboratories: a new organizational form for scientific collaboration. *Psychological Science*, pp. 28–36.

Finholt, T., Sproull, L. & Kiesler, S. (1990). Communication and performance in ad hoc task groups. In J. Galegher, R. Kraut & C. Egido (Eds), *Intellectual Teamwork: Social and Technological Foundations of Cooperative Work*. Hillsdale, NJ: Lawrence Erlbaum.

Finholt, T. A. & Teasley, S. D. (1998). The need for psychology in research on Computer Supported Cooperative Work. *Social Science Computing Review*, 16 (1), 40–52.

Finn, K., Sellen, A. & Wilbur, S. (Eds) (1997). *Video-mediated Communication*. Hillsdale NJ: Lawrence Erlbaum.

Fish, R. S., Kraut, R. E. & Chalfonte, B. L. (1990). The VideoWindow system in informal communications. *Proceedings of the Conference on Computer Supported Cooperative Work*, 1–11.

Fish, R. S., Kraut, R. E., Root, R. & Rice, R. E. (1993). Video as a technology for informal communication. *Communications of the ACM*, 36, 8–61.

Fussell, S. R. & Benimoff, N. I. (1995). Social and cognitive processes in interpersonal communication: implications for advanced telecommunications technologies. *Human Factors*, 37 (2), 228–50.

Gabarro, J. J. (1990). The Development of Working Relationships. In J. Galegher, R. E. Kraut & C. Egido (Eds), *Intellectual Teamwork*. Hillsdale, NJ: Lawrence Erlbaum.

Galegher, J., Kraut, R. E. & Egido, C. (1990). *Intellectual Teamwork: Social and Technological Foundations of Cooperative Work*. Hillsdale, NJ: Lawrence Erlbaum.

Gallupe, R. B., Bastianutti, L. M. & Cooper, W. H. (1991). Unblocking brainstorms. *Journal of Applied Psychology*, 79 (1), 77–86.

Garton, L. & Wellman, B. (1995). Social impacts of electronic mail in organizations: a review of the research literature. In B. R. Burleson (Ed.), *Communication Yearbook* (18). Thousand Oaks, CA: Sage.

Gaver, W. W., Moran, T., MacLean, A., Lovstrand, L., Dourish, P., Carter, K. A. & Buxton, W. (1992). Realizing a video environment: EuroPARC's RAVE system. *Proceeding of the ACM Conference on Human Factors in Computing Systems (CHI '92)*.

Greif, I. (Ed.) (1988). *Computer-Supported Cooperative Work: a Book of Readings*. San Mateo, CA: Morgan Kaufmann Publishers.

Group Technologies, Inc. (1990). Aspects.

Grudin, J. (1988). Why CSCW applications fail: problems in the design and evaluation of organizational interfaces. *Proceedings of the ACM Conference on Computer Supported Cooperative Work (CSCW '88)*, pp. 85–93.

Grudin, J. & Palen, L. (1995). Why groupware succeeds: discretion or mandate? *Proceedings of the European Computer Supported Cooperative Work, ECSCW '95.*
Haake, J. & Wilson, B. (1994). Supporting collaborative writing of hyperdocuments in SEPIA. *Proceeding of the ACM Conference on Computer Supported Cooperative Work (CSCW '94)*, pp. 138–46.
Harrison, S., Bly, S., Anderson, S. & Minneman, S. (1997). The media space. In K. Finn, A. Sellen & S. B. Wilbur (Eds), *Video Mediated Communication* (pp. 273–300). Mahwah, NJ: Lawrence Erlbaum.
Hindus, D., Ackerman, M. S., Mainwaring, S. & Starr, B. (1996). Thunderwire: a field study of an audio-only media space. *Proceeding of the ACM Conference on Computer Supported Cooperative Work (CSCW '96)*, pp. 238–47.
Hinsz, V. B., Tindale, R. S. & Vollrath, D. A. (1997). The emerging conceptualization of groups as information processors. *Psychological Bulletin*, 121 (1), 43–64.
Hirokawa, R. Y. (1990). The role of communication in group decision making efficacy. *Small Group Research*, 21, 190–204.
Hollingshead, A. B., McGrath, J. E. & O'Connor, K. M. (1993). Group performance and communication technology: a longitudinal study of computer-mediated versus face-to-face work. *Small Group Research*, 24 (3), 307–33.
Hudson, S. E. & Smith, I. (1996). Techniques for addressing fundamental privacy and disruption tradeoffs in awareness support systems. *Proceeding of the ACM Conference on Computer Supported Cooperative Work (CSCW '96)*, pp. 248–57.
Hutchins, E. (1990). The technology of team navigation. In J. Galegher, R. E. Kraut & C. Egido (Eds), *Intellectual Teamwork: Social and Technological Foundations of Cooperative Work* (pp. 191–220). Hillsdale, NJ: Lawrence Erlbaum.
Hutchins, E. (1991). The social organization of distributed cognition. In L. B. Resnick, J. M. Levine & S. D. Teasley (Eds), *Perspectives on Socially Shared Cognition* (pp. 283–307). Washington, DC: American Psychological Association.
Hutchins, E. (1995a). *Cognition in the Wild.* Cambridge, MA: MIT Press.
Hutchins, E. (1995b). How a cockpit remembers its speeds. *Cognitive Science*, 19, 265–88.
Hymes, C. M. & Olson, G. M. (1992). Unblocking brainstorming through use of a simple group editor. *Proceedings of the ACM Conference on Computer Supported Cooperative Work (CSCW '92)*, pp. 99–106.
Isaacs, E. A., Morris, T. & Rodriguez, T. K. (1994). A Forum for supporting interactive presentations to distributed audiences. *Proceeding of the ACM Conference on Computer Supported Cooperative Work (CSCW '94)*, pp. 405–16.
Isaacs, E. A., Morris, T., Rodriguez, T. K. & Tang, J. C. (1995). A comparison of face-to-face and distributed presentations. *Proceeding of the ACM Conference on Human Factors in Computing Systems (CHI '95)*, pp. 354–61.
Isaacs, E. A. & Tang, J. D. (1997). Studying video based collaboration in context: from small workgroups to large organizations. In K. Finn, A. Sellen & S. B. Wilbur (Eds), *Video Mediated Communication* (pp. 173–97). Mahwah, NJ: Lawrence Erlbaum.
Ishii, H. & Kobayashi, M. (1994). Integration of interpersonal space and shared workspace: ClearBoard Design and Experiments. *ACM Transactions on Information Systems*, 11 (4), 349–75.
Karsenty, L. (1996). An empirical evaluation of design rationale documents. *Proceeding of the ACM Conference on Human Factors in Computing Systems (CHI '96)*, pp. 150–6.
Kaufer, D. S., Neuwirth, C. M., Chandhok, R. & Morris, J. (1995). Accommodating mixed sensory modal preferences in collaborative writing systems. *Computer Supported Cooperative Work*, 3, 271–95.
Kottemann, J. E., Davis, F. D. & Remus, W. R. (1994). Computer assisted decision making: performance, beliefs, and the illusion of control. *Organizational Behavior and Human Decision Processes*, 57, 26–37.
Knister, M. J. & Prakash, A. (1990). DistEdit: a distributed toolkit for supporting multiple group editors. *Proceedings of Computer Supported Cooperative Work, CSCW '90*, pp. 343–55.
Kraemer, K. L. & Pinsonneault, A. (1990). Technology and groups: assessments of

empirical research. In J. Galegher, R. Kraut & C. Egido (Eds), *Intellectual Teamwork: Social and Technological Foundations of Cooperative Work*. Hillsdale, NJ: Lawrence Erlbaum.

Kraut, R. E., Fish, R. S., Root, R. W. & Chalfonte, B. L. (1990). Informal communication in organizations: form, function, and technology. In S. Oskamp & S. Spacapan (Eds), *People's Reactions to Technology in Factories, Offices, and Aerospace* (pp. 145–99). Sage Publications.

Kraut, R., Lewis, S. & Swezey, L. (1982). Listener responsiveness and the co-ordination of conversation. *Journal of Personality and Social Psychology*, 43, 713–31.

Kraut, R., Scherlis, W., Mukhopadhyay, T., Manning, J. & Kiesler, S. (1996). HomeNet: a field trial of residential internet services. *Proceeding of the ACM Conference on Human Factors in Computing Systems (CHI '96)*, pp. 284–91.

Lange, B. M. (1992). Electronic group calendaring: experiences and expectations. In D. Coleman (Ed.), *Groupware* (pp. 428–32). Morgan Kaufman.

Lave, J. (1988). *Cognition in Practice*. Cambridge: Cambridge University Press.

Lederberg, J. & Uncapher, K. (1989). *Towards a National Collaboratory: Report of an Invitational Workshop at the Rockefeller University*. Washington, DC: National Science Foundation, Directorate for Computer and Information Science.

Leland, M. D. P., Fish, R. S. & Kraut, R. E. (1988). Collaborative document production using Quilt. *Proceedings of the Conference on Computer Supported Cooperative Work, CSCW '88*, pp. 206–15.

Mackay, W. E. (1989). Diversity in the use of electronic mail: a preliminary inquiry. *ACM Transactions on Office Information Systems*, 6 (4), pp. 380–97.

MacLean, A., Young, R. M., Bellotti, V. M. E. & Moran, T. P. (1996). Questions, options, and criteria: elements of a design space analysis. In T. P. Moran & J. M. Carroll (Eds), *Design Rationale: Concepts, Techniques, and Use* (pp. 53–106). Mahwah, NJ: Lawrence Erlbaum.

Malone, T. W., Grant, K. R., Lai, K. Y., Rao, R. & Rosenblitt, D. A. (1989). The information lens: an intelligent system for information sharing and coordination. In M. H. Olson (Ed.), *Technological Support for Work Group Collaboration* (pp. 65–88). Hillsdale, NJ: Lawrence Erlbaum.

Mantei, M., Baecker, R., Sellen, A. J., Wellman, B. & Buxton, W. (1991). Experiences in the use of a media space. *Proceedings of Human Factors in Computing Systems (CHI '91)*, pp. 203–8.

Marca, D. & Bock, G. (1992). *Groupware: Software for Computer Supported Cooperative Work*. Los Alamitos, CA: IEEE Computer Society Press.

March, J. G. & Simon, H. A. (1958). *Organizations*. New York: John Wiley.

Markus, M. L. (1983). *Systems in Organization: Bugs and Features*. San Jose, CA: Pitman.

McCauley, C. C., Stitt, L. & Segal, M. (1980). Stereotyping: from prejudice to prediction. *Psychological Bulletin*, 87, 195–208.

McDaniel, S. E., Olson, G. M. & Magee, J. S. (1996). Identifying and analyzing multiple threads in computer-mediated and face-to-face conversations. *Proceeding of the ACM Conference on Computer Supported Cooperative Work (CSCW '96)*, pp. 39–47.

McGrath, J. E. (1984). *Groups: Interaction and Performance*. Englewood Cliffs, NJ: Prentice-Hall.

McLeod, P. L. (1992). An assessment of the experimental literature on electronic group support: results of a meta-analysis. *Human–Computer Interaction*, 7, 257–80.

Michailidis, A. & Rada, R. (1995). Comparative study on the effects of groupware and conventional technologies on the efficiency of collaborative writing. *Computer Supported Cooperative Work*, 3, 327–57.

Michailidis, A. & Rada, R. (1996). A review of collaborative authoring tools. In R. Rada (Ed.), *Groupware and Authoring* (pp. 9–44). New York: Academic Press.

Minneman, S. L. & Bly, S. A. (1991). Menage a trois: a study of a multi-user drawing tool in distributed design work. *Proceedings of Human Factors in Computing Systems (CHI '91)*, pp. 217–24.

Mitchell, A., Posner, I. & Baecker, R. (1995). Learning to write together using groupware.

Proceeding of the ACM Conference on Human Factors in Computing Systems (CHI '95), pp. 288–95.
Moran, T. & Carroll, J. (1996). *Design Rationale: Concepts, Techniques and Use.* Englewood Cliffs, NJ: Erlbaum.
Moran, T. P., Chiu, P., Harrison, S., Kurtenbach, G., Minneman, S. & van Melle, W. (1996). Evolutionary engagement in an ongoing collaborative work process: a case study. *Proceeding of the ACM Conference on Computer Supported Cooperative Work (CSCW '96)*, pp. 150–9.
Mosier, J. N. & Tammaro, S. G. (1997). When are group scheduling tools useful? *Computer Supported Cooperative Work*, 6, 53–70.
Nardi, B. A., Kuchinsky, A., Whittaker, S., Leichner, R. & Schwarz, H. (1995). Video-as-data: technical and social aspects of a collaborative multimedia application. *Computer Supported Cooperative Work*, 4, 73–100.
National Research Council (1993). *National Collaboratories: Applying Information Technology for Scientific Research.* Washington, DC: National Academy Press.
Neuwirth, C. M., Chandok, R., Charney, D., Wojahn, P. & Kim, L. (1994). Distributed collaborative writing: a comparison of spoken and written modalities for reviewing and revising documents. *Proceedings of the Conference on Human Factors in Computing (CHI '94).*
Neuwirth, C. M., Kaufer, D. S., Chandhok, R. & Morris, J. H. (1990). Issues in the design of computer support for co-authoring and commenting. *Proceedings of Computer Supported Cooperative Work (CSCW '90)*, pp. 183–95.
Nonaka, I. & Takeuchi, H. (1995). *The Knowledge-creating Company: How Japanese Companies Create the Dynamics of Innovation.* New York: Oxford University Press.
Nunamaker, J. F., Dennis, A. R., Valacich, J. S., Vogel, D. R. & George, J. F. (1991). Electronic meeting systems to support group work. *Communications of the ACM*, 34 (7), 40–61.
O'Conaill, B., Whittaker, S. & Wilbur, S. B. (1997). Characterizing, predicting and measuring video-mediated communication: a conversational approach. In K. Finn, A. Sellen & S. B. Wilbur (Eds), *Video Mediated Communication* (pp. 107–31). Mahwah, NJ: Lawrence Erlbaum.
O'Hara-Devereaux, M. & Johansen, R. (1994). *Global Work: Bridging Distance, Culture & Time.* San Francisco: Jossey-Bass.
Olson, G. M., Atkins, D. E., Clauer, R., Finholt, T. A., Jahanian, F., Killeen, T. L., Prakash, A. & Weymouth, T. (1998). The Upper Atmospheric Research Collaboratory. *Interactions.*
Olson, M.H. & Bly, S.A. (1991). The Portland experience: a report on a distributed research group. *International Journal of Man–Machine Studies*, 34, 211–28.
Olson, G. M. & Olson, J. S. (1996). The effectiveness of simple shared electronic workspaces. In R. Rada (Ed.), *Groupware and Authoring* (pp. 105–26). New York: Academic Press.
Olson, G. M. & Olson, J. S. (1997). Research on Computer Supported Cooperative Work. In M. G. Helander, T. K. Landauer & P. V. Prabhu (Eds), *Handbook of Human–Computer Interaction* (pp. 1433–56). Amsterdam: North-Holland.
Olson, G. M. & Olson, J. S. (1997). Making sense of the findings: common vocabulary leads to the synthesis necessary for theory building. In K. Finn, A. Sellen & S. Wilbur (Eds), *Video-mediated Communication* (pp. 75–92). Hillsdale NJ: Lawrence Erlbaum.
Olson, J. S., Olson, G. M. & Meader, D. K. (1995). What mix of video and audio is useful for remote real-time work? *Proceedings of ACM Conference on Human Factors in Computing Systems (CHI '95)*, pp. 362–8.
Olson, J. S., Olson, G. M., Storrøsten, M. & Carter, M. (1993). Groupwork close up: a comparison of the group design process with and without a simple group editor. *ACM Transactions on Information Systems*, 11, 321–48.
Olson, J. S. & Teasley, S. (1996). Groupware in the wild: lessons learned from a year of virtual collocation. *Proceeding of the ACM Conference on Computer Supported Cooperative Work (CSCW '96)*, pp. 419–27.

Orlikowski, W. J. & Gash, D. C. (1994). Technological frames: making sense of information technology in organizations. *ACM Transactions on Information Systems*, 12 (2), 174–207.
Oviatt, S. & Cohen, P. (1991). Discourse structure and performance efficiency in interactive and non-interactive speech modalities. *Computer Speech and Language*, 5, 297–326.
Pedersen, E., McCall, K., Moran, T. P. & Halasz, F. (1993). Tivoli: an electronic whiteboard for informal workgroup meetings. *Proceedings of INTERCHI '93*, pp. 391–98.
Petty, R. E. & Wegener, D. T. (1998). Attitude change: multiple roles for persuasion variables. In D. T. Gilbert, S. T. Fiske & G. Lindzey (Eds), *The Handbook of Social Psychology* (pp. 322–90). Boston, MA: McGraw-Hill.
Plowman, L. (1995). The interfunctionality of talk and text. *Computer Supported Cooperative Work*, 3, 229–46.
Posner, I. R. & Baecker, R. M. (1992). How people write together. *Proceedings of the Twenty-Fifth International Conference on Systems Sciences*. Hawaii, January, 1992, IEEE.
Prinz, W. & Kolvenbach, S. (1996). Support for workflows in a ministerial environment. *Proceedings of the Conference on Computer Supported Cooperative Work*, pp. 199–208.
Rada, R. (1996). *Groupware and Authoring*. New York: Academic Press.
Rocco, E. (1998). Trust disappears over email but it can be repaired with initial face-to-face contact. *Proceeding of the ACM Conference on Human Factors in Computing Systems (CHI '98)*.
Rochlin, G. I. (1997). *Trapped in the Net: The Unanticipated Consequences of Computerization*. Princeton, NJ: Princeton University Press.
Ruhleder, K. & Jordan, B. (1997). Capturing complex distributed activities: video based interaction analysis as a component of workplace ethnography. In A. Lee, J. Liebenau & J. I. DeGross (Eds), *Information Systems and Qualitative Research*. London: Chapman and Hall.
Sakata, S., Maeno, K., Fukuoka, H., Abe, T. & Mizuno, H. (1996). Multimedia and multi-party desktop conference system: MERMAID as groupware platform. In R. Rada (Ed.), *Groupware and Authoring* (pp. 345–60). New York: Academic Press.
Satzinger, J. & Olfman, L. (1992). A research program to assess user perceptions of group work support. *Proceeding of the ACM Conference on Human Factors in Computing Systems (CHI '92)*, pp. 99–106.
Schatz, B. (1991–92). Building an electronic community system. *Journal of Management Information Systems*, 8 (3), 87–107.
Schatz, B. R. & Hardin, J. B. (1994). NCSA Mosaic and the World Wide Web: global hypermedia protocols for the Internet. *Science*, 265, 895–901.
Senge, P. M. (1990). *The Fifth Discipline: the Art and Practice of the Learning Organization*. New York: Doubleday Currency.
Shum, S. B. (1996). Analyzing the usability of a design rationale notation. In T. P. Moran & J. M. Carroll (Eds), *Design Rationale: Concepts, Techniques and Use* (pp. 185–216). Mahwah, NJ: Lawrence Erlbaum.
Sproull, L. & Kiesler, S. (1991). *Connections: New Ways of Working in the Networked Organization*. Cambridge, MA: MIT Press.
Star, S. L. & Ruhleder, K. (1994). Steps toward an ecology of infrastructure: complex problems in design and access for large-scale collaborative systems. *Proceedings of the Conference on Computer Supported Cooperative Work*, pp. 253–64.
Stefik, M., Foster, G., Bobrow, D., Kahn, K., Lanning, S. & Suchman, L. (1987). Beyond the chalkboard: computer support for collaboration and problem solving in meetings. *Communications of the ACM*, 30, 32–47.
Streitz, N., Geissler, J., Haake, J. & Hol, J. (1994). DOLPHIN: integrated meeting support across Live Board, local and remote desktop environments. *Proceedings of the ACM Conference on Computer-Supported Cooperative Work (CSCW '94)*, pp. 345–58.
Suchman, L. (1987). *Plans and Situated Action: the Problem of Human–Machine Communication*. Cambridge University Press.

Tang, J. S., Isaacs, E. A. & Rua, M. (1994). Supporting distributed groups with a montage of lightweight interactions. *Proceeding of the ACM Conference on Computer Supported Cooperative Work (CSCW '94)*, pp. 23–34.

Tang, J. C. & Minneman, S. L. (1990). Videodraw: a video interface for collaborative drawing. *Proceedings of Human Factors in Computing Systems (CHI '90)*, pp. 313–20.

Tenner, E. (1996). *Why Things Bite Back: Technology and the Revenge of Unintended Consequences*. New York: Alfred A. Knopf.

Thagard, P. (1989). Explanatory coherence. *Behavioral and Brain Sciences*, 12, 435–502.

Turkle, S. (1995). *Life on the Screen: Identity in the Age of the Internet*. New York: Simon & Schuster.

Veinott, E. S., Olson, J. S., Olson, G. M. & Fu, X. (1997). Video matters! When communication ability is stressed, video helps. *Short Paper at the ACM Conference on Human Factors in Computing Systems (CHI '97)*. Atlanta, GA: ACM Press.

Vera, A. H. & Simon, H. A. (1993). Situated Action: a symbolic interpretation. *Cognitive Science*, 17 (1), 7–48.

Walsh, J. P. (1995). Managerial and organizational cognition: notes from a trip down memory lane. *Organizational Science*, 6, 280–321.

Walsh, J. P. & Ungson, G. R. (1991). Organizational memory. *Academy of Management Review*, 16, 57–91.

Weick, K. E. (1993). The collapse of sensemaking in organizations: the Mann Gulch disaster. *Administrative Science Quarterly*, 38, 628–52.

Weick, K. E. & Roberts, K. H. (1993). Collective mind in organizations: heedful interrelating on flight decks. *Administrative Science Quarterly*, 38, 357–81.

Wertsch, J. V. (1985). *Vygotsky and the Social Formation of Mind*. Cambridge, MA: Harvard University Press.

Wertsch, J. V. (1991). *Voices of the Mind: a Sociocultural Approach to Mediated Action*. Cambridge, MA: Harvard University Press.

Whittaker, S. & O'Conaill, B. (1997). The role of vision in face-to-face and mediated communication. In K. Finn, A. Sellen & S. B. Wilbur (Eds), *Video Mediated Communication* (pp. 23–49). Mahwah, NJ: Lawrence Erlbaum.

Whittaker, S. & Sidner, C. (1996). Email overload: exploring personal information management of email. *Proceeding of the ACM Conference on Human Factors in Computing Systems (CHI '96)*, pp. 276–83.

Williams, G. (1997). Task conflict and language differences: opportunities for videoconferencing. *Proceedings of the European Computer Supported Cooperative Work (ECSCW '97)*.

Winograd, T. (1988). A language/action perspective on the design of cooperative work. *Human–Computer Interaction*, 3, 3–30.

Wish, M. (1975). User and non-user conceptions of PICTUREPHONE® service. *Proceedings of the 19th Annual Convention of the Human Factors Society*.

Wojahn, P. G., Neuwirth, C. M. & Bullock, B. (1998). Effects of interfaces for annotation on communication in a collaborative task. *Proceeding of the ACM Conference on Human Factors in Computing Systems (CHI '98)*, pp. 456–63.

Chapter 15

Cognitive Engineering Models and Cognitive Architectures in Human–Computer Interaction

Peter Pirolli
Xerox PARC

We engage our physical and social environments through highly evolved technologies, in interactions that often require sophisticated knowledge and virtuoso performance. Finding the order underlying the complexity of these interactions may be one of the most daunting challenges facing science. Over the past few decades, the study of human–computer interaction (HCI) has become an increasingly important arena for pursuing this challenge. HCI is a discipline concerned with the study and design of interactive computing systems used by people towards satisfying their goals. HCI has become an arena in which new computer applications can benefit from new cognitive engineering models that synthesize results from sound cognitive science. It has also become a useful testbed for cognitive architectures, which are integrated theories of psychological mechanisms that aim to predict complex learning, cognition, and performance. This chapter provides an overview of cognitive engineering models and cognitive architectures in the context of HCI.

HCI is a very diverse discipline, as would be revealed by a survey of the proceedings for its major conference, the ACM Conference on Human Factors in Computing Systems, or its major journals, *Human–Computer Interaction* or *ACM Transactions on Computer–Human Interaction*. (ACM stands for the Association for Computing Machinery, which is the major professional association for computer scientists in the USA.) Such a survey would find studies of social organization and work, rules of thumb for computer interface design, and designs

Handbook of Applied Cognition, Edited by F. T. Durso, R. S. Nickerson, R. W. Schvaneveldt, S. T. Dumais, D. S. Lindsay and M. T. H. Chi.

for new input and output technologies, among many other things. The cognitive engineering models and cognitive architectures presented here constitute only a small, but important, slice of this diverse HCI pie.

As a general orientation, consider the word processor on which this chapter was written. It seems reasonable that psychology ought to be able to predict answers to certain questions concerning the effectiveness of its design:

- What is the time it would take to perform elementary tasks, like inserting, deleting, or moving text?
- How long will it take to learn the skills required for basic text editing?
- Will knowledge of other applications, such as a spreadsheet, transfer to the text editor?
- Will a user be able to figure out how to perform tasks (e.g. by exploration of the interface) without explicit instruction?

Of course, one could find the answers to these questions by direct empirical test – for instance, by building a text editor and directly assessing performance, learning, and transfer. Prediction, however, is a sign of understanding and control over the phenomena of interest. In practical terms, it means that a designer can explore and explain the effects of different design decisions on human–computer interaction, before the heavy investment of resources for implementation and testing. This exploration of design space is also more efficient because the choices among different design alternatives are better informed: rather than randomly generating and testing design alternatives, the designer is in a position to know which avenues are better to explore and which are better to ignore. Thirty years ago, when the first textbook on cognitive psychology was written (Neisser, 1967), it would have been impossible to answer the questions listed above based on psychological theory alone. Only the first of the questions could have been answered in a restricted way even fifteen years ago, when the first classic monograph on the psychology of HCI was written (Card, Moran & Newell, 1983). Considerable knowledge has accumulated over this time span to address questions such as these, and this progress is one measure of the fruitfulness of the marriage of psychology and HCI.

Framework of Analysis

The cognitive engineering models and cognitive architectures presented here have a common, though complex, way of approaching the analysis of human behavior, so it is useful to review that basic framework. An analysis of people (users) interacting with systems may involve several interrelated layers of explanation. This is because these models and architectures assume that human activity is:

(a) purposeful and adaptive, which requires a kind of rational analysis
(b) based on knowledge
(c) computed by information processing mechanisms, which are
(d) realized by physical, biological, processes.

Table 15.1 Time-scale on which human action occurs. Different bands are quite different phenomenological worlds

Scale (seconds)	Time unit	Band
10^7	months	Social
10^6	weeks	
10^5	days	
10^4	hours	Rational
10^3	10 minutes	
10^2	minutes	
10^1	10 seconds	Psychological
10^0	1 second	
10^{-1}	100 ms	
10^{-2}	1 ms	Biological

Source: From *Unified Theories of Cognition* (p. 122), by A. Newell, 1990, Cambridge, MA: Harvard University Press. Copyright 1990 by the President and Fellows of Harvard College. Reprinted with permission.

Moreover, different scientific principles enter into the analysis at different time-scales of analysis. Perceptual-motor factors largely govern small-scale activities such as using a computer mouse to point to a menu. Cognitive factors are more evident in larger-scale activities such as reading text. Rational considerations and the analysis of knowledge have larger contributions in even longer-term tasks such as finding a good graduate school or finding the best value for a consumer good.

Phenomena at Different Time-scales of Behavioral Analysis

To understand why the different levels of explanation may be involved in the analysis of behavior, consider the kinds of phenomena that arise at different time-scales of analysis (Newell, 1990; Newell & Card, 1985). The phenomena at each band in Table 15.1 are largely dominated by different kinds of factors. Behavioral analysis at the biological band (approximately milliseconds to tens of milliseconds) is dominated by biochemical, biophysical, and especially neural processes, such as the time it takes for a neuron to fire. The psychological band of activity (approximately hundreds of milliseconds to tens of seconds) has been the main preoccupation of cognitive psychology (Anderson, 1983; Newell, 1990). At this time-scale, it is assumed that elementary cognitive mechanisms play a major part in shaping behavior. The typical unit of analysis is a single response function, involving a perceptual input stage, a cognitive stage, and a stage of action output – for instance, finding a word in the menu of a text editor and moving a mouse to select the menu item. The mechanisms involved at this level of analysis include elementary information processing functions such as memory storage and retrieval, recognition, categorization, comparison of one information element to another, choosing among alternative actions, and so on.

As the time-scale of activity increases, "there will be a shift towards characterizing a system . . . without regard to the way in which the internal processing accomplishes the linking of action to goals" (Newell, 1990, p. 150). This is the rational band of phenomena (minutes to days). The typical unit of analysis at this level is the task, which is defined, in part, by a goal. It is assumed that an intelligent agent will have preferences for actions that it perceives to be applicable in its environment and that it knows will move the current situation towards the goal. So, on the one hand, goals, knowledge, perceptions, actions, and preferences shape behavior. On the other hand, the structure, constraints, and resources of the environment in which the task takes place – called the task environment (Newell & Simon, 1972) – will also greatly shape behavior. Everyday examples of HCI tasks would be editing a manuscript, finding information on the World Wide Web, or designing a spreadsheet.

Explanations at the rational band assume that behavior is governed by rational principles and that it is largely shaped by the structure and constraints of the task environment. It is assumed that people are not infinitely and perfectly rational. Because we have only finite powers and resources – we operate with only limited information and limited computational ability – a more successful hypothesis about humans is that they exhibit bounded rationality or make choices based on satisficing (Simon, 1955). The rationale for behavior at this level is its adaptive fit to its task environment.

Levels of Explanation

Table 15.2 summarizes in a slightly different way the multiple levels of analysis and explanation that might go into the development of a predictive model for HCI. One would not expect to see all levels of analysis to be fully fleshed out for any given HCI problem, but it is useful to see the big picture (for variations on this big picture, see Anderson, 1990; Marr, 1982; Newell, 1982, 1990).

Imagine that a researcher or designer wants to analyze the effects of different computer application interfaces on users' speed in finding information on the World Wide Web. For instance, imagine that two designs are being considered, both requiring that a user type in key words to a search engine, but the results are returned as a list of citations in one case and as a hierarchical hypertext structure in the other. One part of the analyst's task might be to perform a task analysis. One component of this analysis could involve an analysis of the task environment. The task environment consists of the goal of the task (i.e. finding relevant documents) and the structure and constraints of the interaction environment. These might include such things as the time it takes to perform actions with a system (e.g. time to point and click on a hypertext link, the time to scan a list), the value of the results achieved by actions (e.g. the relevance of citations returned by a search engine), the risk involved with an action (e.g. the probability that an action does what was expected), and so on. Analysis of the costs, values, and risks of feasible decisions and actions made by users with respect to their goals and task environment is an explanation at the adaptive analysis level (Table 15.2), where it is assumed that the structure of behavior can be understood in terms of its adaptive fit to the structure and constraints of the environment. At this level, the analyst acts most purely as an engineer concerned with why users' behavior is rational given the task context in

Table 15.2 An integrated framework for ecological and cognitive analysis

Level	Question	Description	Analysis elements
Adaptation	*Why* do they do it that way?	Rational	• States, resources, state dynamics • Optimization criteria • Costs, values, risks, constraints, affordances • Feasible actions, decisions, strategies
Knowledge	*What* do they do?	Intentional	• Environment • Goals, preferences • Knowledge • Perception, action
Cognitive	*How* do they process information to do it?	Mechanistic	• Cognitive states • Cognitive processes
Biological	*How* do they physically do it?	Physical	• Neural processes

which it occurs, and it is assumed that users are optimizing their performance in achieving their goals.

Typically, a task analysis mainly focuses on an analysis of users' knowledge, preferences, perceptions, and actions, with respect to the goal and environment. This is the knowledge level (Newell, 1982) of analysis (Table 15.2). At this level of analysis it is assumed that users deploy their knowledge to achieve their goals, and the focus is on identifying what knowledge is involved. Behavior is assumed to be governed by the principle of rationality: if the user knows that one of his or her actions will lead to a situation preferred according to the goal, then he or she will intend the action, which will then be taken if it is possible. The GOMS analysis method presented below is a way of analyzing the goal, knowledge, preferences, perceptions, and actions involved in expert HCI tasks, as well as the costs and values of different paths of behavior in a task environment. A GOMS task analysis combines adaptive level analysis with knowledge level analysis.

Modern cognitive psychology assumes that the knowledge level can be given a scientific account (i.e. be made predictable) by explaining it in terms of mechanistic information processing (Newell, 1990). This is the cognitive level of explanation. This level of analysis focuses on the properties of the information processing machinery that evolution has dealt to humans to perceive, think, remember, learn, and act in what we would call purposeful and knowledgeable ways. The model human processor discussed below is an engineering attempt to specify this information processing machinery. Cognitive architectures, also discussed below, specify these mechanisms and operating characteristics in a deeper way. These models and architectures attempt to specify the internal information processes of cognition. Ultimately, it is assumed that this abstract information processing machinery is implemented in biological hardware (Table 15.2).

COGNITIVE ENGINEERING: THE GOMS FAMILY OF MODELS

The most influential family of cognitive engineering models for HCI evolved from the work of Card et al. (1983). That seminal work introduced:

1. the Model Human Processor, which is a general characterization of basic information processing (i.e. of the cognitive mechanisms at the psychological time-bands)
2. GOMS techniques for task analysis (i.e. a kind of knowledge-level and adaptation-level analysis spanning the psychological and rational time-bands).

The aim of Card et al. was to provide HCI engineers with a useful model with a sound theoretical base. Such an aim has several entailments. The model and framework of analysis would have to (John & Kieras, 1996b):

- provide qualitative and quantitative predictions with minimum additional empirical validation
- be useful to non-psychologist engineers who receive only some minimum amount of training (e.g. a professional training course, a section in a university course)
- be deliberately approximate and tailorable to the demands of the HCI problem.

These concerns differ from those of the standard research psychologist.

The relationship between a GOMS task analysis and the Model Human Processor is analogous to the relationship between a program and a programming language. The Model Human Processor (Card et al., 1983) is intended to capture, in an approximate way, the basic information processing machinery of human cognition. A GOMS task analysis is like a specification of a computer program that would run on the Model Human Processor. In general, the idea is that an HCI analyst specifies a GOMS task analysis, and can then simulate how it would "run" on the Model Human Processor. Usually, this is done by hand-simulation using the technical specifications for GOMS and the Model Human Processor. Recently, however, there have been attempts to create a version of GOMS that will run as computer simulations (Kieras, 1996).

The Model Human Processor

The Model Human Processor is specified as:

(a) a set of memories and processors
(b) a set of principles of operation.

The processors and memories are summarized schematically in Figure 15.1. There are three subsystems for perceptual input, motor action, and cognition. The processors and memories in Figure 15.1 are characterized by a set of parameters:

μ – the storage capacity in terms of maximum number of items stored
δ – the decay rate of an item (the time an item will reside in memory)
κ – the main type of code (representation type) of information, which may be physical, visual, acoustic, or semantic
τ – the cycle time (the time at which inputs to memory are updated).

The parameters are typical values extracted from the psychological literature. The general idea is that information is input from the world through the perceptual processors, into the visual and auditory stores. Some of this information makes its way into a working memory, which is operated on by the cognitive processor. The cognitive processor uses associations between information in working memory and long-term memory to make decisions and formulate actions. Actions in working memory trigger the motor processor to effect behavior in the world.

Figure 15.2 is a summary of the principles of operation for the Model Human Processor. The cognitive processor works through a recognize–act cycle (Principle P0 in Figure 15.2) on the contents of working memory. Working memory is assumed to be the information that a person is currently heeding – their focus of attention. The contents of working memory are called "chunks" (Miller, 1956; Simon, 1974), which are symbolic structures that themselves may be organized into chunks. For instance, an individual letter "N" may be a chunk, but so might the acronym "NFL", or the word "National", or the phrase "National Football League." In the recognize phase, information in working memory retrieves associated actions in long-term memory. The act phase of the cycle, executes those retrieved actions and changes the contents of working memory. These associations between working memory information and effective actions in long-term memory are built from prior experience. The associations may be organized in the form of plans, such as plans of organized action for operating an interface. In the original Model Human Processor of Card et al. (1983), each recognize–act cycle takes about 70 ms (Figure 15.1), although this varies with task load and degree of uncertainty (Principles P4 and P7, in Figure 15.2). Research since that original formulation has revised the recognize–act cycle time down to 50 ms (John & Kieras, 1996a). Performance time decreases as a power law of practice according to Principle P7, in Figure 15.2.

Working memory is assumed to be of limited capacity and rapid decay rate. For instance, without rehearsal, only about 3 to 7 chunks of information can be held in working memory for about 7 sec (Miller, 1956). On the other hand, long-term memory is of very large capacity (about 10^9 bits: Landauer, 1986) and a very slow decay rate (Figure 15.1). It is the repository of the collective experience and learning of a person. It contains both factual knowledge as well as knowledge of how to perform procedures. Although long-term memory has, effectively, infinite capacity and permanent retention, there are factors that make retrieval less than perfect. These factors have to do with the ability of cues in working memory to retrieve associated information in long-term memory (Principles P2, P3, and P4, in Figure 15.2).

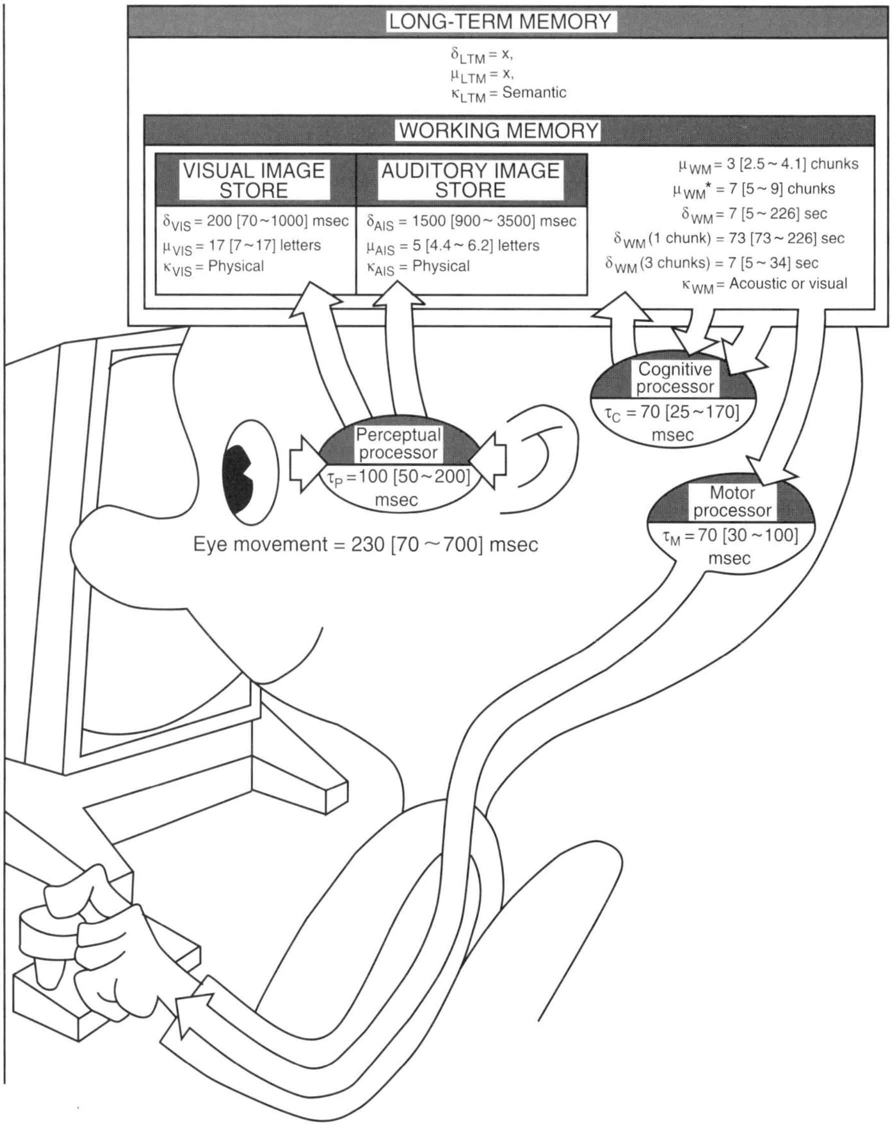

Figure 15.1 The Model Human Processor. Note that some estimates have changed since the original formulation. See text for details. From *The Psychology of Human–Computer Interaction*, (p. 26), by S. K. Card, T. P. Moran & A. Newell, 1983, Hillsdale, NJ: Lawrence Erlbaum Associates. Copyright 1983 by Lawrence Erlbaum Associates. Reprinted with permission.

For the perceptual processor, it is assumed that auditory and visual stimuli trigger the appearance of representations in the auditory and visual memory stores. The representations in these memories encode mostly physical (non-symbolic) characteristics such as the intensity of a sound or the curvature of a line. These memories are also of limited capacity and very rapid decay (items have a half-life of 200 ms in the visual store and about 1500 ms in the auditory

P0 *Recognize–Act Cycle of the Cognitive Processor.* On each cycle of the cognitive processor, the contents of working memory initiate actions associatively linked to them in long-term memory; these actions in turn modify the contents of working memory.

P1 *Variable Perceptual Processor Rate Principle.* The perceptual processor cycle time τ_p varies inversely with stimulus intensity.

P2 *Encoding Specificity Principle.* Specific encoding operations performed on what is perceived determine what is stored, and what is stored determines what retrieval cues are effective in providing access to what is stored.

P3 *Discrimination Principle.* The difficulty of memory retrieval is determined by the candidates that exist in the memory, relative to the retrieval clues.

P4 *Variable Cognitive Processor Rate Principle.* The cognitive processor cycle time τ_c is shorter when greater effort is induced by increased task demands or information loads; it also diminishes with practice.

P5 *Fitt's Law.* The time T_{pos} to move the hand to a target of size S which lies a distance D away is given by:

$$T_{pos} = I_m \log_2(D/S + .5),$$

where $I_m = 100[70{\sim}120]$ msec/bit.

P6 *Power Law of Practice.* The time T_n to perform a task on the nth trial follows a power law:

$$T_n = T_1 n^{-\alpha},$$

where $\alpha = .4[.2{\sim}.6]$.

P7 *Uncertainty Principle.* Decision time T increases with uncertainty about the judgment or decision to be made:

$$T = I_C H,$$

where H is the information-theoretic entropy of the decision and $I_C = 150[0{\sim}157]$ msec/bit. For n equally probable alternatives (called Hick's Law),

$$H = \log_2(n + 1)$$

For $n$alternatives with different probabilities, p_i, of occurence,

$$H = \sum_i p_i \log_2(1/p_i + 1).$$

P8 *Rationality Principle.* A person acts to as to attain his or her goals through rational action, given the structure of the task and his or her inputs of information and bounded by limitations on his or her knowledge and processing ability:

Goals + Task + Operators + Inputs + Knowledge + Process-limits → Behavior

P9 *Problem Space Principle.* The rational activity in which people engage to solve a problem can be described in terms of a set of states of knowledge, operators for changing one state into another, and constraints on applying operators.

Figure 15.2 Principles of operation for the Model Human Processor (from Card et al., 1983). From *The Psychology of Human–Computer Interaction,* (p. 27), by S. K. Card, T. P. Moran & A. Newell, 1983, Hillsdale, NJ: Lawrence Erlbaum Associates. Copyright 1983 by Lawrence Erlbaum Associates. Reprinted with permission.

store). The perceptual processor cycle time of about 100 ms varies according to Principle P1: more intense stimuli, such as those that might occur on a very bright high-contrast display screen are perceived faster than stimuli on a dull blurry screen. The motor processor is assumed to operate with an approximately 70 ms cycle time. Many interactions with computers require movements of the hand or a hand-held mouse to a target location. The time to move the hand, or a mouse pointer, to a target may be calculated by Fitt's Law (Principle P5, in

Figure 15.2), which depends on the distance to be traveled by the movement and the size of the target.

GOMS

A GOMS model is an analysis of the knowledge of how to perform a task in an efficient and effective manner (i.e. assuming Principles P7 and P8, in Figure 15.2). The components of a task analysis forming a GOMS model are:

- goals
- operators
- methods
- selection rules.

Goals specify the state of affairs that a user wants to achieve, such as editing a manuscript on a word processor, or constructing a chart using a spreadsheet. Goals can often be achieved by setting and performing subgoals. Operators specify the perceptual, motor, or cognitive acts that change the task environment (Newell & Simon, 1972). Note that the specification of the "task environment" can vary with the aim of the analysis, and so this can alter the level of detail at which operators are defined. The important features defining operators are (a) that they operate in service of a goal, (b) they change the state of affairs (e.g. the user's mental state, the physical state, or the system state), and (c) the parameters characterizing their operations, such as execution time or error probability are independent of the history of interaction that got the user and system to the current state. In a typical GOMS analysis, the operators are defined by the basic actions that are afforded by the interactive computer system. These may include keyboard commands, menu selections, button presses, and so on.

Methods are the procedures for accomplishing a goal. A method is specified as a conditional sequence of subgoals and operators. For instance, the method for opening a document in a word processor that has a graphical user interface may include subgoals for locating the icon for the document, then performing operators for pointing and clicking on the icon. Often, a user may have learned more than one method for performing a task. For instance, to open a document in a word processor, in addition to the mouse point-and-click method, there may also be a method consisting of a sequence of keyboard commands to find and open the document. In such cases, the analyst must also specify selection rules that determine which method will get used in a particular circumstance. A number of sources are available to provide guidance on how to perform GOMS analyses (Kieras, 1988, 1996).

Example: Time Cost of Performance on a Text Editor

Figure 15.3 is an example GOMS analysis of a hypothetical text editor. Imagine that a user has pages of text containing a draft of a manuscript that has been marked up in pen by a proofreader. The task is to edit the manuscript in

Analysis of overall editing task

```
GOAL: EDIT-MANUSCRIPT
•   GOAL: EDIT-UNIT-TASK . . . repeat until no more unit tasks
•   •   GOAL: ACQUIRE-UNIT-TASK . . . if task not remembered
•   •   •   GOAL: TURN-PAGE . . . if at end of manuscript page
•   •   •   GOAL: GET-FROM-MANUSCRIPT
•   •   GOAL: EXECUTE-UNIT-TASK . . . if a unit task was found
•   •   •   GOAL: MODIFY-TASK
•   •   •       [select: GOAL: MOVE-TEXT . . . if text is to be moved
•   •   •                GOAL: DELETE-PHRASE . . . if a phrase is to be deleted
•   •   •                GOAL: INSERT-WORD . . . if a word is to be inserted]
•   •   •       VERIFY-EDIT
```

Refined analysis of MOVE-TEXT

```
GOAL: MOVE-TEXT
•   GOAL: CUT-TEXT
•   •   GOAL: HIGHLIGHT-TEXT
•   •   GOAL: ISSUE-CUT-COMMAND
•   GOAL: PASTE-TEXT
•   •   GOAL: POSITION-CURSOR-AT-INSERTION-POINT
•   •   GOAL: ISSUE-PASTE-COMMAND
```

Detailed time cost analysis of ISSUE-PASTE-COMMAND

```
GOAL: ISSUE-PASTE-COMMAND
•   MOVE-CURSOR-TO-EDIT-MENU      1.10
•   PRESS-MOUSE-BUTTON             .10
•   MOVE-MOUSE-TO-PASTE-ITEM      1.10
•   VERIFY-HIGHLIGHT              1.35
•   RELEASE-MOUSE-BUTTON           .10
                Total time (sec)  3.75
```

Figure 15.3 A segment of a hypothetical GOMS analysis of editing text using a computer text editor. From "The GOMS Family of User Interface Analysis Techniques: Comparison and Contrast," by B. E. John & D. E. Kieras, 1996, *ACM Transactions on Computer–Human Interaction*, 3, p. 330. Copyright 1996 by ACM. Adapted with permission.

accordance with the proofreader's mark-up. Figure 15.3 presents the top-level task structure according to a GOMS analysis as well as one of the methods for pasting text (i.e. after copying it from elsewhere). The indentation of goals indicates the task goal hierarchy (goals are indicated with GOAL in Figure 15.3). For instance, the EDIT-MANUSCRIPT goal is achieved by repeatedly performing EDIT-UNIT-TASK, which finds and accomplishes the next edit. The italics in Figure 15.3 indicate conditions on the execution of methods or selection rules. Eventually goals are decomposed hierarchically down to operators, such as MOVE-CURSOR-TO-EDIT-MENU and PRESS-MOUSE-BUTTON in Figure 15.3. The column on the right consists of time estimates for the performance of operators. Using these time estimates one may calculate the time it takes to perform a task, such as pasting text in Figure 15.3. Table 15.3 presents a compilation of some recent parameter estimates from a variety of sources.

Varieties of GOMS

John & Kieras (1996a) provide an overview of four varieties of GOMS that have developed over the years:

Table 15.3 Some cognitive engineering parameters used in GOMS analysis

Enter a keystroke		
Best typist	80 ms	CMN
Good typist	120 ms	CMN
Average skilled typist	200 ms	CMN
Average non-secretary	280 ms	CMN
Typing random letters	500 ms	CMN
Worst typist	1200 ms	CMN
Entering spreadsheet formulas (average over applications)	275 ms	ON
Entering spreadsheet commands (average over applications)	305 ms	ON
Entering command abbreviations	230 ms	JN
Expert typing cross-hand digraphs	170 ms	JN
Expert typing same-hand digraphs	220 ms	JN
Point with mouse		
Average value, small screen, menu-shaped target	1100 ms	CMN
Varies with distance (D) and target size (S)	$1 + \log_2(D+S+.5)$ ms	CMN
Move hands to		
Mouse	360 ms	CMN
Joystick	260 ms	CMN
Arrow keys	210 ms	CMN
Function keys	320 ms	CMN
Eye movements		
Travel + fixation time for saccade	230 ms	R
	200 ms	CMN
Scan *k* degrees of visual arc	4 *k* ms	K
Compare two items		
Digits	33 ms	C
Colors	38 ms	C
Letters	40 ms	C
Words	47 ms	C
Shapes	50 ms	C
Forms	69 ms	C

Notes:
CMN = (Card et al., 1983)
JN = (John & Newell, 1990)
R = (Russo, 1978)
K = (Kosslyn, 1983)
C = (Cavanaugh, 1972)

Sources: Lohse, 1993; Olson & Olson, 1990

- CMN-GOMS is the version originally presented by Card et al. (1983) described above.
- KLM is the keystroke-level model. It is a simplified version of GOMS presented by Card et al. (1983) that analyzes a task into keystroke-level operators (e.g. mouse movements, key presses) and a few simple heuristics to analyze mental operators. Goals, methods, and selection rules are not used. Execution time is just calculated as the sum of times performing the operators involved in the task, such as:

Execution time = $K + P + H + M + R$,

where K is the time spent on keystroke operators, P is the time spent on pointing a mouse, H is the time spent homing hands to the keyboard, M is time spent on mental operations, and R is the response of the system. The analysis involves determining the physical operations involved (K, P, H, and R), and then using a set of heuristics to identify the M operators involved (Card et al., 1983; John & Kieras, 1996a; Lane, Napier, Batsell & Naman, 1993). The time cost of the individual operators can be looked up from parameter estimates like those in Table 15.3.

- NGOMSL is the natural GOMS language of Kieras (1996). It is a formal notation for GOMS, along with rules for writing NGOMSL models. Like CMN-GOMS, an NGOMSL analysis involves successively breaking down task goals into methods, until the analysis reaches low-level interaction operators. The methods, however, are represented in a structured notation. In addition to predictions of performance time, the analysis permits predictions of ease of learning and of transfer of skill across tasks (discussed below).
- CPM-GOMS is a parallel-activity version of GOMS (John, 1990; John & Gray, 1995). It involves analyzing a task using cognitive, perceptual, and motor operators in a critical-path method analysis (basically, the network of operators and their dependencies). This kind of analysis is especially useful when a user may be doing several things in parallel. Its most successful application (Gray, John & Atwood, 1993) analyzed a telephone operator workstation on which operators could be talking, reading, and keystroking in parallel.

Figure 15.4 shows an analysis by John & Kieras (1996b) suggesting which GOMS techniques are appropriate for different kinds of tasks.

COGNITIVE ARCHITECTURES AND HCI

The early growth of cognitive psychology during the 1950s and 1960s was characterized by research in largely independent experimental paradigms. Each such paradigm might involve variations on one or a few experimental tasks which were designed to address a few interesting questions about the nature of cognition. A classic example is the Sternberg task (e.g. Sternberg, 1969), in which a participant in an experiment is asked to hold a set of items (e.g. numbers, letters) in short-term memory, then is presented with a target item, and asked to indicate if the target item is a member of the short-term memory set. By measuring the time it takes to respond as a function of the number of items in short-term memory, it is possible to characterize the time it takes for the cognitive processor to scan and compare items in short-term memory (typically around 35 ms per item). A researcher studying the Sternberg task might argue that it is a way to measure the cognitive processor cycle time in Figure 15.1.

In a classic challenge to the field, Allen Newell (1973b) argued that cognitive psychology could not make significant progress by this divide-and-conquer

Design question \ Task type	Sequential actions	Parallel actions
Does application functionality cover needed task operations?	Any GOMS	Any GOMS
Is the interface consistent?	NGOMSL	
What is the sequence of operators to perform task?	CMN-GOMS NGOMSL	CPM-GOMS
What is the time cost?	KLM CMN-GOMS NGOMSL	CPM-GOMS
What is the time to learn a task procedure?	NGOMSL	
Can the user recover from errors?	Any GOMS	Any GOMS

Figure 15.4 GOMS techniques appropriate for different kinds of task type and the kind of design problem being addressed. Sequential actions occur one after the other. Parallel actions may be carried out simultaneously. From "Using GOMS for User Interface Design and Evaluation: Which Technique?," by B. E. John & D. E. Kieras, 1996, *ACM Transactions on Computer–Human Interaction*, 3, p. 294. Copyright 1996 by ACM. Adapted with permission.

approach to research. Understanding cognition could not be parceled out into a set of well-defined independent questions to be answered by different experimental paradigms. Psychologists could not win a "twenty questions" game with nature. Newell believed that understanding cognition, in even simple tasks, required an integrated theory of many cognitive processes and structures. Findings from one paradigm were surely relevant to the analysis of other paradigms. Progress, Newell (1973b) argued, would require the development of theories that provide a unified way of accounting for all the diverse phenomena and tasks found in the individual paradigms. In a sense, the Model Human Processor (Figures 15.1 and 15.2) is such a synthesis of findings from a diverse set of cognitive psychology paradigms (Card et al., 1983). Newell (1973b), however, also argued that the field needed theories that specified the deeper mechanisms that give rise to the diverse phenomena. A deeper account means that the theory is parsimonious – offering the fewest possible structures and mechanisms while giving rise to rich full accounts of human behavior. A mechanistic account means that predictions follow directly from the structures and processes specified by the theory, without guesswork by the theorist (or, equivalently, by "homunculi" processes in the theory which perform complex cognitive processes in unspecified ways). Ideally, such a mechanistic account could be run as a computer simulation of human cognition. A deeper account of the findings summarized in cognitive engineering models is provided by theories of cognitive architecture. Theories of cognitive architecture attempt to provide a deeper account of the mechanisms underlying cognition, learning, and performance.

The relationship between HCI and theories of cognitive architecture should turn out to be a productive one. Complex HCI tasks, such as writing a paper or designing a machine on a computer, are serious tests of cognitive theory and our ability to model the complicated interactions of cognitive, perceptual, and motor processes. For designers of HCI systems, cognitive architectures can act as repositories of accumulated findings that can be the firm foundations of cognitive engineering models.

By their very nature, cognitive architectures are complex and have been applied to a broad range of phenomena. The aim here is to provide an overview of several prominent proposals that have been applied to HCI. In each case, the architecture is summarized and an example of its application is provided. The examples are chosen to be illustrative of the architectures, as well as to illustrate the range of HCI issues addressed by architectures.

EPIC

Of the cognitive architectures reviewed here, the EPIC (Executive Process-Interactive Control) architecture (Kieras & Meyer, 1997; Meyer & Kieras, 1997a, 1997b) is perhaps closest in spirit to the Model Human Processor (Card et al., 1983). One significant advance in EPIC is that it incorporates more recent and detailed results concerning human performance. A second significant advance is that it is actually a computer simulation system. EPIC models are constructed by specifying procedures as production rules. When such a model is presented with the external stimuli for a task (the computer displays, keyboards, etc.) it follows the procedures for the tasks and simulates the time course of events on both the system side and human side of the HCI system.

In large part, EPIC has been developed to yield better models of attention and performance in multiple-task situations. These situations might occur in HCI, for instance, with certain computer operator jobs. Often, computer operators must coordinate and interleave (a) their conversational tasks with a customer with (b) database tasks with a computer. In cognitive psychology, the supervisory processes required to control and supervise other processes have traditionally been called executive processes – a carryover from the terminology of computer operating systems where an executive process oversees the other programs running on a computer. In EPIC, executive processes are considered to be the same as any other well-learned cognitive skill, and like other skills they are represented by production rules.

EPIC has been designed with the realization that perceptual and motor processors are complicated in their own right, and they have important interactions and constraints with cognition and executive control processes. How well people can handle multiple-task situations will depend on the structural constraints on perceptual processors, motor processors, limitations on working memory, etc. In contrast to traditional multi-tasking models, EPIC does not assume a single-

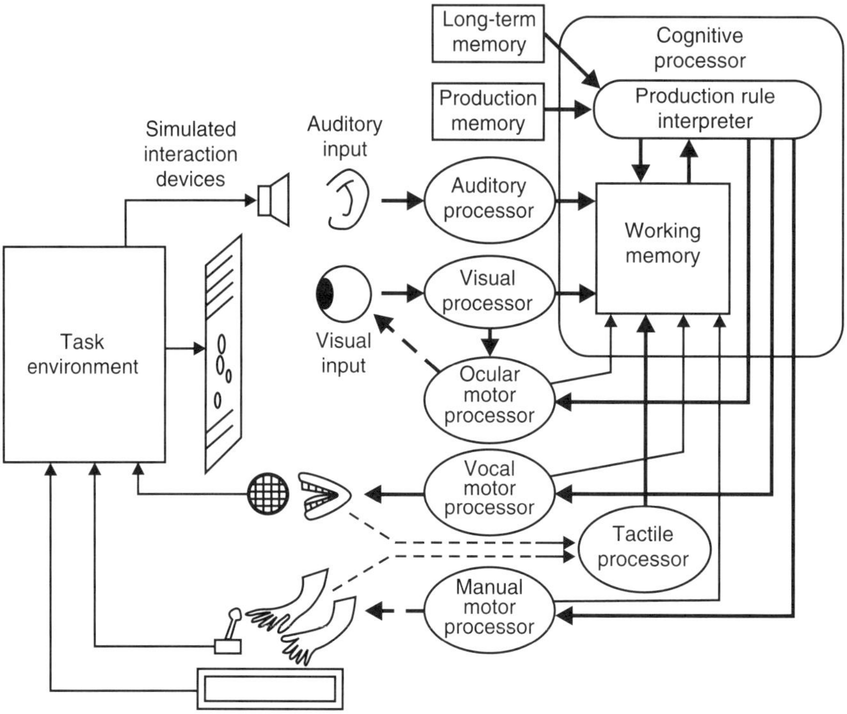

Figure 15.5 A schematic overview of the EPIC architecture. From "An Overview of the EPIC Architecture for Cognition and Performance with Application to Human–Computer Interaction," *Human–Computer Interaction*, 12, p. 399. Copyright 1998 by Lawrence Erlbaum Associates. Reprinted with permission.

channel attentional processor which must be switched from task to task, nor does it assume some limited central resource capacity on cognition. EPIC simply assumes that executive control processes must work around the structural limitations of the perceptual–cognitive–motor system. This assumption has led to successful models of attention and performance covering a large body of multi-task laboratory experiments (Meyer & Kieras, 1997, 1997b).

The Architecture

Figure 15.5 is a schematic for the EPIC architecture. It is a cognitive processor surrounded by perceptual and motor processors. The cognitive processor is controlled by production rules, and information flows through the perceptual processors, to the cognitive processor, and to the motor processors, which have feedback. To develop a specific model of a task situation requires the specification of production rules and the setting of perceptual–motor parameters. When combined with a simulator of the external environment, EPIC will simulate the serial and parallel actions required to perform the task.

The cognitive processor interacts with a working memory. Roughly, this working memory is equivalent to the short-term memory of the Model Human Processor. This working memory can also be thought of as a database that contains information representing goals and knowledge about the current state of affairs. In EPIC notation, for instance,

(GOAL DO MENU TASK)

might represent a goal to perform a task involving finding items on a menu, and

(VISUAL OPEN-FILE-1 IS-ABOVE CLOSE-FILE-1)

might represent knowledge (obtained from visual perceptual processing) that "open file" is above "close file" on a menu.

Production rules (or productions) specify the flow of control of cognitive processing. Productions match to the working memory database and specify changes to the database or other actions to perform. Each production rule is of the form

(<rule-name> IF <condition> THEN <actions>)

The condition of a rule specifies a pattern. When the contents of working memory match the pattern, the rule may be selected for application. The actions of the rule specify additions and deletions of content in working memory, as well as motor commands. These actions are executed if the rule is selected to apply.

The cognitive processor works on a 50 ms cycle. (Note how this figure revises the 70 ms estimate in the Model Human Processor.) At the beginning of the cycle, working memory is updated by inputs from the perceptual processors, and by modifications that result from the application of production rules on the previous cycle. Production rules that match the contents from working memory are applied, and at the end of the cycle any motor commands that were issued are sent to the motor processor. All the production rules that match working memory are applied. The simultaneous application of production rules is a form of parallelism. Many other production systems (such as ACT-R, discussed below) have limits of one production application per cycle. The perceptual and motor processors of EPIC are not necessarily synchronized with the 50 ms cognitive processor cycle. This means that perceptual inputs may have to "wait" on cognitive processing should they arrive before the beginning of the next cognitive cycle.

Working memory is partitioned into stores of different kinds of content. There are partitions of working memory for visual, auditory, and tactile information. These are slaved to the perceptual processors. That is, the outputs of those processors appear as representations in working memory. In addition, there are amodal partitions of working memory. One amodal partition is a control store that contains information about task goals and procedural steps. Another amodal partition is a general working memory that contains miscellaneous information that arises during the execution of a task.

As shown in Figure 15.5, EPIC has several perceptual processors. The time parameters associated with the processing of the perceptual processors may be (a)

standard, which come from surveys of the psychological literature and are felt to be relatively fixed across tasks, or (b) typical, which may vary from task to task.

There is a visual processor, which takes in stimuli from the visual scene and produces outputs in visual working memory. The visual processor has separate processors for the fovea, parafovea, and periphery. Each of these areas will produce different information from the same scene. For instance, the periphery may detect the sudden appearance of objects in the environment, the parafovea may detect the area occupied by a blob of text on a screen, and the fovea may detect the actual characters of the text. Each of these areas may have different time parameters on their processes. Event detection takes about 50 ms (periphery), while shape detection occurs about 100 ms later (parafovea), and pattern recognition about 250 ms later (fovea).

The auditory processor takes in sound stimuli and produces representations in auditory working memory. Again, different kinds of information processing will take different amounts of time to output. The time to process a tone onset is about 50 ms, and a fully discriminated frequency appears about 250 ms later. After these outputs reach auditory working memory, they decay after about 4 s.

There are motor processors controlling the hands, eyes, and vocal tract (Figure 15.5). These can operate simultaneously. The cognitive processor sends commands to a motor processor by specifying the type and parameters of the movement to perform. The motor processor then translates these into a simulated movement. Movements are specified in terms of features. The time to execute a movement depends on movement features and the mechanical properties of the movements (e.g. the trajectory of movement of the hands).

The motor processors work in two phases: (a) preparation, and (b) execution. In the preparation phase, a command is received from the cognitive processor and recoded into a set of movement features. For instance, to specify the peck of a finger on a key may require five features: the peck style, hand, finger, direction of movement, and extent of movement. The generation of each feature takes 50 ms, but features may be re-used from previous movements, or generated in advance. For instance, pecking two different keys will share some features and allow the re-use of features. Pecking the same key twice will re-use all the features. If a movement can be anticipated, then the features can be prepared in advance. The execution phase has a delay of 50 ms to initiate the movement specified in the preparation phase. The physical movement depends on mechanical properties. For instance, the peck motion of a finger to the keyboard depends on a version of Fitt's Law (Figure 15.2). The manual processor is capable of different movement styles such as punching keys, pecking, two-fingered patterns, pointing with a mouse, or pointing with a joystick. The occulomotor system has both voluntary motions (saccades) or involuntary (reflexive) motions. The vocal processor is capable of simple fixed utterances.

Example: Selecting an Item from a Menu

Hornof (Hornof & Kieras, 1997; Kieras & Meyer, 1997) used EPIC to model performance in an HCI task studied in the laboratory by Nilsen (1991). The aim was to understand how people scan and select items from menus using a mouse –

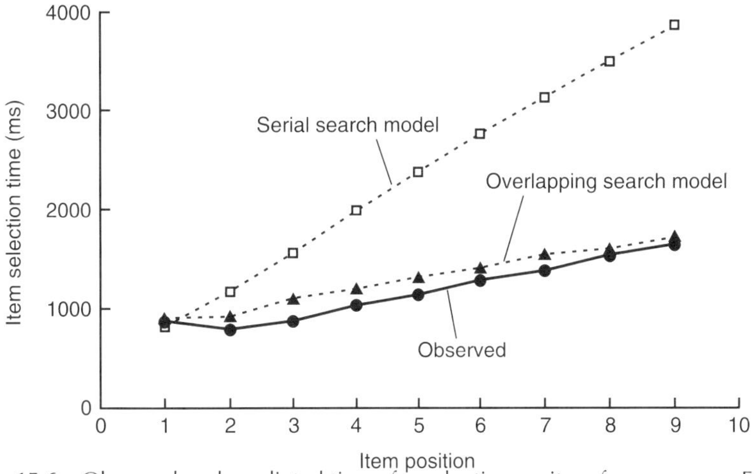

Figure 15.6 Observed and predicted times for selecting an item from a menu. From "An Overview of the EPIC Architecture for Cognition and Performance with Application to Human–Computer Interaction," *Human–Computer Interaction,* 12, p. 415. Copyright 1998 by Lawrence Erlbaum Associates. Reprinted with permission

a task that is ubiquitous in graphical user interfaces. Participants in the Nilsen (1991) study selected items from a pull-down menu. Participants were shown a target digit, 1–9; they clicked on the target; a vertical menu with digits 1–9 in random order appeared below the cursor. The participants then had to use the mouse to point and click on the menu item corresponding to the item they had been shown. Time to select the digit from the menu as function of its location from the top of the menu was linear with a slope of about 100 ms/menu item (see Figure 15.6).

Hornof & Kieras (1997; Kieras & Meyer, 1997) found that the obvious serial search model did not work. The intuitive model of the user is: move the eye to next menu location, if the item matches the target, then initiate a pointing movement using the mouse, otherwise move the eye to the next item. The assumption was that mouse pointing would follow a version of Fitt's Law (Figure 15.2, Principle P5). Figure 15.6 shows that this (serial search) model vastly overpredicted the time cost per menu item with about 380 ms/item slope. The reason for this discrepancy is that the EPIC analysis suggests that 200 ms is required to recognize the item, 50 ms for a production rule to apply to make the decision to point or not, and 50 ms for each eye movement. This lead Hornof & Kieras (1997; Kieras & Meyer, 1997) to propose a somewhat counter-intuitive EPIC model that suggests that the processes of, first, scanning the menu, and second, recognizing and deciding to point are operating partly in parallel (overlapping in time).

There are three EPIC production rules for this overlapped process model developed by Hornof & Kieras (1997; Kieras & Meyer, 1997). The idea is that there is a scanning process that moves the eye from item to item, relying on perceptual pipelining to recognize items. The scanning process is controlled by one production rule that simply recognizes that an item has been scanned and commands the occulomotor system to move the eye to the next item. There is a second production rule that recognizes that a scanned item is one that matches the target item and stops the scan process. A third production initiates the pointing movement. Figure 15.6 shows an excellent match of the model predictions to the data.

EPIC has been developed with a primary emphasis on modeling attention and performance, and especially the subtleties of situations in which people are engaged in multiple tasks that potentially overlap during execution. The architecture has a well-developed set of components modeling motor and perceptual operations. EPIC, however, has not yet been extended to address issues concerning learning. This has been one of the main areas addressed by the ACT architecture, which is discussed next.

ACT

The ACT family of theories has the longest history of the cognitive architectures. The seminal version of the theory was presented in Anderson (1976), shortly after Newell's (1973b) challenge to the field of cognitive psychology, and it has undergone several major revisions since then (Anderson, 1983, 1990, 1993). (ACTE is the version of the theory presented in Anderson (1976), ACT* in Anderson (1983), and ACT-R in Anderson (1993).) Until recently (Anderson & Lebiere, 1998; Anderson, Matessa & Lebiere, 1997), it has been primarily a theory of higher cognition and learning, without the kind of emphasis on perceptual–motor processing found in EPIC or the Model Human Processor. Historically, the success of ACT as a cognitive theory has been in the study of memory (Anderson & Milson, 1989; Anderson & Pirolli, 1984), language (Anderson, 1976), problem solving (Anderson, 1993), and categorization (Anderson, 1991). As a learning theory, ACT has been successful (Anderson, 1993) in modeling the acquisition of complex cognitive skills for tasks such as computer programing, geometry, and algebra, and in understanding transfer of learning across tasks (Singley & Anderson, 1989). ACT has been strongly tested (Anderson, Boyle, Corbett & Lewis, 1990) by application in the development of computer tutors, and less so in the area of HCI. Recently, the ACT group has been extending the architecture to address more about perceptual–motor processing (Anderson & Lebiere, 1998) and this should make ACT even more appealing to HCI researchers.

The Architecture

The architecture presented here corresponds to ACT-R 4.0 as presented in Anderson & Lebiere (Anderson & Lebiere, 1998). Like EPIC, ACT-R is a production system architecture. (It is perhaps more accurate to say that ACT-R is a hybrid architecture, combining production rule processing with neural-like processes such as spreading activation.) ACT-R, like previous versions of the ACT theory, contains three kinds of assumptions about:

1. knowledge representation
2. knowledge deployment (performance)
3. knowledge acquisition (learning).

ACT-R has been recently extended (Anderson et al., in press) to the analysis of visual attention and other perceptual–motor processes, moving it in the direction of EPIC, but strong applications of those aspects of the theory to HCI are just beginning.

The ACT theory assumes there are two kinds of knowledge, declarative and procedural (Ryle, 1949). Declarative knowledge is the kind of knowledge that a person can attend to, reflect upon, and usually articulate in some way (e.g. by declaring it verbally or by gesture). Declarative knowledge includes the kinds of factual knowledge that users can verbalize, such as "The 'open' item on the 'file' menu will open a file." Procedural knowledge is the know-how we display in our behavior, without conscious awareness: knowledge of how to ride a bike, or how to point a mouse to a menu item, are examples of procedural knowledge. Procedural knowledge specifies how declarative knowledge is transformed into active behavior. ACT-R has two kinds of memory for these two different kinds of knowledge.

Declarative knowledge in ACT-R is represented formally in terms of chunks (Miller, 1956; Simon, 1974). These chunks are stored in the declarative memory of ACT-R. One may think of the ACT-R declarative memory as being roughly the same as both the long-term and short-term memories of the Model Human Processor in Figure 15.1. In the Model Human Processor, long-term memory information is dormant, and must be retrieved into short-term memory to have an active effect on behavior. In contrast, declarative chunks in ACT-R have activation values. Chunks with higher activation values take less time to use (and have a greater chance) to have an impact on behavior. Roughly, one could partition ACT-R declarative memory into a high-activation set of chunks and a low-activation set of chunks, and the high-activation set would be like the short-term memory of the Model Human Processor, and the low-activation set like the long-term memory. However, since activation is a continuously valued property in ACT-R, there really are no sharp boundaries between long-term and short-term information. Activation is a way of quantifying the degree of relevance of declarative information to the current focus of attention.

Activation may be interpreted metaphorically as a kind of mental energy that drives cognitive processing. Activation spreads from the current focus of attention, including goals, through associations among chunks in declarative memory. These associations are built up from experience, and they reflect how ideas co-occur in cognitive processing. Generally, activation-based theories of memory predict that more activated knowledge structures will receive more favorable processing. Activation in ACT-R determines the speed of production rule application. Spreading activation is the name of the process that computes activation values. The spread of activation from one cognitive structure to another is determined by weighting values on the associations among chunks. These weights determine the rate of activation flow among chunks (analogous to pipes or wires with specific flow capacities). Figure 15.7 presents a summary of the rational analysis and computation of spreading activation in ACT-R.

Figure 15.8 presents a scenario for a spreading activation analysis (based on Pirolli, 1997). Many information retrieval systems and browsers, such as those developed for the World Wide Web, present small text summaries to represent the

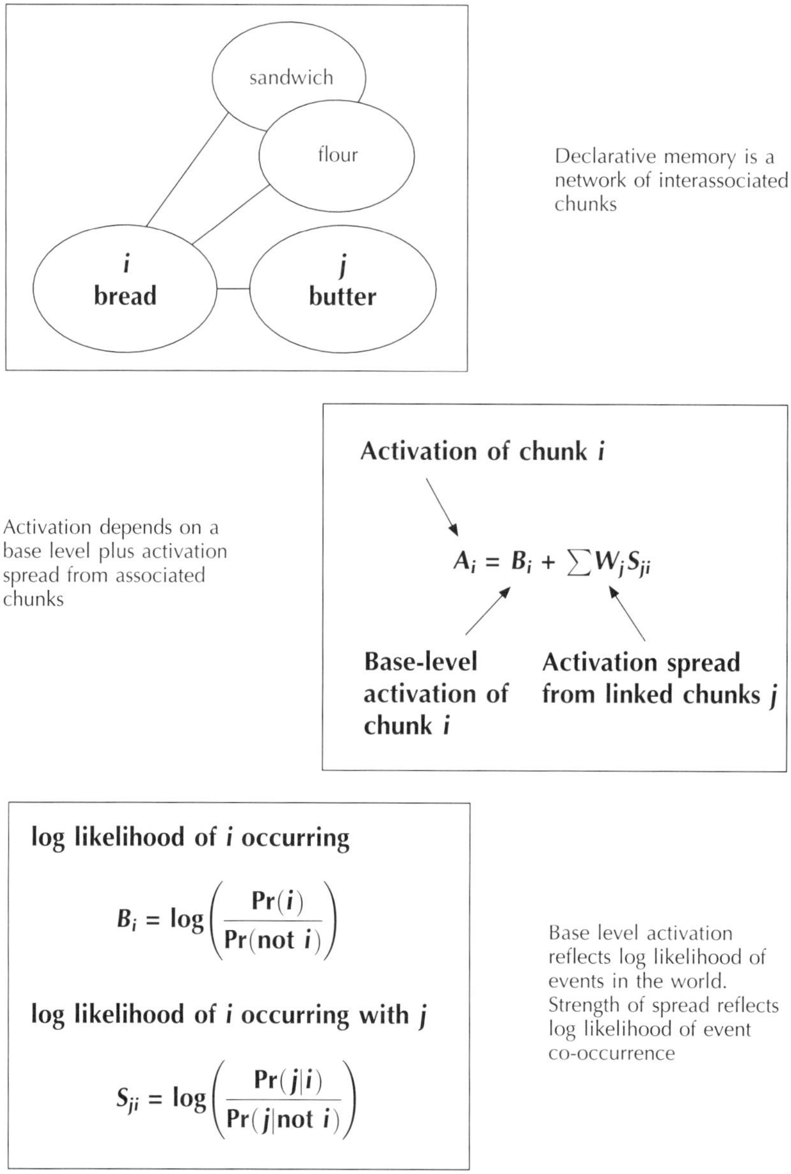
sandwich
flour
i
bread
j
butter
Declarative memory is a network of interassociated chunks
Activation of chunk i
A_i = B_i + ∑W_j S_ji
Base-level activation of chunk i
Activation spread from linked chunks j
Activation depends on a base level plus activation spread from associated chunks
log likelihood of i occurring
B_i = log(Pr(i) / Pr(not i))
log likelihood of i occurring with j
S_ji = log(Pr(j|i) / Pr(j|not i))
Base level activation reflects log likelihood of events in the world. Strength of spread reflects log likelihood of event co-occurrence

Figure 15.7 A summary of spreading activation in ACT-R.

documents that they have retrieved. For instance, suppose a user is looking for "information on medical treatments and procedures for cancer." The representation of this query in declarative memory is depicted by the small set of chunks linked to the concept "QUERY-1" in Figure 15.8 (the nodes labeled medical, treatments, procedures, cancer). These chunks represent the main meaningful concepts making up the user's query. In Figure 15.8, the user is looking at a browser that has retrieved a set of documents. The browser presents short text

Figure 15.8 A scenario for a spreading activation analysis (see text for details).

summaries to indicate the content of the documents. One of the summaries is the text "cell, patient, dose, beam," which summarizes a document that emphasizes those words. The representation of this part of the browser display is depicted by the network of chunks linked to "TEXT-1" in Figure 15.8. Figure 15.8 also shows that there are links between the query chunks and the text summary chunks. These are associations between words that come from past experience. The associations reflect the fact that these words co-occur in the user's linguistic environment. For instance, the word "medical" and "patient" co-occur quite frequently and they would have a high weighting of interassociation. Spreading activation would flow from the query, which is the focus of attention, through the interword associations, to words in the text summary. The stronger the associations (higher weights or strengths that reflect higher rates of co-occurrence) the greater the amount of activation flow. If the query chunks and browser chunks are strongly associated, we expect people to judge them as being highly relevant to one another. At least implicitly, this is what the interface designers of browsers are trying to do when they select small text snippets to communicate the content of large documents to users. They are trying to pick words that people will judge as relevant to their queries. Spreading activation may be used to predict these memory-based judgments of reminding and relevance (Pirolli, 1997) that are key components of surfing the World Wide Web.

Production rules are used to represent procedural knowledge in ACT-R. That is, they specify how to apply cognitive skill (know-how) in the current context, and how to retrieve and use declarative knowledge. Like EPIC, production rules in ACT-R have the basic IF <condition> THEN <action> format (although a more complicated notation is used). In ACT-R, each production rule has conditions that specify which goal information must be matched and which declarative memory must be retrieved. Each production rule has actions that specify behavioral actions and possibly the setting of subgoals.

ACT-R makes a set of assumptions that strongly constrain the analysis of leaning and performance into a production rule representation. Roughly, the idea is that each elemental step of cognition corresponds to a production. The assumptions characterizing the production rule representation of procedural knowledge are:

1. *Modularity* – Production rules are the elemental units by which cognitive skills are learned and deployed. This means that very complex cognitive skills can be analyzed into elemental units (production rules). The acquisition of an entire skill set can be broken down into the analysis of the learning of new production rules and the analysis of transfer of production rules from other skills. An example of this will be discussed below; it concerns how learning new skills for a new text editor, and the transfer of skills from previously learned text editors, can be given a production system analysis. The modularity assumption also means that the performance of a complex cognitive skill (the deployment of procedural knowledge) can be determined by the performance characteristics of each production rule involved in the skill. Thus, ACT-R production rules represent the atomic elements of cognition. As is summarized in Figure 15.9, the performance and learning of each atom of procedural knowledge – each production rule – is strongly predicted by quantitative equations that are motivated by a rational analysis of the problems faced by the human mind in adapting to a complex world.
2. *Abstraction* – Production rules generalize over contexts. A typical experienced user probably has general production rules for using a menu. Such rules would apply (under the appropriate goal situation) once the user recognizes that they are looking at a menu. The production would generalize over menus that have different appearances, so they would be abstract.
3. *Goal structuring* – Production rules are restricted to apply to specific goal types. In this way the goal structure (goals and subgoals) for a task strongly determine which goals may apply. The goal structures in ACT-R typically look very much like those discussed above in GOMS analyses. Sets of production rules that apply to goals and decompose them into subgoals are very much like the methods of a GOMS analysis.
4. *Conditional asymmetry* – Declarative knowledge can be used in many ways. For instance, the declarative knowledge that "Selecting 'file' from a menu opens a file" can be used to answer the questions "How does one open a file?" or "What operation is performed by selecting 'file'?" Procedural knowledge is assumed to have a kind of asymmetry to it that is represented by production rules. The flow of cognition goes from condition to action in a production rule, but not the reverse. Consequently, the knowledge represented by production rules is less flexible and it is use-specific. For instance, skills acquired for comprehending an interface may not transfer immediately to skills for acting on it. Some amount of practice is required to transfer declarative knowledge (e.g. comprehension of an interface) into smooth and fluid procedural knowledge.

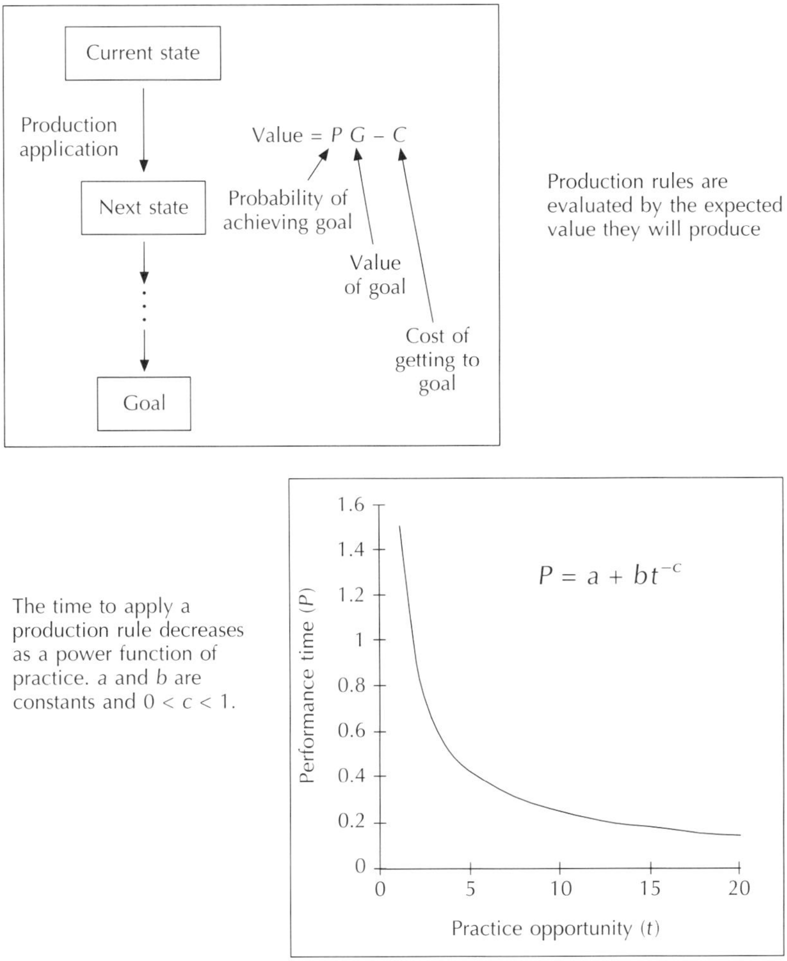

Figure 15.9 A summary of performance and learning assumptions in ACT-R.

Analysis of Cognitive Skill Acquisition and Transfer

A large body of work has accumulated on the acquisition and transfer of cognitive skill using production system models developed in various versions of ACT (Pirolli, 1991; Singley & Anderson, 1989) and in other production system theories (Kieras & Bovair, 1986; Polson, Bovair & Kieras, 1987). The basic idea is that the performance of a task involves the application of some sequence of productions. The performance time, P, associated with the application of each production rule depends on how many times, t, it has been practiced, as indicated in Figure 15.9. Suppose we analyze the performance of a task into the sequence of steps $s = 1, 2, \ldots N$, and for each step we can identify the production rule $r(s)$ that applies at that step, and the amount of practice $t_{r(s)}$ it has acquired prior to that step. We can designate $P_{r(s)}(t_{r(s)})$ as the performance time associated with that rule $r(s)$ which occurs at step s of the task. which will be calculated according to the power function in Figure 15.9,

$$P_{r(s)}(t_{r(s)}) = a + bt_{r(s)}^{-c}$$

Then, the total time to perform the task is basically just the sum of the times for each application of a production rule:

$$\mathit{Total\ Task\ Time} = \sum_{s=1}^{N} P_{r(s)}(t_{r(s)})$$

In many task analyses, the practice curves for the individual productions are relatively similar: for a given level of practice, all production rules will take roughly the same amount of time to perform, but productions with very little practice take substantially longer to perform than productions with greater amounts of practice. In these cases the analysis of total task time can be approximated by:

$$\mathit{Total\ Task\ Time} = (f_{new} \times t_{new}) + (f_{old} \times t_{old})$$

where t_{new} is the performance time of newly acquired productions (those with no practice) and t_{old} is the performance time of more practiced productions, and new productions take longer to perform than practiced ones, $t_{new} > t_{old}$. The number of newly acquired productions on the task is f_{new}, and the number of practiced productions is f_{old}.

Learning a new task, such as a new text editor, may draw upon many cognitive skills learned previously, for example on a previously encountered text editor. In production rule terms, this means that some production rules that apply on the new editor were practiced on the previous editor. If the N steps of tasks on the new editor involve some mixture of new and practiced productions, $N = f_{new} + f_{old}$, then performance on the task is better when there are higher proportions of previously practiced productions, that is higher values of f_{old}/N. By developing a model of the production rules needed to perform the task, one can analyze the acquisition and transfer of the atomic elements of skill set required to perform the task.

Example: Transfer of Text Editor Skill

Singley and Anderson (1989) presented a production system model addressing laboratory studies of the acquisition and transfer of skills across text editors. This example was originally analyzed using the ACT* theory (Anderson, 1983). The participants were hired from a secretarial school, but had no computer experience. The participants in the experimental conditions learned either one or two line editors (called ED and EDT) before transferring to a display-based text editor called EMACS. Participants in control groups either simply typed at a terminal before learning EMACS (to control for perceptual–motor learning), or spent all of their time using EMACS.

Table 15.4 Transfer design for tasks A and B presented over two sequential phases of learning

Group	Phase 1	Phase 2
Experimental	A_1	B_1
Control	B_1	B_2

Participants were asked to make manuscript edits. The goal structure of the tasks, across all text editors, came from a GOMS-style analysis. Although some of the goal structure could be found across all editors, the task analysis for the individual text editors did differ in some of the task subgoals. The goal structure from this task analysis is implemented by production rules such as,

IF the goal is to EXECUTE UNIT TASK
THEN set subgoals to
1. Locate line
2. Modify text.

This rule implements the decomposition of the EXECUTE-UNIT-TASK goal into subgoals to locate lines to edit and then to modify the text on those lines. Singley & Anderson developed production rule models for performing the editing tasks on all three editors (ED, EDT, EMACS).

One of the predictions computed by Singley & Anderson (1989) concerned percent transfer. Percent transfer is a measure of how much improvement on a second task is due to transfer of learning from a previous task. Empirically, this is computed by comparing observed performance measures across different task domains or different domains of subject matter. In this case, Singley & Anderson examined time to perform an editing operation as a function for the kinds of editors they had previously used. The empirical measure of transfer was calculated by a score introduced by Katona (1940). It compares the amount of transfer from one kind of task (A) to another (B). For instance, it might be used to score transfer from the ED editor (task A) to the EMACS editor (task B). It compares data that is arranged as the experimental design in Table 15.4. For instance, the experimental part of the design would correspond to the users who learned ED (task A_1) followed by EMACS (task B_1) and the control group would be those who learned EMACS (task B_1), then practiced more EMACS (task B_2). Katona's score used to gauge the transfer empirically was,

$$Transfer\ Score = \frac{Control\ B_1\ Performance - Experimental\ B_1\ Performance}{Control\ B_1\ Performance - Control\ B_2\ Performance}$$

Singley & Anderson (1989) predicted transfer by calculating:

$$Predicted\ Score = \frac{No.\ productions\ shared\ by\ A\ and\ B}{No.\ productions\ used\ in\ B}$$

Singley & Anderson (1989) found an excellent match of the observed and predicted transfer across text editors. This suggests that ACT-R models of tasks conducted on different HCI applications should be able to make good predictions of transfer of learning.

Other Examples of Production Rule Models of Learning and Transfer

Cognitive Complexity Theory (CCT) has been developed (Kieras, 1988; Kieras & Bovair, 1986; Polson et al., 1987) as a cognitive engineering approach to the analysis of skill acquisition and transfer, again in the domain of text editors (Bovair, Kieras & Polson, 1990). CCT does not provide a detailed theory of learning processes. It does provide a method for analyzing a complex skill into its elements, and determining the learning time for the complex skill and degree of transfer among skills.

As noted above, ACT has been used to develop a wide range of models for learning skills for programing and high school mathematics (Anderson et al., 1990). Often these models were refined in the context of developing intelligent tutoring systems used in real classrooms. Consequently, many of the models address dozens of hours of classroom problem solving. Over and over again, the ACT researchers have found that the complex buzz of behavior involved in tasks like programing become understandable as the application of many simple production rules. When one extracts the experience on individual productions from the buzzing stream of behavior, one finds that performance is predicted by the practice and transfer effects at the production rule level as specified by ACT. Soar, discussed next, has also been used to model a wide range of learning phenomena.

Soar

Responding to his own challenge (Newell, 1973b), Newell (1990) outlined desiderata for a unified theory of cognition, and proposed the Soar architecture as a candidate theory. Again, like EPIC and ACT, it is a production system architecture. The seminal assumptions for Soar can mainly be traced to three sources:

1. Newell's (1973a) original work proposing production systems as a viable theory of cognitive processing
2. Laird's (Laird, 1986) work on a Universal Weak Method, which is a very general problem-solving method, involving universal subgoaling, that may be extended by the addition of knowledge to perform other kinds of problem-solving methods
3. Rosenbloom & Newell's (1987) work on a form of learning called chunking which acquired new production rules based on experience.

Architecture

Soar performs tasks by problem space search using universal subgoaling, and uses a learning mechanism called chunking. Problem spaces consist of sets of states, with operators that move from state to state, or that augment a current problem-solving context. The achievement of desired states within a problem space constitutes task accomplishment. Knowledge is used to define and select problem spaces, to guide progress towards desired states, and to select and apply operators. All long-term knowledge is stored in a content-addressable memory, represented as a production system.

Performance is focused by goal contexts that are stored in a goal stack. A goal context contains a current state and operator that has been selected from operators that apply to that state. The goal stack is stored in working memory. The conditions of production rules test for patterns that occur in the goal stack. Production actions can implement the current operator by changing the current state, or can propose new operators. If an operator is too complex to be implemented directly by productions, the universal subgoaling mechanism recognizes an impasse and creates a new goal context whose purpose is to implement the operator. Similarly, the task of proposing the next operator, or of selecting among competing operators, may be complex enough that Soar must focus on it explicitly with a new goal context. Thus, the full power of problem space search can be applied recursively to any subcomponent of a task.

Soar operates by iterating through decision cycles. Each decision cycle includes an elaboration phase and a decision phase. In the elaboration phase, knowledge relevant to the current task context is retrieved by the parallel firing of productions. The actions of some productions will deposit preferences about possible changes to take. Preferences are basically assertions stated in a domain-independent format concerning the selection, rejection, or comparison of operators for goal contexts on the goal stack. For example, given a particular goal context containing a specific operator, a production may assert that a new operator is "best" for that goal context. Such a preference, in the absence of overriding preferences that reject it, would achieve a step in the problem space search by causing the new operator to be installed in place of the current one. The end of the elaboration phase occurs when all relevant productions have been fired (i.e. quiescence is achieved).

Frequently, the available knowledge is insufficient or conflicting in determining an action. Such a situation gives rise to an impasse, which automatically generates a subgoal. Thus, new goal contexts are added to the goal stack solely through the generation of impasses. In these subgoals, knowledge can be brought to bear in selecting new problem spaces and in guiding search in order to overcome the impasse. When an impasse is overcome, the subgoal disappears from the goal stack. On every decision cycle Soar re-examines each pending impasse in light of the current state of working memory to see if progress is possible. If so, then the goal context corresponding to the impasse, together with all newer impasses on the stack, are terminated. This lets Soar react to unanticipated events in the environment. Chunking summarizes the problem solving (by creating new productions) that lead to the resolution of an impasse by tracing through dependencies from the working memory elements that produced the solution back to the working memory elements that were available in the context that triggered the impasse.

Soar has a declarative working memory, which is assumed to be highly dynamic and transient (i.e. like the short-term memory of the Model Human Processor).

Unlike ACT, Soar does not have a separate long-term storage for declarative knowledge. Soar only stores production rules over the long term. This means that factual information, such as the names of keyboard commands, or the meanings of menu items, must become chunked into production rules that apply at the right time to retrieve needed factual information. Associations between cues in the environment and declarative knowledge happen through production rules, and these associations are formed by the Soar chunking process.

Chunking dictates that declarative knowledge must be learned and recalled by a method of generate-and-recognize (Newell, 1990). During the generate phase, production rules propose declarative elements of information as candidates for recall. During the recognize phase, production rules test the candidates, and those passing the test are tagged as recalled. Chunking learns the rules that recognize the correct declarative items for a particular context and memory problem. A variation on this form of declarative learning is involved in the learning examples described next.

Learning Task–Action Mappings

Howes & Young (1996) implemented a model in Soar called the Task–Action Learner (TAL). TAL assumes that a major hurdle facing users is the learning of task–action mappings. A task–action mapping is an association between the semantics of a task, such as the task of opening a file, and actions, such as moving a mouse and clicking on a menu item. TAL is a model of how instructions about devices and their operation are interpreted and reconstructed to guide action. It addresses several phenomena in HCI that indicate that consistent, interactive, and meaningful devices are easier to learn and use.

TAL is a model of the user who is familiar with some basic aspects of the device (such as the keyboard and mouse) but not specific menu structures, effects of actions, meaning of words, etc. In addition, the user is assumed to have the necessary semantic knowledge to interpret instructions and words and graphics on the system display (e.g. that "file" means file). TAL is given a task which it attempts to perform by interacting with a system display and asking questions of an instructor when it lacks knowledge. On each cycle of operations TAL will examine the display for information about display state. If TAL recalls the appropriate action to take (via a production rule) it performs the action, otherwise it must request instruction. In such situations, instructions from the external instructor are interpreted into actions. After interpreting and performing the instructions, Soar's chunking mechanisms create new production rules that summarize the instructions and actions.

The chunking of instruction works in the following way. Assume that TAL has been given the task of opening a text file and it is working with a display that has a menu item labeled with "file." The system requests instruction (because it has hit an impasse because of a lack of knowledge) and is given "move to 'file'." The instruction is interpreted in the context of the task semantics as meaning to move the mouse to the menu item labeled "file". TAL then executes the action. From this interpretation TAL will chunk the production rule:

C1: IF the task involves a file object
& there is instruction about moving mouse to file
& there is an item "file" on the display
THEN move the mouse pointer to the item "file"

Notice that the instruction is part of the condition of the production rule. This is a result of the way that chunking operates. Basically, all the declarative information that was necessary to produce the action that resolved the impasse is included in the condition of the new production rule. This is related to the data chunking problem (Newell, 1990). Howes & Young (1996) discuss how instruction-based learning in Soar is generally going to have this result: whenever Soar uses an instruction in working memory to overcome an impasse in performance of a task, chunking will create productions that have conditions that test for the presence of the instruction in working memory and actions that recall interpretations of the instructions. The assumption is that users somehow must generate instructions to themselves when task impasses occur. For instance, when attempting to open a file, a user might look at a screen, see a menu item "file," and think the instruction "move the mouse to file." This would then be recognized as the correct action to perform by production rule C1. This would cause a new production rule to be learned:

C2: IF the task involves a file object
& item "file" is on the display
THEN move the mouse pointer to the item "file"

This production rule would apply without the user generating instructions to him or herself.

TAL predicts that interactive, meaningful, and consistent interfaces should be easier to learn because such interfaces facilitate the self-instruction process. Interactive systems are assumed to be easier to learn, in TAL, because the back-and-forth communication of user and machine means that the user can use the system's response to generate the next action. Highly graphical displays, or any sort of interface with a structure that suggests actions (e.g. the card slot on an Automated Teller Machine) may cue the users to generate instructions to themselves. Certain conventions in such displays (e.g. the graying out of menu items to indicate that they cannot be used) may also cue the users to generate instructions to themselves. Meaningful commands for devices, such as command words that suggest their function like "mv" for "move," are easier to learn (Furnas, Landauer, Gomez & Dumais, 1987). When command words cue the users to generate the correct instructions to themselves, the interface is easier to learn. When command words have unintended meanings (are ambiguous) or when tasks do not translate easily into the available command words, then the users will have a poorer chance of generating instructions to themselves and the interface will be more difficult to learn.

When semantically similar tasks share aspects of task–action mappings they are said to be consistent (Payne & Green, 1986). Consistency may arise because there is a common interface metaphor underlying tasks (e.g. the desktop metaphor of the Macintosh interface), a common device model (e.g. the point-and-click operation of many graphical interfaces), some organization of space by semantics (e.g. function keys in one area), and so on. Command structures are usually designed to be consistent, and users assume this consistency: in a system with a command structure such as "delete <filename>" and "save <filename>" (i.e. a command + object order), users would expect other commands to have the same syntax. TAL predicts that interface consistency will result in greater ease of learning because of the transfer of production rule chunks.

GENERAL DISCUSSION

The introduction to this chapter proposed that psychology ought to be able to answer some of the questions facing HCI designers – for instance about the design of application programs such as text editors, spreadsheet systems, or World Wide Web browsers. The survey presented here discussed how skilled performance in HCI could be analyzed using GOMS and the Model Human Processor. Detailed predictions and explanation of performance, especially in multi-tasking applications is provided by EPIC. Production system theories like CCT and ACT can provide predictions about the time it takes to learn an HCI task. These theories also provide ways of making predictions about transfer across HCI tasks and applications. Instructionless learning of interfaces depends on users taking advantage of the ostensive meaning, consistency, and interactivity of interfaces, and Soar has been used in explaining the impact of these properties (see also Kitajima & Polson, 1997).

There are several main differences among the three architectures presented here. Production rules represent cognition at different grain sizes in the three architectures. In ACT-R and EPIC, the application of a production rule corresponds to significant change in cognitive state. Such a rule application corresponds roughly to an entire phase of decision-elaborate cycles in Soar, during which many productions may apply to make a move in problem space search. EPIC has no model of how such rules are acquired, whereas ACT-R and Soar address learning, although they have somewhat different models. ACT-R assumes the serial application of productions – only one may apply at a time. In contrast, EPIC and Soar may apply productions in parallel. This has implications for how the architectures deal with tasks that require divided attention, permit parallel actions, or otherwise have parallel threads of information processing. EPIC has the most refined development and integration of perceptual–motor processing with cognitive activity, but ACT-R and Soar development is moving in this direction also.

Practitioners interested in cognitive engineering models or cognitive architectures should note that to learn and use these frameworks is neither trivial nor does it require several years of intensive graduate training. Tutorials, taking a day or half day, on Model Human Processor and GOMS are often presented at the ACM Computer–Human Interaction Conference. Intensive tutorials and workshops on Soar and ACT are regularly presented over the course of several days. Some example tutorial materials are available on the World Wide Web.

Tutorial materials for ACT-R can be found at http://bk1.psy.cmu.edu/inter/ACT-R-Tutorial.html, which are intended to be used in conjunction with Anderson & Lebiere (1998). Materials for Soar may be found at http://www.psychology.nottingham.ac.uk/staff/Frank.Ritter/pst/pst-tutorial.html.

The study of human psychology is arguably a science of the most complex system we have ever studied. The aim of the cognitive architectures approach to this study is to encompass the full richness of psychological phenomena arising in complex tasks. The success, so far, of this approach highlights the prescience of Newell's (1973b) original challenge to the field of cognitive psychology to specify such architectures. This successful track record is sure to be tested further in the study of human–computer interaction.

ACKNOWLEDGMENTS

This work was supported in part by grant N00014-96-C-0097 from the Office of Naval Research. I would like to thank Bonnie John and Eric Altmann, as well as two anonymous reviewers, for their extensive comments.

REFERENCES

Anderson, J. R. (1976). *Language, Memory, and Thought*. Hillsdale, NJ: Lawrence Erlbaum.

Anderson, J. R. (1983). *The Architecture of Cognition*. Cambridge, MA: Harvard University Press.

Anderson, J. R. (1990). *The Adaptive Character of Thought*. Hillsdale, NJ: Lawrence Erlbaum.

Anderson, J. R. (1991). The adaptive nature of human categorization. *Psychological Review*, 98, 409–29.

Anderson, J. R. (1993). *Rules of the Mind*. Hillsdale, NJ: Lawrence Erlbaum.

Anderson, J. R., Boyle, C. F., Corbett, A. & Lewis, M. W. (1990). Cognitive modelling and intelligent tutoring. *Artificial Intelligence*, 42, 7–49.

Anderson, J. R. & Lebiere, C. (1998). *The Atomic Components of Thought*. Mahwah, NJ: Lawrence Erlbaum.

Anderson, J. R., Matessa, M. & Lebiere, C. (1997). ACT-R: a theory of higher-level cognition and its relationship to visual attention. *Human–Computer Interaction*, 12, 439–62.

Anderson, J. R. & Milson, R. (1989). Human memory: an adaptive perspective. *Psychological Review*, 96, 703–19.

Anderson, J. R. & Pirolli, P. L. (1984). Spread of activation. *Journal of Experimental Psychology: Learning, Memory, and Cognition*, 10, 791–8.

Bovair, S., Kieras, D. E. & Polson, P. G. (1990). The acquisition and performance of text-editing skill: a cognitive complexity analysis. *Human–Computer Interaction*, 5, 1–48.

Card, S. K., Moran, T. P. & Newell, A. (1983). *The Psychology of Human–Computer Interaction*. Hillsdale, NJ: Lawrence Erlbaum.

Cavanaugh, J. P. (1972). Relation between the immediate memory span and the memory search rate. *Psychological Review*, 79, 525–30.

Furnas, G. W., Landauer, T. K., Gomez, L. W. & Dumais, S. T. (1987). The vocabulary problem in human–system communication. *Communcations of the ACM*, 30, 964–71.

Gray, W. D., John, B. E. & Atwood, M. E. (1993). Project Ernestine: a validation of

GOMS for prediction and explanation of real-world task performance. *Human–Computer Interaction*, 8, 237–309.
Hornof, A. J. & Kieras, D. E. (1997). Cognitive modeling reveals menu search is both random and systematic. *Proceedings of the Conference on Human Factors in Computing Systems, CHI '97* (pp. 107–14). New York.
Howes, A. & Young, R. M. (1996). Learning consistent, interactive, and meaningful task–action mappings: a computational model. *Human–Computer Interaction*, 20, 301–56.
John, B. E. (1990). Extensions of GOMS analyses to expert performance requiring perception of dynamic visual and auditory information. *Proceedings of the Human Factors in Computing Systems, CHI '90 Conference* (pp. 107–15). Seattle, WA.
John, B. E. & Gray, W. D. (1995). CPM-GOMS: an analysis method for tasks with parallel activities. *Proceedings of the Human Factors in Computing Systems, CHI '95*. New York.
John, B. E. & Kieras, D. E. (1996a). The GOMS family of user interface analysis techniques: comparison and contrast. *ACM Transactions on Computer–Human Interaction*, 3, 320–51.
John, B. E. & Kieras, D. E. (1996b). Using GOMS for user interface design and evaluation. *AMC Transaction of Computer–Human Interaction*, 3, 287–319.
John, B. E. & Newell, A. (1990). Toward an engineering model of stimulus response compatability. In R. W. Gilmore & T. G. Reeve (Eds), *Stimulus–response compatability: an integrated approach* (pp. 107–15). New York: North Holland.
Katona, G. (1940). *Organizing and Memorizing*. New York: Columbia University Press.
Kieras, D. E. (1988). Towards a practical GOMS model methodology for user interface design. In M. Helander (Ed.), *The Handbook of Human–Computer Interaction* (pp. 135–58). Amsterdam: North-Holland.
Kieras, D. E. (1996). Guide to GOMS model usability evaluation using NGOMSL. In M. Helander & T. Landauer (Eds), *Handbook of Human–Computer Interaction*, 2nd edn. Amsterdam: North-Holland.
Kieras, D. E. & Bovair, S. (1986). The acquisition of procedures from text: a production system analysis of transfer of training. *Journal of Memory and Language*, 25, 507–24.
Kieras, D. E. & Meyer, D. E. (1997). An overview of the EPIC architecture for cognition and performance with application to human–computer interaction. *Human–Computer Interaction*, 12, 391–438.
Kitajima, M. & Polson, P. G. (1997). A comprehension-based model of explorations. *Human–Computer Interaction*, 12, 345–89.
Kosslyn, S. M. (1983). *Ghosts in the Mind's Machine*. New York: Norton.
Laird, J. E. (1986). Universal subgoaling. In J. E. Laird & P. S. Rosenbloom (Eds), *Universal Subgoaling and Chunking: The Automatic Generation and Learning of Goal Hierarchies* (pp. 1–131). Dordrecht, The Netherlands: Kluwer Academic.
Landauer, T. K. (1986). How much do people remember? Some estimates of the quantity of learned information in long-term memory. *Cognitive Science*, 10, 477–93.
Lane, D. M., Napier, H. A., Batsell, R. R. & Naman, J. L. (1993). Predicting the skilled use of hierarchical menus with the Keystroke-Level Model. *Human–Computer Interaction*, 8, 192.
Lohse, G. L. (1993). A cognitive model for understanding graphical perception. *Human–Computer Interaction*, 8, 353–88.
Marr, D. (1982). *Vision*. San Francisco: W. H. Freedman.
Meyer, D. E. & Kieras, D. E. (1997a). A computational theory of executive cognitive processes and multiple-task performance: part 1. Basic mechanisms. *Psychological Review*, 104, 3–65.
Meyer, D. E. & Kieras, D. E. (1997b). A computational theory of executive cognitive processes and multiple-task performance: part 2. Accounts of psychological refractory-period phenomena. *Psychological Review*.
Miller, G. A. (1956). The magical number seven plus or minus two: some limits on our capacity for processing information. *Psychological Review*, 63, 81–97.
Neisser, U. (1967). *Cognitive Psychology*. New York: Appleton-Crofts.

Newell, A. (1973a). Production systems: models of control structures. In W. G. Chase (Ed.), *Visual Information Processing* (pp. 283–308). New York: Academic Press.
Newell, A. (1973b). You can't play 20 questions with nature and win: projective comments on the paper of this symposium. In W. G. Chase (Ed.), *Visual Information Processing*. New York: Academic Press.
Newell, A. (1982). The knowledge level. *Artificial Intelligence*, 18, 87–127.
Newell, A. (1990). *Unified Theories of Cognition*. Cambridge, MA: Harvard University Press.
Newell, A. & Card, S. K. (1985). The prospects for a psychological science in human–computer interactions. *Human–Computer Interaction*, 2, 251–67.
Newell, A. & Simon, H. A. (1972). *Human Problem Solving*. Englewood Cliffs, NJ: Prentice Hall.
Nilsen, E. L. (1991). *Perceptual–Motor Control in Human–Computer Interaction* (Tech. Rep. 37). Ann Arbor, MI: Cognitive Science and Machine Intelligence Laboratory, University of Michigan.
Olson, J. R. & Olson, G. M. (1990). The growth of cognitive modeling in human–computer interaction since GOMS. *Human–Computer Interaction*, 5, 221–65.
Payne, S. J. & Green, T. R. G. (1986). Task–action grammars: a model of the mental representation of task languages. *Human–Computer Interaction*, 2, 93–133.
Pirolli, P. (1991). Effects of examples and their explanations in a lesson on recursion: a production system analysis. *Cognition and Instruction*, 8, 207–59.
Pirolli, P. (1997). Computational models of information scent-following in a very large browsable text collection. *Proceedings of the Conference on Human Factors in Computing Systems, CHI '97* (pp. 3–10). Atlanta, GA.
Polson, P. G., Bovair, S. & Kieras, D. (1987). Transfer between text editors. In J. M. Carroll & P. Tanner (Eds), *Proceedings of CHI '87 Human Factors in Computing Systems and Graphics Interface Conference* (pp. 27–32). New York.
Rosenbloom, P. & Newell, A. (1987). Learning by chunking: a production system model of practice. In D. Klahr, P. Langley & R. Neches (Eds), *Production System Models of Learning and Development*. Cambridge, MA: MIT Press.
Russo, J. E. (1978). Adaptation of cognitive processes to eye movements. In J. W. Senders, D. F. Fisher & R. A. Monty (Eds), *Eye Movements and Higher Psychological Functions*. Hillsdale, NJ: Lawrence Erlbaum.
Ryle, G. (1949). *The Concept of Mind*. London: Hutchinson.
Simon, H. A. (1955). A behavioral model of rational choice. *Quarterly Journal of Economics*, 69, 99–118.
Simon, H. A. (1974). How big is a chunk? *Science*, 183, 482–8.
Singley, M. K. & Anderson, J. R. (1989). *Transfer of Cognitive Skill*. Cambridge, MA: Harvard University Press.
Sternberg, S. (1969). Memory-scanning: mental processes revealed by reaction time experiments. *Acta Psychologica*, 30, 276–315.

Chapter 16

Knowledge Elicitation

Nancy J. Cooke
New Mexico State University

In this chapter the enterprise of knowledge elicitation, the process of explicating domain-specific knowledge underlying human performance, and the cognitive issues that surround this practice are reviewed. Knowledge elicitation had its formal beginnings in the mid to late 1980s in the context of knowledge engineering for expert systems. Expert systems are computer programs that embody domain-specific knowledge and that perform (e.g. decision making, problem solving, design) at levels typical of human experts, but not necessarily in exactly the same manner as human experts. Knowledge engineering is broadly defined here as the process of building knowledge-based systems or applications. These include expert systems, as well as intelligent tutoring systems, adaptive user interfaces, and even knowledge-oriented selection and training devices.

The process of knowledge engineering involves knowledge acquisition which includes knowledge elicitation and other activities such as knowledge explication and conceptual modeling (Regoczei & Hirst, 1992), as well as the coding of the resulting knowledge, the design of a usable interface, and the testing and evaluation of this interface (Diaper, 1989b). Thus, knowledge elicitation is a subprocess of knowledge acquisition, which is itself a subprocess of knowledge engineering. In order to fit knowledge elicitation into the larger context of applied cognitive psychology it is necessary to understand its brief evolution.

SOME BACKGROUND

The push for expert systems in the 1970s and 1980s was motivated by (a) the technological capability, (b) the growing specialization of the workforce and

Handbook of Applied Cognition, Edited by F. T. Durso, R. S. Nickerson, R. W. Schvaneveldt, S. T. Dumais, D. S. Lindsay and M. T. H. Chi.

cognitive complexity of jobs (Howell & Cooke, 1989), (c) the interest in creating artificial intelligence in machines, and (d) rejection of alternative general problem-solving approaches (Feigenbaum, 1989). Instead of relying on search strategies, this new form of machine intelligence was "knowledge-based" or powered by facts and rules. The realization that "knowledge is power," triggered a flurry of interest in knowledge, and particularly in its elicitation and representation (Feigenbaum, 1989). Meanwhile, parallel developments in the psychology of problem solving were taking place. It was becoming clear that expert problem solving could not be attributed to strategy, as much as to domain-specific facts and rules (Glaser & Chi, 1988).

With a new focus on knowledge, questions regarding knowledge elicitation became central to both applied and basic endeavors. How can knowledge be effectively elicited from an expert? Interestingly, the typical (or thought to be typical) transfer of cognitive theory and principles to application did not hold here. Although the cognitive literature had addressed the issue of knowledge, the focus was largely on the question of representation and various theoretical conceptualizations of knowledge structure such as semantic networks, scripts, prototypes, and schemata (e.g. Anderson, 1995; Best, 1995, chapters 5 & 6). The most relevant cognitive research on expert problem solving and memory organization did not directly address elicitation, but provided some hints or guidelines that would help guide the future development of the methods. Additionally, the favored cognitive measures of reaction time and error rate were inadequate as a solution for knowledge elicitation (e.g. Bailey & Kay, 1987).

Thus, researchers and practitioners began to develop knowledge elicitation methods. Many of these techniques were adapted from cognitive methods or methods in other disciplines including anthropology, ethnography, counseling, education, and business management (Boose & Gaines, 1988, 1990; Cooke, 1994; Diaper, 1989a; Hoffman, 1987). Although initial conceptualizations of knowledge elicitation portrayed the process as one of direct "extraction" (e.g. LaFrance, 1992), it quickly became obvious that the problem was not so simple (Cullen & Bryman, 1988). Error and bias were common, and experts' verbal reports and intuitions were often flawed. Thus, more recent conceptualizations of knowledge elicitation view the process as one of constructing a model of the expert's knowledge – the outcome of which may reflect reality to varying degrees (Compton & Jansen, 1990; Ford & Adams-Webber, 1992).

These methodological developments and applied questions fueled research in cognitive psychology and the new field of cognitive engineering (Vicente, 1997; Woods & Roth, 1988). The term "cognitive engineering" is not new. It was introduced by Don Norman (1986) in the context of designing human–computer interfaces. More recently this term has been broadly adopted by those who address applied problems in design and training in which issues of human cognition are critical. This work is also referred to as "applied cognitive psychology" and "cognitive ergonomics." However, the Human Factors and Ergonomics Society technical group, formed in 1996, refers to itself as the "Cognitive Engineering and Decision Making" group. The genesis of cognitive engineering has been in response to the need for research addressing cognition in complex contexts, such as those found in knowledge engineering applications. Similarly, Hoffman, Shadbolt,

Burton & Klein (1995) point out that the study of expertise "has recently gained impetus in part because of the advent of expert systems and related technologies for preserving knowledge" (p. 129). These new developments in research and methodologies no longer neatly fall within the boundaries of the basic or applied.

Concurrently, other applications have surfaced that demand knowledge elicitation, including intelligent tutoring systems, adaptive computer interfaces, and intelligent agents. In addition, developments in human resources and the increasing cognitive complexity of many jobs have led researchers and practitioners in that area to a stronger focus on the cognitive components of job performance (Howell & Cooke, 1989). Training and selection research has looked to knowledge elicitation techniques for answers. Note that unlike performance-critical applications such as expert systems, applications like training that go beyond knowledge use to the transfer of knowledge, require more attention to the psychological validity of the elicited knowledge. Similar emphases on knowledge and cognition underlying complex task performance has surfaced in other areas, such as human–computer interaction, human factors work (e.g. Benysh, Koubek & Calvez, 1993) and cognitive engineering in general. These areas have also made use of knowledge elicitation methods.

This wide array of applications broadened the early focus on knowledge to include other aspects of cognition such as decision making, perception, planning, and design processes. The practitioner's tool kit was once again inadequate, and work was and is being devoted to developing additional methods. Many of these methods were also adapted from cognitive psychology, and are referred to as cognitive task analysis, cognitive engineering, cognitive modeling, or naturalistic decision making methods (e.g. Hutchins, 1995; Klein, 1989; Randel, Pugh & Wyman, 1996; Sundstrom, 1991; Woods & Roth, 1988). Although terms are different, there is substantial overlap among the methods and tools associated with them. In this chapter the focus is on knowledge elicitation, but many of the methods that are described are also used by those who take this broader focus. Before describing these methods and some of the newer developments in knowledge elicitation, the major cognitive issues that have influenced knowledge elicitation are reviewed.

COGNITIVE INFLUENCES

Although mainstream cognitive research and theory offered little in the way of direct solutions to knowledge elicitation, they were nonetheless influential in the development of methods for knowledge elicitation, particularly in the areas of problem-solving expertise and knowledge representation. In addition to the influence from these two content areas, was the influence of verbal report methodology. In this section, each of these three influences is briefly reviewed.

Problem-solving Expertise

Early research on problem solving in the information processing tradition was dedicated to investigating strategies that individuals used to solve problems such as Tower of Hanoi puzzles, or anagrams (Greeno, 1978). This research helped to identify some general strategies of problem solving, such as means–ends analysis and working backwards, and to highlight the importance of problem representation. Then, in the mid 1970s a new problem-solving paradigm emerged that focused on expert problem solving of complex tasks such as chess, bridge, geometry, and physics. In their seminal work, deGroot (1966) and Chase & Simon (1973) found that expertise in chess was associated not so much with search strategies like looking ahead, as with skilled pattern recognition based on the storage of many specific chess configurations in memory. Additionally, it was found that the way in which domain-specific knowledge was organized in memory was critical for expert problem solving. For instance, Chi, Feltovich & Glaser (1981) found that experts in physics categorized physics problems according to laws or principles of physics, whereas those with less physics experience categorized the same problems according to the surface features of the problem. From this result, Chi et al. (1981) inferred that the physics experts represented physics problems according to deep principles, whereas less experienced individuals represented physics problems at a surface level.

A flood of research on expertise followed that replicated the now famous expertise effect (i.e. the finding that experts recall domain-related information better than novices) across many domains (e.g. Engle & Bukstel, 1978; Reitman, 1976; Sloboda, 1976). Other research on expertise explored more fully the actual distinctions between expert and novice knowledge organization (e.g. Cooke & Schvaneveldt, 1988; Gillan, Breedin & Cooke, 1992; Housner, Gomez & Griffey, 1993a; Schvaneveldt, Durso, Goldsmith, Breen, Cooke, Tucker & DeMaio, 1985). One side-effect of experimentation in this area was the need to more clearly define expertise or at least to distinguish experts from novices. This issue also surfaces in knowledge engineering applications (Hoffman et al., 1995) and is addressed in this volume (see Charness & Schultetus, 1999, this volume). Although some of the methodology used in the early expertise experiments to explore knowledge organization (e.g. card sorting, relatedness ratings, think-aloud problem solving) has been adopted by knowledge engineers, the major impact of research on problem-solving expertise was that it provided scientific justification for the knowledge engineering enterprise. That is, it provided evidence for the importance of knowledge, in terms of both its content and structure, for expert performance.

More recently, the literature on problem-solving expertise has included tasks that go beyond puzzles, games, and academic domains to include complex job-related tasks such as radiology (Myles-Worsley, Johnston & Simons, 1988) and avionics troubleshooting (Rowe, Cooke, Hall & Halgren, 1996). This new emphasis has been led by applied researchers, faced with understanding these more complex problems. Indeed, the expertise associated with complex real-world tasks is often impossible for basic researchers to study in factorial experiments due to problems with obtaining experts or studying realistic task scenarios in the laboratory. This is a case, therefore, in which a true synergy is required between the basic and applied in order to understand the complexities of expert problem solving.

Thus problem-solving research, in its attempts to describe and explain problem-solving expertise, revealed the importance of domain-specific knowledge and the organization of this knowledge. This emphasis dovetails nicely with research focusing on knowledge representation.

Knowledge Representation

As the importance of knowledge representation for expert problem solving was recognized, other research in artificial intelligence and the psychology of memory focused on knowledge representation or how meaningful associations are organized in memory (e.g. Minsky, 1975). One of the first network models of memory organization was proposed by Quillian (1969), an artificial intelligence researcher interested in creating a program that could understand language. Psychologists elaborated upon Quillian's model, tested it empirically (Collins & Quillian, 1969) and added processing assumptions (Collins & Loftus, 1975). Other network models of memory organization were developed, as well as feature models in which concepts were represented in terms of a feature list (Smith, Shoben & Rips, 1974).

In order to test these models and to explore knowledge representation empirically, several existing psychometric scaling techniques were employed, including cluster analysis (e.g. Johnson, 1967) and multidimensional scaling (e.g. Shepard 1962a, b). Other techniques were developed specifically for this purpose (e.g. Pathfinder network scaling: Schvaneveldt, 1990; Schvaneveldt, Durso & Dearholt, 1989). These methods were also being used to study knowledge representation underlying expert problem solving (e.g. Schvaneveldt et al., 1985). Knowledge engineers adopted these methods, and others like them such as concept mapping (Sanderson, McNeese & Zaff, 1994) and the repertory grid technique (e.g. Shaw & Gaines, 1987, 1989) for the purpose of knowledge elicitation. However, because the theoretical goals did not focus on elicitation, but rather representation, the methods required some additional tinkering. For instance, in regard to Pathfinder network scaling, it was necessary to develop methods to elicit an initial set of domain concepts (Cooke, 1989) and to identify the meaning of links in a Pathfinder network (Cooke, 1992b). In sum, the theoretical work on memory organization, the methods developed for exploring it empirically, and the concomitant importance of knowledge representation for expert problem solving, provided impetus for new methodological developments in knowledge elicitation.

One other related issue that surfaced simultaneously in both basic and applied camps has to do with the differential access hypothesis (Hoffman et al., 1995) or the assumption that different knowledge elicitation methods may tap different types of knowledge. Along these lines, the phenomena of dissociations in memory performance under different test conditions is a well-studied topic in memory research today (e.g. Roediger, 1990.) Further, some knowledge measures may tap knowledge that is more predictive of performance than others. For example, Broadbent, Fitzgerald & Broadbent (1986) have found dissociations between verbal reports and performance. Similarly, Cooke and Breedin (1994) found dissociations between individuals' written explanations for physics trajectory problems and their predictions of those trajectories. Together, these results suggest that all measures of knowledge are not equal and that, in particular, they may differ in terms of the connection between knowledge and performance.

The connection between knowledge and performance is critical in applications that utilize knowledge to improve or aid performance (e.g. training, expert systems). It has thus become important to map out the relationship between elicitation method and type of knowledge and performance. For example, Rowe et al. (1996) compared various knowledge elicitation methods used to elicit knowledge about an avionics system (i.e. mental models). They found that a relatedness rating method and a hierarchical concept listing interview were superior to diagramming and think-aloud methods at eliciting knowledge that corresponded to avionics troubleshooting performance. Some general assumptions (some untested) about the type of knowledge elicited by various methods is presented later in this chapter in the context of the methods.

One way to systematize the comparison of the numerous knowledge elicitation methods available is to identify one or more dimensions along which they differ. Questions about type of knowledge elicited and connection to performance can then be addressed for these unifying dimensions. One such dimension is the degree to which the method relies on verbal reports, with methods like think-aloud and interviews relying heavily on them compared to other methods such as observations and relatedness ratings. Some cognitive issues relevant to verbal reports shed some light on this dimension.

Verbal Reports

Verbal reports have been used in research ranging from decision making and text comprehension to applications ranging from accounting to user testing in computer systems (Ericsson & Simon, 1996). Although their use in some form dates back to the early 1900s in the heyday of structuralism, verbal reports have been revived recently as a legitimate form of psychological data after a hiatus during the stimulus–response era of psychology.

Throughout this history, verbal report methodologies have undergone much scrutiny. Criticisms of verbal reports have been around as long as verbal reports themselves (e.g. Nisbett & Wilson, 1977). Although some of the earlier critiques were misguided or incorrect, most recent criticisms are based on the grounds that "the TA [think-aloud] procedure changes subjects' thought processes, gives only an incomplete report of them, and mainly reports information that is independent of, hence irrelevant to, the actual mechanisms of thinking" (Ericsson & Simon, 1996, p. 61). Many of these arguments, however, lose their steam when one places verbal reports in the context of other forms of behavioral data, each of which has strengths, weaknesses, and methodological pitfalls.

Ericsson & Simon (1996) have developed a theory of verbalization processes under think-aloud instructions and have been able to account for most of the data suggesting verbal interference, completeness, and relevance within this theoretical framework. Furthermore, their theory suggests conditions under which verbal report procedures should succeed or fail. For instance, verbal reports are not as effective for eliciting knowledge when the problem is novel or the reporter has low verbal ability or is inhibited in some way. Guidelines such as these are relevant to the use of verbal reports by knowledge engineers and are highlighted later in this chapter. Too often, however, practitioners are unaware of or, for practical reasons, fail to adhere to these recommendations, and it is in these cases that the knowledge elicited using verbal report methodology should be questioned.

Summary

Research in cognitive psychology has been influential in the development of knowledge elicitation methods. This research has demonstrated the centrality of knowledge in human performance and, specifically, the importance of the content and structure of knowledge and the context surrounding elicitation of knowledge. Further, some methodologies for studying knowledge organization and utilizing verbal report data have been adopted and adapted by those interested in knowledge elicitation.

In the next section, four groupings of knowledge elicitation techniques are described. Each grouping is illustrated by way of a specific example of knowledge elicitation for the design of an expert system in the area of student advising.

KNOWLEDGE ELICITATION METHODS

Reviews of knowledge elicitation methods and various categorization schemes for these methods abound (Benysh et al., 1993; Boose, 1989; Boose & Bradshaw, 1987; Cooke, 1994; Cordingley, 1989; Geiwitz, Klatsky & McCloskey, 1988; Geiwitz, Kornell & McCloskey, 1990; Hoffman, 1989; Hoffman et al., 1995; Kitto & Boose, 1989; McGraw & Harbison-Briggs, 1989; Meyer & Booker, 1990; Olson & Biolsi, 1991; Olson & Rueter, 1987; Shadbolt & Burton, 1990; Shaw & Woodward, 1989; Wielinga, Schreiber & Breuker, 1992). This preponderance of reviews is probably a reaction to the eclectic nature of the body of methods and the tendency for practitioners to develop methods specifically suited to their application, often with little documentation of their efforts.

In this section, four categories of knowledge elicitation methods are identified and briefly described. Recent methodological developments associated with a particular category are also highlighted. Within each grouping there are a number of knowledge elicitation methods and variations on individual methods. Space precludes the description of each specific method and the variations within each category (for details, see Cooke, 1994, or McGraw & Harbison-Briggs, 1989). Instead, in this chapter, breadth is traded for depth. In particular, each knowledge elicitation category is illustrated through an enumeration of the procedural steps involved in applying a single method within that category to a hypothetical problem. The problem involves the development of an expert system that gives advice to university students regarding course registration. The system should be competent in the mundane aspects of advising such as degree requirements, course availability, and scheduling, as well as some of the more expert issues such as career considerations, course content, and course substitution. Specifically, the illustration focuses on the knowledge elicitation aspect of the development of this system in which knowledge is elicited about university advising from experts (professors, advising staff, experienced students). Although the domain of university advising is not as technologically complex as some other potential knowledge elicitation applications (e.g. avionics troubleshooting, nuclear plant operation), it is assumed that most readers would have some experience or knowledge within this domain, and would therefore be less likely to lose the knowledge elicitation message in the terminology and technical details of the example.

Throughout this section, it is important to keep in mind that due to the wide ranging problems, domains, tasks, and knowledge types, multiple knowledge elicitation methods are warranted for nearly any problem. As mentioned previously, different elicitation methods may tap different types of knowledge (Hoffman et al., 1995), not all of which may correspond to task performance (Rowe et al., 1996). Equally important is the fact that there is no single definitive procedure for applying each of the methods. Although a method and an associated procedure is specified for the hypothetical problem, there are most assuredly other methods and procedures that would also be reasonable. Knowledge elicitation is a modeling enterprise and the methods can be thought of as tools to facilitate the modeling process. These tools may need to be modified to fit the specific situation.

Observations

Knowledge elicitation often begins with observations of task performance within the domain of interest. Observations can provide a global impression of the domain, can help to generate an initial conceptualization of the domain, and can identify any constraints or issues to be dealt with during later phases of knowledge elicitation. Observations can occur in the natural setting, thus providing initial glimpses of actual behavior that can be used for later development of contrived tasks and other materials for more structured knowledge elicitation methods. However, there are some tasks that cannot be observed in the natural settings (e.g. flying a one-seater aircraft) and in these cases it may be necessary to observe performance in a simulated context or through use of a contrived task (Hoffman et al., 1995). Aside from where they occur, observational methods also vary in terms of what is observed (ranging from everything to specific predefined events), the observer's role (ranging from passive and nonintrusive to participatory), and the method of recording (writing, video, photos, audio). See Hoffman (1987), Meyer (1992), and Suen & Ary (1989) for additional information on observational methods.

Observational methods, like other knowledge elicitation methods, are associated with cost–benefit tradeoffs. For instance, on the benefit side, observations tend to interfere minimally with task performance. On the other hand, this is only the case if the observer is nonintrusive. Furthermore, observations can be a rich source of data; however, the interpretation of the data can become unwieldy.

The most recent innovations in this area come from adopting specific observational methods used by other fields such as anthropology and ethnography

(Hutchins, 1995; Suchman & Trigg, 1991). Of most relevance, video analysis tools such as VANNA (Harrison & Baecker, 1991) and MacSHAPA (Sanderson et al., 1994; Sanderson, Scott, Johnston, Mainzer, Watanabe & James, 1994) have been developed to facilitate data analysis of observational videos. In general, these tools allow a video recorder and monitor to interface with a computer so that while the video is viewed, events can be identified and coded or categorized using the computer. Later, summaries of events, their time course, and frequencies can be generated from the software record. In some cases, particular events on the video monitor can be located easily through the software record.

How would observational methods be applied to the advising problem? The most straightforward way to approach this and many other knowledge elicitation problems is to nonintrusively observe experts at work in their natural setting while taking notes with pen and paper. Several types of information should emerge from this process, including the scope of the advising task and the role that an expert system might play in this task. Through observation of several sessions, typical topics that are discussed in advising or specific questions that are asked of the advisor should surface. These topics and questions can provide or refine objectives for the knowledge-based system in terms of areas of knowledge (i.e. facts, rules, strategies) in which a knowledge-based system should be proficient. In other words, observations should provide guidance in generating or refining the functional requirements of the knowledge-based system.

A procedure for implementing the naturalistic passive observation in the context of the advising example is presented in Table 16.1. Some hypothetical data that may be collected in the course of applying this procedure are listed in Table 16.2.

Interviews

The most direct way to find out what someone knows is to ask them. This, in a nutshell, is the approach of unstructured interviews, the most frequently employed of all elicitation methods (Cullen & Bryman, 1988). Like observations, unstructured interviews are good for early stages of elicitation when the elicitor is trying to learn about the domain and does not yet know enough to set up indirect or highly structured tasks.

Unstructured interviews are free-flowing, whereas structured interviews have predetermined content or sequencing. The form of structured interview questions can range from open-ended (e.g. how, what, or why questions) which impose minimal constraints on the response, to closed (e.g. who, where, or when questions), imposing somewhat greater constraints (Shaw & Woodward, 1990). In addition, question content can vary greatly, each type targeting a slightly different type of knowledge (e.g. Ford & Wood, 1992; LaFrance, 1987). Thus, interviews can be used to elicit a wide range of knowledge types depending on the specific interview task.

There are many varieties of structured interviews. Some are focused on a specific topic such as a case, the task goals, or a diagram. For example, forward

Table 16.1 Procedure for using naturalistic passive observation to elicit advising information

1. Select advising experts and advisees and obtain consent from both to observe the advising sessions
2. Identify a room suitable for observations (i.e. natural, like the advisor's office). In addition, the setting should allow the observer to be positioned nonintrusively (e.g. in the back corner outside the field of view, or behind a one-way mirror)
3. Observe two to three advising sessions for each of two to three different advising experts
4. Take notes during the sessions. Record the basic events comprising the session with particular attention to topics discussed, questions raised, and problems encountered
5. Summarize notes by listing events, topics, questions, and problems and any other type of item that may help define the scope and functionality of the expert system
6. For each item recorded (e.g. topic: prerequisites, career guidance), note the frequency with which it was mentioned. This could be the overall number of times it was mentioned or number of sessions in which it was mentioned. The latter measure better controls for talkative dyads
7. Generate functional requirements for the expert system on the basis of these results

Table 16.2 A hypothetical sample of data collected using the procedure outlined in Table 16.1

Notes taken during a segment of one advising session (Step 4):

- Professor D. of History greets the student
- The student requests some help with selecting from three potential history electives
- Professor D. refreshes his memory on HIST 250 by reviewing a recent memo from the instructor of that course
- Professor D. summarizes the content of the three courses and asks the student to state how each corresponds to her interests in European History

Summary of notes (Steps 5 & 6):

- Professor events: greeting (1), information seeking (1), provide course summary (1), probes student interests (1)
- Questions: Selecting electives (1)

scenario simulation interviews, make use of verbal simulation to focus on a case. The expert is walked through the problem verbally by the elicitor who presents system and environmental events to which the expert is asked to respond (Cordingley, 1989; Diederich, Ruhmann & May, 1987; Grover, 1983). This procedure is likely to generate some conditional if–then rules, the "if" part stemming from the elicitor's problem statement and the "then" part comprising the expert's response. Other types of interviews such as goal decomposition involve having the expert work backwards from a single goal to the evidence leading to that goal. A result of this method can be a set of rules associated with each goal (Grover, 1983; Hart, 1986; Schacter & Heckerman, 1987). In other cases, the interview may focus on diagrams. These diagrams may reveal the structure of a task or system. For instance, the elicitor may have the expert draw information flow or functional diagrams (Hall, Gott & Pokorny, 1994), or charts of task activities (Geiwitz et al., 1988), or system state diagrams (Bainbridge, 1979). The information elicited may reveal system or task models held by the experts.

Other structured interview techniques are less focused on a specific type of interview material and instead suggest an interview procedure. The "teachback" method, for example, is a technique in which the expert explains something to the elicitor, who in turn explains the same thing back to the expert for verification. This process continues until the expert is satisfied with the elicitor's explanation (Johnson & Johnson, 1987). This method serves to bring the elicitor up to date with the information in the knowledge base and the way it is presented. Another structured interview technique, the "twenty questions" method, involves having the expert try to guess a domain concept targeted by the elicitor. As in the traditional parlor game, the expert can ask the elicitor yes/no questions about the concept (Breuker & Wielinga, 1987; Cordingley, 1989; Grover, 1983; Shadbolt & Burton, 1990; Welbank, 1990). The yes/no questions that are asked reveal information about distinguishing attributes within the domain.

In general, structured interviews are thought to provide more constraints on the expert's responses and consequently more systematic coverage of the domain. The additional constraints also tend to facilitate the dialogue between the expert and the elicitor as compared to unstructured interviews. Although elicitor training in interview techniques is valuable regardless of interview type, it is much more critical for unstructured interviews than for structured interviews. On the down side, structured interviews require more preparation time and more knowledge of the domain than unstructured interviews.

Interviews, whether structured or unstructured, are relatively easy to administer compared to other knowledge elicitation methods. However, the tradeoff occurs at the data analysis and interpretation phases. The tasks of summarizing and drawing conclusions from open-ended interview responses are not trivial. Depending on the degree of structure inherent in the interview and the amount of preplanning regarding questions that are asked, the analysis of the responses may be relatively straightforward (i.e. frequencies of various responses, similarities of diagrams, lists of features). On the other hand, if the interview is unstructured or structured only slightly, tools and techniques used for observations and protocol analysis (described in the next section) can be helpful. If the interview is recorded on video, then video analysis tools may be used. If it is not taped, then it is still possible to develop and apply a code to audio or written transcripts. Pidgeon, Turner & Blockley (1991) recommend the use of "grounded theory" to analyze interview data. Grounded theory is social science's version of protocol analysis, in which conceptual models are generated from qualitative data.

Recent trends in knowledge elicitation interviews include the development of highly specific interview methodologies in the context of particular domains and problems that target very specific types of knowledge. For instance, the critical decision method (Klein, Calderwood & MacGregor, 1989) requires a series of questions to be asked about an important past event such as a near accident in the case of an aviation domain. This information is used to better understand decision making, and the focus on the specific and real case is said to facilitate elicitation. Another methodology labeled PARI (Hall et al., 1994) is associated with questions to get at each of four aspects of a problem (i.e. Precursors, Actions, Results, Interpretations) that are associated with declarative, procedural, and strategic knowledge. PARI has been used primarily for instructional design in the domain of avionics troubleshooting.

The method illustrated in the advising example is the forward scenario simulation structured interview method. As described previously, this method focuses on one or more cases which the elicitor provides to the expert in an initial form. The expert "walks through" the way in which each case would be handled. The elicitor provides information relevant to the scenario only as it is requested by the expert.

Using forward scenario simulation in the context of the advising example, one would expect to elicit from the expert the relation between relevant features of the situation such as the student's major, career plans, years in college, and grade-point-average and the advice given. These features could comprise the "if" part of some if–then rules. Sequential dependencies among these features may also surface in the order in which the expert requests particular information. This is the information that the knowledge-based system will have to request from the user. The responses of the expert to the information presented by the elicitor should also reveal some "then" parts of the if–then rules. Together, this information is needed by the expert system to give advice using a production rule architecture.

A procedure for implementing the forward scenario simulation in the context of the advising example is presented in Table 16.3. Some hypothetical data that may be collected in the course of applying this procedure are listed in Table 16.4.

Process Tracing

Process tracing involves the collection of sequential behavioral events and the analysis of the resulting event protocols so that inferences can be made about underlying cognitive processes. Thus, these methods are most often used to elicit procedural information, such as conditional rules used in decision making, or the order to which various cues are attended. The popular "think-aloud" technique in which verbal reports associated with task performance are collected and analyzed using protocol analysis is one variation on this general theme (vanSomeren, Barnard & Sandberg, 1994). However, in addition to verbal events, events can also take the form of eye movements, gestures, and other nonverbal behaviors (Altmann, 1974; Sachett, 1977, 1978; Sanderson, James & Seidler, 1989; Scherer & Ekman, 1982; VanHooff, 1982).

Verbal reports can vary in terms of their timing with the task, with concurrent reports occurring in conjunction with the task and retrospective reports occurring after the task (Elstein, Shulman & Sprafka, 1978; Johnson, Zualkerman & Garber, 1987). Ericsson & Simon (1996) recommend concurrent verbal reports over retrospective ones. A possible problem with retrospective reports is that the conditions associated with verbalization are likely to differ from those associated with task performance and, as a result, information processing may differ in the two cases. It is assumed that, the longer the interval between performance and reporting, the more prone the report is to this problem, with immediate retrospective reports being most similar to concurrent reports. Unfortunately, in

Table 16.3 Using a forward scenario simulation to elicit advising information

1. Develop a set of scenarios that represent cases with which the expert advisor typically deals. Each scenario should specify the case in as much detail as possible (i.e. student's background, scheduling details, course availability, etc.). This information may be constructed with the aid of another expert or from information recorded from actual advising sessions (the procedure in Table 16.1, for example)
2. For each scenario, create an initial problem statement in which only some of the case-relevant information is presented. The remaining information will be available only upon request by the expert
3. Pre-test the scenarios with other experts to determine (as much as possible) whether any critical information has been left unspecified
4. Enlist the participation and consent of several expert advisors
5. Describe the forward scenario simulation method to each expert using an example from another area (e.g. career counseling, tax advising)
6. Present the initial information from one scenario to the expert
7. Record the expert's comments (video, audio, or pen and paper), explicitly noting the information requested from the elicitor
8. Present information to the expert as requested, recording the information presented
9. Repeat steps 6 to 8 across the entire set of scenarios (the number depends on the scope of the cases that are targeted)
10. Repeat interviews across all experts. The number of experts depends on their availability and the degree of variability in the responses. If experts are generally in agreement regarding information requested, then little will be gained from additional interviews
11. List the information requested and the advice given across all experts and interviews
12. Organize the list into categories of information separating information requested from advice and noting any sequential dependencies
13. If there are any questions about certain categories, interview additional experts, focusing on these issues
14. Generate if–then rules
15. Show these rules to an expert for verification

applied settings, it is often difficult to obtain the report during task performance (e.g. in the case of air-to-air combat flight maneuvers or in the case of a task that is highly verbal such as our advising example), and in cases like these, practitioners have often attempted to re-enact the performance while collecting verbal reports, often with the aid of video. According to Ericsson & Simon's (1996) position, this practice should produce meaningful reports to the degree that the re-enactment captures the conditions and cognitive processing of the actual task.

Just as important as when the report is collected is how it is collected. Ericsson & Simon (1996) provide detailed procedures for collecting, analyzing, and interpreting verbal reports, including examples of instructions. Reports can be made by the person performing the task or by another individual who provides commentary on the task (Clarke, 1987). In addition, reports can differ in terms of instructions on what to report, and it is argued that only the current contents of consciousness can be accurately reported (Ericsson & Simon, 1996). This would rule out explanations or interpretations of specific thoughts or behaviors. In fact, many of the empirical results that demonstrate interference with verbal reports can be explained in terms of requiring individuals to do more than verbalize the current contents of consciousness (Ericsson & Simon, 1996). The general goal is

Table 16.4 A hypothetical sample of data collected using the procedure outlined in Table 16.3

Interview segment (Steps 6 & 8)	
Elicitor:	The advisee would like to switch majors from history to psychology and would like to know what courses are now required for a BA
Expert:	Well . . . I need to know the year in which the advisee entered the University
Elicitor:	Why?
Expert:	Because the requirements have changed over the years and the year of admission determines the requirements for each individual
Elicitor:	OK. The advisee was admitted in 1997. She is currently finishing her first year
Expert:	Then I need to know what courses she has taken this year
List of information (Step 11)	
Information requested: year of admission, courses taken	
Advice given: none at this point	

to avoid requiring individuals to provide anything in the report that could interfere with or change their thought processes. Instead, individuals should be asked only to verbalize that information that they attend to – that information that is currently heeded. Thus, information regarding perceptual and retrieval processes will not be directly elicited; neither will processes that are compiled or automated. Instead, if this information is of interest, then it would need to be inferred from the information that is elicited.

The data collected using process tracing methods, like observations and interview data, can be costly to analyze, although the results are typically rich in information. The data from verbal reports, for instance, require transcription, segmentation, coding, and summary. Other forms of event data such as on-line event logs collected from computer users also require coding and summary. It is the coding process that is especially labor-intensive. Coding involves categorizing units of the transcribed and segmented protocol. The nature of the categories or code depends on the purpose of the analysis. If the analysis was done to identify procedural rules underlying task performance, then the categories may first consist of condition and action, with subcategories based on type of condition or action under each. Codes can be hierarchical with different levels of abstraction being useful for different analytic purposes (see example in Table 16.6).

Recent advancements have been made to facilitate the analysis of process tracing data. Tools have been developed to facilitate the coding and later summary of verbal transcripts. The field of Exploratory Sequential Data Analysis or ESDA (Sanderson & Fisher, 1994) has recently emerged as a result of a need for better methods for analyzing sequential data of the type collected from video observation or verbal reports. For example, PRONET (PROcedural NETworks: Cooke, Neville & Rowe, 1996) is a method based on Pathfinder network scaling, in which sequential data can be reduced and represented in a graph in which nodes are events and links occur between contiguous events. Others have focused specifically on the identification of repeating patterns in the data (Siochi & Ehrich, 1991). The general goal of such methods is to summarize or reduce the data in a way that preserves its meaning, often providing some graphical way to visualize the data.

It is important to bear in mind that "process" is central to process tracing. That is, the methods are suited for identifying underlying process from data that are thought to reflect it. Therefore, although interviews can be transcribed and coded and frequencies of coded responses examined, the sequential nature of the results would not trace the interviewee's thought processes, but rather the process inherent in the interview itself (i.e. who said what when). Even frequencies with which concepts are mentioned in an interview may simply reflect idiosyncrasies of the interview. This is because think-aloud verbal reports are primarily monologues on that individual's thoughts, whereas interviews are more dialogues between elicitors and the experts in which responses are elicited by elicitor prompts.

Process tracing is illustrated in the context of the advising example using a retrospective think-aloud report procedure, prompted with video tape of performance. This retrospective approach is made necessary by the highly verbal nature of the advising session itself. That is, it is likely that concurrent verbal reports would interfere with the advising process. It is expected that the expert advisor would report the information currently heeded while viewing a video tape of the advising interview. In particular, this method would target conditional (if–then) rules, as well as general strategies applied in advising students.

A procedure for implementing the retrospective think-aloud method in the context of the advising example is presented in Table 16.5. Some hypothetical data that may be collected in the course of applying this procedure are listed in Table 16.6.

Conceptual Methods

Conceptual methods elicit and represent conceptual structure in the form of domain-related concepts and their interrelations. Several steps are generally required, each associated with a variety of methods (Cooke, 1994). The steps are:

1. elicitation of concepts through interviews or analysis of documentation
2. collection of relatedness judgments from one or more experts
3. reduction and representation of relatedness data
4. interpretation of the resulting representation.

Concept elicitation is a critical step upon which the others depend. Cooke (1989) identified four methods of identifying concepts (i.e. concept listing, step listing, chapter listing, and interview transcription) and found that each differed in terms of the quantity and type of concepts elicited. One of the best ways to determine whether the concepts are adequate is to construct a hypothetical structure or structures using the concepts. If, for instance, meaningful distinctions between expert and novice structures cannot be hypothesized using the concept set, then it is most likely inadequate.

Relatedness judgments can be collected from domain experts in a number of ways including pairwise relatedness ratings, sorting techniques, repertory grid, and frequency of co-occurrence (Zachary, Ryder & Purcell, 1990). Relatedness

Table 16.5 Using retrospective think-aloud verbal reports to elicit advising information

1. Determine how many sessions will be recorded. For the most complete coverage of domain rules, the number of advising sessions is not as critical as the range of cases represented in the set of sessions. With inadequate foresight into this issue it may be most prudent to videotape more sessions than are ultimately analyzed
2. Select advisors and advisees and obtain their consent to be tested and videotaped
3. Arrange equipment and room for advising sessions to be videotaped
4. For each session, explain purpose to advisor and advisee and then record on video the advising session. The experimenter should remain nonintrusive, but may take notes on obvious rules or strategies used
5. Invite advisor back at a later time to view the tape while thinking aloud
6. Give each advisor practice in the think-aloud technique using an unrelated task like mental addition, emphasizing the difference between reporting thoughts and reporting explanations of those thoughts
7. Start the videotape
8. Be prepared to remind the advisor to keep talking, but in all other ways the experimenter should remain nonintrusive. Simple prompts like "keep talking" or "think aloud please" are usually adequate
9. Record the verbal protocol (audiotape is sufficient)
10. Repeat Steps 6 to 9 with the appropriate advisors for the set of representative interviews
11. Using a protocol analysis tool like MacSHAPA (Sanderson, Scott et al., 1994), enter the verbal protocol text and begin to generate labels for categories that focus on variations in rules and strategies
12. Iteratively refine the coding scheme using progressively more segments of verbal protocol
13. Identify rules and strategies that were applied. The analysis software may reveal frequent event transitions that may also reflect rules
14. Compile the list of rules and have an expert advisor verify their accuracy

ratings involve presenting pairs of concepts to the expert and requesting a quantitative estimate of the relatedness of the two concepts, usually using a scale that ranges from slightly to very related. This method can become costly in terms of expert time when the number of concepts exceeds 30. In these cases, a sorting method is advised in which concepts are grouped by the expert into piles based on relatedness, and relatedness estimates are then derived in terms of co-occurrence of concepts in the piles (Cordingley, 1989; Geiwitz et al., 1990; Miller, 1969; Schweikert, Burton, Taylor, Cortlett, Shadbolt & Hedgecock, 1987).

An alternative method is the repertory grid approach in which a set of dimensions focuses the ratings (Boose, 1986; Bradshaw, Ford, Adams-Webber & Boose, 1993; Cordingley, 1989; Fransella & Bannister, 1977; Gaines & Shaw, 1992; Mancuso & Shaw, 1988; Shaw, 1980; Shaw & Gaines, 1987, 1989; Zachary et al., 1990). That is, ratings are given for each concept (or element) along each of a set of dimensions (or constructs). So, for instance, the elements may be cars and the constructs along which the cars are rated may be dimensions such as gas mileage, maintenance, and cost. Similarity between a pair of concepts can then be derived by computing the summed difference or correlation between the ratings for each concept.

Once relatedness estimates have been collected they can be summarized using a number of psychometric scaling methods such as MDS (multidimensional

Table 16.6 A hypothetical sample of data collected using the procedure outlined in Table 16.5

Transcribed Protocol Segment (Steps 7 to 9)
"OK . . . This is the part where the student tells me what courses they plan to take. I usually ask the student to back up and tell me about their goals (that is, their major, expected degree date, career visions, etc.). So . . . now the student tells me that they are a computer science major interested in a high-paying career in software design and that they hope to graduate in one year. The "one-year" plan immediately suggests to me that I better do a quick degree check to make sure that the requirements for the degree have been met. I do this on my computer. This is what I'm doing now . . . meanwhile, I'm thinking that this student needs to first complete the requirements for their degree before pursuing the electives they've planned to take next semester. Here . . . this is really typical . . . the student has forgotten the foreign language requirement and therefore needs to enroll in an introductory foreign language course. The student looks despondent and I'm thinking that maybe there is some other way to satisfy this requirement . . ."

Segmented and Coded Protocol Sample (Step 11, code is capitalized)
CONDITION: STUDENT GIVES INFO → COURSE PLAN
OK . . . This is the part where the student tells me what courses they plan to take.

ACTION: ASK ABOUT STUDENT GOALS
I usually ask the student to back up and tell me about their goals (that is, their major, expected degree date, career visions, etc.).

CONDITION: STUDENT GIVES INFO → CS MAJOR, SOFTWARE DESIGN CAREER, ONE YEAR ANTICIPATED GRADUATION
So . . . now the student tells me that they are a computer science major interested in a high-paying career in software design and that they hope to graduate in one year.

ACTION: DO DEGREE CHECK (cued by one-year for expected degree)
The "one-year" plan immediately suggests to me that I better do a quick degree check to make sure that the requirements for the degree have been met. I do this on my computer. This is what I'm doing now . . . meanwhile,

THOUGHTS: NEED FOR DEGREE CHECK
I'm thinking that this student needs to first complete the requirements for their degree before pursuing the electives they've planned to take next semester.

CONDITION: INCOMPLETE DEGREE CHECK → MISSING LANGUAGE REQUIREMENT
Here . . . this is really typical . . . the student has forgotten the foreign language requirement and therefore needs to enroll in an introductory foreign language course.

ACTION (IMPLIED): RECOMMEND COURSE → INTRO FOREIGN LANGUAGE
CONDITION: STUDENT NONVERBAL → DESPONDENT
The student looks despondent and

THOUGHTS: POTENTIAL ALTERNATIVES
I'm thinking that maybe there is some other way to satisfy this requirement . . .

Rules and strategies (Step 13)
- If student initially describes course plan then ask student about goals
- If the student expresses an anticipated degree in a year or less do a degree check
- If degree check is incomplete, then suggest a course to complete it
- If the student is despondent try to find alternatives

scaling: Kruskal, 1977; Kruskal & Wish, 1978; Shepard 1962a, b), Pathfinder network scaling (Schvaneveldt, 1990; Schvaneveldt et al., 1989) or cluster analysis (Corter & Tversky, 1986; Johnson, 1967; Lewis, 1991; Shepard & Arabie, 1979). MDS results in a spatial layout of concepts along dimensions thought to represent features which differentiate the concepts. Pathfinder, on the other hand, results in a graphical structure in which concepts are represented as nodes, and relations as links connecting the nodes. In addition, representations similar to those derived using the methods described above can be generated more directly by having the expert draw the graph or some other representation of a set of concepts (e.g. Olson & Rueter, 1987; Thordsen, 1991). In general, these methods reduce the set of relatedness judgments to a graphical form that is easier to visualize. The resulting representations can then be interpreted qualitatively and quantitatively. For instance, the dimensions represented by MDS can be interpreted qualitatively as features which distinguish concepts, or quantitatively in order to compare two or more individuals according to how concepts are weighted differently along the dimensions.

Conceptual methods have been used to elicit knowledge in order to improve user interface design (McDonald, Dayton & McDonald, 1988; Roske-Hofstrand & Paap, 1986), guide the development of training programs (Rowe et al., 1996), and understand expert–novice differences (Cooke & Schvaneveldt, 1988; Gillan et al., 1992; Housner et al., 1993a; Schvaneveldt et al., 1985). They are considered indirect in that experts are not asked to comment directly on domain facts and rules, but, instead, this information is inferred through their judgments of conceptual relatedness. Some have argued that these methods result in an overly narrow focus that may not relate to performance (Geiwitz et al., 1990). However, recent research (Rowe et al., 1996) has indicated that distinctions between avionics technicians based on Pathfinder network structures of system components, corresponded to performance on a verbal troubleshooting task. Other work has investigated the validity and stability of the outcome of these types of measures with generally favorable results (Cooke, 1992a; Cooke, Durso & Schvaneveldt, 1986; Gammack, 1990; Ricci, Blickensderfer, Cannon-Bowers & Sagi, 1996; Rowe et al., 1996; Rowe, Cooke, Neville & Schacherer, 1992).

Recent research in this area has focused on comparison and assessment using the conceptual structures. For instance, Goldsmith & Davenport (1990) have developed a measure of Pathfinder network similarity based on proportion of shared links and this measure has been used to compare student structures to instructor structures in a classroom context. It is assumed that students who are most like their more experienced counterparts would also be most likely to excel at task performance. Indeed, this assumption has been verified in various classroom domains (Goldsmith, Johnson & Acton, 1991; Housner, Gomez & Griffey, 1993b), and in avionics troubleshooting (Rowe et al., 1996).

In order to make an assessment based on conceptual structures, it is first necessary to derive a referent structure – an expert or ideal structure against which other structures can be compared. Referents can be derived logically by constructing an ideal network structure based on an analysis of the task or an expert's understanding of the task (e.g. Cooke et al., 1996). Unfortunately, not all domains lend themselves to a logical analysis, and in these cases it may be best to derive an empirical referent using relatedness judgments from one or more high performers or experts (e.g. Cooke et al., 1996). Interestingly, there are cases in which knowledge structures are most predictive of performance when assessed by comparison to a high-performing intermediate than an expert referent (Rowe et al. 1996). In other words, the best avionics troubleshooters at beginning levels have knowledge structures that look more like a very good intermediate than an expert troubleshooter.

Interpretations of conceptual structures of groups of individuals can be based on an average of the relatedness judgments of the individuals in that group (as long as interparticipant correlations indicate that the group is cohesive). In cases in which there are discrepancies among individuals, major distortions in the representation can result (Ashly, Maddox & Lee, 1994). In circumstances such as these, the INDSCAL (individual differences scaling) MDS procedure (Carroll & Chang, 1970) can be used, or in the case of network representations, aggregates can be formed by adding or deleting links in the referent network on the basis of that link's presence or absence in the majority of individual networks. Aggregate links can also be weighted according to number of experts who have that link.

Conceptual methods are illustrated in the advising example using pairwise relatedness ratings and Pathfinder network analysis. The resulting network structure is expected to yield information about an advisor's conceptual structure for a set of university courses. In particular, the analysis should reveal courses that are associated to one another and more general structural features that characterize the set.

A procedure for implementing the relatedness ratings and Pathfinder analysis in the context of the advising example is presented in Table 16.7. Some hypothetical data that may be collected in the course of applying this procedure are listed in Table 16.8 and Figure 16.1.

Summary

The groupings described in this section embrace the majority of knowledge elicitation techniques available. However, there are many more techniques per grouping and variations on techniques than could be described in the space of this chapter. The procedures illustrated in the context of the advising application represent only one of many potential approaches.

In general, knowledge elicitation techniques are capable of providing rich information regarding the concepts, relations, facts, rules, and strategies relevant to the domain in question. The techniques differ in terms of their procedures, as well as their emphases on one type of knowledge or another. No technique is guaranteed to result in a complete and accurate representation of an expert's knowledge, although the goal is to model the expert's knowledge, not to extract or reproduce it in its entirety. The major drawback of these methods is that they can be costly. Rich data are associated with lengthy data collection sessions, unwieldy data analysis, and interpretation difficulties. Fortunately, recent methodological developments facilitate the process so that it can be more readily

Table 16.7 Using relatedness ratings and Pathfinder network scaling to elicit advising information

1. Locate and obtain consent from several advisors (around 6 to 10). Although this analysis can be performed on ratings obtained from a single advisor, it may be interesting to collect ratings from multiple advisors and examine cross-advisor differences
2. Generate a list of 25 to 30 courses that are representative of the university courses within the advisors' domains of expertise with the aid of another advisor or from records of advising sessions
3. Obtain or write a computer program to randomly present pairs of courses to each advisor. It is typical to present each pair once (in one direction only) resulting in a total of $(N(N-1))/2$ pairs, where N is equal to the total number of courses. The presentation order of courses in each pair should also be counterbalanced across advisors
4. For each advisor, first present the complete list of courses to the advisor so that the scope of the courses is clear. During this step, identify any courses with which the advisor is unfamiliar. Several unfamiliar courses, especially across multiple advisors may indicate nonrepresentative courses
5. Have advisors each rate the pairs for relatedness on a scale that runs from unrelated to related (a 5 to 10 point scale is typical). Sometimes a discrete option of "unrelated" is also included, as it has been shown that individuals do not discriminate well at the unrelated end of the scale (Roske-Hofstrand & Paap, 1990)
6. For each advisor (and as interparticipant correlation warrants, for the advisors as a group), submit the relatedness ratings (or the mean ratings in the case of the group) to Pathfinder (KNOT software)
7. Use default parameters that relate to minimal network complexity (i.e. r = infinite and q = number of concepts −1). These can be altered under specific conditions (see Schvaneveldt, 1990)
8. Specify data type (similarities or distances depending on rating program data format)
9. Examine the resulting network(s), moving nodes as necessary using the KNOT tools to make the graph more legible
10. Using the similarity metric in the KNOT program, quantitatively compare the advisor networks. In addition, compare them visually for qualitative differences
11. With the aid of an expert advisor, attempt to label the links with a specific relation
12. Identify common features that relate courses and any structural properties of the set of courses

applied to time-critical settings. Additional recent developments in knowledge elicitation are discussed in the next section.

NEW DIRECTIONS

Having amassed methods for eliciting knowledge, the field of knowledge elicitation has recently progressed along two fronts. The first involves research and tool development directed at facilitating the process. For example, there has been work on integrating multiple knowledge elicitation methods and evaluating existing methods. Along the second front has been work that extends the traditional role of knowledge elicitation to other problems or applications. Specifically, there has been a focus on task performance with task analytic and cognitive task analytic methods taking center stage. The most recent work along these two fronts is described in the next two sections.

Table 16.8 A hypothetical sample of data collected using the procedure outlined in Table 16.7

A Sample of courses (Step 2)
HIS 201: American History
LANG 150: Spanish
HIS 301: European History
PSY 310: Experimental Psychology
PSY 325: Abnormal Psychology
CHEM 300: Organic Chemistry
PSY 201: Intro to Psychology
CS 151: Intro to Computer Science
MATH 315: Calculus
PSY 390: Human–Computer Interaction

An example of a pair and rating scale (Step 5)

HIS 201: Amer His
PSY 201: Intro Psy

slightly related								highly related	
1	2	3	4	5	6	7	8	9	10
				↑					

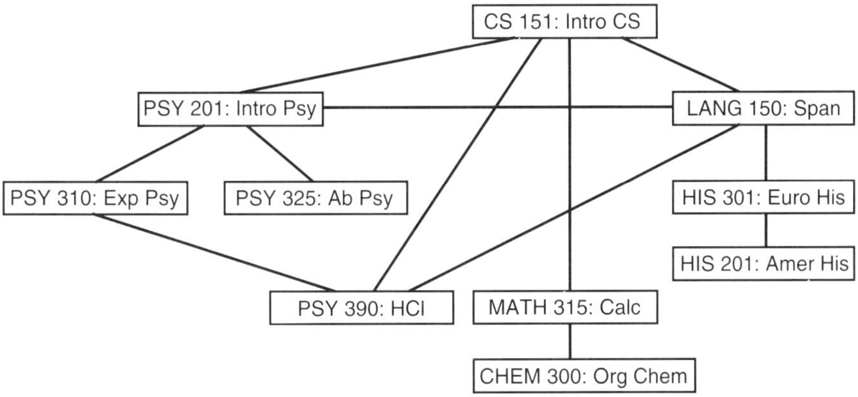

Figure 16.1 Sample Pathfinder network based on concepts in Table 16.8. In it you can see some prerequisite structure in the node-link sequences. In addition, some of the more central nodes are associated with courses that are more interdisciplinary.

Enhancing Existing Methods

The review and cataloging efforts of the late 1980s and early 1990s served to identify the number and variety of knowledge elicitation methods and tools available. It also revealed areas in which additional research and methods were needed. It became increasingly clear that due to the complexity of knowledge and even greater complexity of cognitive skill, that multiple knowledge elicitation methods were probably required for any single application. As a result, research has been directed toward evaluating and comparing methods and devising techniques for managing the results of multiple methods (e.g. Burton, Shadbolt, Rugg & Hedgecock, 1990; Gaines & Shaw, 1997; Hoffman, 1987).

Evaluative efforts in which individual methods are assessed for reliability and validity, and in which two or more methods are compared have increased in the last decade (e.g. Gammack, 1990; Rowe et al., 1996). Dhaliwal & Benbasat (1990) describe a framework which places such evaluation in the context of techniques and tools (the independent variables), the quality of the resulting interface and the efficiency of the process (the dependent variables) and various moderator variables. Then, in the context of this framework, they review the evaluative literature and point out difficulties associated with evaluation. The identification of a satisfactory criterion for the evaluation of a knowledge base is not trivial. Some have proposed that knowledge be evaluated in terms that go beyond reliability and validity, and instead examine knowledge structure and function (Reich, 1995) or utility of that knowledge to the target application (Cooke & Rowe, 1997).

There have been several developments directed toward integrating the results from multiple knowledge elicitation techniques. Mengshoel (1995) describes a Knowledge Reformulation Tool (KRF) that makes use of an intermediary language to translate between two techniques. This procedure is illustrated using the repertory grid and card sorting procedures discussed previously. Gaines & Shaw (1997) approach the knowledge interchange goal through the World Wide Web. They propose that the Web be used to enhance the integration of techniques typically tied to individual laboratories. They illustrate their approach using repertory grid and conceptual network methods also described previously.

Others have addressed some specific shortcomings of existing knowledge elicitation methods. For instance, many of the methods tend to be biased from the perspective of the elicitor or knowledge engineer, neglecting the perspective of the user or expert (e.g. Hale, Sharpe & Haworth, 1996; McNeese, Zaff, Citera, Brown & Whitaker, 1995; Zaff, McNeese & Snyder, 1993). It is thus argued that the result of elicitation efforts can be biased in the same way.

Zaff et al. (1993), for instance, describe a methodology called AKADAM (Advanced Knowledge and Design Acquisition Methodology) which integrates three different knowledge elicitation methods, each revealing a distinct perspective of user requirements and intended to elicit knowledge in the form of concepts, rules, and design. The methodology is user-centered in that information is obtained directly from the expert and elaborated by the expert. The goals of AKADAM include (a) shared communication between the knowledge elicitor and the expert, (b) the facilitation of unconstrained knowledge expression, and (c) resulting knowledge representations compatible with needs, capabilities, and limitations of the stakeholders (McNeese et al., 1995). Similar developments along these lines allow nonprogrammers to edit knowledge structures through the automatic generation of domain-specific knowledge acquisition tools (Eriksson, Puerta & Musen, 1994).

In sum, recent research has provided information for the selection and combination of knowledge elicitation methods from a larger palette. Other efforts have addressed the quality and perspective of the result of elicitation. In addition, new questions have been raised and new methods proposed in response to a broader view of knowledge elicitation.

Broadening the Scope of Knowledge Engineering

As mentioned earlier in this chapter, recent knowledge elicitation efforts have gone beyond the original mission of modeling the knowledge of a single expert, to include cognition and behavior embedded in the context of the actual task. These directions blur distinctions between knowledge elicitation and cognitive engineering or cognitive task analysis, enterprises associated with revealing the cognition underlying complex task performance.

Some of the traditional knowledge elicitation methods (i.e. unstructured interviews, conceptual methods, and contrived tasks in general) remove the expert from the task context, thereby focusing on knowledge at the expense of task and contextual information. They therefore run the risk of generating a knowledge base that is insensitive to context, as opposed to methods that can be applied concurrently with task performance (i.e. observations, some structured interviews, process tracing). Not only have investigators begun to consider methods for eliciting information *in* a broader context, but they are also interested in methods that elicit information *about* the broader context. For instance, methods have been proposed for investigating team as opposed to individual cognition (Cooke, Stout & Salas, 1997).

Interest in the context surrounding the task has been accompanied by interest in the task itself and, in particular, the cognitive and behavioral elements of task performance. This interest was also motivated by the fact that the knowledge elicitation techniques that do consider the task require an initial understanding of it to generate necessary materials (e.g. structured interview questions, task scenarios to perform during think-aloud). Task analysis, which focuses on behavioral aspects of task performance, is one way to satisfy this goal and has long been a mainstay of human factors and applied psychology (Kirwan & Ainsworth, 1992; Meister, 1989). There are numerous variations, but, in general, task analysis involves decomposition of the task goal into subgoals (Cooke, 1994; Hoffman et al., 1995; Wilson, 1989). Investigators have continued to develop new forms of task analysis to meet new goals. For instance, Sutcliffe (1997) has incorporated information needs into the traditional task analysis in order to aid the design of information displays.

Task analysis has also benefited from much of the work associated with the ESDA movement, described previously in the context of process tracing. ESDA is geared toward the understanding of sequential behavior in general, such as the actions taken by surgeons in the operating room or the keystrokes and mouse clicks of a new computer user. ESDA methods can help to reveal subtle patterns and contingencies in sequential behavioral data associated with tasks. These data can be composed of verbal behaviors, as well as nonverbal ones such as gestures, eye movements, and user actions recorded by computer logging software. Unlike traditional knowledge elicitation and task analytic methods, methods that focus on computer-recorded events can amass data in the background, posing little threat of interference to task performance. However, the relation between these kinds of behavioral events and knowledge has been questioned. Rowe et al. (1996) have proposed an approach for exploring the relationship between behavioral patterns and system knowledge (see also Bailey & Kay, 1987).

Knowledge elicitation methods have also moved beyond the traditional conceptualization of knowledge in terms of concepts, relations, rules and strategies. When attempting to build applications using this "knowledge," it becomes clear that there is more to cognition than "knowledge," and probably much more to knowledge than what is captured by traditional knowledge elicitation. In short, much of cognition (e.g. perception) can be left untapped. Recent methods have been adapted or developed to capture other aspects of cognition such as decision making rules (e.g. Klein, 1989) and communication processes (e.g. Bowers, Braun & Kline, 1994). The term "cognitive task analysis" also reflects this more general emphasis on cognition.

CONCLUSION

Knowledge elicitation, once a stage of development of knowledge bases for expert systems, has evolved into a much more ambitious enterprise. Applications continue to include knowledge bases in addition to a variety of other applications in training and software design. Methods no longer focus solely on knowledge, but encompass cognitive processes, task-associated behaviors, and task context as well. This new enterprise is more appropriately labeled cognitive engineering and the methods that are now used may be best referred to as cognitive task analysis methods. These methods continue to be useful, if not critical for solving many applied problems and additionally continue to have an impact on more basic research endeavors.

ACKNOWLEDGMENTS

This chapter benefited from the thoughtful comments of Frank Durso, Robert Hoffman, Thomas Seamster, and several students in Frank Durso's Fall 1997 course on Applied Cognition.

REFERENCES

Altmann, J. (1974). Observational study of behavior: sampling methods. *Behavior*, 49, 227–65.

Anderson, J. R. (1995). *Cognitive Psychology and its Implications*. New York: W. H. Freeman.

Ashly, F. G., Maddox, W. T. & Lee, W. W. (1994). On the dangers of averaging across subjects when using multidimensional scaling or the similarity–choice model. *Psychological Science*, 5, 144–51.

Bailey, W. A. & Kay, D. J. (1987). Structural analysis of verbal data. In J. M. Carroll & P. P. Tanner (Eds), *Human Factors in Computing Systems and Graphics Interface* (pp. 297–301). New York: Association for Computing Machinery.

Bainbridge, L. (1979). Verbal reports as evidence of the process operator's knowledge. *International Journal of Man–Machine Studies*, 11, 411–36.

Benysh, D. V., Koubek, R. J. & Calvez, V. (1993). A comparative review of knowledge structure measurement techniques for interface design. *International Journal of Human–Computer Interaction*, 5, 211–37.

Best, J. B. (1995). *Cognitive Psychology*. St. Paul, MN: West Publishing.
Boose, J. H. (1986). *Expertise Transfer for Expert System Design*. Amsterdam: Elsevier.
Boose, J. H. (1989). A survey of knowledge acquisition techniques and tools. *Knowledge Acquisition*, 1, 3–37.
Boose, J. H. & Bradshaw, J. M. (1987) Expertise transfer and complex problems: using Aquinas as a knowledge-acquisition workbench for knowledge-based systems. *International Journal of Man–Machine Studies*, 26, 3–28.
Boose, J. H. & Gaines, B. R. (Eds) (1988). *Knowledge Acquisition Tools for Expert Systems, Knowledge Based Systems*, Vol. 2. San Diego, CA: Academic Press.
Boose, J. H. & Gaines, B. R. (Eds) (1990). *The Foundations of Knowledge Acquisition, Knowledge Based Systems*, Vol. 4. San Diego, CA: Academic Press.
Bowers, C. A., Braun, C. & Kline, P. B. (1994). Communication and team situational awareness. In R. D. Gilson, D. J. Garland & J. M. Koonce (Eds), *Situational Awareness in Complex Systems* (pp. 305–11). Daytona Beach, FL: Embry-Riddle Aeronautical University Press.
Bradshaw, J. M., Ford, K. M., Adams-Webber, J. R. & Boose, J. H. (1993). Beyond the repertory grid: new approaches to constructivist knowledge acquisition tool development. *International Journal of Intelligent Systems*, 8, 287–333.
Breuker, J. & Wielinga, B. (1987). Use of models in the interpretation of verbal data. In A. Kidd (Ed.), *Knowledge Acquisition for Expert Systems*, pp. 17–43. New York: Plenum Press.
Broadbent, D. E., Fitzgerald, P. & Broadbent, M. H. P. (1986). Implicit and explicit knowledge in the context of complex systems. *British Journal of Psychology*, 77, 33–50.
Burton, A. M., Shadbolt, N. R., Rugg, G. & Hedgecock, A. P. (1990). The efficacy of knowledge elicitation techniques: a comparison across domains and levels of expertise. *Journal of Knowledge Acquisition*, 2, 167–78.
Carroll, J. D. & Chang, J. J. (1970). Analysis of individual differences in multidimensional scaling via an N-way generalization of Eckhart-Young decomposition. *Psychometrika*, 35, 283–319.
Charness, N. & Schultetus, R. S. (1999). Knowledge and expertise. In F. T. Durso, R. S. Nickerson, R. W. Schvaneveldt, S. T. Dumais, D. S. Lindsay & M. T. H. Chi (Eds), *Handbook of Applied Cognition*, chapter 3. Chichester: John Wiley.
Chase, W. G. & Simon, H. A. (1973). The mind's eye in chess. In W. G. Chase (Ed.), *Cognitive Skills and their Acquisition* (pp. 141–89). Hillsdale, NJ: Erlbaum.
Chi, M. T. H., Feltovich, P. J. & Glaser, R. (1981). Categorization and representation of physics problems by experts and novices. *Cognitive Science*, 5, 121–52.
Clarke, B. (1987). Knowledge acquisition for real-time knowledge-based systems. *Proceedings of the First European Workshop on Knowledge Acquisition for Knowledge Based Systems*. September 2–3, Reading University, UK.
Collins, A. M. & Loftus, E. F. (1975). A spreading-activation theory of semantic processing. *Psychological Review*, 82, 407–28.
Collins, A. M. & Quillian, M. R. (1969). Retrieval time from semantic memory. *Journal of Verbal Learning and Verbal Behavior*, 8, 240–7.
Compton, P. & Jansen, R. (1990). A philosophical basis for knowledge acquisition. *Knowledge Acquisition*, 2, 241–57.
Cooke, N. J. (1992a). Predicting judgment time from measures of psychological proximity. *Journal of Experimental Psychology: Learning, Memory, and Cognition*, 18, 640–53.
Cooke, N. J. (1992b). Eliciting semantic relations for empirically derived networks. *International Journal of Man–Machine Studies*, 37, 721–50.
Cooke, N. J. (1994). Varieties of knowledge elicitation techniques. *International Journal of Human–Computer Studies*, 41, 801–49.
Cooke, N. J. & Breedin, S. D. (1994). Constructing naive theories of motion on-the-fly. *Memory and Cognition*, 22, 474–93.
Cooke, N. J. & Neville, K. J. & Rowe, A. L. (1996). Procedural network representations of sequential data. *Human–Computer Interaction*, 11, 29–68.

Cooke, N. J. & Rowe, A. L. (1997). Measures of mental models: a synthesis of evaluative data. *Training Research Journal*, 3, 185–207.

Cooke, N. J., Stout, R. & Salas, E. (1997) Expanding the measurement of situation awareness through cognitive engineering methods. *Proceedings of the Human Factors and Ergonomics Society 41st Annual Meeting*, 215–19.

Cooke, N. M. (1989). The elicitation of domain-related ideas: stage one of the knowledge acquisition process. In C. Ellis (Ed.), *Expert Knowledge and Explanation* (pp. 58–75). England: Ellis Horwood.

Cooke, N. M., Durso, F. T. & Schvaneveldt, R. W. (1986). Recall and measures of memory organization. *Journal of Experimental Psychology: Learning, Memory, and Cognition*, 12 (4), 538–49.

Cooke, N. M. & Schvaneveldt, R. W. (1988). Effects of computer programming experience on network representations of abstract programming concepts. *International Journal of Man–Machine Studies*, 29, 407–27.

Cordingley, E. S. (1989). Knowledge elicitation techniques for knowledge-based systems. In D. Diaper (Ed.), *Knowledge Elicitation: Principles, Techniques, and Applications* (pp. 89–175). New York: John Wiley.

Corter, J. E. & Tversky, A. (1986). Extended similarity trees. *Psychometrika*, 51, 429–51.

Cullen, J. & Bryman, A. (1988). The knowledge acquisition bottleneck: a time for reassessment? *Expert Systems*, 5, 216–25.

deGroot, A. (1966). Perception and memory versus thought: some old ideas and recent findings. In B. Kleinmuntz (Ed.), *Problem Solving*. New York: Wiley.

Dhaliwal, J. S. & Benbasat, I. (1990). A framework for the comparative evaluation of knowledge acquisition tools and techniques. *Knowledge Acquisition*, 2, 145–66.

Diaper, D. (Ed.) (1989a). *Knowledge Elicitation: Principles, Techniques, and Applications*. England: Ellis Horwood.

Diaper, D. (1989b). Designing expert systems – From Dan to Beersheba. In D. Diaper (Ed.), *Knowledge Elicitation: Principles, Techniques, and Applications* (pp. 17–46). England: Ellis Horwood.

Diederich, J., Ruhmann, I. & May, M. (1987). KRITON: a knowledge acquisition tool for expert systems. *International Journal of Man–Machine Studies*, 26, 29–40.

Elstein, A. S., Shulman, L. S. & Sprafka, S. A. (1978). *Medical Problem Solving: An Analysis of Clinical Reasoning*. Cambridge, MA: Harvard Press.

Engle, R. W. & Bukstel, L. (1978). Memory processes among bridge players of differing expertise. *American Journal of Psychology*, 91, 673–89.

Ericsson, K. A. & Simon, H. A. (1996). *Protocol Analysis: Verbal Reports as Data* (rev. edn). Cambridge, MA: MIT Press.

Eriksson, H., Puerta, A. R. & Musen, M. A. (1994). Generation of knowledge acquisition tools from domain ontologies. *International Journal of Human–Computer Studies*, 41, 425–53.

Feigenbaum, E. A. (1989). What hath Simon wrought? In D. Klahr & K. Kotovsky (Eds), *Complex Information Processing: The Impact of Herbert A. Simon* (pp. 165–82). Hillsdale, NJ: Erlbaum.

Ford, K. M. & Adams-Webber, J. R. (1992). Knowledge acquisition and constructivist epistemology. In R. R. Hoffman (Ed.), *The Psychology of Expertise: Cognitive Research and Empirical AI* (pp. 121–36). New York: Springer-Verlag.

Ford, J. M. & Wood, L. E. (1992). Structuring and documenting interactions with subject-matter experts. *Performance Improvement Quarterly*, 5, 2–24.

Fransella, F. & Bannister, D. (1977). *A Manual for Repertory Grid Technique*. London: Academic Press.

Gaines, B. R. & Shaw, M. L. G. (1992). Knowledge acquisition tools based on personal construct psychology. *Knowledge Engineering Review: Special Issue on Automated Knowledge Acquisition Tools*.

Gaines, B. R. & Shaw, M. L. G. (1997). Knowledge acquisition, modelling, and inference through the World Wide Web. *International Journal of Human–Computer Studies*, 46, 729–59.

Gammack, J. G. (1990). Expert conceptual structure: the stability of Pathfinder representations. In R. Schvaneveldt (Ed.), *Pathfinder Associative Networks: Studies in Knowledge Organization* (pp. 213–26). Norwood, NJ: Ablex.

Geiwitz, J., Klatsky, R. L. & McCloskey, B. P. (1988). *Knowledge Acquisition for Expert Systems: Conceptual and Empirical Comparisons*. Santa Barbara, CA: Anacapa Sciences.

Geiwitz, J., Kornell, J. & McCloskey, B. (1990). *An Expert System for the Selection of Knowledge Acquisition Techniques* (Technical Report 785-2). Santa Barbara, CA: Anacapa Sciences, Inc.

Gillan, D. J., Breedin, S. D. & Cooke, N. J. (1992). Network and multidimensional representations of the declarative knowledge of human–computer interface design experts. *International Journal of Man–Machine Studies*, 36, 587–615.

Glaser, R. & Chi, M. T. H. (1988). Overview. In M. T. H. Chi, R. Glaser & M. J. Farr (Eds), *The Nature of Expertise* (pp. xv–xxviii). Hillsdale, NJ: Erlbaum.

Goldsmith, T. E. & Davenport, D. M. (1990). Assessing structural similarity of graphs. In R. Schvaneveldt (Ed.), *Pathfinder Associative Networks: Studies in Knowledge Organization* (pp. 75–87). Norwood, NJ: Ablex.

Goldsmith, T. E., Johnson, P. J. & Acton, W. H. (1991). Assessing structural knowledge. *Journal of Educational Psychology*, 83, 88–96.

Greeno, J. G. (1978). Natures of problem-solving abilities. In W. K. Estes (Ed.), *Handbook of Learning and Cognitive Processes* (Vol. 5, pp. 239–70). Hillsdale, NJ: Erlbaum.

Grover, M. D. (1983). A pragmatic knowledge acquisition methodology. *Proceedings of the 8th International Joint Conference on Artificial Intelligence* (pp. 436–8), Karlsruhe, West Germany, August.

Hale, D. P., Sharpe, S. & Haworth, D. A. (1996). Human-centered knowledge acquisition: a structural learning theory approach. *International Journal of Human–Computer Studies*, 45, 381–96.

Hall, E. M., Gott, S. P. & Pokorny, R. A. (1994). *A Procedural Guide to Cognitive Task Analysis: The PARI Methodology*. Manuscript submitted for publication. Brooks AFB, TX.

Harrison, B. L. & Baecker, R. M. (1991). Designing video automation and analysis systems. *Proceedings Graphics Interface '92*, 209–19.

Hart, A. (1986). *Knowledge Acquisition for Expert Systems*. London: Kogan Page.

Hoffman, R. R. (1987). The problem of extracting the knowledge of experts from the perspective of experimental psychology. *AI Magazine*, 8, 53–67.

Hoffman, R. R. (1989). A survey of methods for eliciting the knowledge of experts. *SIGART Newsletter*, 108.

Hoffman, R. R., Shadbolt, N. R., Burton, A. M. & Klein, G. (1995). Eliciting knowledge from experts: a methodological analysis. *Organizational Behavior and Human Decision Processes*, 62, 129–58.

Housner, L. D., Gomez, R. L. & Griffey, D. C. (1993a). A Pathfinder analysis of expert–novice knowledge. *Proceedings of the Meeting on the National American Alliance for Health, Physical Education, Recreation and Dance*, 64, Supplement, A-88–A-89.

Housner, L. D., Gomez, R. L. & Griffey, D. C. (1993b). Pedagogical knowledge growth in prospective teachers: relationships to performance in a teaching methodology course. *Research Quarterly for Exercise and Sport*, 64, 167–77.

Howell, W. C. & Cooke, N. J. (1989). Training the human information processor: a look at cognitive models. In I. Goldstein (Ed.), *Training and Development in Work Organizations: Frontier Series of Industrial and Organizational Psychology* (Vol. 3, pp. 121–82). New York: Jossey-Bass.

Hutchins, E. (1995). *Cognition in the Wild*. Cambridge, MA: MIT Press.

Johnson, L. & Johnson, N. (1987). Knowledge elicitation involving teachback interviewing. In A. Kidd (Ed.), *Knowledge Elicitation for Expert Systems: A Practical Handbook* (pp. 91–108). New York: Plenum Press.

Johnson, P. E., Zualkerman, I. & Garber, S. (1987). Specification of expertise. *International Journal of Man–Machine Studies*, 26, 161–81.

Johnson, S. C. (1967). Hierarchical clustering schemes. *Psychometrika*, 32, 241–54.

Kirwan, B. & Ainsworth, L. K. (1992). *A Guide to Task Analysis*. London: Taylor & Francis.
Kitto, C. M. & Boose, J. H. (1989). Selecting knowledge acquisition tools and strategies based on application characteristics. *International Journal of Man–Machine Studies*, 31, 149–60.
Klein, G. A. (1989). Recognition-primed decisions. In W. Rouse (Ed.), *Advances in Man–Machine Systems Research*, 5, 47–92.
Klein, G. A., Calderwood, R. & MacGregor, D. (1989). Critical decision method for eliciting knowledge. *IEEE Transactions on Systems, Man & Cybernetics*, 19, 462–72.
Kruskal, J. B. (1977). Multidimensional scaling and other methods for discovering structure. In Enslein, Ralston & Wilf (Eds), *Statistical Methods for Digital Computers*. New York: John Wiley.
Kruskal, J. B. & Wish, M. (1978). *Multidimensional Scaling*. Sage University. Paper Series on Quantitative Applications in the Social Sciences, #07-011. London: Sage Publications.
LaFrance, M. (1987). The knowledge acquisition grid: a method for training knowledge engineers. *International Journal of Man–Machine Studies*, 26, 245–55.
LaFrance, M. (1992). Excavation, capture, collection, and creation: computer scientists' metaphors for eliciting human expertise. *Metaphor and Symbolic Activity*, 7, 135–56.
Lewis, S. (1991). Cluster analysis as a technique to guide interface design. *International Journal of Man–Machine Studies*, 35, 251–65.
Mancuso, J. C. & Shaw, M. L. G. (1988). *Cognition and Personal Structure: Computer Access and Analysis*. New York: Praeger.
McDonald, J. E., Dayton, T. & McDonald, D. R. (1988). Adapting menu layout to tasks. *International Journal of Man–Machine Studies*, 28, 417–36.
McGraw, K. L. & Harbison-Briggs, K. (1989). *Knowledge Acquisition: Principles and Guidelines*. Englewood Cliffs, NJ: Prentice Hall.
McNeese, M. D., Zaff, B. S., Citera, M., Brown, C. E. & Whitaker, R. (1995). AKADAM: Eliciting user knowledge to support participatory ergonomics. *International Journal of Industrial Ergonomics*, 15, 345–63.
Meister, D. (1989). *Conceptual Aspects of Human Factors*. Baltimore, MD: The Johns Hopkins University Press.
Mengshoel, O. J. (1995). A reformulation technique and tool for knowledge interchange during knowledge acquisition. *International Journal of Human–Computer Studies*, 43, 177–212.
Meyer, M. A. (1992). How to apply the anthropological technique of participant observation to knowledge acquisition for expert systems. *IEEE Transactions on Systems, Man, and Cybernetics*, 22, 983–90.
Meyer, M. A. & Booker, J. M. (1990). *Eliciting and Analyzing Expert Judgment: A Practical Guide*. Technical report no. NUREG/CR-5424; LA-11667-MS. Los Alamos National Laboratory, Los Alamos, NM.
Miller, G. A. (1969). A psychological method to investigate verbal concepts. *Journal of Mathematical Psychology*, 6, 169–91.
Minsky, M. (1975). A framework for representing knowledge. In J. Haugeland (Ed.), *Mind Design* (pp. 95–128). Cambridge, MA: MIT Press.
Myles-Worsley, M., Johnston, W. A. & Simons, M. A. (1988). The influence of expertise on x-ray image processing. *Journal of Experimental Psychology: Learning, Memory & Cognition*, 14, 553–7.
Nisbett, R. E. & Wilson, T. D. (1977). Telling more than we can know: verbal reports on mental processes. *Psychological Review*, 84, 231–59.
Norman, D. A. (1986). Cognitive engineering. In D. A. Norman & S. W. Draper (Eds), *User Centered System Design* (pp. 31–61). Hillsdale, NJ: Erlbaum.
Olson, J. R. & Biolsi, K. J. (1991). Techniques for representing expert knowledge. In K. A. Ericsson & J. Smith (Eds), *Toward a General Theory of Expertise* (pp. 240–85). Cambridge: Cambridge University Press.

Olson, J. R. & Rueter, H. H. (1987). Extracting expertise from experts: methods for knowledge acquisition. *Expert Systems*, 4, 152–68.
Pidgeon, N. F., Turner, B. A. & Blockley, D. I. (1991). The use of Grounded Theory for conceptual analysis in knowledge elicitation. *International Journal of Man–Machine Studies*, 35, 151–73.
Quillian, M. R. (1969). The teachable language comprehender. *Communications of the Association for Computing Machinery*, 12, 459–76.
Randel, J. M., Pugh, H. L. & Wyman, B. G. (1996). *Methods for Conducting Cognitive Task Analysis for a Decision Making Task*. Technical report Navy Personnel Research and Development Center, TN-96-10, San Diego, CA.
Regoczei, S. B. & Hirst, G. (1992). Knowledge and knowledge acquisition in the computational context. In R. R. Hoffman (Ed.), *The Psychology of Expertise* (pp. 12–25). New York: Springer-Verlag.
Reich, Y. (1995). Measuring the value of knowledge. *International Journal of Human–Computer Studies*, 42, 3–30.
Reitman, J. (1976). Skilled perception in GO: deducing memory structures from inter-response times. *Cognitive Psychology*, 8, 336–56.
Ricci, K. E., Blickensderfer, E., Cannon-Bowers, J. A. & Sagi, C. (1996). Validity and stability of Pathfinder Indices: a replication and extension. Paper presented at the Annual meeting of the American Psychological Association, Toronto, Canada.
Roediger, H. L. (1990). Implicit memory. *American Psychologist*, 45, 1043–56.
Roske-Hofstrand, R. J. & Paap, K. R. (1986). Cognitive networks as a guide to menu organization: an application in the automated cockpit. *Ergonomics*, 39, 1301–11.
Roske-Hofstrand, R. J. & Paap, K. R. (1990). Discriminating between degrees of low or high similarity: implications for scaling techniques using semantic judgments. In R. W. Schvaneveldt (Ed.), *Pathfinder Associative Networks: Studies in Knowledge Organization* (pp. 61–73). Norwood, NJ: Ablex.
Rowe, A. L., Cooke, N. J., Hall, E. P. & Halgren, T. L. (1996). Toward an on-line knowledge assessment methodology: building on the relationship between knowing and doing. *Journal of Experimental Psychology: Applied*, 2, 31–47.
Rowe, A. L., Cooke, N. J., Neville, K. J. & Schacherer, C. W. (1992). Mental models of metal models: a comparison of mental model measurement techniques. *Proceedings of the Human Factors Society 36th Annual Meeting*, 1195–9.
Sachett, G. P. (1977). *Observing Behavior* (vol. 1). Baltimore: University Park Press.
Sachett, G. P. (1978). *Observing Behavior* (vol. 2). Baltimore: University Park Press.
Sanderson, P. M. & Fisher, C. (1994). Exploratory sequential data analysis: foundations. *Human–Computer Interaction*, 9, 251–317.
Sanderson, P. M., James, J. M., Seidler, K. (1989). SHAPA: an interactive software environment for protocol analysis. EPRL Technical Report no. EPRL-89-08. University of Illinois at Urbana-Champaign, Urbana, IL.
Sanderson, P. M., McNeese, M. D. & Zaff, B. S. (1994). Handling complex real-world data with two cognitive engineering tools: COGENT and MacSHAPA. *Behavior Research Methods, Instruments, and Computers*, 26, 117–24.
Sanderson, P., Scott, J., Johnston, T., Mainzer, J., Watanabe, L. & James, J. (1994). MacSHAPA and the enterprise of exploratory sequential data analysis (ESDA). *International Journal of Human–Computer Studies*, 41, 633–81.
Schacter, R. D. & Heckerman, D. E. (1987). Thinking backward for knowledge acquisition. *The AI Magazine*, 55–61.
Scherer, K. R. & Ekman, P. (1982). *Handbook of Methods in Nonverbal Behavior Research*. Cambridge: Cambridge University Press.
Schvaneveldt, R. W. (1990). *Pathfinder Associative Networks: Studies in Knowledge Organization*. Norwood, NJ: Ablex.
Schvaneveldt, R. W., Durso, F. T. & Dearholt, D. W. (1989). Network structures in proximity data. In G. H. Bower (Ed.), *The Psychology of Learning and Motivation: Advances in Research and Theory* (Vol. 24, pp. 249–84). New York: Academic Press.
Schvaneveldt, R. W., Durso, F. T., Goldsmith, T. E., Breen, T. J., Cooke, N. M., Tucker,

R. G. & DeMaio, J. C. (1985). Measuring the structure of expertise. *International Journal of Man–Machine Studies*, 23, 699–728.
Schweikert, R., Burton, A. M., Taylor, N. K., Cortlett, E. N., Shadbolt, N. R. & Hedgecock, A. P. (1987). Comparing knowledge elicitation techniques: a case study. *Artificial Intelligence Review*, 1, 245–53.
Shadbolt, N. & Burton, M. (1990). Knowledge elicitation. In J. R. Wilson & E. N. Corlett (Eds), *Evaluation of Human Work: A Practical Ergonomics Methodology* (pp. 321–45). London: Taylor & Francis.
Shaw, M. L. G. (1980). *On Becoming a Personal Scientist*. London: Academic Press.
Shaw, M. L. G. & Gaines, B. R. (1987). An interactive knowledge elicitation technique using personal construct technology. In A. Kidd (Ed.), *Knowledge Acquisition for Expert Systems: A Practical Handbook*. New York: Plenum Press.
Shaw, M. L. G. & Gaines, B. R. (1989). Comparing conceptual structures: consensus, conflict, correspondence, and contrast. *Knowledge Acquisition*, 1, 341–63.
Shaw, M. L. G. & Woodward, J. B. (1989). Mental models in the knowledge acquisition process. *Proceedings of the 4th AAAI-sponsored knowledge acquisition for knowledge-based systems workshop*, 29/1–29/24. Banff, Canada, October.
Shaw, M. L. G. & Woodward, J. B. (1990). Modeling expert knowledge. *Knowledge Acquisition*, 2, 179–206.
Shepard, R. N. (1962a). Analysis of proximities: multidimensional scaling with an unknown distance function. I *Psychometrika*, 27, 125–40.
Shepard, R. N. (1962b). Analysis of proximities: multidimensional scaling with an unknown distance function. II *Psychometrika*, 27, 219–46.
Shepard, R. N. & Arabie, P. (1979). Additive clustering: representation of similarities as combinations of discrete overlapping properties. *Psychological Review*, 86, 87–123.
Siochi, A. C. & Ehrich, R. W. (1991). Computer analysis of user interfaces based on repetition in transcripts of user sessions. *ACM Transactions on Information Systems*, 9, 309–35.
Sloboda, J. A. (1976). Visual perception of musical notation: registering pitch symbols in memory. *Quarterly Journal of Experimental Psychology*, 28, 1–16.
Smith, E. E., Shoben, E. J. & Rips, L. (1974). Structure and process in semantic memory: a featural model for semantic decisions. *Psychological Review*, 81, 214–41.
Suchman, L. & Trigg, R. (1991). Understanding practice: video as a medium for reflection and design. In J. Greenbaum & M. Kyng (Eds), *Design at Work*. Hillsdale, NJ: LEA.
Suen, H. K. & Ary, D. (1989). *Analyzing Quantitative Behavioral Observation Data*. Hillsdale, NJ: Erlbaum.
Sundstrom, G. A. (1991). Process tracing of decision making: an approach for analysis of human–machine interactions in dynamic environments. *International Journal of Man–Machine Studies*, 35, 843–58.
Sutcliffe, A. (1997). Task-related information analysis. *International Journal of Human–Computer Studies*, 47, 223–57.
Thordsen, M. L. (1991). A comparison of two tools for cognitive task analysis: concept mapping and the critical decision method. *Proceedings of the Human Factors Society 35th Annual Meeting*, San Francisco, CA, 283–85.
VanHooff, J. A. R. A. M. (1982). Categories and sequences of behavior: methods of description and analysis. In K. R. Scherer & P. Ekman (Eds), *Handbook of Methods in Nonverbal Behavior Research*. Cambridge: Cambridge University Press.
vanSomeren, M. W., Barnard, Y. F. & Sandberg, J. A. C. (1994). *The Think Aloud Method: A Practical Guide to Modeling Cognitive Processes*. London: Academic Press.
Vicente, K. J. (1997). Heeding the legacy of Meister, Brunswick & Gibson: toward a broader view of human factors research. *Human Factors*, 39, 323–8.
Welbank, M. (1990). An overview of knowledge acquisition methods. *Interacting with Computers*, 2, 83–91.
Wielinga, B. J., Schreiber, A. Th. & Breuker, J. A. (1992). KADS: a modelling approach to knowledge engineering. *Knowledge Acquisition*, 4, 5–53.
Wilson, M. (1989). Task models for knowledge elicitation. In D. Diaper (Ed.), *Knowledge*

Elicitation: Principles, Techniques, and Applications (pp. 197–219). Chichester: Ellis Horwood.

Woods, D. D. & Roth, E. M. (1988). Cognitive systems engineering. In M. Helander (Ed.), *Handbook of Human–Computer Interaction* (pp. 3–43). Amsterdam: Elsevier.

Zachary, W. W., Ryder, J. M. & Purcell, J. A. (1990). A computer-based tool to support mental modeling for human–computer interface design. *CHI Systems Technical Report No. 900831-8908*, August 31.

Zaff, B. S., McNeese, M. D. & Snyder, D. E. (1993). Capturing multiple perspectives: a user-centered approach to knowledge and design acquisition. *Knowledge Acquisition*, 5, 79–116.

Section 4

Information and Instruction

Chapter 17

Statistical Graphs and Maps

Stephan Lewandowsky
University of Western Australia
and
John T. Behrens
Arizona State University

Statistical graphs and maps represent numeric data and their summaries by the location and appearance of visual symbols. Statistical graphs are a relatively recent invention, generally being traced back to Playfair (1876). Notwithstanding their short history, graphs have had a profound influence on scientific discovery: nearly a century ago, a single scatterplot arguably changed the course of astronomy by facilitating the detection of "outliers" that escaped detection by simple numerical summary or tabulation (Spence & Garrison, 1993). More recently, the electronic information processing revolution has stimulated exponential growth in graph usage. Practitioners can now easily generate graphs on their personal computers, and the mass media are replete with statistical graphs and maps. After an initial delay, the explosive growth of graph use has, by now, spawned considerable research into how humans perceive, process, and understand statistical displays.

However, that research and the accompanying theoretical efforts have been distributed across several diverse disciplines, including psychology, geography, statistics, education, and business. Correspondingly, major reference works on graphs and maps have been written from different perspectives and targeted at different audiences. Spence & Lewandowsky (1990; see also Lewandowsky & Spence, 1990) provided a comprehensive treatment of graphical perception and the emerging cognitive literature from the perspective of experimental psychologists. Cleveland (1994) provided a detailed account of graphical data analysis as applied in modern statistics. Behrens (1997a) has explored some of the

Handbook of Applied Cognition, Edited by F. T. Durso, R. S. Nickerson, R. W. Schvaneveldt, S. T. Dumais, D. S. Lindsay and M. T. H. Chi.

philosophical justification for these trends in terms of exploratory data analysis (Tukey, 1977). Kosslyn (1985), a cognitive scientist, provided one of the first information processing accounts of graphs for a statistical audience. Finally, MacEachren (1995) produced a comprehensive and scholarly guide to the psychology of cartography that is relevant to all audiences with an interest in the design and perception of maps.

This chapter intends to synthesize those diverse approaches into an integrated overview of the current knowledge, methodology, and issues in the psychological processing of statistical graphs and maps. We organize this chapter in four sections: first, we select and discuss two analytic frameworks in order to foster common conceptualizations and communication across discourse communities; second, we review the empirical literature regarding statistical graph comprehension, progressing from studies that examined elementary perceptual processes towards research that addressed issues of wider scope and broader ecological validity; the third section provides a review of the literature concerning statistical maps, again organized by task complexity; and the final section summarizes the themes that emerged during the review and makes recommendations for additional research.

TWO ANALYTIC FRAMEWORKS

The literature to date has largely evolved without a common approach or uniform conceptualization. Researchers across the various disciplines have seemed united by a shared appreciation of the aesthetic or pragmatic value of graphs and maps, rather than by a common theoretical stance. To help overcome this fragmentation, this chapter is structured around a set of over-arching analytic frameworks.

Existing candidate frameworks cover a wide range of views: at one extreme, there are views that place empirical emphasis on basic perceptual processes in preference to higher level cognition (e.g. Cleveland, 1993). At the other extreme, there are semiotic approaches that prefer extensive interpretation to empirical research (e.g. Bertin, 1983). We chose to frame our discussion within the more balanced and inclusive frameworks of Kosslyn (1989) and Pinker (1990). Both were developed within the tradition of cognitive science, thus combining attention to perceptual details with emphasis on higher-level psychological processes and an awareness of different levels of analysis that is missing in other accounts.

Kosslyn's Analysis of Graph Components

Kosslyn (1989) was among the first to propose an integrated framework for the analysis of graphs and graph-related tasks. His framework rested on two major components: conventional assumptions about human information processing (e.g. a capacity-limited short-term memory) combined with a rational task and component analysis of graphs. From those components, the framework was able to explain success or failure of graph comprehension.

In Kosslyn's approach, graphs were thought to be composed of a background (the paper or screen), a framework (axes and boundaries), specifiers (symbols that convey numeric information), and labels (that explain the framework and specifiers). These elements and their relationships, in turn, were described at the three levels of syntax, semantics, and pragmatics. Syntactic analysis concerns the graph elements as basic perceptual cues: Are they discriminable? Are they distorted? Are they perceived as intended? For obvious reasons, this immediate level of analysis has been the primary focus of research to date. Semantic analysis addresses the meaningfulness of the graph, in particular clarity and effectiveness of the literal meaning conveyed by graph elements. This concerns, for example, whether labels can be readily associated with lines, or whether color is used in a conventional manner (e.g. the danger zone is indicated in red rather than green). There has been comparatively little relevant research. The third level of analysis, pragmatic considerations, addresses the goal of the graph relative to the reader and seeks to assess the connotative aspects of communication. At this level, it may be determined that although some design principles from lower levels of analysis were violated, the reader is still likely to interpret the graph as intended. There has been virtually no empirical research at this level of analysis.

For each level of analysis, Kosslyn postulated a series of questions and recommendations to determine if a graph meets requisite acceptability principles. At the syntactic level, for example, graphs should follow the famous Gestalt principles of continuity, proximity, similarity, and good form. A complete set of pragmatic design recommendations along those lines can be found in Kosslyn's (1994) book.

Pinker's Cognitive Processing of Graphical Information

Pinker's theory had been available in the form of a technical report for nearly 10 years before it was formally published in 1990. During that time, it was circulated widely within the field and stimulated much research in response. In some cases, publication of these responses predates 1990. Pinker (1990) presented a very detailed and distinctly cognitive framework for graph comprehension that relied on the standard information-processing paradigm and in particular the interaction of data driven (bottom-up) and schema-driven (top-down) processing. The bottom-up component involved two steps: first, early processes encode the graph into a visual array, best understood as an unprocessed analog representation. This is followed by the extraction of a "visual description" of the graph, which is a propositional representation that includes variables (which represent objects or entities in the graph) and predicates (relationships among variables). The top-down component consisted of the application of schemas that guide attention and information extraction, to yield a final "conceptual message" or cognitive representation of the graph. Accordingly, the final cognitive representation of a graph is established to satisfy the perceived purpose of the graph (either previously known or deduced) that is represented in the chosen schema. Subsequent performance is facilitated to the degree that the mental representation of the graph is aligned with the required task.

For example, when viewing a bar chart with two vertical bars, the viewer is assumed to first construct a primitive sketch (the visual array), followed by the creation of an associative network of propositions (the visual description) that describe the scene (following the work on basic visual analysis by Marr, 1982). Pinker (1990) assumed that a predicate language described the encoded relationships. Thus, the height of each bar may be encoded directly (e.g. by noting its proximity to the relevant tic-marks), or the length of the bar may be encoded instead (e.g. by noting its extent from the abscissa). Other representations are possible as well, for example information concerning the slope relating the height of the two bars. The actual representation would depend on the precise nature of the schema that embodies the prior knowledge of the viewer. (An analysis of how such knowledge and schemas are acquired during childhood is provided by MacEachren, 1995, pp. 195–8.)

Pinker (1990) argued that when individuals are presented with a specific task, the encoded associative networks are searched using a general matching procedure. If the desired information was not originally encoded, for example because an inappropriate schema guided visual analysis, a mismatch results. In that case, additional processing is required to deduce the answer from the associative net, or by returning to the image and repeating the encoding. The most compelling implication of this model is that performance will vary jointly as a function of the nature of the graph, which affects the encoding process, and the type of task, which drives the retrieval process.

Pinker's (1990) and Kosslyn's (1989) frameworks share some important features but also differ in interesting ways. On the one hand, both assumed that the results of preliminary visual analysis reside in a capacity-limited store (short-term memory in Kosslyn's case and the visual description in Pinker's case). Likewise, both acknowledged the role of prior knowledge in long-term memory and its guiding influence on encoding and information extraction. On the other hand, the frameworks differed in their explanatory emphasis. Whereas Kosslyn was concerned with different levels of analysis and a thorough characterization of early visual processes, Pinker had little to say about early vision but provided a thorough characterization of schemas and the extraction of a conceptual message. In addition, while Pinker focused almost exclusively on computational aspects of cognition, Kosslyn placed graph interpretation in the larger context of the goals of communication.

Role of Analytic Frameworks

Several guiding principles can be derived from the preceding frameworks. First, it is obvious that cognitive psychology provides the rich set of theoretical tools necessary for study and evaluation of statistical graph and map perception. Particularly noteworthy is the way in which these frameworks integrate simple perceptual principles (e.g. the Gestalt laws) with schema-driven higher-level cognition. Second, the frameworks mandate that we consider a *continuum* of perceptual and cognitive processes, ranging from the relatively elementary tasks of color and shape recognition, through the process of categorization and summarization, to goal-directed information integration and extraction.

However, importantly, both frameworks are too loose to permit any but the most general predictions. For example, Kosslyn (1989) cites the Gestalt principle that symbols located close together are likely to be considered as a group. He argues that "if these principles operate to group together elements of a display inappropriately, the display must be changed" (p. 195). This recommendation remains problematic, because although the Gestalt principle captures the psychological issue that perception of groupings is often automatic, no extant model predicts what would constitute inappropriate grouping in a statistical graph. The primary limitation of Pinker's (1990) work, by contrast, is the over-emphasis on the use of a match procedure for memory access, to the exclusion of the specification of other cognitive processes. For example, Pinker's (1990) framework remains mute about the possibilities that graph structure facilitates problem solving, as has been shown in diagrams (Larkin & Simon, 1987), that representations associated with mental models directly affect graph use (Behrens, 1997b), that arithmetic computations are an integral part of some graph comprehension tasks (Gillan, 1995), or that mathematical conceptualizations of the graph structure affect performance on seemingly simple tasks (Leinhardt, Zaslavsky & Stein, 1990).

Despite these limitations, both frameworks provide a valuable global platform to organize relevant research. The formulation and test of predictions involving specific tasks and graphs, however, is the domain of models that combine greater explanatory precision with smaller scope. Several such detailed models of graph perception have been developed within the umbrella of the Kosslyn and Pinker frameworks, and we present some of them later.

We now turn to a review of the empirical literature on statistical graphs and maps that is organized along a continuum of cognitive processes. Use of that continuum mandates that the review begin with statistical graphs and end with statistical maps. The latter necessarily use the two dimensions of the plane to represent geographical information, thus mandating more complex cognitive processes to extract statistical magnitude information.

THE CONTINUUM OF PERCEPTUAL AND COGNITIVE PROCESSES: STATISTICAL GRAPHS

To provide a complete picture of the processing of statistical graphs, we consider the following three major issues: we first discuss the role of the physical display format and outline the research that has sought to extract universal design principles; we then show that effective graph design must additionally consider the perceptual tasks required of the observer; we conclude with a discussion of the interaction between physical display format and the nature of the data being shown in a graph. To foreshadow one of our main conclusions, the analytic frameworks can accommodate at least part of the first two issues, but they cannot illuminate how the particular pattern of data being presented interacts with different display types.

Display Format and Universal Design Principles

Elementary Perceptual Tasks

Cleveland & McGill (1984, 1986) provided one of the first comprehensive treatments of the perceptual aspects of statistical graphs, loosely corresponding to Kosslyn's (1989) syntactic level of analysis. Cleveland & McGill argued that most perceptual processing of graphs involved elementary visual judgments or comparisons using the following graphical coding schemes:

1. position along a common scale
2. position along identical but non-aligned scales
3. length
4. angle
5. slope
6. area
7. volume.

To illustrate, the common bar chart can be understood using judgments of type (1) or (3), whereas the pie chart requires judgment (4) or, possibly, (6).

Cleveland & McGill experimentally compared those elementary tasks, hypothesizing that performance would be best with simple judgments (type 1) and worst with complex judgments (7). Participants viewed a standard graph element and were requested to judge what percentage other elements were of the standard. For example, in the case of judgments of position along a common scale (type 1), subjects were shown four dots at equal horizontal intervals and varying in location along a single vertical scale. For each point, subjects reported what percentage of the standard it represented.

Across conditions, the data were generally consistent with Cleveland & McGill's taxonomy in terms of the ordering of errors from low (position along a common scale) to high (slope, area, and volume). The same results were obtained with high school students, college students, and technically trained professionals, an invariance that would be expected from the large psychophysical literature on magnitude estimation (e.g. Stevens, 1957). Cleveland & McGill also suggested that the elementary tasks of perceiving density (amount of black), color saturation, and color hue constituted additional tasks ordered in terms of quality of perception in positions 8 through 10, respectively. This latter assertion, which will be particularly relevant in the context of statistical maps, was based on analysis of the psychophysical literature and was not tested directly. Table 17.1 summarizes Cleveland & McGill's taxonomy together with representative instantiations in statistical graphs and commonly associated tasks.

A strong corollary of Cleveland & McGill's approach is that graphs provide a computational advantage over numeric representations because they exploit what Cleveland terms pre-attentive visual processes. In particular, unlike numeric displays, which are known to require attentionally-controlled sequential visual search when more than a few values are present, data presented in graphs can often be perceived in parallel.

Table 17.1 Elementary graphical codes and their use in statistical graphics following Cleveland & McGill (1984, 1986)

Rank	Code	Perceptual prototype	Graphic prototype	Task
1.	Position along a common scale			Compare relative height of adjacent bars in bar chart
2.	Position along identical but non-aligned scales	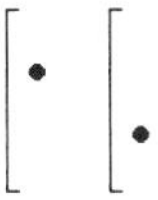	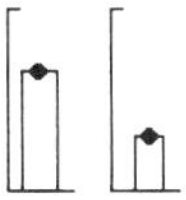	Compare relative height of non-adjacent bars, possibly non-aligned
3.	Length		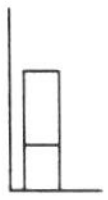	Compare relative lengths of bar-segments in segmented bar chart
4.	Angle		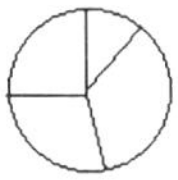	Compare relative size of segmented sections of pie chart
5.	Slope	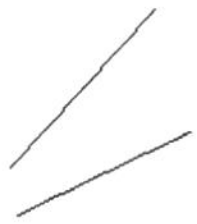	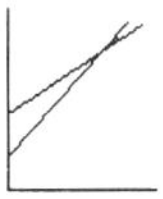	Compare relative rate of increase in two functions
6.	Area	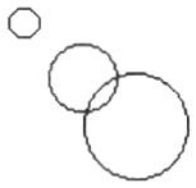	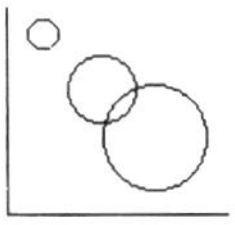	Compare relative size of symbols reflecting magnitude of third variable in a scatterplot
7.	Volume	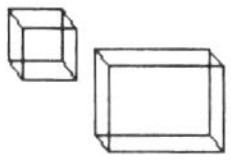		Compare relative magnitude in 3-D bar charts

To illustrate, consider a study by Legge, Gu & Luebker (1989) which compared the efficiency of extracting the mean and variance of samples using scatterplots, tables, and luminance-coded displays. In the scatterplot condition, data were positioned along the y-axis to reflect their value, and jittered along the x-axis in an arbitrary manner to avoid overplotting of symbols. The luminance display consisted of a table whose layout matched the traditional numeric table. However, instead of numbers, bars were shown in the table whose brightness indicated the data value. Performance was found to be highest for scatterplots, which were also immune to a performance decline due to increases in sample size. In contrast, performance with tables suffered as sample size increased.

Legge et al. (1989) concluded that the superiority of graphs arose from their ability to support efficient processing of information. For example, in the scatterplot, the variability in the data can quickly be ascertained by judging the physical spread of the points, and the mean can be judged by picking an approximate center of the symbols. On the other hand, to estimate the mean and variance from a set of numbers requires a number of additional cognitive steps including symbol decoding, short-term memory store, gist extraction, and the possible use of mental arithmetic.

Seeking further confirmation of the Cleveland & McGill taxonomy, Carswell (1992a) conducted a meta-analysis of 36 experiments that compared different visual codes. Effects were considered positive when differences in performance between different codes were in the direction predicted by the taxonomy. The average effect size across all comparisons was a considerable $r = .44$. When analyzed separately by task categories, which comprised point reading, local comparison, global comparison, and synthesis, effects were significantly positive only for point reading ($r = .23$, 95% CI: .02 to .49) and local comparison tasks ($r = .54$, 95% CI: .15 to .78). That is, as predicted by the taxonomy, estimates of a single data point or comparisons of a small set were best when data were coded by position along a common scale, worst when coded by volume, and in between for the intervening levels of the taxonomy.

A different result was obtained for global comparisons, defined as the comparison of multiple parts of a graph against others (e.g. "Is D greater than the average of A and C?"). The average effect size was not significantly different from zero ($r = .15$, 95% CI: –.19 to .45). Finally, for synthesis tasks, such as assessments of variability (e.g. "Is the variability of the data points large?") and interpolation (e.g. "What would the next value in the series be?"), the effect sizes were significantly negative ($r = -.32$, 95% CI: –.57 to –.01). That is, for complex tasks, the taxonomy failed to predict performance.

On balance, the Cleveland & McGill (1984, 1986) taxonomy provides valuable guidance for situations involving perceptually simple tasks. In terms of Kosslyn's (1989) framework, Cleveland & McGill focused extensively on syntax, while omitting considerations of semantics and pragmatics. Hence, the taxonomy must be augmented by other considerations for tasks that are more complex.

Interaction of Perceptual and Cognitive Information

There are several suggestions that even some of the very basic, supposedly pre-attentive processes considered by Cleveland & McGill (1984, 1986) are subject to top-down intervention. For example, Tversky & Schiano (1989; see also Schiano & Tversky, 1992) reported a series of studies in which participants viewed stimuli consisting of an L-frame, with a single line emanating from the origin. The stimuli were described to subjects either as maps that contained a river or graphs that contained a function. When subjects reconstructed the lines from memory, a bias toward a 45° angle was observed for those stimuli that were described as graphs, whereas that bias was absent when the same stimuli were presented as maps.

Tversky & Schiano concluded that these distortions arose from cognitive activity associated with interpretation of the meaning of the stimulus, rather than as the result of pre-attentive perception. This is difficult to accommodate by Cleveland & McGill's (1984) taxonomy, but it is entirely consistent with Pinker's (1990) framework, which underscored the importance of schemas and also the involvement of bottom-up processes in their selection. Hence, even "elementary" graph perception is a composite of "bottom-up" perceptual and "top-down" cognitive mechanisms. By implication, models of graph perception must combine perceptual and cognitive components in order to provide a plausible and comprehensive account of human performance. Several such models have been developed during the past decade, loosely conforming to our analytic frameworks.

Extensions of Classical Psychophysics

Turning first to models formulated as extensions of classical psychophysics, Spence (1990) demonstrated that errors in judgments of proportion (e.g. "What proportion is A of B?") could be predicted from the perceived absolute magnitudes that were expected, from Stevens' "power law", for the standard (B) and comparison (A) stimulus. Stevens' power law (e.g. Stevens, 1957) states that the perceived absolute magnitude of a stimulus (e.g. line lengths or the volume of 3-D objects) is equal to its physical magnitude raised to an exponent. The exponent remains invariant across stimulus magnitudes within a modality, but varies across modalities. For example, exponents for estimates of length are approximately 1.0, whereas exponents for volume are around 0.8. Exponents of less than 1.0 indicate that the perceived absolute magnitude is smaller than the physical extent of the stimulus, whereas an exponent of 1.0 indicates that perceived and physical magnitudes are identical. Cleveland & McGill's (1984) taxonomy incorporated the rank ordering of exponents, with tasks whose exponents are closest to 1.0 at the top of the hierarchy. By mathematically combining these expected absolute magnitude judgments, then, Spence (1990) was able to account for much of the average error observed in relative (or proportional) judgments.

However, Spence's (1990) model could not account for the error pattern at a more fine-grained level of analysis. When the average judgment errors were separated by stimulus magnitude, a cyclical pattern was revealed, such that the prevalence of over-estimations and under-estimations alternated across stimulus magnitudes. This pattern was present in Spence's (1990) own data and in related psychometric work (e.g. Huttenlocher, Hedges & Duncan, 1991). Hollands & Dyre (1997, 1998) were able to account for the cyclical error pattern by considering that the stimulus attributes underlying Spence's (1990) model may not be the physical graph elements, but rather perceptual anchors such as the 25% or 50% location. For example, when judging the proportion of the area of a pie-shaped wedge to the entire circle, the perceiver may imagine a 25% wedge that subtends a quadrant of the circle and compare the actual shape to this mental anchor. Likewise, when comparing bar lengths in bar graphs, the perceiver may bisect the longer bar at the 50% mark and compare the shorter bar against this anchor position, rather than the total length of the bar.

This extension of the Spence (1990) model allowed Hollands & Dyre to predict a variety of cyclical patterns in proportion judgment. Such patterns are found in many contexts including judgments of the relative angles of lines in function plots

(Schiano & Tversky, 1992), relative lengths of bars in bar charts (Spence & Lewandowsky, 1991), and lengths of different portions of box-plot displays (Behrens, Stock & Sedgwick 1990; Stock & Behrens, 1991). Direct application of the Hollands & Dyre approach to the data of Huttenlocher, Hedges & Duncan (1991), Spence (1990), and Spence & Krizel (1994) provided significant improvements in fit. This model thus represents the most powerful extension of classical psychophysics to modern graphical perception. However, being tied to tradition of psychophysical functions, it is unlikely to be a candidate for application to other, more complex graphical tasks that go beyond simple estimation or comparison. Those tasks are best described by componential models that rely on the flexible interaction between a variety of visual and mental processes.

Componential Models of Graph Perception

Simkin & Hastie (1987) conducted a task analysis that aimed to isolate and identify the cognitive sub-processes underlying performance in a variety of experimental tasks. In contrast to Cleveland & McGill's emphasis on basic perception, Simkin & Hastie (1987) introduced the term elementary mental processes to describe the components putatively identified by the task analysis. These processes included:

1. anchoring (selecting a standard such as the 25% mark, akin to Hollands & Dyre, 1998)
2. scanning (sweeping across an image)
3. projection (cognitively extending a comparison line from one point to another)
4. superimposition (cognitively moving elements across the display in order to make comparisons of size or shape)
5. detection operators (comparison procedures such as larger/smaller).

Consider the task of judging the height of bar B relative to the height of bar A, akin to Spence's (1990) procedure, that is shown in panel (a) of Figure 17.1. As illustrated in panel (b), the elementary processes proposed by Simkin & Hastie (1987) to accomplish this task include (1) segmenting the left bar into anchors, (2) projecting the 25% location on the left bar onto the parallel location on the right bar, and (3) scanning the length from the projection of the 25% anchor to the end of the right bar. While this simple task can be accommodated by the psychophysical models of Spence (1990) and Hollands & Dyre (1998), Simkin & Hastie's (1987) model additionally captures more complex tasks. For example, comparison of the sums of two pairs (e.g. "Are A and B together greater than the sum of C and D?") would first involve superimposition, where the visual objects representing bars A and C would be cognitively "stacked" onto B and D, respectively, before the resulting compounds are compared as for the simpler A–B comparison.

The resemblance between those processes and other existing metaphors for mental (Kosslyn, 1980) and visual images (Ullman, 1984) is apparent. Superimposition is a variant of mental rotation processes (e.g. Cooper & Shepard, 1973),

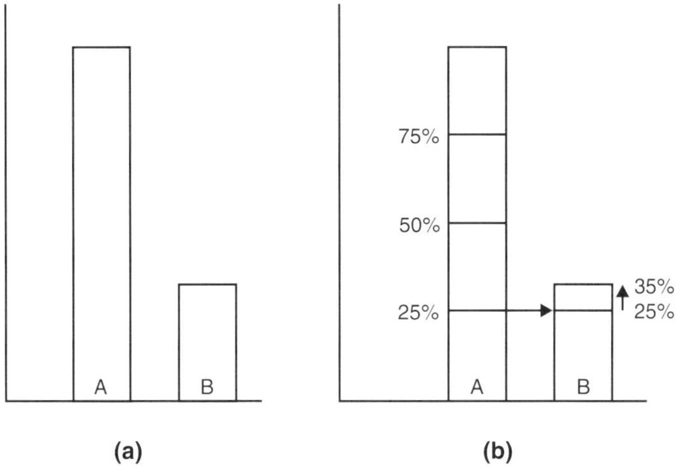

Figure 17.1 (a) Typical bar chart format for comparing bar lengths, and (b) Anchoring, projection and scanning tasks involved in estimating relative length

whereas projection resembles the well-known attentional spotlight (e.g. Posner, Snyder & Davidson, 1980). The principal contribution of Simkin & Hastie (1987) was that the model provided a "cognitive grammar" that allowed analysis and description of performance in a variety of situations. However, the flexibility of the model also reduced the possibility of serious empirical test and falsification. Models that were developed more recently strike a better balance between flexibility and falsifiability.

Lohse (1993) developed a detailed computational model of graph reading that was based on findings from the memory literature and data about the time required for fundamental processes such as scanning, comparing, or keyboard data entry. Lohse's model was instantiated in a LISP program that predicted the precise sequence and duration of gaze fixations during inspection of a graph. The program simultaneously created an image for the subjects to view and an accompanying propositional representation as suggested by Pinker's (1990) framework. When given a graphical task, the program then searched those propositional representations and extracted information in a manner consistent with the literature on visual search and short-term memory, thus predicting human response time in that situation.

To test the model, Lohse (1993) presented subjects with bar graphs, line graphs, or tables together with questions of varying difficulty. The questions involved reading of single values, comparing values, and assessing an overall trend. When data were averaged across subjects, 37% of the variance in response times was accounted for by the model. For individual response times, the model accounted for 10% of the variance. It is notable that the model made specific reaction time predictions across a range of tasks, and accounted for a significant amount of variance even at the level of individual participants. This constituted a major increase in theoretical precision compared to the work of Pinker (1990), Kosslyn (1989), and Simkin & Hastie (1987).

Among the many interesting results of this study, Lohse (1993) found that tables led to faster performance than graphs across several levels of task difficulty. In the corresponding simulation, the superiority of the table arose because individual data values were identified more quickly than in a graph. By contrast, graphs supported a quicker assessment of the overall pattern of data. The partial superiority of tables contradicted the widespread recommendation to use graphs for data sets of more than 20 observations (Tufte, 1983) or for complex data patterns (Jarvenpaa & Dickson, 1988; Wainer & Thissen, 1981). It is important to note, however, that Lohse's (1993) most difficult task consisted of determining whether a trend between two points was increasing or decreasing. By comparison to tasks undertaken in natural settings, this represents a relatively simple question because it can be reduced to a simple data look-up problem. In general, the conditions under which tables should be preferred over graphs continue to be debated. Interested readers should consult the meta-analysis conducted by Schaubroeck & Muralidhar (1991, 1992) as well as the critique provided in response by Montazemi (1991).

Another componential model of graph reading was proposed by Gillan & Lewis (1994). In contrast to Lohse's (1993) low-level analysis of information processing, Gillan & Lewis (1994) asked subjects to "think aloud" while performing several graphical tasks, and subsequently used those protocols to guide model development. Briefly, the model relied on a small set of component processes (e.g. search, encoding, spatial comparison) identified during protocol analysis. The model assumed that people apply those component processes sequentially, and in the order required for a particular graph–task combination. The model was found to account for more than 70% of the variance among response times across experimental conditions, involving eleven tasks, three different graphs, and two subject populations.

Overall, the field now has access to several well-defined models of graph reading that provide impressive predictive power, sometimes at the level of individual subjects. One important attribute of those models is the universal recognition that performance is not only a function of the type of graph, but also of the particular task that is required of the observer.

Display Format and Perceptual Task

Interaction of Design Features and Task Demands

Early work on graphs (e.g. Cleveland, 1985; Cleveland & McGill, 1984) was characterized by sweeping statements concerning the relative merits of different display designs. For example, the finding that judgments of proportion were more accurate for two aligned lines than for angles led Cleveland to conclude that bar charts should be universally preferred over pie charts, and that pie charts were fundamentally flawed because of their reliance on angle judgments. Global conclusions of this type are now considered inadequate, and there is much evidence to suggest that different perceptual tasks may favor different graphs. We first present studies that explicitly manipulated the observer's task, before turning to an examination of the default expectations and processes with which people approach statistical graphs.

Simkin & Hastie (1987) were among the first to point to the importance of the task. They noted that Cleveland & McGill's (1984, 1985) experiment on judgment of proportions, although aimed at comparing graphs under identical circumstances, actually involved very different uses of the stimuli. In the case of aligned line segments, participants had to judge what proportion one line was of the larger, a task that is consistent with common bar-graph reading. In the case of angles, participants were asked the same question of two different angles. The judgment of two angles, however, is not commonly involved in the analysis of the pie chart. Instead, the pie chart requires a judgment of a single angle out of a larger whole. Hence, Cleveland & McGill's results may have no bearing on the everyday use of statistical graphs, an expectation that Simkin & Hastie (1987) confirmed by experimentation.

Simkin & Hastie (1987) first replicated Cleveland & McGills's (1984, 1985, 1986) results, that for the task of judging what proportion one stimulus was of another, lines (as represented in bar charts) were superior to angles. However, when the task was to judge the proportion of a whole, performance on pie and bar charts was statistically undistinguishable and both were superior to segmented bar charts. This result was easily accommodated by Simkin & Hastie's (1987) model introduced earlier. Specifically, when comparing two separate angles, a graph reader must create a mental image of one angle and superimpose it on the other, which is quite a difficult task. By contrast, when comparing a subcomponent against the whole, the size of the subcomponent can be directly compared with cognitive anchors (cf. Hollands & Dyre, 1998).

Extending this work, Spence & Lewandowsky (1991) examined performance in a forced-choice task in which participants indicated the larger of two values in bar charts, pie charts, tables, or horizontal divided bar charts. Tasks included the direct comparison of values (e.g. A vs. B) and simple combinations (A vs. B + C) or compound combinations (A + B vs. C + D). On each trial, subjects compared different combinations of segments, specified by letters presented below the graph. Again, contrary to the conclusions of Cleveland & McGill (1984), Spence & Lewandowsky (1991) discovered an interaction between type of task and type of graph. Simple tasks (A vs. B and A vs. B + C) led to a joint superiority of pie and bar charts over tables, whereas compound comparisons (A + B vs. C + D) led to statistically superior performance for pie charts over bar charts and bar charts over tables. These results are shown in the top panel of Figure 17.2. (The bottom panel will be discussed later.)

Spence & Lewandowsky (1991) explored several potential reasons for this effect. First, they considered the possibility that the advantage of the pie chart was limited to cases in which segments that needed to be combined (e.g. A + B) happened to be visually adjacent. This possibility was ruled out by analysis of performance as a function of segment order. A second possibility involved the ease of visually locating graph elements: perhaps the pie chart afforded faster and more accurate identification of the segments involved in the comparison. In a further experiment, Spence & Lewandowsky (1991) therefore colored the relevant segments in the stimuli, thus allowing their instant identification. Moreover, color

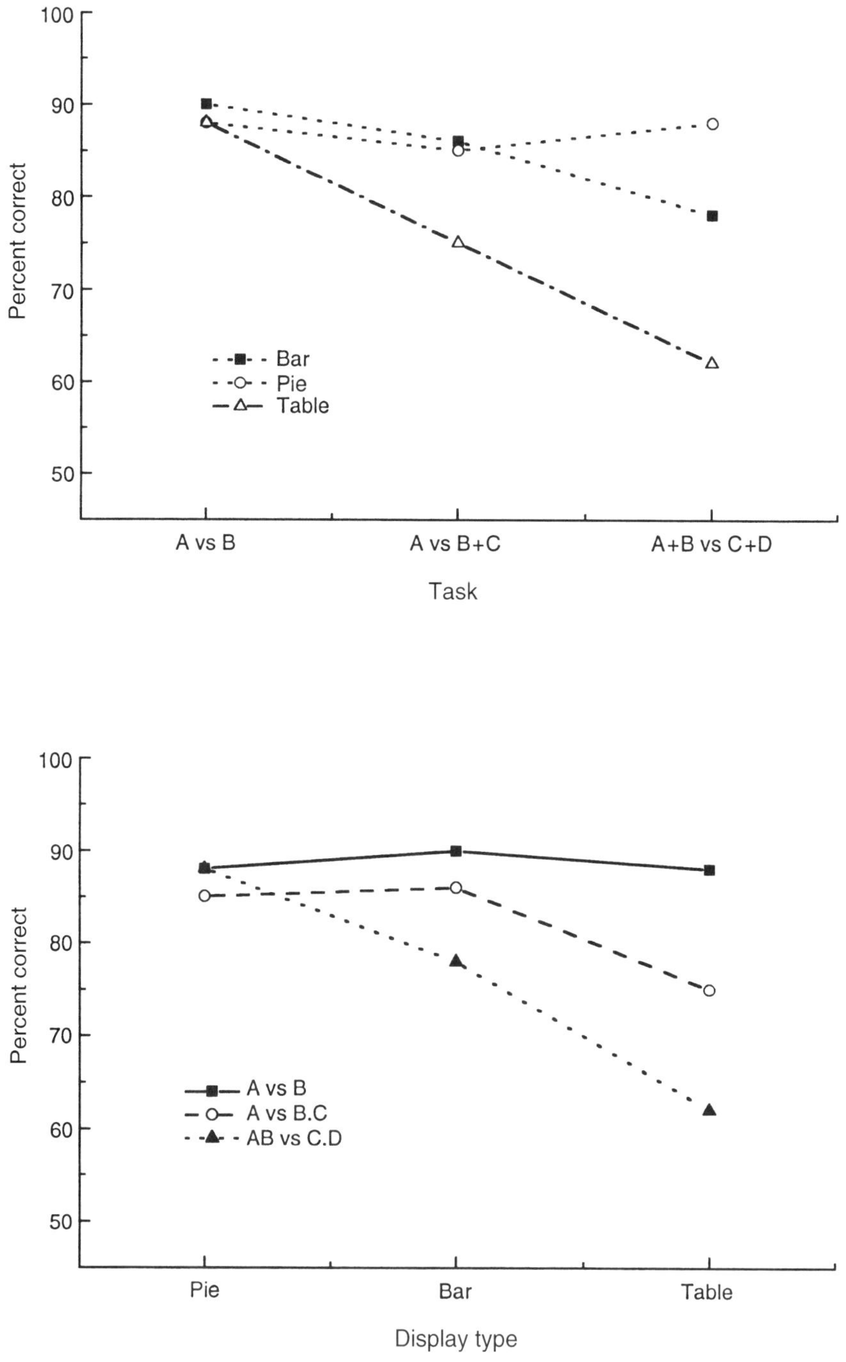

Figure 17.2 Line plot depicting interaction effect in factorial design. Data from Spence & Lewandowsky (1991)

was consistently mapped to response keys, thus obviating the need for any trial-by-trial matching of letters, segments, and response keys. Performance was unaffected, suggesting that higher-level cognitive processing, rather than early perception, was responsible for the superiority of the pie chart for compound comparisons.

Hollands & Spence (1992) further extended this paradigm to tasks that required processing of information from several graphs simultaneously. Subjects were asked to judge the rate of change in quantitative variables across several pie charts, grouped bar charts, or line charts. Direction of change judgments (increase, decrease, or constant) were most accurate when judged from line or bar charts as opposed to pie charts. Hollands & Spence concluded that the presence of vertical bars supported the extension of horizontal scan paths, akin to the projection operator proposed by Simkin & Hastie (1987), to form virtual line plots across the tops of the bars. These virtual line plots directly supported judgments of slope and rate of change. Pie charts, on the other hand, could not support such direct image-based processing and therefore required additional computation. Accordingly, the advantage of bar charts in rate-of-change estimation could be eliminated when they were stacked on non-aligned scales. Contrary to previous research (Simkin & Hastie, 1987), bar and line charts were also superior for answering questions concerning proportions of a whole (e.g. "What proportion is A of the whole at time 2?"). Further experimentation confirmed that this result was a consequence of the availability of tic-marks in the bar and line charts: when explicit scales and tic-marks were omitted from all displays in a second study, the results were reversed and pie charts and stacked bar charts led to superior proportion of whole performance.

Overall, there is no doubt that the observer's task plays a crucial role in determining the efficacy of various graphs. What, then, are the tasks most frequently performed in a naturalistic setting? Gillan & Lewis (1994) reported a survey of graph users that identified the following five tasks to be the most common ones:

1. comparison of two or more values
2. determining trends in the data
3. computing the mean of a sample
4. determining the difference between values
5. identifying a single observed value.

Clearly, the tasks chosen for the studies just reviewed were representative of practical applications.

Task Demands, Default Expectations, and Encoding Specificity

Thus far, we have focused on experimental manipulations of the observer's task. However, equally important may be the default expectations that observers bring to bear based on prior experience. The importance of expectation was represented in Pinker's (1990) framework, which predicted a degradation in performance when observers had to perform tasks that were inconsistent with the original encoding. This issue was explored in a series of studies by Simcox (1981, 1983a, b) that varied the aspect of the graph that was most likely to be spontaneously encoded. All stimuli contained two values, represented by one of the following:

- two vertical lines with dots on the end in separate frames (suggestive of two separate bar charts)
- two such vertical lines in a single frame
- two dots alone
- two dots connected horizontally by a slanted line.

Simcox (1981) hypothesized that subjects would spontaneously focus on encoding of individual data values when the graphs resembled bar charts, but would focus on encoding of slope when the stimuli looked more like line graphs.

The stimuli in Simcox's studies orthogonally varied the absolute magnitudes of the left and right data value and the slope between them. Participants were instructed to sort stimuli by magnitude of only one aspect of the graph (e.g. the slope). Simcox argued that sorting would be faster when the stimuli only varied in the relevant dimension (homogeneous set), whereas interference would result if stimuli varied in the second dimension also (heterogeneous). The extent of that interference, in turn, was expected to differ according to whether or not subjects spontaneously encoded the irrelevant dimension, depending on the default expectations brought to bear on the various graphs. Defining interference as the difference in sorting speed between heterogeneous and homogeneous card sets, Simcox (1981) found decreased interference for sorting by slope as the displays looked less like bar charts and more like line plots. Conversely, also as predicted, when sorting by the magnitude of the two data values, Simcox found decreased interference as subjects sorted card sets that more closely resembled bar charts. Subsequent studies (Simcox, 1983a, b) extended this basic finding to other graphs (e.g. line graphs showing a two-way interaction), demonstrating that people used default encoding strategies with considerable generality. Interference resulted whenever subsequent tasks did not match the encoded representation.

In another demonstration of people's default understanding of graphs, Gattis & Holyoak (1996) found that comprehension of straight-line function graphs was affected by the way in which increases in magnitude were represented. In some instances, graphs were shown in which descending lines indicated faster chemical processes, whereas in other instances, ascending lines indicated the faster process. Superior performance resulted when the slope mapping function of faster = steeper was retained. When the faster = steeper correspondence was not maintained, performance was degraded.

Shah (1997) reported a related instance, in which people's expectations of likely relationships in the data overrode what was actually presented. Graphs contained trivariate data involving the number of car accidents, distance between cars, and the number of drunk drivers. Even though in one condition the data did not show an association between drunk driving and number of accidents, 93% of novice graph viewers inaccurately reported its presence.

Finally, Tversky, Kugelmass & Winter (1991) conducted a cross-cultural comparison of the understanding of graph representations, in this case patterns of change over time. Comprehension was facilitated when the temporal order of the graph matched the left-to-right or right-to-left reading pattern of the participant's language. In cultures with a right-to-left reading pattern, interpretation was facilitated by organizing the graph to show temporal ordering from right to left. At the same time, regardless of language, culture, and age, individuals universally associated the terms "more" and "better" with an upward graphical direction, paralleling the result by Gattis & Holyoak (1996).

Overall, the results of Simcox (1981, 1983a, b), Gattis & Holyoak (1996), Shah (1997), and Tversky et al. (1991) lend considerable support to Pinker's (1990) contention that the original encoding of a graph is driven by default expectations and schemas. Concerning the nature of these expectations and schemas, Gattis & Holyoak and Tversky at al. revealed the seemingly universal graphic-to-semantic association between "up" and "more." Tversky et al. additionally demonstrated that other graphic-to-semantic associations are culture-specific. Simcox additionally showed that interference results when subsequent task demands do not match the encoded representation. Shah, finally, showed how expectations about causal relationships can override perception.

CONCEPTUAL GRAPHICAL TASKS: INTERPRETING FACTORIAL EXPERIMENTS

Most of the studies reviewed so far have focused on the use of relatively direct tasks and simple graphical forms. That is, the tasks tended to rely primarily on visual read-out of information available in the graph itself, even in cases where judgments involved compounds (e.g. Spence & Lewandowsky, 1991) or recognition of trends (e.g. Hollands & Spence, 1992; Lohse, 1993). In Pinker's (1990) framework, this corresponds to applying the matching process to compare previously encoded information with currently queried information. We now turn to the perception of *conceptual* graphical tasks, defined here as requiring the translation of visual features into abstract conceptual relations before the data can be interpreted (Shah & Carpenter, 1995, p. 45). (Shah & Carpenter (1995) used the term complex to refer to those tasks. However, in distinction to other usages of that term, we prefer to label those tasks as "conceptual.") We can think of this in terms of Pinker's (1990) framework by considering tokens and associative nodes of great complexity and abstraction that are connected not only with the visual surface features of the graph, but also with rich mathematical and spatial information. Conceptual graphical tasks exert a great demand for cognitive resources, as indicated by the fact that they may take up to 30 seconds to complete, or about the time required to understand a paragraph of text (Shah, 1997).

Although many conceptual graphical tasks exist, primary interest here is on the interpretation of factorial experiments, in particular of interactions between experimental variables. The research literature abounds with factorial experiments whose results are displayed in line graphs. Typically, the response variable is plotted on the ordinate, one of the experimental variables is assigned to the x-axis, and the other (known as the z-variable) serves as parameter.

Consider again the earlier Figure 17.2, which showed the results of the study by Spence & Lewandowsky (1991): the two panels used the same type of graph to provide two alternative perspectives of the same data. The only difference between panels was that different experimental variables serve as x- and z-variable in each case. The top panel replicated the original presentation format of Spence & Lewandowsky and illustrated the result they emphasized; namely, that the pie chart was superior to the bar chart for comparisons involving two pairs of data values, whereas it was indistinguishable for the simpler comparisons. This result was seemingly obscured in the bottom panel, which emphasized instead that performance with the table was far more variable across tasks than with the other displays. It is clear from comparison of the panels that interpretation of a given data set depends not only on the visual properties of a graph – since both panels used identical graphical techniques – but on the way in which people form an abstract representation of the pattern of results. This again supports Pinker's (1990) distinction between encoding of a graph into a propositional network and its subsequent interpretation, and the importance of a default interpretative schema.

Surprisingly, notwithstanding the ubiquity of factorial experiments, a search of the literature reveals only a single paper that has investigated the comprehension of line graphs with more than one experimental variable (Shah & Carpenter, 1995). The consistent result of the study was that people have difficulty extracting precise quantitative information from the z-variable. That is, when presented with line graphs containing separate lines for each level of the z-variable, people could not readily distinguish between linear and exponential increases of the z-variable. By contrast, the corresponding judgment involving values along the x-axis is trivial.

When asked to decide whether two graphs depicted the same or different results from a factorial experiment, people erroneously considered the same data to be different on nearly half the trials involving two different views, as in the two panels in Figure 17.2. Moreover, when instructed to draw a previously presented interaction from memory, people were quite accurate when perspective remained the same, but performance dropped to about 24% when the alternative perspective had to be drawn. This occurred despite the fact that participants were actively encouraged to use spatial encoding when viewing the graph. Shah & Carpenter (1995) tested advanced graduate students and spatially trained architecture students in addition to novices, and found the same performance deficits in all groups.

Overall, Shah & Carpenter (1995) demonstrated convincingly that people's understanding of standard experimental outcomes was significantly affected by the way in which the data were displayed. This is particularly noteworthy in light of the fact that little if any abstract guidance exists on which perspective of the data is the "correct" or "better" one. For example, there are no *a priori* reasons to prefer one panel in Figure 17.2 to the other, and Spence & Lewandowsky (1991) chose the representation that underscored their particular interpretative emphasis. By implication, situations may arise in which data are interpreted very differently by different researchers, depending on the perspective chosen for graphing.

Shah & Carpenter (1995) focused exclusively on x–y plots, in which the z-variable was represented as parameter (i.e. by different lines in the x–y space). An alternative display involves the use of "3-D" graphs, in which both the x- and z-variables have metric properties, with the z-axis inflected to simulate visual depth. Can 3-D displays avoid perspective-bound interpretations? Notwithstanding the popularity of such 3-D graphs, Shah & Carpenter (1995, p. 59) presented several arguments against their use. Shah (1997) discussed a further study that compared 3-D representations to line graphs and found that, although people provided a more exhaustive description of the data landscape with 3-D representations, their accuracy of point estimates suffered. Lewandowsky & Myers (1993) provided further evidence against the applicability of 3-D graphs by showing that perceptual thresholds for differences between data values were dramatically greater if an axis was inflected by 30° (akin to a z-axis) rather than horizontal (as in a conventional x-axis). Taken together, the results of Shah (1997) and Lewandowsky & Myers (1993) recommend against the use of 3-D displays: later on, we discuss situations in which this recommendation does not apply.

In summary, the scarcity of research on a topic as important as the interpretation of common experimental results must give rise to concern, in particular since the data suggest serious limitations in peoples' abstract graphical abilities. For the data analyst and graph designer, it follows that experimental results should be explored and presented in numerous different ways. For the graph consumer, it follows that the skills of recognizing the relationships between different perspectives should be rehearsed and improved.

Interaction of Design Features and Data Structure

So far, we have focused on two major themes: we first examined the role of the physical attributes of the graph, and we then considered various manifestations of the interaction between graphs and perceptual task. We now turn to our third and final major theme, the role of the particular patterns in the data being shown and their interaction with the type of graph. To illustrate with an obvious case, consider the x–y scatterplot, which can reveal outliers in two-dimensional space that cannot possibly be detected in separate univariate graphs of the x and y distributions (cf. Spence & Garrison, 1993). Accordingly, Yu & Behrens (1995) proposed the alignment framework, which holds that overall performance is the result of the tripartite alignment between the type of graph, the observer's task, and the underlying pattern of the data.

Working from this viewpoint, Yu (1995) reviewed the literature concerning the efficacy of interactive 3-D data visualization tools. Despite their increasing popularity in applied statistical analysis, a number of studies had concluded there was no advantage to such 3-D visualizations (Marchak & Marchak, 1991; Marchak & Whitney, 1990; Marchak & Zulager, 1992; Wickens, Merwin & Lin, 1994; Wickens & Todd, 1990). Following the alignment framework, Yu (1995) argued that the failure to find an additional benefit from these more complex techniques reflected the use of data sets whose structure was extremely simple and therefore not well aligned with the complexity of the 3-D graphs. In terms of the alignment framework, because 3-D rotating plots are designed to perceive 3-D structure without perspective dependence, data that are inherently two-dimensional, or consist of only few values, should not be expected to reveal the utility of 3-D plots. As a case in point, consider the study by Wickens & Todd (1990), in which the 3-D surface was defined by only four data points – hardly enough to justify the complexity of a 3-D visualization tool.

To test the alignment framework, Yu (1995) presented subjects with data sets comprising 8, 50 or 100 points, using either histograms, x–y scatterplots, 3-D rotating plots that appeared as point clouds, or 3-D rotating plots with smoothed mesh surfaces added within the point clouds to emphasize the data structure. Participants were asked to describe the shape of the function (e.g. "What is the value of z when x and y are low?") and to identify outliers. Yu used data that exhibited a 3-D saddle shape in which a plane had been modified with one set of opposite corners peaked in the positive direction, and the remaining corners peaked in a negative direction. In data of such complexity, a given data point may appear to lie in the bulk of the data, on the edge of the data, or squarely separated from the data, depending on the viewpoint of the observer in the three-dimensional space. Representative stimulus data from Yu (1995) are presented in Figure 17.3. Each panel shows the same data from a different viewpoint. Consider the single observation marked with a '+' character: in panel (a), the observation appears to be extreme, but not an outlier, whereas in (b) it looks more deviant, and in panel (c), the observation clearly does not conform to the underlying saddle-shaped function.

For the task of outlier detection, Yu found both 3-D rotating plots and 3-D mesh plots to be superior to 2-D plots. In fact, performance on 3-D plots improved with an increase in plotted symbols, but became worse for 2-D plots. For the task of judging function shape, the 3-D mesh plots were superior to the other plots across all data set sizes. The superior performance for 3-D plots in high dimensional data, along with the converse finding of superiority of 2-D plots for low dimensional data (Wickens & Todd, 1990), supported the alignment framework.

While the importance of the underlying data pattern has received relatively little attention in the psychological literature, the statistical literature on graph design includes emphasis on an iterative process of test and refinement using many different datasets (Tukey, 1982, cited in Cleveland, 1987).

Summary: Status of Theoretical Frameworks

We suggest that the plethora of findings reviewed so far can be distilled into two main themes. Both fit within the frameworks by Pinker (1990) and Kosslyn (1989) proposed at the outset, while at the same time also revealing their limitations. None of the analytic frameworks introduced at the outset, nor any of the specific models we reviewed, can address the issues presented in the last two sections. We do not currently have access to theories that describe how people perform

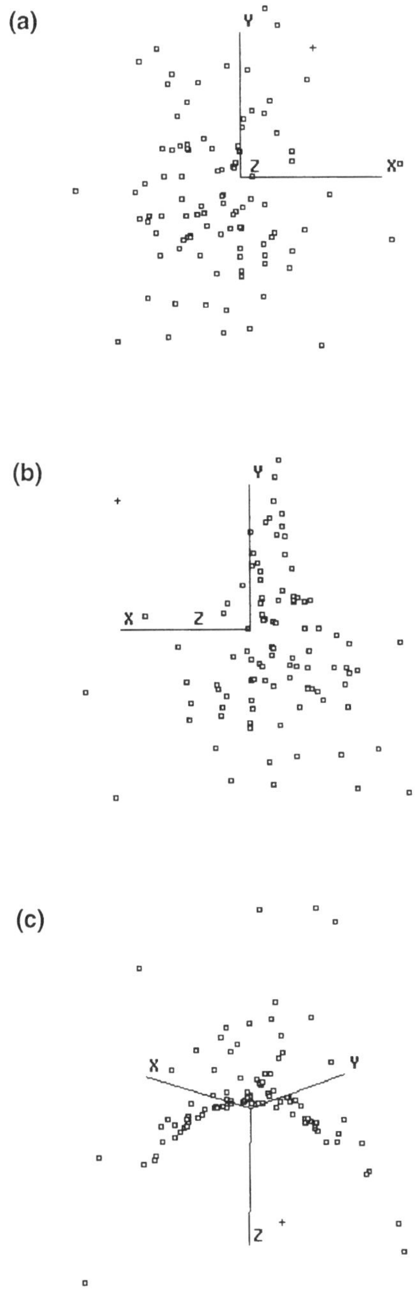

Figure 17.3 Three-dimensional representation of data used by Yu (1995) to assess the value of three-dimensional displays. Each plot depicts the same data from a different viewpoint in the coordinate system

conceptual graphical tasks, such as interpreting factorial experiments, on abstract mental representations of the data. Although Pinker (1990) has presented a predicate language that may allow description of these processes in principle, his framework has yet to be formally applied to the interpretation of factorial experiments. Progress in this direction would be particularly helpful given the ubiquity of those data and given people's consistently poor performance.

Likewise, no current theory can precisely specify the conditions of alignment between the pattern in the data, the type of graph, and the observer's task necessary to support satisfactory performance. Again, Pinker's (1990) framework may provide the requisite flexibility, although it remains unclear how it would represent different data patterns in such a way as to predict the performance differences observed by Yu (1995).

We believe that exploration of these two themes provides a useful guide towards necessary future research.

COGNITIVE COMPLEXITY IN THE FACE OF APPARENT SIMPLICITY: STATISTICAL MAPS

Statistical maps are indispensable tools for the analysis and presentation of data whose geographic distribution is of interest. Compared to graphs, maps present some unique additional challenges to the graph designer. First, the two dimensions of the plane are taken up with the display of geographic information, which prevents the coding of magnitude through vertical or horizontal position. By implication, magnitude must be coded in other ways, for example by use of symbols or shading of areas. Earlier, we noted some support for the taxonomy of elementary perceptual tasks proposed by Cleveland & McGill (1984). In their taxonomy, judgments of position formed the most accurate perceptual task, whereas judgments of density (e.g. shadings of gray) were among the least accurate. This mandates that particular care is taken during the design of statistical maps. Second, statistical maps may show many hundreds or even thousands of data points. This imposes great demands on the map-reader who may be asked to assess the overall pattern.

Notwithstanding these challenges, statistical maps, especially those representing mortality data, have had a unique influence on public policy: the earliest known case involved mapping of cholera deaths in London in 1854, which allowed the water-borne illness to be traced to a contaminated water pump (discussed in Gilbert, 1958; Wainer, 1992). To this date, statistical maps have been central to epidemiological efforts directed at controlling the spread of diseases. In particular, cancer research would have taken a very different path if detailed mortality atlases (e.g. Pickle, Mungiole, Jones & White, 1996) had not been available during the past few decades. A specific case that demonstrates the utility of statistical maps involves the identification of a particularly high incidence of cervical cancer in West Virginia from the 1987 cancer atlas (Pickle, Mason, Howard, Hoover & Fraumeni, 1987). Detection of this cluster prompted the allocation of extra funds towards early detection and treatment of this often curable disease, with the result that mortality subsequently declined (Maher, 1995).

Statistical Maps: Pre-experimental Considerations

Practitioners can choose from a large number of statistical mapping techniques. We limit discussion here to choropleth and symbol maps, two of the most popular types of statistical maps.

Choropleth Maps

Choropleth maps use shading or coloring of individual regions on the map to represent magnitudes. Most choropleth maps are classed; that is, data values are aggregated into few (typically 5–8) class intervals that sub-divide the overall range of magnitudes (for discussion of unclassed maps, see e.g. Gale & Halperin, 1982; MacEachren, 1995, p. 156). The three maps shown in Figure 17.4 are examples of such "classed" choropleth maps.

Monochrome choropleth maps use increasingly dense shadings or fills of a single color to represent increasing numerical magnitude. Double-ended choropleth maps, also known as bipolar or two-opposing colors maps, use increasingly dense shadings of one color to represent high (above-midrange) magnitudes and increasingly dense shadings of another color to represent low (below-midrange) magnitudes. Categorical color or multi-hue maps, finally, assign a different fully-saturated hue to each class of magnitudes.

The use of choropleth maps has several perceptual and cognitive implications: first, for all choropleth maps, a given numerical magnitude will be given greater visual prominence if it happens to fall into a larger region because a greater physical area on the page will be shaded or colored. Second, color-coded maps may lose intelligibility when perceived in black and white – either because monochrome photocopies have been made or because the viewer is among the non-trivial proportion (7%) of males who are colorblind. Third, color-coding requires the presence and use of a legend: whereas ordinal understanding of a monochrome map is possible without any explanation, a categorical or double-ended scale is meaningless without accompanying legend.

Symbol Maps

A symbol map represents magnitudes by superimposing some graphical symbol, such as a pie chart or a framed rectangle, onto each map area. In consequence, symbol maps are not susceptible to areal bias because the symbol size is unaffected by the size of map areas (although complications may arise for areas that are too small to allow superimposition of the symbol).

These pre-experimental considerations are in large part confirmed by the available data. We now selectively review those results, again in the order of complexity of experimental task. We limit discussion to point estimates and cluster detection.

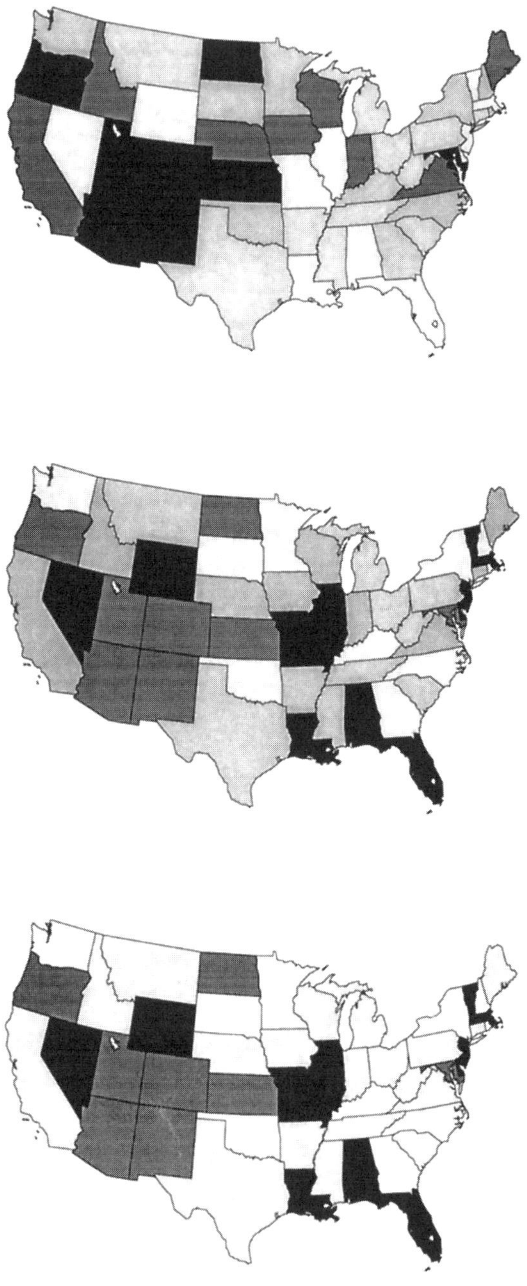

Figure 17.4 Examples of classed choropleth maps

Reviews that are more comprehensive can be found in Herrmann & Pickle (1996), and Lewandowsky & Behrens (1996). A particularly thorough treatment of the cognitive aspects of cartography in general, rather than just statistical mapping, can be found in MacEachren (1995).

Point Estimation Tasks

Maps, like graphs, can be used to estimate a single data value, for example when asking observers to report mortality for the state of Maine. Kimerling (1985) investigated perceived magnitude as a function of density of gray shading and found a strikingly non-linear relationship between physical and perceived density. That is, in contrast to the straightforward power law for other graphical judgments (cf. Spence, 1990), shades of gray obey a more complex relationship, in particular when texture becomes noticeable owing to technical limitations in reproduction. This suggests that other means of magnitude representation might lead to more accurate point estimates.

Using a point estimation task, Dunn (1988) compared framed-rectangle maps (in which a small framed bar chart is superimposed on each area to represent magnitude) to a conventional monochrome choropleth map. The framed-rectangle maps yielded far more accurate point estimates of individual magnitudes. The error associated with subjects' estimates (in this case of murder rates) was almost twice as large with the choropleth map than the framed-rectangle map. Moreover, as expected from the foregoing discussion, areal bias (i.e. the tendency for larger states to yield inflated estimates) was eliminated with framed rectangles. In a related study, Meihoefer (1973) showed that circles of varying sizes, when superimposed on map regions, can also support accurate numerical estimates in the presence of a legend, an observation further supported by Cleveland, Harris & McGill (1982).

In summary, there is fairly consistent evidence that symbol maps engender more accurate estimates of individual values than choropleth maps. Additionally, unlike choropleth maps, symbol maps can represent two variables simultaneously, for example by using the width of framed rectangles to represent absolute size of population, while murder or mortality rate is represented by the height of each framed bar (Dunn, 1987).

On the more negative side, it is unclear how distinct symbols support the formation of a perceptual "gestalt" across a number of map regions. For example, how would one perceive a set of three distinct pie charts or framed rectangle charts as a single perceptual entity? Slocum (1983) addressed this issue using circles as symbols and found that people tended to form a perceptual gestalt based on proximity of the circles, rather than circle size or similarity. This introduced a new variant of the areal bias, thought to be eliminated by use of symbols, since neighborhoods of small areas necessarily give rise to greater proximity among symbols than large areas. This is likely to cause problems when observers have to integrate information across map regions, for example when searching for clusters of data values.

Complex Map Reading Tasks: Cluster Detection

Epidemiologists are among the most ardent users of statistical maps, although their interest is rarely on the estimation of individual values. Instead, in the majority of epidemiological applications, emphasis is on the detection of "clusters," contiguous areas of particularly high (or low) mortalities that represent unusual situations. Visual analysis is often the preferred way to detect clusters because mathematical approaches cannot model all relevant features of geographical space (Marshall, 1991). In light of the importance and ubiquity of cluster detection, the paucity of relevant research is quite striking.

Symbol Maps

In one of the few published studies on cluster detection, Lewandowsky, Herrmann, Behrens, Li, Pickle & Jobe (1993) asked participants to identify and mark high and low mortality clusters by drawing their outlines on the stimulus maps. Additionally, clusters had to be ordinally ranked according to their perceived size and importance. Lewandowsky et al. found that pie maps, similar to those shown in Figure 17.5, were consistently judged to contain fewer clusters than a variety of choropleth maps displaying the same mortality data.

In confirmation of the earlier considerations regarding symbol maps and cluster detection, the finding suggested that subjects had difficulty perceiving the full complexity of the stimulus data when presented in a symbol map.

Double-ended vs. Monochrome Scales

Turning to choropleth coding schemes, the case for color has been stated very eloquently by Carswell, Kinslow, Pickle & Herrmann (1995). Given that humans typically cannot differentiate more than 3–5 levels of gray or brightness (Sanders & McCormick, 1993), the double-ended scale provides an opportunity to double the number of available categories through concatenation of two hues, each with its own set of shadings. In addition, because low and high magnitudes are typically represented by identical scales of saturation, the double-ended scale affords the opportunity to correct the known human bias of attending primarily to the confirming presence of critical information (i.e. high mortalities), even though its absence (i.e. low mortalities) may be equally relevant to understanding the etiology of a disease.

On the other hand, valid psychological reasons can also be cited against the double-ended scale, in particular if one assumes that pre-attentive processes engaged in visual search also underlie map inspection. There is widespread agreement among cognitive psychologists that visual detection of a target is qualitatively more difficult and time-consuming if conjunctions of features must be formed (e.g. Treisman, 1991). For example, if the features "red" and "triangle" must be detected and combined to identify a target (because red squares and green triangles are also present) a qualitatively different perceptual process appears to be engaged than when the task is to pick out a red object among green distractors or a triangle among squares. Applied to the context of mortality maps, it follows that

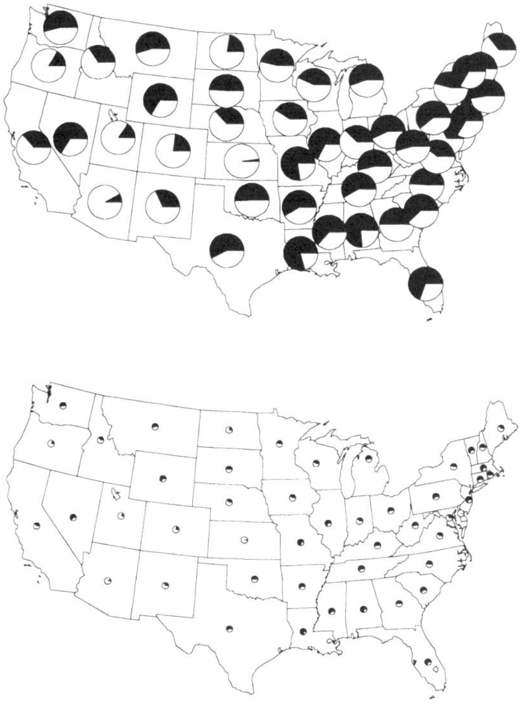

Figure 17.5 Examples of the use of pie chart symbols in statistical maps

a monochrome scale may be more readily perceived than the double-ended scale, which relies on formation of the conjunction of saturation and hue.

The available empirical evidence mirrors the theoretical ambivalence surrounding the double-ended scales. Consider first the more negative results, provided by Lewandowsky et al. (1993). In that study, the double-ended scale was found to lead to somewhat greater perceptual variability (i.e. less agreement among participants about perceived cluster locations, suggesting less consistent data communication) than two monochrome scales involving shades of blue and black. At least in part, that result was due to the non-negligible number of scale reversals for the double-ended scale, exactly as one might expect from the visual search literature. Specifically, four (out of 31) participants placed a high mortality cluster in regions that were identified as having the lowest incidence of the disease by the remaining subjects. These observations, representing more than 10% of the subjects, are best interpreted as scale-reversals. Perceptual difficulties associated with the double-ended scale are not confined to the study by Lewandowsky et al. (1993). Mersey (1990) also reported occasional scale reversals by participants, and Cuff (1973) found that subjects often chose the lightest class interval (that is, the midpoint of the double-ended scale) when asked to identify the region with the lowest data value. Although each study in isolation is subject to limitations arising from the choice of participants or details of the design (Carswell et al., 1995), there can be little doubt that scale reversals occur in a non-negligible number of cases.

Turning to the more supportive evidence, Carswell et al. (1995) conducted a particularly thorough investigation of several different double-ended schemes in comparison to a gray scale. Performance with a red–yellow opposing scale was found to be consistently better than with a monochrome gray scale. At the same time, a blue–yellow opposing scale was found inferior to shades of gray, with a third double-ended scale, red–blue, taking up the middle ground. Fortunately, Carswell et al. (1995) were able to provide principled explanations for the observed differences between color pairings, which otherwise would have formed a confusing array of seemingly arbitrary outcomes. Carswell et al. (1995) suggested that the success of the red–yellow scale was in large part due to the decoupling of perceived brightness and saturation. Specifically, for that scale, brightness increased monotonically from the lowest (saturated red) to the highest category (saturated yellow), thus providing an additional perceptual cue for estimation of magnitudes and also eliminating the problems otherwise associated with black-and-white reproduction. The failure of the blue–yellow scale at first appears puzzling because it, too, decoupled brightness and saturation. Carswell et al. (1995) suggested that the blue–yellow scale failed because of its conflicting use of two opposing graphical conventions; "darker-for-more" (shades of blue) and "warmer-for-more" (shades of yellow). Earlier, in the context of graphs, the importance of conforming to graphical conventions was noted in the context of the study by Gattis & Holyoak (1996).

On balance, the available experimental results are best summarized as follows:

1. Double-ended scales that decouple brightness and saturation are suitable for cluster detection (Carswell et al., 1995).
2. Other double-ended scales are at best comparable to monochrome scales (Carswell et al., 1995; Lewandowsky et al., 1993).
3. The occurrence of scale reversals with a double-ended scale cannot be ruled out (Cuff, 1973; Lewandowsky et al., 1993; Mersey, 1990).
4. On a theoretical note, the double-ended scale supports a "residual" approach to data analysis, in which a tentative model is applied to the data – whether visual or by statistical means – and focus is on the residuals. The double-ended scale supports residual analysis by subtracting the mean of the data and emphasizing deviations from that "model."

Categorical Color Scales

Unlike monochrome scales, sets of different colors are not immediately perceived as an ordinal sequence of magnitudes: green does not necessarily represent "more" (or "less") than blue or red. In consequence, for most categorical color scales, hues are assigned to magnitudes either arbitrarily or in spectral sequence. There is evidence that, for a given set of colors, assignment to magnitudes has no effect on performance in a variety of tasks (Hastie, Hammerle, Kerwin, Croner & Herrmann, 1996).

However, assignment to magnitudes aside, choice of the set of colors is important. Cleveland & McGill (1983) showed that the number and size of red areas was consistently overestimated in comparison to areas filled in green. Similarly, in their cluster detection task, Lewandowsky et al. (1993) found that performance with a categorical color scale differed depending on which set of colors observers had to attend. If the task required observers to focus primarily on areas whose hues were highly discriminable, performance was good, whereas performance was relatively poor for areas filled with less discriminable colors.

THE ROLE OF THE PATTERN IN THE DATA

During our discussion of graphs, we noted the importance of the alignment between the particular pattern of data that is being displayed and the type of graph (e.g. Yu, 1995; Yu & Behrens, 1995). For statistical maps, similar alignment considerations are likely to apply, although we know of only one study that investigated the issue. Muehrcke (1973, cited in MacEachren, 1995) presented participants with a set of ten maps that had to be ranked by their correlation with an eleventh comparison map. The study orthogonally manipulated the type of map (i.e. choropleth vs. several other display formats) and the level of data complexity. Data complexity here referred to the degree of the polynomial (first through fifth) that was used to produce the data shown on the map. Muerhcke discovered a complex interaction between data structure and map type, suggesting once again that questions about the "best" type of display can only be answered in the context of a specific alignment between data, task, and display type. Alas, as in the case of graphs, relevant research is scarce.

A COGNITIVE MODEL OF STATISTICAL MAP READING

In contrast to the work on statistical graphs, where the past few years have witnessed the arrival of strong and testable models, research on statistical map perception has proceeded largely without theory. Accordingly, the data just reviewed predate the only model of statistical map reading known to us (Herrmann & Pickle, 1996). MacEachren's (1995) cognitive and semiotic analysis of cartography is an important scholarly and theoretical effort; however, it addresses the broader aspects of cartography with little specific reference to the unique properties of statistical maps. Hence, we limit discussion to the model by Hermann & Pickle (1996).

Herrmann & Pickle (1996) proposed that map reading involves four stages that are typically executed in sequence:

1. orienting to the map
2. comprehension of the legend
3. integration of information gathered during the first two stages
4. extraction of statistical information.

Within each stage, a variety of cognitive subprocesses (e.g. sensation, perception, memory retrieval) is engaged to accomplish the objective of that stage. The first stage, orienting, refers to the exploration of global and very basic questions: What does the map represent? What is the map designed to communicate? The following stage, legend comprehension, consists of answering questions about how the symbolization scheme should be interpreted. The third, integrative stage consists of exploring the data values that are associated with various geographic regions. The fourth and final stage, extraction of information, culminates in an overt response to the observer's task.

Broad support for the model arises from the fact that the durations of the substages have been shown to be additive (Hastie et al., 1996) and from the fact that verbal protocols mirror the presumed division into four stages (e.g. Pickle, Herrmann, Kerwin, Croner & White, 1993). However, the model is not without its limitations. To date, it has been limited to choropleth maps and its extension to symbol maps and other schemes is by no means assured. In addition, although Herrmann & Pickle (1996, pp. 176–7) tabulate a lengthy list of model predictions, their largely intuitive character renders future falsification unlikely. For example, it is difficult to think of a theoretical alternative to the assertion that "error and latency of response increase with linguistic difficulty of legend" (Herrmann & Pickle, 1996, p. 177).

The theoretical maturity of the Herrmann & Pickle model – and by implication of statistical map research overall – can be further assessed by comparing it to the models of graph reading discussed earlier. That comparison suggests that Herrmann & Pickle's model resembles, in terms of theoretical detail, testability, and scope, the work by Simkin & Hastie (1987). Assuming that the history of the graph arena is predictive of the likely progress of work on statistical maps, we can expect stronger models to be put forward within the next few years. Interestingly, MacEachren's (1995) recent treatise of cartography relied extensively on Pinker's (1990) framework, suggesting it may also influence future, more detailed models of statistical map perception.

SUMMARY AND RECOMMENDATIONS

This chapter has shown that the last two decades have witnessed a dramatic increase in our knowledge of the cognitive processes involved in the comprehension of statistical graphs and maps. Moreover, the principal elements of that knowledge can be readily summarized and condensed into specific recommendations for graph construction; however, because this review was necessarily selective, we first mention our omissions before turning to a final summary.

Issues Omitted from the Review

We decided to omit discussion of research conducted outside our current theoretical frameworks (i.e. Kosslyn, 1989; Pinker, 1990). That is, we only considered research that could be clearly anchored in our frameworks, and omitted work that examined visual details of graphs and maps for purely pragmatic reasons. The latter type of work can be illustrated with a study by Poulton (1985), which showed that reading of point values in a line graph was detrimentally affected when observers had to scan over sloped lines between the point and the scaled axis. This situation occurs when the point cloud in a scatterplot is superimposed by, say, a regression line, and subjects must report the value of a specific point located on the side of the regression line away from the axis. Poulton suggested that this effect represented an instantiation of the familiar Poggendorf illusion. Accordingly, in a condition in which scales and tic-marks were placed on axes on both sides of the graph, such that no lines needed to be traversed during scanning, the error was negligible. (Given those results, it is unfortunate that publication guidelines for most scientific societies do not require labeled axes on both sides of the graph.) A parallel example involving statistical maps involves a study by DeLucia & Hiller (1982), which found that small changes in the format of the legend could alter perception of the pattern of data presented on the map.

Both examples are noteworthy in the present context because, even though they have little bearing or connection to our stated frameworks, they had a significant and large effect on performance. It follows that numerous other such effects may await serendipitous discovery.

In addition to pragmatic research into details of graph and map design, we also did not consider the research concerning separable and integral displays and the role of emergent features in object recognition. This research has sought to identify the circumstances when graphs are interpreted as single integral objects (akin to, say, a human face) as opposed to a series of separate independent indicators. There seems to be little consensus on the issue, and the interested reader may consult Carswell (1992b) or Sanderson, Flach, Buttigieg & Casey (1989) for different views on this type of research.

The Principal Elements of Graphs and Maps

Turning now to a summary of our review, we believe that the following findings and issues are most central:

1. Graph and map comprehension is the result of a complex interaction of bottom-up (perceptual) and top-down (cognitive/memorial) processes. Even seemingly pre-cognitive activities may be influenced by the interpretation of graph elements in terms of their role in the display. Researchers must avoid excessive focus on perceptual interpretations of graph reading that overlook the multi-layered processing of information.
2. The efficacy of graph comprehension cannot be tied exclusively to graph format, but must also be considered in terms of the task to be undertaken, and the pattern of data underlying the appearance of the display.
3. The quality of graph comprehension is dependent on the interpretation of the meaning of the graph and the schema driven encoding that follows.

4. Graph comprehension involves encoding of both propositional and analog (visual–graphic) mental representations. The interaction of these systems is poorly understood.
5. Statistical maps are qualitatively different from the bulk of other statistical graphs because the spatial extent constrains the symbols that can be associated with individual regions, and because the proximity of the symbols leads to perceptual interactions.

Targets for Further Research Effort

In addition to these general advances, a few notable lapses exist in the literature. We take that as an opportunity to issue recommendations for areas of future research.

1. The earlier calls for systematic verification and extension of the alignment framework (e.g. Yu & Behrens, 1995) deserve to be repeated here.
2. Compared to the complexity of real-world graph reading, tasks studied in the laboratory have been, in most cases, extremely simple. In the early stages of programmatic research, the use of well-defined and precisely operationalized tasks may be advisable because it fosters slow but sure advancement. This has been the case to date with tasks that mimic component processes subsumed in more global tasks. For example, the majority of studies examining bar charts (Cleveland & McGill, 1984, 1985; Simkin & Hastie, 1987; Spence & Lewandowsky, 1991) did not place tic-marks on the vertical axis. While this simplification helps to isolate mental component processes such as scanning or projection, it cannot mirror the richness of real-world tasks. In consequence, confusion may arise regarding the generalizability of findings to more authentic tasks. Interestingly, Gillan & Richman (1994) manipulated the presence of tic-marks on the y-axis of graphs and found complex interactions in which tic-marks appeared to slow performance on simple tasks.
3. Closely related to the problem of task complexity is the issue of the range of graph formats examined. Most of the studies reviewed here examined bar charts, pie charts, and scatterplots. Other displays have received relatively less attention, notwithstanding the increased usage of complex statistical graphs that is evident in the data analytic literature (e.g. Behrens, 1997a).
4. The role of propositional knowledge representation has been undervalued relative to its importance in general information processing. Most studies have conceptualized graph comprehension in terms of analog (visual-graphic) representation and processing. Intra- and inter-personal communication, however, is primarily a verbal activity. Accordingly, cognition and meta-cognition concerning statistical graphs are likely to be rich in propositional form, which in turn are likely to constrain the operations that act on the analog representations (cf. Simcox, 1981). It follows that our understanding of the propositional aspects of graph processing must advance in parallel with the growing understanding of analog visual processes.

Particularly relevant in this context is the role of the observer's content knowledge, both concerning the design of graphs and the subject matter of the data being presented. We therefore call for further studies involving highly practiced data analysts, both those who specialize in the use of statistical graphs and those with advanced mathematical knowledge but little training in graphical representation. Similarly, examination of the move from novice to expert conceptualizations deserves to receive more empirical attention.

5. The social role of graphs, and the situational context that motivates their use, have so far been largely overlooked. This is inadvisable because social and situational context can point to important theoretical issues. For example, the alignment framework was motivated by the apparent incongruity between laboratory-based failures to demonstrate the usefulness of 3-D rotating plots (Marchak & Zulager, 1992; Wickens & Todd, 1990; Wickens et al., 1994) and the ecological fact that 3-D plots were obtaining widespread use among graphically oriented data analysts (Cleveland & McGill, 1988).
6. In the theoretical arena, attention should turn to the development of strong models of statistical map reading, in order to go beyond the initial proposal by Herrmann & Pickle (1996). MacEachren's (1995) comprehensive work on cartography may usefully guide this process.
7. Finally, the frameworks by Kosslyn (1989) and Pinker (1990) need to be reassessed in light of recent results and theoretical developments. Notwithstanding their utility to date, it is already clear that the frameworks fail to accommodate the complete alignment framework.

To conclude, our knowledge of statistical graph and map comprehension has advanced markedly in the last few decades. The field now seems ready to move from the original focus on elementary tasks that are examined in restricted situations, to a broader focus that examines the integration of different types of information in a wider range of data analytic circumstances and social contexts.

ACKNOWLEDGMENTS

Preparation of this article was facilitated by Large Research Grants No. A79600016 and A79701143 from the Australian Research Council to the first author. The first author also gratefully acknowledges the support received from the University of Potsdam, where this chapter was completed, through a grant from the Deutsche Forschungsgemeinschaft (German Research Foundation; Grant INK 12/A1, Project C).

We wish to thank John Dugan for his assistance with bibliographic aspects of this work.

REFERENCES

Behrens, J. T. (1997a). Principles and procedures of exploratory data analysis. *Psychological Methods*, 2, 131–60.

Behrens, J. T. (1997b). Toward a theory and practice of using interactive graphics in statistical education. In J. B. Garfield & G. Burrill (Eds), *Research on the Role of*

Technology in Teaching and Learning Statistics (pp. 111–22). Voorburg, Netherlands: International Statistical Institute.
Behrens, J. T., Stock, W. A. & Sedgwick, C. E. (1990). Judgment errors in elementary box-plot displays. *Communications in Statistics B: Simulation and Computation*, 19, 245–62.
Bertin, J. (1983). *Semiology of Graphics: Diagrams, Networks, Maps*. Madison, WI: University of Wisconsin Press, Translation of the French edition.
Carswell, M. C. (1992a). Choosing specifiers: an evaluation of the basic task model of graphical perception. *Human Factors*, 34, 535–54.
Carswell, M. C. (1992b). Reading graphs: interactions of processing requirements and stimulus structure. In B. Burns (Ed.), *Percepts, Concepts, and Categories* (pp. 605–45). Amsterdam: Elsevier.
Carswell, C. M., Kinslow, H. S., Pickle, L. W. & Herrmann, D. J. (1995). Using color to represent magnitude in statistical maps: the case for double-ended scales. Manuscript submitted for publication.
Cleveland, W. S. (1985). *Elements of Graphing Data*. Monterey, CA: Wadsworth Advanced Books and Software.
Cleveland, W. S. (1987). Research in statistical graphics. *Journal of the American Statistical Association*, 82 (398), 419–23.
Cleveland, W. S. (1993). A model for studying display methods of statistical graphics. *Journal of Computational and Graphical Statistics*, 2, 323–43.
Cleveland, W. S. (1994). *Visualizing Data*. Summit, NJ: Hobart Press.
Cleveland, W. S., Harris, C. S. & McGill, R. (1982). Judgments of circle sizes on statistical maps. *Journal of the American Statistical Association*, 77, 541–7.
Cleveland, W. S. & McGill, R. (1983). A color-caused optical illusion on a statistical graph. *The American Statistician*, 37, 101–5.
Cleveland, W. S. & McGill, R. (1984). Graphical perception: theory, experimentation, and application to the development of graphical methods. *Journal of the American Statistical Association*, 79, 531–53.
Cleveland, W. S. & McGill, R. (1985). Graphical perception and graphical methods for analyzing and presenting scientific data. *Science*, 214, 93–4.
Cleveland, W. S. & McGill, R. (1986). An experiment in graphical perception. *International Journal of Man–Machine Studies*, 25, 491–500.
Cleveland, W. S. & McGill, M. E. (Eds) (1988). *Dynamic Graphics for Statistics*. New York: Chapman & Hall.
Cooper, L. A. & Shepard, R. N. (1973). The time required to prepare for a rotated stimulus. *Memory & Cognition*, 1, 246–50.
Cuff, D. J. (1973). Colour on temperature maps. *The Cartographic Journal*, 10, 17–21.
DeLucia, A. A. & Hiller, D. W. (1982). Natural legend design for thematic maps. *Cartographic Journal*, 19, 46–52.
Dunn, R. (1987). Variable-width framed rectangle charts for statistical mapping. *The American Statistician*, 41, 153–6.
Dunn, R. (1988). Framed rectangle charts or statistical maps with shading. *The American Statistician*, 42, 123–9.
Gale, N. & Halperin, W. C. (1982). A case for better graphics: the unclassed choropleth map. *The American Statistician*, 36, 330–6.
Gattis, M. & Holyoak, K. J. (1996). Mapping conceptual to spatial relations in visual reasoning. *Journal of Experimental Psychology: Learning, Memory and Cognition*, 22, 231–9.
Gilbert, E. W. (1958). Pioneer maps of health and disease in England. *Geographical Journal*, 124, 172–3.
Gillan, D. J. (1995). Visual arithmetic, computational graphics and the spatial metaphor. *Human Factors*, 37, 766–80.
Gillan, D. J. & Lewis, R. (1994). A componential model of human interaction with graphs: 1. Linear regression modeling. *Human Factors*, 36, 419–40.

Gillan, D. J. & Richman, E. H. (1994). Minimalism and the syntax of graphs. *Human Factors*, 36, 619–44.

Hastie, R., Hammerle, O., Kerwin, J., Croner, C. M. & Herrmann, D. J. (1996). Human performance reading statistical maps. *Journal of Experimental Psychology: Applied*, 2, 3–16.

Herrmann, D. J. & Pickle, L. W. (1996). A cognitive subtask model of statistical map reading. *Visual Cognition*, 3, 165–90.

Hollands, J. G. & Dyer, B. P. (1997). Bias in proportion judgements with pie charts: the cyclical power model. In *Proceedings of the Human Factors and Ergonomics Society 41st Annual Meeting* (pp. 1357–61). Santa Monica, CA: Human Factors and Ergonomics Society.

Hollands, J. G. & Dyre, B. P. (1998). Bias in proportion judgments: the cyclical power model. Manuscript submitted for publication.

Hollands, J. G. & Spence, I. (1992). Judgments of change and proportion in graphical perception. *Human Factors*, 34, 313–34.

Huttenlocher, J., Hedges, L. V. & Duncan, S. (1991). Categories and particulars: prototype effects in estimating spatial location. *Psychological Review*, 98, 352–76.

Jarvenpaa, S. L. & Dickson, G. W. (1988). Graphics and managerial decison making: research based guidelines. *Communications of the ACM*, 31, 764–74.

Kimerling, A. J. (1985). The comparison of equal-value gray scales. *American Cartographer*, 12, 132–42.

Kosslyn, S. M. (1980). *Image and Mind*. Cambridge, MA: Harvard University Press.

Kosslyn, S. M. (1985). Graphics and human information processing: a review of five books. *Journal of the American Statistical Association*, 80, 499–512.

Kosslyn, S. M. (1989). Understanding charts and graphs. *Applied Cognitive Psychology*, 3, 185–225.

Kosslyn, S. M. (1994). *The Elements of Graph Design*. New York: W. H. Freeman.

Larkin, J. & Simon, H. (1987). Why a diagram is (sometimes) worth a thousand words. *Cognitive Science*, 11, 65–99.

Legge, G. E., Gu, Y. & Luebker, A. (1989). Efficiency of graphical perception. *Perception & Psychophysics*, 46, 365–74.

Leinhardt, G., Zaslavsky, O. & Stein, M. K. (1990). Functions, graphs, and graphing: tasks, learning, and teaching. *Review of Educational Research*, 60, 1–64.

Lewandowsky, S. & Behrens, J. T. (1996). Visual detection of clusters in statistical maps. In *Proceedings of the 1995 Annual Meeting of the American Statistical Association* (pp. 8–17). Alexandria, VA: American Statistical Association.

Lewandowsky, S., Herrmann, D. J., Behrens, J. T., Li, S.-C., Pickle, L. & Jobe, J. B. (1993). Perception of clusters in statistical maps. *Applied Cognitive Psychology*, 7, 533–51.

Lewandowsky, S. & Myers, W. E. (1993). Magnitude judgments in 3D bar charts. In R. Steyer, K. F. Wender & K. F. Widaman (Eds), *Psychometric Methodology. Proceedings of the 7th European Meeting of the Psychometric Society in Trier* (pp. 266–71). Stuttgart: Gustav Fischer Verlag.

Lewandowsky, S. & Spence, I. (1990). The perception of statistical graphs. *Sociological Methods and Research*, 18, 200–42.

Lohse, G. E. (1993). A cognitive model for understanding graphical perception. *Human–Computer Interaction*, 8, 353–88.

MacEachren, A. M. (1995). *How Maps Work: Representation, Visualization, and Design*. New York: Guilford.

Maher, R. J. (1995). A history of the influence of statistical maps on public policy. In L. W. Pickle & D. J. Herrmann (Eds), *Cognitive Aspects of Statistical Mapping* (pp. 13–20). National Center for Health Statistics, Working Paper Series, No. 18.

Marchak, F. M. & Marchak, L. C. (1991). Interactive versus passive dynamics and the exploratory analysis of multivariate data. *Behavior Research Methods, Instruments & Computers*, 23, 296–300.

Marchak, F. M. & Whitney, D. A. (1990). Dynamic graphics in the exploratory analysis of multivariate data. *Behavior Research Methods, Instruments & Computers*, 22, 176–8.
Marchak, F. M. & Zulager, D. D. (1992). The effectiveness of dynamic graphics in revealing structure in multivariate data. *Behavior Research Methods, Instruments & Computers*, 24, 253–7.
Marr, D. (1982). *Vision*. San Francisco: Scott Foresman.
Marshall, R. J. (1991). A review of methods for the statistical analysis of spatial patterns of disease. *Journal of the Royal Statistical Society A*, 154, 421–41.
Meihoefer, H.-J. (1973). The visual perception of the circle in thematic maps/experimental results. *The Canadian Cartographer*, 10, 63–84.
Mersey, J. E. (1990). Colour and thematic map design: the role of colour scheme and map complexity in choropleth map communication. *Cartographica*, 27 (3), Monograph No. 41, 1–182.
Montazemi, A. R. (1991). Comments on "A meta-analysis of the relative effectiveness of tabular and graphic display format on decision making performance." *Human Performance*, 4, 147–53.
Muehrcke, P. (1973). Visual pattern comparison in map reading. *Proceedings, Association of American Cartographers* (pp. 190–4). Atlanta, GA.
Pickle, L. W., Herrmann, D. J., Kerwin, J., Croner, C. M. & White, A. A. (1993). The impact of statistical graphic design on interpretation of disease rate maps. *Proceedings of the Statistical Graphics Section, American Statistical Association.*
Pickle, L. W., Mason, T. J., Howard, N., Hoover, R. & Fraumeni, J. F. Jr (1987). *Atlas of US Cancer Mortality among Whites: 1950–1980*. Washington, DC: National Institutes of Health.
Pickle, L. W., Mungiole, M., Jones, G. K. & White, A. A. (1996). *Atlas of United States Mortality*. Hyattsville, MD: US Department of Health and Human Services.
Pinker, S. (1990). A theory of graph comprehension. In R. Freedle (Ed.), *Artificial Intelligence and the Future of Testing* (pp. 73–126). Hillsdale, NJ: Erlbaum.
Playfair, W. (1876). *The Commercial and Political Atlas*. London: Corry.
Posner, M. I., Snyder, C. R. R. & Davidson, B. J. (1980). Attention and the detection of signals. *Journal of Experimental Psychology: General*, 109, 160–74.
Poulton, E. C. (1985). Geometric illusions in reading graphs. *Perception & Psychophysics*, 37, 543–8.
Sanders, M. S. & McCormick, E. J. (1993). *Human Factors in Engineering and Design*. New York: McGraw-Hill.
Sanderson, P. M., Flach, J. M., Buttigieg, M. A. & Casey, E. J. (1989). Object display does not always support better integrated task performance. *Human Factors*, 31, 183–98.
Schaubroeck, J. & Muralidhar, K. (1991). A meta-analysis of the relative effects of tabular and graphic formats on decision-making performance. *Human Performance*, 4, 127–45.
Schaubroeck, J. & Muralidhar, K. (1992). Does display format really affect decision quality? *Human Performance*, 5, 245–8.
Schiano, D. & Tversky, B. (1992). Structure and strategy in encoding simplified graphs. *Memory & Cognition*, 20, 12–20.
Shah, P. (1997). A model of the cognitive and perceptual processes in graphical display comprehension. In *Proceedings of the 1997 Fall Symposium of The American Association for Artificial Intelligence. Reasoning with Diagrammatic Representations* (pp. 94–101). Menlo Park, CA: AAAI Press.
Shah, P. & Carpenter, P. A. (1995). Conceptual limitations in comprehending line graphs. *Journal of Experimental Psychology: General*, 124, 43–61.
Simcox, W. (1981). *Cognitive Considerations in Display Design* (400-79-006). Washington, DC: National Institute of Education. (ERIC Document Reproduction Service No. ED 222 191.)
Simcox, W. A. (1983a). *Configural Properties of Graphic Displays and their Effects on Processing* (NIE 400-79-0066). Washington, DC: National Institute of Education. (ERIC Document Reproduction Service No. ED 238 685.)

Simcox, W. A. (1983b). *Memorial Consequences of Display Coding* (NIE 400-79-0066). Washington, DC: National Institute of Education. (ERIC Document Reproduction Service No. ED 238 683.)

Simkin, D. & Hastie, R. (1987). An information-processing analysis of graph perception. *Journal of the American Statistical Association*, 82, 454–65.

Slocum, T. A. (1983). Predicting visual clusters on graduated circle maps. *American Cartographer*, 10, 59–72.

Spence, I. (1990). Visual psychophysics of simple graphical elements. *Journal of Experimental Psychology: Human Perception and Performance*, 16, 683–92.

Spence, I. & Garrison, R. F. (1993). A remarkable scatterplot. *The American Statistician*, 47, 12–19.

Spence, I. & Krizel, P. (1994). Children's perception of proportion in graphs. *Child Development*, 65, 1193–213.

Spence, I. & Lewandowsky, S. (1990). Graphical perception. In J. Fox & S. Long (Eds), *Modern Methods of Data Analysis* (pp. 13–57). Newbury Park, CA: Sage.

Spence, I. & Lewandowsky, S. (1991). Displaying proportions and percentages. *Applied Cognitive Psychology*, 5, 61–77.

Stevens, S. S. (1957). On the psychophysical law. *Psychological Review*, 64, 153–81.

Stock, W. A. & Behrens, J. T. (1991). Box, line, and mid-gap plots: effects of display characteristics on accuracy and bias of estimates of whisker length. *Journal of Educational Statistics*, 16, 1–20.

Treisman, A. M. (1991). Search, similarity, and integration of features between and within dimensions. *Journal of Experimental Psychology: Human Perception and Performance*, 17, 652–76.

Tufte, E. R. (1983). *The Visual Display of Quantitative Information*. Cheshire, CT: Graphics Press.

Tukey, J. W. (1977). *Exploratory Data Analysis*. Reading, MA: Addison Wesley.

Tukey, J. W. (1982). Thoughts on the evolution of dynamic graphics for data modification display. In W. S. Cleveland (Ed.), *The Collected Works of John W. Tukey: Graphics* (Vol. 5). Monterey, CA: Wadsworth.

Tversky, B., Kugelmass, S. & Winter, A. (1991). Cross-cultural and developmental trends in graphic productions. *Cognitive Psychology*, 23, 515–57.

Tversky, B. & Schiano, D. J. (1989). Perceptual and cognitive factors in memory for graphs and maps. *Journal of Experimental Psychology: General*, 118, 387–98.

Ullman, S. (1984). Visual routines. *Cognition*, 18, 97–159.

Wainer, H. (1992). Understanding graphs and tables. *Educational Researcher*, 21, 14–23.

Wainer, H. & Thissen, D. (1981). Graphical Data Analysis. *Annual Review of Psychology*, 32, 191–241.

Wickens, C. D., Merwin, D. H. & Lin, E. L. (1994). Implications of graphics enhancements for the visualization of scientific data: dimensional integrality, stereopsis, motion and mesh. *Human Factors*, 36, 44–61.

Wickens, C. D. & Todd, S. (1990). Three dimensional technology for aerospace and visualization. Paper presented at the Human Factors Society 34th Annual Meeting, Santa Monica.

Yu, C. H. (1995). The interaction of research goal, data type, and graphical format in multivariate visualization. Unpublished Doctoral Dissertation, Arizona State University, Tempe.

Yu, C. H. & Behrens, J. T. (1995). The alignment framework for data visualization: relationships among research goals, data type, and multivariate visualization techniques. Paper presented at the Annual meeting of the Society for Computers in Psychology, Los Angeles, CA.

Chapter 18

Instructional Technology

Richard E. Mayer
University of California, Santa Barbara

Instructional technology – or educational or learning technology – refers to tools that are used for the purpose of helping people to learn. This definition is broad enough to include classic technologies such as books and chalkboards, as well as twentieth-century innovations such as film, radio, and television. It includes widely available modern technologies such as videotape recorders, graphing calculators, and overhead projectors; it also includes emerging, newer technologies such as interactive video, computer projection, satellite TV, videoconferencing, virtual reality and the World Wide Web.

In addition, this definition of instructional technology is broad enough to include both hardware (such as computers or communication satellites) and software (such as instructional material available for the hardware). For example, computer hardware can be used to support multimedia programs whereas communication hardware can be used to support distance learning programs. Gallini & Gredler (1989, p. 3) argue that "hardware does not operate without courseware" so "the term educational technology refers to both components."

Advances in instructional technology can shape educational practice. It seems clear that the future of education will become increasingly intertwined with the development of technology. In particular, advances in information technologies (such as the World Wide Web), communication technologies (such as satellite-based distance learning and videoconferencing), and visualization technologies (such as computer-based multimedia and virtual reality) hold potential for shaping the schools of the future. For example, a recent review noted that "computer, video, and telecommunications systems available today were hard to imagine even 10 years ago" (Cognition and Technology Group at Vanderbilt, 1996, p. 807).

Handbook of Applied Cognition, Edited by F. T. Durso, R. S. Nickerson, R. W. Schvaneveldt, S. T. Dumais, D. S. Lindsay and M. T. H. Chi.

The interaction among cognitive psychology, educational psychology, and computer technology represents one of the main venues for applied cognitive psychology, and includes the field of instructional technology. The motivating issue for research on instructional technology concerns how technology can be used to support student learning. The outcome of learning can be measured in retention tests (such as determining how much of the presented material a student can remember) and transfer tests (such as determining the degree to which students can apply what they have learned to solve a new problem) (Mayer & Wittrock, 1996). Therefore, the study of instructional technology depends on whether the goal is to promote retention or transfer. (Tests to assess learning outcomes constitute a continuum ranging from near transfer to far transfer. In many cases, the ideal situation is to test along the whole continuum.) In this chapter, I focus on problem-solving transfer as a major educational goal.

TWO APPROACHES TO INSTRUCTIONAL TECHNOLOGY

Two approaches to instructional technology involve what can be called a technology-centered approach and a learner-centered approach.

Technology-centered Approach

Adherents of the technology-centered approach focus on the capabilities of technology, and tend to emphasize cutting-edge advances in technology. Technology is the starting point for educational reform, and the major challenge is to help students to have access to it. For example, a technology-centrist might say: "The World Wide Web will revolutionize education, so let's make sure students have access to it." In short, the motivating question for the technology-centered approach is, "What can technology do?" The goal of technology-centered proponents is to improve teaching, a goal that is often expressed as "revolutionizing" the way school subjects are taught.

The underlying theory of learning can be called the information transmission view (Mayer, 1996a) in which information is a commodity that can be transferred from the teacher to the student. According to this view, the student's mind is an empty vessel into which the teacher pours new information. Instructional technology is simply the delivery system for information, such that improvements in instructional technology offer more efficient ways of delivering information to students. It follows that the main task of an educational technology system is to present information to students.

"Does technology improve student learning?" This is the classic research question in the field of educational technology. Put more generally, the research issue concerns the role of media in learning: "Do students learn more with one presentation medium than with another?" Such questions have dominated – and in the opinion of many scholars, hindered – the study of technology in education (Clark, 1983, 1994; Clark & Salomon, 1986; Salomon, 1994).

The methods employed in media research involve experimental paradigms comparing how much students learn from two or more delivery systems. The independent variable is the medium of instruction (such as one group learning on a computer-based system versus another group learning on a textbook-based system). The dependent measure focuses on how much is learned (such as a multiple-choice test covering the major facts presented during instruction). The research venue may be controlled laboratory settings or more authentic settings such as classrooms or larger educational communities.

Learner-centered Approach

In contrast, adherents of the learner-centered approach focus on how student learning can be fostered through the use of technology, and tend to emphasize advances in our understanding of the learning process. The learner is the starting point for educational reform, and the major challenge is to use technology in ways that help students learn. A learner-centrist might be concerned with how student learning can be improved through access to the World Wide Web. In short, the motivating question for the learner-centered approach is, "How can we foster student learning with technology?" The goal of learner-centered proponents is to improve learning, a goal that is often expressed as fostering appropriate cognitive processing.

The underlying theory of learning can be called the knowledge construction view (Mayer, 1996a) in which learners actively build their learning outcomes by selecting incoming information, organizing it into coherent structures, and connecting it with existing knowledge. According to this view, the outcome of learning depends both on what is presented and the cognitive processes that the learner performs, including relating the material to existing knowledge. It follows that the main task of an educational technology system is to help the learner process the presented information in productive ways.

The motivating research questions in the learner-centered approach concern how and what students learn in technology-based environments, for example "How can we help students understand a new concept, principle, or system using technology?" The overarching research issue concerns how to use technologies to foster meaningful learning and improve human cognitive processing (Lajoie & Derry, 1993).

The methods employed involve both experimental and observational paradigms and occur in both laboratory and school settings. In experimental research, the independent variable is likely to be a feature of the technology, such as the degree of interactivity or amount of guidance provided, whereas the dependent measures are likely to include both retention and problem-solving transfer (Mayer & Wittrock, 1996). Observational research includes interviews of students as they learn from a technology-based system.

Table 18.1 summarizes the technology-centered and learner-centered approaches to instructional technology. In this chapter, I present a case for

Table 18.1 Two approaches to instructional technology

Characteristic	Technology-centered approach	Learner-centered approach
Focus	What technology can do	How can student learning be fostered by technology
Starting-point	Technology's power	Learner's cognitive processing
Goal	Improve teaching	Improve learning
Theory of learning	Information transmission	Knowledge construction
Role of technology	Delivery system	Cognitive aid
Research issue	Compare computers to humans	Compare ways to use computers

choosing the learner-centered approach over the technology-centered approach. First, I present an example of what can happen when the technology-centered approach is applied to education by reviewing the somewhat disappointing history of LOGO in schools. Second, I present an example of how the learner-centered approach can be used to improve education by deriving principles of multimedia design based on cognitive research.

THE LOGO SYNDROME: AN EXAMPLE OF TECHNOLOGY-CENTERED INNOVATION

The LOGO syndrome refers to the recurring pattern in the history of instructional technologies in which strong claims are made for the educative value of a technology, educators attempt to use the technology, and eventually educators find that the initial promises were not met. In this section, I review the cases of three classic educational technologies of the twentieth century – film, radio, and television – and then take a more in-depth look at the LOGO movement of the 1980s.

The Disappointing History of Educational Technologies

Part of the historic heritage of the instructional technology movement in education is the tendency to create grand expectations that are not met. For example, when the motion picture was invented in the early 1900s, hopes were high that the new technology would improve education. In 1922, the famous inventor Thomas Edison stated: "I believe that the motion picture is destined to revolutionize our educational system and that in a few years it will supplant largely, if not entirely, the use of textbooks" (cited in Cuban, 1986, p. 9). Edison's justification for this prediction is not unlike current claims concerning the power of computer graphics: "Scholars will soon be instructed through the eye. It is possible to touch every branch of human knowledge with the motion picture" (cited in Cuban, 1986, p. 11). Yet, in reviewing the role of motion pictures in schools over the decades since Edison's grand predictions, Cuban (1986, p. 17) concluded that "most teachers used films infrequently in classrooms." In short, the predicted educational revolution in which movies would replace books failed to materialize.

As another example, consider the sad case of education by radio. William Levenson, director of the Ohio School of the Air, predicted in 1945 that a "radio receiver will be as common in the classroom as the blackboard" and "radio instruction will be integrated into school life" (cited in Cuban, 1986, p. 19). Not unlike current calls for distance education through the creation of a virtual school (either on TV or on the World Wide Web), the potential magic of textbooks of the air was justified on the grounds that radio would expand the world of the student. For example, in 1932, Benjamin Darrow, founder of the Ohio School of the Air, proclaimed (cited in Cuban, 1986, p. 19): "The dominant aim of education by radio is to bring the world to the classroom, to make universally available the services of the finest teachers, the inspiration of the greatest leaders . . ." Yet, in spite of heroic efforts by teachers around the nation to use radio in their classes, subsequent research revealed that "radio has not been accepted as a full-fledged member of the educational family" (cited in Cuban, 1986, p. 24).

Finally, the history of educational television is no more rosy than that of movies and radio. By the early 1950s, educational television was introduced as a way of creating a continental classroom. Consistent with modern justifications for distance education, educational television was promoted as a way of "providing a richer education and at less cost than was possible by conventional methods of instruction" (cited in Cuban, 1986, p. 33). Yet, in spite of its great potential, research in the ensuing decades revealed that educational television was seldom used by teachers and "when teachers do use television, they do so infrequently and for only a tiny fraction of the instructional day" (Cuban, 1986, p. 40).

In the case of film, radio, and television, the technologies were different but all experienced the same cycle of grand promises, attempted implementation in schools, and, ultimately, unmet expectations. What went wrong? The disappointing results may be traced to the technology-centered approach taken by each technology's promoters. Instead of basing instructional technology innovations on the needs of students, the capabilities of the technologies themselves were the driving force behind instructional technology innovation. Instead of asking, "How can we help students to learn by using technology?", proponents of educational technology seemed to be asking, "How can we use the latest instructional technology in schools?"

Are these experiences relics of the past that cannot be repeated? Are the advances in modern technology so powerful that they are insulated from the disappointments of earlier, less sophisticated technologies? In order to address these questions, I briefly examine the more recent history of a popular educational technology – the LOGO movement of the 1980s (Mayer, 1988; Papert, 1980).

The LOGO Movement

LOGO is a programming language that includes turtle graphics in which the user may issue instructions to move a turtle-shaped cursor around a screen (see

Papert, 1980). For example, when the cursor is in the middle of the screen facing to the top, the program:

```
PD
RT 180
FD 10
LT 90
FD 5
```

causes the cursor to put its pen down (to leave a line were it moves), to rotate 180° (to face downward), to move forward ten turtle steps (creating a vertical line), to rotate 90° to its left (to face the right side of the screen), and to move forward five turtle steps (creating a horizontal line). The result of this program is the creation of an L-shaped figure on the screen.

During the 1980s, LOGO was used increasingly in schools and was recognized as an exciting tool for helping children to become programmers. One would be hard pressed to find a piece of 1980s educational software that had more impact on elementary school than LOGO (De Corte, Greer & Verschaffel, 1996; Mayer, 1988). The LOGO environment can be recognized today as one of the most influential applications of computer-based technology in schools in the 1980s.

LOGO's inventor, Seymour Papert (1980) took a learner-centered approach by focusing on how the mind of the learner could be improved through participation in a LOGO environment. However, the application of LOGO into schools was often based on a technology-centered approach in which LOGO was taught for its own sake. The original goals of LOGO included the improvement of children's problem-solving skills but learning LOGO quickly became an educational end in itself.

In some ways, the LOGO movement demonstrates the pattern of earlier instructional technologies – including phases of powerful claims, school implementation, and disappointing results.

Phase 1: Powerful Claims

What if we could create an instructional technology that would improve the way that children think? This is the vision of instructional technology advanced by early proponents of LOGO.

Consistent with the introduction of earlier technological innovations in schools, LOGO was introduced with a flurry of strong claims. In his influential book, *Mindstorms*, Papert (1980, p. 19) called for "free contact between children and computers" in which students learn to use LOGO on their own. In learning to program computers, children must "teach the computer how to think" and in the process "children embark on an exploration about how they themselves think" (Papert, 1980, p. 19). The computer aids learning because "the computer allows, or obliges, the child to externalize expectations" so "when the intuition is translated into a program it becomes . . . more accessible to reflection" (Papert, 1980, p. 145). The expected cognitive outcome of learning to use LOGO is that "powerful intellectual skills are developed in the process" (Papert, 1980, p. 60).

In short, in learning how to program, children would also learn how to think (Mayer, Dyck & Vilberg, 1986).

Abelson & di Sessa (1981, p. xiii) foresaw an educational revolution: "Today we are approaching a new technological revolution, one whose impact on education may be as far-reaching as that of the printing press: the emergence of powerful computers that are sufficiently inexpensive to be used by students for learning, play, and exploration."

As you can see, the 1980s began with strong claims that children's cognitive development could be promoted by allowing them to learn computer programming in a discovery environment. Accordingly, the new curriculum of the computer age should include computer programming such as LOGO and the new instructional method should be pure discovery in which children work with LOGO computers on their own.

Phase 2: Large-scale Implementation

If scale of implementation is the standard of success, LOGO has been fabulously successful. Resnick (1988) notes that LOGO is widely used in schools, although not in the way that Papert proposed. In particular, school use of LOGO is largely restricted to turtle graphics and has been institutionalized mainly within the mathematics curriculum (Gurtner, 1992; Kilpatrick & Davis, 1993; Resnick, 1988).

Phase 3: Disappointing Results

As schools increasingly incorporated LOGO, it became clear that student performance did not always support the powerful claims (Clements & Gullo, 1984; Nickerson, Perkins & Smith, 1985; Pea & Kurland, 1984). Mayer (1988, p. 3) notes that the "vision of students becoming better problem solvers due to hands-on LOGO learning collided with the documented reality of students' difficulties in learning even the fundamentals of LOGO." Similarly, De Corte, Greer & Verschaffel (1996, pp. 526–7) noted that a considerable research literature "has documented the difficulty of realizing Papert's vision" and shown that "children, left to themselves, do not, in general, construct powerful mathematical ideas latent in the LOGO environment." For example, in a survey of early studies, Perkins (1985, p. 12) concluded that exposure to LOGO resulted in "no transfer of skill and poor learning within LOGO itself." In another early review of LOGO research, Dalbey & Linn (1985, p. 267) found "students who learn LOGO fail to generalize this learning to other tasks." De Corte, Greer & Verschaffel (1996, p. 526) concur that "early optimism that experience with LOGO would lead to major changes in general problem solving skills such as planning and monitoring . . . was not supported in a series of studies carried out in the early 1980s."

Phase 4: Revised Vision

The failure to achieve the promise of LOGO could have spelled the complete demise of LOGO in schools. Although LOGO use is attenuated, it still exists in somewhat revised form. In particular, the modern uses of LOGO include a revised vision of both the instructional method and the curricular content. First, instead of relying on discovery as the primary method of instruction, successful implementations of LOGO rely on more structure and guidance from the teacher. For example, students who participated in a highly structured LOGO curriculum that explicitly emphasized planning showed improvements in their planning skills in domains outside LOGO (De Corte, Verschaffel & Schrooten, 1992; Fay & Mayer, 1994; Mayer, 1992). Second, the curricular goal shifted from the teaching of computer programming as a means to improve thinking to using LOGO as a tool for teaching mainline mathematical topics. For these reasons, "more recent investigations with more focused aims have produced positive results" (De Corte, Greer & Verschaffel, 1996, p. 527). In recognition of the changing use of LOGO in schools, Papert (1992, p. xv) noted the need to put "the dream on the back burner" and to "look for things to do with LOGO that have a better chance in the short run than recreating mathematics." In retreating from the original goal of students learning programming in order to become better problem solvers, LOGO proponents have substituted LOGO as a tool for teaching standard topics in the mathematics curriculum.

Today, computer programming is no longer part of the curriculum for most students. Partly because of unsupported claims, many educators no longer view computer programming as a means of promoting students' problem-solving ability. With the exception of some exciting – but somewhat isolated – demonstration projects and teacher innovations, most students do not use computers to improve their problem-solving skills. Instead, computers are used mainly for applications such as word processing, or an occasional educational game.

What can we learn from the saga of LOGO in schools, which I characterize as the LOGO syndrome? Like other innovations before it, the promises for LOGO outdistanced what could be delivered. When strong claims about the revolutionary power of a new technology fail to be met in real classrooms, then a backlash develops that greatly attenuates the use of that technology. When technology is naïvely viewed as some sort of magical delivery system that will provide learners with knowledge, skills, and intellectual power, then failure is a likely outcome. When changes are made without an understanding of how students learn, the potential power of educational technology can be completely lost.

Is it time to bury computers in the educational-technology graveyard next to film, radio, and TV? I hope that the answer is "No". When technology is used to support student learning based on a solid research-based theory of how students learn and when the projected claims are focused and realistic, then educational technology has a chance of success. In the next section, I provide an example of how computer technology can be used in the service of fostering student learning.

THE POTENTIAL OF MULTIMEDIA: AN EXAMPLE OF LEARNER-CENTERED INNOVATION

What can be done to avoid the LOGO syndrome? That is, how can we avoid a trail of broken promises concerning the educational benefits of each new technology that comes along? A reasonable solution is to use instructional technology in ways that are grounded in research-based theory. The overarching theme of this chapter is that effective use of a new instructional technology must be guided by a research-based theory of how students learn. Fortunately, advances in cognitive psychology provide the starting point for such theories. It follows that one of the most important avenues of cognitive psychology is to understanding how technology can be used to foster student learning. As an example, in this section I provide a research-based review of five principles of multimedia design.

We can begin with a cognitive theory of multimedia learning (Mayer, 1997), which draws on Paivio's (1986; Clark & Paivio, 1991) dual coding theory, Baddeley's (1992) model of working memory, Sweller's (Chandler & Sweller, 1991; Sweller, Chandler, Tierney & Cooper, 1990) cognitive load theory, Wittrock's (1989) generative theory, and Mayer's (1996b) SOI model of meaningful learning. According to the theory, the learner possesses a visual information-processing system and a verbal information-processing system, such that auditory narration goes into the verbal system whereas animation goes into the visual system.

In multimedia learning, the learner engages in three important cognitive processes. The first cognitive process, selecting, is applied to incoming verbal information to yield a text base and is applied to incoming visual information to yield an image base. The second cognitive process, organizing, is applied to the word base to create a verbally based model of the to-be-explained system and is applied to the image base to create a visually based model of the to-be-explained system. Finally, the third process, integrating, occurs when the learner builds connections between corresponding events (or states or parts) in the verbally based model and the visually based model. The theory is explained more fully in Mayer (1997), and has generated a series of experiments yielding five major principles of how to use multimedia to help students understand a scientific explanation. Each principle of multimedia design is subject to further research.

Multiple Representation Principle

Principle: It is better to present an explanation in words and pictures than solely in words. That is, it is better to present an explanation using two modes of representation rather than one. For example, students who listened to a narration explaining how a bicycle tire pump works while also viewing a corresponding animation generated twice as many useful solutions to subsequent problem-solving transfer questions than did students who listened to the same narration without viewing any animation (Mayer & Anderson, 1991, 1992). Similarly, students who read a text containing captioned illustrations placed near the corresponding words generated about 65% more useful solutions on a subsequent problem-solving transfer test than did students who simply read the text (Mayer, 1989; Mayer & Gallini, 1990). I call this result a multimedia effect, and similar results have been obtained using other materials (Plass, Chun, Mayer & Leutner, 1998). The multimedia effect is consistent with a cognitive theory of multimedia learning because students given multimedia explanations are able to build two different mental representations – a verbal model and a visual model – and build connections between them.

Contiguity Principle

Principle: When giving a multimedia explanation, present corresponding words and pictures contiguously rather than separately. That is, students better understand an explanation when corresponding words and pictures are presented at the same time than when they are separated in time. For example, students who listened to a narration explaining how a bicycle tire pump works while also viewing a corresponding animation generated 50% more useful solutions to subsequent problem-solving transfer questions than did students who viewed the animation before or after listening to the narration (Mayer & Anderson, 1991, 1992; Mayer & Sims, 1994). Similarly, students who read a text explaining how tire pumps work that included captioned illustrations placed near the text generated about 75% more useful solutions on problem-solving transfer questions than did students who read the same text and illustrations presented on separate pages (Mayer, 1989; Mayer, Steinhoff, Bower & Mars, 1995). We call this result a continuity effect, and similar patterns have been noted by other researchers (Chandler & Sweller, 1991; Paas & Van Merrienboer, 1994; Sweller & Chandler, 1994; Sweller, Chandler, Tierney & Cooper, 1990). This result is consistent with the cognitive theory of multimedia learning because corresponding words and pictures must be in working memory at the same time in order to facilitate the construction of referential links between them.

Split-Attention Principle

Principle: When giving a multimedia explanation, present words as auditory narration rather than as visual on-screen text. That is, words should be presented auditorily rather than visually. For example, students who viewed an animation depicting the formation of lightning while also listening to a corresponding narration generated approximately 50% more useful solutions on a subsequent problem-solving transfer test than did students who viewed the same animation with corresponding on-screen text consisting of the same words as the narration (Mayer & Moreno, 1998). Sweller and his colleagues call this a split-attention effect (Chandler & Sweller, 1991; Mousavi, Low & Sweller, 1995; Sweller, Chandler, Tierney & Cooper, 1990). This result is consistent with the cognitive theory of multimedia learning because the on-screen text and animation can overload the visual information processing system whereas narration is processed in the verbal information processing system and animation is processed in the visual information processing system. The split-attention effect is strong when students do not have as much time as they want to replay or study the presented material; it may be diminished or eliminated when these options are available to students.

Individual Differences Principle

Principle: The foregoing principles are more important for low-knowledge than high-knowledge learners, and for high-spatial rather than low-spatial learners. That is, multimedia effects, contiguity effects, and split-attention effects depend on individual differences in the learner. For example, students who lack prior knowledge tended to show stronger multimedia effects and contiguity effects than students who possessed high levels of prior knowledge (Mayer & Gallini, 1990; Mayer, Steinhoff, Bower & Mars, 1995). According to a cognitive theory of multimedia learning, students with high prior knowledge may be able to generate their own mental images while listening to an animation or reading a verbal text so that having a contiguous visual presentation is not needed. Additionally, students who scored high on tests of spatial ability showed greater multimedia effects than did students who scored low on spatial ability (Mayer & Sims, 1994). According to a cognitive theory of multimedia learning, students with high spatial ability are able to hold the visual image in visual working memory and thus are more likely to benefit from contiguous presentation of words and pictures.

Coherence Principle

Principle: When giving a multimedia explanation, use few rather than many extraneous words and pictures. That is, students learn better from a coherent summary which highlights the relevant words and pictures than from a longer version of the summary. For example, students who read a passage explaining the steps in how lightning forms along with corresponding illustrations generated 50% more useful solutions on a subsequent problem-solving transfer test than did students who read the same information with additional details inserted in the materials (Harp & Mayer, 1997; Mayer, Bove, Bryman, Mars & Tapangco, 1996). Sweller and his colleagues refer to this as a redundancy effect and they have found a similar pattern of results (Bobis, Sweller & Cooper, 1993; Chandler & Sweller, 1991). This result is consistent with a cognitive theory of multimedia learning, in which a shorter presentation primes the learner to select relevant information and organize it productively. A summary is effective when the goal of instruction is for the student to build a coherent mental model of main ideas; when the goal of instruction is for the student to be able to remember many details in the presented material, then a summary is not appropriate.

By beginning with a theory of how learners process multimedia information, we have been able to conduct focused research that yields some preliminary principles of multimedia design. Although all of the principles are subject to further testing, this work demonstrates how it is possible to take a learner-centered approach to instructional technology. This line of research can be considered a success to the extent that it contributes to the implementation of successful multimedia instruction.

EXPANDING THE LEARNER-CENTERED APPROACH TO COMPUTER TUTORING SYSTEMS

Perhaps, the best documented shift from a technology-centered to learner-centered approach is occurring within the field of computer tutoring systems. A computer tutoring system is a computer program intended to take the role of a teacher. As conceptions of the role of the teacher have changed, so has the nature of computer tutoring systems. Three important elements in a computer tutoring system that reflect the technology-centered-to-learner-centered shift involve:

- educational objective – i.e. what changes the teacher wishes to encourage in the learner
- educational methods – i.e. how the teacher seeks to accomplish this goal
- educational knowledge – i.e. who the learner is and how to adapt to his or her needs.

In this section, I briefly review three phases in the development of computer tutoring systems: the computer-assisted instruction (CAI) systems of the 1960s and 1970s, intelligent tutoring systems of the 1980s, and computer-supported cognitive apprenticeship systems of the 1990s.

Phase 1: Computer-assisted Instruction

The first large-scale implementation of computer tutoring machines occurred under the banner of computer-assisted instruction (CAI). Based largely on the programmed instruction principles of behaviorism (Holland & Skinner, 1961), CAI involved presenting short frames which elicited a response with each response followed by some sort of right–wrong feedback. The educational objective in CAI focuses solely on curricular content, that is helping students acquire specific pieces of knowledge. The educational method is generally some form of drill and practice in which students are prompted to give a short response which is rewarded if it is correct and is punished if it is wrong. Eberts (1997) points out that CAI courseware can use four types of instructional methods: drill and practice, tutorials, simulations, and games. However, the latter methods are more commonly found in intelligent computer-assisted instruction (ICAI). The educational knowledge is either none at all or simply a record of the learner's accuracy on each question or type of question.

Taking a technology-centered approach, research on CAI sought to determine whether "instruction delivered by computer would be as good or better than instruction delivered by a teacher" (Cognition and Technology Group at Vanderbilt, 1996, p. 811). Consistent with the knowledge-transmission metaphor, researchers focused on whether knowledge could be delivered more efficiently by computers than by teachers. The research methods generally involved comparing how much was learned by students who learned via CAI or in a traditional teacher-based setting.

In spite of the heavy costs of CAI, early results often failed to show that computers were more effective than teachers. For example, a large-scale CAI program aimed at teaching mathematics failed to produce larger learning gains than traditional methods, but was helpful when used as an adjunct to traditional teacher-based instruction (Suppes & Morningstar, 1968; Jamison, Suppes & Wells, 1974). Similarly, evaluations of the two largest computer-based instructional systems that emerged in the 1970s – PLATO (Alpert & Bitzer, 1970; Eastwood & Ballard, 1975) and TICCIT (Bunderson, 1975) – failed to provide conclusive evidence for the superiority of CAI over traditional teacher-based instruction (Cognition and Technology Group at Vanderbilt, 1996). Later reviews – such as meta-analyses carried out in 1980s – reported small but significant effects favoring CAI over teacher-based instruction, particularly for well-defined curricula such as mathematics (Burns & Bozeman, 1981; Kulik, Bangert & Williams, 1983).

Research on CAI has been criticized on methodological, conceptual, and theoretical grounds. First, CAI studies are methodologically confounded because students who receive CAI treatments may spend more time studying the material than students who receive teacher-based instruction (Bright, 1983; Lepper & Chabay, 1985). Second, CAI studies are conceptually confounded because the delivery system (computers versus humans) cannot be separated from the instructional method (Clark, 1983; Clark & Salomon, 1986). Clark (1983, p. 445) argues that it is not possible to conclude that media affect learning because media "do not influence student achievement any more than the truck that delivers our groceries causes changes in our nutrition." Third, CAI studies are based on an outmoded view of learning as knowledge transmission that is inconsistent with the idea that learning involves active knowledge construction by the learner (Mayer, 1997).

In summary, CAI research failed because it addressed the wrong question, namely, "Is learning with technology better than learning without technology?" The central goal was to determine whether computers could be used to get information in to learners' heads more effectively than traditional teacher-based systems. By taking a technology-centered approach, CAI researchers failed to address the more fundamental issue of how technology can be used to aid human learning. According to a learner-centered approach, it is not computers *per se* that influence learning but rather how computers are used. Instead of focusing on how to get pieces of information into the learner's head, the learner-centered approach focuses on how students construct knowledge and the role that computer tutors can play as aids to knowledge construction.

Phase 2: Intelligent Tutoring Systems

Research on intelligent tutoring systems (ITS) represents a transition from a technology-centered to a learner-centered approach. An intelligent tutoring system is a computer program aimed at simulating expert teaching of problem-solving processes in various domains (Psotka, Massey & Mutter, 1988; Sleeman & Brown, 1982). The educational objective, like that of CAI, is to help students acquire both the content knowledge and the cognitive processes involved in reasoning in a certain domain. The educational methods simulate those of expert teachers and generally involve some sort of guided practice in which students work on problems with some coaching or modeling. Coaching involves hints for how to carry out the task, and modeling involves a step-by-step description of how a mentor carries out the task. The educational knowledge involves information concerning the learner's error patterns, so that the system can infer what the student has mastered and what the student still needs to learn. By having a model of what the student knows and a model of what an expert should know, the system can adapt to the student by focusing on those areas that the student has not yet mastered.

During the 1980s intelligent tutors were developed for dozens of subject areas ranging from electronic troubleshooting (Brown, Burton & de Kleer, 1981) to medical diagnosis (Clancey, 1981) to geometry (Anderson, Boyle & Reiser, 1985; Anderson, Boyle & Yost, 1985). Importantly, work on intelligent tutors was often guided by cognitive theories of learning (Anderson, Corbett, Koedinger & Pelletier, 1995; Corbett, Koedinger & Anderson, 1997). Most of the research involved cognitive task analyses of the knowledge required to solve problems in various domains as well as the instructional methods used by expert teachers. For example, Koedinger & Anderson's (1993, p. 15) geometry tutor attempts to teach the "thought processes of successful students" to novices, by giving them problems to solve. Based on a student's performance, the tutor determines which aspects of the process the student has not mastered and provides coaching and modeling of those aspects of the problem-solving processes.

In a review, Derry & Lajoie (1993, p. 5) noted that "although the ITS movement of the eighties spawned development of many pioneering systems, most of these required years of development and a relatively small number were actually finished and used." On the positive side, the ITS research helped shift the focus towards the cognitive processes of the learner. By carefully analyzing the cognitive processes of successful students, ITS researchers were able to develop systems that help novices acquire those processes. On the negative side, ITS has been criticized for failing to address the larger learner-centered issues of metacognitive control, self-regulated learning, and development of appropriate dispositions for learning (Lajoie & Derry, 1993).

Phase 3: Technology-supported Learning Environments

The transition to a learner-centered approach is most fully reflected in the development of technology-supported learning environments (Vosniadou, De Corte, Glaser & Mandl, 1996) during the 1990s. The educational goal of instruction is not solely the acquisition of well-defined pieces of knowledge, but also to help the learner develop metacognitive and self-regulation skills for learning. According to this view, "unintelligent cognitive tools supplied by computer technologies can serve as powerful catalysts for facilitating the development of generalized self-regulatory skills" (Derry & Lajoie, 1993, p. 6). The educational method is a form of cognitive apprenticeship in which students work on authentic academic tasks along with a more expert mentor, such as a computer coach.

Consistent with constructivist visions of learning, technology is used within the context of authentic academic tasks to help in the process of cognitive apprenticeship (Collins, Brown & Newman, 1989). In contrast to ITS research which uses computer technology to create expert teachers that teach specific problem-solving processes, research on technology-supported learning environments uses computers as mind-extending cognitive tools. The educational knowledge is somewhat more limited than for the expert teaching of intelligent tutoring systems, but may be enhanced by using the technology in a social context.

During the 1990s dozens of technology-supported learning environments were developed ranging from workplace simulations (Hoc, Cacciabue & Hollnagel, 1995) to exploratory environments for learning geometry (Yerushalmy, 1991) to microworlds for exploring physics (White, 1993). Although it is too early to assess the contribution of this approach to student learning, there is some promising evidence that learning is enhanced when students have the opportunity to work in a social context such as being able to talk with others (Cognition and Technology Group at Vanderbilt, 1996). Katz & Lesgold (1993) point out that tutors still have a role to play, even in collaborative learning situations, by providing advice on demand, quality control over peer critiquing, and management of learning activities.

A promising direction for research on computer-based learning concerns the integration of technology-supported learning environments in educational settings. The development of virtual reality learning environments offer another exciting venue for future research. However, research on computer-supported learning environments needs to be subjected to the same level of theory-based research and intense scientific evaluation as was earlier research in the CAI tradition.

CONCLUSION

Instructional technology refers to tools for fostering student learning, including both hardware (e.g. machines) and software (e.g. instructional programs). In a technology-centered approach to instructional technology, the focus is on what advanced technologies can do; in a learner-centered approach to instructional technology, the focus is on how to improve student learning by using technology.

Technology-centered implementations of instructional technology tend to begin with strong claims, followed by attempted implementation in schools, and ultimately unfulfilled promises. Examples through the twentieth century include film, radio, and television. A more recent example is the LOGO movement of the 1980s: first, there were strong claims that unfettered learning to program in LOGO would produce improvements in students' thinking skills; then, there was widespread implementation of LOGO in schools; finally, there was a pattern of disappointing results in which students who learned LOGO by discovery methods often failed to show evidence of transfer. This pattern can be called the LOGO syndrome.

Learner-centered implementations follow from research-based theories of how students learn and process information. For example, research on multimedia learning yields five principles of multimedia design which can be used to guide the construction of instructional technology involving multimedia. There is promising preliminary evidence that multimedia instruction based on these principles can significantly enhance students' problem-solving transfer in which they apply what they have learned to solving new problems.

Research and development in computer-based instruction has followed a transition from a technology-centered approach focusing on computer-assisted learning (CAI) in which computers are used to deliver information, to a compromise approach focusing on intelligent tutoring systems (ITS) in which computers are used as expert teachers, to a learner-centered approach focusing on technology-supported learning environments in which computers are used as cognitive tools.

The future value of instructional technology may depend on whether its implementation is based on a technology-centered approach or a learner-centered approach.

REFERENCES

Abelson, H. & di Sessa, A. A. (1981). *Turtle Geometry: The Computer as a Medium for Exploring Mathematics*. Cambridge, MA: MIT Press.

Alpert, D. & Bitzer, D. L. (1970). Advances in computer-based education. *Science*, 167, 1582–90.

Anderson, J. R., Boyce, C. F. & Reiser, B. J. (1985). Intelligent tutoring systems. *Science*, 228, 456–568.

Anderson, J. R., Boyle, C. F. & Yost, G. (1985). The geometry tutor. In *Proceedings of the International Joint Conference on Artificial Intelligence*. Los Angeles: International Joint Conference on Artificial Intelligence.

Anderson, J. R., Corbett, A. T., Koedinger, K. & Pelletier, R. (1995). Cognitive tutors: lessons learned. *The Journal of the Learning Sciences*, 4, 167–207.

Baddeley, A. (1992). Working memory. *Science*, 255, 556–9.

Bobis, J., Sweller, J. & Cooper, J. (1993). Cognitive load effects in a primary-school geometry task. *Learning and Instruction*, 3, 1–21.

Bright, G. (1983). Explaining the efficiency of computer-assisted instruction. *Association for Educational Data Systems Journal*, 16, 144–52.

Brown, J. S., Burton, R. R. & de Kleer, J. (1981). Pedagogical, natural language and knowledge engineering techniques in SOPHIE I, II and III. In D. Sleeman & J. S. Brown (Eds), *Intelligent Tutoring Systems* (pp. 227–82). London: Academic Press.

Bunderson, C. V. (1975). The TICCIT project: design strategy for educational innovation. In S. A. Harrison & L. M. Stolurow (Eds), *Improving Instructional Productivity in Higher Education* (pp. 91–111). Englewood Cliffs, NJ: Educational Technology.

Burns, P. & Bozeman, W. (1981). Computer-assisted instruction and mathematics achievement: is there a relationship? *Educational Technology*, 10, 32–9.

Chandler, P. & Sweller, J. (1991). Cognitive load theory and the format of instruction. *Cognition and Instruction*, 8, 293–332.

Clancey, W. J. (1981). Tutoring rules for guiding a case method dialogue. In Sleeman, D. & J. S. Brown (Eds), *Intelligent Tutoring Systems* (pp. 201–25). London: Academic Press.

Clark, J. M. & Paivio, A. (1991). Dual coding theory and education. *Educational Psychology Review*, 3, 149–210.

Clark, R. E. (1983). Reconsidering research on learning from media. *Review of Educational Research*, 53, 445–59.

Clark, R. E. (1994). Media will never influence learning. *Educational Technology Research and Development*, 42, 21–30.
Clark, R. E. & Salomon, G. (1986). Media in teaching. In M. C. Wittrock (Ed.), *Handbook of Research on Teaching* (3rd edn) (pp. 464–78). New York: Macmillan.
Clements, D. H. & Gullo, D. F. (1984). Effects of computer programming on young children's cognition. *Journal of Educational Psychology*, 76, 1051–8.
Cognition and Technology Group at Vanderbilt (1996). Looking at technology in context: a framework for understanding technology and education research. In D. C. Berliner & R. C. Calfee (Eds), *Handbook of Educational Psychology* (pp. 807–40). New York: Macmillan.
Collins, A., Brown, J. S. & Newman, S. E. (1989). Cognitive apprenticeship: teaching the craft of reading, writing, and mathematics. In L. Resnick (Ed.), *Knowing, Learning, and Instruction: Essays in Honor of Robert Glaser* (pp. 453–94). Hillsdale, NJ: Erlbaum.
Corbett, A. T., Koedinger, K. R. & Anderson, J. R. (1997). Intelligent tutoring systems. In M. G. Helander, T. K. Landauer & P. V. Prabhu (Eds), *Handbook of Human–Computer Interaction* (pp. 849–74). Amsterdam: Elsevier.
Cuban, L. (1986). *Teachers and Machines: The Classroom Use of Technology Since 1920*. New York: Teachers College Press.
Dalbey, J. & Linn, M. C. (1985). The demands and requirements of computer programming: a literature review. *Journal of Educational Computing Research*, 1, 253–74.
De Corte, E., Greer, B. & Verschaffel, L. (1996). Mathematics teaching and learning. In D. C. Berliner & R. C. Calfee (Eds), *Handbook of Educational Psychology* (pp. 491–549). New York: Macmillan.
De Corte, E., Verschaffel, L. & Schrooten, H. (1992). Cognitive effects of learning to program in LOGO: a one-year study with sixth graders. In E. De Corte, M. C. Linn, H. Mandl & L. Verschaffel (Eds), *Computer-based Learning Environments and Problem Solving* (pp. 207–28). Berlin: Springer-Verlag.
Derry, S. J. & Lajoie, S. P. (1993). A middle camp for (un)intelligent instructional computing: an introduction. In S. P. Lajoie & S. J. Derry (Eds), *Computers as Cognitive Tools* (pp. 1–11). Hillsdale, NJ: Erlbaum.
Eastwood, L. F. & Ballard, R. J. (1975). The PLATO IV CAI system: Where is it now? Where can it go? *Journal of Educational Technology Systems*, 3, 267–83.
Eberts, R. E. (1997). Computer-based instruction. In M. G. Helander, T. K. Landauer & P. V. Prabhu (Eds), *Handbook of Human–Computer Interaction* (pp. 825–47). Amsterdam: Elsevier.
Fay, A. L. & Mayer, R. E. (1994). Benefits of teaching design skills before teaching LOGO computer programming: evidence for syntax-independent learning. *Journal of Educational Computing Research*, 11, 187–210.
Gallini, J. K. & Gredler, M. E. (1989). *Instructional Design for Computers*. Glenview, IL: Scott, Foresman.
Gurtner, J. (1992). Between LOGO and mathematics: a road of tunnels and bridges. In C. Hoyles & R. Noss (Eds), *Learning Mathematics and LOGO* (pp. 247–68). Cambridge, MA: MIT Press.
Harp, S. & Mayer, R. E. (1997). Role of interest in learning from scientific text and illustrations: on the distinction between emotional interest and cognitive interest. *Journal of Educational Psychology*, 89, 92–102.
Hoc, J.-M., Cacciabue, P. C. & Hollnagel, E. (Eds) (1995). *Expertise and Technology: Cognition and Human–Computer Cooperation*. Hillsdale, NJ: Erlbaum.
Holland, J. G. & Skinner, B. F. (1961). *The Analysis of Behavior: A Program for Self-instruction*. New York: McGraw-Hill.
Jamison, D., Suppes, P. & Wells, S. (1974). The effectiveness of alternative instructional media: a survey. *Review of Educational Research*, 44, 19–26.
Katz, S. & Lesgold, A. (1993). The role of the tutor in computer-based collaborative learning situations. In S. P. Lajoie & S. J. Derry (Eds), *Computers as Cognitive Tools* (pp. 289–317). Hillsdale, NJ: Erlbaum.
Kilpatrick, J. & Davis, R. B. (1993). Computers and curriculum change in mathematics.

In C. Keitel & K. Ruthgven (Eds), *Learning from Computers: Mathematics Education and Technology* (pp. 203–21). Berlin: Springer-Verlag.
Koedinger, K. R. & Anderson, J. R. (1993). Reifying implicit planning in geometry: guidelines for model-based intelligent tutoring system design. In S. P. Lajoie & S. J. Derry (Eds), *Computers as Cognitive Tools* (pp. 1–11). Hillsdale, NJ: Erlbaum.
Kulik, J. A., Bangert, R. L. & Williams, G. W. (1983). Effects of computer-based teaching on secondary school students. *Journal of Educational Psychology*, 75, 19–26.
Lajoie, S. P. & Derry, S. J. (Eds) (1993). *Computers as Cognitive Tools*. Hillsdale, NJ: Erlbaum.
Lepper, M. R. & Chabay, R. W. (1985). Intrinsic motivation and instruction: conflicting views on the role of motivation in computer-based education. *Educational Psychologist*, 20, 217–30.
Mayer, R. E. (1988). Introduction to research on teaching and learning computer programming. In R. E. Mayer (Ed.), *Teaching and Learning Computer Programming: Multiple Research Perspectives* (pp. 1–12). Hillsdale, NJ: Erlbaum.
Mayer, R. E. (1989). Systematic thinking fostered by illustrations in scientific text. *Journal of Educational Psychology*, 81, 240–6.
Mayer, R. E. (1992). Teaching for transfer of problem-solving skills to computer programming. In E. De Corte, M. C. Linn, H. Mandl & L. Verschaffel (Eds), *Computer-based Learning Environments and Problem Solving* (pp. 193–206). Berlin: Springer-Verlag.
Mayer, R. E. (1996a). Learners as information processors: legacies and limitations of educational psychology's second metaphor. *Educational Psychologist*, 31, 3/4, 151–62.
Mayer, R. E. (1996b). Learning strategies for making sense out of expository text: the SOI model for guiding three cognitive processes in knowledge construction. *Educational Psychology Review*, 8, 357–71.
Mayer, R. E. (1997). Multimedia learning: are we asking the right questions. *Educational Psychologist*, 32, 1–19.
Mayer, R. E. & Anderson, R. B. (1991). Animations need narrations: an experimental test of a dual-coding hypothesis. *Journal of Educational Psychology*, 83, 484–90.
Mayer, R. E. & Anderson, R. B. (1992). The instructive animation: helping students build connections between words and pictures in multimedia learning. *Journal of Educational Psychology*, 84, 444–52.
Mayer, R. E., Bove, W., Bryman, A., Mars, R. & Tapangco, L. (1996). When less is more: meaningful learning from visual and verbal summaries of science textbook lessons. *Journal of Educational Psychology*, 88, 64–73.
Mayer, R. E., Dyck, J. L. & Vilberg, W. (1986). Learning to program and learning to think: what's the connection? *Communications of the ACM*, 29, 605–10.
Mayer, R. E. & Gallini, J. K. (1990). When is an illustration worth ten thousand words? *Journal of Educational Psychology*, 82, 715–26.
Mayer, R. E. & Moreno, R. (1998). A split-attention effect in multimedia learning: evidence for dual information processing systems in working memory. *Journal of Educational Psychology*, 90, 312–20.
Mayer, R. E. & Sims, V. K. (1994). For whom is a picture worth a thousand words? Extensions of a dual-coding theory of multimedia learning. *Journal of Educational Psychology*, 86, 389–401.
Mayer, R. E., Steinhoff, K., Bower, G. & Mars, R. (1995). A generative theory of textbook design: using annotated illustrations to foster meaningful learning of science text. *Educational Technology Research and Development*, 43, 31–44.
Mayer, R. E. & Wittrock, M. C. (1996). Problem-solving transfer. In D. C. Berliner & R. C. Calfee (Eds), *Handbook of Educational Psychology* (pp. 47–62). New York: Macmillan.
Mousavi, S. Y., Low, R. & Sweller, J. (1995). Reducing cognitive load by mixing auditory and visual presentation modes. *Journal of Educational Psychology*, 87, 319–34.
Nickerson, R. S., Perkins, D. N. & Smith, E. E. (1985). *The Teaching of Thinking*. Hillsdale, NJ: Erlbaum.

Paas, F. G. W. & Van Merrienboer, J. G. (1994). Instructional control of cognitive load in the training of complex cognitive tasks. *Educational Psychology Review*, 6, 351–72.
Paivio, A. (1986). *Mental Representations: A Dual Coding Approach*. Oxford: Oxford University Press.
Papert, S. (1980). *Mindstorms: Children, Computers, and Powerful Ideas*. New York: Basic Books.
Papert, S. (1992). Foreword. In C. Hoyles & R. Noss (Eds), *Learning Mathematics and LOGO* (pp. xi–xvi). Cambridge, MA: MIT Press.
Pea, R. D. & Kurland, D. M. (1984). On the cognitive effects of learning computer programming. *New Ideas in Psychology*, 2, 137–68.
Perkins, D. N. (1985). The fingertip effect: how information-processing technology shapes thinking. *Educational Researcher*, 14, 11–17.
Plass, J. L., Chun, D. M., Mayer, R. R. & Leutner, D. (1998). Supporting visual and verbal learning preferences in a second-language multimedia learning environment. *Journal of Educational Psychology*, 90, 25–36.
Psotka, J., Massey, L. D. & Mutter, S. A. (Eds) (1988). *Intelligent Tutoring Systems: Lessons Learned*. Hillsdale, NJ: Erlbaum.
Resnick, M. (1988). Lego, LOGO, and life. In C. Langton (Ed.), *Artificial Life* (pp. 143–77). Hillsdale, NJ: Erlbaum.
Salomon, G. (1994). *Interaction of Media, Cognition, and Learning*. Hillsdale, NJ: Erlbaum.
Sleeman, D. & Brown, J. S. (Eds) (1982). *Intelligent Tutoring Systems*. London: Academic Press.
Suppes, P. & Morningstar, M. (1968). Computer-assisted instruction. *Science*, 166, 343–50.
Sweller, J. & Chandler, P. (1994). Why some material is difficult to learn. *Cognition and Instruction*, 12, 185–233.
Sweller, J., Chandler, P., Tierney, P. & Cooper, M. (1990). Cognitive load as a factor in the structure of technical material. *Journal of Experimental Psychology: General*, 119, 176–92.
Vosniadou, S., De Corte, E., Glaser, R. & Mandl, H. (Eds) (1996). *International Perspectives on the Design of Technology-supported Learning Environments*. Hillsdale, NJ: Erlbaum.
White, B. Y. (1993). ThinkerTools: causal models, conceptual change, and science education. *Cognition & Instruction*, 10, 1–100.
Wittrock, M. C. (1989). Generative processes of comprehension. *Educational Psychologist*, 24, 345–76.
Yerushalmy, M. (1991). Enhancing acquisition of basic geometric concepts with the use of the Geometric Supposer. *Journal of Educational Computing Research*, 7, 407–20.

Chapter 19

Cognition and Instruction

Martin J. Dennis and Robert J. Sternberg
Yale University

Sue is a high school psychology teacher who wishes to base her instructional design on the theoretical principles she teaches. Some psychological research appears to be directly relevant to design; for instance, she begins to outline her lectures so that they are organized into more easily remembered chunks (Miller, 1956). After a while, however, she begins to realize that she desires a more complete description of the chaotic and messy world in her classroom. She wants to test for understanding, but it is becoming clearer that a psychological definition of "understanding" is eluding her. And so it has been for the field of cognition and instruction. When applying cognitive psychology to the classroom, it is often important to have a view of learning and knowledge that is broader than the operational definitions that serve in the laboratory. Settling on such a definition therefore becomes a central concern, one which strongly influences the design of educational interventions.

In this chapter, we will cover current perspectives on the issue of the nature of knowledge. First, we will review and attempt to resolve the debate about which approach is the proper one to define the nature of knowledge and learning. One's perspective on these issues strongly influences the type of research done and the educational implications drawn from that research. We suggest, however, that each perspective may be better used to understand different types of activities. That is, we hope to move the debate from an epistemological standpoint to a more pragmatic one.

To illustrate this idea, we next review some of the evidence on the question of transfer. This question is, do people take lessons learned from one situation or problem and apply them to other situations or problems? Although an affirmative answer seems to be intuitive – after all, it seems to be the very definition of

Handbook of Applied Cognition, Edited by F. T. Durso, R. S. Nickerson, R. W. Schvaneveldt, S. T. Dumais, D. S. Lindsay and M. T. H. Chi.

learning – evidence is accumulating to show that transfer is a difficult phenomenon to obtain. Nevertheless, it is possible to set up conditions under which learners do employ their previous experience in novel situations. The conditions that one specifies depend on the perspective on learning one brings to the problem. Again, the conditions implied by the different perspectives are not necessarily contradictory. In other words, instructional design for transfer may be aided, not hindered, by using multiple perspectives.

Throughout the chapter, we will occasionally illustrate the various theoretical perspectives using examples of specific educational interventions. Often studies in the field of cognition and instruction have two purposes: to provide evidence in support of a particular theory, and to serve as actual aids to instruction. In this way, it can become clear both what the strengths of a theory are, and how that theory could be implemented in the classroom.

There is much in the field of instruction and cognition that is not covered in this chapter. For instance, although some educational researchers have claimed that cognition and motivation are inseparably intertwined (Pintrich, Marx & Boyle, 1993), it would be impossible to give a complex topic such as motivation due consideration within the allotted space. By focusing on the fundamental issue which motivates many of the other topics, we hope to give a general overview of the area that will help orient our readers to the many more specialized topics within the area of cognitive psychology and instructional design. Those readers who are then interested in further information may refer to a recent publication by the American Psychological Association, Division 15 (Berliner & Calfee, 1996), which covers all areas of educational psychology, beyond instruction and cognition.

THREE TRADITIONAL PERSPECTIVES ON THE NATURE OF KNOWLEDGE AND LEARNING

Before one can apply theories from cognitive psychology to instructional design, there are fundamental questions that must be answered. The most fundamental question is simply, "What does learning mean?" Does it mean rote memorization, skill acquisition, or comprehension? The perspective one takes on this question constrains the psychological theories one develops, and the educational interventions one designs. There are three general intellectual traditions which lay claim to differing perspectives on the issue of knowledge and learning: the associative/empiricist, cognitivist/rationalist, and situative/sociohistoric traditions (Case, 1992; Greeno, Collins & Resnick, 1996). Briefly, the empiricist tradition (historically dominated by behaviorist animal learning research) emphasizes the strengthening of associations between units of knowledge or skill components. The cognitivist tradition focuses on conceptual understanding of a given content domain and on general cognitive skills. The situative tradition places an emphasis on analyzing the relationship between a learner and the learner's physical and social environments.

Figure 19.1 illustrates the conceptual relationships between the three traditions. Note that the associative and cognitivist traditions share a common theme, in that

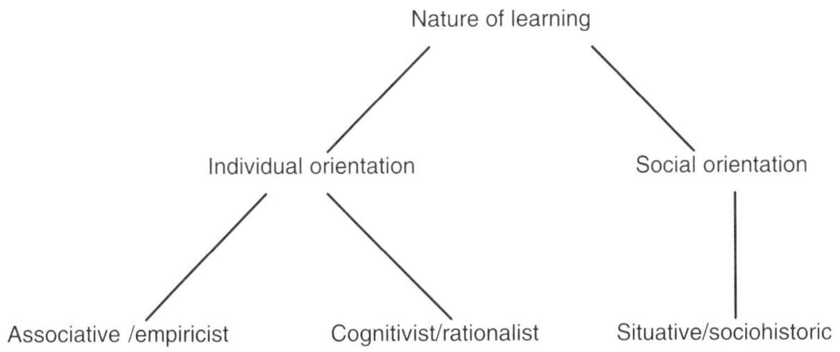

Figure 19.1 Conceptual relationships between three traditional theoretical perspectives on the nature of learning

they are oriented towards analyses of learning as a process within the learner; the situative tradition, in contrast, is oriented towards analyses of learning as a process within a social milieu. Although the orientation of both the associative and cognitivist traditions towards the individual sometimes makes it difficult to clearly distinguish the two (especially when they are contrasted with the situative tradition), there are enough differences between the two to differentiate them for expository convenience. We note this to emphasize the fact that any schematic view of the philosophical underpinnings of cognition and instruction will oversimplify some details, and thus be open to debate. Instead of attempting to provide an impossibly complex formal definition of each tradition, it is better that each reader forms his or her own "prototypical" conceptual understanding of the different perspectives based on the thumbnail sketches provided here.

Although the boundaries between the three traditions are sometimes fuzzy, each one at its core brings a different view of learning and knowing to research on cognitive and educational phenomena. Sometimes these views appear to be incommensurable, with debates springing up regarding which view is the best able to explain current findings, and to impact educational reforms most effectively (see Anderson, Reder & Simon, 1996; Greeno, 1997). These debates are useful, in that they encourage all parties to define their own positions more carefully (and hence help to reduce the fuzziness in the boundaries). However, the incommensurability between the approaches arises not because they offer competing theoretical accounts of the same phenomenon, but rather because they define the phenomenon of interest differently. Therefore, such debates may be needlessly divisive. Each tradition brings with it theoretical issues and methods of analysis which, we believe, operate at different levels. The debate may then shift from the issue of best defining "learning" to identifying those activities to which each tradition best applies.

The Associative/Empiricist Perspective

The empiricist perspective on the nature of learning is based on the idea of association; association between stimuli and responses (e.g. Hull, 1942; Skinner,

1938), association between conditions – including problem-solving goals – and actions (e.g. Anderson, 1993), or association between nodes in a connectionist network (e.g. Rumelhart, McClelland & the PDP Research Group, 1986). In this perspective, learning occurs as associations are formed between stimuli in the environment and responses to those stimuli. Such associations could be formed according to a variety of models of the processes by which the stimuli and responses are paired.

For example, one popular model of how associations form, the Rescorla–Wagner rule (Rescorla & Wagner, 1972; Wagner & Rescorla, 1972), is based on the proposal that individual conditioned stimuli (CS) compete for associative strength in repeated pairings with an unconditioned response (UR). In cognitive terms, organisms selectively attend to stimuli that are more contingent with the unconditioned stimulus (US), and that are therefore more informative than other stimuli in the environment. The associations including those stimuli are then learned better than those with less informative stimuli. As learning goes on, the CS with the higher associative strength manages to "block" the other CS (Kamin, 1969). Besides explaining a variety of learning phenomena in animals (cf. Miller, Barnet & Grahame, 1995), the Rescorla–Wagner rule has been used to explain how humans learn the diagnosticity of symptoms of diseases (Gluck & Bower, 1988) and the relative strengths of causes (Wasserman, Kao, Van Hamme, Katagiri & Young, 1996). It is also formally equivalent to the delta, or LMS, rule, a popular learning algorithm in connectionist models (Gluck & Bower, 1988). All of these models are based on differentially increasing the relative strengths of associations with experience.

One common implication of the associative view is that knowledge of complex skills or knowledge structures can be decomposed into simpler associations. For example, animals can be trained to perform complex sequences of actions. Each sequence, however, is composed of much simpler actions that are chained during training, so that the animal learns to perform each component action in order. Likewise, task analyses of complex human skills, such as arithmetic operations, can specify simpler components on which those skills are built (e.g. Gagné, 1966). For instance, in solving for x in the equation $3x + 15 = 25$, the operations of subtraction and division are prerequisites for calculating the correct answer, three and one-third. This view of skills as assemblies of simpler responses is one aspect of modern intelligent tutoring systems, such as those based on the ACT-R model of cognition (Anderson, 1993). These tutoring systems guide a learner's practice of a skill so that the appropriate components (e.g. using constants as arguments in conditional statements in Pascal; Anderson, 1993, p. 207) are strengthened as the learner works on training problems. In line with the associative tradition, learners gain mastery of complex skills through strengthening of the component actions.

Another implication of the associative/empiricist perspective is that incidental, or unintended, learning may occur. Because the empiricist perspective explains learning as the formation of associations – any associations – it is possible for students to form associations that are unintended, or incidental. For instance, students in a mathematics class may associate specific features of stimuli, such as having a minus sign in the problem, with an inappropriate strategy for solving the problem, such as taking the smaller number from the larger regardless of order (Schoenfeld, 1988). Because the co-occurrence of any two events could possibly lead to association of those events in memory, incidental associations, especially those that may be misleading, should be avoided. This implication lay behind attempts to perfect "error-free" learning techniques (e.g. Terrace, 1966). As sports coaches and music instructors know, associations with "error-prone" responses can be difficult to undo.

In summary, the associative/empiricist tradition implies instructional methods that are designed to help students acquire the knowledge and component skills for mastery of routine skills. Such instructional programs are designed to present information to learners efficiently, allow students to practice component skills, provide clear feedback to avoid strengthening error-prone performance, and organize instruction so that students do not move to more complex activities until they have acquired the requisite component skills. Many traditional learning environments are founded on associative/empiricist principles (Greeno et al., 1996). All of these environments are based on the idea that learning to perform a task relies on the association of the component elements within that task.

Cognitive/Rationalist Perspective

The second perspective views learning as the acquisition of conceptual understanding, rather than simple associations. Cognitive theories appeal to knowledge structures and symbolic processes to explain learners' conceptual growth in domains such as physics or mathematics, and the general processes presumed to underlie problem solving and reasoning (e.g. Piaget, 1983). A common theme among most cognitive research is that learners actively construct understanding based on their experiences. Passive knowledge acquisition processes such as rote memorization have little place in most cognitive theories.

One branch of cognitive research examines the course of development of conceptual understanding throughout childhood. Although some of this research focuses on the development of general reasoning schemata (Case, 1985; Piaget, 1983), most current work has examined conceptual development in a variety of specific domains, including number (Resnick, 1989), biological kinds (Keil, 1989), physical forces (Spelke, Breinlinger, Macomber & Jacobson, 1992), and mental phenomena (Wellman, 1990). For example, Keil (1989) found a shift between kindergarten and second grade in the features children used to classify a strange animal (e.g. a tiger that looked like a lion) into the appropriate natural kind. Younger children tended to base their categorization on the appearance of the animal – whether it had stripes or not, for example – whereas older children used information about the internal organs or parents of the animal. The older children seem to have formed a theory about the biological functioning of animals, so that the "essence" of a particular kind of animal is seen to inhere in its physiology (Carey, 1985). This theory can then guide children to make inferences about one animal (e.g. that an animal has a certain skeletal structure) based on knowledge of another (Gelman & Markman, 1987). As children develop, their conceptual understanding becomes more elaborated and coherent.

A similar phenomenon has been observed in another branch of research focused on the adult acquisition of cognitive skills. This research has highlighted the importance not only of the quantity of knowledge acquired as part of the skill (Chase & Simon, 1973), but also the organization of that knowledge. Experts at a particular skill have representations of the domain based on more abstract principles, and with more interconnections between principles, than do novices (Bédard & Chi, 1992). The literary analyses of novice critics, for instance, are confined primarily to factual information and superficial relationships in stories, whereas experts provide both more connections and more abstract correspondences between story elements (Zeitz, 1994). Knowledge of a domain aids in skilled levels of problem solving in a variety of ways. First, that knowledge helps the skilled problem solver to define a useful representation of a problem. For example, a physicist can use his or her knowledge of mechanical principles to derive abstract features, such as "mass," from descriptions of concrete objects (Chi, Feltovich & Glaser, 1981). When working with less well-defined problems, such as those found in the field of international relations, an expert's knowledge can aid in the formation of constraints on the problem, changing a messy question to one more straightforwardly answered (Voss, Wolfe, Lawrence & Engle, 1991). Second, knowledge of a domain seems to guide the use of different problem-solving strategies. As expertise with a skill develops, learners are less likely to work backwards from the desired solution, and more likely to move forwards from the given problem state towards a possible solution (Greeno & Simon, 1988). For instance, a novice programmer in a computer language may successfully solve problems by first writing the code to produce the desired output, then using that routine to decide what information needs to be input. An expert programmer, in contrast, may draw on similar, previously encountered problems to outline the procedures necessary for successful solution. This outline then guides the creation of code directly from input to output. Although working forwards increases the risk of following fruitless paths, it may be more efficient as it allows the production of one clear path to solution. In terms of the course of development of expertise, Ericsson and his colleagues (Ericsson, Krampe & Tesch-Römer, 1993) have noted that the acquisition of complex skills in real life seems to require extended periods (about ten years) of deliberate practice, involving tasks designed specifically to increase the quality of performance.

A third branch of cognitive research has investigated general cognitive processes, especially those involved in problem solving. For example, several models of problem solving have been devised. In some of these models, the problem solving process is imagined to consist of operators that transform information within a problem space, and strategies that determine how well the problem solver is coming towards solution (Newell & Simon, 1972). The particular operators used in solving problems can be learned in a variety of ways: for instance, from following general heuristics such as means–ends analysis (Newell, 1990), or from interpreting information given in instructions or examples (Anderson, Conrad, Corbett, Fincham, Hoffman & Wu, 1993). Some researchers propose that people form mental models of the problem-solving situation (Halford, 1993; Johnson-Laird, 1983). By transforming mental models, learners may then "run" a simulation of the problem until a solution is found (Lajoie &

Lesgold, 1992). These models of problem solving provide frameworks within which tasks from many different domains may be analyzed.

One instructional implication of the cognitive perspective is that learners need experience with the materials of a domain so that they can construct appropriate conceptual understandings. For example, in the Jasper series of multimedia presentations, students learn to formulate mathematical solutions to specific problems (e.g. "Does Jasper have enough gasoline to reach a landing upriver?") within the context of a complex story line (Cognition and Technology Group at Vanderbilt, 1994). The presentations allow students to explore a variety of mathematical relationships within the general context, from rate of consumption to volumes of solid objects. Other instructional programs present students with the opportunity to control objects in a simulated frictionless world for learning Newtonian physics (White, 1993), and to construct a variety of geometric diagrams (Schwartz, Yarushalmy & Wilson, 1993). By providing opportunities to manipulate objects (or computer simulations of objects), students can change their conceptualizations of a variety of domains. This conceptual development is integral to the cognitive perspective on the nature of learning.

The Situative/Sociohistoric Perspective

In contrast to both the associative and cognitive perspectives, the situative view does not see knowledge as a decontextualized entity which exists only in the learner's mind. Instead, knowledge and learning are inextricably linked to activities and situations (Brown, Collins & Duguid, 1989). For instance, an associative theory of mathematical reasoning might include the specification of abstract mental algorithms which can be applied to any content, constrained by limitations of working memory or the probability of accurate recall of the algorithm when cued. Learning to reason mathematically, then, would focus on the acquisition and practice of those algorithms in order to increase the chances that a student would use them correctly with the appropriate type of problems.

In contrast, a situative theory of mathematical reasoning might emphasize both the ways in which practicing mathematicians use intuition, negotiate meaning, and invent solution strategies, and the ways in which the context supports those activities in everyday life (Lave, 1988). Learning to reason mathematically, in this view, becomes a matter of finding ways to use the physical and social environment to reach solutions to meaningful problems. This learning occurs by a process of increased participation in a community of practice (Lave & Wenger, 1991). A community of practice is a group of people who are engaged in a common activity, such as weaving, navigation, or scientific inquiry. As a person becomes enculturated in a community, he or she becomes more adept at the practices within that community. This increased facility at the central activity in the community is the hallmark of learning. Research on learning then focuses on the activities of practitioners, as well as the tools and artifacts they use in the course of their activity (Keller & Keller, 1996; Resnick, Levine & Teasley, 1991).

For example, analyses of various forms of apprenticeships have revealed commonalities among those situations in which learners successfully advance throughout the course of their careers (Lave & Wenger, 1991; Rogoff, 1990). One important factor in the advancement of the learner is the opportunity to observe and practice those activities that are defined as being more central to the community (i.e. more indicative of mastery). For example, quartermasters on board US Navy vessels generally begin their careers as navigators at stations removed from the navigation chart on the bridge (Hutchins, 1993). The duty at these stations is simply to collect information from a specific source: say, by taking fathometer readings. After rotating among the peripheral stations, the "apprentice" navigators advance to more central stations where the basic information is integrated, until they reach a point in their careers where their duty is to plot the ship's position, based on the information passed up from the other stations. By gaining experience with precisely those tasks that are valued in the community – in this case, the navigation crew – learners are afforded the skills that allow them to take part in the community more fully.

Instructional interventions based on the situative perspective emphasize the organization of the classroom environment so that students are allowed to participate in common activities. For example, the CSILE (Computer Supported Intentional Learning Environments) computer environment is designed to allow students to engage in dialogues of inquiry among themselves, in the same way that the practice of scientific inquiry is carried out among groups of researchers (Scardamalia, Bereiter & Lamon, 1994). CSILE, much like an Internet newsgroup, is a communal database in which students can raise questions, respond to other students, or report on further research they have done. In the course of responding to each other's questions and comments, sixth-grade students using CSILE have developed answers to such questions as "Why do sponges have three ways to reproduce, and humans have only one?" without guidance from the teacher. Other students, in a section on history, constructed working models of various medieval artifacts, applying knowledge of physical principles learned in another section. By interacting with their peers in a common activity of inquiry, students learn not only concepts in biology or history, but also become attuned to the practices by which groups extend knowledge. This process of attunement is, of course, at the heart of the situative view of learning.

Discussion

Although there are obvious differences between the three traditional perspectives on the nature of learning (especially between the situative, and behaviorist and cognitivist views), these differences do not necessarily mean that they are mutually exclusive. Indeed, if we shift the focus of the discussion to one of practical applications, it becomes clear that the theoretical perspectives have different pragmatic implications.

To illustrate this idea, let us ask the question, "For what sorts of tasks is each tradition best suited as an explanation?" The *associative* tradition is best suited to explain the acquisition of routine skills, that is, those skills for which a premium is placed on accurate and timely performance. Examples of such skills include writing code to create computer programs that match given specifications, solving math problems with few errors, acquiring new vocabulary through rote memorization, or re-sawing lumber without deviation from a straight line. The *cognitive* tradition is best suited to explain the acquisition of an understanding of the principles of a domain, that is, when success in a domain depends on having appropriate representations of problem spaces, theoretical constructs, or texts. Examples of such skills include making inferences about a scientific phenomenon based on theoretical knowledge, constructing correct equations to solve arithmetic word problems, or comprehending arguments for or against an advocated course of action. Finally, the *situative* tradition is not suited to any particular set of tasks, or rather, is suited to all. The focus of the situative tradition is on structuring the social environment. In such structuring, students acquire the skills or understandings necessary for mastery of a domain: by fostering a spirit of inquiry in students, or by organizing the community of practice so that every learner has the opportunity to contribute to the common activity. Because each theoretical perspective largely covers a range of activities different from the others, it is more appropriate to think of them as being complementary, rather than exclusive.

THE QUESTION OF TRANSFER

To further exemplify the complementary qualities of the three traditions, we will examine the issue of transfer of previously learned skills and knowledge to new tasks and problems. In this section, we will describe the different perspectives on transfer: the associative perspective, the Gestalt/cognitive psychological perspective, and the situative perspective, in addition to a view of transfer as being based in a particular formal discipline (Mayer & Wittrock, 1996). In general, transfer of learning between problems has been difficult to obtain reliably, so much so that several researchers have wondered whether transfer as a phenomenon exists at all (Detterman, 1993; Salomon & Perkins, 1989). The difficulty of obtaining transfer makes it a good "test case" for comparisons between the different traditions; within each tradition, the conditions under which transfer will occur must be well specified for any effect to be found. The level of specification required to predict transfer effectively provides an opportunity for the elaboration of the various theories of transfer which arise from the different perspectives. We should note that, within almost all of the traditions, researchers have made strides in more regularly obtaining transfer. Although the theories arising from each perspective are quite different, their success implies that each one does not necessarily compete with the others, but rather may cover a different range of phenomena.

Formal Disciplines Perspective

The first perspective on transfer is not related to any of the epistemological traditions discussed in the previous section. It is, however, a recurrent perspective within educational psychology, and thus needs to be addressed in any discussion of transfer. This particular view equates a specific, formal discipline with general skill. The given discipline is seen as a sort of mental exercise, so that the general skills learned in that discipline could transfer to a wide range of other activities (Angell, 1908). For example, the Latin school movement in the United States in the nineteenth century was aimed at teaching students classical subjects, which were thought to promulgate good mental habits and orderly thinking. More recently, the study of a programming language such as LOGO (Papert, 1980) has been thought to lead to general skills, such as planning and precise thinking, which would transfer to a wide variety of domains. In both examples, the claim is made that learning a specific discipline also leads to the acquisition of general mental skills, which in turn will transfer to other disciplines.

The evidence for this general view of transfer has not been encouraging. Returning to the Latin school example, students who studied Latin and other classical subjects did no better on tests of reasoning than other students (Thorndike, 1924). Furthermore, learning the programming language LOGO did not transfer to a planning task as expected (Pea & Kurland, 1984), except when learners received intensive guidance from an instructor (Clements & Gullo, 1984). The evidence is weak that general skills learned in a particular discipline transfer to other unrelated tasks.

Indeed, some evidence exists that students rarely even apply the lessons learned in the classroom to appropriate situations in real life (Lave, 1988). For instance, students in mathematics classes learn specific methods of comparison (e.g. taking unit prices of items in a grocery store). Outside of the classroom, however, those skill-taught strategies are likely to be abandoned in favor of such "homemade" strategies as ratio comparison (i.e. comparing the ratio of sizes of cans with the ratio of their prices). If knowledge of a discipline is not applied, even within the domain that the discipline covers, it seems unlikely that that discipline will undergird any general ability that transfers to other domains.

The formal disciplines view does not serve as an adequate model of transfer. Most researchers, therefore, have turned to examining the particular mental processes that might help to explain how prior experience with specific skills or knowledge will transfer to other specific tasks. We now turn to two perspectives that attempt to explain how a particular skill or concept can transfer to other situations.

Associative Perspective

A second view of transfer arose from the behaviorist tradition in response to the formal disciplines view of transfer (Cox, 1997). In this perspective, identical elements in behavior could be generalized from one learning situation to another (Rescorla, 1976; Thorndike & Woodworth, 1901). For example, one-column addition is a component of two-column addition; insofar as the procedures of one-column addition are used in two-column addition, training in one-column addition will transfer to two-column. This view of transfer was the basis of the notion of "vertical" transfer (Gagné, 1966), in which the learning of high-level skills depended on mastery of the low-level skills. For instance, solution of a mathematical equation should depend on the learner being able to carry out more basic arithmetic operations such as addition or division. The skills involved in solving an equation can be organized into a hierarchy, with mastery of lower-level skills a requisite for mastery of higher-level skills. A modern incarnation of an identical elements theory of transfer may be seen in computerized intelligent tutoring systems, such as those based on Anderson's ACT-R cognitive architecture (Anderson, 1993).

These tutoring systems were originally an attempt by researchers in artificial intelligence to develop computer instruction systems that were able to respond to students much as human tutors would (Anderson, 1993; Wenger, 1987). Earlier programs for computer-assisted instruction (e.g. Suppes & Morningstar, 1972) worked simply to drill learners in problem tasks. Tutoring systems based on ACT-R (Anderson, 1993), for example, attempt to determine which of a set of production rules an individual student is using to solve example problems in a domain. (A production rule is simply an "IF–THEN" rule; once a certain condition is met a particular bit of behavior is produced.) The system may then present further examples to strengthen the student's grasp of particular rules, as well as point out errors and provide explanations. In this way, the computerized tutor can respond flexibly to an individual student's weaknesses. These tutoring systems guide students to learn and strengthen specific condition–action rules, so that they will be more likely to use that same rule when it is appropriate in future problem solving. Transfer will obtain to the extent that two tasks use identical productions (i.e. the conditions triggering productions are identical between the two tasks, and the actions learned in one task will lead to successful problem solving in the other). The heart of transfer is the sharing of common elements among the different tasks.

As with the formal discipline view, evidence for this form of transfer is also mixed (VanPatten, Chao & Reigeluth, 1986). For example, an instructional program based on vertical transfer was generally ineffective (Gagné & Paradise, 1961). Although learners showed joint mastery (or lack thereof) of both higher-level skills and their lower-level components, learners showed a high percentage of failures at both levels. Furthermore, learners showed a fair number of transitions in which they demonstrated mastery of the lower-level skill but not the higher-level skill. The problem seems to be one of specifying just what the overlapping or component operations should be (Singley & Anderson, 1989). That is, a single high-level skill may rest at the top of several different skill hierarchies. When learners fail to show transfer from a low-level skill to a higher level, we cannot be sure if indeed they are unable to transfer. It may be that the instructional program does not use the best skill hierarchy to promote transfer, or that the learner is using the component skills correctly, but as part of a skill hierarchy that does not lead to correct higher-level solutions.

Production rule theories of transfer (Anderson, 1993; Singley & Anderson, 1989) have been more successful at avoiding these problems than older versions within the associative tradition. For instance, students who had recently learned to edit text in one-line computer text editors performed modestly better on a screen-based editor than students who had been practicing typing (Singley & Anderson, 1985; reported in Singley & Anderson, 1989). In another study, learning one programming language, such as LISP, has been shown to reduce the time it takes to design, code, and debug a function in a second language (Anderson, et al., 1993). Two factors might have led to this increased success at observing transfer. First, identical productions are more powerful than identical elements, because of the increased level of abstractness: identical elements only match surface features of two tasks, whereas identical productions match any number of intermediate steps in processing those surface features. Second, the tasks involved in these studies had been extensively analyzed (Card, Moran & Newell, 1980; Card, Moran & Newell, 1983) so that the researchers had descriptions of more possible paths to solution than had been available to previous researchers (Singley & Anderson, 1989). As noted above, tutoring systems made use of these additional paths to provide flexible training. There is some evidence that training can transfer, at least in those cases where learners are properly instructed so that whole sequences can be automatized.

The key to transfer, from the associative perspective, lies in the presence of shared elements between two tasks. Because the shared element has been associated with features of the previously learned task, it is more likely to be activated in the new situation, and thus will more likely lead to success. The next view of transfer, in contrast, emphasizes the abstraction and mapping of relationships between the learned and novel situations.

Gestalt/Cognitive Perspective

A third view of transfer traces its heritage to the Gestaltists, who, not surprisingly, believed that people could learn by gaining understanding of the structural relations among problem elements. This understanding could then transfer to new problems, if the structural relations learned from previous problems were related to the requirements of the new problems. Note that the two problems, in this view, do not have to share identical elements for transfer to occur. For example, students who learned to make rectangles out of parallelograms (by cutting off one end and then placing the two slanted sides together) and then to find the area of the rectangle were later better able to solve problems involving other distortions of rectangles than were students who had simply learned the routine formula for finding the area (Wertheimer, 1959). According to this view of transfer, students learned a general principle (i.e. some shapes were distortions of rectangles) and were able to apply that principle to find the area of other objects.

The Gestalt view, by itself, did not specify the cognitive mechanisms underlying transfer. Recent work in cognitive psychology has pointed to several areas where models of cognitive processes might help to understand how learners extract principles from instances, and when they are likely to use those principles successfully with novel problems. One class of processes seems to be particularly critical for the study of transfer: analogy. Analogy is central to the cognitive view of transfer because it specifies how people are able to bridge the gap between previously acquired conceptual understanding and novel situations, by mapping the relations among features of the prior concepts to relationships in the new situation (Sternberg, 1985).

Current theories of analogy may also help to explain how understanding for transfer is gained (and why it is so difficult to obtain). Analogy is "the process of understanding a novel situation in terms of one that is already familiar" (Gentner & Holyoak, 1997, p. 32). In the process of analogy, a familiar situation, or analogue, is accessed (Seifert, McKoon, Abelson & Ratcliff, 1986); corresponding elements between the familiar situation and the novel, or target, situation are mapped onto each other (Gentner, 1983); and new inferences about the target situation are drawn (Lassaline, 1996). For example, an analogue might be an algebra story problem, which a student remembers concerned the rate of flow in inlet and outlet pipes on a water tank. The analogue may then help to solve a problem involving buckets of grain being dumped in and scooped out of a bin, if the student realizes the correspondence between the problems – both concern the rate of input and output of some material in a storage container. The principles involved in solving the first problem may then be applied to the second.

A structure mapping model of analogy (Gentner, 1983; Gentner, 1989; Gentner & Markman, 1997) explains how analogical processes allow the comparison between two problems. In this model, the comparison is based on the number of similar relationships between features in the analogue and the target. For example, the solar system can serve as an analogue for an atom: just as the planets revolve around a more massive sun, electrons revolve around a more massive nucleus (Gentner, 1983). The structure mapping model consists of several steps on the way to formation of an analogy (see Forbus, Gentner & Law, 1995; Gentner & Markman, 1997; cf. Holyoak & Thagard, 1989; Holyoak & Thagard, 1997). First, all of the local matches between attributes of the analogue and target are found (e.g. the fact that the sun and nucleus are at the center of their respective systems). Second, relationships among those attributes in the local matches are structured into consistent clusters (e.g. planets revolve around the sun, and electrons revolve around the nucleus). These clusters are systematically combined into higher-order relations. At this point, if the analogy is deemed acceptable, inferences can be drawn about unknown qualities of the target, based on the analogous qualities in the analogue (Clement & Gentner, 1991).

There may be several possible analogues for a target problem; the particular solution attempted for the target may depend on the analogue used. For instance, during the 1991 Persian Gulf War (stemming from Iraq's invasion of Kuwait) the Iraqi leader Saddam Hussein was often portrayed as analogous to Hitler. Former President Bush could then be viewed as analogous either to Franklin Roosevelt or Winston Churchill. Note that the role of the USA in this analogy depends on the mapping of George Bush to the leaders of the Second World War. Students preferred to map the US in 1991 to the USA in 1941 when George Bush was analogous to FDR; and to Great Britain if Bush was analogous to Churchill (Spellman & Holyoak, 1992). The attributes were mapped, not only to be consistent between each pair (e.g. between Kuwait–Poland and Iraq–Germany), but to be consistent within the entire system.

The model helps to explain how people may use analogies to solve problems. For example, students learning about electricity may picture the flow of electrons using either a water-flow model or a moving-crowd model (Gentner & Gentner, 1983). The particular analogy used influences problem-solving performance; for instance, students who learned a moving-crowd model (in which mice are seen as electrons and gates as resistors) performed better on questions about serial resistors than did students who learned a flowing-water model (Gentner & Gentner, 1983). The students tended to use the model of electricity they had learned as an analogue to solve problems in a novel domain.

Although analogy sometimes seems to play a role in problem solving (Gentner & Gentner, 1983), people seem to use it only under certain conditions. When left to their own devices, students seem rarely to apply what they have learned to new problems. For instance, after learning to solve the famous missionaries and cannibals problem – in which the learner had to figure out how to move two groups across a river following strict rules for combining the groups – students failed to employ the previous experience in solving an analogous husbands and wives problem (Reed, Ernst & Banerji, 1974). This problem also involved moving two groups between banks of a river; furthermore, it shared similar combination rules to the missionaries and cannibals problem. In another example, students who had successfully solved a problem that involved attacking a fortress by simultaneously converging small numbers of troops from many different directions failed to transfer that strategy to solve Duncker's (1945) radiation problem. This latter problem can be solved by converging small doses of radiation from multiple directions (Gick & Holyoak, 1980; Gick & Holyoak, 1983). In both of these failures to transfer, the learners had simply been given the second problem without reference to the first. It appears that they failed to take advantage of their previous experience in solving the new problems.

Despite this general failure to exploit previous experiences, learners can be pushed to use analogous situations to solve novel problems. First, they can be helped to notice that their prior experience is helpful; they may normally simply not have *encoded* the current problem in such a way as to recognize the applicability of the analogous problems (Sternberg, 1985). For example, if learners are told explicitly that the problem they have just completed will help them to solve the current problem, they are more likely to transfer their previous experience successfully (Brown & Kane, 1988; Gick & Holyoak, 1983; Reed et al., 1974). Students may also recognize the relevance of a prior analogue if the analogue and target are superficially similar to each other (Holyoak & Koh, 1987; Ross, 1987; Ross, 1989). For instance, subjects were more likely to solve the radiation problem if they summarized an analogous story with which it shared surface features, than if they summarized the same story, but with different surface features (Holyoak & Koh, 1987). Presumably the surface similarity reminds learners of the analogue, making it more likely that they will use it to solve the target problem.

Second, they can be helped to *infer* the appropriate structural features from the analogues (Sternberg, 1985). If learners do not understand the key relationships within the analogue, they will not be able to apply that analogue to new situations. One could, for example, teach the appropriate inferences directly (Nisbett, Krantz, Jepson & Kunda, 1983). Another way to increase the likelihood of inference is to make learners compare a number of dissimilar examples, all of which share the same structural properties. For instance, subjects who compared two stories – one about a general attacking a fortress, the other about a fire chief putting out a fire, both of which involved converging small amounts of people or water from many directions – were more likely to solve the radiation problem (Duncker, 1945) than were subjects who received only one relevant story (Gick & Holyoak, 1983), or who did not explicitly make the comparison (Cantrambone & Holyoak, 1989). Note that expertise in a domain (discussed under the "Cognitivist/Rationalist Perspective" heading in the previous section) implies that these structural features have already been abstracted (VanLehn, 1996). For example, expert physicists are more likely to use an appropriate representation, such as the abstract principle of Newton's Second Law, to solve problems, whereas novices focus on irrelevant superficial features, such as the presence of an inclined plane (Chi, Feltovich & Glaser, 1981). With effort, learners can abstract the appropriate structure from analogous problems, thus increasing the likelihood that experience with those problems will transfer to new ones.

One of the most important educational implications of analogical transfer concerns the role of example problems with the solutions given, such as would be found in a mathematics textbook. Such worked-out examples are an efficient way (from the teacher's or textbook writer's point of view) to present instances for later use as problem-solving analogues. Students, however, use those worked-out examples to solve new problems with varying degrees of success. Learners profit more from worked-out examples to the extent that they explain the given solutions to themselves (Chi, Bassok, Lewis, Reimann & Glaser, 1989; Novick, 1988; Pirolli & Recker, 1994; Renkl, 1997). For example, Renkl (1997) found that students' performance on a test of probability calculation was predicted from specific strategies for using examples given before that test. These strategies included: basing self-explanations on principles of probability, using goal–operator combinations to understand the example (see also Catrambone, 1995), trying to anticipate the next step in the example before it was presented, and not paying attention to impasses in comprehension. The best "self-explainers" especially tended to use general principles and goal–operator combinations to understand the examples; the worst group used few of those strategies. Clearly, the quality of study of analogues affects the success of transfer to new problems.

The key to analogical transfer, in the cognitive approach, is the ability to match the relationships from previous learning to new concepts. Like the associative approach, this view focuses on processes going on within the minds of individual learners. The last approach to be discussed implies that the analysis of physical and social environments is important for understanding the phenomenon of transfer.

Situative Perspective

Unlike the more established associative and cognitive perspectives, researchers in the situative tradition have not yet thoroughly studied the question of transfer (Greeno, 1997). One recent analysis, however, provides a rough sketch of what a future situative theory of transfer might look like (Greeno, Smith & Moore, 1993). According to this sketch, transfer involves the learner becoming sensitive to invariant features in the environment. Echoing Gibson ([1979] 1986), a class of these invariant features includes constraints in the environment that afford, or support, a particular activity. For example, the finger-sized depressions and labels on a large dictionary afford opening that dictionary to a desired section. A learner becomes attuned to the affordances in a situation as he or she begins to perceive the possibilities of activity that situation supports. Transfer occurs when that learner happens to become attuned to those affordances that apply to novel situations. Note that Greeno et al. (1993) expand the notion of affordance from the perceptual world to the conceptual world. Just as percepts in the physical world support certain types of activities, such as walking through doorways and opening dictionaries, concepts (as defined in the social world) support other types of activities, such as adding numbers or forming an argument.

As an example of attunement to affordances, consider the analysis of Greeno et al. to the results of some of the first transfer studies (Hendrickson & Schroeder, 1941; Judd, 1908). In both of these studies, a group of boys was asked to throw a dart (Judd, 1908) or shoot an air rifle (Hendrickson & Schroeder, 1941) at a target under water. Because of the refraction of light by the water, the target would appear to be horizontally displaced, so that aiming directly at the target would cause the missile to land beyond the actual target. After an initial training phase with the water at one depth, the water level was changed, thus changing the amount of displacement caused by refraction. One group of boys, which had received an explanation of the refraction of light before the initial training, was better able to adapt to the new water level than was another group of boys, which had not received any such explanation. An additional group in Hendrickson & Schroeder's (1941) study that received explicit information that deeper water causes more horizontal displacement performed better in the transfer task than the other two groups.

According to the analysis of Greeno et al., there are multiple affordances for adjusting aim to which the boys could have become attuned during the initial training phase. These affordances include aiming short of the target and getting to the center through trial and error, paying attention to the angular rotation of the path of the missile as it entered the water, or focusing on the relation between the distance the missile landed from the target and the apparent depth of the water. Either of the last two affordances for adjustment (or both in conjunction) could support transfer from the initial water level to the new water level. The effect of the instructions was to aid the boys in becoming attuned to those constraints that better supported transfer.

In summary, a situative view of transfer could be based on the idea that people become attuned to certain invariances in the environment that support particular activities. Some of these affordances also exist in different situations. To the extent that a learner becomes attuned to these affordances, he or she will be better able to perform in novel situations.

Conclusion

The different perspectives certainly seem to lead to different explanations of transfer. For example, associative theories of transfer emphasize the proceduralization of complex patterns of behavior. Cognitive theories of transfer emphasize the processes which create mappings between relationships in prior concepts and novel situations. A situative theory of transfer would emphasize the ways in which particular features in different physical or social environments afford a common activity. The different traditions obviously point to different explanatory mechanisms for transfer, yet theories arising from the three perspectives are able to explain successfully or predict conditions under which transfer occurs (in contrast to the formal disciplines approach).

Again, note that the different perspectives focus on different aspects of those situations in which transfer occurs. In line with the discussion from the previous section of this chapter, an associative analysis is best suited to those tasks in which a particular automatized skill is expected to play a role in the transfer situation. A cognitivist analysis helps to predict when transfer between specific conceptual understanding and a novel situation will occur. Finally, a situative perspective moves the analysis of transfer to a different level; the key, in this view, is a thorough exploration of the features in different situations that support a common activity.

A SYNTHESIS

From the foregoing discussion, it should be clear that the traditional perspectives on the nature of learning explain different aspects of the same phenomenon; each tradition can help fill in different pieces of the puzzle. For instance, the different perspectives can be put to use in designing instructional programs for learning second languages. An associative perspective is well-suited to devising schedules of vocabulary drill, or to organizing introductions to grammar so that simple notions like present and past tenses of verbs are mastered before more complex verbal forms, such as gerunds and participles, are introduced. The cognitive perspective could add more value to the analysis by describing how learners try to infer the meanings of unknown words, or interpret idiomatic expressions by analogy. Finally, the situative perspective could additionally describe how to arrange classroom activities to draw students into using the second language with one another in a natural manner, so that their language skills could be effectively practiced. That is, by using tools and theories from each perspective, a more holistic description of the instructional program could be developed. When the three traditions stop being viewed as competing explanations of the same phenomenon, it becomes clear that they can provide complementary views that capture a wider description of behavior.

Finally, we would like to offer a description of our own research program in intelligence and instruction as a rough example of a synthesis of the different perspectives. The contextual subtheory of the triarchic theory of human intelligence (Sternberg, 1985) includes an examination of lay conceptions of intelligence in the United States (Sternberg, Conway, Ketron & Bernstein, 1981), in line with the situative perspective's emphasis on defining those activities that are valued by the culture. An analysis of those activities that people labeled as "intelligent" revealed three kinds of abilities involved in intelligent behavior.

Analytic abilities play a large role in solving inductive and deductive problems, learning vocabulary, and comprehending text. Note that these abilities are the ones most often emphasized in traditional school classrooms. In addition to these traditional analytic skills, the triarchic theory specifies a *creative* component to intelligence. This component is concerned with dealing effectively with novelty, both in skill acquisition and task execution, and with the automatization of skills. The triarchic theory also includes a *practical* component, which is concerned with successfully fulfilling pragmatic needs. These latter two components expand the view of intelligence to include activities in a culture that are not normally covered by the traditionally academic perspective. Although the triarchic theory is, therefore, sensitive to the social situation in which an individual was raised, it also attempts to specify the universal cognitive processes involved in each of the components. For example, although actions which may be considered expedient vary from culture to culture, general abilities to adapt to, select, or shape a person's environment operate across cultures. In this way, the situative concern with the sociocultural situation is merged with the cognitive concern to specify mental processes.

The triarchic theory also informs instructional design. Because people vary in the extent to which they are analytically, creatively, or practically endowed, it is possible that instruction that is matched to a particular student's abilities will be more efficacious than a "one size fits all" approach (Sternberg, 1996). That is, instruction that emphasizes the practical activities of a discipline will be more efficacious for those students who are high in practical abilities. Note that, because traditional instruction primarily focuses on analytic activities, students high in practical or creative ability might normally be under-served by their education. A series of studies is confirming that, indeed, matching students' patterns of abilities to classroom instruction and performance assessment leads to better learning than does using a traditional instructional approach (Sternberg, Ferrari, Clinkenbeard & Grigorenko, 1996). In particular, high school participants were chosen for patterns of analytical, creative, and practical abilities. One group was ranked high only in analytical abilities, another only in creative abilities, another only in practical abilities, another high in all three abilities, and another low in all three abilities. The students then came to Yale to take a college-level psychology course. They were placed in course sections that emphasized either memory, analytical, creative, or practical instruction. Some participants were instructed in ways that matched their patterns of abilities; other participants were placed in ways that mismatched. All participants were evaluated in their achievement for memory, analytical, creative, and practical achievements. Students who were placed in course sections that matched their patterns of abilities performed better than did students who were mismatched.

In another series of studies (Sternberg, Torff & Grigorenko, 1998), it was found that instruction that emphasizes analytic, creative, *and* practical abilities serves students well, regardless of their strengths. In one part of this study, third-graders in North Carolina went through a classroom unit on communities. In another part, eighth-graders studying in California and Maryland studied psychology. In each part, students received either memory-based instruction alone, critical thinking (analytic) instruction alone, or triarchic (analytic, creative, and practical) instruction. Examples of creative and practical instruction included activities such as inventing a government agency and finding a solution to a problem with litter. Students who received triarchic instruction generally performed better on a variety of assessments (including memory-based tests; analytic, creative, and practical essay assignments; and classroom portfolios) than did students who received the other types of treatments. These results suggest that the triarchic theory is a useful basis for instructional design. Indeed, triarchic instruction even improved performance relative to other conditions in the memory condition. More broadly, the results also suggest that a synthesis of theoretical perspectives allows an enhanced understanding of the processes involved in learning. This enhanced understanding can then be used successfully to design instructional interventions.

ACKNOWLEDGMENTS

The authors gratefully acknowledge the support received from Yale University and the US Office of Educational Research (Grant R206R50001) during the preparation of this chapter. The positions taken in this chapter do not necessarily reflect those of OERI or of the United States government.

REFERENCES

Anderson, J. R. (1993). *Rules of the Mind.* Hillsdale, NJ: Lawrence Erlbaum.

Anderson, J. R., Conrad, F., Corbett, A. T., Fincham, J. M., Hoffman, D. & Wu, Q. (1993). Computer programming and transfer. In J. R. Anderson (Ed.), *Rules of the Mind* (pp. 205–234). Hillsdale, NJ: Lawrence Erlbaum.

Anderson, J. R., Reder, L. M. & Simon, H. A. (1996). Situated learning and education. *Educational Researcher*, 25 (4), 5–11.

Angell, J. R. (1908). The doctrine of formal discipline in the light of the principles of general psychology. *Educational Review*, 36, 1–14.

Bédard, J. & Chi, M. T. H. (1992). Expertise. *Current Directions in Psychological Science*, 1 (4), 135–9.

Berliner, D. C. & Calfee, R. C. (Eds) (1996). *Handbook of Educational Psychology*. New York: Simon & Schuster Macmillan.

Brown, A. L. & Kane, L. R. (1988). Preschool children can learn to transfer: learning to learn and learning from example. *Cognitive Psychology*, 20, 493–523.

Brown, J. S., Collins, A. & Duguid, P. (1989). Situated cognition and the culture of learning. *Educational Researcher* (January–February), 32–42.

Catrambone, R. & Holyoak, K. J. (1989). Overcoming contextual limitations on problem-solving transfer. *Journal of Experimental Psychology: Learning, Memory, and Cognition*, 15, 1147–56.

Card, S. K., Moran, T. P. & Newell, A. (1980). Computer text-editing: an information processing analysis of a routine cognitive skill. *Cognitive Psychology*, 12, 32–74.

Card, S. K., Moran, T. P. & Newell, A. (1983). *The Psychology of Human–Computer Interaction.* Hillsdale, NJ: Lawrence Erlbaum.

Carey, S. (1985). *Conceptual Change in Childhood.* Cambridge, MA: MIT Press.

Case, R. (1985). *Intellectual Development: Birth to Adulthood.* Orlando, FL: Academic Press.

Case, R. (1992). Neo-Piagetian theories of child development. In R. J. Sternberg & C. A.

Berg (Eds), *Intellectual Development* (pp. 161–96). New York: Cambridge University Press.
Catrambone, R. (1995). Aiding subgoal learning: effects on transfer. *Journal of Educational Psychology*, 87 (1), 5–17.
Chase, W. G. & Simon, H. A. (1973). The mind's eye in chess. In W. G. Chase (Ed.), *Visual Information Processing* (pp. 215–81). New York: Academic Press.
Chi, M. T. H., Feltovich, P. J. & Glaser, R. (1981). Categorization and representation of physics problems by experts and novices. *Cognitive Science*, 5, 121–52.
Chi, M. T. H., Bassok, M., Lewis, M. W., Reimann, P. & Glaser, R. (1989). Self explanations: how students study and use examples in learning to solve problems. *Cognitive Science*, 13, 145–82.
Clement, C. A. & Gentner, D. (1991). Systematicity as a selection constraint in analogical mapping. *Cognitive Science*, 15, 89–132.
Clements, D. H. & Gullo, D. F. (1984). Effects of computer programming on young children's cognition. *Journal of Educational Psychology*, 76 (6), 1051–8.
Cognition and Technology Group at Vanderbilt (1994). From visual word problems to learning communities: changing conceptions of cognitive research. In K. McGilly (Ed.), *Classroom Lessons: Integrating Cognitive Theory and Classroom Practice* (pp. 157–200). Cambridge, MA: MIT Press.
Cox, B. D. (1997). The rediscovery of the active learner in adaptive contexts: a developmental-historical analysis of transfer of training. *Educational Psychologist*, 32 (1), 41–55.
Detterman, D. K. (1993). The case for the prosecution: transfer as an epiphenomenon. In D. K. Detterman & R. J. Sternberg (Eds), *Transfer on Trial: Intelligence, Cognition, and Instruction*. Norwood, NJ: Ablex.
Duncker, K. (1945). On problem-solving. *Psychological Monographs*, 58 (5), Whole No. 270.
Ericsson, K. A., Krampe, R. Th. & Tesch-Römer, C. (1993). The role of deliberate practice in the acquisition of expert performance. *Psychological Review*, 100 (3), 363–406.
Forbus, K. D., Gentner, D. & Law, K. (1995). MAC/FAC: a model of similarity-based retrieval. *Cognitive Science*, 19, 141–205.
Gagné, R. M. (1966). *The Conditions of Learning*. New York: Holt, Rinehart & Winston.
Gagné, R. M. & Paradise, N. E. (1961). Abilities and learning sets in knowledge acquisition. *Psychological Monographs*, 75 (14).
Gelman, S. A. & Markman, E. (1987). Young children's inductions from natural kinds: the role of categories and appearances. *Child Development*, 58, 1532–41.
Gentner, D. (1983). Structure-mapping: a theoretical framework for analogy. *Cognitive Science*, 7, 155–70.
Gentner, D. (1989). The mechanisms of analogical learning. In S. Vosniadou & A. Ortony (Eds), *Similarity and Analogical Reasoning*. Cambridge: Cambridge University Press.
Gentner, D. & Gentner, D. R. (1983). Flowing waters or teeming crowds: mental models of electricity. In D. Gentner & A. L. Stevens (Eds), *Mental Models* (pp. 99–130). Hillsdale, NJ: Erlbaum.
Gentner, D. & Holyoak, K. J. (1997). Reasoning and learning by analogy: an introduction. *American Psychologist*, 52 (1), 32–4.
Gentner, D. & Markman, A. B. (1997). Structure mapping in analogy and similarity. *American Psychologist*, 52 (1), 45–56.
Gibson, J. J. ([1979] 1986). *The Ecological Approach to Visual Perception*. Hillsdale, NJ: Erlbaum.
Gick, M. L. & Holyoak, K. J. (1980). Analogical problem solving. *Cognitive Psychology*, 12, 306–55.
Gick, M. L. & Holyoak, K. J. (1983). Schema induction and analogical transfer. *Cognitive Psychology*, 15, 1–38.
Gluck, M. A. & Bower, G. H. (1988). From conditioning to category learning: an adaptive network model. *Journal of Experimental Psychology: General*, 117 (3), 227–47.

Greeno, J. G. (1997). On claims that answer the wrong questions. *Educational Researcher*, 26 (1), 5–17.
Greeno, J. G., Collins, A. M. & Resnick, L. B. (1996). Cognition and learning. In D. C. Berliner & R. C. Calfee (Eds), *Handbook of Educational Psychology* (pp. 15–46). New York: Simon & Schuster Macmillan.
Greeno, J. G. & Simon, H. A. (1988). Problem solving and reasoning. In R. C. Atkins, R. J. Herstein, G. Lindzey & R. D. Luce (Eds), *Steven's Handbook of Experimental Psychology*. New York: Wiley.
Greeno, J. G., Smith, D. R. & Moore, J. L. (1993). Transfer of situated learning. In D. K. Detterman & R. J. Sternberg (Eds), *Transfer on Trial: Intelligence, Cognition, and Instruction*. Norwood, NJ: Ablex.
Halford, G. S. (1993). *Children's Understanding: The Development of Mental Models*. Hillsdale, NJ: Lawrence Erlbaum.
Hendrickson, G. & Schroeder, W. H. (1941). Transfer of training in learning to hit a submerged target. *Journal of Educational Psychology*, 32, 205–13.
Holyoak, K. J. & Koh, K. (1987). Surface and structural similarity in analogical transfer. *Memory & Cognition*, 15, 332–40.
Holyoak, K. J. & Thagard, P. (1989). Analogical mapping by constraint satisfaction. *Cognitive Science*, 13, 295–355.
Holyoak, K. J. & Thagard, P. (1997). The analogical mind. *American Psychologist*, 52 (1), 35–44.
Hull, C. L. (1942). *Principles of Behavior: An Introduction to Behavior Theory*. New York: Appleton-Century.
Hutchins, E. (1993). Learning to navigate. In S. Chaikin & J. Lave (Eds), *Understanding Practice: Perspectives on Activity and Context* (pp. 35–63). Cambridge: Cambridge University Press.
Johnson-Laird, P. N. (1983). *Mental Models: Towards a Cognitive Science of Language, Inference, and Consciousness*. Cambridge, MA: Harvard University Press.
Judd, C. H. (1908). The relation of special training to general intelligence. *Educational Review*, 36, 28–42.
Kamin, L. J. (1969). Predictability, surprise, attention and conditioning. In B. A. Campbell & P. M. Church (Eds), *Punishment and Aversive Behavior*. New York: Appleton-Century-Crofts.
Keil, F. C. (1989). *Concepts, Kinds, and Cognitive Development*. Cambridge, MA: MIT Press.
Keller, C. M. & Keller, J. D. (1996). *Cognition and Tool Use: The Blacksmith at Work*. Cambridge: Cambridge University Press.
Lajoie, S. P. & Lesgold, A. M. (1992). Dynamic assessment of proficiency for solving procedural knowledge tasks. *Educational Psychologist*, 27 (3), 365–84.
Lassaline, M. E. (1996). Structural alignment in induction and similarity. *Journal of Experimental Psychology: Learning, Memory & Cognition*, 22, 754–70.
Lave, J. (1988). *Cognition in Practice*. Cambridge: Cambridge University Press.
Lave, J. & Wenger, E. (1991). *Situated Learning: Legitimate Peripheral Participation*. Cambridge: Cambridge University Press.
Mayer, R. E. & Wittrock, M. C. (1996). Problem-solving transfer. In D. C. Berliner & R. C. Calfee (Eds), *Handbook of Educational Psychology* (pp. 47–62). New York: Simon & Schuster Macmillan.
Miller, G. A. (1956). The magical number seven plus or minus two: some limits on our capacity for processing information. *Psychological Review*, 63, 81–97.
Miller, R. R., Barnet, R. C. & Grahame, N. J. (1995). Assessment of the Rescorla–Wagner model. *Psychological Bulletin*, 117 (3), 363–86.
Newell, A. (1990). *Unified Theories of Cognition*. Cambridge, MA: Harvard University Press.
Newell, A. & Simon, H. A. (1972). *Human Problem Solving*. Englewood Cliffs, NJ: Prentice Hall.

Nisbett, R. E., Krantz, D. H., Jepson, D. & Kunda, Z. (1983). The use of statistical heuristics in everyday inductive reasoning. *Psychological Review*, 90, 339–63.
Novick, L. R. (1988). Analogical transfer, problem similarity, and expertise. *Journal of Experimental Psychology: Learning, Memory, and Cognition*, 14, 510–20.
Papert, S. (1980). *Mindstorms*. New York: Basic Books.
Pea, R. D. & Kurland, D. M. (1984). On the cognitive effects of learning computer programming. *New Ideas in Psychology*, 2 (2), 137–68.
Piaget, J. (1983). Piaget's theory. In P. H. Mussen (Ed.), *Handbook of Child Psychology*. New York: John Wiley.
Pintrich, P. R., Marx, R. W. & Boyle, R. A. (1993). Beyond cold conceptual change: the role of motivational beliefs and classroom contextual factors in the process of conceptual change. *Review of Educational Research*, 63 (2), 167–99.
Pirolli, P. & Recker, M. (1994). Learning strategies and transfer in the domain of programming. *Cognition & Instruction*, 12 (3), 235–75.
Reed, S. K., Ernst, G. W. & Banerji, R. (1974). The role of analogy in transfer between similar problem states. *Cognitive Psychology*, 6, 436–50.
Renkl, A. (1997). Learning from worked-out examples: a study on individual differences. *Cognitive Science*, 21 (1), 1–29.
Rescorla, R. A. (1976). Stimulus generalization: some predictions from a model of Pavlovian conditioning. *Journal of Experimental Psychology: Animal Behavior Processes*, 2, 88–96.
Rescorla, R. A. & Wagner, A. R. (1972). A theory of Pavlovian conditioning: variations in the effectiveness of reinforcement and nonreinforcement. In A. Black & W. F. Prokasy (Eds), *Classical Conditioning: II. Current Research and Theory* (pp. 64–99). New York: Appleton-Century-Crofts.
Resnick, L. B. (1989). Developing mathematical knowledge. *American Psychologist*, 44, 162–9.
Resnick, L. B., Levine, J. M. & Teasley, S. D. (Eds) (1991). *Perspectives on Socially Shared Cognition*. Washington, DC: American Psychological Association.
Rogoff, B. (1990). *Apprenticeship in Thinking*. New York: Oxford University Press.
Ross, B. H. (1987). This is like that: the use of earlier problems and the separation of similarity effects. *Journal of Experimental Psychology: Learning, Memory, and Cognition*, 13, 629–39.
Ross, B. H. (1989). Distinguishing types of superficial similarities: different effects on the access and use of earlier problems. *Journal of Experimental Psychology: Learning, Memory, and Cognition*, 15, 456–68.
Rumelhart, D. E., McClelland, J. L. & the PDP Research Group (Eds) (1986). *Parallel Distributed Processing: Explorations in the Microstructure of Cognition: Vol. 1. Foundations*. Cambridge, MA: MIT Press.
Salomon, G. & Perkins, D. N. (1989). Rocky roads to transfer: rethinking mechanisms of a neglected phenomenon. *Educational Psychologist*, 24, 113–42.
Scardamalia, M., Bereiter, C. & Lamon, M. (1994). The CSILE project: trying to bring the classroom into World 3. In K. McGilly (Ed.), *Classroom Lessons: Integrating Cognitive Theory and Classroom Practice*. Cambridge, MA: MIT Press.
Schoenfeld, A. H. (1988). When good teaching leads to bad results: the disasters of "well-taught" mathematics courses. *Educational Psychologist*, 23, 145–66.
Schwartz, J. L., Yarushalmy, M. & Wilson, B. (Eds) (1993). *The Geometric Supposer: What is it a Case of?* Hillsdale, NJ: Lawrence Erlbaum.
Seifert, C. M., McKoon, G., Abelson, R. P. & Ratcliff, R. (1986). Memory connections between thematically similar episodes. *Journal of Experimental Psychology: Learning, Memory & Cognition*, 12, 220–31.
Singley, M. K. & Anderson, J. R. (1985). The transfer of text-editing skill. *Journal of Man–Machine Studies*, 22, 403–23.
Singley, M. K. & Anderson, J. R. (1989). *The Transfer of Cognitive Skill*. Cambridge, MA: Harvard University Press.
Skinner, B. F. (1938). *The Behavior of Organisms*. New York: Appleton-Century-Crofts.

Spelke, E. S., Breinlinger, K., Macomber, J. & Jacobson, K. (1992). Origins of knowledge. *Psychological Review*, 99 (4), 605–32.

Spellman, B. A. & Holyoak, K. J. (1992). If Saddam is Hitler then who is George Bush? Analogical mapping between systems of social roles. *Journal of Personality and Social Psychology*, 62, 913–33.

Sternberg, R. J. (1985). *Beyond IQ: A Triarchic Theory of Human Intelligence*. Cambridge: Cambridge University Press.

Sternberg, R. J. (1996). Matching abilities, instruction, and assessment: reawakening the sleeping giant of ATI. In I. Dennis & P. Tapsfield (Eds), *Human Abilities: Their Nature and Measurement* (pp. 167–82). Mahwah, NJ: Lawrence Erlbaum.

Sternberg, R. J. (1997). Cognitive conceptions of expertise. In P. J. Feltovich, K. M. Ford & R. R. Hoffman (Eds), *Expertise in Context: Human and Machine* (pp. 149–62). Menlo Park, CA: AAAI Press.

Sternberg, R. J., Conway, B. E., Ketron, J. L. & Bernstein, M. (1981). People's conceptions of intelligence. *Journal of Personality and Social Psychology*, 41, 37–55.

Sternberg, R. J., Ferrari, M., Clinkenbeard, P. & Grigorenko, E. L. (1996). Identification, instruction, and assessment of gifted children: a construct validation of a triarchic model. *Gifted Child Quarterly*, 40 (3), 129–37.

Sternberg, R. J., Torff, B. & Grigorenko, E. L. (1998). Teaching triarchically improves achievement. *Journal of Educational Psychology*, 90, 374–84.

Suppes, P. & Morningstar, M. (1972). *Computer-assisted Instruction at Stanford, 1966–68*. New York: Academic Press.

Terrace, H. S. (1966). Stimulus control. In W. K. Honig (Ed.), *Operant Behavior: Areas of Research and Application* (pp. 271–344). New York: Appleton-Century-Crofts.

Thorndike, E. L. (1924). Mental discipline in high school studies. *Journal of Educational Psychology*, 15, 1–22, 83–98.

Thorndike, E. L. & Woodworth, R. S. (1901). The influence of improvement in one mental function upon the efficiency of other functions. *Psychological Review*, 8, 247–61.

VanLehn, K. (1996). Cognitive skill acquisition. *Annual Review of Psychology*, 47, 513–39.

VanPatten, J., Chao, C. & Reigeluth, C. M. (1986). A review of strategies for sequencing and synthesizing instruction. *Review of Educational Research*, 56, 437–71.

Voss, J. F., Wolfe, C. R., Lawrence, J. A. & Engle, R. A. (1991). From representation to decision: an analysis of problem solving in international relations. In R. J. Sternberg & P. A. Frensch (Eds), *Complex Problem Solving: Principles and Mechanisms* (pp. 119–58). Hillsdale, NJ: Lawrence Erlbaum.

Wagner, A. R. & Rescorla, R. A. (1972). Inhibition in Pavlovian conditioning: application of a theory. In R. A. Boakes & M. S. Halliday (Eds), *Inhibition and Learning* (pp. 301–36). New York: Academic Press.

Wasserman, E. A., Kao, S.-F., Van Hamme, L. J., Katagiri, M. & Young, M. E. (1996). Causation and association. In D. R. Shanks, D. L. Medin & K. J. Holyoak (Eds), *Causal Learning: The Psychology of Learning and Motivation*, Vol. 34 (pp. 208–64). San Diego, CA: Academic Press.

Wellman, H. M. (1990). *The Child's Theory of Mind*. Cambridge, MA: MIT Press.

Wenger, E. (1987). *Artificial Intelligence and Tutoring Systems: Computational and Cognitive Approaches to the Communication of Knowledge*. Los Altos, CA: Morgan Kaufmann.

Wertheimer, M. (1959). *Productive Thinking*. Chicago, IL: University of Chicago Press.

White, B. Y. (1993). ThinkerTools: causal models, conceptual change, and science education. *Cognition and Instruction*, 10, 1–100.

Zeitz, C. M. (1994). Expert–novice differences in memory, abstraction and reasoning in the domain of literature. *Cognition and Instruction*, 12, 277–312.

Chapter 20

Design Principles for Instruction in Content Domains: Lessons from Research on Expertise and Learning

Susan R. Goldman
Vanderbilt University
Anthony J. Petrosino
University of Wisconsin, Madison
and
Cognition and Technology Group at Vanderbilt
Vanderbilt University

A primary goal of instruction in any content area is to encourage the acquisition of the knowledge, practices, and ways of thinking that constitute the domain. Important insights on the mature forms of these are provided by research on domain expertise. Less is known about how these mature forms are learned. There is, however, research on the cognitive and social aspects of learning that identifies several processes and conditions necessary for successful learning. In this chapter, we present a set of principles for designing instruction that are consistent with this research. Learning environments designed in accordance with these principles can foster learning that reflects what we know about domain expertise. The goal of such learning environments is not to make experts of students. Rather it is to help students develop the types of knowledge

Handbook of Applied Cognition, Edited by F. T. Durso, R. S. Nickerson, R. W. Schvaneveldt, S. T. Dumais, D. S. Lindsay and M. T. H. Chi.

representations, ways of thinking, and social practices that define successful learning in specific domains.

To accomplish this goal we first summarize research on domain experts in a variety of disciplines. We then consider design principles for learning environments that show promise for supporting the development of expertise. In doing so we draw on a set of design principles that support learning with understanding (Barron et al., in press). These principles have evolved from work conducted at our center over the past ten years (Cognition and Technology Group at Vanderbilt (CTGV), 1997) and are consistent with ideas emanating from a number of other research projects (e.g. Blumenfeld et al., 1991; Edelson, Pea & Gomez, 1996; Schauble, Glaser, Duschl, Schulze & John, 1995; White & Frederiksen, 1998). In discussing the design principles, we provide relevant examples from ongoing research and implementation activities in the field of cognition and instruction. Given space constraints we are able to discuss only a small selection of the interesting ongoing implementation and research projects related to learning in the content areas.

Evidence exists for the importance of these principles to instruction in a number of content areas, although their specific realization is shaped by the organization of knowledge and the epistemology of the particular domain. The design principles are consistent with a perspective on instruction that reflects two major shifts in thinking about learning that have occurred over the past 25 years. The first shift is reflected in the "cognitive revolution" (e.g. Dennis & Sternberg, in press; Gardner, 1985; Resnick & Klopfer, 1989). Instead of knowledge being something to be received, accumulated and stored, it is now viewed as an active construction by learners through interaction with their physical and social environments and through the reorganization of their own mental structures (e.g. Cobb, 1994; Cobb, Yackel & Wood, 1992; Collins, Brown & Newman, 1989; De Corte, Greer & Vershaffel, 1996; Greeno, 1998; Harel & Papert, 1991). The second shift involves relocating individual cognitive functioning within its social, cultural and historical contexts (e.g. Bransford, Goldman & Vye, 1991; J. Brown, Collins & Duguid, 1989; Pea, 1993; vonGlaserfeld, 1989; Wheatley, 1993).

CHARACTERISTICS OF DOMAIN EXPERTS AND SUCCESSFUL LEARNERS

Experts have Well-developed Knowledge in their Domains of Expertise

Research conducted on the characteristics of expertise in a variety of domains has revealed a number of important principles about memory, knowledge representation, and processing (e.g. Bransford, Sherwood, Vye & Rieser, 1986; Charness & Shultetus, 1999, this volume; Chi, Glaser & Farr, 1988). Areas investigated include physics, mathematics, computer programming, writing, social studies, and teaching (e.g. Anzai, 1991; Berliner, 1991; Chi, Feltovich & Glaser, 1981; Hayes, 1990; Larkin, McDermott, Simon & Simon, 1980). The deep knowledge that experts have in their domain has important implications for what they notice, represent and remember when processing information in the domain, and for the flexibility with which they can adapt to different tasks and learning situations in the domain. We elaborate on these claims below.

Differences in Noticing

Differences in experts' and novices' patterns of noticing have been found in a number of domains, including medical diagnosis (e.g. Lesgold et al., 1988) and teaching. In looking at expertise in teaching, Sabers, Cushing & Berliner (1991) found that expert and novice teachers differed in what they monitored and in how they interpreted what they saw on a videotaped lesson. The novice teachers noticed less and did not set what they did notice in an interpretive frame. They tended to provide simple descriptions of isolated events and tended not to make inferences about the underlying structure of the instruction and student behavior. Experts paid more attention to a greater range of activities that were going on simultaneously in the classroom and used verbalizations to help them interpret events they saw.

Differences in Processing and Problem Solving Strategies

Many studies of expert problem solving in different content areas show that domain experts process information and approach problem solving differently than novices in the domain. Here we specifically discuss work in history and science, highlighting processes of evidence-based reasoning and problem solving.

In history, experts and novices approach problem solving and essay writing tasks differently. These differences reflect the experts' understanding of the kinds of knowledge that are useful, meaningful, and necessary for interpreting historical events. Wineburg (1991, 1994) identified three heuristics that historians used significantly more often than students when processing historical documents. These heuristics related the information in the document to (a) the historians' prior knowledge or information in other documents (corroboration), (b) concrete temporal and spatial contexts (contextualization), and (c) the document's source or author, particularly the bias and the rhetorical intent the source might have had (sourcing). Wineburg emphasized the differences in sourcing because they reflected the different epistemic stances experts and novices brought to text. For historians, the belief system and historical context of the document's author was critical to the interpretation of the information in the document and its meaningfulness in historical interpretation (Wineburg, 1994). Consistent with this, Greene (1993) found that historians related documents to prior knowledge and context whereas students tended to focus on the information in the particular document, summarizing sources rather than submitting them to critical examination. Greene (1993, 1994) emphasized that historians' knowledge of argument construction in history made certain kinds of information and processing more meaningful to historians than it was to students. Different views of the historical task, strategies for using knowledge, and efforts to relate information across documents result in different representations and evaluations of historical events (Leinhardt, Stainton & Virji, 1994; Perfetti, Rouet & Britt, 1999; Rouet, Favart, Britt & Perfetti, 1997).

A parallel set of differences have been described for experts working in various fields of science. Researchers point out that discipline specialists recognize the need to evaluate information against an established set of criteria for reliable and valid data (e.g. Chinn & Brewer, 1996; Dunbar, 1995; Koslowski, 1996; Schauble et al., 1995). These criteria (e.g. replicability, appropriate sampling, nonbiased observation) serve the same function as sourcing and corroboration do in history, namely, establishing the trustworthiness and importance of the information.

Differences in Representation and Memory

Experts' disciplinary knowledge is characterized by rich mental representations that present a coherent and consistent mental model of the relationships among sets of events or phenomena (Glaser & Chi, 1988). These representations tend to reflect deeper, principled understandings whereas novices' representations tend to be more superficial and fragmentary. The seminal work of Chase & Simon (1973) with chess experts revealed that experts' superior memory for layouts of chess pieces on a board was limited to patterns that were meaningful in the context of the game. This effect of expertise is sufficient to overcome frequently observed age differences in recall performance: 10-year-old chess experts outperformed the adult novices when asked to remember "legal" chess board configurations (Chi, 1978).

Differences between physics experts and novices also reflect the operation of principled ways of representing information. Chi et al. (1981) showed that when physics experts sorted physics problems, they based their clusters on underlying concepts and principles of physics, whereas novices sorted on the basis of superficial features of the problems. Other evidence for principled organization comes from a study of differences in experts' and novices' interpretations of a report about the air war in South Vietnam (Britton & Gulgöz, 1991): Military experts understood the report by creating a more consistent and coherent representation than the army recruits.

A number of researchers report that expert scientists and good science students construct alternative representations as they think about scientific problems (Ben-Zvi, Eylon & Silberstein, 1987; Bowen, 1990; Kozma & Russell, 1997; Miller, 1984). In contrast, Ben-Zvi et al. (1987; Yarroch, 1985) found that typical students did not construct multiple representations for chemical reactions.

Effects of expertise on memory and representation are also very specific. Chi & Koeske (1983) investigated the organization of knowledge about dinosaurs in a child who was highly knowledgeable about some species. The child's knowledge representation of familiar species, as compared to unfamiliar, was more coherent, with two clearly defined clusters, a greater number of within-cluster links, and fewer between-cluster links.

The highly specific nature of expertise has been replicated in several other domains often by comparing effects on memory of high versus low knowledge about the domain or topic (e.g. Spilich, Vesonder, Chiesi & Voss, 1979). For example, Kuhara-Kojima & Hatano (1991) found domain-specific effects: students with high knowledge in both music and baseball learned information about both equally well. However, students with high knowledge in only one area learned the information in that area better than the information in the low-knowledge domain. Finally, students with low knowledge in both areas did not learn much in either domain.

The coherence and elaborateness of memorial representations are important because they have powerful effects on how we process information. They enable fast and accurate retrieval of information, guide what we notice in new situations, differentiate new from known information, and provide information that helps us interpret new input as consistent or inconsistent with what we already "know." The detection and resolution of inconsistencies in knowledge is a metacognitive skill that can be a powerful cognitive force for conceptual change (e.g. Clement, 1991). Experts display strong self-monitoring skills that in conjunction with deep knowledge allow them to successfully evaluate and resolve relationships among different sources of information.

Flexibility and Transfer

Strategy, process, and representation differences between experts and novices in a domain have implications for the ability to use and interpret facts and procedures flexibly and to transfer to new situations. Flexibility and transfer involve being able to recognize how strategies, procedures or conceptual knowledge acquired previously might be used when dealing with a new situation. Flexibility implies adapting prior knowledge to a new situation, although the degree of adaptation varies with the specific type of transfer situation. The many studies of the processes and sources of difficulty involved in flexibility and transfer are too numerous to review here but there are several excellent sources (e.g. Detterman & Sternberg, 1993; Gentner, 1989; Schwartz, Lin, Brophy & Bransford, in press).

In the present context, we note that there are clear indications of greater flexibility on the part of domain experts and successful learners. For example, expert and good readers show greater flexibility than less successful readers (e.g. Dee-Lucas & Larkin, 1988; Goldman & Saul, 1990). In a problem solving task, Dörner & Schölkopf (1991) found that expertise in coping with a complex, dynamic system involved flexible and adaptive selection and application of strategies. Experienced executives of companies were more successful than university students on a simulation task that involved caring for the welfare of a fictitious tribe over a 25-year period. The locus of the differences between the groups was in knowing when to use particular strategies. Dörner & Schölkopf (1991) concluded that expert performance in dealing with the complex system involved examining configurations of conditions, adaptively selecting appropriate combinations of strategies for the conditions, and reflecting on the actions.

Adaptation to task constraints and greater flexibility in experimentation and scientific reasoning strategies also distinguishes among more and less successful learners of DC circuits (Schauble, Glaser, Raghavan & Reiner, 1991). In this learning situation, the better learners were sensitive to the fact that some strategies, e.g. control of variables, were useful for discovering certain laws (e.g. laws of resistance in parallel circuits) but were not useful for other laws. The poorer learners tended to rotely misapply strategies.

In the teaching domain, Borko & Livingston (1989) reported that expert mathematics teachers were more flexible than novice teachers in their instruction. They were more aware of when and how to interweave explanation and demonstration versus rapid coverage (as in direct instruction) of material. But the critical difference was in the greater ability of the expert teachers to improvise in the course of their instruction. Borko and Livingston attributed these differences to experts' knowledge of students' learning and their flexible adaptation of prior knowledge to the teaching situation. Teachers' modeling of flexibility in thinking is one characteristic of effective social studies classrooms (Newmann, 1990).

Domain specificity applies to flexibility and transfer as well as to representation and memory. In an interesting demonstration of this specificity, Voss, Greene, Post & Penner (1983) compared the solutions to a problem in political science of a political science expert and an expert chemist. The former produced a sophisticated solution; the latter a very simplistic one. Among history experts, Leinhardt & Young (1996) found that historians read documents in areas of high familiarity differently than they read documents in areas of low familiarity.

Finally, we note that there may be multiple kinds of expertise with different implications for transfer and flexibility. Hatano (1988; Hatano & Inagaki, 1986) made the distinction between two kinds of expertise: routine and adaptive. Routine experts are very good at solving routine problems but when faced with novel problems they demonstrate only modest skill. Adaptive experts can invent new procedures for novel circumstances because of their deeper conceptual understanding of the domain. These distinctions suggest that experts may display some of the previously mentioned characteristics of expertise but not others.

Implications

The domain-specificity of expertise implies that there are many circumstances where more superficial, non-expert-like understanding is adequate for our learning goals. Recognizing these situations is adaptive and reflects flexibility in adjusting to task demands. For example, when reading or listening to news reports, we usually do not have deep understanding goals. Rather, our goal is more likely to be one of having an awareness of the major local, national, and global events. This level is often sufficient for everyday conversational purposes and reflects relatively shallow processing of the information. Shallow processing may account for an interesting empirical phenomenon, the failure to update information (Tapiero & Otero, 1999; Van Oostendorp & Bonebakker, 1999). Johnson & Seifert (1999) reported that adult readers participating in an experiment failed to notice and update inaccurate reports of news that were later corrected in the media. Van Oostendorp & Bonebakker (1999; Tapiero & Otero, 1999) have recently proposed that readers do not process news information at a level sufficiently deep to notice the inconsistency between the two reports, let alone update it. Much of the time these inconsistencies have few if any consequences for our lives although they do reduce the chances of attitude or belief change.

A second way in which superficial knowledge is important is that it provides us with at least a surface level awareness of the language of particular disciplines. Familiarity with the vocabulary provides an entry point into the domain. Learning the language of the content area is a first step toward deeper understanding. In short, if we understand the appropriate contexts of use for superficial knowledge it can contribute in important ways to learning (CTGV, 1997).

Finally, the importance of deep disciplinary knowledge for effective thinking and problem solving has led to reconceptualizations of intelligence (Glaser, 1991). Deep knowledge in a domain is not the same thing as generalized "thinking skills" or general intelligence, as shown in domains as diverse as soccer (Schneider, Körkel & Weinert, 1989) and horseracing (Ceci & Liker, 1986).

These demonstrations of the power of domain-specific expertise stand in stark contrast to more classic views of intelligence. Expanded views of intelligence are especially important because people's beliefs about the nature of intelligence can affect their assessment of their own capabilities and their actual performance. For example, Dweck (1989) distinguishes between an incremental view of intelligence and an entity view. Children who hold incremental views emphasize skill development and mastery orientations whereas those who hold entity views are oriented toward demonstrating how smart they are and react to failure with "helplessness" responses. Although we know of no research that has specifically examined domain experts' views of intelligence, Bereiter & Scardamalia (1993) characterize experts as operating at the edge of their own understanding. They are motivated by new problems to solve, new tasks to master. Such an orientation seems more consistent with an incremental as compared to an entity view of intelligence.

Expertise in Context

We have characterized expertise from an individual, cognitive perspective. It is important to point out, however, that experts typically function in social contexts such as teams and communities of practice (Bereiter & Scardamalia, 1993; Lave, 1988; Lave & Wenger, 1991; Newman, Griffin & Cole, 1989). Studies of these social systems of activity using ethnographic, microethnographic, and discourse analytic techniques have increasingly informed cognitive perspectives. These types of analyses reveal that people participate with the intent of achieving objectives that are valued in relation to their identity and membership within a community of practice. Furthermore, they allow us to examine expertise as a process that can be carried out by an individual, a group of individuals, a machine, or a combination of individuals and machines (Bereiter & Scardamalia, 1993). Typical studies within this paradigm include the communication between members as they plan, execute and evaluate their activities as well as organize interactions with each other and resource material.

From this theoretical perspective, expertise develops as one becomes more effective in participating in activities that are essential to a community's practice (Lave & Wenger, 1991). This participation includes understanding the concepts that are vital in the community's discourse about its activities. Indeed, communities establish criteria that define expertise within the domain and roles within the community are often based on level of expertise. Many communities develop and adopt consensually agreed upon symbol systems and representational conventions. They invent tools (e.g. clocks, calendars, and sales tax tables) that eliminate the need to solve repetitive sets of problems (Lave, 1988). These conventions legitimize certain discourse patterns over others, define what counts as evidence and acceptable argumentation, and what is evaluated as "good work" (Bereiter, 1994; Chinn & Brewer, 1996).

Hence, expertise in a domain entails understanding the norms and values of the community and how to function successfully in that community. Becoming a member of the community means coming to adopt these conventions of successful practice in the community (e.g. Cobb, 1994; Driver, Asoko, Leach, Mortimer & Scott, 1994; Gee, 1992; Saxe, 1991). However, the conventions and criteria of successful practice sometimes require understanding concepts that incorporate adjustments to constraints and affordances that are not always explicit (Hall, 1996). An important function of schooling or other learning environments is to make those constraints and affordances explicit and manageable, and thereby foster the development of expertise and expert-like practice.

Specifying the characteristics of learning environments that will foster the development of expertise and expert-like performance is a much less well-developed endeavor than is the effort to understand characteristics of expertise (cf. Charness & Shultetus, 1999, this volume). We know that the development of expertise takes a lot of practice over a long period of time (Glaser & Chi, 1988), and that domain-specific expertise is learned (Ericsson & Smith, 1991). In the remainder of this chapter, we propose a set of design principles that seem promising for creating learning environments that foster the development of powerful domain knowledge. In discussing each principle, we briefly summarize expert-like performance relevant to the principle and provide additional research that supports each principle.

DESIGN PRINCIPLES FOR CREATING POWERFUL LEARNING ENVIRONMENTS IN CONTENT DOMAINS

Learning environments that support the acquisition of powerful domain knowledge depend on a variety of cognitive and social practices (Collins, Greeno & Resnick, 1994). Many "cognitive" approaches now recognize and incorporate a sociocultural perspective and attempt to understand learning and the development of expertise situated in particular social and cultural contexts (e.g. Greeno, 1998).

Collins et al. (1994) outline three observable functions that are essential to effective learning and that distinguish among learning environments: (a) participation in discourse (what learners do); (b) participation in activities (instruction that teachers model); and (c) presentation of examples of work (what is evaluated and assessed). Using these functions, Collins et al. (1994) contrast traditional schooling and schooling that is more likely to support the development of expertise (cf. Bereiter & Scardamalia, 1993). The former emphasize the discourse of information transmission, and training in which learners practice to improve specific skills and knowledge in order to recite or "present" them back to the teacher. In contrast, the latter emphasize communicative discourse among all the participants in the learning environment, problem solving contexts in which learners work on projects and problems, and performances for authentic purposes and audiences.

Environments that are more likely to support the development of expert-like performance represent a departure from classroom cultures dominated by textbook-driven instruction and accountability systems pegged solely to performance on standardized tests. Furthermore, alternative cultures do not emerge without explicit attention to their design (Collins, 1996; CTGV, 1997). The four design principles we describe in this section are concerned with establishing alternative cultures for effective learning. They deal with learning goals, and the resources and processes that support achieving the goals while learners become self-reflective about their learning and participate in communities of learners. Thus, the design principles reflect both cognitive and sociocultural perspectives on learning. The four design principles are:

1. Instruction is organized around meaningful learning and appropriate goals
2. Instruction provides scaffolds for achieving meaningful learning
3. Instruction provides opportunities for practice with feedback, revision, and reflection
4. Instruction is arranged to promote collaboration, distributed expertise, and entry into a discourse community of learners.

Although we discuss each principle separately, in operation the principles mutually support one another to achieve two objectives. One objective is the acquisition of content and skills. The other objective is to help students become aware of their learning activities so they may take on more responsibility and ownership of their learning. In this manner both individual and social aspects of acquiring expert-like knowledge are bridged. This "bridging" includes many aspects of what has been characterized as "metacognition," including knowing the goal of learning, self-assessing progress toward the stated goal, understanding revision as a natural component of achieving a learning goal, and recognizing the value of scaffolds, resources, and social structures that encourage and support revision (Barron et al., 1998; Vye et al., 1998).

Instruction is Organized Around Meaningful Learning and Appropriate Goals

Earlier we indicated that experts know a lot in their domain, and this information is organized so that they can bring the knowledge to bear in new situations, making appropriate adaptations. Adaptation of knowledge implies sensitivity to noticing features of situations that cue the applicability of previously learned information. Adaptation also implies domain understanding that goes deeper than a set of superficial facts to important domain concepts and principles, sometimes referred to as "deep principles" (A. Brown & Campione, 1994) or "big ideas" (AAAS, 1993). These concepts and principles support flexible use of knowledge and transfer (Bransford et al., in press). Flexible knowledge is a more likely outcome when learning is meaningful and related to appropriate goals, as we discuss below. The accumulation of a large body of information that is organized around deep principles takes in-depth study and a substantial amount of time (Bereiter & Scardamalia, 1993; Ericsson & Smith, 1991). This has important implications for issues of motivation, the second topic we discuss in this section.

Meaningful Learning

Research on learning suggests that when learning occurs in the context of meaningful situations and appropriate goals, it is more likely to lead to knowledge that is represented coherently and can be accessed flexibly under appropriate conditions. This contrasts with "inert" knowledge, defined by Whitehead (1929) as knowledge previously learned but unavailable in contexts where it would be potentially useful. Simon (1980) pointed out that usefulness relies on recognizing the conditions that make knowledge relevant, i.e. the contexts in which particular facts are useful or actions appropriate (cf. Anderson, 1987). Indeed, analyses of learning in everyday settings show sophisticated reasoning and problem solving that are not typically evident in more formal settings or traditional assessment venues. When children or adults are engaged in authentic or meaningful everyday tasks such as selling candy on the streets of Brazil or measuring correct portions of ingredients for a recipe, they display much more adaptable learning than is visible in formal educational settings (Carraher, Carraher & Schliemann, 1985; Lave, 1988; Lave & Wenger, 1991; Resnick, 1987; Rogoff, 1990; Rogoff & Lave, 1984; Saxe, 1988; Schliemann & Acioly, 1989).

The meaningfulness of problem solving and learning in everyday settings contrasts sharply with learning in school settings. Across a number of content areas, researchers have analyzed school materials and concluded that there is little support for meaningful learning. For example, science textbooks are a compendium of facts and have too much in them (Chambliss & Calfee, 1989). Learning occurs in fragmented, unrelated activities that are divorced from meaningful contexts (Koballa, 1988; Ross, 1988; Schauble et al., 1995). The result is that students often see the content area as a bunch of unrelated facts and content areas are distinguished only by the titles on the textbooks (Bloome, Goldman, Bransford, Hasselbring & CTGV, 1997). The contrast between informal and formal environments is particularly important in light of observations that students who perform poorly in school often seem to learn well in informal learning environments (e.g. Holt, 1964).

One way in which learning can be made more meaningful is through authentic problems. Problem-based instruction in medicine, law, and other professions is being used increasingly to situate content learning in the solution of problems authentic to the profession (e.g. Barrows, 1985; Bridges & Hallinger, 1995; Williams, 1992). These kinds of curricula help students develop conditionalized knowledge, i.e. knowledge that is connected to its circumstances of use (Anderson, 1987; Simon, 1980), rather than disembodied facts. Conditionalized knowledge is more likely to be available in circumstances encountered "on the job." Furthermore, learning in the context of solving problems makes knowledge less inert (e.g. Adams et al., 1988; Bransford et al., 1989; Sherwood, Kinzer, Bransford & Franks, 1987).

In an effort to focus learning around authentic and meaningful goals, project- and problem-based curriculum units are being introduced into grade K-12 settings (Blumenfeld et al., 1991; CTGV, 1997, 1998; Krajcik, 1991; Secules, Cottom, Bray, Miller & CTGV, 1997; Sherwood, Petrosino, Lin, Lamon & CTGV, 1995). Initial results of these kinds of activities indicate high levels of involvement on the part of students (Carver, Lehrer, Connell & Erickson, 1992) and increased learning of important content (Barron et al., 1998).

A second way in which learning can be made more meaningful is through learning strategies that foster interconnected and coherent knowledge. There are a variety of techniques that promote learning by stimulating connections to prior knowledge, some designed into materials (e.g. advance organizers, pictures, titles, and headings) and others that learners engage in when they interact with the material (e.g. elaborating, summarizing, and explaining). Pressley & McCormick (1995) provide a very informative review of these techniques.

The type of connection to prior knowledge is also a critical determiner of the success of the technique or strategy. Across a variety of types of material, research indicates that learners who construct causal relations among events learn the information better than those who do not (e.g. Beck & Dole, 1992; Coté, Goldman & Saul, 1998). For example, Martin & Pressley (1991) found that "Why" questions that activated prior knowledge relevant to causal explanations helped learning but those that more indirectly focused attention on prior knowledge showed little evidence of improving learning. Another strategy that leads to improved learning in problem solving and text comprehension situations is self-generated explanations. Chi, Bassok, Lewis, Reimann & Glaser (1989) showed that learners who generated self-explanations while studying worked-out examples of physics problems learned better than learners who did not use this technique frequently. Pirolli & Bielaczyc (1989) found a similar effect on learning the LISP programming language. Finally, a number of learning-from-text studies show that greater degrees of self-explanation during reading positively predict learning in a variety of content areas (Chan, Burtis, Scardamalia & Bereiter, 1992; Chi, de Leeuw, Chiu & La Vancher, 1994; Coté & Goldman, 1999; Coté et al., 1998; Trabasso, Suh, Payton & Jain, 1995). In short, strategies that lead to active processing of new information in relation to prior knowledge help establish the kind of richly interconnected knowledge bases characteristic of experts.

Motivation and Interest

One characteristic of authentic problems is that they often require extended periods of time to solve, leading some critics of inquiry learning to question whether students are capable of this kind of engagement. Extended engagement with a problem is consistent with the fact noted earlier that experts spend a great deal of time acquiring the information and deep understanding of their domains. If we expect students to devote lengthy periods of time to learning tasks, students need to be motivated and interested in the task. Recent conceptualizations of motivation suggest that instruction organized around meaningful learning and appropriate goals will create and maintain student motivation and interest. For example, McCombs (1991, 1996) provides an analysis of motivation for lifelong learning that includes an emphasis on meaningful learning, appropriate goals, and authentic tasks that students perceive as real work for real audiences. This emphasis contrasts with earlier emphases on elaborate reinforcements for motivation (Collins, 1996).

Learners are also willing to work hard and for long periods of time on tasks that they find interesting or challenging (CTGV, 1997; Goldman, Mayfield-Stewart, Bateman, Pellegrino & CTGV, in press). Other research on the relationship between interest and learning indicates that personal interest in a topic or domain positively impacts academic learning in that domain (Alexander, Kulikowich & Jetton, 1994). For example, in a study of learning from expository text, Schiefele & Krapp (1996) found that topic interest was positively related to depth of learning, including recall of main ideas and coherence of recall. These effects of the interest variable were independent of prior knowledge and intelligence. In addition, students judge texts interesting to the degree that they perceive the information to be relevant to their interests (Wade, Buxton & Kelly, 1993). Finally, a number of studies indicate that adolescent learners are very interested in tasks that are perceived by them as authentic and useful, even though these tasks are challenging and require a great deal of effort (e.g. Blumenfeld et al., 1991; Bransford et al., in press; A. Brown & Campione, 1994; Carver et al., 1992; CTGV, 1994b, 1997; Goldman et al., 1996; Hickey, 1996; Lamon, et. al., 1996).

To "hook" or stimulate learners' interests in the topic of study several contemporary educational reform efforts use dilemmas, puzzles, and paradoxes (A. Brown & Campione, 1994, 1996; CTGV, 1997; Lamon et al., 1996; Scardamalia, Bereiter & Lamon, 1994). For example, A. Brown and colleagues began a science unit on animal/habitat interdependence by reading second-grade students a story called *The Tree of Life* (Bash, 1989), an engaging children's book. Children began their research by picking an animal or plant that interested them and writing about how it was dependent on the tree (A. Brown & Campione, 1996). Science projects for older students also begin by posing dilemmas such as "How far does light go?" (Linn, Bell & Hsi, in press), "How could we identify and clean up a chemical spill?" (Goldman et al., 1996; Sherwood et al., 1995), and "How do we account for the behavior of moving objects?" (White & Frederiksen, 1998). Similar approaches are also being taken in other content areas (cf. Goldman, Williams, Sherwood & Hasselbring, 1998).

Interest in providing opportunities for learners to work on meaningful learning activities and appropriate goals has led to a rapid increase in project-based and inquiry learning activities as a means of students acquiring and using domain-specific knowledge. Experiences with these kinds of projects are making researchers and educators aware of the need to provide scaffolds, feedback and opportunities for reflection, and classroom participation structures that allow learners access to the content as they develop expertise in the domain. The remaining three design principles deal with each of these issues.

Instruction Provides Scaffolds for Achieving Meaningful Learning

Meaningful problems are often more complex than typical school tasks. Learners need support for dealing with this complexity. A traditional approach to dealing with complexity is to break down a complex task into components that are "simpler" (e.g. Gagné, 1968). The task is learned by mastering each of the simpler components. One problem with this technique is that too frequently the components become the ends in themselves. Learners never see the big picture or understand the meaningfulness of the complex task. At the other extreme, J. Brown et al. (1989) proposed that a useful analogy could be drawn between learning in complex situations and the apprenticeship system common in many trades. In an apprenticeship, learning is situated in the authentic practices of the discipline, trade, or art. Initially, learners are legitimate peripheral participants in the community, but with exposure to, and learning of, the culture they may become full participants (Lave & Wenger, 1991). According to this situated cognition perspective, moving from novice to expert in a content area involves a cognitive apprenticeship in the culture and practice of the discipline (Cobb, 1994; Collins et al., 1989; Driver et al., 1994; Rogoff, 1990). Rogoff (1990) indicates that this process involves *guided* participation by the master of the apprentice with a gradual transfer of responsibility.

Cognitive Scaffolds

We use the general notion of scaffolds to encompass the various possible forms of guidance and support. Cognitive scaffolds are analogous to actual physical scaffolds used in constructing buildings. A scaffold around a building under construction provides a temporary framework within which building can occur. The supports are temporary and are removed as the building is completed. Likewise, cognitive scaffolding provides a support structure for thinking. The concept of cognitive scaffolding is most closely related to the Vygotskyan theoretical construct "zone of proximal development (ZPD)" (Vygotsky, 1978). The ZPD is the distance between children's actual and potential levels of development. Interactions with adults and more capable peers are one form of scaffolding that enables children to perform at their potential levels (Bakhtin, 1981; Vygotsky, 1962; Wood, Bruner & Ross, 1976). The purpose of the interactions is to help children develop strategies that replace the support structure, allowing children to think on their own and generalize their knowledge. During the interactions, adults model good thinking and hint and prompt children who cannot "get it" on their own. They stimulate interest, maintain motivation, and control frustration and risk associated with the activity. Children eventually adopt the patterns of thinking reflected by the adults by internalizing the processes that were scaffolded.

Cobb (1994) noted that this view of scaffolding brings with it the problem of accounting for how things external to the child become internalized. He pointed out that Rogoff's (1990) position on internalization provided a solution to the problem. For Rogoff (1990), whenever children are actively observing or participating in social interaction practices they are developing internalized, joint understandings of the situation. These joint understandings are "appropriations of the shared understanding by each individual that reflects the individual's understanding of and involvement in the activity" (1990, p. 156). In other words, there is always internalization but the relationship between (alignment of) the learner's internalized representation and that of other participants in the interaction may vary.

In general, then, scaffolds are needed to help learners become more expert. They function to bridge between experts' ways of organizing and using knowledge, including their problem representations and visualizations, and those of novices. As we discussed above, interactions with more knowledgeable others are one way of realizing cognitive scaffolding. Other forms of scaffolding include modeling; visualization and representation tools; and guides and reminders about the concepts, procedures and steps that are important for the task (Collins et al., 1989).

Interactions with More Knowledgeable Others

Coaching and tutoring are common ways in which learners interact with more knowledgeable others.There is a large literature on tutoring, especially regarding computer-assisted tutoring (e.g. Anderson, Corbett, Koedinger & Pelletier, 1995; Graesser & Person, 1994; Graesser, Person & Magliano, 1995; Lepper, Wolverton, Mumme & Gurtner, 1993; McArthur, Stasz & Zmuidzinas, 1990). In the present context we can only summarize some of the important issues that have arisen regarding coaching and tutoring.

Studies of human coaching and tutoring indicate that effective tutoring techniques are very subtle and provide as much social validation for the learner as cognitive input (Graesser & Person, 1994; Lepper, Aspinwall, Mumme & Chabay, 1990; McArthur et al. 1990). For example, Graesser and colleagues (Graesser & Person, 1994; Graesser et al., 1995) analyzed tutorial dialogues in a college research methods course and in seventh-grade mathematics. They found that 70% of tutors' questions were driven by a curriculum script, which consisted of a partially ordered, preselected set of topics, example problems and questions. Tutors also followed politeness norms that minimized face-threatening acts such as negative feedback and criticism.

In the context of computer-based tutoring, a major issue concerns when to intervene and how much information to provide in responding to the learner. Highly directive approaches seem to work best for students who are learning simple procedures and formal notations (Anderson, Boyle & Reiser, 1985; Reiser, Copen, Ranney, Hamid & Kimberg, 1994). For achieving conceptual understanding, it seems to be important for students to be able to explore and develop their own alternative mental models (Jungck, 1991; White, 1993). Clearly, tutorial interactions also provide feedback to students, a point we take up in discussing the third design principle.

Modeling/Prompting

Modeling is realized in many forms. Teachers commonly use demonstrations as a way to help students understand various concepts and procedures in content domains. Increasingly, educators are calling for teachers to model the processes of thinking in the domain as well as the procedures (e.g. Putnam & Borko, 1997; Schoenfeld, 1985; Wineburg, 1994).

Other types of modeling include worked examples (e.g. Chi et al., 1989; Sweller & Cooper, 1985) and videotaped models of people's solutions (Bielaczyc, Pirolli & Brown, 1995). Both have been shown to be effective scaffolds for college-aged students. The mathematical problem solving series, *The Adventures of Jasper Woodbury*, also uses video-based models. For difficult-to-master content, teaching scenes are embedded into the video as a natural part of the story (CTGV, 1997). For example, in one scene in *The Big Splash*, a business planning adventure that uses statistics, Jasper demonstrates the calculation of a cumulative distribution and illustrates principles of sampling and extrapolation to the population. In other work on mathematics problem solving, student actors have been videotaped presenting their solution plans (Barron et al., 1995). The students in the classroom play the role of "friendly critic" and provide helpful feedback on how to improve the plans. Students find these sessions highly motivating and teachers report that they provide excellent opportunities for content-based discussions (Barron et al., 1995; CTGV, 1997).

A number of projects are looking at scaffolds for argumentation processes and building computer tools that prompt learners to construct appropriate arguments (Linn et al., in press; Suthers, Weiner, Connelly & Paolucci, 1995). Argumentation is a central discourse genre in inquiry-based projects. Learners need to understand what counts as a sound argument in the various domains they study; they need to understand what goes across domains as compared to what is specific to a domain. In other words, how is argumentation in science similar and different from argumentation in history? For example, what counts as evidence? Research indicates that argumentation skills are not well-developed generally (e.g. Kuhn, 1989). A major issue for work on argumentation is the degree to which prompts for argument structures need to be content-specific versus domain-general.

Increasingly Complex Microworlds

White and Frederiksen (White, 1993; White & Frederiksen, 1998) have developed a different approach to scaffolding in complex domains, namely increasingly complex microworlds. They use this approach as a way to scaffold the inquiry process in the domain of the physics of force and motion. In one implementation (White & Frederiksen, 1998), students in seventh-, eighth-, and ninth-grade classrooms progressed through a series of seven modules. The modules were instantiated in a computer microworld called ThinkerTools. In the early modules, the inquiry process was highly scaffolded, decreasing across successive modules. For example, in module 1, students were given the experiments to do and the alternative possible laws to evaluate. By module 3, they designed their own experiments and constructed their own laws. In addition, the complexity of the microworld increased from module 1 to module 7, beginning with a simplifying case (a world with no friction), and adding factors with each module. These scaffolds, plus elements of the model consistent with the three other design principles discussed in this chapter, led to physics learning that was equivalent to that of juniors and seniors in high school (White & Frederiksen, 1998). This conclusion was based on performance on qualitative problems that required application of basic principles of Newtonian mechanics in real-world contexts (e.g. "If you kick a ball off a cliff, what path does it take as it falls to ground? Explain your answer").

Working with children at a much younger age level, we are taking an approach that is similar to White & Frederiksen's (1998). We are embedding science process skills in decreasingly constrained design spaces. We introduce research skills by building on five- and six-year-olds' familiarity with a highly engaging video-based story, *The Magic Hats*. Students develop familiarity with the story through language arts activities that build comprehension and writing skills (CTGV, 1998). The research skills of observation and data collection are introduced through the "Create a Creature" task. This task challenges children to draw and name new creatures to live on the Little Planet where *The Magic Hats* story takes place. To do so, they must follow the design constraints that teachers give in the form of clues. The clues allow the teacher to adjust the difficulty of the task in a manner analogous to White & Frederiksen's (1998) module progression. For example, simple clues may not require research but only knowledge of shape words, e.g. "The head is a rectangle." More complex clues may require children to search through the video story, collect relevant data, and perform computations on the information they find. For example, children might read the clue, "It has two more toes than Ribbit." To use the clue, students must find pictures of Ribbit in the video story that show all his toes (observation), count the toes (data collection), and then construct and solve the implied mathematical representation.

Problem-based to Project-based Inquiry

Another approach to scaffolding children's efforts to deal with the complexity and open-endedness of authentic projects is to begin with a problem and then proceed to projects (Barron et al., 1998). Problem-based learning provides a big picture without entailing the ill-defined complexity often associated with open-ended projects. Our version of problem-based learning (see Williams, 1992; for extended discussions of this topic, see CTGV, 1992) involves the use of authentic but designed problems that students and teachers can explore collaboratively. The problems are designed to tap important content in the domain. Solving the problem exposes the learner to content knowledge that will be needed to work on the project that follows. Our project-based learning experiences are typically centered in everyday settings with tangible outcomes. Examples of problem-to-project progressions that we have investigated are working with a simulated river problem to prepare for active monitoring of a real river; designing a playground to prepare for designing a playhouse; planning for an imaginary fair to prepare for planning and carrying out an actual fun fair (Barron et al., in press; CTGV, 1997; Schwartz, Goldman, Vye, Barron & CTGV, 1998).

Visualizations and Representations

Other forms of scaffolds provide students with visualizations and representations of concepts and their relationships. These techniques provide a framework that learners can use to organize their knowledge. They have been found to improve learning in a variety of domains (for reviews, see Lewandowsky & Behrens, 1999, this volume, and Pressley & McCormick, 1995). As well, dynamic visualizations help learners understand a variety of relationships in the physical world (e.g. Mayer, 1999, this volume; Mayer, 1997; Mayer & Sims, 1994). A number of researchers are developing computer-based systems that make it relatively easy for students to see the same concept represented in multiple ways (e.g. Crews, Biswas, Goldman & Bransford, 1997; Goldman, Zech, Biswas & Noser, in press; Kozma, in press). Explanations of the benefits of alternative representation are that they (a) highlight different dimensions of the same situation, (b) make obvious the critical functional relations, or (c) create multiple encodings and increased depth of processing.

Representations and visualizations seem particularly important in science and mathematics where relationships among sets of variables are key to understanding important domain concepts (Bransford et al., in press). For example, the Geometric Supposer (Schwartz, Yerushalmy & Wilson, 1993) allows students to create and manipulate geometric objects and relationships. In science, there are a number of web-based visualization tools to support investigations of weather (e.g. Gordin & Pea, 1995; NOAA/Forecast Systems Laboratory, 1998), and ecosystems, nutrition, and photosynthesis (Jackson, Stratford, Krajcik & Soloway, 1996). Important issues to explore with respect to these types of scaffolds concern (a) the importance to learning of having learners generate such representations as opposed to having them generated for them (Schwartz & Bransford, in press); and (b) understanding the processes by which learners acquire the ability to notice in these representations the features that make the representations useful to domain experts (Lowe, in press).

Instruction Provides Opportunities for Feedback, Revision, and Reflection

As we noted earlier, experts exhibit strong self-monitoring skills that enable them to regulate their learning goals and activities. Feedback, revision, and reflection are aspects of metacognition and are critical to developing the ability to regulate one's own learning. Self-monitoring requires sufficient knowledge to evaluate thinking, to provide feedback to oneself, and to access knowledge of how to make necessary revisions. In other words, learners cannot effectively monitor what they know and make effective use of feedback for revision unless they have deep understanding in the domain. The idea that monitoring is highly knowledge dependent creates a "catch-22" for novices. How can they regulate their own learning without the necessary knowledge to do so? Scaffolds for monitoring and self-regulation skills are needed so that deep understanding and reflective learning can develop hand-in-hand.

We are not the first to highlight the importance of reflection, feedback, and revision activities. Dewey (1933) noted the importance of reflecting on one's ideas, weighing ideas against data, and predictions against obtained outcomes. Some twenty years ago, A. Brown (1978) and Flavell (1976) defined metacognition as "the active monitoring and consequent regulation and orchestration of [cognitive] processes" (Flavell, 1976, p. 232). Self-regulated learners take feedback from their performance and adjust their learning in response to it. There is also evidence that higher levels of self-regulation are associated with a greater willingness to participate in situations where feedback, reflection, and revision are part of the process. In a study of first-year veterinary students, Ertmer, Newby & MacDougal (1996) found that students high in self-regulation tended to value problem-based instruction and used reflective strategies that enabled strategic approaches to difficult cases. Students low on self-regulation were more lukewarm toward the problem-based approach and were more concerned about learning facts and being right than in approaching problem solving strategically.

Other research indicates that self-regulated learners have high perceived self-efficacy and believe they are capable of doing well on academic tasks (Bandura, 1977; Schunk, 1990, 1991; Zimmerman, 1990). However, self-efficacy is highly domain specific and "false" praise is easily detected (Marsh & Craven, 1991; Stipek & MacIver, 1989). Schunk (1991) reported that evidence from one's own efforts is the most effective form of feedback for developing self-efficacy. Thus, the social norms in the learning environment need to help students understand that opportunities to identify ideas that seem unclear and to discover errors in one's own thinking, are signs of success rather than failure and are keys to effective learning (Dweck, 1989).

Monitoring and reflection on one's thinking have featured prominently in considerations of learning in a variety of content areas. In the context of teaching, Schön (1983) emphasized the importance of reflection in creating new mental models. In history, experts routinely reflect on their historical reasoning processes (Leinhardt & Young, 1996) and effective social studies classrooms allow time for students to reflect, think, and explain their thinking by providing reasons for their conclusions (Newmann, 1990). Scientists subject their hypotheses to rigorous critical examination; feedback, revision, and reflection are cultural norms in the scientific community (Chinn & Brewer, 1996). With respect to science learning, Smith, Maclin, Grosslight & Davis (1997) reported that modifications to a curriculum that made it possible for eighth-grade students to get feedback that enabled them to reflect on and revise their initial ideas about density led to marked improvements in qualitative reasoning. This improvement was relative to a comparable group using the unmodified curriculum.

Indeed, a frequent criticism of "hands-on" science is that it is not "minds-on." That is, hands-on science activities often lack opportunities for reflection. Rather, activities are often short, unrelated to one another and inordinately focused on the manipulation of objects and events rather than on principled understanding of a phenomenon (Schauble et al., 1995). Bettencourt (1993) argued that "unless hands-on science is embedded in a structure of questioning, reflecting, and re-questioning probably very little will be learned." Petrosino (1998) argued similarly that frequent cycles of doing experiments followed by reflection and revision were necessary if learners were to achieve the goals of experimentation (see also Edelson, Pea & Gomez, 1996).

Consistent with these arguments for multiple opportunities to revisit concepts, a number of interventions in science learning provide evidence for the value added by cycles of doing research (e.g. conducting experiments or gathering information), reflecting on feedback or data, and revising the approach based on new questions, hypotheses, or revised learning goals (Barron et al., 1998; A. Brown & Campione, 1996; Duschl & Gitomer, 1997; Kuhn, Schauble & Garcia-Mila, 1992; Minstrell & Stimpson, 1996; Petrosino, 1998; Roth & Bowen, 1995; Schauble et al. 1995; Vye et al., 1998; White & Frederiksen, 1998). For example, in a recently completed study Petrosino (1998) found significant improvement in 10-year-old students' understanding of the variables determining the height a model rocket would achieve only after multiple cycles of design, data collection, reflection, and revision of the designs. He also observed increased understanding of the purpose of hands-on activities, the importance of design, and of how to design an experiment. Similarly, Kuhn et al. (1992) found that over repeated experiences with the same task involving toy boats and toy cars there was significant improvement in the adequacy of the evidence children provided in defense of their conclusions.

White & Frederiksen's (1998) work on the ThinkerTools project, discussed earlier with respect to scaffolds, also included an assessment of the impact of multiple opportunities for reflective self-assessment and repetitions of the inquiry cycle. One group of students was given a set of criteria for judging scientific research, including reasoning carefully, being systematic, and so forth. At the end of each module, they reflected on their work by evaluating it on all the criteria. These students increased both the quality of their research projects and their performance on an inquiry post-test over a comparison group of students who participated in all the activities except for those involving reflection and self-assessment.

The effects apply in the mathematics domain as well. The SMART (Science and Mathematical Arenas for Refining Thinking) instructional model, developed for mathematics as well as science, includes explicit cycles of solving, feedback, reflection on that feedback, and opportunities for revision (with needed informational resources available) (CTGV, 1997). Students who participated in the SMART model showed improved mastery of the mathematical concepts involved in constructing business plans (e.g. sampling and extrapolation from a sample to a population, expenses, revenue, and net profit) and provided justifications for correct answers that were substantially better than students who had not had feedback and revision opportunities (CTGV, 1997).

Finally, simulation environments not only provide representations and visualizations for learners but they also provide opportunities for feedback and revision. Crews et al. (in press) compared the effects of two versions of a computer-based simulation environment (*Jasper AdventurePlayer*) on students' problem solving and learning in a trip planning situation. In one version (full system), the simulation provided feedback and coaching; the other version used the system without these functionalities (core system). Students who worked with the full system made fewer errors and developed more complete and optimal trip planning solutions than those who worked with the core system. In a related study, Goldman et al. (in press) found that students' interpretations of the feedback from simulations and their use of this feedback to guide subsequent question generation were indicative of their level of understanding of the relationships among distance, rate, and time.

We mentioned earlier that the development of expertise takes a great deal of practice over a long period of time. Cycles of feedback, reflection, and opportunities for revision provide students with opportunities to practice using the skills and concepts they are trying to master. Cognitive theories of skill acquisition place importance on practice because it leads to fluency and a reduction in the amount of processing resources needed to execute the skill (e.g. Anderson, 1987; Schneider & Shiffrin, 1977). Practice with feedback produces better learning than practice alone (Lhyle & Kulhavy, 1987). Indeed, in a complex learning situation such as learning LISP programming, no feedback on performance produced significantly worse learning than providing feedback immediately or on demand (Anderson et al., 1995). In more complex learning situations, information must often be provided to learners in order for them to know what steps to take to improve their performance. Two unresolved issues with respect to feedback, whether delivered by a human tutor as discussed above or by a computer-based tutor, are (a) how much information to include in a feedback message, and (b) whether to state the information immediately or successively prompt learners to generate the information on their own.

Instruction is Arranged to Promote Collaboration, Distributed Expertise, and Entry into a Discourse Community of Learners

The view of cognition as socially shared rather than individually owned is an important shift in the orientation of cognitive theories of learning. It reflects the idea that thinking is a product of several heads in interaction with one another (Bereiter, 1990; Hutchins, 1991). Earlier we discussed the domain-specificity of expertise. In the work environment this specificity leads to the need for teams of experts to work together to solve important problems (Bereiter & Scardamalia, 1993). Likewise, in classroom learning environments, meaningful and authentic contexts for learning are often quite complex. Learners have to work together to accomplish goals that would be too difficult if they worked by themselves. In other words, collaboration can make complexity more manageable (A. Brown & Campione, 1996; Bereiter & Scardamalia, 1993; CTGV, 1997; Pea 1993, 1994; Salomon, 1993).

Working together cooperatively results in better learning than competitive or individualistic learning (Johnson, Maruyama, Johnson, Nelson & Skon, 1981) and facilitates problem solving and reasoning (CTGV, 1994a; Kuhn, Shaw &

Felton, 1997; Yackel, Cobb & Wood, 1991). For example, Vye et al. (1997) found that middle school students who worked in dyads to solve a complex mathematical problem explored multiple solutions and tested solutions against constraints. In contrast, when middle school students worked this problem alone, they did not exhibit these problem solving behaviors. Furthermore, among the dyads in the Vye et al. (1997) study, the dyads who produced more accurate and complete solutions explored more dimensions of the problem and exhibited more accurate mathematical formulations than did dyads who had less complete and accurate problem solutions. The more successful dyads were more likely to build on each other's problem solving behaviors than were the less successful.

Collaborative environments also make excellent venues for making thinking visible, generating and receiving feedback, and revising (Barron et al., 1995; CTGV, 1994a; Hatano & Inagaki, 1991; Vye et al., 1997; Vye et al., 1998). As noted in our discussion of monitoring and reflection, an important property of most academic disciplines is that members of the community provide feedback to one another. Productive collaborative work depends on participants serving this role for one another. For example, when college students as well as middle school students engaged in a series of discussions on capital punishment, the quality of reasoning increased relative to either a single dyadic interaction or repeated elicitation of a participant's own opinions (Kuhn et al., 1997). What seemed to be responsible for the increase was a greater awareness of multiple viewpoints, leading to reasoning that reflected more two-sided arguments. There were limitations to the improvement: few participants offered evidence that was differentiated from the argument claim itself (Kuhn et al., 1997).

However, not all collaborations work effectively (Eichinger, Anderson, Palincsar & David, 1991; Goldman, Cosden & Hine, 1992; Linn & Burbules, 1993; Salomon & Globerson, 1989). For example, Eichinger et al. (1991) found that discussions among students were often not at a precise enough level to achieve conceptual understanding. As well, those who participated intellectually learned more than those who stayed at the fringes of the group work. Others have also found that the type of interaction impacts learning outcomes: learners who "just listen" and do not actively engage in discussions by elaborating and explaining ideas learn less from these interactions than students who actively participate in them (Hatano & Inagaki, 1991; Webb, 1989). One of the most important issues regarding collaborative groups is participation by all members of the group and how to deal with learners who do not want to participate.

In instructional settings, there are several conditions that make it more likely that cooperative as opposed to competitive interactions will result. As outlined by Johnson & Johnson (1985):

1. learning should be interdependent, with tasks needing more than one student to complete them
2. face-to-face interactions among students in small groups make participation more likely
3. interpersonal and small group skills need to be taught
4. students must be individually accountable for work but there must also be incentives for the group as a whole.

Collaborations having these four characteristics are a cornerstone of the Fostering Communities of Learners (FCL) model developed by A. Brown and colleagues (A. Brown et al., 1993; A. Brown & Campione, 1994, 1996). The distributed expertise model is a central concept for organizing instructional activities in these learning communities (A. Brown et al., 1993; Pea, 1993, 1994; Salomon, 1993). Originally developed for science investigations that would build literacy skills, FCL has been extended to all areas of the curriculum in the Schools for Thought program (Lamon et al., 1996; Secules et al., 1997). Students work as part of a research team and each team is responsible for learning about different parts of a complex problem. Each member of the team needs to learn the information deeply so they can be the experts who teach others in the community about that aspect of the problem. The research teams are interdependent and in order for the whole group to solve the problem, learners must pool their deep knowledge and cooperate to integrate the information and develop a problem solution. This is done in a structured fashion using the jigsaw procedure (Aaronson, 1978) wherein one member of each research team regroups with members from each of the other research teams. As each "expert" presents in the jigsaw group, other members of the group provide feedback that helps set new learning goals for the "expert." Often the feedback helps the "expert" realize where concepts need to be more clearly understood, more explanation needs to be provided, or other modifications made that deepen and enhance knowledge. The distributed expertise model of research thus establishes conditions for learners to function like experts: they learn something deeply but do it in the context of a complex task. Thus, complexity is reduced but meaningful learning and deep understanding are not sacrificed.

Important to the successful functioning of the distributed expertise model are community norms that recognize the interdependence among members of the learning community and value the participation of all. Students learn to listen to one another because they have a need to know: the outcome task requires the exchange of information among all groups. For example, a second-grade class might be studying habitats and adaptation. Small groups might look at different animal needs (e.g. food, shelter, protection, reproduction). For a habitat to be suitable for an animal it must satisfy all of these vital needs. To complete the outcome task, which might be designing an animal and suitable habitat for it, children must have mastered the information researched by all of the groups, not just their own. Learning environments organized around a distributed expertise model facilitate the development of social norms that help students feel valued and respected, and that encourage diversity.

SUMMARY AND CONCLUSIONS

Research on the characteristics of expertise and those of effective learning environments suggest four principles important to content area instruction that produces in-depth understanding of important and meaningful content, as opposed to memorization of lists of facts. This type of understanding is necessary for flexible and adaptive learning that supports transfer. Meaningful content often requires that learners deal with complex situations. The instructional environment needs to provide support for learning despite the complexity. The provision of scaffolds as well as opportunities for feedback, reflection, and revision and the opportunity to work collaboratively as a community of learners are important sources of support for dealing with complex learning situations. Finally, school environments that are organized so that learners work as a community enable them to develop the kinds of cognitive and social skills that are necessary to participate in discipline-based communities.

We hope it is evident that expert characteristics do not bear a one-to-one relationship to the design principles of learning environments. Different principles support the development of multiple characteristics of expertise and multiple characteristics of expertise provide the rationale for individual principles.

Given this, we emphasize the importance of seeing the design principles as a *system* rather than a checklist of independent features. A. Brown & Campione (1996) point out the dangers of the "check-off" model of instructional design. In this model, educators go through a list of activities such as group work, projects, and so forth, indicating "We do that. We do that, etc." However, unintegrated implementation of a grab bag of instructional features will not necessarily produce instruction consistent with the four principles that we have discussed, nor support the development of expert-like learning and understanding. The four design principles must be integrated into a system and operate in concert. Finally, there are a number of ways to realize these underlying principles in instruction. Powerful instruction that leads to learning with understanding will not look the same in every content area and in every learning situation.

ACKNOWLEDGMENT

The Cognition and Technology Group at Vanderbilt (CTGV) comprises researchers from a variety of disciplines, including cognitive science, developmental psychology, computer science, curriculum and instruction, and video and graphic design. We are fortunate to be members of the group. Many of the ideas about learning presented herein reflect the collaborative research and development activities of this group, in conjunction with teachers and students. These activities have been funded by a number of organizations, including the James S. McDonnell Foundation, the Department of Education Office of Research and Improvement and Office of Special Education, the Mellon Foundation, and the Russell Sage Foundation. However, no official endorsement by these organizations of the ideas presented in this chapter should be inferred.

REFERENCES

AAAS (American Association for Advancement of Science) (1993). *Benchmarks for Science Literacy*. NY: Oxford University Press.

Aaronson, E. (1978). *The Jigsaw Classroom*. Beverly Hills, CA: Sage.

Adams, L., Kasserman, J., Yearwood, A., Perfetto, G., Bransford, J. & Franks, J. (1988). The effects of facts versus problem-oriented acquisition. *Memory & Cognition*, 16, 167–75.

Alexander, P. A., Kulikowich, J. M. & Jetton, T. L. (1994). The role of subject-matter knowledge and interest in the processing of linear and nonlinear texts. *Review of Educational Research*, 64 (2), 201–52.

Anderson, J. R. (1987). Skill acquisition: compilation of weak-method problem solutions. *Psychological Review*, 94, 192–210.

Anderson, J. R., Boyle, C. F. & Reiser, B. J. (1985). Intelligent tutoring systems. *Science*, 228, 456–62.

Anderson, J. R., Corbett, A. T., Koedinger, K. R. & Pelletier, R. (1995). Cognitive tutors: lessons learned. *Journal of the Learning Sciences*, 4, 167–207.

Anzai, Y. (1991). Learning and use of representations for physics expertise. In K. A. Ericsson & J. Smith (Eds), *Toward a General Theory of Expertise: Prospects and Limits* (pp. 64–92). NY: Cambridge University Press.

Bakhtin, M. M. (1981). *The Dialogic Imagination: Four Essays by M. M. Bakhtin*. M. Holquist (Ed.). Translated by C. Emerson & M. Holquist. Austin, TX: University of Texas Press.

Bandura, A. (1977). Self-efficacy: toward a unifying theory of behavioral change. *Psychological Review*, 84, 191–215.

Barron, B., Schwartz, D., Vye, N., Bransford, J., Moore, A., Petrosino, T. & the Cognition and Technology Group at Vanderbilt (1998). Doing with understanding: lessons from research on problem and project based learning. *Journal of Learning Sciences*, 1, 271–311.

Barron, B., Vye, N. J., Zech, L., Schwartz, D., Bransford, J. D., Goldman, S. R., Pellegrino, J., Morris, J., Garrison, S. & Kantor, R. (1995). Creating contexts for community-based problem solving: the Jasper Challenge Series. In C. N. Hedley, P. Antonacci & M. Rabinowitz (Eds), *Thinking and Literacy: The Mind at Work* (pp. 47–71). Hillsdale, NJ: Lawrence Erlbaum.

Barrows, H. S. (1985). *How to Design a Problem-based Curriculum for the Preclinical Years*. New York: Springer.

Bash, B. (1989). *The Tree of Life: The Life of the African Baobab*. San Francisco: Sierra Club Books, Little Brown.

Ben-Zvi, R., Eylon, B. & Silberstein, J. (1987). Students' visualization of a chemical reaction. *Education in Chemistry*, July, 117–20.

Beck, I. L. & Dole, J. A. (1992). Reading and thinking with history and science text. In C. Collins & J. M. Mangieri (Eds), *Teaching Thinking: an Agenda for the Twenty-first Century* (pp. 3–22). Hillsdale, NJ: Erlbaum.

Bereiter, C. (1990). Aspects of an educational learning theory. *Review of Educational Research*, 60, 603–24.

Bereiter, C. (1994). Constructivism, socioculturalism, and Popper's world 3. *Educational Researcher*, 23 (7), 21–3.

Bereiter, C. & Scardamalia, M. (1993). *Surpassing Ourselves*. Chicago, IL: Open Court.

Berliner, D. C. (1991). Educational psychology and pedagogical expertise: new findings and new opportunities for thinking about training. *Educational Psychologist*, 26 (2), 145–55.

Bettencourt, A. (1993). The construction of knowledge: a radical constructivist view. In K. Tobin (Ed.), *The Practice of Constructivism in Science Education* (pp. 39–50). Washington, DC: American Association for Advancement of Science.

Bielaczyc, K., Pirolli, P. & Brown, A. L. (1995). Training in self-explanation and self-regulation strategies: investigating the effects of knowledge acquisition activities on problem solving. *Cognition & Instruction*, 13, 221–53.

Bloome, D. M., Goldman, S. R., Bransford, J. D., Hasselbring, T. & CTGV (1997). Theoretical perspective on a Whole Day Whole Year Approach to Student Achievement. Paper presented at the American Educational Research Association meetings, Chicago, IL, July.

Blumenfeld, P. C., Soloway, E., Marx, R. W., Krajcik, J. S., Guzdial, M. & Palincsar, A. (1991). Motivating project-based learning: sustaining the doing, supporting the learning. *Educational Psychologist*, 26 (3 & 4), 369–98.

Borko, H. & Livingston, C. (1989). Cognition and improvisation: differences in mathematics instruction by expert and novice teachers. *American Educational Research Journal*, 26, 473–98.

Bowen, C. W. (1990). Representational systems used by graduate students while problem solving in organic synthesis. *Journal of Research in Science Teaching*, 27, 351–70.
Bransford, J. D., Franks, J. J., Vye, N. J. & Sherwood, R. D. (1989). New approaches to instruction: because wisdom can't be told. In S. Vosniadou & A. Ortony (Eds), *Similarity and Analogical Reasoning* (pp. 470–97). NY: Cambridge University Press.
Bransford, J. D., Goldman, S. R. & Vye, N. J. (1991). Making a difference in peoples' abilities to think: reflections on a decade of work and some hopes for the future. In L. Okagaki & R. J. Sternberg (Eds), *Directors of Development: Influences on the Tevelopment of Children's Thinking* (pp. 147–80). Hillsdale, NJ: Lawrence Erlbaum.
Bransford, J. D., Sherwood, R. S., Vye, N. J. & Rieser, J. (1986). Teaching thinking and problem solving: research foundations. *American Psychologist*, 41, 1078–89.
Bransford, J. D., Zech, L., Schwartz, D., Barron, B., Vye, N. & the Cognition and Technology Group at Vanderbilt (in press). Designs for environments that invite and sustain mathematical thinking. In P. Cobb (Ed.), *Symbolizing, Communicating, and Mathematizing: Perspectives on Discourse, Tools, and Instructional Design*. Hillsdale, NJ: Lawrence Erlbaum.
Bridges, E. M. & Hallinger, P. (1995). *Implementing Problem Based Learning in Leadership Development*. Eugene, OR: Eric Publishing.
Britton, B. K. & Gulgöz, S. (1991). Using Kintsch's computational model to improve instructional text: effects of repairing inference calls on recall and cognitive structures. *Journal of Educational Psychology*, 83, 329–45.
Brown, A. (1978). Knowing when, where, and how to remember: a problem of metacognition. In R. Glaser (Ed.), *Advances in Instructional Psychology* (Vol. 1, pp. 77–165). Hillsdale, NJ: Erlbaum.
Brown, A., Ash, D., Rutherford, M., Nakagawa, K., Gordon, A. & Campione, J. C. (1993). Distributed expertise in the classroom. In G. Salomon (Ed.), *Distributed Cognitions: Psychological and Educational Considerations* (pp. 188–228). New York: Cambridge University Press.
Brown, A. & Campione, J. C. (1994). Guided discovery in a community of learners. In K. McGilly (Ed.), *Classroom Lessons: Integrating Cognitive Theory and Classroom Practice* (pp. 229–72). Cambridge, MA: MIT Press.
Brown, A. & Campione, J. C. (1996). Psychological theory and the design of innovative learning environments: on procedures, principles, and systems. In L. Schauble & R. Glaser (Eds), *Innovations in Learning: New Environments for Education* (pp. 289–325). Mahwah, NJ: Erlbaum.
Brown, J., Collins, A. & Duguid, P. (1989). Situated cognition and the culture of learning. *Educational Researcher*, 18 (1), 32–42.
Carraher, T. N., Carraher, D. W. & Schliemann, A. D. (1985). Mathematics in the streets and in schools. *British Journal of Developmental Psychology*, 3, 21–9.
Carver, S. M., Lehrer, R., Connell, T. & Erickson, J. (1992). Learning by hypermedia design: issues of assessment and implementation. *Educational Psychologist*, 27, 385–404.
Ceci, S. J. & Liker, J. K. (1986). A day at the races: a study of IQ expertise, and cognitive complexity. *Journal of Experimental Psychology: General*, 115, 255–66.
Chambliss, M. J. & Calfee, R. C. (1989). Designing science textbooks to enhance student understanding. *Educational Psychologist*, 24, 307–22.
Chan, C. K. K., Burtis, P. J., Scardamalia, M. & Bereiter, C. (1992). Constructive activity in learning from text. *American Educational Research Journal*, 29, 97–118.
Charness, N. & Schultetus, S. (1999). Knowledge and expertise. In F. Durso, R. S. Nickerson, R. W. Schvaneveldt, S. T. Dumais, D. S. Lindsay & M. T. H. Chi (Eds), *Handbook of Applied Cognition* (chapter 3). Chichester: John Wiley.
Chase, W. G. & Simon, H. A. (1973). Perception in chess. *Cognitive Psychology*, 1, 33–81.
Chi, M. T. H. (1978). Knowledge structure and memory development. In R. S. Siegler (Ed.), *Children's Thinking: What Develops?* (pp. 73–96). Hillsdale, NJ: Erlbaum.
Chi, M. T. H., Bassok, M., Lewis, M., Reimann, M. & Glaser, R. (1989). Self-explanations: how students study and use examples in learning to solve problems. *Cognitive Science*, 13, 145–82.

Chi, M. T. H., de Leeuw, N., Chiu, M. & La Vancher, C. (1994). Eliciting self-explanations improves understanding. *Cognitive Science*, 18, 439–77.

Chi, M. T. H., Feltovich, P. & Glaser, R. (1981). Categorization and representation of physics problems by experts and novices. *Cognitive Science*, 5, 121–52.

Chi, M. T. H., Glaser, R. & Farr, M. (1988). *The Nature of Expertise*. Hillsdale, NJ: Erlbaum.

Chi, M. T. H. & Koeske, R. (1983). Network representation of a child's dinosaur knowledge. *Developmental Psychology*, 19, 29–39.

Chinn & Brewer, (1996). Mental models in data interpretation. *Philosophy of Science*, 63 (Proceedings), S211–S219.

Clement, J. (1991). Nonformal reasoning in experts and in science students: the use of analogies, extreme cases, and physical intuition. In J. F. Voss, D. N. Perkins & J. W. Segal (Eds), *Informal Reasoning and Education* (pp. 345–62). Hillsdale, NJ: Lawrence Erlbaum.

Cobb, P. (1994). Where is the mind? Constructivist and sociocultural perspectives on mathematical development. *Educational Researcher*, 23 (7), 13–20.

Cobb, P., Yackel, E. & Wood, T. (1992). A constructivist alternative to the representational view of mind in mathematics education. *Journal for Research in Mathematics Education*, 19, 99–114.

Collins, A. (1996). Design issues for learning environments. In S. Vosniadou, E. De Corte, R. Glaser & H. Mandl (Eds), *International Perspectives on the Psychological Foundations of Technology-based Learning Environments* (pp. 347–62). Hillsdale, NJ: Erlbaum.

Collins, A., Brown, J. S. & Newman, S. E. (1989). Cognitive apprenticeship: teaching the crafts of reading, writing and mathematics. In L. B. Resnick (Ed.), *Knowing, Learning and Instruction: Essays in Honor of Robert Glaser* (pp. 453–94). Hillsdale, NJ: Erlbaum.

Collins, A., Greeno, J. G. & Resnick, L. B. (1994). Learning environments. In T. Husen & T. N. Postlewaite (Eds), *International Encyclopedia of Education* (2nd edn, pp. 3297–302). Oxford: Pergamon.

Coté, N. & Goldman, S. R. (1999). Building representations of informational text: evidence from children's think-aloud protocols. To appear in H. van Oostendorp & S. R. Goldman (Eds), *The Construction of Mental Representations during Reading*, (pp. 169–94). Mahwah, NJ: Erlbaum.

Coté, N., Goldman, S. R. & Saul, E. U. (1998). Students making sense of informational text: relations between processing and representation. *Discourse Processes*, 25, 1–53.

Crews, T. R., Biswas, G., Goldman, S. R. & Bransford, J. D. (1997). Anchored interactive learning environments. *International Journal of AI in Education*, 8, 142–78.

CTGV (Cognition and Technology Group at Vanderbilt) (1990). Anchored instruction and its relationship to situated cognition. *Educational Researcher*, 19 (6), 2–10.

CTGV (Cognition and Technology Group at Vanderbilt) (1992). The Jasper experiment: an exploration of issues in learning and instructional design. *Educational Technology Research and Development*, 40, 65–80.

CTGV (Cognition and Technology Group at Vanderbilt) (1994a). From visual word problems to learning communities: changing conceptions of cognitive research. In K. McGilly (Ed.), *Classroom Lessons: Integrating Cognitive Theory and Classroom Practice* (pp. 157–200). Cambridge, MA: MIT Press.

CTGV (Cognition and Technology Group at Vanderbilt) (1994b). Multimedia environments for developing literacy in at-risk students. In B. Means (Ed.), *Technology and Educational Reform: The Reality Behind the Promise* (pp. 23–56). San Francisco: Jossey-Bass.

CTGV (Cognition and Technology Group at Vanderbilt) (1997). *The Jasper Project: Lessons in Curriculum, Instruction, Assessment, and Professional Development*. Mahwah, NJ: Erlbaum.

CTGV (Cognition and Technology Group at Vanderbilt) (1998). Designing environments to reveal, support, and expand our children's potentials. In S. A. Soraci & W. McIlvane (Eds), *Perspectives on Fundamental Processes in Intellectual Functioning: a Survey of Research Approaches* (Vol. 1, pp. 313–50). Stamford, CT: Ablex.

De Corte, E., Greer, B. & Verschaffel, L. (1996). Mathematics teaching and learning. In D. C. Berliner & R. C. Calfee (Eds), *Handbook of Educational Psychology* (pp. 491–549). NY: Macmillan.

Dee-Lucas, D. & Larkin, J. H. (1988). Novice rules for assessing importance in scientific texts. *Journal of Memory and Language*, 27, 288–308.

Dennis, M. J. & Sternberg, R. J. (1999). Cognition and instruction. In F. T. Durso, R. S. Nickerson, R. W. Schvaneveldt, S. T. Dumais, D. S. Lindsay & M. T. H. Chi (Eds), *Handbook of Applied Cognition* (chapter 19). Chichester: John Wiley.

Detterman, D. K. & Sternberg, R. J. (1993). *Transfer on Trial: Intelligence, Cognition and Instruction*. Norwood, NJ: Ablex.

Dewey, S. (1933). *How We Think, "a Restatement" of the Relation of Reflective Thinking to the Educative Process*. Boston, MA: Heath.

Dörner, D. & Schölkopf, J. (1991). Controlling complex systems; or, expertise as "grandmother's know-how." In K. A. Ericsson & J. Smith (Eds), *Toward a General Theory of Expertise: Prospects and Limits* (pp. 218–39). NY: Cambridge University Press.

Driver, R., Asoko, H., Leach, J., Mortimer, E. & Scott, P. (1994). Constructing scientific knowledge in the classroom. *Educational Researcher*, 23 (7), 5–12.

Dunbar, K. (1995). How scientists really reason: scientific reasoning in real-world laboratories. In R. J. Sternberg & J. Davidson (Eds), *Mechanisms of Insight* (pp. 365–95). Cambridge, MA: MIT Press.

Duschl, R. & Gitomer, D. H. (1997). Strategies and challenges to changing the focus of assessment and instruction in science education. *Educational Assessment*, 4 (1), 37–73.

Dweck, C. S. (1989). Motivation. In A. Lesgold & R. Glaser (Eds), *Foundations for a Psychology of Education* (pp. 87–136). Hillsdale, NJ: Lawrence Erlbaum.

Edelson, D. C., Pea, R. D. & Gomez, L. (1996). Constructivism in the collaboratory. In B. Wilson (Ed.), *Constructivist Learning Environments: Case Studies in Instructional Design* (pp. 151–64). Englewood Cliffs, NJ: Educational Technology Publications.

Eichinger, D. C., Anderson, C. W., Palincsar, A. S. & David, Y. M. (1991). An illustration of the roles of content knowledge, scientific argument, and social norms in collaborative problem solving. Paper presented at the annual meeting of the American Educational Research Association. Chicago, IL, July.

Ericsson, K. A. & Smith, J. (1991). Prospects and limits of the empirical study of expertise: an introduction. In K. A. Ericsson & J. Smith (Eds), *Toward a General Theory of Expertise: Prospects and Limits* (pp. 1–38). NY: Cambridge University Press.

Ertmer, P. A., Newby, T. J. & MacDougal, M. (1996). Students' responses and approaches to case-based instruction: the role of reflective self-regulation. *American Educational Research Journal*, 33 (3), 719–52.

Flavell, J. C. (1976). Metacognitive aspects of problem solving. In L. B. Resnick (Ed.), *The Nature of Intelligence* (pp. 231–6). Hillsdale, NJ: Erlbaum.

Gagné, R. M. (1968). Contributions of learning to human development. *Psychological Review*, 75, 177–91.

Gardner, H. (1985). *The Mind's New Science: A History of the Cognitive Revolution*. New York: Basic Books.

Gee, J. P. (1992). *The Social Mind*. New York: Bergin & Garvey.

Gentner, D. (1989). The mechanisms of analogical learning. In S. Vosniadou & A. Ortony (Eds), *Similarity and Analogical Reasoning* (pp. 199–241). Cambridge: Cambridge University Press.

Glaser, R. (1991). Intelligence as an expression of acquired knowledge. In H. A. H. Rowe (Ed.), *Intelligence: Reconceptualization and Measurement* (pp. 47–56). Hillsdale, NJ: Lawrence Erlbaum.

Glaser, R. & Chi, M. T. H. (1988). Introduction: what is it to be an expert? In M. T. H. Chi, R. Glaser & M. J. Farr (Eds), *The Nature of Expertise* (pp. xv–xxiix). Hillsdale, NJ: Erlbaum.

Goldman, S. R., Cosden, M. A. & Hine, M. S. (1992). Working alone and working together: individual differences in the effects of collaboration on learning handicapped students' writing. *Learning and Individual Differences*, 4, 369–93.

Goldman, S. R., Mayfield-Stewart, C., Bateman, H. V., Pellegrino, J. W. & the Cognition and Technology Group at Vanderbilt (in press). Environments that support meaningful learning. To appear in *Proceedings of the Seeon-Conference on Interest and Gender*.

Goldman, S. R., Petrosino, A., Sherwood, R. D., Garrison, S., Hickey, D., Bransford, J. D. & Pellegrino, J. (1996). Anchoring science instruction in multimedia learning environments. In S. Vosniadou, E. De Corte, R. Glaser & H. Mandl (Eds), *International Perspectives on the Design of Technology-supported Learning Environments* (pp. 257–84). Hillsdale, NJ: Erlbaum.

Goldman, S. R. & Saul, E. U. (1990). Flexibility in text processing: a strategy competition model. *Learning and Individual Differences*, 2, 181–219.

Goldman, S. R., Williams, S. M., Sherwood, R., Hasselbring, T. (1998). Technology for teaching and learning with understanding. In J. Cooper (Ed.), *Classroom Teaching Skills* (pp. 181–219). NY: Houghton-Mifflin.

Goldman, S. R., Zech, L. K., Biswas, G. & Noser, T. (in press). Computer technology and complex problem solving: issues in the study of complex cognitive activity. *Instructional Science*.

Graesser, A. C. & Person, N. K. (1994). Question asking during tutoring. *American Educational Research Journal*, 31, 104–37.

Graesser, A. C., Person, N. K. & Magliano, J. P. (1995). Collaborative dialogue patterns in naturalistic one-on-one tutoring. *Applied Cognitive Psychology*, 9, 359–87.

Greene, S. (1993). The role of task in the development of academic thinking through reading and writing in a college history course. *Research in the Teaching of English*, 27, 46–75.

Greene, S. (1994). The problems of learning to think like a historian: writing history in the culture of the classroom. *Educational Psychologist*, 29 (2), 89–96.

Greeno, J. G. & the Middle School Mathematics Through Applications Project Group (1998). The situativity of knowing, learning, and research. *American Psychologist*, 53, 5–26.

Hall, R. P. (1996). Representation as shared practice: situated cognition and Dewey's cartography of experience. *Journal of the Learning Sciences*, 5, 211–40.

Harel, I. & Papert, S. (Eds) (1991). *Constructionism*. Norwood, NJ: Ablex.

Hatano, G. (1988). Social and motivational bases for mathematical understanding. In G. G. Saxe & M. Gearhart (Eds), *Children's Mathematics* (pp. 55–70). San Francisco: Jossey-Bass.

Hatano, G. & Inagaki, K. (1986). Two courses of expertise. In H. Stevenson, H. Azuma & K. Hakuta (Eds), *Child Development and Education in Japan* (pp. 262–72). San Francisco: Freeman.

Hatano, G. & Inagaki, K. (1991). Sharing cognition through collective comprehension activity. In L. Resnick, J. M. Levine & S. D. Teasley (Eds), *Perspectives on Socially Shared Cognition* (pp. 331–48). Washington, DC: American Psychological Association.

Hayes, J. R. (1990). Individuals and environments in writing instruction. In B. F. Jones & L. Idol (Eds), *Dimensions of Thinking and Cognitive Instruction* (pp. 241–63). Hillsdale, NJ: Lawrence Erlbaum.

Hickey, D. T. (1996). Constructivism, motivation & achievement: the impact of classroom mathematics environments & instructional programs. Unpublished doctoral dissertation, Vanderbilt University, Nashville, TN.

Holt, J. (1964). *How Children Fail*. New York: Dell.

Hutchins, E. (1991). The social organization of distributed cognition. In L. Resnick, J. M. Levine & S. D. Teasley (Eds), *Perspectives on Socially Shared Cognition* (pp. 283–307). Washington, DC: American Psychological Association.

Jackson, S., Stratford, S. J., Krajcik, J. S. & Soloway, E. (1996). Making system dynamics modeling accessible to pre-college science students. *Interactive Learning Environments*, 4, 233–57.

Johnson, D. W. & Johnson, R. (1985). Classroom conflict: controversy over debate in learning groups. *American Educational Research Journal*, 22, 237–56.

Johnson, D., Maruyama, G., Johnson, R., Nelson, C. & Skon, L. (1981). The effects of

cooperative, competitive, and individualistic goal structures on achievement: a meta-analysis. *Psychological Bulletin*, 89, 47–62.
Johnson, H. M. & Seifert, C. M. (1999). Modifying mental representations: comprehending corrections. In H. Van Oostendorp & S. R. Goldman (Eds), *The Construction of Mental Representations During Reading* (pp. 303–18). Mahwah, NJ: Erlbaum.
Jungck, J. R. (1991). Constructivism, computer exploratoriums, and collaborative learning: constructing scientific knowledge. *Teaching Education*, 3, 151–70.
Koballa, T. R. (1988). Persuading girls to take elective physical science courses in high school: who are the credible communicators? *Journal of Research in Science Teaching*, 25, 465–78.
Koslowski, B. (1996). *Theory and Evidence: The Development of Scientific Reasoning*. Cambridge, MA: MIT Press.
Kozma, R. B. (in press). The use of multiple representations and the social construction of understanding in chemistry. In M. Jacobson & R. Kozma (Eds), *Learning the Sciences of the 21st Century: Research, Design, and Implementing Advanced Technology Learning Systems*. Mahwah, NJ: Erlbaum.
Kozma, R. & Russell, J. (1997). Multimedia and understanding: expert and novice responses to different representations of chemical phenomena. *Journal of Research in Science Teaching*, 43 (9), 949–68.
Krajcik, J. S. (1991). Developing students' understanding of chemical concepts. In S. M. Glynn, R. H. Yeany & B. K. Britton (Eds), *The Psychology of Learning Science* (pp. 117–47). Hillsdale, NJ: Erlbaum.
Kuhara-Kojima, K. & Hatano, G. (1991). Contribution of content knowledge and learning ability to the learning of facts. *Educational Psychology*, 83, 253–63.
Kuhn, D. (1989). Children and adults as intuitive scientists. *Psychological Review*, 96, 674–89.
Kuhn, D., Schauble, L. & Garcia-Mila, M. (1992). Cross-domain development of scientific reasoning. *Cognition and Instruction*, 9 (4), 285–327.
Kuhn, D., Shaw, V. & Felton, M. (1997). Effects of dyadic interaction on argumentative reasoning. *Cognition & Instruction*, 15, 287–315.
Lamon, M., Secules, T. J., Petrosino, T., Hackett, R., Bransford, J. D. & Goldman, S. R. (1996). Schools for thought: overview of the project and lessons learned from one of the sites. In L. Schauble & R. Glaser (Eds), *Innovations in Learning: New Environments for Education* (pp. 243–88). Mahwah, NJ: Erlbaum.
Larkin, J., McDermott, J., Simon, D. P. & Simon, H. A. (1980). Expert and novice performance in solving physics problems. *Science*, 208, 1335–42.
Lave, J. (1988). *Cognition in Practice: Mind, Mathematics, and Culture in Everyday Life*. Cambridge: Cambridge University Press.
Lave, J. & Wenger, E. (1991). *Situated Learning: Legitimate Peripheral Participation*. Cambridge, MA: Cambridge University Press.
Leinhardt, G., Stainton, C. & Virji, S. M. (1994). A sense of history. *Educational Psychologist*, 29 (2), 79–88.
Leinhardt, G. & Young, K. M. (1996). Two texts, three readers: distance and expertise in reading history. *Cognition and Instruction*, 14 (4), 441–86.
Lepper, M. R., Aspinwall, L. G., Mumme, D. L. & Chabay, R. W. (1990). Self-perception and social-perception processes in tutoring: subtle social control strategies of expert tutors. In J. M. Olson & M. P. Zanna (Eds), *Self-inference Processes: The Ontario Symposium* (pp. 217–37). Hillsdale, NJ: Erlbaum.
Lepper, M. R., Wolverton, M., Mumme, D. L. & Gurtner, J.-L. (1993). Motivational techniques of expert human tutors: lessons for the design of computer-based tutors. In S. P. Lajoie & S. J. Derry (Eds), *Computers as Cognitive Tools* (pp. 75–106). Hillsdale, NJ: Erlbaum.
Lesgold, A. (1988). Problem solving. In R. J. Sternberg & E. E. Smith (Eds), *The Psychology of Human Thought* (pp. 188–213). NY: Cambridge University Press.
Lesgold, A., Glaser, R., Rubinson, H., Klopfer, D., Feltovich, P. & Wang, Y. (1988).

Expertise in a complex skill: diagnosing x-ray pictures. In M. T. H. Chi, R. Glaser & M. J. Farr (Eds), *The Nature of Expertise* (pp. 311–42). Hillsdale, NJ: Erlbaum.
Lewandowsky, S. & Behrens, J. T. (1999). Statistical maps and graphs. In F. T. Durso, R. S. Nickerson, R. W. Schvaneveldt, S. T. Dumais, D. S. Lindsay & M. T. H. Chi (Eds), *Handbook of Applied Cognition* (chapter 17). Chichester: John Wiley.
Lhyle, K. G. & Kulhavy, R. W. (1987). Feedback processing and error correction. *Journal of Educational Psychology*, 79, 320–2.
Linn, M. C., Bell, P. & Hsi, S. (in press). Using the Internet to enhance student learning in science: the knowledge integration environment. *Interactive Learning Environments.*
Linn, M. C. & Burbules, N. C. (1993). Construction of knowledge and group learning. In K. Tobin (Ed.), *The Practice of Constructivism in Science Education* (pp. 121–34). Washington, DC: AAAS.
Lowe, R. (in press). Extracting information from an animation during complex visual learning. *European Journal of Psychology of Education.*
Marsh, H. W. & Craven, R. G. (1991). Self–other agreement on multiple dimensions of preadolescent self-concept: inferences by teachers, mothers, and fathers. *Journal of Educational Psychology*, 83, 393–404.
Martin, V. L. & Pressley, M. (1991). Elaborative-interrogation effects depend on the nature of the question. *Journal of Educational Psychology*, 83, 113–19.
Mayer, R. E. (1997). Multimedia learning: are we asking the right questions? *Educational Psychologist*, 31, 1–19.
Mayer, R. E. (1999). Instructional technology. In F. Durso, R. S. Nickerson, R. W. Schvaneveldt, S. T. Dumais, D. S. Lindsay & M. T. H. Chi (Eds), *Handbook of Applied Cognition* (chapter 18). Chichester: John Wiley.
Mayer, R. E. & Sims, V. K. (1994). For whom is a picture worth a thousand words? Extensions of a dual-coding theory of multimedia learning. *Journal of Educational Psychology*, 86, 389–401.
McArthur, D., Stasz, C. & Zmuidzinas, M. (1990). Tutoring techniques in algebra. *Cognition and Instruction*, 7, 197–244.
McCombs, B. L. (1991). Motivation and lifelong learning. *Educational Psychologist*, 26 (2), 117–27.
McCombs, B. L. (1996). Alternative perspectives for motivation. In L. Baker, P. Afflerbach & D. Reinking (Eds), *Developing Engaged Readers in School and Home Communities* (pp. 67–87). Mahwah, NJ: Erlbaum.
Miller, A. I. (1984). *Imagery in Scientific Thought: Creating 20th-century Physics*. Boston, MA: Birkhaüser.
Minstrell, J. & Stimpson, V. (1996). A classroom environment for learning: guiding students' reconstruction of understanding and reasoning. In S. Vosniadou, E. De Corte, R. Glaser & H. Mandl (Eds), *International Perspectives on the Design of Technology-supported Learning Environments* (pp. 175–202). Hillsdale, NJ: Erlbaum.
Newman, D., Griffin, P. & Cole, M. (1989). *The Construction Zone: Working for Cognitive Change in School.* NY: Cambridge University Press.
Newmann, F. (1990). Qualities of thoughtful social studies classes: an empirical profile. *Journal of Curriculum Studies*, 22, 253–75.
NOAA/Forecast Systems Laboratory (1998). <http://netcast.noaa.gov>
Pea, R. D. (1993). Practices of distributed intelligence and designs for education. In G. Salomon (Ed.), *Distributed Cognitions: Psychological and Educational Considerations* (pp. 47–87). New York: Cambridge University Press.
Pea, R. D. (1994). Seeing what we build together: distributed multimedia learning environments for transformative communications. *The Journal of the Learning Sciences*, 3, 285–301.
Perfetti, C. A., Rouet, J.-R. & Britt, M. A. (1999). Toward a theory of document representation. In H. Van Oostendorp & S. R. Goldman (Eds), *The Construction of Mental Representations During Reading* (pp. 99–122). Mahwah, NJ: Erlbaum.
Petrosino, A. J. (1998). At-risk children's use of reflection and revision in hands-on

experimental activities. Unpublished doctoral dissertation, Vanderbilt University, Nashville, TN.
Pirolli, P. & Bielaczyc, K. (1989). Empirical analyses of self-explanation and transfer in learning to program. *Proceedings of the Ninth Annual Conference of the Cognitive Science Society* (pp. 450–7). Hillsdale, NJ: Erlbaum.
Pressley, M. & McCormick, C. B. (1995). *Advanced Educational Psychology for Educators, Researchers, and Policymakers*. NY: HarperCollins.
Putnam, R. T. & Borko, H. (1997). Teacher learning; implications of new views of cognition. In B. J. Biddle, T. L. Good & I. F. Goodson (Eds), *International Handbook of Teachers and Teaching* (Vol. II, pp. 1223–96).
Reiser, B. J., Copen, W. A., Ranney, M., Hamid, A. & Kimberg, D. Y. (1994). *Cognitive and Motivational Consequences of Tutoring and Discovery Learning*. (Technical Report No. 54). The Institute for the Learning Sciences, Northwestern University.
Resnick, L. (1987). *Education and Learning to Think*. Washington, DC: National Academy Press.
Resnick, L. B. & Klopfer, L. E. (Eds) (1989). *Toward the Thinking Curriculum: Current Cognitive Research*. Alexandria, VA: ASCD.
Rogoff, B. (1990). *Apprenticeship in Thinking*. New York: Oxford University Press.
Rogoff, B. & Lave, J. (Eds) (1984). *Everyday Cognition: Its Development in Social Context*. Cambridge, MA: Harvard University Press.
Ross, J. A. (1988). Controlling variables: a meta-analysis of training studies. *Review of Educational Research*, 58, 405–37.
Roth, W. M. & Bowen, G. M. (1995). Knowing and interacting: a study of culture, practice and resources in a grade 8 open-inquiry science classroom guided by a cognitive apprenticeship metaphor. *Cognition & Instruction*, 13, 73–128.
Rouet, J.-F., Favart, M., Britt, M. A. & Perfetti, C. A. (1997). Studying and using multiple documents in history: effects of discipline expertise. *Cognition and Instruction*, 15 (1), 85–106.
Sabers, D. S., Cushing, K. S. & Berliner, D. C. (1991). Differences among teachers in a task characterized by simultaneity, multidimensionality, and immediacy. *American Educational Research Journal*, 28 (1), 63–88.
Salomon, G. (Ed.) (1993). *Distributed Cognitions: Psychological and Educational Considerations*. New York: Cambridge University Press.
Salomon, G. & Globerson, T. (1989). When teams do not function the way they ought to. *International Journal of Educational Research*, 13, 89–99.
Saxe, G. B. (1988). Children's mathematical thinking: a developmental framework for preschool, primary, and special education teachers by A. J. Broody. *Contemporary Psychology*, 33, 997.
Saxe, G. B. (1991). *Culture and Cognitive Development: Studies in Mathematical Understanding*. Hillsdale, NJ: Erlbaum.
Scardamalia, M., Bereiter, C. & Lamon, M. (1994). The CSILE Project: trying to bring the classroom into world 3. In K. McGilly (Ed.), *Classroom Lessons: Integrating Cognitive Theory and Classroom Practice* (pp. 201–28). Cambridge, MA: MIT Press/Bradford Books.
Schauble, L., Glaser, R., Duschl, R. A., Schulze, S. & John, J. (1995). Students' understanding of the objectives and procedures of experimentation in the science classroom. *Journal of Learning Sciences*, 4, 131–66.
Schauble, L., Glaser, R., Raghavan, K. & Reiner, M. (1991). Causal models and experimentation strategies in scientific reasoning. *The Journal of the Learning Sciences*, 1, 201–38.
Schiefele, U. & Krapp, A. (1996). Topic interest and free recall of expository text. *Learning and Individual Differences*, 8, 141–60.
Schliemann, A. D. & Acioly, N. M. (1989). Mathematical knowledge developed at work: the contribution of practice versus the contribution of schooling. *Cognition and Instruction*, 6, 185–222.

Schneider, W. A. & Shiffrin, R. M. (1977). Controlled and automatic processing: detection, search, and attention. *Psychological Review*, 84, 1–66.
Schneider, W., Körkel, J. & Weinert, F. E. (1989). Domain-specific knowledge and memory performance: a comparison of high- and low-aptitude children. *Journal of Educational Psychology*, 81, 306–12.
Schoenfeld, A. H. (1985). *Mathematical Problem Solving*. Orlando, FL: Academic Press.
Schön, D. A. (1983). *The Reflective Practitioner: How Professionals Think in Action*. New York: Basic Books.
Schunk, D. H. (1990). Goal setting and self-efficacy during self-regulated learning. *Educational Psychologist*, 25, 71–86.
Schunk, D. H. (1991). Self-efficacy and academic motivation. *Educational Psychologist*, 26, 207–32.
Schwartz, D. L. & Bransford, J. D. (in press). A time for telling. *Cognition and Instruction*.
Schwartz, J. L., Yerushalmy, M. & Wilson, B. (Eds) (1993). *The Geometric Supposer: What is it a Case of?* Hillsdale, NJ: Erlbaum.
Schwartz, D. L., Lin, X. D., Brophy, S. & Bransford, J. D. (in press). Towards the development of flexibly adaptive instructional design. In C. Reigeluth (Ed.), *Instructional Design Theories and Models, Volume II*. Mahwah, NJ: Erlbaum.
Schwartz, D. L., Goldman, S. R., Vye, N. J., Barron, B. J. & The Cognition and Technology Group at Vanderbilt (1998). Aligning everyday and mathematical reasoning: the case of sampling assumptions. In S. P. Lajoie (Ed.), *Reflections on Statistics: Learning, Teaching, and Assessment in Grades K-12* (pp. 233–73). Mahwah, NJ: Erlbaum.
Secules, T., Cottom, C. D., Bray, M. H., Miller, L. D. & the Cognition and Technology Group at Vanderbilt (1997). Schools for thought: creating learning communities. *Educational Leadership*, 54 (6), 56–60.
Sherwood, R. D., Kinzer, C. K., Bransford, J. D. & Franks, J. J. (1987). Some benefits of creating macro-contexts for science instruction: initial findings. *Journal of Research in Science Teaching*, 24 (5), 417–35.
Sherwood, R. D., Petrosino, A. J., Lin, X., Lamon, M. & the Cognition and Technology Group at Vanderbilt (1995). Problem-based macro contexts in science instruction: theoretical basis, design issues, and the development of applications. In D. Lavoie (Ed.), *Towards a Cognitive-science Perspective for Scientific Problem Solving* (pp. 191–214). Manhattan, KS: National Association for Research in Science Teaching.
Simon, H. A. (1980). Problem solving and education. In D. T. Tuma & R. Reif (Eds), *Problem Solving and Education: Issues in Teaching and Research* (pp. 81–96). Hillsdale, NJ: Erlbaum.
Smith, C., Maclin, D., Grosslight, L. & Davis, H. (1997). Teaching for understanding: a study of students' preinstruction theories of matter and a comparison of the effectiveness of two approaches to teaching about matter and density. *Cognition and instruction*, 15 (3), 317–93.
Spilich, G. J., Vesonder, G. T., Chiesi, H. L. & Voss, J. F. (1979). Text processing of domain-related information for individuals with high and low domain knowledge. *Journal of Verbal Learning and Verbal Behavior*, 18, 275–90.
Stipek, D. & MacIver, D. (1989). Developmental change in children's assessment of intellectual competence. *Child Development*, 60, 521–38.
Suthers, D., Weiner, A., Connelly, A. & Paolucci, M. (1995). Belvedere: engaging students in critical discussion of science and public policy issues. Paper presented at AI-Ed 95, The 7th World Conference on Artificial Intelligence in Education, Washington, DC, August.
Sweller, J. & Cooper, G. A. (1985). The use of worked examples as a substitute for problem solving in learning algebra. *Cognition and Instruction*, 2, 59–89.
Tapiero, I. & Otero, J. (1999). Distinguishing between textbase and situation model in the processing of inconsistent information: elaboration vs. tagging. In H. Van Oostendorp & S. R. Goldman (Eds), *The Construction of Mental Representations During Reading* (pp. 341–66). Mahwah, NJ: Erlbaum.
Trabasso, T., Suh, S., Payton, P. & Jain, R. (1995). Explanatory inferences and other

strategies during comprehension and their effect on recall. In R. F. Lorch & E. J. O'Brien (Eds), *Sources of Coherence in Reading* (pp. 219–39). Hillsdale, NJ: Erlbaum.

Van Oostendorp, H. & Bonebakker, C. (1999). Difficulties in updating mental representations during reading news reports. In H. Van Oostendorp & S. R. Goldman (Eds), *The Construction of Mental Representations During Reading* (pp. 319–40). Mahwah, NJ: Erlbaum.

vonGlaserfeld, E. (1989). Cognition, construction of knowledge, and teaching. *Synthese*, 80, 121–40.

Voss, J. F., Blais, J., Means, M. L., Greene, T. R. & Ahwesh, E. (1986). Informal reasoning and subject matter knowledge in the solving of economics problems by naive and novice individuals. *Cognition and Instruction*, 3, 269–302.

Voss, J. F., Greene, T. R., Post, T. A. & Penner, B. C. (1983). Problem-solving skill in the social sciences. In G. H. Bower (Ed.), *Psychology of Learning and Motivation*, 17 (pp. 165–213). NY: Academic Press.

Vye, N. J., Goldman, S. R., Voss, J. F., Hmelo, C., Williams, S. & the Cognition and Technology Group at Vanderbilt (1997). Complex mathematical problem solving by individuals and dyads. *Cognition and Instruction*, 15, 435–84.

Vye, N. J., Schwartz, D. L., Bransford, J. D., Barron, B. J., Zech, L. & the Cognition and Technology Group at Vanderbilt (1998). SMART environments that support monitoring, reflection, and revision. In D. Hacker, J. Dunlosky & A. C. Graesser (Eds), *Metacognition in Educational Theory and Practice* (pp. 305–46). Mahwah, NJ: Erlbaum.

Vygotsky, L. S. (1962). *Thought and Language*. Cambridge, MA: MIT Press.

Vygotsky, L. S. (1978). *Mind in Society: the Development of Higher Psychological Processes*. Cambridge, MA: Harvard University Press.

Wade, S., Buxton, W. & Kelly, M. (1993, April). What text characteristics create interest for readers. Paper presented at the annual meeting of the American Educational Research Association, Atlanta, GA.

Webb, N. (1989). Peer interaction and learning in small groups. *International Journal of Educational Research*, 13, 21–39.

Wheatley, G. (1993). The role of negotiation in mathematics learning. In K. Tobin (Ed.), *The Practice of Constructivism in Science Education* (pp. 121–34). Washington, DC: AAAS.

White, B. (1993). ThinkerTools: causal models, conceptual change, and science education. *Cognition and Instruction*, 10, 1–100.

White, B. & Frederiksen, J. (1998). Inquiry, modeling, and metacognition: making science accessible to all students. *Cognition and Instruction*, 16 (1), 3–118.

Whitehead, A. N. (1929). *The Aims of Education*. New York: Macmillan.

Williams, S. M. (1992). Putting case-based instruction into context: examples from legal and medical education. *The Journal of the Learning Sciences*, 2 (4), 367–427.

Wineburg, S. S. (1991). Historical problem solving: a study of the cognitive processes used in the evaluation of documentary and pictorial evidence. *Journal of Educational Psychology*, 83, 73–87.

Wineburg, S. S. (1994). The cognitive representation of historical texts. In G. Leinhardt, I. L. Beck & C. Stainton (Eds), *Teaching and Learning in History* (pp. 85–135). Hillsdale, NJ: Lawrence Erlbaum.

Wood, S. S., Bruner, J. S. & Ross, G. (1976). The role of tutoring in problem solving. *Journal of Child Psychology and Psychiatry*, 17, 89–100.

Yackel, E., Cobb, P. & Wood, T. (1991). Small group interactions as a source of learning opportunities in second grade mathematics. *Journal for Research in Mathematics Education*, 22 (5), 390–408.

Yarroch, W. L. (1985). Student understanding of chemical equation balancing. *Journal of Research in Science Teaching*, 22, 449–59.

Zimmerman, B. J. (1990). Self-regulating academic learning and achievement: the emergence of a social-cognitive perspective. *Educational Psychology Review*, 2, 173–201.

Chapter 21

Cognitive Psychology Applied to Testing

Susan E. Embretson
University of Kansas

Cognitive psychology has seemingly held great potential for ability testing. Carroll & Maxwell (1979), in their *Annual Review of Psychology* chapter, heralded cognitive psychology as the breath of fresh air in intelligence measurement. Many others have concurred about the significance of cognitive psychology for testing (e.g. Embretson, 1985; Mislevy, 1993; Wittrock & Baker, 1991). Yet, more than two decades after Carroll & Maxwell's (1979) enthusiastic prognosis, actual applications to ability tests have been limited; some longstanding incompatibilities between cognition and testing need resolution. So, to date, a major impact of cognitive psychology on testing involves fundamental testing principles, such as the conceptual and procedural framework for test development, and psychometric models for estimating abilities. Although few tests have been developed with extended applications of cognitive psychology principles, several partial applications to specific testing issues do exist.

This chapter contains five major sections. First, the conceptual and procedural issues for applying cognitive psychology principles to testing are elaborated. A cognitive design system that centralizes cognitive psychology in test development is described. The design system contains a series of stages which differ qualitatively from traditional test development. Second, the impact of cognitive psychology on psychometric models is reviewed and several cognitive psychometric models are described. Third, the chapter overviews three tests which have employed cognitive design principles extensively. Fourth, several partial applications of cognitive psychology principles are reviewed. Fifth, the future impact of cognitive psychology is considered from the perspective of current issues in testing.

Handbook of Applied Cognition, Edited by F. T. Durso, R. S. Nickerson, R. W. Schvaneveldt, S. T. Dumais, D. S. Lindsay and M. T. H. Chi.

CONCEPTUAL AND PROCEDURAL ISSUES

Two Approaches for Relating Cognitive Psychology to Measurement

There are several different paradigms for interfacing cognitive theory with cognitive measurement. The two major paradigms are the cognitive correlates approach and the cognitive components approach. Although the cognitive correlates approach was developed earliest, the cognitive components approach dominated theoretical research on aptitude during the 1980s.

In the cognitive correlates approach, often attributed to Hunt and collaborators (Hunt, Frost & Lunneborg, 1973; Hunt, Lunneborg & Lewis, 1975), the meaning of ability for cognitive processing is established by correlations. That is, individual differences in performing laboratory tasks of information processing are correlated with ability test measures. Hunt and colleagues found that verbal ability scores correlated with several aspects of information processing, including speed of lexical access, speed in analyzing elementary sentences, size of memory span for words and digits, and adeptness in holding memory information while manipulating simple sentences.

In the cognitive component approach (e.g. Sternberg, 1977), test items are decomposed into a set of more elementary information processing components. Ability is explicated by the nature and strength of the underlying processes involved in item solving. Many item types that appear on ability tests were studied as cognitive tasks (e.g. see Sternberg, 1985) but verbal analogies have been, perhaps, the most intensively studied item type. Verbal analogies have had a special status in both ability measurement and cognitive psychology. Verbal analogies appear routinely on many ability tests and, in fact, Spearman's (1927) early theory of intelligence regarded analogies as the prototype of intelligent thought processes. Several studies have concerned the processes, strategies or knowledge structures involved in solving analogy items (e.g. Klix & van der Meer, 1982; Mulholland, Pellegrino & Glaser, 1980; Pellegrino & Glaser, 1980; Sternberg, 1977).

Bejar, Chaffin & Embretson (1991) connect diverse results from cognitive component studies on verbal analogies to psychometric analyses. Bejar et al. (1991) also include studies that are directed specifically toward testing issues, such as the prediction of item difficulty. Although cognitive component results seem useful for generating verbal analogies to reflect specific sources of difficulty, several shortcomings were observed. The shortcomings included:

1. most studies used simple verbal analogies that are unlikely to represent the processes required on more difficult psychometric analogies
2. most studies concerned processing rather than the semantic characteristics of analogies
3. semantic features, when studied, included only global characteristics, which did not predict item difficulty very well.

Incompatibilities between Cognitive Psychology and Testing

A deeper problem is reflected in Pellegrino's (1988) conclusion that cognitive psychology has become "wittingly or unwittingly, a form of construct validation." In other words, cognitive component results, as well as cognitive correlate results, further explicate the meaning of the construct(s) involved in test performance. This is unfortunate, according to Pellegrino (1988), because a more exciting potential for cognitive psychology is designing, rather than validating, tests.

This section elaborates a major source of incompatibility between cognitive psychology and measurement; namely, the traditional view of construct validation. Then, an alternative two-part conceptualization of construct validity is presented.

Traditional Conceptualization of Construct Validation

Cronbach & Meehl (1955) conceptualized construct validation research as establishing meaning empirically *after* the test is developed. According to Cronbach & Meehl (1955, p. 289) "the vague, avowedly incomplete network gives the constructs whatever meaning they do have." To explicate the nomological network, test scores are correlated with external variables, such as external criteria and other test scores. As noted by Pellegrino (1988), cognitive correlate and cognitive component results fit well within the validity framework as another aspect of the nomological network.

However, the traditional view of construct validation limits the role of theory (e.g. cognitive theory) in test development. Relying on the nomological network to elaborate meaning entails developing a test *prior to* determining its theoretical meaning. Because a test must meet many other psychometric criteria (scalability, reliability, norms, etc.), considerable effort is expended prior to validation studies. Thus, item content is usually relatively insensitive to results from construct validation studies. It is easier to recommend new test interpretations than to develop a new test. So, the main impact of cognitive theory in traditional construct validation is guiding test interpretations. That is, the question asked by Hunt et al. (1975) "What does it mean to be high verbal?" can be answered by referring to information processing capabilities, as well as to traditional nomological network results, such as success on various criteria and scores on other traits.

Because the theoretical nature of the ability construct is established after a test already exists, cognitive theory has no real role or advantage in test design. The link of any test design system to construct meaning falls outside the test validation process. Consequently, the impact of item specifications on the psychometric properties of the test is often unknown. Test developers employ item specifications that are often general content considerations (e.g. topic area, abstractness of content etc.).

Theory also has had a limited role in the design of typical nomological network studies. Although Cronbach & Meehl (1955) anticipated a strong program for construct validation in which studies are designed to evaluate specific hypotheses about construct meaning, in fact, a much weaker program is typical (see Cronbach, 1988). In the weak program, test intercorrelations from many studies are accumulated, irrespective of initial hypotheses. Thus, theory *follows from* the empirical findings.

In contrast, theory strongly influences the design of cognitive psychology studies. Task conditions are explicitly manipulated to test hypotheses about specific constructs. Theory *precedes* the development of tasks that reflect specific constructs. Thus, the role of theory differs sharply between testing and cognitive psychology.

The traditional construct validity concept, as noted by Bechtoldt (1959), confounds meaning with significance. According to Bechtoldt (1959), meaning and significance should depend on different aspects of the research process. Meaning concerns the nature of the construct in characterizing behavior. Bechtoldt emphasized operational definitions as determining meaning. Significance, in contrast, concerns the relationship of the construct to other constructs or variables, which is established by empirical relationships. Bechtoldt notes that in Cronbach & Meehl's (1955) conceptualization of construct validity, both meaning and significance are elaborated by the (empirical) nomological network. Thus, meaning depends on significance.

Two-part Conceptualization of Construct Validity

The two-part conceptualization distinguishes two aspects of construct validation: construct representation and nomothetic span (see Embretson, 1983). These two aspects are empirically separable because the supporting data is qualitatively different. Construct representation concerns the meaning of test scores. Construct meaning is elaborated by understanding the processes, strategies and knowledge that are used to solve items. Construct representation is supported by research that utilizes the methods of contemporary cognitive psychology. For example, alternative cognitive processing models for item solving can be examined by mathematical modeling of item difficulty and response time. Nomothetic span, in contrast, concerns construct significance. Here, the utility of the test for measuring individual differences is elaborated by the correlations of test scores with other measures. Nomothetic span research does not define test meaning, however. Instead, the correlations are a consequence of construct representation.

The two-part distinction in construct validation permits a direct role for cognitive theory. That is, since test score meaning is established in the construct representation phase, test items can be designed to reflect specified cognitive constructs. Consequently, items can be developed with stimulus features that have been shown to influence certain processes, strategies and knowledge structures. Nomothetic span, in turn, is influenced by test design because varying cognitive processes relate differentially to external variables.

Cognitive Design Systems

The cognitive design system framework (Embretson, 1988, 1995b, in press) utilizes the two-part conceptualization of construct validity to guide test development. In this framework, cognitive theory guides not only item development and selection,

Table 21.1 Overview of cognitive design systems

- I. Goals of measurement
  - Specify intended construct representation (meaning)
  - Specify intended nomothetic span (significance)
- II. Construct representation
  - Identify and operationalize cognitive constructs
    - Develop a cognitive model
      - Review cognitive process literature
      - Identify task-general and task-specific features
      - Empirically evaluate model
    - Evaluate operationalizations for psychometric potential
    - Specify item distributions on stimulus features
  - Generate items to fit specifications
  - Psychometric calibrations
    - Evaluate cognitive construct model for generated items
    - Calibrate items on underlying cognitive variables
    - Estimate processing abilities, strategies or knowledge for persons
- III. Nomothetic span
  - Hypothesize specific correlational structures, based on cognitive model
  - Test expectations with confirmatory approaches

but also the estimation of item and person parameters and the design of nomothetic span studies. Bejar (1993) elaborated a generative response modeling approach which is compatible with the cognitive design system framework. It will be described below.

Cognitive Design System Framework

The stages in the cognitive design system approach are shown in Table 21.1. The first stage, specifying the goals of measurement, is typical in traditional test development. In the cognitive design system framework, however, both construct representation and nomothetic span are specified. Construct representation refers explicitly to the processes, strategies and knowledge structures that should be involved in solving the items. Nomothetic span refers to the criteria that the test is expected to predict or diagnose. Here, expectations for test score correlations are developed from the intended construct representation.

The next stage concerns the construct representation of the test. A great diversity of effort falls within this stage. The cognitive constructs to be measured are identified and operationalized within this stage. A cognitive model is developed. Cognitive theory and literature are reviewed to select tasks and to define stimulus features that influence processing complexity. Once an item type is selected, further empirical studies may be needed. For example, a cognitive model can be evaluated by predicting item performance (i.e. accuracy or response time) from the item stimulus features. Of course, the psychometric potential, such as item fit to a psychometric model must also be evaluated. Taken together, these results impact the item specifications.

The results from the identification and operationalization stage are crucial to implementing cognitive theory in test design. First, item specifications result from interfacing the measurement goals with the cognitive modeling results. Item specifications contain details about the relative representation of item stimulus properties. Thus, stimulus properties that influence difficulty on targeted processes can be manipulated to control both the level and the source of item difficulty. Item stimulus properties that prompt irrelevant processes are controlled or eliminated. Second, construct validity is elaborated. Understanding the processing mechanisms that are involved in item solving establishes construct representation.

Once specifications have been determined, items can be generated to represent item specifications. A very complete set of specifications may allow for computerized item generation. Artificially generating items not only is efficient, but also further supports the cognitive model.

Although the construct representation stage seems similar to cognitive experimental research, two major differences exist. First, the research goals differ. In cognitive psychology, competing theories often are compared. In test development, the operationalization of the target constructs is evaluated. Second, the task domain is probably broader for psychometric items than for laboratory research tasks. Test items must have appropriate difficulty levels for measuring persons precisely at various ability levels. In contrast, cognitive psychology research tasks are often unrepresentative of the task domain. If tasks are selected to show differences between competing theories, tasks that are well explained under each theory would be excluded.

In the next substage, psychometric calibrations, the cognitive modeling results can be directly incorporated. Items are banked by their cognitive demands. This is a possibility because many cognitive psychometric models have been developed in item response theory (IRT). In IRT models, a person's response pattern is predicted from parameters for items and persons. The cognitive IRT models can incorporate a cognitive model into the psychometric calibrations.

The last stage shown in Table 21.1 is nomothetic span research. Like traditional construct validation research, nomothetic span research concerns individual differences correlations. However, unlike traditional construct validation, the strong program of construct validation (Cronbach, 1988) is emphasized. Specifically, the construct representation results provide strong hypotheses about the correlates of test scores. For example, if the items on alternative tests have been equated for cognitive demands, then equal correlations with other variables can be hypothesized. Or, for another example, if the processes underlying some reference tests have been studied as well, then correlations may be hypothesized from the shared common processes.

Generative Response Modeling

Bejar's (1993) generative response modeling focuses intensively on item development and the role of computerization. Bejar (1993) emphasizes both computer composed items and computer-assisted item generation. In both cases, cognitive specifications are formulated and operationalized. Then, items are composed to fulfill the specifications. He reports special success in generative modeling of spatial ability items. Mental rotation problems, for example, can be generated by specifying varying degrees and directions of rotation between a figure and target.

Other item types studied by Bejar (1993) for generative response modeling include hidden figure items, verbal analogies, vocabulary and the assessment of writing (Bejar, 1988).

Unlike the cognitive design system framework, Bejar (1993, 1996) focuses intensively on the item development phase. He is concerned with feedback systems to item writers, to influence not only specific item features, but also the design system that underlies item specifications. Traditionally, feedback to item writers is quite limited; delays of several months are typical and results are not accumulated systematically.

Bejar (1993) notes several advantages of a design-driven approach, including increased validity (i.e. construct representation), increased efficiency, increased synergy of psychological and instruction theories, and increased feasibility for automated scoring of constructed responses.

COGNITIVE PSYCHOMETRIC MODELS

In the last two decades, a very active area of psychometric research has been developing item response theory (IRT) models to incorporate cognitive variables. IRT is the psychometric basis for increasingly many ability tests. IRT is rapidly replacing classical test theory due to its many theoretical and practical advantages. Before presenting the cognitive IRT models, a very brief introduction to IRT is given below. More extended treatments are available in textbooks such as Hambleton, Swaminathan & Rogers (1991).

The traditional IRT models do not incorporate cognitive psychology variables. The cognitive IRT models, however, include parameters to represent cognitive theory variables. For example, some cognitive IRT models include parameters for the cognitive processing demands behind item difficulty, while other models include parameters for person differences on the underlying processes, strategies or knowledge structures. The advantages of the cognitive IRT models include (a) measurement of abilities that more closely reflect underlying cognitive processes, and (b) test assembly and item banking by the cognitive demands of items.

A Simple IRT Model

IRT models are mathematical models of the responses of persons to items or tasks. The IRT model contains parameters that represent the characteristics of the item and the abilities of the person. The probability that a person will pass or endorse a particular item depends jointly on ability level and on the item characteristics. In typical models, ability level and item difficulty combine additively, according to some function, to produce the probability that the item is endorsed or passed.

Many IRT models are based on the logistic distribution which gives the probability of a response in a simple expression. Specifically, if w_{ij} represents the parameters in the model, then the probability of success for person j on item i (i.e. $P(X_{ij} = 1|w_{ij})$), is given as follows:

$$P(X_{ij} = 1|w_{ij}) = \frac{\exp(w_{ij})}{1 + \exp(w_{ij})} \quad (1)$$

The exponent w_{ij} includes parameters to represent both the person and the item.

For example, the Rasch (1960) model predicts response potential as the simple difference between the item's difficulty, b_i, and the person's ability, θ_j, as follows:

$$w_{ij} = \theta_j - b_i \quad (2)$$

When plugged into equation 1, it can be seen that if the person's ability exceeds item difficulty, then the probability of passing is greater than .50. Conversely, if the person's ability falls below item difficulty, then the probability of passing is less than .50.

The Rasch (1960) IRT model is usually written as follows, combining equation 1 and equation 2:

$$P(X_{ij} = 1|\theta_j, b_i) = \frac{\exp(\theta_j - b_i)}{1 + \exp(\theta_j - b_i)} \quad (3)$$

The Rasch model is a very simple IRT model because it includes only one item parameter (i.e. item difficulty) to represent differences in items. Other models may add item characteristics, such as item discrimination and guessing to further model differences between items.

Item Characteristics Curves (ICC)

Equation 1 above will produce a probability of passing or endorsing the item for a person at any ability level. The predictions given by IRT models are typically summarized in an item characteristics curve (ICC) which regresses item solving probabilities on ability level. Figure 21.1 shows ICCs for four dichotomous items as specified from the two parameter logistic model. The ICCs are S-shaped. In the middle of the curve, large changes in item solving probability are observed for small ability changes, while at the extremes, item solving probabilities change very slowly with ability changes.

Although all the four ICCs have the same general shape, they differ in both location and slope. Location is indicated by item difficulty; however, notice that location is directly linked to ability level. For example, the ability level which has a probability of .50 for solving item 1 is much lower than for solving the other three items. Slope is indicated by item discrimination. It describes how rapidly the probabilities change with ability level. For item 2, the change is much slower. Thus, item 2 is less discriminating because item response probabilities are less responsive to changes in ability level. Notice also that the ICCs have upper and lower bounds (i.e. .00 to 1.00). In some IRT models, however, a more restricted range of probabilities is specified to accommodate features like guessing.

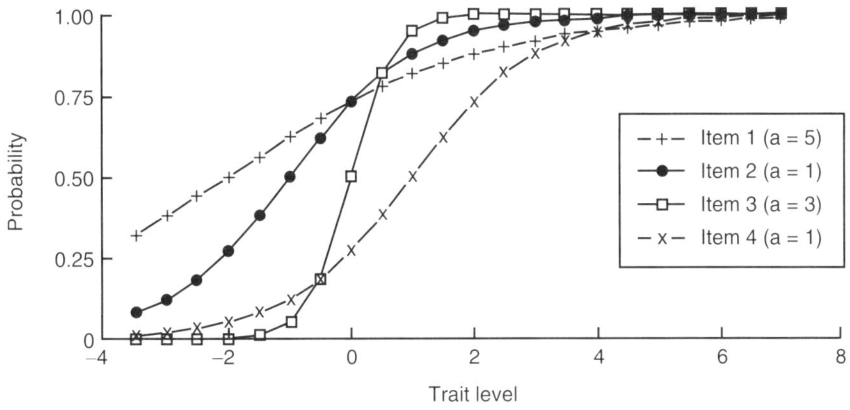

Figure 21.1 Item characteristics curves for four items

Advantages

The theoretical advantages of IRT models include:

1. conjoint scaling of items and persons
2. justifiable interval or ratio level scaling of persons
3. ability levels have item-referenced meaning which does not require norm distributions.

First, conjoint scaling means that persons and items are located on the same continuum, as shown in Figure 21.1. Item solving probabilities, such as in equation 1, depend on how much the person's ability level exceeds the item's difficulty. The same increase in item probabilities results from either increasing ability or decreasing item difficulty. Second, justification for interval level scaling derives from the conjoint measurement of persons and items. Andrich (1988) points out that conjoint additivity criterion for fundamental measurement is met directly by successful scaling with the Rasch model. Further, it can readily be shown that ability differences have invariant meaning across items (see Hambleton et al., 1991), a property which also derives from conjoint additivity. Third, ability level meaning may be referenced directly to the items. Probabilities can be predicted for each item that has been calibrated, including items that were not administered. Thus, ability levels have meaning by describing which items are at the person's threshold (where passing is as likely as failing) and which items are relatively easy or relatively hard.

The practical advantages of IRT stem from its capacity to handle missing data as well as its optimal theoretical properties. For example, a practical advantage that derives from interval level scaling is measuring individual change to reflect treatment or developmental effects. When interval level scaling is not obtained, as true for tests developed under classical test theory, change scores have paradoxical reliabilities, spurious correlations with initial scores and non-monotonic relationships to true change (see Bereiter, 1963). Another practical advantage derives from the link of ability level to item performance. Diagnostic feedback may be given about item or skill clusters that persons at an ability level find hard or easy. The practical advantages for missing data result from the conjoint measurement of persons and items. First, ability level estimates are readily comparable over different item sets, such as from different test forms or from computerized adaptive testing. Because item parameters are included in the model, person ability level estimates are implicitly controlled for the properties of the items that were administered. Second, population equating becomes less important in item calibration. Because ability levels are included in the model, item parameter estimates are implicitly controlled for the abilities of the calibration sample.

Cognitive IRT Models with a Single Ability

Notice that neither ability nor item difficulty in the Rasch model above is explicitly connected to cognitive parameters. The Rasch model will reflect cognitive processing only if the test items involve a single processing component. However, most ability test items are complex problem-solving tasks that involve multiple processing stages. If so, the Rasch model parameters will reflect a confounded composite of these influences, thus yielding parameters with unclear construct representation.

Linear Logistic Latent Trait Model

The linear logistic latent trait model (LLTM; Fischer, 1973) incorporates item stimulus features into the prediction of item success. For example, if the item stimulus features that influence processes are specified numerically (or categorically) for each item, as in a mathematical model of item accuracy, then the impact of processes in each item may be estimated directly:

$$w_{ij} = \theta_j - \textstyle\sum_k \tau_m q_{ik} \tag{4}$$

where q_{ik} is the value of stimulus feature k in item i, τ_k is the weight of stimulus feature k in item difficulty and θ_j is the ability for person j.

To give an example, consider the three cube folding items presented in Figure 21.2 from the Spatial Learning Ability Test (SLAT; Embretson, 1994a). Cube folding items are not only a well regarded task to measure of spatial visualization ability (Carroll, 1993), but they have long been studied by experimental methods (e.g. Shepard & Feng, 1971). In general, many studies support processing of spatial items as a mental analogue of a physical process. For SLAT items, a processing model with two spatial processing components, rotation and folding, as well as encoding and decision processing was supported (see Embretson, 1994a). Rotation involves aligning the stem and the response options. For the bottom item, the unfolded stem may be overlaid directly on the correct answer (#2), while the unfolded stem on the middle item must be rotated 90 degrees to be

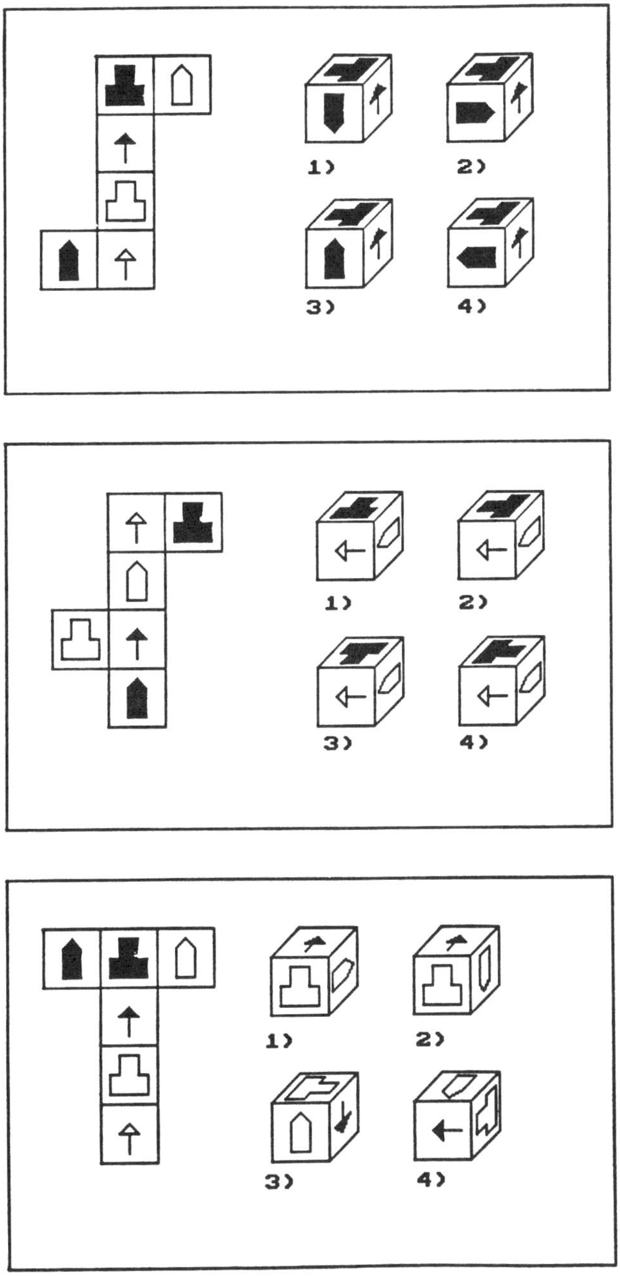

Figure 21.2 Three items from the Spatial Learning Ability Test

Table 21.2 LLTM Estimates for Spatial Visualization Items (SLAT)

Processing variable	Scored variable	LLTM Weight τ_m	LLTM SE
Confirmation processing			
Folding	Number of surfaces	.81**	.07
Rotation	Degrees rotation	.17**	.03
Falsification processing			
Folding	Number of surfaces	.01	.06
Rotation	Degrees rotation	−.13**	.03

** $p < 0.01$

overlaid on the correct answer (#2). Folding involves moving the third side into position. For the middle item all three surfaces in the correct answer are adjacent on the stem. Thus, only surface is carried in folding. In the top item, however, one surface is three surfaces away from the other two surfaces. Thus, three surfaces are carried to confirm the correct answer. Similarly, the distractors can also be characterized on these variables to determine the difficulty of falsifying them.

Multiple choice items involve both confirmation processing, for the correct answer, and falsification processing, for the distractors. For each SLAT item, the degree of rotation and the number of surfaces carried were scored for both the correct answer and the maximum distractor. Table 21.2 shows the LLTM estimates that were obtained (for details, see Embretson, 1994a). LLTM estimates are similar to regression weights for predicting item difficulty. Both spatial processes had significant weights in confirmation processing, while only degrees of rotation was significant for falsification. For a particular SLAT item, the weight times the scored value of a processing variable, $\tau_m q_{ik}$, describes the impact of the process on item difficulty. Thus, for an item requiring two surfaces to be carried, the contribution to difficulty from the folding process is 1.62 (i.e. (.81)(2)).

Models for Combining Speed and Accuracy

For many tests, performance depends on both accuracy and speed. For cognitive tests with tight time limits, for example, mental ability is a combination of power and speed. Several models have been proposed to incorporate speed and accuracy into the estimation of ability level. The probability of a correct response depends partly on the time involved in answering the item. Roskam (1997) & Verhelst, Verstralen & Jansen (1997) present various models which incorporate item response time into the prediction of item success. For some variants of these models, the only additional observation required is average or total item response time.

Cognitive IRT Models with Several Abilities

If ability test items are complex tasks with multiple processing stages, each stage may require a different ability. Multidimensional IRT models contain two or more abilities for each person. The cognitive IRT models contain design structures or mathematical models to link items to underlying cognitive variables. These design structures can be derived from cognitive psychology research to identify processes, strategies or knowledge structures from item responses. In this section, only a few models will be presented. Cognitive IRT modeling is a rapidly expanding area. This section cannot review all these developments, but several models will be mentioned here. The reader is referred to van der Linden & Hambleton's (1994) *Handbook of Modern Item Response Theory* for more details on several models.

Models for Independent Processing Components

MLTM and GLTM

The general component latent trait model (GLTM, Embretson, 1984) measures (a) persons' abilities on covert processing components, (b) item difficulties on covert processing components, and (c) the impact of item stimulus features on difficulty in processing components. GLTM, a generalization of MLTM (Whitely, 1980), is a non-compensatory model that is appropriate for tasks which require correct outcomes on several processing components.

GLTM combines a mathematical model of the response process with an IRT model. Item success is assumed to require success on *all* underlying components. If any component is failed, then the item is not successfully solved. Thus, GLTM gives the probability of success for person j on item i, X_{ijT}, as the product of successes on the underlying components, X_{ijm} as follows:

$$P(X_{ijT} = 1) = \Pi_m \, P(X_{ijm}) \tag{5}$$

Although the component outcomes are covert, they may be operationalized by subtasks or by special constraints on the GLTM model (i.e. without subtasks). Each component probability, in turn, depends on the person's ability and the item's difficulty on the component; that is, a Rasch model is behind each component probability. Further, like LLTM, GLTM includes a model of item (component) difficulty from the stimulus features. So, combining terms, GLTM is the following:

$$P(X_{ijT} = 1|w_{ijm}) = \Pi_m \frac{\exp(w_{ijm})}{1 + \exp(w_{ijm})} \tag{6}$$

And

$$w_{ijm} = \theta_{jm} - \textstyle\sum_k \tau_{km} q_{ikm}$$

where τ_{km} is the weight of stimulus factor k in component m, q_{ikm} is the score of stimulus factor k on component m for item i and θ_{jm} is the ability level of person j on component m.

To give an example, Maris (1995) applied MLTM to estimate two components that were postulated to underlie success on synonym items, generation and evaluation. The results had several implications. First, Maris' results further elaborated the construct representation of synonym items; the generation component was much stronger than the evaluation component in contributing to item solving. Second, overall ability on synonym items was decomposed into two more fundamental abilities, generation ability and evaluation ability. Thus, diagnostic information about the source of performance was differentiated by the relative strength of the two abilities. Third, the contributions of each component to the difficulty of each item could also be described. Such information is useful for selecting items to measure specified sources of difficulty.

Originally, both MLTM and GLTM required component responses, as well as the total item response, to estimate the component parameters. Now, however, GLTM can be applied to the total item task directly, without subtasks, if a strong cognitive model of item difficulty is available. An example will be given in the section on partial applications of cognitive theory.

Models for Contrasting Experimental Task Conditions

Several IRT models can identify abilities by contrasting a person's performance over varying conditions. These IRT models interface well with contemporary cognitive experiments that use within-subject designs in which each person receives several conditions. In these experiments, construct impact is estimated by comparing performance across conditions. A similar approach can be applied in testing to measure individual differences in construct impact. Calculating performance differences directly for a person, say by subtracting one score from another, has well-known psychometric limitations (see Bereiter, 1963). Some new cognitive IRT models, however, can provide psychometrically defensible alternatives. Several general models have been proposed including Adams & Wilson (1996), DiBello, Stout & Roussos (1995), Embretson (1994b, 1997a) and Meiser (1996). Like all structured IRT models, performance under a certain condition or occasion is postulated to depend on a specified combination of underlying abilities. Like confirmatory factor analysis, the specification is determined from theory.

These models may be illustrated by elaborating a special case, the multidimensional Rasch model for learning and change (MRMLC; Embretson, 1991). MRMLC measures a person's initial ability and one or more modifiabilities from repeated measurements. MRMLC contains a Wiener process design structure to relate the items to initial ability and the modifiabilities. The Wiener process structure is appropriate if ability variances increase or decrease across conditions, because it specifies increases (or decreases) in the number of dimensions. Complex cognitive data often have increasing variances over time (see Embretson, 1991).

In MRMLC, w_{ijk} refers to the potential for person j to pass item i when administered under condition k, as follows:

$$w_{i(k)j} = \sum_m \lambda_{i(k)m}\, \theta_{jm} - b_i \tag{7}$$

where θ_1 is initial ability level and $\theta_2, \ldots, \theta_M$ are modifiabilities between successive occasions or conditions and b_i is difficulty for item i. The weight $\lambda_{i(k)m}$

is the weight of ability m in item i under occasion k. In MRMLC the weight is specified as 0 or 1, depending on the occasion. The Wiener process design structure determines which ability is involved on each occasion. For three occasions the structure, Λ, is specified as follows:

		Ability		
	Occasion	θ_1	θ_2	θ_3
	1	1	0	0
$\Lambda =$	2	1	1	0
	3	1	1	1

Thus, on the first occasion, only initial ability is involved. On the second occasion, both initial ability and the first modifiability are involved.

Obviously, in the general models mentioned above, other design structures can be developed to represent specific comparisons or contrasts between conditions, such as trends, Helmert comparisons and more.

Models for Distinct Classes of Persons

Several IRT models can identify groups of persons that differ qualitatively in their response patterns. In many cognitive experiments, persons who have different knowledge bases or who apply different strategies differ in which tasks are passed or failed. That is, the relative difficulty of the task depends on which knowledge structure or strategy is being applied. For example, in many spatial ability tests, items may be solved by either a spatial or a verbal strategy. Or, for another example, suppose that the source of knowledge for an achievement test differs between persons (e.g. formal education versus practical experience). In both cases, what distinguishes groups is a different pattern of item difficulties.

Mixed Rasch Model

The mixed population Rasch model (MIRA; Rost, 1990) (a) defines the latent classes from response patterns, and (b) estimates class membership for the person, as well as ability level. In MIRA, IRT is combined with latent class analysis. The meaning of the ability level depends on the class because the item difficulties are ordered differently. The classes are mixed in the observed sample, according to a proportion, γ_h, for each latent class, as follows:

$$P(X_{ij} = 1|\theta_{jh}, b_{ih}) = \textstyle\sum_h \gamma_h \frac{\exp(w_{ijh})}{1 + \exp(w_{ijh})} \tag{8}$$

And

$$w_{ijh} = \theta_{jh} - b_{ih}$$

where θ_{jh} is the ability for person j in class h and b_{ih} is the difficulty of item i in class h. Advantages of applying MIRA include (a) increased knowledge of construct representation for the test, and (b) identification of a possible moderate variable (i.e. the latent class), that influences the prediction of criterion behaviors or other tasks.

McCollam (in press) applied MIRA to analyze item response data from SLAT (as shown on Figure 21.1) on a sample of young adults. Two latent classes were required to adequately model the response patterns that were observed. In the first class, the pattern of item difficulties was consistent with spatial processing demands, hence this class was interpreted as a spatial processing strategy. The data indicated that 65% of the sample belonged to this class. In the second class, the pattern of item difficulties were consistent with a verbal-analytic processing strategy. The remaining 35% of the sample belonged to this class. Thus, these results suggested qualitative, as well as quantitative, differences between persons. That is, for a large percentage of the sample, spatial abilities reflect successful verbal-analytic processing rather than spatial processing. The results not only reflect a widely held hypothesis about spatial processing, but further allow assessment of individuals for processing strategies.

SALTUS

Another model that combines traits and classes is the SALTUS model. SALTUS (which means to "leap" in Latin) was proposed for developmental or mastery data (Wilson, 1989). Such data does not fit a traditional IRT model because stage attainment implies a sudden increase in success on an entire class of items. For example, some developmental tasks, such as the balance task, involve distinctly different types of rules at different stages. When a rule is mastered, the probabilities for solving items that involve the rule shifts dramatically. SALTUS extends IRT to cognitive task data that otherwise would not fit the models.

Cognitive Diagnostic Assessment

The rule space methodology (Tatsuoka, 1983, 1984, 1985) classifies persons on the basis of their knowledge states, as well as measures overall ability level. For example, a person's score on a mathematical test indicates overall performance levels, but does not usually diagnose processes or knowledge structures that need remediation. The rule space methodology provides diagnostic information about the meaning of a person's response pattern. The meaningfulness of the diagnostic assessment depends directly on the quality of the cognitive theory behind the attributes and resulting knowledge states. The rule space methodology has been applied to both ability and achievement tests, and to both verbal (Buck, Tatsuoka & Kostin, in press) and non-verbal tests (Tatsuoka, Solomonson & Singley, in press).

A basic rule space is defined by two dimensions, the ability level (namely, θ_j from an IRT model), and by a fit index (ζ_j). Ability, of course, represents overall

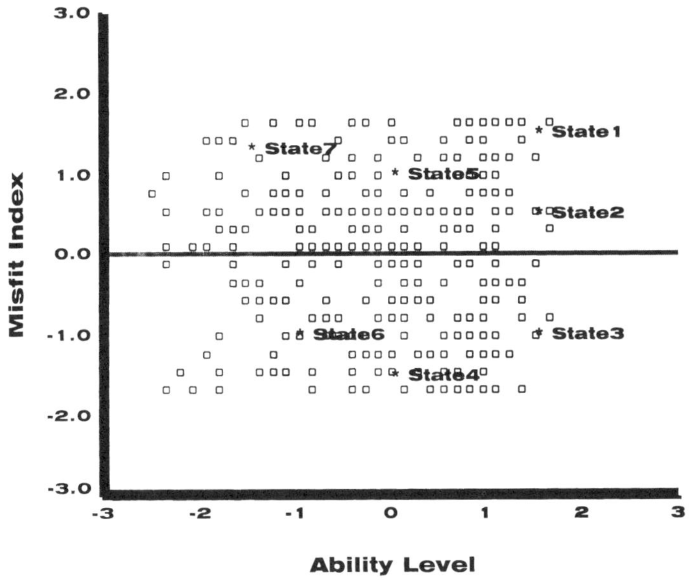

Figure 21.3 A hypothetical rule space with three hundred examinees and seven knowledge states

performance, and the fit index measures the typicality of the person's response pattern. For example, passing hard items and failing easy items is an atypical response pattern that would yield an extreme value for a fit index. Fit indices are calculated by comparing the person's response pattern to the predictions given by the IRT model.

Figure 21.3 plots both persons and knowledge states into the rule space from ability level and fit. Persons are classified into knowledge states by the distances of their response patterns from the locations of the knowledge states. Obviously, persons are plotted directly on the rule space because both ability level and fit are estimated. Locating a knowledge state requires some intermediate steps. First, an attribute incidence matrix is scored to reflect which attributes are required to solve each item. This is the first step in which cognitive theory is implemented. Second, knowledge states are defined from patterns of attributes. Knowledge states are extracted empirically by applying a Boolean clustering algorithm to the attribute incidence matrix. Third, an ideal response pattern is generated for each knowledge state; that is, the ideal response pattern specifies the items that are passed and failed by someone in the knowledge state. Fourth, the ideal response pattern is located in the rule space to represent the knowledge state. Like a person, an ideal response pattern can be scored for ability (i.e. from total number of items passed) and for a fit index.

An alternative method for extracting knowledge states from item attribute patterns has been developed recently. Sheehan (in press) uses a tree-based regression to clusters of items that reflect knowledge states. The classes of items are located on the item difficulty scale. Diagnostic meaning for a person's ability is derived from the attributes in items that lie above, below and just at their ability level.

APPLICATIONS: PARTIAL

Cognitive psychology is influencing testing in many areas. However, most applications must be classified as partial. That is, the application does not extend over the full range of test development activities, such as shown on Table 21.1. Many partial applications, however, are significantly changing testing operations and such applications eventually may become more extended. In this section, prototypic applications of cognitive theory in several areas are elaborated.

Specifying Goals of Measurement

Support for traditional construct validation was derived primarily from individual differences relationships; hence, the goals of measurement often emphasized the expected correlations of test scores. So, for example, the Scholastic Aptitude Test was developed to measure the cognitive skills that were important in first year college grades. Or, the goals of measurement emphasized expected factorial structure, which again reflects test score correlations.

More recently, however, construct representation has become a central issue. For example, in education, Wittrock & Baker (1991, p. 1) view cognitive psychology as important for measurement because "students' thought processes mediate the effects of teaching upon achievement." Measurement goals that reflect cognitive psychology include learning strategies and metacognition (Weinstein & Meyer (1991), mathematical thinking skills, organization and structure (Collis & Romberg, 1991), critical aspects of expert performance (Glaser, 1991) and components of intelligence, including metacomponents, performance components and knowledge-acquisition components (Sternberg, 1991). To operationalize these goals effectively, measurement tasks that require constructed responses, such as performance tasks, completion and open response tasks and writing samples, have been emphasized.

Similarly, in psychology, construct representation is increasingly emphasized in ability measurement. For example, Sternberg's (1985) triarchic theory of intelligence emphasizes both cognitive components and learning, both of which are connected to cognitive psychology. One influence of Sternberg's (1985) and other cognitive theories, has been to enhance descriptions of measurement goals and interpretations for test scores. For example, ability test scores are described as reflecting parallel versus serial processing, cognitive consistency, executive processing and so forth (e.g. Kaufman & Kaufman, 1993). However, by and large, for most tests the items were not developed explicitly to operationalize cognitive psychology constructs. Further, the relative representation specific cognitive constructs in the items is unknown.

Identifying and Operationalizing Cognitive Components

Developing Cognitive Models: General Versus Specific Item Features

In several studies, cognitive theory models are used to explicate differences between alternative measurement tasks. Research on mathematical ability and achievement testing has been particularly active. For example, Katz, Friedman, Bennett & Berger (1996) compared the multiple choice format to a constructed response format (i.e. the answer must be supplied by the examinee) for items with the same stem. Katz et al. (1996) compared the formats for the frequency with which various problem-solving strategies are applied. Similarly, Sebrechts, Enright, Bennett & Martin (1996) modeled the difficulty of both constructed response and multiple choice word problems (from the Graduate Record Exam (GRE)) by problem-solving strategies, complexity of mathematical structure and linguistic complexity. Some differences in the relative importance of the underlying variables was observed.

Another constructed response item, underdetermined algebra word problems, was compared to traditional well-defined word problems by using cognitive modeling (Nhouyvanisvong, Katz & Singley, 1997). In underdetermined word problems, a unique solution is not possible; instead, the examinee is asked to produce examples of possible solutions. Nhouyvanisvong et al. (1997) compared the two versions of the task for six cognitive processes, according to postulated task models. Their results suggested that the constructed response format not only taps new processes, but also places greater emphasis on processes that are under represented in existing assessments of mathematical ability.

Cognitive theory also can guide the development of new item types. For example, the cognitive literature on mathematical problem solving has often emphasized schema or quantitative representations. Bennett & Sebrechts (1997) developed a computerized sorting task to measure quantitative representations. In this task, examinees sort mathematical word problems into categories by underlying mathematical structures. Bennett & Sebrechts (1997) results supported task validity, because sorting accuracy was highly correlated with other ability measures.

Generating Items to Fit Specifications

Computerized generation of items is currently an active area in testing. Computerized item generation is most successfully implemented when a strong cognitive theory underlies the items. Such a theory must not only specify the stimulus features that impact processing difficulty, but also should predict item difficulty. The several advantages for testing include:

1. generation of items for a specific difficulty level, as needed for optimal measurement of each examinee
2. support for the construct representation aspect of validity

3. exclusion of stimulus features that influence processes that are irrelevant to the goals of measurements
4. practical economy, items are generated quickly and inexpensively.

Some item types that have been successfully generated include mental rotation items (Bejar, 1990; Embretson, 1994b), progressive matrix problems (Embretson, in press; Hornke & Habon, 1986), hidden figures (Bejar & Yocom, 1991), mathematical items (Hively, Patterson & Page, 1968) and many others. In fact, in the United Kingdom, item generation has been applied on operational tests (see Irvine, Dunn & Anderson, 1989).

To illustrate item generation, consider a spatial visualization task in which a complex visual figure must be compared for identity to a rotated target, such as shown on Figure 21.2. Various cognitive theories have been developed (e.g. Just & Carpenter, 1985; Kosslyn, 1978) for mental rotation tasks. Most theories postulate a mental analogue process to explain why physical angular disparity between the initial and target figures predicts processing difficulty. Bejar & Yocom (1991) generated spatial visualization items with well predicted item difficulties by (a) specifying a set of three-dimensional figures, and (b) systematically varying the angular disparity.

Other item types involve more elaborate specifications. Generating complex non-verbal items, such as progressive matrices, requires a design system for relationships, as well as a theory about how the relationships influence processing difficulty (see ART in complete applications below). Generating verbal item types, such as verbal analogies, will require specifying some semantic features, which in turn requires more detailed knowledge about semantic memory (see Bejar, Chaffin & Embretson, 1991). Generating verbal comprehension items, in which questions are answered about a paragraph, requires viable theories about propositional meaning and syntactic processing difficulty, as well as comprehension processing.

Psychometric Calibrations

Evaluating Cognitive Models on Test Items

For many item types, specific cognitive models have been evaluated. Stimulus features that operationalize sources of processing difficulty are the independent variables in mathematical modeling item difficulty or response time. If sufficiently good prediction is obtained, several potential advantages for testing include:

1. increasing construct validity by elaborating construct representation
2. providing a set of stimulus features that may be useful for computerized item generation
3. providing cognitive indices for item banking. This advantage results from applying an appropriate cognitive psychometric model, which will be elaborated below.

Sheehan & Mislevy (1990) apply cognitive modeling to explain performance on a complex verbal item type, document literacy items. In these items, examinees locate and use information from a non-prose document (e.g. labels, forms, tables and so forth) to answer questions (i.e. the task directive). Table 21.2 shows three types of variables that were operationalized, materials (MAT, the document), task directives (DIR, the question asked) and processes (PROC). Kirsch & Mosenthal's (1988) four-stage processing model was applied to characterize processing difficulty. Operationalized processing variables included degree of correspondence between the document and the directive (DEGCORR), type and number of restricting features that must be maintained in working memory (TYPINFO), and amount of semantic information shared between document and directive (DEGPLAUS). Mosenthal's (1985) taxonomic grammar of exposition was applied to parse the documents and the task directive into organizational categories (OCs) and specific categories (SPEs). Number of categories was scored for both the document and directive, and the number of embedded categories (EMB) was also scored for the document.

Table 21.2 shows that good prediction was obtained from the complete model, with an overall R^2 of .81. Table 21.2 also shows that the largest prediction weights were observed for the amount of shared semantic information (DEGPLAUS) and the number of specific semantic categories (SPEs). Since these weights are derived from LLTM, the semantic and processing features may be used to bank the items by sources of difficulty.

Numerous other item types have been modeled. To mention just a few examples, difficulties have been modeled for paragraph comprehension (Embretson & Wetzel, 1987), verbal analogies (Embretson, Schneider & Roth, 1985; Sternberg, 1977), verbal classifications (Whitely, 1981), geometric analogies (Mulholland, Pellegrino & Glaser, 1980), mathematical word problems (Embretson, 1995a; Sheehan, in press) and synonym tasks (Janssen & de Boeck, 1997).

Calibrating Items on Underlying Cognitive Variables

A special advantage of cognitive psychometric modeling is that items may be banked by their sources of cognitive demand. This information is useful for maintaining representation of various cognitive demands in different tests. Models such as LLTM, GLTM and SALTUS, as discussed above, contain indicators that are useful for balancing processes or strategies across items.

For LLTM, obtaining the cognitive demands is computed by multiplying the LLTM weight by the value of the stimulus feature in the item. On Table 21.2, for example, the item's score on DEGPLAUS multiplied by .36 indicates the contribution of this processing feature to item difficulty. Similarly, the impact of the other eight features shown on Table 21.2 can be obtained for each item. These indices are useful for test assembly and item selection. Features can be balanced to best reflect the desired construct representation across test forms. Similarly, results from applying GLTM and SALTUS models, respectively, permits items to be balanced for component difficulty or stage-wise sensitivity. For each item type that was mentioned above, at least one study specifically applied a cognitive psychometric model to complex psychometric items.

Person Measurement

Cognitive psychology theories can influence psychometric calibrations for persons in two ways: (a) the type of variables that can be measured from test responses, and (b) the use of artificial intelligence in scoring constructed responses. Although the potential applicability of cognitive theory to person measurement seemingly is significant, actual operational applications are difficult to find.

New types of variables may be measured when cognitive psychology theory is implemented in a cognitive psychometric model. Individual differences in response patterns (i.e. the exact items that are passed or failed) can assess strategies, knowledge structures or processing components. As shown in the section on cognitive psychometric models, assessments of strategy probabilities (mixed Rasch model), developmental level (SALTUS), component processing abilities (GLTM), and so forth, are possible. To date, however, the cognitive psychometric models have been applied mainly for construct validity research rather than for person measurement in existing tests.

In some ways, obtaining multiple measurements from the same items defies conventional practice in selecting items for cognitive ability tests. That is, ability items are selected for their high saturation on a single dimension. Scoring multiple indicators from the same items is feasible only if two or more dimensions are reflected in item solution. Although IRT models for multidimensional data have long been available, only recently has implementation of multidimensional psychometric models in computerized adaptive testing been seriously considered (see Segall, 1996).

Cognitive theories, of course, view complex problem-solving tasks as requiring multiple processing components, strategies and knowledge structures. Individuals may differ in their pattern of component capabilities; thus, item responses would be multidimensional. Rather different cognitive capabilities can be measured from the same item type. For example, the primary source of difficulty for verbal analogies could be encoding (if items have high vocabulary levels), relational inferences (if the relationships are obscure) or response evaluation (if the response options are similar).

Traditional test development handles multidimensionality by selecting items that are highly intercorrelated. Items fit unidimensional IRT models not necessarily because they measure a single aspect of processing. Items with similar patterns of skills also will fit unidimensional models. But, because the item specifications for most tests have not considered such skills explicitly, cognitive psychometric modeling provides useful elaborations of their construct representation. Cognitive psychometric models results are even more useful for guiding item selection. However, rarely have they been applied during item development.

Several examples of cognitive psychometric modeling for enhanced construct representation are available. Birenbaum & Tatsuoka (1993) applied the rule space method to diagnose procedural bugs in basic mathematical skills, such as elaborated by Brown & Burton (1978). Students' knowledge states and their overall performance level was assessed on exponential operations. The 25 most frequent knowledge states varied not only in the number of buggy operations, but also in which operations were not mastered. Embretson & McCollam (in press) applied GLTM to measure the relative impact of working memory capacity versus executive processes on age-related declines in spatial visualization. Contrary to some previous studies, executive processing was an important source of individual differences in performance. Embretson (1995c) applied GLTM to estimate the relative impact of working capacity versus executive processing differences on abstract reasoning. Again, executive processes were the most important source of individual differences. McCollam (in press) applied MIRA to spatial visualization items. Two classes of examinees that differed qualitatively in solution strategies were identified. The patterns of item difficulties within the two classes reflected the well-known distinction in cognitive psychology between spatial analogue and verbal-analytic processing strategies. Thus, performance on the same test may reflect qualitatively different abilities for different examinees.

For constructed response items, in which the examinee produces rather than chooses a response, cognitive psychology theories can provide meaningful frameworks for computerized scoring. For example, Singley & Bennett (1995) applied cognitive theory in a computer-based scoring system for mathematical word problems. In these word problems, examinees supplied the work leading to their solution, as well as their answer. Schema theory was applied to score work leading to solution. Two advantages of Singley & Bennett's approach are (a) partial credit may be given for right components (even with an erroneous outcome), and (b) diagnostic information is available about the solution process. Similarly, Burstein et al. (1997) applied a computer-based scoring system for writing samples. Writing samples are now included on some large volume tests. Writing samples are expensive because human raters must be hired to evaluate them. Burstein et al. (1997) developed empirical indices of writing, including syntactic complexity, topical content, and so forth, that had agreement as high as 95% with human raters. It should be noted that the Burstein et al. (1997) indices are *not* tied to cognitive psychology or psycholinguistic constructs. Consequently, it would be difficult to justify the indices as defining writing quality. However, many indices seem highly related to operationalizations of cognitive constructs, so additional theoretical work could increase construct representation.

Nomothetic Span and Test Interpretation

Increasingly, cognitive constructs are guiding nomothetic span studies on existing tests. To give one example, Kyllonen & Christal (1990) examine the role of working memory capacity in the general intelligence, a factor that underlies many ability test batteries. In a series of four studies, Kyllonen & Christal (1990) applied confirmatory factor analysis to evaluate hypotheses about the relationship of working memory capacity to general intelligence. Many different tasks were used to measure working memory capacity, including tasks borrowed from cognitive psychology experiments. They found very high correlations between working memory and general intelligence (.90s), which suggested that intelligence is little more than working memory capacity. For other examples, the studies mentioned above on person measurement also include results that are relevant to nomothetic span.

APPLICATIONS: EXTENSIVELY DESIGNED TESTS

In this section, tests and test batteries that were developed by applying cognitive theory extensively in both the construct representation and the nomothetic span phases of construct validation will be described. The three examples described below represent systematic approaches to incorporating cognitive psychology into test development. As will be shown, these applications differ substantially in the type of cognitive theory that is applied, the method for operationalizing cognitive theory and the relative emphasis of the various stages in the cognitive design system framework. It should be noted that, with the exception of the Das*Naglieri Cognitive Assessment System, these tests are not yet available to test users.

This section is not intended to exhaustively review tests for application of cognitive theory. Literally thousands of ability tests have been developed and reviewing the role of cognitive theory is a substantial undertaking, which is clearly beyond the scope of this chapter.

Cognitive Abilities Measurement (CAM) from Project LAMP

The Learning Abilities Measurement Project (LAMP) is a large scale effort by the Air Force Armstrong Laboratory to develop cognitive ability measures that are grounded in cognitive theory. A major goal was measuring abilities that are closely related to learning. According to Kyllonen (1994), LAMP has met its goal. Not only does Cognitive Abilities Measurement (CAM) battery predict various learning tasks, but it does so better than the military ability selection test, the Armed Services Vocational Aptitude Battery (ASVAB). Unfortunately, some details of CAM are not readily accessible for two reasons: (a) CAM is still under development and has not yet been implemented, and (b) CAM is a military test and certain testing details may be unavailable to maintain test security.

The construct representation of CAM was clearly based on cognitive theory. Initially, a four source global model was postulated to span various aspects of cognitive theory. The four sources are processing speed, working memory, declarative knowledge, and procedural knowledge. Further, to represent factor analytic findings on the importance of modality, the CAM taxonomy also included three content modalities; verbal, quantitative, and spatial. Thus, the original 4×3 CAM taxonomy included twelve different types of tests. Later, declarative learning and procedural learning sources were added to the CAM model, which became a 6×3 taxonomy. Tests were developed to fit within the categories. Many tests reflected task paradigms that were applied in cognitive experimental research while many others were adaptations (see Kyllonen, 1993).

The processing speed and working memory categories were designed to reflect information processing resources, and hence employed simple, overlearned stimulus material. For example, Baddeley's (1968) ABCD order task measures working memory in the verbal modality. For example, sentences such as "A precedes B" and "C does not precede D" are contained on the task. Alternative tests were developed for each category. For example, Daneman & Carpenter's (1980) reading span task and a word span task are also verbal working memory tests.

The declarative knowledge and procedural knowledge tests were designed to represent information resources that are available to a person. Kyllonen & Christal (1989) note that knowledge can vary between persons in several ways, including depth, breadth, accessibility and organization.

Although many CAM item types were drawn from cognitive psychology research, the details of item development are unclear. For example, item specifications to define varying and constant features across items are not available. Consequently, the impact of specific item features on item difficulty are unknown.

Psychometric calibrations of CAM tests varied across categories in the taxonomy. According to Kyllonen (1994), CAM scores are number correct for tests in which deadlines are unimportant (e.g. knowledge tests) and for tests with fixed deadlines (e.g. working memory tests). Normative standard scores can be derived from linear transformations of number correct scores. To date, CAM has applied classical test theory rather than IRT to calibrate persons and items. For tests with no deadlines, but where speed is important (e.g. the processing speed tests), indices that combine both speed and accuracy have been developed. For example, percentage correct divided by mean latency is one such index.

Nomothetic span studies on CAM were clearly derived from construct representation. Several predictions can be derived (Kyllonen, 1994; Kyllonen & Christal, 1990) based on the construct representation of CAM. These predictions are implemented in confirmatory factor analyses of the correlations of CAM with various external measures. The 4×3 cognitive resources model was not only supported, but correlations with external measurements (namely, ASVAB) supported the generality of the functions measured by CAM (Kyllonen, 1993).

Das*Naglieri Cognitive Assessment System

The Das*Naglieri Cognitive Assessment System (CAS, Das & Naglieri, 1997) represents the PASS theory (Das, Naglieri & Kirby, 1994) of cognitive processing. The PASS theory combines both theoretical and applied psychology concerns. Theoretically, PASS is based on Luria's (1966) neurologically based theory of functional units in the brain rather than on information-processing theories, like CAM above. PASS also was designed to address applied issues, such as the assessment of learning disabilities and retardation, as well as remedial interventions in education.

The PASS theory includes four areas of cognitive functioning; planning, attention, successive processing, and simultaneous processing, which are elaborated by Das & Naglieri (1997, pp. 140–3), as follows. *Planning* involves determining, selecting, and using efficient solutions to problems. Planning includes executive processes in problem solving, such as formulating alternatives, monitoring and evaluating processes. Tasks that require conscious processing or a solution strategy require planning. *Attention*, on the other hand, involves selectively attending to a particular stimulus and not attending to competing stimuli. High levels of attentional processing are involved when the non-target stimuli are more salient than the target stimuli. *Simultaneous processing* involves integrating stimuli into groups. Non-verbal tasks, such as progressive matrices and block designs, as well as logical verbal questions, involve simultaneous processing. Finally, *successive processing* involves integrating stimuli into a serial order. Linguistic tasks that require processing stimulus order involve successive processing.

In contrast to CAM, in which many item types were based on task paradigms in experimental cognitive psychology, item types for the CAS were designed or selected to fit the PASS definitions. However, like CAM, the contribution of specific stimulus features to item difficulty is unclear. Thus, the operationalization of the theory is not specific.

Nomothetic span studies on PASS and on the various CAS tasks have included diverse data, such as sensitivity to remediation, group differences, and correlations with external measurements (Das & Naglieri, 1997). The studies primarily involve confirmatory approaches, in which hypotheses about relationships are derived directly from PASS.

Tests from the Cognitive Design System Approach: ART and SLAT

Two tests, the Abstract Reasoning Test (ART; Embretson, in press) and the Spatial Learning Ability Test (SLAT; Embretson, 1994a) were developed to illustrate the cognitive design system approach shown on Table 21.1. The item types for ART and SLAT were selected from psychometric research, rather than from cognitive theory. They have been used on several popular cognitive ability tests. ART contains progressive matrix items, which have been used for several decades to measure fluid or abstract intelligence (see Raven, Court & Raven, 1992). SLAT contains cube folding items, which have appeared routinely on tests for spatial visualization, such as the spatial test on the differential ability test. However, the specific items on ART and SLAT were designed by cognitive theory. ART and SLAT items were generated analytically by specifying design features that were known to control processing difficulty.

The test development process for ART and SLAT began with developing cognitive models that predicted item difficulty. The cognitive model for ART is a simplification of Carpenter, Just & Shell's (1990) theory of processing progressive matrix problems. A single variable, working memory load, predicts item difficulty quite well (Embretson, in press). For SLAT, the cognitive model was based on spatial processing theories that stress mental rotation and folding as analogue processes. A cognitive model that quantified the degrees of rotation and the number of surfaces carried in folding provided strong prediction of item difficulty (Embretson, 1994a).

For both ART and SLAT, item generation followed from item specifications that included specific sources of processing difficulty. In ART, the number and types of relationships for each problem were specified in a formal notational system for each matrix item. Five structurally equivalent items were generated by combining objects and attributes to fulfill the notational specifications. Certain drawing features were also specified for the structurally equivalent items. In SLAT, items were generated by crossing features in a 3 (degrees of rotation) × 3 (number of surfaces carried) design. Thus, SLAT contains nine structurally different problem types. The perceptual markings that uniquely identified each side of the cube varied across problems.

Psychometric calibrations for both ART and SLAT reflected the design principles directly. Cognitive psychometric models were applied to estimate cognitive demand in each item. Thus, both ART and SLAT items were banked by design features, as well as by empirical item difficulty levels.

Nomothetic span studies for both ART and SLAT were guided by construct representation. For ART, hypotheses about both factor structure (Embretson, in press) and processing salience (Embretson, 1995c) were derived from ART's representation of working memory load. For SLAT, the specifications were designed to elimination verbal processing strategies. A series of studies showed that SLAT was a more pure measure of spatial processing than other available spatial visualization tests (Embretson, 1997b).

SUMMARY AND CONCLUSION

As shown in this review, cognitive psychology principles have rarely been applied extensively in testing. Although cognitive psychology has inspired new frameworks to guide testing, as well as many new psychometric models for calibrating persons and items, extensive applications to actual tests have been few and far between. More often, cognitive theory has been applied to specific research issues in testing, such as enhancing construct validity or specifying goals of measurement. Although, on the surface, the current impact seems discouraging, the situation could change soon.

Although testing is often slow to apply new developments, tests do indeed change. New methods are applied slowly in testing because stable methods benefit testing by yielding scores that are comparable across time. Consider, for example, the history of item response theory in testing. IRT models have been available since the 1960s (Lord & Novick, 1968; Rasch, 1960) and a solid research base for applications was available by 1980. However, only recently has IRT been applied extensively. But, now IRT applications are snowballing due primarily to computer administration of tests. That is, computerized test administration is now the practical and efficient method of test delivery. Some major advantages of IRT, such as adaptive testing, now may be fully realized.

The role of cognitive psychology in testing seems analogous to the role of IRT in testing several years ago. Like IRT, the basic developments for applying cognitive psychology to testing are now available. More than half of this chapter reviewed research on methodological frameworks and psychometric models needed to implement cognitive psychology in testing. Also, like IRT, technology is creating opportunities that are best addressed by cognitive psychology.

Several factors are currently impacting testing. First, computerized versions of paper and pencil items sometimes significantly change the task. When computerization of a test must be implemented rapidly, cognitive psychology principles can guide design issues in the computerized version. Consider the case of the test of English as a foreign language (TOEFL) which is being fully computerized soon. Computerizing the long text comprehension items, for example, requires decisions about how to display the text and the questions. On the paper and pencil version, the long text appears over two pages, followed by the questions. On the computerized version, viewing a long text requires scrolling. On the paper and pencil version, questions can be read by a quick glance to the next page. Where should the questions be placed? If the questions follow the text on the computerized version, scrolling will be required. If the questions appear on the right side of a split screen, do scanning and searching become more salient processes? Which processes are most consistent with the goals of measurement? Second, computerized adaptive testing is creating demand for large numbers of new items. To maintain test security and to measure examinees precisely, many items at each difficulty level are needed. Methods to generate items by computer are being seriously considered to help create the vast number of items that are needed. Again, applying cognitive psychology models to generate items can yield items with known difficulty levels and validity. Third, diagnostic feedback about test performance is becoming increasingly demanded by examinees. Information about why items are failed is desired. Embedding cognitive psychology principles in items provides a meaningful basis for interpreting performance deficits. That is, the failures of specific processes, strategies or knowledge structures can be indicated, and examples can be provided.

Taken together, these influences suggest a prediction. Ten years hence, when perhaps another "Handbook of Applied Cognitive Psychology" appears, cognitive psychology could be mainstream in test development.

NOTE

Susan Embretson has published previously as Susan E. Whitely.

REFERENCES

Adams, R. A. & Wilson, M. (1996). Formulating the Rasch model as a mixed coefficients multinomial logit. In G. Engelhard & M. Wilson (Eds), *Objective Measurement III: Theory into Practice*. Norwood, NJ: Ablex.

Andrich, D. (1988). *Rasch Models for Measurement*. Newbury Park, CA: Sage.

Baddeley, A. C. (1968). A 3 min reasoning test based on grammatical transformation. *Psychonomic Science*, 10, 341–2.

Bechtold, H. (1959). Construct validity: a critique. *American Psychologist*, 14, 619–29.

Bejar, I. I. (1988). A sentence-based automated approach to the assessment of writing: a feasibility study. *Machine-Mediated Learning*, 2, 321–32.

Bejar, I. I. (1990). A generative analysis of a three-dimensional spatial task. *Applied Psychological Measurement*, 14, 237–46.

Bejar, I. I. (1993). In N. Frederiksen, R. Mislevy & I. Bejar (Eds), *Test Theory for a New Generation of Tests*. Hillsdale, NJ: Lawrence Erlbaum.

Bejar, I. I. (1996). Generative response modeling: leveraging the computer as a test delivery medium. (Research Report No. RR-96-13). Princeton, NJ: Educational Testing Service.

Bejar, I. I., Chaffin, R. & Embretson, S. E. (1991). *Cognitive and Psychometric Analysis of Analogical Problem Solving*. New York: Springer-Verlag.

Bejar, I. I. & Yocom, P. (1991). A generative approach to the modeling of isomorphic hidden-figure items. *Applied Psychological Measurement*, 15, 129–38.

Bennett, R. E. & Sebrechts, M. M. (1997). A computer-based task for measuring the representational component of quantitative proficiency. *Journal of Educational Measurement*, 34, 211–19.

Bereiter, C. (1963). Some persisting dilemmas in the measurement of change. In C. W. Harris (Ed.), *Problems in Measuring Change* (pp. 3–20). Madison: University of Wisconsin Press.

Birenbaum, M. & Tatsuoka, K. K. (1993). Applying an IRT-based cognitive diagnostic model to diagnose students' knowledge states in multiplication and division with exponents. *Applied Measurement in Education*, 6, 255–68.

Brown, J. S. & Burton, R. R. (1978). Diagnostic models for procedural bugs in basic mathematical skills. *Cognitive Science*, 2, 155–92.

Buck, G., Tatsuoka, K. & Kostin, I. (in press). Exploratory rule space analysis of the test of English for international communication. *Journal of Language and Teaching*.

Burstein, J., Braden-Harder, L., Chodorow, M., Hua, S., Kaplan, B., Kukich, K., Lu, C., Nolan, J., Rock, D. & Wolff, S. (1997). Computer analysis of essay content for automated score prediction. Final Report for Graduate Record Exam. Princeton, NJ: Educational Testing Service.

Carpenter, P. A., Just, M. A. & Shell, P. (1990). What one intelligence test measures: a theoretical account of processing in the Raven's Progressive Matrices Test. *Psychological Review*, 97.

Carroll, J. B. (1994). *Human Cognitive Abilities: A Survey of Factor-analytic Studies*. New York: Cambridge University Press.

Carroll, J. B. & Maxwell, S. (1979). Individual differences in ability. *Annual Review of Psychology*, 603–40.

Collis, K. & Romberg, T. A. (1991). Assessment of mathematical performance: an analysis of open-ended test items. In M. C. Wittrock & E. L. Baker (Eds), *Testing and Cognition* (pp. 82–130). Englewood Cliffs, NJ: Prentice Hall.

Cronbach, L. (1988). Five perspectives on the validity argument. In H. Wainer & H. I. Brown (Eds), *Test Validity*. Hillsdale, NJ: Erlbaum.

Cronbach, L. J. & Meehl, P. E. (1955). Construct validity in psychological tests. *Psychological Bulletin*, 52, 281–302.

Daneman, M. & Carpenter, P. A. (1980). Individual differences in working memory and reading. *Journal of Verbal Learning & Verbal Behavior*, 19 (4), 450–66.

Das, J. P., Naglieri, J. A. & Kirby, J. R. (1994). *Assessment of Cognitive Processes*. Needham Heights, MA: Allyn & Bacon.

Das, J. P. & Naglieri, J. A. (1997). Intelligence revised: the planning, attention, simultaneous, successive (PASS) cognitive processing theory. In R. F. Dillon (Ed.), *Handbook on Testing* (pp. 136–63). Westport, CT: Greenwood Press.

DiBello, L. V., Stout, W. F. & Roussos, L. (1995). Unified cognitive psychometric assessment likelihood-based classification techniques. In P. D. Nichols, S. F. Chipman & R. L. Brennan (Eds), *Cognitively Diagnostic Assessment*. Hillsdale, NJ: Erlbaum.

Embretson, S. E. (1983). Construct validity: construct representation versus nomothetic span. *Psychological Bulletin*, 93, 179–97.

Embretson, S. E. (1984). A general multicomponent latent trait model for response processes. *Psychometrika*, 49, 175–86.

Embretson, S. E. (1985). *Test Design: Developments in Psychology and Psychometrics*. New York: Academic Press.

Embretson, S. E. (1988). Psychometric models and cognitive design systems. Paper presented at the annual meeting of the Psychometric Society, Los Angeles, CA, June.

Embretson, S. E. (1991). A multidimensional latent trait model for measuring learning and change. *Psychometrika*, 56, 495–516.
Embretson, S. E. (1994a). Application of cognitive design systems to test development. In C. R. Reynolds (Ed.), *Cognitive Assessment: A Multidisciplinary Perspective* (pp. 107–35). New York: Plenum Press.
Embretson, S. E. (1994b). Structured multidimensional IRT models for measuring individual differences in learning or change. Paper presented at the annual meeting of the American Educational Research Association. New Orleans, LA, April.
Embretson, S. E. (1995a). A measurement model for linking individual change to processes and knowledge: application to mathematical learning. *Journal of Educational Measurement*, 32, 277–94.
Embretson, S. E. (1995b). Developments toward a cognitive design system for psychological tests. In D. Lupinsky & R. Dawis (Eds), *Assessing Individual Differences in Human Behavior*. Palo Alto, CA: Davies-Black.
Embretson, S. E. (1995c). The role of working memory capacity and general control processes in intelligence. *Intelligence*, 20, 169–90.
Embretson, S. E. (1997a). Structured ability models in tests designed from cognitive theory. In M. Wilson, G. Engelhard & K. Draney (Eds), *Objective Measurement III* (pp. 223–36). Norwood, NJ: Ablex.
Embretson, S. E. (1997b). The factorial validity of a cognitively designed test: the Spatial Learning Ability Test. *Educational and Psychological Measurement*, 57, 99–107.
Embretson, S. E. (in press). A cognitive design system approach to generating valid tests: application to abstract reasoning. *Psychological Methods*.
Embretson, S. E. & McCollam, K. M. (in press). A multicomponent Rasch model for measuring covert processes. In M. Wilson & G. Engelhard (Eds), *Objective Measurement V*.
Embretson, S. E., Schneider, L. M. & Roth, D. L. (1985). Multiple processing strategies and the construct validity of verbal reasoning tests. *Journal of Educational Measurement*, 23, 13–32.
Embretson, S. E. & Wetzel, D. (1987). Component latent trait models for paragraph comprehension tests. *Applied Psychological Measurement*, 11, 175–93.
Fischer, G. H. (1973). Linear logistic test model as an instrument in educational research. *Acta Psychologica*, 37, 359–74.
Glaser, R. (1991). Expertise and assessment. In M. C. Wittrock & E. L. Baker (Eds), *Testing and Cognition* (pp. 17–30). Englewood Cliffs, NJ: Prentice Hall.
Hambleton, R., Swaminathan, H. & Rogers, J. (1991). *Fundamentals of Item Response Theory*. Newbury Park, CA: Sage Publishers.
Hornke, L. F. & Habon, M. W. (1986). Rule-based item bank construction and evaluation within the linear logistic framework. *Applied Psychological Measurement*, 10, 369–80.
Hively, W., Patterson, H. L. & Page, S. (1968). A "universe-defined" system of arithmetic achievement tests. *Journal of Educational Measurement*, 5, 275–90.
Hunt, E. B., Frost, N. & Lunneborg, C. L. (1973). Individual differences in cognition: a new approach to intelligence. In G. Bower (Ed.), *Advances in Learning and Motivation*, Vol. 7. New York: Academic Press.
Hunt, E. B., Lunneborg, C. & Lewis, J. (1975). What does it mean to be high verbal? *Cognitive Psychology*, 7, 194–227.
Irvine, S. H., Dunn, P. L. & Anderson, J. D. (1989). *Towards a Theory of Algorithm-Determined Cognitive Test Construction*. Devon, UK: Polytechnic South West.
Janssen, R. & De Boeck, P. (1997). Psychometric modeling of componentially designed synonym tasks. *Applied Psychological Measurement*, 21, 37–50.
Just, M. & Carpenter, P. (1985). Cognitive coordinate systems: accounts of mental rotation and individual differences in spatial ability. *Psychological Review*, 92, 137–72.
Katz, I. R., Friedman, D. E., Bennett, R. E. & Berger, A. E. (1996). Differences in strategies used to solve stem-equivalent constructed-response and multiple-choice SAT-mathematics items. College Board Report No. 95-3. New York: The College Board.

Kaufman, A. S. & Kaufman, N. L. (1993). *Manual for the Kaufman Adolescent & Adult Intelligence Scale*. Minneapolis, MN: American Guidance Service.
Kirsch, I. & Mosenthal, P. B. (1988). Understanding document literacy: variables underlying the performance of young adults. (RR-88-62). Princeton, NJ: Educational Testing Service.
Klix, F. & van der Meer, E. (1982). The role of different modes of knowledge representation in analogical reasoning process. In F. Klix, J. Hoffman & E. Van der Meer (Eds), *Cognitive Research in Psychology*. Amsterdam: North Holland.
Kosslyn, S. M. (1978). Measuring the visual angle of the mind's eye. *Cognitive Psychology*, 10, 356–89.
Kyllonen, P. (1993). Aptitude testing inspired by information processing: a test of the four-sources model. *Journal of General Psychology*, 120, 375–405.
Kyllonen, P. (1994). Cognitive abilities testing: an agenda for the 1990s. In M. G. Rumsey, C. B. Walker & J. H. Harris (Eds), *Personnel Selection and Classification*. Mahwah, NJ: Erlbaum.
Kyllonen, P. & Christal, R. (1989). Cognitive modeling of learning abilities: a status report of LAMP. In R. Dillon & J. W. Pellegrino (Eds), *Testing: Theoretical and Applied Perspectives*. New York: Freeman.
Kyllonen, P. & Christal, R. (1990). Reasoning ability is (little more than) working memory capacity? *Intelligence*, 14, 389–434.
Lord, F. N. & Novick, M. R. (1968). *Statistical Theories of Mental Test Scores*. Reading, MA: Addison-Wesley.
Luria, A. R. (1966). *Human Brain and Psychological Processes*. New York: Harper & Row.
Luria, A. R. (1970). The functional organization of the brain. *Scientific American*, 222, 66–78.
Luria, A. R. (1973). *The Working Brain: An Introduction to Neuropsychology*. New York: Basic Books.
Maris, E. M. (1995). Psychometric latent response models. *Psychometrika*, 60, 523–47.
McCollam, K. M. Schmidt (in press). Latent trait and latent class models. In G. M. Marcoulides (Ed.), *Modern Methods for Business Research*. Mahwah, NJ: Erlbaum.
Meiser, T. (1996). Loglinear Rasch models for the analysis of stability and change. *Psychometrika*, 61, 629–45.
Mislevy, R. (1993). Foundations of a new test theory. In N. Frederiksen, R. Mislevy & I. Bejar (Eds), *Test Theory for a New Generation of Tests*. Hillsdale, NJ: Lawrence Erlbaum.
Mosenthal, P. B. (1985). Defining the expository discourse continuum: towards a taxonomy of expository text types. *Poetics*, 14, 387–414.
Mulholland, T., Pellegrino, J. W. & Glaser, R. (1980). Components of geometric analogy solution. *Cognitive Psychology*, 12, 252–84.
Nhouyvanisvong, A., Katz, I. R. & Singley, M. K. (1997). Toward a unified model of problem solving in well-determined and under-determined algebra word problems. Paper presented at the annual meeting of the National Council on Measurement in Education. Chicago, IL, March.
Pellegrino, J. W. (1988). Mental models and mental tests. In H. Wainer & H. I. Brown (Eds), *Test Validity*. Hillsdale, NJ: Erlbaum.
Pellegrino, J. W. & Glaser, R. (1980). Components of inductive reasoning. In R. E. Snow, P.-A. Federico & W. E. Montague (Eds), *Aptitude, Learning and Instruction: Cognitive Process Analyses of Aptitude* (vol. I, pp. 177–217). Hillsdale, NJ: Erlbaum.
Rasch, G. (1960). *Probabilistic Models for Some Intelligence and Attainment Tests*. Chicago, IL: University of Chicago Press.
Raven, J. C., Court, J. H. & Raven, J. (1992). *Manual for Raven's Progressive Matrices and Vocabulary Scale*. San Antonio, TX: The Psychological Corporation.
Roskam, E. E. (1997). Models for speed and time-limit tests. In W. J. Van der Linden & R. Hambleton (Eds), *Handbook of Modern Item Response Theory* (pp. 187–208). New York: Springer-Verlag.

Rost, J. (1990). Rasch models in latent classes: an integration of two approaches to item analysis. *Applied Psychological Measurement*, 3, 271–82.
Sebrechts, M. M., Enright, M., Bennett, R. E. & Martin, K. (1996). Using algebra word problems to assess quantitative ability: attributes, strategies, and errors. *Cognition and Instruction*, 14, 285–341.
Segall, D. O. (1996). Multidimensional adaptive testing. *Psychometrika*, 61, 331–54.
Sheehan, K. M. (in press). A tree-based approach to proficiency scaling and diagnostic assessment. *Journal of Educational Measurement.*
Sheehan, K. M. & Mislevy, R. J. (1990). Integrating cognitive and psychometric models in a measure of document literacy. *Journal of Educational Measurement*, 27, 255–72.
Shepard, R. N. & Feng, C. (1971). A chronometric study of mental paper folding. *Cognitive Psychology*, 3, 228–43.
Singley, M. K. & Bennett, R. E. (1995). Toward computer-based performance assessment in mathematics. (RR-95-34). Princeton, NJ: Educational Testing Service.
Spearman, C. (1927). *The Abilities of Man: Their Nature and Measurement*. London: MacMillan.
Sternberg, R. J. (1977). *Intelligence, Information Processing, and Analogical Reasoning: the Componential Analysis of Human Abilities*. Hillsdale, NJ: Erlbaum.
Sternberg, R. J. (1985). *Beyond IQ: a Triarchic Theory of Human Intelligence*. New York: Cambridge University Press.
Sternberg, R. J. (1991). Toward better intelligence tests. In M. C. Wittrock & E. L. Baker (Eds), *Testing and Cognition* (pp. 31–9). Englewood Cliffs, NJ: Prentice Hall.
Tatsuoka, K. K. (1983). Rule space: an approach for dealing with misconceptions based on item response theory. *Journal of Educational Measurement*, 20, 34–8.
Tatsuoka, K. K. (1984). Caution indices based on item response theory. *Psychometrika*, 49, 94–110.
Tatsuoka, K. K. (1985). A probabilistic model for diagnosing misconceptions in the pattern classification approach. *Journal of Educational Statistics*, 12, 55–73.
Tatsuoka, K. K., Solomonson, C. & Singley, K. (in press). The new SAT I mathematics profile. In G. Buck, D. Harnish, G. Boodoo & K. Tatsuoka (Eds), *The New SAT*.
Van der Linden, W. & Hambleton, R. (1994). *Handbook of Modern Item Response Theory*. New York: Springer-Verlag.
Verhelst, N. D., Verstralen, H. H. F. M. & Jansen, M. G. H. (1997). A logistic model for time-limit tests. In W. J. van der Linden & R. Hambleton (Eds), *Handbook of Modern Item Response Theory* (pp. 169–86). New York: Springer-Verlag.
Weinstein, C. E. & Meyer, D. K. (1991). In M. C. Wittrock & E. L. Baker (Eds), *Testing and Cognition* (pp. 40–61). Englewood Cliffs, NJ: Prentice Hall.
Whitely, S. E. (1980). Multicomponent latent trait models for ability tests. *Psychometrika*, 45, 479–94.
Whitely, S. E. (1981). Measuring aptitude processes with multicomponent latent trait models. *Journal of Educational Measurement*, 18, 67–84.
Wilson, M. (1989). SALTUS: a psychometric model of discontinuity in cognitive development. *Psychological Bulletin*, 105, 276–89.
Wittrock, M. C. & Baker, E. L. (1991). *Testing and Cognition*. Englewood Cliffs, NJ: Prentice Hall.

Section 5

Health and Law

Chapter 22

Medical Cognition

Vimla L. Patel, Jose F. Arocha and David R. Kaufman
McGill University

We dance around in a ring and suppose,
But the secret sits in the middle and knows.
Robert Frost

Medicine is the science and art of evaluating, treating, and managing illness, as well as maintaining health. This discipline permeates many facets of our lives and provides a source of considerable fascination. Everyone, from lay people to policy-makers to television drama writers, has some insight into how medical practitioners think. Yet the vastness, complexity, and uncertainties embodied in the domain of medicine continue to perplex medical educators, health care professionals, and those of us who are committed to understanding the process of medical cognition. Although theories about the nature of medical thought and practice can be traced back for many centuries, the systematic study of medical cognition has been the subject of formal inquiry for only about twenty-five years.

The origin of contemporary research on medical thinking is associated with the seminal work of Elstein, Shulman & Sprafka (1978) who studied the problem-solving processes of physicians by drawing on then contemporary methods and theories of cognition. When we speak of medical cognition, we refer to a discipline devoted to the study of cognitive processes, such as perception, comprehension, reasoning, decision making, and problem solving, both in medical practice itself and in tasks representative of medical practice. These studies examine subjects who work in medicine, including medical students, physicians, and biomedical scientists. Cognitive science in medicine refers to a broader discipline encompassing medical artificial intelligence, philosophy in medicine, medical linguistics, medical anthropology, and cognitive psychology.

Handbook of Applied Cognition, Edited by F. T. Durso, R. S. Nickerson, R. W. Schvaneveldt, S. T. Dumais, D. S. Lindsay and M. T. H. Chi.

The study of medical cognition has traditionally drawn on information processing psychology as well as on methods and theories in other cognitive science disciplines. The research approaches and objectives in the study of medical cognition have mirrored those used in other cognitive disciplines. For example, early research in problem solving emphasized general processes and strategies, exemplified by performance in knowledge-lean tasks. As the interest of cognitive researchers shifted towards more complex domains of inquiry such as physics (e.g. Chi, Feltovich & Glaser, 1981), domain knowledge was found to be the most important determinant of skilled performance. Early research on medical cognition, typified by the work of Elstein, Shulman & Sprafka (1978), looked at general quantitative parameters such as the number of hypotheses used during problem-solving activity. Knowledge structures became one of the central foci in the study of medical cognition with consistent results reported by a number of researchers (e.g. Feltovich, Johnson, Moller & Swanson, 1984; Patel & Groen, 1986).

Much of the early research in the study of complex cognition in domains such as medicine was carried out in laboratory or experimental settings (Lesgold, Rubinson, Feltovich, Glaser, Klopfer & Wang, 1988; Norman, Feightner, Jacoby & Campbell, 1979; Patel, Groen & Frederiksen, 1986). In recent years, there has been a growing body of research examining cognitive issues in naturalistic medical settings, such as work by medical teams in intensive care units (Patel, Kaufman & Magder, 1996), anesthesiologists working in surgery (Gaba, 1992), and nurses providing emergency telephone triage (Leprohon & Patel, 1995). This research has been informed by work in the area of dynamic decision making (Klein, Orasanu, Calderwood & Zsambok, 1993), complex problem solving (Frensch & Funke, 1995; Sternberg & Frensch, 1991), human factors (Hoffman & Deffenbacher, 1992; Vicente & Rasmussen, 1990), and cognitive engineering (Rasmussen, Pejtersen & Goodstein, 1994). Studies of the workplace (Hunt, 1995) are beginning to reshape our views about cognition in profound ways. Current perspectives on distributed thinking have shifted the onus of cognition from being the unique province of the individual to being distributed across social and technological contexts (Salomon, 1993).

Cognitive research in medicine has employed the expert–novice paradigm contributing to our understanding of the nature of expertise and skilled performance (Patel & Groen, 1991). The expert–novice paradigm contrasts individuals at varying levels of competency and training in order to characterize differences in cognitive processes (e.g. reasoning strategies, memory) and knowledge organization. Typically, three levels of expertise are distinguished: novices (medical students), intermediates (medical residents), and experts (practicing physicians). Although this paradigm has yielded valuable insights into domains of complex cognition, it has not greatly informed the process of learning or instruction. In recent years, however, a growing number of investigations of medical learning and instruction (Norman, Trott, Brooks & Smith, 1994; Patel, Groen & Norman, 1993) have uncovered forms of knowledge required for successful performance in a variety of educationally relevant tasks (Patel, Kaufman & Arocha, in press).

The study of medical cognition has a dual purpose: the first purpose is to develop theoretical models of medical cognition, which may also be used towards practical goals of medical instruction and training. The second purpose is to engage in empirical research, exploiting the domain of medicine as a knowledge-rich and semantically complex domain. The empirical research has served to modify theoretical models, strengthening in this way the relationship between theory and experiment, and facilitating the bridging from the academic environment to the world of practical applications in social and educational settings (Kassirer & Kopelman, 1991). This in turn has had a synergistic effect in reshaping theory and charting new directions in research experimentation and methodologies.

In the first section of this chapter, we present a critical survey of the major issues researched in the field of clinical case comprehension, problem solving and conceptual understanding in medicine. In the second section, we discuss research on the processes of clinical case comprehension as evidenced in the recall and explanation of patient data. Informed by theories of discourse comprehension, this area of research examines the relationship between memory for clinical cases and the development and maintenance of diagnostic expertise. This section also explores the nature of knowledge development from novice to expert, and its relationship to learning in medicine. The third section explores research in medical problem solving, characterized by the reasoning process and strategies used by physicians and medical trainees to solve clinical problems. In addition, the relationship of problem solving to decision making in complex settings, including naturalistic environments, is discussed. In the fourth section, we examine conceptual understanding of biomedical concepts, considering theoretical, methodological, and empirical issues involved in the acquisition of complex concepts. This includes detailed characterization of students' and physicians' patterns of understanding and misunderstanding of complex basic science concepts. The final section provides the summary and conclusions from the studies of medical cognition.

CLINICAL CASE COMPREHENSION

The study of clinical case comprehension has been one of the most active in medical cognition. It has been carried out using a variety of tasks, such as recall and explanation. Performance on these tasks, used as indicators of comprehension, reveal the way memory and knowledge structures are organized in the minds of novices and experts. The questions addressed in this section are the following: How do physicians and medical students differ in their memory for medical information? Does expertise in the medical domain improve memory? Are physicians superior to medical students in recalling patient data? After an overview of some of the more important issues in clinical case comprehension, we present a brief historical development of this research, followed by a description of studies demonstrating the importance of the clinical case comprehension approach for understanding medical cognition.

The study of clinical case comprehension in medicine has been highly influenced by research in other complex domains, such as chess (Charness, 1992; Chase & Simon, 1973) and physics (Chi, Feltovich & Glaser, 1981; Larkin, McDermott, Simon & Simon, 1980). This research demonstrated distinct differences in the way in which domain information was represented in memory by experts and novices. For instance, novices represented physics problems based on surface-level aspects, such as the objects involved (e.g. springs, blocks, pulleys), while experts represented problems according to physics principles or abstract solution procedures (e.g. conservation of energy, Newton's Second Law).

In attempts to replicate these studies in medicine, investigations were conducted (Muzzin, Norman, Jacoby, Feightner, Tugwell & Guyatt, 1982; Norman, Feightner, Jacoby & Campbell, 1979) examining expert–novice differences in the free recall of clinical cases. The experimental paradigm used consisted of giving novices and experts written patient descriptions, usually including the main complaint, past medical history, results from physical examination and laboratory data. Recall was measured in terms of the number of sentences accurately reproduced, and chunk size was estimated in terms of the number of words between pauses. However, these early studies failed to replicate the recall differences found in the domains of chess and physics. Specifically, no differences were found between experts and novices in the amount of information recalled, although experts took less time to read and process the cases. This anomalous finding has been replicated in several studies (Claessen & Boshuizen, 1985; Hassebrock, Johnson, Bullemer, Fox & Moller, 1993) and suggests that recall of clinical cases is unique and unlike recall in other domains.

These results were also at variance with the theory of text comprehension (Kintsch & van Dijk, 1978) as applied to medical tasks (Coughlin & Patel, 1987; Patel & Groen, 1986). According to comprehension theory, clinical information consists of a process involving both bottom-up and top-down processes. The interpretation of a text reflects the distinction between the textbase, which is constructed in a bottom-up fashion, and the situation model, which is constructed in a top-down fashion (Kintsch & van Dijk, 1978). The textbase consists of the representation of the input text in memory, whereas the situation model is the representation of the events, actions, and the general situation referred to by the text. Comprehension results from the integration of the person's general and specific prior knowledge with the textbase.

A comprehension-based approach to medical cognition suggests a hybrid rule-based and instance-based model, embedded into a discourse processing framework where various processes interact (Arocha & Patel, 1995a). The model builds on the construction–integration theory (Kintsch & Welsch, 1991), given in Figure 22.1. This model views the process of clinical understanding as composed of two stages: a rule-based construction process of text representation (e.g. a clinical case), and an integration process. In the former stage, rules are triggered by the clinical problem, generated to form a loose textbase (case description). In the latter, the rules are consolidated into a coherent representation of the problem. In this view, disease schemata (memory structures representing a particular disease with associated signs, symptoms, and underlying pathophysiological processes) are not fixed in memory, but are constantly built from the interaction between prior knowledge and current case understanding.

Research (Arocha & Patel, 1995b; Patel, Arocha & Kaufman, 1994) suggests that expert knowledge is hierarchically organized into concepts of an increasingly abstract nature, ranging from clinical observations of a patient to conceptual

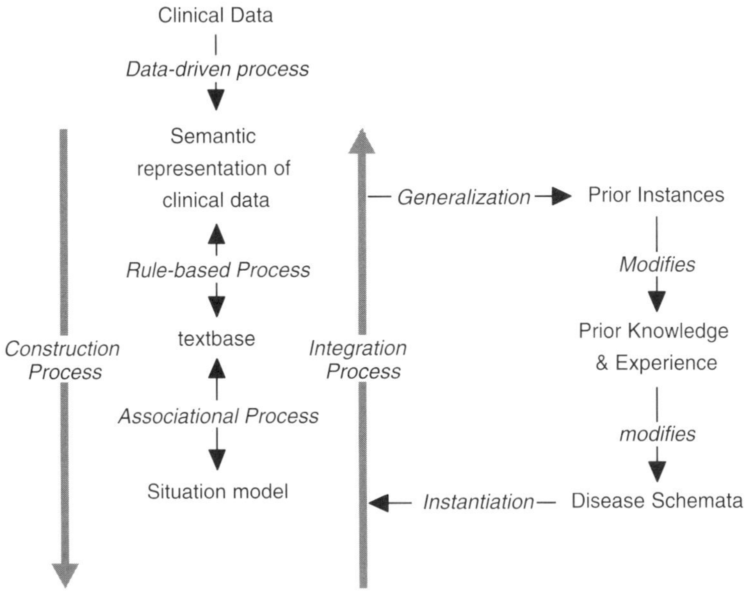

Figure 22.1 Model of clinical comprehension for problem solving

structures referring to physiological processes and diagnoses. This knowledge organization leads to understanding by providing a basis for the development of the situation model. Kintsch's construction–integration theory (Kintsch & Welsch, 1991; Weaver, Mannes & Fletcher, 1995) suggests that the expert's understanding of a clinical case goes through a cycle of construction of a broad representation of a patient's signs and symptoms, followed by a process of integration of this representation with prior knowledge into a coherent whole, resulting in the situation model. Support for this hypothesis is presented elsewhere (Arocha & Patel, 1995a), and is consistent with the notion advanced by Ericsson & Staszewsky (1989) that experts make use of intermediate memory structures that allow them to store whole patterns of cues, rather than relying on the analysis of individual cues. This allows experts to interpret clinical information in a flexible manner (Ericsson & Kintsch, 1995).

Patel, Groen & Frederiksen (1986) hypothesized that the inconsistent findings between medicine and other domains were the result of some fundamental differences in the methods of analysis used. By focusing on the subjects' ability to reconstruct the explicit information in the case (verbatim recall), the previous research was limited to uncovering only the contribution of bottom-up processing and not the interaction between bottom-up and top-down processes. Unless the method captures the underlying semantic information in the verbal reports, one is not likely to find differences between experts and novices.

One method of analysis (Patel, Groen & Frederiksen, 1986) delineated two basic types of responses in recalling clinical case information, "recalls" – which are reconstructions of portions of a clinical case drawn directly from the original text – and "inferences" – which consist of transformations performed on the original text based on the subject's specific or general world knowledge. These transformations, which involve high level processes, provide evidence that people's mental representations are based on prior knowledge and experience. The basic methodology for the study of comprehension and problem solving involves the use of some form of propositional analysis (Hassebrock & Prietula, 1992), or some combination of propositional (Kintsch & van Dijk, 1978) and protocol analysis (Ericsson & Simon, 1993). The first stage of analysis involves generating a propositional representation of the reference text which is used for comparison. Then, a subject's response protocol is transformed into a semantic network representation. The network consists of propositions that describe attribute information, which form the nodes of the network, and those that describe relational information, which form the links. A distinction is made between attributes that appear in the description of the clinical case (recall) and those that are spontaneously generated by subjects (inference). The methodology used by Patel and colleagues and Schmidt and colleagues makes use of labels to identify the types of relations in the protocol. The more common relations are dependency (e.g. causal, and conditional), algebraic (e.g. greater than), and categorical (i.e. category membership, part–whole relations). The causal and conditional links that form a major part of the semantic network resemble the rules used in an expert system, such as NEOMYCIN (Clancey, 1985). In the semantic networks one can identify rules of two types, data-directed or hypothesis-directed rules. Capturing the directionality of medical reasoning, forward reasoning consists of data-directed rules, and backward reasoning consists of hypothesis-directed rules (Patel & Groen, 1986).

Using the theory of text comprehension as a framework, Patel, Groen & Frederiksen (1986) reanalyzed some of the data from the study by Muzzin et al. (1982). Patel and colleagues (Coughlin & Patel, 1987; Patel, Groen & Frederiksen, 1986) hypothesized that when a distinction is made between recall and inference, and between various types of information in clinical cases indicating degrees of importance (e.g. critical, relevant, and irrelevant information to a particular clinical case), fundamental differences should be observed between novices and experts, similar to those found in other domains (Chase & Simon, 1973; Larkin, McDermott, Simon & Simon, 1980). The results of this reanalysis showed significant differences as a function of level of expertise across typical and atypical cases. Experts made more inferences than novices, whereas novices made more verbatim recalls.

The differences between recall and inferences indicate that novices and experts encode clinical case information at different levels of abstraction (Lemieux & Bordage, 1992). An inference involves the generation of a concept or a proposition that captures a large portion of a clinical case description (a set of signs and symptoms) with a high-level concept. The generation of inferences depends on prior knowledge (involving top-down processing). In contrast, recall consists of the retrieval of information already present in the clinical case description, which is dependent on other factors, such as general memory. In a study by Norman, Brooks & Allen (1989), it was found that the recall of laboratory data was better for experts when the goal was to diagnose the case, but not when the goal was to memorize the case information. This result is consistent with that of

Hassebrock, Johnson, Bullemer, Fox & Moller (1993), who found that, although experts had fewer "recalls" and inferences, they showed a positive increase for those case items that were consistent with the line of reasoning (a representation of a clinical case constructed in response to specific patient data) that they had used to reach the diagnosis. In contrast, novices did not show any such pattern.

The level of abstraction at which experts approach a clinical case is also dependent on prior knowledge, constraining the way information is interpreted. This is supported by research results (Coughlin & Patel, 1987) showing that experts are insensitive to the order of presentation of information at the time of recall. A study was conducted where the natural patient description was disrupted by randomizing the sequence of information presented in the case. The hypothesis was that, in contrast to novices, experts impose a structure to the randomized case making sense of such information. This hypothesis, however, was supported in only one of the two cases used where the order of information was not decisive for interpreting it correctly. In another case, where the sequence of events was important, no such superiority was observed. This suggests that although prior domain knowledge may be necessary for medical comprehension, it may not be sufficient. Other factors that are contextual to the clinical case, but are not part of its medical description, may be needed. Indeed, some research (Hobus, Schmidt, Boshuizen & Patel, 1987) found evidence that contextual information (e.g. risk factors) was used by expert physicians much more often to reach a diagnosis than by medical students.

In summary, although earlier investigation of clinical case comprehension as measured in recall tasks showed some inconclusive results, further research demonstrated that these results could be due, at least in part, to the use of inappropriate measures of comprehension (surface measures, such as words or phrases) instead of measures such as propositions or other semantic and pragmatic units (Hassebrock & Prietula, 1992; Lemieux & Bordage, 1992; Patel, Groen & Frederiksen, 1986). Using such measures, it has been shown that the memory structures of novices and experts differ substantially. The apparent superiority of expert memory resides not in the amount of recall, but in the relevance of the information recalled to the goals of the particular task (e.g. diagnosis), and the level of abstraction of the recalled information. This indicates that a critical factor in clinical case comprehension lies in the way knowledge is organized in memory, rather than in the amount of medical knowledge retrieved from memory (since novices and intermediates recall more "facts" than experts). The nature of knowledge organization and the mechanisms by which medical trainees develop the highly organized memory structures of the expert have been active areas of research in medical cognition.

The Nonmonotonic Nature of Knowledge Growth in Medical Expertise Research

The expertise literature in domains such as chess (Chase & Simon, 1973) shows an increasing monotonic relationship between recall performance and expertise. Consistent with this finding, an assumption in medicine has traditionally been that the development of expertise is monotonic. That is, as the expertise level of medical trainees (e.g. students, residents) and expert physicians increases, they develop increasingly complex rules that serve to making finer discriminations among clinical cases, leading to better recall and more accurate diagnoses. As far as diagnostic accuracy is concerned, the development of expertise in medicine shows a monotonic growth (i.e. the accuracy of diagnosis increases with expertise). However, as far as recall is concerned, this assumption has been questioned. It has been shown that the expertise continuum does not consist of a monotonic improvement in recall performance.

The case against a monotonic growth of recall with the development of medical expertise has been made in a series of investigations employing various tasks. The major finding from this research is known as the "intermediate effect". The finding refers to the observation of an inverse U-shaped pattern in several performance measures when novices, intermediates, and experts are compared. Intermediate subjects – those between novices and experts in an expertise continuum – perform worse in clinical recall tasks than either novices or experts (Patel & Groen, 1991; Schmidt & Boshuizen, 1993). Intermediates typically generate more irrelevant information in clinical case recall (Patel, Groen & Frederiksen, 1986), make more interpretation errors of dermatology disorders (Norman, Brooks & Allen, 1989), make more diagnostic errors of radiological images (Lesgold, 1984), and generate a higher number of inaccurate diagnostic hypotheses in case explanations (Arocha, Patel & Patel, 1993). Thus, after many studies by different researchers showing the robustness of the intermediate effect, it is now accepted that the development towards expertise is not linear, but that it is characterized by drops in performance at intermediate levels.

Schmidt & Boshuizen (1993) carried out a study investigating the intermediate effect in clinical case recall in more detail. They explored the relationship between time for case processing, recall, and explanation. To this end, a recall and explanation task was developed that varied the time of case exposure (3'30", 1'15", and 30"). The results showed that as the processing time decreased, the intermediate effect tended to disappear. It was strongest in the longest time case exposure and least in the shortest time exposure. In a second study reported in the same paper, they hypothesized that the intermediate effect was found because the longer processing time allowed the activation of prior knowledge needed by intermediate subjects, something that experts would not need. To address this issue, they asked subjects at several levels of expertise to recount everything they knew about a disease within 30" or 3'30". The hypothesis was that when intermediate subjects were given the longer time to recall everything they knew about a disease, they would activate more knowledge than when given the shorter time. After this activation task, they were given a clinical case to solve and to recall the information in the case. The results showed, as expected, an inverted U-shaped pattern of clinical recall, with the intermediate subjects recalling much more information when given the case after the longer activation time. Experts, however, recalled the same amount of information regardless of activation time.

In summary, research on the development of medical expertise has revealed that the growth of medical knowledge does not proceed in a linear fashion. Rather, it shows an inverted U-shape phenomenon, where a decrease in performance indicated through a variety of measures is observed in intermediate subjects when compared with novices or experts. This finding disconfirms the assumption usually made in the medical education literature that the process of knowledge acquisition increases in a linear fashion with medical training. Research findings suggest that such a process of knowledge acquisition is more complex than the one traditionally assumed. The nonmonotonic nature of the development of expertise can be explained, however, as the result of a more extensive search through the problem space by intermediates (cf. Saariluoma, 1990). As intermediates do not possess a highly organized knowledge structure, they perform unnecessary searches, accessing information that is not directly relevant to the clinical problem. Novices and experts do not perform such an extensive search. Novices lack the knowledge base to search, whereas experts possess an organized knowledge base which is sufficient to sort out the relevant from the irrelevant information.

MEDICAL PROBLEM SOLVING

This section presents a general overview of the literature on medical problem solving. This work has largely addressed the process of clinical diagnosis by experts and novices, although some studies have been conducted on the process of patient management and therapy. Although this body of research has an intimate connection to clinical case comprehension, it has focused on the reasoning processes and the strategies used in clinical diagnosis. The section begins with a brief historical review, followed by an overview of research on directionality of the reasoning as a function of medical knowledge. Next, we review the literature on diagnostic performance in visual domains in medicine (e.g. interpretation of X-ray films). The section ends with a brief review of research literature on clinical decision making as it relates to medical problem solving and to the development of medical text understanding.

The first major work in medical problem solving in the cognitive tradition was carried out by Elstein, Shulman & Sprafka (1978). Their research transformed the field of medical cognition in much the same way that Newell & Simon's (1972) pioneering work was instrumental in the evolution of problem-solving research. The cognitive approach was characterized by the study of the processes of cognitive activity based on the information-processing theory of problem solving developed by Newell & Simon (1972) and work in Gestalt psychology (deGroot, 1965). Although Elstein, Shulman & Sprafka's (1978) work focused on problem solving and judgment, its influence spread over other areas of medical cognition by emphasizing a cognitive approach that relies on different types of verbal reports as data (e.g. concurrent and retrospective protocols).

The major results from Elstein, Shulman & Sprafka's (1978) work can be summarized as follows. First, physicians generated a small set of hypotheses very early in the case, as soon as the first pieces of data became available. Second, they were selective in the data they collected, focusing only on the relevant data. Third, physicians made use of a hypothetico-deductive method of diagnostic reasoning. The hypothetico-deductive process was viewed as consisting of four stages: cue acquisition, hypothesis generation, cue interpretation, and hypothesis evaluation. Attention to initial cues led to the rapid generation of a few select hypotheses. According to the authors, each cue was interpreted as positive, negative or non-contributory to each hypothesis generated. They were unable to find differences between superior physicians (as judged by their peers) and other physicians (Elstein, Shulman & Sprafka, 1978). Others (Barrows, Feightner, Neufeld & Norman, 1978), using a very similar approach, found no differences between students and clinicians in their use of diagnostic reasoning strategies except for the quality of the hypotheses and the accuracy of diagnosis.

The characterization of hypothetico-deductive reasoning as an expert strategy seemed anomalous as it was widely regarded as a "weak" method of problem solving useful in cases where little knowledge was available (Groen & Patel, 1985) and more characteristic of novice problem solving in other domains (Simon & Simon, 1978). Further research suggested that experts possess an elaborate, highly structured knowledge base capable of supporting efficient reasoning (Bordage & Zacks, 1984; Feltovich, Johnson, Moller & Swanson, 1984). Gale & Marsden (1983) provided an additional insight when they suggested that Elstein, Shulman & Sprafka (1978) had collapsed all hypotheses into the category of diagnoses, but in fact most hypotheses generated by physicians were not diagnoses (e.g. myocardial infarction) but prediagnostic interpretations (e.g. potential cardiac problem). Gale & Marsden suggested that diagnostic reasoning involves an incremental solution process rather than the generation of the correct diagnosis from the start, as implied by the use of a hypothetico-deductive strategy.

In contrast, a study by Patel & Groen (1986) showed that when diagnosis was accurate, all expert physicians explained routine problems by means of an inductive process of pure forward reasoning as opposed to a deductive process of backward reasoning. With inaccurate diagnoses, however, a mixture of forward and backward reasoning was used. In forward reasoning, the pattern of inferences go from the data presented in the case towards the hypothesis. This differs from backward reasoning, a form of reasoning that goes from a hypothesis (e.g. a diagnosis) towards the clinical data. Examples of forward- and backward-directed inferences are given in Table 22.1. Forward reasoning is highly error prone in the absence of adequate domain knowledge and is only successful in situations where one's knowledge of a problem can result in a chain of inferences from the initial problem statement to the problem solution. In contrast, backward reasoning is most likely to be used when domain knowledge is inadequate. Backward reasoning is most often used when a specific solution to the problem is not readily at hand. This suggests that Elstein, Shulman & Sprafka's (1978) findings result from the nature of the tasks used which may have encouraged the utilization of backward reasoning strategies. For example, physicians were offered the opportunity to suggest hypotheses while working on a problem, thereby providing the opportunity to explicitly generate and test hypotheses.

A hypothesis for reconciling these seemingly contradictory results is that forward reasoning is used in clinical problems in which the physician has ample experience. However, when unfamiliar or difficult cases are used, physicians resort to backward reasoning since their knowledge base does not support a pattern-matching process. Patel, Groen & Arocha (1990) investigated the conditions under which forward reasoning breaks down. Cardiologists and endocrinologists were

Table 22.1 Types of inferences used during clinical diagnosis (the arrows represent the directionality of reasoning)

Type of inference	Direction of inference	Example from a protocol
Forward	*Data* → Hypothesis	"This patient is very *short of breath,* which suggests that he's having respiratory failure"
		shortness of breath → respiratory failure
Backward	Hypothesis → *Data*	"The blocking of the thyroxing release mechanism is causing a respiratory failure, which accounts for the patient's *shortness of breath*"
		blocking of the thyroxing release → respiratory failure → *shortness of breath*

asked to solve diagnostic problems both in cardiology and in endocrinology. They showed that under conditions of case complexity and uncertainty, the pattern of forward reasoning was disrupted. Structural properties of the clinical case resulted in this breakdown of forward reasoning. More specifically, the breakdown occurred when nonsalient cues in the case were tested for consistency against the main hypothesis, even in subjects who had generated the correct diagnosis. Otherwise, the results supported previous studies in that subjects with accurate diagnoses used pure forward reasoning.

In this study, as in most research on clinical diagnosis, the clinical problems were presented in the form of whole case descriptions where physicians read a complete case before they generated a diagnosis. In studies where clinical problems were presented in segments a few sentences at a time (Joseph & Patel, 1990; Patel, Arocha & Kaufman, 1994), it was shown that the presentation of partial information was not sufficient for disrupting the pattern of forward reasoning if the case was routine – i.e. familiar to the physicians. However, this pattern was disrupted in a more complex, unfamiliar case. It was the "loose ends" in the complex cases, which did not fit the familiar pattern of disorder, that were responsible for disrupting the forward-directed reasoning.

The notion that experts utilize forward reasoning in routine cases suggests a type of processing that is fast enough to be able to lead to the recognition of a set of signs and symptoms in a patient and generate a diagnosis based on such recognition. This has triggered a wealth of research investigations that explore the role of perceptual processes in medical tasks. It has been an implicit assumption that expertise is the result of having accumulated a vast body of rules relating signs and symptoms to disease categories as a function of years of extensive practice. According to this assumption, experts can use such rules to diagnose routine and non-routine cases in an efficient manner. However, empirical research lends support to an alternative hypothesis which states that experts use knowledge of specific instances (e.g. particular patients with specific disease presentations), rather than abstract rules when diagnosing clinical cases. This hypothesis has been advocated by Norman and colleagues (Brooks, Norman & Allen, 1991; Norman, Brooks, Coblentz & Babcook, 1992).

In summary, the study of problem solving in medicine has been investigated by comparing the reasoning processes used during clinical diagnosis. The methodology used consisted of the presentation of either whole problem descriptions at one time or segments of the problem in sequence. This research has shown that when solving familiar problems, experts utilize a form of reasoning characterized by the generation of inferences from the given patient data in the clinical problem to the diagnosis (hypothesis). This form of reasoning is called forward-driven reasoning or data-driven reasoning. This contrasts with backward-driven or hypothesis-driven reasoning, where the direction of inference is from a diagnosis (hypothesis) to the explanation of given patient data. The pattern of forward-driven reasoning breaks down when experts solve complex clinical cases, where there is uncertainty about the likely diagnosis. In these cases, experts, like novices, resort to backward-directed reasoning. The distinction between forward- and backward-driven reasoning is related to the notions of strong and weak methods in Artificial Intelligence, where the former make use of an extensive knowledge base, whereas the latter use general purpose heuristics and do not rely on domain specific knowledge.

Expertise and Problem Solving in Visual Diagnostic Tasks

Research on visual diagnosis has provided evidence that seems to question the forward nature of expert reasoning. Visual diagnosis involves the interpretation of images, such as X-rays, dermatological slides, and electrocardiograms. In one study (Norman, Brooks, Coblentz & Babcook, 1992), it was found that the errors made by experts in identifying abnormalities in X-ray films were dependent on the prior history associated with the films. If the prior history mentioned a possible abnormality, expert physicians more often identified abnormalities in the films even when none were there. Novice subjects did not show such a differential pattern of response to the prior history, performing in a similar way regardless of prior history. These results argue for the experts using a top-down approach to radiological diagnosis, consistent with a hypothetico-deductive strategy. However, since forward reasoning proceeds from known (e.g. any input to the problem-solving process) to unknown (e.g. the diagnosis), the results presented by Norman, Brooks, Coblentz & Babcook (1992) can be interpreted as forward reasoning. The prior history information provided to the physicians in their study acts as data in this case, since it was not generated as hypothesis by the physicians. Furthermore, evidence for forward reasoning has been found with tasks involving the interpretation of the patient's history, which is the first step in the evaluation of any patient problem. Interpretation of laboratory data (such as X-ray films) and other information gathered from physical examination is used only to confirm or disconfirm a diagnosis that has already been made (Joseph & Patel, 1990; Patel, Arocha & Kaufman, 1994). Recent studies (Patel, Groen & Patel, 1997) show that schemata for patient problems develop very early in clinical encounters. These schemata are used as guides to generating and interpreting laboratory data.

Norman and colleagues have investigated visual diagnosis in dermatological (Norman, Brooks, Rosenthal, Allen & Muzzin, 1989), radiological (Norman, Brooks, Coblentz & Babcook, 1992), and ECG representations (Regehr, Cline, Norman & Brooks, 1994). The main motivation for the study of the visual aspects of diagnosis is the hypothesis that a great deal of experts' superiority in diagnosis is accounted for by highly developed "perceptual" abilities, rather than highly developed analytical skills (e.g. logical reasoning). Furthermore, Norman and colleagues have argued for a non-analytic basis for medical diagnosis. By non-analytic, they mean a form of diagnostic reasoning that relies on unanalyzed retrieval of previous cases seen in medical practice. This argues against the hypothesis that expert physicians diagnose clinical cases by analyzing the signs and symptoms present in a patient and by developing correspondences between those signs, symptoms and diagnoses. Instead, it is suggested that previous cases resembling the current case are remembered, and that the same or a similar diagnosis is then retrieved from memory (Weber, Bockenholt, Hilton & Wallace, 1993).

Other research in visual diagnostic tasks has been carried out (Lesgold, Rubinson, Feltovich, Glaser, Klopfer & Wang, 1988). The abilities of radiologists (at various levels of expertise) to interpret chest X-ray pictures and provide a diagnosis was investigated (Lesgold, 1984; Lesgold et al., 1988). The authors found that experts were able to detect a general pattern of disease. This resulted in a gross anatomical localization (e.g. affected lung area) and served to constrain possible interpretations. With the forward–backward reasoning hypothesis, forward reasoning is initially used to deflect the familiar pattern of disease. The pattern of disease is used to interpret the loose ends in the unfamiliar data by a process of backward reasoning. This process continues (moving between forward and backward reasoning) until all of the loose ends are accounted for (for review, see Patel & Ramoni, 1997). The loose ends trigger the shift in directionality.

The study of problem solving in visual domains, such as radiology and dermatology, has produced results that seem to be in opposition to those of more verbal domains of medical problem solving. Evidence from this research seems to suggest that experts use some form of backward reasoning in the interpretation of radiological images. We have attempted to reconcile the differences by proposing that "prior information" used in this study was "given information", which was used as data to solve the problem. According to the definition of forward reasoning, the experts used given information to generate the unknown (problem solution). Research evidence also shows that laboratory data is often interpreted in the context of diagnosis. Laboratory test requests are made based on the diagnostic hypothesis after the patient's medical history and results of the physical examination are gathered, and thus, the test results are mostly used to confirm a diagnosis or to rule-out alternatives (Patel, Groen & Patel, 1997).

Medical Reasoning and the Development of Clinical Problem-Solving Skills

Although most investigations of the "intermediate effect" have been carried out using recall tasks, other research has found evidence of this intermediate effect using such tasks as "on-line" explanations, where the number of propositions generated was used as a measure of performance. This research provides evidence that the intermediate effect extends beyond simple recall tasks. One research study (Arocha & Patel, 1995b) explored the strategies medical students used when confronted with clinical case information that was inconsistent with a previously generated explanation. The intermediate subjects tended to generate the largest number of hypotheses to account for different findings, frequently generating different explanations for the same finding but failing to reach a conclusion. Like the intermediate subjects, advanced novices generated and evaluated multiple hypotheses, but retained only a handful in their evaluation process. In summary, the pattern that developed consisted of an inverted U-shape, with intermediates generating and evaluating more hypotheses than advanced subjects.

The differential use of reasoning strategies deployed by physicians and medical students are probably a consequence of the amount and quality of the knowledge available to them. For intermediate subjects, this knowledge becomes almost unmanageable, as they have accumulated a great deal of information from both basic medical training and some practical experience but have not had the opportunity to consolidate it into coherent structures. We may argue, following the construction integration theory (Kintsch & Welsch, 1991), that experts' experience in the practical environment has served to "prune" their knowledge structures, discarding weak or unlikely associations among concepts, and acquiring implicit practical knowledge in the process.

Although we can find differences in terms of the strategies used by more novice and less novice subjects, the findings suggest that the key to an explanation may be not in the differential use of cognitive strategies, but in the different knowledge available to experts and novices and the way that such knowledge is organized. It is generally agreed that medical knowledge consists of two types of knowledge: (a) clinical knowledge, including knowledge of diseases and associated findings, and (b) basic science knowledge (e.g. biochemistry, anatomy, and physiology). The existence of these two types of knowledge has given rise to the development of two different models of diagnostic reasoning based on the considered relevance of each type of knowledge in clinical diagnostic reasoning. These are the fault model and the heuristic classification model, respectively. The first model suggests that medical diagnosis is akin to diagnostic troubleshooting in electronics, with a primary goal of finding the structural fault or systemic perturbation (Boshuizen & Schmidt, 1992; Feinstein, 1973). From this perspective, clinical and biomedical knowledge become intricately intertwined, providing medical practice with a sound scientific basis. This model suggests that biomedical and clinical knowledge could be seamlessly integrated into a coherent knowledge structure that supports all cognitive aspects of medical practice, such as diagnostic and therapeutic reasoning.

The second model views diagnostic reasoning as a process of heuristic classification (Clancey, 1985) involving the instantiation of specific slots in a disease schema. The primary goal of diagnostic reasoning is to classify a cluster of patient findings as belonging to a specific disease. From this perspective, the diagnostic reasoning process is viewed as a process of coordinating theory and evidence rather than one of finding fault in the system (Patel, Arocha & Kaufman, 1994). As expertise develops, a clinician's disease models become more dependent on clinical experience and problem solving is guided more by the use of exemplars and analogy and less by an understanding of the biological system. That is not to say that basic science does not play an important role in medicine but that the process of diagnosis, particularly in dealing with routine problems, is essentially one of classification. Basic science knowledge is important in resolving anomalies and is essential in therapeutic contexts.

In summary, the process of medical problem solving relies heavily on the development of knowledge and knowledge structures. This development should not be viewed as the increasingly more sophisticated deployment of problem-solving strategies. Rather, the differential use of strategies and skills is the result of more advanced and better organized knowledge structures with increase in medical training.

THE RELATIONSHIP BETWEEN COMPREHENSION, PROBLEM SOLVING AND DECISION MAKING IN MEDICINE

Comprehension processes are an integral part of problem solving and decision making in semantically complex domains. Physicians need to understand the nature of clinical findings before a medical problem can be solved. Similarly, therapeutic and patient management decisions are framed within the constrains of the problem representation which is guided by comprehension processes. In this section, we examine the relationship between comprehension, problem solving, and decision making.

The study of medical decision making began in the late 1960s within a normative, statistical framework (through the use of either regression or Bayesian models). The research conducted under this framework focused on finding ways to predict clinical performance, using models that do not describe the cognitive processes but that parallel a physician's performance in clinical judgment tasks. Issues of relevance to this framework are exemplified by questions such as: How do physicians use clinical data to make a diagnosis or to recommend a treatment? How do they weigh evidence? Statistical models are used as a criterion against which the clinician's performance is measured.

Most medical decision making research conducted within this framework focused on methods of decision analysis and subjective expected utility (Weinstein, 1980), where the main approach consists of comparing a normative model (e.g. expected utility) with human performance. This research revealed weaknesses in human judgment and decision making. In particular, two findings were emphasized: people's judgment seemed to be strongly affected by patterns of evidence and did not show rational procedures for weighing evidence. However, studies under the normative approach revealed little about the underlying reasoning processes in making decisions.

Significant research has been conducted using a more descriptive perspective influenced by the seminal work of Tversky & Kahneman (1974). This research has investigated factors that affect decision making, such as the number of additional alternatives (Redelmeier & Shafir, 1995) – physicians use different strategies to make decisions when they choose with more or fewer alternatives; the explication of implicit possibilities (Redelmeier, Koehler, Liberman & Tversky, 1995) – this increases the judgment of its probability.

Results from several studies (e.g. Elstein, 1984) have shown that medical practitioners are not experts in probability or decision analysis. They interpret statements phrased in the language of decision theory using naive common sense schemata. For instance, using protocol analysis to study the decision making strategies of physicians in hormone replacement therapy, Elstein, Holzman, Belzer & Ellis (1992) found that physicians considered levels of risks in terms of categories rather than in terms of continuous probability scales. This supports previous findings (Kuipers, Moskowitz & Kassirer, 1988) suggesting that physicians do not reason probabilistically. Although probability and decision analysis are powerful techniques, it seems reasonable to conclude that this power will frequently be lost when medical practitioners attempt to interpret clinical results (McNeil, Pauker, Sox & Tversky, 1982).

A different approach to decision making is characterized by the research conducted in naturalistic settings, which combines the study of medical comprehension and problem solving addressing the reasoning processes and strategies used during complex decision making tasks. The next section provides a summary of this research.

Problem Solving and Decision Making in Naturalistic Settings

The investigation of naturalistic problem solving and decision making is a relatively new area of research. This research crosses boundaries between theoretical and applied research, and incorporates different methods and assumptions. It recognizes that decision making occurs under a set of constraints of a cognitive (e.g. memory, knowledge, inferences, and strategies), socio-cultural (e.g. norms), and situational nature. It also recognizes the importance of assessing the problem-solving situation before decisions are made. Situations of uncertainty and urgency affect the decision making process in such a way that the conventional approach to decision making and judgment is not applicable. Different strategies are used depending on the type of decision situation, including pattern recognition strategies for situations of high urgency and severe time pressure; focused problem solving, where the goal frequently is achieved through a process of "satisficing" (Simon, 1990); and deliberate problem solving, where there is a careful assessment of evidence before decisions are made (Leprohon & Patel, 1995; Patel, Arocha & Kaufman, 1994).

Decision making in naturalistic settings is goal-driven and situationally-driven. A critical situation demands immediate attention superseding any prior goals. It may be also complex and uncertain, given the number of interconnected aspects involving many different decisions and possible courses of action. Frequently, there is also risk involved. The actions of the decision maker may result in unintended, and often unpredictable, consequences. Instances of such research include decision making by anesthesiologists (Gaba, 1992) and dispatchers of emergency medical services (Leprohon & Patel, 1995). In this regard, recent decision making research differs substantively from the conventional decision making research which most often focuses on the making of decisions by selecting the best alternative from a fixed set of choices in a stable environment (Klein, Calderwood & McGregor, 1989). In contrast, in realistic situations decisions are embedded in a broader context and are part of a complex decision–action process. This is especially true in environments such as those in complex workplaces (e.g. intensive care unit), where knowledge structures, processes, and skills interact with modulating variables, such as stress, time pressure, and fatigue, as well as communication patterns in team performance.

Leprohon & Patel (1995) investigated the decision making strategies used by nurses (front-end call receivers) in 911 emergency telephone triage settings. The study was based on an analysis of transcripts of nurse–patient telephone conversations of different levels of urgency (low, medium, and high) and in problems of different levels of complexity. The authors found that in high urgency situations, data-driven heuristic strategies were used to make decisions. In this situation, decisions were mostly accurate. With an increase in problem complexity more causal explanations were used and the decisions were very often inaccurate. However, even with accurate decisions the supporting explanations were often inaccurate, showing a decoupling of knowledge and action. Alternative decisions were considered in moderate to low urgency conditions, where contextual knowledge of the situations (e.g. the age of the patient, whether the patient was alone or with others) was exploited to identify the needs of the patients and to negotiate the best plan of action to meet these needs.

The results from the Leprohon & Patel (1995) study are consistent with three patterns of decision making that reflect the perceived urgency of the situation. The first pattern corresponds to immediate response behavior as reflected in situations of high urgency. In these circumstances, decisions are made with great rapidity. Actions are typically triggered by symptoms or the unknown urgency level in a forward-directed manner. The nurses in this study responded with perfect accuracy in these situations. The second pattern involves limited problem solving and typically corresponds to a situation of moderate urgency and to cases which are of some complexity. The behavior is characterized by information seeking and clarification exchanges over a more extended period of time. These circumstances resulted in the highest percentage of decision errors (mostly false positives). The third pattern involves deliberate problem solving and planning and typically corresponds to low urgency situations. This involved evaluating the whole situation and exploring alternative solutions (e.g. identifying the basic needs of a patient, referring the patient to an appropriate clinic). In this situation, nurses made fewer errors than in situations of moderate urgency and more errors than in situations requiring immediate response behavior.

A similar study of decision making in an intensive care unit (ICU) environment was carried out by Patel, Kaufman & Magder (1996). This involved a collaborative team effort between health care professionals to solve urgent and sensitive patient problems. Consistent with research by Leprohon & Patel (1995) and Gaba (1992), they showed the use of two different kinds of strategies under urgent and less urgent conditions. The first is characterized by the use of a high-level organization of knowledge such that reasoning is driven in a forward direction toward action, with no underlying justification. In the second, attempts are made to use causally-directed, backward reasoning to explain the relevant patient information with the use of detailed pathophysiology.

In summary, decision making in naturalistic settings is emerging as an important new area of research. This research informs and calls into question some of the framing assumptions of the traditional decision-making approach. Models of decision making must take into account both the responsive and deliberative character of solution processes. Similarly, cognition in "real-world" settings is often a socially-driven process that extends beyond the boundaries of individuals.

One of the central themes in studies of clinical reasoning is the effect that basic science knowledge has in furthering or hindering diagnostic performance. However, reasoning tasks offer only a glimpse at the sort of biomedical models held by subjects at different levels of expertise. This is the subject of the next section.

CONCEPTUAL UNDERSTANDING

Medicine is a domain of advanced knowledge in the sense that it builds on the mastery of basic knowledge acquired during an introductory learning phase (Feltovich, Spiro & Coulson, 1989). Students in most medical schools are expected to have acquired sufficient fluency in human biology, biochemistry, physiology, and anatomy. Research in many different scientific domains indicates that students begin their study of science with misconceptions of scientific phenomena (Eylon & Linn, 1988). Several studies in medicine have similarly documented the range of misconceptions that students acquire and the adverse impact that this has on clinical reasoning (Dawson-Saunders, Feltovich, Coulson & Steward, 1990; Feltovich, Spiro & Coulson, 1989; Kaufman, Patel & Magder, 1996; Patel, Kaufman & Magder, 1991). What gives rise to misconceptions? How can instructors foster robust productive knowledge? Answers to these questions can be partially provided by a theory of conceptual understanding. Conceptual understanding refers to acquiring a level of competency in employing knowledge across a range of contexts, including novel situations. One of the central goals of medical school is to impart a level of conceptual competency such that future practicing physicians can draw on this knowledge in diverse clinical tasks. However, there is considerable debate over the best pedagogical method for imparting this knowledge (Patel, Groen & Norman, 1993).

In this section, we explore different theoretical and methodological perspectives on acquiring biomedical knowledge. We first characterize two different views on knowledge acquisition and consider how it can be used to justify different curricular approaches (Bruer, 1993). The second part of the section describes approaches for investigating and characterizing conceptual understanding, using cardiovascular and circulatory medicine as exemplary biomedical domains.

Perspectives on the Acquisition of Basic Science Knowledge

As discussed previously, medical knowledge consists of two categories of knowledge: clinical knowledge, including knowledge of disease entities and associated findings; and basic science knowledge, incorporating subject matter such as biochemistry, anatomy, and physiology. Basic science or biomedical knowledge is supposed to provide a scientific foundation for clinical reasoning. The conventional view is that basic science knowledge can be seamlessly integrated into clinical knowledge analogous to the way that learning the rules of the road can contribute to one's mastery of driving a car. In this capacity, a particular piece of biomedical knowledge (e.g. oxygen-hemoglobin saturation) could be automatically elicited in a range of clinical contexts and tasks in more or less the same fashion.

How can basic science knowledge become integrated with clinical knowledge? Boshuizen & Schmidt (1992) proposed a learning mechanism, knowledge encapsulation, for explaining how biomedical knowledge becomes subsumed under clinical knowledge as a function of training. When medical students commence clinical training, typically after two years of medical school, they have already acquired a sizable body of basic science and clinical knowledge. They have also learned about methods of history taking, physical examinations, and treatment and management. Knowledge encapsulation is a learning process that involves the subsumption of biomedical propositions, concepts and their interrelations in an associative network, under a small number of higher level clinical propositions of equal explanatory power. Through exposure to clinical training, biomedical knowledge becomes encapsulated and integrated into clinical knowledge. Boshuizen & Schmidt cite a wide range of clinical reasoning and recall studies that support this kind of learning process. Of particular importance is the well-documented finding that with increasing levels of expertise, physicians produce explanations at higher levels of generality, using fewer and fewer biomedical concepts while producing consistently accurate responses. The intermediate effect can also be accounted for as a stage in the encapsulation process in which a trainee's network of knowledge has not yet become sufficiently differentiated, thus resulting in more extensive processing of information.

Knowledge encapsulation provides an appealing account of a range of developmental phenomena in the course of acquiring medical expertise. However, the integration of basic science in clinical knowledge is a rather complex process, and encapsulation is likely to play only part of the knowledge development process. Basic science knowledge plays a different role in different clinical domains. For example, clinical expertise in perceptual domains, such as dermatology and radiology, necessitate a relatively robust model of anatomical structures which is the primary source of knowledge for diagnostic classification. In other domains, such as cardiology and endocrinology, basic science knowledge has a more distant relationship with clinical knowledge. The misconceptions evident in physicians' biomedical explanations would argue against well-developed encapsulated knowledge structures where basic science knowledge could easily be retrieved and applied when necessary.

Biomedical knowledge represents a complex multi-leveled hierarchical structure from ultra cellular to systems levels. Can the nature of basic science knowledge and the structure of basic science curricula provide us with some insights in the development of students' knowledge structures? It is clear that neither conventional nor problem-based curricula are entirely successful at fostering conceptual understanding. There is a successful integration of basic science knowledge into clinical structure with problem-based curriculum. However, it has also created the problem of students' inability to decontextualize it once it is integrated (Patel, Groen & Norman, 1993). This problem should be attended to if one assumes that relevant basic science knowledge is naturally embedded into clinical knowledge. Indeed, this appears to be a basic assumption of the clinical rationale for medical education. On the other hand, the basic sciences have a structure that is quite different from that of the clinical sciences. If this is correct, then one would expect an inability to decontextualize basic science knowledge learned in a clinical context.

It is our view that the results of research into medical problem solving are consistent with the idea that clinical medicine and the biomedical sciences constitute two distinct and not completely compatible "worlds," with distinct modes of reasoning and quite different ways of structuring knowledge (see Patel, Arocha & Kaufman, 1994). Clinical knowledge is based on a complex taxonomy that relates disease symptoms to underlying pathology. In contrast, the biomedical sciences are based on general principles defining chains of causal mechanisms. Thus, learning to explain how a set of symptoms is consistent with a diagnosis may be very different from learning how to explain what causes a disease.

Recently, the notion of the progression of mental models (White & Frederiksen, 1990) has been used as an alternative framework for characterizing the development of conceptual understanding in biomedical contexts. Mental models are dynamic knowledge structures that are composed to make sense of experience and to reason across spatial and/or temporal dimensions. An individual's mental models provide predictive and explanatory capabilities of the function of a given system. The running of a model corresponds to a process of mental simulation that can generate possible future states of a system from observed or hypothetical states. To use a simple example, one can mentally simulate the process of driving home from work and create a set of expectations corresponding to each turn along the way. Similarly, a physician can construct a model to reason about the effects of an obstruction of blood flow in the pulmonary artery. White & Frederiksen (1990) employed the progression of mental models to explain the process of understanding increasingly sophisticated electrical circuits. This notion can be used to account for differences between novices and experts in understanding circulatory physiology, describing misconceptions (Kaufman & Patel, 1994) and explaining the generation of spontaneous analogies in causal reasoning (Kaufman, Patel & Magder, 1996).

Running a mental model is a potentially powerful form of reasoning but it is also cognitively demanding. It can require an extended chain of reasoning and the use of complex representations. It is apparent that skilled individuals learn to circumvent long chains of reasoning and chunk or compile knowledge across intermediate states of inference (Chandrasekaran, 1994; Newell, 1990). This results in shorter, more direct, inferences that are stored in long term memory and are directly available to be retrieved in the appropriate contexts. Chandrasekaran (1994) refers to this sort of knowledge as compiled causal knowledge. This refers to knowledge of causal expectations that people compile directly from experience and partly by chunking results from previous problem-solving endeavors (Kaufman & Patel, 1994). The goals of the individual and the demands of recurring situations largely determine which pieces of knowledge get stored and used. For example, if a physician has to reason about the effects of a pulmonary embolism on liver function, she may initially reason through an extended series of inferences that account for how certain vessels are blocked. This blockage may result in inadequate gas exchange (insufficient oxygenation of blood) and subsequently poor perfusion of tissues and organs as well as incomplete elimination of carbon dioxide resulting in certain urinary findings indicative of liver dysfunction. Through experience, this chain can be reduced to a cause–effect relation in which pulmonary embolism can result in liver dysfunction given the goal of explaining certain urinary findings. When a physician is confronted with a similar situation, she can employ this compiled knowledge in an efficient and effective manner. The development of compiled knowledge is an integral part of the acquisition of expertise.

The idea of compiling declarative knowledge bears a certain resemblance to the idea of knowledge encapsulation. However, the claim differs in two important senses. The process of compiling knowledge is not one of subsumption or abstraction, and the original knowledge (uncompiled mental model) may no longer be available in a similar form (Kuipers & Kassirer, 1984). The second difference is that mental models are composed dynamically out of constituent pieces of knowledge rather than pre-stored unitary structures. The use of mental models is somewhat opportunistic and the learning process less predictable. The compilation process can work in reverse as well. That is to say, discrete cause and effect relationships (for example, as acquired by students from reading medical texts) can be integrated into a mental model as a student reasons about complex physiological processes.

Evaluating Understanding in Conceptually Complex Domains

Olson & Biolsi (1991) reviewed the methods available to researchers interested in the nature of expertise, including both direct methods such as interviews and think-aloud protocols, and indirect methods that are more detailed in processes and narrower in their conclusions. The authors suggest choosing methods that fit the kinds of assumptions one has about the way experts organize information. For the domains in which there is an availability of associations among concepts, either network analysis, such as Pathfinder (McGaghie, Boerger, McCrimmon & Ravitch, 1996; Schvaneveldt, 1990) or qualitative methodologies that can uncover overlapping categories, such as influence network analysis (Feltovich, Spiro & Coulson, 1993; Kaufman, Patel & Magder, 1996) can be used. In this section, we consider both direct and indirect methodologies for evaluating student's understanding of biomedical concepts, with examples from the work of Feltovich and colleagues as well as our own research into conceptual understanding.

Feltovich and colleagues have developed a framework for investigating medical students' understanding of complex concepts (Feltovich, Spiro & Coulson, 1993; Feltovich, Spiro & Coulson, in press). The framework includes a methodological scheme for analyzing conceptual structure which can be used to identify areas of potential cognitive difficulty. Concepts are decomposed into their most basic elements. For each concept studied, a probe set of questions is developed. The first questions tend to be open-ended and very general. The following questions address the basic elements or components of the concept. Subsequent questions require more complex kinds of integration and synthesis. The final items of a probe set focus on applying the concepts in applied contexts. The objective is to identify the kinds of conceptual models exhibited by students and their limitations. This method allows an investigator to examine student understanding from multiple perspectives. While this method has been developed in the context of studying students' biomedical knowledge, it can be applied to any domain of science.

The framework has been used to characterize serious misconceptions in cardiology (Feltovich, Spiro & Coulson, 1989). Misconceptions can be decomposed into component misconceptions. The components are interdependent and have multiple sources that converge and reinforce the erroneous knowledge. These sources include one or more psychological "reductive biases" that favor the development of simplified conceptual models. The authors also suggest that specific instructional practices and materials can contribute to these biases. A clear example of their research is reflected in a misconception related to congestive heart failure (Feltovich, Spiro & Coulson, 1989). This is a syndrome in which the heart's effectiveness as a pump can diminish greatly and as a result the rate of blood flow slows dramatically. The misconception that was expressed by over 60% of first and second year medical students and by some medical practitioners, suggest that heart failure is caused by the heart getting too big which in turn stretches the cardiac muscle fibers. Several component misconceptions were also identified. As these misconceptions interact and support each other yielding a robust conceptual structure, they lead to an inappropriate analogy that an individual cardiac muscle fiber is like an individual skeletal fiber. In fact, these two kinds of fibers differ on the dimensions of importance (length–tension). However, students have a better acquaintance with skeletal muscle fiber and instructors use the analogy to introduce the subject matter.

The discussion of this misconception amplifies several important themes. Misconceptions emanate from multiple converging sources of students' knowledge. The sources or pieces of knowledge by themselves can be partially correct or fully correct, but may be inappropriately inserted as a causal mechanism. The second important theme is that instructional practice and resources (textbooks) can be primary contributors to a component misconception. This could be as a result of an educator's own misconception, or more frequently, is a result of simplifying a complex concept so that students may grasp it more easily.

The research of Feltovich and colleagues suggests the need for a comprehensive framework for characterizing conceptual understanding in a biomedical domain. This framework incorporates an investigative method and method of analysis for identifying sources of conceptual difficulties. These sources have multiple origins, including the students' knowledge base and a tendency to reduce complexity by the student, which is reinforced by methods of formal instruction. These investigators have extended this framework to consider issues of cognitive assessment (Feltovich, Spiro & Coulson, 1993) and to predict the difficulty of conceptual change for a given body of biomedical concepts (Feltovich, Spiro & Coulson, in press).

Kaufman, Patel, and colleagues developed a framework for characterizing conceptual understanding in biological domains, drawing on the construct of progression of mental models, the epistemological distinction in basic biomedical science, and the work of Feltovich and colleagues (Kaufman, Patel & Magder, 1996; Kaufman & Patel, 1994). The broad objective of this research is to investigate individuals' knowledge structures and to identify productive and counterproductive forms of knowledge. In this section, the focus is on presenting the framework. Results of this research are described in the aforementioned papers and are summarized elsewhere (Patel, Kaufman & Arocha, in press).

The notion of knowledge structures is undergoing some degree of change in cognitive psychology. The schema approach emphasizes a set of relatively fixed structures (transformed through learning experiences) that are applied to problems as needed. Certain emerging perspectives view knowledge as a process (rather than a fixed structure) that provide potential to engage in activities and participate in discourse (Greeno, 1997). We tend to take an intermediate stance, in that we view knowledge as highly malleable structures that can be dynamically composed to respond to a problem or an explanation. For example, we would not expect an expert cardiologist to use a stored mental model (or a fixed set of mental models) of the circulatory and cardiovascular system to reason about blood flow. Rather, the knowledge that is applied would depend on the particular level of explanation (e.g. cellular vs. systemic), the locality of the problem (e.g. pulmonary artery, left ventricle), and the context of use (i.e. nature of the problem and task). An expert can draw on constituent component structures and compose a model dynamically, constructing an explanation. This allows for much greater flexibility in the use of knowledge to confront anomalous or previously unseen medical problems. The explanation would differ if the expert were reasoning about a complex problem than if he were explaining the physiology to a group of medical students.

The methodological framework is based on the use of a semi-structured interview and related explanation tasks to probe understanding of a set of interrelated biomedical concepts. There is a need to expose and analyze understanding of a concept in diverse and more extended contexts that offer a subject the opportunity to express his or her apprehension domains (Spiro, Feltovich, Coulson & Anderson, 1989). The methods employ a systematic domain analysis, identifying pertinent concepts, and their interrelations. We draw on certain distinctions such as the difference between device-centered (emphasis on structure and function) and process-centered models. Most of our research within this framework has focused on the circulatory and cardiovascular systems, which can be described in terms of structure–function relations (e.g. blood vessels and chambers of the heart) or in terms of process-centered models (e.g. blood flow). In particular, we have studied subjects' understanding of cardiac output, which is

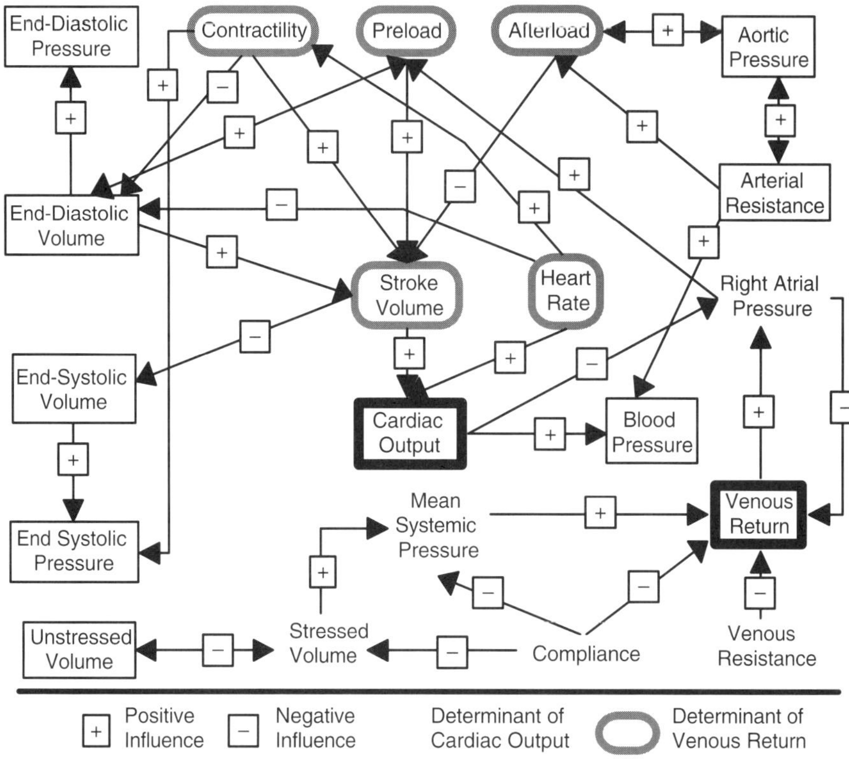

Figure 22.2 Reference qualitative influence graph representing relationships between variables

a measure of the blood ejected from the heart per unit time and venous return, and the blood returning to the heart per unit time. We are principally interested in characterizing the pressure–volume and pressure–flow relations and their role in regulating cardiac output and venous return. In our view, this can be more effectively expressed in terms of a process-centered model. The concepts pertaining to the regulation of cardiac output lack explicit structure–function correspondences. For example, venous resistance is distributed across different structures (e.g. large and small veins, venules, etc.). The regulation of cardiac output can be described in terms of a set of interacting processes or variables that determine the net outflow and inflow of blood into the heart.

A qualitative influence graph was generated to represent the set of variables and influences involved in the problem set (Kaufman & Patel, 1994). This method allows us to characterize aspects of students' or physicians' mental models of the mechanics of the cardiovascular system, and to diagnose conceptual errors. The directional influences or dependencies between the primary variables included in the study are illustrated in a reference qualitative influence graph in Figure 22.2.

The variables represent quantities that when changed can initiate a process that will affect other variables in predictable ways. A variable can exert a positive, negative or neutral (no) influence on another variable. If an independent variable increases and exerts a positive influence, then the dependent measure will be more likely to increase. Conversely, if the relationship is negative, the dependent variable will be more likely to decrease. For example, preload positively influences and afterload negatively influences cardiac output. Therefore, an increase in preload will tend to produce an increase in cardiac output, and an increase in afterload tends to result in a decrement in cardiac output. There are 20 variables and 30 relationships illustrated in Figure 22.2. We could also divide this model into a set of component models and study in greater depth, for example, students' and physicians' understanding of variables that influence venous return (blood returning to the heart).

The structured interview requires subjects to respond to questions and problems of graded complexity involving the factors that affect cardiac output and venous return. The first set of questions is open-ended to elicit their beliefs about these factors. The second set consisted of basic physiology questions that asked directly about specific factors influencing cardiac output, venous return, pressure–volume, and pressure–flow relationships. These questions require subjects to make predictions and provide explanations. The third and fourth set of questions require subjects to apply their knowledge to explain situations involving normal physiological processes (e.g. physiological changes due to exercise) and problems involving patient descriptions. This method allows one to investigate subjects' understanding of concepts and relations from multiple converging perspectives. Their explanations are coded for the accuracy of predictions and explanations. We also look for various patterns across subjects that are suggestive of misconceptions and reasoning biases.

The results of the study are reported elsewhere (Kaufman, Patel & Magder, 1996). To briefly summarize, we were able to characterize a progression of mental models corresponding to levels of expertise on the basis of assessing predictions and explanations. Accuracy of prediction and explanation tend to increase as a function of expertise. However, there were interesting individual differences with subjects at a certain level performing well above or well below expectations. In addition, certain component processes such as factors affecting venous return (e.g. resistance and compliance) were not as well understood as factors influencing cardiac output. The study documented four misconceptions that were observed in subjects at varying levels of training.

Misconceptions, and to a lesser extent errors of analysis, propagated through subjects' models and produced consistent patterns of errors of prediction and explanation. This is most apparent when an individual's model is otherwise coherent and consistent. Misconceptions by more novice subjects may have been more isolated due to a lack of connections in a fragmentary knowledge base. In other words, misconceptions in a more advanced trainee may be more deleterious than in a rank novice. Misconceptions, at more advanced levels of training, became firmly entrenched in one's network of knowledge and were supported by elaborate justifications.

In summary, the framework outlined in this section is based on the belief that advanced domains of knowledge acquisition required methods sufficiently sensitive for diagnosing complex conceptual problems. Standard problem-solving or clinical interview methods are likely to be of limited utility in characterizing and understanding in these domains. The approach is predicated on: (a) a systematic analysis of domain content and the kinds of reasoning required; (b) a set of probes that converge on common themes; (c) methods for formally representing students' mental models (e.g. qualitative influence graphs); and (d) a means for identifying sources of misconceptions. This approach was developed in the context of medicine, but we believe it to be broadly applicable to other applied scientific contexts like engineering and architecture. Both of these domains require the development of complex mental representations and require substantial formal knowledge in physics and mathematics. Although these domains substantively differ from medicine, students are likely to be challenged by similar kinds of hurdles in applying (less than fully formed) basic science concepts towards solving complex problems.

SUMMARY AND CONCLUSION

This chapter has provided an overview of the field of medical cognition as it has developed in the last 20 years. Several approaches have provided different views of what is medical expertise and how it develops. Major theoretical and methodological influences have come from the study of comprehension, first via the basic recall paradigms and later through the study of comprehension and concept understanding, which encompass more complex phenomena and are informed by more sophisticated theories. The superior performance of experts has been shown to reside not in the amount of information they possess, but in the organization of knowledge in memory. This is achieved by a process of knowledge acquisition which is characterized by an inverted U-shaped performance curve, where the vertical and horizontal axes are level of performance and level of expertise, respectively. This challenges the usual assumption in medical education that the process of knowledge acquisition increases linearly as a function of expertise.

Medical problem solving also has a foundational role in the study of medical cognition, given that clinical problem solving and, in particular, clinical diagnosis, is a critical component of medical practice. A great deal of research has been devoted to the investigation of how physicians and medical trainees diagnose clinical cases. This research began by examining general strategies used during diagnosis, and evolved to considering the role that knowledge plays in reasoning. Findings such as the utilization of forward reasoning in routine cases and backward, hypothetico–deductive reasoning in complex clinical cases has given rise to a number of competing theories attempting to provide a coherent explanation of clinical diagnosis in various medical domains ranging from the more conceptual domains (e.g. cardiology) to more perceptual domains (e.g. radiology).

The study of decision making began within the normative framework where human decision making is compared to a normative model. However, changes have ensued that have shifted the attention to the investigation of heuristics and biases and more recently to decision making in naturalistic settings. This has provided yet another shift in perspective by emphasizing the study of "real world" and complex processes. This recent research has dramatically changed the field of medical decision making by redirecting efforts toward the investigation of decision making as a "situated" cognitive activity and towards a unification of the various fields of medical cognition, including comprehension, reasoning, and problem solving.

Finally, conceptual understanding research has focused the attention on the investigation of medical trainees, with an emphasis on the problems faced when understanding complex biomedical concepts. Such problems are exemplified by the use of analogies in biomedical concept understanding. The identification of misconceptions have direct relevance to the design of instruction and the learning of medical students.

The study of medical cognition presents a fascinating set of real world problems and immense theoretical challenges, which makes it a rich and fertile area of research in applied cognitive psychology. Despite the variety of cognitive issues investigated in the medical domain, we believe that a theoretical and applied science of cognition would benefit greatly from an enlarged framework covering the various forms of advanced knowledge acquisition.

ACKNOWLEDGMENTS

The writing of this chapter was supported in part by awards from the Social Sciences and Humanities Research Council of Canada to Vimla L. Patel (410-95-1206) and Jose F. Arocha (410-95-1208). This manuscript has benefited greatly from valuable comments and suggestions by our colleagues, Vanessa Allen and Kayla Cytryn, and from several anonymous reviewers.

REFERENCES

Arocha, J. F. & Patel, V. L. (1995a). Construction–integration theory and clinical reasoning. In I. C. A. Weaver, S. Mannes & C. R. Fletcher (Eds), *Discourse Comprehension: Essays in Honor of Walter Kintsch* (pp. 359–82). Hillsdale, NJ: Lawrence Erlbaum.

Arocha, J. A. & Patel, V. L. (1995b). Novice diagnostic reasoning in medicine: accounting for clinical evidence. *Journal of the Learning Sciences*, 4, 355–84.

Arocha, J. F., Patel, V. L. & Patel, Y. C. (1993). Hypothesis generation and the coordination of theory and evidence in novice diagnostic reasoning. *Medical Decision Making*, 13, 198–211.

Barrows, H. S., Feightner, J. W., Neufeld, V. R. & Norman, G. R. (1978). *Analysis of the clinical methods of medical students and physicians* (Final Report). Hamilton, Ontario: Ontario Department of Health.

Bordage, G. & Zacks, R. (1984). The structure of medical knowledge in memories of medical students and practitioners: categories and prototypes. *Medical Education*, 18, 406–16.

Boshuizen, H. P. A. & Schmidt, H. G. (1992). On the role of biomedical knowledge in clinical reasoning by experts, intermediates, and novices. *Cognitive Science*, 16, 153–84.

Brooks, L. R., Norman, G. R. & Allen, S. W. (1991). Role of specific similarity in a medical diagnostic task. *Journal of Experimental Psychology: General*, 120, 278–87.

Bruer, J. T. (Ed.) (1993). *Schools for Thought: A Science of Learning in the Classroom*. Cambridge, MA: MIT Press.

Chandrasekaran, B. (1994). The functional representation and causal process. In M. Yovitz (Ed.), *Advances in Computing*. New York: Academic Press.

Charness, N. (1992). Expertise in chess: the balance between knowledge and search. In K. A. Ericsson & J. Smith (Eds), *Toward a General Theory of Expertise: Prospects and Limits* (pp. 39–63). New York: Cambridge University Press.

Chase, W. G. & Simon, H. A. (1973). Perception in chess. *Cognitive Psychology*, 4, 55–81.

Chi, M. T. H., Feltovich, P. J. & Glaser, R. (1981). Categorization and representation of physics problems by experts and novices. *Cognitive Science*, 5, 121–52.

Claessen, H. F. A. & Boshuizen, H. P. A. (1985). Recall of medical information by students and doctors. *Medical Education*, 19, 61–7.

Clancey, W. J. (1985). Heuristic classification. *Artificial Intelligence*, 27, 289–350.

Coughlin, L. D. & Patel, V. L. (1987). Processing of critical information by physicians and medical students. *Journal of Medical Education*, 62, 818–28.

Dawson-Saunders, B., Feltovich, P. J., Coulson, R. L. & Steward, D. (1990). A survey of medical school teachers to identify basic biomedical concepts medical students should understand. *Academic Medicine*, 7, 448–54.

deGroot, A. D. (1965). *Thought and Choice in Chess*. The Hague: Mouton.

Elstein, A. S. (1984). Introducing the cognitive and decision sciences to medical education. In C. P. Friedman & E. F. Purcell (Eds), *The New Biology and Medical Education* (pp. 198–208). New York: Josiah Macy Jr Foundation.

Elstein, A. S., Holzman, D. B., Belzer, L. J. & Ellis, R. D. (1992). Hormonal replacement therapy: analysis of clinical strategies used by residents. *Medical Decision Making*, 12, 165–73.

Elstein, A. S., Shulman, L. S. & Sprafka, S. A. (1978). *Medical Problem Solving. An Analysis of Clinical Reasoning*. Cambridge, MA: Harvard University Press.

Ericsson, K. A. & Kintsch, W. (1995). Long-term working memory. *Psychological Review*, 102, 211–45.

Ericsson, K. A. & Simon, H. A. (1993). *Protocol Analysis: Verbal Reports as Data*. Cambridge, MA: MIT Press.

Ericsson, K. A. & Staszewski, J. J. (1989). Skilled memory and expertise: mechanisms of exceptional performance. In D. Klahr & K. Kotovsky (Eds), *Complex Information Processing: The Impact of Herbert A. Simon* (pp. 235–67). Hillsdale, NJ: Lawrence Erlbaum.

Eylon, B. & Linn, M. C. (1988). Research perspectives in science education. *Review of Educational Research*, 58, 251–301.

Feinstein, A. R. (1973). An analysis of diagnostic reasoning. I. The domains and disorders of clinical macrobiology. *Yale Journal of Biology & Medicine*, 46, 212–32.

Feltovich, P. J., Johnson, P. E., Moller, J. H. & Swanson, D. B. (1984). LCS: the role and development of medical knowledge in diagnostic expertise. In W. J. Clancey & E. H. Shortliffe (Eds), *Readings in Medical Artificial Intelligence: The First Decade* (pp. 275–319). Reading, MA: Addison-Wesley.

Feltovich, P. J., Spiro, R. & Coulson, R. L. (1989). The nature of conceptual understanding in biomedicine: the deep structure of complex ideas and the development of misconceptions. In D. A. Evans & V. L. Patel (Eds), *Cognitive Science in Medicine: Biomedical Modeling* (pp. 113–72). Cambridge, MA: MIT Press.

Feltovich, P. J., Spiro, R. J. & Coulson, R. L. (1993). Learning, teaching, and testing for complex conceptual understanding. In N. Frederiksen, R. J. Mislevy & I. I. Bejar (Eds), *Test Theory for a New Generation of Tests* (pp. 181–217). Hillsdale, NJ: Lawrence Erlbaum.

Feltovich, P. J., Spiro, R. J. & Coulson, R. L. (in press). A scheme for predicting the difficulty of conceptual change: an example application to the concepts of opposition to blood flow in the cardiovascular system (cardiovascular impedance). In A. Pace (Ed.), *Beyond Prior Knowledge: Issues in Text Processing and Conceptual Change*. Mawah, NJ: Lawrence Erlbaum.

Frensch, P. A. & Funke, J. (1995). *Complex Problem Solving: The European Perspective.* Hillsdale, NJ: Lawrence Erlbaum.

Gaba, D. (1992). Dynamic decision-making in anesthesiology: cognitive models and training approaches. In D. A. Evans & V. L. Patel (Eds), *Advanced Models of Cognition for Medical Training and Practice* (pp. 123–48). Heidelberg, Germany: Springer-Verlag.

Gale, J. & Marsden, P. (1983). *Medical Diagnosis from Student to Clinician.* Oxford: Oxford University Press.

Greeno, J. (1997). On claims that answer the wrong questions. *Educational Researcher*, 26, 5–17.

Groen, G. J. & Patel, V. L. (1985). Medical problem-solving: some questionable assumptions. *Medical Education*, 19, 95–100.

Hassebrock, F. & Prietula, M. (1992). A protocol-based coding scheme for the analysis of medical reasoning. *International Journal of Man–Machine Studies*, 37, 613–52.

Hassebrock, F., Johnson, P. E., Bullemer, P., Fox, P. W. & Moller, J. H. (1993). When less is more: representation and selective memory in expert problem solving. *American Journal of Psychology*, 106, 155–89.

Hobus, P. O. M., Schmidt, H. G., Boshuizen, H. P. A. & Patel, V. L. (1987). Contextual factors in the activation of first diagnostic hypotheses: expert–novice differences. *Medical Education*, 21, 471–6.

Hoffman, R. R. & Deffenbacher, K. A. (1992). A brief history of applied cognitive psychology. *Applied Cognitive Psychology*, 6, 1–48.

Hunt, E. B. (1995). *Will we be Smart Enough?: a Cognitive Analysis of the Coming Workforce.* New York: Russell Sage Foundation.

Joseph, G.-M. & Patel, V. L. (1990). Domain knowledge and hypothesis generation in diagnostic reasoning. *Medical Decision Making*, 10, 31–46.

Kassirer, J. P. & Kopelman, R. I. (1991). *Learning Clinical Reasoning.* Baltimore: Williams & Wilkins.

Kaufman, D. R. & Patel, V. L. (1994). Cognitive models for characterizing biomedical knowledge and expertise. In S. Spyrou, S. Christofides, C. S. Pattichis, E. Keravnou, C. N. Schizas & G. Christodoulides (Eds), *Proceedings of the International Conference on Medical Physics & Biomedical Engineering, vol. 2* (pp. 398–407). Nicosia, Cyprus: The Department of Computer Science, University of Cyprus.

Kaufman, D. K., Patel, V. L. & Magder, S. (1996). The explanatory role of spontaneously generated analogies in reasoning about physiological concepts. *International Journal of Science Education*, 18, 369–86.

Kintsch, W. & van Dijk, T. A. (1978). Toward a model of text comprehension and production. *Psychological Review*, 85, 363–94.

Kintsch, W. & Welsch, D. M. (1991). The construction–integration model: a framework for studying memory for text. In W. E. Hockley & S. Lewandowsky (Eds), *Relating Theory and Data: Essays on Human Memory in Honor of Bennett B. Murdock* (pp. 367–85). Hillsdale, NJ: Lawrence Erlbaum.

Klein, G. A., Calderwood, R. & McGregor, D. (1989). Critical decision method for eliciting knowledge. *IEEE Systems, Man, and Cybernetics*, 19 (3), 462–72.

Klein, A., Orasanu, J., Calderwood, R. & Zsambok, C. E. (Eds) (1993). *Decision Making in Action: Models and Methods.* Norwood, NJ: Ablex Publishing.

Kuipers, B. J. & Kassirer, J. P. (1984). Causal reasoning in medicine: analysis of a protocol. *Cognitive Science*, 8, 363–85.

Kuipers, B. J., Moskowitz, A. J. & Kassirer, J. P. (1988). Critical decisions under uncertainty: representation and structure. *Cognitive Science*, 12, 177–210.

Larkin, J. H., McDermott, J., Simon, D. P. & Simon, H. A. (1980). Expert and novice performance in solving physics problems. *Science*, 208, 1335–42.

Lemieux, M. & Bordage, G. (1992). Propositional versus structural semantic analyses of medical diagnostic thinking. *Cognitive Science*, 16, 185–204.

Leprohon, J. & Patel, V. L. (1995). Decision making strategies for telephone triage in emergency medical services. *Medical Decision Making*, 15, 240–53.

Lesgold, A. (1984). Acquiring expertise. In J. R. Anderson & S. M. Kosslyn (Eds),

Tutorials in Learning and Memory: Essays in the Honor of Gordon Bower (pp. 31–60). San Francisco, CA: W. H. Freeman.

Lesgold, A., Rubinson, H., Feltovich, P., Glaser, R., Klopfer, D. & Wang, Y. (1988). Expertise in a complex skill: diagnosing x-ray pictures. In M. T. H. Chi, R. Glaser & M. J. Farr (Eds), *The Nature of Expertise* (pp. 311–42). Hillsdale, NJ: Lawrence Erlbaum.

McGaghie, W. C., Boerger, R. L., McCrimmon, D. R. & Ravitch, M. M. (1996). Learning pulmonary physiology: comparison of student and faculty knowledge structures. *Academic Medicine*, 71 (January Supplement), S13–S15.

McNeil, B., Pauker, S. G., Sox, M. C. & Tversky, A. (1982). On the elicitation of preferences for alternative therapies. *New England Journal of Medicine*, 306, 1259–62.

Muzzin, L. J., Norman, G. R., Jacoby, L. L., Feightner, J. W., Tugwell, P. & Guyatt, G. H. (1982). Manifestations of expertise in recall of clinical protocols. *Research in Medical Education: 1982 Proceedings of the 21st Annual Conference* (pp. 163–8). Washington, DC: Association of American Medical Colleges.

Newell, A. (1990). *Unified Theories of Cognition*. Cambridge, MA: Harvard University Press.

Newell, A. & Simon, H. A. (1972). *Human Problem Solving*. Englewood Cliffs, NJ: Prentice-Hall.

Norman, G. R., Brooks, L. R., Allen, S. W. (1989). Recall by expert medical practitioners and novices as a record of processing attention. *Journal of Experimental Psychology: Learning, Memory & Cognition*, 15, 1166–74.

Norman, G. R., Brooks, L. R., Coblentz, C. L. & Babcook, C. J. (1992). The correlation of feature identification and category judgments in diagnostic radiology. *Memory & Cognition*, 20, 344–55.

Norman, G. R., Brooks, L. R., Rosenthal, D., Allen, S. W. & Muzzin, L. J. (1989). The development of expertise in dermatology. *Archives of Dermatology*, 125, 1063–8.

Norman, G. R., Feightner, J. W., Jacoby, L. L. & Campbell, G. J. M. (1979). Clinical experience and the structure of memory. *Research in Medical Education: 1979 Proceedings of the 18th Annual Conference* (pp. 214–18). Washington, DC: Association of American Medical Colleges.

Norman, G. R., Trott, A. D., Brooks, L. R. & Smith, E. K. M. (1994). Cognitive differences in clinical reasoning related to postgraduate training. *Teaching and Learning in Medicine*, 6, 114–20.

Olson, J. R. & Biolsi, K. J. (1991). Techniques for representing expert knowledge. In K. A. Ericsson & J. Smith (Eds), *Toward a General Theory of Expertise: Prospects and Limits* (pp. 240–85). New York: Cambridge University Press.

Patel, V. L., Arocha, J. F. & Kaufman, D. R. (1994). Diagnostic reasoning and expertise. *The Psychology of Learning and Motivation*, 31, 137–252.

Patel, V. L. & Groen, G. J. (1986). Knowledge-based solution strategies in medical reasoning. *Cognitive Science*, 10, 91–116.

Patel, V. L. & Groen, G. J. (1991). The general and specific nature of medical expertise: a critical look. In K. A. Ericsson & J. Smith (Eds), *Toward a General Theory of Expertise: Prospects and Limits* (pp. 93–125). New York: Cambridge University Press.

Patel, V. L., Groen, G. J. & Arocha, J. F. (1990). Medical expertise as a function of task difficulty. *Memory & Cognition*, 18, 394–406.

Patel, V. L., Groen, G. J. & Frederiksen, C. H. (1986). Differences between students and physicians in memory for clinical cases. *Medical Education*, 20, 3–9.

Patel, V. L., Groen, G. J. & Norman, G. R. (1993). Reasoning and instruction in medical curricula. *Cognition & Instruction*, 10, 335–78.

Patel, V. L., Groen, G. & Patel, Y. C. (1997). Cognitive aspects of clinical performance during patient workup: the role of medical expertise. *Advances of Health Science Education*, 2, 95–114.

Patel, V. L., Kaufman, D. R. & Arocha, J. F. (in press). Conceptual change in the biomedical and health sciences domain. In R. Glaser (Ed.), *Advances in Instructional Psychology*. Mahwah, NJ: Lawrence Erlbaum.

Patel, V. L., Kaufman, D. R. & Magder, S. (1991). Causal reasoning about complex physiological concepts by medical students. *International Journal of Science Education*, 13, 171–85.
Patel, V. L., Kaufman, D. R. & Magder, S. A. (1996). The acquisition of medical expertise in complex dynamic environments. In K. A. Ericsson (Ed.), *The Road to Excellence: The Acquisition of Expert Performance in the Arts and Sciences, Sports and Games* (pp. 127–65). Hillsdale, NJ: Lawrence Erlbaum.
Patel, V. L. & Ramoni, M. F. (1997). Cognitive models of directional inference in expert medical reasoning. In P. J. Feltovich, K. M. Ford & R. R. Hoffman (Eds), *Expertise in Context: Human and Machine* (pp. 67–99). Cambridge, MA: MIT Press.
Rasmussen, J., Pejtersen, A. M. & Goodstein, L. P. (1994). *Cognitive Systems Engineering*. New York: John Wiley.
Redelmeier, D. A., Koehler, D. J., Liberman, V. & Tversky A. (1995). Probability judgment in medicine: discounting unspecified possibilities. *Medical Decision Making*, 15, 227–30.
Redelmeier, D. A. & Shafir, E. (1995). Medical decision making in situations that offer multiple alternatives. *Journal of the American Medical Association*, 273, 302–5.
Redelmeier, D. A. & Tversky, A. (1990). Discrepancy between medical decisions for individual patients and for groups. *New England Journal of Medicine*, 322, 1162–4.
Regehr, G., Cline, J., Norman, G. R. & Brooks, L. R. (1994). Effects of processing strategy on diagnostic skill in dermatology. *Academic Medicine*, 69 (Supp), S34–6.
Saariluoma, P. (1990). Apperception and restructuring in chess players' problem solving. In K. J. Gilhooly, M. T. G. Keane, R. H. Logies & G. Erdos (Eds), *Lines of Thinking: Reflections on the Psychology of Thought, vol. 2: Skills, Emotion, Creative Processes, Individual Differences and Teaching Thinking* (pp. 41–57). Chichester: John Wiley.
Salomon, G. (Ed). (1993). *Distributed Cognition: Psychological and Educational Considerations*. New York: Cambridge University Press.
Schmidt, H. G. & Boshuizen, H. P. (1993). On the origin of intermediate effects in clinical case recall. *Memory & Cognition*, 21, 338–51.
Schvaneveldt, R. W. (Ed.) (1990). *Pathfinder Associative Networks: Studies in Knowledge Organization*. Norwood, NJ: Ablex Publishing.
Simon, H. A. (1990). Invariants of human behavior. *Annual Review of Psychology*, 41, 1–19.
Simon, D. P. & Simon, H. A. (1978). Individual differences in solving physics problems. In R. Siegler (Ed.), *Children's Thinking: What Develops?* (pp. 325–48). Hillsdale, NJ: Lawrence Erlbaum.
Spiro, R. J., Feltovich, P. J., Coulson, R. L. & Anderson, D. K. (1989). Multiple analogies for complex concepts: antidotes for analogy-induced misconceptions in advanced knowledge acquisition. In S. Vosniadou & R. Ortony (Eds), *Similarity and Analogical Reasoning* (pp. 498–531). Cambridge, MA: Cambridge University Press.
Sternberg, R. J. & Frensch, P. A. (1991). *Complex Problem Solving: Principles and Mechanisms*. Hillsdale, NJ: Lawrence Erlbaum.
Tversky, A. & Kahneman, D. (1974). Judgment under uncertainty: heuristics and biases. *Science*, 185, 1124–31.
Vicente, K. J. & Rasmussen, J. (1990). The ecology of human–machine systems. II: Mediating "direct perception" in complex work domains. *Ecological Psychology*, 2, 207–50.
Weaver, C. A., Mannes, S. & Fletcher, C. R. (Eds) (1995). *Discourse Comprehension. Essays in Honor of Walter Kintsch*. Hillsdale, NJ: Lawrence Erlbaum.
Weber, E. U., Bockenholt, U., Hilton, D. J. & Wallace, B. (1993). Determinants of diagnostic hypothesis generation: effects of information, base rates, and experience. *Journal of Experimental Psychology: Learning, Memory & Cognition*, 19, 1151–64.
Weinstein, M. C. (1980). *Clinical Decision Analysis*. Philadelphia, PA: W. B. Saunders.
White, B. Y. & Frederiksen, J. R. (1990). Causal model progressions as a foundation for intelligent learning environments. *Artificial Intelligence*, 24, 99–157.

Chapter 23

Designing Healthcare Advice for the Public

Patricia Wright
Cardiff University

PUBLIC HEALTHCARE ADVICE

Advice about Medicines and Healthcare Options

Advice about healthcare ranges from general encouragement of hygienic practices, such as brushing teeth, to personal details of exercises to assist recovery from surgery. The sources of healthcare advice range from clinically qualified experts, through self-help groups, to magazines, the popular press and the World Wide Web. This diversity is too great to be encompassed within a single chapter, so this discussion will focus on two categories of healthcare advice, one involving procedural instructions and the other supporting informed choice. It is important to realise that even procedural instructions are often treated by readers as "advice" rather than as imperatives. For example, the medicine label may say clearly "Not to be given to children under twelve", but if my son will be 12 in 2 weeks' time and he's a big lad for his age and the rest of the family respond well to this medication, then I may choose to ignore the advice. Compliance with instructions is perhaps the most important outcome from reading medical text (see the section "Designing for compliance").

There is a growing appreciation among the medical profession of the need to involve patients in decisions about their healthcare because treatment benefits and risks are not the only criteria that people use in making healthcare decisions (Entwistle, Sheldon, Sowden & Watt, 1996). Patients' decisions about therapy may need to take into account non-medical considerations, such as the financial

Handbook of Applied Cognition, Edited by F. T. Durso, R. S. Nickerson, R. W. Schvaneveldt, S. T. Dumais, D. S. Lindsay and M. T. H. Chi.

consequences of time away from work or the additional demands of the disabled child. Furthermore, there are numerous sources of information that can help people decide about healthcare options such as whether to have a malaria injection before going on holiday or whether to make an appointment for a breast-screening examination.

Medication instructions are important because the size of the market for over-the-counter medication is growing rapidly (Hoy, 1994). Consequently the leaflets accompanying these medicines will play an increasingly vital role in determining health outcomes. European Union directives stipulated that by the end of 1998 all packs of licensed medicines had to include patient information leaflets. This effort will be wasted if the contents of the leaflet are misunderstood or the leaflets are printed in such small type that many people cannot read them easily. The usability criterion is reflected in the US Federal mandate that by the year 2000 *useful* information must be delivered to 75% patients receiving new prescriptions. It is hoped this will rise to 95% by 2006. Hammond (1995) gives examples of how pharmaceutical companies are responding to the need to better inform people about their medication. But legislation about the provision of information is only the first step. That information must be usable if the aims of the legislation are to be attained. In Australia it has been recognised that achieving adequate usability will rcquirc thc adoption of performance-based design procedures (Sless & Wiseman, 1994). This chapter will illustrate both why this is so and how it can be accomplished.

The area of healthcare procedures is important as a research domain because it challenges existing theories of reading to enlarge their scope. They need to encompass the way people search the material, as well as their interpretation of it; the theories also need to address issues surrounding how this interpretation is translated into a set of actions. The advantages of this broader view of reading have been recognised in other areas of public information (Wright, 1980, 1988a). Nevertheless, the domain of healthcare advice raises special problems because readers can be emotionally involved when their own health is at issue. They may also have strong, though possibly faulty, prior knowledge and beliefs about the causes and remedies of illness.

Another facet of patient choice concerns the explanations given to hospital patients of the procedures they will undergo, perhaps describing what to expect as a consequence of surgical intervention. Mason (1993) suggests that informing patients before an operation makes them less anxious and more co-operative during their period in hospital. Several meta-analyses of research in this area have demonstrated that psycho-educational interventions can reduce the length of stay in hospital (Devine & Cook, 1982; Matthews & Ridgeway, 1984; Mumford, Schlesinger & Glass, 1982). Hospitals can support communication options other than, or in addition to, printed leaflets. So although the present review will focus on print materials for explaining medication procedures, it will also consider video cassettes and interactive multi-media displays.

Not everyone finds reading an easy option, either through physical disability (Rayner & Yerassimou, 1997), unfamiliarity with the language, or learning problems (Weiss & Coyne, 1997). Replacing reading with listening may help some people; material can be provided on an audio cassette or via a telephone line. In the UK since 1993, a national telephone number has been available free of charge for people to access information on several hundred health topics (Entwistle, Watt & Herring, 1996, p. 36). In large shops it would be feasible to think of the product bar code being used in conjunction with, perhaps, small palmtop computers to give customers access to auditory details about healthcare products on sale. A different set of problems arises from not being a fluent speaker of the dominant language in the location where the medical advice is sought, a phenomenon that increases as travel for business or leisure becomes more frequent. Travellers might benefit from international standardisation in the way certain categories of information are given (e.g. dosage and contra-indications).

Some studies have found people reluctant to read leaflets. For example, 600 patients visiting the surgery of a rural practice in the South of England were given a questionnaire to return by post as they left the building (Wicke, Lorge, Coppin & Jones, 1994). From the 327 replies received (a 55% response rate) fewer than 20 reported having read any of the leaflets available on a table while they were waiting to see the doctor. Nor had the patients attended to the wall notices. As Mayberry & Mayberry (1996) point out, "Unfortunately the sophistication of today's society is not always accompanied by equivalent reading ability". In contrast, from an overview of 11 empirical studies, Ley (1988) concluded that it seemed reasonable to expect that just under three-quarters of patients would read leaflets if they were personally handed them. This greater willingness to study the leaflets may result from the patients' assessment of personal relevance. When readers see themselves as part of the intended audience this may influence not only their willingness to read information but also to comply with it.

Even in Ley's review, the proportion reading leaflets varied across the studies from 47% to 95%. Either leaflets are not suitable for some topics or some people. Perhaps other technologies, such as video cassettes or CD-ROMs or the World Wide Web, would be more successful in communicating healthcare advice in contemporary society (Randall, 1993).This raises concerns about the quality of such advice (Impicciatore, Pandolfini, Castella & Bonatti, 1997) and how the public can distinguish good advice from bad (Wyatt, 1997), a problem that also applies to telephone helplines (Dickinson, 1998) and popular print media such as magazines. Non-print media present new challenges to information design professionals who need to know which medium to choose for specific healthcare messages and the critical design features within these media.

Differences from Mass Media Campaigns

This chapter will not discuss health education campaigns which involve mass media advertising in order to reach an audience that may have little interest in the message content. Instead, the present focus will be on healthcare advice where the decision making is time-limited. You can decide to think about changing your diet next month, but you cannot postpone until tomorrow the decision about whether wine with dinner would be risky given the cold remedy you took earlier in the day. Even within this constraint the medical topics are diverse. They include pre-natal screening, child vaccination, purchasing cough mixture, deciding if it is safe to take another tablet for a persistent headache. Time pressure may enhance people's willingness to attend to written materials. So this is a fruitful domain for exploring factors that enhance information usability.

Even for procedures and decision making, the audience for healthcare advice varies widely. It includes hospital in-patients who may be concerned about surgery and post-operative recovery, as well as out-patients for whom additional information may enhance the quality of their consultation by enabling them to ask questions or to better understand and remember what the clinician says. The audience also includes people who are not patients but may be purchasing medical remedies on their own initiative. This diversity of audience and contexts is one reason why care is needed in generalising from empirical studies. Inevitably researchers will have studied a particular audience and medical topic. Yet topics vary along three major dimensions: the threat they pose to life (e.g. cancer versus colds); the age and sex of the patients (e.g. pregnancy versus prostate surgery); the complexity of the concepts being explained. Such factors can have implications for the design of healthcare advice. A video in which a young female nurse discusses prostate cancer, or a young male physician explains hormone replacement therapy, may not be ideal mappings of topic and information source.

A meta-analysis of the research on healthcare communication would be helpful (Chalmers & Altman, 1995) but is not easily achieved because relevant studies come from several different disciplines (health promotion, information design, educational research, cognitive psychology, visual ergonomics, communication studies, human–computer interaction). Researchers in different disciplines work within different theoretical frameworks and use different methodologies. This divergence is not unique to healthcare advice but applies to the design of most functional materials that people read in order to use (Wright, 1988a). Greater interchange across disciplinary boundaries could be beneficial, both to people wanting healthcare advice and to the medical and pharmaceutical services that seek so valiantly to provide it.

A Framework for Designing Communications

When the content of a leaflet is determined predominantly by clinicians, it may fail to meet patients' information needs. Meredith, Emberton, Wood & Smith (1995) examined 25 leaflets or fact sheets about prostate surgery and contrasted the information given with the information wanted by 5361 patients. They reported that much of the information distributed had considerable shortcomings. It lacked uniformity in form and content, topics of relevance to patients were omitted, terminology was often poor and patients' experience was at variance with what their surgeon said. To give just one example, only six of these 25 leaflets mentioned the possibility of changes in sexual sensation after the operation and all six said that this would not occur. In contrast, 24% of patients reported a constant change and a further 12% reported an occasional change. There were 500 patients (12%) who said they were worried about these changes in sensation. Such data indicate that there can be considerable scope for improving the information content given to patients. Meredith et al. stressed the need to

Table 23.1 Summary of how people read healthcare information

ACCESS	• Reader formulates one or more questions • Reader scans the available information seeking locations where answer(s) may be found
INTERPRETATION	• Reader understands the literal meaning of the verbal and graphic information provided • Reader integrates the verbal and graphic information • Literal meaning is combined with the reader's pre-existing schemas and personal values • Reader infers author's agenda and relates this to own personal goals
APPLICATION	• Reader takes decison(s) about appropriate actions (forms an intention) • An action plan, consisting of subgoals and the steps necessary for achieving these, is devised • Reader implements the steps for each subgoal, monitoring outcomes • A mismatch between subgoal and attainment may lead to a new question and the process may then recycle from ACCESS

Source: Adapted from Wright, in press.

involve previous patients in specifying this content. The need for evaluation techniques to be incorporated into design procedures is discussed later in this chapter. The point being made here is that good intentions are not enough to ensure successful communication.

Information design needs to be reader-based rather than text-based (Schriver, 1997). A framework that characterised how people read functional documents was proposed by Wright (1994) and can be extended to healthcare materials. This framework subdivided readers' activities into those occurring before what is conventionally thought of as reading, those occurring during the reading episode itself, and those occurring subsequently (see Table 23.1). When people are trying to use written materials, Wright has shown that readers begin by formulating a question. Instructions will be ignored if people believe there is nothing they need to ask (Wright, Creighton & Threlfall, 1982). For healthcare materials, the questions people ask may concern the suitability of the product for a specific user, or the frequency of dosage or possible side-effects. The design implication is that the answers to such questions need to be found easily.

Having formulated a question, readers search for an answer using their understanding of the document structure to skip straight to places where this is likely to be found. Readers then interpret the information they find. This can involve both understanding the literal meaning and also drawing inferences on several levels. When readers think they know what advice the writer is giving then they must decide what to do. They may seek more information, either within the document or elsewhere, or decide they can now answer their question(s). Finally, readers will formulate an intention that gives rise to a plan for action. While carrying out the plan, people monitor the outcomes and may respond to a mismatch between goal and outcome by re-reading the healthcare advice. The activities just described do not always occur in the same linear sequence. Readers may move backwards and forwards across these activity clusters as they formulate different questions.

Each cluster of reading activities involves a wide range of cognitive processes such as attention, perception, comprehension, memory and planning. Theories of how people orchestrate their cognitive resources are being developed for tasks in which one of these activity clusters dominates, e.g. search tasks (Pirolli & Card, 1995) or interpretation tasks (Otero & Kintsch, 1992; Pressley, Ghatala, Woloshyn & Pirie, 1990). Current theories of reading contribute more to our knowledge of how texts are interpreted than to how readers access information or modify their reading strategies.

Other frameworks also have implications for the design of healthcare advice. Much of the theoretical work on message presentation has been concerned with the formation of beliefs and their determination of patterns of behaviour, such as the Health Belief Model (Becker, 1974). Social learning theory has been influential with its emphasis on learning through modelling and imitation (Bandura, 1986). Such theories can have important implications for the content and style of healthcare advice. So too can the theoretical formulations of decision-making theory, since the action readers often take is in the form of a decision (e.g. Yates, 1992). Here, we adopt a different but complementary theoretical approach, looking at healthcare materials from the reader's perspective because of the evidence that readers are influenced by the cognitive demands that arise from the message structure and also by the verbal and visual features of its presentation (Schriver, 1997). From this reader perspective there are distinctly separate sets of activities that information designers need to support: (a) speedy access to specific details, (b) ease of understanding the advice and its credibility, and (c) help in carrying out subsequent actions.

Related to credibility is the evidence that readers interpret not only the literal content but also the message-giver's agenda (Hatch, Hill & Hayes, 1993; Hayes, 1996). Readers will ask themselves "Is he trying to sell me something?" Similarly they will assess whether they think the writer is intending to address people such as themselves. Studies of young people's reaction to drug information leaflets found that people could respond very negatively to their perception of the implied role-relationship between the message-giver and the reader (Schriver, 1997). These issues will be explored in more detail in the next section.

Because healthcare materials are used by people to make trade-offs across several dimensions (health, social, economic) it becomes important to know which design features influence attitudes or support decision-making (Morrow, Leirer & Sheik, 1988). This offers considerable scope for the imaginative information designer to show that appropriate design features can make a real difference to people's behaviour.

Articulating the activities of readers or viewers from a cognitive perspective highlights the value of understanding the communication process and not just the outcome. The solutions to problems arising from different reading activities have little in common. For example, solving problems caused by readers' forgetfulness while carrying out the planned actions may entail designing a calendar-based package so that people can check whether they have taken today's dose. Such packaging refinements would have no effect if readers misinterpreted the writer's intention. For example, the potential for ambiguity in the instruction "Take one tablet three times a day at mealtimes" may not be apparent to either writer or reader. Nevertheless the writer may intend that the tablets are taken with food whereas a reader may think that the important factor is the time of day and will take a tablet at breakfast time even though the reader never eats breakfast. Misinterpretations of this kind can be very difficult for writers to detect and illustrate that performance-based evaluation of healthcare materials is essential (see the section entitled "Incorporating Evaluation into Design Procedures", below).

MEDICATION INSTRUCTIONS

No matter whether medicines have been prescribed by a clinician or purchased over the counter they will specify a procedure to be followed and possibly list side-effects from taking the medication. These details will interest those scanning healthcare products in a shop, before deciding which to purchase. Shoppers may read manufacturers' warnings about not exceeding the stated dose and people for whom the product is not suitable (e.g. children under five years old or people with high blood pressure). The advantage of making these information categories visually distinct on medication labels comes from the fact that readers will want to access these categories at different times. Warnings and exclusion criteria may be of most interest before purchase. The focus shifts to procedural details later when the medicine is being taken. Flagging these various categories will therefore be helpful. Critical design factors extend beyond the verbal text to include non-verbal material such as tables and illustrations.

The Text

People's access to healthcare information depends on its legibility. However, legibility is necessary but not sufficient. The writer's choice of words can have many subtle effects on readers' interpretations, a point sometimes illustrated with bogus conjugations such as "I'm persistent, You're obstinate, He's bloody-minded". The visual appearance of the text can also have important consequences for ease of use. For example, replacing prose paragraphs with a list of steps can be helpful when giving procedural information (Morrow, Leirer & Altieri, 1995). In spite of this evidence that in functional materials, language and layout often dynamically interact, for convenience the issues of visual presentation and the choice of language will be considered separately below.

Legibility and Visual Presentation

For the manufacturers, one of the difficulties about the information accompanying drugs is that the packet itself is often small. If considerable detail has to be given within a small space, this can lead to the choice of condensed typefaces, printed in a very small size, which inevitably reduces the proportion of the public who can read the information easily. The people excluded are not only the elderly and the visually handicapped, but also members of the public who do not wear their reading glasses when they are shopping or in normal daily activities around the house. Hartley (1994a), in overviewing the text-design features that are helpful for the visually impaired, suggests that in Britain with approximately 60 million adults there are almost 1 million partially sighted people over 16 years old, the age at which most people are likely to assume responsibility for their own medication. A review of 85 leaflets available in GPs' practices in Britain found only nine (11%) conformed to the minimum size of typeface recommended by the Royal National Institute for the Blind (Albert & Chadwick, 1992). This suggests that legibility problems are widespread even though leaflets are less constrained in size than are the labels on medication containers. So, the failure rate for information accompanying medication is probably much higher.

Ingenuity and lateral thinking may be needed to find solutions to the problems of communicating about proprietary medicines with the visually impaired. Possibilities include distributing the details over a wider area of the packaging. Wogalter, Magurno, Scott & Dietrich (1996) found that fins attached to the caps of medicine containers provided a useful additional surface area that could be used to repeat crucial information and so enhance memory for the information. In a previous study he had shown that people preferred the containers with enhanced writing areas (Wogalter & Dietrich, 1995). Other solutions may include providing further information at the point of sale, where details from the packaging could be enlarged, or supplementary leaflets provided. When leaflets are inside the package, purchasers may not have access to that information until after purchasing the product. In time, we may have a small pocket computer that enables this bar code information to be displayed in whatever ways the palmtop owner chooses.

For research purposes, analysis of drug information is made easier by annual publications such as Walker (1995), sponsored by the Association of the British Pharmaceutical Industry which reproduces over 400 of the leaflets issued by its members. Hartley (in press) has drawn on this resource to highlight the characteristics of patient information leaflets and to relate these to the needs of the elderly. He points out that relatively few research studies examining the comprehension and retention of material by the elderly check whether people can read the text. Only three of the ten studies Hartley reviews have included this elementary precaution. It is easy for legibility issues to be overlooked by those for whom legibility is not a problem.

General design features which enhance legibility include the type size being at least 12 or 14 point (Poulton, 1967a, 1969; Vanderplas & Vanderplas, 1980), but it becomes counter-productive if the print is so large that very few words will fit on a line. Moreover, in healthcare materials it is important that the typeface chosen differentiates clearly among digits such as 3, 5, 8. The white space between the lines, plus a clear contrast between the color of text and its background can be more influential in promoting ease of reading than the small differences between serif and non-serif fonts (Poulton, 1967b). The importance of a clean background seems to be forgotten when text is printed over graphics, or if the paper is so thin that details show through from the reverse side (Spencer, Reynolds & Coe, 1977). Very thin paper is sometimes used if leaflets have to be folded several times to fit inside small packets. Increasing the container size could be more cost-effective than reducing the weight of the paper.

Extensive passages written in capital letters slow readers down because the capitals do not provide the differentiated word outlines that lower case letters offer (Poulton, 1968). It is a corollary of this need for differentiation that typefaces having clear ascending strokes on letters such as b, d, h, t, and clear descending strokes on letters such as p, j, g, y, will be easier to read. The thickness of the strokes in the typeface is also important, with bold text usually being more legible than normal text. These legibility factors become critical when the information is read in poor ambient light or by the visually impaired. Hartley (1994b) points out that medication advice should not be printed in fonts having thin strokes or low contrast with the background colour.

A uniform spacing between words, although it results in a ragged right-hand edge, helps older readers where line length is short (Gregory & Poulton, 1970). It is for short line lengths, such as newspaper columns, that the process of aligning text at both left- and right-hand margins can result in very odd spacing between and within words. This happens because the space left behind by a word that did not fit on the line is distributed among the relatively few words remaining on that line. This unusual spacing impairs normal reading processes. Hartley (1994a) suggests that reading difficulties caused by legibility factors will be exacerbated by the cognitive deficits associated with aging. This leads him to suggest that elderly people should be included in any testing of healthcare materials. Design features that assist older people rarely hinder younger readers although the reverse is not necessarily the case.

Language

Problems with the language of healthcare advice can arise at several levels: words, sentences, paragraphs, document structure. At the word level, healthcare advice may use medical terms that are not familiar to readers. The word "contra-indications" seldom crops up in casual conversation. Even familiar words such as "sometimes" or "seldom" may imply different frequencies for clinicians and the public. Pander Maat & Klaassen (1994) asked 39 patients waiting in a Dutch health centre to read statements about side-effects occurring "seldom" or "sometimes" or "regularly" then fill in the blank in the following statement: "In saying this, the author means that this side-effect will occur for . . . out of every 100 patients." They found patients over-estimated the frequency with which these side-effects would occur. The Dutch authority responsible for producing many drug labels (7000) was using "seldom" to mean less than 1%, but the patients' mean estimate was about 6%. This frequency could be reduced by preceding the details about side-effects with a short paragraph explaining that they did not reduce the effectiveness of the medicine, were usually not dangerous and were only temporary. This is evidence that the meanings assigned to some words are easily modified, wittingly or unwittingly, by the writer.

Content is known to have a strong influence on people's interpretation of quantifiers (Hartley, Trueman & Rodgers, 1984; Moxey & Sanford, 1993). Seeing a rainbow sometimes is a much less frequent event than getting a busy signal sometimes when dialling a telephone number. One consequence of this contextual dependency may be that the coupling of quantifiers with specific side-effects (e.g.

nausea) results in similar estimates across languages and cultures. Studies are needed in medical contexts involving several language communities before such conclusions can be safely drawn.

In another study, Pander Maat & Klaassen (1994) compared three versions of a leaflet for a non-steroid anti-inflammatory drug which had many potential side-effects. They interviewed 97 patients by telephone during the week after these people had visited the pharmacy and collected the drug for the first time. Although there was no overall change in patients' attitudes to their medication, when "sometimes" was replaced by "seldom" (thereby coming closer to the pharmacist's intended frequency) this change not only decreased the number of side-effects that patients recalled as being mentioned in the leaflet, but it also decreased the number of side-effects that people reported they had personally experienced – a drop from 24% to 7%. Such data strongly suggest that the reader's interpretation of healthcare advice can be a powerful determinant of a range of subsequent behaviours.

Interpretation involves not only the words and sentence structure but also the way the information is organised at a higher level, the discourse structure. There is evidence that people prefer medication information to be in a particular sequence, and that the material is better remembered when presented in this sequence (Morrow, Leirer, Andrassy, Tanke & Stine-Morrow, 1996). Certainly, reorganising the discourse can influence readers' assessment of the quality and effectiveness of written health materials (Lambert & Gillespie, 1994; O'Keefe, 1988).

When written procedures are being studied in a laboratory setting, people are usually willing to demonstrate their understanding by doing whatever the text asks of them. In real life, readers may compute several parallel interpretative strands as part of their understanding of a text, and some of these interpretations may conflict rather than converge on a specific course of action. For example, readers may decide the writer is addressing an audience that does not include themselves. This is a characteristic of the interpretation of much public advice, not just healthcare. In a literal sense readers understand the meaning of a written message saying, "Do not stand near the edge", but they assume it is intended for people who are either young or old and have uncertain motor control, rather than for themselves. Similarly, the label in a synthetic garment saying that it should be hand-washed may be seen as the manufacturer hedging against legal liability rather than giving good advice. These examples illustrate that readers impute to the author a set of communicative intents in addition to conveying the content. For healthcare materials readers may be sceptical about certain information sources, perhaps drug companies, if they anticipate an underlying intention to sell a product. Similarly, the credibility of the advice-giver (e.g. medical expert or other patients) might be an important factor in the persuasiveness of videos or multi-media communications where there is a personal presence of the message-giver. This seems less salient in print, where conveying authentically different voices within the text is harder to do.

Medical leaflets may adopt a tone that some readers dislike. Readers may be put off by the mental picture of the author that they are forming as they read (Hatch, Hill & Hayes, 1993; Hayes, Hatch & Hill, 1992; Schriver, 1997). Monahan (1995) has argued for the value of authors adopting a positive approach. Since the emotional response to a leaflet can have many determinants, isolating the separate effects of each may not be meaningful if they interact dynamically. This difficulty may have contributed to the lack of empirical study that emotional tone has received. It is a factor missing from most models of reading although it may have an important influence on whether people continue to read or decide to stop (Wright, 1988b). At least such emotive elements are now being incorporated into models of writing (Hayes, 1996).

The need to develop models of text interpretation that take greater account of the readers' emotional involvement with the material has been highlighted by studies of Berry & Michas (in press) on the written information accompanying drugs. People more accurately remembered the details of how the drug should be taken if this information preceded details of possible side-effects; whereas memory for the details about side-effects varied with their severity, not with their position in the leaflet. Memory theories have long grappled with explaining the better retention of material encountered first (Baddeley, 1993). Models predicting the trade-off between serial position and other textual features, such as interest or emotional impact, have yet to be formulated (Cohen, 1996).

Fine-tuning the verbal language will not have much effect when complex concepts are involved, as is the case for illnesses having both chronic and acute phases (Masson & Waldron, 1994). Here, intervention and re-design at the discourse level will be needed in order to achieve adequate understanding. Rogers, Shulman, Sless & Beach (1995) made a similar point when stressing the need for performance-centred design rather than the routine application of rules, algorithms or house styles. Moreover, for some kinds of healthcare advice a combination of communication media may be more effective than any one alone (see the section "Alternatives to print").

Tables

Medication advice can include tables, perhaps specifying dosage in different circumstances. People can easily make mistakes when looking up details in a table and the likelihood of error is a function of the number of decisions that must be made in order to locate a specific cell (Wright, 1977). For tables having 16 cells, errors were greater when the column headings required four binary decisions rather than two decisions each made among four options. Errors were also greater when decisions were distributed across row and column headings rather than confined to just one of the spatial dimensions. It appears that co-ordinating information from two spatially separate axes makes greater demands on readers' memory. So this study identifies two of the factors contributing to the complexity of tabular information, decision making and memory. There are others. Even in completely numeric tables, linguistic factors can be influential. It is easier for people to decide that some referent value, such as their temperature or a child's age, is *more than* the appropriate cell value in the table, than to decide that it is *less than* the tabulated value (Wright & Barnard, 1975). If writers are aware of the cognitive processing that readers undertake when using tables, they can design their information to reduce the demands being made.

Fortunately, many of the tables that are given within healthcare advice are simpler than those which occur in other domains of public information – e.g. transport timetables have to deal with parallel events and have many irregularities and exceptions. Nevertheless, even simple tables need clear headings to the rows and columns, plus a good visual gestalt indicating which items belong together. When numerical data are given, mistakes are less likely if the numbers are vertically aligned about the decimal point and the units represented by these numbers are unambiguous. For fuller reviews of the many information design factors known to influence the ease of using, see Chapman & Mahon, 1986; Simmonds & Reynolds, 1994.

Illustrations

Another way in which the tone of a printed text can be changed is through the use of illustrations. Analysis of the compendium of patient information leaflets compiled by Walker (1995) was carried out with the first leaflets from the 45 different pharmaceutical companies included in that publication. This constraint of just one leaflet from each manufacturer prevents the analysis being biased by the graphic style of any one company, but does not necessarily reflect the likelihood of people encountering leaflets in a particular style because some leaflets are much more common than others. Within this sample of leaflets, 19 (45%) included illustrations of some kind: 16 (84%) were in the form of line drawings; only 2 (11%) included photographs. So nearly half the patient information leaflets accompanying medication may contain line drawings. Since research suggests that for both young and older readers illustrations enhance the success in following procedural instructions (Morrell & Park, 1993) this would seem to be a helpful design feature.

Advice is available on the drawing of illustrations (e.g. Lowe, 1993) and research has explored the cognitive processes by which people interpret illustrations, particularly in educational texts where graphics are used for explanation (Mandl & Levin, 1989). However, graphics can be used in texts for many purposes. Reviewing 46 studies, Levie & Lentz (1982) found that, in 45, people learned better when illustrations were included. In domains other than text books the findings are less clear-cut. After reviewing the mixed results from six studies of illustrations in patient information leaflets, Ley concluded: "At best the verdict of 'not proven' must be brought in concerning the usefulness of adding illustrations to written materials for patients" (Ley, 1988, p. 138).

There are several potential reasons for this discrepancy between education and healthcare materials. Research on graphics is a difficult area in which to attempt a meta-analysis since illustrations can differ greatly in their style (photographs versus line drawings) as well as in their clarity of expressing the intended meaning (it may be an excellent drawing of an internal organ but still be unrecognised by readers). Furthermore, the way the illustrations are visually and verbally linked to the text can be crucial. This linkage may be caption-style, with text under or alongside each picture. Alternatively, the author may refer to "fig. 1" during the course of writing. Readers may not heed such directions from authors unless the illustration can be studied without disruption to the continued reading of the main text (Whalley & Flemming, 1975). Attempts to specify whether a picture might be worth a thousand words have not always taken into account this variation in the text–picture relation (Larkin & Simon, 1987). This is among the reasons why extending the work on printed materials to encompass the role of graphics in interactive documents is not always straightforward (Wright, Milroy & Lickorish, in press).

In a scholarly discussion of the many ways in which illustrations can be used for communicating, Twyman (1985) has pointed out that there are at least eight variables that need to be considered whenever graphics are used. These factors include the purpose, content, the spatial organisation of the graphic elements, graphic style (e.g. pictorial or schematic), production method, available expertise and other resources, the audience and the circumstances in which the material will be used. These circumstances can vary from relaxed consideration to stressful urgency, from passive indifference to anxious concern. These dimensions of readers' emotional state can be difficult to capture in evaluation studies.

As Twyman points out, illustrations differ not only in style but also in purpose. They can be used to embellish the visual appearance of the page even though they add nothing to the content itself. Three of the leaflets (7%) in the sample from Walker (1995) contained small illustrations of this kind. These visual tokens can be used to break the text on the page into smaller chunks which may make the page seem less daunting to reluctant readers. Care is needed when graphics are used for purposes other than explanation because they may risk appearing to trivialise a serious subject or may discourage readers in other ways. Schriver (1997, p. 172) reports that teenagers thought the line drawings in one leaflet were intended for a younger age group, so assumed that their own age group was not part of the intended audience for that leaflet. It is one of the potential drawbacks of illustrations that they make concrete what a verbal description can leave imprecise. The word "person" does not denote a particular age, race or sex, whereas illustrations have difficulty avoiding such unwanted constraints. The use of non-human, cartoon characters may sometimes offer a solution where a graphic's only function is to embellish the page.

A third communicative purpose of illustrations can be to emphasise part of the content by re-stating the message in a different way – for example, through visual puns (Abed, 1994). They offer an opportunity to introduce humour when using graphics for emphasis, and so prevent the message sounding too strident. Few readers like to be shouted at. Both embellishment and emphasis may change the tone that is detected by readers and this may influence their willingness to engage with the material or follow the advice given. However there are wide individual differences in people's sense of humour, and some people may find an illustration childish or patronising rather than amusing.

Designing for Compliance

A crucial measure of the effectiveness of healthcare communication is often whether people comply with the advice given. Understanding the written message is undoubtedly an important part of achieving compliance, and healthcare materials are not always easy to understand (Albert & Chadwick, 1992). In addition, it may be important to address conflicting goals and prior beliefs (DiMatteo, Reiter & Gambone, 1994). There have been suggestions that the word "compliance" would be better replaced by words such as "consensus" or "concordance" which remove the power asymmetry implicit in the older term (Marinker, 1997; Mullen, 1997; Royal Pharmaceutical Society of Great Britain, 1996). This conceptual shift seems more appropriate for discussion between clinicians and patients than for procedures that need to be followed once a decision has been reached about a particular course of treatment. If the manufacturer stipulates that no more than six tablets can be taken within 24 hours, this leaves no room for reaching a consensus with the person who wants to take more. Nevertheless, as was noted earlier, some readers will view such instructions as general advice for the average person rather than as a strict command that applies to them.

Re-designing the instructions to increase compliance may require specifying the health risks that are run by taking too many tablets, or there may be a need to clarify that the count does not re-set to zero at bedtime. Pills taken yesterday evening have implications for how many can be taken on waking. Non-compliance can result from conceptual mistakes such as this. Design solutions might add the word "consecutively" or use a time unit (e.g. 8 h) that does not have a common verbal label such as "day" that can introduce ambiguities

Table 23.1 indicates how failures of compliance could result from mishaps at numerous points in the communication process. There can be problems with patients not finding the information. For example, Rogers et al. (1995) observed that when people were given a medicine container and asked about information on the wrap-around label, 18% failed to turn the bottle round. This study involved 68 people in their 60s and 70s. Since two-thirds of older people take non-prescription drugs regularly (Hammond & Lambert, 1994) it is not appropriate to dismiss these data as simply reflecting a decline in the cognitive abilities of older people. There is a serious healthcare advice problem that can successfully be addressed by re-designing the label (Rogers et al., 1995).

Access to written information can be a problem even for prescription drugs, as some studies have shown that doctors in general practice may forget to give relevant leaflets to patients (Gibbs, Waters & George, 1987). Even if leaflets are distributed, they may become lost or their contents mis-remembered by the time patients have obtained the medication. Such problems lead Gibbs et al. (1987) to suggest that it might be better if leaflets were distributed by pharmacists at the same time as the medication.

Even if the procedural information is accessible, there can be problems of comprehension and interpretation that can lead to unintentional failures of compliance. These problems are likely to be detectable and correctable if performance-based design and evaluation techniques are used. Ingenuity can be needed to devise performance measures that will detect the problems of compliance that arise from people's attempts at problem solving (e.g. "What do I do if I miss a dose?"), or the distortions that arise from memory processes operating in contexts that trigger other, inappropriate recall schemas.

ALTERNATIVES TO PRINT

If it were true that people now watch more information on screens but read less printed material, then there might be a case for replacing print with other media, such as video cassette or an interactive CD-ROM. The benefits and risks of communicating healthcare advice via these newer technologies are considered below.

Can Video Replace Print?

Many of the evaluation studies of patient information videos go little further than establishing that viewers liked the video and from this concluding that the videos must be a good alternative to print (Eiser & Eiser, 1996; Gagliano, 1988). The design of the video itself is rarely considered, yet this "magic bullet" approach runs counter to the evidence that listeners' perceptions of bias in a broadcast can be influenced by the text structure not just the content (Berry, Scheffler & Goldstein, 1993). Videos need to be assessed by many of the same factors as print, since understanding will be influenced by the choice of vocabulary and sentence styles, together with the overall discourse structure. For example, the benefits of therapy can be expressed in different ways which can dramatically influence patients' willingness to undergo the therapy. Hux & Naylor (1995) asked people about their willingness to undergo a hypothetical medical regime. They found 88% of those told that the treatment offered a 34% reduction in heart attacks said they would be willing to have it, whereas only 42% agreed to the treatment when the difference in risk was expressed in absolute terms (i.e. 1.4% fewer patients had heart attacks). The same patterns of responding emerged with a hypothetical anti-hypertensive drug. There is no reason for thinking this pattern will change across media. The critical factor seems to be how the messages are anchored to a conceptual framework for their interpretation.

Although some design features overlap for print and video, others will be media-specific – such as the way verbal and graphic materials are integrated (e.g. whether a voice-over is used on the video or preliminary explanation is given of unfamiliar concepts). Presentation factors may affect the perceived tone of a video. For instance, perhaps talking heads become less boring if the talk is shared among more heads, or this may confuse viewers who have trouble keeping track of who is who. There may even be the risk that distributing the talk reduces thematic continuity, instead of reinforcing all speakers' concordance with the message. We do not yet know whether advice from other patients appears more credible than advice from medical experts. One Australian study has reported that increasing the emotional content of a video produces longer lasting effects on people's intention to reduce skin cancer risks from exposure to the sun (Cody & Lee, 1990). This is a very useful starting point but emotional content can be varied in many ways and it would be helpful to know in what contexts it matters whether the emotional tone is positive or negative.

Comparisons across media have been made in educational settings but healthcare advice may differ in important ways from materials for student learning. The patient's emotional involvement with a healthcare topic may influence their reaction to different media, and for some medical topics people may prefer media affording privacy. In order to explore whether medical topic influences people's preference for particular media we distributed a small questionnaire to 189 women members of the volunteer panel at the Applied Psychology Unit in Cambridge UK (Wright, Lickorish & Green, 1996). These volunteers were predominantly white, middle class, articulate women, most of whom were not in full-time employment. They were asked a hypothetical question about how they would like to receive information on five healthcare topics: childhood vaccination, asthma treatment, hip replacement, recovery from strokes and speech therapy for children. For each medical topic three alternatives were given: print, audio and video, the order being counterbalanced across questionnaires. More than 80% of these volunteers chose print for vaccination, but fewer than 40% did so for speech therapy. These data strongly suggest that media preference varies with medical topic. The audio cassette option was rarely chosen – fewer than 2% across all topics. This may reflect the context in which these people usually listened to audio cassettes – perhaps in the car which might not be appropriate for listening to healthcare information. A subsidiary analysis showed that media preference did not vary with the age of the people completing the questionnaire. So videos may not be ideal solutions for giving healthcare advice on all topics.

If videos are only preferred where precise movements must be shown (e.g. correcting speech problems) perhaps message-givers need to think carefully before moving from print to more expensive media. Of course, preference data are not necessarily valid predictors of communication effectiveness, and performance data from the same message presented in different media are needed in order to assess understanding, retention and compliance. But these preference data are not irrelevant, and may reflect people's willingness to access the material in the first instance.

Conducting any meta-analysis of the research done on patient information videos is hampered by the fact that seldom are any details reported about the style adopted for the video. There is advice available on how to write medical leaflets for the public (e.g. Morrow, Von Leirer & Sheikh, 1988; Morrow et al., 1996; Secker & Pollard, 1995). However, nothing similar exists for the development of patient information videos. Some research suggests that the role-modelling components of videos are among their most important features (Gagliano, 1988; Melamed et al., 1978). Other researchers advocate that healthcare videos should have a content and discourse structure reflecting contemporary theories of attitude change (Eisser & Eisser, 1996). Theoretical foundations are certainly to be welcomed in this area but may not be sufficient for the development of effective videos if other design issues are overlooked. As with printed materials there can be no substitute for performance-based evaluation that sheds light on specific cognitive processes involved in attending to, understanding and remembering video materials.

Combining Media

Having recognised the many cognitive activities that people engage in when reading or viewing, it is no surprise to find that combining print and video, or using the video as a basis for group discussions, can be more successful than using a video alone (Odonnell, Doval, Duran & Odonnell, 1995). Different media may have a complementarity that is seldom explored by researchers. If readers have questions or want to refer back to an earlier point, this is more easily done in print than with video; but the pace of a video may carry viewers towards grasping the bigger picture rather than getting bogged down in details as may happen when reading. Posing research issues in terms of whether one medium is better than another, or more cost-effective when taking account of production and distribution costs, may obscure important questions about how media can be combined and which design features enhance these combinations. The notion of enhancement raises further questions about whether this is assessed in terms of ease of access, understanding or retention, or may be assessed by its effects on attitudes, beliefs and compliance. The multi-dimensional nature of assessment is considered in the section on "Incorporating Evaluation into Design Procedures", but the impact of print and video media on changing attitudes will be considered below.

Attitude Change

Information alone can sometimes change attitudes and lower anxiety. Loumidis, Hallam & Cadge (1991) found that a two-page leaflet giving factual reassurance about tinnitus resulted in greater acceptance of the condition by patients. The measure of acceptance was the number of unfulfilled needs recorded via a questionnaire, when comparison was made with a group of patients attending the same audiometry clinic who had not read the leaflet. A similar finding with a very different medical topic was reported by Kai (1994) who interviewed 42 inner-city parents with babies under six months old. These parents had been given a booklet to help them assess the severity of any ill health their baby might show. Kai reports that these parents found the booklet reduced anxiety and increased their confidence in coping with infant illness. The effect is not confined to printed materials. A recent audit reported by Dickinson (1997) found that roughly one-third of those people telephoning a healthline for advice subsequently decided that they need not trouble their GP. So there is clear potential for the provision of information being highly cost-effective.

Watching a video can be a social event. When friends watch a video together they will make comments both positive and negative during and after watching. In contrast, readers are less likely to interrupt each other to share a reaction to something the author says. But if videos are provided as stand-alone sources of healthcare advice, they may be little more effective than leaflets would be – if people bothered to read them. In which case it might be cheaper to encourage people to read, perhaps by asking them to read the leaflet while in the clinic and offering to return and answer questions, rather than making and distributing videos.

The emotional tone of a video can influence attitude change. Rook (1987) contrasted a vivid case history with a more matter of fact presentation of the same content, and found the case history video appeared more effective in changing attitudes as reflected in viewers' reported intentions about future behaviour. However, a six-week follow-up suggested these intentions had not been realised, although these people were still better at remembering the information than those who had the more abstract video message. Such findings underline the point made above that assessment must be made along several dimensions if an adequate profile of the relative effectiveness of different media is to be obtained.

While new information may change attitudes based on ignorance, the evidence suggests that it fares less well with changing attitudes based on false beliefs (Chambliss & Garner, 1996). Strong opinions lead people to focus on the details they agree with and to dismiss as biased any contradictory material, with the consequence that they strengthen their previous views no matter what material they encounter. So there will be instances where patients' prior attitudes and beliefs are much more powerful determinants of attitude change, or the lack of it, than any design features of healthcare materials (Gaskins, 1996). The expense of video would seem wasted in such circumstances. Nevertheless, this could be an area where sophisticated analysis of individual differences would repay greater dividends than the more conventional research focus on group mean effects. For similar reasons, this may provide the incentive for developing computer-based, interactive materials that can accommodate individual differences in prior knowledge as well as variation in the desire for new knowledge.

INTERACTIVE MULTI-MEDIA AND HEALTHCARE ADVICE

There are several reasons for wanting to explore computer-based, multi-media presentations. It is known that patients are more responsive to information that has been personalised for them, and this increases compliance (Campbell, DeVellis, Strecher, Ammerman, DeVellis & Sandler, 1994). It is also the case that reading is onerous for people with visual impairments or learning difficulties. Computer-based information can be multi-lingual, and can offer expanded explanations of points not understood. Not only will a computer display tend to chunk the presentation into small portions but, if well designed, it will help users quickly locate information relevant to their own concerns, something which is not always easy to do with printed materials.

Interactive displays in hospitals may be better located in a public area rather than a quiet, secluded place (Jones, Edgerton, Baxter, Navon, Ritchie, Bell & Murray, 1993). This apparent contrast with the earlier comments about the success of telephone healthcare advice because of the privacy and anonymity it affords, may reflect potential users' thinking how their behaviour will be interpreted by bystanders. Seeking privacy may be thought to suggest that the medical topic is of a highly sensitive nature rather than just suggesting that the information-seeker prefers peace and quiet. Making a phone call carries no such implications.

The ambient noise in public areas may suggest the need for a hand-held earpiece but this reduces the opportunity for social sharing of information with others, which has already been mentioned as a potentially important feature of multi-media presentations. Multi-media raises issues about whether verbal messages should be read or listened to, and whether graphics should be still or animated. Such issues are more often addressed in the context of school or college learning rather than healthcare. As was mentioned earlier, caution is needed when generalising from high school to healthcare, or even in generalising from studies of touch-screen information kiosks, because people's emotional involvement with healthcare materials can be much stronger than for other topics.

With an interactive computer-based display, tone can be conveyed by all the design features mentioned for print and video and, in addition, by the style of interaction facilitated by the interface. Difficulty in navigating within the document will suggest an unsympathetic author if people make no distinction between the content provider and the interface designer. Unpredictability in the interface (e.g. when going back does not take you to the preceding screen but to an earlier choice point) may lead patients to have doubts about the reliability of the information itself, with perceived carelessness in presentation being over-generalised and attributed to the content.

On the other hand, the public may feel that the computer-as-expert is more neutral than messages conveyed through other media. This too may influence compliance. But when people actively select small sections of a document, they may miss some of the crucial information either inadvertently or through faulty navigation decisions. Careful interface design can reduce this risk (e.g. drawing people's attention to material they have overlooked). Once again this underlines the importance of performance-based evaluation as part of the design process (Nielsen, 1993).

INCORPORATING EVALUATION INTO DESIGN PROCEDURES

Although a great deal is known about how to enhance the communication effectiveness of print and other media, this knowledge does not deliver a set of fail-safe guidelines. It may be better to think of the research literature as flagging the trouble spots, since factors such as illegibility always need to be avoided, whereas adequate legibility can be achieved by various routes. This is fortunate because the process of design usually involves trade-offs. For example, in order to fit information within a specific area, either the print size or interline spacing may need to be reduced. Indeed some information design principles are inherently dynamic, such as the need for larger print and greater interline spacing as the length of the line of print increases.

When considering the procedures for evaluating healthcare information, it is important to realise that this is not a procedure analogous to a filter, letting through the good information and keeping out the bad. Rather, it is a process that is intimately involved with the development of the material, the specification of its content, together with its visual and linguistic form (Mayberry & Mayberry, 1996). Because miscommunication results from the subtleties of both verbal language and graphic presentation, detecting and removing trouble spots will require more than just showing the material to a few people and asking them if they like it or find it helpful. Instead, performance-based criteria are needed, where the author specifies what readers should be able to do on the basis of the information provided, and evaluators check that such performances are achieved. Typical criteria might be that 70% of readers can locate relevant dosage information within 20 seconds; 80% of readers can demonstrate correct understanding for responding to a hypothetical scenario; 90% of readers can identify circumstances in which the medicine should not be taken. In this illustration the criterion rises with the importance of correct performance by readers. It is a matter of judgement that will inevitably vary with the product, to decide what these criteria should be for specific communication goals.

In the domain of education a distinction is drawn between formative evaluation, which is an iterative process whereby problems are identified, the text revised and re-evaluated, and summative evaluation which determines how closely the material achieves the intended goals for the target audience. Both types of evaluation are necessary, for there is no value in ironing out all the creases if you never notice that the garment has shrunk. However, these two kinds of evaluation require different techniques, different sample sizes and different measures. The summative evaluation occurs at the end of the process of information development and needs large samples that are representative of the intended audience. It will also need measures of outcome that can be related to the cost-effectiveness of producing and disseminating the material. None of this applies during the formative stages of evaluation. The samples can be small, especially if they represent some of the more vulnerable subgroups within the intended audience, and the measures need to be heterogeneous, including performance, attitude and preference.

Historically, thinking of evaluation as a filter may have led to the continued popularity of readability formulae (Flesch, 1948). Unfortunately, many of the aspects of language that need to be taken into account by those writing healthcare advice are missed by global assessments of text difficulty. Readability formulae take into account only a few features of the language used, such as the number of words in a sentence and the number of syllables in words. Nevertheless, Ley (1988) reviewed evidence from eight studies, six being his own, showing that revising medical leaflets to produce better scores on readability formulae can improve reading speed and increase understanding, together with retention of the information in the leaflet. In one study, where 160 patients had either no leaflet or a leaflet at one of three levels of "readability", Ley compared the number of tablets a patient should have taken with the number actually taken, and found the two numbers grew closer as the readability of the leaflet increased (Ley, Jain & Skilbeck, 1975). He concluded that, "despite the probably high motivation of the subjects and the probably high level of interest in the materials for them, an increase in readability often has desirable results" (Ley, 1988, p. 133). However, caution is necessary because there is an underlying predictive asymmetry here. A leaflet with a poor readability index will almost certainly benefit from revision, whereas a leaflet with a good readability index may still contain ambiguities or misleading expressions.

Sample Characteristics

While specifying the content that the leaflet should cover, it can be valuable to obtain input from a wide diversity of people, such as former patients and nursing staff as well as the intended audience and the clinical experts. These different groups may have an informed awareness of information needs relating to this medical topic that may simply not occur to medical professionals. For example, the procedure may involve some routine clinical activity such as taking a blood sample; but this activity is not routine for members of the public. So people may want to know whether it will be painful, how long it takes, whether there are side-effects or some precautions they should take.

Sophistication may be needed in eliciting content information from patients who may not have the knowledge to respond to a completely open-ended question ("What do you want to know?"), and may be over-enthusiastic in accepting whatever material is offered because they feel that any information is better than no information. One way around this dilemma is to ask people to rate the importance of specific items of information. If there is consensus about items receiving low ratings these will be a strong candidates for pruning if space is tight. The procedure of determining content is not necessarily separate from, nor logically prior to, taking decisions about presentation issues. As the content structure is made clearer through careful design of the presentation, so gaps in the content can become apparent.

Measures: Converging Methods that Focus on Process

The framework of how people read functional materials outlined in the section "Medical instructions" offers a basis for deciding which reading processes the evaluation should focus on during the design of the material. People need to be able to find the information that answers the questions they ask. Having found it, they need to understand it in the way the message-giver intended. Having understood it, they may need to remember it and formulate a plan for acting on it. During the design process these issues can be addressed separately, so that design solutions can be implemented when problems are found. For example, there is no point in showing that everyone correctly interprets the wording of a typewritten warning if, when this message is included on the box packaging, it is printed where many readers do not look, or is thought by readers to be some additional advertising and is ignored. Conversely, there is no point in assuming inattention or deliberate non-compliance when the message has been read, understood but misremembered. Improving the design of healthcare advice requires understanding what has caused the problems. Only from such an understanding can revisions be made safely.

As an example of the need for a detailed understanding of the reasons for communication failure, consider a study in which leaflets warning about the relation between skin cancer and sunburn were placed in the seat pockets for holiday passengers travelling with Air UK from Manchester in England. The researchers found no differential frequency of reporting sunburn among the

6276 people who completed the questionnaire on their return, when compared with the 6109 people who had travelled on flights not having the leaflet (Dey, Collins, Will & Woodman, 1995). However, the researchers did not ascertain whether passengers had not read the leaflet, whether they disbelieved the advice, or whether they forgot the message or disregarded it because they thought it inappropriate to them personally. The researchers decided against asking such questions in case they influenced people's response to other items in the questionnaire. This is understandable, but it is clearly hard to make progress in remedying communication problems if vital data are not collected. So the use of convergent methodologies, perhaps combining a postal questionnaire with a structured interview of a smaller sample, might have yielded more insight into the reasons for peoples' responses – or lack of them – to this healthcare advice and so have suggested what kinds of changes might be more successful.

The evaluation of people's success in locating information has to be made for specific categories of information (e.g. exclusion criteria; how to take the medicine; who should not take the medicine; possible side-effects) and also for details within these categories. As an illustration of why it is helpful to separate finding the category from finding the detail within it, consider the possibility that using colour for a category, or boxing the information, may make it easy to identify, but the spacing within this demarcated section generates a gestalt that confuses readers. Only by separating these two issues can the data collected be used to highlight the kind of revision that is needed. Relevant methodologies include asking readers to "find and underline" target information, or to report the next word after some target detail. As was mentioned earlier in this section, an ideal design procedure would stipulate a percentage of readers who could locate target information within a specified time, where this time may vary with the product or information category. This is at the heart of a technique known as a "performance-based design" (Sless & Wiseman, 1994).

Care also needs to be taken when assessing whether people have understood what they read. In one study of cystic fibrosis leaflets, 90% of the 312 people returning a questionnaire said they found it easy to understand, but nevertheless more than one-third gave the wrong answer when asked about the risk that they personally might have the CF gene (Livingstone, Axton, Mennie, Gilfillan & Brock, 1993). Failure to correctly understand or interpret information is such an obvious reason for medication not being taken correctly that one might imagine all healthcare materials would be carefully evaluated. It is difficult to obtain data on how widely this is done by any method but there exists evidence that some instructions could be improved. Morrell, Park & Poon (1989) assessed comprehension by asking groups of younger and older people to write plans describing how they would take the medicine they were shown. In this study it was found that revising the information given on a medicine bottle resulted in a 21% drop in errors for the group with an average age of 70 years. Even the 20 year olds showed a 14% decrease in errors. The important design feature concerned the organisation of the material.

Morrell's technique captures important facets of readers' understanding. In contrast, many aspects of comprehension can be completely missed by the use of question and answer methods. If questions can be answered with words or phrases taken directly from the healthcare advice this offers no evidence that anything has been understood. For example, after reading a leaflet saying that "when empty the franzzle must be thrown away", many people would correctly answer a question about what must be thrown away and none would know what a "franzzle" is. Asking for a paraphrase or offering multiple-choice alternatives that do not repeat the word "franzzle" would be more informative.

Readers' understanding needs to be assessed at several levels. The easiest assessment is to check on the details, but it is important to evaluate how well readers are combining the details to give a higher level representation of the gist of the message. This gist level may be all that is remembered when readers return to take a second dose of medication. At that time they may no longer feel the need to re-read the instructions. The material that readers consider to be lower level detail is forgotten most easily, particularly by older people (Rice, Meyer & Miller, 1989). So, it is important that the discourse structure correctly signals the most important information. Techniques such as asking people to underline the *n* most important points is one way of approaching this.

Assessment also needs to include readers' inferences about whether the writer really means what is written or is just feeling obliged to say it. Here, indirect evaluation procedures may reveal more than direct questions. Scenario techniques, which have been developed to assess understanding in non-medical contexts (Young & Barnard, 1987), can be extended to healthcare materials. For example, if a character is described as having missed a dose or mistakenly taken too much, the volunteer can be asked to say what the person should do now. Scenarios offer a useful way of assessing whether readers think it is important to comply with specific details. Since attributed unimportance can be one reason for non-compliance, it is obviously helpful to discover during the course of evaluation whether this is a potential trouble spot. Again the point being made is that evaluation within the design procedure needs to be more discriminative than just yielding a pass/fail verdict on the information as a whole. The scenarios will be chosen to discriminate between a misinterpretation of what was read and a discounting of it. Achieving adequate discriminations usually requires using a combination of evaluation techniques. These performance measures cannot all be taken from the same volunteers because the techniques themselves will perturb the nature of the person's interaction with the material. But large numbers of volunteers are not needed; the need is for data that are richly informative about readers' underlying processes, in order that the text can be modified in the light of this new knowledge.

Performance-based evaluation procedures have several advantages over qualitative measures, e.g. asking people if they found the information clear or informative. One of the snags with techniques relying on rating-scale answers is that the people being asked may feel that it is their competence in understanding the material that is being assessed (Schriver, 1997). So they are keen to give a positive response rather than risk the interviewer thinking they are stupid. On other occasions politeness conventions may constrain people from making negative comments about materials they feel the questioner has given time to producing. They respect the good intention, and do not wish to discourage efforts to make healthcare information available.

Evaluation as Feedforward

Formative evaluation dragoons empiricism to the service of improving communication. If no similar messages will ever be produced then this data-driven approach will suffice. However, messages about medication procedures or healthcare options are not unique. They are variants of many similar messages that will be produced in the future, dealing with other medical topics or new therapies. This foreseeable demand makes it valuable to learn lessons from the development of one set of materials that can be applied in the development of others. This longer-term perspective can benefit from supplementary research undertaken in order to isolate critical communication design factors.

Any corporate memory also requires mechanisms for passing on the lessons learned. Yet surprisingly often, an individual who has never before produced information for the general public will feel capable of tackling the job without needing to acquire new skills or consult with those having any special expertise in communication and evaluation. It seems to be a widespread belief that anyone can write a leaflet or specify the content and style of a video. This myth persists in spite of considerable evidence to the contrary (Wright, 1998).

CONCLUSIONS

This chapter has examined evidence that the way people respond to healthcare advice can critically depend on how the information is designed and presented. The chapter has also illustrated the value of subdividing reading into processes relating to accessing the material, interpreting it and reaching decisions that lead to action. Media differ in the way they impact upon access, understanding and persuasion. So different medical topics may be best suited to different media.

The readers' processes of interpretation involve not only understanding the content but also making inferences about the message-giver's agenda and responding to the emotional tone in which the material is presented. Since tone may influence willingness to further access the material, there is a dynamic interdependency among the parallel strands of interpretation. In some instances people may prematurely abandon a leaflet or video whose tone they find distasteful. It seems probable that several parallel processes of interpretation (understanding the content, imputing the author's agenda and responding to the tone of the message) combine to influence people's decisions about how to follow procedural recommendations or deciding about which healthcare options to pursue. Nevertheless, studies demonstrating this interdependence among discourse interpretation processes remain to be done in a clinical context.

This chapter has emphasised that readers treat healthcare information as advice, to be weighed against other factors, incorporated with other knowledge. The writers of healthcare materials may not always realise that they are in this sense negotiating compliance. The risks to health from non-compliance are well documented. Incorporating a range of sophisticated evaluation techniques into the design process, could enable potential causes of non-compliance to be identified and addressed through re-design. This may seem an expensive option but providing the public with healthcare advice in a form they find acceptable and can use easily is almost certainly cost-effective. Coulter (1997) has argued that some forms of information for patients may be as cost-effective as a new drug or surgical procedure, but, because healthcare materials also have potential for harm, that "it is important they are carefully developed and rigorously evaluated". The procedures for doing this are not trivial but can be taught, once the need for specialist skills have been recognised.

ACKNOWLEDGMENTS

I am indebted to Dr Jeremy C. Wyatt for drawing my attention to many of the studies to which I refer and to anonymous referees for many helpful suggestions.

REFERENCES

Abed, F. (1994). Visual puns as interactive illustrations: their effects on recognition memory. *Metaphor and Symbolic Activity*, 9, 45–60.

Albert, T. & Chadwick, S. (1992). How readable are practice leaflets? *British Medical Journal*, 1305, 1266–8.

Baddeley, A. D. (1993). *Your Memory: A User's Guide* (2nd edn). London: Prion Multimedia Books Ltd.

Bandura, A. (1986). *Social Foundations of Thought and Action: a Social Cognitive Theory*. Englewood Cliffs, NJ: Prentice-Hall

Becker, M. H. (Ed.) (1974). The health belief model and personal health behavior. *Health Education Monographs*, 2, 324–473.

Berry, C., Scheffler, A. & Goldstein, C. (1993). Effects of text structure on the impact of heard news. *Applied Cognitive Psychology*, 7, 381–95.

Berry, D. C. & Michas, I. (in press). Evaluating explanations about drug prescriptions: effects of varying the nature of the information about side effects and its relative position within leaflets. *Psychology and Health*.

Campbell, M. K., DeVellis, B. M., Strecher, V. J., Ammerman, A. S., DeVellis, R. F. & Sandler, R. S. (1994). Improving dietary behavior: the effectiveness of tailored messages in primary care settings. *American Journal of Public Health*, 84, 783–7.

Chalmers, I. & Altman, D. G. (Eds) (1995). *Systematic Reviews*. London: British Medical Journal Publishing Group.

Chambliss, M. J. & Garner, R. (1996). Do adults change their minds after reading persuasive text? *Written Communication*, 13, 291–313.

Chapman, M. & Mahon, B. (1986). *Plain Figures*. London: Her Majesty's Stationery Office.

Cody, R. & Lee, C. (1990). Behaviors, intentions and beliefs in skin cancer prevention. *Journal of Behavioral Medicine*, 13, 373–89.

Cohen, G. (1996). *Memory in the Real World* (2nd edn). Sussex, UK: Psychology Press.

Coulter, A. (1997). Developing evidence-based patient information. In M. Dunning, G. Needham & S. Weston (Eds) *But Will it Work, Doctor?* (pp. 30–2). Oxford: The But Will It Work, Doctor? Group.

Devine, E. C. & Cook, T. D. (1982). A meta-analysis of the effects of psycho-educational interventions on length of postsurgical hospital stay. *Nursing Research*, 32, 267–74.

Dey, P., Collins, S., Will, S. & Woodman, C. B. J. (1995). Randomised control trial assessing effectiveness of health education leaflets in reducing incidence of sunburn. *British Medical Journal*, 311, 1062–3.

Dickinson, D. (1997). Get on the phone to get informed: health information by telephone. *Patient* i, 5, August, 6–7.
Dickinson, D. (1998). Patient helplines on trial. *Patient* i, 12, 10–11.
DiMatteo, M. R., Reiter, R. C. & Gambone, J. C. (1994). Enhancing medication adherence through communication and informed collaborative choice. *Health Communication*, 6, 253–66.
Eiser, J. R. & Eiser, C. (1996). *Effectiveness of Video for Health Education: a Review*. London: Health Education Authority.
Entwistle, V. A., Sheldon, S. A., Sowden, A. J. & Watt, I. S. (1996). Supporting consumer involvement in decision making: what constitutes quality in consumer health information? *International Journal for Quality in Health Care*, 8, 425–37.
Entwistle, V., Watt, I. S. & Herring, J. E. (1996). *Information About Healthcare Effectiveness*. London: King's Fund Publishing.
Flesch, R. (1948). A new readability yardstick. *Journal of Applied Psychology*, 32, 221–33.
Gagliano, M. E. (1988). A literature review of the efficacy of video in patient edcuation. *Journal of Medical Education*, 63, 785–92.
Gaskins, R. W. (1996). "That's just how it was": the effect of issue-related emotional involvement on reading comprehension. *Reading Research Quarterly*, 31, 386–405.
Gibbs, S., Waters, W. E. & George, C. F. (1987). The design of prescription information leaflets and feasibility of their use in general practice. *Pharmaceutical Medicine*, 2, 23–33.
Gregory, M. & Poulton, E. C. (1970). Even versus uneven right-hand margins and the role of comprehension in reading. *Ergonomics*, 13, 427–34.
Hammond, L. S. (1995). Supplementing health campaign messages: recent developments in informing patients about their prescription drugs. In E. Maibach & R. L. Parrott (Eds), *Designing Health Messages: Approaches from Communication Theory and Public Health Practice* (pp. 249–69). Thousand Oaks, CA: Sage Publications.
Hammond, S. L. & Lambert, B. L. (1994). Communicating about medications: directions for research. *Health Communication*, 6, 247–52.
Hartley, J. (1994a). *Designing Instructional Text* (3rd edn). London: Kogan Page.
Hartley, J. (1994b). Designing instructional text for older readers. *British Journal of Educational Technology*, 25, 172–88.
Hartley, J. (in press). What does it say? Text design, medical information and older readers. In D. C. Park, R. W. Morrell & K. Shifren (Eds), *Processing Medical Information in Aging Patients: Cognitive and Human Factors Perspective*. Mahwah, NJ: Lawrence Erlbaum.
Hartley, J., Trueman, M. & Rodgers, A., (1984). The effects of verbal and numerical quantifiers on questionnaire responses. *Applied Ergonomics*, 15, 149–55.
Hatch, J., Hill, C. & Hayes, J. R. (1993). When the messenger is the message: readers' impressions of writers. *Written Commuication*, 10, 569–98.
Hayes, J. R. (1996). A new framework for understanding cognition and affect in writing. In C. M. Levy & S. Ransdell (Eds), *The Science of Writing: Theories, Methods, Individual Differences and Applications* (pp. 1–27). Mahwah, NJ: Lawrence Erlbaum.
Hayes, J. R., Hatch, J. & Hill, C. (1992). Reading the writer's personality: the functional impact in communication. In M. Steehouder, C. Jansen, P. van der Poort & R. Verheijen (Eds), *Quality of Technical Documentation* (pp. 33–44). Amsterdam: Rodopi.
Hoy, M. G. (1994). Switch drugs vis-a-vis RX and OTC – policy, marketing and research considerations. *Journal of Public Policy and Marketing*, 13, 85–96.
Hux, J. E. & Naylor, C. D. (1995). Communicating the benefits of chronic preventive therapy: does the format of efficacy data determine patients' acceptance of treatment? *Medical Decision Making*, 15, 152–7.
Impicciatore, P., Pandolfini, C., Castella, N. & Bonatti, M. (1997). Reliability of health information for the public on the world wide web: systematic survey of advice on managing fever in children at home. *British Medical Journal*, 314, 1879–81.
Jones, R. B., Edgerton, E., Baxter, I., Navon, L. M., Ritchie, J., Bell, G. & Murray, K.

(1993). Where should a public-access health information system be sited? *Interacting with Computers*, 4, 413–21.
Kai, J. (1994). "Baby Check" in the inner city – use and value to parents. *Family Practice*, 11, 245–50.
Lambert, B. L. & Lee Gillespie, J. (1994). Patient perceptions of pharmacy students' hypertension compliance-gaining messages: effect of message design logic and content themes. *Health Communication*, 6, 311–25.
Larkin, J. H. & Simon, H. A. (1987). Why a diagram is (sometimes) worth ten thousand words. *Cognitive Science*, 11, 65–99.
Levie, W. H. & Lentz, R. (1982). Effects of text illustrations: a review of research. *Educational Communciation and Technology Journal*, 30, 185–232.
Ley, P. (1988). *Communicating with Patients: Improving Communication, Satisfaction and Compliance*. London: Chapman Hall.
Ley, P., Jain, V. K. & Skilbeck, C. E. (1975). A method for decreasing patients' medication errors. *Psychological Medicine*, 6, 599–601.
Livingstone, J., Axton, R. A., Mennie, M., Gilfillan, A. & Brock, D. J. H. (1993). A preliminary trial of couples screening for cystic fibrosis: designing an appropriate information leaflet. *Clinical Genetics*, 43, 57–62.
Loumidis, K. S., Hallam, R. S. & Cadge, B. (1991). The effect of written re-assuring information on out-patients complaining of tinnitus. *British Journal of Audiology*, 25, 105–9.
Lowe, R. (1993). *Successful Instructional Diagrams*. London: Kogan Page.
Mandl, H. & Levin, J. R. (Eds) (1989). *Knowledge Acquisition from Text and Pictures*. Amsterdam: North Holland.
Marinker, M. (1997). Personal paper: Writing prescriptions is easy. *British Medical Journal*, 314, 747–8.
Mason, P. (1993). Honest admissions. *Nursing Times*, 89, 14–15.
Masson, M. J. & Waldron, M. E. (1994). Comprehension of legal contracts by non-experts: effectiveness of plain language redrafting. *Applied Cognitive Psychology*, 87, 67–85.
Matthews, A. & Ridgeway, V. (1984). Psychological preparation for surgery. In A. Matthews & A. Steptoe (Eds), *Healthcare and Human Behaviour*. London: Academic Press.
Mayberry, J. F. & Mayberry, M. K. (1996). Effective instructions for patients. *Journal of Royal College of Physicians of London*, 30, 205–8.
Melamed, B. G., Yurcheson, R., Fleece, E. L., Hutcherson, S. & Hawes, R. (1978). Effects of film-modelling on the reduction of anxiety-related behaviours in individuals varying in level of previous experience in the stress situation. *Journal of Consulting Clinical Psychology*, 46, 1357–67.
Meredith, P., Emberton, M., Wood, C. & Smith, J. (1995). Comparison of patients' needs for information on prostate surgery with printed materials provided by surgeons. *Quality in Health Care*, 4, 18–23.
Monahan, J. L. (1995). Thinking positively: using positive affect when designing health messages. In E. Maibach & R. L. Parrott (Eds), *Designing Health Messages: Approaches from Communication Theory and Public Health Practice* (pp. 81–98). London: Sage.
Morrell, R. W., Park, D. C. & Poon, L. W. (1989). Quality of instructions on prescription drug labels: effects of memory and comprehension in young and old adults. *The Gerontologist*, 29, 345–54.
Morrell, R. W. & Park, D. C. (1993). The effects of age, illustrations and task variables on the performance of procedural assembly tasks. *Psychology and Aging*, 8, 389–99.
Morrow, D., Leirer, V. O. & Altieri, P. (1995). List formats improve medication instructions for older adults. *Educational Gerontology*, 21, 163–78.
Morrow, D., Leirer, V. O., Andrassy, J. M., Tanke, D. & Stine-Morrow, E. A. L. (1996). Medication information design: younger and older adult schemas for taking medication. *Human Factors*, 38, 556–73.

Morrow, D., Leirer, V. O. & Sheik, J. (1988). Adherence and medication instructions: review and recommendations. *Journal of the American Geriatrics Society*, 36, 1147–60.
Moxey, L. & Sanford, A. J. (1993). Prior expectation and the interpretation of natural language quantifiers. *European Journal of Cognitive Psychology*, 5, 73–91.
Mullen, P. D. (1997). Compliance becomes concordance. *British Medical Journal*, 314.
Mumford, E., Schlesinger, H. J. & Glass, G. V. (1982). The effects of psychological intervention on recovery from surgery and heart attacks: analysis of the literature. *American Journal of Public Health*, 72, 141–51.
Nielsen, J. (1993). *Usability Engineering*. NJ: Academic Press
Odonnell, L. N., San Doval, A., Duran, R. & Odonnell, C. (1995). Video-based sexually transmitted disease patient education: its impact on condom acquisition. *American Journal of Public Health*, 85, 817–22.
O'Keefe, B. J. (1988). The logic of message design: individual differences in reasoning about communication. *Communication Monographs*, 55, 80–103.
Otero, J. & Kintsch, W. (1992). Failures to detect contradictions in a text: what readers believe versus what they read. *Psychological Science*, 3, 229–35.
Pander Maat, H. & Klaassen, R. (1994). Side effects of side effect information in drug information leaflets. *Journal of Technical Writing and Communication*, 24, 389–404.
Pirolli, P. & Card, S. (1995). Information foraging in information access environments. In I. R. Katz, R. Mack, L. Marks, M. B. Rossen & J. Nielsen (Eds), *Mosaic of Creativity* (pp. 51–8). Proceedings of CHI '95. NY: ACM Inc.
Poulton, E. C. (1967a). Skimming (scanning) news items printed in 8 point and 9 point letters. *Ergonomics*, 10, 713–16.
Poulton, E. C. (1967b). Searching for newspaper headlines printed in capitals or lower case letters. *Journal of Applied Psychology*, 51, 417–25.
Poulton, E. C. (1968). Rate of comprehension of an existing teleprinter output and of possible alternatives. *Journal of Applied Psychology*, 52, 16–21.
Poulton, E. C. (1969). Skimming lists of food ingredients printed in different sizes. *Journal of Applied Psychology*, 53, 55–8.
Pressley, M., Ghatala, E. S., Woloshyn, V. & Pirie, J. (1990). Sometimes adults miss the main ideas and do not realise it: confidence in response to short-answer and multiple-choice questions. *Reading Research Quarterly*, 25, 2332–49.
Randall, T. (1993). Producers of videodisc programs strive to expand patient's role in medical decision-making process. *Journal of the American Medical Association*, 270, 160–2.
Rayner, D. K. & Yerassimou, N. (1997). Medicines information – leaving blind people behind? *British Medical Journal*, 315, 268.
Rice, G. E., Meyer, B. J. F. & Miller, D. C. (1989). Using text structure to improve older adults' recall of important medical information. *Educational Gerontology*, 15, 527–42.
Rogers, D., Shulman, A., Sless, D. & Beach, R. (1995). *Designing Better Medicine Labels*. Canberra, Australian Capital Territory: Communication Research Institute of Australia.
Rook, K. (1987). Effects of case-history versus abstract information on health attitudes and behaviors. *Journal of Applied Social Psychology*, 17, 533–53.
Royal Pharmaceutical Society of Great Britain (1996). *From Compliance to Concordance: Towards Shared Goals in Medicine Taking*. London: Royal Pharmaceutical Society.
Schriver, K. A. (1997). *Dynamics in Document Design*. Chichester: John Wiley & Sons.
Secker, J. & Pollard, R. (1995). *Writing Leaflets for Patients: Guidelines for Producing Written Information*. Edinburgh: Health Education Board for Scotland.
Simmonds, D. & Reynolds, L. (1994). *Data Presentation and Visual Literacy in Medicine and Science*. Oxford: Butterworth-Heinemann Ltd.
Sless, D. & Wiseman, R. (1994). *Writing about Medicines for People*. Canberra, Australian Capital Territory: Communication Research Institute of Australia.
Spencer, H., Reynolds, L. & Coe, B. (1977). The effects of show-through on the legibility of printed text. Report 9. London: Royal College of Art, Readability of Print Research Unit.

Twyman, M. (1985). Using pictorial language: a discussion of the dimensions of the problem. In T. M. Duffy & R. Waller (Eds), *Designing Usable Texts* (pp. 245–312). New York: Academic Press.

Vanderplas, J. M. & Vanderplas, J. H. (1980). Some factors affecting the legibility of printed materials for older adults. *Perceptual and Motor Skills*, 50, 923–32.

Walker, G. (Ed.) (1995). *Compendium of Patient Information Leaflets 1995–96*. London: Datapharm Publications.

Weiss, B. D. & Coyne, C. (1997). Communicating with patients who cannot read. *New England Journal of Medicine*, 337, 272–4.

Whalley, P. C. & Flemming, P. W. (1975). An experiment with a simple recorder of reading behaviour. *Programmed Learning & Educational Technology*, 12, 120–3.

Wicke, D. M., Lorge, R. E., Coppin, R. J. & Jones, K. P. (1994). The effectiveness of waiting room notice-boards as a vehicle for health education. *Family Practice*, 11, 292–5.

Wogalter, M. S. & Dietrich, D. A. (1995). Enhancing label readability for over-the-counter pharmaceuticals by elderly consumers. Proceedings of the Human Factors and Ergonomics Society 39th Annual Meeting (pp. 143–7). Santa Monica, CA: Human Factors and Ergonomics Society.

Wogalter, M. S., Magurno, A. B., Scott, K. L. & Dietrich, D. A. (1996). Facilitating information acquisition for over-the-counter drugs using supplemental labels. Proceedings of the Human Factors and Ergonomics Society 40th Annual Meeting. Santa Monica, CA: Human Factors and Ergonomics Society.

Wright, P. (1977). Decision making as a factor in the ease of using numerical tables. *Ergonomics*, 20, 91–6.

Wright, P. (1980). Usability: the criterion for designing written information. In P. A. Kolers, M. E. Wrolstad & H. Bouma (Eds), *Processing of Visible Language 2* (pp. 183–206). New York: Plenum Press.

Wright, P. (1988a). Functional literacy: reading and writing at work. *Ergonomics*, 31, 265–90.

Wright, P. (1988b). The need for theories of NOT reading: some psychological aspects of the human–computer interface. In B. A. G. Elsendoorn & H. Bouma (Eds), *Working Models of Human Perception* (pp. 319–40). London: Academic Press.

Wright, P. (1994). Quality or usability? Quality writing provokes quality reading. In M. Steehouder, C. Jansen, P. van der Poort & R. Verheijen (Eds), *Quality of Technical Documentation* (pp. 7–38). Amsterdam: Rodopi.

Wright, P. (1998). Printed instructions: can research make a difference? In H. Zwaga, T. Boersema & H. Hoonout (Eds), *Visual Information for Everyday Use; Design and Research Perspectives* (pp. 45–66). London: Taylor & Francis

Wright, P. (in press). Writing and information design of healthcare materials. In C. Candlin & K. Hyland (Eds), *Writing: Texts Processes and Practices*. London: Addison Wesley Longman.

Wright, P. & Barnard, P. (1975). Effects of "more than" and "less than" decisions on the use of numerical tables. *Journal of Applied Psychology*, 60, 606–11.

Wright, P., Creighton P. & Threlfall, S. M. (1982). Some factors determining when instructions will be read. *Ergonomics*, 25, 225–37.

Wright, P, Lickorish, A. & Green, H. (1996). For many health topics women prefer print to video. Poster presented at annual meeting of the BPS Special Group in Health Psychology, York.

Wright, P, Milroy, R. & Lickorish, A. (in press). Static and animated graphics in learning from interactive texts. *European Journal of Psychology of Education*.

Wyatt, J. C. (1997) Commentary: measuring quality and impact of the world wide web. *British Medical Journal*, 314, 1875–9.

Yates, J. F. (1992). *Risk-Taking Behavior*. Chichester: John Wiley.

Young, R. & Barnard, P. J. (1987). The use of scenarios in human–computer interaction research: turbocharging the tortoise of cumulative science. In J. M. Carroll & P. P Tanner (Eds), *Proceedings of CHI+GI'87*: Human Factors in computing systems and graphics interface (pp. 291–6). New York: ACM Press.

Chapter 24

Cognitive Contributions to Mental Illness and Mental Health

Catherine Panzarella
MCP Hahnemann University
Lauren B. Alloy
Temple University
Lyn Y. Abramson
University of Wisconsin
and
Karen Klein
MCP Hahnemann University

A COGNITIVE PERSPECTIVE ON MENTAL ILLNESS AND MENTAL HEALTH

It has long been recognized that different people can perceive the same event differently. Psychologists focus on the characteristic ways that individuals perceive situations and how their perceptions, in turn, relate to their behaviors and emotions. From the cognitive perspective, emotional reactions to events are determined by a combination of characteristics of the event itself and the cognitive construal processes of the perceiver (e.g. Landau, 1980). In the case of relatively extreme emotional reactions considered to be hallmarks of mental dysfunction or illness, cognitive processes take on heightened importance. According to the cognitive perspective on mental illness, most psychological disorders have at their core the misperception or misinterpretation of events.

Handbook of Applied Cognition, Edited by F. T. Durso, R. S. Nickerson, R. W. Schvaneveldt, S. T. Dumais, D. S. Lindsay and M. T. H. Chi.

It was once thought that good mental health could be defined in terms of the absence of misperceptions or misinterpretations. Many lay people still think of mental illness as "losing touch with reality." However, the scientific literature now supports the idea that people considered mentally healthy can also be characterized by biases and misperceptions that are essential to maintaining positive mental health (Alloy & Abramson, 1988; Kahneman & Miller, 1986; Taylor, 1989). Thus, it is not the mere presence of distortions that defines mental illness or health from the cognitive perspective. Rather, it is the type and frequency of misperceptions or misinterpretations (cognitive content) as well as the manner in which information is processed (cognitive processes) that distinguishes the two.

In this chapter, we review theory and evidence pointing to particular cognitive biases and the attentional, memorial, and interpretive processes that underlie these biases for a range of psychological disorders as well as psychological health. First, we discuss a few basic theoretical constructs utilized in cognitive studies. Then, we review some of the more promising methods borrowed from basic research in cognitive psychology that have been used to discover cognitive distortions and processes associated with various mental conditions. Finally, we describe the results of studies that have used innovative methods to discover the cognitive biases and processes that distinguish some psychological disorders as well as good mental health. Given that it is impossible in a single chapter to cover the full array of cognitive research on any mental disorder, let alone all of them, we have sampled disorders that present different challenges to cognitive researchers. We focus heavily on mood and anxiety disorders, particularly unipolar depression and panic, because they are highly prevalent problems and the cognitive research in these areas has been prolific and innovative. We examine eating disorders because they present unique challenges to cognitive researchers. Finally, we discuss dissociative disorders because the related controversy regarding "repressed" and subsequently recovered memories of childhood abuse is currently the subject of much media attention.

BASIC CONCEPTS UTILIZED IN THE STUDY OF COGNITIVE MODELS OF MENTAL HEALTH

A few basic concepts are sufficient for an introductory understanding of cognitive research on mental health. Most cognitive researchers distinguish between the content of thought and the underlying structures that organize thought processes (e.g. see Craik & Lockhart, 1972). Some cognitive psychologists do not draw a sharp distinction between process and content. For example, see Kolers & Roediger (1984) for a procedural view of information processing. Thought content consists of the actual events or situations that are the substance of thoughts. Both thoughts that are deliberative or conscious and thoughts that are fleeting and not in full awareness contain content that is of interest to cognitive psychologists. In mental health research, the fleeting, automatic self-dialogue that people engage in is often of most interest. These rapid, stream-of-consciousness type thoughts are often referred to as automatic thoughts (e.g. Beck, Rush, Shaw & Emery, 1979). The content of these automatic, surface-level cognitions is hypothesized to be influenced by deeper organizational structures. The deeper organizational structures contain generalized beliefs about the self and the world, sometimes called core beliefs (e.g. Beck, Rush, Shaw & Emery, 1979), as well as functional processing mechanisms for handling the wide variety of information that is available to a person at any one time. (See Williams, Watts, MacLeod & Mathews (1997) for a discussion of the limits of Beck's schema theory and alternative models.) These structures are referred to as schemata. Schemata are conceptualized as cognitive structures, but not necessarily in the literal sense that they occupy particular loci in the brain. Many researchers do indeed explore the physical and neurochemical correlates of schemata, but in this chapter, our interest is in functional aspects of schemata.

Schemata assist people in processing complex environmental information by:

1. selecting only a fraction of incoming stimuli for processing
2. abstracting meaning from incoming information and favoring storage of the meaning rather than a veridical representation of the original stimulus
3. using prior knowledge to assist in processing and interpreting information
4. integrating information to favor creation of internal consistency over external veracity (Alba & Hasher, 1983).

Schemata pertaining to the self are of greatest interest to mental health researchers. Markus (1977) defines self-schemata as "cognitive generalizations about the self, derived from past experience, that organize and guide the processing of self-related information contained in the individual's social experiences" (p. 64). Researchers have identified characteristics of self-schemata uniquely associated with different disorders. For example, depressed individuals show evidence of self-schemata characterized by a negative view of the self and information processing biased toward pessimistic interpretations of events. People with dissociative identity disorder have more than one self-schema that operate independently and without mutual awareness. Before describing the research on self-schemata and cognitive content associated with various mental disorders, we briefly describe some methods that have been developed for studying cognitive phenomena in mental disorders.

METHODS USED TO STUDY COGNITIVE CONTRIBUTIONS TO MENTAL HEALTH

One of the oldest and most basic methods for studying people's cognitions is simply to ask them about their thoughts (e.g. Lana, 1991). Self-report is still one of the most widely used methodologies for studying cognition. However, the field has also developed more sophisticated laboratory methods for examining thought content and processes. These alternative information processing paradigms are particularly important if one believes that people are not always accurate reporters of their own cognitive experience. Self-reports can be inaccurate either because individuals may not be aware of all of their thoughts, or because they are unwilling to report certain thoughts. Thus, there are serious limitations to self-report alone for studying cognition. Some of the more promising methodologies that attempt to circumvent the problems of direct self-report are briefly described below.

Reaction-time Measures

Many studies measure the time it takes participants to react to a particular stimulus or to make a decision. Differences in reaction time are presumed to be an indication of differences in underlying cognitive processes. In particular, stimuli that are congruent with the content of an individual's self-schema are hypothesized to be processed faster than stimuli incongruent with the schema (Markus, 1977; Rogers, Kuiper & Kirker, 1977). For example, participants might be asked to press a button labeled "me" or "not me" depending on whether each of several adjectives is self-descriptive or not. Adjectives that fit with a person's self-view will be processed quickly as compared to adjectives that do not fit with an already developed self-schema. For example, consistent with the hypothesis that they have negative self-schema, depressed people respond very quickly to words like "inferior" but more slowly to words like "adept" (e.g. Alloy, Abramson, Murray, Whitehouse & Hogan, 1997; Greenberg & Alloy, 1989; Rogers, Kuiper & Kirker, 1977).

Ambiguous Stimuli Tasks

A popular method for examining interpretive biases is to ask people to respond to a stimulus that could be interpreted in different ways. The Rorschach Inkblot test is one of the classic tests in psychology based on the idea that responses to an ambiguous stimulus reveal something about the cognitive organization that the viewer imposes on the situation (e.g. Exner, 1986). Cognitive psychologists have used the same basic idea in a more circumscribed manner to uncover processes of cognitive interpretation associated with various disorders. For example, anxiety researchers have successfully used homophones (words that sound the same but are spelled differently and have different meanings) to deduce that anxious people have a general cognitive bias to perceive threat in an ambiguous stimulus. For example, the sound "slay/sleigh" was presented to participants who were asked to write the word. Anxious persons were more likely to write "slay" than "sleigh" and to make this threat-biased choice more frequently than normal controls (Mathews, Richards & Eysenck, 1989).

Competing Stimuli Tasks

Another way to infer individuals' cognitive biases is to present two different stimuli simultaneously forcing participants to attend to only one of them. Ideally, the presentation is so rapid that participants are not aware of making a choice, thereby providing some information about automatic processing presumably influenced by underlying schemata. For example, in the dichotic listening task, participants wearing earphones are presented with a different message in each earpiece and are asked to attend to and shadow (repeat) the message in one of their ears and to press a button when they hear certain words in either ear (Treisman & Geffen, 1967). This methodology allows researchers to attribute differences between groups to cognitive differences by controlling for simultaneous responding limitations. Burgess and colleagues (Burgess, Jones, Robertson, Radcliffe & Emerson, 1981) used this task to compare phobics (social phobia and agoraphobia) with normal controls on detection of words pertinent to the phobics' feared situations (e.g. public speaking, being alone). The anxious participants and normal controls did not differ in their detection of neutral or depressive words (e.g. failure), but did differ in detection of fear words. Anxious participants detected significantly more fear relevant phrases in the unattended passage than did controls, suggesting that they had a heightened proclivity for perceiving fear-related information. MacLeod and colleagues (MacLeod, Mathews & Tata, 1986; MacLeod & Mathews, 1988) used the competing stimuli task to learn that anxious individuals shift their attention toward threatening words and nonanxious individuals actually shift their attention away from threatening words.

Emotional Stroop Tests

In the Stroop task (Stroop, 1935), individuals are shown a series of words printed in color and are asked to name the ink color of each word. If the word "green" is printed in red, people are slower to name the ink color than when a random series of letters is printed in red. Presumably, automatic processing of the meaning of the word interferes with color naming. The emotional Stroop task uses words likely to be of relevance to certain people so that investigators can make inferences about the attentional processing of people with particular psychological profiles. For example, dysphoric students take longer to name the ink colors when the words are negative than when they are neutral or positive, suggesting that depressive words are attended to more than non-depressive words. Non-dysphoric students do not show a difference in response time depending on the nature of the word (Gotlib & McCann, 1984). Such studies provide some indication that dysphoric individuals may be highly attentive to negative information and may have difficulty tuning out negative information in the environment.

Williams, Mathews & MacLeod (1996) concluded from a literature review on the emotional Stroop Test that interference with color-naming reliably occurs across a wide range of mental disorders. They also ruled out the possibility that the attentional bias observed in the Stroop is due to artifacts such as priming (presentation of early words causes the person to attend more to later words of the same theme) or practice. However, further research is needed to understand more precisely the mechanisms underlying the attentional bias. (Williams, Mathews &

MacLeod (1996) suggest that a connectionist model might provide a good framework for better understanding attentional bias for emotional stimuli as seen in the Stroop.)

Priming Studies

Priming or construct activation procedures are analogous to biological challenge studies in that they involve activating a putative vulnerability in someone (cognitive in this case) and then studying the effects of a stressor ("challenge") to the system (e.g. Segal & Ingram, 1994). For example, one would not learn much about causes of asthma attacks by having people with and without asthma blow up balloons, because much of the time, people with asthma can blow up balloons as well as people without asthma. However, one would learn a great deal about asthma attacks by asking asthmatics and non-asthmatics to blow up balloons after administering a drug that causes bronchial spasms in people vulnerable to asthma, but has no effect on people without the underlying biological vulnerability. Likewise, people prone to a disorder such as depression or anxiety may behave like others except when their vulnerabilities are primed.

Priming tasks used to test cognitive models rely on the assumption that cognitive and affective information are interconnected so that activating one type of information makes the other more accessible (Bower, 1981). For example, activating a sad mood would make negative memories more likely to be recalled than positive memories. In priming tasks, participants are typically presented with a stimulus that activates hypothetical mental structures (e.g. depressive self-schemata) without the participant being fully aware of the activation (Segal & Ingram, 1994). Teasdale & Dent (1987) used a mood induction priming procedure to study cognitive vulnerability to depression by having recovered depressives and never-depressed controls complete an adjective recall measure while in a normal mood state and after a negative mood induction (listening to a depressing piece of music). The groups did not differ in recall of negative self-descriptive adjectives while in a normal mood state, but the formerly depressed group recalled more negative adjectives than the never-depressed group after the negative mood induction.

Judgment of Covariation Studies

Cognitive researchers have noted for years that people often make mistakes in judging contingencies between events and that such mistakes tend to be consistent with the *a priori* beliefs of the observer (Nisbett & Ross, 1980). Thus, the types of errors that occur in judging covariation can provide an indication of an individual's cognitive biases. For example, one who believes he or she is a powerful agent of action in the world will likely infer greater contingency between his or her own actions and events than one who generally believes that he or she is an unwitting victim of events. In judgment of covariation tasks, participants are asked to judge the contingency between two stimuli or between their own responses and outcomes so that cognitive biases associated with inaccurate judgments can be examined (e.g. Alloy & Abramson, 1988). For example, Alloy & Abramson (1979, Experiments 1–4) presented depressed and non-depressed participants with a task in which the goal was to turn on a green light by pressing a button. In fact, the actual degree of contingency between button pressing and green light onset was varied by the experimenters. The experimenters also made green light onset either a positive or negative outcome by having participants either win or lose money. Depressed participants were more accurate than non-depressed participants in estimating the degree of control they had over the green light in all conditions. Non-depressed participants showed a bias, dubbed an "illusion of control," to overestimate the control they had when outcomes were desirable.

Tomarken, Mineka & Cook (1989) used a judgment of covariation task to examine cognitive biases involved in fear. Individuals who showed either high or low fear of snakes and spiders were shown fear-relevant (snakes and spiders) and fear-irrelevant (mushrooms and flowers) slides that were randomly and equally paired with three possible outcomes: (a) electric shock; (b) a tone; or (c) nothing. The high-fear participants showed a bias to overestimate the co-occurrence of fear-relevant slides with the aversive outcome (shock). The low-fear participants accurately judged the association between the fear-relevant stimuli and aversive outcome. Covariation studies such as these have contributed greatly to our understanding of the tendency for anxiety-prone individuals to overestimate the relationship between the object of their fears and aversive outcomes.

Below, we review studies that have used these and other methodologies adapted from basic research in cognition to understand the cognitive biases central to some forms of mental illness and mental health.

APPLYING THE COGNITIVE PERSPECTIVE TO PARTICULAR DISORDERS

Anxiety Disorders

Anxiety disorders involve excessive fears, worries, or time spent trying to control worrisome thoughts (American Psychiatric Association, 1994). Cognitive theorists suggest that two cognitive biases are central to the development and maintenance of anxiety disorders: (a) a selective attention toward threatening stimuli; and (b) an overestimation of the threat inherent in relatively benign stimuli. The stimuli can be either external, such as exaggerated fear of a plane crashing in phobia, or internal, such as exaggerated fear of heart attack in panic disorder. Substantial research has been conducted on cognitive biases in anxiety disorders. Here, we will present some of the findings from research on panic disorder and phobias.

Panic Disorder

Panic attacks are a fairly common experience reported by as many as two-thirds of the general population (for a review, see Margraf & Ehlers, 1988). A panic attack is characterized by the sudden onset of somatic symptoms such as racing heart, chest pain, dizziness and sweating as well as cognitive symptoms such as fear of dying or going crazy (American Psychiatric Association, 1994). One might have a panic attack involving rapid heartbeat and breathing, sweaty palms, and intense apprehension while experiencing the floor shaking, walls cracking, and dishes from the kitchen cabinet suddenly taking to flight during an earthquake. This response is considered *normal* given that such conditions pose a realistic threat of injury or death. The same reaction is not considered normal when there is no realistic threat. Panic disorder is characterized by frequent, debilitating panic attacks and persistent worry about the consequences of panic (American Psychiatric Association). Typical worries include catastrophic thinking such as believing that one will die, faint, or go crazy if the panic occurs again. (Of course, panic attacks that can be explained by the physiological effects of a substance (e.g. crack cocaine, caffeine intoxication), a general medical condition (e.g. hyperthyroidism) or another mental disorder (e.g. social phobia) are not considered part of panic disorder.) Many people with panic disorder also meet criteria for a condition known as agoraphobia due to attempts to avoid situations in which a panic attack is likely or in which it might be difficult to get help if a panic attack occurs. In Latin, agoraphobia means fear of open spaces, and clinicians have adopted this term because some people with panic avoid so many situations that they literally become housebound.

Researchers have noted that stimuli such as sodium lactate, hyperventilation, carbon dioxide inhalation, and phobic stimuli can all trigger panic (Aronson, Carasiti, McBane & Whitaker-Azmitia, 1989; Nutt & Lawson, 1992). In spite of the wide variety of biochemical and physical stimuli that can produce panic in vulnerable people, from the cognitive perspective, all pathological panic involves the catastrophic misinterpretation of threat. For example, in the case of Klein's (1994) biologically based suffocation false-alarm theory, the panicker identifies certain somatic cues as indicating suffocation when, in fact, the person is not suffocating (Panzarella, 1995).

People with panic disorder are more likely than others to perceive *internal* cues, especially bodily sensations, as threatening. People with specific phobias described below also experience frequent panic attacks, but it is the *external* stimulation associated with the feared object that they perceive as threatening. Panic disorder patients believe that benign bodily sensations such as tachycardia and lightheadedness after drinking caffeine could be a signal of a catastrophic change; therefore, they attend carefully and selectively to minor bodily sensations to which most people are indifferent. As one pays attention to mild tachycardia, for instance, and thinks, "I may be having a heart attack," not surprisingly, the symptoms and discomfort actually increase, thereby seemingly confirming the catastrophic interpretation (Beck, 1988; Clark, 1988, 1993). In other words, the catastrophic cognition (heart attack) initiates a positive feedback loop in which anxiety increases, thereby intensifying the bodily sensation (rapid heartbeat) that triggered the catastrophic cognition (heart attack). An even more rapidly beating heart seems, in turn, to confirm the notion that something is very wrong and anxiety further increases, resulting in panic (Clark et al., 1997). The panicker may further aggravate matters by trying to do something to stop the symptoms and then attributing relief from the purported catastrophe to his or her action. For example, someone who is exercising and becomes overly concerned about increased heart rate and sweating, thinking "I'm having a heart attack" may stop exercising immediately. As heartbeat slows, the person thinks "thank goodness I stopped, I may have had a heart attack," thereby reinforcing him or herself for hypervigilance and avoidance. This "vicious cycle" of panic is nicely depicted in a diagram by Beck (1997), reproduced in Figure 24.1.

Considerable experimental support exists for the cognitive model of panic. For example, people with panic disorder recalled more anxiety-related than nonanxiety-related words (explicit memory test) from a previous rating task, whereas normal controls showed the opposite pattern (McNally, Foa & Donnell, 1989). Moreover, this threat-related memory bias was somewhat (nonsignificantly) enhanced for panic participants who received a priming manipulation (physiological arousal induction via a stepping exercise) prior to the rating and recall tasks. Another study examined implicit memory biases of people with panic (Amir, McNally, Riemann & Clements, 1996). Participants with panic disorder and normal controls listened to a series of neutral and panic-related sentences and then listened to a series of sentences while also rating the loudness of white noise. Some of the sentences in this stage of the study were previously presented (old) and others were new. Implicit memory is supposedly revealed when the noise level is rated as less loud for old sentences than for new sentences. Panic patients differed from normal controls in that they rated the white noise accompanying panic-related sentences as less loud than neutral sentences, thereby exhibiting enhanced implicit memory for threat-related sentences. Thus, people with panic disorder have been shown to exhibit a memory bias for threat-related material on both explicit and implicit memory tasks.

Other studies have used an emotional Stroop test to demonstrate that people with panic disorder show an attentional preference for threat information (e.g. Ehlers, Margraf, Davies & Roth, 1988; Hope, Rapee, Heimberg & Dombeck, 1990; Maidenberg, Chen, Craske, Bohn & Bystritsky, 1996; McNally et al., 1994). In one study, panickers and normal controls were shown cards containing color words, non-threat words, and threat words related to physical harm, social embarrassment, and separation (Ehlers et al., 1988). Compared to normal controls, the panickers were slower in naming the ink color for threat words, suggesting that processing of the threat word was interfering with color naming. Furthermore, the attentional bias was particularly strong for physical threat words as compared to other types of threat, suggesting that panickers show a particular bias toward somatic threats. Similarly, Hope et al. used an emotional Stroop task to show that panickers had more response interference with color naming when the words were physical threat words than when they were social threat words.

Self-report research has also corroborated the finding that panic disorder patients are more likely than other anxiety disorder patients or normal controls to apply a catastrophic misinterpretation to ambiguous bodily sensations (Clark et al., 1988, 1997; Foa, 1988). For example, Clark et al. (1997) found that while both panic patients and those with other anxiety disorders overestimate threat as compared to normal controls, only the panic patients showed the specific bias for overestimating threat from bodily sensations (internal stimuli). In addition, panic

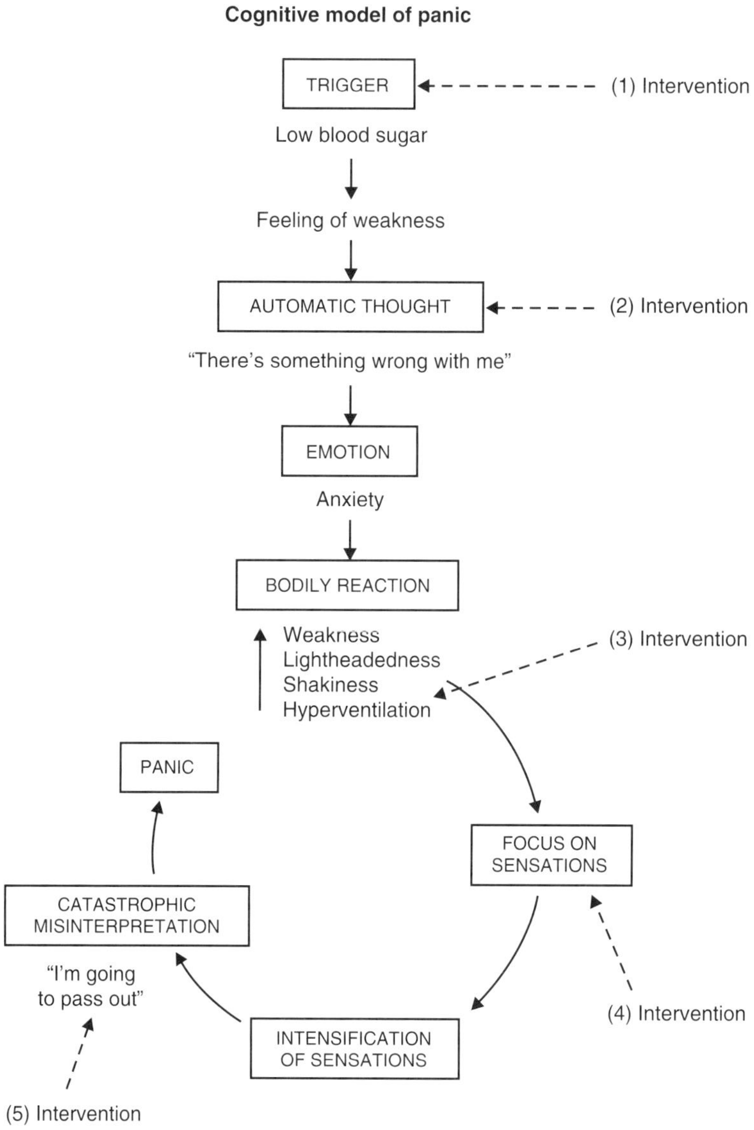

Figure 24.1 Panic disorder can begin with misinterpretations of bodily sensations, leading to a cycle that perpetuates heightened anxiety. Reproduced with permission, © 1997 Judith S. Beck PhD.

patients, but not normal controls, were likely to have panic attacks when researchers attempted to prime negative interpretations of bodily sensations by having the participants read word pairs such as "breathless–suffocate" (Clark et al., 1988). Other supporting evidence comes from studies that have shown that panic attacks can be prevented by teaching patients not to misinterpret bodily sensations as catastrophic (Beck, Sokol, Clark, Berchick & Wright, 1992; Clark, Gelder, Salkovskis & Anastasiades, 1991).

Some studies, however, have not corroborated the finding that panickers are more responsive to somatic threats than other types of threat. For example, Maidenberg et al. (1996) compared social phobics, panickers, and normal controls on an emotional Stroop test using neutral, positive, and threat words related to panic, social concerns, and general concerns. Compared to the other groups, panickers exhibited delayed response times (attentional bias) for all threat words, whereas social phobics displayed the bias for social-threat words only. McNally (McNally, Riemann, Louro, Lukach & Kim, 1992) used an emotional Stroop test after a priming exercise to examine cognitive processing in panic. The researchers randomly assigned participants to a high or low arousal condition. The high arousal condition involved having the participants exercise on a stationary bike in order to heighten somatic symptoms of arousal, such as increased heart rate, that panickers tend to be concerned about. Participants then engaged in an emotional Stroop test that involved neutral, positive, and threat words. The threat words pertained to bodily sensations, fear, and catastrophes. Panickers exhibited the greatest attentional bias (Stroop interference) for catastrophic words. Positive words, fear words, and bodily sensation words all produced more interference than neutral words but not as much as catastrophic words. Note, however, that the catastrophic words all had to do with going crazy or with bodily catastrophes such as heart attack, collapse, or brain tumor. The physiological prime did not seem to enhance the bias for threat words in this study. The authors suggested that this may be due to using an obvious prime (riding a stationary bike) instead of one in which the participants are less aware of its effects. Although panickers showed more Stroop interference than normal controls in this study, they did not differ from people with another anxiety disorder (obsessive–compulsive disorder), suggesting that the biases observed may be associated with anxiety disorders in general rather than panic disorder in particular. Yet, a later study by the same group that also used an emotional Stroop test found that panic patients did differ from patients with obsessive–compulsive disorder in showing a bias for panic-related threat words having to do with bodily sensations or catastrophes, but did not differ for positive words related to panic or neutral words (McNally et al., 1994). This study differed from the earlier study in that it attempted to improve the sensitivity of the emotional Stroop test by selecting threat words for each participant idiographically from words that they had previously rated as "most disturbing."

Thus, interpretive bias with regard to threat from internal bodily sensations has been shown to distinguish panic patients from normal controls. The evidence regarding whether panic disorder patients show a unique cognitive bias for bodily threat when compared to people with other anxiety disorders is more conflicting.

Another question for researchers and clinicians is how well cognitive bias to perceive threat predicts actual panic-related avoidance (agoraphobic) behavior. Some research indicates that self-efficacy beliefs (beliefs about one's ability to cope) predict avoidance behavior better than perceived threat. One study showed that increasing the panicker's perceived control over a physical trigger without increasing actual control reduced panic (Sanderson, Rapee & Barlow, 1989). Thus, agoraphobia may be especially characterized by a negative appraisal of coping ability, for example, "I can't cope with panic." In fact, Telch, Brouillard,

Telch, Agras & Taylor (1989) directly examined self-efficacy beliefs and found that they significantly correlated with panic-related avoidance. If self-efficacy beliefs are more important than danger-related cognitions in predicting actual behavior, they may also be a more important target of psychotherapeutic interventions, even if they are not uniquely identifying features of a particular disorder.

Specific Phobia

Specific phobia is a persistent, marked fear of some clearly identifiable object or situation such as animals or heights. Often, people with phobias attempt to avoid exposure to their feared stimuli, which may cause some interference with functioning (American Psychiatric Association, 1994). For example, one of the authors' clients was often late for work or appointments, as he would cross the street and go well out of his way to avoid pigeons. The word "specific" distinguishes these phobias from more pervasive phobias such as social phobia (fear and avoidance of social situations in which one might be the object of others' scrutiny) and agoraphobia (fear and avoidance of multiple places in which panic might occur).

Cognitively, specific phobias involve the perception of danger or threat in situations that most people consider benign. Unlike other anxiety disorders, the biased perceptions in specific phobia are fairly circumscribed and thereby provide a good opportunity to examine some of the intricacies of anxious thinking. For example, Landau (1980) found that dog-phobic individuals tended to evaluate dogs based simply on ferocity rather than also including criteria such as size that non-phobic individuals used. Thus, the dog phobics seemed to process information about dogs in a simplistic way that facilitated maximizing potential threat.

Tomarken, Sutton & Mineka (1995) employed a judgment of covariation task to examine whether people prone to specific fears show a bias to overestimate the association between the feared object and an aversive outcome. Students with either high or low fear of snakes were shown slides of snakes (fear-relevant), damaged electrical outlets (possibly fear inducing and conceptually related to the experience of electric shock), flowers, and mushrooms (fear-irrelevant). The slides were randomly and equally paired with three possible outcomes: (a) electric shock; (b) noise, or (c) nothing. Although participants rated damaged electrical outlets and shocks as belonging together more than shocks and snakes, high snake fear participants significantly overestimated the pairing of electric shock with snake slides but did not show this bias for damaged outlets. Thus, phobics or other people with heightened fears may overestimate the correlation between the object of their fears and aversive outcomes, and even favor this association over one that makes more conceptual sense (damaged electrical outlets and shock). However, this finding has not been entirely consistent. In a similar study involving people high or low in fear of blood and injuries (analogous to blood–injury phobia), Pury & Mineka (1997) failed to find a difference in covariation estimates for the two groups. Rather, everyone, regardless of fear level, showed a tendency to overestimate the association between injury slides (the fear stimulus) and electric shock (the aversive outcome). They suggested that perhaps blood–injury stimuli are more likely to evoke negative reactions in people in general than are slides of stimuli such as snakes and spiders. Thus, more research is needed to determine which phobic stimuli are likely to produce heightened covariation estimates in phobic participants rather than in the general population.

Other research has shown that the cognitive bias to perceive phobic threat is especially associated with high levels of anticipatory anxiety. Andrews, Freed & Teesson (1994) compared phobics to normal controls as they approached a feared situation. For the phobic participants, the feared situation was the object of their phobia. For the normal participants, the feared situation was a gondola ride over a ravine that many people found anxiety-provoking. Although both groups found the stimulus somewhat threatening, the phobics differed from the normal controls in the timing of their highest anxiety ratings. Phobics gave their highest fear ratings before entering the situation; whereas, normal controls gave their highest fear ratings when actually in the situation. The authors surmised that before actually encountering the phobic stimulus, the situation is rather ambiguous. Therefore, high anticipatory anxiety in phobics may be consistent with previous literature showing that ambiguous situations are likely to activate cognitive biases to perceive threat in people with highly developed anxiety schemata.

Some researchers have suggested that inaccurately predicting the magnitude of anxiety one is likely to experience in a feared situation contributes to increased fear behavior in similar future situations, regardless of whether the misestimates are underestimates or overestimates of actual anxiety (Telch, Ilai, Valentiner & Craske, 1994). Telch et al. reasoned that the mismatch between predicted and actual fear leads to greater fear-related behavior in the future because unpredicted outcomes are more aversive than predicted ones.

As with panic, self-efficacy beliefs rather than danger cognitions *per se* may be an important predictor of phobic behavior. For example, Williams & Watson (1985) conducted an innovative study that found that perceived danger was a poor predictor of actual phobic behavior whereas self-efficacy beliefs (confidence in ability to approach the feared situation) were good predictors of phobic behavior and of response to an intervention. Acrophobics were asked to rate their anxiety level, perceived danger, and confidence in their ability to approach the railings of balconies at various heights in a multistory building. Ratings were given on the ground and at each new height. Self-efficacy was a strong predictor of approaching balcony railings at ascending heights when perceived danger and anxiety arousal were held constant. On the other hand, perceived danger and anxiety arousal did not significantly predict approaching balcony railings with self-efficacy held constant.

Mood Disorders

Mood disorders involve excesses of low or high moods or their combination. Manic states, which involve overly positive, grandiose thinking, typically do not occur without a person also experiencing depressive states. Thus, depressive disorders either involve the experience of low moods (unipolar depression) or a combination of low and high moods (bipolar disorder; American Psychiatric Association, 1994). Bipolar disorders traditionally have been thought to be heavily influenced by genetic and biological causes, with cognitive processes playing a smaller role. However, recent evidence suggests that attributional styles and life events may contribute to the severity and timing of depressive and manic episodes among bipolar individuals (e.g. Hammen, Ellicott & Gitlin, 1992; Reilly-Harrington, Alloy & Fresco, 1998). Nonetheless, because little work has examined the role of such cognitive factors in bipolar disorders, we will focus on cognitive research in unipolar depression.

Unipolar Depression

Most people can identify with a blue mood or temporary loss of interest in usual activities. Depressive disorders, however, are characterized by persistent depressed mood or loss of interest (most of the time for at least two weeks) and at least four other symptoms such as sleep disturbance, change in eating patterns or appetite, fatigue, feelings of worthlessness or excessive guilt, trouble concentrating, or persistent thoughts of death or suicide (American Psychiatric Association, 1994).

A prominent feature of most cases of depression is a cognitive bias to view the self, world and future negatively (Beck et al., 1979; Engel & DeRubeis, 1993). Beck and colleagues have identified several types of biases that characterize depressive thinking (e.g. Beck et al., 1979; Burns, 1980). For example, depressives tend to overgeneralize negative events, seeing one bad experience as a pattern of failure or defeat. Depressives also tend to focus on negative information and disqualify or ignore positive information. They also tend to take responsibility for negative events that are not in their control. Like panickers, depressives are in a vicious cycle in which low moods are maintained by negative beliefs: generalized negative expectations about self, world, and future lead to a proclivity to process information in a negatively biased manner, which then confirms the negative expectations.

One cognitive theory of depression, hopelessness theory, posits that consistently negatively biased cognition (a depressive inferential style) in interaction with negative life events plays a causal role in the development of some depressions (Abramson, Metalsky & Alloy, 1989). The depressive inferential style involves attributing negative events to global and stable causes, inferring that negative consequences will follow from a negative event, and that the occurrence of the negative event indicates flaws in oneself. Many studies have obtained promising support for the potential causal role of negative inferential style in the development of depression (e.g. Alloy & Clements, in press; Alloy, Just & Panzarella, 1997; Metalsky, Halberstadt & Abramson, 1987; Metalsky, Joiner, Hardin & Abramson, 1993; Nolen-Hoeksema, Girgus & Seligman, 1992). The work on cognitive structures as a potential causal factor in depression has interesting implications for the treatment of depression. Cognitive therapy, which aims to modify depressive belief systems, should be more effective in preventing relapse than treatments targeted primarily at more superficial aspects of depression (Segal, 1988). In fact, there is some evidence that cognitive therapy is associated with lower relapse rates than medication for the treatment of depression (Hollon, DeRubeis & Evans, 1996; Hollon, DeRubeis & Seligman, 1992).

In addition, some research suggests that attributional style for interpreting *positive* rather than negative events may be important in predicting recovery from depression as well as lower rates of relapse. Needles & Abramson (1990) found that depressives who showed a tendency to attribute positive events to internal, stable, and global causes were more likely to recover from depressive symptoms following the occurrence of positive life events. Similarly, Ilardi, Craighead and Evans (1997) found that depressed patients with an internal, stable, global attributional style for positive events were less likely to relapse in the year following hospital discharge than depressives who did *not* show this attributional style. In other words, depressed persons who did not show the tendency to minimize or discount positive information were more likely to recover and were less vulnerable to relapse.

In addition to the work on the role of inferential styles as vulnerability and invulnerability factors for depression, much research has focused on documenting the nature of cognitive processes exhibited by depressed persons. For example, Bargh & Tota (1988) used an innovative reaction-time procedure for assessing automatic cognitive processes in depression. Participants were asked to hold six digits in working memory while determining how descriptive a series of positive and negative adjectives were of themselves and a friend. Based on reaction times, the authors found that memory load interfered less with endorsements of negative content than with positive content for dysphoric persons. The opposite was true for non-dysphoric persons, leading to the conclusion that processing negative self-referent information was less effortful and more automatic for the dysphoric participants, whereas processing positive self-referent material was more automatic for non-dysphoric participants.

Depression is also associated with a memory bias in which negative memories are more easily consolidated and accessed than positive memories. Given that people with depression may be depressed because they have, in fact, had more negative events happen to them, it is important to control for this possibility in testing memory bias. Clark & Teasdale (1982) controlled for history of negative life events by asking patients who experienced diurnal variation in their mood to recall pleasant and unpleasant memories at their more depressed time of day and at their better time of day. Patients remembered more unpleasant memories when feeling more depressed and more happy experiences when they were less depressed.

Although empirical studies have consistently demonstrated that depressive thinking is more negative than cognition in non-depressed people, it is not clear whether depressives actually distort information in a negative direction, or whether their negative thinking is realistic. Many studies have found that while negative in content, depressives' perceptions and inferences about themselves are actually more accurate than those of non-depressed persons, who typically show optimistic biases and distortions in self-perception (for a review of "depressive realism" studies, see Alloy & Abramson, 1988). Alternatively, it may be that people who are dysphoric or mildly depressed process information about themselves more accurately than either non-depressives who show optimistic biases or more severely depressed persons who display negative distortions (Ackerman & DeRubeis, 1991).

One important issue in the cognitive literature on depression is whether or not negative cognition precedes, and possibly causes, depressed mood. While the hopelessness theory described above suggests a causal role for depressive inferential styles, other cognitive theories suggest that depressed mood may occur first and serve as a "prime" for depressive thought processes (Persons & Miranda, 1992; Teasdale, 1988). Several researchers have activated a negative or positive mood in individuals and then examined participants' thought processes. Activation of pleasant moods leads to greater recall of pleasant memories, whereas activation of dysphoric mood leads to better recall of unpleasant ideas (see Segal (1988) for a review of social cognition and mood). A basic finding of social cognition research is that the more often a belief system is accessed, the more readily available it becomes, making it more likely to be activated in an increasingly wide variety of circumstances. Thus, depressed people may activate negative belief systems about self, world, and future more frequently than non-depressives, making it more likely, in turn, that these negative belief systems will be called upon when interpreting ambiguous stimuli.

Segal (1988) suggested that to sort out whether affect simply primes congruent cognitive structures or cognitive structures influence mood, one needs to use experimental paradigms that attempt to uncover putative cognitive structures. Along these lines, Rogers et al. (1977) adapted a task developed by cognitive psychologists for studying schemata to the study of self-schemata in depression. Participants were presented with a series of adjectives and asked to decide if each described them or not. Response times for making these decisions were also assessed, as were participants' delayed recall of the words. Response times for making the judgments and recall accuracy were used to infer the content of self-schemata, based on the idea that quicker reaction times and greater recall should be associated with more developed schemata. This self-schema task battery has been used in many studies to show that compared to normals, depressed participants make decisions more quickly about negative than about positive words, rate more negative adjectives as self-descriptive, and recall more negative adjectives, suggesting that they do indeed have a negatively biased cognitive information processing system (e.g. Greenberg & Alloy, 1989; MacDonald & Kuiper, 1984).

However, it is still possible in these studies that depressed mood serves as a prime that leads depressed persons to process negative information more quickly (Segal, 1988). In a more rigorous test of whether or not negative self-schemata exist independently of mood state and contribute to development of depression, initially non-depressed participants identified as high or low risk for depression based on their inferential styles were administered the self-schema task battery and followed prospectively for two years with assessments every six weeks of dysphoria and clinically significant depressive episodes (Alloy et al., 1997). Cognitively high-risk participants exhibited more negative self-referent information processing than cognitively low-risk participants at Time 1, despite the fact that all participants were not clinically depressed and they controlled for initial depressive symptoms. In addition, participants' negative self-referent processing at Time 1 predicted onsets of major and minor depressive episodes during the two-year follow-up period.

Emotional Stroop tests, described earlier, have also been employed by depression researchers to examine whether depressive self-schemata exist independently of depressive mood. Gotlib & McCann (1984) presented depressive, neutral, and manic words in the Stroop task and found that dysphoric undergraduates took longer to name the ink color when a depressive word was presented than when other types of words were presented. Non-dysphoric students showed no difference in color naming time depending on type of word. Then, to rule out the possibility that transient mood rather than a stable depressive cognitive schema accounted for the results, the authors conducted a second study in which undergraduates were randomly assigned to a depression, elation, or neutral mood priming induction before participating in the Stroop task. In this case, there were no differences between groups on the Stroop task, so transient mood did not seem sufficient to create interference with color naming in response to depressive words. Of course, it is likely that there is a reciprocal relationship between mood and thinking such that negative thinking can cause depressed mood, and depressed mood can prime negative thinking and memories (Teasdale & Fogarty, 1979).

In sum, cognitive research on depression supports the idea that depressives have highly developed negative self-schemata that lead to memory biases for negative events and attentional biases for negative stimuli. Although it is likely that there is a reciprocal relationship between depressed thinking and mood, there is some evidence that negative schemata in non-depressed persons are a risk factor for the development of future depressive episodes. Furthermore, treatments that directly target depressive cognition are more effective than those that target mood and symptoms in preventing relapse (for a review, see Engel & DeRubeis, 1993).

Eating Disorders

Problems with eating behavior are classified as mental health conditions when it has been established that a psychological syndrome is implicated. Obesity, for example, is not considered a mental health disorder because there is not a clear association between psychological factors and the problem of obesity. Anorexia and bulimia nervosa, described below, are two syndromes that involve problematic eating behaviors that have been classified as mental health disorders (American Psychiatric Association, 1994).

Anorexia and Bulimia Nervosa

Anorexia nervosa is characterized by refusal to maintain a minimally normal body weight (less than 85% of expected weight) by restricted eating, purging food, or excessive exercise. Bulimia nervosa is binge eating combined with compensatory strategies for avoiding weight gain, including purging by inducing vomiting or taking laxatives, fasting, and excessive exercise. Both anorexics and bulimics typically have distorted perceptions of body shape and weight, and these perceptions have great influence on their self-esteem (American Psychiatric Association, 1994). Because cognitive models of anorexia and bulimia are quite similar, we will discuss them together (Vitousek & Orimoto, 1993).

According to Vitousek & Orimoto (1993), eating disorders often evolve when a young woman faced with stress attributes her distress to "fatness." She then starts to engage in behaviors to control body fat because she believes that if thin, she will be happy. Vitousek & Orimoto point out that "The equation of slenderness and happiness is a delusion that eating-disordered individuals share with much of western society" (p. 196). Vitousek and colleagues suggested that although beliefs about the importance of weight and shape are shared with much of the normal population, they are more elaborated, inflexible, and emotionally laden among people with eating disorders (Vitousek & Hollon, 1990; Vitousek & Orimoto, 1993). Furthermore, many of the eating disordered person's moment-to-moment thoughts (automatic thoughts) have to do with food, purging calories, exercising, and body shape (Clark, Feldman & Channon, 1989; Vitousek & Ewald, 1992). For example, compared to normals and dieting controls, bulimics report spending more time thinking about food and weight and report greater elation or upset at the loss or gain of trivial amounts of weight (cited in Vitousek & Orimoto, 1993).

Vitousek & Orimoto, 1993 proposed four key types of beliefs that distinguish a person with eating disorder from others:

1. perception of being overweight (or potentially overweight)
2. evaluation of being overweight as bad
3. attribution of the means of weight control to the self
4. expectation of weight loss as a result of specific behaviors.

Unlike people with anxiety or depression who are often distressed by their fearful or negative thoughts, people with eating disorders often do not regard excessive thinness and other eating-related problems as an "affliction but as an accomplishment in which they feel a complete emotional and moral investment" (Vitousek & Orimoto, 1993, p. 196). For example, one way in which bulimics differ from normal controls is that they believe that inducing vomiting and diarrhea (with laxatives) purifies the body (Garner & Bemis, 1982).

Although there is much clinical lore to suggest that anorexics are characterized by beliefs associated with negative self-image and perfectionistic ideals, careful research has not shown these characteristics to distinguish eating disorders from other psychiatric disorders (Cooper, Cooper & Fairburn, 1985; Fairburn & Garner, 1988; Phelps & Wilczenski, 1993). Thus, in terms of content of thought, it seems to be only beliefs about eating and weight that reliably distinguish people with eating disorders from those with other mental disorders. Furthermore, Vitousek & Hollon (1990) proposed that the cognitive schemata associated with eating disorders are not radically different in content from those of other disorders and normal functioning, but rather are remarkable because of extreme simplicity and rigidity: "anorexics and bulimics have a particularly urgent need for these simplifying, organizing, and stabilizing functions of schematic processing, and the focus on weight is 'chosen,' valued, and defended in part because it has unusually potent schematic properties" (p. 193). The authors labeled this phenomenon the "New Year's resolution cognitive style" in which there is a great preference for simplicity, certainty, and achieving control through one's own behavior. For example Lingswiler, Crowther & Stephens (1989) found that bulimics differed from both binge eaters and normal controls in displaying extremely polarized dichotomous thinking prior to overeating episodes.

An important complexity in considering the cognitive model applied to eating disorders involves cognitive dysfunction due to starvation. Starvation is associated with cognitive phenomena such as rigidity and faulty information processing (Demitrack et al., 1990; Laessle, Bossert, Hank, Hahlweg & Pirke, 1989). Thus, although rigidity of beliefs about weight and shape may contribute to development of eating disorders, physiological changes associated with sequelae of the disorders further contribute to these cognitive dysfunctions. To date, research on cognitions in eating disorders has relied heavily on self-report. The problems with self-report described earlier are of even greater concern with an eating disorder sample because these patients are especially prone to deliberate distortion in order to try to preserve their symptomatology. In addition, starvation may contribute to impoverishment of thought content and difficulty with abstraction, which also impede self-report methodologies (Vitousek & Orimoto, 1993).

There have, however, been a handful of studies that have used alternative methodologies for discovering cognitive processes in people with eating disorders. For example, Schotte, McNally & Turner (1990) used a dichotic listening task to show that bulimics selectively attend more than normal controls to words pertaining to body weight. Vitousek and colleagues (cited in Vitousek & Orimoto, 1993) found that participants with eating disorders were more likely than normal or subclinical control participants to report a food or body-related meaning of homophones (e.g. wait/weight). Several investigators have used the Stroop test to examine cognitive processing in people with eating disorders. One would expect that people with eating disorders would show greater response times than others when the words are related to food *or* weight. However, response times have been greater only when the Stroop cards contained food-related words, suggesting that hunger rather than eating disorder interfered with color naming (Vitousek & Orimoto, 1993). In fact, Channon & Hayward (1990) found support for hunger-producing interference in color naming food-related words by having normals fast for 24 hours before completing the Stroop test. Normal participants showed greater processing time for food words but not body image words when hungry. Vitousek & Hollon (1990) suggest that it is important for future studies to use control groups of dieters to help control for the possibility that hunger and/or a general preoccupation with food account for the findings.

Thus, although cognitive research in eating disorders is in its infancy, it seems that people with eating disorders differ from others not only in the content of their thoughts about eating and weight, but – perhaps even more importantly – in the frequency of these thoughts and the rigidity of their cognitive processing.

Dissociative Disorders

Dissociative disorders are characterized by a splitting apart of cognitive functions that are usually integrated (American Psychiatric Association, 1994). In these disorders, aspects of self-schema including autobiographical memory may be entirely excluded from consciousness. As with other cognitive functions, some dissociation occurs as part of normal experience and can even be adaptive (Rauschenberger & Lynn, 1995). For example, one can talk on the phone and wash dishes by dissociating or screening out many of the stimuli related to washing the dishes. However, if the water becomes too hot, one quickly reallocates attention to the dishwashing task. Thus, in normal functioning, dissociated elements of experience are easily called back. In the dissociative disorders, the screened out aspects of experience are not readily called back into consciousness. Furthermore, the dissociation associated with mental disorders is often of critical functions like memory of past events rather than incidental aspects of the environment. This section will focus on dissociative identity disorder, formerly known as multiple personality disorder.

Dissociative Identity Disorder

Diagnosis of dissociative identity disorder (DID) is made when someone exhibits two or more distinct personalities. At least one of the personalities is amnesic for the experiences of the other(s). Typically, the personality most closely associated with premorbid functioning is referred to as the "host" personality and the later-developing personalities are referred to as "alters" (Putnam, 1989).

From the cognitive perspective, DID is fundamentally a disorder of explicit episodic (autobiographical) memory. Procedural memory (skills that have been learned) and semantic memory (general knowledge) are typically intact. Furthermore, implicit memory may exist but the patient is impeded in his or her ability to call this material into consciousness (explicit memory; Kihlstrom, Tataryn & Hoyt, 1993).

Cognitive research on the causes and mechanisms of DID is in its infancy. However, one promising avenue of inquiry has to do with state-dependent memory. A number of studies have shown that recall is enhanced when a person is in the same mood state as they were when the event occurred (for a review, see Blaney, 1986). It may be that memories established in an extreme emotional state, such as might accompany trauma, are dissociated from other memories simply because they are linked to a mood state that does not typically recur (Bower, 1981). In DID, the different personalities are frequently characterized by different mood states (e.g. a calm, passive host and an angry alter). Thus, the amnesia of one personality for another may be consistent with the phenomenon of state-dependent memory (Bower, 1994).

Most people with DID report severe trauma such as sexual abuse in childhood and the appearance of their first alter at a traumatic time (Atchison & McFarlane, 1994; Loewenstein, 1994). It has been hypothesized that dissociated personalities may develop as terrified children try to distance themselves from the reality of their lives (Atchison & McFarlane, 1994). However, because almost all of the evidence of childhood abuse in people with DID is based on retrospective report, there is concern that many claims of abuse may be inaccurate or even entirely fabricated (Piper, 1994). Given that many psychotherapists who specialize in recovering memories believe that childhood abuse is a cause of DID, they may operate under a bias to seek confirmatory information for the hypothesis of childhood sexual abuse and may inadvertently lead patients to develop plausible but unfounded memories (Lindsay & Read, 1994; Loftus, 1993). The difficulty in confirming reports of childhood abuse has led to a great deal of debate regarding adults' memories of childhood traumas, particularly memories of sexual abuse that have been "repressed" and subsequently recovered. (Forgotten and subsequently remembered memories of childhood trauma are commonly referred to as "repressed and recovered." However, it should be noted that further research is needed to clarify the differences between repression and other memory phenomena such as suppression and natural processes such as forgetting. See Brewin (1997) for more information.)

Psychologists have begun to explore the phenomenon of repressed and recovered memories empirically. Concerns about the possibility of completely fabricated stories of childhood abuse have led some researchers to explore whether amnesia for childhood trauma actually occurs. Prospective studies in which there is clear documentation of actual episodes of abuse are the only means to definitively answer this question. There have been only a few such studies conducted to date (Widom, 1997; Williams, 1994). Williams contacted 129 women with previously documented histories of sexual abuse. (These women were ages 18 to 31 and had been victims of childhood sexual abuse 17 years earlier (ages 10 months to 12 years at the time of abuse). All of the women had been examined at a particular hospital at the time of abuse, and details of the abuse and sexual assault were recorded when the incident was reported.) The women were told that they were participating in a study on women's lives and health, and were not aware that the focus of the study was memories of childhood trauma. An extensive interview was conducted with each woman, which included questions about her childhood sexual experiences, particularly those involving older or authority figures or unwanted sexual contact. The researchers found that 38% of the women did not report the episode of abuse that had been previously recorded. The women may not have reported the abuse because they had amnesia for it or because they did not wish to disclose it. Williams discounted the possibility that women who did not report abuse were simply reluctant to discuss sensitive issues because many of these same women reported different instances of abuse as well as other personal life events. In addition, 16% of the women who reported the documented abuse said that there had been a time in their lives when they did not remember the event.

Such findings provide evidence that amnesia for traumatic childhood events can occur and that recovery of the forgotten memories is also possible. However, there are still questions as to the accuracy of memories of abuse that have been forgotten and later recalled. We know that memory in general is subject to error, and memory for childhood trauma is not particularly infallible (Christianson, 1992). One common source of memory error is misattribution about the source of a memory. Johnson & Raye (1981) define "real" memories as those that have been obtained externally (through perceptual processes), whereas "imagined" memories develop through internal thought processes or imagination. People often have trouble distinguishing real from imagined memories because they confuse things they have heard, thought, or imagined with actual perceptions or experiences. For example, people have been found to confuse what they say in a conversation with what others say (Raye & Johnson, 1980).

The tendency to misattribute the source of information suggests that new information may be accepted by people as actual memories. Loftus has explored the impact of misleading information on memories and found that when people are provided with new and misleading information, they incorporate this information when reporting the original event (Loftus & Hoffman, 1989). In one study, people were shown a video involving an assault and a blue car (Loftus, Levidow & Duensing, 1992). After viewing the video, inquiries to one group contained misinformation that the car involved was white, while inquiries to another group did not contain the misleading information. People in the misled group were more likely to later report that the vehicle was white, while the other group tended to remember accurately that the vehicle was blue.

In an analog study that may have more relevance to memories of childhood trauma, students were given a booklet describing four events from their childhood (Loftus & Pickrell, 1995). Three of the events were real and had been provided by a close relative of the student. One event was a fabricated story about the participant being lost in a department store or shopping mall as a child. Fabricated stories were developed with the help of relatives using details about probable locations and people involved. Participants were asked to read each story, write their memories of the event, and indicate how clear their memory was for the event. In two interviews held after completion of the booklets, 25% of participants reported that they at least partially remembered the false event. Although memories for the fabricated event were generally less clear than memories for the true events, clarity for the false events tended to increase from the first interview to the second. Not only did the students accept false memories as their own, but they became more clear about these memories as time passed and they were interviewed about details. Thus, in some cases of "false memories," the rememberer may not be entirely fabricating the remembered event, but rather may simply misattribute something they heard or witnessed to their own lives (Lindsay & Read, 1994).

In sum, it has been established that amnesia for childhood trauma can occur. However, given the malleable nature of memory, it is quite possible that some memories that are recovered after many years are inaccurate and even completely fabricated. This possibility is heightened when people are prompted with misinformation and encouraged to remember details.

APPLYING THE COGNITIVE PERSPECTIVE TO ABSENCE OF DISORDER OR MENTAL HEALTH

The preceding sections illustrate the types of cognitive biases that characterize several of the psychological disorders and show how various misperceptions can undermine healthy psychological functioning. Early researchers in social cognition believed that healthy cognition was largely unbiased, logical, and accurate (Ross & Anderson, 1982). Consistent with the traditional view of mental health, this model saw social perception as competent and reality-based. This idealistic view of human evaluative capacities, however, has not been supported by empirical evidence. In contrast, research has pointed to the existence of widespread distortion and bias in healthy cognitive functioning (e.g. Alloy & Abramson, 1988; Nisbett & Ross, 1980). People who are characterized by positively biased views of themselves, the world, and their ability to exert control over events seem to be more resilient to anxiety and depression than people who are realistic or have negatively biased perceptions (e.g. Alloy & Abramson, 1988; Alloy, Abramson & Viscusi, 1981; Taylor & Brown, 1988).

Theorists have identified three positive biases that seem to be particularly important for positive mental health: (a) unrealistically positive self-evaluation; (b) an exaggerated belief in personal control and mastery; and (c) unrealistic optimism (Taylor & Brown, 1988, 1994). The presence of positive biases in normal people appears to be associated with criteria of mental health such as the ability to be happy, care about others, engage in productive work, and manage adversity (Taylor & Brown, 1988, 1994; Taylor, Lichtman & Wood, 1984). It has been suggested that positive biases protect mental health by minimizing negative affect and maximizing positive affect (Taylor, Wayment & Collins, 1993). With respect to the ability to establish relationships, overly positive self-evaluation has been associated with perceived and actual popularity among peers (Bohrnstedt & Felson, 1983). There is also evidence that both partners of married couples in a college community hold an idealized image of their spouse, and that this image is partly maintained by attributing positive behaviors of the spouse to personal qualities and negative behaviors to situational factors (Hall & Taylor, 1976). Further, positive biases may promote productivity and creativity by enhancing functioning and increasing motivation (Taylor & Brown, 1988).

Positive biases may also serve as moderators of psychosocial stress by increasing individuals' ability to cope with stressful life events (Taylor & Aspinwall, 1996). In one study of gay men at risk of AIDS, unrealistic optimism about the possibility of avoiding AIDS was associated with psychological benefits such as less hopelessness and dysphoria (Taylor et al., 1992). It may be that positive biases play a particularly important role in the context of threatening events because feeling in control may help people adjust (Taylor & Armor, 1996). For example, a study conducted with breast cancer patients showed that patients who held an exaggerated sense of personal control over their disease course adjusted better than those who did not (Taylor, Lichtman & Wood, 1984). Our understanding of the benefits of exaggerated perceptions of personal control has been greatly enhanced through the study of depressive cognitions, in which illusions of control are markedly absent.

Research comparing depressed to non-depressed persons on judgment of covariation tasks described earlier has provided evidence not only for the existence of illusions of control among non-depressed people, but also for the notion that the absence of these illusions is associated with poorer mental health (see earlier section on unipolar depression). Whereas non-depressed people overestimate the relationship between their actions (e.g. pressing a button) and a target outcome (e.g. turning on a green light) in positive situations (e.g. turning on the light wins money), depressives tend to more accurately judge their personal control (Alloy & Abramson, 1982; for a review, see Alloy & Abramson, 1988). One study found that an inflated sense of control buffered depressive reactions to adversity both in laboratory and in real-life situations (Alloy & Clements, 1992). Undergraduates were given a computerized judgment of covariation test to assess realistic versus inflated judgments of personal control. Then, participants were given a laboratory stressor in the form of an unsolvable block design task. Participants were also interviewed one month later and reported naturally occurring stressors over the intervening time period. Participants who exhibited illusions of control at Time 1 were less likely to display negative mood reactions immediately after the unsolvable block designs and less likely to become discouraged after the occurrence of negative life events. Furthermore, illusions of control also predicted fewer depressive symptoms at follow-up for those participants who experienced many negative life events in the intervening period. The authors concluded that illusions of control helped people to cope with adversity in part by reducing discouragement in the face of negative life events.

The fact that healthy functioning is characterized by positive bias raises a question: What happens when an individual's unrealistic beliefs are challenged or disconfirmed? Taylor & Armor (1996) argued that people may exert control in a variety of areas and that those who experience a loss of control in one domain may adapt by gaining it in another. For example, patients with chronic illness who do not have much actual control over the disease's course may enhance their perception of control by exerting control over their emotional reactions (Thompson, Sobolew-Shubin, Galbraith, Schwankovsky & Cruzen, 1993). Thus, people with optimistic biases may not always assume personal control in areas where they are likely to fail, but instead show flexibility in terms of where and when they apply the illusion of control.

Flexibility seems to be adaptive in that it allows people to process negative information when it has important implications for adaptive behavior change but to screen out negative information when it has a pernicious effect on mood and sense of well-being (Taylor et al., 1992). Taylor & Gollwitzer (1995) found that healthy people tend to be realistic in their perceptions when they are involved in decision making, but utilize positive illusions when implementing goals. These findings suggest that positive mental health might be particularly characterized by adaptive and flexible processes whereby cognitive attributions adjust to the situation. While pursuing goals, it may be most beneficial to maintain very positive impressions of oneself and one's efforts, even if illusory, because of their salutory effect on motivation. However, when making important decisions, it may be more critical to even-handedly evaluate both positive and negative information.

In sum, flexible deployment of positive cognitive biases such as inflated self-esteem, exaggerated beliefs in personal control, and unrealistic optimism all seem to enhance mental health by protecting one from depression and anxiety and assisting with adjustment to stressful circumstances.

CONCLUSION

Although human cognition represents only one domain of functioning, the interplay between cognitive processes and social and personal environments explains much about psychological functioning. The common thread throughout this chapter is the idea that it is not the accuracy of one's perception of the environment that accounts for good or poor mental health. Rather, cognitive biases are ubiquitous across the various mental disorders as well as in good mental health. In fact, most of the mental disorders and good mental health can be partly defined in terms of particular key cognitive biases. Whereas people with anxiety disorders have a bias to perceive and process threat-related information, those with depressive disorders have a bias to perceive and process negative information, particularly about themselves. Individuals with eating disorders have biased perceptions of their body weight and shape as well as rigid and extreme views about the importance of thinness. Finally, good psychological adjustment is characterized by a positive bias to see oneself and one's effects on the environment in an enhanced perspective.

If both mental disorders and mental health are characterized by cognitive bias, how are we to distinguish the two? Although many factors undoubtedly contribute to mental health, cognitive flexibility may importantly distinguish adaptive from maladaptive functioning. Taylor & Gollwitzer (1995) suggested that healthy individuals show flexibility in calling upon cognitive biases. Participants maintained unrealistic positively biased cognitions while pursuing goals but showed less bias and more evenhandedness when engaged in decision making. Thus, mentally healthy individuals may adjust their cognitions depending on circumstances in order to interact more effectively with the environment. Another study found that people who responded to hypothetical scenarios with different cognitive strategies depending on the situation functioned better socially (Chiu, Hong, Mischel & Shoda, 1995).

While further work is needed to determine if cognitive rigidity is characteristic of mental disorders, certainly much of the research we presented suggests that this may be the case. For example, eating disordered individuals were not notably different from normals in the types of cognitions entertained but rather in the rigidity with which they maintained them (e.g. Vitousek & Orimoto, 1993). People with dissociative identity disorder change personalities in response to different stimuli because the host's sense of self is not flexible enough to integrate certain experiences. Furthermore, many researchers and clinicians would suggest that anxiety and depressive disorders can range greatly in severity, with more severe manifestations characterized by more consistent application of the prototypical maladaptive schema to a wide variety of situations (e.g. Abramson et al., 1989; Beck et al., 1979).

Thus, the particular type and frequency of cognitive biases define various mental disorders as well as good mental health. Furthermore, rigidity of cognitive processing may be generally characteristic of mental illness whereas flexibility is a hallmark of positive mental health.

ACKNOWLEDGMENTS

Many thanks for assistance to Celeste Bethea, Thelma Carson, Joia Copeland, Roseanne DeFronzo, and Pat Panzarella.

REFERENCES

Abramson, L. Y., Metalsky, G. & Alloy, L. B. (1989). Hopelessness depression: a theory-based subtype of depression. *Psychological Review*, 96 (2), 358–72.

Ackerman, R. & DeRubeis, R. J. (1991). Is depressive realism real? *Clinical Psychology Review*, 11, 565–84.

Alba, J. W. & Hasher, L. (1983). Is memory schematic? *Psychological Bulletin*, 93 (2), 203–31.

Alloy, L. B. & Abramson, L. Y. (1979). Judgment of contingency in depressed and nondepressed students: sadder but wiser? *Journal of Experimental Psychology: General*, 108, 441–85.

Alloy, L. B. & Abramson, L. Y. (1982). Learned helplessness, depression, and the illusion of control. *Journal of Personality and Social Psychology*, 42 (6), 1114–26.

Alloy, L. B. & Abramson, L. Y. (1988). Depressive realism: four theoretical perspectives. In L. B. Alloy (Ed.), *Cognitive Processes in Depression* (pp. 223–65). New York: Guilford.

Alloy, L. B., Abramson, L. Y. & Viscusi, D. (1981). Induced mood and the illusion of control. *Journal of Personality and Social Psychology*, 41 (6), 1129–40.

Alloy, L. B., Abramson, L. Y., Murray, L. A., Whitehouse, W. G. & Hogan, M. E. (1997). Self-referent information processing in individuals at high and low cognitive risk for depression. *Cognition and Emotion*, 11, 539–68.

Alloy, L. B. & Clements, C. M. (1992). Illusion of control: invulnerability to negative affect and depressive symptoms after laboratory and natural stressors. *Journal of Abnormal Psychology*, 101 (2), 234–45.

Alloy, L. B. & Clements, C. M. (in press). Hopelessness theory of depression: tests of the symptom component. *Cognitive Therapy and Research*.

Alloy, L. B., Just, N. & Panzarella, C. (1997). Attributional style, daily life events, and hopelessness depression: subtype validation by prospective variability and specificity of symptoms. *Cognitive Therapy and Research*, 21 (3), 321–44.

American Psychiatric Association (1994). *Diagnostic and Statistical Manual of Mental Disorders* (4th edn). Washington, DC: Author.

Amir, N., McNally, R., Riemann, B. C. & Clements, C. (1996). Implicit memory bias for threat in panic disorder: application of the "white noise" paradigm. *Behavior Research and Therapy*, 34 (2), 157–62.

Andrews, G., Freed, S. & Teesson, M. (1994). Proximity and anticipation of a negative outcome in phobias. *Behavior Research and Therapy*, 32 (6), 643–5.

Aronson, T. A., Carasiti, I., McBane, D. & Whitaker-Azmitia, P. (1989). Biological correlates of lactate sensitivity in panic disorder. *Biological Psychiatry*, 26, 463–77.

Atchison, M. & McFarlane, A. C. (1994). A review of dissociation and dissociative disorders. *Australian and New Zealand Journal of Psychiatry*, 28, 591–9.

Bargh, J. A. & Tota, M. E. (1988). Context-dependent automatic processing in depression: accessibility of negative constructs with regard to self but not others. *Journal of Personality and Social Psychology*, 54, 925–39.

Beck, A. T. (1988). Cognitive approaches to panic disorder: theory and therapy. In S. Rachman & J. D. Maser (Eds), *Panic: Psychological Perspectives*. Hillsdale, NJ: Erlbaum.

Beck, J. S. (1997). Panic scenario. Unpublished figure.

Beck, A. T., Rush, A. J., Shaw, B. F. & Emery, G. (1979). *Cognitive Therapy of Depression*. New York: Guilford.

Beck, A. T., Sokol, L., Clark, D. A., Berchick, R. & Wright, F. (1992). A crossover study of focused cognitive therapy for panic disorder. *American Journal of Psychiatry*, 149 (6), 778–83.

Blaney, P. H. (1986). Affect and memory: a review. *Psychological Bulletin*, 99, 229–46.

Bohrnstedt, G. W. & Felson, R. B. (1983). Explaining the relations among children's

actual and perceived performances and self-esteem: a comparison of several causal models. *Journal of Personality and Social Psychology*, 45, 43–56.
Bower, G. H. (1981). Mood and memory. *American Psychologist*, 36, 129–48.
Bower, G. H. (1994). Temporary emotional states act like multiple personalities. In R. M. Klein & B. K. Doane (Eds), *Psychological Concepts and Dissociative Disorders* (pp. 207–34). Hillsdale, NJ: Erlbaum.
Brewin, C. R. (1997). Clinical and experimental approaches to understanding repression. In J. D. Read & D. S. Lindsay (Eds), *Recollection of Trauma: Scientific Evidence and Clinical Practice*. New York: Plenum.
Burgess, I. S., Jones, L. M., Robertson, S. A., Radcliffe, W. N. & Emerson, E. (1981). The degree of control exerted by phobic and non-phobic verbal stimuli over the recognition behavior of phobic and non-phobic subjects. Behavior of phobic and non-phobic subjects. *Behavioral Research and Therapy*, 19, 233–43.
Burns, D. D. (1980). *Feeling Good: The New Mood Therapy*. New York: Signet.
Channon, S. & Hayward, A. (1990). The effect of short-term fasting on processing of food cues in normal subjects. *International Journal of Eating Disorders*, 9 (4), 447–52.
Chiu, C. Y., Hong, Y. Y., Mischel, W. & Shoda, Y. (1995). Discriminative facility in social competence: conditional versus dispositional encoding and monitoring–blunting of information. *Social Cognition*, 13 (1), 49–70.
Christianson, S. (1992). Emotional stress and eyewitness memory: a critical review. *Psychological Bulletin*, 112 (2), 284–309.
Clark, D. A., Feldman, J. & Channon, S. (1989). Dysfunctional thinking in anorexia and bulimia nervosa. *Cognitive Therapy and Research*, 13 (4), 377–87.
Clark, D. M. (1988). A cognitive model of panic attacks. In S. Rachman & J. D. Maser (Eds), *Panic: Psychological Perspectives*. Hillsdale, NJ: Erlbaum.
Clark, D. M. (1993). Cognitive mediation of panic attacks induced by biological challenge tests. *Advances in Behaviour Research and Therapy*, 15 (1), 75–84.
Clark, D. M., Gelder, M., Salkovskis, P. M. & Anastasiades, P. (1991). Cognitive mediation of lactate-induced panic. Paper presented at the annual conference of the American Psychiatric Association, New Orleans, LA.
Clark, D. M., Salkovskis, P. M., Gelder, M., Koehler, C., Martin, M., Anastasiades, P., Hackmann, A., Middleton, H. & Jeavons, A. (1988). Tests of a cognitive theory of panic. In I. Hand & H. V. Wittchen (Eds), *Panic and Phobias 2*. Berlin: Springer-Verlag.
Clark, D. M., Salkovskis, P. M., Ost, L. G., Breitholtz, E., Koehler, K. A., Westling, B. E., Jeavons, A. & Gelder, M. (1997). Misinterpretation of body sensations in panic disorder. *Journal of Consulting and Clinical Psychology*, 65 (2), 203–13.
Clark, D. M. & Teasdale, J. D. (1982). Diurnal variation in clinical depression and accessibility of memories of positive and negative experiences. *Journal of Abnormal Psychology*, 91, 87–95.
Cooper, A., Cooper, P. J. & Fairburn, C. G. (1985). The specificity of the Eating Disorders Inventory. *British Journal of Clinical Psychology*, 24, 129–30.
Craik, F. I. M. & Lockhart, R. S. (1972). Levels of processing: a framework for memory research. *Journal of Verbal Learning and Verbal Behavior*, 11, 671–84.
Demitrack, M. A., Lesem, M. D., Listwak, S. J., Brandt, H. A., Jimerson, D. C. & Gold, P. W. (1990). CSF Osytocin in anorexia nervosa and bulimia nervosa: clinical and pathophysiologic considerations. *American Journal of Psychiatry*, 147 (7), 882–6.
Ehlers, A., Margraf, M., Davies, S. & Roth, W. T. (1988). Selective processing of threat cues in subjects with panic attacks. *Cognition and Emotion*, 2 (3), 201–19.
Engel, R. A. & DeRubeis, R. J. (1993). The role of cognition in depression. In K. S. Dobson and P. C. Kendall (Eds), *Psychopathology and Cognition* (pp. 83–119). San Diego: Academic Press.
Exner, J. E. (1986). *The Rorschach: A Comprehensive System*. New York: John Wiley.
Fairburn, C. G., Garner, D. M. (1988). Diagnostic criteria for anorexia nervosa and bulimia nervosa: the importance of attitudes to shape and weight. In D. M. Garner & P. E. Garfinkel (Eds), *Diagnostic Issues in Anorexia Nervosa and Bulimia Nervosa* (pp. 36–55). New York: Brunner/Mazel.

Foa, E. B. (1988). What cognitions differentiate panic disorder from other anxiety disorders? In I. Hard & H. Wittchen (Eds), *Panic and Phobias* 2. New York: Springer-Verlag.

Garner, D. M. & Bemis, K. M. (1982). A cognitive-behavioral approach to anorexia nervosa. *Cognitive Therapy and Research*, 6, 123–50.

Gotlib, I. H. & McCann, C. D. (1984). Construct accessibility and depression: an examination of cognitive and affective factors. *Journal of Personality and Social Psychology*, 47 (2), 427–39.

Greenberg, M. S. & Alloy, L. B. (1989). Depression versus anxiety: processing of self- and other-referent information. *Cognition and Emotion*, 3 (3), 207–23.

Hall, J. A. & Taylor, S. E. (1976). When love is blind: maintaining idealized images of one's spouse. *Human Relations*, 29 (8), 751–61.

Hammen, C., Ellicott, A. & Gitlin, M. J. (1992). Stressors and sociotropy/autonomy: a longitudinal study of their relationship to the course of bipolar disorder. *Cognitive Therapy and Research*, 16 (4), 409–18.

Hollon, S. D., DeRubeis, R. J. & Evans, M. D. (1996). Cognitive therapy in the treatment and prevention of depression. In P. M. Salkovskis (Ed.), *Frontiers of Cognitive Therapy* (pp. 293–317). New York: Guilford.

Hollon, S. D., DeRubeis, R. J. & Seligman, M. E. P. (1992). Cognitive therapy and prevention of depression. *Applied and Preventive Psychology*, 1 (2), 89–95.

Hope, D. A., Rapee, R. M., Heimberg, R. G. & Dombeck, M. J. (1990). Representations of the self in social phobia: vulnerability to social threat. *Cognitive Therapy and Research*, 14 (2), 177–89.

Ilardi, S. S., Craighead, W. E. & Evans, D. D. (1997). Modeling relapse in unipolar depression: the effects of dysfunctional cognitions and personality disorders. *Journal of Consulting and Clinical Psychology*, 65 (3), 381–91.

Johnson, M. K. & Raye, C. L. (1981). Reality monitoring. *Psychological Review*, 88 (1), 67–85.

Kahneman, D. & Miller, D. T. (1986). Norm theory: comparing reality to its alternatives. *Psychological Review*, 93 (2), 136–53.

Kihlstrom, J. F., Tataryn, D. J. & Hoyt, J. P. (1993). Dissociative disorders. In P. B. Sutker & H. E. Adams (Eds), *Comprehensive Handbook of Psychopathology* (2nd edn, pp. 203–34). New York: Plenum.

Klein, D. F. (1994). Testing the suffocation false alarm theory of panic disorder. *Anxiety*, 1 (1), 1–7.

Kolers, P. A. & Roediger, H. L. (1984). Procedures of mind. *Journal of Verbal Learning and Verbal Behavior*, 23, 425–49.

Laessle, R. G., Bossert, S., Hank, G., Hahlweg, K. & Pirke, K. M. (1989). Cognitive processing in bulimia nervosa: preliminary observations. *Annals of New York Academy of Sciences*, 575, 543–4.

Lana, R. E. (1991). *Assumptions of Social Psychology: A Reexamination*. New Jersey: Lawrence Erlbaum.

Landau, R. J. (1980). The role of semantic schemata in phobic word interpretation. *Cognitive Therapy and Research*, 4 (4), 427–34.

Lindsay, D. S. & Read, J. D. (1994). Psychotherapy and memories of childhood sexual abuse: a cognitive perspective. *Applied Cognitive Psychology*, 8, 281–338.

Lingswiler, V. M., Crowther, J. H. & Stephens, M. A. P. (1989). Affective and cognitive antecedents to eating episodes in bulimia and binge eating. *International Journal of Eating Disorders*, 8 (5), 533–9.

Loewenstein, R. J. (1994). Diagnosis, epidemiology, clinical course, treatment, and cost effectiveness of treatment for dissociative disorders and MPD: Report submitted to the Clinton administration Task Force on Health Care Financing Reform. *Dissociation*, 7, 3–11.

Loftus, E. F. (1993). The reality of repressed memories. *American Psychologist*, 48, 518–37.

Loftus, E. F. & Hoffman, H. G. (1989). Misinformation and memory: the creation of new memories. *Journal of Experimental Psychology: General*, 118 (1), 100–4.

Loftus, E. F., Levidow, B. & Duensing, S. (1992). Who remembers best? Individual differences in memory for events that occurred in a science museum. *Applied Cognitive Psychology*, 6, 93–107.

Loftus, E. F. & Pickrell, J. E. (1995). The formation of false memories. *Psychiatric Annals*, 25 (12), 720–5.

MacDonald, M. R. & Kuiper, N. A. (1984). Self-schema decision consistency in clinical depressives. *Journal of Social and Clinical Psychology*, 2 (3), 264–72.

MacLeod, C. & Mathews, A. (1988). Anxiety and the allocation of attention to threat. *Quarterly Journal of Experimental Psychology*, 40A, 653–70.

MacLeod, C., Mathews, A. & Tata, P. (1986). Attentional bias in emotional disorders. *Journal of Abnormal Psychology*, 95 (1), 15–20.

Maidenberg, E., Chen, E., Craske, M., Bohn, P. & Bystritsky, A. (1996). Specificity of attentional bias in panic disorder and social phobia. *Journal of Anxiety Disorders*, 10 (6), 529–41.

Margraf, J. & Ehlers, A. (1988). Panic attacks in nonclinical subjects. In I. Hand and H. U. Wittchen (Eds), *Panic and Phobias* 2. New York: Springer-Verlag.

Markus, H. (1977). Self-schemata and processing information about the self. *Journal of Personality and Social Psychology*, 35, 63–78.

Mathews, A., Richards, A. & Eysenck, M. (1989). Interpretation of homophones related to threat in anxiety states. *Journal of Abnormal Psychology*, 98, 31–4.

McNally, R. J., Foa, E. B. & Donnell, C. D. (1989). Memory bias for anxiety information in patients with panic disorder. *Cognition and Emotion*, 3 (1), 27–44.

McNally, R. J., Riemann, B. C., Louro, C. E., Lukach, B. M. & Kim, E. (1992). Cognitive processing of emotional information in panic disorder. *Behavior Research and Therapy*, 30 (2), 143–9.

McNally, R. J., Amir, N., Louro, C. E., Lukach, B. M., Riemann, B. C. & Calamari, J. E. (1994). Cognitive processing of idiographic emotional information in panic disorder. *Behavior Research and Therapy*, 32 (1), 119–22.

Metalsky, G. I., Halberstadt, L. J. & Abramson, L. Y. (1987). Vulnerability to depressive mood reactions: toward a more powerful test of the diathesis-stress and causal mediation components of the reformulated theory of depression. *Journal of Personality and Social Psychology*, 52 (2), 386–93.

Metalsky, G. I., Joiner, T. E., Hardin, T. S. & Abramson, L. Y. (1993). Depressive reactions to failure in a naturalistic setting: a test of the hopelessness and self-esteem theories of depression. *Journal of Abnormal Psychology*, 102, 101–9.

Needles, D. J. & Abramson, L. Y. (1990). Positive life events, attributional style, and hopefulness: testing a model of recovery from depression. *Journal of Abnormal Psychology*, 99 (2), 156–65.

Nisbett, R. & Ross, L. (1980). *Human Inference: Strategies, and Shortcomings of Social Judgment*. New Jersey: Prentice-Hall.

Nolen-Hoeksema, S., Girgus, J. S. & Seligman, M. E. P. (1992). Predictors and consequences of childhood depressive symptoms: a 5-year longitudinal study. *Journal of Abnormal Psychology*, 101 (3), 405–22.

Nutt, D. & Lawson, C. (1992). Panic attacks: a neurochemical overview of models and mechanisms. *British Journal of Psychiatry*, 160, 165–78.

Panzarella, C. (1995). Klein's suffocation false alarm theory: another perspective. *Anxiety*, 1, 144–9.

Persons, J. B. & Miranda, J. (1992). Cognitive theories of vulnerability to depression: reconciling negative evidence. *Cognitive Therapy and Research*, 16, 485–502.

Phelps, L. & Wilczenski, F. (1993). Eating disorders inventory – 2: cognitive-behavioral dimensions with nonclinical adolescents. *Journal of Clinical Psychology*, 49 (4), 508–15.

Piper, A., Jr. (1994). Multiple personality disorder. *British Journal of Psychiatry*, 164, 600–12.

Pury, C. L. S. & Mineka, S. (1997). Covariation bias for blood-injury stimuli and aversive outcomes. *Behavior Research and Therapy*, 35 (1), 35–47.

Putnam, F. W. (1989). *Diagnosis and Treatment of Multiple Personality Disorder*. New York: Guilford.

Rauschenberger, S. L. & Lynn, S. J. (1995). Fantasy proneness, DSM-III-R axis I psychopathology, and dissociation. *Journal of Abnormal Psychology*, 104, 373–80.

Raye, C. L. & Johnson, M. K. (1980). Reality monitoring vs. discrimination between external sources. *Bulletin of the Psychonomic Society*, 15, 405–8.

Reilly-Harrington, N., Alloy, L. B., Fresco, D. & Whitehouse, W. G. (1998). Cognitive styles and life events as predictors of bipolar and unipolar symptomatology. Temple University.

Rogers, T. B., Kuiper, N. A. & Kirker, W. S. (1977). Self-reference and the encoding of personal information. *Journal of Personality and Social Psychology*, 35, 677–88.

Ross, L. & Anderson, C. A. (1982). Shortcomings in the attribution process: on the origins and maintenance of erroneous social assessments. In D. Kahneman, P. Slovic & A. Tversky (Eds), *Judgment under Uncertainty: Heuristics and Biases*. New York: Cambridge University Press.

Sanderson, W. C., Rapee, R. M. & Barlow, D. H. (1989). The influence of an illusion of control on panic attacks induced via inhalation of 5.5% carbon dioxide-enriched air. *Archives of General Psychiatry*, 46, 157–62.

Schotte, D. E., McNally, R. & Turner, M. L. (1990). A dichotic listening analysis of body weight concern in bulimia nervosa. *International Journal of Eating Disorders*, 9 (1), 109–13.

Segal, Z. V. (1988). Appraisal of the self-schema construct in cognitive models of depression. *Psychological Bulletin*, 103 (2), 147–62.

Segal, Z. V. & Ingram, R. E. (1994). Mood priming and construct activation in tests of cognitive vulnerability to unipolar depression. *Clinical Psychology Review*, 14 (7), 663–95.

Stroop, J. R. (1935). Studies on interference in serial verbal reactions. *Journal of Experimental Psychology*, 18, 643–62.

Taylor, S. E. (1989). *Positive illusions: Creative Self-deception and the Healthy Mind*. United States: Basic Books.

Taylor, S. E. & Armor, D. A. (1996). Positive illusions and coping with adversity. *Journal of Personality*, 64 (4), 874–98.

Taylor, S. E. & Aspinwall, L. G. (1996). Mediating and moderating processes in psychosocial stress: appraisal, coping, resistance, and vulnerability. In H. B. Kaplan (Ed.), *Psychosocial Stress*. Academic Press, Inc.

Taylor, S. E. & Brown, J. D. (1988). Illusion and well-being: a social psychological perspective on mental health. *Psychological Bulletin*, 103 (2), 193–210.

Taylor, S. E. & Brown, J. D. (1994). Positive illusions and well-being revisited: separating fact from fiction. *Psychological Bulletin*, 116 (1), 21–7.

Taylor, S. E. & Gollwitzer, P. M. (1995). Effects of mindset on positive illusions. *Journal of Personality and Social Psychology*, 69 (2), 213–26.

Taylor, S. E., Kemeny, M. E., Aspinwall, L. G., Schneider, S. G., Rodriguez, R. & Herbert, M. (1992). Optimism, coping, psychological distress, and high-risk sexual behavior among men at risk for Acquired Immunodeficiency Syndrome (AIDS). *Journal of Personality and Social Psychology*, 63 (3), 460–73.

Taylor, S. E., Lichtman, R. R. & Wood, J. V. (1984). Attributions, beliefs about control, and adjustment to breast cancer. *Journal of Personality and Social Psychology*, 46 (3), 489–502.

Taylor, S. E., Wayment, H. A. & Collins, M. A. (1993). Positive illusions and affect regulation. In D. M. Wegner & J. W. Pennebaker (Eds), *Handbook of Mental Control. Century psychology series*. Englewood Cliffs, NJ: Prentice Hall.

Teasdale, J. D. (1988). Cognitive vulnerability to persistent depression. *Cognition and Emotion*, 2, 247–74.

Teasdale, J. D. & Dent, J. (1987). Cognitive vulnerability to depression: an investigation of two hypotheses. *British Journal of Clinical Psychology*, 26, 113–26.
Teasdale, J. D. & Fogarty, S. J. (1979). Differential effects of induced mood on retrieval of pleasant and unpleasant events from episodic memory. *Journal of Abnormal Psychology*, 88, 248–57.
Telch, M. J., Brouillard, M., Telch, C. F., Agras, W. S. & Taylor, C. B. (1989). Role of cognitive appraisal in panic-related avoidance. *Behavior Research and Therapy*, 27, 373–83.
Telch, M. J., Ilai, D., Valentiner, D. & Craske, M. G. (1994). Match–mismatch of fear, panic and performance. *Behavior Therapy and Research*, 32 (7), 691–700.
Thompson, S. C., Sobolew-Shubin, A., Galbraith, M. E., Schwankovsky, L. & Cruzen, D. (1993). Maintaining perceptions of control: finding perceived control in low-control circumstances. *Journal of Personality and Social Psychology*, 64, 293–304.
Tomarken, A. J., Mineka, S. & Cook, M. (1989). Fear-relevant selective associations and covariation bias. *Journal of Abnormal Psychology*, 98 (4), 381–94.
Tomarken, A. J., Sutton, S. K. & Mineka, S. (1995). Fear-relevant illusory correlations: what types of associations promote judgmental bias? *Journal of Abnormal Psychology*, 104 (2), 312–26.
Treisman, A. & Geffen, G. (1967). Selective attention: perception or response? *The Quarterly Journal of Experimental Psychology*, XIX (part1), 1–17.
Vitousek, K. B. & Ewald, L. S. (1992). Self-representation in eating disorders: a cognitive perspective. In A. Segal & S. Blatt (Eds), *Self-representation in Emotional Disorders: Cognitive and Psychodynamic Perspectives*. New York: Guilford.
Vitousek, K. B. & Hollon, S. D. (1990). The investigation of schematic content and processing in eating disorders. *Cognitive Therapy and Research*, 14 (2), 191–214.
Vitousek, K. B. & Orimoto, L. (1993). Cognitive-behavioral models of anorexia nervosa, bulimia nervosa, and obesity. In K. S. Dobson & P. C. Kendall (Eds), *Psychopathology and Cognition*. New York: Academic Press Inc.
Widom, C. S. (1997). Accuracy of adult recollections of early childhood abuse. In J. D. Read & D. S. Lindsay (Eds), *Recollections of Trauma* (pp. 49–78). New York: Plenum.
Williams, J. M. G., Mathews, A. & MacLeod, C. (1996). The emotional Stroop task and psychopathology. *Psychological Bulletin*, 120, 3–24.
Williams, J. M. G., Watts, F. N., MacLeod, C. & Mathews, A. (1997). *Cognitive Psychology and Emotional Disorders* (2nd edn). New York: John Wiley.
Williams, L. M. (1994). Recall of childhood trauma: a prospective study of women's memories of child sexual abuse. *Journal of Consulting and Clinical Psychology*, 62 (6), 1167–76.
Williams, S. L. & Watson, N. (1985). Perceived danger and perceived self-efficacy as cognitive determinants of acrophobic behavior. *Behavior Therapy*, 16, 136–46.

Chapter 25

The Natural Environment: Dealing with the Threat of Detrimental Change

Raymond S. Nickerson
Tufts University

ASPECTS OF ENVIRONMENTAL CHANGE

The problem of detrimental environmental change has received much attention from scientists and policy makers, and from the media. Scientific periodicals, as well as news magazines and daily newspapers, have provided a constant stream of warnings of environmental changes the long-term consequences of which could be unpleasant, if not disastrous. The problem has many aspects – global warming, acidic precipitation, stratospheric ozone loss, air pollution and urban smog, water contamination and depletion, deforestation, desertification, wetland loss, decreasing biodiversity, excessive waste production – the list goes on.

The various aspects of the problem are not distributed uniformly around the globe. Clean water is abundant in some areas and scarce in others; air pollution is especially severe in parts of eastern Europe; acid rain is problematic in the northeastern United States, eastern Canada, and in parts of Europe; stratospheric ozone loss has been most noticeable over Antarctica; waste production and disposal are most problematic in the most highly industrialized and affluent societies. But all aspects of the problem have worldwide implications, especially in view of the growing interdependencies among national economies and the effective shrinkage of the globe that has been caused by modern means of travel and communication. Moreover, the areas that are directly affected by specific

Handbook of Applied Cognition, Edited by F. T. Durso, R. S. Nickerson, R. W. Schvaneveldt, S. T. Dumais, D. S. Lindsay and M. T. H. Chi.

difficulties are likely to grow in number and extent if their precipitating causes are not checked.

Inasmuch as many types of environmental change are caused by human behavior, which is shaped in large part by attitudes and beliefs, cognitive psychology should have an important role to play in addressing the problem. Psychological research has been done on some aspects of it, but there are many unrealized opportunities for additional research in this area. In this chapter I note a variety of ways in which human behavior contributes to environmental change, review some of the psychological studies that have been addressed to one or another aspect of the problem, and consider what appear to be some of the opportunities for further work on it.

HUMAN BEHAVIOR AS AN AGENT OF ENVIRONMENTAL CHANGE

Human behavior affects the environment in many ways. I will mention some of them briefly here, but fuller accounts are readily accessible (e.g. Gardner & Stern, 1996; Geller, Winett & Everett, 1982; Stern, 1992a). Some of what follows has been discussed also in Nickerson (1992) and in Nickerson & Moray (1995).

Energy Use

An increase in world population by a factor of about 3.5 combined with a per capita increase in energy consumption by a factor of about 4 has meant nearly a factor-of-15 increase in worldwide energy consumption since the beginning of the twentieth century (Gibbons, Blair & Gwin, 1989). Both world population and per capita energy use are expected to continue to grow rapidly for the foreseeable future.

The percentage of the world's total energy expenditure that comes from the burning of oil, coal, and natural gas is high, probably well over 75 (Davis, 1990; Gibbons, Blair & Gwin, 1989). This is a major source of problems associated with the emission of greenhouse gases and air pollutants into the atmosphere (National Research Council, 1981), and with the dispersal of toxic metals (Bertine & Goldberg, 1971).

The problem of vehicle emissions illustrates the roles both of technology and human behavior as causal agents in effecting change. Because of emission control regulations, late model vehicles emit less, on average, than older models; however, measurements of on-road vehicle emissions suggest that differences due to states of vehicle maintenance can be greater than differences attributable to vehicle age (Beaton, Bishop, Shang, Ashbaugh, Lawson & Stedman, 1995).

Land Use

Shrinkage of the world's forests, which has been occurring at an alarming rate especially in the tropics (Myers, 1989; Terborgh, 1992) has been attributed to a variety of activities, notably appropriation of forest land for agriculture and cattle ranching or for industrial, commercial or residential development (Myers, 1995) and the harvesting of timber in ways that make the land less conducive to forest growth or that delay reforestation (Repetto, 1990).

Wetlands, like forests, are disappearing, especially in industrialized countries. In the United States, wetlands are being lost to farms, shopping centers, highway corridors, airport runways, marinas, industrial parks, and housing tracks at a rate of 300,000 to 500,000 acres a year (Steinhart, 1990). Wallace (1985) has estimated that over half of the wetlands of the contiguous 48 states had already been "reclaimed" for such purposes by 1985.

Many practices in agriculture and in the harvesting of forest products are considered nonsustainable. Effects of nonsustainable agricultural practices include soil erosion, ground water contamination from pesticide and fertilizer runoff, and destruction of wildlife habitat (Holmes, 1993). Overharvesting of natural products – harvesting products in amounts that exceed their replenishment rates – has had severe environmental impact in certain parts of the world (Repetto & Gillis, 1988; Vincent, 1992).

Irrigation and Other Fresh Water Uses

The amount of irrigated land worldwide tripled between 1950 and 1985 (Postel, 1985). While essential for agriculture in many places, irrigation, when not properly controlled, can not only deplete aquifers from which water is drawn, but can degrade the quality of soil for future use (la Riviere, 1989). Irrigation-caused salinization of once-arable lands has been credited with the demise of several ancient civilizations (Pillsbury, 1981).

Industrial and household uses of water in some areas of the United States are sufficiently high relative to the aquifer reserves to cause problems, especially during dry seasons, and the shortage of potable water is chronic in some parts of the developing world (Myers, 1997).

CFC Production and Use

An ozone "hole" has been detected over Antarctica almost every spring since the 1970s (Stolarski, 1988), but the thinning of stratospheric ozone may not be restricted to this region (Stolarski, Bojkov, Bishop, Zerefos, Staehelin & Zawodny, 1992). A 20-kilometer thick (but extremely diffuse) blanket of ozone shields the earth from ultraviolet radiation. The decrease in ozone concentration is widely believed to be due in part to an increase of chlorofluorocarbons (CFCs) in the atmosphere (Molina & Rowland, 1974).

CFCs have been used for several decades as refrigerants, aerosol propellants, foam-blowing agents, and solvents. There appears to be general agreement among governments that CFC emissions must be reduced, and there is some evidence that concerted efforts to ensure their reduction are having an effect (French, 1994).

Consumption

According to one estimate, more nonfuel mineral resources have been consumed worldwide during the latter half of the twentieth century than during all preceding human history (Wellmer & Kursten, 1992). Durning (1992) claims that "since 1940, Americans alone have used up as large a share of the earth's mineral resources as did everyone before them combined" (p. 38). This upward trend in consumption clearly cannot continue indefinitely, although projected population growth and industrialization of developing countries provide a basis for the expectation that it will continue for the foreseeable future.

Some observers see the problem as less that of general overconsumption than as that of consumption unguided by environmental concerns (Vincent & Panayotou, 1997). Myers (1997) makes a distinction between using resources and using them up, and argues that what poses a threat to the environment is use of resources that are not easily recycled as though they were inexhaustible.

Waste Production

Waste is unavoidable, but the amount generated depends on many factors, some of which are not beyond control. That members of relatively affluent societies generate more waste than is either necessary or desirable is not debatable. Unnecessary waste is problematic in two ways: it squanders limited resources, and it creates problems of disposal.

Hazardous (toxic, radioactive) waste poses special difficulties, but even disposal of "run-of-mill" household trash is also difficult in view of the limited land available in some areas for this use – as in some urban centers that can get rid of trash only by exporting it – and the problems associated with incineration. Reduction of waste production is one preferred method of waste management, and recycling is another. The potential for improvement in waste management is considered by some to be great (Daniels, 1992).

Inadequate Recycling

Most people, when asked, express support for the idea of recycling (DeYoung, 1989), but the correspondence between approval in principle and participation in practice appears to be somewhat less than complete (Hopper & Nielsen, 1991). Early studies indicated that efforts to get people voluntarily to recycle paper (Couch, Garber & Karpus, 1978–79; Geller, Chaffee & Ingram, 1975) or plastics (Powell, 1990) were less than spectacularly successful.

Within some industries, recycling has increased fairly regularly over several decades; however, Ross & Steinmeyer (1990) estimate that only about 20% of the paper, plastic, glass and metal goods that are made in the United States are made from recycled materials, whereas roughly 50% could be, and with less energy than required to make the same goods from new raw materials. More and more communities are sponsoring recycling programs involving either curbside pickup or collection sites, and there are encouraging reports of high levels of consumer resident participation in these programs (Knickerbocker, 1995), but the number of communities yet participating is a minority of the total in the nation.

Population Growth

The natural environment is affected adversely by human behavior in numerous ways, only a few of which have been mentioned here. Many of the problems have become noteworthy only because of the size that the world's population has attained. Many behaviors that are problematic when practiced by a population the size of the current one, would not be so with a population of much more limited size.

The rate of increase in population growth has been declining in recent years and stood at about 1.4% per year as of 1995. At this level the population would double again, reaching over 10 billion, before the middle of the twenty-first century. The downward trend in growth rate could continue to the point of effecting no growth or even population decline, but the prevailing assumption among demographers appears to be that although the rate of increase will continue to decline, it will remain positive for the foreseeable future. The 1997 *Statistical Abstract of the United States* (US Bureau of the Census, 1997, Table 1331) shows the expected growth rate decreasing steadily from the 1995 level to 0.61% in 2040. This yields an expected world population of about 9.3 billion in 2050, an increase of about 64% over the population in 1995. This picture of population trends is rather less alarming than some of the more dire predictions that have been made, but given the evidence that a population of the present size is able to have a considerable detrimental impact on the environment, one can hardly be sanguine about what further increases will mean.

RESEARCH ON BEHAVIOR AND THE NATURAL ENVIRONMENT

The following review of psychological research on behavior and the natural environment is necessarily selective. It focuses on research that has been motivated specifically by a desire to understand how behavior affects the natural environment or how behavior might be made more environmentally beneficial or benign. There has been much psychological research that is relevant to environmental issues but not motivated by environmental concerns; some of this work is mentioned here, but no effort is made to cover it systematically. There also have been numerous studies within the general domain of environmental psychology addressing questions of the effects of the built environment (workspaces, living spaces, hospital rooms) on human behavior and well-being; that work also is outside the scope of this review. In many instances it would be possible to cite references in addition to those cited in connection with specific points. I have limited the number of citations in most such cases, because of space considerations.

Attitude Assessment

Attitude assessment and the relationship between attitudes and behavior have been the focus of a great deal of research (Eagly & Chaiken, 1993; Petty & Rosnick, 1995). Several questionnaire instruments have been developed for assessing attitudes toward environmental issues (e.g. Fridgen, 1994; McKechnie, 1974; Weigel & Weigel, 1978). Here I will mention some of the methodological problems involved in the assessment of environmental attitudes and then review some of the research results that have been obtained.

Methodological Difficulties

All attitude surveys are subject to effects of question wording; stated preferences among essentially the same alternatives vary with how alternatives are expressed (Dawes, 1988; Kahneman & Tversky, 1984). In the environmental context, different results may be obtained depending on whether questions are couched in terms of potential losses or potential gains (Tversky & Kahneman, 1981) and on whether respondents are required to reveal preferences among alternatives by choosing some or by rejecting some (Shafir, 1993). Interpretation of expressed-attitude data is complicated also by the difficulty, if not impossibility, of telling whether an answer to a survey query reflects a genuine attitude or only what the respondent believes to be socially correct (Milstein, 1977).

How people respond to specific aspects of an environment depends in part on what they have come to consider normal. People accustomed to living in smog are less sensitive to this form of pollution than are those who are not accustomed to it (Evans, Jacobs & Frazer, 1982). Recent migrants from rural areas are likely to judge a city to be noisier than are recent migrants from urban areas (Wohlwill & Kohn, 1973). Affective responses to specific scenes can be influenced by the immediate context in which those scenes are viewed; for example, in keeping with adaptation-level theory (Helson, 1964), how attractive a particular forest scene is considered is likely to depend on the relative attractiveness of other scenes that are judged in the same session (Brown & Daniel, 1987). How a place is perceived affectively can be influenced by the perceiver's expectations (Baum & Greenberg, 1975) or prior mood (Sherrod, Armstrong, Hewitt, Madonia, Speno & Teruya, 1977).

Environmental Attitudes

Despite the methodological difficulties, attitude studies have yielded results that bear on the question of how behavior might be made more environmentally friendly. An encouraging finding from polling is that a majority of Americans are concerned about the environment (Gutfeld, 1991). Polls in many other countries also have revealed high levels of environmental concern (Dunlap, Gallup & Gallup, 1993).

Attitudes that people have toward animals, especially wild animals, have been of interest to researchers for some time (Kellert, 1983; King, 1947). This work is germane to the psychology of environmental change insofar as change has implications for species' habitat. Attitudes toward animals appear to be affected by several variables, including value of the species in terms of aesthetics, cultural and historical importance, and economics; degree of socioeconomic impact involved in protecting the species; and phylogenetic relation (similarity) of the species to human beings (Kellert, 1983). Other lists of attributes that might be used in species valuation have been proposed (e.g. Adamus & Clough, 1978; Ramsay, 1976).

How people judge the quality of various aspects of the natural environment has also been the focus of some research (Craik & Zube, 1976; Ulrich, 1983). Researchers have attempted to determine the dependence of perceived quality on such variables as the presence of power lines (Jackson, Hudman & England, 1978), optical conditions of the atmosphere (Latimer, Hogo & Daniel, 1981), and intended uses of surveyed scenes (Peterson, 1974).

Many of the judgments that have been obtained have been of photographs rather than actual scenes. Although there appears to be a consensus among investigators that this approach produces valid results (Bosselmann & Craik, 1989) and studies using both photographs and actual scenes have evoked similar reactions (Shafer & Richards, 1974; Zube, Pitt & Anderson, 1975), the question is still a topic of debate (Hull & Stewart, 1992). Various types of simulation – photographs, scale models, computer-based video presentations – have been used widely in environmental studies and the problem of ensuring the generalizability of the results obtained to the corresponding real environments has received some attention (Weinstein, 1976).

Work on environmental quality perception has yielded a surprising degree of consistency, even among judgments obtained from different interest groups and with the use of different methods, as to what constitutes scenic beauty or landscape quality (Daniel, Anderson, Schroeder & Wheeler, 1977; Ward & Russell, 1981).

The importance of trees and plants for the maintenance of a life-supporting atmosphere, through their production of oxygen and absorption of carbon dioxide, is widely recognized; their importance from a psychological point of view has received some attention (Alexander, Ishikawa & Silverstein, 1977; Thayer & Atwood, 1978). Trees and other forms of vegetation tend to be valued elements of out-of-window views of people who can see them (Herzog, Kaplan & Kaplan, 1982; Kaplan, 1983).

Ease of access to nature is a major determinant of how satisfied many people are with their residences (Fried, 1982; Ulrich & Addoms, 1981). Despite the fact that under certain conditions, especially those that lead to disuse (Whyte, 1980), parks and wooded areas in urban settings have been scenes of violence, "nearby nature" appears to be valued by urban residents for a variety of reasons, aesthetic appreciation and recreation among them (Kaplan, 1985; Talbot, Bardwell & Kaplan, 1987).

Behavior Change

A major reason for interest in the assessment of attitudes regarding the environment is the belief that attitudes help shape behavior and that changing attitudes is one means of effecting behavior change. It needs to be acknowledged that the relationship between attitudinal variables and behavior is complex and still not completely understood (Chaiken & Stangor, 1987; Tesser & Shaffer, 1990), and that expressed attitudes about environmental issues are not invariably accurate indicators of how people will act relative to those issues (Bickman, 1972; Seligman, Kriss, Darley, Fazio, Becker & Pryor, 1979). On the other hand, attitudes generally are predictive of behavior to some degree (Fazio, 1986; Schuman & Johnson, 1976), and the relationship is strong enough to justify the assumption that changing attitudes is one, among other reasonable ways to attempt to modify behavior that has implications for the environment.

The position can also be taken that it is sometimes more cost effective to try to change behavior directly than to do so via a change in attitudes. That changes in attitude sometimes follow changes in behavior that have been induced by persuasion or coercion (Tesser & Shaffer, 1990) prompts consideration of the possibility of motivating environmentally beneficial behavior not only by encouraging the adoption of environmentally favorable attitudes, but by means of inducements, incentives, or pressures as well.

Fortunately, the question of whether to attempt to change attitudes or to attempt to change behavior directly does not require an either–or answer; the targeting of both attitudes and behavior would seem to be the best strategy in general. It may be that attitudes and behavior must be consistent if the desired behavior is to be sustained. Short-term behavior changes may be effected by experimental interventions of various sorts, but the persistence of those changes much beyond the durations of the interventions seems unlikely in the absence of attitudes that support them (Dwyer, Leeming, Cobern, Porter & Jackson, 1993).

Increasing Energy-conserving Behavior

If historical trends continue unabated, the current level of worldwide energy use could quadruple by the middle of the twenty-first century (Starr, Searl & Alpert, 1992). This is worrisome in view of Oppenheimer & Boyle's (1990) contention that if a 3° rise in global temperature is to be avoided, the 80 trillion kilowatt-hours of fossil-fuel energy that the world was using annually as of 1990 will have to be cut in half by 2030.

The only ways to reduce the use of fossil-fuel energy are to develop alternative sources and to find ways to increase energy efficiency. Psychology is not likely to play a leading role in developing new energy sources or more energy-efficient systems, but perhaps it has something to offer to the problem of finding ways to reduce energy use.

Some technologists believe that the technology exists to permit large improvements in the efficiency of energy use and that the challenge is to convince people to avail themselves of the possibilities (Cherfas, 1991). Studies aimed at determining the effectiveness of various methods of encouraging energy conservation have focused on education, persuasion, inducements and incentives, and feedback regarding the effectiveness of conservation efforts.

Education

Simply providing people with information about ways in which household or automotive energy use can be reduced appears to have had limited success in evoking energy-conserving behavior (Dennis, Soderstrom, Koncinski & Cavanaugh, 1990). On the other hand, the evidence indicates that many consumers do not have a very precise understanding of the relative effectiveness of different forms of energy conservation (Kempton, Harris, Keith & Weihl, 1985; Milstein, 1977); they may lack accurate knowledge of how the energy used by one appliance (a fan) compares with that used by another (an air conditioner), or how the electricity used by specific appliances compares with that used for purposes of lighting (Costanzo, Archer, Aronson & Pettigrew, 1986; Kempton & Montgomery, 1982). It may be that the failure of educational approaches to have the desired behavioral effects is that the approaches have not effectively provided the intended education. One educational technique that has shown promise is that of using televised demonstrations of what constitutes effective energy-conserving behavior (Winett, Leckliter, Chinn & Stahl, 1984; Winett, Leckliter, Chinn, Stahl & Love, 1985). A challenge to research is to find other ways to ensure a well-informed public regarding the environmental implications of various types of behavior.

Persuasion

Efforts to persuade people through media campaigns to conserve energy have also had limited success (Dwyer et al., 1993). Studies have shown, however, that the effectiveness of persuasion may depend on several other variables. The persuasiveness of a message depends in part on the reliability, credibility, or expertise of its source, as perceived by the message's recipients (Hass, 1981; McGuire, 1969). A message that comes from a source that is believed to have a vested interest in effecting a specific change in the recipients' behavior is likely to be given less credence than one that comes from a more "disinterested" source (Miller & Ford, 1985).

Steps that make it easy for consumers to participate in energy-conserving projects – providing them with energy-conserving devices free of charge – or that make it difficult for them to forget to do what they are supposed to do – posting of conspicuous signs to encourage desired actions – have been effective in some instances (Delprata, 1977; Hutton, 1982; Zolik, Jason, Nair & Peterson, 1982–83). Multiple requests to turn off unused classroom lights proved to be more effective than a single such request (Luyben, 1982–83). Daily reminders in the form of thank-you notes from cleaning staff appeared to be effective in sustaining the lowering of venetian blinds at night (to inhibit the radiative cooling of classrooms), in compliance with a request from college administration (Luyben, 1984).

Inducements and Incentives

The use of inducements and incentives has sometimes led to decreased energy consumption at least over short periods (Slavin, Wodarski & Blackburn, 1981;

Stern, Aronson, Darley, Hill, Hirst, Kempton & Wilbanks, 1986), although sometimes other variables, such as feedback, have also been involved, making the effects of the incentives difficult to isolate. In some cases, the cost of incentives has exceeded the immediate monetary value of the energy saved (Hake & Foxx, 1978; McClelland & Canter, 1981); however, to the extent that unnecessary energy use is drawing down a resource that is at risk of being depleted, or contributing to environmental pollution, the long-term value of conservation may be greater than it is typically considered to be.

The use of disincentives to decrease energy consumption has been explored less than the use of incentives for the same purpose. Evidence that disincentives can work in certain contexts comes from a study by Van Houten, Nau and Merrigan (1981), who showed that elevator use could be reduced considerably by the simple measure of increasing the door-closing delay from 10 to 26 seconds.

Feedback

Several studies have attempted to determine the effectiveness of providing feedback regarding actual energy use at considerably shorter intervals than those of typical billing cycles. Substantial decreases in consumption have been observed in some instances (Hutton, Mauser, Filiatrault & Ahtola, 1986; Seligman & Darley, 1977; Winett, Neale & Grier, 1979), but not in others (Katzev, Cooper & Fisher, 1980–81; Midden, Meter, Weening & Zieverink, 1983).

In one study, homes were equipped with a device for signalling whenever the household's use of electricity exceeded 90% of its peak level, and a metered display of electricity cost. Continuous feedback did not lead to less use of electricity, but it did result in a shifting of a greater percentage of the total usage to off-peak hours, when costs were less (Sexton, Johnson & Konakayama, 1987). In another study, even monthly feedback, in the form of a letter comparing that month's usage with the amount used during the same month in past years, was enough to effect modest decreases in consumption (Hayes & Cone, 1981). A possibility worth exploring is that of providing consumers with fine-grained feedback on a short-term or continuing basis regarding the implications of moment-to-moment behavior – say with resettable meters on electrical appliances showing the cumulative cost of their operation.

In the aggregate, the results of studies of energy use have shown that modification in the interest of conservation is possible, but their generality is limited by several considerations – the use (often) of volunteers as study participants, relatively small effects, and uncertainty about the permanence of observed behavior changes. The use of volunteer participants in many studies of attitudes and behavior relating to environmental change is problematic in general, because people who volunteer for such studies may differ in important ways from those who do not (Nitzel & Winett, 1977). The fact that many studies rely on questionnaire data is also a problem, because there is little assurance that people's behavior corresponds exactly to their reports of same (Geller, 1981; Luyben, 1982).

There are many opportunities for research on behavior as it relates to energy use and conservation. If such research is to be effective in helping to bring about practically significant savings, there is a need to be sensitive to large differences in impact that different types of changes in behavior would have. Stern & Gardner (1981) argue that, for the most part, research on energy conservation has focused on actions with limited potential for environmental benefit, and that actions with much greater potential have been ignored. They contend that the magnitude of the effect that could be obtained by focusing on personal transportation and home heating swamps the potential effects of all other possible changes in household energy uses combined. Although any increases in efficiency that result from changes in behavior are positive from an environmental point of view, there is an obvious social benefit to focusing research on how to effect the more consequential changes.

Increasing Transportation Efficiency

In the United States, about one-fourth of all energy used is for transportation (Transportation Research Board, 1988), and over half of that is used to fuel private automobiles (Andrle & Dueker, 1974). Worldwide, the population of cars is increasing faster than the population of people; one prediction has the total number quadrupling between the late 1980s and 2025 (Keyfitz, 1989).

So, an obvious reason for interest in increasing transportation efficiency is the impact this could have on energy conservation. There are other compelling reasons for focusing on transportation as well: automotive emissions contribute to air pollution and the accumulation of greenhouse gases in the atmosphere, traffic congestion is a serious problem in many urban areas, and highway accidents remain the single greatest cause of accidental death in industrialized countries.

Car pooling or ride sharing, especially for commuting to and from work, has been promoted for some time as an effective means of responding to several of these problems. Despite considerable effort by companies and municipalities to encourage the practice, it has not been adopted as widely as had been hoped. What little evidence there is on the question of why people do or do not participate in car pooling programs suggests that such decisions are not made strictly on the basis of the economics involved (Margolin & Misch, 1978); social factors appear to be major determinants of these decisions (Reichel & Geller, 1981). A major challenge is that of finding ways of making public transportation, which accounts for a very small percentage of personal trips in the United States (Klinger & Kuzmyak, 1986), a more attractive alternative to the use of personal cars, especially for travel in urban areas.

Increasing Recycling and Reducing Waste

Recycling is used here as a relatively broad term to include reusing products for their intended purposes (as with returnable bottles, or reused building materials), finding uses for products other than their intended ones, using discarded or waste materials (paper, metals, glass) to manufacture more of the same materials, and converting discarded or waste materials to other types of materials (which is sometimes referred to as "reclamation" or "conversion").

People may fail to participate voluntarily in recycling programs because of lack of knowledge, indifference, or the perceived inconvenience of participation (Howenstine, 1993). Providing information regarding the purpose and details of recycling programs has been moderately effective in some cases (Hopper & Nielsen, 1991; Jacobs, Bailey & Crews, 1984) as has the use of prompting and reminders to recycle (Jacobs & Bailey, 1982–83; Luyben & Cummings, 1981–82). In the aggregate, studies show that providing information, as well as prompting and reminding, can have at least small effects, but they also make it clear that the situation is somewhat more complicated than this simple statement makes it appear, inasmuch as the targeted effects are not always obtained (Jacobs, Bailey & Crews, 1984; Pardini & Katzev, 1983–84).

Participation has sometimes been increased, at least temporarily, through the use of explicit goals or incentives (Couch, Garber & Karpus, 1978–79; Jacobs & Bailey, 1982–83). Logistic factors, such as the design and placement of receptacles for deposit of recyclables can have an effect on recycling behavior (Jacobs, Bailey & Crews, 1984; Reid, Luyben, Rawers & Bailey, 1976). Simplifying participation by providing clear instructions to recyclers and locating collection receptacles in many convenient places produced a very high rate of recovered paper waste in one study (Humphrey, Bord, Hammond & Mann, 1977).

The results of many of these studies, like those of the studies of energy use, are somewhat limited in generality inasmuch as they were obtained with students living in college housing facilities, the behavioral changes tended to be small and of limited duration, and other investigations of the same variables sometimes found no effects. Stern & Oskamp (1987) have estimated that behavioral techniques have typically motivated only about 10% to 15% of the people who are eligible to participate in the recycling programs to do so. On the other hand, the determinants of success in community-sponsored pickup programs appear to be increasingly well-understood, and include such user-convenient characteristics as having recyclables picked up the same day as the conventional trash, containers provided by the town, and little sorting required by residents (paper of all types versus all other categories of recyclables) (Gardner & Stern, 1996).

Importance of Commitment

The importance of an overt commitment as a determinant of future participation in an environmental program, such as energy conservation or recycling, has been documented in many studies (Burn & Oskamp, 1986; Wang & Katzev, 1990). Sometimes a modest commitment has been enough to have a behavioral effect; agreement by participants in one household energy conservation project to have their names appear on a published list was enough to ensure a significant reduction in energy use (Pallak, Cook & Sullivan, 1980). In another case the signing of pledge cards was enough to guarantee participation in a recycling program, at least during the duration of the experiment (Katzev & Pardini, 1987–88).

Acceptance of an explicit goal has also been found to influence subsequent behavior. Accepting a goal of returning a specific number of cans per day ensured participation in an on-campus aluminum-can recycling program (McCaul &

Kopp, 1982); setting a specific goal was effective also in a paper-recycling effort (Hamad, Bettinger, Cooper & Semb, 1980–81).

Although studies on the effects of commitment on environmentally relevant behavior have shown that even modest types of overt expressions of commitment can have measurable behavioral consequences, the conclusions that can be drawn are limited by the relatively low levels of commitment that study participants have been asked to make. Most of the effects that have been reported have been small and evidence that they persist much beyond the durations of the experiments is sparse. There is a need for data regarding the effects that major commitments to environmental causes have on environmentally relevant behavior over the long term, and regarding what personal values tend to find expression in long-term environmental concerns (Neuman, 1986).

Some investigators have emphasized the importance of a sense of moral obligation and the personal satisfaction that can come from doing something that is intended to benefit others as determinants of environmentally protective behavior (DeYoung, 1985–86; DeYoung & Kaplan, 1985–86). Some have argued that certain types of environmentally beneficial behaviors should be viewed as acts of altruism (Black, Stern & Elworth, 1985; Hopper & Nielsen, 1991). People may participate in recycling, for example, despite the fact that there is no immediate benefit to them for doing so and may even incur some cost in time and inconvenience, because of their desire to do something that will benefit society in general in the future.

Intrinsic motivation is generally recognized to be more effective than extrinsic motivation in sustaining any particular behavior over the long run (Deci & Ryan, 1985). And there is evidence to suggest that intrinsically motivated people are more likely than extrinsically motivated people to participate in environmentally beneficial activities in the first place (DeYoung, 1996; Trigg, Perlman, Perry & Janisse, 1976).

Change versus Effective Lasting Change

Perhaps the most discouraging aspect of the considerable work that has been done on the modification of attitudes and behavior for the sake of the environment is the lack of evidence of lasting effects of many of the approaches that have been tried. Most of the positive effects that have been obtained in experimental studies have been small and temporary (DeYoung, 1993; Dwyer, Leeming, Cobern, Porter & Jackson, 1993; Geller, 1987).

Lasting change in environmentally relevant behavior is likely to occur only as an adjunct to substantive changes in social norms and values relating to the environment. People's day-to-day stable behavior, as it relates to environmental preservation, is likely to be greatly influenced by what they perceive to be acceptable within their culture generally, and especially by the opinions and values of those who matter to them personally (Black, Stern & Elworth, 1985; Vining & Ebreo, 1990.) The greater likelihood for people to litter in an already littered area than in a clean one (Krauss, Freedman & Whitcup, 1978; Reiter & Samuel, 1980) serves as a metaphor for this influence.

Notwithstanding its limitations, the work that has been done on attitude and behavior change has demonstrated the possibility of effecting change at least of modest magnitude and duration. And it has produced many leads that need to be followed up with further research. The work also highlights, however, the need to find additional ways to bring psychology to bear on the problem of environmental change. It demonstrates the folly of relying on behavior change alone to solve the problem. Moreover, there is probably a limit to what can be accomplished in this way under the best of circumstances. It is not reasonable to expect, for example, to be able to convince most people to give up large personal benefits that come from specific types of behavior (relying on the private automobile as one's major means of transportation) in order to decrease by a very small amount a widely shared future cost (increased air pollution) (Stern & Kirkpatrick, 1977). The tragedy of the commons (about which more later), in its countless guises, is a powerful incentive to the development of approaches, in addition to behavior modification, to the problem of environmental change.

The Psychology of Risk

Environmental change is a matter of concern because many of the trends and predicted developments pose threats to health and comfort, if not to life. This being so, work that has been done on the assessment and communication of risk, and on human response to risk is relevant to the general topic.

The Assessment, Communication, and Perception of Risk

When the risk is one for which incidence statistics exist, assessment means using the statistics as indications of probabilities of occurrence, perhaps contingent on the presence or absence of specified contributing factors (highway fatalities associated with excessive speed, with drunken driving, etc.). When the risk is one for which appropriate statistics do not exist (the possibility of global warming), assessment is usually based on expert opinion and on calculations based on estimated probabilities of events that would have to occur in concert to effect the event of interest. Risk communication involves conveying information about specific risks to various audiences, especially the general public. Risk perception refers to what people consider, rightly or wrongly, specific risks to be.

The assessment, communication, and perception of risk have received considerable attention from psychological researchers (National Research Council, 1989; Stern & Fineberg, 1996). Gardner & Stern (1996) have reviewed research on how people perceive risks of various types, including those associated with environmental change, and have given several theoretical accounts of why people systematically over or underestimate risks in specific instances.

Perceptions of the relative riskiness of various situations often do not correspond closely to the actual riskiness of those situations, as reflected in incidence statistics (Lichtenstein, Slovic, Fischhoff, Layman & Combs, 1978; Slovic, Fischhoff & Lichtenstein, 1979.) Environmental risks are perceived differently, in many cases, by the general public than by experts (Burton, Kates & White, 1978;

Gould, Gardner, DeLuca, Tiemann, Doob & Stolwijk, 1988). Objective assessment and accurate perception of situations are impeded in some instances, such as nuclear power generation, by the intensity of the emotional reactions of people on all sides of the issue (Levi & Holder, 1986; van der Pligt, Eiser & Spears, 1986).

Inasmuch as policy decisions are often made on the basis of perceived risks, such findings are troublesome. It is important to attempt to ensure that the perception of specific risks by the public, and especially by policy makers, is reasonably accurate. In part for this reason, researchers have shown interest not only in the question of how to assess risks but in that of how to communicate effectively the results of those assessments (Allen, 1987; National Research Council, 1989).

Misestimation of readers' comprehension ability has been a problem in the design of brochures intended to help people make informed decisions about certain environmental risks (Atman, Bostrom, Fischhoff & Morgan, 1994). Risks are conventionally expressed in several different ways, and this may contribute to the difficulty the public has in understanding them. Risk data are more likely to be seen by individuals as personally relevant when framed in terms of personal risk than when presented in the form of population statistics (Jeffery, 1989; Sharlin, 1986).

The problems of risk assessment, communication, and perception are compounded by the fact that the perception of risk can itself be injurious, independent of the environmental reality. Some people who live in the proximity of nuclear power plants or hazardous landfills may experience chronic stress-related symptoms stemming from continuous worry about the perceived threat (Baum & Fleming, 1993). There is some concern that health-promotion programs can, in some instances, have the undesirable effect of causing "epidemics of apprehension" about the specific risks that are targeted by the programs (Thomas, 1983). Baum & Fleming (1993) have urged that attempts to quantify risks should take such effects into account, but they acknowledge that this is very difficult to do.

Human Response to Perceived Risk

Wandersman & Hallman (1993) have summarized the findings regarding how people respond to perceived risks:

> [G]iven two risks of equal magnitude, a risk that is voluntary is more acceptable than an involuntary risk. Similarly, risks under individual control are seen as more acceptable than those under government control. Risks that seem fairly distributed are more acceptable than those that seem unfairly distributed. Natural risks are more acceptable than artificial risks. Familiar risks are more acceptable than exotic risks. Risks that are detectable are more acceptable than risks that are undetectable. Risks that are well understood by science are more acceptable than those that are not. Risks that are associated with other memorable events (like Love Canal or Chernobyl) are seen as more risky. Risks that seem ethically wrong are less acceptable. (p. 683)

In addition to these types of factors, personality variables, character traits, and personal values help determine how individuals respond to perceived risks.

Values and attitudes toward risks are strongly influenced by the social and cultural contexts in which people live (Bradbury, 1989; Vaughn & Nordenstam, 1991); beliefs about fate and luck can also contribute to people's estimates of their personal vulnerabilities to risks (Weinstein, Klotz & Sandman, 1988; Weinstein, Sandman & Roberts, 1991).

Slovic, Fischhoff & Lichtenstein (1981) make the important point that the evaluation of risks requires an appreciation of the probabilistic nature of the world and an ability to think in probabilistic terms. In view of this and the fact that many people have difficulty in dealing with probabilities, research on probabilistic thinking has considerable relevance to environmental issues and the question of how to make behavior more environmentally benign.

Cost–benefit Analyses

Closely associated with the problems of risk assessment, communication, and perception is that of understanding the costs and benefits associated with courses of action that might be taken in the interest of protecting the environment against detrimental change. Without adequate cost–benefit analyses that provide a basis for comparisons between alternative solutions to specific problems, it is very easy to jump to conclusions based on thinking that focuses on the more salient aspects of situations and overlooks less obvious, but critical, facts.

The quantification of costs and benefits relating to environmental change has proved to be difficult. Assigning specific values to such factors as human life and health (MacLean, 1990; Russell, 1990) is a delicate matter. Resistance to the idea of quantifying such things is sufficiently strong in some instances to translate into objection to the use of cost–benefit analyses as a basis for decision making or policy setting at all. This attitude is sometimes reflected in claims that the environment must be protected at any cost. Such extreme positions cannot be translated into feasible policies, however, and when faced with the prospect of actually bearing the costs, people usually back off from them (Melnick, 1990).

Even when the variables involved do not evoke objections to quantification in principle, assigning values can be very difficult How much, for example, are clean air and clean water worth? How does one quantify the benefit of climate stabilization, or the cost of runaway warming? How does one determine what the benefits derived, or derivable, from the world's forests are worth, or the value of a given degree of species biodiversity? How does one attach a number to the avoidance of chronic stress and stress-related disorders that have been observed among people who live with the threat of industrial or agricultural toxins in their neighborhoods? Or to the value of the emotional and affective benefits that people derive from natural environments and the many recreational uses that are made of them.

Some have argued that the problem of developing a satisfactory way to weight the benefits on which environmental preservation programs focus is at least as much a philosophical and ethical issue as an economic one, and that the "good" of economics and the "good" of ethics may not be the same (MacLean, 1990; Morowitz, 1991). The problem is compounded by the fact that what one person sees as a benefit may be viewed with indifference, or even disdain, by another.

Such differences may be based, in part, on different degrees of understanding of the implications of specific types of environmental change; but this consideration aside, it is not reasonable to assume that all people attach the same value to any given property of the environment (Fischhoff, 1991; Pearce & Turner, 1990).

Another complication is the considerably less-than-perfect match between the people who realize the benefits from goods and services and those who pay the costs of their production, use, and eventual disposal. One does not, for example, pay for the cost of the contribution of burning a gallon of gasoline to air pollution or global warming when one buys the gas. This complicates the problem of determining total costs and benefits in particular cases, but it also establishes the importance of doing so. Only a reasonably accurate understanding of what the actual total costs and benefits are can provide a basis for pricing policies that permit rational decisions about whether specific goods and services are worth what they really cost.

Determining costs and benefits, both short- and long-range, of various actions, or inactions, pertaining to the environmental change remains a major challenge to research. A special challenge to psychology is that of finding ways to express such costs and benefits in terms of consequences for quality of life – the satisfaction of basic human needs and preferences.

Social Dilemmas

An important factor contributing to the perpetuation of behavior that is detrimental to the environment is conflict between self-interest and the common good. A closely related factor is the difficulty that people have in seeing their personal behavior as mattering: how can what one out of over 5 billion souls currently on the planet does possibly have any appreciable impact on the future quality of the environment?

The Nature of Social Dilemmas

The clash between self-interest and the common good is captured by Hardin's (1986) metaphor of the "tragedy of the commons," according to which a herdsman can realize a substantial personal benefit at little personal cost by adding an animal to his herd that is grazing on common land. The benefit that comes from having an additional animal is his alone, whereas the cost, in terms of slightly less grazing land per animal is shared by all. But every herdsman sees the situation the same way, and when each works in what appears to be his own best short-term interest, they collectively ruin the land.

The tragedy of the commons illustrates the more general idea of a social trap (Platt, 1973) or social dilemma (Glance & Huberman, 1994; Komorita & Parks, 1996), which includes any situation that, because of short-term benefits, entices individuals or groups to do things that, if done by many, will eventually yield undesirable consequences. A characteristic of social dilemmas, which typically have to do either with the preservation of public resources or the maintenance of public services, is that the positive short-term benefits are typically enjoyed by individual members or subsets of a group, whereas the long-term costs are borne by the group as a whole. Many of the behavioral causes of detrimental environmental change mentioned in the foregoing sections of this chapter can be viewed as examples of ways in which social traps or the commons tragedy can be played out.

Platt (1973) discusses several possible ways to facilitate escape from social traps, including making long-term negative consequences of behavior more salient, offsetting short-term benefits by increasing the behavior's immediate cost, and incentivizing competing behavior that does not have long-term negative consequences. Messick & Brewer (1983) describe several approaches to the resolution of social dilemmas. Other treatments of the problem are given by Ostrom (1990); van Vugt (1997); and Gardner & Stern (1996, chapter 6).

The tragedy of the commons and the idea of social traps illustrate the lure of the possibility of trading distributed costs for individual gain. The other side of this coin is the reluctance that people may show to incur individual costs for the sake of an increase in the public good that has relatively little benefit to the individual who incurs the cost. If everyone were willing to incur the cost, the increase in the public good could be great enough to ensure a favorable cost–benefit ratio for all. Unfortunately, if most people incur the cost, those who do not will benefit as much as those who do, so again, there is a disincentive to act in an environmentally responsible way, when the situation is seen from a narrow egocentric view.

Social Dilemma Research

A considerable amount of research has dealt with social dilemmas directly, usually with computer simulations (Fusco, Bell, Jorgensen & Smith, 1991; Gifford & Wells, 1991) or other laboratory analogs of real-life problems (Brechner & Linder, 1981; Dawes, 1980). Many studies of this sort use variations of prisoner's dilemma situations in which participants have to decide whether to cooperate (for mutual good) or to defect (to gain at the other's expense) (Dawes, 1988; Orbell, Dawes & van de Kragt, 1995). The likelihood of conserving, or cooperating, in the situations of interest is greatly influenced by one's expectations – e.g. trust (Mosler, 1993) – regarding the behavior of others.

An approach to the commons dilemma that has received a lot of attention is that of partitioning the commons into smaller units each of which is used by only a subset of the population (privatization). Olson (1965) emphasized group size as an important variable in early work on social dilemmas. The theory behind privatization is that relatively small groups of users of a shared resource should find it easier to cooperate in the management of the resource and to share responsibility for its preservation. The results of both laboratory studies and real-world experiments have shown that the approach can work (Stern, 1978; Stern & Kirkpatrick, 1977), although it is not feasible in all cases (it is hard to privatize air and water, for example) and it is not without problems even when it is feasible.

Brechner & Linder (1981) have suggested that social-trap analysis could be useful as a tool for training purposes; simulations involving social traps could be used to sensitize people to the long-term consequences of certain types of behavior. Others have also suggested the use of simulations of commons dilemmas and other social traps to educate people to the existence of such situations and to the relative effectiveness of alternative ways of dealing with them (Powers, Duus & Norton, 1979).

As environmental problems increase and their consequences become evermore apparent around the globe, as it seems they are bound to do, the chances of conflicts centered on these problems are also likely to increase. Especially if there are pressures on third-world countries to moderate energy use and to limit activities that the rest of the world views as contributing to global environmental problems, conflicts seem inevitable. There is a need for better techniques both for anticipating conflicts so they can be avoided, and for resolving those that do occur so they do not escalate to crisis proportions. Especially needed are approaches that can restructure zero–sum and win–lose conflicts into non zero–sum and win–win situations, and those that can work despite a reluctance on the part of parties to compromise.

TECHNOLOGY ENHANCEMENT

The argument has been made that limited progress should be expected on the problem of environmental change through attempts to modify consumers' attitudes and behavior, so long as the technology facilitates environmentally detrimental behavior (Crabb, 1992). As long as automobiles are built to consume lots of fuel, people will use lots of fuel in operating them. As long as products are designed to be used for a short time and then discarded, the problem of waste disposal will continue. An approach complementary to that of attempting to change attitudes and behavior is to attempt to modify technology so as to make it more environmentally benign.

Leverage in Technological Changes

Stern (1992b) points out that more energy was saved when automobile manufacturers were forced to meet standards of fuel economy than could have been saved by any conceivable effort to change the behavior of automobile purchasers. He notes too the beneficial effect of forcing appliance manufacturers to provide energy use information on appliance labels, which came less from the influence the labels had on consumers than on the motivation they provided to manufacturers to produce more energy-efficient models. Stern and Gardner (1981; Gardner & Stern, 1996) argue that, in general, the adoption of more energy-efficient technology appears to offer greater opportunities for energy conservation than does decreased use of existing energy systems. Commoner (1991) makes a similar point in arguing that degradative environmental trends have been slowed or reversed primarily as a consequence of technological changes that have prevented the entry of polluting substances into the environment, and seldom as a result of efforts to modify behavior or to clean up pollution after the fact.

Changes in technology and changes in behavior are, of course, not mutually exclusive possibilities. A question of interest is whether psychology has anything to offer toward the objective of making technology more environmentally friendly. I want to argue that it does. Increasing the environmental friendliness of technology, as distinct from making it more useful and usable, has not been an explicit objective of much psychological research to date, but, in my view, there is a need, and opportunities, for psychological research with this objective.

The Environmental Challenge to Cognitive Technologies

In the penultimate section of this chapter, I want to focus on information technology and the potential that its rapid development may hold for helping to address some aspects of detrimental environmental change. This technology is of special interest to cognitive psychology because many of the artifacts that have emerged, or are emerging, from it have cognitive, or cognition-like capabilities. It also provides many new tools that are intended to enhance human performance of cognitive tasks.

The aspect of information technology that I want to emphasize in this context is the potential it appears to have for substituting energy-light and material-light processes for energy-intense and material-heavy processes in satisfying human needs and desires. I do not mean to suggest that greater use of information technology will necessarily result in decreased demand for energy and material resources; it could have precisely the opposite effect. I want only to suggest that the potential for decreasing the demand for energy and materials seems to be there, and that the challenge is to realize it.

If the expectations of many technologists are realized, facilities will exist in the not-distant future for delivering digitally encoded information of any type nearly anywhere and for linking offices, schools, and homes to information resources around the world. People will have immediate access to information on a scale unknown before (Nickerson, 1995). They will be able to browse through the world's libraries or to direct automatic searches for specific information, to visit "virtual" museums and other places of interest, to dial up movies for home viewing on their own schedules, to read interactive newspapers and view "tell-me-more" television. The "books" they read may contain not only conventional text and graphics, but animations, process simulations, voice and other sound, and question-answering capabilities.

There is, in this technology, the potential for satisfying many human needs in ways that are more environmentally benign than are the traditional means of satisfying them. Some needs may be met by the transmission of information equally as well as by the transportation of people or material, and the movement of information over an electronic (or optical) network has little, if any, adverse environmental effect, whereas the transporting of people and material, in contrast, consumes fuel, and contributes to air pollution. I do not mean to suggest that the transmission of information can always be an acceptable substitute for the movement of people and material, but sometimes it can.

Newspapers, of which about 63 million are published and distributed daily in the United States, represent an extraordinarily inefficient utilization of resources for the purpose of conveying information, as compared to technologically feasible alternative means, especially inasmuch as any given newspaper is likely to be read by very few people, and then only in part, and will be obsolete within hours of its production. Similar observations could be made with respect to the publication of magazines, professional journals, and books. To the extent that electronic mail can substitute for conventional paper mail, this too could result in a reduction in the use of material resources and the production of solid waste. Greater use of "virtual offices" connected by computer networks could decrease the need for travel to centralized office buildings.

The fact that information technology has the potential for providing resource-light alternatives to resource-heavy means of meeting many human needs or desires does not guarantee that greater use of this technology will automatically result in a net reduction in the burden we place on the environment. Although there has been much talk of the "paperless office" that computer technology would make possible, there is little evidence that, to date, the use of computers in the workplace has resulted in decreased use of paper. Total paper consumption increased by over 50% in the United States between 1970 and 1988, and the amount of paper used for printing and writing more than doubled (US Bureau of the Census, 1990). It is not clear to what extent information technology has been a causal factor in this development, but it is possible that the growing dependency on this technology has actually increased the demand for paper rather than lessened it.

Apparently, many people prefer to read from a printed page than to read from a computer display terminal. The extent to which this preference is contingent on the quality of existing display terminals and will disappear when better terminals are in place is not known; it may be in part a matter of psychological attachment to a familiar medium that has served so well for so long and a reluctance to transfer to a new one. Perhaps, with the help of imaginative design and experimentation, electronic books could, in time, come to be at least as acceptable as their paper counterparts. Moreover, electronic books have the potential to provide capabilities for their users that paper books cannot offer.

Research is needed to determine why people use one medium for information representation rather than another when more possibilities than one exist. We need to understand, in particular, why people continue to use paper in those instances in which its use would appear to be unnecessary – why, for example, do people print out electronic mail messages or journal articles that are continuously available in electronic form?

The use of information technology to support interperson communication has been a topic of research for some time. Studies have focused on teleconferencing, electronic mail, electronic bulletin boards, and computer-supported work by groups or teams (Nickerson, 1986; Sproull & Kiesler, 1991). Various forms of computer-mediated communication have been compared with other types of communication (face-to-face, telephone, conventional mail) in efforts to identify relative strengths and weaknesses, or advantages and disadvantages. The environmental implications of greater utilization of these types of resources remain to be determined, but they appear to be great.

There is much interest among computer scientists and others in the emerging technology that deals with what are sometimes referred to as artificial or "virtual" realities (Durlach & Mavor, 1995; Hamilton, 1992; Pool, 1992). A virtual reality is a simulated object, situation or other aspect of the physical world with which one can interact much as one would with the real thing, except without the inconvenience or perhaps danger that would be involved in doing so (Foley, 1987). It is too early to tell whether the development of this technology will match the expectations of its more enthusiastic supporters, but if it comes at all close to doing so it should offer many opportunities to substitute energy-light and material-light resources for energy-heavy and material-heavy ones.

Among the problems that must be solved in order to make virtual-reality technology a practical reality are many of a psychological nature. An abiding question is: "How real is real enough?" Problems arise from the conflicting sensory cues that observers of virtual realities sometimes receive. What effects short- or long-term exposure to virtual worlds will have on human perception, cognition, and motor control is still another question requiring research. Beyond such specific problems, there is the general challenge of finding ways to apply this technology effectively to the problem of environmental change, among other desirable ends.

CONCLUDING COMMENTS

Detrimental environmental change is a matter of substantial and growing concern among scientists and lay people alike. Inasmuch as human behavior has become a major agent of environmental change, there are good reasons for research aimed at finding ways to make behavior more environmentally benign or to lessen the severity of its effects.

A substantial part of the difficulty of effecting substantive changes in behavior that has environmental implications is the fact that most of the environmental consequences of behavior are greatly delayed as compared to the goals and objectives toward which people typically work. Many of the most important types of improvement in the environment that can be expected to result from modifications of behavior are likely to be realized only after several years, or, in some cases, decades; similarly, the most serious consequences of environmentally detrimental behavior also tend to be threats to the long-term future rather than to the here and now.

How can people be convinced of the importance of what they perceive to be inconsequential behavior? Are there psychological approaches that could be effective in averting the tragedy of the commons in the countless contexts in which it occurs? A more complete understanding of behavior that leads to commons tragedies and social traps, and of how it can be modified effectively, remain significant challenges to psychology, and especially to psychologists with an interest in the implications of behavior for environmental change.

The need for a better understanding by the general public of the relationship between human behavior and environmental change is one that cognitive psychology should be able to help address. In the context of a discussion of attempts to increase energy-conserving behavior, the point was made that simply providing people with information about ways in which energy use can be reduced has not proved to be very effective in producing energy-conserving behavior. It is worth noting, however, that in most of the studies that support this conclusion the environmental information was provided in a compressed form (lecture, discussion, pamphlet) over a very short period of time. We should not conclude from the limited effectiveness of this approach that substantive consistent education about environmental change and the role of human behavior in causing it would be equally ineffective. There is evidence that, at least in the case of efforts to change risky behavior such as smoking, sustained educational programs can have considerable influence (Flay, 1987).

Finding effective ways to educate the public regarding the various aspects of environmental change, the role that human behavior plays in it, and what can be done to improve the situation, must be considered a major continuing challenge. The public is concerned about the quality of the environment in general, but there appears to be widespread confusion regarding many aspects of the problem. Many people are not aware, for example, of what causes air pollution or of the effects that such pollution can have on human health (Kromm, Probald & Wall, 1973). I have noted the general lack of a very precise understanding of the relative effectiveness of various forms of energy conservation (Kempton, Harris, Keith & Weihl, 1985; Milstein, 1977). Reports of ozone loss in one part of the atmosphere and ozone accumulation in another provide the basis for confusion. And so on. These are problems that cognitive psychology should be able to help solve.

Finally, noteworthy among the opportunities for research by cognitive psychologists is the potential that information technology appears to offer for substituting energy-light and material-light processes for energy-intense and material-heavy processes to serve human ends and meet human needs. The extent to which such substitutions can be made remains to be determined, but many of the constraining factors are psychological in nature.

ACKNOWLEDGMENTS

I am grateful to Frank Durso, Gerald Gardner, Kelly Henry, Richard Reardon, and Paul Stern for very helpful comments on a draft of this chapter.

REFERENCES

Adamus, P. R. & Clough, G. C. (1978). Evaluating species for protection in natural areas. *Biological Conservation*, 13, 165–78.

Alexander, C., Ishikawa, S. & Silverstein, M. A. (1977). *Pattern Language*. New York: Oxford University Press.

Allen, F. W. (1987). Towards a holistic appreciation of risk: the challenges for communicators and policy makers. *Science, Technology, and Human Values*, 12, 138–43.

Andrle, S. & Dueker, K. J. (1974). Attitudes toward and evaluation of carpooling

(Technical Report N. 32). Iowa City, IA: Center for Urban Transportation Studies, University of Iowa.

Atman, C. J., Bostrom, A., Fischhoff, B. & Morgan, M. G. (1994). Designing risk communications: completing and correcting mental models of hazardous processes, Part I. *Risk Analysis*, 14, 779–88.

Baum, A. & Fleming, I. (1993). Implications of psychological research on stress and technological accidents. *American Psychologist*, 48, 665–72.

Baum, A. & Greenberg, C. I. (1975). Waiting for a crowd: the behavioral and perceptual effects of anticipating crowding. *Journal of Personality and Social Psychology*, 32, 671–9.

Beaton, S. P., Bishop, G. A., Zhang, Y., Ashbaugh, L. L., Lawson, D. R. & Stedman, D. H. (1995). On-road vehicle emissions: regulations, costs, and benefits. *Science*, 268, 991–2.

Bertine, K. K. & Goldberg, E. D. (1971). Fossil fuel combustion and the major sedimentary cycle. *Science*, 173, 233–5.

Bickman, L. (1972). Environmental attitudes and actions. *Journal of Social Psychology*, 87, 323–4.

Black, J. S., Stern, P. C. & Elworth, J. T. (1985). Personal and contextual influences on household energy adaptations. *Journal of Applied Psychology*, 70, 3–21.

Bosselmann, P. & Craik, H. K. (1989). Perceptual simulations of environments. In R. Bechtal, R. Marans & W. Michelson (Eds), *Methods in Environmental and Behavioral Research* (pp. 162–90). New York: Van Nostrand Reinhold.

Bradbury, J. A. (1989). The policy implications of differing concepts of risk. *Science, Technology, and Human Values*, 14, 380–99.

Brechner, K. C. & Linder, D. E. (1981). A social trap analysis of energy distribution systems. In A. Baum & J. E. Singer (Eds), *Advances in Environmental Psychology, vol. 3: Energy Conservation: Psychological Perspectives* (pp. 27–51). Hillsdale, NJ: Erlbaum.

Brown, T. C. & Daniel, T. C. (1987). Context effects in perceived environmental quality assessment: scene selection and landscape quality ratings. *Journal of Environmental Psychology*, 7, 233–50.

Burn, S. M. & Oskamp, S. (1986). Increasing community recycling with persuasive comunication and public commitment. *Journal of Applied Social Psychology*, 16, 29–41.

Burton, I., Kates, R. W. & White, G. R. (1978). *The Environment as Hazard*. New York: Oxford University Press.

Chaiken, S. & Stangor, C. (1987). Attitudes and attitude change. *Annual Review of Psychology*, 38, 575–630.

Cherfas, J. (1991). Skeptics and visionaries examine energy saving. *Science*, 251, 154–6.

Commoner, B. (1991). The failure of the environmental effort. In A. B. Wolbrast (Ed.), *Environment in Peril* (pp. 38–63). Washington, DC: Smithsonian Institution Press.

Costanzo, M., Archer, D., Aronson, L. & Pettigrew, T. (1986). Energy conservation behavior: the difficult path from information to action. *American Psychologist*, 41, 521–8.

Couch, J. V., Garber, T. & Karpus, L. (1978–79). Response maintenance and paper recycling. *Journal of Environmental Systems*, 8, 127–37.

Crabb, P. B. (1992). Comment: effective control of energy-depleting behavior. *American Psychologist*, 47, 815–16.

Craik, K. H. & Zube, E. H. (Eds) (1976). *Perceiving Environmental Quality*. New York: Plenum.

Daniel, T. C., Anderson, L. M., Schroeder, H. W. & Wheeler, L. W., III. (1977). Mapping the scenic beauty of forest landscapes. *Leisure Sciences*, 1, 35–53.

Daniels, J. E. (Ed.) (1992). *1993 Earth Journal: Environmental Almanac and Resource Directory*. Boulder, CO: Buzzworm Books.

Davis, G. R. (1990). Energy for planet earth. *Scientific American*, 263 (3), 54–62.

Dawes, R. M. (1980). Social dilemmas. *Annual Review of Psychology*, 31, 169–93.

Dawes, R. M. (1988). *Rational Choice in an Uncertain World*. New York: Harcourt Brace Jovanovich.

Deci, E. L. & Ryan, R. M. (1985). *Intrinsic Motivation and Self-determinism in Human Behavior*. New York: Plenum.

Delprata, D. J. (1977). Prompting electrical energy conservation in commercial users. *Environment and Behavior*, 9, 433–40.

Dennis, M. L. & Sonderstrom, E. J. (1988). Application of social psychological and evaluation research: lessons from energy information programs. *Evaluation and Program Planning*, 11, 77–84.

Dennis, M. L., Sonderstrom, E. J., Koncinski, W. S. Jr. & Cavanaugh, B. (1990). Effective dissemination of energy-related information: applying social psychology and evaluation research. *American Psychologist*, 45, 1109–17.

DeYoung, R. (1985–1986). Encouraging environmentally appropriate behavior: the role of intrinsic motivation. *Journal of Environmental Systems*, 15, 281–92.

DeYoung, R. (1989). Exploring the difference between recyclers and non-recyclers: the role of information. *Journal of Environmental Systems*, 18, 341–51.

DeYoung, R. (1993). Changing behavior and making it stick: the conceptualization and management of conservation behavior. *Environment and Behavior*, 25, 485–505.

DeYoung, R. (1996). Some psychological aspects of reduced consumption behavior: the role of intrinsic satisfaction and competence motivation. *Environment and Behavior*, 28, 358–409.

DeYoung, R. & Kaplan, S. (1985–1986). Conservation behavior and the structure of satisfactions. *Journal of Environmental Systems*, 15, 233–42.

Dunlap, R. E., Gallup, G. H. Jr. & Gallup, A. M. (1993). Of global concern: results of the Health of the Planet Survey. *Environment*, 39, 6–15, 33–9.

Durlach, N. I. & Mavor, A. S. (1995). *Virtual Reality: Scientific and Technological Challenges*. Washington, DC: National Academy Press.

Dwyer, W. O., Leeming, F. C., Cobern, M. K., Porter, B. E. & Jackson, J. M. (1993). Critical review of behavioral interventions to preserve the environment: research since 1980. *Environment and Behavior*, 25, 275–321.

Eagly, A. H. & Chaiken, S. (1993). *The Psychology of Attitudes*. New York: Harcourt Brace Jovanovich.

Evans, G. W., Jacobs, S. V. & Frager, N. B. (1982). Adaptation to air pollution. *Journal of Environmental Psychology*, 2, 99–108.

Fazio, R. H. (1986). How do attitudes guide behavior? In R. M. Sorrentino & E. T. Higgins (Eds), *The Handbook of Motivation and Cognition: Foundations of Social Behavior* (pp. 204–43). New York: Guilford Press.

Fischhoff, B. (1991). Eliciting values: is there anything in there? *American Psychologist*, 46, 835–47.

Flay, B. R. (1987). Mass media and smoking cessation: a critical review. *American Journal of Public Health*, 77, 153–60.

Foley, J. D. (1987). Interfaces for advanced computing. *Scientific American*, 257 (4), 126–35.

French, H. F. (1994). Making environmental treaties work. *Scientific American*, 271 (6), 94–7.

Fridgen, C. C. (1994). Human disposition toward hazards: testing the environmental appraisal inventory. *Journal of Environmental Psychology*, 14, 101–11.

Fried, M. (1982). Residential attachment: sources of residential and community satisfaction. *Journal of Social Issues*, 38, 107–19.

Fusco, M. E., Bell, P. A., Jorgensen, M. D. & Smith, J. M. (1991). Using a computer to study the commons dilemma. *Simulation Games*, 22, 67–74.

Gardner, G. T. & Stern, P. C. (1996). *Environmental Problems and Human Behavior*. Boston, MA: Allyn & Bacon.

Geller, E. S. (1981). Evaluating energy conservation programs: is verbal report enough? *Journal of Consumer Research*, 8, 331–5.

Geller, E. S. (1987). Environmental psychology and applied behavior analysis: from strange bedfellows to a productive marriage. In D. Stokols & I. Altman (Eds), *Handbook of Environmental Psychology* (pp. 361–88). New York: Wiley.

Geller, E. S., Chaffee, J. L. & Ingram, R. (1975). Promoting paper-recycling on a university campus. *Journal of Environmental Systems*, 5, 39–57.
Geller, E. S., Winett, R. R. & Everett, P. B. (1982). *Preserving the Environment: New Strategies for Behavior Change*. Elmsford, NY: Pergamon Press.
Gibbons, J. H., Blair, P. D. & Gwin, H. L. (1989). Strategies for energy use. *Scientific American*, 261 (3), 136–43.
Gifford, R. & Wells, J. (1991). FISH: a commons dilemma simulation. *Behavioral Research Methods, Instrumentation and Computing*, 23, 437–41.
Glance, N. S. & Huberman, B. A. (1994). The dynamics of social dilemmas. *Scientific American*, 279 (3), 76–81.
Gould, L. C., Gardner, G. T., DeLuca, D. R., Tiemann, A. R., Doob, L. W. & Stolwijk, J. A. J. (1988). *Perceptions of Technological Risks and Benefits*. New York: Russell Sage Foundation.
Gutfeld, R. (1991). Eight of 10 Americans are environmentalists, at least so they say. *Wall Street Journal*, 218 (24), A1–A4.
Hake, D. F. & Foxx, R. M. (1978). Promoting gasoline conservation: the effects of reinforcement schedules, a leader and self-recording. *Behavior Modification*, 2, 339–69.
Hamad, C. D., Bettinger, R., Cooper, D. & Semb, G. (1980–81). Using behavioral procedures to establish an elementary school paper recycling program. *Journal of Environmental Systems*, 10, 149–56.
Hamilton, D. P. (1992). Envisioning research with virtual reality. *Science*, 256, 603.
Hardin, G. (1968). The tragedy of the commons. *Science*, 162, 1243–8.
Hass, R. G. (1981). Effects of source characteristics on cognitive responses in persuasion. In R. E. Petty, T. M. Ostrom & T. C. Brock (Eds), *Cognitive Responses in Persuasion* (pp. 141–72). Hillsdale, NJ: Erlbaum.
Hayes, S. C. & Cone, J. D. (1981). Reduction of residential consumption of electricity through simple monthly feedback. *Journal of Applied Analysis of Behavior*, 14, 81–8.
Helson, H. (1964). *Adaptation Level Theory*. New York: Harper & Row.
Herzog, T. R., Kaplan, S. & Kaplan, R. (1982). The prediction of preference for unfamiliar urban places. *Population and Environment*, 5, 43–59.
Holmes, B. (1993). Can sustainable farming win the battle of the bottom line? *Science*, 260, 1893–5.
Hopper, J. R. & Nielsen, J. McC. (1991). Recycling as altruistic behavior: normative and behavioral strategies to expand participation in a community recycling program. *Environment and Behavior*, 23, 195–220.
Howenstine, E. (1993). Market segmentation for recycling. *Environment and Behavior*, 25, 86–102.
Hull, R. B. & Stewart, W. P. (1992). Validity of photo-based scenic beauty judgments. *Journal of Environmental Psychology*, 12, 101–14.
Humphrey, C. R., Bord, R. J., Hammond, M. M. & Mann, S. (1977). Attitudes and conditions for cooperation in a paper recycling program. *Environment and Behavior*, 9, 107–24.
Hutton, R. B. (1982). Advertising and the Department of Energy's campaign for energy conservation. *Journal of Advertising*, 11 (2), 27–39.
Hutton, R. B., Mauser, G. A., Filiatrault, P. & Ahtola, O. T. (1986). Effects of cost-related feedback on consumer knowledge and consumption behavior: a field experimental approach. *Journal of Consumer Research*, 13, 327–36.
Jackson, R. H., Hudman, L. E. & England, J. L. (1978). Assessment of the environmental impact of high voltage power transmission lines. *Journal of Environmental Management*, 6, 153–70.
Jacobs, H. E. & Bailey, J. S. (1982–83). Evaluating participation in a residential recycling program. *Journal of Environmental Systems*, 12, 141–52.
Jacobs, H. E., Bailey, J. S. & Crews, J. I. (1984). Development and analysis of a community-based resource recovery program. *Journal of Applied Behavior Analysis*, 17, 127–45.

Jeffery, R. W. (1989). Risk behaviors and health: contrasting individual and population perspectives. *American Psychologist*, 44, 1194–202.

Kahneman, D. & Tversky, A. (1984). Choices, values and frames. *American Psychologist*, 39, 341–50.

Kaplan, R. (1983). The role of nature in the urban context. In I. Altman & J. F. Wohlwill (Eds), *Behavior and the Natural Environment* (pp. 127–61). New York: Plenum.

Kaplan, R. (1985). Nature at the doorstep: residential satisfaction and the nearby environment. *Journal of Architectural Planning Research*, 2, 115–28.

Katzev, R. D., Cooper, L. & Fisher, P. (1980–81). The effect of feedback and social reinforcement on residential electricity consumption. *Journal of Environmental Systems*, 10, 215–27.

Katzev, R. D. & Pardini, A. U. (1987–88). The comparative effectiveness of reward and commitment approaches in motivating community recycling. *Journal of Environmental Systems*, 17, 93–113.

Kellert, S. R. (1983). Affective, cognitive, and evaluative perceptions of animals. In I. Altman & J. F. Wohlwill (Eds), *Behavior and the Natural Environment* (pp. 241–67). New York: Plenum.

Kempton, W., Harris, C. K., Keith, J. G. & Weihl, J. S. (1985). Do consumers know what works in energy conservation? *Marriage and Family Review*, 9, 115–33.

Kempton, W. & Montgomery, L. (1982). Folk quantification of energy. *Energy*, 7, 817–27.

Keyfitz, N. (1989). The growing human population. *Scientific American*, 261 (3), 118–26.

King, R. T. (1947). The future of wildlife in forest use. *Transactions of the North American Wildlife Conference*, 12, 454–66.

Klinger, D. & Kuzmyak, R. (1986). *Personal travel in the United States: 1983–1984 nationwide personal transportation study*, 1, FHWA. Washington, DC: US Department of Transportation.

Knickerbocker, B. (1995). Earthday at 25: a US environmental report card. *Christian Science Monitor*, 18 April, p. 10.

Komorita, S. S. & Parks, C. D. (1996). *Social Dilemmas*. Boulder, CO: Westview Press.

Krauss, R., Freedman, J. & Whitcup, M. (1978). Field and laboratory studies of littering. *Journal of Experimental Social Psychology*, 14, 109–22.

Kromm, D. E., Probald, F. & Wall, G. (1973). An international comparison of response to air pollution. *Journal of Environmental Management*, 1, 363–75.

La Riviere, J. W. M. (1989). Threats to the world's water. *Scientific American*, 261 (3), 80–94.

Latimer, D. A., Hogo, H. & Daniel, T. C. (1981). The effects of optical conditions on perceived scenic beauty. *Atmospheric Environment*, 15, 1865–74.

Levi, D. J. & Holder, E. E. (1986). Nuclear power: the dynamics of acceptability. *Environment and Behavior*, 18, 385–95.

Lichtenstein, S., Slovic, P., Fischhoff, B, Layman, M. & Combs, B. (1978). Judged frequency of lethal events. *Journal of Experimental Psychology: Human Learning and Memory*, 4, 551–78.

Luyben, P. D. (1982). Prompting thermostat setting behavior: public response to a presidential appeal for conservation. *Environment and Behavior*, 14, 113–28.

Luyben, P. D. (1982–83). A parametric analysis of prompting procedures to encourage electrical energy conservation. *Journal of Environmental Systems*, 12, 329–39.

Luyben, P. D. (1984). Drop and tilt: a comparison of two procedures to increase the use of venetian blinds to conserve energy. *Journal of Community Psychology*, 12, 149–54.

Luyben, P. D. & Cummings, S. (1981–82). Motivating beverage container recycling on a college campus. *Journal of Environmental Systems*, 11, 235–45.

MacLean, D. E. (1990) Comparing values in environmental policies: moral issues and moral arguments. In P. B. Hammond & R. Coppock (Eds), *Valuing Health Risks, Costs, and Benefits for Environmental Decision Making* (pp. 83–106). Washington, DC: National Academy Press.

Margolin, J. B. & Misch, M. R. (1978). *Incentives and Disincentives for Ridesharing: A Behavioral Study*. Washington, DC: US Government Printing Office.

McCaul, K. D. & Kopp, J. T. (1982). Effects of goal setting and commitment on increasing metal recycling. *Journal of Applied Psychology*, 67, 377–9.

McClelland, L. & Canter, R. J. (1981). Psychological research on energy conservation: context, approaches, methods. In A. Baum & J. E. Singer (Eds), *Advances in Environmental Psychology, vol. 3: Energy Conservation: Psychological Perspectives* (pp. 1–25). Hillsdale, NJ: Erlbaum.

McGuire, W. J. (1969). The nature of attitudes and attitude change. In G. Lindzey & E. Aronson (Eds), *The Handbook of Social Psychology* (2nd edn, vol 3). Reading, MA: Addison-Wesley.

McKechnie, G. E. (1974). *Environmental Response Inventory Manual.* Palo Alto, CA: Consulting Psychologists Press.

Melnick, R. S. (1990). The politics of benefit–cost analysis. In P. B. Hammond & R. Coppock (Eds), *Valuing Health Risks, Costs, and Benefits for Environmental Decision Making* (pp. 23–54). Washington, DC: National Academy Press.

Messick, D. M. & Brewer, M. B. (1983). Solving social dilemmas. In L. Wheeler & P. Shaver (Eds), *Review of Personality and Social Psychology* (vol. 4). Beverly Hills, CA: Sage.

Midden, C. J., Meter, J. E., Weening, M. H. & Zieverink, H. J. (1983). Using feedback, reinforcement and information to reduce energy consumption in households: a field experiment. *Journal of Economic Psychology*, 3, 65–86.

Miller, R. D. & Ford, J. M. (1985). *Shared Savings in the Residential Market: A Public/Private Partnership for Energy Conservation.* Baltimore, MD: Urban Consortium for Technology Initiatives, Energy Task Force.

Milstein, J. S. (1977). *How Consumers Feel about Energy: Attitudes and Behavior During the Winter and Spring of 1976–77.* Washington, DC: Federal Energy Administration.

Molina, M. J. & Rowland, F. S. (1974). Stratospheric sink for chlorofluoromethanes: Chlorine atom catalysed destruction of ozone. *Nature*, 249, 810–12.

Morowitz, H. J. (1991). Balancing species preservation and economic considerations. *Science*, 253, 752–4.

Mosler, H. J. (1993). Self-dissemination of environmentally-responsible behavior: the influence of trust in a commons dilemma game. *Journal of Environmental Psychology*, 13, 111–23.

Myers, N. (1989). *Deforestation Rates in Tropical Forests and their Climatic Implications.* London: Friends of the Earth.

Myers, N. (1995). The world's forests: need for a policy appraisal. *Science*, 268, 823–4.

Myers, N. (1997). Consumption: challenge to sustainable development. *Science*, 276, 53–5.

National Research Council (1981). *Atmosphere–Biosphere Interactions: Toward a Better Understanding of the Ecological Consequences of Fossil Fuel Combustion.* Washington, DC: National Academy Press.

National Research Council (1989). *Improving Risk Communication.* Committee on Risk Perception and Communication, National Research Council. Washington, DC: National Academy Press.

Neuman, K. (1986). Personal values and commitment to energy conservation. *Environment and Behavior*, 18, 53–74.

Nickerson, R. S. (1986). *Using Computers: Human Factors in Information Technology.* Cambridge, MA: MIT Press.

Nickerson, R. S. (1992). *Looking Ahead: Human Factors Challenges in a Changing World.* Hillsdale, NJ: Erlbaum.

Nickerson, R. S. (1995). Human interaction with computers and robots. *The International Journal of Human Factors in Manufacturing*, 5, 5–27.

Nickerson, R. S. & Moray, N. (1995). Environmental change. In R. S. Nickerson (Ed.), *Emerging Needs and Opportunities for Human Factors Research* (pp. 158–76). Washington, DC: National Academy Press.

Nitzel, M. T. & Winett, R. A. (1977). Demographics, attitudes, and behavioral responses to important environmental events. *American Journal of Community Psychology*, 5, 195–206.

Olson, M. (1965). *The Logic of Collective Action*. Cambridge, MA: Harvard University Press.
Oppenheimer, M. & Boyle, R. H. (1990). *Heat Death: The Race Against the Greenhouse Effect*. New York: Basic Books.
Orbell, J., Dawes, R. & van de Kragt, A. (1995). Cooperation under laissez faire and majority decision rules in group-level social dilemmas. In D. A. Schroeder (Ed.), *Social Dilemmas: Perspectives on Individuals and Groups* (pp. 105–16). Westport, CT: Praeger.
Ostrom, E. (1990). *Governing the Commons*. New York: Cambridge University Press.
Pallak, M. S., Cook, D. A. & Sullivan, J. J. (1980). Commitment and energy conservation. In L. Bickman (Ed.), *Applied Social Psychology Annual* (vol. 1, pp. 235–54). Beverly Hills, CA: Sage.
Pardini, A. U. & Katzev, R. D. (1983–84). The effect of strength of commitment on newspaper recycling. *Journal of Environmental Systems*, 13, 245–54.
Pearce, D. W. & Turner, R. K. (1990). *Economics of Natural Resources and the Environment*. Baltimore, MD: Johns Hopkins University Press.
Peterson, G. L. (1974). Evaluating the quality of the wilderness environment: congruence between perceptions and aspirations. *Environment and Behavior*, 6, 169–93.
Petty, R. E. & Rosnick, J. A. (Eds) (1995). *Attitude Strength: Antecedents and Consequences*. Mahwah, NJ: Erlbaum.
Pillsbury, A. F. (1981). The salinity of rivers. *Scientific American*, 245 (1), 54–65.
Platt, J. (1973). Social traps. *American Psychologist*, 28, 641–51.
Pool, R. (1992). A visit to a virtual world. *Science*, 256, 45.
Postel, S. (1985). Thirsty in a water-rich world. *International Wildlife*, 15 (6), 32–7.
Powell, C. S. (1990). Science and business: plastic goes green. *Scientific American*, 263 (2), 101.
Powers, R. B., Duus, R. E. & Norton, R. S. (1979). The commons game: teaching students about social traps. Paper presented at the meeting of the Rocky Mountain Psychological Association, Las Vegas.
Ramsay, W. (1976). Priorities in species preservation. *Environmental Affairs*, 5, 595–616.
Reichel, D. A. & Geller, E. S. (1981). Applications of behavioral analysis for conserving transportation energy. In A. Baum & J. E. Singer (Eds), *Advances in Environmental Psychology, vol. 3: Energy Conservation: Psychological Perspectives* (pp. 53–91). Hillsdale, NJ: Erlbaum.
Reid, D. H., Luyben, P. D., Rawers, R. J. & Bailey, J. S. (1976). Newspaper recycling behavior: the effects of prompting and proximity of containers. *Journal of Environmental Systems*, 13, 245–54.
Reiter, S. M. & Samuel, W. (1980). Littering as a function of prior litter and the presence or absence of prohibitive signs. *Journal of Applied Social Psychology*, 10, 45–55.
Repetto, R. (1990). Deforestation in the tropics. *Scientific American*, 262 (4), 36–42.
Repetto, R. & Gillis, M. (Eds) (1988). *Public Policies and the Misuse of Forest Resources*. New York: Cambridge University Press.
Ross, M. H. & Steinmeyer, D. (1990). Energy for industry. *Scientific American*, 263 (3), 88–98.
Russell, M. (1990). The making of cruel choices. In P. B. Hammond & R. Coppock (Eds), *Valuing Health Risks, Costs, and Benefits for Environmental Decision Making* (pp. 15–22). Washington, DC: National Academy Press.
Schuman, H. & Johnson, M. P. (1976). Attitudes and behavior. *Annual Review of Sociology*, 2, 161–297.
Seligman, C. & Darley, J. M. (1977). Feedback as a means of decreasing residential energy consumption. *Journal of Applied Psychology*, 64, 363–8.
Seligman, C., Kriss, M., Darley, J. M., Fazio, R. H., Becker, L. J. & Pryor, J. B. (1979). Predicting residential energy consumption from homeowners' attitudes. *Journal of Applied Social Psychology*, 9, 70–90.
Sexton, R. J., Johnson, N. B. & Konakayama, A. (1987). Consumer response to continuous-display electricity-use monitors in a time-of-use pricing experiment. *Journal of Consumer Research*, 14, 55–62.

Shafer, E. L. & Richards, T. A. (1974). A comparison of viewer reactions to outdoor scenes and photographs of those scenes. USDA Forest Service Research Paper NE-302. Upper Darby, PA: Northeastern Forest Experiment Station.
Shafir, E. (1993). Choosing versus rejecting: why some options are both better and worse than others. *Memory and Cognition*, 21, 546–56.
Sharlin, H. I. (1986). EDB: a case study in communicating risk. *Risk Analysis*, 6, 61–8.
Sherrod, D. R., Armstrong, D., Hewitt, J., Madonia, B., Speno, S. & Teruya, D. (1977). Environmental attention, affect, and altruism. *Journal of Applied Social Psychology*, 7, 359–71.
Slavin, R. E., Wodarski, J. S. & Blackburn, B. L. (1981). A group contingency for electricity conservation in master-metered apartments. *Journal of Applied Behavior Analysis*, 14, 357–63.
Slovic, P., Fischhoff, B. & Lichtenstein, S. (1979). Rating the risks. *Environment*, 21 (3), 14–20, 36–9.
Slovic, P., Fischhoff, B. & Lichtenstein, S. (1981). Perception and acceptability of risk from energy systems. In A. Baum & J. E. Singer (Eds), *Advances in Environmental Psychology: vol. 3. Energy: Psychological Perspectives* (pp. 155–69). Hillsdale, NJ: Erlbaum
Sproull, L. & Kiesler, S. (1991). *Connections: New Ways of Working in the Networked Organization*. Cambridge, MA: MIT Press.
Starr, C., Searl, M. F. & Alpert, S. (1992). Energy sources: a realistic outlook. *Science*, 256, 981–6.
Steinhart, P. (1990, July). No net loss. *Audobon*, 18–21.
Stern, P. C. (1978). When do people act to maintain common resources: a reformulated psychological question of our times. *International Journal of Psychology*, 13, 149–58.
Stern, P. C. (1992a). Psychological dimensions of global environmental change. *Annual Review of Psychology*, 43, 269–302.
Stern, P. C. (1992b). What psychology knows about energy conservation. *American Psychologist*, 47, 1224–32.
Stern, P. C., Aronson, E., Darley, J. M., Hill, D. H., Hirst, E., Kempton, W. & Wilbanks, T. J. (1986). The effectiveness of incentives for residential energy conservation. *Evaluation Review*, 10, 147–76.
Stern, P. C. & Fineberg, H. V. (Eds) (1996). *Understanding Risk: Informing Decisions in a Democratic Society*. Washington, DC: National Academy Press.
Stern, P. C. & Gardner, G. T. (1981). Psychological research and energy policy. *American Psychologist*, 36, 329–42.
Stern, P. C. & Kirkpatrick, E. M. (1977). Energy behavior. *Environment*, 19, 10–15.
Stern, P. C. & Oskamp, S. (1987). Managing scarce environmental resources. In D. Stokols & I. Altman (Eds), *Handbook of Environmental Psychology*, vol 2 (pp. 1043–88). New York: Wiley.
Stern, P. C., Young, O. R. & Druckman, D. (Eds) (1992). *Global Environmental Change: Understanding the Human Dimensions*. Washington, DC: National Academy Press.
Stolarksi, R. S. (1988). The Antarctic ozone hole. *Scientific American*, 258 (1), 30–6.
Stolarski, R. S., Bojkov, R., Bishop, L., Zerefos, C., Staehelin, J. & Zawodny, J. (1992). Measured trends in stratospheric ozone. *Science*, 256, 342–9.
Talbot, J. F., Bardwell, L. V. & Kaplan, R. (1987). The functions of urban nature: uses and values of different types of urban nature settings. *Journal of Architectural Planning Research*, 4, 47–63.
Terborgh, J. (1992). Why American songbirds are vanishing. *Scientific American*, 266 (5), 98–104.
Tesser, A. & Shaffer, D. R. (1990). Attitudes and attitude change. *Annual Review of Psychology*, 41, 479–523.
Thayer, R. L. & Atwood, B. G. (1978). Plants, complexity, and pleasure in urban and suburban environments. *Environmental Psychology and Nonverbal Behavior*, 3, 67–76.
Thomas, L. (1983). An epidemic of apprehension. *Discover*, 4, 78–80.
Transportation Research Board (1988). Transportation in an aging society: improving

mobility and safety for older persons, vol. 1, Special Report 218. Washington, DC: Transportation Research Board, National Research Council.

Trigg, L. J., Perlman, D., Perry, R. P. & Janisse, M. P. (1976). Antipollution behavior: a function of perceived outcome and locus of control. *Environment and Behavior*, 8, 307–13.

Tversky, A. & Kahneman, D. (1981). The framing of decisions and the psychology of choice. *Science*, 211, 453–8.

Ulrich, R. S. (1983). Aesthetic and affective response to natural environment. In I. Altman & J. F. Wohlwill (Eds), *Behavior and the Natural Environment* (pp. 85–125). New York: Plenum.

Ulrich, R. S. & Addoms, D. L. (1981). Psychological and recreational benefits of a residential park. *Journal of Leisure Research*, 13, 43–65.

US Bureau of the Census (1990). *Statistical Abstract of the United States*. Washington, DC: Government Printing Office.

US Bureau of the Census (1997). *Statistical Abstract of the United States*. Washington, DC: Government Printing Office.

Van der Pligt, J., Eiser, J. R. & Spears, R. (1986). Attitudes toward nuclear energy: familiarity and salience. *Environment and Behavior*, 18, 75–94.

Van Houten, R., Nau, P. A. & Merrigan, M. (1981). Reducing elevator use: a comparison of posted feedback and reduced elevator convenience. *Journal of Applied Behavior Analysis*, 14, 377–87.

van Vugt, M. (1997). Concerns about the privatization of public goods: a social dilemma analysis. *Social Psychology Quarterly*, 60, 355–67.

Vaughn, E. & Nordenstam, B. (1991). The perception of environmental risks among ethnically diverse groups. *Journal of Cross-Cultural Psychology*, 22, 29–60.

Vincent, J. R. (1992). The tropical timber trade and sustainable development. *Science*, 256, 1651–5.

Vincent, J. R. & Panayotou, T. (1997). . . . or distraction? *Science*, 276, 53–7.

Vining, J. & Ebreo, A. (1990). What makes a recycler? A comparison of recyclers and nonrecyclers. *Environment and Behavior*, 22, 55–73.

Wallace, D. R. (1985). Wetlands in America: labyrinth and temple. *Wilderness*, 49, 12–27.

Wandersman, A. H. & Hallman, W. K. (1993). Are people acting irrationally? Understand public concerns about environmental threats. *American Psychologist*, 48, 681–6.

Wang, T. H. & Katzev, R. D. (1990). Group commitment and resource conservation: two field experiments on promoting recycling. *Journal of Applied Social Psychology*, 20, 265–75.

Ward, L. M. & Russell, J. A. (1981). The psychological representation of molar physical environments. *Journal of Experimental Psychology: General*, 110, 121–52.

Weigel, R. & Weigel, J. (1978). Environmental concern: the development of a measure. *Environment and Behavior*, 10, 3–15.

Weinstein, N. D. (1976). The statistical prediction of environmental preferences: problems of validity and application. *Environment and Behavior*, 8, 611–26.

Weinstein, N. D., Klotz, M. L. & Sandman, P. (1988). Optimistic biases in public perception of the risk from radon. *American Journal of Public Health*, 78, 796–800.

Weinstein, N. D., Sandman, P. M. & Roberts, N. E. (1991). Perceived susceptibility and self-protective behavior: a field experiment to encourage home radon testing. *Health Psychology*, 10, 25–33.

Wellmer, F. W. & Kursten, M. (1992). *Episodes*, 15, 182.

Whyte, W. H. (1980). *The Social Life of Small Urban Spaces*. Washington, DC: The Conservation Foundation.

Winett, R. A., Neale, M. S. & Grier, H. C. (1979). The effects of self-monitoring and feedback on residential electricity consumption. *Journal of Applied Behavior Analysis*, 12, 173–84.

Winett, R. A., Leckliter, I. N., Chinn, D. E. & Stahl, B. (1984). Reducing energy consumption: the long-term effects of a single TV program. *Journal of Communication*, 34, 37–51.

Winett, R. A., Leckliter, I. N., Chinn, D. E., Stahl, B. & Love, S. Q. (1985). Effects of television modeling on residential energy conservation. *Journal of Applied Behavior Analysis*, 18, 33–44.

Wohlwill, J. F. & Kohn, I. (1973). The environment as experienced by the migrant: an adaptation level approach. *Representative Research in Social Psychology*, 4, 135–64.

Zolik, E. S., Jason, L. A., Nair, D. & Peterson, M. (1982–83). Conservation of electricity on a college campus. *Journal of Environmental Systems*, 12, 225–8.

Zube, E. H., Pitt, D. G. & Anderson, T. W. (1975). *Perception and Measurement of Scenic Resources in the Southern Connecticut River Valley*. Institute of Man and His Environment Publication R-74-1. Amherst, MA: University of Massachusetts.

Chapter 26

Eyewitness Testimony

Daniel B. Wright
University of Bristol
and
Graham M. Davies
University of Leicester

On December 3, 1996, Mrs Duncan, a former policewoman living deep in the Worcestershire countryside, opened her door late at night to a distraught caller, whose clothing was soaked in blood. The woman, 28-year-old Tracy Andrews, explained that she and her fiancé, Lee Harvey, had been driving home from a public house when they overtook an F-registration Ford Sierra. She said the driver of the Sierra pursued them for three miles along country lanes, bumper to bumper, with headlights flashing, until they had come to a stop outside Mrs Duncan's house. When her fiancé emerged from their car, he had a violent argument with the passenger in the pursuing vehicle which culminated in a frenzied knife attack. Lee Harvey died. The man then turned on Miss Andrews, kicking and punching her and leaving her with a wound over her eye. Police pathologists found some 15 stab wounds to Mr Harvey's face, neck and body. The officer in charge of the case told the press it was "a road-rage-type incident" and continued "this was a vicious crime, one of the most vicious I've seen in thirty years."

Over the next two days, police interviewed Miss Andrews four times. They obtained a full verbal description of her attacker who she described as "a porky man" around 25 years old, between 5'9" and 6'0" tall with "chubby cheeks" and "big staring eyes." With the assistance of a police technician, she compiled an "E-fit" picture of her attacker's face. She estimated it to be 70% accurate. The police asked for any witnesses who had noticed either the dark Sierra or the white Escort Turbo driven by Mr Harvey to come forward. A tearful Miss Andrews appeared at a police press conference where she led police appeals for further witnesses.

Handbook of Applied Cognition, Edited by F. T. Durso, R. S. Nickerson, R. W. Schvaneveldt, S. T. Dumais, D. S. Lindsay and M. T. H. Chi.

When witnesses were found, the story they told did not correspond with Miss Andrews' version of events. Two witnesses described how, on the crucial night, they had seen Mr Harvey reverse his car after overshooting his turning home, but there was no sign of a pursuing Sierra. A nine-year-old girl living close to the crime scene had been awakened by the sound of an argument between a man and a woman, but she told the police there was just the single male voice. When forensic evidence suggested that the blood stains on Miss Andrews' clothing were consistent with her having stabbed her fiancé rather than cradling him as he lay dying, police moved to arrest Miss Andrews and charge her with murder. In July 1997, after a three-week trial, at which the conflicting eyewitness accounts were aired before the jury, Miss Andrews was found guilty and sentenced to life imprisonment (Chaudhury, 1997).

Particularly in cases where there are conflicting accounts, it is often impossible to know the truth of what happened. In some cases people may purposefully deceive the police investigators. We discuss this in a later section on credibility assessment. Fortunately, most witnesses will set out to tell the truth rather than to deceive. But this does not mean that all statements made by well-meaning witnesses are accurate or complete. They will frequently contain *errors of omission* and *commission*; details which occurred are not spontaneously reported and, more damaging, events will be described which did not in fact occur in the way reported. The demonstration of such witness errors were among the earliest achievements of applied cognitive psychology (Bartol & Bartol, 1987) and recent years have seen a renewal of interest in the variables influencing a witness's account. Such variables can usefully be divided into what Wells (1978) terms *estimator* and *system variables*. By estimator variables, we mean factors inherent in the setting and nature of the crime, and the character and circumstances of the witness. By system variables, we refer to factors that are under the control of the police, such as how a witness is questioned. In this chapter we review existing research on estimator and system variables before turning to three issues which are at the cutting edge of current debate: the reliability of child witnesses; the role that psychologists and psychological research should play when the courts hear eyewitness testimony, and the credibility of memories "recovered" after long delays.

ESTIMATOR VARIABLES

To understand eyewitness testimony, it is necessary to understand the psychology of memory. Memory is a remarkable facility. An event occurs and somehow this facility translates the event into a representation which is later used as a basis to construct a memory for the event. However, research on memory conclusively shows that it is not perfect. The transition from event to memory can be divided into three stages: encoding, storing and retrieving a memory of an event. At each of these stages memories can distort. The stress in estimator variable research is on the encoding and storage of information because these are often out of the control of the judicial system and thus qualify as estimator variables.

For a participant in a memory experiment a failure to recognize a previously seen nonsense syllable or incorrectly recognize one has no serious consequences.

In relation to eyewitness testimony, a single error can allow a guilty person to be freed or an innocent person to be incarcerated (Connors, Lundregan, Miller & McEwan, 1996; further examples in Loftus & Ketchum, 1991). To give an indication of the magnitude of the problem, a survey of lineups in the London area found that in at least 20% of cases an innocent person was chosen (Wright & McDaid, 1996). Further, in over 40% of those lineups no identification was made. In many of these cases the suspect was released, although it is likely some did commit the crime. Psychologists often focus on cases where innocent people are convicted based on eyewitness testimony. This may be due to following William Blackstone's adage that it is better that ten guilty people are set free than one innocent man is imprisoned, or perhaps it is because of imagining oneself being falsely incarcerated. However, memory errors affect both sides of the scales of justice.

There is much discussion about the applicability of much "eyewitness" research to actual eyewitness situations. Some argue that the laboratory analog is too distant from real crime situations to be applicable (for example, Egeth & McCloskey, 1984; Yuille, 1993). Others feel that laboratory eyewitness research is sufficiently advanced to inform legal proceedings (Faigman, 1995; Loftus, 1986). For the field to advance it is clearly best to draw upon laboratory studies and real crime situations since both approaches have drawbacks and advantages (Davies, 1993). In a laboratory, it is impractical and unethical to mimic the emotion levels of some crimes. While it is possible to manipulate emotion in the laboratory (see Christianson, 1992a), the levels of terror experienced in some crimes cannot be approached. Also, some eyewitnesses are not traumatized. For example, witnessing fraud or a narcotic transaction is unlikely to heighten unduly most people's emotional state. The main drawback for archival studies of real-world crimes, or case studies of crimes, is the lack of experimental control in a highly complex situation. This makes it difficult to make causal attributions, although some information can still be gleaned (for discussion, see Wright & McDaid, 1996).

In the next few pages we describe some estimator variables explored by eyewitness research: own race (and more generally own group) bias, weapon focus and memory for emotional events, the effects of postevent information, and memory for automobiles. This is not an exhaustive list. Other topics include the relatively low association between witness confidence and accuracy (Penrod & Cutler, 1995; Sporer et al., 1995), identification from clothes and body shape (Lee & Geiselman, 1994; MacLeod, Frowley & Sheperd, 1994), voice memory (Yarmey, 1995), and time estimation (Burt & Popple, 1996).

Own Race Bias

Several studies have demonstrated that people from one race are better at recognizing people from their own race than those of others (cf. Brigham & Malpass, 1985; Brigham & Ready, 1985). While the effects are not always large, it is a reliable finding, which is generally accepted in the research community (Kassin, Ellsworth & Smith, 1989). This is important for determining the reliability of an eyewitness's report if the culprit is from a different race and for constructing fair lineups. One influential hypothesis for this effect is that increased contact with people from your own race leads to different, and more diagnostic, encoding strategies and thus better memory (Brigham & Malpass, 1985; see also Chiroro & Valentine, 1995). An early exposition of this hypothesis was provided by Feingold (1914): "individuals of a given race are distinguishable from each other in proportion to our familiarity, to our contact with the race as a whole. Thus to the un-initiated American all Asiatics look alike, while to the Asiatic all white men look alike" (p. 50).

Experiments of the "contact" hypothesis have failed to find consistent support and as such this hypothesis does not appear to be able to account for the complete effect. Further, there are other "own group" effects which are not easily explained by this hypothesis. For instance, men appear better at recognizing men, and women are better recognizing women (for example, Shaw & Skolnick, 1994). Since men and women have much contact with each other it is not clear why this effect should occur if the contact hypothesis is the complete explanation for it.

There appears also to be an own age bias. Yarmey (1993) had one of two young women approach members of the public and talk to them about some lost jewellery. The other young woman came up to them later and asked them about the woman with whom they had previously spoken. Yarmey found that people of about the same age as the woman were more accurate than older adults. This is consistent with some previous research (Adams-Price, 1992). One conclusion could be that young adults are simply better at recognizing people than older adults. However, Yarmey recognized that "since the two culprits were young adults, it is possible that a same age effect occurred" (p. 1929). This has recently been explored and observed: young people are better at recognizing other young people than they are older adults (Stroud & Wright, 1997). These results suggest we must search elsewhere for an explanation of the "own race" effect.

Emotion, Memory and Weapon Focus

Some crimes, like being physically assaulted or witnessing an armed robbery, are likely to be traumatic. When people experience events like these, which are both traumatic and important, they are likely to remember them better than non-traumatic and unimportant events (see Christianson & Hubinette, 1993, for memories of a bank robbery). They can produce what are sometimes called flashbulb memories (Brown & Kulik, 1977; Wright & Gaskell, 1995; and papers in Winograd & Neisser, 1992). The problem is that these vivid memories are not necessarily accurate (for discussion, see Neisser, 1982). One explanation is that there is an inverted U-curve between arousal and memory: the Yerkes–Dodson law. When arousal is low, memory performance (and in indeed most cognitive abilities) are poor. As arousal increases, performance improves, but there is some optimal point of arousal, beyond which performance deteriorates.

It is uncontroversial that when arousal is low, memory performance is poor. There is more debate about what happens as arousal rises. The general view is that beyond some level performance deteriorates for at least some aspects, an inverted U-shaped curve. However, memory for some central details improves at the cost of memory for peripheral details (Christianson et al., 1991; Easterbrook, 1959; for a review, see Christianson, 1992b). This has the effect that in a highly emotive situation, like being robbed at gun point, a witness may remember details about the weapon but not the assailant's face. This is called *weapon focus* (Loftus, Loftus & Messo, 1987). Many factors are likely to be involved in this phenomenon beyond just the high levels of emotion. An example is the uniqueness of the stimuli (see Mitchell, Livosky & Mather, 1998).

There is another theory about memory and trauma that is popular among many therapists and derives, in part, from Freud's theory of repression. The idea is that when someone experiences a very traumatic event, the memory for the event is repressed, banished from consciousness. This is different from just having a poor memory for the crime; the person denies that the crime ever occurred. We discuss this notion briefly when considering legal aspects of recovered/false memories.

Postevent Information

After viewing a crime, and before describing it to a police officer or in court, a witness may hear or read about the crime; this is termed postevent information. There are several ways in which this information can be encountered, including being asked questions about the event (by police officers, friends, lawyers, etc.), reading about the crime in a newspaper, and talking to other witnesses. The question is does this postevent information affect witness memory?

Loftus, Miller & Burns (1978) conducted a series of studies that mimicked the first of these situations. Participants were shown a series of slides in which a car hit a pedestrian after turning right at an intersection. There were two versions of the slide showing the corner where the car turned. In one there was a stop sign, in the other a yield sign. Half of the participants saw the stop sign and half saw the yield sign. If this had been a real accident and had gone to litigation, which sign was there could be critical for establishing negligence. After seeing the slides, participants answered several questions. For some participants this included a question implying that the sign was a stop sign. Other participants had it implied that a yield sign was at the corner and some had no mention of the sign. Participants were then asked if it was a stop sign or a yield sign. Those given consistent information were the most accurate; the question seemed to enhance their memories. However, those given errant information, what is often called misinformation, had the worst memories. People incorporated this misinformation into their memories.

Even questions that are not errant can affect memory. Loftus & Palmer (1974, exp. 2) showed people several car crashes and asked them how fast the cars were going when they "hit" or when they "smashed" into each other. Both are technically accurate but "smashed" suggests a more violent collision. Not only were speed estimates higher with "smashed," but also when asked if there was any broken glass at the scene (there was none), those given "smashed" were more likely to say there was.

The second way postevent information may be encountered is through reading about it, possibly in a newspaper report. There has been much research simulating this. For example, in Wright & Stroud (1998), participants were shown pictures of a shoplifting incident. They then read a brief summary of the crime in which some details were in error. Just as information in biasing questions can be incorporated into people's memory, so some of the errant details entered participants' memory.

The third way that information can be encountered is by talking to other witnesses. Much laboratory research in social psychology demonstrates how what one person says can affect another person's responses (Bond & Smith, 1996). Schneider & Watkins (1996) showed how one person's response on a memory test for previously seen words can affect another person's response. Hyman, Husband & Billings (1995) and Loftus & Pickrell (1995) have shown how what one person says can even be used to create an entire memory for a non-existent event. This memory conformity research is particularly important for crimes which are witnessed by many people, like a child abduction from outside a school or a robbery in a crowded bank. If the witnesses talk, and for important events like this they probably will, they should not be treated as independent observations. This means that the police and the courts should not treat having five witnesses all agreeing on some details necessarily being more informative than if only a single witness remembered that detail.

There is still dispute on the precise explanation of how postevent information influences memory: do some aspects of the original memory remain intact, or is the total memory destroyed (Wright, 1995)? Recent reviews of the possible explanations for the misinformation effect include Brainerd & Reyna's (in press) discussion of source monitoring, blending and fuzzy trace theory, and Ayers & Reder (1998) on activation spread explanations. This is an example of research on a real-world topic raising a fundamental question about basic memory processes.

Eyewitnessing Automobiles

Most of the existing eyewitness testimony research has focused on memory for people's faces, which is clearly important for identifying the culprit. However, police may rely on people's memory for many other aspects of the crime: for instance memory for automobiles. Western society is an automotive culture (Giuliano, 1996). Criminals share this culture and its "automobility." Some crimes directly involve automobiles like road rage, hit-and-run accidents, car theft, "ram-raiding", and "car-jacking". In others automobiles are used to transport criminals ("getaway cars") or in abductions.

Consider the situation of Constable Simon Grantham of the Dorset Police. In 1987 he was investigating a series of attempted child abductions. Often several people observed the automobiles involved in these attempts but people also saw other automobiles in the vicinity being driven suspiciously. The problem was knowing what the automobiles were and which of the "suspicious" cars were also seen being used in the abductions. Grantham (1989) produced a computer program called MotorFit that is an analog to the computerized face identification kits, like the one used with Tracy Andrews to create a composite of her alleged attacker. The police could have used MotorFit with Tracy Andrews, or with other witnesses, to help the police to know if the car being described really was a Ford Sierra.

The fact that the police were interested enough in automobile memory to fund MotorFit is testament to its applied importance, yet, there has been relatively little academic research on this topic. One aspect which has been explored is gender differences (Davies & Robertson, 1993; McKelvie et al., 1993). Males do better than females. Davies and colleagues (Davies et al., 1996; Davies & Robertson, 1993) showed how some differences exist with children as young as seven. It appears that this is due to automobiles being, in most contemporary western cultures, male-oriented objects (Powers, Andriks & Loftus, 1979). It is worth stressing that the gender effects are not large and therefore care must be taken when (and if) incorporating them into a trial setting (Davies et al., 1996).

Another area of automobile memory is estimating the velocity at which they are traveling. This can be important for assessing blame in collisions. Recall that in Loftus & Palmer's (1974) study people were asked, with differently worded questions, to estimate the velocity of automobiles in several films. Four of the films they used came from the police. These were designed to illustrate the amount of destruction at different velocities and therefore the velocities were known: one at 20 mph, one at 30 mph and two at 40 mph. The means of the estimated velocities were 37.7 mph, 36.2 mph, 39.1 mph and 36.1 mph, respectively. Thus, in line with other research in this area, Loftus & Palmer concluded that "people are not very good at judging how fast a vehicle was actually traveling" (p. 586).

SYSTEM VARIABLES

Interview Procedures

Tracy Andrews was interviewed four times by the police. Despite the advances in forensic science of recent years, statements from witnesses remain the most important source of information to the police. In recent years, psychologists have made major contributions toward the development of forensic interviewing. At one stage, hypnosis was advocated as a solution (Reiser, 1989). However, later work employing both experimental studies and more realistic field studies suggest that hypnotized witnesses may be suggestible and prone to fabrication, thereby greatly increasing the risks of miscarriages of justice (for a recent review, see Lynn, Myers & Malinoski, 1997).

The goal of interviewing research has been to find a method of interviewing which genuinely increases the amount of useful information provided without the confabulation associated with hypnosis. One very promising tool is the Cognitive Interview or CI (Fisher & Geiselman, 1992). This technique has undergone numerous refinements and additions since its inception, fuelled in part by the experiences of officers trained in its use. At the core of the original CI is the idea of applying techniques of memory retrieval derived from laboratory research based on two contrasting theories of memory.

The first theory views memory as a bundle of attributes: remembering is more probable when many of the retrieval cues generated by the subject are the same as those defining the original event (Tulving, 1983). According to the CI, one way of achieving this in an interview situation is to encourage witnesses to reinstate the context of the event. Such context will include the physical environment, time of day and the witnesses' own thoughts and emotions at the time of the incident (for a review of experimental research on reinstatement, see Davies, 1988). A second way is to encourage witnesses to recall everything about the incident, rather than to limit their recall to what they believe the officer requires: recall of trivial details such as the robber's undone shoelace may lead to recall of important details such as the color and style of shoe worn.

The second theory views memory as a network of associations. According to this view, successful retrieval involves activating as many linked pathways as possible (Bower, 1981). The two mnemonic devices advocated to achieve this are: recall events repeatedly in a varied order, for instance beginning at a key moment and moving backward and forward from that point and to encourage the witness to look at events from a changed perspective. For example, a customer who is witness to a bank robbery might consider what the bank teller could have seen.

While laboratory research could justify advocating these four techniques (Geiselman, 1988), research was necessary to demonstrate that the basic principles of the interview would translate into a field setting. A series of studies conducted by Geiselman and colleagues demonstrated impressive effectiveness of the original CI, relative to other forms of interviewing. For instance, Geiselman, Fisher, MacKinnon & Holland (1985) compared the efficacy of the original CI relative to a conventional police interview and a hypnotic interview. Groups of students watched an FBI training film depicting a violent robbery, before being questioned about the content by experienced detectives who were trained in one of the three interview procedures. Relative to the conventional police interview, both the CI and the hypnotic interview increased the amount of information recalled by witnesses by some 35%, with no significant difference in outcome between the latter. Moreover, this increased information was accompanied by no significant increase in errors. Thus, the CI appeared to offer all the claimed advantages of improved access to memory associated with hypnotic interviewing without any of the problems of suggestibility and confabulation associated with hypnosis. Subsequent studies by Geiselman and colleagues demonstrated comparable improvements in recall performance with the CI when members of the public, rather than students, served as witnesses, and when live rather than televised events were being recalled (for a review, see Geiselman, 1988). Bekerian & Dennett (1993) reviewed a range of studies conducted both by Geiselman and by other research groups and found improvements in recall of between 12% and 92% for the original CI compared to the standard police interview, with accuracy rates exceeding 90%.

As knowledge of the encouraging results of the CI spread through the police community, Fisher and Geiselman became increasingly involved in police training. They noted that much conventional police interviewing was formulaic and rigid, involving a string of questions concerning the appearance of the suspect and incident details with little opportunity for the witness to construct their own narrative. One study (Fisher, Geiselman & Amador, 1989) suggested that US police officers waited an average of only 7 seconds before interrupting a witness's account with a question! Fisher & Geiselman (1992) encapsulated their experiences in a training manual which emphasized the social dynamic as much as the cognitive aspects of the interviewing process. There was a new stress on the importance of listening skills and of not interrupting the witness prematurely. Officers were told to allow the witness to dictate the pace and direction of questioning and to avoid a "tick box" approach which could rapidly reduce witnesses to monosyllabic replies. Further, while context reinstatement and recalling everything were still strongly emphasized, the importance of varied recall order and perspective change were subordinated to a more general emphasis on the importance of repeated recall attempts. Results from laboratory trials suggested that the "revised CI" might be as much as 45% more effective compared to the original CI (Fisher, Geiselman, Raymond, Jurkevich & Warhaftig, 1987).

The most effective demonstration of the potential of the new interview package came from a field study with the Hertfordshire police reported by George & Clifford (1995). Officers tape recorded an interview with an actual witness which served as a base level for allocating subjects to control and CI conditions. The CI subjects then received intensive training in the use of the revised interview procedure before recording a second interview using the new technique. Relative to the controls who had also recorded a second interview, CI trained officers asked many fewer questions than the other officers, but secured five times as much information per question. According to the authors, the reason for this lay in the type of questions asked by the CI trained officers: they employed less than half the number of closed questions ("What colour was his hair?") and many fewer leading questions ("He was clean shaven, wasn't he?") than the untrained officers. This study suggests that CI interviewing can be taught rapidly and effectively to police professionals, that it can impact directly on their interviewing of actual witnesses and can pay dividends in increases in information of use to the police. Shortly after this research was completed, a decision was taken to circulate, to all serving detectives in England and Wales, a handbook outlining the value of the CI and other innovative interviewing procedures developed by psychologists.

While the value of the CI training seems well established, research continues on the importance of specific mnemonic elements. Attempts to partial out the relative importance of the original four mnemonic components have led to inconclusive results, with context reinstatement producing the most consistent effects, though it is the technique which officers seem least ready to employ in practice (Memon, Wark, Holley, Bull & Koehnken, 1994). One obvious concern is that encouraging victim witnesses to recreate their own rape or violent assault may produce secondary trauma. Fisher & Geiselman (1992) suggest that if such witnesses are to be interviewed, they should be encouraged to use a third person narrative to distance themselves from the events.

It can be argued that some of the dramatic demonstrations of the superiority of the original CI relative to the conventional interview said more about the poverty of police training in interviewing than the effectiveness of the specific cognitive mnemonics (Davies, 1993). The original CI involved up to three attempts at recall, while the standard police interview would involve only a single attempt (Fisher & Geiselman, 1992). It is well established that repeated attempts at recall in themselves produce improvements in recall or hypermnesia (Erdelyi, 1984). When researchers have sought to equate the number of recall attempts for control and CI conditions, the advantages of the latter have on occasion been eliminated entirely (Memon, Wark, Holley, Bull & Koehnken, 1997), though a more common finding has been a smaller, but still operationally significant improvement in performance (Koehnken, Schimmossek, Aschermann & Hofer, 1995). A recent meta-analysis of the outcome of field studies with CI confirmed the general improvement in witness recall, but also found a small but significant increase in error rate relative to the standard police interview (Koehnken, Milne, Memon & Bull, in press). This has led to suggestions that any improvement in the recall of witnesses with CI might be caused by social facilitation: witnesses just try harder with a more empathic interviewer (Memon & Stevenage, 1996). However, as Koehnken et al. (1995) point out, a 35% increase in recall at the expense of only a 2% drop in accuracy is a bargain most police officers readily accept.

Adapted forms of the CI have been proven to be useful in interviewing children (Saywitz, Geiselman & Bornstein, 1992) and those with mild learning difficulties (Milne, Clare & Bull, 1996). However, a concern has arisen as to whether increases in recall for both these groups may be accompanied by unacceptable rises in error rate (Memon & Stevenage, 1996). Recent miscarriages of justice associated with overzealous interviewing of child complainants of sexual abuse have focused attention on the need to develop interviewing techniques which minimize the risk of such errors (Ceci & Bruck, 1995). In England and Wales, social workers and police officers interviewing children are expected to follow the guidelines set out in the *Memorandum of Good Practice* (Home Office, 1992). This advocates a form of the stepwise interview (Yuille, 1988), where emphasis is placed on the child providing a free account with the minimum of prompting; the use of focused or direct questioning is only resorted to if all other methods fail (Bull, 1995). Research suggests that interviewers can be readily trained in the use of the "Memorandum" interview (Davies & Wilson, 1997). However, much more research is required on special techniques for interviewing those with learning and communication difficulties (Brennan & Brennan, 1994; Marchant & Page, 1997).

Identification Procedures: Lineups

As described in the last section, when a crime occurs the police interview witnesses to try to assist their investigation. In many cases the important part is the description of the culprit. If the police have a suspect, they may want the witness to view this person to help them decide if this suspect is the culprit. In these circumstances police will often conduct what is called a lineup in the US or an identification parade in the UK. In this section we describe some of the considerations in conducting lineups and mention some alternatives.

The traditional "live" lineup is where the suspect stands with several foils (people known to be innocent). The witness views the lineup and is asked if the culprit is present, and if so, which person it is. These can be costly and in many parts of North America have been replaced by photo spreads or video lineups. For example, Tollestrup, Turtle & Yuille (1994) surveyed robbery and fraud cases in Vancouver, Canada, and found photo spreads were used in about 90% of cases. Here we use the word lineup to refer to live lineups, photo spreads and video lineups. Cutler, Berman, Penrod & Fisher (1994) compared these mediums and found they produce similar identification rates.

It has long been known that people can and do make errors in lineups, both of false identifications and not identifying the culprit (Wright & McDaid, 1996). There are some examples in judicial history where a lineup is clearly unfair, where the suspect stands out from the other people by race or other obvious physical characteristic (Ellison & Buckout, 1981). Some of these may arise through intent, described as "noble cause corruption," where the officers involved are confident that the suspect is guilty (Lindsay, 1994). However, many more biases can arise through more subtle effects. Wells and colleagues (Wells & Seelau, 1995; Wells, Seelau, Rydell & Luus, 1994) have made several recommendations for good practice, which we summarize.

First, it is critical that witnesses are aware that the culprit may not be in the lineup. Many witnesses assume that the culprit is in the lineup, and therefore the task is to choose which of the people in the lineup is the culprit, using what Wells calls the relative judgement heuristic. One method to assess whether the witness is doing this is to show them a suspect-absent, or "blank," lineup first. If the witness picks someone, then the value of any latter identification would be compromised. This procedure is costly with live lineups, but could easily be implemented with photo spreads and video lineups. However, if suspect-absent lineups were always shown first, witnesses might become aware of this and respond accordingly.

The second set of recommendations concern deciding who the foils should be. There has been much discussion and research about whether the foils should be chosen for similarity to the suspect or the description given by the witness at the original interview. The research (for example, Wells, Rydell & Seelau, 1993) shows that the "similar to description" approach is preferred. For the moment assume that the description is accurate and the initial interview gathered all details the witness could recall. For the lineup to add additional information, the witness will need to discriminate among people fitting the description. Suppose a description says that the culprit is a 6-foot tall male with brown curly hair, and the suspect meets this description but he has a large scar across his face. The foils should be chosen to fit the physical description, but not the scar. If the suspect is innocent, the scar should help as the witness should not remember it (providing the culprit did not have a similar scar which happened to be omitted in the description). If the suspect is guilty, being the sole person with a large facial scar should increase the likelihood of him being chosen. This relates to what Wells and colleagues call propitious heterogeneity. This means the foils and the suspect should match on the description but otherwise be as different as possible to maximize the additional information which can be gained from a lineup.

Because the initial description is not always accurate, and multiple witnesses can disagree, there are sometimes problems using just description similarity. Consider, for example, if the description does not match the suspect, so that in the example above the suspect was only 5'6". If the foils are all about 6', the suspect would stand out. If the witness is simply bad at height estimation, s/he may think that a 5'6" person is about 6' and choose this person solely because his height discriminates him from the others. For this reason Wells and colleagues recommend that the suspect does not "stand out" in the lineup.

Some of their recommendations focus more on procedural aspects. For example, that all lineups should be video recorded and that different lineups should be used for different witnesses. Another recommendation is that the person conducting the lineup should not know who the suspect is. One of Wells et al.'s more controversial recommendations is that witnesses should be asked how certain they are about their choice immediately after they have made an identification, even before they are told whether they have picked the suspect (see Wells & Bradfield, in press). This is despite there being frequently a low association between confidence and accuracy (Wells & Murray, 1984; but see Lindsay, Read & Sharma, in press). However, the association is strongest immediately after the identification and before other information has had the opportunity to distort confidence estimates and lower their predictive accuracy.

Several alternatives to the standard lineup have been proposed. One is a showup. This is where the police show the suspect to the witness without any foils. It is generally frowned upon as being overly suggestive, although the small amount of empirical research that exists which compares lineups and showups does not support this (Gonzalez, Ellsworth & Pembroke, 1993). Clearly further research is warranted.

Lindsay & Wells (1985) proposed having a sequential lineup, which is like a series of showups. The witness is shown the first potential culprit and is asked if the person is the culprit. If the witness says "yes" the procedure stops. If s/he says "no" then the next potential culprit is shown. Research has shown that the sequential lineup is a useful procedure for minimizing the use of the relative judgement heuristic and does not have any obvious drawbacks.

Credibility Assessment

How can we be sure that what witnesses tell us is an honest account of what they remember? As the Tracy Andrews case illustrates, some witnesses interviewed by the police subsequently turn out to be suspects. Are there any signs in the behavior of a witness which suggest that the person is lying? When witnesses describe events they provide a range of cues which are potential sources of information on credibility. Koehnken (1989) has classified these cues into behavioral, paralinguistic, physiological, and statement content.

Behavioral and paralinguistic cues have traditionally been thought to be a rich source of information for establishing whether a person is telling the truth. The rationale for this belief is that to be a convincing liar requires a person to maintain a façade of behavior characteristic of truth telling. Such simultaneous monitoring cannot be accomplished continuously and there will be "leakage": a liar may manage to maintain an even tone of voice but lose control of pitch. Accordingly, the seeker of truth must learn to detect such leakage (Ekman, 1985).

Research evidence suggests that the ability of members of the public to detect deception under experimental conditions rarely rises much above chance. If, for instance, volunteers view video sequences of people either telling the truth or lies about their likes and dislikes of persons or products, their detection accuracy is at chance or just above chance levels, but certainly not at a level which would be practically useful. Observers tend to show a "truth bias": they label more deceptive statements as true than vice versa (DePaulo, Stone & Lassiter, 1985).

Are children any more transparent than adults? Westcott, Davies & Clifford (1991) had children age 7–8 and 10–11 years old testify on camera about a school trip they had allegedly taken part in: half had attended while the remainder had merely seen a video of the trip. Overall accuracy at detecting those who had really been on the trip was 59%, but rates were better with the younger children: the most accurately detected group being 7–8 year old boys. Chahal & Cassidy (1995) replicated these findings and reported that parents were the most reliable judges and trained social workers did no better than students!

Are any professional groups more likely to be accurate than members of the public? Experimental studies of the lie detection skills of customs officers (Kraut & Poe, 1980) and police officers (Vrij & Winkel, 1993) suggest that in practice they do no better than the general public, but they make their decisions with greater confidence. It could be argued that the experimental task is not a realistic reflection of how officers go about detecting deception in reality. However, even when police officers were given a preliminary opportunity to view the target telling the truth and a prolonged opportunity to gauge the truthfulness or otherwise of the statement, performance was still at chance levels (Koehnken, 1987).

One reason for the poor performance may be that people just look for the wrong cues. Diary studies suggest that lying is a routine exercise in daily life (DePaulo & Kirkendol, 1989) and we may only be aware of the most blatant lies which are told to us and thus miss out on the tell tale signs. Studies suggest a mismatch between the behaviors which people believe characterize lying and the actual cues which research demonstrates are present in lying communications (Koehnken, 1989). In these circumstances it is not surprising that the human lie detector should be fallible.

Will a machine do any better? "Voice stress analyzers" are supposedly able to detect whether a person is lying from low frequency stress changes in the voice. Such machines can be used on recorded interviews or attached to telephones. However, existing research suggests that such devices are ineffective. People can show stress in their voice because they are lying, but also for a variety of other reasons, not least in response to the accusation they that they are telling lies (the "Othello" error, Ekman, 1989).

While the idea of telling whether you are being lied to on the phone is an attractive one, a practical device remains a dream. A much more widespread device for establishing truth is the lie detector or polygraph. This instrument simultaneously measures a person's respiration, blood pressure and galvanic skin response (perspiration). The device is widely used in the interrogation of suspects in the United States, Canada and Israel, though not in the United Kingdom or other parts of Europe. The effectiveness of the machine is dependant on how it is used. Two common questioning procedures are the control question technique and the guilty knowledge test.

The control question technique is the most widely used in the United States and involves comparing the physiological reaction of the accused to questions about the offense to control questions which are either innocuous (personal details) or are designed to arouse some emotion in even innocent persons ("Have you ever traveled on public transport without a ticket?"). The rationale is that while the innocent will show no systematic differences in reactance, the guilty will show an increased response on the offense-related questions. Laboratory tests employ a mock crime paradigm when, for instance, some subjects enter a room and "steal" cash from a drawer while others are merely told about it. Trained polygraph operators correctly identified 97% of the "guilty" persons, and only misclassified 7% of the innocent people as guilty (Raskin, 1989).

Most studies demonstrate a lie-bias in that more innocent people are labeled guilty than vice versa. There are limitations on the realism achievable with laboratory tests (Lykken, 1988) and field research paints a less optimistic picture. When output from actual cases of individuals who have been subsequently proven to be entirely innocent and those who are demonstrably guilty are compared, even highly trained operators working from the output alone classified only 52% of the truthful witnesses correctly (Horvath, 1984): they mislabeled 9% as guilty and returned 39% of the records as inconclusive (corresponding figures for the guilty were 65% correct, 4% wrong and 31% inconclusive).

The guilty knowledge test operates by measuring a suspect's reaction to items connected to the crime but not publicly known. If, say, a bloodied glove was found at the crime scene, the suspect will be asked about this item alongside other decoy items. If the suspect shows a specific physiological reaction to mention of the glove, this will be taken as a sign of guilt. It is a technique widely used in Israel and has the advantage of not displaying the strong lie-bias associated with the control question method (Elaad, 1990). However, such privileged information is not available on many crimes and there is always the danger that the suspect may have acquired the critical information through entirely innocent means. In the meantime, the search continues for new and even more foolproof measures of lie detection, such as examining evoked potentials (Iacono, 1995; Rosenfeld, 1995).

Controversy also surrounds the use of the final source of information, the verbal content of the statement. Statement validity analysis (SVA) has been used in Germany since 1954 as a semi-objective procedure for establishing the validity or otherwise of children's allegations of sexual abuse (Undeutsch, 1989). The central tenet of statement analysis is that there are differences in content and quality which differentiate a true statement from one which is fabricated. These relate to both the cognitive and motivational aspects of the statement. From a cognitive standpoint, a child who has experienced an event is likely to describe it in more detail, contain more irrelevancies, locate the event in a specific time and place, use reported speech and make reference to their own subjective experiences. As regards motivation, it is argued that the child who is lying would not, for instance, readily admit to doubts about their own testimony, make spontaneous corrections to their story, or admit to a lack of memory for aspects of the event. Transcripts of children's statements are scored according to the presence of such criteria.

There are a number of different lists of such criteria of which the criteria-based content analysis (CBCA) advocated by Raskin & Esplin (1991) is among the best known (see Table 26.1). These authors were among the first to conduct an objective assessment of the effectiveness of SVA. A clinician trained in the use of SVA made "blind" assessments of 40 transcripts of interviews with child complainants of sexual abuse, half of which were supported by other evidence and the remainder involved allegations which were classified as "doubtful" (e.g. child recounted, case dismissed, accused passed polygraph test).

When scored for the presence of CBCA criteria, there was no overlap in total scores between the two groups. Moreover, seven of the criteria were always present in the "confirmed" cases and a further seven were never present in the "doubtful" cases. Wells & Loftus (1991) have criticized the study, suggesting that perhaps the "doubtful" cases fell into that category precisely because the children's accounts lacked the realistic qualities which CBCA sets out to measure. There was thus an element of circularity about the whole exercise. However, more recent studies, which have used more precise criteria for allocation of statements have still found evidence for the effectiveness of some of the SVA criteria (Lamb et al., 1997).

However, SVA has some way to go before becoming a universally accepted legal tool. A recent review by Rudy & Brigham (1998) sets down some of the unanswered questions. They include:

- no clear threshold for the number of criteria a statement must fulfil to be accepted as true
- the strong correlation between the mental age of the child and the number of criteria present in a statement
- potential cross-cultural differences in the indicators of reliability for statements
- poor or doubtful reliability in scoring some of the criteria.

In Britain and the USA, the adversarial system of justice makes it difficult to introduce expert evidence on credibility into the criminal court. SVA, though a potentially promising development, currently falls well short of the criteria set down in *Daubert* for the admission of such evidence. For the foreseeable future, in matters of credibility, the jury will continue to decide.

SPECIAL TOPICS

The Reliability of Child Witnesses

The nine-year old girl in the Tracy Andrews case provided evidence in a murder trial. However, most children who give evidence in court will be appearing in cases of alleged sexual abuse. The last decade has seen a mushrooming of such

Table 26.1 Criteria-based content analysis. (Reprinted from Raskin & Esplin, Copyright 1991, with permission from Elsevier Science)

GENERAL CHARACTERISTICS

1. *Logical Structure* Is the statement coherent? Is the content logical? Do the different segments fit together? (Note: Peculiar or unique details or unexpected complications do not diminish logical structure.)
2. *Unstructured Production* Are descriptions unconstrained? Is the report somewhat unorganized? Are there digressions or spontaneous shifts of focus? Are some elements distributed throughout? (Note: This criterion requires that the account is logically consistent.)
3. *Quantity of Details* Are these specific descriptions of place or time? Are persons, objects, and events specifically described? (Note: Repetitions do not count.)

SPECIFIC CONTENTS

4. *Contextual Embedding* Are events placed in spatial and temporal context? Is the action connected to other incidental events, such as routine daily occurrences?
5. *Interactions* Are there reports of actions and reactions or conversations composed of a minimum of three elements involving at least the accused and the witness?
6. *Reproduction of Speech* Is speech or conversation during the incident reported in its original form? (Note: Unfamiliar terms or quotes are especially strong indicators, even when attributed to only one participant.)
7. *Unexpected Complications* Was there an unplanned interruption or an unexpected complication or difficulty during the sexual incident?
8. *Unusual Details* Are there details of persons, objects, or events that are unusual, yet meaningful in this context? (Note: Unusual details must be realistic.)
9. *Superfluous Details* Are peripheral details described in connection with the alleged sexual events that are not essential and do not contribute directly to the specific allegation? (Note: If a passage satisfies any of the specific criteria 4–18, it probably is not superfluous.)
10. *Accurately Reported Details Misunderstood* Did the child correctly describe an object or event but interpret it incorrectly?
11. *Related External Associations* Is there reference to a sexually-toned event or conversation of a sexual nature that is related in some way to the incident but is not part of the alleged sexual offenses?
12. *Subjective Experience* Did the child describe feelings or thoughts experienced at the time of the incident? (Note: This criterion is not satisfied when the witness responds to a direct question, unless the answer goes beyond the question.)
13. *Attribution of Accused's Mental State* Is there reference to the alleged perpetrator's feelings or thoughts during the incident? (Note: Descriptions of overt behavior do not qualify.)

MOTIVATION-RELATED CONTENTS

14. *Spontaneous Corrections or Additions* Were corrections offered or information added to material previously provided in the statement? (Note: Responses to direct questions do not qualify.)
15. *Admitting Lack of Memory or Knowledge* Did the child indicate lack of memory or knowledge of an aspect of the incident? (Note: In response to a direct question, the answer must go beyond "I don't know" or "I can't remember".)
16. *Raising Doubts About One's Own Testimony* Did the child express concern that some part of the statement seems incorrect or unbelievable? (Note: Merely asserting that one is telling the truth does not qualify.)
17. *Self-Deprecation* Did the child describe some aspect of his/her behavior related to the sexual incident as wrong or inappropriate?
18. *Pardoning the Accused* Did the child make excuses for or fail to blame the alleged perpetrator, minimize the seriousness of the acts, or fail to add to the allegation when the opportunity occurred?

allegations and a greater readiness of the police and the judiciary to bring such cases to court (Myers, 1997). This growth has inevitably revived the debate over the reliability of the evidence of juveniles: can children be accurate witnesses and how vulnerable are they to the suggestions of committed interviewers?

Early researchers had little doubt that children were thoroughly unreliable witnesses. In 1910, the Belgian psychologist Varendonck was consulted on a child murder case where the principle witnesses were aged 8 and 9 years. As part of his investigations he arranged for a class of 9-12 year olds to listen to a brief talk by a stranger. Later, the children were asked in which hand the man had held his hat: 17 said his right hand, 7 his left and only 3 correctly reported that he had no hat. Varendonck concluded, "Those who are in the habit of living with children do not attach the least value to their testimony because children cannot observe and because their suggestibility is inexhaustible" (Varendonck, 1911, cited in Goodman, 1984, p. 27). Varendonck used no adult controls who were asked the same leading questions to see what proportion also misreported the presence of the hat. There is an implicit assumption that adults are not vulnerable to suggestive questioning which has been shown to be wrong (see earlier discussion on postevent information). The view that children are a separate and inferior class of witness still permeates some legal textbooks (e.g. Heydon, 1984), but it is one which is increasingly challenged by contemporary researchers such as Gail Goodman.

Goodman was among the first to exploit naturally occurring stressors in children's lives as a source of data on the likely impact of abuse on children's memory. In one study (Goodman, Aman & Hirschman, 1987) children aged 3–4 and 5–6 years, attending a health clinic to receive inoculations, were questioned about their experiences. Both objective ("What color was the nurse's hair?") and leading questions ("The nurse had black hair didn't she?") were employed. Objective questions led to higher overall accuracy than leading questions and older children were more accurate in their answers than younger. Goodman asserted that questions dealing with "central" events (the actions of the nurse) were more accurately answered than those on "peripheral" events (the color and furnishings of the room). Moreover, suggestions of a kind which might be asked in an abuse investigation ("Did the person put anything in your mouth?") were in general rejected by children of all ages. When this same cohort were re-questioned a year later, children continued to reject the "abuse" questions (Goodman, Hirschman & Rudy, 1987). Goodman concluded that young children's memory was altogether more robust and resistant to suggestion than had been implied by earlier research, which had failed to use events grounded in the child's life and where the child was a participant rather than a passive witness. Children were more likely to omit details of body touch than to elaborate upon them in a spurious way (Saywitz, Goodman, Nicholas & Moan, 1991).

However, Goodman's more optimistic picture of the child witness was challenged by a number of high profile cases where apparently innocent adults had been convicted of sexual abuse on a child's word (e.g. Bruck & Ceci, 1995). In general, the child witnesses involved had not made spontaneous allegations, but rather, incriminating statements had emerged from investigative interviews. In a series of ingenious experiments, Stephen Ceci has demonstrated how witness motivation and over-zealous questioning can dramatically increase the rates of error in young children's statements.

In one study, children aged 3–6 years were interviewed about a brief visit from a stranger ("Sam Stone") to their nursery. When interviewed ten weeks later as to whether Stone had damaged a book or a teddy bear, 90% of even the youngest children accurately reported that he had not. However, if the visit was preceded by tales of Sam's clumsiness (negative stereotyping), the proportion of children claiming that Sam had damaged the playthings rose to 40% among the youngest children and this in turn increased to 70% if the visit was followed by a series of interviews in which damage was implied by the interviewer. Frequently, positive responding was accompanied by spontaneous elaborations and spurious detail which gave an aura of authenticity to the children's statements sufficient to convince unprepared audiences of experts of their truth (Leichtman & Ceci, 1995).

Ceci, Loftus, Leichtman & Bruck (1994) were able to demonstrate that such elaborations could be elicited under some circumstances by repeatedly questioning (see also Zaragoza & Mitchell, 1996). Children were asked repeatedly about a mixture of real and fictitious (getting their finger caught in a mouse trap and going to hospital to have the mouse trap removed) life events. When children were encouraged to imagine each event and were told that their parents had confirmed it had taken place, by the seventh iteration, some 32% of 6-year-olds were prepared to believe a non-existent event had occurred.

Ceci's work has been quoted as justifying renewed skepticism concerning the testimony of children in general and young children in particular. Yet it is open to the same criticism as Varendonck's, that adults may be vulnerable to similar pressures. Ceci's work compliments Goodman's in demonstrating that under neutral conditions, even very young children can be accurate witnesses to events. However, any child's statement must be judged by the context from which it is derived: interview procedures must be employed which avoid the dangers which his work has demonstrated. In England and Wales under the 1992 Criminal Justice Act, children who make an allegation of abuse are likely to be interviewed as soon as possible after the complaint by officers trained in the use of the "Memorandum" or stepwise interview and this will be videotaped. The videotape forms the basis for the prosecution's case and further interviewing is discouraged. By minimizing risks in this way, the rights of both the innocent adult and the abused child are most likely to be safeguarded.

Expert Scientific Testimony

Many court cases, both criminal and civil, require an understanding of science to reach a proper verdict. In these cases, scientific experts are often called to educate the court. In adversarial systems of justice, such as the US and UK, this can mean scientific experts for each side describing their own theory in an attempt to influence the judge and/or jury. Rules are necessary for deciding when expert testimony can be presented. Here we describe those used in the U.S.A. and how expert testimony on eyewitness research has developed. There are four basic prerequisites for deciding whether testimony can be accepted. We will go through these and their relevance to eyewitness testimony. Then we will describe a recent court case and its importance for deciding whether testimony can be accepted.

The first prerequisite for admitting expert testimony is that there is a need for education. This was one of the original hurdles for accepting expert testimony on eyewitness memory. Some judges argued that what psychologists could tell them about memory was just common sense. This is not a surprising attitude given that it was voiced by prominent memory experts also (Neisser, 1978). To counter this, general population surveys were conducted which demonstrated that to the lay person much is unknown and other beliefs are incorrect (see, for example, Deffenbacher & Loftus, 1982).

The second prerequisite is that the testimony will not unduly bias the jury or take too much of the court's time. Judges often feel that if the testimony is on the reliability of a particular minutia of evidence which itself has only minor probative significance, then this will be unfair. The time constraint is also important given the backlog in most court systems and the mounting costs associated with each additional day that a trial takes.

The third criterion is that the person testifying is in fact an expert. For scientific testimony this is usually satisfied by publications, grants/contracts, degrees and membership of societies and committees.

The most important – though not the only – prerequisite for accepting testimony is whether the evidence given is true. This seems obvious, but how is it decided? How is a judge supposed to decide whether a particular theory is accurate? Most judges and lawyers are not specifically trained in science. According to Moenssens, Inbau & Starrs (1986, p. 7) "lawyers as a group evidence an appalling degree of scientific illiteracy . . . [and] many judges simply do not understand evidence based on scientific principles."

In the USA, for most of this century, judges used the *Frye* or general acceptance test to assess whether a theory is valid. The critical passage in that judgment is:

> Just when a scientific principle or discovery crosses the line between the experimental and demonstrable stages is difficult to define. Somewhere in this twilight zone the evidential force of the principle must be recognized, . . . [it] must be sufficiently established to have gained general acceptance in the particular field in which it belongs. (*Frye v. United States*, 1923, p. 1014)

Thus, if a theory was "generally accepted" by one's colleagues, then it was assumed true. The judge in effect is using the relevant scientific community to decide the worth of the testimony, rather than having to assess the validity directly. Of course, examples exist where generally accepted theories are shown to be wrong and where unaccepted theories ultimately prove their worth. When Einstein first proposed his theory of general relativity it had not gained general acceptance and therefore would have been excluded. Of course new theories which do not gain acceptance, like the "discovery" of cold fusion in the late 1980s, are also excluded. This conservatism is valuable since "for every Einstein there are hundreds of Ponses and Fleishmanses" (Faigman, 1995, p. 969).

One problem with the *Frye* test occurs if opposing testimony comes from two different communities, and within each community there is agreement, but disagreement exists between the communities. In the next section, on recovered/false memories, the communities of mental health professionals and experimental psychologists have been shown to disagree.

There is also the question of what "general acceptance" means. While there were some courts accepting expert eyewitness testimony in the 1970s (for history of the acceptance of expert eyewitness testimony, see Loftus, 1986), it was not until the 1980s that it was more commonplace in the USA. However, even now it is not universally accepted either by the courts or by some cognitive psychologists. While a survey by Kassin et al. (1989) showed that many topics within eyewitness testimony had reached "general acceptance" in the scientific community, there was still some dissent. McCloskey & Zaragoza (1985, p. 387) claimed that "situations involving eyewitnesses are essentially guesswork and as such should have no place in scientific expert testimony." Egeth & McCloskey (1984, p. 283) felt a different standard for evidence was necessary. They suggested it should be "similar to the one adopted by the Food and Drug Administration in its assessment of drugs: We think expert testimony should be offered only if it clearly is 'safe and effective'" (p. 283). While there were clearly problems with the *Frye* test, it does not seem the place of psychologists to advise the courts on rules on the admissibility of evidence.

In 1993, the Justices of the US Supreme Court in 1993 did change the admissibility rules. There had been a series of cases against Merrell Dow Pharmaceuticals on whether Bendectin caused birth defects. Particularly when a jury decided, the battling of experts using different methods caused confusion (Sanders, 1993, on the Pre-Daubert Bendectin cases). In 1993, in *Daubert v. Merrell Dow Pharmaceuticals*, the court produced what is now called the validity test. For expert testimony to be admitted four criteria should be considered. The testimony does not have to satisfy each of these.

1. The theory must be falsifiable and attempts must have been made to falsify it. The court cites Popper's philosophy.
2. The error rate should be known. For example, beyond knowing that people are better at recognizing people of their own race, the court would want to know how much better they are. While there are likely to be difficulties estimating effect sizes across contexts for many psychological phenomena, examining the size of effects goes along with the advice of the APA working party on statistical inference.
3. The research should be in peer reviewed scientific journals. Judges are also allowed to discriminate among journals. This, like the *Frye* test, is allowing scientists in the relevant community to decide the validity and scientific rigor of a finding. Of course, this will only be a handful of reviewers and editors for any given paper. These reviewers and editors are likely, however, to be particularly knowledgeable and respected in their scientific communities.
4. The theory should be generally accepted. However, unlike *Frye*, this is only one of four criteria, and is neither necessary nor sufficient for admissibility.

With *Daubert*, judges are required to understand more about science than under *Frye*. This does not mean judges should become experts in every scientific discipline, but that they should be good "consumers" of science. Faigman (1995) concludes that much research on eyewitness memory satisfies these four *Daubert* criteria. He contrasts this with the research on recovered memories which he claims fails to meet these scientific standards. We now consider some legal aspects of this debate.

Recovered and False Memories

As discussed above, from the mid-1970s to the present, many US courts and those in some other countries have accepted expert testimony on the unreliability of human memory. There was a growing awareness that memories are not unblemished accounts of reality. Another kind of memory testimony made its first appearance in a courtroom in 1990. It was argued that a different kind of memory existed which was accurate although it remained undetected for decades (Terr, 1994).

In 1969 and days before her ninth birthday, Susan Nason disappeared. Her body was later found. She had been brutally murdered. Eileen Lipsker (née Franklin) was a friend of Susan's at the time and was presumably quite distraught by her friend's tragic death. In fact, their entire town would have been affected both by the death and that the killer remained at large. Over twenty years later Eileen began recovering memories of Susan's death. She eventually came to believe that her father, George Franklin, committed the atrocity. While there is some dispute about the circumstances in which these images emerged (Maclean, 1993; see also Loftus, 1993; Loftus & Ketchum, 1994; Ofshe & Watters, 1994; Terr, 1994), the result was that the police arrested George Franklin in November 1989. Lenore Terr testified for the prosecution, arguing that Eileen's memory was accurate and that much of her childhood had been "repressed." Based on these memories, in November 1990 George Franklin was found guilty of murder and in January 1991 sentenced to life. After spending six years in prison, US District Judge Lowell Jensen ordered a retrial. The prosecution dropped the charges in July 1996, largely for two reasons:

1. Eileen's sister said that Eileen had been hypnotized before recovering the memories – memories brought about during or after hypnosis are generally regarded as inadmissible, with a few exceptions (for example, *Rock v. Arkansas*, 1987).
2. Eileen accused George Franklin of another murder, which DNA tests showed he did not commit (for discussion of DNA evidence, see Connors et al., 1996).

Hundreds of cases involving recovered memories have gone to court since the Franklin case. Most have dealt with memories of child sexual abuse which have surfaced in the context of therapy or counseling. The debate about the veracity of these memories has become the psychology debate of the 1990s. Numerous journal articles, journal special issues, books and conferences have been devoted to the topic (for example, Conway, 1997; Lindsay & Read, 1994; Read & Lindsay, 1997; Schacter, 1995). Here we deal just with two aspects of this situation that differentiate recovered memory cases from other eyewitness testimony situations: statute of limitations and patient–client privilege.

The statute of limitations refers to the amount of time after the event that a person has to begin legal action. Some crimes, like murder, have no statute of limitations so that the Nason case could still be tried if another suspect is found. However, with child sexual abuse there are statutes of limitations in the US states and in many countries in Europe. These limit the time since the event (or the age of majority of the alleged victim) that a person can be charged (or that civil proceedings can be brought). There are exceptions to this. If a surgeon leaves an instrument in your stomach, you might not notice it until years later when you again have surgery. The courts have ruled that this "delayed discovery" should not prevent legal action. Many courts have argued that someone recovering a memory is in an analogous situation (see Pope & Brown, 1996, appendix B, for a list of the state decisions). Some states have not and others are re-evaluating their previous decisions. For example, the Maryland Court of Appeals (*Doe et al. v. Maskell et al.*, 1996) found insufficient evidence to say repression was not different from forgetting, and therefore the delayed discovery doctrine does not apply.

It is important to realize that the statute of limitations exists for several reasons. One is that as time increases most forms of evidence deteriorate. This makes it difficult for the defendant to be represented. Therefore, the delayed discovery doctrine was, before the 1990s, usually only invoked in exceptional circumstances. In recovered memory cases, where the alleged abuse may have happened decades before, there is unlikely to be any physical evidence remaining which can confirm or disconfirm the abuse. All that often exists is one person's recovered memories of abuse versus another person's belief that these alleged events never happened.

As said before, the court cases involving recovered memories tend to also involve therapy. Several psychology and psychiatry societies have warned their members against using so called "recovered memory" techniques (including hypnosis, "truth" drugs, guided imagery, etc.) because these can create false memories. In recovered memory cases the accused often argues that the memory was created in therapy sessions. Restricting access to the therapist's notes makes it extremely difficult for the accused to put forward the case of implantation (Loftus, Paddock & Guernsey, 1996). When the accused is a defendant in a criminal trial, this denies the defendant due process. In many US states there is some form of patient–client privilege. While it is often not absolute, judges can be reluctant to use their powers to force therapists to testify or to present their case notes to the court. In the UK there is no patient–client privilege, but still courts seldom force therapists to break the confidentiality pledge that many psychotherapists feel is critical for therapeutic success. Many worry that defense lawyers would trawl through these notes, bringing up aspects of no probative value and discussing them in court, thus needlessly prolonging the trial. Procedures like *in camera* reading, where the court looks for relevant passages, could maintain a satisfactory balance of the defendant's right to due process and the confidentiality of the patient–client relationship (Loftus et al., 1996).

There are several other types of cases involving recovered memories that have come to court. A growing number are retractor cases. Retractors are people who recover memories and then later retract them. For example, Patricia Burgess believed that she had multiple personality disorder (MPD) (now called dissociative identity disorder) and was royalty in a Satanic cult. She had gone on television to say how Dr Bennett Braun had helped her to survive. After leaving therapy (see Pendergrast, 1996, for description of this case), she came to realize that she was not part of a Satanic cult. She sued Dr Braun and the hospital where he worked. In late 1997 she received a settlement of over $10 million. Another type involves "third party" cases. The most famous of these is of Gary Ramona who successfully sued his daughter's therapist for implanting memories (see Johnston, 1997). Finally, there have also been criminal charges brought against some mental health professionals. In late 1997, Dr Judith Peterson and some of her colleagues were indicted on 60 criminal counts (59 fraud and one for conspiracy) in relation to their dissociative disorder unit (for description of the case, see Pendergrast, 1996).

While recovered memory cases involve memory of a crime, the debate about recovered memories has often moved onto more political issues than are discussed with regards to other eyewitness testimony. Child sexual abuse is a heinous crime. While the reasons for it, the treatment of it, its tolerance in some cultures, and many other aspects about it are intertangled in political, cultural and societal issues, the evidential status of these recollections should be a debate about science and memory.

CONCLUSION

Eyewitness testimony has both a substantial impact on jury decision making and for guiding police investigations. In the Tracy Andrews case, eyewitness testimony changed her from a bereaved victim to a suspect in the police investigation, and was part of the evidence that led to her conviction. For many cases eyewitness testimony is the only evidence available. Without it, numerous crimes would be unsolvable. If courts gave a blanket exclusion to memory testimony this would be tantamount to legalizing these crimes and of much harm to society. However, as Connors et al.'s (1996) report demonstrates, numerous people have been falsely incarcerated because of eyewitness testimony errors.

Eyewitness research, on both adults and children, has been conducted to identify particular situations in which the testimony is less reliable and to discover ways of gathering information that maximize reliability. Much of the estimator variable research examines the first of these. The results can be used so that police investigators, judges and jurors can assess the probative value of an identification or description. Research on system variables tends to focus on ways of maximizing the reliability of testimony. Lineup construction and interviewing techniques are prime examples of this, where researchers try to find techniques that increase the amount of accurate information reported while reducing the chance of inaccurate information being reported. The research we describe has made considerable progress in achieving both these goals, although clearly there is much scope for refining experimental procedures and acheiving greater realism while retaining ethical constraints.

REFERENCES

Adams-Price, C. (1992). Eyewitness memory and aging: predictors of accuracy in recall and person recognition. *Psychology and Aging*, 7, 602–8.

Ayers, M. S. & Reder, L. M. (1998). A theoretical review of the misinformation effect: predictions from an activation-based memory model. *Psychonomic Bulletin & Review*, 5, 1–21.

Bartol, C. R. & Bartol, A. M. (1987). History of forensic psychology. In I. B. Weiner & A. K. Hess (Eds), *Handbook of Forensic Psychology* (pp. 3–21). New York: Wiley.

Bekerian, D. A. & Dennett, J. L. (1993). The cognitive interview: reviving the issues. *Applied Cognitive Psychology*, 7, 275–98.

Bond, R. & Smith, P. (1996). Culture and conformity: a meta-analysis of studies using Asch's (1952b, 1956) line judgement task. *Psychological Bulletin*, 119, 111–37.

Bower, G. H. (1981). Mood and memory. *American Psychologist*, 36, 129–48.

Brainerd, C. J. & Reyna, V. F. (in press). Fuzzy-trace theory and children's false memories. *Journal of Experimental Child Psychology*.

Brennan, M. & Brennan R. (1994). *Cleartalk: Police Responding to Intellectual Disability*. Wagga Wagga, NSW: School of Education, Charles Sturt University.

Brigham, J. C. & Malpass, R. S. (1985). The role of experience and contact in the recognition of faces of own-race and other-race persons. *Journal of Social Issues*, 41, 139–55.

Brigham, J. C. & Ready, D. J. (1985). Own-race bias in lineup construction. *Law and Human Behavior*, 9, 415–24.

Brown, R. & Kulik, J. (1977). Flashbulb memories. *Cognition*, 5, 73–99.

Bruck, M. & Ceci, S. J. (1995). Amicus brief for the case of *State of New Jersey versus Margaret Kelly Michaels* presented by a committee of concerned social scientists. *Psychology, Public Policy and Law*, 1, 272–322.

Bull, R. (1995). Good practice for video recorded interviews with child witnesses for use in criminal proceedings. In G. Davies, S. Lloyd-Bostock, M. McMurran & C. Wilson (Eds), *Psychology, Law and Criminal Justice: International Developments in Research and Practice* (pp. 100–17). Berlin: De Gruyter.

Burt, C. D. B. & Popple, J. S. (1996). Effects of implied action speed on estimation of event duration. *Applied Cognitive Psychology*, 10, 53–63.

Ceci, S. J. & Bruck, M. (1995). *Jeopardy in the Courtroom*. Washington DC: American Psychological Association.

Ceci, S. J., Loftus, E. F., Leichtman, M. & Bruck, M. (1994). The role of source misattributions in the creation of false beliefs among preschoolers. *International Journal of Clinical and Experimental Hypnosis*, 62, 304–20.

Chahal, K. & Cassidy, T. (1995). Deception and its detection in children: a study of adult accuracy. *Psychology, Crime and the Law*, 1, 237–45.

Chaudhury, V. (1997, 30 July). Road rage attack that never was. *Guardian*, p. 8.

Chiroro, P. & Valentine, T. (1995). An investigation of the contact hypothesis of the own-race bias in face recognition. *Quarterly Journal of Experimental Psychology: A (Human Experimental Psychology)*, 48, 879–94.

Christianson, S.-Å. (1992b). Emotional memories in laboratory studies versus real-life studies: do they compare? In M. A. Conway, D. C. Rubin, H. Spinnler & W. A. Wagenaar (Eds), *Theoretical Perspectives on Autobiographical Memory* (pp. 339–52). Netherlands: Kluwer Academic Publishers.

Christianson, S.-Å. (1992a). Emotional stress and eyewitness memory: a critical review. *Psychological Bulletin*, 112, 284–309.
Christianson, S.-Å. & Hubinette, B. (1993). Hands up: a study of witnesses emotional reactions and memories associated with bank robberies. *Applied Cognitive Psychology*, 7, 365–79.
Christianson, S.-Å., Loftus, E. F., Hoffman, H. & Loftus, G. R. (1991). Eye fixations and memory for emotional events. *Journal of Experimental Psychology: Learning, Memory and Cognition*, 17, 693–701.
Connors, E., Lundregan, T., Miller, N. & McEwen, T. (1996). Convicted by juries, exonerated by science: case studies in the use of DNA evidence to establish innocence after trial. NIH Research Report: US Department of Justice.
Conway, M. A. (Ed.) (1997). *Recovered Memories and False Memories*. Oxford: Oxford University Press.
Cutler, B. L., Berman, G. L., Penrod, S. & Fisher, R. P. (1994). Conceptual, practical, and empirical issues associated with eyewitness identification test media. In D. F. Ross, J. D. Read & M. P. Toglia (Eds), *Adult Eyewitness Testimony: Current Trends and Developments* (pp. 163–81). Cambridge, UK: Cambridge University Press.
Daubert v. Merrell Dow Pharmaceuticals, Inc., 113 S CT. 2786. (1993).
Davies, G. M. (1988). Faces and places: laboratory research on context in face recognition. In G. M. Davies & D. M. Thomson (Eds), *Memory in Context: Context in Memory* (pp. 35–54). Chichester: John Wiley.
Davies, G. M. (1993). Witnessing events. In G. M. Davies & R. H. Logie (Eds), *Memory in Everyday Life* (pp. 367–401). Amsterdam: North Holland.
Davies, G. M., Kurvink, A., Mitchell, R. & Robertson, N. (1996). Memory for cars and their drivers: a test of the interest hypothesis. In D. J. Herrmann, C. McEvoy, C. Hertzog, P. Hertel & M. K. Johnson (Eds), *Basic and Applied Memory Research: Practical Applications* (Vol. 2). New Jersey: Lawrence Erlbaum.
Davies, G. M. & Robertson, N. (1993). Recognition memory for automobiles: a developmental study. *Bulletin of the Psychonomic Society*, 31, 103–6.
Davies, G. M. & Wilson, C. (1997). Implementation of the *Memorandum*: an overview. In H. Westcott & J. Jones (Eds), *Perspectives on the 'Memorandum'* (pp. 1–12). Aldershot, Hants: Arena.
Deffenbacher, K. A. & Loftus, E. F. (1982). Do jurors share a common understanding concerning eyewitness behavior? *Law and Human Behavior*, 6, 15–30.
DePaulo, B. & Kirkendol, S. E. (1989). The motivational impairment effect in the communication of deception. In J. C. Yuille (Ed.), *Credibility Assessment* (pp. 51–70). Dordrecht, The Netherlands: Kluwer.
DePaulo, B. M., Stone, J. I. & Lassiter, G. D. (1985). Deceiving and detecting deceit. In B. R. Schlenker (Ed.), *The Self in Social Life* (pp. 320–70). New York: McGraw-Hill.
Doe v. Maskell, 679 A.2d 1087 (Md., 1996), cert denied 117 S.Ct. 770 (1997).
Easterbrook, J. A. (1959). The effect of emotion on cue utilization and the organization of behavior. *Psychological Review*, 66, 249–80.
Egeth, H. E. & McCloskey, M. (1984). The jury is still out: a reply. *American Psychologist*, 39, 1068–9.
Ekman, P. (1985). *Telling lies: Clues to Deceit in the Marketplace, Politics and Marriage*. New York: Norton.
Ekman, P. (1989). Why lies fail and what behaviours betray a lie. In J. C. Yuille (Ed.), *Credibility Assessment* (pp. 71–82). Dordrecht, The Netherlands: Kluwer.
Elaad, E. (1990). Detection of guilty knowledge in real-life criminal investigations. *Journal of Applied Psychology*, 75, 521–9.
Ellison, K. W. & Buckout, R. (1981). *Psychology and Criminal Justice*. New York: Harper and Row.
Erdelyi, M. (1984). The recovery of unconscious (inaccessible) memories: laboratory studies of hypermnesia. In G. Bower (Ed.), *The Psychology of Learning and Motivation* (vol. 18) (pp. 95–127). New York: Academic Press.
Faigman, D. L. (1995). The evidentiary status of social science under Daubert: is it

"scientific", "technical", or "other" knowledge? *Psychology, Public Policy, and Law*, 1, 960–79.

Feingold, G. A. (1914). The influence of environment on the identification of persons and things. *Journal of Criminal Law and Police Science*, 5, 39–41.

Fisher, R. P. & Geiselman, R. E. (1992). *Memory-enhancing Techniques for Investigative Interviewing: the Cognitive Interview*. Springfield, IL: C. C. Thomas.

Fisher, R. P., Geiselman, R. E. & Amador, M. (1989). Field test of the cognitive interview: enhancing the recollections of actual victims and witnesses of crime. *Journal of Applied Psychology*, 74, 722–7.

Fisher, R. P., Geiselman, R. P., Raymond, D. S., Jurkevich, L. M. & Warhaftig, M. L. (1987). Enhancing eyewitness memory: refining the cognitive interview. *Journal of Police Science and Administration*, 15, 291–7.

Frye v. United States 293 F.1013 (D.C. Cir. 1923).

Geiselman, R. E. (1988). Improving eyewitness memory through mental reinstatement of context. In G. M. Davies & D. M. Thomson (Eds), *Memory in Context: Context in Memory* (pp. 245–66). Chichester: John Wiley.

Geiselman, R. E., Fisher, R. P., MacKinnon, D. P. & Holland, H. L. (1985). Eyewitness memory enhancement in the police interview: cognitive retrieval mnemonics versus hypnosis. *Journal of Applied Psychology*, 70, 401–12.

George, R. C. & Clifford, B. R. (1995). The cognitive interview – Does it work? In G. Davies, S. Lloyd-Bostock, M. McMurran & C. Wilson (Eds), *Psychology, Law and Criminal Justice; International Developments in Research and Practice* (pp. 146–56). Berlin: De Gruyter.

Giuliano, G. (1996). Transporting Los Angeles. In M. J. Dear, H. E. Schockman & G. Hise (Eds), *Rethinking Los Angeles* (pp. 231–47). Thousand Oaks, CA: Sage Publications.

Gonzalez, R., Ellsworth, P. C. & Pembroke, M. (1993). Response biases in lineups and showups. *Journal of Personality and Social Psychology*, 64, 525–37.

Goodman, G. S. (1984). Children's testimony in historical perspective. *Journal of Social Issues*, 40, 9–31.

Goodman, G. S., Aman, C. J. & Hirschman, J. (1987). Child sexual and physical abuse: children's testimony. In S. J. Ceci, M. P. Toglia & D. F. Ross (Eds), *Children's Eyewitness Memory* (pp. 1–23). New York: Springer Verlag.

Goodman, G. S., Hirschman, J. & Rudy, L. (1987). *Children's Testimony: Research and Policy Implications*. Paper presented at the Society for Research on Child Development, Baltimore, MD.

Grantham, S. (1989). *MotorFit*. London: Home Office Police Research Group.

Heydon, J. (1984). *Evidence, Cases and Materials*. London: Butterworth.

Home Office and the Department of Health (1992). *Memorandum of Good Practice on Video Recorded Interviews with Child Witnesses for Criminal Proceedings*. London: Her Majesty's Stationery Office.

Horvath, F. (1984). Detecting deception in eyewitness cases: problems and prospects in the use of polygraph. In G. L. Wells & E. F. Loftus (Eds), *Eyewitness Testimony: Psychological Perspectives* (pp. 214–55). Cambridge: Cambridge University Press.

Hyman, I. E., Husband, T. H. & Billings, F. J. (1995). False memories of childhood experiences. *Applied Cognitive Psychology*, 9, 181–97.

Iacono, W. G. (1995). Offender testimony: detection of deception and guilty knowledge. In N. Brewer & C. Wilson (Eds), *Psychology and Policing* (pp. 155–71). Hillsdale, NJ: Erlbaum.

Johnston, M. (1997). *Spectral Evidence. The Ramona Case: Incest, Memory and Truth on Trial in Napa Valley*. Boston, MA: Houghton Mifflin.

Kassin, S. M., Ellsworth, P. C. & Smith, V. L. (1989). The general acceptance of psychological research on eyewitness testimony: a survey of the experts. *American Psychologist*, 44, 1089–98.

Koehnken, G. (1987). Training police officers to detect deceptive eyewitness statements. *Social Behaviour*, 2, 1–17.

Koehnken, G. (1989). Behavioural correlates of statement credibility: theories, paradigms and results. In H. Wegener, F. Losel & H. Jochen (Eds), *Criminal Behaviour and the Justice System: Psychological Perspectives* (pp. 271–89). New York: Springer.

Koehnken, G., Milne, R., Memon, A. & Bull, R. (in press). A metaanalysis of the effects of the cognitive interview. *Psychology, Crime and the Law*.

Koehnken, G., Schimmossek, E., Aschermann, E. & Hofer, E. (1995). The cognitive interview and the assessment of credibility of adults' statements. *Journal of Applied Psychology*, 80, 671–84.

Kraut, R. E. & Poe, D. (1980). Behavioural roots of person perception: the deception judgements of custom inspectors and laymen. *Journal of Personality and Social Psychology*, 39, 784–98.

Lamb, M. E., Sternberg, K. J., Esplin, P. W., Hershkowitz, I., Orbach, Y. & Hovav, M. (1997). Criterion-based content analysis: a field validation study. *Child Abuse and Neglect*, 21, 255–61.

Lee, T. & Geiselman, R. E. (1994). Recall of perpetrator height as a function of eyewitness and perpetrator ethnicity. *Psychology, Crime & Law*, 1, 11–19.

Leichtman, M. D. & Ceci, S. J. (1995). The effects of stereotypes and suggestions on preschoolers' reports. *Developmental Psychology*, 31, 568–78.

Lindsay, D. S. & Read, J. D. (1994). Psychotherapy and memories of childhood sexual abuse: a cognitive perspective. *Applied Cognitive Psychology*, 8, 281–338. See also the replies.

Lindsay, D. S., Read, J. D. & Sharma, K. (in press). Accuracy and confidence in person identification: the relationship is strong when witnessing conditions vary widely. *Psychological Science*.

Lindsay, R. C. L. (1994). Biased lineups: where do they come from? In D. F. Ross, J. D. Read & M. P. Toglia (Eds), *Adult Eyewitness Testimony: Current Trends and Developments* (pp. 182–200). Cambridge: Cambridge University Press.

Lindsay, R. C. L. & Wells, G. L. (1985). Improving eyewitness identifications from lineups: simultaneous versus sequential lineup presentation. *Journal of Applied Psychology*, 70, 556–64.

Loftus. E. F. (1986). Ten years in the life of an expert witness. *Law and Human Behavior*, 10, 241–63.

Loftus, E. F. (1993). The reality of repressed memories. *American Psychologist*, 48, 518–37.

Loftus, E. F. & Ketcham, K. (1991). *Witness for the Defense: the Accused, the Eyewitness, and the Expert who Puts Memory on Trial*. New York: St Martin's Press.

Loftus, E. F. & Ketcham, K. (1994). *The Myth of Repressed Memory: False Memories and Allegations of Sexual Abuse*. New York: Griffin.

Loftus, E. F., Loftus, G. R. & Messo, J. (1987). Some facts about weapon focus. *Law and Human Behavior*, 11, 55–62.

Loftus, E. F., Miller, D. G. & Burns, H. J. (1978). Semantic integration of verbal information into a visual memory. *Journal of Experimental Psychology: Human Learning and Memory*, 4, 19–31.

Loftus, E. F., Paddock, J. R. & Guernsey, T. F. (1996). Patient–psychotherapist privilege: access to clinical records in the tangled web of repressed memory litigation. *University of Richmond Law Review*, 30, 109–54.

Loftus, E. F. & Palmer, J. C. (1974). Reconstruction of automobile destruction: an example of the interaction between language and memory. *Journal of Verbal Learning and Verbal Behavior*, 13, 585–9.

Loftus, E. F. & Pickrell, J. E. (1995). The formation of false memories. *Psychiatric Annals*, 25, 720–5.

Lykken, D. T. (1988). The case against polygraph testing. In A. Gale (Ed.), *The Polygraph: Lies, Truth and Science* (pp. 111–25). London: Sage.

Lynn, S. J., Myers, B. & Malinoski, P. (1997). Hypnosis, pseudomemories and clinical guidelines: a sociolinguistic perspective. In J. D. Read & D. S. Lindsay (Eds),

Recollections of Trauma: Scientific Evidence and Clinical Practice (pp. 305–36). New York: Plenum Press.

Maclean, H. (1993). *Once Upon a Time*. New York: HarperCollins.

MacLeod, M. D., Frowley, J. N. & Sheperd, J. W. (1994). Whole body information: its relevance to eyewitnesses. In D. F. Ross, J. D. Read & M. P. Toglia (Eds), *Adult Eyewitness Testimony: Current Trends and Developments* (pp. 125–43). Cambridge: Cambridge University Press.

Marchant, R. & Page, M. (1997). The Memorandum and disabled children. In H. Westcott & J. Jones (Eds), *Perspectives on the 'Memorandum'* (pp. 67–79). Aldershot: Arena.

McCloskey, M. & Zaragoza, M. (1985). Misleading postevent information and memory for events: arguments and evidence against memory impairment hypotheses. *Journal of Experimental Psychology: General*, 114, 1–16.

McKelvie, S. J., Standing, L., St. Jean, D. & Law, J. (1993). Gender differences in recognition memory for faces and cars: evidence for the interest hypothesis. *Bulletin of the Psychonomic Society*, 31, 447–8.

Memon, A. & Stevenage, S. (1996). Interviewing witnesses: what works and what doesn't? *Psycholoquy*, 96.7.06.witness-memory.1.memon.

Memon, A., Wark, L., Holley, A., Bull, R. & Koehnken, G. (1994). Towards understanding the effects of interviewer training in evaluating the cognitive interview. *Applied Cognitive Psychology*, 8, 641–59.

Memon, A., Wark, L., Holley, A., Bull, R. & Koehnken, G. (1997). Eyewitness performance in cognitive and structured interviews. *Memory*, 5, 639–55.

Milne, R., Clare, I. & Bull, R. (1996). How effective is the cognitive interview as an investigative tool for use with adults with mild intellectual disabilities (mental retardation)? Poster presented at the American Psychology–Law Society Conference, Hilton Head, SC, March.

Mitchell, K., Livosky, M. & Mather, M. (1998). The weapon focus effect revisited: the role of novelty. *Legal and Criminological Psychology*, 3, 287–303.

Moenssens, A. A., Inbau, F. E. & Starrs, J. E. (1986). *Scientific Evidence in Criminal Cases* (3rd edn). New York: Foundation Press.

Myers, J. E. B. (1997). *Evidence in Child Abuse and Neglect Cases* (3rd edn). New York: John Wiley.

Neisser, U. (1978). Memory: what are the important questions? In M. M. Gruneberg, P. E. Morris & R. N. Sykes (Eds), *Practical Aspects of Memory* (pp. 3–24). London: Academic Press.

Neisser, U. (1982). Snapshots or benchmarks? In Neisser, U. (Ed.), *Memory Observed: Remembering in Natural Contexts* (pp. 43–8). San Francisco: Freeman.

Ofshe, R. & Watters, E. (1994). *Making Monsters: False Memories, Psychotherapy, and Sexual Hysteria*. New York: Scribner.

Pendergrast, M. (1996). *Victims of Memory: Incest, Accusations and Shattered Lives* (UK edition). London: HarperCollins.

Penrod, S. & Cutler, B. (1995). Witness confidence and witness accuracy: assessing their forensic relation. *Psychology, Public Policy and Law*, 1, 817–45.

Pope, K. S. & Brown, L. S. (1996). *Recovered Memories of Abuse: Assessment, Therapy, Forensics*. Washington, DC: American Psychological Association Press.

Powers, P. A., Andriks, J. L. & Loftus, E. F. (1979). Eyewitness accounts of males and females. *Journal of Applied Psychology*, 64, 339–47.

Raskin, D. C. (1989). Polygraph techniques for the detection of deception. In D. C. Raskin (Ed.), *Psychological Methods in the Detection of Criminal Investigation and Evidence* (pp. 247–95). New York: Springer-Verlag.

Raskin, D. C. & Esplin, P. W. (1991). Statement validity assessment: interview procedures and content analysis of children's statements of sexual abuse. *Behavioural Assessment*, 13, 265–91.

Read, J. D. & Lindsay, D. S. (Eds) (1997). *Recollections of Trauma: Scientific Evidence and Clinical Practice*. London: Plenum Press.

Reiser, M. (1989). Investigative hypnosis. In D. Raskin (Ed.), *Psychological Methods in Criminal Investigation and Evidence* (pp. 151–90). New York: Springer.

Rock v. Arkansas (1987). 483 US 44, 97 L Ed 2d 37, 107 S. Ct 2704.

Rosenfeld, J. P. (1995). Alternative views of Bashore and Rapp's (1993) alternatives to traditional polyography: a critique. *Psychological Bulletin*, 117, 159–66.

Rudy, C. L. & Brigham, J. C. (1998). The usefulness of the criteria-based content analysis technique in distinguishing between truthful and fabricated allegations: a critical review. *Psychology, Public Policy and Law*, 3, 705–37.

Sanders, J. (1993). From science to evidence: the testimony on causation in the Bendectin cases. *Stanford Law Review*, 46, 1–86.

Saywitz, K., Geiselman, R. E. & Bornstein, G. K. (1992). Effects of the cognitive interview and practice on children's recall performance. *Journal of Applied Psychology*, 77, 744–56.

Saywitz, K., Goodman, G. S., Nicholas, E. & Moan, S. (1991). Children's memories of physical examinations involving genital touch: implications for reports of child sexual abuse. *Journal of Consulting and Clinical Psychology*, 59, 682–91.

Schacter, D. L. (Ed.) (1995). *Memory Distortion: How Minds, Brains and Societies Reconstruct the Past*. Cambridge, MA: Harvard University Press.

Schneider, D. M. & Watkins, M. J. (1996). Response conformity in recognition testing. *Psychonomic Bulletin & Review*, 3, 481–5.

Shaw, J. I. & Skolnick, P. (1994). Sex-differences, weapon focus, and eyewitness reliability. *Journal of Social Psychology*, 134, 413–20.

Sporer, S. L., Penrod, S., Read, D. & Cutler, B. (1995). Choosing, confidence, and accuracy: a metaanalysis of the confidence–accuracy relation in eyewitness identification studies. *Psychological Bulletin*, 118, 315–27.

Stroud, J. N. & Wright, D. B. (1997). Identifying your own age: an own-age bias in lineup identifications. Paper presented to the Society of Applied Research in Memory and Cognition, Toronto, July.

Terr, L. (1994). *Unchained Memories: True Stories of Traumatic Memories, Lost and Found*. New York: Basic Books.

Tollestrup, P. A., Turtle, J. W. & Yuille, J. C. (1994). Actual victims and witnesses to robbery and fraud: an archival study. In D. F. Ross, J. D. Read & M. P. Toglia (Eds), *Adult Eyewitness Testimony: Current Trends and Developments* (pp. 144–60). Cambridge: Cambridge University Press.

Tulving, E. (1983). *Elements of Episodic Memory*. Oxford: Oxford University Press.

Undeutsch, U. (1989). The development of statement reality analysis. In J. Yuille (Ed.), *Credibility Assessment* (pp. 101–20). Dordrecht, The Netherlands: Kluwer.

Varendonck, J. (1911). Les temoingnages d'enfants dans un proces retentissant [The testimony of children in a famous trial]. *Archives de Psychologie*, 11, 129–71.

Vrij, A. & Winkel, F. W. (1993). Objective and subjective indicators of deception. *Issues in Criminological and Legal Psychology*, 20, 51–7.

Wells, G. L. (1978). Applied eyewitness testimony research: system variables versus estimator variables. *Journal of Personality and Social Psychology*, 36, 1546–57.

Wells, G. L. & Bradfield, A. L. (in press). "Good, you identified the suspect:" feedback to eyewitnesses distorts their reports of the witnessing experience. *Journal of Applied Psychology*.

Wells, G. L. & Loftus, E. F. (1991). Commentary: is this child fabricating? Reactions to a new assessment technique. In J. Doris (Ed.), *The Suggestibility of Children's Recollections* (pp. 168–71). Washington: American Psychological Society.

Wells, G. L. & Murray, D. M. (1984). Eyewitness confidence. In G. L. Wells & E. F. Loftus (Eds), *Eyewitness Testimony: Psychological Perspectives* (pp. 155–70). Cambridge: Cambridge University Press.

Wells, G. L. & Seelau, E. P. (1995). Eyewitness identification: psychological research and legal policy on lineups. *Psychology, Public Policy and Law*, 1, 765–91.

Wells, G. L., Rydell, S. M. & Seelau, E. P. (1993). The selection of distractors for eyewitness lineups. *Journal of Applied Psychology*, 78, 835–44.

Wells, G. L., Seelau, E. P., Rydell, S. M. & Luus, C. A. E. (1994). Recommendations for properly conducted lineup identification tasks. In D. F. Ross, J. D. Read & M. P. Toglia (Eds), *Adult Eyewitness Testimony: Current Trends and Development* (pp. 223–44). New York: Springer-Verlag.

Westcott, H., Davies, G. M. & Clifford, B. R. (1991). Adults' perceptions of children's truthful and deceptive statements. *Children and Society*, 5, 123–35.

Winograd, E. & Neisser, U. (Eds) (1992). *Affect and Accuracy in Recall: Studies of Flashbulb Memories*. New York: Cambridge University Press.

Wright, D. B. (1995). Misinformation methodologies: explaining the effect of errant information. In G. M. Davies, S. Lloyd-Bostock, M. McMurran & J. C. Wilson (Eds), *Psychology, Law and Criminal Justice: International Developments in Research and Practice* (pp. 39–45). Berlin: De Gruyter.

Wright, D. B. & Gaskell, G. D. (1995). Flashbulb memories: conceptual and methodological issues. *Memory*, 3, 67–80.

Wright, D. B. & McDaid, A. T. (1996). Comparing system and estimator variables using data from real line-ups. *Applied Cognitive Psychology*, 10, 75–84.

Wright, D. B. & Stroud, J. N. (1998). Memory quality and misinformation for peripheral and central objects. *Legal and Criminological Psychology*, 3, 273–86.

Yarmey, A. D. (1993). Adult age and gender differences in eyewitness recall in field settings. *Journal of Applied Social Psychology*, 23, 1921–32.

Yarmey, A. D. (1995). Earwitness speaker identification. *Psychology, Public Policy and Law*, 1, 792–816.

Yuille, J. C. (1988). The systematic assessment of children's testimony. *Canadian Psychologist*, 29, 247–62.

Yuille, J. C. (1993). We must study forensic eyewitnesses to know about them. *American Psychologist*, 48, 572–3.

Zaragoza, M. S. & Mitchell, K. J. (1996). Repeated exposure to suggestion and the creation of false memories. *Psychological Science*, 7, 294–300.

Chapter 27

Perspectives on Jury Decision-making: Cases with Pretrial Publicity and Cases Based on Eyewitness Identifications

Jennifer L. Devenport
California State University, Fullerton
Christina A. Studebaker
Castleton State College
and
Steven D. Penrod
University of Nebraska – Lincoln

During a trial, jurors face many judgment and decision-making tasks. They must evaluate the credibility of each witness, evaluate the evidence presented by each witness, judge the evidence presented throughout the trial as a whole, and apply the judge's instructions to arrive at a final verdict and sometimes a sentence. Cognitive processes – memory, judgment, and the applications of decision rules – are thus at the heart of jurors' tasks. Cognitive approaches to the jury provide us with the tools needed to examine jurors' and juries' judgment and decision-making processes.

We know jurors do not come to trial as blank slates. They have beliefs and knowledge – about the defendant, the world, the perceptual and memory

Both J. L. Devenport and C. A. Studebaker were supported as post-doctoral fellows by an NINH Training Grant (MH16156) during the preparation of this manuscript.

Handbook of Applied Cognition, Edited by F. T. Durso, R. S. Nickerson, R. W. Schvaneveldt, S. T. Dumais, D. S. Lindsay and M. T. H. Chi.

capabilities of people, and about their own decision-making capabilities and processes – which may influence their decision-making, sometimes in undesired or unexpected ways. Furthermore, jurors may be unaware of the ways in which their beliefs and knowledge are influencing their decisions. This sometimes creates problematic situations, because judges and attorneys often rely on and treat jurors' self-reports as accurate descriptions of jurors' cognitive processes and capabilities.

Research methods common to cognitive and social psychology allow us to examine juror decision-making from multiple perspectives and obtain a better understanding of what jurors are actually doing. First, self-reports can be used to assess jurors' beliefs and knowledge as well as the effects jurors believe these factors will have on their decision-making. Second, experimental methods can be used to systematically manipulate a variety of factors – those included in self-reports as being influential as well as others hypothesized to be influential – to determine whether they do, in fact, influence juror decision-making. These factors may include such things as pretrial knowledge about the defendant, assessments of the credibility of one or more witnesses testifying at trial, the probative value of evidence presented by one or more witnesses at trial, the standards of proof to be used by jurors, and many others. The results of self-report studies and empirical studies can be compared to determine whether jurors' prior knowledge and beliefs are influencing their verdict decision-making in unexpected or undesired ways. When factors are found to influence juror decision-making in undesired ways, cognitive approaches may suggest possible aids or other ways of dealing with the problems. Furthermore, cognitive methods may then be used to test the efficacy of these proposed aids and solutions. In this chapter we highlight research in two areas of juror decision-making that underscore these points – studies of the influence of pretrial publicity on juror and jury decisions and studies of the influence of prior knowledge and beliefs about eyewitness reports on jurors' witness credibility judgments at trial.

ASSESSING THE EFFECTS OF PRETRIAL PUBLICITY

As media becomes more pervasive and accessible in our society, concerns about pretrial publicity and its effects on juror decision-making and a defendant's right to a fair trial grow. One need only consider the recent developments of 24-hour news networks such as CNN and MSNBC, specialized cable channels such as Court TV, and the public's widespread access to cable television and satellite broadcasting to recognize that the media environment in which Americans now live is profoundly different from the environment that prevailed just a few years ago. With these changes have come increased access to pretrial publicity that may be biasing to a defendant or civil litigant when a case goes to trial.

The overwhelming publicity surrounding recent cases involving Oprah, Ted Kaczynski, Timothy McVeigh and Terry Nichols, Lyle and Eric Menendez, OJ Simpson, and a host of others underscores the ready availability of pretrial publicity and the possible prejudice it may produce in the population in general and potential jurors in particular. Although the nationwide publicity devoted to these cases makes them easily recognizable, it is important to note that the presentation of prejudicial information may affect juror decision-making in any case that receives substantial media coverage whether it is at the local or national level. It should also be noted that although it is possible for pretrial publicity to create bias both for and against a defendant, pro-defendant bias is typically not of concern to the courts. The criminal trial process is designed to provide a defendant with a fair trial and to decrease the chance of erroneous conviction. To understand this better consider various elements of a criminal trial such as the presumption of the defendant's innocence at outset of trial, the burden of proof resting on the prosecution, the high standard of proof that must be met before a guilty verdict can be reached (i.e. beyond a reasonable doubt), and decision rules that require at least a majority of the jury and sometimes the entire jury to agree on the verdict. Bias against the defendant at the outset of the trial (which may result from exposure to pretrial publicity) is of concern because of its potential to interfere with or remove the presumption of the defendant's innocence before the trial has ever begun. Thus, pretrial publicity is of particular concern when it contains information that would be inadmissible at trial (e.g. prior convictions of the defendant, a confession made by the defendant) or information that is so biasing against the defendant that it may interfere with the defendant's right to receive a fair trial.

Examining the effects of pretrial publicity on people's attitudes and decision-making is important, because even if prejudicial pretrial publicity about a case has been voluminous, judges may not see it as producing significant bias against the defendant. In criminal cases the United States Supreme Court currently uses a "totality of the circumstances" test to assess claims of prejudicial pretrial publicity (*Murphy v. Florida*, 1975). Under this test, the court examines the atmosphere of the trial, the transcript of the jury selection process, and other "indicia of impartiality" to determine if the defendant did indeed have a fair trial. The courts also consider jurors' representations about their ability to disregard prejudicial pretrial publicity when assessing whether prejudice was likely to exist in a case. If potentially prejudicial information about a case has been presented in the newspapers or on television, the judge or the attorneys might ask potential jurors during *voir dire* (the jury selection phase of the trial) whether they can disregard the pretrial publicity to which they have been exposed and whether they can serve as fair and impartial jurors. Potential jurors typically report that they are able to disregard pretrial publicity and to be fair and impartial. These statements are routinely taken as sufficient proof that they can and will do so if selected as jurors (Minow & Cate, 1991; Moran & Cutler, 1991; *Mu'Min v. Virginia*, 1991).

Although it may be difficult to prove that pretrial publicity has biased potential jurors against the defendant, courts realize that the problem may arise. When persuaded there is a problem of bias produced by pretrial publicity, courts may go so far as to move an entire trial to another location where bias against the defendant is less prevalent. This is referred to as changing the venue of the trial and one illustration is the removal of the Timothy McVeigh and Terry Nichols trials from Oklahoma to Denver, Colorado.

Researchers have examined the influence of pretrial publicity on case-relevant attitudes and verdicts, people's beliefs about the influence of pretrial publicity on juror decision-making, and the effectiveness of procedures designed to uncover, reduce, or eliminate bias resulting from exposure to pretrial publicity. Traditionally, two methods have been used to study various aspects of pretrial publicity – public opinion surveys and experimental studies.

Opinion Surveys

Field surveys of jury-eligible individuals are commonly employed to examine the effect of pretrial publicity on pretrial judgments about particular real-life cases. Respondents are typically asked questions about how many news sources (e.g. newspapers, cable news programs, prime-time news programs) they attend to and how often they use these sources (e.g. daily). In addition, respondents are often asked to recall or recognize information about a particular case, to report opinions they might have formed about the case, and to evaluate the strength of the case and the likelihood the defendant is guilty (or, in a civil case, that one party or the other ought to prevail). Questions about the defendant's ability to receive a fair trial in the surveyed community are often also included. Statistical analyses are based on correlations between exposure to pretrial publicity and prejudgments about the case.

In an early example of such an approach, Simon & Eimermann (1971) conducted a telephone survey of potential jurors a week before a scheduled murder trial. During the two-month period from the time of the murder to the time of the survey, one local paper had carried articles about the case on 13 days, and the other local paper had carried articles on 12 days. Although none of the articles contained potentially prejudicial information according to guidelines of the American Bar Association (e.g. there was no mention of prior criminal records, no opinion was expressed as to the guilt or innocence of the defendants), the defense claimed that the circumstances of the case led to a "natural" antagonism towards the defendants and that the newspaper stories strongly suggested that there were witnesses who saw exactly what happened during the crime.

Of the 130 survey respondents, 100 indicated that they had read or heard something about the case. Of the 100 respondents who were aware of the case, three-quarters were able to supply details about the crime. Of those who were able to recall details, 65% favored the prosecution and 28% reported indifference (favoring neither the prosecution nor the defense). Despite the large proportion favoring the prosecution, 59% of those who knew details thought they could serve as a juror with an open mind in this case. In comparison, 41% of the respondents who could not recall details about the case favored the prosecution, and 53% reported that they were indifferent. When asked whether the defendants could receive a fair trial in the community, there was little difference between the groups. Of those who could supply details, 67% thought a fair trial was possible, and 76% of those who could not supply details thought so.

Similar result patterns were detected by Nietzel & Dillehay (1983) in five separate public opinion surveys conducted to assess community beliefs and knowledge about five capital murder trials. Comparisons were made between the venue counties (i.e. the counties in which the trials were scheduled to be held) and alternate counties. Overall, survey respondents in the venue counties had more knowledge about the case in question than respondents in alternate counties. Thus, respondents in the venue counties were more likely to know the defendant by name and to believe that the defendant was probably guilty than respondents from alternative counties. In contrast to the differences between venue and alternate counties on knowledge and prejudgment about the cases, there was little difference in the perceived ability of the defendant to receive a fair trial. Of the respondents in the venue counties, 58% thought the defendant could receive a fair trial in their county, and 69% of the respondents in alternate counties believed the defendant could receive a fair trial in their county. These results clearly suggest that the possibility of juror bias would be greater in the venue counties than in other counties. This study as well as the Simon & Eimermann (1971) study, however, show that people may not consider knowledge or prejudgment about a case an impediment to fairness.

Although early survey research indicated that community beliefs and knowledge are related to prejudgments about a case, this research failed to examine the impact of other potential correlates such as attitudinal and demographic factors on juror judgments. Costantini & King (1980/81) addressed this issue while surveying jury-eligible adults' knowledge regarding two different murder cases and a rape case. As part of the survey, respondents were asked questions concerning their general attitudes toward crime and punishment, their social background, their exposure to news media, their recall of the cases, their knowledge about case-relevant details, and their level of prejudgment about the cases including whether they thought the defendants were guilty. In each of these cases, Costantini & King found a strong relationship between the amount of information a respondent could supply about a case and the measures of prejudice. Thus, the more media sources to which respondents reported attending, the more they knew about a case. In turn, the more respondents knew about a case, the more likely they were to consider the defendant guilty. Furthermore, respondents' opinions about the defendant's guilt were correlated with several variables including gender, educational level, general attitudes about crime, and knowledge about the specific case Although the results suggested that each of these variables was a significant indicator of the respondents' tendencies to presume the defendant guilty, by far the best predictor was knowledge about the case. Specifically in the three different cases, 30%, 2%, and 2% of "poorly informed" respondents thought the defendants were guilty, whereas 54%, 66%, and 61% of "well informed" respondents thought so. Consistent with the findings of Simon & Eimermann (1971), respondents with greater knowledge about a case were found to be more pro-prosecution. Costantini and King concluded from these results that pretrial knowledge was the best predictor of prejudgment.

The relation between exposure to pretrial publicity and prejudgment about a case was also recently examined by Moran & Cutler (1991) in two large survey studies. In the first survey, 604 individuals were questioned about a case involving the distribution of drugs that had received moderate newspaper coverage, much of which was prejudicial toward the defendant. In the second survey, 100 individuals were questioned about a highly publicized case concerning the murder of a police officer that had received a large amount of emotional publicity. For each case, survey respondents were asked about their knowledge of the case, their attitudes toward crime in general, and their attitudes about the case in particular. In both surveys, amount of knowledge about the case and ratings of how much evidence there was against the defendant(s) were significantly correlated. Results from the larger of the two studies showed that the proportion of respondents who said there was "A lot of evidence" against the defendant rose as a function of the number of items of case-relevant information about which the respondent was aware. Neither of the studies showed a significant relationship between prejudgment about the case and self-reported ability to be impartial. Regardless of the amount of knowledge about the case, a significant proportion of individuals thought they could be fair and impartial. In fact, in the larger study the group that most strongly endorsed the proposition that there was a lot of evidence against the defendant also had the highest proportion of respondents who thought that they could be fair and set aside what they had learned from the media.

These survey studies consistently show a relationship between knowledge about a case (most likely gained from pretrial publicity) and prejudgment about the case, specifically a belief in the defendant's guilt. Furthermore, self-reports of impartiality or the ability to serve as a fair and open-minded juror are not related to knowledge about the case or prejudgment. But perhaps these findings need not cause alarm about a defendant's ability to receive a fair trial in cases receiving prejudicial pretrial publicity as long as judges are aware of the potential bias caused by the publicity and the unreliability of individuals' self-reports about their ability to be fair and disregard the publicity.

Judicial Perspectives

In addition to public opinion surveys, another source of views about the influence of pretrial publicity on juror decision-making is appellate court opinions. These opinions are particularly important, because they are the source of the legal guidelines by which the impact of pretrial publicity in future cases will be judged. There are several notable Supreme Court cases touching on pretrial publicity which establish the framework for judicial evaluations of the prejudicial potential of pretrial publicity (for a detailed consideration of the case law, see Campbell, 1994).

Irvin v. Dowd (1961) was the first case in which the US Supreme Court struck down a state conviction on the grounds of prejudicial pretrial publicity. The Court held that a defendant could secure a change of venue by demonstrating actual juror prejudice during *voir dire*. The Court observed that a "pattern of deep and bitter prejudice shown to be present throughout the community . . . was clearly reflected in the sum total of the *voir dire* examination of a majority of the jurors finally placed in the jury box." (p. 727). Of the 430 persons examined as potential jurors for the case, 268 were excused by the court because they had fixed opinions of Irvin's guilt. Furthermore, eight of the 12 individuals who served as jurors in the case indicated sometime during *voir dire* a belief that Irvin was guilty. The Court stated that "[w]here so many, so many times, admitted prejudice," statements indicating an ability to serve as impartial jurors "can be given little weight" (p. 728). The Court, however, also noted that prejudgment alone is not sufficient to rebut a prospective juror's presumed impartiality and that "[i]t is sufficient if the juror can lay aside his impression or opinion and render a verdict based on the evidence presented in court" (p. 723).

In *Rideau v. Louisiana* (1963), the Supreme Court elaborated on the conditions under which a defendant might be granted a change of venue based on the existence of prejudicial pretrial publicity in the community. In a case where the community "had been exposed repeatedly and in depth to the spectacle of Rideau personally confessing in detail to the crimes with which he was later to be charged" (p. 726), the Court reversed a lower court conviction on the basis of presumed prejudice without even considering whether *voir dire* resulted in the removal of individuals prejudiced against the defendant.

In *Sheppard v. Maxwell* (1966), the Court observed in language that has even more force 30 years later: "Given the pervasiveness of modern communications and the difficulty of effacing prejudicial publicity from the minds of the jurors, the trial courts must take strong measures to ensure that the balance is never weighed against the accused" (p. 362). The Court reversed Sheppard's murder conviction because the defendant had been the target of a "deluge of publicity" (p. 357) before the trial and the trial itself was conducted in a "carnival atmosphere" (p. 358).

Although prejudicial pretrial publicity was found to interfere with the defendant's right to a fair trial in each of the cases discussed above, the Court has said that these cases "cannot be made to stand for the proposition that juror exposure to information about a state defendant's prior convictions or to news accounts of the crime with which he is charged alone presumptively deprives the defendant of due process" (*Murphy v. Florida*, 1975, p. 2036). Rather the "totality of the circumstances" must be examined. In Murphy the court found that qualified jurors need not be totally ignorant of the facts and issues involved in a case and that it remains to the defendant to demonstrate the actual existence of a preconceived opinion of guilt in the mind of jurors.

More recently, the Supreme Court decided the case of *Mu'Min v. Virginia* (1991) in which the defendant was convicted and sentenced to death. The defendant was a prison inmate who was serving time for first-degree murder when he committed another murder while out of prison on work detail. Eight of the twelve jurors in Mu'Min had admitted during *voir dire* to some prior exposure to the case. In his change of venue motion, Mu'Min submitted 47 newspaper articles which had discussed the case. One or more of the articles discussed details of the murder, the subsequent investigation, and included information about Mu'Min's prior criminal record, the fact that he had been rejected for parole six times, accounts of alleged prison infractions, details about the prior murder for which Mu'Min was currently serving a sentence, and indications that Mu'Min had confessed to killing the victim (including headlines such as one proclaiming "Murderer Confesses to Killing Woman"). The trial court denied the defendant's request for a change of venue as well as his request for the prospective jurors to be questioned individually during *voir dire*. The Supreme Court affirmed and held that the Due Process Clause does not mandate that prospective jurors be screened about the specific content of the pretrial publicity to which they have been exposed. The Court stated that although questioning jurors about the content of pretrial publicity might be helpful in determining whether potential jurors can be impartial, helpfulness is not enough. Rather, the defendant must show that the trial court's failure to ask these questions caused his or her own trial to be fundamentally unfair. The standard for establishing bias set forth in this case is a fairly high one.

The beliefs about the influence of pretrial publicity on juror decision-making as reflected in the appellate court opinions and the public opinion surveys are similar. In the public opinion surveys, pretrial knowledge about a case is consistently associated with beliefs about the defendant's guilt; however, beliefs about the defendant's guilt are not related to self-reports of impartiality. Regardless of their opinion about the defendant, most people believed they could serve as an impartial juror. In comparison, appellate court opinions indicate a recognition of the potential anti-defendant bias that may be associated with prejudicial pretrial publicity in a community, but have consistently held that pretrial publicity exposure alone is not enough on which to presume that potential jurors from the community cannot be impartial. The weight given to jurors' assurances of impartiality depends on the "totality of the circumstances" surrounding the case.

Experimental Studies of the Effects of Pretrial Publicity

Opinion data provide only a partial picture of pretrial publicity effects on juror decision-making. Although a relationship between knowledge about a case (presumably gained through pretrial publicity) and prejudgment about a case has been consistently found, the data are correlational. They do not allow causal inferences to be made about the effects of pretrial publicity on juror beliefs and their decision-making. Experimental studies which randomly assign individuals to conditions in which they are exposed or not exposed to pretrial publicity permit causal conclusions to be drawn about its effects. In addition various aspects of pretrial publicity, such as the amount to which individuals are exposed and the nature of the publicity, can be systematically manipulated so that the effects of different forms of pretrial publicity can be determined. Of course, the enhanced control over extraneous variables that is available in the laboratory comes at the cost of some artificiality, which may be of particular concern when the results are likely to be generalized to real-world cases and trials. But, despite their artificiality, experimental simulations shed light on behavior in real trial settings. Furthermore, a number of studies have determined that the artificialities of the typical trial simulation study generally do not bias verdicts (e.g. Kerr, Nerenz & Herrick, 1979; Kramer & Kerr, 1989; MacCoun & Kerr, 1988; Miller, 1975; Simon & Mahan, 1971; Stasser, Kerr & Bray, 1982). For these reasons, laboratory research on pretrial publicity effects on mock juror behavior is highly relevant to "real-world" courtroom settings.

Contrary to people's naive beliefs, as gleaned from public opinion surveys, the results of empirical research indicate that pretrial publicity is influential to jurors' judgments and verdict decisions. Prejudicial pretrial publicity has been found to influence evaluations of the defendant's likability, feelings of sympathy for the defendant, perceptions of the defendant as a typical criminal, pretrial judgments of the defendant's guilt, and final verdicts (Costantini & King, 1980/81; DeLuca, 1979; Hvistendahl, 1979; Kline & Jess, 1966; Moran & Cutler, 1991; Otto, Penrod & Dexter, 1994; Padawer-Singer & Barton, 1975; Simon & Eimermann, 1971; Sue, Smith & Gilbert, 1974; Sue, Smith & Pedroza, 1975; Tans & Chaffee, 1966).

Psychologists began the empirical investigation of the effects of pretrial publicity by manipulating the presence and nature of information that would most likely be inadmissible as evidence in a jury trial. Consequently, past convictions for criminal offenses and confessions of guilt that may later be recanted are two types of pretrial information that were examined by experimenters early on. Tans & Chaffee (1966), for example, gave student participants newspaper stories about crimes that varied along a number of dimensions: seriousness of the crime, favorable or unfavorable statements by the district attorney, a confession or denial by the suspect, and whether the defendant was released or kept in custody. After reading the stories, participants were asked to evaluate the defendant on several measures including an item assessing guilt. When the stories consisted of unfavorable information about the defendant, 65% of the participants rated the defendant guilty. The conditions in which all the unfavorable information about the defendant was presented and in which the suspect's confession alone was presented elicited the highest percentage of guilty judgments, 76% and 80% respectively. When the stories consisted of favorable information or no information about the defendant, the defendant was judged guilty approximately 50% of the time.

Studies using trial simulation methodology allowed researchers to further explore the impact of pretrial publicity on mock-jurors' judgments of guilt within the context of the evidence presented at trial. In an elaborate and well-designed trial stimulation study conducted by Padawer-Singer and Barton (1975), for example, mock-jurors read a version of a newspaper story which either stated that the suspect had a criminal background and had retracted an alleged confession (information that would be inadmissible in court) or did not mention the suspect's criminal background or alleged confession. After reading the newspaper stories, jurors listened to a three-hour audiotaped trial that was based on the edited transcript of a real murder trial and then deliberated in groups until they reached a verdict or declared the group deadlocked. More than 72% of jurors exposed to the newspaper story containing inadmissible information voted to convict, whereas fewer than 44% of the jurors exposed to the newspaper story not containing inadmissible information voted to convict. These data indicate that juror knowledge of inadmissible information obtained from exposure to pretrial publicity can have a profound impact on later assessments of defendant guilt.

Another form of information often included in pretrial publicity is the naming or identification of a suspect. Hvistendahl (1979) investigated the impact of identifying a suspect in a news story on mock-jurors' assessments of guilt using four different identification techniques: a fictional address (control group), race, gang membership, and a prior criminal record. The placement of the suspect identification information within the article was then manipulated such that the suspect's identification was placed in the lead or the conclusion of the news story.

Although the author found no effects for placement of the identification, the type of information presented did influence jurors' judgments of guilt. Reporting that the suspect was a member of a gang or that he had a prior criminal record resulted in more judgments of guilt than reporting the defendant's address regardless of whether the information appeared in the lead or the conclusion of the news story.

More recent research has examined the effects of pretrial publicity containing negative characterizations of the defendant or emotionally charged information. One such study conducted by Kramer, Kerr & Carroll (1990) examined the influence of factual and emotional pretrial publicity on pre- and post-deliberation verdicts. In this study, the factual pretrial publicity consisted of news reports detailing the defendant's previous convictions for armed robbery and the discovery of incriminating evidence at his girlfriend's apartment. In comparison, the emotional pretrial publicity identified the defendant as a suspect in a fatal hit-and-run of a child involving the same motor vehicle used in the robbery for which he was currently being tried.

After being presented with television and newspaper reports in which the presence of "factual" and "emotional" pretrial publicity was manipulated, participants viewed a 51-min re-enactment of an actual armed robbery trial. Post-deliberation verdicts indicated a 20% higher conviction rate by juries exposed to the emotional publicity than juries exposed to factual publicity, and this difference in conviction rates was even greater (41%) when hung juries were not considered in the analysis. In addition, judicial instructions were ineffective at reducing the impact of pretrial publicity despite the fact that whenever pretrial publicity was mentioned during deliberation it was almost always followed by a reminder from other jurors that the jury should not consider such information. These results demonstrate the power of pretrial publicity to bias jurors against a defendant even when they recognize the influence of pretrial publicity as inappropriate.

Otto, Penrod & Dexter (1994) used a somewhat different trial simulation procedure in which they explored the differential impact of various types of pretrial publicity on verdicts rendered both before and after the presentation of the trial evidence. In this study, student jurors were presented with one of several different forms of pretrial publicity concerning a defendant who was accused of disorderly conduct in an actual case. The pretrial publicity included negative information about the defendant's character, statements about the defendant's prior police record, mention of the defendant's low-status job, or strong or weak inadmissible statements by a neighbor. Jurors' verdicts were significantly affected by the pretrial publicity even after they had heard the trial evidence. The strongest effects were for the negative pretrial publicity about the defendant's character. Participants who read this type of pretrial publicity were more likely to say the defendant was guilty both before they had seen the trial and at the completion of the trial. In addition, pretrial publicity containing inadmissible statements by a neighbor about the defendant significantly increased participants' belief in the guilt of the defendant before viewing the trial.

Not surprisingly, empirical research has also demonstrated that the effects of pretrial publicity are not limited to verdict decisions made by jurors in criminal cases. Using trial simulation methodology, Kline & Jess (1966) examined the effect of pretrial publicity on jurors' judgments in a civil case by presenting mock-jurors with either a prejudicial news story or a non-prejudicial news story. A few days after reading the news story, participants listened to an audiotaped trial and participated in mock jury deliberations. Although juries that had received the prejudicial news story made reference to this information during their deliberations, it could not be determined whether discussion of this information influenced their final verdicts.

What are the psychological processes through which these effects operate? Penrod, Otto & Dexter (1990) examined possible mediational processes utilizing a criminal case arising from a very well-publicized racial incident that involved members of two campus fraternities. One of the fraternities had been the subject of well-publicized allegations of misconduct in prior incidents and these incidents received new reporting at the time of the incident in question. The researchers assessed participants' exposure to pretrial publicity about the case (e.g. by testing recognition of actual newspaper headlines) and the inferences and judgments participants had made about the case. Participants then viewed a two-hour videotape of a mock trial that was based on actual statements made by witnesses and the defendant during discovery proceedings. After viewing the trial, participants' verdict preferences and other judgments were measured. Assessments of mock jurors' pretrial knowledge revealed high levels of case awareness and well-structured attitudes about fraternities, ethnic jokes and racial slurs, drinking, and personal experiences with fraternities. Dependent measures assessed the defendant's culpability, strength of the defense and prosecution evidence, belief in a self-defense claim, the degree of injury to the victim, and the ability to identify with the defendant. There were significant relationships among measures of pretrial publicity recall, measures of bias in recall, a number of pretrial attitudes (e.g. attitudes about fraternities), and the ratings of the defendant's culpability.

Otto, Penrod & Hirt (1990) also drew upon an actual case to examine the possible effects of pretrial publicity on juror decision-making in a civil trial. Student participants viewed a four-hour edited videotape of a two-day trial involving claims of personal injury arising from an automobile/pedestrian accident. Prior to viewing the videotape, participants were presented a "newspaper article" containing one of nine possible combinations of pretrial publicity including such information as prior police record, negative character statements assessed from hearsay, or neutral information about each party. The pretrial publicity influenced not only the judgments of negligence, but also mock-jurors' memories for the trial evidence, impressions of the parties, and inferences from the trial – all of which were examined as possible mediators of the pretrial publicity effects on negligence judgments. Specifically, pretrial publicity regarding the negative character and prior police record of the plaintiff influenced participants' judgments of the defendant's negligence. Thus, participants who read either of these types of pretrial publicity about the plaintiff were less likely to judge the defendant as negligent and provided more positive ratings of both the defendant and his witnesses.

As can be seen from this collection of studies, prejudicial pretrial publicity can create bias against a defendant which can result in a higher probability of judgments of guilt or wrongdoing. The effect of prejudicial pretrial publicity on final judgments appears to operate via pretrial inferences about the defendant, memory for facts about the case, and inferences made during trial. In addition, the influence of prejudicial pretrial publicity on people's perceptions of a defendant and their verdict decisions appears to be robust and generalizable to real-life cases. Despite the consistency of both survey and empirical studies, however, concern about pretrial publicity effects in real cases may be downplayed because of various safeguards the courts have implemented in an attempt to eliminate the influence of media on juror and jury decision-making. These safeguards include a trial continuance (i.e. delaying a trial), extended *voir dire*, judicial admonitions to disregard pretrial publicity, jury deliberation, change of venire (i.e. selecting the pool of potential jurors from a jurisdiction different from that where the trial is being held), and change of venue. All of these safeguards except change of venire and change of venue have been found to be less than fully effective (Dexter, Cutler & Moran, 1992; Kerr, Kramer, Carroll & Alfini, 1991; Kramer, Kerr & Carroll, 1990; Otto, Penrod & Dexter, 1994; Sue, Smith & Gilbert, 1974; Sue, Smith & Pedroza, 1975). Some similarities among the ineffective safeguards may provide some insight as to why they do not overcome the problems introduced by exposure to prejudicial pretrial publicity. For example, all of the ineffective safeguards are based on removing bias after it has developed, and three of them (*voir dire*, judicial instructions, and deliberation) require jurors to disregard pretrial publicity immediately after attention has been brought to it. This suggests that examination of the encoding of pretrial publicity and continued research on the mediating processes may be the key to a better understanding of pretrial publicity including the conditions under which exposure to it does and does not result in bias and whether this bias can be overcome once it has developed (for a more thorough discussion, see Studebaker & Penrod, 1997).

This section of the chapter has focused on the impact of pretrial publicity (information obtained prior to the trial) on jurors' beliefs, knowledge, and decision-making processes. The following section examines how jurors' prior beliefs and knowledge and experiences regarding something as common as memory may affect their perceptions of evidence presented during the trial and their subsequent verdict decisions. As we illustrate in the next section, the psychological research examining the impact of eyewitness identification evidence on juror decision-making has also drawn upon the breadth of methods and knowledge provided by cognitive psychology.

EYEWITNESS IDENTIFICATION EVIDENCE: JUROR KNOWLEDGE ABOUT FACTORS THAT INFLUENCE EYEWITNESS PERFORMANCE

Although eyewitness identifications are one of the most important forms of evidence presented in criminal trials, a substantial amount of eyewitness research suggests that these identifications are not always accurate (e.g. Brigham, Maass, Snyder & Spaulding, 1982; Krafka & Penrod, 1985; Pigott, Brigham & Bothwell, 1990; Platz & Hosch, 1988) and that a variety of factors may influence a witness's memory for the perpetrator or the event at various stages of memory – for example, the presence of a weapon at the encoding stage (Kramer, Buckhout & Eugenio, 1990; Loftus, Loftus & Messo, 1987; Steblay, 1992), the viewing of mugshots during the storage stage (Brown, Deffenbacher & Sturgill, 1977; Gorenstein & Ellsworth, 1980) or the wording of questions presented to the witness during the retrieval stage (Cutler, Penrod & Martens, 1987; Loftus & Zanni, 1975; Malpass & Devine, 1981).

The conclusions posited by the eyewitness research regarding the fallibility of eyewitness memory (for a more thorough discussion, see Wright & Davies, 1999, this volume) is further underscored by the fact that mistaken identifications appear to be the most frequent source of error accounting for wrongful convictions. In fact, a recent study conducted by Connors, Lundregan, Miller & McEwen (1996) reported that in an investigation of 28 cases of erroneous convictions in which defendants were subsequently cleared with scientific DNA evidence, all convictions were predicated, at least in part, on mistaken eyewitness identifications. Furthermore, Huff (1987; Huff, Rattner & Sagarin, 1996) implicated mistaken eyewitness identifications in 60% of the more than 500 erroneous convictions he studied. Overall, these studies raise concerns regarding the accuracy of eyewitness identifications and, more importantly, jurors' knowledge of the factors that influence eyewitness identification performance and the impact of eyewitness identification evidence on jurors' verdict decisions.

As in the case of pretrial publicity, researchers have taken multiple methodological approaches to assessing juror knowledge and the use of factors that influence eyewitness identification accuracy. These approaches include juror surveys, post-dictions studies which assess juror ability to predict (actually post-dict) the outcome of eyewitness identification experiments, and the use of trial simulations to examine the influence of various types of eyewitness evidence on jury decision-making.

Juror Surveys

Several studies using survey methodology have attempted to assess juror knowledge about the factors that influence eyewitness identification accuracy by administering the knowledge of eyewitness behavior questionnaire (KEBQ) to a variety of respondents including undergraduates, law students and community members from the USA, UK, and Australia (Deffenbacher & Loftus, 1982; McConkey & Roche, 1989; Noon & Hollin, 1987). Overall, the results are remarkably similar across all respondents. Respondents appear to be moderately aware of the influence of both cross-race recognition and prior photo-array identifications on identification accuracy. Thus, a majority of the respondents are aware of the fact that, regardless of guilt or innocence, a person who has been identified from a previous photo-array is likely to be identified during a subsequent lineup and that cross-race identifications are more difficult than same-race identifications. Respondents, however, appear to be less aware of the detrimental effects of age and retention interval. Respondents inaccurately believe that an individual's ability to recognize faces increases up to early school age and then remains constant throughout old age and that memory for faces remains extremely accurate even after a period of several months. Also, in contrast to psychological research, respondents believe that police officers have more experience and are better at making eyewitness identifications than the general public (for a discussion on experts' beliefs about factors affecting eyewitness reliability, see Kassin, Ellsworth & Smith, 1989).

Post-diction Studies of Juror Knowledge

Juror knowledge of the factors influencing eyewitness identification performance has also been assessed by having students and prospective jurors post-dict the outcome of previously conducted eyewitness identification experiments (Brigham & Bothwell, 1983; Kassin, 1979; Wells, 1984). During post-diction studies, participants are provided with a written description of the methodology used in eyewitness identification experiments and are asked to post-dict the identification accuracy rates of the witnesses who participated in the original experiment. By comparing the post-dicted identification accuracy rates with the results from the original experiment, researchers are able to assess whether prospective jurors are aware of the effect of the specific factors manipulated in the experiment on eyewitness identification performance. For example, a post-diction study by Kassin (1979) was conducted using a written summary of an eyewitness identification experiment originally conducted by Leippe, Wells & Ostrom (1978). The Leippe et al. study had manipulated crime seriousness by staging the theft of an item that was considered to be either valuable (high seriousness) or less valuable (less seriousness). In addition, participants were either made aware of the value of the stolen item prior to the theft or were informed of the item's value immediately after the theft. In the low seriousness condition, 19% of the witnesses versus 56% of the witnesses in the high seriousness condition correctly identified the thief when they knew the value of the item prior to the theft. When witnesses were unaware of the item's value prior to the theft, however, 35% of the witnesses in the low seriousness and 12.5% of the witnesses in the high seriousness conditions correctly identified the thief. In contrast to the actual experiment, participants in Kassin's study predicted that witnesses who knew the value of the item prior to the theft would make fairly accurate identifications in both the high seriousness (66%) and low seriousness conditions (65%) and would perform similarly to those witnesses who were unaware of the value of the item prior to the theft, 53% and 60% respectively.

Brigham & Bothwell (1983) also had subjects predict eyewitness identification accuracy rates for Leippe et al.'s (1978) study of crime seriousness as well as Brigham, Maass, Snyder & Spaulding's (1982) field study of cross-race recognition. Consistent with findings of other post-diction research, Brigham & Bothwell found that respondents overestimated the accuracy of eyewitness identifications. For example, in Leippe et al.'s study, 12.5% of the eyewitness identifications were accurate, whereas Brigham & Bothwell's respondents believed that 70.6% of the identifications would be correct. Similarly, the results of Brigham et al.'s (1982) field study revealed that 32% of white clerks correctly identified black customers, and 31% of black clerks correctly identified white customers.

Participants in Brigham & Bothwell's post-diction study, however, estimated that 51% of the black clerks had made correct identifications and that 70% of the white clerks had done so.

Other factors that have been examined in order to assess their relationships with eyewitness identification accuracy are the witness's level of confidence and the instructions presented to the eyewitness prior to the viewing of the lineup. These factors have also been the subjects of post-diction studies. Wells (1984) conducted two post-diction studies in order to assess lay persons' knowledge of eyewitness identification performance in situations involving eyewitness confidence and instruction bias. In the first study, students read the method section of the Leippe, Wells & Ostrom (1978) experiment and were asked to predict the identification accuracy rate for an eyewitness who was described as being either "completely certain" or "somewhat uncertain" about his/her identification. Although the results of the Leippe et al. study had indicated that confidence was not related to identification accuracy, Wells' participants predicted that more confident witnesses would produce greater identification accuracy.

In Wells' second study, students read a description of Malpass & Devine's (1981) study of instruction bias and were asked to predict the identification accuracy of witnesses who had been shown either target absent or target present photo-arrays. In vandal-absent conditions in the original study, biased instructions produce a 78% false identifications rate versus a 33% false identifications rate with unbiased instructions. Wells' students, however, predicted 16% and 18%, respectively – they were insensitive to a factor that clearly contributes to the suggestiveness of identification procedures: instruction bias.

In summary, post-diction research suggests that prospective jurors tend to predict higher identification accuracy rates than those generally found among participants of eyewitness research (Brigham & Bothwell, 1983; Kassin, 1979; Wells, 1984). In addition, prospective jurors appear to be insensitive to a number of factors influencing eyewitness identification accuracy such as crime seriousness (Kassin, 1979), cross-racial identifications (Brigham & Bothwell, 1983), and instruction bias (Wells, 1984). Furthermore, post-diction studies reveal that lay persons appear to place too much emphasis on eyewitness confidence (Brigham & Bothwell, 1983; Wells, 1984).

Trial Simulations as Tests of Juror Knowledge

Juror knowledge has also been examined by manipulating factors that have been shown to influence an eyewitness's identification accuracy during simulated trials while other evidence and testimony are held constant (e.g. Bell & Loftus, 1989; Cutler, Dexter & Penrod, 1990; Cutler, Penrod & Stuve, 1988; Devenport, Stinson, Cutler & Kravitz, 1996; Lindsay, Lim, Marando & Cully, 1986). Rather than testing whether laypersons can second-guess the results of experiments, these studies are designed to assess the degree to which jurors are sensitive to factors known to influence eyewitness performance. Participants in these studies are asked to assume the role of jurors while either reading a written summary of a trial, hearing an audiotaped simulation, or viewing a videotape simulation, after which they complete questionnaires assessing their verdicts and other reactions to the trial. Juror knowledge is gauged by significant effects for factors that are known to influence identification accuracy and non-significant effects for factors that are known to not predict identification accuracy (e.g. Cutler, Dexter & Penrod, 1990).

There have been two distinct approaches to studying juror knowledge: the first examines jurors' abilities to discriminate between accurate and inaccurate eyewitnesses and the second examines mock-juror sensitivity to the factors that influence identification accuracy.

Differentiating Accurate from Inaccurate Witnesses

In cases where an eyewitness identification is the primary evidence presented at trial, jurors have the important task of determining whether the witness is accurate in his/her identification of the defendant. In order to assess jurors' abilities to distinguish between accurate and inaccurate eyewitnesses, Wells, Lindsay & Ferguson (1979) staged a crime in view of witnesses who then attempted identifications of the perpetrator from six-person photo-arrays. Eyewitnesses who had made either accurate or inaccurate identifications were then asked to participate in a simulated cross-examination which was conducted in a leading manner for half of the witnesses and a nonleading manner for the other half. The testimony presented during the cross-examination of each eyewitness was videotaped and later shown to and evaluated by students serving as mock jurors. The results indicated that leading questions may improve juror assessments of eyewitness identification accuracy. Specifically, inaccurate eyewitnesses were believed by more jurors (86%) than were accurate eyewitnesses (76%) when nonleading questions were used during witness cross-examination. During the leading cross-examination, however, accurate eyewitnesses were believed by more jurors (84%) than were inaccurate eyewitnesses (73%).

Unfortunately, the non-significant interaction between accuracy of the eyewitness and method of questioning used during cross-examination suggests that mock jurors were actually quite poor at differentiating accurate and inaccurate eyewitnesses. Thus, among jurors exposed to nonleading cross-examination, 76% correctly identified accurate eyewitnesses but only 14% correctly determined which eyewitnesses were inaccurate. Among jurors exposed to leading cross-examination, 84% correctly identified accurate eyewitnesses and 27% correctly determined which eyewitnesses were inaccurate.

In addition to having difficulty distinguishing between accurate and inaccurate eyewitnesses, Wells, Lindsay & Ferguson (1979) also found that jurors appeared to place too much weight on eyewitness confidence. Although witness confidence was not significantly correlated (r = .05) with accuracy of the juror's decision, confidence was significantly correlated (r = .53) with whether or not a juror believed the eyewitness. Thus, jurors were more likely to believe confident eyewitnesses, but confident eyewitnesses simply were not more likely to be accurate than less confident eyewitnesses. These findings were replicated in a study by Lindsay, Wells & Rumpel (1981) who also tested jurors' abilities to discriminate accurate from inaccurate eyewitnesses using similar methods. In this study, jurors were also more likely to believe confident witnesses (77%) than less confident witnesses (59%) even though witness confidence was again found to be only weakly related to witness accuracy.

Using a more elaborate and realistic trial simulation, Lindsay, Wells & O'Connor (1989) also tested whether mock jurors could differentiate accurate from inaccurate eyewitnesses. Similar to Wells, Lindsay & Ferguson's (1979) study, witnesses viewed a staged crime and tried to identify the perpetrator from target-present or target-absent photo-arrays. Witnesses were then asked to participate in a mock trial which involved direct examination by a prosecutor, cross-examination by a defense attorney, and redirect examination by the prosecutor. The eyewitness testimony was videotaped and 16 "trials" were created using eight eyewitnesses who made correct identifications and eight who made false identifications. The videotaped trials were then shown to undergraduates who viewed one trial and rendered a verdict. The conviction rate did not vary as a function of eyewitness accuracy (i.e. jurors could not differentiate accurate from inaccurate eyewitnesses); thus, the methodological realism of the examination/cross-examination led to findings consistent with those from Wells & Lindsay's earlier study.

In summary, studies using trial simulation methodology to examine jurors' abilities to differentiate accurate from inaccurate eyewitnesses converge on rather dismaying conclusions about jurors' abilities. Specifically, jurors overestimate the accuracy of identifications (Wells, Lindsay & Ferguson, 1979), fail to distinguish accurate from inaccurate eyewitnesses (Lindsay, Wells & O'Connor, 1989), and base their decisions in part on witness confidence, a poor predictor of identification accuracy (Lindsay, Wells & Rumpel, 1981; Wells, Lindsay & Ferguson, 1979).

Juror Evaluations of Eyewitness Identification Evidence

Trial simulation methodology has also been used to determine whether jurors are sensitive to factors known to influence eyewitness identification performance and whether jurors use this information appropriately when rendering their verdict decisions. For example, Lindsay, Lim, Marando & Cully (1986) conducted a series of four experiments examining the effect of various factors on jurors' evaluations of eyewitness testimony. In the first experiment, Lindsay et al. examined the influence of consistency of identification testimony across eyewitnesses by manipulating three factors: strong versus weak physical evidence, the number of eyewitnesses for the prosecution (0, 1, or 2), and the number of eyewitnesses for the defense (0, 1, or 2). Although jurors' decisions were not significantly influenced by the physical evidence presented during the mock trial, jurors' verdicts were influenced by the number of eyewitnesses who testified for the prosecution and the defense. Convictions were most likely, however, when the prosecution's witnesses were unopposed (50%) and least likely when defense's witnesses were unopposed (2%) which suggests that the number of eyewitnesses is less important than whether or not there is conflicting eyewitness identifications.

The second Lindsay et al. experiment examined the impact of defense witness testimony on subsequent juror evaluations of the eyewitness identification testimony. Using a videotaped enactment of an assault trial, this study tested the following five conditions: no additional evidence; a second eyewitness identification of the defendant; a defense eyewitness who testified that the defendant was not the perpetrator; an alibi witness for the defendant; and an alibi witness who was a relative of the defendant. The results revealed that the highest conviction rates were obtained when either one or two prosecution eyewitnesses testified unopposed by a defense witness (80% and 60%, respectively). In contrast, the lowest conviction rates were obtained when a defense eyewitness either provided an alibi for the defendant or testified that the defendant was not the perpetrator (27% in each condition). When compared with the no-defense witness conditions, an alibi provided by a relative did not significantly reduce the conviction rate (57% guilty).

The third Lindsay et al. experiment examined whether inconsistent eyewitness testimony would lead jurors to assign less weight to the eyewitness evidence when rendering their verdict decisions. During the trial simulation, the eyewitness's testimony was either consistent or inconsistent such that the witness testified that she (a) originally said the criminal was blond but did not think the defendant was blond; (b) but did not know whether the defendant altered her hair color; (c) recalled the defendant's hair was dark at the lineup, but (d) was still confident about her identification. The consistency of the eyewitness's testimony, however, was not found to significantly influence jurors' verdicts.

Lindsay et al.'s fourth experiment examined the impact of viewing conditions at the scene of the crime on juror's evaluations of the eyewitness evidence. In this study, jurors heard a version of an audiotaped trial which indicated that the witness had observed the crime at either 9 a.m. on a sunny day or at 1 a.m., 60 ft from the nearest streetlight, and that the witness had viewed the perpetrator for a duration of either 5 seconds, 30 minutes, or 30 minutes including interactions with the perpetrator. In all versions of the audiotaped trial, the eyewitness was highly confident in his identification. Surprisingly, neither the time of day nor the viewing duration of the eyewitness had a significant effect on juror verdicts. These results indicate a lack of juror sensitivity to witnessing conditions that have been shown to influence eyewitness identification performance.

Although Lindsay et al. found that consistency of the witness' testimony did not influence jurors' verdicts, the consistency of an eyewitness' testimony may vary with respect to the type of information (central versus peripheral) being described. A study conducted by Berman & Cutler (1996) also examined the effect of witness consistency on juror evaluations of eyewitnesses, but in contrast to Lindsay et al., Berman & Cutler manipulated whether the witness gave inconsistent testimony on peripheral versus central information. As predicted, jurors exposed to inconsistencies concerning central details, perceived the eyewitness as less credible and the defendant as less culpable. These jurors were less likely to convict.

In addition to the consistency of a witness's testimony, a number of factors such as eye contact (Hemsley & Doob, 1978), confidence (Wells et al., 1979) and speech patterns (Miller, Maruyama, Beaber & Valone, 1976) have been shown to affect jurors' perceptions of a witness' credibility. Along these same lines, Bell & Loftus (1989) examined whether the level of detail provided in an eyewitness' testimony influenced jurors' verdict decisions. In this study, mock jurors read a written summary of a criminal trial within which the degree of the detail provided by a prosecution witness (high versus low), and a defense witness (high versus low) were manipulated. In addition, the degree of relation between the detail and the perpetrator (high versus low), and the relatedness of the testimony were also manipulated by having the witness's statements describe either the actions of the perpetrator or another individual. Although no effect of the relatedness of the testimony was found, the detail of the testimony significantly influenced mock jurors' verdicts. Thus, 33% of mock-jurors convicted when the prosecution eyewitness's testimony was high in detail (versus 21% when the detail was low), and 23% convicted when the defense eyewitness's testimony was high in detail (versus 31% when it was low – this difference was only marginally significant).

Although these studies indicate that exposing inconsistencies and probing about details in the witness's testimony may be an effective way to raise doubts about the reliability of an eyewitness identification, these strategies may not be as effective as initially thought given that eyewitness studies suggest that description accuracy and consistency are not related to identification accuracy. Thus, an argument can be made that jurors should not rely on inconsistencies in witness testimony as a basis for devaluing eyewitness identification evidence (see Cutler & Penrod, 1995).

Trial simulation methodology has also been used to examine whether jurors are sensitive to the impact of various witnessing and identification conditions that influence eyewitness identification accuracy. For example, a trial simulation study conducted by Cutler, Penrod & Stuve (1988) assessed juror knowledge of a number of factors that vary in the extent to which they influence eyewitness identification performance (e.g. whether the perpetrator wore a disguise, produced a weapon, or used violence while perpetrating the crime, the length of retention interval, the presence and/or absence of instruction bias, foil bias, and the level of witness confidence). After viewing one version of a simulated videotaped trial, mock-jurors estimated the probability that the identification was correct and rendered an individual verdict decision. The results revealed that when presented with testimony that should call into question the identification accuracy of an eyewitness, jurors appear to be insensitive to the importance of this information and to pay little attention to it when evaluating the accuracy of an eyewitness. Specifically, juror verdicts were not influenced by such factors as a disguise, the presence of a weapon, violence, retention interval, instruction bias, or foil bias. Of the factors studied, jurors relied most on expressions of confidence from the identifying witness ($d = .34$) – although research indicates the relation between witness confidence and identification accuracy is fairly modest (Bothwell, Deffenbacher & Brigham, 1987; Cutler & Penrod, 1989; Penrod & Cutler, 1995; Sporer, Penrod, Read & Cutler, 1995). Using the same methodology and materials as Cutler, Penrod & Stuve, a subsequent study conducted by Cutler, Dexter & Penrod (1990) supplemented the earlier student sample with eligible and experienced jurors and found that both college students and experienced jurors appear to be comparably insensitive to factors influencing eyewitness identification performance.

Another factor that has consistently been shown by the eyewitness research to influence eyewitness identification accuracy is level of lineup suggestiveness present during the identification procedure. Elements of the lineup procedure that may contain suggestiveness or encourage a specific response include the selection of the foils (Lindsay & Wells, 1980; Wells & Lindsay, 1980; for a review, see Wells, 1993), the instructions given to the witness prior to viewing the lineup (Cutler, Penrod & Martens, 1987; Malpass & Devine, 1981), and the manner of presentation of the lineup members (Cutler & Penrod, 1989; Lindsay & Wells, 1985). A study conducted by Devenport, Stinson, Cutler & Kravitz (1996) assessed juror knowledge of lineup suggestiveness by manipulating the presence of foil, instruction, and presentation bias. In this study, students and experienced jurors watched a version of a simulated videotaped trial and rendered individual verdicts and rated the suggestiveness of the foils, instructions, presentation, and overall lineup procedure. The results revealed that when asked to rate the suggestiveness of the specific lineup biases, jurors were sensitive to evidence of foil, and instruction biases but insensitive to the beneficial nature of sequential lineups (which have been shown to reduce false identification rates, Cutler & Penrod, 1989; Lindsay & Wells, 1985). Specifically, jurors who were presented with evidence of biased foils rated both the foils and the overall identification procedure as more suggestive than jurors who were presented with evidence of unbiased foils. In addition, jurors who were presented with evidence of biased lineup instructions rated the instructions as more suggestive than jurors who were presented with evidence of unbiased lineup instructions. Significantly however, juror verdicts were not influenced by jurors' sensitivity to foil or instruction biases. These results suggest that jurors possess some common sense knowledge about the deleterious effects of both foil and instruction biases as demonstrated by their awareness of these biases when asked about them directly, but have difficulty applying their knowledge of these biases in their decision-making, as indexed by their verdicts.

In summary, jurors appear to be unaware of the harmful effects of various witnessing conditions (e.g. whether the perpetrator wore a disguise, displayed a weapon, or exerted violence while committing the crime) on eyewitness identification accuracy. Jurors, however, appear to be only somewhat aware of the deleterious effects of lineup suggestiveness in the form of foil and instruction bias. When asked to evaluate lineup foils and instructions, jurors can successfully identify bias in these lineup procedures, but fail to use this information in their decision-making as indicated by their verdicts.

The Impact of Expert Psychological Testimony on Juror Decision-making

Although jurors tend to rely on factors that are not indicative of eyewitness accuracy, the situation is not entirely hopeless. In cases where the information being presented is outside the ken of the jury, the judicial system has established a legal safeguard which may permit an expert psychologist to testify about factors that influence identification accuracy as a way of educating jurors and assisting them with the interpretation and the evaluation of eyewitness evidence (for a thorough discussion on legal safeguards in cases involving eyewitness identifications, see Devenport, Penrod & Cutler, 1997). Expert psychological testimony on eyewitness memory, however, has been accepted only reluctantly by the courts (Cutler & Penrod, 1995; Penrod, Fulero & Cutler, 1995).

Studies Involving Expert Testimony

Although early research showed that the presence of expert psychological testimony reduced conviction rates, it was unclear whether this reduction was due to a simple increase in juror skepticism about eyewitness testimony as feared by some (McCloskey & Egeth, 1983; McCloskey, Egeth & McKenna, 1986) or to improved juror sensitivity to the factors influencing eyewitness identification performance. Juror skepticism refers to a tendency to doubt the eyewitness identification evidence, whereas juror sensitivity refers to both a general awareness or knowledge regarding the factors that influence eyewitness memory as well as an ability to use the information accordingly when rendering a verdict – i.e. to be skeptical or credulous – as appropriate to the evidence.

By simultaneously manipulating both expert psychological testimony and factors that have been shown to influence a witness's identification accuracy, a few studies have been able to separate juror skepticism from juror sensitivity and thus, determine whether the presence of expert testimony actually sensitizes jurors to the specific factors mentioned during the course of the trial – as evidenced by an interaction between the factors affecting eyewitness memory and expert testimony such that the factors have a larger effect among mock jurors exposed to expert testimony (Cutler, Dexter & Penrod, 1989; Cutler, Dexter & Penrod, 1990; Loftus, 1980; Wells, Lindsay & Tousignant, 1980). One of the first studies to examine both juror skepticism and juror sensitivity was Loftus (1980). This study examined the impact of expert testimony on juror judgments by manipulating the level of violence associated with the crime and the presence of expert testimony. Participants read a version of a trial transcript and rendered individual verdict decisions. Overall, the results indicated that exposure to expert testimony led jurors to be both skeptical of the eyewitness identification evidence and sensitive to the effect of violence on eyewitness memory. Thus, participants who were exposed to expert testimony were less likely to convict the defendant (39%) than participants who were not exposed to expert testimony (58%). In addition, participants who read a violent version of a trial transcript were more likely to convict (56%) than participants who read a nonviolent version (41%). Furthermore, the results revealed a trend toward enhanced juror sensitivity when expert testimony was presented during the trial. Specifically, among participants who were not exposed to expert testimony, there was a larger difference in conviction rates among those who read the nonviolent transcript (47%) and those who read the violent transcript (68%) than among participants exposed to expert testimony (35% versus 43%).

A study conducted by Wells, Lindsay & Tousignant (1980) also assessed both juror skepticism and juror sensitivity to factors known to influence witness viewing conditions. In this study, participants viewed the videotaped cross-examination of four eyewitnesses from the same viewing condition filmed during a previous eyewitness identification study (Lindsay, Wells & Rumpel, 1981). These witnesses in the previous study had made identifications under either poor, moderate, or good witness viewing conditions and had been either accurate or inaccurate in their identifications. This trial simulation differed from typical trial proceedings in that participants were only presented with the cross-examination of the eyewitness; and those who were exposed to expert testimony heard the testimony *prior* to viewing the videotaped cross-examination of the eyewitness. After viewing the videotaped cross-examinations, jurors were asked whether or not they believed the eyewitnesses' testimony. Consistent with the results found by Loftus (1980), the presence of expert testimony produced juror skepticism of the eyewitness testimony as well as juror sensitivity to the effect of witnessing conditions on identification accuracy. Thus, mock jurors who were exposed to expert testimony prior to the eyewitnesses testimony were less likely to believe the eyewitnesses (41%) than mock jurors who were not exposed to expert testimony (62%). However, the trend toward enhanced juror sensitivity by expert testimony (62%, 58%, and 73% believed identifications to be accurate when no expert testimony was presented versus 42%, 28%, and 50% believed identifications to be accurate when expert testimony was presented for poor, moderate, and good viewing conditions, respectively) was not statistically significant.

Several studies conducted to examine the effect of expert testimony on jurors' evaluations of eyewitness identification evidence have incorporated more elaborate and realistic trial simulation methodologies. For example, Cutler, Dexter and Penrod (1989) had mock-jurors watch a version of a videotaped simulated trial which examined the influence of expert testimony (presence versus absence) on mock-jurors' sensitivity to witnessing and identification conditions (good versus poor), and levels of witness confidence (high versus moderate). The primary dependent measures included in this study were jurors' memory of the trial evidence, jurors' knowledge regarding the factors influencing eyewitness identification accuracy, the probability that the identification was correct, and verdict. When asked whether a specific factor influences identification accuracy, jurors were sensitive to the harmful effects of disguises, retention interval, and lineup instructions on identification accuracy but insensitive to the effect of weapon focus and to the trivial relation between eyewitness confidence and identification accuracy. Expert testimony did not enhance juror sensitivity to the factors to which jurors displayed some awareness, but did increase juror sensitivity to the factors of which they were unaware – weapon focus and eyewitness confidence. With respect to juror verdicts, jurors who were exposed to expert testimony appeared to be more sensitive to the witnessing and identification conditions and to use this information accordingly when rendering a verdict (36% versus 58% convictions for poor and good witnessing and identification conditions, respectively) than jurors who were not exposed to expert testimony (38% v. 48% convictions for poor and good witnessing and identification conditions, respectively).

The trial simulation study conducted by Devenport et al. (1996) also examined the impact of expert testimony on jurors' evaluations. This study, however, manipulated the presence of expert testimony and the presence of lineup suggestiveness in the form of foil, instruction, and presentation biases. Although jurors were sensitive to the harmful effects of foil and instruction biases when asked about them directly, they were insensitive to the harmful effects of these factors as indexed by their verdicts. In this instance expert testimony did not improve juror sensitivity to foil, or instruction biases with respect to jurors' verdicts, ratings of lineup suggestiveness, or ratings of defendant guilt.

Overall, the research examining the impact of eyewitness identification evidence on juror decision-making suggests that jurors lack knowledge regarding the factors that influence the reliability of eyewitness testimony. Although these findings are quite discouraging, the presentation of expert psychological testimony generally appears to increase juror sensitivity to factors influencing eyewitness identification performance and to improve their decision-making (Cutler, Dexter & Penrod, 1989; Loftus, 1980; Wells, Lindsay & Tousignant, 1980).

CONCLUSIONS

As underscored throughout this chapter, trial simulations are one of the most effective and commonly used methods of studying juror decision-making. Trial simulation research examining the effect of pretrial publicity and eyewitness identification evidence on juror decision-making has consistently demonstrated that jurors' beliefs and knowledge influence their decision-making in a number of undesirable ways. Numerous studies have shown that jurors obtain a substantial amount of knowledge (and sometimes erroneous information) regarding a case from the media and that this exposure to prejudicial pretrial publicity affects both pre- and post-deliberation verdicts. In fact, the impact of prejudicial pretrial publicity has been demonstrated with various types of publicity including minimal information (e.g. race), information that would be inadmissible at trial (e.g. defendant's confession), and information that has no direct evidentiary relevance (e.g. "emotional" publicity), as well as with a variety of materials and procedures, some of which were quite realistic. In contrast to the empirical findings, however, jurors consistently believe that they can set aside this prejudicial information and render impartial and fair verdicts.

Similarly, jurors enter a courtroom with personal knowledge and experiences with memory and factors they believe might influence memory. Psychological research, however, suggests that a juror's knowledge and experience do not always appear to assist him/her with evaluations of eyewitness identification evidence. In fact, empirical research suggests that jurors tend to over-estimate eyewitness accuracy (Brigham & Bothwell, 1983; Kassin, 1979; Wells, 1984) and to rely on factors that are not diagnostic of eyewitness accuracy such as an eyewitness's memory for peripheral details (Bell & Loftus, 1989) and eyewitness confidence (Wells, 1984). In addition, jurors appear to be insensitive to factors influencing witnessing and identification conditions (Cutler, Penrod & Stuve, 1988) and to have difficulty applying their knowledge of lineup suggestiveness to their verdict decisions (Devenport et al., 1996). Expert testimony regarding the factors that influence eyewitness identification performance, however, does appear to improve juror knowledge and awareness of some of these factors.

One of the notable features of the empirical findings in these two research arenas is the contrast between what jurors (and sometimes judges and attorneys) believe about the impact that pretrial publicity or eyewitness identification evidence has had upon them and the impact that these factors appear to have when methods other than self-report are employed. The application of cognitive perspectives and methodologies in the area of jury and juror decision-making has equipped researchers to compare jurors' self-predicted behaviors with the behaviors of jurors in experimental trial settings. A more formidable challenge for the future is to use similar methods to remedy the deficiencies in decision-making and legal procedures revealed by the research reviewed here.

REFERENCES

Bell, B. E. & Loftus, E. F. (1989). Trivial persuasion in the courtroom: the power of (a few) minor details. *Journal of Personality and Social Psychology*, 56, 669–79.

Berman, G. L. & Cutler, B. L. (1996). Effects of inconsistencies in eyewitness testimony on mock-jurors' decisionmaking. *Journal of Applied Psychology*, 81, 170–7.

Bothwell, R. K., Deffenbacher, K. A. & Brigham, J. C. (1987). Correlation of eyewitness accuracy and confidence: optimality hypothesis revisited. *Journal of Applied Psychology*, 72, 691–5.

Brigham, J. C. & Bothwell, R. K. (1983). The ability of prospective jurors to estimate the accuracy of eyewitness identifications. *Law and Human Behavior*, 7, 19–30.

Brigham, J. C., Maass, A., Snyder, L. D. & Spaulding, K. (1982). Accuracy of eyewitness identifications in a field setting. *Journal of Personality and Social Psychology*, 42, 673–80.

Brown, E. L., Deffenbacher, K. A. & Sturgill, W. (1977). Memory for faces and the circumstances of encounter. *Journal of Applied Psychology*, 62, 311–18.

Campbell, D. S. (1994). *Free Press v. Fair Trial: Supreme Court Decisions since 1807*. Praeger.

Connors, E., Lundregan, T., Miller, N. & McEwen, T. (1996). *Convicted by Juries, Exonerated by Science: Case Studies in the Use of DNA Evidence to Establish Innocence After Trial*. US Department of Justice Office of Justice Programs.

Costantini, E. & King, J. (1980/81). The partial juror: correlates and causes of prejudgment. *Law and Society Review*, 15, 9–40.

Cutler, B. L. & Penrod, S. D. (1989). Forensically relevant moderators of the relation between eyewitness identification accuracy and confidence. *Journal of Applied Psychology*, 74, 650–2.

Cutler, B. L. & Penrod, S. D. (1995). *Mistaken Identifications: The Eyewitness, Psychology, and the Law*. New York: Cambridge University Press.

Cutler, B. L., Dexter, H. R. & Penrod, S. D. (1989). Expert testimony and jury decision making: an empirical analysis. *Behavioral Sciences and Law*, 7, 215–25.

Cutler, B. L., Dexter, H. R. & Penrod, S. D. (1990). Nonadversarial methods for improving juror sensitivity to eyewitness evidence. *Journal of Applied Social Psychology*, 20, 1197–207.

Cutler, B. L., Penrod, S. D. & Martens, T. K. (1987). The reliability of eyewitness identifications: the role of system and estimator variables. *Law and Human Behavior*, 11, 223–58.

Cutler, B. L., Penrod, S. D. & Stuve, T. E. (1988). Jury decision making in eyewitness identification cases. *Law and Human Behavior*, 12, 41–56.

Deffenbacher, K. A. & Loftus, E. F. (1982). Do jurors share a common understanding concerning eyewitness behavior? *Law and Human Behavior*, 6, 15–30.

DeLuca, A. J. (1979). Tipping the scales of justice: the effects of pretrial publicity. Unpublished master's thesis, Iowa State University, Ames. IA.

Devenport, J. L., Penrod, S. D. & Cutler, B. L. (1997). Eyewitness identification evidence: evaluating commonsense evaluations. *Psychology, Public Policy, and Law*, 3, 338–61.

Devenport, J. L., Stinson, V., Cutler, B. L. & Kravitz, D. A. (1996). Does cross-examination and expert psychological testimony improve juror sensitivity to lineup suggestiveness? Unpublished doctoral dissertation, Florida International University, Miami.

Dexter, H. R., Cutler, B. L. & Moran, G. (1992). A test of voir dire as a remedy for the prejudicial effects of pretrial publicity. *Journal of Applied Social Psychology*, 22, 819–32.

Fox, S. G. & Walters, H. A. (1986). The impact of general versus specific expert testimony and eyewitness confidence upon mock juror judgment. *Law and Human Behavior*, 10, 215–28.

Gorenstein, G. W. & Ellsworth, P. C. (1980). Effect of choosing an incorrect photograph on a later identification by an eyewitness. *Journal of Applied Psychology*, 65, 616–22.

Hemsley, G. D. & Doob, A. N. (1978). The effect of looking behavior on perceptions of a communicator's credibility. *Journal of Applied Social Psychology*, 8, 136–44.

Hosch, H. M., Beck, E. L. & McIntyre, P. (1980). Influence of expert testimony regarding eyewitness accuracy on jury decisions. *Law and Human Behavior*, 4, 287–96.

Huff, C. R. (1987). Wrongful conviction: societal tolerance of injustice. *Research in Social Problems and Public Policy*, 4, 99–115.

Huff, C. R., Rattner, A. & Sagarin, E. (1996). *Convicted but Innocent: Wrongful Conviction and Public Policy*. Thousand Oaks, CA: Sage.

Hvistendahl, J. K. (1979). The effect of placement of biasing information. *Journalism Quarterly*, 56, 863–5.

Irvin v. Dowd, 366 U.S. 717, 727 (1961).

Kassin, S. M. (1979). Personal communication cited by Wells, G. L. (1984). How adequate is human intuition for judging eyewitness testimony. In G. L. Wells & E. F. Loftus (Eds), *Eyewitness Testimony: Psychological Perspectives* (pp. 256–72). New York: Cambridge University Press.

Kassin, S. M., Ellsworth, P. C. & Smith, V. L. (1989). The 'general acceptance' of psychological research on eyewitness testimony: a survey of the experts. *American Psychologist*, 44, 1089–98.

Kerr, N. L., Kramer, G. P., Carroll, J. S. & Alfini, J. (1991). On the effectiveness of voir dire in criminal cases with prejudicial pretrial publicity: an empirical study. *American University Law Review*, 40, 665–701.

Kerr, N. L., Nerenz, D. & Herrick, D. (1979). Role playing and the study of jury behavior. *Social Methods and Research*, 7, 337–55.

Kline, F. G. & Jess, P. H. (1966). Prejudicial publicity: its effects on law school mock juries. *Journalism Quarterly*, 43, 113–16.

Krafka, C. & Penrod, S. (1985). Reinstatement of context in a field experiment on eyewitness identification. *Journal of Personality and Social Psychology*, 49, 58–69.

Kramer, G. P. & Kerr, N. L. (1989). Laboratory simulation and bias in the study of juror behavior: a methodological note. *Law and Human Behavior*, 13, 89–100.

Kramer, G. P., Kerr, N. L. & Carroll, J. S. (1990). Pretrial publicity, judicial remedies, and jury bias. *Law and Human Behavior*, 14, 409–38.

Kramer, T. H., Buckhout, R. & Eugenio, P. (1990). Weapon focus, arousal, and eyewitness memory: attention must be paid. *Law and Human Behavior*, 14, 167–84.

Leippe, M. R., Wells, G. L. & Ostrom, T. M. (1978). Crime seriousness as a determinant of accuracy in eyewitness identification. *Journal of Applied Psychology*, 63, 345–51.

Lindsay, R. C. L., Lim, R., Marando, L. & Cully, D. (1986). Mock-juror evaluations of eyewitness testimony: a test of metamemory hypotheses. *Journal of Applied Social Psychology*, 16, 447–59.

Lindsay, R. C. L. & Wells, G. L. (1980). What price justice? Exploring the relationship of lineup fairness to identification accuracy. *Law and Human Behavior*, 4, 303–14.

Lindsay, R. C. L. & Wells, G. L. (1985). Improving eyewitness identifications from

lineups: simultaneous versus sequential lineup presentations. *Journal of Applied Psychology*, 70, 556–64.
Lindsay, R. C. L., Wells, G. L. & O'Connor, F. J. (1989). Mock juror belief of accurate and inaccurate eyewitnesses: a replication and extension. *Law and Human Behavior*, 13, 333–9.
Lindsay, R. C. L., Wells, G. L. & Rumpel, C. M. (1981). Can people detect eyewitness identification accuracy within and across situations? *Journal of Applied Psychology*, 66, 79–89.
Loftus, E. F. (1980). Impact of expert psychological testimony on the unreliability of eyewitness identification. *Journal of Applied Psychology*, 65, 9–15.
Loftus, E. F., Loftus, G. R. & Messo, J. (1987). Some facts about "weapon focus." *Law and Human Behavior*, 11, 55–62.
Loftus, E. F. & Zanni, G. (1975). Eyewitness testimony: the influence of the wording of a question. *Bulletin of the Psychonomic Society*, 5, 86–8.
Maass, A., Brigham, J. C. & West, S. G. (1985). Testifying on eyewitness reliability: expert advice is not always persuasive. *Journal of Applied Social Psychology*, 15, 207–29.
MacCoun, R. & Kerr, N. L. (1988). Asymmetric influence in mock jury deliberation: jurors' bias for leniency. *Journal of Personality and Social Psychology*, 54, 21–33.
Malpass, R. S. & Devine, P. G. (1981). Eyewitness identification: lineup instructions and the absence of the offender. *Journal of Applied Psychology*, 66, 482–9.
McCloskey, M. & Egeth, H. (1983). Eyewitness identification: what can a psychologist tell a jury? *American Psychologist*, 38, 550–63.
McCloskey, M., Egeth, H. & McKenna, J. (1986). The experimental psychologist in court: the ethics of expert testimony. *Law and Human Behavior*, 10, 1–13.
McConkey, K. M. & Roche, S. M. (1989). Knowledge of eyewitness memory. *Australian Psychologist*, 24, 377–84.
Miller, N. (1975). Jurors' responses to videotaped trial materials. *Personality and Social Psychology Bulletin*, 1, 561–9.
Miller, N., Maruyama, G., Beaber, R. J. & Valone, K. (1976). Speed of speech and persuasion. *Journal of Personality and Social Psychology*, 34, 615–24.
Minow, N. N. & Cate, F. H. (1991). Who is an impartial juror in an age of mass media? *American University Law Review*, 40, 631–64.
Moran, G. & Cutler, B. L. (1991). The prejudicial impact of pretrial publicity. *Journal of Applied Social Psychology*, 21, 345–67.
Mu'Min v. Virginia, 500 U.S. 415 (1991).
Murphy v. Florida, 421 U.S. 794, 799-802 (1975).
Nietzel, M. T. & Dillehay, R. C. (1983). Psychologists as consultants for changes of venue. *Law and Human Behavior*, 7, 309–55.
Noon, E. & Hollin, C. R. (1987). Lay knowledge of eyewitness behaviour: a British survey. *Applied Cognitive Psychology*, 1, 143–53.
Otto, A. L., Penrod, S. & Dexter, H. (1994). The biasing impact of pretrial publicity on juror judgments. *Law and Human Behavior*, 18, 453–70.
Otto, A., Penrod, S. & Hirt, E. (1990). The influence of pretrial publicity on juror judgments in a civil case. Unpublished manuscript.
Padawer-Singer, A. & Barton, A. H. (1975). The impact of pretrial publicity on jurors' verdicts. In R. J. Simon (Ed.), *The Jury System in America: A Critical Overview* (pp. 123–39). Beverly Hills: Sage.
Penrod, S. & Cutler, B. (1995). Witness confidence and witness accuracy: assessing their forensic relation. *Psychology, Public Policy & Law*, 1, 817–45.
Penrod, S. D., Fulero, S. & Cutler, B. (1995). Expert psychological testimony on eyewitness reliability before and after *Daubert*. *Behavioral Sciences and the Law*, 13, 229–60.
Penrod, S., Otto, A. & Dexter, H. (March 1990). Assessing the impact of pretrial publicity on jury decisionmaking. American Psychology-Law Society, Williamsburg, VA.
Pigott, M. A., Brigham, J. C. & Bothwell, R. K. (1990). A field study of the relationship

between quality of eyewitnesses' descriptions and identification accuracy. *Journal of Police Science and Administration*, 17, 84–8.
Platz, S. J. & Hosch, H. M. (1988). Cross racial/ethnic eyewitness identification: a field study. *Journal of Applied Social Psychology*, 18, 972–84.
Rahaim, G. L. & Brodsky, S. L. (1982). Empirical evidence versus common sense: juror and lawyer knowledge of eyewitness accuracy. *Law and Psychology Review*, 7, 1–15.
Rideau v. Louisiana, 373 U.S. 723 (1963).
Seltzer, R., Lopes, G. M. & Venuti, M. (1990). Juror ability to recognize the limitations of eyewitness identifications. *Forensic Reports*, 3, 121–37.
Sheppard v. Maxwell, 384 U.S. 333, 362 (1966).
Simon, R. J. & Eimermann, T. (1971). The jury finds not guilty: another look at media influence on the jury. *Journalism Quarterly*, 48, 343–4.
Simon, R. J. & Mahan, L. (1971). Quantifying burdens of proof: a view from the bench, the jury, and the classroom. *Law and Society Review*, 5, 319–30.
Sporer, S., Penrod, S. D., Read, D. & Cutler, B. L. (1995). Gaining confidence in confidence: a new meta-analysis on the confidence–accuracy relationship in eyewitness identification studies. *Psychological Bulletin*, 118, 315–27.
Stasser, G., Kerr, N. L. & Bray, R. M. (1982). The social psychology of jury deliberations: structure, process, and product. In N. L. Kerr & R. M. Bray (Eds), *The Psychology of the Courtroom* (pp. 221–56). New York: Academic Press.
Steblay, N. M. (1992). A meta-analytic review of the weapon focus effect. *Law and Human Behavior*, 16, 413–24.
Studebaker, C. A. & Penrod, S. D. (1997). Pretrial publicity: the media, the law, and common sense. *Psychology, Public Policy, and the Law*, 3, 428–60.
Sue, S., Smith, R. E. & Gilbert, R. (1974). Biasing effect of pretrial publicity on judicial decisions. *Journal of Criminal Justice*, 2, 163–71.
Sue, S., Smith, R. E. & Pedroza, G. (1975). Authoritarianism, pretrial publicity and awareness of bias in simulated jurors. *Psychological Reports*, 37, 1299–302.
Tans, M. & Chaffee, S. (1966). Pretrial publicity and juror prejudice. *Journalism Quarterly*, 43, 647–54.
Wells, G. L. (1984). How adequate is human intuition for judging eyewitness testimony. In G. L. Wells & E. F. Loftus (Eds), *Eyewitness Testimony: Psychological Perspectives* (pp. 256–72). New York: Cambridge University Press.
Wells, G. L. (1993). What do we know about eyewitness identification? *American Psychologist*, 48, 553–71.
Wells, G. L. & Lindsay, R. C. L. (1980). On estimating the diagnosticity of eyewitness nonidentifications. *Psychological Bulletin*, 88, 776–84.
Wells, G. L., Lindsay, R. C. L. & Ferguson, T. J. (1979). Accuracy, confidence, and juror perceptions in eyewitness identification. *Journal of Applied Psychology*, 64, 440–8.
Wells, G. L., Lindsay, R. C. L. & Tousignant, J. P. (1980). Effects of expert psychological advice on human performance in judging the validity of eyewitness testimony. *Law and Human Behavior*, 4, 275–85.
Wright, D. B. & Davies, G. M. (1999). Eyewitness testimony. In F. T. Durso, R. S. Nickerson, R. W. Schvaneveldt, S. T. Dumais, D. S. Lindsay & M. T. H. Chi (Eds), *Handbook of Applied Cognition* (chapter 26). Chichester: John Wiley.

Author Index

AAAS, 604
Aaker, D.A., 346
Aaronson, E., 616
Abbott, K.R., 431
Abe, T., 414
Abed, F., 707
Abelson, H., 557
Abelson, R.P., 583
Abernethy, B., 292, 295
Abramson, L.Y., 726, 728, 731, 738, 739, 740, 747, 749
Acioly, N.M., 604
Ackerman, M.S., 415, 433
Ackerman, P., 315, 323
Ackerman, P.L., 48, 50
Ackerman, R., 739
Acton, W.H., 24, 496
Adam, J., 396
Adams, J.A., 42, 47, 48
Adams, L., 605
Adams, M.J., 153, 154, 264, 265, 285, 286
Adams, R.A., 642
Adams-Price, C., 792
Adams-Webber, J.R., 480, 494
Adamus, P.R., 763
Addoms, D.L., 763
Adelman, L., 126
Agras, W.S., 735
Ahtola, O.T., 766
Ainsworth, L.K., 222, 501
Ajzen, I., 185, 186, 187, 188, 358
Alba, J.W., 344, 345, 347, 349, 352, 353, 354, 355, 356, 357, 359, 365, 702, 708, 727
Albright, C.A., 399
Alexander, C., 763
Alexander, P.A., 605
Alexander, R.A., 323
Alfini, J., 830
Allard, F., 296
Allen, C.K., 65
Allen, F.W., 771
Allen, S.W., 668, 670, 673
Allen, T.J., 9,10,13
Alloy, L.B., 726, 728, 731, 738, 739, 740, 747, 748, 749
Alpert, D., 563
Alpert, S., 764
Altieri, P., 701
Altman, D.G., 698
Altmann, J., 490
Altom, M.W., 10
Alton, J., 255, 256
Amador, M., 795, 797, 798
Aman, C.J., 805
Amir, N., 733, 735
Ammerman, A.S., 712
Anastasiades, P., 733, 734
Anderson, A.H., 425
Anderson, C.A., 746
Anderson, C.W., 615
Anderson, D.K., 150, 152, 688
Anderson, J.D., 648
Anderson, J.R., 5, 7, 8, 38, 39, 60, 64, 65, 126, 130, 176, 295, 422, 445, 446, 462, 463, 467, 468, 469, 470, 480, 564, 573, 574, 576, 581, 582, 604, 605, 608, 614
Anderson, L.M., 763
Anderson, N.H., 358, 359
Anderson, R.C., 96
Anderson, R.B., 559, 560
Anderson, R.H., 427, 428
Anderson, S., 415
Anderson, T.W., 763
Anderson, U., 130
Anderson-Garlach, M.M., 40
Andrassy, J.M., 704, 710
Andre, A.D., 288, 306
Andrews, G., 737
Andrich, D., 637
Andriks, J.L., 795
Andrle, S., 767
Andrzejewski, S.J., 393, 396
Angell, J.R., 580
Angus, R.G., 43
Antunano, M.J., 255
Anzai, Y., 596
Apa, 731, 732, 736, 738, 741, 743
Arabie, P., 22, 496
Archer, D., 765
Aretz, A.J., 255, 256
Argyris, C., 422
Arkes, H.R., 124, 130, 347
Armor, D.A., 747, 748
Armstrong, D., 762
Armstrong, G.M., 357
Arocha, J.F., 70
Arocha, J.F., 300
Arocha, J.F., 664, 666, 667, 670, 672, 673, 674, 676, 677, 678, 682, 685, 689
Aronson, E., 766
Aronson, L., 765, 766
Aronson, T.A., 732
Arrow, H., 428
Arthur, W., 48, 49
Arvey, R.D., 318
Ary, D., 486
Aschermann, E., 798
Ash, D., 616
Ashbaugh, L.L., 758
Ashly, F.G., 497
Asoko, H., 602, 607
Aspinwall, L.G., 608
Aspinwall, L.G., 747
Atchison, M., 744
Atkins, D.E., 424, 434
Atkinson, R.C., 86, 295
Atlas, R.S., 128

Atman, C.J., 771
Atwood, B.G., 763
Atwood, M.E., 455
Aveni, A.F., 379, 396
Avolio, B.J., 333
Axton, R.A., 716
Ayers, M.S., 794

Babcook, C.J., 105, 673, 674, 675
Bacdayan, P., 422
Backer, T.E., 181
Baddeley, A., 399, 559
Baddeley, A.C., 652
Baddeley, A.D., 290, 295, 705
Baecker, R., 425, 426
Baecker, R.M., 426, 429, 435, 487
Bagozzi, R.P., 18, 358
Bahrick, L., 94
Bailey, G., 6,14
Bailey, J.S., 768
Bailey, W.A., 480, 501
Bain, D., 399
Bainbridge, L., 72, 73, 213, 222, 225, 226, 237, 274, 488
Bajo, M., 24
Baker, E., 414
Baker, E.L., 629, 646
Baker, P., 6
Baker, S.M., 195
Bakhtin, M.M., 607
Baldwin, M.W., 180
Ball, G.A., 331
Ball, K., 47
Ballard, R.J., 563
Ballas, J.A., 302
Baltes, P.B., 58
Banaji, M.R., 17, 104
Bandura, A., 612, 700
Banerji, R., 584
Bangert, R.L., 563
Bank, B.J., 188
Banks, D., 389
Bannister, D., 329, 494
Bardwell, L.V., 763
Bareket, T., 49
Barfield, W., 294, 307
Bargh, J.C., 739
Barile, A.L., 399
Barley, S.R., 332
Barlow, D.H., 735
Barnard, C.I., 328
Barnard, P., 379, 705, 717
Barnard, Y.F., 490
Barnes-Farrell, 315, 319, 320
Barnet, R.C., 574
Barnett, B., 263
Barns, H., 77
Baron, J., 145, 146
Barr, R., 94
Barr, S.H., 321
Barron, B., 596, 603, 604, 605, 606, 609, 611, 613, 615
Barron, B.J., 611
Barron, F.H., 118
Barrows, H.S., 604
Barrows, H.S., 672
Barry, R., 429
Barsalou, L.W., 353, 355
Bartol, A.M., 790
Bartol, C.R., 790
Barton, A.H., 827
Bash, B., 606
Bass, B.M., 325
Bassili, J.N., 186, 176
Bassok, M., 585, 605, 609
Bastianutti, L.M., 420
Bateman, H.V., 606
Batsell, R.R., 455
Battiste, V., 49
Baum, A., 762
Baumeister, R.F., 102
Baumgardner, M.H., 18, 354
Baxter, I., 712
Bayarri, S., 6
Baynes, T.H., 293, 300
Beaber, R.J., 836
Beach, L.R., 117, 118, 123, 321, 322, 350
Beach, R., 705, 708
Beal, C.R., 396
Beard, B., 47
Beard, D., 389
Beaton, S.P., 758
Bechtel, W., 4
Bechtold, H., 632
Beck, A.T., 727, 732, 734, 738, 749
Beck, I.L., 605
Becker, L.J., 764
Becker, M.H., 700
Becklen, R., 253
Bedard, J., 77, 576
Begeman, M., 414, 430
Behrens, J.T., 7,513, 517, 522, 531, 532, 534, 538, 539, 540, 541, 544, 611
Beishon, R.J., 225, 236
Bejar, I.I., 630, 633, 634, 635, 648
Bell, B.E., 833, 836, 841
Bell, G., 712
Bell, H.H., 303
Bell, P., 606, 609
Bell, P.A., 774
Bellenkes, A.H., 248, 252, 265
Bellotti, V.M.E., 414, 430
Beltracchi, L., 234
Belzer, L.J., 678
Bemis, K.M., 742
Ben Shaul, O., 292, 293, 300
Benbasat, I., 500
Bendapudi, N., 102
Bendiksen, I., 396
Bendiksen, M., 396
Benimoff, N.I., 421
Bennett, J.L., 411
Bennett, K.B., 229, 230
Bennett, R.E., 647, 651
Bentler, P.M., 188
Benysh, D.V., 481, 485
Ben-Zvi, R., 598
Berchick, R., 734
Berdahl, J.L., 428
Bereiter, C., 578, 601, 602, 603, 604, 605, 606, 614, 638, 642
Berent, M.K., 183
Berger, A.E., 647
Berger, R.C., 128
Beringer, D., 294
Berkely, D., 119
Berkerian, D.A., 796
Berliner, D.C., 572, 596, 597
Berliner, H.J., 62
Berliner, L., 99
Berman, G.L., 799, 836
Berner, E., 122
Bernstein, M., 587
Berntson, G., 180
Berry, C., 709
Berry, D.C., 705
Berryman, R.G., 119, 154, 155, 156, 161
Bertin, J., 514
Bertine, K.K., 758
Best, J.B., 480
Bettencourt, A., 613
Bettinger, R., 769
Bettman, J., 117, 127
Bettman, J.R., 152, 359, 363, 364
Bewley, T.L., 5,10
Beyth, R., 116
Beyth-Marom, R., 130
Bias, R.G., 8, 10, 11, 14, 20
Bibby, P.A., 225
Bickman, L., 764
Biddle, B.J., 188
Biederman, I., 256
Biehal, G., 353, 364
Bielaczyc, K., 605, 609
Bieman-Copland, S., 64
Bien, W., 22
Bieser, M., 119
Bikson, T.K., 427, 428, 429
Billings, C., 270, 272
Billings, C.E., 143, 163, 165, 226, 302
Billings, F.J., 101, 794
Binning, J.F., 325
Biolsi, K.J., 70, 485, 683
Birenbaum, M., 650
Birnbaum, M.H., 122
Birren, J.E., 66
Bishop, G.A., 758

Bishop, L., 759
Biswas, G., 611, 613, 614
Bitzer, D.L., 563
Bjork, R.A., 92, 292, 300, 303
Black, F.W., 401
Black, J.S., 769
Blackburn, B.L., 765
Blackwell, J.M., 17, 91, 100, 105
Blair, J.H., 429
Blair, P.D., 758
Blaney, P.H., 744
Blaxton, T.A., 89
Blickensderfer, E., 305, 496
Bliss, M.E., 396
Blockley, D.I., 489
Bloome, D.M., 604
Blumenfeld, P.C., 596, 605, 606
Blumer, C., 124, 347
Bly, S.A., 414, 425, 433
Bobis, J., 561
Bobrow, D., 414, 426
Bobrow, D.G., 269
Bock, G., 435
Bockenholt, U., 130, 675
Boerger, R.L., 683
Boes, J.O., 131
Bohn, P., 733, 735
Bohrnstedt, G.W., 747
Boje, D.M., 331
Bojkov, R., 759
Bolger, F., 349
Bolstad, C.A., 289
Bonatti, M., 697
Bond, R., 794
Bonebakker, C., 600
Boninger, D.S., 183
Bonto, M.A., 94
Booker, J.M., 485
Boorman, L., 288
Boose, J.H., 480, 485, 494
Bord, R.J., 768
Bordage, G., 668, 669, 672
Borgeaud, P., 295
Boring, E.G., 142
Borko, H., 600, 609
Borman, W.C., 330
Born, D.G., 65
Bornstein, G.K., 798
Bosart, L.F., 129
Boschelli, M.M., 288
Boshuizen, H.P.A., 666,669, 670, 676, 681
Bosselmann, P., 763
Bossert, S., 743
Bostrom, A., 771
Bothwell, R.K., 93, 830, 832, 833, 837, 841
Bouas, K.S., 428
Bourgeois, M., 396
Bourne, L.E. Jr, 125
Bourne, L.E., 353
Bovair, S., 148, 467, 470
Bove, W., 561
Bowen, C.W., 598
Bowen, G.M., 613
Bower, G.H., 85, 96, 730, 744, 574, 796
Bower, G., 560, 561
Bowers, C.A., 502
Boyce, C.F., 564
Boyle, C.F., 462, 564, 608
Boyle, R.A., 572
Boyle, R.H., 764
Bozeman, W., 563
Bradbury, J.A., 772
Braden-Harder, L., 651
Bradfield, A.L., 95, 800
Bradley, R.A., 360
Bradshaw, J.M., 485, 494
Brainerd, C.J., 296, 299, 794
Branaghan, R., 25
Brandimonte, M.A., 379, 380, 381, 400
Brandsford, J.D., 87
Brandt, H.A., 743
Brannan, M., 798
Brannon, L.A., 178
Bransford, J., 151, 596, 603, 605, 610, 611, 613
Bransford, J.D., 87, 596, 599, 604, 605, 606, 609, 611, 613, 615, 616
Braun, C., 502
Braune, R., 257, 270
Braunstein, D.N., 328
Braverman, E.P., 324
Bray, M.H., 605, 616
Brechner, K.C., 774
Breckler, S.J., 177, 180
Breedin, S.D., 22,25, 482, 483, 496
Breen, T., 23
Breen, T.J., 25, 220, 291, 482, 483, 496
Breinlinger, K., 575
Breitholtz, E., 732, 733
Brennan, R., 798
Brennan, S.E., 421
Bresley, B., 268
Breuker, J., 489
Breuker, J.A., 485
Brewer, M.B., 774
Brewer, W., 384
Brewer, W.F., 298
Brewer, ***, 598, 602, 612
Brewin, C.R., 745
Bridges, E.M., 604
Bridgwater, C., 178
Briere, J., 100, 101
Brigham, J.C., 93, 791, 802, 830, 832, 833, 837, 841
Bright, G., 563
Britt, M.A., 598
Britton, B.K., 598
Broadbent, D.E., 11, 17, 18, 36, 290, 396, 483
Broadbent, M.H.P., 483
Brock, D.J.H., 716
Brock, J.F., 49
Brock, R., 223, 234
Brock, T.C., 178
Bromer, P., 180
Bronfenbrenner, U., 378, 385, 386
Broniarczyk, S., 347, 349, 356
Brookings, J.B., 45
Brooks, L., 356
Brooks, L.R., 105, 664, 668, 670, 673, 674, 675
Brophy, S., 599
Brouillard, M., 735
Brown, A.L., 584, 604, 606, 609, 612, 613, 614, 616, 617
Brown, C.E., 500
Brown, D.W., 186, 196
Brown, D.J., 326, 327
Brown, E.L., 831
Brown, J., 596, 607, 608
Brown, J.D., 747
Brown, J.S., 298, 563, 564, 565, 577, 650, 810
Brown, R., 792
Brown, S.P., 345
Brown, S.W., 91
Brown, T.C., 762
Browne, A., 100
Brubaker, B., 383, 384, 385, 392, 395
Bruce, R., 427
Bruck, M., 94, 798, 805, 806
Brucks, M., 352, 357
Bruer, J.T., 680
Bruner, J.S., 607
Bruni, J.R., 47
Brunswick, E., 132
Bryan, W.L., 35, 37, 39
Bryman, A., 480, 487, 561
Bryson, S., 6
Buck, G., 644
Buckhout, R., 831
Buckout, R., 799
Bukstel, L., 482
Bull, R., 797, 798
Bullemer, P., 666, 669
Bullen, C.V., 411
Bullock, B., 430
Bunderson, C.V., 563
Burbules, N.C., 615
Burdick, M., 262, 274
Burgess, I.S., 729
Burgess-Yanemovic, K.C., 414, 430
Burke, R.R., 344
Burn, S.M., 768
Burns, D.D., 738
Burns, H.J., 793

Burns, P., 563
Burr, B.J., 6
Burrows, D., 396, 400
Burstein, J., 651
Burt, C.D.B., 791
Burtis, P.J., 605
Burton, A.M., 71, 128, 480, 482, 483, 485, 486, 489, 494, 499, 501
Burton, I., 770
Burton, R.R., 564, 650
Busemeyer, J.R., 123
Bushyhead, J.B., 129
Busquets, A.M., 288
Buss, T., 236, 239
Butler, K.A., 22
Butterfield, E.C., 17
Butterfield, K.D., 331
Buttigieg, M., 232, 543
Button, C.M., 176
Buxton, W., 414, 415, 425, 433, 606
Buxton, W.A.S., 414, 425
Byrne, M.D., 148
Bystritsky, A., 733, 735

Cacciabue, P.C., 565
Cacioppo, J.T., 131, 180, 184, 186, 196
Cadge, B., 711
Cafferty, T.P., 318, 319, 320
Caird, J., 234
Calamari, J.E., 733, 735
Calderwood, R, 121, 145, 149, 163, 220, 228, 293, 300, 489, 664, 679
Calfee, R.C., 572, 604
Calvez, V., 481, 485
Camerer, C.F., 77, 130, 362
Camp, C.J., 99, 104, 396, 401
Campbell, D.S., 824
Campbell, D.T., 417
Campbell, G.J.M., 664, 666
Campbell, J.I.D., 62
Campbell, M.K., 712
Campbell, R.L., 5,7
Campion, J.E., 318
Campion, M.A., 318, 322
Campione, J.C., 606, 613, 614, 616, 617
Canas, J., 24
Cannella, A.A., 328
Cannon-Bowers, J.A., 303, 305, 496
Canter, R.J., 766
Cantor, N., 325
Cantril, H., 183
Caplan, L.J., 386
Caplan, R., 146
Carasiti, I., 732
Carbonnell, J.R., 265
Card, S., 700
Card, S.K., 6, 13, 61, 77, 424, 444, 445, 448, 449, 454, 455, 456, 457, 582
Cardosi, K.M., 259
Cardy, R.L., 318
Carey, S., 575
Carley, K., 428
Carmody, M.A., 302
Carpenter, P., 648
Carpenter, P.A., 266, 529, 530, 531, 653, 654
Carr, H.A., 9
Carraher, D.W., 604
Carraher, T.N., 604
Carretta, T.R., 288, 294
Carroll, J., 430
Carroll, J.B., 629, 638
Carroll, J.D., 358, 359, 497
Carroll, J.M., 5, 7, 11, 14, 435
Carroll, J.S., 828, 830
Carroll, L.A., 284
Carron, A.V., 188
Carswell, C.M., 12, 45, 232, 257
Carswell, M.C., 520, 538, 539, 540, 543
Carter, K.A., 414, 415, 433
Carter, M., 417, 426
Carver, C.S., 322
Carver, S.M., 605, 606
Case, R., 572, 575
Casey, E.J., 232, 543
Casey, J.T., 300
Casey, S., 283
Cashman, T.J., 378
Cassidy, T., 801
Castella, N., 697
Cate, F.H., 821
Catrambone, R., 585
Cavanaugh, J.C., 98
Cavanaugh, J.P., 454
Ceci, S.J., 94, 101, 378, 385, 601, 798, 805, 806
Cellier, M.-M., 222
Cermak, L.S., 86, 97, 98
Chabay, R.W., 563, 608
Chadwick, S., 702, 708
Chaffee, S., 760, 827
Chaffin, R., 378, 630, 648
Chahal, K., 801
Chaiken, S., 120, 176, 179, 180, 182, 183, 184, 190, 191, 193, 194, 416, 762, 764
Chakravarti, D., 353, 364
Chalfonte, B.L., 88, 90, 414, 433
Chalmers, I., 698
Chambliss, M.J., 604, 712
Chan, C.K.K., 605
Chance, J.E., 95
Chandhok, R., 430
Chandler, C.C., 94
Chandler, P., 559, 560, 561
Chandok, R., 430
Chandrasekaran, B., 682, 683
Chang, J.J., 497
Chang, T.M., 69
Channon, S., 742, 743
Chao, C., 581
Chapanis, A., 11, 387, 389, 396, 424
Chapman, M., 706
Charness, N., 57, 58, 59, 61, 62, 63, 64, 128, 285, 297, 482, 596, 602, 665
Charney, D., 430
Chase, W.G., 23, 57, 64, 68, 128, 260, 482, 576, 665, 668, 669
Chatterjee, R., 351
Chatterjee, S., 364
Chattopadhyay, A., 344, 345, 353, 354
Chaudhury, V., 790
Cheit, R., 101
Chen, E., 733, 735
Cheney, F., 146
Cherfas, J., 764
Cherry, E.C., 34, 35, 36
Cheung, B., 283
Chi, M.T.H., 23, 58, 69, 77, 150, 357, 480, 482, 576, 585, 596, 598, 602, 605, 609, 664, 665
Chiesi, H.L., 598
Child, J., 328
Childers, T.L., 103
Chinn, D.E., 765
Chinn, ***, 598, 602, 612
Chipman, S., 69
Chiroro, P., 792
Chiu, C.Y., 749
Chiu, M., 605
Chiu, P., 427
Chodorow, M., 651
Choi, J.-I., 16
Chou, C., 269
Christal, R., 651, 653
Christal, R.E., 48
Christensen-Szalanski, J.J.J., 129
Christhilf, D.M., 252
Christianson, S., 95, 744, 791, 792, 793
Chun, D.M., 559
Chute, D.L., 396
Chute, R.D., 258
Citera, M., 500
Claessen, H.F.A., 666
Clancey, W.J., 564, 668, 676
Clare, I., 798
Clark, D.A., 734, 742
Clark, D.M., 732, 733, 734, 739, 742
Clark, H.H., 260, 421
Clark, J.M., 559
Clark, R.E.., 553, 563

Clarke, B., 491
Clauer, R., 424, 434
Cleghorn, A., 379
Clement, C.A., 583
Clement, J., 599
Clements, C.M., 733, 738, 748
Clements, D.H., 557, 580
Cleveland, J.N., 320
Cleveland, W.S., 513, 514, 518, 520, 524, 525, 532, 537, 540, 545
Clifford, B.R., 797, 801
Clifford, B.R.,
Cline, J., 675
Clinkenbeard, P., 588
Clough, G.C., 763
Cobb, L., 327
Cobb, P., 596, 602, 607, 615
Cobern, M.K., 764, 765, 769
Coblentz, C.L., 105, 673, 674, 675
Cockburn, J., 396, 400
Cody, R., 704
Coe, B., 702
Coekin, J.A., 232
Cohen, G., 705
Cohen, M.D., 422
Cohen, M.S., 303
Cohen, P., 426
Cole, M., 377, 379, 601
Collins, A., 23, 69, 73, 483, 565, 572, 575, 577, 596, 602, 603, 606, 607, 608
Collins, M.A., 747
Collins, S., 716
Collis, K., 646
Combs, B., 770
Commoner, B., 775
Companion, M.A., 292
Compton, P., 480
Cone, J.D., 766
Conklin, E., 414, 430
Conlon, A.B., 119
Connell, T., 605, 606
Connelly, A., 609
Connolly, T., 127
Connors, E., 791, 804, 811, 831
Conrad, F., 576, 582
Conrad, F.G., 7
Constanzo, M., 765
Conte, J., 101
Conway, B.E., 587
Conway, M.A., 104, 810
Cook, D.A., 768
Cook, M., 731
Cook, R.I., 144, 146, 147, 148, 149, 150, 158, 162, 164, 165, 168
Cook, T.D., 417, 696
Cooke, A.D.J., 118
Cooke, D.J., 116
Cooke, F.W., 212, 221
Cooke, N., 22, 23, 25, 39, 76, 128, 220, 291, 299, 323, 480, 481, 482, 483, 484, 485, 486, 492, 493, 496, 497, 500, 501
Cooksey, R.W., 115, 123
Cooper, A., 742
Cooper, D., 769
Cooper, G.A., 609
Cooper, J., 561
Cooper, L., 359, 766
Cooper, L.A., 255, 276, 522
Cooper, M., 559, 560
Cooper, P.F., 396
Cooper, P.J., 742
Cooper, W.H., 420
Copen, W.A., 608
Coppin, R.J., 697
Corban, J.M., 153
Corbett, A., 462
Corbett, A.T., 564, 576, 582
Cordingley, E.S., 485, 488, 489, 494
Corfman, K.P., 131
Corlett, E.N., 494
Corstjens, M.L., 360
Corteen, R.S., 36
Corter, J.E., 22, 496
Corvette, M., 393, 396
Cosden, M.A., 615
Cosier, R., 157
Costantini, E., 823, 826
Cote, N., 605
Cottom, C.D., 605, 616
Cotton, J.L., 182
Couch, J.V., 760, 768
Coughlin, L.D., 666, 668, 669
Coulson, R., 150, 152
Coulson, R.L., 150, 152, 680, 683, 684, 685, 688
Coulter, A.,
Coupey, E., 152
Courage, M.L., 94
Court, J.H., 654
Coury, B.G., 44
Covi, L., 434
Cowan, D.A., 328, 329
Cowan, N., 37, 88
Cox, B.D., 580
Cox, J., 126
Coyne, C., 696
Crabb, P.B., 775
Crabtree, M.S., 287, 304
Craig, K.M., 428
Craighead, W.E., 739
Craik, F.I.M., 86, 91, 106, 726
Craik, H.K., 763
Craik, K.H., 763
Crandall, B., 117, 121, 292, 293, 300, 303
Craske, M.G., 733, 735, 737
Craven, R.G., 612
Creighton, P., 699
Crews, J.I., 768
Crews, T.R., 611, 613
Crites, S.L. Jr., 177
Cronbach, L.J., 49, 631, 632, 634
Croner, C.M., 540, 542
Cronshaw, S.F., 326, 327
Crossman, E.R., 212, 221, 222
Crotteau-Huffman, M., 101
Crowder, R.G., 17, 104
Crowley, T., 414
Crowther, J.H., 743
Crutchfield, J., 275, 283, 284, 288, 291, 301
Cruzen, D., 748
Ctgv, 603, 605, 606, 611, 613, 615, 616
Cuban, L., 554, 555
Cuff, D.J., 539, 540
Cullen, J., 480, 487
Cully, D., 833, 835
Culter, B.L., 93
Cummings, A., 428
Cummings, S., 768
Cunnungham, J.P., 22
Curry, D.J., 131
Curry, R.E., 213, 226, 237, 270
Curtis, P., 414, 424
Cushing, K.S., 597
Cutler, B., 791
Cutler, B.L., 799, 821, 823, 826, 830, 831, 833, 834, 836, 837, 838, 839, 840, 841
Cutshall, J.L., 94, 95, 104
Cyert, R.M., 422

D'amico, M., 379
Dalbey, J., 557
Dallenbach, K.M., 35
Damos, D.L., 45
Daneman, M., 653
Daniel, T.C., 762, 763
Daniels, J.E., 760
Danko, N., 275
Darby, M.R., 345
Dark, V., 260
Dark, V.J., 289
Darley, J.M., 764, 766
Darnell, M., 14
Das, J.P., 653, 654
Davenport, D.M., 486, 496
David, Y.M., 615
Davidson, A.R., 179, 185, 186
Davies, D.R., 33, 42
Davies, G., 97
Davies, G.M., 791, 795, 796, 798, 801, 831
Davies, S., 733
Davis, F.D., 18, 416
Davis, G.R., 758
Davis, H., 612

Davis, R.B., 557
Davis, T.J., 263
Dawes, R.M., 116, 120, 129, 174, 762, 774
Dawson-Saunders, B., 680
Day, D.V., 320, 321, 326, 327, 328, 329
Day, L., 292
Dayton, T., 299, 496
De Vlaminck, M., 287
Deanda, A., 155
Dearborn, D.C., 329
Dearholt, D.W., 22, 23, 25, 299, 483, 496
Deboeck, P., 649
Debreu, G., 360
Debreuil, S.C., 91
Deci, E.L., 769
Decorte, E., 556, 557, 558, 564, 596
Decortis, F., 222, 227
Deelucas, D., 599
Deffenbacher, K.A., 93, 664, 807, 831, 837
Degani, A., 262, 266, 267, 268
Degroot, A.D., 128, 482, 671
Deighton, J., 345, 352, 355
Dekeyser, V., 154, 155, 222, 223, 227
Dekleer, J., 298, 564
Delaney, R., 389, 396, 400
Deleeuw, N., 605
Dellarosa, D., 353
Delprata, D.J., 765
Deluca, A.J., 826
Deluca, D.R., 771
Delucia, A.A., 543
Demaio, J., 23
Demaio, J.C., 482, 483, 496
Demitrack, M.A., 743
Dempster, F.N., 90
Denisi, A.S., 318, 319, 320
Dennett, J.L., 796
Denning, R., 73
Dennis, A.R., 423
Dennis, M.J., 596
Dennis, M.L., 765
Dent, J., 730
Depaulo, B.M., 801
Derry, S.J., 553, 564
Derubeis, R.J., 738, 739, 741
Desanctis, G., 414
Desessa, A.A., 557
Deshon, R.P., 323
Deshpande, S.P., 322
Dessouky, M.I., 222
Detterman, D.K., 579, 599
Detweiler, M.C., 294
Deutsch, D., 36
Deutsch, J.A., 36
Devader, C., 325
Devenport, J.L., 833, 838, 839, 840, 841
Devillis, B.M., 712
Devillis, R.F., 712
Devine, E., 696
Devine, P.G., 173, 831, 833, 838
Dewey, S., 612
Dewsbury, D.A., 38
Dexter, H.R., 826, 828, 829, 830, 833, 834, 837, 839
Dey, P., 716
Deyoung, R., 760, 769
Dhaliwal, J.S., 500
Dhar, R., 352
Diaper, D., 479, 480
Dibello, L.V., 642
Dickinson, D., 697, 711
Dickson, G.W., 414, 524
Dickson, P.R., 349
Diederich, J., 488
Diehl, E., 125
Diehl, M., 180
Dietrich, D.A., 702
Dillehay, R.C., 822
Dimatteo, M.R., 708
Dimges, 300
Dipboye, R.L., 318
Dipboye, R.L., 318
Djemil, T., 223, 234
Dobbins, G.H., 318
Dodson, J.D., 94
Doerner, D., 380
Doherty, M.E., 125, 301
Doherty, M.L., 321, 364
Doherty-Sneddon, G., 425
Dole, J.A., 605
Dombeck, M.J., 733
Dominguez, C., 264, 283, 284
Donchin, E., 49, 304
Donnell, C.D., 733
Doob, A.N., 836
Doob, L.W., 771
Dorner, D., 154, 157, 599
Dougherty, M.R.P., 123, 283, 295
Dourish, P., 414, 415, 433
Downing, J.W., 180
Downs, J., 122
Doyle, D.J., 296, 300
Drake, R.A., 180
Driskell, J.E., 304
Driver, R., 602, 607
Druckman, D., 292, 300, 303, 775
Drury, C.G., 229
Dueker, K.J., 767
Duensing, S., 746
Duffy, S.A., 44
Dugdale, B., 50, 323
Duguid, P., 577, 596, 607
Dukerich, J.M., 334
Dulin, J., 127
Dumais, D.S., 596, 602
Dumais, S.T., 39, 66, 473
Dunbar, K., 598
Duncan, J., 254
Duncan, K., 148
Duncan, S., 521, 522
Duncker, K., 66, 584, 585
Dunegan, K.J., 118
Dunlap, R.E., 763
Dunn, C.P., 330
Dunn, P.L., 648
Dunn, R., 537
Dunning, D., 93
Duran, A.S., 155
Duran, R., 711
Durlach, N.I., 778
Durso, F.T., 22, 23 153, 154, 220, 250, 264, 265, 275, 283, 284, 288, 291, 299, 301, 482, 483, 496
Duschl, R.A., 596, 598, 599, 604, 613
Dutta, R., 67
Dutton, J.E., 330, 334
Dutton, J.M., 225, 235
Duus, R.E., 775
Dweck, C.S., 601, 612
Dwyer, W.O., 764, 765, 769
Dyck, J., 24
Dyck, J.L., 557
Dyer, B.P., 521, 522, 525
Dywan, J., 105
Dzubia-Leatherman, J., 100

Eagly, A.H., 176, 177, 180, 182, 183, 184, 190, 191, 416, 762
Easterbrook, J.A., 793
Eastwood, L.F., 563
Ebbinghaus, H., 90
Eberts, R.E., 49, 562
Ebreo, A., 769
Echabe, A.E., 184
Eco, U., 332
Edelson, D.C., 596, 613
Edgerton, E., 712
Edwards, E., 209, 213, 222, 223, 225, 228, 232
Edwards, J.R., 323
Edwards, K., 177
Edwards, M.B., 302
Edwards, M.U., 429
Edwards, W., 118
Egeth, H., 839
Egeth, H.E., 791, 808
Eggemeier, F.T., 41, 46, 268
Egido, C., 424, 435
Ehlers, A., 731, 733
Ehrich, R.W., 492
Ehrlich, D., 182
Ehrlich, S.B., 326
Ehrlich, S.F., 433
Eich, J.M., 86

Eichinger, D.C., 615
Eimermann, T., 822, 823, 827
Einhorn, H.J., 117
Einstein, G.O., 99, 378, 379, 380, 396, 398, 400
Eisenhardt, K.M., 331
Eiser, C., 709, 710
Eiser, J.R., 709, 710, 771
Ekman, P., 490, 801
Elaad, E., 802
Eliashberg, J., 351
Elie, C.J., 90, 91
Elkind, J.I., 13
Ellicott, A., 738
Ellis, C.A., 414
Ellis, J.A., 378, 379, 380, 382, 385, 393, 398
Ellis, R.D., 294, 678
Ellis, S.R., 257
Ellison, K.W., 799
Ellsworth, P.C., 791, 800, 808, 831, 832
Elo, A.E., 63
Elrod, S., 427
Elstein, A.S., 128, 490, 663, 664, 671, 678
Elworth, J.T., 769
Emberton, M., 698
Embretson, S.E., 629, 630, 632, 638, 640, 642, 648, 649, 650, 651, 654, 655
Emerson, E., 729
Emery, G., 727, 738, 749
Endsley, M.R., 213, 234, 250, 264, 274, 283, 284, 287, 289, 291, 298, 295, 296, 302, 303
Engel, R.A., 738
England, J.L., 763
Engle, R.A., 575
Engle, R.W., 482
Englestadt, P.H., 222
English, W.K., 6
Ensing, M., 290
Ensing, M.J., 253
Entwistle, V.A., 695, 697
Epstein, W., 92
Erdelyi, M., 798
Erdener, C.B., 330
Erickson, J., 605, 606
Ericsson, K.A., 57, 58, 59, 61, 70, 73, 128 , 250, 265, 292, 296, 484, 490, 491, 500, 576, 602, 604, 667, 668
Ernst, G.W., 584
Ertmer, P.A., 612
Erzberger, H., 263
Esplin, P.W., 803
Eugenio, P., 831
Euston, D., 23
Evans, E., 401
Evans, G.W., 762
Evans, M.D., 738, 739
Everett, P.B., 758
Ewald, L.S., 741, 742, 743
Exner, J.E., 728
Eylon, B., 598, 680
Eysenck, M.W., 395, 728

Fabrigar, L.R., 176, 177, 183
Fadden, D.M., 257
Fader, P.S., 363
Faigman, D.L., 791, 807, 809
Fairburn, C.G., 742
Farr, J.L., 318
Farr, M.J., 58, 150, 596
Farr, M.J., 357
Fathi, D.C., 96
Favart, M., 598
Fay, A.L., 558
Fazio, R.H., 176, 180, 184, 185, 186, 189, 764
Federico, P., 283, 293
Feger, H., 22
Feigenbaum, E.A., 57, 64, 65, 480
Feightner, J.W., 664, 666, 668, 672
Feinberg, F.M., 351
Feinstein, A.R., 676
Feldman, J., 742
Feldman, J.M., 319, 354, 363
Feldman, M.S., 331, 332, 333
Felson, R.B., 747
Felton, M., 614, 615
Feltovich, P.J., 23, 69, 145, 150, 152, 155, 482, 576, 585, 596, 597, 598, 664, 665, 672, 675, 676, 680, 683, 684, 685, 688
Feng, C., 638
Ferguson, J., 378
Ferguson, T.J., 834, 835, 836
Fernandez, M., 6
Ferrari, M., 588
Ferrell, W.R., 225, 228
Festinger, L., 180, 181, 182, 183, 184
Filiatrault, P., 766
Fillenbaum, S., 126
Fincham, J.M., 576, 582
Fineberg, H.V., 770
Finholt, T.A., 414, 416, 417, 424, 428, 434
Finkelhor, D., 100
Finn, K., 421, 425, 435
Finnie, S., 287, 299, 301, 303
Fiol, C.M., 332
Fiol, M.C., 328
Fischer, G.H., 638
Fischer, K., 126
Fischer, U., 155, 263, 269, 300
Fischhoff, B., 116, 117, 122, 126, 129, 130, 145, 146, 262, 770, 771, 772, 773
Fish, R.S., 414, 415, 429, 433
Fishbein, M., 185, 186, 187, 188, 358
Fisher, C., 492
Fisher, D.L., 44
Fisher, P., 766
Fisher, R.P., 96, 104, 795, 796, 797, 798, 799
Fisk, A.D., 38, 39, 40, 41, 42
Fiske, S.T., 173, 191, 193
Fitts, P.M., 38, 142, 252
Fitzgerald, P., 396
Fitzgerald, P., 483
Fivush, R., 94
Flach, J., 229, 230, 232, 234, 252, 289, 543
Flascher, O.M., 234
Flavell, J.C., 612
Flay, B.R., 779
Fleece, E.L., 710
Fleishman, E.A., 48
Fleming, A.M., 425
Fleming, I., 771
Flemming, P.W., 707
Flesch, R., 714
Fletcher, C.R., 667
Fletcher, J.F., 176
Fletcher, S.W., 399
Flores, F., 164
Flores, F., 16
Foa, E.B., 733
Fodor,J., 9
Fogarty, S.J., 741
Foley, J.D., 778
Folkard, S., 395
Folleso, K., 283, 287, 300
Forbes, S.M., 239
Forbus, K.D., 583
Ford, J.M., 71, 72, 487, 765
Ford, J.K., 315, 321, 323, 324, 319, 364
Ford, K.M., 145, 150, 480, 494
Forgas, J., 193
Forsdick, H., 414
Foss, J.W., 99, 104, 396
Foster, G., 414, 426
Foti, R.J., 325
Fournier, J., 97, 98, 379
Foushee, H.C., 259, 261
Fowler, R., 396
Fox, P.W., 666, 669
Foxx, R.M., 766
Foyle, D.C., 301
Frager, N.B., 762
Fraisse, P., 380, 394
Francouer, E., 94
Franks, J.J., 87, 605
Fransella, F., 329, 494
Fraumeni, J.R., 534

Frazier, L., 74
Frederiksen, C.H., 664, 667, 668, 682
Frederiksen, J., 596, 606, 609, 610, 613
Fredrickson, R.,
Freed, S., 737
Freedman, J., 769
Freedman, M.R., 130
Freeman, J.T., 121, 303
French, H.F., 759
Frensch, P.A., 664
Fresco, D., 738
Freud, S., 100
Frey, D., 182
Fridgen, C.C., 762
Fried, M., 763
Friedman, A., 297
Friedman, D.E., 647, 658
Friedman, W., 383
Frost, N., 630
Frowley, J.N., 791
Fu, X., 411
Fukuoka, H., 414
Fulero, S., 839
Fuller, D.K., 302
Fullilove, M.T., 101
Funk, K., 269, 270
Funke, J., 664
Furnas, G.W., 473
Furness, T.A., 294
Fusco, M.E., 774
Fussell, S.R., 421

Gaba, D., 664, 679, 680
Gaba, D.M., 155, 283
Gabarro, J.J., 411
Gabriel, R.F., 257
Gaeth, G.J., 119, 120, 121
Gagliano, M.E., 709, 710
Gagne, R.M., 574, 580, 581, 607
Gaines, B.R., 480, 483, 494
Galbraith, M.E., 748
Gale, J., 672
Gale, N., 535
Galegher, J., 435
Gallini, J.K., 551, 559, 561
Gallup, A.M., 763
Gallup, G.H., 763
Gallupe, R.B., 420
Gambone, J.C., 708
Gammack, J.G., 23, 496, 500
Garber, S., 490
Garber, T., 760, 768
Garcia-Mila, M., 613
Gardner, G.T., 758, 767, 768, 770, 771, 774, 775
Gardner, H., 596
Gardner, W.L., 180, 333
Garland, D.J., 250
Garner, D.M., 742
Garner, R., 712
Garner, W.R., 260
Garrison, R.F., 513, 531
Garrison, S., 606, 609, 615
Garry, M., 91, 102
Garton, L., 428
Gash, D.C., 411, 431
Gaskill, G.D., 792
Gaskins, R.W., 712
Gati, I., 131
Gattis, M., 528, 529, 540
Gautschi, D.A., 360
Gaver, W.W., 414, 415, 433
Gee, J.P., 602
Geffen, G., 36, 729
Geiselman, R.E., 96, 104, 791, 795, 796, 797, 798
Geissler, J., 414, 415
Geiwitz, J., 75, 485, 488, 494, 496
Gelder, M., 733, 734
Geller, E.S., 758, 760, 766, 767, 769
Gelman, S.A., 575
Gentner, D., 19, 150, 151, 225, 583, 584, 599
Gentry, M., 390
George, C.F., 708
George, J.F., 423
George, R.C., 797
Gescheider, G.A., 359
Getchell-Reiter, K, 121
Getty, D.J., 154
Gettys, C.F., 123, 299, 300
Ghatala, E.S., 700
Gibbons, J.H., 758
Gibbs, S., 708
Gibbs, S.J., 414
Gibson, J.J., 234, 251, 585
Gibson,W., 6
Gick, M.L., 584, 585
Gifford, R., 774
Gigerenzer, G., 122, 123, 351
Gilbert, E.W., 534
Gilbert, R., 827, 830
Gilfillan, A., 716
Gillan, D.J., 8, 10, 11, 12, 14, 22, 25, 482, 496, 524, 527, 544, 545
Gilligan, S.G., 96
Gilliland, K., 395
Gilliland, S.W., 321, 323
Gillis, M., 759
Gilmartin, K., 58
Gilson, R.D., 155
Giner-Sorolla, R., 179, 180
Gioia, D.A., 334
Girgus, J.S., 738
Gitlin, M.J., 738
Gitomer, D., 613
Givon, M ., 131
Glance, N.S., 773
Glaser, 482
Glaser, B.G., 331
Glaser, R., 7, 23, 58, 69, 150, 357, 480, 564, 576, 585, 596, 597, 598, 601, 602, 604, 605, 609, 613, , 630, 646, 649, 664, 665, 675
Glass, G.V., 696
Glenberg, A.M., 92, 102
Glgvz, S., 604
Glisky, E.L., 104
Globerson, T., 615
Gluck, M.A., 85, 574
Gluckman, J.P., 302
Gobet, F., 68
Goff, M., 48
Gold, P.W., 743
Gold, R., 427
Goldberg, D., 427
Goldberg, E.D., 758
Goldberg, M.E., 357
Goldman, S.R., 596, 604, 605, 606, 609, 611, 613, 614, 615, 616
Goldsmith, M., 90
Goldsmith, T.E., 23, 24, 482, 483, 486, 496
Goldstein, A.G., 95
Goldstein, C., 709
Goldstein, D., 122, 123
Goldstein, I.L., 39, 324
Gollwitzer, P.M., 748, 749
Gomez, L., 596, 613
Gomez, L.W., 473
Gomez, R.L., 24, 482, 496
Gomez-Meza, M., 292
Gonthier, D., 154
Gonzalez, R., 800
Gonzalvo, P., 24
Goodenough D.R., 289
Goodman, G.S., 94, 805
Goodstein, L., 209, 210, 215, 223, 224, 226, 275
Goodstein, L.P., 664
Goossens, L., 97
Gopher, D., 37, 48, 49, 153, 250, 266, 268, 269
Gorayska, B., 388, 398
Gordon, A., 616
Gordon, P.C., 355
Gorenstein, G.W., 831
Gosbee, J.W., 255
Goschke, T., 383, 384
Gotlib, I.H., 729, 741
Gott, S.P., 488, 489
Gould, L.C., 771
Graesser, A.C., 608
Graf, P., 88, 273
Grafman, J., 396
Grahame, N.J., 574
Grant, K.R., 414, 429
Grant, M.J., 176
Grantham, C.E., 429

Grantham, S., 794
Grassia, J., 132
Gravelle, M., 286
Gray, J.A., 36
Gray, W.D., 455
Grazioli, S., 156
Gredler, M.E., 551
Green, P.E., 359
Green, S., 263
Green, T.R.G., 473
Greenberg, C.I., 762
Greenberg, M.S., 728, 740
Greene, S., 597
Greene, T.R., 600
Greeno, J., 16, 685
Greeno, J.G., 482, 572, 573, 575, 576, 585, 586, 596, 602
Greenwald, A.G., 18, 77, 354
Greer, B., 556, 557, 558, 596
Gregory, M., 703
Greier, H.C., 766
Greif, I., 435
Greimas, A.J., 332, 333
Grether, D.M., 351
Grewal, D., 352
Grief, I., 389, 392
Grier, M., 122
Griffey, D., 24
Griffey, D.C., 482, 496
Griffin, P., 601
Griffin, W.C., 262
Griggs, D., 47
Grigorenko, E.L., 588
Groen, G.J., 70, 664, 666, 667, 668, 670, 672, 674, 675, 680
Gronlund, S.D., 153, 154, 250, 264, 265 283, 295
Grosslight, L., 612
Grossman, L.R., 7
Grote, G.S., 237
Group Tech, 426
Grover, M.D., 488, 489
Grudin, J., 430, 433
Gruen, D.M., 296
Gruneberg, M.M., 97, 98
Gu, Y., 519, 520
Guadagni, P.M., 361
Guernsey, T.F., 810, 811
Gugerty, L.J., 283, 287, 295
Gullo, D.F., 557, 580
Gupta, S., 131
Gurtner, J., 557
Gurtner, J.-L., 608
Gutfeld, R., 762
Guttman, I., 182
Guyatt, G.H., 666, 668
Guynn, M.E., 99
Guzdial, M., 596, 605, 606
Gwin, H.L., 758

Ha, H.-Y., 345
Ha, Y.-W., 345
Haake, J., 414, 415, 429
Habon, M.W., 648
Hackett, R., 606, 616
Hackworth, C.A., 275, 283, 284, 288, 291, 301
Hadfield, O.D., 24
Hahlweg, K., 743
Hahn, E.C., 260
Hake, D.F., 766
Halasz, F., 16, 414, 427
Halberstadt, L.J., 738
Hale, D.P., 500
Halford, G.S., 576
Halgren, T.L., 23, 482, 484, 486, 496, 497, 500, 501
Hall, E.M., 488, 489
Hall, E.P., 23, 482, 484, 486, 496, 497, 500, 501
Hall, J.K., 304
Hall, J.-A., 747
Hall, P.D., 328
Hall, R.P., 602
Hallam, R.S., 711
Hallinger, P., 604
Hallman, W.K., 771
Halperin, W.C., 535
Hamad, C.D., 769
Hambleton, R., 635, 637
Hambrick, D.C., 328
Hamid, A., 608
Hamilton, D.L., 173
Hamilton, D.P., 778
Hamm, R.M., 127, 132
Hammen, C., 738
Hammerle, O., 540, 542
Hammond, K.R., 125, 126, 132
Hammond, L.S., 696, 708
Hammond, M.M., 768
Hancock, P.M.A., 40
Hancock, P., 234
Hancock, P.A., 292, 294
Hanes, L.F., 155, 157, 232
Hanges, P.J., 326, 327
Hank, G., 743
Hannafin, M., 16
Hanowski, R.J., 77
Hansen, J.-P., 232
Hansman, R.J., 258, 260, 287
Happ, A., 24
Harbison-Briggs, K., 485
Hardie, B.G.S., 363, 368
Hardin, G., 773
Hardin, J.B., 428
Hardin, T.S., 738
Harel, I., 596
Harkins, S.G., 195
Harma, M.I., 395
Harp, S., 561
Harris, C.K., 765, 779
Harris, C.S., 537
Harris, J.E., 98, 99, 378, 379, 384, 385, 386, 387, 390
Harris, J.L., 396
Harris, R.J., 119
Harris, R.L., 252, 266
Harris, R.P., 399
Harrison, B.L., 487
Harrison, P., 124
Harrison, S., 415, 427
Hart, A., 488
Hart, J.T., 92
Hart, J., 396
Hart, S.G., 49, 269, 270
Harter, N., 35, 37, 39
Hartman, B.O., 292
Harvey, N., 349
Hasher, L., 67, 299, 727
Hashtroudi, S., 91, 105
Hass, R.G., 180, 765
Hassebrock, F., 155, 666, 668, 669
Hasselbring, T., 604, 606
Hastie, R., 131, 321, 354, 522, 523, 525, 527, 540, 542, 544
Hastorf, A., 183
Hatano, G., 599, 600, 615
Hatch, J., 700, 702, 703, 704
Haugtvedt, C.P., 196, 197
Hausenblas, H.A., 188
Hauser, J.R., 346, 351, 365
Hawes, R., 710
Hawkins, F.H., 259, 268
Haworth, D.A., 500
Hayes, J.R., 596, 700, 704
Hayes, S.C., 766
Hayward, A., 743
Heath, T.B., 364
Heckerman, D.E., 488
Heckler, S.E., 103, 118
Hedgecock, A.P., 494, 499
Hedges, D.G., 90
Hedges, L.V., 521, 522
Heers, S., 262, 274
Heiman, M., 86
Heimberg, R.G., 733
Helmreich, R.L., 259, 261, 275
Helson, H., 762
Hempel, W.E., 48
Hemsley, G.D., 836
Hendrickson, G., 586
Hendy, K.C., 269
Herbert, M., 747
Herman, J.L., 101
Hermann, D.J., 537, 538, 539, 540, 541, 542, 545
Herrick, D., 826
Herring, J.E., 697
Herrmann, D.J., 7, 86, 90, 103, 104, 378, 383, 384, 385, 390, 391, 392, 393, 395, 396, 398, 400, 401
Herschler, D.A., 292
Hershey, J., 119, 145, 146
Hershkowitz, I., 803

Hertel, P., 7
Hertzog, C., 7, 40
Herzog, T.R., 763
Hess, S.M., 294
Hewitt, J., 762
Heydon, J., 805
Hickey, D., 606
Hickey, D.T., 606
Hickox, J., 255, 256
Hicks, J.L., 99
Hicks, L., 153
Highhouse, S., 119
Hill, C., 700, 704
Hill, D.H., 766
Hiller, D.W., 543
Hilton, D.J., 130, 145, 675
Hindus, D., 415, 433
Hine, M.S., 615
Hinkle, R., 188
Hinsz, V.B., 58, 418, 420
Hintzman, D.L., 90, 102
Hirokawa, R.Y., 420
Hirschhorn, L., 163
Hirschman, J., 805
Hirst, E., 766
Hirst, G., 479
Hirt, E., 829
Hirtle, S.C., 23
Hiskes, D., 224
Hitch, G., 378
Hitt, M.A., 321
Hively, W., 648
Hmelo, C., 615
Ho, T.-H., 362
Hobus, P.O.M., 669
Hoc, J.-M., 223, 565
Hoch, S.J., 345, 352, 355
Hochberg, J, 13
Hodge, K.A., 40
Hodges, S.D., 176
Hodh, 793
Hofer, E., 798
Hoffman, D., 576, 582
Hoffman, H., 793
Hoffman, H.G., 746
Hoffman, R.R., 71, 128, 145, 150, 286, 480, 482, 483, 486, 485, 486, 499, 501, 664
Hoffrage, U., 351
Hogan, M.E., 728, 740
Hogarth, R.M., 117, 124
Hogg, D.N., 283, 287, 300
Hogo, H., 763
Hol, J., 414, 415
Holder, E.E., 771
Holland, H.L., 96, 796
Hollands, J.G., 12, 521, 522, 525, 527, 529, 562
Hollenbeck, J.R., 322
Holley, A., 797, 798
Hollin, C.R., 831
Hollingshead, A.B., 423, 428
Hollnagel, E., 144, 156, 221, 565
Hollon, S.D., 738, 742, 743
Holmes, B., 759
Holmes, J., 415
Holmes, D.S., 100
Holt, J., 604
Holyoak, K.J., 64, 355, 528, 529, 540, 583, 584, 585
Holzman, D.B., 678
Hong, Y.Y., 749
Hoover, R., 534
Hope, D.A., 733
Hopkin, D., 273, 275
Hopper, J.R., 760, 768, 769
Hornke, L.F., 648
Hornof, A.J., 460, 461
Horvath, F., 802
Hosch, H.M., 830
Houser, L.D., 482, 496
Housiaux, A., 222, 227
Housner, L.D., 24
Houston, D.A., 184
Houston, M.J., 103
Hovav, M., 803
Hovland, C., 327
Howard, J.A., 362, 363
Howard, N., 534
Howard, S.K., 283
Howe, M.L., 94
Howell, W.C., 39, 323, 480, 481
Howenstine, E., 768
Howes, A., 472, 473
Hoy, C., 287, 299, 301, 303
Hoy, M.G., 696
Hoyer, W.D., 345
Hoyt, J.P., 744
Hsi, S., 606, 609
Hsu, J.P., 210
Hua, S., 651
Huber, J., 351, 364
Huberman, B.A., 773
Hubinette, B., 792
Hudman, L.E., 763
Hudson, S.E., 433
Hueser, M., 237
Huey, B.M., 13
Huff, A.S., 328
Huff, C.R., 831
Hughes, H.D., 128
Hughes, J., 164
Hull, C.L., 573
Hull, R.B., 763
Hults, B.M., 321, 364
Humm, A., 389
Hummel, J.E., 64
Humphrey, C.R., 768
Humphreys, M.S., 395
Humphreys, P., 118, 119, 123
Hunt, E., 295
Hunt, E.B., 630, 631, 664
Hunter, I.M.L., 378
Hurwitz, S., 255
Husband, T.H., 101, 794
Hutcherson, S., 710
Hutchins, E., 7,16, 163, 164, 165, 168, 209, 210, 296, 332, 335, 417, 418, 421, 481, 578, 614
Hutchinson, J.W., 22, 352, 353, 355, 357, 359, 361, 362
Hutchinson, S., 255, 256
Huttenlocher, J., 521, 522
Hutton, R.B., 355, 765, 766
Hux, J.E., 709
Hvistendahl, J.K., 826, 827
Hyman, F., 263
Hyman, I.E., 101, 794
Hymes, C.M., 417, 418, 420

Iacono, W.G., 802
Ickes, W.J., 305
Ilai, D., 737
Ilardi, S.S., 739
Ilgen, D.R., 315, 317, 319
Illmarinen, J., 395
Impicciatore, P., 697
Inagaki, K., 600, 615
Inagaki, T., 224, 237
Inbau, F.E., 807
Ingaki, T., 237
Ingram, R.E., 730, 760
Intons-Peterson, M.J., 97, 98, 379, 390
Iosif, G., 228
Irvine, S.H., 648
Isaacs, E.A., 414, 415, 426, 432
Isen, A.M., 127
Isenberg, D.J., 330
Ishii, H., 414, 425
Ishikawa, S., 763

Jaccard, J.J., 185
Jackson, J.L., 384
Jackson, J.M., 764, 765, 769
Jackson, R.H., 763
Jackson, S., 611
Jackson, S.E., 330, 334
Jacobs, H.E., 768
Jacobs, S.V., 762
Jacobs, T.O., 292, 300, 303
Jacobson, A., 254, 258
Jacoby, L.L., 67, 91, 105, 664, 666, 668
Jahanian, F., 424, 434
Jain, R., 605
Jain, V.K., 714
Jamal, K., 119, 154, 155, 156, 161
James, J., 487, 490
James, W., 9, 35, 39, 293
Jamison, D., 563
Janis, I., 327
Janisse, M.P., 769
Janiszewski, C., 365

Jansen, M.G.H., 640
Jansen, R., 480
Janssen, R., 649
Janssen, W., 427
Jarvenpaa, S.L., 524
Jason, L.A., 765
Javaux, D., 287
Jeavons, A., 732, 733
Jeffery, R.W., 771
Jennings, J.M., 67
Jensen, R.S., 262, 263
Jepson, D., 584
Jerison, H.J., 42, 229
Jess, P.H., 826, 828
Jetton, T., 605
Jimerson, D.C., 743
Joaquim, S.G., 92
Jobe, J.B., 538, 539, 540, 541
Johannesen, L., 144, 146, 147, 148, 158, 162, 164, 165, 168
Johansen, R., 427
John, B.E., 448, 449, 453, 454, 455
John, J., 596, 598, 599, 604, 613
Johnson, B. T., 184, 191
Johnson, D., 614, 615
Johnson, E.J., 77, 117, 119, 122, 130, 152, 363
Johnson, E.N., 288
Johnson, H.M., 600
Johnson, L., 489
Johnson, M.K., 88, 90, 91, 105, 745, 746
Johnson, M., 7, 89
Johnson, M.P., 764
Johnson, N., 489
Johnson, N.B., 766
Johnson, P.J., 24
Johnson, P.E., 119, 154, 155, 156, 161, 490, 664, 666, 669, 672
Johnson, P.J., 496
Johnson, R., 614, 615
Johnson, S.C., 22, 483, 496
Johnson-Laird, P.N., 220, 225, 228, 297, 324, 576
Johnston, M., 811
Johnston, T., 487
Johnston, W.A., 289, 482
Joiner, T.E., 738
Jonas, K., 180
Jones, B.G., 223, 234
Jones, D.G., 264, 283, 291
Jones, G., 396
Jones, G.K., 534, 542
Jones, K.P., 697
Jones, L.M., 729
Jones, R.B., 712
Jones, R.E., 142, 252
Jordan, B., 425
Jordan, J.A., 48, 49
Jorgensen, M.D., 774
Joseph, G.M., 130, 673
Jou, J., 119
Judd, C.M., 125, 180, 184
Judd, C.H., 586
Jungck, J.R., 604
Jungermann, H., 124, 126
Jurkevich, L.M., 797
Just, M.,
Just, M.A., 266, 648, 654
Just, N., 738

Kadar, E.E., 234
Kaempf, G.L., 121, 247, 261, 275, 300
Kahn, B.E., 127
Kahn, K., 414, 426
Kahneman, D., 36, 50, 77,119, 131, 228, 262, 678, 726, 762
Kai, J., 711
Kallgren, C.A., 186
Kamin, L.J., 574
Kane, L.R., 584
Kanfer, A., 331
Kanfer, R., 48, 50, 315, 322, 323
Kanki, B.C., 259, 261, 275
Kantor, R., 609, 615
Kantowitz, B.H., 77
Kantowitz, S.C., 77
Kao, C.F., 131, 186, 196
Kao, S.-F., 574
Kaplan, B., 651
Kaplan, K.J., 179
Kaplan, R., 763
Kaplan, S., 763, 769
Kapur, N., 396, 400, 401
Karni, E., 345
Karpus, L., 760, 768
Karsenty, L., 430
Karwoski, W., 237
Kass, S.J., 292
Kasserman, J., 605
Kassin, S.M., 791, 808, 832, 833, 841
Kassirer, J.P., 665, 678, 683
Katagiri, M., 574
Kates, R.W., 770
Katona, G., 469
Katz, D., 177, 178
Katz, I., 180
Katz, I.R., 647, 658
Katz, S., 565
Katzev, R.D., 766, 768
Kaufer, D.S., 430
Kaufman, A.S., 646
Kaufman, D.R., 70, 300, 664, 666, 673, 674, 677, 678, 679, 680, 682, 683, 685, 686, 687
Kaufman, N.L., 646
Kay, D.J., 480, 501
Keil, F.C., 575
Keith, J.G., 765, 779
Keller, C.M., 577
Keller, J.D., 577
Keller, K.L., 102, 103
Kellert, S.R., 763
Kelley, C.M., 89, 91, 105
Kelley, H.H., 145, 327
Kellogg, W.A., 25
Kelly, C., 212, 232
Kelly, G.A., 329
Kelly, J.F., 387, 389, 396
Kelly, M., 606
Kelman, H.C., 178
Kemeny, J.G., 226, 227, 228
Kemeny, M.E., 747
Kemper, K., 263, 292, 296, 300, 303
Kempton, W., 765, 766, 779
Keppel, G.,
Keren, G., 75
Kerns, K., 260
Kerr, N.L., 826, 828, 830
Kerr, R., 153
Kerwin, J., 540, 542
Kessel, C., 274
Kessel, C.J., 299
Ketcham, K., 95, 100, 791
Ketron, J.L., 587
Keyfitz, N., 767
Kidder, D.P., 99
Kidder, D.P., 385, 399
Kieras, D.E., 7, 37, 45, 295, 302, 448, 449, 451, 452, 453, 455, 457, 458, 460, 461, 467, 470
Kiesler, S., 416, 427, 428, 434, 777
Kihlstrom, J.F., 744
Kijowski, B., 222
Kilduff, M., 333
Killeen, T.L., 424, 434
Kilpatrick, J., 557
Kim, E., 735
Kim, L., 430
Kimberg, D.Y., 608
Kimerling, A.J., 537
King, J., 823, 826
King, R.T., 763
Kinslow, H.S., 538, 539, 540
Kintsch, W., 7, 61, 250, 265, 296, 298, 666, 667, 676, 668, 700
Kinzer, C.K., 605, 606
Kirby, J.R., 653
Kiris, E.O., 213, 234, 274, 287, 302
Kirkendol, S.E., 801
Kirker, W.S., 728, 740
Kirkpatrick, E.M., 770, 774
Kirlik, A., 41, 42
Kirsch, I., 649
Kirschenbaum, S.S., 130
Kirwan, B., 222, 501

Kitajima, M., 474
Kite, K., 263, 292, 296, 300, 303
Kitto, C.M., 485
Klaassen, R., 703, 704
Klatsky, R.L., 485,488
Klein, D.F., 732
Klein, G., 59, 71, 121, 128, 117, 121, 145, 149, 163, 220, 228, 263, 293, 294, 300, 303, , 480, 481, 482, 483, 485, 486, 489, 501, 502, 664, 679
Klein, H., 322
Kleinmuntz, D.N., 119, 121
Kline, F.G., 826, 828
Kline, P.B., 502
Klinger, D., 767
Klix, F., 630
Klopfer, D., 597, 664, 675
Klopfer, L.E., 596
Klotz, M.L., 772
Knauth, P., 395
Knickerbocker, B., 761
Knight, B.P., 399
Knister, M.J., 414
Knowlton, B., 9
Koballa, T.R., 604
Kobayashi, K., 390
Kobayashi, M., 414, 425
Koedinger, K., 564
Koehler, D.J., 678
Koehler, K.A., 732, 733, 734
Koehnken, G., 797, 798, 801
Koeske, R., 598
Koffka, K., 12
Koh, K., 584
Kohn, I., 762
Kolers, P.A., 726
Kolvenbach, S., 432
Komorita, S.S., 773
Konakayama, A., 766
Kopelman, R.I., 665
Kopp, J.T., 768
Koriat, A., 90, 268
Koritas, E., 287
Kornell, J., 75, 485, 494, 496
Koslowski, B., 598
Kosslyn, S.M., 11, 69, 513, 514, 516, 515, 517, 518, 520, 522, 523, 532, 542, 545
Kosslyn, S.M., 648
Kostin, I., 644
Kottermann, J.E., 416
Koubek, R.J., 481, 485
Kozlowski, S.W.J., 319
Kozma, R.B., 598, 611
Kraemer, K.L., 423
Krafka, C., 830
Kragt, H., 229
Kraiger, K., 315, 323, 324
Krajcik, J.S., 596, 605, 606, 605, 611
Kramer, A.F., 254, 258
Kramer, G.P., 826, 828, 830
Kramer, T.H., 831
Krampe, R., 57, 59
Krampe, R.T., 576
Krantz, D.H., 584
Krapp, A., 606
Krauss, R., 769
Kraut, R.E., 414, 415, 425, 429, 433, 434, 435, 801
Kravitz, D.A., 833, 838, 840, 841
Krendel, E., 221, 225
Kriss, M., 764
Krizel, P., 522
Kromm, D.E., 779
Krosnick, J.A., 175, 176, 179, 180, 183
Kruskal, J.B., 22, 496
Kuchar, J.K., 258
Kuchinsky, A., 427
Kugelmass, S., 528, 529
Kuhara-Kojima, K., 599
Kuhberger, A., 120
Kuhl, J., 383, 384
Kuhn, D., 609, 613, 614, 615
Kuhn, T., 9
Kuiper, N.A., 728, 740
Kuipers, B.J., 678, 683
Kukich, K., 651
Kulhavy, R.W., 614
Kulik, J., 792
Kulik, J.A., 563
Kulikowich, J.M., 605
Kunda, Z., 584
Kunreuther, H., 119, 124
Kuo, W., 210
Kurland, D.M., 429, 557, 580
Kurlychek, R.T, 396
Kursten, M., 769
Kurtenbach, G., 427
Kurvink, A., 795
Kuzmyak, R., 767
Kvalseth, T., 228
Kvavilshvi, L., 378, 379
Kvrkel, J., 601
Kyllonen, P.C., 48
Kyllonen, P., 651, 652, 653

Laberge, D.L., 37
Lachman, J.L., 17
Lachman, R., 17
Laessle, R.G., 743
Lafrance, M., 480, 487
Lai, K.Y., 414, 429
Laird, J.E., 470
Lajoie, S.P., 553, 564, 577
Lakoff, G., 89
Lamb, M.E., 803
Lambert, B.L., 704, 708
Lamon, M., 578, 605, 606, 616
Lampinen, J.M., 91
Lana, R.E., 727
Landau, J.D., 99
Landau, R.J., 725, 736
Landauer, T.K., 8, 66
Landauer, T., 20
Landauer, T.K., 449, 473
Landis, R.S., 323
Landy, F.J., 318
Lane, D.M., 128, 455
Lange, B.M., 433
Langton, S., 425
Lanir, Z., 226
Lanning, S., 414, 426
Laporte, T., 222
Laporte, T.R., 160, 163, 168
Larish, J.F., 252
Lariviere, J.W.M., 759
Larkin, J., 517, 596
Larkin, J.H., 599, 665, 668, 707
Lassaline, M.E., 583
Lassiter, G.D., 801
Latham, G.P., 322
Latimer, D.A., 763
Laudeman, I.V., 270
Laughery, K.R., 227
Lavancher, C., 605
Lave, J., 16, 417, 577, 578, 580, 601, 602, 604, 607, 608
Law, J., 795
Law, K., 583
Law, S.A., 427, 428
Lawrence, J.A., 575
Lawson, C., 732
Lawson, D.R., 758
Layman, M., 770
Layton, C., 158, 263
Leach, J., 602, 607
Leatherberry, T., 119
Lebei, L., 428
Leberge, D., 153
Lebiere, C., 462, 463
Leckliter, I.N., 765
Lederberg, J., 434
Lee, A., 259, 260
Lee, C., 704
Lee, D., 427
Lee, F.J., 295
Lee, J., 274, 386
Lee, J.D., 223, 224, 237, 239
Lee, M.D., 40
Lee, T., 791
Lee, T.W., 321
Lee, W.W., 497
Leegillespie, J., 704
Leeming, F.C., 764, 765, 769
Leermakers, T., 228
Lees, F., 209, 213, 222, 223, 225, 228, 232
Legge, G.E., 519, 520
Lehmann, A.C., 58, 292
Lehrer, R., 605, 606
Leibowitz, H., 252

Leichner, R., 427
Leichtman, M., 806
Leiman, B., 379
Leinhardt, G., 517, 598, 600, 612
Leippe, M.R., 18, 354, 832, 833
Leirer, V.O., 385, 395, 399, 701
Leland, M.D.P., 415, 429
Lemieux, M., 668, 669
Lemley, R.E., 300
Lenat, D.B., 76
Lentz, R., 706
Leplat, J., 148
Lepper, M.R., 563, 608
Leprohon, J., 664, 678, 679, 680
Lesem, M.D., 743
Lesgold, A., 565, 597, 664, 670, 675, 678
Lesgold, A.M., 577
Leutner, D., 559
Levi, D.J., 771
Levidow, B., 746
Levie, W.H., 706
Levin, I.P., 119, 120, 125, 126, 131
Levin, J.R., 706
Levine, J.M., 195
Levine, J.A., 429
Levine, J.M., 305, 577
Levitt, M., 94
Lewandowsky, S, 7, 237, 239, 513, 522, 525, 529, 530, 513, 531, 537, 538, 539, 540, 541, 611
Lewis, J., 24, 630, 631
Lewis, M., 605, 609
Lewis, M.W., 462, 585
Lewis, R., 12
Lewis, S., 425, 496
Lewis, V., 399
Ley, P., 697, 706, 714
Lhyle, K.G., 614
Li, S.-C., 538, 539, 540, 541
Liang, C.-C., 256, 257
Liao, J., 269
Liberman, A., 191
Liberman, V., 678
Lichtenstein, S., 262, 770, 772
Lichtman, R.R., 747
Lickorish, A., 707
Liker, J.K., 601
Lim, R., 833, 835
Lin, E.L., 531, 545
Lin, X., 599, 605, 606
Linder, D.E., 774
Lindsay, D.S., 85, 89, 91, 97, 100, 101, 102, 105, 745, 746, 800, 810
Lindsay, M.T.H., 596, 602
Lindsay, P.H., 229
Lindsay, R.C.L., 799, 800, 833, 834, 835, 838, 839, 840, 841
Lingswiler, V.M., 743
Linn, M.C., 557
Linn, M.C., 606, 609, 615
Linn, M.C., 680
Linville, D., 102
Lipman, P.D., 386
Lipshitz, R., 146, 292, 293, 300
Listwak, S.J., 743
Little, J.D.C., 361
Livingston, C., 600
Livingstone, J., 716
Livosky, M., 793
Locke, E.A., 322
Lockhart, R.S., 86, 91, 106, 726
Loewenstein, R.J., 744
Loftus, E.F., 23, 69, 91, 93, 95, 96, 100, 101, 102 483, 745, 746, 791, 793, 794, 795, 803, 806, 807, 808, 809, 810, 811, 826, 831, 833, 834, 840, 841
Loftus, G., 260
Loftus, G.R., 94, 791, 793, 794, 795, 808, 809, 810, 811, 831
Logan, G.D., 39
Lohse, G.E., 523, 524, 529
Lohse, G.L., 13
Long, J., 8, 253, 254
Lootsteen, P., 212, 221
Lopes, L.L., 131
Lord, F.N., 655
Lord, R.G., 315, 322, 325, 326, 327, 328, 329
Lorge, R.E., 697
Loumidis, K.S., 716
Louro, C.E., 733, 735
Love, S.Q., 765
Lovstrand, L., 414, 415, 433
Low, R., 560
Lowe, R., 611, 706
Lu, C., 651
Luce, M., 127
Luckhardt Redfield, C., 77
Luebker, A., 519, 520
Lukach, B.M., 733, 735
Lundregan, T., 791, 804, 811, 831
Lundy, B., 94
Lunneborg, C.L., 630, 631
Luria, A.R., 653
Lutz, D.A., 103
Lutz, R.J., 103
Lutz, R., 365
Luus, C.A.E., 799
Luyben, P.D., 765, 766, 768
Lykken, D.T., 802
Lynch, J.G., 352, 354, 363, 365
Lynch, W.J., 392, 396, 401
Lynn, S.J., 8, 744, 795

Maass, A., 830, 832
Macan, T.M., 318
Maccoun, R., 826
Macdonald, M.R., 740
Macdougall, M., 612
Maceachren, A.M., 514, 516, 535, 537, 541, 542, 545
Macgregor, D., 121, 489
Maciver, D., 612
Mack, D.E., 188
Mack, I., 43
Mackay, W.E., 428
Mackinnon, D.P., 96, 796
Maclean, A., 414, 415, 430, 433
Maclean, D.E., 772
Maclean, H., 809
Maclean, N., 332, 335
Macleod, C., 727, 729, 730
Macleod, M.D., 791
Maclin, D., 612
Macomber, J., 575
Macwan, A.P., 239
Maddox, W.T., 497
Madhavan, D., 269
Madonia, B., 762
Maeno, K., 414
Magder, S., 664, 679, 680, 682, 683, 685, 687
Magee, J.S., 424
Magurno, A.B., 702
Mahajan, J., 129
Mahan, L., 826
Maher, K.J., 315, 325
Maher, R.J., 535
Maheswaran, D., 193, 194
Mahon, B., 706
Maidenberg, E., 733, 735
Mainwaring, S., 415, 433
Mainzer, J., 487
Major, D.A., 317, 320
Malcus, L., 24
Malinoski, P., 795
Malone, T.W., 414, 429
Malpass, R.S., 791, 831, 833, 838
Mancuso, J.C., 494
Mandl, H., 564, 706
Mane, A., 49
Mann, S., 768
Mannes, S., 667
Manning, C.A., 275, 283, 284, 288, 291, 295, 300, 301, 302, 399
Manning, J., 434
Mano, H., 127
Mantei, M., 425
Mantrala, M., 353, 359
Mantyla, T., 396
Marando, L., 833, 835
Marble, T.A., 118
Marca, D., 435
Marcelo, R.A.Q., 287
March, J.G., 315, 329, 422
Marchak, F.M., 531, 545, 531

Marchak, L.C., 531
Marchant, G., 130
Marchant, R., 798
Marcoen, A., 97
Margolin, J.B., 767
Margraf, J., 731
Margraf, M., 733
Marinker, M., 708
Maris, E.M., 641
Markman, A.B., 583
Markman, E., 575
Markus, H., 727, 728
Markus, M.L., 432
Marmorstein, H., 352, 354
Marqvardsen, P., 415
Marr, D., 446, 516
Mars, R., 560, 561
Marsden, P., 672
Marsh, H.W., 612
Marsh, R.L., 99
Marshall, R.J., 538
Martens, T.K., 838
Martin, F., 151
Martin, J., 333
Martin, M., 733, 734
Martin, V.L., 605
Martin-Emerson, R., 254
Maruno, S., 390
Maruyama, G., 614, 836
Marx, R.W., 572, 596, 605, 606
Mason, P., 328, 696
Mason, T.J., 534
Massey, L.D., 563
Masson, M.J., 705
Mateer, C., 401
Matessa, M., 462, 463
Matessa, M.P., 295
Mather, M., 793
Mathews, A., 696, 727, 728, 729, 730
Maurer, T.J., 40
Mauser, G.A., 766
Mavor, A.S., 260, 261, 263, 271, 275, 294, 778
May, M., 488
Mayberry, J.F., 697, 713
Mayberry, M.K., 697, 713
Mayer, R.E., 552, 553, 555, 556, 557, 558, 559, 560, 561, 563, 579, 611
Mayer, R.R., 559
Mayfield-Stewart, C., 606
Mayhew, D.J., 11, 20
Maylor, E., 396
Mayr, U., 57, 59
Mcarthur, D., 608
Mcbane, D., 732
Mccall, K., 414, 427
Mccann, C.D., 729, 741
Mccann, R.S., 301
Mccarty, D.L., 97
Mccaul, K.D., 768
Mccauley, C.C., 421
Mcclelland, G.H., 125
Mcclelland, J.L., 8, 64, 69, 85, 574
Mcclelland, L., 766
Mccloskey, B., 75
Mccloskey, B.P., 485, 488, 494, 496
Mccloskey, M., 94, 791, 808, 839
Mccollam, K.M., 644, 650, 651
Mccombs, B.L., 606
Mcconkey, K.M., 831
Mccormick, C.B., 605
Mccormick, E.J., 538
Mccoy, A.L., 287, 304
Mccoy, C.E., 263
Mccoy, E., 158
Mccrimmon, D.R., 683
Mcdaid, A.T., 791, 799
Mcdaniel, M., 97, 99, 378, 379, 380, 396, 398, 400
Mcdaniel, R.R., 330
Mcdaniel, S.E., 424
Mcdemott, K.B., 89
Mcdermott, J., 596, 665, 668
Mcdermott, K.B., 90, 91
Mcdonald, D.R., 496
Mcdonald, J.E., 25, 496
Mcevoys, C., 7
Mcewen, T., 791, 804, 811, 831
Mcfarlane, A.C., 744
Mcgaghie, W.C., 683
Mcgee, J.P., 260, 261, 263, 271, 275, 294
Mcgill, R., 518, 520, 525, 537, 540, 545
Mcgrath, J.E., 423, 428
Mcgraw, K.L., 485
Mcgreevy, M.W., 257
Mcgregor, D., 679
Mcguire, W.J., 765
Mckechnie, G.E., 762
Mckeithen, K.B., 23
Mckellin, D.B., 315, 319, 320
Mckelvie, S.J., 795
Mckenna, J., 839
Mckitrick, L.A., 401
Mckoon, G., 583
Mcleod, P.L., 423
Mcmillan, G., 283
Mcnally, R., 733
Mcnally, R.J., 733, 735, 743
Mcneese, M.D., 483, 487, 500
Mcneil, B.J., 131
Mcneil, B., 678
Mcruer, D.T., 221, 225
Meacham, J.A., 378, 379
Meader, D.K., 425, 426
Means, B., 292, 300, 303
Means, M.L., 128
Mecham, M., 274
Meehl, P.E., 631, 632
Meglino, B.M., 318
Meihoefer, H.-J., 537
Meindl, J.R., 326
Meiser, T., 642
Meister, D., 501
Melamed, B.G., 710
Mellers, B.A., 116, 118, 122
Melnick, R.S., 772
Memon, A., 94, 797, 798
Mengshoel, O.J., 500
Mennie, M., 716
Meredith, P., 698
Merrigan, M., 766
Mersey, J.E., 539, 540
Merwin, D., 257
Merwin, D.H., 531, 545
Messick, D.M., 774
Messo, J., 793, 831
Meszaros, J., 119
Metacalfe, J., 92
Metalsky, G., 738, 749
Metcalfe, J., 86, 92
Meter, J.E., 766
Mey, L., 388, 398
Meyer, B.J.F., 717
Meyer, D.E., 23, 37, 45, 293, 295, 302, 451,457, 458, 460, 461
Meyer, D.K., 646
Meyer, M.A., 485, 486
Meyer, R.J., 361, 362
Meyerowitz, B.E., 120
Mezzanotte, R.J., 256
Michailidis, A., 415, 429
Michas, I., 705
Michon, J.A., 384
Midden, C.J., 766
Milazzo, P., 414
Milgram, P., 269, 296, 300
Miller, A.I., 598
Miller, D.C., 717
Miller, D.G., 793
Miller, D.T., 726
Miller, F.D., 326
Miller, G.A., 61, 67, 295, 449, 463, 494, 571
Miller, L.D., 605, 616
Miller, N., 791, 804, 811, 826, 831, 836
Miller, R., 47
Miller, R.D., 765
Miller, R.R., 574
Miller, T., 121
Mills, J., 182
Milne, R., 798
Milroy, R., 12, 707
Milson, R., 462
Milstein, J.S., 762, 765, 779
Milton, E., 252
Mineka, S., 731, 736

Minneman, S.L., 414, 415, 425, 427
Minow, N.N., 821
Minsky, M., 483
Minsky, M.L., 297
Minstrell, J., 613
Miranda, J., 740
Misch, M.R., 767
Mischel, W., 325, 749
Mishra, S., 102
Mislevy, R., 629, 649
Mitchell, A., 426
Mitchell, B.M., 427, 428
Mitchell, K., 793, 806
Mitchell, R., 795
Mitchell, T.R., 321, 322
Mizuno, H., 414
Mladinic, A., 177
Moan, S., 805
Modigliani, V., 90
Moen, J.B., 154, 155, 156, 161
Moenssens, A.A., 807
Moertl, P.M., 283
Mogford, R.H., 299
Mohler, S.R., 255
Molina, M.J., 759
Moller, J., 155
Moller, J.H., 664, 666, 669, 672
Molloy, R., 261, 274, 302
Monahan, J.L., 704
Monan, W.P., 260, 261
Money, K., 283
Monk, T.H., 395
Monroe, M.J., 328
Montano, D.E., 186
Montazemi, A.R., 524
Monteiro, K.P., 96
Montgomery, L., 765
Montvalo, M., 155
Moore, A., 596, 603, 605, 610, 611, 613
Moore, C., 396, 400
Moore, C.M., 393, 396
Moore, J.L., 585, 586
Moore, J., 16
Moran, G., 821, 823, 826, 830
Moran, T.P., 16, 61, 77, 414, 415, 424, 427, 430, 433, 444, 448, 449, 454, 455, 456, 457, 582
Moray, N., 36, 163, 212, 221, 222, 224, 225, 226, 228, 229, 235, 237, 239, 248, 261, 270, 274, 275, 289, 290, 297, 299, 758
Moreland, R.L., 305
Moreno, R., 560
Morgan, M.G., 771
Morningstar, M., 563, 581
Morowitz, H.J., 772
Morrell, R.W., 700, 706, 719
Morris, C.D., 87, 92
Morris, J., 430, 609, 615
Morris, N.M., 298
Morris, P.E., 379
Morris, T., 414, 426
Morrow, D., 259, 260, 701, 704, 710
Morrow, D.G., 385, 395, 399
Mortimer, E., 602, 607
Morton, J., 260
Mosenthal, P.B., 649
Moshansky, V.P., 159
Mosier, J.N., 433
Mosier, K.L., 262, 268, 274
Moskowit, A.J., 678
Mosler, H.J., 774
Moss, S.M., 44
Mount, M.K., 320
Mousavi, S.Y., 560
Moxey, L., 703
Mpofu, E., 379
Msmtapg, 596, 602
Muehrcke, P., 541
Muir, B.M., 224, 237, 239
Mukhopadhyay, T., 434
Mulholland, T., 630, 649
Mullen, P.D., 708
Mulligan, R.M., 10
Mullin, J., 425
Mullin, P., 395
Mumford, E., 696
Mumford, M.D., 48, 131
Mumme, D.L., 608
Mungiole, M., 534, 542
Muralidhar, K., 524
Murphy, A.H., 129
Murphy, K.R., 320
Murray, D.M., 93, 800
Murray, K., 712
Murray, L.A., 728, 740
Murtha, T.C., 50
Murtha, T.C., 323
Musa, J., 121
Musen, G., 9
Musen, M.A., 500
Mutter, S.A., 563
Muzzin, L.J., 666, 668, 675
Myers, B., 795
Myers, J.E.B., 805
Myers, N., 758, 759, 760
Mykityshyn, M.G., 258
Myles-Worsley, M., 482
Mynatt, C.R., 125, 301
Myscielska, K., 148

Nagel, K., 41, 42
Naglieri, J.A., 653, 654
Nair, A., 389
Nair, D., 765
Nakagawa, K., 616
Naman, J.L., 455
Napier, H.A., 455
Nardi, B.A., 427
Nat'l Transp Safety Brd., 160
Nau, P.A., 766
Naugle, R., 389, 396, 400
Navon, D., 37
Navon, L.M., 712
Naylor, C.D., 709
Naylor, G., 118
Neale, M.S., 766
Neary, M., 12
Needles, D.J., 739
Neisser, U., 16, 103, 104, 153, 253, 444, 792, 807
Nelson, C., 614
Nelson, D.L., 103
Nelson, L., 50, 323
Nelson, T.O., 75
Nerenz, D., 826
Neufeld, V.R., 672
Neuman, K., 769
Neuschatz, J.S., 90, 91
Neuwirth, C.M., 415, 429, 430
Neville, K.J., 492, 496, 497
Newby, T.J., 612
Newell, A., 60, 61, 62, 54, 64, 66, 69, 77, 148, 424, 444, 445, 446, 447, 448, 449, 452, 454, 455, 456, 457, 462, 470, 576, 582
Newlands, A., 425
Newman, D., 601
Newman, L.S., 102
Newman, S.E., 565, 596, 607, 608
Newmann, F., 600, 612
Newsome, G.L., 379
Nhouyvanisvong, A., 647
Nibett, R.E., 484
Nicholas, E., 805
Nickerson, R.S., 557, 758, 769, 776, 777
Nielsen, J., 19, 713, 760, 768, 769
Nietzel, M.T., 822
Nikolic, D., 283
Nilsen, E.L., 461
Nimmo-Smith, I., 399
Nisbett, R., 730, 747
Nisbett, R.E., 286, 300, 584
Nitzel, M.T., 766
Noaa/Fsl, 611
Nolan, J., 651
Nold, D.E., 288
Nolen-Hoeksema, S., 738
Nonaka, I., 422
Noon, E., 831
Nordenstam, B., 772
Norman, D.A., 7, 8, 9,14, 19, 36, 77, 144, 148, 154, 164, 168, 226, 266, 269, 378, 402, 480

Norman, G.R., 105, 664, 666, 668, 670, 672, 673, 674, 675, 680, 682
Normore, L.F., 73
Norton, R.S., 775
Norwood, M., 186
Noser, T., 611, 614
Noseworthy, J., 176
Novick, L.R., 585
Novick, M.R., 655
Nowak, A., 327
Nrc, 434, 758, 770, 771
Nunamaker, J.F., 423
Nutt, D., 732
Nye, L.G., 284
Nye, N., 596, 603, 605, 610, 611, 613
Nygren, T.E., 127

O'brien, J., 155, 157
O'brien, J.V., 257
O'conaill, B., 421, 425
O'connor, F.J., 835
O'connor, K.M., 423, 428
O'donnell, L.N., 711
O'hanlon, A.M., 396
O'hara-Devereaux, M., 427
O'hare, D., 262, 263
O'keefe, B.J., 704
O'malley, C., 425
O'malley, M.S., 399
Ochsman, R.N., 424
O'connor, M.J., 129
O'donnell, R.D., 46
Ofshe, R., 809
Ogden, E.E., 123
O'hanlon, A.M., 99
Ohrt, D., 283, 295
Oldfield, R.C., 67
Olfman, L., 427
Olmos, O., 256, 257
Olson, G.M., 411, 414, 417, 418, 420, 424, 425, 426, 434
Olson, J.R., 485, 496, 683
Olson, J.S., 411, 414, 417, 425, 426, 431, 432
Olson, M., 774
Olson, M.H., 415, 433
Oltman, P.K., 289
On Armed Services, 160
O'neill, P., 43
Oppenheimer, M., 764
Orasanu, J., 145, 149, 163, 155, 220, 228, 250, 262, 263, 269, 300, 305
Orbach, Y., 803
Orbell, J., 774
Ordonez, L.D., 122
Orimoto, L., 742, 743, 749
Orlikowski, W.J., 411, 431
Ornstein, P.A., 97
Osipow, S.H., 131
Oskamp, S, 128, 768
Ost, L.G., 732, 733
Ostrom, E., 774
Ostrom, T.M., 173, 832, 833
Otero, J., 600, 700
Otto, A.L., 826, 828, 829, 830
Otto, S., 177
Oviatt, S., 426
Owen, D.H., 252
Owsley, C., 47

Paap, K.R., 24, 25, 44, 261, 496
Paas, F.G.W., 560
Padawer-Singer, A., 827
Paddock, J.R., 810, 811
Paese, P.W., 119
Page, M., 798
Page, S., 648
Paivio, A., 559
Pajak, J., 212, 221
Palanianppan, M., 389
Palen, L., 433
Palincsar, A., 596, 605, 606, 615
Pallak, M.S., 768
Palmer, D.K., 318
Palmer, E.A., 262, 268, 270
Palmer, J.C., 91, 93, 791, 795
Panayotou, T., 760
Pandermaat, H., 703, 704
Pandolfini, C., 697
Panzarella, C., 732, 738
Paolucci, M., 609
Papert, S., 555, 556, 558, 596
Paradise, N.E., 581
Parasuraman, R., 33, 42, 224, 237, 239, 261, 263, 271, 272, 274, 302
Pardini, A.U., 768
Parente, R., 378, 396, 400
Pariante, G.M., 385, 399
Park, B., 321, 354
Park, C.W., 364
Park, D.C., 98, 99, 385, 399, 700, 706, 719
Parker, J.F., 94
Parkes, A.M., 290
Parkes, K.R., 396
Parks, C.D., 773
Parlett, J.W., 77
Parrish, R.V., 288
Pashler, H., 45
Patel, V.L., 70, 130, 300, 664, 666, 667, 668, 669, 670, 672, 673, 674, 675, 676, 678, 670, 679, 680, 682, 683, 685, 686, 687
Patel, Y.C., 670, 674, 675
Paton, D., 331
Patterson, E.S., 153
Patterson, H.L., 648
Pauker, S.G., 131
Pauker, S.G., 678
Payne, D.G., 8, 17, 90, 91, 94, 100, 105
Payne, J.W., 117, 121, 127, 152, 364
Payne, S.J., 392, 393, 394, 473
Payton, P., 605
Pdp Research Grp, 574
Pea, R.D., 557, 580, 596, 613, 614, 616, 624
Pearce, D.W., 773
Pearson, T., 132
Pedersen, E., 414, 427
Pedroza, G., 827, 830
Pejtersen, A., 275
Pejtersen, A.M., 209, 210, 215, 222, 223, 224, 226, 233, 234, 664
Pellegrino, J., 295, 606, 609, 615, 630, 631, 649
Pelletier, R., 564
Pembroke, M., 800
Pendergrast, M., 811
Penner, B.C., 600
Penrod, S., 93, 791, 799, 826, 828, 829, 830, 831, 833, 834, 837, 838, 839, 840, 841
Pepert, S., 580
Perez, M., 6
Perfetti, C.A., 598
Perfetto, G., 605
Perkins, D., 151
Perkins, D.N., 557, 579
Perlman, D., 769
Perrow, C., 162, 167, 211
Perry, D.C., 288, 294
Perry, J.L., 283, 295
Perry, R.P., 769
Person, N.K., 608
Persons, J.B., 740
Peters, D.P., 94
Peters, L.H., 318, 320
Petersen, P.T., 37
Peterson, C., 94
Peterson, G.L., 763
Peterson, M., 765
Petro, S., 378, 396, 400
Petrosino, A.J., 605, 606, 613
Petrosino, T., 596, 603, 605, 606, 610, 611, 613, 616
Petroski, H., 9
Pettigrew, T., 765
Petty, R.E., 131, 175, 176, 177, 179, 184, 186,195, 196,197, 416, 762
Pew, R.W., 153, 154, 264, 265, 285, 286
Pfister, H., 126
Phegley, L., 389, 390, 393
Phelps, L., 742
Phillips, J.S., 325
Phipps, D., 42
Piaget, J., 575

Pichert, J.W., 96
Pickett, R., 229
Pickett, R.M., 154
Pickle, L., 534, 537, 538, 539, 540, 541, 542, 545
Pickrell, J.E., 746, 794
Pidgeon, N.F., 489
Pier, K., 427
Pigeau, R.A., 43
Pigott, M.A., 830
Pillsbury, A.F., 759
Pinker, S., 9, 74, 514, 515, 516, 517, 521, 522, 527, 529, 530, 532, 534, 542, 545
Pinsonneault, A., 423
Pintrich, P.R., 572
Piper, A., 744
Pirie, J., 700
Pirke, K.M., 743
Pirolli, P., 68, 462, 463, 465, 467, 585, 605, 609, 700
Pitre, E., 334
Pitt, D.G., 763
Plass, J.L., 559
Platt, J., 773, 774
Platz, S.J., 830
Playfair, W., 513
Pleasants, F., 292
Pliske, R.M., 300
Plowman, L., 430
Plude, D.J., 396, 400
Poe, D., 801
Pokorny, R.A., 488, 489
Pollard, R., 710
Polonskym S., 101
Polson, P.G., 7, 467, 470, 474
Pomerantz, E.M., 179, 180
Pomerantz, J.R., 69
Pool, R., 778
Poole, D.A., 97
Poole, M.S., 414
Poon, L.W., 700, 719
Pope, K.S., 810
Pople, H.E., 156, 161, 162
Popple, J.S., 791
Porac, J.F., 331
Porter, B.E., 764, 765, 769
Posner, I., 426
Posner, I.R., 426, 429
Posner, K., 146
Posner, M.I., 37, 252, 255, 274, 523
Post, T.A., 600
Postel, S., 759
Postka, J., 563
Poulton, E.C., 12, 543, 702, 703
Pounds, J., 121
Powell, C.S., 760
Powell, M.C., 186
Powers, P.A., 795
Powers, R.B., 775
Prakash, A., 414, 424, 434
Pratkanis,A.R., 18
Pressley, M., 7, 97, 605, 700
Prevett, T., 257
Prevey, M., 389, 396, 400
Priester, J.R., 176
Prietula, M., 155, 668, 669
Prince, C., 305
Prinz, W., 432
Pritchett, A., 287, 288
Probald, F., 779
Pryor, J.B., 764
Puerta, A.R., 500
Pugh, H.L., 283, 293, 300
Pugh, H.L., 481
Purcell, J.A., 493, 494
Pury, C.L.S., 736
Putnam, F.W., 744
Putnam, R.T., 609
Puto, C.P., 118
Puto, C., 364
Pylyshyn, Z.W., 8

Quillian, M.R., 23, 69, 73, 483

Raaijmakers, J.G.W., 86
Rabinowitz, J.C., 256
Raby, M., 269, 270
Rada, R., 415, 429, 435
Radcliffe, W.N., 729
Raghavan, K., 599
Raman, K., 353, 359
Ramoni, M.F., 675
Ramsay, W., 763
Randall, D., 164
Randall, T., 697
Randel, J.M., 283, 293, 300, 481
Ranney, M., 608
Rao, R., 414, 429
Rapee, R.M., 733, 735
Rasch, G., 636, 655
Raskin, D.C., 802, 803
Rasmussen, J., 144, 145, 148, 152, 261, 162, 167, 209, 210, 215, 218, 221, 223, 224, 226, 228, 234, 261, 275, 297, 664
Ratcliff, R., 583
Rattner, A., 831
Rauschenberger, S.L., 744
Raven, J.C., 654
Ravitch, M.M., 683
Rawers, R.J., 768
Raybeck, D., 103, 390, 391, 393, 396
Raye, C.L., 745, 746
Raymond, D.S., 797
Raymond, J.E., 304
Rayner, D.K., 696
Raynor, K., 74
Read, D., 837
Read, J.D., 85, 93, 102, 100, 101, 745, 746, 791, 800, 810
Ready, D.J., 791
Reason, J., 143, 144, 148, 163, 167, 168, 220, 221, 224, 226, 396
Recker, M., 585
Redding, R.E., 247, 260, 261, 275
Redelmeier, D.A., 678
Reder, L.M., 92, 573, 794
Ree, M.J., 288, 294
Reed, S.K., 584
Reed, V.S., 103
Regehr, G., 675
Reger, R.K., 329
Regian, J.W., 48, 49
Regoczei, S.B., 479
Reich, Y., 500
Reichel, D.A., 767
Reid, D.H., 768
Reigeluth, C.M., 581
Reilly-Harrington, N., 738
Reimann, M., 605, 609
Reimann, P., 585
Rein, G.L., 414
Reiner, M., 599
Reiser, B.J., 5, 564, 608
Reiser, M., 795
Reising, D.V.C., 223
Reiter, R.C., 708
Reiter, S.M., 769
Reiter-Palmon, R., 131
Reitman Olson, J., 70
Reitman, J.S., 23
Reitman, J., 482
Remus, W.R., 416
Renkl, A., 585
Renner, G.J., 255, 256
Repetto, R., 759
Rescorla, R.A., 574, 580
Resnick, L., 163, 168
Resnick, L.B., 572, 575, 577, 596, 602
Resnick, M., 557
Revelle, W., 395
Reyna, V.F., 296, 299, 794
Reynolds, L., 702, 706
Rhoades, J.A., 428
Ribot, Th., 35
Ricci, K.E., 496
Rice, G.E., 717
Rice, R.E., 414, 415
Richards, A., 728
Richards, T.A., 763
Richman, E.H., 544
Richman, H.B., 62, 64, 69
Ridgeway, V., 696
Riedl, T.R., 121
Riemann, B.C., 733, 735
Rieser, J., 151, 596
Riley, V., 224, 237, 239, 272, 274
Rips, L.J., 73

Rips, L., 483
Ritchie, J., 712
Ritov, I.,
Robbins, T., 319
Roberts, K., 222
Roberts, K.H., 145, 155, 160, 163, 168, , 422
Roberts, N.E., 772
Roberts, T.L., 5,10
Robertson, M.M., 303
Robertson, N., 795
Robertson, S.A., 729
Robinson, H.A., 98
Robinson, J., 130
Rocco, E., 411, 429
Roche, S.M., 831
Rochlin, E., 222
Rochlin, G., 160, 163, 168
Rochlin, G.I., 416
Rock, D., 651
Rockwell, T.H., 262
Rodgers, A., 703
Rodgers, M.D., 284, 287
Rodriguez, R., 186, 196, 747
Rodriguez, T.K., 414, 426
Rodvold, M., 259, 260
Roebber, P.J., 129
Roeder, K.D., 285
Roediger, H.L. III, 89, 90, 91
Roediger, H.L., 483, 726
Roenker, D.L., 47
Rogers, D., 705, 708
Rogers, E.M., 181
Rogers, J., 635, 637
Rogers, T.B., 728, 740
Rogers, W.A., 39, 40
Rogers, Y., 225
Rogoff, B., 577, 604, 607, 608
Rohrbaugh, C.C., 130, 321
Romberg, T.A., 646, 657
Ronis, D.L., 354
Rook, K., 711
Root, R., 414, 415
Rosch, E., 325
Roscoe, S.N., 253, 257, 262, 263, 268
Rosen, L.D., 396
Rosenberg, C., 294
Rosenberg, S., 328
Rosenblitt, D.A., 414, 429
Rosenbloom, P.S., 60, 66
Rosenbloom, P., 470
Rosenfeld, J.P., 802
Rosenthal, S.W., 675
Roskam, E.E., 640
Roske-Hofstrand, R.J., 24, 44, 261, 496
Rosnick, J.A., 762
Ross, B.H., 584
Ross, G., 607
Ross, J.A., 604
Ross, L., 730, 746, 747
Ross, M.H., 760
Rosson, M.B., 435
Rost, J., 643
Rotella, J., 24
Rotenberg, I., 226, 289, 290
Roth, D.L., 649
Roth, E.M., 156, 161, 162, 220, 223, 224, 300, 480
Roth, W.M., 613
Roth, W.T., 733
Rouet, J.-F., 598
Rouet, J.-R., 598
Rouse, W., 261
Rouse, W.B., 224, 226, 228, 237, 298
Rousseau, D.M., 155
Roussos, L., 642
Rovira, D.P., 184
Rowe, A.L., 23, 482, 484, 486, 492, 496, 497, 500, 501
Rowland, F.S., 759
Rpsgb, 708
Rua, M., 414, 415, 432
Rubinson, H., 597, 664, 675
Rudy, C.L., 802
Rudy, L., 805
Rueter, H.H., 23, 485
Rugg, G., 499
Ruhleder, K., 425, 434
Ruhmann, I., 488
Rumelhart, D.E., 8, 64, 69, 85, 574
Rumpel, C.M., 834, 835, 840
Runco, M.A., 131
Rush, A.J., 727, 738, 749
Rush, M.C., 325
Russell, D.G., 284, 286
Russell, J., 598
Russell, J.A., 763
Russell, M., 772
Russo, J.E., 454
Rutenfranz, J., 395
Ruth, J., 66
Rutherford, A., 225, 297
Rutherford, M., 616
Ryan, R.M., 769
Rydell, S.M., 799
Ryder, J.M., 493, 494
Ryle, G., 463
Rypma, B., 67

Saariluoma, P, 66, 671
Sabers, D.S., 597
Sachett, G.P., 490
Sagan, S.D., 332
Sagarin, E., 831
Sagi, C., 496
Sakata, S., 414
Saks, M.J., 131
Salas, E., 40, 292, 300, 303, 304, 305, 308, 315, 323, 324, 501
Salas, R., 305
Salkovskis, P.M., 732, 733, 734
Salomon, G., 553, 563, 579, 614, 615, 616, 664
Salvendy, G., 209, 237
Sampson, E.E., 334
Samuel, W., 769
Sandberg, J.A.C., 490
Sanders, A.F., 47
Sanders, G.S., 96
Sanders, J., 802
Sanders, M., 538
Sanderson, P.M., 222, 223, 232, 236, 239, 483, 487, 490, 492, 543
Sanderson, W.C., 735
Sandler, A., 396
Sandler, R.S., 712
Sandman, P., 772
Sandoval, A., 711
Sanford, A.J., 703
Sanocki, T., 92
Sarin, S.K., 431
Sarkar, P., 283
Sarter, N.B., 78, 143, 144, 146, 147, 148, 158, 162, 163, 164, 165, 168, 226, 260, 264, 265, 266, 270, 272, 286, 287, 288, 302, 303
Sattath, S., 22, 120, 121
Satzinger, J., 427
Saufley, W.H.,
Saul, E.U., 605
Sawyer, A., 349, 365
Saxe, G.B., 602, 604
Saywitz, K., 798, 805
Scardamalia, M., 578, 601, 603, 604, 605, 606
Scerbo, M.S., 224
Schaaf, J.M., 94
Schacherer, C., 496
Schacter, D.L., 88, 89, 104, 810
Schacter, R.D., 488
Schadewald, M., 130
Schaie, K.W., 67
Schank, R.C., 297
Schatz, B.R., 428, 434
Schatzow, E., 101
Schauble, L., 596, 598, 599, 604, 613
Schaubroeck, J., 524
Schechtman, S., 321
Schechtman, S.L., 364
Scheffler, A., 709
Scheffler, S., 396
Scheier, M.F., 322
Scherer, K.R., 490
Scherlis, W., 434
Schiano, D., 520, 522
Schiavo, M.B., 125
Schiefele, U., 606
Schimmossek, E., 798
Schkade, D.A., 119, 121

Schlesinger, H.J., 696
Schliemann, A.D., 604
Schlosser, A., 428
Schmidt, F.L., 322
Schmidt, H.G., 669, 670, 676, 681
Schmitt, N, 315, 318, 321, 364
Schneider, D.M., 794
Schneider, L.M., 649
Schneider, S.L., 119, 120
Schneider, S.G., 747
Schneider, W., 37, 38, 39, 40, 41, 220, 290, 601, 614
Schneller, G.R., 95
Schoenfeld, A., 575
Schoenfeld, A.H., 604
Scholkopf, J., 599
Schon, D.A., 612
Schonbach, P., 182
Schooler, C., 386
Schopper, A.W., 286
Schotte, D.E., 743
Schreiber, A.T., 485
Schreiber, B.T., 255, 256
Schriver, K.A., 699, 700, 704, 707, 717
Schroeder, H.W., 763
Schroeder, W.H., 586
Schroit, D., 5,10
Schrooten, H., 558
Schultetus, R.S., 482
Schultetus, S., 128, 596, 602
Schulze, S., 596, 598, 599, 604, 613
Schumann-Hengsteler, R., 396
Schunk, D.H., 612
Schutte, P.C., 251
Schutz, H., 126
Schvaneveldt, R.W., 22, 23, 25, 220, 291, 293, 299, 305, 482, 483, 496, 683
Schwankovsky, L., 748
Schwartz, A., 116
Schwartz, B.L., 92
Schwartz, D., 577, 596, 599, 603, 605, 604, 606, 609, 610, 611, 613, 615
Schwartz, L.K., 396, 400
Schwarz, H., 427
Schweikert, R., 494
Schweitzer, M., 119
Schwenk, C., 157
Schwenk, C.R., 328
Scott, J., 487
Scott, K.L., 702
Scott, P., 602, 607
Seamster, T.L., 247, 261, 275
Searl, M.F., 764
Searleman, A., 90, 104, 378, 391, 395, 396, 400
Sebrechts, M.M., 647
Secker, J., 710
Secrist, G.E., 292
Secules, T., 605, 606, 616
Seelau, E.P., 799
Segal, L.D., 261
Segal, M., 421
Segal, Z.V., 730, 738, 740
Segall, D.O., 650
Seidler, K., 490
Seifert, C.M., 165, 583, 600
Seigel, K., 261, 270
Seiler, M., 236, 239
Seiple, W., 47
Sekigawa, E., 274
Selcon, S.J., 287
Seligman, C., 764, 766
Seligman, M.E.P., 738
Sellen, A., 421, 425, 435
Sellen, A.J., 414, 425
Semb, G., 769
Senders, J.W., 228, 265
Senge, P.M., 422
Sexton, R.J., 766
Shadbolt, N.R., 71,128, 480, 482, 483, 485, 486, 489, 494, 499
Shafer, E.L., 763
Shaffer, D.R., 764
Shafir, E., 678, 762
Shah, P., 528, 529, 530, 531
Shan, Y.P., 389
Shanteau, J., 119, 121, 122, 124, 125, 128, 129, 131, 295, 321
Shapiro, D., 164
Shapiro, K.L., 304
Sharlin, H.I., 771
Sharma, K., 800
Sharpe, S., 500
Shaughnessy, J.J., 91
Shaw, B.F., 727, 738, 749
Shaw, J.I., 792
Shaw, M.L.G., 483, 487, 494, 499, 500, 504, 506
Shaw, R.E., 234
Shaw, V., 614, 615
Sheasby, M.C., 414, 425
Shebilske, W.L., 48, 49
Sheehan, K.M., 645, 649
Sheehan, M., 396
Sheets, V., 383, 384, 385, 391, 392, 393, 395, 396
Sheik, J., 710
Sheikh, J.I., 399
Sheldon, S.A., 695
Shell, P., 654
Shelly, G.B., 378
Shepard, R.N., 22, 30, 69, 255, 483, 496, 498, 522, 638
Sheperd, J.W., 791
Sheridan, T., 265, 270, 271
Sheridan, T.B., 213, 223, 224, 225, 228, 232, 237, 270
Sherrod, D.R., 762
Sherwood, R., 151
Sherwood, R.D., 596, 605, 606
Sheth, J.N., 362, 363
Shiffrin, R.M., 37, 38, 39, 44, 37, 86, 220, 290, 295, 614
Shimp, T.A., 349
Shoben, E.J., 73, 483
Shoda, Y., 749
Shortliffe, E.H., 70
Shulman, A., 705, 708
Shulman, L.S., 490, 663, 664, 671, 672
Shum, S.B., 430
Shuman, H., 764
Shute, V.J., 48
Sidner, C., 428
Siegel, D., 49
Silberstein, J., 598
Silverstein, M.A., 763
Simcox, W., 528, 529, 544
Simkin, D., 522, 523, 525, 527, 542, 544
Simkin, D.K., 10
Simmons, D., 706
Simon, D.P., 61, 596, 665, 668, 672
Simon, H., 148, 210, 228, 233, 517
Simon, H.A., 9, 23, 57, 58, 60, 61, 62, 64, 65, 66, 68, 69, 70, 73, 122, 128, 315, 329, 417, 422, 446, 449, 452, 463, 482, 484, 490, 491, 573, 576, 596, 598, 604, 605, 665, 668, 669, 671, 672, 678, 707
Simon, L., 395
Simon, R.J., 822, 823, 826, 827
Simons, M.A., 482
Simonson, I.,
Simonson, I., 118
Simonton, D.K., 66
Sims, V.K., 560, 561, 611
Sinclair, M.A., 229
Singalewitch, H., 236, 237
Singer, J., 379
Singh, I.L., 261, 274
Singh, I.L., 302
Singh, S.N., 102
Singleton, W.T., 209, 213
Singley, M.K., 14, 66, 462, 467, 468, 469, 470, 581, 582, 644, 647, 651
Siochi, A.C., 492
Sipe, W.P., 326, 327
Skilbeck, C.E., 714
Skinner, B.F., 562, 574
Skitka, L.J., 262, 274
Skolnick, P., 792
Skon, L., 614
Slamecka, N.J., 273
Slavin, R.E., 765

Slavings, R.L., 188
Sleeman, D., 563
Sless, D., 696, 705, 708, 710
Sloane, M.E., 47
Sloboda, J.A., 482
Slocum, T.A., 537
Slovic, P., 120, 121, 228, 262, 770, 772
Small, S.D., 283
Smilowitz, E.D., 6
Smith, A.D., 98
Smith, C., 612
Smith, D., 16
Smith, E.E., 73, 483, 557
Smith, E.K.M., 664
Smith, E.R., 326
Smith, I., 433
Smith, J., 58, 602, 604, 698
Smith, J.M., 774
Smith, K., 292
Smith, M., 96
Smith, P., 158, 794
Smith, P.J., 73, 263
Smith, R.E., 827, 830
Smith, S.M., 131
Smith, T.L., 174
Smith, V.L., 791, 808, 832
Smith, W., 101
Smith, W.C., 326, 327
Smith, D.R., 585, 586
Snow, R.E., 49
Snyder, D.E., 500
Snyder, K., 24
Snyder, L.D., 830, 832
Sobolew-Shubin, A., 748
Sohlberg, M.M., 401
Sokol, L., 734
Solomons, L., 35, 37, 39
Solomonson, C., 644
Soloway, E., 596, 605, 606, 611
Sonderstrom, E.J., 765
Sopory, P., 181
Sowden, A.J., 695
Sox, H.C., 131
Sox, M.C., 678
Spaulding, K., 830, 832
Spearman, C., 630
Spears, R., 771
Speckart, G., 188
Spelke, E.S., 575
Spellman, B.A., 583
Spence, I., 513, 521, 522, 525, 527, 529, 530, 531, 537
Spence, M.T., 129
Spencer, H., 702
Speno, S., 762
Sperandio, J.C., 269, 295
Spilich, G.J., 598
Spiro, R., 680, 683, 684, 685, 688
Spiro, R.J., 150, 152
Sporer, S.L., 93, 791
Sporer, S., 837
Sprafka, S.A., 490, 663, 664, 671, 672
Sproull, L., 416, 427, 428, 777
Squire, L.R., 9, 88, 89
Srinivasan, V., 359
Srivastava, J., 127
Srull, T.K., 344
St.Jean, D., 795
Staehelin, J., 759
Stahl, B., 765
Stainton, C., 598
Standing, L., 795
Stangor, C., 764
Stanton, N., 227
Star, S.L., 434
Starbuck, W., 225, 235
Stark, H.A., 88
Starkes, J.L., 296
Starr, B., 415, 433
Starr, C., 764
Starrs, J.E., 807
Stassen, H.G., 299
Stasser, G., 826
Stasz, C., 608
Staszewski, J.J., 62, 64, 69, 667
Staudinger, U.M., 58
Steblay, 831
Steckel, J.H., 131
Stedman, D.H., 758
Stefik, M., 414, 426
Stein, B.S., 87
Stein, G., 35, 37, 39
Stein, M.K., 517
Steinhart, P., 759
Steinhoff, K., 560, 561
Steinmeyer, D., 760
Stephens, D.L., 48
Stephens, M.A.P., 743
Sterman, J.D., 125
Stern, L.B., 93
Stern, P.C., 758, 766, 767, 768, 769, 770, 774, 775
Sternberg, K.J., 803
Sternberg, R.J., 90, 582, 584, 587, 588, 596, 599, 630, 646, 649, 664
Sternberg, S., 61, 455
Stevenage, S., 798
Stevens, A.B., 99, 396
Stevens, A.L., 150, 151, 225
Stevens, C.K., 321
Stevens, S.S., 518, 521
Steward, D., 680
Stewart, B.E., 125
Stewart, T.R., 129
Stewart, W.P., 763
Stimpson, V., 613
Stine-Morrow, E.A.L., 704, 710
Stinson, L., 305
Stinson, V., 833, 838, 840, 841
Stipek, D., 612
Stitt, L., 421
Stock, W.A., 522
Stogdill, R.M., 325
Stokes, A.F., 263,292, 296, 300, 303
Stolarksi, R.S., 759
Stolwijk, J.A.J., 771
Stolzfus, E.R., 67
Stone, J.I., 801
Storrosten, M., 417, 426
Stotland, E., 177
Stout, R., 501
Stout, R.J., 299, 305
Stout, W.F., 642
Strand-Volden, F., 283, 287, 300
Stratford, S.J., 611
Strathman, A., 197
Strauch, B., 254, 264, 269, 274
Strauss, A.L., 331
Strecher, V.J., 712
Streitz, N., 414, 415
Strong, M.H., 48, 49
Stroop, J.R., 729
Stroud, J.N., 792, 794
Stubbart, C.I., 328
Studebaker, C.A., 830
Sturgill, W., 831
Stuve, T.E., 93
Stuve, T.E., 833, 837, 841
Suchman, L., 414, 417, 426, 487
Suchman, L.A., 16
Sue, S., 827, 830
Suen, H.K., 486
Suh, S., 605
Sujan, M., 359
Sullivan, J.J., 768
Sulsky, L.M., 320, 321
Sundstrom, G.A., 481
Suppes, P., 563, 581
Sutcliffe, A., 501
Sutcliffe, K.M., 331
Suthers, D., 604
Sutton, S.K., 736
Svenson, O., 125, 131
Swaminathan, H., 635, 637
Swanson, D.B., 155, 664, 672
Sward, D., 23
Sweller, J., 559, 560, 561, 609
Swets, J., 229
Swets, J.A., 154
Swezey, L., 425
Sykes, R.N., 97
Szlyk, J.P., 47

Takeuchi, H., 422
Talbot, J.F., 763
Tammaro, S.G., 433
Tan, G., 237, 239
Tang, J., 427
Tang, J.C., 425
Tang, J.D., 414, 426
Tang, J.S., 414, 415, 432

Tanke, D., 704, 710
Tanke, E.D., 385, 395, 399
Tans, M., 827
Tansley, B.W., 299
Tapangco, L., 561
Tapiero, I., 600
Tasca, L., 146, 147
Tata, P., 729
Tataryn, D.J., 744
Tatsuoka, K.K., 644, 650
Taylor, C.B., 735
Taylor, M., 229
Taylor, N.K., 494
Taylor, P.J., 127
Taylor, R.M., 286, 287, 299, 301, 303
Taylor, S.E., 173, 191, 193, 726, 747, 748, 749
Teague, K.W., 24
Teasdale, J.D., 730, 739, 740, 741
Teasley, S., 431, 432
Teasley, S.D., 416, 417, 577
Teesson, M., 737
Telch, M.J., 735, 737
Tengs, T.O., 44
Tenner, E., 416
Tenney, Y.J., 153, 154, 264, 265, 285, 286
Terborgh, J., 758
Terr, L., 809
Terrace, H.S., 575
Terry, M.E., 360
Teruya, D., 762
Tesch-Romer, C., 57, 59, 576
Tesser, A., 764
Thagard, P., 421, 583
Thayer, R.L., 763
Theunissen, E., 253
Thissen, D., 524
Thom, R., 327
Thomas, E.L., 98
Thomas, H., 331
Thomas, J.B., 334, 330
Thomas, J.C., 325
Thomas, L., 771
Thompson, B.B., 303
Thompson, D., 320
Thompson, S.C., 748
Thompson, W.B., 154, 155, 156, 161
Thomson, D.M., 96, 103
Thordsen, M., 121
Thordsen, M.L., 300, 496
Thorndike, E.L., 580
Threlfall, S.M., 699
Thuring, J., 124
Thuring, M., 126
Tiemann, A.R., 771
Tierney, P., 559, 560
Tilling, L., 7
Tindale, R.S., 58, 418, 420
Tio, A., 391, 397
Tirre, W.C., 48
Titchener, E.B., 35
Todd, S., 545, 531, 532
Tollestrup, P.A., 799
Tomarken, A.J., 731, 736
Tomlinson, R., 414
Torff, B., 588
Torralba, B., 283, 287, 300
Tota, M.E., 739
Tousignant, J.P., 839, 841
Towers, S.L., 317, 320
Townsend, J.T., 123
Trabasso, T., 605
Treisman, A., 36, 729
Treisman, A.M., 36, 538
Trevino, L.K., 331
Trigg, L.J., 769
Trigg, R., 487
Trollip, S.R., 263
Trotscher, B., 396
Trott, A.D., 664
Trueman, M., 703
Truitt, T.R., 275, 283, 284, 288, 291, 301, 399
Trujillo, A.C., 251
Tsang, P., 46, ,268, 269
Tubbs, M.E., 119
Tucker, R., 23
Tucker, R.G., 482, 483, 496
Tufte, E.R., 524
Tugwell, P., 666, 668
Tulga, M.K., 270
Tullis, T.S., 13,14
Tulving, E., 9, 87, 88, 96, 103, 383, 398, 796
Turkey, J.W., 514, 532
Turkle, S., 424
Turner, B.A., 489
Turner, M.L., 743
Turner, R.K., 773
Turtle, J.W., 799
Tversky, A., 22, 77, 118, 119, 120, 121, 131, 228, 262, 496, 678, 762
Tversky, B., 520, 522, 528, 529
Tweney, R.D., 125, 301, 707

Ullman, S., 522
Ulrich, R.S., 763
Uncapher, K., 434
Underwood, B.J., 65, 96
Underwood, G., 37
Undeutsch, U., 802
Ungson, G.R., 328, 422
Unrein, J.T., 299
Urban, G.L., 365
Urbany, J.E., 349
US Dept Defense, 160
US Bureau Census, 761, 777
Uytterhoeven, G., 287

Valacich, J.S., 423
Valentine, T., 792
Valentiner, D., 737
Vallacher, R.R., 327
Valone, K., 836
Valot, C., 222
Van Dijk, T., 298
Van Heuvelen, D, 23
Van Lehn, K., 58
Van Melle, W., 427
Vandaele, A., 222, 227
Vandekragt, A., 774
Vanderbilt, 551, 562, 563, 565, 577, 596, 601, 603, 604, 605, 606, 609, 610, 611, 613, 614, 615
Vandermeer, E., 630
Vanderplas, J.H., 702
Vanderplas, J.M., 702
Vanderpligt, J., 771
Vandervelden, J., 425
Vandijk, T.A., 666, 668
Vangent, R.N.H.W., 273
Vanhamme, L.J., 574
Vanhooff, J.A.R.A.M., 490
Vanhouten, R., 766
Vanlehn, K., 585
Vanmerrienboer,J.G., 560
Vanoostendorp, H., 600
Vanpatten, J., 581
Vansomeren, M.W., 490
Vanvugt, M., 774
Vaughan, D., 331
Vaughn, E., 772
Veinott, E.S., 411
Veldhuyzen, W., 299
Vera, A.H., 417
Verhaeghen, P., 97
Verhelst, N.D., 640
Verity, J.W., 19
Verplanck, W., 237
Verplank, W.L., 5,10
Verschaffel, L., 556, 557, 558, 596, 621
Verstralen, H.H.F.M., 640
Vesonder, G.T., 598
Viana, M., 47
Vicente, K., 234
Vicente, K.J., 17, 210, 222, 223, 233, 234, 295, 303, 480, 664
Vidulich, M., 283, 286, 287, 303
Vidulich, M.A., 287
Vierling, A.E., 210
Vilberg, W., 557
Vincent, J.R., 759, 760
Vipond, D., 7
Virji, S.M., 598
Viscusi, D., 747
Viswesvaran, C., 322
Vitousek, K.B., 741, 742, 743, 749
Vogel, D.R., 423

Vogel, E., 283
Vollrath, D.A., 58, 418, 420
Von Hippel, W., 177
Vonglaserfeld, E., 596
Vortac, O.U., 302, 399
Vosniadou, S., 564
Voss, J.F., 128, ,575, 598, 600, 615
Vrij, A., 801
Vye, N., 151
Vye, N.J., 596, 603, 604, 605, 606, 609, 611, 613, 615, , , 626, 627
Vygotsky, L.S., 607

Wade, S., 606
Wafler, T., 237
Wagenaar, W.A., 384
Waggoner, G.A., 378
Waggoner, W.C., 378
Wagner, A.R., 574
Wagner, A.R., 574
Wainer, H., 524, 534
Waldron, M.E., 705
Walker, G., 702, 706, 707
Walker, N., 38, 41, 42
Wall, G., 779
Wallace, B., 130, 675
Wallace, D.R., 759
Wallace, H.A., 128
Walling, J.R., 103
Wallsten, T.S., 126
Wallsten, T.S., 262
Walsh, J.P., 315, 328, 422
Wandersman, A.H., 771
Wang, T.H., 768
Wang, Y., 597, 664, 675
Ward, J.L., 265
Ward, L.M., 763
Ward, N.J., 290
Warhaftig, M.L., 797
Wark, L., 797, 798
Warm, J.S., 42, 43
Warnecke, H.J., 237
Warren, R., 251
Warren, R.M., 297
Warrington, E.K., 88
Warshaw, P.R., 18
Wasserman, E.A., 574
Watanabe, L., 487
Waters, W.E., 708
Watkins, M., 87
Watkins, M.J., 794
Watson, N., 737
Watt, I.S., 695, 697
Watters, E., 809
Watts, F.N., 727
Watts, J.C., 153
Wayment, H.A., 747
Weatherly, K.A., 321
Weaver, C.A., 667
Webb, N., 615
Weber, E.U., 129, 130, 675
Weber, E.U.,
Wedderburn, A.A.I., 36
Weening, M.H., 766
Wegener, D.T., 176, 197, 416
Wei, Z.-G., 226, 237, 239
Weick, K.E., 145, 334, 335, 422
Weigel, J., 762
Weigel, R., 762
Weihl, J.S., 765, 779
Weik, T., 237
Weil, M., 49
Weil, M.M., 396
Weinberg, B.W., 365
Weiner, A., 609
Weiner, E.L., 43
Weinert, F.E., 601
Weinstein, C.E., 646
Weinstein, M.C., 677
Weinstein, N.D., 763, 772
Weintraub, D.J., 253
Weintraub, D.J., 290
Weiringa, P.A., 237, 239
Weiskrantz, L., 88
Weiss, B.D., 696
Weitz, B., 365
Weitzenfeld, J.S., 121
Welbank, M., 489
Welch, B., 427
Wellens, A.R., 290
Wellman, B., 425, 428
Wellman, H.M., 575
Wellmer, F.W., 769
Wells, G.L., 93, 95, 790, 799, 800, 803, , 832, 833, 834, 835, 836, 838, 839, 840, 841
Wells, J., 383, 384, 385, 390, 391, 392, 393, 395, 396, 774
Wells, S., 563
Welsch, D.M., 666, 667, 676
Wendt, K., 428
Wenger, E., 577, 578, 581, 601, 602, 604, 607
Wenger, M.J., 90
Werner, A., 75
Werner, J.M., 319
Wernerfelt, B., 351
Wertheim, A.H., 251
Wertheimer, M., 582
Wertsch, J.V., 417
West, R.L., 396
Westcott, H., 801
Westling, B.E., 732, 733
Wetzel, D., 649
Weymouth, T., 424, 434
Whalley, P.C., 707
Wheatley, G., 596
Wheeler, L.W., 763
Whitaker, R., 500
Whitaker-Azmitia, P., 732
Whitcup, M., 769
White, A.A., 534, 542
White, B., 596, 606, 608, 609, 610, 613
White, B.Y., 565, 577, 682
White, G.R., 770
White, O., 401
Whitehead, A.N., 604
Whitehouse, W.G., 728, 740
Whitely, S.E., 641, 649
Whitney, D.A., 531
Whittaker, S., 421, 425, 427, 428
Whittrock, M.C., 559
Whyte, W.H., 763
Wicke, D.M., 697
Wickens, C.D., 6, 12, 37, 101, 213, 225, 232, 250, 253, 254, 255, 256, 257, 260, 261, 262, 263, 264, 265, 269, 270, 271, 272, 274, 275, 286, 287, 288, 290, 294, 298, 299, 301, 305, 531, 532, 545, 745
Wickens, D.D., 65
Wiedemann, J., 257
Wieling, B.J., 485
Wielinga, B., 489
Wiener, E.L., 213, 226, 237, 254, 258, 259, 261, 266, 267, 268, 269, 270, 275
Wiers, V.C.S., 236
Wierwille, W.W., 268
Wiggins, E.C., 177
Wilbanks, T.J., 766
Wilbur, S., 421, 425, 435
Wilcox, S.B., 9, 421
Wilczenski, F., 742
Wilkins, A.J., 266, 378, 386
Will, S., 716
Williams, C.J., 184, 185, 186
Williams, D., 260
Williams, G., 411
Williams, G.W., 563
Williams, H., 255, 256
Williams, J.M.G., 727, 729, 730
Williams, L.M., 92, 95, 101, 745
Williams, S.L., 737
Williams, S.M., 604, 606, 610, 615
Williams, S.P., 288
Williamson, J.E., 48, 49
Williges, R.C., 268
Willis, S.L., 67
Wilson, B., 414, 415, 429, 577, 611
Wilson, C., 798
Wilson, F., 331
Wilson, G.F., 46
Wilson, G., 268, 269
Wilson, J.R., 225, 297
Wilson, M., 68, 501, 642, 644
Wilson, T.D., 176 286, 484
Wineburg, S.S., 597, 609
Winett, R.A., 765, 766

Winett, R.R., 758
Winkel, F.W., 801
Winkler, P., 129
Winograd, E., 379, 792
Winograd, T., 16, 164, 428
Winter, A., 528, 529
Wise, J.A., 232
Wiseman, D.B., 125, 126
Wiseman, R., 696, 710
Wish, M., 424, 496
Witken, H.A., 289
Wittrock, M.C., 552, 553, 579, 629, 646
Wodarski, J.S., 765
Wogalter, M.S., 227, 702
Wohlwill, J.F., 762
Wojahn, P., 430
Wojahn, P.G., 430
Wolf, S., 121, 300
Wolfe, C.R., 575
Wolff, S., 651
Woloshyn, V., 700
Woltz, D.J., 48
Wolverton, M., 608
Wood, B., 36
Wood, C., 698
Wood, J.V., 747
Wood, L., 321
Wood, L.E., 71, 72, 487
Wood, S., 365
Wood, S.S., 607
Wood, T., 596, 615
Wood, W., 186
Woodhouse, R., 284
Woodhouse, R.A., 284
Woodman, C.B.J., 716
Woods, D.D., 78, 143, 144, 146, 147, 148, 149, 150, 152,153, 154, 155, 156, 157, 158, 161, 162, 163, 164, 165, 220, 223, 224, 226, 227, 232, 237, 260, 264, 265, 266, 270, 272, 286, 287, 288, 302, 303, 480
Woodward, J.B., 483, 487
Woodworth, R.S., 580
Wright, D.B., 791, 792, 794, 799, , 831
Wright, D.L., 292
Wright, F., 734
Wright, O.R., 318
Wright, P., 696, 698, 699, 702, 705, 707
Wu, Q., 576, 582
Wyatt, J.C., 697
Wyman, B.G., 481

Xiao, Y., 296, 300

Yackel, E., 596, 615
Yantis, S., 153, 186
Yarney, A.D., 791, 792
Yarroch, W.L., 598
Yarushalmy, M., 577
Yates, J.F., 124, 262, 700
Yearwood, A., 605
Yee, P.L., 295
Yerassimou, N., 696
Yerkes, R.M., 94
Yerushalmy, M., 565, 611
Yntema, D.B., 294
Yocom, P., 648
Yoder, C., 383, 384, 385, 390, 391, 392, 393, 395, 396
Yost, G., 564
Young, K.M., 600, 612
Young, L.R., 225
Young, M.E., 16, 574
Young, O.R., 775
Young, R., 717
Young, R.M., 414, 430
Young, R.M., 472, 473
Young, S.L., 227
Yu, C.H., 531, 532, 534, 541, 544
Yuille, J.C., 94, 95, 104, 791, 798, 799
Yungkurth, E.J., 44
Yurcheson, R., 710

Zachary, W.W., 493, 494
Zacks, R., 672
Zacks, R.T., 67, 299
Zaff, B.S., 483, 487, 500
Zanna, M.P., 180
Zanni, G., 831
Zaragoza, M., 808
Zaragoza, M.S., 94, 806
Zaslavsky, O., 517
Zawodny, J., 759
Zbslaw, A., 415
Zech, L., 604, 606, 611, 614
Zech, L., 609, 615
Zechmeister, E.B., 91
Zeitz, C.M., 576
Zerefos, C., 759
Zhang, J., 154, 168
Zhang, Y., 758
Ziambok, 293, 294, 300
Zieverink, H.J., 766
Zimmerman, B.J., 612
Zmuidzinas, M., 608
Zolch, M., 237
Zolik, E.S., 763, 765
Zsambok, C.E., 59, 220, 228, 263, 664
Zualkernan, I., 156, 490
Zube, E.H., 763
Zuboff, S., 221, 224
Zukier, H., 300
Zulager, D.D., 545, 531

Subject Index

3-D
graphs, 531, 532
perspective, 256, 257
6-o'clock problem, 286

abilities, 3, 4, 18, 19, 21, 24, 48, 49, 50, 70, 76, 93, 128, 209, 224, 237, 290, 357, 531, 587, 588, 629, 635, 640, 641, 642, 644, 651, 652, 675, 708, 792, 834, 835
abstract function, 215
abstract syllogism, 297
abstraction hierarchy, 215
access, 64
accuracy-confidence in eyewitness memory, 93
acid rain, 757
acquisition, 65
acrophobics, 737
ACT, 5, 64, 65, 215, 459, 462, 463, 465, 466, 467, 468, 470, 472, 474, 574, 581
adaptation, 446, 599, 600, 603, 652, 749
advertising, 102, 174, 181, 343, 344, 345, 348, 351, 353, 355, 363, 715
affect, 116, 120, 122, 127, 177, 193
affordances *see* Gibsonian
age-related, 47, 702, 703, 708
agoraphobia, 735
air pollution, 757, 758, 767, 779
air traffic controller, 258, 259, 263, 264, 269, 273, 299
aircraft, 3, 39, 43, 50, 78, 121, 247, 248, 250, 251, 252, 253, 256, 257, 258, 260, 261, 264, 265, 266, 268, 270, 271, 272, 274, 275, 288, 290, 294, 296, 299, 301, 302, 486
alarm, 226
alignment, 531, 532, 534, 541
altruism, 769
ambivalence, 179, 180, 539
amnesia, 744, 745, 746
analogical problem solving, 583, 590
analytic abilities, 588
analytic modeling, 291
anesthesiologist, 283, 300
anorexia, 741, 742
anxiety, 731, 749
APA, 808
appellate court opinions, 824
application sharing, 414
apprenticeships, 577
argument, 192, 193, 194, 195, 196, 198, 597, 602, 609
arousal, 36, 182, 733, 735, 737, 792
ART, 648, 654, 655
artificial intelligence, 223, 263
Aspects, 414, 426, 438
ASRS, 291
assessment, 770
association, 572, 573, 574, 575, 592
attention, 17, 19, 33, 34, 35, 36, 37, 38, 39, 40, 42, 43, 44, 45, 46, 47, 48, 49, 50, 51, 74, 98, 127, 128, 153, 173, 182, 183, 184, 223, 224, 227, 228, 250, 253, 258, 261, 265, 266, 269, 275, 284, 285, 286, 289, 290, 291, 292, 293, 297, 300, 301, 302, 304, 305, 315, 316, 318, 319, 320, 323, 344, 349, 380, 384, 385, 388, 398, 417, 418, 419, 423, 425, 426, 433, 449, 457, 458, 462, 463, 465, 474, 481, 514, 515, 518, 523, 560, 561, 585, 586, 597, 603, 605, 653, 700, 713, 715, 726, 729, 731, 732, 733, 735, 741, 744, 798, 830, 837, 843
attitude(s), 770, 764
accessibility, 176
assessment, 762
behavior consistency, 181, 186, 360
change, 711
functions, 178
persistence, 197
strength, 185
structure, 175, 176
toward animals, 763
attributional style, 739
audience, 704

audio and video conferencing, 424
auditory processing, 450, 460
authentic problems, 604, 605
autobiographical memory, 744
automatic process, 37, 39, 40, 41, 42, 93, 118, 220, 285, 291, 294, 363, 727, 729, 739
automation, 43, 210, 213, 214, 226, 236, 237, 239, 254, 258, 264, 268, 270, 271, 273, 274, 301, 302, 303
aviation psychology, 264, 283
awareness, 284
  servers, 415
  of the situation *see* situation awareness

backward reasoning, 672
Bad Design Web Site, 14
basic research, 9, 10, 681
Bayesian learning, 351
behavior(al), 778
  and the natural environment, 761
  change, 764, 770
  decision theory, 362
  intentions, 186, 188
belief, 129, 130, 187, 328, 345, 356, 600, 687, 700, 708, 712, 718, 727, 735, 736, 737, 738, 740, 743, 747, 810, 824, 828, 829
binge eaters, 743
biological band, 445
biomedical knowledge, 680
bipolar disorder, 738
Blacksburg Electronic Village, 435, 436
blocking, 574
blood-injury, 737
bodily sensations, 732
bottom-up *see* data-driven
bounded rationality, 148, 315, 329, 446
brand(s), 191, 345, 346, 347, 352, 353, 354, 356
  equity, 345
  loyalty, 347, 351, 361
  switching, 347, 361
buggy knowledge, 150
bulimia nervosa, 741, 742, 743

calibration, 129
career choice, 130
catastrophic (mis)interpretation, 732, 733
categorical color, 535, 540
categorization, 76, 105, 250, 293, 306, 318, 325, 326, 327, 331, 356, 421, 445, 462, 485, 517, 575
causal attribution, 145, 167
causality, 213, 214, 218
caveat emptor, 345
CAVECAT, 425
central route, 191, 363
CFCs, 759
CFIT, 254, 283
chain analysis, 332
changed trace hypothesis, 94
ChatBoxes, 414
chess, 58, 59, 61, 63, 66, 68, 70, 80, 128, 288, 482, 598
child(ren)
  interviewing, 798, 805
  sexual abuse, 96, 802, 809
  trauma, 745, 746
  witness, 96, 790, 803, 805
Choropleth maps, 535
chronic illness, 748
chunking, 67, 269, 295, 296, 449, 463, 470, 471, 472, 473, 683
clinical case comprehension, 665
clinical knowledge, 681
closed loop, 212
clumsy automation, 213
cluster detection, 538
clutter, 257, 261
CMN-GOMS, 454
coaching, 608
cognition
  cultural, 209
  danger, 737
  distributed, 417
  ecological, 16, 719
  in the wild, 168, 335
  situated, 16, 607
  socially shared, 614
  structuralism, 9
cognitive
  apprenticeship, 303, 607, 624
  architectures, 443
  artifacts, 3, 7, 11, 13, 15, 16, 19
  bias, 731, 735, 746, 749
  Complexity Theory, 470
  continuum theory, 132
  design, 629, 632, 633, 635, , 652, 654
  diagnostic assessment, 644
  dysfunction, 743
  engineering models, 443
  factors, 147, 148, 167
  flexibility, 749
  interview, 96, 795
  level, 447
  load, 211
  lockup, 228
  rigidity, 228, 262, 743, 749
  science, 663
  skill, 465, 467
  task analysis, 121, 299, 481, 501, 502
  therapy, 738
  tunnel vision *see* cognitive rigidity
cognitively compatible, 253
cognitivist/rationalist, 572
Cognoter, 414, 426
collaboration, 409, 424, 434, 440, 596, 603, 615, 621
commitment, 768, 769
common ground, 421
commons dilemmas, 775, 778
commune, 414, 425
communication, 211, 212, 222, 224, 237, 239, 271, 290, 299, 770, 771, 777
community of practice, 577, 579
competitive interactions, 615

compiled causal knowledge, 683
compliance, 687, 707, 708, 710, 711, 712, 713, 715, 717, 718
component action, 574
componential models of graph perception, 522
compromise effect, 364
computational modeling, 37, 523
computer, 5, 6, 8, 16, 19, 20, 43, 60, 61, 80, 84, 85, 176, 389, 409, 410, 428, 451, 513, 551, 556, 557, 558, 562, 563, 565, 566, 697, 777
  assisted instruction (CAI), 562
  mediated communication, 777
  Supported Cooperative Work (CSCW), 410, 435
  Supported Intentional Learning Environments (CSILE), 578
  supported work, 777
  tutoring system, 562
  Whiteboards, 414
conceptual
  competency, 680
  development, 575, 577
  graphical tasks, 529, 534
  sorting, 71
  understanding, 572, 573, 575, 582, 587, 685
conceptually driven, 250, 266, 290, 291, 297, 299, 515
conjoint analysis, 359, 360
conjunctions of features, 538
connectionist models, 85, 86, 105, 574
consciousness, 744
consequences of elaboration, 196
conservation, 766
consideration sets, 352
consistent mapping, 220
constraint, 210, 223, 233
construct validation, 631, 632, 634, 646, 652
construction–integration theory, 666, 667
consumer memory, 102
consumer welfare, 345, 346, 365
consumption, 760
content analysis, 330, 803
context, 16, 17, 35, 40, 57, 66, 67, 72, 74, 87, 96, 98, 104, 106, 115, 116, 117, 118, 119, 120, 121, 122, 123, 125, 126, 127, 129, 130, 132, 174, 178, 180, 185, 186, 188, 191, 192, 193, 195, 196, 197, 218, 219, 221, 222, 225, 239, 255, 266, 293, 294, 297, 304, 317, 321, 334, 336, 344, 349, 350, 351, 352, 354, 359, 360, 363, 365, 411, 413, 417, 419, 421, 423, 424, 428, 443, 446, 465, 466, 470, 471, 472, 479, 480, 484, 485, 486, 487, 489, 490, 493, 496, 497, 500, 501, 502, 516, 518, 521, 538, 540, 541, 543, 545, 565, 577, 587, 596, 597, 598, 599, 601, 602, 603, 604, 605, 608, 610, 612, 614, 616, 664, 669, 675, 677, 679, 680, 681, 682, 683, 684, 685, 688, 698, 703, 708, 709, 710, 713, 717, 718, 747, 762, 766, 772, 776, 778, 796, 797, 806, 808, 809, 827
control question technique, 802
control room, 211
control theory, 214, 322, 323
controlled process, 39, 40, 49, 118
conversational conventions, 421
cooperative, 614, 615, 622
cooperative learning, 614
core belief, 727
corporate memory, 718
cost–benefit analyses, 772, 773
coupling, 161, 162, 167, 211
covariation estimates, 736
creative abilities, 588
Criteria-Based Content Analysis, 803
cross-racial identifications, 791, 833
Cruiser, 414, 415, 432
cultural cognition, 209
cycles, 613

danger, 737
Das*Naglieri, 652, 653
data driven, 266, 290, 291, 515, 521, 543, 666, 667
data limits, 269
Daubert, 808
decision
  aids, 263
  ladder, 215
  making, 40, 59, 79, 85, 106, 113, 115, 116, 117, 118, 119, 121, 122, 123, 127, 128, 129, 130, 131, 132, 135, 137, 173, 186, 212, 219, 220, 223, 224, 227, 229, 248, 250, 262, 263, 275, 284, 285, 293, 294, 300, 303, 304, 315, 316, 317, 318, 321, 322, 324, 328, 330, 331, 336, 338, 343, 344, 347, 350, 351, 353, 354, 356, 357, 361, 362, 363, 365, 411, 418, 420, 422, 423, 431, 479, 481, 484, 489, 490, 502, 663, 665, 671, 677, 678, 679, 680, 688, 749, 811
  rules, 821
  support, 414
declarative knowledge, 71, 72, 266, 463, 465, 466, 472, 683
deconstruction analytical technique, 333
decoy effects, 364
deep understanding, 600, 606
default expectations, 525, 527, 528, 529
defense in depth, 226
degree of automation, 214
degrees of freedom, 211
delayed discovery, 810
deliberate practice, 57, 59, 65, 77, 576, 590
depression, 737, 738, 739, 741, 747, 748, 749
design
  analysis models, 13
  designer-initiated, 6
  guidelines, 11, 12
  need-based, 5
  of user interface, 24
  principles, 596, 602, 603, 617
  rationale, 414, 430, 436, 439, 440, 442
  spaces, 610
  technology transfer, 4
desktop audio/video, 414
diagnostic performance, 671
diagnosticity, 132
dichotic listening task, 729, 743

dichotomous thinking, 743
dieting, 742
dilemmas, 166, 606, 773, 774, 775
dimensional analysis, 234
direct pattern recognition, 228
direction of elaboration, 192
discourse, 596, 601, 602, 609, 618
discrete manufacturing systems, 209
disincentives, 766
displays, 6, 7, 13, 19, 121, 211, 214, 215, 219, 222, 223, 225, 227, 228, 229, 232, 233, 234, 253, 257, 258, 260, 261, 263, 265, 266, 269, 272, 274, 275, 289, 291, 364, 424, 457, 473, 501, 513, 518, 519, 522, 527, 528, 530, 531, 543, 544, 696, 712
disposal, 757, 760
dissociated personalities, 744
dissociative identity disorder (DID), 744, 749, 811
distributed
  cognition, 417, 418, 427
  cognitive system, 164
  control, 212
  expertise, 603, 616
distribution of practice, 90
divide and conquer, 126
divided attention, 17, 253, 285, 289, 474
domain-specific expertise, 596, 601, 602
double-ended choropleth maps, 535
dramaturgical analysis, 333
driving, 34, 39, 45, 47, 48, 124, 185, 220, 233, 261, 295, 302, 681, 682
dyadic interaction, 615, 622
dynamic environment, 285, 290, 291, 294, 296, 301, 303
dynamic visualizations, 611
dynamical systems theory, 327
dynamics, 212
dysphoria, 747

eating behavior, 741, 742, 749
ecological, 16, 43, 252, 514, 545
  displays, 232, 233
  psychology, 234
  validity, 791
education, 765
educational technology, 551, 552, 553, 555, 558
effortful, 739
elaboration, 186
  amount of, 186, 191, 192, 193, 195, 196
  ELM, 190, 191, 193, 195, 196, 197, 198
elderly *see* aging
electronic
  books, 777
  bulletin boards, 777
  calendars, 413, 415
  mail, 414, 427, 428, 435, 437, 439, 442, 777
elementary perceptual tasks, 518
emergencies, 224, 290
emergent feature displays, 232
emergent features, 232, 543
emotional
  content, 709
  involvement, 709
  pretrial publicity, 828
  Stroop test, 729, 733, 735
  tone, 711, 718
encoding, 419, 584, 831
  specificity, 87, 103, 527
endowment effects, 348
energy
  conservation, 765, 767, 775, 779
  consumption, 758
  efficiency, 764
  efficient technology, 775
  intense, 779
  light, 776, 779
  use, 764, 766
environmental
  attitudes, 762
  change, 757, 778
  psychology, 761
EPIC, 457, 458, 459, 460, 461, 462, 463, 465, 470, 474
episodic memory, 87
ergonomics, 209, 698
error(s), 220, 259, 260, 262, 284, 291, 299
  signal, 213
  tolerance, 144
escalation, 161, 162, 167
ESDA, 492, 501
estimator variables, 790
ethnography, 331
evaluation, 716
evaluative consistency, 179
exaggerated beliefs, 748
executive processes, 457
expectancies, 248, 250, 259
experience, 6, 9, 15, 17, 20, 21, 22, 34, 44, 45, 49, 59, 60, 69, 76, 86, 87, 88, 90, 91, 100, 106, 115, 116, 121, 124, 127, 128, 129, 130, 131, 132, 137, 179, 211, 225, 228, 229, 236, 250, 259, 272, 289, 293, 295, 297, 300, 304, 305, 315, 345, 352, 356, 359, 378, 383, 393, 396, 400, 401, 424, 427, 431, 434, 449, 463, 465, 466, 468, 470, 482, 486, 496, 527, 555, 557, 572, 574, 575, 577, 578, 580, 584, 585, 610, 613, 643, 668, 672, 676, 677, 682, 683, 685, 698, 704, 727, 731, 732, 736, 737, 738, 739, 744, 745, 746, 748, 749, 771, 791, 792, 793, 795, 796, 797, 802, 805, 829, 830, 832, 837, 838, 841
experience attributes, 345
experimental economics, 362
experimental studies, 821
expert(ise), 23, 38, 39, 48, 57, 58, 59, 60, 61, 62, 63, 64, 65, 66, 67, 68, 69, 70, 71, 72, 73, 74, 75, 76, 77, 98, 117, 121, 126, 128, 129, 130, 132, 180, 194, 211, 212, 220, 224, 225, 234, 250, 252, 263, 265, 266, 283, 287, 288, 289, 292, 293, 295, 296, 297, 298, 300, 301, 303, 304, 329, 330, 344, 345, 357, 359, 410, 480, 481, 482, 483, 484, 485, 487, 488, 489, 490,

expert(ise), (*cont.*)
493, 496, 497, 500, 501, 502, 545, 563, 564, 566, 576, 585, 595, 596, 597, 598, 599, 600, 601, 602, 603, 605, 606, 607, 608, 611, 612, 614, 616, 617, 618, 619, 620, 621, 623, 624, 646, 664, 665, 666, 667, 668, 669, 670, 671, 672, 673, 674, 675, 676, 677, 678, 680, 681, 682, 683, 685, 687, 688, 695, 704, 707, 709, 713, 715, 718, 765, 770, 803, 806, 807, 808, 809, 832, 838, 839, 840, 841
aquisition, 225
chess, 598
compared to novices, 597, 598, 599, 619, 664
in context, 601
in teaching, 597
knowledge, 666
performance, 58, 60, 70, 76, 482, 599
testimony, 806, 839
systems, 57, 70, 76, 77, 78, 220, 479, 481
expert–novice differences, 666
explanation task, 685
explicit memory, 88, 89, 106, 733, 744
expository text, 606, 624
extrinsic motivation, 769
eye movement, 73, 74, 227, 228, 289, 304, 461, 490, 501
eyewitness identification, 95, 830, 831, 832, 833, 834, 835, 836, 837, 838, 839, 840, 841, 842
eyewitness testimony, 92, 790, 791, 794, 807, 808, 810, 811, 835, 836, 839, 840, 841

false identification, 799, 838
false memories, 7, 91, 101, 102, 105, 746, 793, 808, 809, 810
fast and frugal algorithms, 123
fault, 210, 226, 290, 676
faulty information processing, 743
feedback, 12, 13, 14, 19, 41, 42, 85, 92, 116, 122, 125, 132, 214, 227, 303, 322, 323, 357, 411, 419, 420, 425, 426, 428, 458, 562, 575, 596, 603, 606, 608, 609, 611, 612, 613, 614, 615, 616, 617, 635, 638, 656, 732, 765, 766
feeling of knowing, 92
field studies, 220, 237
filters for email, 414
final causality, 213
first-mover advantage, 353
Fitt's law, 451, 461
Fitts' List, 224
fixation, 154, 155, 156, 157, 228
flexibility, 597, 599, 600, 748, 749
flight management system, 258
flight progress strip, 302
focused attention, 34, 258, 605, 798
forests, 758
forgetting, 74, 89, 94, 95, 100, 101, 228, 260, 274, 377, 393, 394, 395, 398, 428, 745, 810, 843
formal disciplines, 579
formative evaluation, 714
forward reasoning, 300, 668, 672, 673, 674, 675, 688
breakdown of, 673
frame, 120, 528
of reference, 255
rectangle maps, 537
system, 297
work, 410, 417, 419
framing effects, 117, 119, 120
Frye, 807
function allocation, 213, 237
functional models, 86
functionalism, 9
functionality, 18, 19
fundamental surprises, 226
future, 229, 232, 253, 263, 264, 284, 291, 292, 293, 296, 298, 300, 301, 302, 306

garden path, 156
gaze duration, 289, 290
general acceptance test, 807
general function, 215
George Franklin murder case, 809
Gestalt/Cognitive, 582
gIBIS, 414, 430, 436
Gibsonian, 290, 292, 586
gistification, 296, 297, 299
global temperature, 764
GLTM, 641, 642, 649, 650, 651
goal, 452
conflicts, 158, 159, 160, 165, 166, 167
setting theory, 322, 323
GOMS, 447, 448, 452, 453, 454, 455, 466, 469, 474
good mental health, 749
graph comprehension, 7, 514, 515, 517, 543, 544
graphical user interface, 5, 452, 461
greenhouse gases, 758, 767
group authoring, 415
group cognition, 212
Group Decision Support Systems(GDSS), 423, 426
Group Embedded Figures Test, 289
group polarization, 196
groups as information processors, 418
GUI, 5, 6
guided participation, 607
guidelines, 713
guilty knowledge test, 802

H & B, 115, 133, 135
Health Belief Model, 700
healthy functioning, 748
heterogeneity, 358, 361, 799, 843
heuristics (and biases), 59, 70, 115, 123, 135, 151, 262, 263, 344, 355, 363, 431, 454, 455, 576, 591, 597, 674, 676, 688
high reliability organizations, 167
hindsight, 146, 147, 159, 162, 165, 166
history, 597, 598, 600, 609, 618, 621, 622, 623, 624, 626
HomeNet, 434, 439
homomorphs, 225
hopelessness, 740, 747
hostile media bias, 184

how people read, 699
human–computer interaction, 4, 5, 8, 21, 43, 443, 444, 481, 698
human–machine, 209, 214
Hydra, 414, 425
hypnosis, 795, 810
hypothetico-deductive reasoning, 672

ICC, 563, 636
identification parade, 798
illusions of control, 731, 747, 748
illustrations, 706, 707
image theory, 117, 118
impasse, 471
implanting memories, 811
implicit leadership theories, 325
implicit learning, 323
implicit memory, 88, 90, 733
incentives, 765, 768
incidental learning, 574
independence from irrelevant alternatives, 360, 363
individual differences, 45, 47, 48, 49, 50, 99, 117, 127, 130, 131, 132, 133, 328, 390, 398, 497, 561, 632, 634, 642, 646, 651, 687, 707, 712
industrial automation, 210
inert knowledge, 150, 151, 162, 604
inferences, 68, 296, 325, 327, 584, 590, 667, 668, 717, 718
inferential styles, 739
inflated self-esteem, 748
informal information, 223
information
  acquisition, 316, 318, 319, 321, 351, 352, 358, 365
  search, 350
  technology, 20, 128, 365, 422, 776, 777, 779
  transmission, 603
instruction, 15, 16, 22, 34, 49, 50, 57, 97, 130, 131, 221, 259, 260, 262, 323, 444, 472, 473, 484, 490, 491, 551, 552, 553, 554, 555, 556, 557, 558, 559, 561, 562, 563, 564, 565, 566, 571, 572, 573, 575, 576, 577, 581, 586, 587, 588, 593, 595, 596, 597, 600, 602, 603, 604, 606, 612, 613, 615, 616, 617, 635, 664, 684, 685, 689, 695, 696, 700, 706, 708, 716, 717, 768, 819, 828, 830, 833, 837, 838, 840, 841
instructional design, 571, 572, 588, 589
instructional technology, 551, 552, 565
intelligent tutoring systems (ITS), 563, 566
interactive displays, 712
inter-attitudinal consistency, 180
intermediate effect, 670, 675, 676, 681
internal cues, 732
internalizing, 607
interpersonal communication, 777
interpretation of factorial experiments, 529, 534
interpretive bias with regard to threat, 735
interviewing, 96, 317, 336, 795, 796, 797, 798, 806, 811
  children, 798, 805
interviews, 71, 72, 74, 96, 121, 129, 185, 235, 315, 317, 318, 331, 335, 484, 487, 489, 493, 501, 553, 683, 746, 801, 803, 805, 806
intra-attitudinal consistency, 179, 180
intrasystem coupling, 214
intrinsic motivation, 769
invariances, 234, 292, 585
ironies of automation, 226
irrelevant information, 121, 122, 125, 128, 300, 668, 670, 671
irrigation, 759
IRT, 634, 635, 636, 637, 638, 640, 641, 642, 643, 644, 650, 653, 655
isomorphs, 225

Jasper series, 577
jigsaw, 616, 617
judging contingencies, 730
judgment of covariation, 730, 736, 747, 748
judgment-referral, 354
judicial evaluations, 824
juror
  decision-making, 820
  knowledge, 834
  sensitivity, 834, 839
  skepticism, 839
justification, 124

keystroke-level model, 454
knowledge, 9, 12, 15, 16, 17, 22, 23, 24, 48, 57, 58, 59, 60, 61, 62, 63, 64, 65, 66, 67, 68, 69, 70, 71, 72, 73, 74, 75, 76, 77, 80, 83, 87, 88, 98, 106, 117, 119, 124, 127, 128, 130, 178, 179, 180, 184, 186, 192, 223, 225, 234, 252, 259, 265, 269, 284, 285, 290, 293, 297, 298, 299, 304, 305, 306, 316, 318, 319, 323, 329, 344, 347, 348, 350, 351, 354, 355, 356, 402, 416, 420, 422, 430, 431, 443, 444, 446, 447, 448, 449, 452, 459, 462, 463, 465, 466, 470, 471, 472, 479, 480, 481, 482, 483, 484, 485, 486, 487, 489, 490, 496, 497, 498, 499, 500, 501, 502, 516, 542, 544, 545, 554, 558, 561, 562, 563, 564, 571, 572, 574, 575, 576, 577, 578, 579, 580, 595, 596, 597, 598, 599, 600, 601, 602, 603, 604, 605, 606, 607, 608, 610, 611, 616, 630, 632, 633, 635, 641, 643, 644, 645, 646, 648, 650, 653, 656, 664, 665, 666, 668, 669, 670, 671, 672, 673, 674, 676, 677, 678, 679, 680, 681, 682, 683, 684, 685, 687, 688, 689, 696, 712, 715, 718, 727, 744, 765, 768, 819, 820, 823, 824, 826, 827, 829, 830, 831, 832, 833, 834, 837, 838, 839, 840, 841
  assessment, 23, 24
  based behavior, 220
  construction, 553, 563, 568
  encapsulation, 681
  level, 447
  organization, 71, 323, 482, 485, 667, 669

LAMP, 652
language skills, 411

latent, 144, 330
Latin school movement, 580
lattice theory, 299
lay conceptions of intelligence, 587
leadership perceptions, 325, 326, 327, 339
learner-centered approach, 552, 553, 554, 556, 561, 562, 563, 564, 565, 566
learning environments, 595, 602, 620
  situated, 607
  technology, 551
legal safeguards, 839
legibility, 701, 702
LENS, 414, 429
levels of processing framework, 86
lie detection, 801
lineup suggestiveness, 838
lineups, 798
listening, 696
LiveBoard, 414, 427, 437
LLTM, 638, 640, 641, 649
local rationality, 160
logical positivism, 4, 7
LOGO, 554, 555, 556, 557, 558, 565, 567, 568, 569, 580
long-term memory, 61, 84, 87, 95, 225, 296, 418, 449, 463, 516
long-term working memory, 61, 72, 296
lookup tables, 236
Lotus Notes, 409, 414, 415, 428, 430
lying, 800

maintenance, 211
majority/minority sources, 195
management, 211
manic states, 737
manifest content, 330
manual control, 234
maps, 513, 514, 517, 518, 520, 534, 535, 537, 538, 541, 542, 543, 544, 546, 547, 548, 549
massed practice, 91, 92
material causality, 213
material-light processes, 776, 779
material-heavy processes, 779
mathematical models, 352, 353, 357, 358, 359, 360, 361, 362, 638, 641
MAU, 115
meaningful learning, 596, 603, 604, 606, 621
means-ends hierarchy, 215
media preference, 710
medical cognition, 664
medical decision making, 677
medical problem solving, 671
medicine, 664
Meeting Maker, 415, 433
memories, 745
  of childhood trauma, 746
memory, 3, 4, 5, 6, 7, 9, 19, 21, 42, 61, 63, 64, 68, 69, 72, 83, 84, 85, 86, 87, 88, 89, 90, 91, 92, 93, 94, 95, 96, 97, 98, 99, 100, 101, 102, 103, 104, 105, 106, 107, 122, 123, 125, 127, 128, 132, 135, 175, 176, 177, 178, 179, 180, 182, 184, 220, 225, 250, 257, 259, 260, 263, 265, 266, 270, 273, 285, 286, 287, 288, 289, 291, 294, 295, 296, 298, 299, 302, 303, 306, 316, 319, 321, 323, 343, 344, 346, 349, 350, 352, 353, 354, 357, 361, 365, 377, 378, 379, 381, 382, 383, 384, 385, 387, 388, 390, 391, 392, 393, 394, 396, 397, 398, 399, 400, 401, 402, 418, 421, 422, 424, 430, 445, 449, 450, 455, 457, 459, 460, 462, 463, 464, 466, 471, 472, 473, 480, 482, 483, 514, 516, 517, 520, 523, 530, 542, 559, 560, 561, 575, 577, 588, 596, 598, 600, 630, 648, 649, 651, 652, 653, 654, 655, 664, 665, 666, 667, 668, 669, 675, 678, 682, 688, 700, 702, 705, 708, 718, 733, 739, 741, 744, 745, 746, 790, 791, 792, 793, 794, 795, 796, 803, 805, 807, 809, 810, 811, 819, 830, 831, 839, 840, 841, 843
  aid, 99, 378, 387
  and confidence, 800
  and emotion, 792
  for automobiles, 794
  illusions, 91
  in legal settings, 95
  metaphor, 84, 86, 89, 106
mental disorders, 749
mental health, 749
mental model, 4, 116, 123, 124, 214, 222, 225, 228, 233, 234, 235, 236, 248, 252, 261, 265, 266, 272, 297, 298, 299, 303, 304, 305, 306, 324, 419, 484, 517, 576, 598, 608, 612, 682, 683, 685, 686, 687, 688
mental representations, 598, 620, 625
mental rotation, 255, 256
mere exposure effect, 355
mere-possession, 348
message-giver's agenda, 700
meta-analysis, 93, 120, 520, 524, 698, 706, 710, 798
metamemory, 92
metarecognition, 303
methods, 4, 10, 21, 22, 25, 45, 46, 47, 67, 68, 69, 71, 74, 75, 117, 118, 130, 132, 173, 286, 287, 317, 319, 321, 322, 323, 324, 327, 328, 331, 332, 333, 334, 335, 336, 343, 358, 359, 360, 362, 363, 364, 393, 410, 417, 427, 452, 453, 454, 455, 466, 470, 480, 481, 483, 484, 485, 486, 487, 489, 490, 492, 493, 494, 496, 497, 498, 499, 500, 501, 502, 553, 555, 562, 563, 564, 565, 573, 575, 580, 608, 632, 638, 655, 663, 664, 667, 674, 677, 678, 681, 683, 685, 687, 716, 726, 727, 763, 764, 798, 808, 820, 822, 830, 834, 841, 842
micro side of management, 316, 335
microworlds, 239, 565, 609, 620
mindset, 149, 167
misconceptions, 680, 684, 687
misinformation, 93, 793
misperceptions, 746
mistake, 220
MLTM, 641, 642
mnemonic, 97
MODE model, 188
mode of control, 210

Model Human Processor, 448
modeling, 4, 135, 263, 327, 358, 360, 462, 479, 481, 486, 501, 564, 600, 608, 609, 622, 626, 632, 633, 634, 635, 641, 647, 648, 649
monitoring, 48, 223, 261, 294, 612
monochrome choropleth maps, 535
montage, 414, 415, 432, 442
mood, 127, 175, 193, 726, 730, 737, 738, 739, 740, 741, 744, 748, 762
mood disorders, 737
motivation, 34, 38, 43, 50, 51, 59, 77, 90, 179, 183, 187, 188, 191, 192, 194, 197, 198, 224, 268, 315, 316, 317, 322, 323, 324, 335, 336, 351, 355, 358, 395, 572, 604, 606, 607, 714, 747, 748, 769, 802, 806
motor processors, 460
MRMLC, 642, 643
MUDs and MOO, 414, 423, 424
multidimensional scaling, 22, 24, 70, 328, 359, 496
multimedia, 260, 712
  learning, 559, 560, 561, 568
  presentations, 577
multinominal logit model of choice, 361
multiple personality disorder, 744, 811
multiple resources, 37
multiple sources, 195, 684
multiple targets, 195
multiple tasks, 45, 46, 269, 462
multiple trace hypothesis, 94
multiple-fault failure, 290

naturalistic decision making, 59, 220, 263, 293, 294, 481
naturalistic problem solving, 678
naturalistic settings, 678
nature of knowledge and learning, 572
navigation, 222, 248, 250, 256, 258, 260, 269, 272
need for cognition, 131, 186, 192, 196, 197
negative beliefs, 738, 739, 740, 741, 749
neoGibsonian view, 285
NetMeeting, 414, 426
networks, 22, 23, 24, 37, 64, 69, 70, 85, 102, 176, 480, 497, 516, 668
neural network *see* parallel distributed processing
neurophysiological assessments, 37
New Year's resolution cognitive style, 742
newspapers, 777
NGOMSL, 455
non-analytic basis for medical diagnosis, 675
nonsustainable agricultural practices, 759
norms and values, 602
noticing, 597
novice, 23, 34, 38, 39, 44, 48, 58, 59, 61, 66, 68, 69, 128, 129, 130, 252, 265, 266, 288, 292, 293, 294, 295, 296, 297, 300, 301, 304, 329, 352, 357, 359, 482, 493, 496, 528, 530, 545, 564, 576, 585, 597, 598, 599, 600, 607, 608, 611, 664, 665, 666, 667, 668, 669, 670, 671, 672, 674, 676, 682, 687
nuclear power plant, 3, 43, 211, 233, 283, 300, 301
nurses, 679

Object Camera, 414
observability, 214
older people *see* age-related
on-line impression formation, 321
on-line processing, 327
open loop, 212
operational errors, 291
operators, 43, 121, 211, 212, 213, 215, 221, 225, 239, 290, 291, 299, 301, 399, 452, 802
optimistic biases, 739, 748
organization of knowledge, 57, 596, 598, 680, 688
organizational cognition, 422
organizational routines, 422, 436
organizational sensemaking, 334, 338
out of the loop syndrome, 213
outcome bias *see* hindsight
output interference, 344
overload, 237
oversimplifications, 150, 152
oversimplify, 166
own race bias, 791
ozone (loss), 757, 759, 779

panic attacks, 731, 732, 733
parallel distributed processing, 64, 65, 85, 574
participation in instructional activities, 602
part-list cuing, 353
part-task training, 41
part-whole decomposition, 215
Pathfinder, 23, 24, 25, 305, 483, 492, 496, 497, 683
patient choice, 696
patient information leaflets, 696
patient–client privilege, 810
pattern matching, 220
pattern recognition, 223, 225, 228, 229, 285, 291, 292, 293, 303, 460, 482, 678
PDP *see* parallel distributed processing
perceived behavioral control, 188, 190
perceived quality of environment, 763
perception of control, 748
perception of risk, 770
perception/re-perception model, 105, 106
perceptual
  anchors, 521
  cycle, 153
  processor, 450
  Task, 524
  -motor skills, 220
performance
  appraisal, 318, 338
  based evaluation, 713
  -based criteria, 714
  -based design, 708, 716
  -based evaluation, 710
  -centred design, 705
  cue effect, 325
  not SA, 284

peripheral route *see* elaboration: ELM
persistence, 66
personal control, 748
persuasion, 176, 177, 179, 180, 181, 190, 191, 192, 193, 194, 195, 197, 344, 354, 363, 718, 764, 765
  four roles in, 192
phobias, 732, 735, 736, 737
photo spreads, 799
physical form & function, 215
physiological measures, 46
picture superiority effect, 103
pie maps, 538
piloting, 39, 48, 220
planning, 214, 222, 257, 263, 270, 300, 302, 305, 328, 330, 396, 397, 412, 481, 557, 558, 580, 653, 679, 700
Point-to-Point, 426
policy capturing, 321
policy use, 116, 127
politeness conventions, 717
pollution, 757, 758, 759, 760, 767, 779
polygraph, 801
pop-out, 289
Popper, 808
population growth, 760, 761
positive biases, 747, 749
positive cognitive biases, 748
post-dictions studies, 831
postevent information, 793
postevent misinformation effect, 94
power function, 449, 468, 521, 537
practical abilities, 588
practical relevance, 35, 51
practice, 12, 35, 36, 37, 39, 40, 41, 44, 48, 49, 50, 57, 59, 65, 66, 73, 77, 90, 91, 92, 220, 224, 236, 290, 291, 295, 303, 392, 396, 449, 466, 467, 468, 469, 470, 545, 562, 564, 574, 575, 576, 577, 578, 579, 587, 596, 601, 602, 603, 607, 614, 618, 619, 621, 622, 624, 626, 673, 729, 760
pragmatism, 9
pre- and post-deliberation verdicts, 841
predictability of the system, 285
predictor displays, 232
preference, 357, 358
preference reversal, 120, 121, 360
prejudicial pretrial publicity, 826, 829
PREP Editor, 429
pretrial publicity, 820, 821
price sensitivity, 347, 353
pricing, 348
prime, 290, 730, 734, 735, 740, 741, 811, 822
principle of rationality, 148, 447
principled organization, 598
principled understandings, 598
prior attitudes, 712
prior knowledge, 130, 319, 516, 561, 597, 599, 600, 605, 606, 667, 668, 820
prisoner's dilemma, 429, 774
privatization, 774
pro-active interference, 344
problem demands, 161
problem solving, 218, 597, 599, 601, 604, 605, 609, 612, 614, 615, 617, 618, 620, 621, 625, 626, 677
  -based instruction, 604
  -solving strategies, 576
  space, 223
procedural instructions, 695
procedural knowledge, 60, 71, 72, 252, 259, 261, 463, 465, 466, 744
process control systems, 209
process tracing, 73, 319, 321, 322, 364, 492, 493, 501
production rule, 457, 459, 461, 462, 463, 465, 466, 467, 468, 469, 472, 473, 474, 490, 581
production systems, 220
PROFs, 415, 433
project based inquiry, 610
project management, 415, 432
project-based learning, 610, 618
prominence hypothesis, 120
propitious heterogeneity, 799
propositional representation, 668
ProShare, 414, 425, 426
prospective memory, 99, 266, 378, 379, 381, 382, 383, 385, 390, 392, 393, 394, 396, 397, 398, 400, 401, 402
psychological band, 445
psychometric model, 629, 634, 648, 649, 650
psychophysics, 521, 522, 549
psychotherapy and memory, 99
public opinion surveys, 821

QOC, 414, 430
quality of the environment, 779
quantifiers, 703
quartermasters, 578

Rasch model, 636, 637, 638, 641, 642, 643, 650
rational band, 446
rational expectations model, 349
RAVE, 433, 438
reaction time, 71, 73, 74, 104, 289, 480, 523, 556, 728, 739, 740
reactions to failure, 146
readability formulae, 714
readers' emotional involvement, 705
real time, 62, 64, 211, 212, 214, 215, 220, 237, 260, 409, 412, 424, 432, 433
realistic behavior, 239
real-world systems, 212
reasoning strategies, 676
recall, 24, 44, 68, 69, 70, 86, 87, 88, 91, 92, 95, 97, 99, 101, 102, 103, 123, 128, 184, 296, 319, 320, 321, 344, 345, 346, 349, 353, 354, 356, 358, 395, 418, 420, 472, 482, 577, 598, 606, 665, 666, 667, 668, 669, 670, 675, 688, 704, 708, 730, 733, 739, 740, 745, 796, 797, 798, 822, 823, 829, 836
recognition primed decision making, 263
recognition-based processes, 325

recognize-act cycle, 449
recovered memories, 7, 100, 726, 745, 809, 810, 811
recycling, 760, 767, 768
reference points, 349, 350
reference price, 348, 350
reflection, 596, 603, 612, 617, 624, 626
remedial training, 41, 42
remembering, 712
repertory grid technique, 329, 330, 483
representation effect, 154
representation tools, 608
repression, 100, 745, 793, 810
Rescorla–Wagner rule, 574
research life cycle, 336
reservation value, 351
resident pathogens, 226
resource allocation model, 322, 323
resources, 7, 14, 16, 37, 39, 40, 50, 188, 191, 269, 286, 288, 289, 290, 292, 295, 302, 346, 420, 446, 529, 603, 613, 614, 652, 653, 684, 700, 776
retractor cases, 811
retrieval, 420, 831
retro-active interference, 344
revision, 596, 603, 611, 612, 617, 624, 626
revision control, 414
risk, 125, 212, 226, 262, 271, 292, 770, 771, 772
  assessment, 771
  aversion, 348
robotics, 213
routine experts, 600
RT *see* reaction time
rule-based, 220

safeguards, 830
SAGAT, 287, 288, 295, 304, 305
salinization, 759
SALTUS, 644, 649, 650
sampling, 228
SART, 286, 301, 304
satisficing, 9, 122, 354, 446, 678
scaffolds, 596, 603, 606, 607, 608, 609, 617
scale-reversals, 539
scaling methods, 22, 25
scanner panel data, 361
scenario techniques, 717
scheduling, 212, 222
schema theory, 727
schema-driven *see* conceptually driven
scientific reasoning, 599, 622, 624
search, 6, 40, 43, 44, 57, 60, 61, 62, 63, 70, 73, 123, 135, 218, 289, 299, 318, 319, 321, 323, 329, 343, 345, 347, 350, 351, 352, 353, 357, 365, 383, 461, 470, 480, 524, 671, 699
security-potential, 131
selection rules, 452
selective attention, 34, 48, 250, 265, 266, 731
selective exposure, 182, 183
selective perception, 182, 183, 184, 329
self
  -confidence, 239
  -efficacy beliefs, 735, 737
  -explanations, 605, 619
  -monitoring skills, 599, 611
  -organizing properties, 224
  -regulated learners, 612
  -report, 286, 727, 733, 820
  -schema, 727, 744
  -schema task battery, 740
semantics, 66, 87, 88, 472, 515, 667
semiotics, 220, 332
semi-structured interview, 685
SEPIA, 414, 415, 429, 438
sequential lineup, 800
shared editors, 414
shared file server, 415
Shared-X, 414, 426
short-term memory *see* working memory
ShrEdit, 414, 426
side effects, 162, 482, 701, 702
signals *see* semiotics
signs *see* semiotics
similarity effect, 360, 363
simulation, 4, 6, 42, 43, 50, 69, 76, 117, 124, 263, 287, 288, 289, 295, 299, 301, 302, 303, 304, 420, 448, 456, 457, 488, 490, 524, 565, 576, 577, 599, 613, 682, 763, 774, 776, 826, 827, 828, 831, 833, 835, 836, 837, 840, 841
simulator, 41, 42, 47, 239, 303
situated cognition *see* cognition, situated
situation awareness, 40, 41, 121, 234, 248, 250, 262, 263, 264, 265, 266, 268, 269, 274, 283, 284, 286, 305
situative, 572, 577, 585
size, 210, 211
skill, 5, 15, 17, 34, 38, 39, 41, 42, 43, 44, 48, 49, 51, 58, 59, 60, 61, 66, 68, 75, 77, 83, 92, 117, 128, 130, 131, 188, 213, 220, 221, 226, 228, 232, 234, 236, 250, 252, 265, 266, 269, 270, 274, 283, 289, 290, 292, 293, 303, 306, 323, 392, 393, 395, 396, 401, 411, 416, 431, 444, 455, 457, 462, 465, 466, 467, 468, 470, 474, 482, 499, 531, 556, 557, 558, 564, 565, 572, 574, 575, 576, 578, 579, 580, 581, 587, 588, 599, 600, 601, 603, 609, 610, 611, 614, 615, 616, 617, 638, 646, 650, 664, 675, 677, 679, 682, 718, 719, 744, 797, 801
skill acquisition, 220, 470, 614
SLAT, 638, 640, 644, 654, 655
slips, 220
SMART, 118, 135, 613
SOAR, 470
social cognition, 173, 174, 193, 198, 275, 740, 746
social dilemmas *see* dilemmas
social learning theory, 700
social perception, 746
social practices, 596, 602
social trap(s), 773, 774, 775, 778
sociocultural perspective, 602
sociotechnical, 215, 221

source attractiveness, 194
source expertise, 194
source monitoring model, 105
spacing effect, 90, 91
SPAM, 288
spatial ability, 255, 561
sports players, 283, 288, 292, 295, 296, 300
spreading activation, 463, 464, 465
star diagram, 232
starvation, 743
state identification, 229
state space, 223
state-dependent memory, 744
statement validity analysis, 802
statistical graphs, 513
statistical maps, 534, 535, 541
status quo bias, 347
statute of limitations, 810
stimulus–response compatibility, 220
storybuilding, 300, 301
strategic leadership, 325, 327, 328, 330
strategies, 234, 237, 263, 265, 269, 270, 289, 290, 295, 296, 297, 304, 305
Stroop, 729, 733, 735, 741, 743, 843 *see also* emotional Stroop
structure mapping, 583
Structured conversational database, 414
structured interview, 687
subjective, 187, 188, 190, 286 *see also* self-reports
successful learners, 596
suffocation false-alarm theory, 732
summative evaluation, 714
sunk cost, 124, 347, 348
supervisory control, 223
suppression, 745
sustained attention, 34, 42, 43, 51
switching attention, 34
symbol maps, 535
symbols, 220
symptomatic search, 218
syntactic analysis, 515
systems, 214, 795

tables, 519, 523, 524, 525, 549, 705
task analysis, 222
task environment, 210, 446
task–action mappings, 472
teaching, 596, 597, 600, 609, 620, 621, 624, 625, 626
technological gatekeepers, 13
technologies, 6, 44, 45, 410, 411, 412, 413, 415, 416, 420, 421, 422, 426, 427, 428, 429, 431, 432, 434, 435, 443, 444, 481, 551, 553, 554, 555, 556, 564, 565, 697, 709, 775, 776
technology transfer, 4
technology-centered approach, 552, 554, 555, 556, 562, 563, 565, 566
technology-supported learning environments, 564, 565, 566, 569
teleconferencing, 777
temporal, 210, 211, 212, 222, 232
text comprehension, 666
The Coordinator, 414, 428
thematic vagabonding, 154
Theory of Planned Behavior, 186, 188, 843
Theory of Reasoned Action, 186, 188, 843
theory of signal detection, 229
threat-related information, 749
threat-related memory, 733
Timbuktu, 414, 426
time-sharing, 45, 46
tone, 704, 713
top-down *see* conceptually driven
topic interest, 606
topographic search, 218
tradeoffs, 149, 157, 158, 160, 166
tragedy of the commons, 770, 773, 774
training, 5, 15, 17, 21, 38, 39, 40, 41, 42, 47, 48, 49, 50, 51, 57, 59, 75, 77, 92, 96, 99, 117, 121, 122, 221, 224, 225, 260, 263, 266, 268, 274, 286, 290, 292, 294, 299, 301, 303, 304, 306, 315, 316, 317, 318, 320, 323, 324, 329, 336, 396, 400, 401, 434, 448, 474, 479, 481, 484, 489, 496, 502, 531, 545, 574, 580, 582, 586, 603, 664, 671, 676, 677, 681, 687, 774, 796, 797, 798
training in cognitive psychology, 15
transaction utility, 348
transfer, 467, 469, 470, 571, 579, 580, 581, 582, 583, 584, 585, 586, 587, 589, 590, 591, 592, 599, 600, 604, 624
transportation efficiency, 767
trauma, 744
traumatic memories, 99, 792
trend displays, 232
trial simulations, 831
triarchic theory of human intelligence, 587, 592
trust, 239, 411, 412, 424, 429
tutoring, 608, 617, 621, 623, 624, 626
tutoring systems, 574, 581, 582, 593

UCIE, 13
understanding of biomedical concepts, 683
unipolar depression, 737, 738
universal subgoaling, 470, 471
Universal Weak Method, 470
unrealistic optimism, 748
Upper Atmospheric Research Collaboratory, 434
usability, 4, 6, 8, 14, 15, 17, 19, 20, 21, 22, 75, 696, 698
Useful Field of View, 47
user interface metaphors, 6
user interface prototyping tools, 12
users' models, 25
utility theory, 117, 358

vehicle emissions, 758
veiled processes, 284
venue, 821, 822
verbal protocol, 121, 222, 235, 330, 364, 542
verbal reports, 70, 71, 72, 73, 480, 483, 484, 490, 491, 492, 493, 667, 671
vertical transfer, 580

video, 709
conferencing, 411, 412, 423, 425
email, 414
game, 283, 304
lineups, 799
Window, 414, 415, 433, 437
viewpoint independent features, 256
vigilance, 34, 40, 42, 43, 51, 385, 733
violations, 224
virtual reality, 6, 551, 565, 778
visual, 608, 617
diagnosis, 674, 675
impairment, 702
processor, 460
search, 40, 41, 44, 51, 252, 518, 523, 538, 539
store, 450
Voice stress analyzers, 801
voir dire, 821

waste management, 760
waste production, 757, 760
water, 757
weapon focus, 792
wetlands, 759
witness credibility, 820
work, examples of, 602
worked-out examples, 585, 591
workflow applications, 431
workflow systems, 415
working memory, 19, 42, 61, 72, 220, 225, 250, 257, 259, 260, 265, 285, 289, 294, 296, 418, 449, 457, 459, 460, 471, 473, 559, 560, 561, 577, 649, 651, 652, 653, 654, 655, 739
workload, 45, 46, 51, 232, 236, 237, 248, 259, 261, 262, 265, 268, 269, 270, 273, 284, 287, 301, 302, 303
workplace, 5, 16, 43, 224, 296, 565, 664, 679, 777
Worm Community, 434

xerox star, 5

Yerkes-Dodson, 94, 95, 792